DATE DUE

PRINTED IN U.S.A.

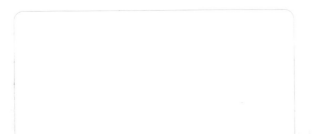

CONTRIBUTING EDITORS

Louise Alexander

Molly Cernicek

Harry Huiping Dai

Thistle I. Elias

Hanna Y. Freij

Donald M. Goldstein

Mary E. Lennon

J. Steven Ott

Sam J. Shafritz

David T. Twining

Kenneth C. Wenzer

Ken Zapinski

THE DICTIONARY OF
20TH-CENTURY
WORLD POLITICS

JAY M. SHAFRITZ
PHIL WILLIAMS
RONALD S. CALINGER

A HENRY HOLT REFERENCE BOOK

HENRY HOLT AND COMPANY
NEW YORK

A Henry Holt Reference Book
Henry Holt and Company, Inc.
Publishers since 1866
115 West 18th Street
New York, New York 10011

Henry Holt® is a registered trademark
of Henry Holt and Company, Inc.

Library of Congress Cataloging-in-Publication Data
Shafritz, Jay M.
The dictionary of 20th-century world politics / Jay M. Shafritz,
Phil Williams, Ronald S. Calinger. —1st ed.
p.   cm. —(Henry Holt reference book)
1. Political science—Dictionaries.   I. Williams, Phil.
II. Calinger, Ronald S.   III. Title.   IV. Title: Dictionary of
twentieth-century world politics.   V. Series.
JA61.S53   1993   93-15204
909.82—dc20   CIP
ISBN 0-8050-1976-6 (alk. paper)

Henry Holt books are available for special
promotions and premiums. For details contact:
Director, Special Markets.

First Edition—1993

DESIGNED BY LUCY ALBANESE

Printed in the United States of America
All first editions are printed on acid-free paper. ∞

10 9 8 7 6 5 4 3 2 1

Contents

Preface

This is a dictionary of the history, people, theories, and ideas that have impacted and transformed international politics in the twentieth century. It contains accounts of all of the obvious events—the wars, the treaties, the conferences, and the crises—that have shaped this century. It also includes the intellectual events—the major theories, doctrines, and concepts—that have equally influenced the century.

With more than 4,000 entries, this is the most comprehensive single-volume reference book on all of the concerns of contemporary international relations. It captures and codifies the living language of contemporary world politics and modern diplomacy. Because the concerns of international politics are anything but pure and limited to one discipline, judgments constantly had to be made about how extensively to cover related fields such as economics, history, law, military science, and sociology, among others. Beyond including generally accepted and established terms, we have specifically included political terms found in newspapers and mass-market journals that have not yet found their way into text, reference, and scholarly books. Generally excluded were those terms whose meaning in the context of world politics does not differ from definitions to be found in any college-level dictionary of the English language. However, when a word has multiple meanings, we often thought it useful to provide a brief standard English meaning first.

Writing the dictionary was akin to doing a gargantuan jigsaw puzzle in which one has to make up the pieces as one goes along and has no idea how large it will be in the end. The first task in completing this jigsaw puzzle was to find the pieces. For a subject as commonly taught and written about as world politics, many terms were obvious entries. But as a check on comprehensiveness, we systematically reviewed each issue of several dozen scholarly journals in the field for the last three decades. If a political scientist or historian took the trouble to write an article on a concept, theory, practice, law, or individual, we seriously considered including an entry on it. Next we roamed the stacks and reference sections of a variety of university libraries, finding new puzzle pieces here and there. Periodically we gathered up all the newfound pieces, gave them form and polish, and then placed them on the puzzle board—in this case, the hard disk of a computer. Especially useful were a variety of public domain materials published by government agencies, especially the U.S. Department of State.

Alphabetization

The dictionary is arranged in continuous alphabetical order. This organization is especially useful for comparing entries that sound similar. It also allows for quick comparison of terms with the same root. For example, the entry for diplomacy is followed by more than a dozen variants: "diplomacy, bilateral," "diplomacy, checkbook," "diplomacy, dollar," and so on. The entry for democracy is followed by "democracy, direct," "democracy, guided," "democracy, people's," and so on. This format is followed as often as possible so that if the root of a term is known, all of its variants can be found readily. When numbers are used in the name of an entry, they are treated as if they are spelled out. Thus "U-2 incident" is alphabetized as if the letter U were followed by the letters TWO.

Key Concept List

At the back of the book is a key concept list. If you are not quite sure of a word you are seeking but know, for example, that it has something to do with diplomacy, scan the diplomacy section in the key entry list to see if something looks familiar. If not, find some key words that are close, look them up, and follow the cross-references. The key entry list also is useful if you wish to examine all of the major concepts of an area of world politics. Remember that the key concept list does not contain all of the definitions to be found in the dictionary, only the core terms in each of the following substantive and geographical areas:

Africa
Central America and the
Caribbean
Central and South-Central
Asia
China
Cold War
Diplomacy
East Asia and the Pacific
Eastern Europe
Environment
European Integration
Foreign Policy
France
Germany
Intelligence and Espionage
International Law
International Organizations
International Relations
Theorists
International Relations Theory
International Trade

Italy
Middle East
National Security Policy
North America
North Atlantic Treaty
Organization
Nuclear Weapons Policy
Political Economy
Political Theory
Scandinavia
South America
Soviet Union
Spain
Terrorism
Third World Development
Treaties and International
Agreements
United Kingdom
United Nations
World War I
World War II

Cross-References

No event or term of world politics is an island unto itself. No dictionary of this size would be optimally useful if it did not suggest the related terms, laws, treaties, or personalities significant to a fuller understanding of the initial term. The many hundreds of cross-references provide threads the reader can use to follow the connections between and evolution of political concepts and events. Cross-references to related and comparable terms often follow the end of an entry. When a cross-reference is needed for a fuller understanding of a word within the body of the definition, it is indicated by putting the word in SMALL CAPITALS.

Biographical Entries

Hundreds of entries are identifications of people, living and dead, who have been significant in the history, writing, and practice of world politics. These entries are designed merely to identify individuals; they are not a substitute for reading works by or about them. We readily concede that some notable individuals may have been excluded and other individuals may have been described in words too brief to do them justice. For the most part, biographical entries are limited to presidents, kings, prime ministers, foreign ministers, and assorted dictators—the key actors in the twentieth-century political arena. But also included are a large number of identifications of those who have made an intellectual contribution to international thinking about the great issues of war, peace, economic development, and international organizations. This latter group includes foreign policy analysts, historians, journalists, and political theorists—even if they lived in an earlier century, such as Thucydides from ancient Greece and Niccoló Machiavelli from the Italian Renaissance. If their ideas still influence the politics of the twentieth century, they have been included.

Historical Entries

Included are all of the major political events of the twentieth century— such as brief summaries of treaty provisions and accounts of all major wars, as well as little ones that had international implications. Also covered are important internal coups d'état and international conferences that have shaped today's world. Because twentieth-century world politics cannot be understood outside of the context of its history, this dictionary of world politics is, in effect, also a dictionary of twentieth-century political history.

International Relations

Included are entries on the core concepts, theories, practices, and institutions of diplomacy and international relations, as well as entries on all the major international organizations—from the League of Nations to all of the specialized agencies of the United Nations. Comprehensive coverage is given to all the concerns of national security in the nuclear age.

Foreign Words

Foreign terms, most of which have now come into English (if only recently), are an inherently important part of a world politics dictionary. Here you will find the difference between *realpolitik* and *machtpolitik*, between a *coup d'état* and a *coup de main*, and between a *raison d'être* and a *raison guerre*. We have included not just translations of the foreign words, but brief discussions and analysis when appropriate.

Boxes

As the dictionary grew, many tidbits surfaced that seemed to deserve a spot of their own in the manuscript to help shed light or humor on an entry. These irresistible asides became the many boxes you will find on subjects as diverse as Edward R. Murrow's description of the London Blitz and Mohandas K. Gandhi's analysis of passive resistance. Other boxes contain lists of British prime ministers, United Nations members, U.S. National Security Advisors, and so on. Chronologies also are provided in boxes to detail the histories of wars (such as the Afghanistan intervention, the Chinese Civil War, or World War II) or of institutions (such as the League of Nations or NATO). Each box is located near the entry for its key term.

Contributing Editors

The various contributing editors listed opposite the title page helped produce this book in a wide variety of ways, from suggesting entries, to drafting entries, to revising entries and providing countless bits of advice and information that made this book far more comprehensive than it would have been otherwise. We thank them and are pleased to acknowledge their friendship and assistance. This is also a good place to thank our editors at Henry Holt and Company, Ken Wright and Mary Kay Linge—and the wonderful agent who brought us together, Mitchell Rose. Others deserving of mention because of their assistance along the way include Harry A. Bailey, Jr., of Temple University; Albert C. Hyde and David H. Rosenbloom of American University; Davis Bobrow, Tony Demaso, E. F. Gibbons, Alice Kaiser, Mary Sheila Kelly, Simon Reich, Greg Scott, Marshall Singer, and Tim Tipperman of the University of

Pittsburgh; Arthur Marsh of Oxford University; the late John Vincent of the London School of Economics and Political Science; Roger H. Davidson of the University of Maryland; and Barry D. Karl of the University of Chicago.

This work was designed to include definitions of everything that anyone interested in twentieth-century world politics might reasonably wish to look up. If you do not find a term that you feel should be included, we can only mimic Samuel Johnson's explanation when a woman made a similar complaint about his 1755 English *Dictionary*: "Ignorance, Madam, pure ignorance." Naturally, all omissions, mistakes, or other flaws to be found herein are solely our responsibility. It is still true today as Johnson wrote in 1755 that while "every other author may aspire to praise; the lexicographer can only hope to escape reproach." Yet we remain hopeful that as the years go by, this work will warrant subsequent editions. We would therefore encourage those readers who might care enough to help us do it "right" the next time around to write to us. Suggestions for enhancements, new entries, and additional citations will always be welcome.

Jay M. Shafritz
Graduate School of Public and International Affairs
University of Pittsburgh
Pittsburgh, Pennsylvania 15260

Phil Williams
Graduate School of Public and International Affairs
University of Pittsburgh
Pittsburgh, Pennsylvania 15260

Ronald S. Calinger
Department of History
The Catholic University of America
Washington, D.C. 20064

ABC powers Argentina, Brazil, and Chile. This term was first used in 1914 when these states sought to use their GOOD OFFICES to mediate a conflict between Mexico and the United States.

ABC warfare The use of atomic, biological, and chemical weapons. *Compare to* NBC WARFARE.

abdication 1. The formal act of giving up a hereditary office. A document stating this intention is an Act of Abdication. Historically monarchs have abdicated in the wake of a revolution, such as the Russian czar in the Russian Revolution of 1917. Sometimes rulers have abdicated to allow a younger heir to assume the duties of the monarchy, such as the Netherlands' Queen Wilhelmina in favor of her daughter Juliana in 1948. Another famous twentieth-century abdication was that of EDWARD VIII, king of England (later known as the Duke of Windsor), who gave up his throne to marry a commoner, the twice-divorced American socialite Wallis Simpson. 2. In more recent usage, a resignation from high public office. For example, Richard M. Nixon was said to have abdicated when he resigned his office as president of the United States in 1974 3. The informal leaving of a public office, as opposed to submitting a formal resignation; in effect, abdicating a position.

abdication crisis The political dispute within the British Empire occasioned by Edward VIII's announcement in November 1936 that he wanted to marry Wallis Simpson, an American divorcée. This crisis was resolved by his abdication the following month.

Abdullah I, Ibn Hussein (1882–1951) The first king of Jordan. As a reward for being one of the leaders of the World War I Arab revolt against the Ottoman Empire, the British allowed his forces to occupy Transjordan in 1920. Thereupon he was recognized as ruler by the British, who controlled the area by virtue of a League of Nations mandate. (*See* MANDATES SYSTEM.) During World War II his army, the ARAB LEGION, helped the British in Iraq and Syria. In 1946 he was rewarded with independence from Great Britain, renamed his country Jordan, and made himself a king. Considered by many Arab political hard-liners to be a collaborator with the Israelis and the British, Abdullah made enemies in the Arab world by annexing the West Bank of the Jordan River into the Hashemite Kingdom of Jordan following the 1948 war with Israel. He was assassinated in Jerusalem by a Palestinian on July 20, 1951, and was succeeded by his son, TALAL. Abdullah I was the grandfather of the current ruler of Jordan, King HUSSEIN IBN TALAL.

Abel, Rudolf (1902–1971) The Soviet spy sentenced to 30 years in prison by a U.S. court in 1957 for conspiring to obtain defense secrets. In 1962 he was exchanged for Francis Gary Powers, the U.S. reconnaissance pilot who was shot down over the Soviet Union in the 1960 U-2 INCIDENT.

Abgrenzung German word for "separation"; was used by the East German government to indicate the policy of totally formal division between East and West Germany. First used in this sense in 1971 to indicate the limits of the West German policy of OST-POLITIK, *Abgrenzung* was gradually eroded by West

Germany's stance and was eventually destroyed by German reunification in 1990.

ABM (antiballistic missile)   A missile designed to shoot down intercontinental ballistic missiles (ICBMs); also referred to as a missile defense, defensive, or antimissile missile. An ABM system was formally defined in the ABM TREATY of 1972 as a system (consisting of launchers, missiles, and radar) designed to counter (make ineffective or destroy) strategic ballistic missiles or parts of them in flight.

ABM Treaty   The treaty signed in 1972 between the United States and the Soviet Union on the deployment of defensive antiballistic missiles. The treaty allowed each side two ABM systems, one centered on the national capital (Washington or Moscow) and the other around an intercontinental ballistic missile site. Each site was limited to 100 launchers and missiles. A 1974 PROTOCOL to the treaty restricted both sides to one ABM site each. The Soviet Union deployed an ABM system around Moscow. While the United States has not yet deployed an ABM system, in 1983 President Ronald Reagan placed considerable emphasis on the development of a defense against strategic missiles through the STRATEGIC DEFENSE INITIATIVE (SDI). This initiative seemed to contradict the ABM Treaty by calling for what amounts to ABMs in space; Article 5 of the ABM Treaty pledged each side "not to develop, test or deploy ABM systems or components which are sea based, air based, space based, or mobile land based." During the Reagan Administration there was a major policy dispute between the supporters of SDI, who had a "permissive" interpretation of the ABM Treaty, and the supporters of the treaty (mainly members of Congress), who adhered to a much more restrictive interpretation. The Reagan Administration claimed that the treaty allowed for research and testing of exotic weapons (such as lasers). But this view was rejected by critics, including some of the officials involved in the negotiation of the treaty itself. The PERSIAN GULF WAR rekindled interest in defenses against ballistic missiles. On September 27, 1991, when U.S. President George Bush announced major changes in strategic nuclear forces, he also stated that he wanted to negotiate an amending of the ABM Treaty to allow ABM deployments to protect against accidental nuclear missile launches or nuclear missile attacks by small countries on the United States. This reorientation of the SDI program was known as GPALS, or Global Protection Against Limited Strikes. *See also* ALPS, SALT.

abrogation   1. The formal cancellation of a law. 2. The ending of an agreement (such as a treaty or contract) by the mutual consent of the parties to it. 3. The ending of a formal agreement by one side only. For example, the United States abrogated its defense agreement with Taiwan in 1979 even though Taiwan was eager for it to continue.

absolute advantage   A concept that provides the basis for international economic specialization and division of labor. It was first formulated by Adam Smith (1723–1790), who contended that one nation has an absolute advantage over another when, using the same amount of resources, it can produce more of a product than another nation. *Compare to* COMPARATIVE ADVANTAGE.

absolute gain   The level of benefit that is obtained by a single state from a cooperative venture seen only in its own terms and not considered relative to the gains of any other state. This concept is often used in relation to the problems of cooperation in an anarchic world. Although all parties gain from cooperation in an absolute sense, the concern with the relative gains or who gains more than whom can sometimes undermine cooperation. NEOINSTITU- TIONALISTS tend to argue that states are interested only in absolute gain.

absolutism   1. A government that recognizes few limits to its power and offers no guaranteed or constitutional rights to its people. The term was first used to describe the monarchies of rulers such as Louis XIV of France (1638–1715) who claimed a divine right to rule. The last phase of absolutism in the eighteenth century was known as enlightened despotism or reform absolutism in which rulers began to make efforts to improve the welfare of their people.   2. In *The Devil's Dictionary* (1911) Ambrose Bierce described an absolute monarchy as "one in which the sovereign does as he pleases so long as he pleases the assassins." *Compare to* AUTOCRACY; DICTATOR.

abstention   Refraining from voting even though one is entitled to do so. In some circumstances, such as at the United Nations, this can be a diplomatic expedient. It is a way of finessing an issue when acting more decisively would have undesirable consequences. Article 27 of the UN Charter states that Security Council decisions "shall be made by an affirmative vote of nine members including the concurring votes of the permanent members" but does not deal with abstention by the five permanent members of the Security Council who must concur. In practice, however, an abstention has not been regarded as a veto, which would bar passage of a proposal or prevent a decision from being implemented.

abstraction   A conceptual or intellectual model. Such abstractions as the BALANCE OF POWER, the DETERRENT EFFECT, and SYSTEMS ANALYSIS are often used by political scientists and historians to explain the behavior of politicians, diplomats, and nations.

Abu Abbas (1948–   )   The NOM DE GUERRE of Mohammed Abbas Zaidan, the head of the PALESTINE LIBERATION FRONT who organized the October 1985 siege of the Italian cruise liner ACHILLE LAURO, during which Leon Klinghoffer, an elderly, wheelchair-bound Jewish-American, was murdered. In the summer of 1986, Abbas was convicted in absentia by an Italian court for his role in the hijacking and sentenced to life imprisonment. In a November 1988 interview with the *New York Times*, Abbas, who was attending the Palestine National Council meeting, joked openly about the death of Klinghoffer, suggesting that "maybe he was trying to swim for it." NBC News telecast an interview with Abbas in May 1986. This was widely criticized as irresponsible journalism by the U.S. Department of State and various media sources because it showed an acknowledged pirate and murderer in a favorable light.

Abu Amar   The NOM DE GUERRE of YASIR ARAFAT, from the Arabic term meaning "to build."

Abu Nidal (1935–   )   The NOM DE GUERRE (meaning "Father of the Struggle" in Arabic) of Sabri al-Banna, a Palestinian terrorist whose disenchantment with YASIR ARAFAT's policies led him to form the Fatah Revolutionary Council (FRC) in 1974. A PALESTINE LIBERATION ORGANIZATION tribunal has imposed a death sentence on Nidal in absentia. Nidal's operatives have assassinated various PLO representatives in Paris, London, and other cities. Groups under Nidal's direction have included Black June (used against Jordanian targets) and the Revolutionary Organization of Socialist Muslims (used against British targets). The U.S. State Department now puts these groups under the umbrella classification of the Abu Nidal Organization (ANO). This organization has conducted terrorist activities in at least 20 nations. Among the more than 90 attacks of which it is accused are the Rome Airport and the Vienna Airport murders in 1985. The 1986 ISTANBUL SYNAGOGUE MASSACRE is widely thought to have been an ANO operation. In 1988 Nidal operatives were responsible for the attack on the Greek cruise ship CITY OF POROS. Syria, Iraq, Libya, and Saudi Arabia have supported the Nidal organization both financially and logistically.

abuse of right   The INTERNATIONAL LAW precept that one party should not exercise a right to do something if in so doing it violates the rights of other parties.

Abwehr   The military intelligence service of NAZI Germany's Armed Forces High Command prior to and during World War II. It was responsible for espionage, counterespionage, and sabotage. Its leader, Admiral Wilhelm Canaris (1887–1945), seemed to HEINRICH HIMMLER of the SS insufficiently committed to the Nazi cause, so his organization was taken over by the SD (the Nazi party's intelligence service). After the July 1944 plot to kill ADOLF HITLER failed, Canaris was arrested. After a Nazi trial he was hanged for treachery in April 1945.

Abyssinian-Italian War   The 1935–1936 military conquest of Ethiopia (then known as Abyssinia) by Fascist Italy. This was part of Italy's grand scheme for a neo-Roman Empire around the Mediterranean. Great Britain and France had not objected to Italian intimidations of Ethiopia in early 1935 and even recognized a privileged economic position for Italy in Ethiopia's civil service. Though Italian dictator Benito Mussolini could have gotten all he wanted by patient diplomacy (Great Britain and France were in their appeasing period), he followed a major doctrine of FASCISM, the desirability of war, and invaded Ethiopia in October 1935. In a poignant plea for help to the LEAGUE OF NATIONS in 1936, Ethiopian Emperor HAILE SELASSIE showed that the League was incapable of coping even with small wars. Besides, the British, who allowed the Italians to send all their troops and equipment through the Suez Canal, did not want to annoy the Italians too much. They were more concerned that Italy, an ally in World War I against Germany, might be needed again as an ally against Germany. The Ethiopians put up a spirited defense but modern weapons, especially air power and poison gas, routed their forces by the spring of the following year. In 1941, as part of their defeat in World War II, the Italians lost Ethiopia to the British Army, which returned control to Haile Selassie, the previous ruler.

acceptable casualties   1. The number of dead and wounded that one side in a military conflict is willing to endure before deciding to withdraw and accept a defeat. **2.** In STRATEGIC PLANNING, the number (in the tens of millions) of civilian deaths one side might be willing to accept to "win" a nuclear war. In this context, this is a highly abstract concept and one that had little relevance beyond the esoteric process of strategic planning. There is little evidence that it intruded into real decision making. Indeed, during the Cold War the governments of the United States and the Soviet Union made great efforts to ensure that they did not get into war. In this sense, the level of acceptable casualties was very low—whatever the strategic planners might argue.

acceptance   1. ACCESSION. **2.** RATIFICATION of a treaty. Treaties are often accepted rather than ratified so that some states can avoid the formal ratification processes required by their constitutions. **3.** Broadly, any agreement to purchase goods at a stated price and under specified terms.

accession   1. Taking possession of a right, title, or office. Historically this most commonly refers to the rise of a new monarch to the throne. **2.** The ACCEPTANCE of the terms of a multilateral agreement by a party who was not an original signer. An Act of Accession passed by an acceding state normally contains the full text of the agreement or treaty and a statement that it is unreservedly acceded to. The

government(s) or international organization in charge of the treaty accepts the accession (assuming that the treaty has a clause providing for subsequent accessions) on behalf of all signatories and then formally notifies all other signatories. The terms *accession* and *adhesion* are often used interchangeably to describe this process. But adhesion is the more limiting word; it implies that the party desires to become a signatory of only certain articles of a treaty or convention. This is not possible when the original document is declared to be "whole, one, and indivisible." **3.** Admission to an international organization.

**Accession, Treaties of   **The formal documents by which new states have joined the European Community. For example, by the Treaty of Accession (sometimes known as the Brussels Treaty) signed in Brussels in 1972, Denmark, the Irish Republic, and the United Kingdom joined the EC.

**accidental war   ***See* WAR, ACCIDENTAL.

**accommodation   **A tactic in foreign affairs designed to lessen tensions in a crisis by allowing other parties to a negotiation or a dispute the room to maneuver into face-saving positions. The essence of accommodation is to give someone a way out—not to back an opponent into a diplomatic, political, or military corner. Glenn Snyder and Paul Diesing in *Conflict Among Nations* (1977) argue that in crises, policymakers not only have to decide on the appropriate mix between COERCION and accommodation but must also try to ensure that they accommodate cheaply and keep concessions to a minimum. *Compare to* APPEASEMENT; *see also* CRISIS MANAGEMENT.

accord   1. An informal diplomatic agreement achieved through specific negotiations or established custom. **2.** An international agreement that is for all practical purposes a TREATY, except that it is not politic to call it one. **3.** An agreement reached by two previously conflicting parties (such as labor and management). **4.** An agreement by one side to pay, and another side to accept, less than full payment of a debt or obligation. **5.** Sometimes used as a synonym for the idea of broad agreement or consensus, for example, in a statement that "states are *in accord* about a particular issue."

accreditation   **1.** The formal process by which an individual is invested with rights as a diplomatic representative. Heads of state typically sign a LET-TRES DE CRÉANCE, which is personally presented by an AMBASSADOR to the head of the receiving state. Although the action of accreditation is a diplomatic formality, the process does mean that an ambassador's credentials as the representative of his or her government are accepted by the receiving state. Lower-ranking diplomats usually present their letters merely to a foreign minister.   **2.** The actual letter of credence itself.

accretion   **1.** Any gradual accumulation.   **2.** The concept of international law that a state automatically acquires rights to new land created by the gradual deposits of soil by a river or ocean that extends a riverbank or a seacoast. *Compare to* AVULSION.

acculturation   The process by which an individual or, more significantly, a group learns about and is assimilated into a new culture. Traditionally the means by which an immigrant group adapts to a new social environment. In the context of the Third World, acculturation refers to the installation of Western cultural values during colonialism and the continuing cultural imperialism of today. *See also* IMPERIALISM, CULTURAL.

ACE   *See* ALLIED COMMAND EUROPE.

Acheson, Dean Gooderham (1893–1971)   U.S. secretary of state (1949–1953) under President Harry S Truman. Acheson was one of the creators of the policy of CONTAINMENT of Soviet expansion. He was a major influence on the development of the MARSHALL PLAN, the NORTH ATLANTIC TREATY ORGANIZATION, and the subsequent commitment of American troops to Western Europe. According to James Chace and Caleb Carr in *America Invulnerable* (1988): "It was Acheson who was primarily the author of the doctrine that would bear Truman's name, filling much the same role that John Quincy Adams had played for James Monroe in 1823—and producing the most important American foreign policy declaration since

Dean Acheson (Library of Congress)

that same Monroe Doctrine." Ironically, although Acheson was extremely anti-Soviet and played a major role in transforming containment from a political to a military policy, he was subject to intense criticism from conservative Republicans for being soft on communism. In part, this was because Acheson was secretary of state when the Chinese Communists defeated Chiang Kai-shek and his KUOMINTANG forces, which had been supported by the United States. Acheson contended that nothing that the United States did or could have done, within reasonable limits, could have changed the end result. Nevertheless, he was blamed for the "loss of China" to the Communists (even though China was never America's to lose). In a period of intense partisanship, Acheson not only was severely criticized but was castigated as a traitor by Republican partisans such as Senators Joseph McCarthy and Richard M. Nixon. The attacks intensified with the outbreak of the Korean War in June 1950. In January of that year, in a speech to the National Press Club, Acheson had excluded Korea from the American "defense perimeter"—a statement that, his critics subsequently argued, had given the green light for North Korea to invade the South. Ironically it was this invasion that allowed Acheson to implement his conception of *military* containment in Europe and Asia—as opposed to GEORGE F. KENNAN's idea of *political* containment. Acheson was one of the key figures in shaping the postwar world. That he saw his own role in this way was evident in the title of his 1969 memoirs, *Present at the Creation.*

ACHESON STUDIES NUCLEAR PHYSICS

When later I achieved a wholly undeserved reputation for expertise in nuclear matters, no one knew better than Robert Oppenheimer how fraudulent this was. At the beginning of our work he came to stay with us and after dinner each evening would lecture [John J.] McCloy and me with the aid of a borrowed blackboard on which he drew little figures representing electrons, neutrons, and protons, bombarding one another, chasing one another about, dividing and generally carrying on in unpredictable ways. Our bewildered questions seemed to distress him. At last he put down the chalk with gentle despair, saying "It's hopeless! I really think you two believe neutrons and electrons are little men!" We admitted nothing.

SOURCE: Dean Acheson, *Present at the Creation* (1969).

Acheson-Lilienthal Plan   The proposal made in 1946 by Dean Acheson (as U.S. undersecretary of state) and David Lilienthal (as head of the U.S. Atomic Energy Commission) for the international control of nuclear materials and means of production. Just as with the BARUCH PLAN, which it followed, it came to nothing because of Soviet intransigence.

Acheson's Rule   The precept that a memorandum is written not so much to inform the reader as it is to protect the writer. U.S. Secretary of State Dean Acheson wrote in his memoirs, *Present at the Creation* (1969): "I have never yet read a memorandum of conversation in which the writer came off second best."

Achille Lauro   The Italian cruise liner hijacked in the Mediterranean by four members of the PALES-TINE LIBERATION FRONT on October 7, 1985. During the crime, an elderly wheelchair-bound Jewish-American, Leon Klinghoffer, was murdered and his body thrown overboard. Italian authorities successfully requested that Syria, Cyprus, and Tunisia deny port to the hijacked vessel and arranged with the Egyptian government to facilitate the release of the ship in exchange for the hijackers' freedom. The U.S. government, dissatisfied with Egypt's refusal to hold the hijackers and aware that ABU ABBAS (the leader of the PLF) was to accompany them on their bartered flight to freedom, staged a midair interception of the Egyptian airliner carrying the terrorists. U.S. fighter planes forced the jet to land at a North Atlantic Treaty Organization airfield at Signolla, Sicily. A potentially explosive situation ensued there as the U.S. DELTA FORCE, under orders to capture the terrorists, faced off against Italian carabinieri, who knew nothing of the Americans' instructions. This standoff was defused only upon direct orders from the White House, and the five PLF members entered Italian custody. An Italian magistrate released Abbas because of insufficient evidence, despite American pleas for his extradition. Abbas fled the country using an Iraqi diplomatic passport. An Italian court later convicted him, in absentia, of being the mastermind of the hijacking. The four other hijackers were sentenced to long terms in Italian prisons.

acid rain   Contaminated rainfall (or any precipitation) caused by industrial pollution. The sources of these contaminants are as varied as coal-burning electric power plants, metal smelters, and automobile emissions. Because of its acidity, such rain adversely affects inland aquatic life and forests. Since the pollutants that cause acid rain come from one place and the rain itself falls on another, this has become an important interregional and international environmental issue. A case in point is the damage to the lakes and forests of upstate New York by acid rain from the industrial Midwest. Acid rain has been an especially contentious issue between the United States and Canada. Canadians contend that their lakes and forests are increasingly damaged by acid rain of U.S. origin. But the problem of acid rain is not limited to North America. It also is a major problem in Europe (where it is decomposing ancient statues and monuments) and the Third World. This will undoubtedly be the leading transboundary pollution issue addressed by the United Nations in the 1990s. *See also* EARTH SUMMIT.

ACP countries **1.** The developing countries of Africa, the Caribbean, and the Pacific that cooperate in trade with the European Economic Community under the LOMÉ CONVENTIONS. Most of these states were former colonies of Belgium, France, Great Britain, and Portugal. **2.** Atom-controlling powers; a 1950s term for those countries that had "the bomb."

Acquired Immune Deficiency Syndrome *See* AIDS.

acte authentique French term for a notarized or authenticated, usually diplomatic, document.

acte final French term for a formal summary of proceedings of an international conference.

Action Directe (AD) "Direct Action," a French Marxist terrorist group formed in 1979 to combat "international imperialism and capitalism." AD has a history of bombings, arson, robberies, and assassinations against French, U.S., Israeli, and North Atlantic Treaty Organization targets. It is believed to have evolved from French radical groups of the 1970s, including the *Groups d'action revolutionnaire internationaliste* (Revolutionary International Action Group), or GARI, and the *Noyaux armés pour l'autonomie populaire* (Armed Nuclei for Popular Autonomy), or NAPAP. These groups occasionally resorted to terrorist tactics but never demonstrated the organizational sophistication and operational capability displayed by the AD. In March 1980 AD bombed and destroyed the Toulouse police station and in May of that year injured eight in a bombing at Orly Airport. Bombings against banks, businesses, and other targets identified with capitalist interests dominated AD terrorism until 1985. In that year AD claimed joint responsibility with the RED ARMY FACTION for the bombing of Rhein-Main Air Force Base in Germany in which two American servicemen were killed. The two groups, possibly with others, then formed an ANTI-IMPERIALIST ARMED FRONT to combat the "Americanization of Europe." In 1986 the group

assassinated Georges Besse, chairman of the Renault automobile company. AD financed its operations primarily through bank robberies. By 1989 all of the organization's major leaders had been arrested and sentenced to life imprisonment.

Action Française **1.** A French far right, monarchist, anti-Semitic, Catholic political movement founded in 1899 by Charles Maurias (1868–1952). Because of its collaboration with the occupying Nazis during World War II, it was outlawed by the French government after the war. Maurias was sentenced to life imprisonment, pardoned for medical reasons in 1952, and died later that year. **2.** The title of the periodical publication of the *Action Française* political movement. It ceased publication in 1944 in a general ban on all periodicals that had supported the German occupation. However, in 1992 the far right monarchist weekly *Aspects de la France,* published since 1947, changed its name to *L'Action Française.*

Action Front for National Socialists (*Aktionsfront Nationaler Sozialisten*) German NEO-NAZI organization that is a violent offshoot of the right-wing National Democratic Party. The Action Front was formed during the 1970s and was responsible for some of the West German right-wing extremist violence of the 1980s, much of which was racially motivated vandalism against immigrants, Jews, and leftists.

action-reaction **1.** An explanation of how states behave during an international CRISIS. Because each state responds to the actions of others with preplanned moves, the military and diplomatic actions that are taken do not necessarily reflect long-term policy goals or actual motivation. The term originated in Isaac Newton's (1642–1727) third law of motion, which states that "For every action there is an equal and opposite reaction." The classic example of the political action-reaction phenomenon is the beginning of World War I. The response of the two main European alliances to the assassination of Archduke FRANZ FERDINAND of Austria in 1914 was a continuing action-reaction, or what is called a chain reaction: mobilization by Russia caused mobilization by Germany, which in turn led to mobilization by France and Great Britain. Because of the increasingly inflexible nature of the alliances, participants reacted largely in an automatic way rather than making deliberate decisions. **2.** The deployment of a new weapons system by one side, which leads to the development of an equivalent or superior system by the other side in an ARMS RACE. According to Robert S. McNamara, writing in a *Department of State Bulletin* (October 9, 1967), "The Soviet Union and the United States mutually influence one another's strategic plans. Whatever their intentions or our intentions, actions . . . on either side relating to the build-up of nuclear forces necessarily trigger reactions on the other side. It is precisely this action-reaction phenomenon that fuels an arms race." But Edward N. Luttwak, in *Strategy* (1987), warns that while the action-reaction sequence is familiar, "slightly less obvious is the relationship (inevitably paradoxical) between the very success of new devices and the likelihood of their eventual failure [since] any sensible enemy will focus his most urgent efforts on countermeasures meant to neutralize whatever opposing device seems most dangerous at the time." In fact, the reactions can take the form of similar or imitative moves or can be designed to counter or offset the capabilities of the adversary. An offense-defense race involves the latter kind of reactions. The action-reaction phenomenon is sometimes further complicated by efforts at preemptive reactions; for example, one side believes that the other is about to initiate a certain action and responds in ways designed to offset this, even though it has not yet taken place. **3.** A series of moves and counter-moves by the Soviet Union and the United States during the COLD WAR, as each side sought an advantage over the other.

active legation *See* LEGATION, RIGHT OF.

active measures **1.** Covert actions by one state designed to influence the policies of other states. Active measures are distinct from traditional DIPLOMACY and ESPIONAGE because they include the use of false FRONT organizations abroad, dissemination of rumors (DISINFORMATION), forgery of documents, manipulation of the press, and personal and economic blackmail. The KGB had primary responsibility for developing and implementing the Soviet Union's active measures during the COLD WAR.

Its active measures directed against the United States included campaigns "sponsored" by local Communist parties to have U.S. military bases removed in Greece and Spain. Of course, the CENTRAL INTELLIGENCE AGENCY of the United States had parallel responsibilities; it, for example, encouraged and helped to fund the 1980s prodemocracy, anti-Soviet movements in Eastern Europe that eventually forced the Soviets to withdraw their forces and grant freedom to these onetime SATELLITES. **2.** Active defense measures such as ABM systems, as opposed to passive defenses such as civilian bomb shelters. Traditionally, defensive measures against enemy attacks are twofold: passive measures, which seek to minimize the damage created by an attack on both military and civilian elements; and active measures, such as defensive systems or stratagems designed as a military response to an enemy attack.

act of state Actions by a government for which its citizens cannot be held accountable, such as declaring war or passing laws that only a state has the legal right to enact.

act of state doctrine The judicial policy that a court in one state should not issue decisions on the legality of the internal acts of another state.

act of war An action that is regarded by others as the equivalent of a declaration of hostilities or as indicating that a state of hostilities already exists. States often seek to perform hostile acts that are legally short of an act of war. For example, during the CUBAN MISSILE CRISIS in 1962 the United States imposed a naval "quarantine" rather than a blockade of Cuba because a blockade would have been widely regarded as an act of war.

actor A player in the "game" of international or domestic politics. Actors can be individuals who play their roles as presidents or prime ministers, or states (which, according to the school of REALISM, are the most important actors). But they also can be international organizations such as the United Nations or nongovernmental organizations such as privately controlled multinational corporations. While *actor* is a term that is inherently vague, it is extremely useful to international affairs analysts and practitioners because it furthers a dispassionate systems view of events and avoids the word *state*, which is too limiting. At the same time, it cannot obscure the fact that a certain amount of the debate about international politics centers around differences over precisely who should be regarded as the primary actors.

adaptation Those activities whereby an ACTOR responds to a changing environment. Sometimes seen as a key element in foreign policy, it is a concept that has been developed most fully by JAMES ROSENAU in *The Study of Political Adaptation* (1981).

ADB *See* ASIAN DEVELOPMENT BANK.

Addams, Jane (1860–1935) The American social worker who shared the 1931 Nobel Peace Prize (with NICHOLAS MURRAY BUTLER) for her work as a founder and first president (1919–1929) of the Women's International League for Peace and Freedom.

Adee, Alvery Augustus (1824–1924) A U.S. assistant secretary of state from 1882 to 1924 who often functioned as acting secretary of state and provided bureaucratic continuity through various presidential administrations. In the 1880s he brought the first typewriters into American diplomatic service.

Adenauer, Konrad (1876–1967) The chancellor of West Germany from 1949 to 1963. He had been the chief burgomaster (mayor) of Cologne (1917–1933) who was dismissed by the Nazis. In the postwar period he guided West Germany to economic recovery and political independence after the devastation of World War II. Known as "der Alte" because of his age and longevity in office, Adenauer and the Christian Democrats were firm anti-Communists who used COLD WAR tensions to get the Western allies to treat West Germany as a partner rather than as a conquered foe. He described West Germany as "the rare case where the conquered is very satisfied with the conqueror" (*New York Times,* March 21, 1960). Under Adenauer's leadership West Germany joined the North Atlantic Treaty Organization in 1955 and became a charter member of the European Community in 1957. He was a strong advo-cate of European unity. During the late 1950s and early 1960s, Adenauer and France's CHARLES DE GAULLE were Western Europe's leading statesmen. In foreign relations, Adenauer's government followed the HALLSTEIN DOCTRINE, refusing to have diplomatic relations with any nation (except the Soviet Union) that recognized East Germany. This reflects the fact that although Adenauer gave priority to restoring the legitimacy of the Federal Republic within the West, he never abandoned the objective of GERMAN REUNIFICATION. He did not retire until 1963, at the age of 87. His retirement came only after a scandal caused by his defense minister, who improperly arrested the editors of the news magazine *Der Spiegel* for revealing NATO military maneuvers. LUDWIG ERHARD followed Adenauer as chancellor.

adhesion *See* ACCESSION.

adjudication 1. An attempt to ensure the peaceful settlement of disputes through the application of international law in such a body as the World Court. 2. A loose term that refers to myriad forms of third-party settlement, including ARBITRATION. The difficulty with all such approaches to peaceful settlement is that they require the consent of the states involved. More often than not such consent is not forthcoming, and compulsory adjudication is not a characteristic of a state system that continues to be based predominantly on self-help.

adjustment assistance Financial and technical help for workers, firms, and communities to help them adapt to competition from imported products. Workers adversely affected by imports are eligible for special unemployment compensation, retraining to develop new skills, and job search and relocation assistance; affected firms can receive technical assistance and loan guarantees to finance modernizations or shifts to other product lines. Communities threatened by increasing imports can receive loans and other assistance to attract new factories or to enable existing ones to move into more competitive fields. Adjustment assistance programs began in the United States with the Trade Expansion Act of 1962. Since then other states such as Canada, Japan, Norway, Sweden, and the United Kingdom have adopted similar programs.

administered territories   The former colonial possessions of Germany and Turkey, which were placed under the MANDATES SYSTEM of the League of Nations established in Article 22 of its Covenant. Particular states were given the mandate for these territories and controlled and administered them on behalf of the League of Nations, even though they did not have SOVEREIGNTY over them. The assumption was that these territories would progress to self-government. The most famous and troubled mandate system was the British mandate over Palestine. Another troublesome area was South-West Africa, which was given to South Africa to control. At the end of World War II those mandates that were not yet independent were placed under the UN TRUSTEESHIP system. South Africa refused to place South-West Africa under this system, and it took a protracted struggle before Namibia finally became independent. *See also* NAMIBIAN INDEPENDENCE.

admiral   A high-ranking, or flag, officer of a navy; comparable to a general in an army. It was Voltaire in his 1759 novel *Candide* who first observed that "an admiral has to be put to death now and then to encourage the others." (Of course, he was referring to the presumed policy of the British Royal Navy.)

admiralty   1. Maritime law; the general laws of the sea. Article III, Section 2, of the U.S. Constitution provides that the federal courts will have exclusive jurisdiction in all cases of admiralty law. However, many other countries operate independent admiralty courts.   2. A court that handles maritime cases, such as collisions at sea.   3. The naval agency in the United Kingdom roughly parallel to the U.S. Department of the Navy.   4. The specific office or jurisdiction of an admiral.

admission   In the context of international relations, the process whereby a state becomes a member of an international organization. In the case of the UNITED NATIONS, admission requires the approval of the General Assembly upon receipt of a recommendation from the Security Council. The latest wave of admissions in the early 1990s occurred when the former states of the Soviet Union and Yugoslavia were admitted to the United Nations after an increasing number of states had recognized their independence. In the aftermath of the breakdown and demise of the Soviet Union, new states also have been admitted to the Conference on Security and Cooperation in Europe, and some of those in Eastern Europe have made clear that they would like to join the North Atlantic Treaty Organization and the European Community. Joining these two organizations, however, is likely to be a much slower process. EC members are divided between those who believe that the EC should be widened by the admission of new members and those who believe that new members should not be admitted until after existing members deepen their levels of cooperation and integration.

adoption   Agreement on the exact wording of a proposed treaty by the parties to it. This does not always mean that a state urging the adoption of a proposed treaty will subsequently allow itself to be bound by it. Indeed, an executive branch of a government often adopts treaties that are not subsequently ratified by its legislative branch. According to Article 9, Section 2, of the Vienna Convention on the Law of Treaties of 1969, "The adoption of the text of a treaty at an international conference takes place by the vote of two-thirds of the states present and voting, unless by the same majority they shall decide to apply a different rule." *Compare to* ACCEPTANCE; ACCESSION.

adoption, doctrine of   1. The policy that INTERNATIONAL LAW cannot become part of a state's statutory or common law without specific legislation by that state. This means that international law cannot be binding on a state unless it formally agrees to be bound. This is also known as the doctrine of *transformation*.   2. The doctrine of *incorporation*, whereby international law becomes part of municipal law unless there is conflicting national legislation. This is generally accepted under English and American law. Note that the term *doctrine of adoption* has two meanings that are directly opposed.

ad referendum   1. Being subject to subsequent confirmation. Diplomats accept a proposal or sign a treaty ad referendum when it is understood that such approval is conditional because it needs to be further approved by their governments. The Vienna Convention on the Law of Treaties of 1969 recognizes in Article 12, Section 2(b), that "The signature ad referendum of a treaty by a representative, if confirmed by his State, constitutes a full signature of the treaty." **2.** A diplomat's review of an issue not covered by existing instructions from his or her government. The matter is then "considered" by seeking instructions that deal with the new issue.

ad valorem duty   *See* DUTY, AD VALOREM.

advance against documents   A loan made on the security of the documents covering a shipment.

adventurism   State actions that are provocative or dangerous, that are liable to precipitate either a major confrontation or the outbreak of conflict. The term often is used in conjunction with the idea of expansionism and generally carries with it the notion of high-risk behavior. The word comes from the Russian *avantyurizm*. During the Cold War it was often used by the Soviet Union both to describe and denounce U.S. foreign policies and actions. Ironically, it was sometimes used by the Chinese to refer to such Soviet actions as the installation of missiles in Cuba in 1962. According to Soviet analyst Marshall D. Shulman: "The Soviets hope that the world will view their withdrawal [from Afghanistan] as a sign that they've turned away from adventurism, that they mean it when they say that force no longer drives their foreign policy" (*New York Times,* February 5, 1989).

advising bank   Any bank operating in an exporter's country that handles letters of credit for a foreign bank by notifying the exporter that the credit has been opened in his or her favor. The advising bank fully informs the exporter of the conditions of the letter of credit without necessarily bearing responsibility for payment.

advisors   **1.** Military units, or civilian or military experts, from one state sent to "advise" the military forces of another. While the tasks of such advisors are often limited to training missions, they sometimes become more like "lead workers" and demonstrate to their "students" how to operate against insurgents or other enemies. Since the U.S. experience in Vietnam in the 1960s, there has been great concern that sending advisors into a conflict can lead all too easily to deeper involvement.   **2.** A

euphemism for military forces of one country that openly intervene in the affairs of another country. **3.** Technical experts. The classic statement on the advice of experts is contained in a letter the British Secretary of India Lord Salisbury wrote on June 15, 1877, to Lord Lytton, Viceroy of India: "No lesson seems to be so deeply inculcated by the experience of life as that you never should trust in experts. If you believe the doctors nothing is wholesome; if you believe the theologians nothing is innocent; if you believe the soldiers nothing is safe. They all require to have their strong wine diluted by a very large admixture of insipid common sense."

advisory opinion   A statement by a judge or court about a question that has been informally submitted. The International Court of Justice (the World Court) is empowered to issue advisory opinions. Article 96 of the United Nations Charter states that any organ of the UN may ask the World Court for an advisory opinion on a dispute. While the World Court is so authorized, it has no obligation to issue advisory opinions. And should the same case come before the World Court for actual settlement, a previous advisory opinion is not binding on it. Commissions of CONCILIATION also commonly issue advisory opinions on international disputes.

Aegean dispute   The long-standing opposing positions of Greece and Turkey on the status of the territorial waters of the Aegean Sea. The dispute concerns oil-drilling and navigation rights, air traffic control, and North Atlantic Treaty Organization command and control arrangements in the area. Greece has proposed that the issues be submitted to the International Court of Justice. Turkey has called for bilateral talks. Settlement has been complicated by the harsh feelings over the CYPRUS CONFLICT.

Afghanistan intervention   The invasion of Afghanistan by the Soviet Union. When the Democratic Republic of Afghanistan, a Marxist regime, was unable to deal with an insurgency and the Afghan Army began to collapse, the Soviet Union intervened. On the night of December 24, 1979, large numbers of Soviet airborne forces began to land in the capital of Kabul. This was the BREZHNEV DOCTRINE in action; the Soviets were intervening to protect a socialist state from its enemies. The Western and particularly the American interpretation of the intervention was that it marked the culmination of a major and very successful geopolitical offensive by the Soviet Union in the Third World during the 1970s, and that it was a move to control Western oil supplies coming from the Persian Gulf. In fact, it seems to have been prompted by the Soviet inability to control HAFIJULLAH AMIN, the Afghan leader who was supposedly a Soviet puppet, and by concerns that the unrest in Afghanistan could be exploited by hostile powers. This paranoia was combined with unrealistic expectations of the prospects for a successful intervention. In any event Soviet troop strength in Afghanistan grew to over 120,000. But the Soviets and the puppet regime they maintained were unable to make good the Soviet conquest. Afghan freedom fighters, or MUJAHEDIN, with supplies from the United States, waged a successful war of ATTRITION and forced the Soviets to begin a military withdrawal in May 1988, which was completed in February 1989. The war, often referred to as the Soviet Union's Vietnam, cost over a million Afghan and some 15,000 Soviet lives. In initial response to the invasion, U.S. President Jimmy Carter canceled U.S. participation in the 1980 Moscow Olympics and embargoed shipments of American wheat to the Soviet Union. He also withdrew the SALT II agreement from consideration by the U.S. Senate. In addition to providing humanitarian aid to Afghan refugees in Pakistan, the United States gave extensive clandestine military assistance to the Afghan resistance. This included hundreds of Tennessee mules for mountain transport and Stinger antiaircraft missiles. The portable Stingers, small enough to be carried and used by a single fighter, transformed the military situation by allowing the Afghan guerrillas to shoot down hundreds of Soviet aircraft. This is one of the few instances in which a small tactical weapon had strategic significance. On January 27, 1989, the *New York Times* quoted an anonymous aide to the Soviet Union's Communist Party's Central Committee who offered this analysis: "It's a defeat, no question about it. We had your experience in Vietnam right before our eyes, and we still went in like fools."

Afghanistan–USSR Friendship Treaty of 1978 The Treaty of Friendship, Good-Neighborliness and Cooperation between the Union of Soviet Socialist Republics and the Democratic Republic of Afghanistan in which the "high contracting parties solemnly declare their determination to consolidate and deepen the unshakable friendship between the two countries and to develop cooperation in all fields on the basis of equality of rights, respect for national sovereignty and territorial integrity, and non-interference in each other's internal affairs." This treaty became effective on January 7, 1979. Later that year the Soviets invaded Afghanistan.

African Crisis **1.** The drought and associated famine beginning in the 1970s that affected those states on the southern rim of the Sahara. **2.** The food shortages in more than half of the states of Africa beginning in the 1980s caused by civil wars, poor weather, and ineffectual government policies that brought death to hundreds of thousands and led to large-scale relief efforts by the West. **3.** The inability of many African states to pay their international debts, caused in part by a decline in commodity prices, an unmanageable debt service (interest and principal) burden, and a consequent decline in capital infusion.

African Development Bank (AFDB) A regional bank formed in 1963 by 33 independent African countries headquartered in Abidjan, Ivory Coast. In 1973 non-African countries joined with AFDB to establish the African Development Fund (AFDF), the concessional lending affiliate of AFDB, which loans only to the poorest African countries. Membership in the bank was limited to African nations (except South Africa) until late 1982, when 24 non-regional countries began to join.

African Group The United Nations caucus of African states (excluding South Africa) that often presents a united front on issues of African interest. Its 50 votes make up the largest single UN voting bloc.

African horn *See* HORN OF AFRICA.

Africanization **1.** The postcolonial-era process of replacing European experts and bureaucrats with African nationals. This includes efforts by local businesses as well as multinational corporations to bring Africans to the forefront of management and

THE SOVIET INVASION OF AFGHANISTAN: A Chronology

1978	April	Soviet-backed coup installs hard-line Communist regime.
	December	Soviet Union and Afghanistan sign Friendship Treaty.
1979	February	U.S. Ambassador to Afghanistan, Adolph Dubs, is kidnapped and murdered.
	March	Anti-Communist guerrillas kill a dozen Soviet "advisors."
	December	Over 100,000 Soviet troops invade by land and air.
1980	January	U.S. President Jimmy Carter announces sanctions that include a U.S. grain embargo.
	February	Anti-Soviet demonstrators in Kabul crushed. *Mujahedin* resistance grows stronger.
	April	While Soviet troops control the cities, *mujahedin* guerrillas control the countryside.
	July	The United States and more than 50 other states boycott the Moscow Olympic Games in protest.
1981	April	U.S. President Ronald Reagan lifts grain embargo.
	December	Over 2 million Afghan refugees in Pakistan.
1984	November	U.S. aid to guerrillas estimated at $260 million per year.
1985	May	Seven guerrilla groups form united front.
1986	February	Gorbachev tells 27th Soviet Party Congress that withdrawal will begin shortly.
	July	Gorbachev announces that six regiments will return home by end of the year.
	September	United States provides guerrillas with Stinger antiaircraft missiles.
1987	January	Moscow calls for a cease-fire to be followed by a withdrawal.
1988	January	Soviet Foreign Minister Eduard Shevardnadze says withdrawal should be complete by end of year.
	April	It is estimated that U.S. aid to guerrillas totals more than $2 billion. Accord on Soviet withdrawal is signed in Geneva by Afghanistan, Pakistan, the Soviet Union, and the United States; it calls for a neutral, nonaligned Afghanistan.
1989	February	Last Soviet troops leave after suffering 15,000 dead during the campaign. Kabul regime, having assisted in the killing of a million of its citizens, continues to fight on against a mosaic of guerrilla groups.
1992	April	Kabul regime falls as guerrillas occupy capital.

ownership.   **2.** A euphemism for the EXPROPRIA-TION of foreign assets in Africa.

African National Congress (ANC)   The dominant black opposition group in South Africa. It was founded initially in 1912 to protect the rights of the black population following the transfer of political authority from Britain to the newly created Union of South Africa. In response to an unyielding policy of APARTHEID (the rigid legal separation of the races), the ANC adopted a more radical program of boycotts, strikes, and civil disobedience. The South African Government banned the ANC following a protest demonstration in 1960 that ended in the massacre known as the SHARPEVILLE INCIDENT. Then the group began a period of operating as an underground guerrilla organization, surviving on subsidies from other African states, the ORGANIZATION OF AFRICAN UNITY (OAU), and the Soviet Union.

The ANC was dedicated to passive and nonviolent resistance for much of its history. Chief Albert Luthuli, a longtime ANC leader, was even awarded the Nobel Peace Prize in 1960. After the Sharpeville Incident, the ANC moved toward industrial sabotage and guerrilla attacks. The U.S. Department of Defense even included the ANC in its 1988 listing of world terrorist groups. This inclusion prompted heated reaction from the group's supporters, as well as from the U.S. Department of State, which does not classify the ANC as a terrorist organization. NELSON MANDELA, in prison from 1962 to 1990, is the ANC president and the most enduring and internationally recognized symbol of the anti-apartheid movement. The South African government released Mandela from prison in 1990, made the ANC a legal opposition party, and initiated negotiations to end apartheid. While talks continued with the South African government, supporters of the ANC and its principal black political rival organization, the Zulu-based INKATHA FREEDOM PARTY, were involved with many instances of deadly COMMUNAL CONFLICT during 1991 and 1992.

THE AFRICAN NATIONAL CONGRESS
A Chronology

1912 South African Native National Congress (SANNC) founded.

1923 SANNC renamed African National Congress (ANC).

1944 Nelson Mandela becomes secretary of ANC Youth League.

1949 ANC adopts a policy of noncooperation with government.

1960 ANC calls for a general strike in response to Sharpeville Incident; is banned by government.

1961 ANC President Albert J. Luthuli awarded Nobel Peace Prize; Nelson Mandela leads campaign of sabotage.

1964 Nelson Mandela sentenced to life in prison.

1987 Oliver Tambo, representing an outlawed ANC, meets with U.S. Secretary of State George Shultz in Washington.

1990 Thirty-year prohibition on ANC lifted. Mandela released from prison. ANC starts talks with government on future of South Africa.

1992 In a national referendum, the white minority votes to draft a new constitution that would share power with the black majority.

African socialism   A localized form of socialism derived from tribal customs and traditions, as opposed to the European-derived socialism based on CLASS STRUGGLE as espoused in the works of Karl Marx (1818–1883). African socialism thus sees the nation as an extension of the tribe. The problem with this is that many African states are amalgams of conflicting tribes that have had great difficulties working in harmony with one another.

Afrikaans   The language of the Dutch settlers of South Africa, known as the Boers. Since 1915 this has been the official language of the Union of South Africa.

Afrika Korps   The WORLD WAR II German military forces fighting the British and Americans in North Africa from 1941 to 1943. They were led by General ERWIN ROMMEL (the "Desert Fox"). The Korps could have made a major difference in the outcome of the war had it been able to capture Egypt and, more important, the Suez Canal, but it was soundly rebuffed by the British in 1942 at EL ALAMEIN and fought a retreat until the 150,000 left alive were forced to surrender to the Allies in May 1943. Only Rommel and some of his staff escaped.

Afrikaners   The Afrikaans word for white citizens of the Union of South Africa, especially those of Boer descent.

Afro-Asian   A term indicating unity between the THIRD WORLD states of Africa and Asia. Many international organizations, such as the Afro-Asian Peoples' Solidarity Organization (headquartered in Cairo), are Afro-Asian in name and character.

Agadir crisis   A crisis that occurred in 1911 and can be understood as the result of imperial rivalry between Germany and France over Morocco. It was precipitated by the deployment of a German gunboat, the *Panther,* in the Moroccan port of Agadir in response to French intervention that centered around Fez. Although the crisis was resolved without war, it confirmed British fears about German ambitions and encouraged Great Britain and France to diplomatically move closer to each other. It was both a warning of the dangers of war in Europe and part of what is sometimes termed a

CRISIS SLIDE as the European powers moved toward war in 1914.

Agca, Mehmet Ali (1956–   ) The would-be assassin of Pope JOHN PAUL II. Using a pistol, he wounded the pope in St. Peter's Square, Rome, on May 13, 1981. He had been convicted in the 1979 murder of a Turkish newspaper editor but had escaped from a Turkish prison. Arrested immediately after his attempt on the pope, he sought to implicate the Bulgarian Secret Service and the KGB in a plot to kill the pope. He was sentenced to life in prison by an Italian court after a trial in which he maintained that he was Jesus. This claim undermined the credibility of his accusations against the Bulgarians and the Soviets. Although Italian courts acquitted the Bulgarians named by Agca as coconspirators due to a lack of substantive evidence, the presiding magistrates proclaimed: "We have evidence that this man, Agca, did not act alone."

agency 1. Any formally established unit of a government. 2. A legal relationship whereby one person is authorized to act for another. 3. In intelligence usage, an organization engaged in collecting and/or processing information. 4. A slang term for the U.S. Central Intelligence Agency.

Agency for International Development (AID) The primary U.S. government agency for THIRD WORLD assistance programs. It is part of the U.S. International Development Cooperation Agency and is authorized by the Foreign Assistance Act of 1961 to carry out assistance programs designed to help the people of certain less-developed countries develop their human and economic resources, increase their productive capacities, and improve their quality of life. AID was a part of the U.S. Department of State until 1979, when it was made a semiautonomous organization.

agent 1. A person given authority to act on behalf of another. 2. In intelligence usage, a person who is recruited, trained, controlled, and employed to obtain and report information. 3. An INTELLIGENCE agent employed in a covert operation; a spy. 4. A saboteur, or one who carries out acts of SABOTAGE.

agent, consular *See* CONSUL.

agent authentication 1. The technical support task of providing an intelligence agent with personal documents, accoutrements, and equipment that have the appearance of authenticity as to their claimed origin and that support and are consistent with the agent's cover story. 2. The prearranged items and signals employed to identify one secret intelligence agent to another.

agent-in-place A person employed in a position with access to secret information who spies (for money or ideological reasons) for an enemy. An agent-in-place is inherently a traitor to his or her state and is in an extremely dangerous situation. Such a person differs from a MOLE in that the agent-in-place is a volunteer as opposed to one who has been planted deliberately.

agent net A clandestine organization of intelligence agents that operates under the direction of a principal agent.

agent of influence 1. An individual of one presumed loyalty who is under the control of a competitor, not for purposes of espionage or other illegal activities but to influence overall public opinion. Sometimes the control is so subtle that the "agent" does not realize he or she is being used—as when an academic from one state plants misinformation with counterparts in other states. And sometimes the intent is limited to influencing the opinion of a single individual, as when the lover of an ambassador seeks to impart certain views. 2. Pat Choate's term, from his 1990 book *Agents of Influence,* for Japanese agents who buy influence in Washington (and in universities and think tanks) to support U.S. trade and economic policies favorable to Japan.

Agent Orange The chemical used by the U.S. military during the VIETNAM WAR to defoliate jungle areas and destroy enemy food supplies. While the U.S. government asserted that the chemical was "not harmful," it was later blamed for deformed or stillborn children of Vietnamese and U.S. Vietnam veterans as well as for high cancer rates among these groups. In 1984 the manufacturers of Agent

Orange, after extended legal action, agreed to pay $180 million for the medical costs of U.S. Vietnam veterans and their families. Many veterans continue to campaign for compensation from the federal government.

AGENT ORANGE IN ACTION

The fetuses, many of them stillborn after eight or nine months in utero, continue to be collected from women suffering the effects of Agent Orange. The tiny, surreal figures stare out of glass jars displayed on three walls of a fairly large room, bearing witness to the wonders of modern military science. I saw a child with three faces superimposed on a single head, another with a large eye instead of a nose, still others with webbed feet or hands and ears protruding from their chests.

SOURCE: Lewis A. Lapham, "Vietnam Diary" (*Harpers,* May 1989).

---

agent provocateur French term for a person hired to create trouble for an opposing country or organization by inducing the members of rival organizations to do things that are ultimately contrary to their interests.

aggression 1. An unprovoked, unjustified, and thus illegal attack by one state on another. It may or may not be preceded by a DECLARATION OF WAR. But what one state may see as unprovoked, another may view as justifiable retaliation. Ultimately, each state defines aggression in its own interest. The Charter of the United Nations pointedly does not define aggression. However, Article 39 holds that the "Security Council shall determine the existence of any threat to the peace, breach of the peace, or act of aggression . . ." But this provision did not stop the UN General Assembly from defining aggression in a 1974 resolution (3313/XXIX): "Aggression is the use of armed force by a State against the sovereignty, territorial integrity or political independence of another State, or in any other manner inconsistent with the Charter of the United Nations." According to this General Assembly definition, "the first use of armed force by a State in contravention of the Charter shall constitute prima facie evidence of an act of aggression although the Security Council may, in conformity with the Char-

ter conclude that a determination that an act of aggression has been committed would not be justified in the light of other relevant circumstances, including the fact that the act concerned or their consequences are not of sufficient gravity." But in the end this resolution backs down from its assertion that "no consideration of whatever nature, whether political, economic, military or otherwise, may serve as a justification for aggression," when it sanctions specified categories of aggression by asserting that "nothing in the definition in any way prejudices the right to self-determination, freedom and independence of peoples forcibly deprived of that right . . . particularly peoples under colonial and racist regimes or other forms of alien domination; nor the right of these peoples to struggle to that end and to seek and receive support." 2. ECONOMIC WARFARE. 3. Something less than a full military attack, such as an unauthorized overflight for reconnaissance purposes over another state's territory or a formal mobilization of forces at a frontier. The danger of such intimidating tactics is that they might encourage a preemptive strike. 4. A traditional naval blockade, which under international law has long been considered an act of war. 5. The peaceful takeover of land and business assets by foreign individuals and corporations. Domestic companies, whose stock is for sale in capital markets, often find themselves fighting foreign takeover. There is much truth to the joke about the Japanese signers of the World War II surrender document whispering to each other: "Next time, we'll *buy* Pearl Harbor."

aggression, naked A totally unambiguous and unprovoked attack by one state upon another; military conquest in the classic manner.

agitprop A contraction of the Russian term *agitatsiya propaganda* ("agitation propaganda"); Communist propaganda disseminated through journalism and entertainment, especially by drama on the stage and cinema.

agonizing reappraisal A major reevaluation of a government's foreign policy. Its coinage is usually credited to U.S. Secretary of State John Foster Dulles, who said in a speech at the National Press Club on December 22, 1953: "When I was in Paris last week, I said that . . . the United States would have to undertake an agonizing reappraisal of basic foreign policy in relation to Europe." Since then there has been a tendency for every American reappraisal of its commitment to Europe to be described by analysts as "agonizing."

Agreement on the Prevention of Nuclear War   *See* PREVENTION OF NUCLEAR WAR AGREEMENT.

agree to disagree   A stalemate in diplomatic negotiations; both sides realize that it is impossible to reconcile opposing views on a matter.

agrément   French term for the formal agreement by a receiving state that a particular individual is acceptable as the head of a diplomatic mission of the sending state. This is usually a confidential and pro forma procedure. According to Article 4 of the 1961 Vienna Convention on Diplomatic Relations, "The sending State must make certain that the agrément of the receiving State has been given for the person it proposes to accredit as head of the mission to that state." No state is obligated to give a reason for the refusal of agrément. The processes of agrément, known as agreation, concerns only the head of a diplomatic mission. A state is always free to object to any individual member of a mission by declaring him or her to be PERSONA NON GRATA. According to David Wise in *The Spy Who Got Away* (1988): "Under a little-known practice the chief of the CIA's Moscow station is, in effect, subject to an *agrément* by Moscow, in much the same fashion that a new American ambassador must be approved before being dispatched to the Soviet Union. In turn, the CIA approves the KGB resident in Washington."

Agricultural Trade Development and Assistance Act of 1954   *See* FOOD FOR PEACE.

Ahidjo, Ahmadov (1924–1989)   The premier of the French Cameroons who became the first president of the independent Republic of Cameroon (1960–1982).

ahimsa   The Hindu ethical teaching of nonviolence preached by MOHANDAS K. GANDHI in the struggle for Indian independence. Gandhi, quoted in E. Easwaran's *Gandhi the Man* (1978), held that *ahimsa* meant "conscious suffering. It does not mean meek submission to the will of the evil-doer, but it means pitting of one's whole soul against the will of the tyrant. Working under this law of our being, it is possible for a single individual to defy the whole might of an unjust empire and lay the foundation for that empire's fall." Thus Gandhi stood in marked contrast to older leaders of the Indian independence movement who stressed the heroic, conquering traditions of Hinduism as the road to independence. Gandhi and MARTIN LUTHER KING, JR., are the two leading exponents of nonviolence and passive resistance in the twentieth century.

AID   *See* AGENCY FOR INTERNATIONAL DEVELOPMENT.

aid, foreign   *See* FOREIGN AID.

aide-memoire   French for "an aid to the memory"; an informal summation of a diplomatic event, an interview, a conversation at a social gathering, or any other matter for which it is worthwhile to create a record.

AIDS   Acquired Immune Deficiency Syndrome, a disease unknown until 1981. Since then it has killed more than a million persons throughout the world. In 1991 the WORLD HEALTH ORGANIZATION estimated that 40 million people will be infected with the human immunoficiency virus (HIV) by the year 2000 and that at least 10 million will develop AIDS (which is almost always fatal). AIDS has considerable political significance because governments have been forced to respond to the disease by funding massive research, treatment, and prevention programs. Because AIDS is spread through contact with HIV-infected blood, the developed world has responded with massive public education campaigns that are increasingly slowing the overall rate of infection. However, in the THIRD WORLD AIDS deaths continue to increase. Indeed, the World Health Organization estimates that 90 percent of all new AIDS cases will be in sub-Saharan Africa, South America and the Caribbean, and Asia.

Because the AIDS virus is often transmitted during sexual relations, British politician Edwina Currie offered this advice: "My message to the businessmen of this country when they go abroad on business is that there is one thing above all they can take with them to stop them catching AIDS—and that is their wife" (*Guardian,* February 13, 1987).

Ailleret Doctrine   *See* TOUS AZIMUTHS.

Air America   The U.S. Central Intelligence Agency's cover name for its covert airline, which operated during the VIETNAM WAR.

air attaché   *See* ARMY ATTACHÉ.

Airborne Warning and Control Systems   *See* AWACS.

aircraft carrier   A CAPITAL SHIP that transports military aircraft and is therefore able to add another dimension to traditional forms of naval power. Carrier-based aircraft can be used for both land attack and military action against surface ships and submarines. They also are a very effective way of showing the flag or signaling military presence. They provide flexibility and mobility and can apply force of varying levels. Nuclear-powered aircraft carriers can move to crisis areas fairly rapidly. During the COLD WAR the United States had many more carriers than the Soviet Union; this was the basis for U.S. supremacy at sea. The carriers were organized into carrier battle groups, each of which, critics argued, was necessary to defend the carrier itself, which is actually a very vulnerable weapons platform. With the end of the Cold War the United States has decided to reduce the number of its carriers. Nevertheless, it remains the major proponent of the carrier. The latest versions of the Nimitz-class nuclear-powered carriers weigh just over 100,000 tons when fully loaded. In future crises the carrier will remain one of the most important means whereby the United States can intervene or project its power into regional conflicts. *See also* CORAL SEA, BATTLE OF THE; *compare to* BATTLESHIP.

air force   **1.** Air power; whatever destructive capability can be brought to an enemy by air.   **2.** A military service that focuses on air and space operations regardless of whether it is independent (such as the U.S. Air Force or the U.K. Royal Air Force) or part of another service (such as naval aviation).   **3.** A subunit within a larger air force.

Distinctions are sometimes made, for example, between the strategic and tactical components of air forces, with the former focusing on strategic bombing and the latter engaged in other tasks such as air-to-air combat, support for land operations, and suppression of enemy defenses.

Air India explosion   The June 23, 1985, destruction of an Air India 747 jet with 329 people on board. The wreckage, found off the coast of Ireland, indicated a midair explosion. Both the DASHMESH REGIMENT, a Sikh terrorist group, and the KASHMIR LIBERATION ARMY claimed responsibility.

air-launched cruise missile   *See* ALCM.

airlift   **1.** The use of air forces to move military personnel and equipment or other supplies to a critical area, usually in a response to some kind of crisis. The most famous example of an airlift of nonmilitary supplies is the shipment of food and fuels to West Berlin in 1948 in response to the Soviet blockade of the city. *See also* BERLIN BLOCKADE.   **2.** The capability for lifting people and material to a critical area rapidly. Airlift is important for rapid responses to all sorts of contingencies, but in terms of the deployment of heavy armor and other equipment, it generally has to be supplemented by SEALIFT.

air piracy   *See* SKYJACKING.

air power   **1.** The capability to inflict harm on others or to coerce them through the use of ballistic missiles or aircraft carrying appropriate weapons systems. The early twentieth-century prophet of air power was the Italian general GIULIO DOUHET. He wrote in *The Command of the Air* (1921): "I have mathematical certainty that the future will confirm my assertion that aerial warfare will be the most important element in future wars, and that in consequence not only will the importance of the Independent Air Force rapidly increase, but the importance of the army and the navy will decrease in proportion."   **2.** The totality of a nation's air forces that may be used for strategic or tactical purposes.   **3.** The airborne weapons systems that can be used to destroy an enemy's armed forces, to inflict harm on its civilian population, and to degrade its military and civilian infrastructure. The PERSIAN GULF WAR in 1991 involved an impressive display of air power by the United States and its allies against Iraq. In this case the use of air power proved particularly successful because Iraqi air defenses were suppressed early in the conflict, thereby allowing allied air power to operate with virtual impunity over Iraq. The other development that added to the effectiveness of these operations was the use of "smart" lasers and computer-guided bombs.

air raid Traditionally a single bombing and/or strafing attack from a formation of enemy aircraft. However, the term has been extended to include any attack from the air from any combination of airborne weapons including missiles and rockets. *Compare to* RAID.

airspace reservation or restriction 1. The airspace located above an area on the surface of the land or water, designated and set apart by a state, commonwealth, or territory, over which the flight of aircraft is prohibited or restricted for the purpose of national defense or for other governmental purposes. 2. An agreement with an air traffic control agency for special use of airspace at a particular time and point; usually for a limited duration and for a specific purpose, such as aerial refueling.

air strike An attack on specific objectives by aircraft on an offensive mission. Strikes are composed of sorties; a *sortie* is one operational flight by a single aircraft.

air superiority That degree of dominance in an air battle of one force over another that permits the conduct of operations by the former and its related land, sea, and air forces at a given time and place without prohibitive interference by the opposing air force. Air superiority consists of two elements: (1) the ability to prevent enemy aircraft, especially bombers and reconnaissance planes, from operating over one's own lines, which requires a sizable interceptor or "fighter" force; and (2) the ability to fly missions over the enemy's lines, attacking its troop concentrations and supply network, and observing military movements. *Compare to* COMMAND OF THE AIR.

air warfare 1. A fight for command of the air. This generally involves a battle between offensive forces designed to bomb the enemy and defensive forces that are seeking to prevent the bombers from getting through, or at least from inflicting serious damage. The BATTLE OF BRITAIN is a good example of air warfare in which the defensive forces were decisive. 2. The use of the air to deliver munitions against the armed forces or civilian population of an enemy. The more precise term is *strategic bombing*. This form of warfare became potentially much more destructive with the development of nuclear weapons. There are still arguments about its effectiveness when restricted to conventional weapons, however. In both World War II and the Vietnam War it failed to destroy the morale of the population under attack. In the 1991 war against Iraq, however, strategic and tactical bombing destroyed the morale of the Iraqi ground forces and prepared the way for a short and decisive land campaign.

Akihito, Tsugu no Miya (1933–   ) The emperor of Japan (a CONSTITUTIONAL MONARCH) since the death of his father, Emperor HIROHITO, in 1989.

Alamein, El *See* EL ALAMEIN, BATTLE OF.

Alamogordo The New Mexico city near which the United States exploded the first ATOMIC BOMB. William L. Laurence reported this event in the *New York Times* on September 26, 1945, as follows: "The Atomic Age began at exactly 5:30 Mountain War Time on the morning of July 16, 1945, on a stretch of semi-desert land about fifty airline miles from Alamogordo, New Mexico. At that great moment in history, ranking with the moment in the long ago when man first put fire to work for him and started on his march to civilization, the vast energy locked within the hearts of the atoms of matter was released for the first time in a burst of flame such as had never before been seen on this planet." Len Giovannitti and Fred Freed in *The Decision to Drop the Bomb* (1965) quote J. Robert Oppenheimer, the scientist in charge of building the bomb, on what happened next: "We waited until the blast had passed, walked out of the shelter . . . A few people laughed, a few people cried. Most people were silent. I remembered the line from the Hindu scripture, the *Bhagavad-Gita:* Vishnu is trying to persuade the Prince that he should do his duty and to impress him he takes on his multi-armed form and says, 'Now I am become Death, the destroyer of worlds.' I suppose we all thought that, one way or another."

Albanian isolationism Albania's estrangement from most of the world in the post–World War II period. For four and one-half centuries, Albania was ruled by the Ottoman Turks. Then in 1912 at the height of the first of the BALKAN WARS, Albania declared its independence from Turkey. After World War I Albania was recognized as an independent state by the Paris Peace Conference, largely through the efforts of U.S. President Woodrow Wilson. In 1920 Albania was admitted to the League of Nations and remained a member until Italy conquered the country in 1939. Occupied during World War II (first by the Italians, then by the Germans), by the end of 1944 the Communist-led National Liberation Front (NLF) gained control of the country and established the regime that ruled until 1990. Under Communist rule, Albania went through four general stages in its foreign relations. In the first phase from 1944 to 1948, its foreign policy was tied closely to Yugoslavia's. The second phase began with the expulsion of Yugoslavia's leader, JOSIP BROZ TITO, from the COMINFORM in June 1948 and lasted until 1960; during this time, Albanian foreign policy dovetailed that of the Soviet Union. But in 1960, as Soviet leader NIKITA S. KHRUSHCHEV sought to have world Communist parties condemn China, Albania refused to collaborate. In 1961 the two countries severed relations, Soviet aid ceased, and Soviet advisors and technicians left Albania. After the break with the Soviet Union, Albania entered the third stage in its foreign policy orientation: the alliance with China, which lasted until 1978. After China's reapprochement with the United States, Albania then entered the fourth phase of its relations with the outside world: it chose to "go it alone" and was at odds with all major powers. Albania was one of the last states of Eastern Europe to respond to the wave of post–Cold War democratization. In 1991 the Communist Party changed its name to the Socialist Party and held the first contested elections since World War II. Even though the Socialists got a majority of the seats in the new parliament the power of the socialists, along with the economy,

continued to erode and the country began to drift into a state of anarchy in that it lacked effective political leadership. By 1992 Albania had become the poorest country in Europe, with more than half of its work force unemployed. Humanitarian aid has become Albania's leading import. In 1992 the Democratic Party of Albania crushed the former Communists in parliamentary elections. Sali Berisha (1944–   ), a heart surgeon and one-time loyal Communist, became Albania's first non-Communist president since World War II and faced the twin tasks of increasing stability and attracting investment.

ALCM (air-launched cruise missile) One of three variants of CRUISE MISSILES developed by the United States since the mid-1970s. Its main purpose was to maintain the utility of the B-52 bomber, which had a very old airframe and was highly vulnerable to Soviet antiaircraft defenses. ALCMs, with a range of about 2,500 kilometers (1,500 miles), are capable of being carried to within range of their targets and launched while the aircraft are still at a safe distance from even the most sophisticated antiaircraft defenses. U.S. nuclear strategy (like the French, but unlike the British) has always held that missiles launched from piloted aircraft form an indispensable part of the deterrent force, along with ICBMS and SLBMS. (The three together are known as the deterrent TRIAD).

Aldermaston The location of the United Kingdom's atomic weapons establishment. It has been a common target of antinuclear demonstrations.

Aldo Moro Affair *See* MORO, ALDO.

alert 1. Readiness for action, defense, or protection. 2. A warning signal of a real or threatened danger, such as an air attack. 3. The period of time during which troops stand by in response to an alarm. 4. A warning received by a military unit or a headquarters that apprises it of an impending operational mission. 5. A system of increasing military readiness and preparation for war. Alert systems can have several levels. In the United States they are known as DEFCONs or Defense Conditions, and during the Cold War the North Atlantic Treaty Organization had its own alert system, which began at the level of military vigilance and went right up to a war footing. Placing forces on alert can be both a precaution should a situation deteriorate and a signal of resolve to an adversary. In alerting during crises there are many dilemmas and tradeoffs, perhaps the most important of which is the desire to demonstrate resolve and ensure preparedness while avoiding actions that will be seen by adversaries as provocative or make them believe that war is inevitable.

Alexander I (1888–1934)   The king of Yugoslavia (1921–1934) who was assassinated in Marseilles, France, in 1934 during a state visit. Louis Barthou, the French foreign minister, also was killed when a Bulgarian in the employ of the Croatian separatist leader Ante Pavelic (1889–1959) boarded the king's open parade car and opened fire. During World War II the Germans made Pavelic head of a puppet Croat state after the Axis conquest of the Balkans in 1941. That state brutally killed thousands of Serbians. After the war Pavelic fled to the Nazi safe haven of Argentina.

Alexander, Harold (1891–1969)   The British Army officer who was in overall command of the World War II North African campaign; he commanded the Allied forces in the invasion of Sicily and spent the remainder of the war in an offensive in Italy. After the war he served as governor-general of Canada (1946–1952) and minister of defense (1952–1954).

Al-Fatah   *See* FATAH, AL-.

Alfonsin Foulkes, Raúl   *See* ARGENTINE FASCISM.

Algerian War of Independence   The revolt against French rule by indigenous Arab Algerians that began in 1954 and ended when France, under CHARLES DE GAULLE, declared Algeria to be independent in 1962. The nationalists, who called themselves the National Liberation Front (FLN), fought a guerrilla war in which both sides used terrorist and counterterrorist tactics. Eventually protracted negotiations led to a formal cease-fire and referendum on self-determination. By the time the struggle ended more than 250,000 Algerians had been killed, making this the worst of the post-1945 colonial wars. The savagery with which the French Army sought to suppress the insurgency generated so much bitterness on the part of the population that 91 percent voted for independence. About 800,000 *colons* (French settlers) fled as refugees to France. *See also* EVIAN AGREEMENTS.

alien   1. A temporary visitor or permanent resident living in a state of which he or she is not a citizen; a citizen of one state who lives in another. Because no state can insist that its nationals be allowed to visit or reside in another state, the laws governing the rights and obligations of aliens are internal matters for every state.   2. A creature from another planet; any earthling on another planet.

alien, enemy   A national of an enemy state who is outside his or her state's boundaries and is in the territory of, or territory occupied by, a belligerent power.

alien, illegal   A person from one country who is living or working in another country unlawfully. (In the United States the Department of Labor prefers to refer to these people as *undocumented workers,* a term that preserves the presumption of innocence and sounds less criminal.) In every state a noncitizen without a valid visa or entry permit is an illegal alien. Aliens who entered legally as tourists become illegal the moment they seek or obtain employment.

alien, resident   One who lives legally in a country of which he or she is not a citizen. In most states resident aliens have the full protection of the laws but do not have all of the privileges of citizenship, such as the right to vote, the opportunity to hold many government jobs, and the right to certain welfare benefits. According to international law, during wartime alien citizens of belligerent states may have their property seized and may be arrested or expelled.

alienation   The notion of disaffection from government or of estrangement from the political system of which the individual is a member. The notion of alienation is a key element in MARXISM but also has wide applicability in psychology and sociology as well as political science.

alignment   An arrangement of things usually in a straight line. During the COLD WAR the term referred

A pro-Allende demonstration in Chile. (Library of Congress)

to the division of the world into the FREE WORLD led by the United States and its Western European allies on one side and the Communist bloc of the Soviet Union and its Eastern European satellites. States not taking either side formed the NONALIGNED MOVEMENT.

aliya   Hebrew for "going-up"; the migration of Jews from all parts of the world to Israel.

allegiance   **1.** The loyalty that each citizen owes his or her country; the customary obligation that a citizen has to protect the interests of his or her state. **2.** The emotional, coercive, or legal bond that binds a subject to a state's sovereign.

Allenby, Edmund (1861–1936)   The British general who forced the Turks out of their middle eastern Ottoman Empire and back into Turkey during World War I. Thereafter he served as British high commissioner in Egypt (1919–1925).

Allende, Salvador (1908–1973)   The Marxist president of Chile (1970–1973) who was overthrown and killed during a military coup. In the 1970 election, Popular Unity (*Unidad Popular,* or UP) candidate Allende won only 36.3 percent of the vote but

was nevertheless confirmed as president by the Chilean Congress over strong conservative opposition. He immediately froze prices and raised wages. He nationalized industries and expropriated mineral resources, including those of the copper industry. His government took over large estates and divided land among the peasants, further alienating the conservative upper class. But Allende's government began to lose control as the economy took a downturn, and peasants and workers took over estates and industrial plants without government approval. High inflation, civil unrest, a truckers' strike, and the cutoff of U.S. loans contributed to the alienation of the middle class. A military coup led by General AUGUSTO PINOCHET (and supported by the U.S. CENTRAL INTELLIGENCE AGENCY) resulted in the death of Allende and the installation of an authoritarian regime.

alliance   **1.** A coalition of states that have agreed to help each other in the event of war or crisis. Alliances involve not only cooperation and aggregation of capabilities but are generally directed toward an actual or potential enemy and the actual or potential use of force. The agreement on which an alliance is based is often embodied formally in a TREATY, but it also can be based on a tacit or informal agreement. Alliances can be between states that are relatively equal in power and involve mutual security guarantees or they can be between unequal states, in which case the more powerful state generally extends a unilateral guarantee to the less powerful one and displays a willingness to protect and preserve the smaller state's independence and territorial integrity. Alliances differ in duration, number of members, and the extent to which there are common interests among the members. The greater the common interest, the stronger and more durable the alliance is likely to be. Alliances also can differ in terms of their purpose. Historically there have been two kinds of alliances: aggressive and defensive. Since World War II aggressive alliances (such as the AXIS, which was created to wage war) were deemed conspiracies against peace and invalid under international law. In consequence all subsequent alliances have been branded by their makers to be defensive (such as the North Atlantic Treaty Organization, which was designed to deter aggression).

M. Small and J. D. Singer in "Formal Alliances, 1818–1965" (*Journal of Peace Research* 3, 1969) classify alliances into three categories: defensive alliances such as NATO, which obligate members to assist other members militarily in the event of an attack; NONAGGRESSION PACTs, which obligate members not to fight each other even when war breaks out with a nonmember nation; and ENTENTES, which only obligate governments to consult each other in the event of an attack on either party. Alliances provide a great measure of structure and predictability in the international system; they make clear to potential aggressors that an attack may force them to confront more than one state. There is great variety to the membership, cohesion, commitment, and durability of alliances. In a multipolar international system, such as existed in nineteenth-century Europe, alliances were fluid; an ally of today could easily become tomorrow's adversary, and vice versa. Alliances were thus the major element in the BALANCE OF POWER system. They were the vehicles that maintained the equilibrium among the major powers. In the post–World War II period the major alliances of NATO and the Warsaw Pact clustered around the superpowers of the United States and the Soviet Union. The 1990s began with great uncertainty over the future of the existing alliances in Europe. The Warsaw Pact disintegrated and NATO seemed to be an alliance in search of an enemy. **2.** Any of a vast array of cooperative agreements among states for peaceful purposes such as economic development.

Alliance for Progress U.S. President John F. Kennedy's name for his administration's policies toward Latin America, which sought mutual economic cooperation. The alliance was a formal pact among the United States and the 19 other American republics established by the Punta del Este Charter in 1961. The goals of the $20 billion, ten-year cooperative program were to bring political stability, representative government, and economic and social development to Latin America. The alliance tried to foster development of the private sector and to expand U.S. trade and investment through loans from the U.S. government, international lending agencies, and private sources. However, countries could use aid money only to purchase U.S. products, and much of the money was wasted through corruption and mismanagement, never reaching the intended recipients. FIDEL CASTRO, whose Communist Cuba was not included in the alliance's largesse, dismissed it as "an alliance between one millionaire and many beggars" (*New York Times,* November 7, 1964). A more effective component of the alliance was U.S. assistance to the Latin American military, focusing especially on counterinsurgency tactics. But overall the alliance did not have a significant impact because Latin American leaders were reluctant to make major political and economic reforms and the interest and financial aid from the United States lessened as the 1960s advanced and the VIETNAM WAR became the dominant U.S. foreign policy concern.

allied commander A leader of a military command composed of elements of two or more allied nations working together.

Allied Command Europe (ACE) NORTH ATLANTIC TREATY ORGANIZATION's major military command, which would have had the responsibility for organizing NATO's forces in Europe had there ever been a conflict against the WARSAW PACT. As the main land and air war organization for NATO, it comes under the command of SACEUR (Supreme Allied Command

Europe), which has always been headed by an American general.

allied staff A staff or headquarters composed of two or more allied nations working together.

allied states States bound to each other by a military alliance.

allies 1. States legally obligated by a mutual defense treaty to aid each other in time of war. Thus North Atlantic Treaty Organization countries refer to themselves as allies. Former U.S. Secretary of State DEAN ACHESON, writing in the *New York Times Magazine* (December 15, 1963), mused on the nature of allies: "Unhappily, amity is not the inevitable result of close relations between either people or peoples. Marriage and war lock both into close embrace. Sometimes the parties live happily ever after; sometimes they don't. So it is with allies." 2. The Allies in WORLD WAR II, the association of nations led by the United States, the United Kingdom, and the Soviet Union against the AXIS powers. In World War I the Allies were the coalition of the United States, the United Kingdom, France, and Italy.

Alliluyeva, Svetlana (1926–   ) The daughter of JOSEPH STALIN who fled the Soviet Union to the West in 1967. This defection received enormous publicity and was considered a great propaganda victory for the West. She returned to the Soviet Union in 1984 but left again in 1986 for Western Europe.

Allison, Graham T., Jr. (1940–   ) The Harvard University professor who wrote a classic study of government decision making, *Essence of Decision: Explaining the Cuban Missile Crisis* (1971). It showed the inadequacies of the view that policies are made by a "single calculating decisionmaker" who has complete control over the organizational units and individual officials within his or her government. Instead, Allison demonstrated that differing bureaucratic viewpoints fight over policy. Although Allison's ideas were not new, he helped to crystallize thinking about foreign policymaking by dealing with the different approaches in terms of three models. The dominant model, which, he argued, obscured more than it illuminated, was

described as the "Rational Actor Model," or Model One. He believed that this needed to be replaced by two other models. Allison's Model Two, the "Organizational Processes Model," basically held that government action could be understood as the output of large organizations that operate according to standard procedures. Model Three was described by Allison as a "Governmental Politics Model," the essence of which is that decisions are the outcome of a bargaining process between different groups and individuals with different bureaucratic perspectives and different political interests. Allison's thesis first appeared in the article "Conceptual Models and the Cuban Missile Crisis" (*American Political Science Review,* September 1969). Allison later became associated with those who argued for massive Western economic aid to the Soviet Union in the wake of the COLD WAR.

Almond, Gabriel (1911–   ) One of the pioneers in the analysis of political culture and political attitudes and coauthor of *The Civic Culture Study* (1974), a pathbreaking work in this area. One of Almond's other famous works was *The American People and Foreign Policy* (1960), which extended some of his previous studies to cover attitudes toward foreign policy. In this study he not only explored the American character and foreign policy but also developed the concept of *mood:* Because the foreign policy attitudes of the mass public have little factual content or intellectual structure, Almond said, they are best described in terms of moods, which are unstable. He traced some of the changes in them over time and related mood to social groupings.

ALPS Accidental Launch Protection System. A term coined by the chairman of the U.S. Senate Armed Services Committee, Sam Nunn, to describe a light antimissile defense system that in his view is more realistic than the total defense system envisaged by the STRATEGIC DEFENSE INITIATIVE. The rationale for ALPS is that such a system could protect the United States against not only an accidental launch of a small number of missiles but also against a strike by a new or emerging and relatively small nuclear weapons state. The rationale for such a system may well grow stronger as further nuclear PROLIFERATION occurs. *Compare to* GPALS.

Alsace-Lorraine   Northeastern provinces of France that were taken by Germany in 1871 after the Franco-Prussian War, regained by France after World War I, reconquered by Germany during World War II, and restored to France in 1945. In 1949 the Federal Republic of Germany (West Germany) recognized French sovereignty over the area. Many of the inhabitants of these provinces have found it useful to be bilingual.

alternat   The customary right of a head of state to be the first to sign on his or her personal copies of treaties. This tradition is fading; the more recent practice is for states to be listed in alphabetical order.

alternate   1. A deputy to a state representative at an international conference; the second in command to a state's primary delegate.   **2.** One who is an understudy for a delegate to an international meeting. She or he is entitled to participate formally only if the designated delegate is unable or chooses not to attend.   **3.** An associate member in a Communist Party central committee or POLITBURO who is in line to become a full member when a seat is vacated.

alternative technology   *See* APPROPRIATE TECHNOLOGY.

alternative world futures   General term for studies that attempt to identify a variety of possible directions for the international system. Although such studies are often based on the projection of current trends, they generally involve prescriptions designed to reform the international system and encourage a move away from the preoccupation with national interests and national security. In this sense the notion of alternative futures generally implies some idea of preferable futures. Such prescriptions have taken strength from the idea that many of the problems now facing humankind—such as environmental pollution, degradation of the ozone layer, population growth, and the spread of weapons of mass destruction—can be dealt with only through concerted action by the international community.

Alvor Accord   An agreement sponsored by Portugal and the Organization for African Unity that attempted to bring together the various factions fighting for independence in Angola. Signed on January 15, 1975, the Alvor Accord provided for a transitional government in which the three independence movements—the MPLA, the FNLA, and UNITA—would share power with the Portuguese until November 11, 1975, the date set for independence. Elections were to be held in October to determine the postindependence government. The accord broke down because of the hostility among the groups. Some critics of U.S. policy argue that if the United States had given more support to the accord and had worked harder to promote an African solution to an African problem, the subsequent civil war, the Cuban and South African interventions, and the victory of the MPLA could have been avoided. *See also* ANGOLAN CIVIL WAR.

Amal   "Hope" (in Arabic), one of the two primary SHI'ITE Muslim militia organizations in Lebanon, the other being HEZBOLLAH. It was founded in the mid-1970s to gain a more equitable share of power for the Shi'ites in their struggle with the Maronite Christians and SUNNI Muslims, who have dominated the Lebanese state since independence from the French in 1943. Amal often functions as a proxy army of Syria.

Amazon Pact   The 1978 treaty signed by Bolivia, Brazil, Colombia, Ecuador, Guyana, Peru, Surinam, and Venezuela to protect the ecology and promote the responsible development of the Amazon River basin.

ambassador   The highest ranking of all diplomats; one who is sent as the personal representative of one head of state to another. Not all ambassadors are equal, however. The most powerful is an *ambassador extraordinary and plenipotentiary,* who has the broadest mandate of authority. Then follows an *ambassador extraordinary,* who has lesser powers, an *ambassador plenipotentiary,* who has authority of a specific nature, and an *ambassador ordinary,* who is the chief of a diplomatic mission without specifications as to authority. Sir Henry Wotton (1568–1639), Queen Elizabeth I's ambassador to Venice, was the first of many wits to write that "an ambassador is an honest man sent to lie abroad for the commonwealth." (Wotton has long been misjudged: He did "lie abroad," but his statement referred to a sexual rather than to an ethical escapade.) Often ambassadors are not trusted to lie well enough; their governments purposely misinform them to ensure that their false representations will seem all the more sincere. Thus the Japanese ambassador to the United States in 1941 did not know of the impending PEARL HARBOR attack, the German ambassador to the Soviet Union in 1941 was not told of the coming invasion, and the U.S. ambassador to the United Nations in 1961 was not told of the BAY OF PIGS landing.

The modern ambassadorship dates from the fifteenth century, when Italian city-states began establishing permanent representatives in each other's capitals. By the next century all the monarchies of Europe were exchanging resident ambassadors. The 1815 CONGRESS OF VIENNA first codified modern diplomatic ranks with ambassadors (along with papal nuncios and legates) at the top. (This ordering was reaffirmed by the 1961 Vienna Convention on Diplomatic Relations.) At first the title of ambassador was reserved for representatives of one monarch to another; republics sent "ministers." But by the end of the nineteenth century the title lost its royalist taint and became used universally.

The job of modern ambassadors has been downgraded somewhat in this era of instant communications. But they still are the chief executives of diplomatic missions, still negotiate (if not finalize) agreements, and still function as the political and social representatives of their nations. *See also* COUNTRY TEAM; DIPLOMATIC PRIVILEGES AND IMMUNITIES.

ambassadress An ambassador's wife. This term should never be used to refer to a female ambassador, whose title is "ambassador."

America First The ISOLATIONIST motto first used during World War I by U.S. President Woodrow Wilson in a speech on April 20, 1915. During World War II it was used by those who did not want the United States to help Great Britain before the United States formally entered the war. Later it was used to describe those who supported former President Herbert Hoover's opposition to sending U.S. troops to Europe in the post–World War II period. In the 1990s the phrase has been heard once again on the U.S. campaign trail by both presidential and congres-

sional candidates. In its contemporary variant, it is used less to denote isolationism than two other things: the need for the United States to deal more effectively with its domestic problems and a more hard-headed approach to foreign policy that asks how a particular action will benefit the United States.

America First Committee The organization created in September 1940 to halt the movement of the United States toward involvement in World War II in Europe. Charles A. Lindbergh, Jr. (1902–1974), the first pilot to make a solo flight over the Atlantic in 1927 and subsequently a recipient of a Nazi medal during a visit to Germany, was one of the committee's major spokesmen for nonintervention. U.S. President Franklin D. Roosevelt never forgave the world's most famous aviator for his defeatist speeches and isolationist views. Even when the committee dissolved after the Japanese attack on Pearl Harbor on December 7, 1941, Roosevelt would never allow Lindbergh the honor of having a formal combat role in the war. Nevertheless, as an aviation expert for government contractors, Lindbergh visited the Pacific theater of war and "informally" flew combat missions. He even shot down some Japanese planes.

American, ugly Any U.S. citizen in a THIRD WORLD nation who inadvertently exploits and alienates the very people he or she means to help. The phrase comes from the title of a popular 1959 novel by Eugene Burdick and William Lederer. Ironically, in the book, the ugly American was the opposite of what the term has come to mean; the character was merely ugly in a physical sense.

American Academy of Diplomacy A U.S. organization created in 1984 to review the qualifications of presidential nominees for ambassadorships. Many former secretaries of state are among the academy's members. The academy is designed to function in the diplomatic field in the same way as the American Bar Association functions in the judicial field—by providing an independent assessment of presidential nominees. In 1985 a six-member bipartisan group of the U.S. Senate Foreign Relations Committee announced that it would seek information from the academy to assist its committee in considering ambassadorial nominees.

American Committee on East-West Accord A non-profit U.S. citizens' group founded in 1974 as the American Committee on U.S.-Soviet Relations; it formally became the American Committee on East-West Accord in 1977 to encourage the United States to proceed with SALT talks as well as scientific, cultural, and educational exchanges with the Soviet Union. *See also* COMMITTEE ON THE PRESENT DANGER; TEAM A/TEAM B.

American Committee on U.S.-Soviet Relations *See* AMERICAN COMMITTEE ON EAST-WEST ACCORD.

American Expeditionary Force The formal name of the U.S. military forces (army and marines) that fought in France during World War I. They were commanded by General JOHN J. PERSHING.

American Foreign Service Association (AFSA) A professional organization for members of the United States Foreign Service, founded in 1924. AFSA functions as the exclusive representative and bargaining unit for Foreign Service employees in the U.S. Department of State and the Agency for International Development. AFSA, located in Washington, D.C., publishes the *Foreign Service Journal*.

American Friends Service Committee *See* QUAKERS.

American Political Science Association (APSA) The major academic organization for U.S. political scientists, founded in 1903. APSA, located in Washington, D.C., publishes the *American Political Science Review, PS* (a quarterly newsletter) and various other materials relating to the political science profession.

American selling price (ASP) U.S. system under which the tariff rate on imported goods, principally benzenoid chemicals, is based on the price of the competitively produced U.S. products rather than on the actual import price. Foreign exporters and U.S. importers are especially critical of this form of nontariff barrier, claiming it causes uncertainty at the time of shipment as to what the tariffs will be and creates an artificially high level of protection. A conditional agreement was reached during the 1964–1967 KENNEDY ROUND among the United States, the countries of the European Economic Community, and Switzerland to eliminate the ASP system in return for tariff concessions and liberalization of some nontariff barriers, but the U.S. Congress did not approve the agreement.

Amin Dada, Idi (1925–   ) The president of Uganda who took power during a 1971 military coup and ruled with a degree of terror unusually severe even for Third World dictators. He assisted the hijackers of Air France Flight 139 in 1976 by giving them a safe haven in his capital city, leading to the ENTEBBE RAID and the dramatic rescue of 106 mostly Jewish hostages by the Israeli military. In 1977 the heads of 33 British Commonwealth nations condemned his regime. He was deposed by a Tanzanian invasion in 1979 and escaped to Saudi Arabia, where he was given refuge.

Amin, Hafijullah (1929–1979) Leader of the Afghan government when the Soviet Union intervened in 1979. Although Amin was nominally pro-Soviet, he was unwilling to be influenced by Moscow and his social and economic policies in Afghanistan increasingly alienated the population and provoked violent opposition. The Soviet Union tried to control Amin and was involved in efforts to assassinate him. When these failed Moscow concluded that the situation could be brought under control only by direct intervention. The December 1979 invasion may well have aimed at capturing Amin and taking him back to Moscow (as had been done with ALEXANDER DUBCEK in Czechoslovakia in 1968). It failed, however, and on December 27 a special unit of Soviet forces stormed Amin's palace and the Afghan leader was killed—a development that added to the international condemnation of the Soviet invasion. *See also* AFGHANISTAN INTERVENTION.

Amman Agreement A 1985 agreement (named after the capital of Jordan) between the PALESTINE LIBERATION ORGANIZATION and Jordan that called for a "peaceful and just settlement" to the Arab-Israeli conflict by advocating that a joint Jordanian-Palestinian delegation to an international peace conference gain self-determination for the Palestinians within the context of proposed confederated states of Jordan and Palestine.

amnesty The act of "forgetfulness" by a government for crimes committed by a group of people.

This is commonly done after a civil war in order to help reunite a country. For example, after the U.S. Civil War, President Andrew Johnson granted amnesty to all Confederate soldiers. An amnesty is usually a group action granted for political offenses. U.S. President Jimmy Carter granted an amnesty to all Vietnam-era draft evaders (but not to military deserters) in 1977. Uruguay has granted amnesty to both the TUPAMAROS and to members of the Uruguayan Armed Forces in order to help heal the wounds that the left-wing insurgency of the 1960s and 1970s, and the military response to the guerrillas, left on that South American nation. A pardon, in contrast, is usually applied to individuals for criminal acts.

Amnesty International   A worldwide organization that aims to secure "throughout the world the observance of the provisions of the United Nations UNIVERSAL DECLARATION OF HUMAN RIGHTS." Thus it seeks to gain the release of political and religious prisoners by publicizing their plight and lobbying governments. It often uses letter-writing and other campaigns to seek the freedom of individuals and groups. Since its founding in 1961 it has grown to over half a million members in over 150 countries. It has been especially effective in exposing cases of government-sanctioned torture. In 1972 it was awarded the Nobel Peace Prize.

Amritsar Massacre   1. An incident that occurred in the northern Punjab region of India in 1919. An unsuspecting crowd of roughly 10,000 gathered in an enclosed square in Amritsar to celebrate a Hindu festival. The British commander, who had banned public meetings, marched in Gurkha troops. They fired into the crowd, killing 379 and wounding over 1,130. The Amritsar Massacre, as it came to be remembered, shattered the hopes for gradual reforms and transformed India's Congress Party into one demanding independence from Great Britain.   **2.** The 1984 attack on the GOLDEN TEMPLE OF AMRITSAR during which Indian troops killed more than 500 Sikh extremists.

Amur-Ussuri River incidents   Series of Russo-Chinese disputes stemming at least from 1850 when China ceded the north bank of the Amur River to Imperial Russia and 1860 when China gave Russia the maritime provinces between the Ussuri River and the Pacific. Border clashes in 1969 increased tensions between the two military giants. *See also* SINO-SOVIET BORDER DISPUTE.

anarchism   The belief that governments and their administrative institutions are inherently evil and therefore should be abolished (typically by violence) so they can be replaced by arrangements not "corrupted" by exploitative and oppressive structures. The word is derived from the ancient Greek *anarkhia,* meaning "nonrule." Anarchism as a political movement first came to light in late nineteenth-century Russia. It was heavily influenced by the writings of Mikhail Bakunin (1814–1876), who called for the violent overthrow of all societal institutions. The justification for anarchistic terrorist attacks is often "propaganda by deed," a phrase coined by French writer Paul Brousse (1844–1912) to describe individual acts of terror. James Joll, in *The Anarchists* (1964), quotes Pierre Joseph Proudhon's (1809–1865) famous 1851 invective against all governments: "To be governed is to be watched over, inspected, spied on, directed, legislated at, regulated, docketed, indoctrinated, preached at, controlled, assessed, weighed, censored, ordered about, by men who have neither the right nor the knowledge nor the virtue." The basic problem with anarchism was summed up by British playwright Alan Bennett (1934–   ) in his 1972 play *Getting On:* "We started off trying to set up a small anarchist community, but people wouldn't obey the rules."

anarchy   1. A system characterized by lack of order.   **2.** Chaos.   **3.** The absence of a centralized overriding authority. The international system is often said to be in a state of anarchy in this third sense of the word. Indeed, anarchy is often seen as the defining characteristic of politics among states, as opposed to politics within states. As Kenneth Waltz noted in his *Theory of International Politics* (1979):

National politics is the realm of authority, of administration, and of law. International politics is the realm of power, of struggle and accommodation. The international realm is preeminently a political one. . . . No appeal can be made to a higher entity clothed with the authority and equipped with the ability to act on its own initiative. Under such conditions, the possibility that force will be used by one or other of the parties looms always as a threat in the background. In politics force is said to be the ULTIMA RATIO. In international politics force serves, not only as the ultima ratio but indeed as the first and constant one.

None of this should suggest that because there is anarchy there are no rules. Alongside the elements of anarchy in international politics there are certain elements of society such as norms, international institutions, diplomacy, and the like. This juxtaposition of the forces of anarchy with those of society led HEDLEY BULL to title his book on international politics *The Anarchical Society* (1977).

ANC *See* AFRICAN NATIONAL CONGRESS.

ancien régime **1.** French term for "the old order" or "the previous government"; specifically the monarchy in France prior to the French Revolution of 1789. **2.** The absolutist regimes of Europe between the 1648 Treaty of Westphalia and the French Revolution of 1789. This ancien régime structure evolved the classic BALANCE OF POWER. **3.** A regime existing prior to a current government. **4.** Any obsolete system of governance even though it is still in power for the time being. **5.** Any regime so incapable of reform that it is ripe for REVOLUTION.

Andean Group Also known as the Andean Common Market, a subregional group of the LATIN AMERICAN FREE TRADE ASSOCIATION organized in 1969 by the Andean Pact or Cartagena Agreement. This group has as its purpose the economic integration of the region, partially to be accomplished through restrictions imposed on external influences such as foreign investment. The group has created an Andean Development Corporation to assist in the financing of development projects and is signatory to a cooperation agreement with the European Community. In 1991 the group announced that it had formed a FREE TRADE ZONE and CUSTOMS UNION to further the economic integration of Latin America. Members include Bolivia, Colombia, Ecuador, Peru, and Venezuela.

Andean Strategy A term used to describe the recent U.S. approach to the governments of Bolivia, Colombia, and Peru in its efforts to contain the smuggling of cocaine into the United States. In 1989 the Bush Administration first completed a comprehensive five-year plan to work with these governments to disrupt and destroy the growing, processing, and transportation of coca and coca products to reduce the supply of cocaine entering the United States. The goal of over $2 billion in assistance was to strengthen the "political will and institutional capability" of the three governments to deal with the coca trade; to increase the effectiveness of their intelligence, military, and law enforcement activities, partly through the provision of greater air mobile assets; and to inflict significant damage on the trafficking organizations. As well as emphasizing more vigorous efforts in counternarcotic activities by the military and law enforcement agencies in Bolivia, Colombia, and Peru, the Andean Strategy also provides greater economic assistance in order to offset the economic dislocation associated with disruption of the drug trade. In February 1992 U.S. President George Bush met with the leaders of the South American states involved in the drug trade in an effort to consolidate and extend the patterns of cooperation established at the previous drug summit held in Cartagena, Colombia, two years earlier. On this occasion, however, the Latin American states pressed for more economic assistance and less emphasis on the military and law enforcement responses to the problem. The Andean Strategy has been, at best, only a partial success.

Andorran Agreement The thirteenth-century compromise of the French count of Foix and the Spanish bishop of Seo de Urgel to recognize each other as coprinces of the Andorran valleys, which gave the small state of Andorra, located in the Pyrenees Mountains between France and Spain, its political form and territorial integrity continuously to the present. Over the years, the title of prince of Andorra on the French side passed to the kings of Navarre, then to the kings of France, and is now held by the presidents of France. The president of France and the bishop of Seo de Urgel, Spain, as coprinces, are charged with the conduct of Andorra's foreign affairs, defense, and judicial system. In 1993

Andorra adopted its first constitution, which restructures its government as a parliamentary co-principality. Because Andorra is a major TAX HAVEN Andorran citizens are now outnumbered three-to-one by resident foreign nationals.

Andropov, Yuri Vladimirovich (1914–1984) General secretary of the COMMUNIST PARTY OF THE SOVIET UNION from 1982 to 1984. As the Soviet ambassador to Hungary (1954–1957), he helped suppress the HUNGARIAN UPRISING OF 1956. As the head of the KGB (1967–1982), he was a major suppressor of Soviet dissidents. According to historian Edward Crankshaw, "Today's dissenters now languishing in camps and lunatic asylums were put where they are now by Andropov himself who also presided over the expulsion of Solzhenitsyn and the sequestration in Gorky of Sakharov. It will take a lot of enlightened action on his part to reduce skepticism about his intentions" (*The Observer,* June 26, 1983). From his base in the KGB he was well positioned to gain the general secretaryship following LEONID BREZHNEV's death in 1982. But after all those years of suppressing people Andropov was not in good health himself. He died a little over a year later.

angary The right of a belligerent state, during wartime, to destroy or use property belonging to neutrals when that property is in the belligerents' own or in enemy territory, or on the open seas. Under customary international law, the belligerent state is obligated to pay compensation for any damage done to the neutral's property.

Angell, Norman (1874–1967) British writer who was most famous for *The Great Illusion* (1910), in which he argued that it was no longer possible for advanced industrialized states to fight with one another because the economic linkages among them had become so strong that the economic and financial costs of war would be prohibitive. The limitations of Angell's analysis were evident as the major European powers not only went to war with one another in 1914 but continued to fight for the next four years. Yet in some respects the upheaval caused by World War I proved that Angell was correct. Moreover, it is clear that his thesis was one of the most important antecedents of contemporary theo-

ries of INTERDEPENDENCE. It is not surprising, therefore, that in the latter half of the 1980s a new generation of international analysts began to suggest that Angell was not the misguided idealist he had often been made out to be.

Anglo-Chinese Treaty of 1984 The agreement between the United Kingdom and China that provides that, when Britain's 99-year lease on Hong Kong and nearby lands expires in 1997, these areas will revert to Chinese sovereignty. The treaty provides that Hong Kong will be allowed to continue its capitalistic system for 50 years, that Hong Kong will continue as a free port, and that the current rights of Hong Kong citizens will be maintained.

Anglo-French Channel Agreement The 1964 treaty for the construction of the "Chunnel"—the 32-mile (23 miles under water) railroad tunnel beneath the English Channel that, when it opens in the mid-1990s, will provide a direct rail link between France and England.

Anglo-French-Russian Agreement *See* SYKES-PICOT AGREEMENT.

Anglo-French Union The proposed political joining of Great Britain and France, offered by the British in June 1940 so that if France was overrun by the Germans during World War II, which seemed likely (and did occur), it would not be defeated unless Great Britain also was conquered. The French cabinet rejected the proposal and a few days later capitulated to the Germans. *See also* FRANCE, BATTLE OF.

Anglo-German Naval Agreement of 1935 The accord that Great Britain secretly negotiated with Germany that permitted the Germans to exceed the arms limitations of the Versailles Treaty of 1919 in exchange for their pledge not to exceed 35 percent of the total tonnage of the combined British Commonwealth fleets. Britain thus acquiesced to Germany's repudiation of the last disarmament restriction from the treaty. This British effort to limit German naval construction, and thus maintain British naval superiority, did not inhibit Nazi Germany in its naval construction. This bilateral agreement destroyed all efforts to resurrect a World War

I coalition of France, Britain, Russia, and Italy to prevent further German transgressions against the Versailles Treaty.

Anglo-Irish Accord of 1985   A partial solution to the political-religious conflict in NORTHERN IRELAND. This agreement between the governments of the Republic of Ireland and the United Kingdom gives increased rights to Catholics in Northern Ireland (ULSTER) and gives Ireland a limited role in governing that area. It seems to be a temporary solution because it was imposed on Northern Ireland against the wishes of both indigenous sides: The 900,000-person Protestant majority has been opposed to a formal voice in their affairs from Roman Catholic Ireland, and the 600,000-person Catholic minority complains that the agreement does not provide for a united Ireland. (At the same time, the Protestants complain that the agreement is the first step toward a united Ireland.)

Anglo-Irish Treaty of 1921   The document that gave Ireland—except for the six counties of Northern Ireland—its independence from Great Britain and ended the ANGLO-IRISH WAR OF 1919–1921. MICHAEL COLLINS, a leader of the Irish Republican Army during the war, believed the arrangement was the best that could be gained under the circumstances. EAMON DE VALERA, a rival nationalist leader, disagreed. Consequently the signing of the treaty triggered an 11-month civil war between supporters of the treaty and opponents, led by de Valera, who disliked the splitting off of the six northern counties as well as the requirement that the leaders of the new Irish Free State (a DOMINION of the BRITISH EMPIRE) swear allegiance to the British crown. Collins was killed during the 1922–1923 civil war, which his protreaty forces won.

Anglo-Irish War of 1919–1921   The revolt against British rule in Ireland that led to the Anglo-Irish Treaty of 1921, which gave independence to Ireland. The executions of the Irish leaders of the EASTER RISING of 1916 so alienated the Irish public that SINN FEIN, the Irish nationalist political party, gained massive public support. When the British sought to suppress the party, sporadic outbursts of violence eventually led to general war between the nationalists and the British forces. The British, war

weary from World War I, had no stomach for a drawn-out conflict and conceded independence except for the largely Protestant six counties of the north.

Anglo-Polish Treaty   The mutual assistance pact of August 25, 1939, between Great Britain and Poland. Earlier that year, on March 31, British Prime Minister Neville Chamberlain told the House of Commons: "I have to inform the House that . . . in the event of any action which clearly threatened Polish independence and which the Polish government accordingly considered it vital to resist with their national forces, His Majesty's Government would feel themselves bound at once to lend the Polish government all support in their power." By this treaty Britain guaranteed Poland's independence. Thus when Germany and the Soviet Union invaded Poland on September 1, Britain was honor-bound to enter World War II. Ironically, the freedom of Poland was one of the major objectives that Britain did *not* achieve by the war.

Anglo-Soviet Treaty of 1942   The mutual aid pact between Great Britain and the Soviet Union, signed in response to the German invasion of the Soviet Union in 1941. It prohibited either party from making a separate peace with Germany—something that the Soviets had done under duress in World War I in the BREST-LITOVSK TREATY.

Angolan Civil War   The fighting that began immediately after Portugal granted Angola its independence in 1975. Following World War II, Portuguese unwillingness to concede eventual independence led to the outbreak of two separate guerrilla insurgencies in 1961. While initially hard-pressed, Portuguese forces gradually reduced the guerrilla efforts of the *Movimento Popular de Libertacao de Angola* (Popular Movement for the Liberation of Angola), or MPLA, and the *Fronte Nacional de Libertacao de Angola* (National Front for the Liberation of Angola), or FNLA, to relatively low levels. The *Uniao Nacional para a Independencia Total de Angola* (National Union for the Total Independence of Angola), or UNITA, began a third movement against the Portuguese in the late 1960s and generally was no more effective than the others. But when elements of the Portuguese armed forces overthrew the regime of Portuguese dictator Marcelo Caetano in April 1974, they decided to grant immediate independence to their African colonies. In January 1975 the Portuguese and the three liberation movements worked out a complicated agreement—the ALVOR ACCORD—that provided for a transitional government composed of all three groups and for elections in preparation for independence in November 1975. The transitional government collapsed before elections could be held, and fighting began among MPLA, FNLA, and UNITA forces.

In 1975 the MPLA, a self-proclaimed Marxist movement, began receiving considerable amounts of Soviet weapons and Cuban military ADVISORS. The United States then began supplying arms to both the FNLA and UNITA. The FNLA, led by Holden Roberto (1925–   ), and UNITA, led by Jonas Savimbi (1934–   ), had indicated a pro-Western orientation. In August South African forces occupied Angolan territory along the Namibian border, ostensibly to protect a hydroelectric project. Soon 5,000 South African troops were fighting alongside UNITA and FNLA forces. At the MPLA's request, Cuban combat troops began landing in response. Thus the MPLA, with its Cuban forces and modern Soviet-supplied weaponry, was able to stop the pro-Western combatants from capturing the capital city. The MPLA was therefore in control of Luanda on November 11 when Portugal ceded power without recognizing an Angolan government.

U.S. assistance to the FNLA and UNITA ceased following congressional votes—by the Senate in December 1975 and by the House in January 1976—prohibiting all direct and indirect military or paramilitary assistance to any group in Angola. South African forces withdrew, and by March Cuban and Soviet support for the MPLA proved decisive. The MPLA established control over most of Angola. The FNLA reverted to guerrilla warfare in northern Angola. UNITA retreated to the southeastern corner and carried out intermittent guerrilla operations with the aid of South African troops.

Since independence, Angola has depended on the Soviet Union and Cuba for military assistance. During the mid-1980s the Soviets supplied extensive amounts of military hardware to Angola. In addition to military personnel (mostly Cuban), numerous Soviet and Cuban civilian advisors were in Angola as well. In 1988 U.S. mediation led to an agreement whereby Cuba, which by then had some 40,000 troops in Angola, and South Africa would withdraw their forces by stages. UNITA stated that it would fight on in spite of the fact that the agreement also called for South Africa to halt its military aid to UNITA. But Western support for UNITA has waned with the collapse of the Soviet Union and the end of the COLD WAR. The 16-year civil war, which cost 500,000 dead (two-thirds of them children), ended with a May 1992 peace accord. United Nations–supervised elections held in late 1992 declared the MPLA to be the clear winner in fair elections. But UNITA, refusing to accept the results, resumed guerrilla warfare.

Animal Farm   George Orwell's (1903–1950) satirical 1945 novel on Soviet communism. It also is a warning that all revolutions, and especially the Russian Revolution, eventually betray their original ideals. On the farm the revolutionary ideal was that "all animals are equal." But after the pigs took over, they decided that "some animals [pigs] are more equal than others."

animus belligerendi   Latin term meaning "the intention to wage war." It is sometimes asserted that a state of war cannot exist unless there are specific acts of warfare committed with *animus belligerendi,* that is, with intent.

animus dispunendi   Latin term meaning "the intention to renounce sovereignty over specified territory."

animus occupandi   Latin term meaning "the intention to gain sovereignty over a specified territory by occupying it."

annexation   1. A state's formal extension of sovereignty over new territory. Traditionally this has been done by force or by the threat of the use of force. Historically annexations have been generally recognized under the LAW OF WAR. But after World War I the right of self-determination of nations became a competing interest in international law. Even peaceful annexation may not be agreeable to all sides. For example, when Israel annexed East Jerusalem in 1980, most of the Arab residents were not pleased. When Iraq announced on August 8, 1991, that it had annexed Kuwait, this alienated the international community as much as had Iraq's initial invasion on August 2 and encouraged the development of a coalition to eject Iraq from Kuwait. On August 9 the United Nations Security Council voted unanimously to declare the annexation of Kuwait "null and void." **2.** The acquisition of adjacent settlements by a city. After annexation, these settlements are part of the city. While most U.S. cities grew by annexation, it is difficult for most cities to annex now because their suburbs are often incorporated entities that may not be subject to involuntary annexation.

Anschluss **1.** German word meaning "union" or "annexation"; specifically the union of Germany and Austria in 1938. Article 80 of the 1919 Treaty of Versailles prohibited this union, which ended with the defeat of both countries during World War II. Beginning in 1937 the Germans increased pressure on Austria's government to align its domestic and foreign policies with those of the GERMAN REICH. Following Adolf Hitler's orders, Austrian Nazis stepped up subversive activities aimed at a peaceful takeover in Vienna that would lead to a voluntary unification. When Austrian Chancellor Kurt Schuschnigg found evidence of this collusion through police raids on the Austrian Nazi headquarters, Hitler moved to direct intimidation of Vienna. When Schuschnigg called for a plebiscite, German troops marched into Austria in March 1938. They met no resistance. Hitler had obtained the tacit consent of Italy to this move on its neighbor. The British and the French had refused Schuschnigg advice or help, for neither was prepared to risk war to enforce the Versailles Treaty provision. A rigged plebiscite in Austria in April 1940 led to an overwhelming vote for unification.

Since Austria was incorporated as a German province during World War II because of the *Anschluss,* it has long evaded its share of responsibility for the war. This evasion is problematic when it is remembered that leading Nazis such as Hitler and Adolf Eichmann were Austrians. According to writer Geoffrey Wheatcroft, "National Socialist Party membership was proportionately higher in

'Ostmark' (Austria) than the rest of Germany, and Austria provided a disproportionately high number of the Reich's worst criminals" (*The New Republic,* March 28, 1988). The AUSTRIAN STATE TREATY prohibits any future *Anschluss.* **2.** A word now used informally to refer to the de facto economic union of Germany and its Eastern European neighbors. The word has a negative connotation because it implies a fear of German economic domination.

Antarctic Club   The original 12 signatories to the Antarctic Treaty, signed in Washington, D.C., in December 1959: Argentina, Australia, Belgium, Chile, France, Japan, New Zealand, Norway, South Africa, the Soviet Union, the United Kingdom, and the United States. Twenty additional countries have acceded to the treaty, and four of these (Brazil, India, Poland, and West Germany) have become full treaty partners.

Antarctic Treaty   **1.** The agreement that internationalized and outlawed the militarization of Antarctica in 1959. All signatory states, including the United States and the Soviet Union, retained the right to inspect the facilities of other signatories to make sure the continent is used solely for peaceful purposes. The treaty opened the Antarctic continent for scientific research and proscribes any nuclear tests or disposal of nuclear wastes in Antarctica. **2.** A 1988 treaty that sought to govern the development of the natural resources of Antarctica. The accord was to take effect after 16 members of a 20-state governing group formally ratified it. But because many environmental groups opposed the treaty's effect of opening up the continent and its fragile ecosystem to mineral exploration and extraction, it was not only defeated but, in effect, denounced: In 1991, 24 states including the United States signed an agreement (in the form of a PROTOCOL to the 1959 treaty) that bans mineral and oil exploration in the Antarctic for at least 50 years.

antiballistic missile   *See* ABM.

anticlericalism   Opposition to traditional religion; usually expressed as antipathy toward the power of the Roman Catholic Church. Anticlericalism has been a recurrent theme in the histories of France, Germany, and Spain.

Anti-Comintern Pact The 1936 treaty between Japan and Germany, ostensibly directed against the spread of international communism. It was a critical step toward World War II. Japan at the time admired Nazi Germany and wanted an alliance against the Soviet Union. Germany wanted Japan to sign an alliance against the United States and Great Britain, but the Japanese refused. When Japanese troops fought Soviet soldiers in an undeclared mini-war on the Mongolian border in 1939, Japanese sentiment favored an alliance with Germany, but Japan felt betrayed by the signing of the NAZI-SOVIET NONAGGRESSION PACT later in 1939. Italy joined the Anti-Comintern Pact in 1937; Hungary, Manchuria, and Spain joined in 1939. This pact paved the way for subsequent alliances among Germany, Italy, and Japan. *See also* AXIS; COMINTERN.

antidumping duty *See* DUTY, ANTIDUMPING.

antidumping law *See* DUMPING.

anti-imperialism **1.** Opposition to the acquisition and exploitation of colonies. Every European state that sought a colonial empire had a minority anti-imperialist movement or sentiment that opposed IMPERIALISM on moral or practical grounds. **2.** The U.S. political movement (1870–1900) that opposed the acquisition of colonies, the Spanish-American War, and the reelection of President William McKinley. The movement dissipated after 1900. *Compare to* DECOLONIZATION.

Anti-Imperialist Armed Front (AIAF) A now-defunct Western European alliance of left-wing terrorist groups, banded together to form a common front against North Atlantic Treaty Organization targets. The AIAF was founded in the early 1980s by the French ACTION DIRECTE and the West German RED ARMY FACTION.

Anti-Imperialist International Brigade (AIIB) A left-wing terrorist group suspected of being a front for the JAPANESE RED ARMY. In 1986 and 1987 terrorists claiming to represent the AIIB carried out a series of rocket and mortar assaults against U.S. embassies in Jakarta, Rome, and Madrid. The AIIB also claimed responsibility for several other minor bombing incidents in Rome against U.S. and British diplomatic targets in 1987.

antisatellite weapon (ASAT) A device designed to destroy satellites in space. During the COLD WAR, ASATs were seen by many as extremely dangerous because they threatened to destabilize the nuclear balance. Satellites had become crucial to the military command and control functions, intelligence gathering, navigation, and targeting operations of both the United States and the Soviet Union. A clear and unrivaled capacity for one side to destroy the other's orbiting satellites quickly would give it a considerable advantage and would produce a very real fear on the part of the vulnerable power that it could be subject to a first-strike attack. If the United States suddenly lost many of its satellites, it would be unable to detect signs of an impending nuclear attack and might not even know that a strike had been launched until a few minutes before it suffered the resulting damage. In a nonnuclear warfare scenario, loss of satellites would seriously impair both communications with one's own forces and the tracking of the enemy's, resulting in a major strategic and probably tactical advantage to the enemy. But with the end of the Cold War this problem has declined in its immediacy and importance. *See also* COMMAND, CONTROL, COMMUNICATIONS AND INTELLIGENCE.

anti-Semitism **1.** Animosity ranging from irrational dislike to hatred of Jews. It can be passive and subtle or aggressive and gross. Anti-Semitism is a prejudice that reaches back to the Middle Ages and has been a formal part of European politics since the nineteenth century. It reached its height in this century with the NAZI effort to murder all Jews. During the HOLOCAUST the Germans killed 6 million, about one-third of the world's Jewish population. Anti-Semitism thus spurred the creation of the state of Israel as a refuge for Jews. Even today, despite the fact that there are relatively few Jews in Europe, anti-Semitism remains a significant element in Austria, France, Germany, Poland, and other states. **2.** Anti-ZIONISM. Since the creation of the state of Israel in 1948, hostility from Arab states toward Zionism has given a political dimension to traditional anti-Semitism. **3.** Hatred of all peoples of Semitic origin—both Arabs and Jews.

antisubmarine warfare   *See* SUBMARINE WARFARE.

Anti-Terrorism Assistance   *See* ATA.

Antonescu, Ion (1882–1946)   The Romanian dictator who brought his country into World War II on the side of the Germans. He was overthrown in 1944 and later executed as a war criminal.

ANZAC   The Australia and New Zealand Army Corps of World War I. By analogy subsequent groupings of forces from these two states also have been called, informally, Anzacs.

ANZAC Pact   The 1944 bilateral treaty between Australia and New Zealand signed in Canberra, Australia (thus it is also known as the Canberra Pact) to create a framework for dealing with mutual concerns in defense and general welfare.

ANZUS Pact   The 1951 Pacific Security Treaty binding Australia, New Zealand, and the United States. The organ of the ANZUS pact is the Pacific Council, established by Article 7 of the treaty and composed of the foreign ministers (or their deputies) of the signatory powers, who generally meet once a year. The council has no permanent staff. The alliance worked harmoniously until the victory of the New Zealand Labour Party in a 1984 election. The new government was strongly committed to antinuclear policies and decided to ban U.S. nuclear-powered or nuclear-capable ships from New Zealand waters. The United States, which has maintained a policy of neither confirming nor denying the presence of nuclear weapons on board specific ships, strongly objected to this policy. The issue came to a head in 1985, when the Labour government refused a U.S. request for port facilities in New Zealand for the USS *Buchanan,* a destroyer with potential nuclear capability. The United States, concerned that this might be a precedent that could be followed in Europe should left-wing opposition parties ever come to power there, reacted strongly.

New Zealand was accused of breaching Article 2 of the pact, in which the partners pledged to develop their capacity to resist armed attack through self-help and mutual aid. A proposed pact meeting and joint exercises in the Pacific were cancelled. But the nonnuclear policy had considerable public support, stemming in part from the sensitivity of New Zealanders to nuclear issues, a stance that had been generated by the use of the South Pacific for nuclear testing. It also reinforced the government's belief that the main danger was not Soviet aggression in the Pacific but the possibility that New Zealand might be entangled in a conflict between the two superpowers. Thus New Zealand Prime Minister David Lange (1942–   ) stated on September 27, 1985, that his government would "not accept the proposition that the ANZUS alliance requires us to accept nuclear weapons." He also said: "We do not ask the United States to defend New Zealand with nuclear weapons. We do intend to exercise greater self-reliance in our own defence." The policy was directed only against the nuclear elements of ANZUS. The New Zealand government wanted to ensure that the alliance was based on conventional forces only. A New Zealand law of December 10, 1985, established a New Zealand zone free of nuclear arms and biological weapons and implemented the South Pacific Nuclear Free Zone Treaty, signed in 1985 by Australia, New Zealand, and other South Pacific states, which renounced the manufacture, possession, or control of nuclear weapons. Although the legislation forbids nuclear-armed ships from docking in New Zealand ports, the ships are allowed to pass through its territorial waters. On August 12, 1986, the United States formally suspended all its security obligations to New Zealand under the ANZUS Pact until New Zealand was prepared to restore unrestricted port and air access to U.S. warships and military aircraft. Australia ultimately sided with the United States on the whole issue but clearly was not as opposed to New Zealand's policy as was Washington. The end result is that ANZUS, if not formally defunct, is effectively suspended.

apartheid   **1.** An Afrikaans word meaning "separate development." **2.** South Africa's policy of racial segregation, formally adopted in 1948. Apartheid classified all South Africans into one of four racial groups: white, black, colored, or Asian. A person's political and economic rights follow from this classification. White supremacy was maintained by laws limiting the political participation and economic advancement of the other groups. Apartheid has been formally denounced by the United Nations in various resolutions. For example, a 1966 resolution (2202/XXI) called it a "crime against humanity." Since 1962, the UN General Assembly has repeatedly called for economic and diplomatic sanctions against South Africa. Today many states have imposed such sanctions to encourage the dismantling of apartheid. The combination of international and domestic pressure has only gradually had an effect on apartheid. The release of NELSON MANDELA and the reforms of the South African government have marked the increasing breakdown of the system. This collapse was made certain in 1992, when a national referendum approved government negotiations with the AFRICAN NATIONAL CONGRESS (ANC) and other groups representing the black majority population. These negotiations are expected to lead to a new constitution that will share power among racial groups. Though the ANC and its main rival, the Zulu-based INKATHA FREEDOM PARTY, sit together in talks with the South African government, supporters of these two main black factions carry on murderous COMMUNAL CONFLICTs in the black townships as the sides vie for political primacy.

apocalypse   **1.** An event of universal destruction; a euphemism for full-scale nuclear war.   **2.** A major battle to come in which, some believe, the forces of good will triumph over evil. *Compare to* ARMAGEDDON.

Apollo   **1.** The ancient Greek god of the sun, of light, of music, and of poetry.   **2.** The name for the series of U.S. space flights that achieved President John F. Kennedy's goal of landing a man on the moon as part of the space race with the Soviet Union. *Apollo XI* (1969) made NEIL ARMSTRONG the first human to step on the moon.

Apollo-Soyuz   The first international space mission, in which a U.S. Apollo spaceship linked up with a Soviet Soyuz spaceship in 1975 for two days of joint experiments. Then both ships separated and returned safely to earth. The mission had more political than scientific significance. It was an effort by the Nixon and Ford administrations to extend their policy of DÉTENTE with the Soviet Union into space.

apostolic   Something of or related to the pope of the Roman Catholic Church.

U.S. and Soviet astronauts pose with a model of their linked spaceships. (NASA)

apostolic delegate A diplomatic envoy from the pope to a state that does not have formal diplomatic relations with Vatican City in Rome.

Apostolic See Also known as the Holy See; the headquarters of the Roman Catholic Church, located in Vatican City in Rome. "Apostolic" refers to the continuous line of Church leaders from the apostles of Jesus. "See" comes from the Latin word *sedes,* meaning "seat"—thus, the place or location that emits the supreme authority of the pope.

apparatchik Russian word for "bureaucrat," now used colloquially to refer to any administrative functionary. The word as used in the United States seems to have no political connotations; it merely implies that the individual mindlessly follows orders and is a petty manager. However, in Communist countries it usually means a member of the Communist Party who is in some intermediate position in the bureaucracy. The apparatchiki formed the bulk of MILOVAN DJILAS's *New Class.* The term is often used pejoratively in the West for administrators and bureaucrats who bully those in their power and truckle to their superiors and has an unpleasant connotation when used about former officials in Eastern Europe and the former Soviet Union.

appeasement 1. Giving in to the demands of those making threats. The term is famously associated with Great Britain and France's permitting Germany to occupy the Sudetenland of Czechoslovakia in 1938. No strategy in twentieth-century European affairs has had more disastrous consequences. When British Prime Minister Neville Chamberlain (1869–1940) returned to England in September 1938 with the MUNICH AGREEMENT, which ceded Sudeten areas of Czechoslovakia to Adolf Hitler's Germany, he gained a hero's welcome because it seemed he had avoided war. Thereupon, Chamberlain said there would be "peace in our time," and German Chancellor Hitler (1889–1945) declared that he had no further territorial ambitions in Europe.

Prior to Chamberlain, appeasement had two meanings: making peace through bringing about agreement or making peace by offering concessions. Although Chamberlain may have had the former meaning in mind, Hitler had the latter. The policy of appeasement only encouraged Hitler's aggression, which directly led to World War II. The word *appeasement* (which was once merely descriptive of a policy of accession) has since taken on a decidedly negative connotation. When Chamberlain returned from Munich, the farsighted Winston Churchill (1874–1965) told him in the House of Commons on November 24, 1938: "Prime Minister, you had the choice between war and dishonor. You have chosen dishonor, and you will get war." 2. A foreign policy in which aggressive acts by a potential enemy are allowed to pass without resistance or punishment. But as writer George Orwell warned in *New Leader,* "In international politics . . . you must either be ready to practice appeasement indefinitely, or at some point you must be ready to fight" (March 29, 1947). Appeasement has been seen as an intrinsic evil by U.S. politicians ever since President Franklin D. Roosevelt warned in a message to Congress on January 6, 1941 that "we must always be wary of those who . . . preach the 'ism' of appeasement." President Dwight D. Eisenhower made the rhetorical dislike of appeasement bipartisan in his first inaugural address (January 20, 1953): "Realizing that common sense and common decency alike dictate the futility of appeasement, we shall never try to placate an aggressor by the false and wicked bargain of trading honor for security. Americans, indeed all free men, remember that in the final choice a soldier's pack is not so heavy a burden as a prisoner's chains." 3. Acceding to the demands of terrorists. According to political pundit William Safire: "One difference between French appeasement and American appeasement is that France pays ransom in cash and gets its hostages back while the United States pays ransom in arms and gets additional hostages taken" (*New York Times,* November 13, 1986).

appelation d'origine French term for the name of the place of origin of a commodity or product.

appreciations Assumptions, estimates, and facts about an opponent's intentions and military capabilities used in planning and decision making.

approbation Official but not formal approval of a treaty; the taking of a favorable disposition toward a treaty by a state without formally signing it.

appropriate technology   A concept that rejects centralized control or direction for the use of technology and replaces it with local determination of which technologies best fit the local environment. Proponents stress the democratizing, populist thrust of appropriate (also called *alternative*) technology, as opposed to a centralized decision-making process. According to the proponents of the growing appropriate technology movement, the technology developed during periods when unemployment was low and natural resources were considered unlimited is not necessarily the right technology when resources are scarce and unemployment is high, especially if the technology is to be transferred to developing countries. Other terms used synonymously with appropriate technology and alternative technology are *intermediate technology* and *soft technology.* E. F. Schumacher's *Small Is Beautiful* (1973) has popularized the concept in the United States. *See also* TECHNOLOGY TRANSFER.

approximation of laws   The process whereby governments align their laws concerning commercial transactions to facilitate international trade. The goal of approximation is to make laws more similar but not identical as in HARMONIZATION.

Apter, David E. (1924–   )   A leading academic analyst on the transfer of power and authority from colonial governments to the new states of Africa. He used the structural-functional approach of the behavioral sciences to analyze political change during African regime transitions. He was especially concerned that charismatic leaders would sidetrack institutionalization, the creation and legitimization of a central governing authority. Charisma (so often rooted in religion as well as the personality of the leader), he wrote, is "dysfunctional to the maintenance of secular systems of authority." His major works include *The Gold Coast in Transition* (1955; 2d ed. 1963); *The Political Kingdom of Uganda: A Study of Bureaucratic Nationalization* (1961); *Ghana in Transition* (1963); *The Politics of Modernization* (1965); *Some Conceptual Approaches to the Study of Modernization* (1968).

Aquinas, Thomas (1224–1274)   The Italian theologian and philosopher whose most famous work was *Summa Theologica* (1266–1273) and who believed that politics should be conducted according to moral and religious principles. Aquinas was a key figure in the development of NATURAL LAW theory and JUST WAR THEORY. He believed that true morality was the same as true rationality and true prudence. His ideas have been used occasionally as the basis for a critique of nuclear strategy.

Aquino, Benigno S., Jr. (1932–1983)   Popular Filipino opposition leader who was assassinated by agents of the FERDINAND E. MARCOS regime at Manila International Airport as he returned from exile on August 21, 1983. His assassin, Rolando Golman, was in turn killed immediately by security officers. While the military sought to portray Golman as a Communist revolutionary, too much evidence pointed to a murder planned and carried out by the Filipino military, with the direct involvement of General Fabian Ver, the armed forces chief of staff. Aquino's widow, CORAZON AQUINO, subsequently sought election as president of the Philippines. After an election rife with fraud, Marcos announced his own reelection; however, Aquino assumed her rightful position as president after a popular uprising forced the discredited Marcos to flee the country. Aquino's government then brought to light clear evidence of the Marcos regime's engineering and cover-up of her husband's assassination.

Aquino, Corazon (1933–   )   President of the Philippines from 1986 to 1992. She took over the Liberal Party after her husband, BENIGNO AQUINO, was assassinated in 1983. She attempted to make her country more responsive to republican institutions, contained a Communist insurgency, defeated various military coup attempts, and was forced to negotiate (at the insistence of the legislature) the removal of U.S. military bases. Aquino was succeeded by Fidel V. Ramous (1928–   ), the former defense secretary, in a tightly fought multicandidate election in which he won with 23.5 percent of the vote.

Arab   The ethnic designation first used for the people of the Arabian peninsula, now applied as well to the people of all those states whose primary language is Arabic: Algeria, Egypt, Iraq, Jordan, Lebanon, Libya, Morocco, Syria, and Yemen. The religion of most (but not all) Arabs is ISLAM.

Arab boycott   *See* BOYCOTT.

Arab funds   Agencies created by the oil-rich states of the Middle East to funnel financial aid (mostly loans on concessional terms) to favored developing states of the THIRD WORLD. Examples include the Abu Dhabi Fund for Arab Economic Development, the Arab Fund for Economic and Social Development, the Arab Monetary Fund, and the Saudi Development Fund.

Arab-Israeli Peace Talks   The direct negotiations among Israel, its Arab neighbors (Jordan, Lebanon, and Syria), and the Palestinians of the OCCUPIED TERRITORIES that began with the October 1991 MADRID CONFERENCE and have continued intermittently since—mainly in Washington, D.C. Various states, especially the United States, Egypt (with whom Israel has a peace treaty), and Saudi Arabia, have been using their good offices to facilitate this process. The talks were given new impetus in mid-1992 when general elections in Israel replaced the hard-line government of YITZHAK SHAMIR with the outwardly more flexible government of YITZHAK RABIN.

Arab-Israeli Wars   The series of four major wars between Israel and much of the Arab world. While Israel has been constantly at war with its Arab neighbors since its independence in 1948 through countless minor skirmishes, full-scale military conflict has also occurred in November 1948 to July 1949 (ISRAELI WAR OF INDEPENDENCE); October to November 1956 (SUEZ CRISIS); June 1967 (SIX-DAY WAR); October 1973 (YOM KIPPUR WAR). *See also* LEBANESE CIVIL WAR; PALESTINE.

Arab League   A loose alliance of Arab states founded in 1945 to promote military, economic, and cultural cooperation. Its governing body, which meets in Cairo, Egypt, is a council consisting of one voting member from each of the 21 member states. Unanimous decisions are binding on all members. Otherwise members are bound only if they vote with the majority. The league's original activity was the coordination of opposition to Israel. But it has since expanded into other areas through specialized agencies such as the Arab Educational, Scientific and Cultural Organization; the Arab Fund for Economic and Social Development; the Arab Labor Organization; the Arab Monetary Fund; and the Industrial Development Centre for the Arab States.

Arab Legion   An obsolete name for the army of Jordan. Organized by the British in 1930 as a police force, by the end of World War II it had become, under British tutelage, a professional mechanized army. Its last British officer left in 1956. Then the legion was disbanded as a separate force and merged with the Jordanian army.

Arab Maghreb Union Treaty   The 1989 agreement among Algeria, Libya, Mauritania, Morocco, and Tunisia that seeks to create a common market for these five North African states. Initial progress has been slow in part because of the difficulty of integrating Algeria's state-run system with the freer markets of Morocco and Tunisia. Tensions in the region have increased as well with United Nations SANCTIONS against Libya and the rising influence of ISLAMIC FUNDAMENTALISM in Algeria.

Arab oil embargo   *See* OIL EMBARGO.

Arab option   The name given to the diplomatic efforts of the Arab states to find a peaceful solution to the PERSIAN GULF CRISIS in 1990 and 1991. Jordan's King HUSSEIN led the search for a face-saving mechanism that would satisfy all the parties involved. But when the Arab option proved ephemeral, the PERSIAN GULF WAR became real.

Arab Revolt   The WORLD WAR I insurgency within the Ottoman Empire of the Middle East. With the help of British officers such as T. E. LAWRENCE (better known as Lawrence of Arabia), the revolt helped drive the Turks out of the area. But since the ensuing peace left France in control of Syria and Great Britain in control of Palestine, the Arabs, with some justice, felt bitter about the outcome. *See also* FAISAL I.

Arab Revolution   Pseudonym of the POPULAR FRONT FOR THE LIBERATION OF PALESTINE.

Arab Revolutionary Brigades or Arab Revolutionary Council   Cover names used by the ABU NIDAL Organization.

Arafat, Yasir (1929–   )   Chairman of the PALES-
TINE LIBERATION ORGANIZATION (PLO) and leader of
its largest constituent organization, AL-FATAH. A
founding member of Fatah in the mid-1950s, he
became well known as the organizer of Fatah raids
into Israeli territory in the mid-1960s. Fatah was
one of the Palestinian groups that formed the PLO
in 1964. In 1969 Arafat ascended to leadership of a
PLO humbled by its defeat in the SIX-DAY WAR in
1967. He stated then, as he continues to state today,
that the PLO is the "sole, legitimate representative
of the Palestinian people." In November 1974
Arafat addressed the United Nations General
Assembly, becoming the first nongovernmental representative to be accorded such an opportunity. He
has been criticized by many Palestinian activists and
the Syrian government, which find him to be too
"moderate." In 1982 he fled to Tunisia as a result of
the Israeli invasion of Lebanon. Arafat returned to
southern Lebanon in 1983 but was forced to flee
again when rebel PLO forces mutinied. Mediation
by Syria and Saudi Arabia contributed to a UN-
sponsored escort of Arafat and his forces to a safe
haven in Tunisia and North Yemen. After this setback the PLO adopted a new strategy. The
INTIFADA, begun in December 1987, has recast the
plight of Palestinians in a more favorable light,
while the response of the Israeli army somewhat
weakened support for Israel in the United States.
During December 1988 Arafat made a series of
statements regarding his willingness to accept RESO-
LUTIONS 242 and 338 and to renounce terrorism.
These were preconditions that the United States had
set before any dialogue could begin between it and
the PLO. The discussions began in Tunis shortly
thereafter but were broken off in May 1990, when
PLO terrorists attempted a seaborne assault on
Israeli beaches.

Arafat's sudden willingness to negotiate a settlement to the Palestinian question bears testament to
his diplomatic skill and the political pragmatism
that have characterized his long leadership of the
Palestinian cause. Still, many hard-line members of
the Palestinian movement, such as the REJECTION
FRONT groups, have been angered by his apparent
readiness to compromise. During the PERSIAN GULF
WAR Arafat politically and literally embraced Iraq's
Saddam Hussein. Arafat's support of Iraq's conquest of Kuwait cost him much of his financial support from other Arab states and made it impossible
for him to participate directly in the ARAB-ISRAELI
PEACE TALKS that began in Madrid in 1991.

Arbeit Macht Frei   German phrase meaning "work
brings freedom"; the cynically deceptive slogan that
the Germans placed on the gates of some World
War II CONCENTRATION CAMPS—most notably at
AUSCHWITZ and Dachau.

Arbenz Guzmán, Jacobo (1913–1971)   The president of Guatemala from 1951 to 1954 who continued the reform program of Guatemala's first
democratically elected president, Juan José Arevalo
(1945–1951). Arbenz passed laws aimed at expropriating uncultivated land belonging to multinational companies, which prompted officials of the
U.S.-owned United Fruit Company, 80 percent of
whose Guatemalan land lay fallow, to appeal to
U.S. Secretary of State John Foster Dulles for assistance. The reforms, along with the interception of a
Czech arms shipment to Guatemala, convinced the
U.S. government that the Arbenz government was
aligned with Communists. A U.S.-funded rebel
organization, assisted by an intense propaganda
campaign, overthrew Arbenz in the GUATEMALAN
COUP of 1954.

arbitrage   The process of buying foreign exchange,
stocks, bonds, and other commodities in one market and immediately selling them in another market
at higher prices.

arbitration   1. A method of dispute settlement in
which an impartial third party, the *arbitrator,* holds
a formal hearing and renders a decision that may or
may not be binding on both sides. The arbitrator
may be a single individual or a board of three, five,
or more (usually an uneven number). 2. A process sometimes used to peacefully resolve a dispute
between two or more states. Basically the parties
agree to submit their case to a third party for resolution and at the same time agree to be bound by
the decision. The formal agreement to use arbitration is called the *compromis* or *compromis d'arbitrage.* The decision or verdict in the case is called
the *award.* Arbitration has been much discussed as
a conflict resolution technique in international
affairs but is seldom used on truly important issues.

Arbitration, Permanent Court of   A continuously extant panel of available arbitrators from which parties to an international dispute, usually states, may select judges to settle their cases. It was first created by the 1899 Hague Convention for the Pacific Settlement of International Disputes and revised by the Second Hague Conference of 1907. The "court" is neither permanent nor a court. It is simply a list of qualified jurists, appointed by states party to the conventions, whose main value is the fact that it is a readily available machinery. Indeed, in its whole history the "court" has decided only a few dozen cases. It is headquartered in the Hague, the Netherlands.

arbitration acts   Laws that encourage (and sometimes demand) the submission of many types of problems, often labor-management disputes, to an arbitrator.

archives   **1.** The records that document the day-to-day operations of an organization. These include all internal and external communications of whatever nature, no matter how insignificant they may seem. **2.** Any repository of documentary records.

archives, diplomatic   All of the documents and papers of a formal diplomatic mission. Article 24 of the Vienna Convention on Diplomatic Relations asserts: "The archives and documents of the mission shall be inviolable at any time and wherever they may be." In the event of the breaking of diplomatic relations, the archives of the departing mission, if they do not leave with the diplomats, are usually put under seal and put in the custody of a neutral state's mission pending for the time being.

arc of crisis   An area of great political instability (sometimes called the *crescent of crisis*) that stretches from Ethiopia through the Arabian peninsula and the Persian Gulf to Afghanistan, Pakistan, and India. In the late 1970s and 1980s crises in the area included the civil war in Ethiopia, the IRANIAN REVOLUTION after the fall of the shah, the Soviet invasion of Afghanistan and the IRAN-IRAQ WAR. It was U.S. President Jimmy Carter's National Security Advisor, Zbigniew Brzezinski, who popularized this concept in the late 1970s to link disparate events and areas characterized by instability; he saw the common factor as Soviet involvement designed to undermine Western, especially the United States', influence. The arc of crisis encompassed the HORN OF AFRICA, where the Soviet Union had changed alliances and supported Ethiopia in its war against Somalia in the Ogaden in 1977–1978, and Afghanistan, where pro-Soviet forces took control in a coup in 1978. The idea of the arc was both persuasive and controversial. Many were easily convinced that the Soviets were behind all upheaval in the Third World and that there was a pattern of Soviet geopolitical advancement, as Brzezinski indicated. But others focused on the indigenous causes of these conflicts. In subsequent years this latter view has gained in credence.

Ardennes, Battle of   **1.** The August 20–25, 1914, World War I battle wherein the Germans stopped a French offensive in the wooded area of northern France.   **2.** The May 12–15, 1940, World War II battle wherein the Germans invaded northern France and quickly defeated the French and their British allies. *See also* DUNKIRK.   **3.** The unexpected December 1944–January 1945 World War II offensive by the Germans. Also known as the BATTLE OF THE BULGE, this was the last major effort by the Germans to forestall an invasion of Germany from the west.

area studies   Social science examinations of a given geographical area that explores its culture, economy, history, political institutions, and so on.

ARENA   "Republican National Alliance," a right-wing political party that has been responsible for assassinations and many other forms of political violence in El Salvador. The party was founded in 1982 by a coalition of wealthy businessmen and right-wing politicians. In March 1989 ARENA candidate Alfredo Christiani emerged victorious in the Salvodoran presidential election. He professes to represent a party that is more moderate and practical than its earlier incarnation.

Arendt, Hannah (1906–1975)   The German-born American political philosopher who argued in *The Origins of Totalitarianism* (1951; 2d ed. 1958) that the TOTALITARIANISM of Adolf Hitler's Germany and Joseph Stalin's Soviet Union were "novel form[s] of government" with critical differences "from other forms of political oppression known to us such as despotism, tyranny, and dictatorship." It was the alienation of modern life, she held, that made people vulnerable to ideological movements such as National Socialism or communism—movements that, through terror, encompass all aspects of life in a totalitarianist embrace. But the one concept for which Arendt is best known comes from her account of the trial of Adolf Eichmann (1906–1962), the high-ranking GESTAPO leader who oversaw the NAZI persecution of the Jews. He was kidnapped by Israeli agents in Argentina in 1960 and tried in Israel in 1961. In the provocative *Eichmann in Jerusalem: A Report on the Banality of Evil* (1963) Arendt, herself a Jewish refugee from the Nazis, looks at the murderer of millions of innocent civilians during the HOLOCAUST of World War II and discovers him to be merely a banal bureaucrat, a functionary who might otherwise have been perfectly harmless and led a normal life. This highly controversial analysis implied that too many other "normal" people might have done the same under the circumstances. In a stinging rebuttal, historian Barbara W. Tuchman wrote in *The New York Review of Books* that "Eichmann was an extraordinary, not an ordinary man, whose record is hardly one of the 'banality' of evil. For the author of that ineffable phrase—as applied to the murder of six million—to have been so taken in by Eichmann's version of himself as just a routine civil servant obeying orders is one of the puzzles of modern journalism. From a presumed historian it is inexplicable" (May 29, 1966).

Argentine Anti-Communist Alliance Known as "Triple A," this right-wing Argentine DEATH SQUAD had strong ties to the military junta, which ruled that country from 1976 to 1983. A paramilitary organization, it played a major role in Argentina's DIRTY WAR, in which many of the nation's liberals, leftists, Jews, and members of the intelligentsia joined the ranks of the DISAPPEARED.

Argentine fascism Dictatorial rule as practiced in Argentina. Modern Argentine fascism was imitative of the European models provided by BENITO MUSSOLINI and ADOLF HITLER with policies of nationalistic industrialization directed by an authoritarian

leader. It began with a 1943 military coup led by Colonel JUAN DOMINGO PERON, which ousted the constitutional government. Elections in 1946 brought Peron to the presidency. His dynamic wife, Eva Duarte Peron (1919–1952), helped develop his appeal to labor and women's groups. (Women obtained the right to vote in 1947.) Reelected in 1952, Peron was ousted by the military in 1955 and went into exile, eventually settling in Spain. In the 1950s and 1960s, the government passed between military and civilian administrations, as each sought to deal with diminishing economic growth and continuing social and labor unrest. In 1973 Peron returned as president; his third wife, Isabel de Peron, was made vice president. When Peron died in 1974, he was succeeded by his wife, the first female president in the Western Hemisphere. Mrs. Peron's administration was undermined by economic deterioration, Peronist intraparty struggles, and growing terrorism from both left and right. She was removed from office by a 1976 military coup. Serious economic problems, defeat by the British in 1982 after an unsuccessful Argentine attempt to establish sovereignty over the Falklands/Malvinas Islands (during the FALKLANDS WAR), human rights abuses, and charges of growing corruption eventually discredited the military. This resulted in a period of gradual transition leading the country toward democratic rule. Previous bans on political parties and other basic political liberties were lifted, and a successful and generally peaceful process for the return to elected government was implemented.

During the years of military rule from 1976 to 1983, the Argentine military and right-wing DEATH SQUADS directed an era of state terror officially known as the "Process of National Reorganization." This period is better known as the DIRTY WAR, in which perhaps 20,000 citizens—women, men, and children—"disappeared." Many of the DISAPPEARED were incarcerated for long periods of time before being tortured and killed at the hands of the military or the paramilitary death squads. The dirty war was the right wing's response to the pervasive Argentine left-wing guerrilla violence of the late 1960s and early and mid-1970s. The dirty war, however, was directed not only against the violent left, but against moderates and liberals, Jews, and other perceived and potential opponents of the right-wing regime. When the democratic government of Raul Alfonsin Foulkes (1926–) ascended to power in December 1983, the new president appointed the National Commission on Disappeared Persons (CONADEP) to uncover the specific fates of the thousands of disappeared persons. CONADEP issued a report in September 1984 that documented a level of state repression that may be the most glaring example of state terrorism in a Western nation since NAZI Germany—an appropriate comparison when it is remembered that since World War II Argentina has had the well-earned reputation of being hospitable to Nazi war criminals.

Argov, Slomo (1929–) Israeli ambassador to Great Britain who was severely wounded on June 3, 1982, in an assassination attempt by Black June, a radical Palestinian group led by ABU NIDAL. This attack helped prompt Israeli Prime Minister MENACHEM BEGIN to launch the 1982 invasion of Lebanon, an attempt by Israel to drive the PALESTINE LIBERATION ORGANIZATION out of that country. The PLO denied any complicity in the Argov incident. Three Arabs, including the nephew of Abu Nidal, were arrested by London police following the shooting; in March 1983 the three were sentenced to prison terms ranging from 30 to 35 years.

Ariana The district in Geneva, Switzerland, in which the European headquarters of the United Nations has been located since 1946.

Arianespace The European consortium of aerospace companies that in 1980 became the world's first commercial space transportation business. Since then it has placed dozens of satellites into earth orbit with Ariane rockets.

Arias Peace Plan The arrangements for peace in Central America primarily created by Oscar Arias Sanchez, president of Costa Rica, and signed in Guatemala on August 7, 1987, by the presidents of Costa Rica, El Salvador, Guatemala, Honduras, and Nicaragua. The accord was drafted mainly to bring peace to Nicaragua, but all signatories agreed to end censorship, grant amnesty to political prisoners, hold elections with international observers, negotiate cease-fires with rebels, and prevent their

territories from being used as bases for guerrilla operations in neighboring states. Arias won the 1987 Nobel Peace Prize for this. This award was in the best Nobel tradition of giving peace prizes not to those who actually achieved peace but to those who at least made an effort. While the Arias Peace Plan was not successful when it was first proposed, it helped establish the framework and create the political conditions by which peace was later achieved with the end of the NICARAGUAN CIVIL WAR in 1990 and the EL SALVADOR CIVIL WAR in 1992.

armageddon 1. A full nuclear exchange between the superpowers that would destroy all life and civilization. Armageddon has been often referred to by U.S. military and political leaders. General Douglas MacArthur in his speech (reprinted in his 1964 *Reminiscences*) just after accepting the surrender of Japan on September 2, 1945, said: "Military alliances, balances of power, leagues of nations, all in turn failed, leaving the only path to be by way of the crucible of war. The utter destructiveness of war now blocks out this alternative. We have had our last chance. If we will not devise some greater and more equitable system, Armageddon will be at our door." More recently President Ronald Reagan, in Gwynne Dyer's *War* (1985), shared his thoughts on nuclear war: "I turn back to your ancient prophets in the Old Testament and the signs foretelling Armageddon, and I find myself wondering if—if we're the generation that's going to see that come about. . . . There have been times in the past when we thought the world was coming to an end, but never anything like this." A final word goes to General Bruce Holloway, quoted in Michael Parfit's *The Boys Behind the Bombs* (1983): "I don't think there'll be an Armageddon war, but I'll put it this way. There has never been any weapon yet invented or perfected that hasn't been used." 2. A great last battle between good and evil that the Bible (Revelation 16:14–16) predicts will precede the end of the world. 3. A decisive major battle.

armaments-tension dilemma The argument whether armaments result from underlying tensions or themselves are an independent source of tension. In fact, they are probably both. States engage in an

ARMS RACE when they have serious political differences, but the arms race itself will usually exacerbate tensions.

armed neutrality   *See* NEUTRALITY.

armed propaganda   A kinder, gentler name for traditional TERRORISM.

Armed Services Committees   The permanent standing committees in the Senate and the House of Representatives of the U.S. Congress where most debate, analysis, and amendment of legislation concerning military policy takes place. Their primary function is to review the military budget and, in particular, procurement plans. More recently they also have used their power to influence military doctrine and strategy—especially as it affects the NORTH ATLANTIC TREATY ORGANIZATION. The membership of both committees always has been heavily unrepresentative of their respective legislative houses. They tend to be dominated by representatives and senators from southern states who, whether Democrat or Republican, are notably more conservative than other members of Congress. Therefore the committees have had a general ideological inclination to be sympathetic toward Pentagon requests for high defense expenditures. Furthermore, the members typically have major military bases or defense industry plants in their districts or states, and they tend not only to accept any Pentagon requests benefiting those areas but also to increase procurement where it will help their constituents. The overall consequence has been general inability of the committees to form consistent long-range policy or to deal with defense budgets comprehensively, rather than on a piecemeal basis. Nevertheless, the committees contribute to informed debates about defense policy. In the early 1990s the chairmen of House and Senate committees, Representative Les Aspin of Wisconsin and Senator Sam Nunn of Georgia, played crucial roles in the efforts to adjust U.S. national security policy to the post–Cold War environment, with Aspin in particular devising his own blueprint for downsizing as an alternative to that of the Pentagon. Aspin would have an even greater influence on restructuring the U.S. military beginning in 1993 when he became Secretary of Defense in the administration of President WILLIAM J. CLINTON.

Armenian-Azerbaijani Civil War   *See* AZERBAIJANI-ARMENIAN CIVIL WAR.

Armenian earthquake   The December 7, 1988, earthquake in Soviet Armenia that killed over 50,000 and left ten times that number homeless. This was the first time that the Soviet Union welcomed international help in the aftermath of a national disaster. The West responded with substantial disaster relief and medical aid.

ARMENIANS SURRENDER

It happened during the international rescue effort in earthquake-stricken Armenia. A uniform-wearing French military contingent, aided by a team of trained dogs, detected the presence of a group of people trapped underneath the rubble. The rescuers summoned a crane, and, as the rubble was cleared, they kept talking among themselves in French. When the Armenians finally surfaced, they looked at the dogs, saw the uniforms, listened to the conversations in a strange language and assumed they were victims of a foreign attack. They put their arms up in the air and "surrendered" to the French.

SOURCE: Charles Fenyvesi, "Washington Whispers" (*U.S. News & World Report,* February 20, 1989).

Armenian genocide   The systematic murder of an estimated 1.5 million Armenians by the Turkish government in 1915. At the outbreak of World War I, the rulers of the Ottoman Empire perceived the Armenians as a dangerous foreign element within their borders and decided to rid the entire country of its Armenian residents. Even Armenians serving in the Ottoman armies were murdered. Those who were not killed were forced to travel for weeks over mountains and deserts to Syria, Mesopotamia, and other neighboring areas. This was the last of a series of massacres going back to the 1870s.

Armenian terrorism   Campaigns of violence launched in the name of Armenian nationalism. Armenian terrorism is a relatively recent phenomenon, having emerged in 1975. Its perpetrators, while varying in some specific aims and motivations, generally seek autonomy for the

Armenian people and revenge for the deaths of an estimated 1.5 million members of their minority Christian community at the hands of the Ottoman Turks during what has come to be known as the ARMENIAN GENOCIDE. Much of Armenian terrorism is directed against members of the Turkish government, especially Turkish diplomats at international posts. The present-day Turkish government both disputes the factual basis of the GENOCIDE and denies any responsibility for the actions of the Ottomans. Armenian radicals refuse to dismiss what they claim is the historical case and the present reality of a scattered people without an autonomous homeland. In January 1988 the Turkish government announced its intention to open the Ottoman archives, in an effort to disprove the claims of government-directed genocide. Since then Turkish officials have conceded that 300,000 perished during the forcible relocation of the Armenian population during wartime. Members of Armenian terrorist organizations have repeatedly stated that they have resorted to violence only after the complete failure of 60 years of seeking a peaceful settlement. The principal terrorist organizations are the Armenian Revolutionary Army, the Armenian Secret Army for the Liberation of Armenia, and the Justice Commandos of the Armenian Genocide. *See also* YANIKIAN, GURGEN.

armistice An agreement on the cessation of hostilities between warring parties. A *capitulary armistice* leads to a surrender. An armistice does not affect the legal status of the war. Only those terms set out in the agreement are legally binding according to international law. If an armistice is not agreed to by the highest political authorities of the belligerent states, it will not have legal force. Thus agreements reached only by military commanders may have no legal force. The scope, purpose, and duration of an armistice agreement can range from a temporary halt to hostilities in a specific area for a limited time to a complete cessation of all hostilities in anticipation of a peace treaty. Purposes of an armistice vary from a brief respite to tend to the wounded and bury the dead to an opportunity to negotiate peace (as in World War I), or to the end of fighting without a peace treaty (as in the Korean War).

Armistice, the The document signed in a railway car in Compiegne, France, by Germany and the Allies on November 11, 1918. When the Germans conquered France in 1940 they made the French government sign their surrender to the Germans in this very same railway car, which had been resting in a museum. The railway car was later taken to Berlin where it was destroyed during a wartime air raid.

Armistice Day November 11, 1918; the day World War I ended on the western front. Germany accepted this agreement in order to negotiate a peace before the ALLIES overran its armies and invaded the country, thereby avoiding an unconditional surrender. The failure of Allied armies to enter Germany led to conservative and reactionary claims in the WEIMAR REPUBLIC era that their army had not been defeated in the field of battle but stabbed in the back by liberal politicians. Once a holiday celebrating the end of the "war to end all wars" in the United States, Armistice Day has since been converted to a day to commemorate the veterans of all wars.

arms control 1. The idea that international agreements may govern the numbers, types, and performance characteristics of weapons systems or armed forces. Note that arms control (limiting weapons) is not DISARMAMENT (giving up or destroying weapons). The modern concept of arms control evolved in the late 1950s and early 1960s as a response to the total failure of all efforts for disarmament. The basic rationale behind arms control is that potential enemies have a common interest in reducing uncertainty connected with weapons developments by adopting certain restraints. Thus arms control frequently is analyzed as a restraint on the development, deployment, control, and use of armaments in an effort to promote national security and lessen international tensions. From an analytical point of view, arms control can be formal or tacit, unilateral or mutual. Arms control measures include the PARTIAL TEST-BAN treaty of 1963, the NUCLEAR NON-PROLIFERATION treaty of 1968, the SALT treaty of 1972, the ABM treaty of 1972, the Intermediate Nuclear Forces Treaty of 1987, and the START treaty of 1991. 2. A general name for measures taken to reduce international military instability. Arms control can be divided into two types: controls over existing weapons systems and preemptive arms control, which tries to prevent the deployment of a new or potential weapon. Arms control may be self-imposed or unilateral, but more often it is the result of bilateral or multilateral agreements or treaties. 3. Any measures taken by potential adversaries to reduce the likelihood or scope of a future war. David P. Barash in *The Arms Race and Nuclear War* (1987) quotes Albert Einstein giving this opinion on arms control efforts in the 1920s: "What would you think about a meeting of a town council which is concerned because an increasing number of people are knifed to death each night in drunken brawls, and which proceeds to discuss just how long and how sharp shall be the knife that the inhabitants of the city may be permitted to carry?" If Einstein were alive today, he would probably agree with Alva Myrdal, who writes in *The Game of Disarmament* (1977): "I wish it were not too late to start a boycott against the use of 'arms control' as an overall term. It is nothing but a euphemism, serving regrettably to lead thinking and action towards the acceptance as 'arms control measures' of compromises with scant or nil disarmament effect." Former U.S. Secretary of Defense Caspar W. Weinberger rejected such attitudes when he observed, "Wishful thinking is equally as effective for arms control as it is for birth control"(*USA Today*, October 6, 1986). Nevertheless, as strategic analyst Stanley Hoffmann noted in *Newsweek* (October 1, 1984): "Arms control has to have a future, or none of us does."

With the end of the Cold War and the demise of the Soviet Union, however, the days of bilateral arms control may be largely over. The United States and Russia, however, have carried on where the United States and the Soviet Union left off. On June 16, 1992, Russian President Boris Yeltsin and U.S. President George Bush produced an accord that will bring about more significant reductions in strategic nuclear forces than those agreed to in START. The accord proposed to cut nuclear weapons to one-third of their existing levels and to eliminate all land-based MIRV missiles. Warhead limits would be cut to 4,250 (United States) and 3,800 (Russia) by 1999 and to 3,500 (United States) and 3,000 (Russia) by 2003. This could well be the last of the bilateral nuclear arms control agreements. Nor is it clear

that there will be future multilateral arms control in Europe of the kind that led to the 1990 CONVENTIONAL FORCES EUROPE TREATY. This is not to suggest that arms control has no future; simply that there will be a refocusing of effort toward multilateral efforts to halt the spread of ballistic missiles and chemical, biological, and nuclear capabilities to states in the Third World.

Arms Control and Disarmament Act of 1961　The law that created the U.S. Arms Control and Disarmament Agency to conduct research, aid in arms control and disarmament negotiations, and provide public information. The act specifically states that "adequate verification of compliance should be an indispensable part" of any arms control treaty. The act was amended in 1975 to require an annual submission to Congress of an "Arms Control Impact Statement" with all budget requests for new weapons developments. But the effectiveness of this amendment in alerting Congress and the public to the adverse consequences of new weapons developments is diminished by the fact that the report is prepared by the very same agencies that would be primarily responsible for the development of these new weapons.

Arms Control and Disarmament Agency (ACDA)　The U.S. government agency established in 1961 to formulate and implement arms control policy within the framework of overall national security policy. While ACDA is located in the State Department, its director is the "principal advisor" to the secretary of state and the president on arms control and disarmament matters. The ACDA itself has four primary functions: operation of control systems (monitoring), where it has been less important than the Central Intelligence Agency; the dissemination and coordination of public information concerning arms control and disarmament; conduct of research for arms control; and preparation for and management of U.S. arms control negotiations. Because of its limited size and capabilities, it has generally had a supporting rather than a dominant role in formulating and implementing arms control policy. With the end of the Cold War and questions about the future relevance of arms control, the future of the ACDA itself is in some doubt.

arms control paradox   The argument that arms control is most attainable when it is unnecessary and least feasible when it is most needed. This paradox was developed by HEDLEY BULL in *The Control of the Arms Race* (1961).

arms conversion   The retooling and reorganization of a nation's industry from military to domestic civilian production. This is always a matter of degree. The United States had a major arms conversion after World War II but nevertheless continued to maintain war production capacities as a matter of policy. With the end of the Cold War, arms conversion—or, as it is widely termed, *defense conversion*—has once again become a major item on the domestic agenda in the United States and in the countries of Eastern and Western Europe. In the United States it is estimated that by 1995 there could be up to 1 million fewer defense-related jobs than there were in 1989. The states of the former Soviet Union are having an especially difficult time converting their defense industries because, unlike the West, their managerial infrastructure is only beginning to develop a consumer focus and capitalistic orientation. Thus many of their factories, instead of converting, are seeking to sell products such as helicopters and fighter aircraft to the rest of the world at cut-rate prices.

arms race   1. The vigorous competition between rival states or alliances to bolster military and/or naval capabilities to gain PARITY with or superiority over the opposition. The usual reasons for engaging in an arms race are age-old and intertwined with concepts of defense, deterrence, national honor, prestige, and the elusive glory of war. This is not without dire consequences. For example, the naval race between Great Britain and Germany was one of the factors leading to World War I.   2. A process whereby potential enemies adjust their arms procurement policies to each other's military development, with the intention of gaining a specific level of comparative military strength. Critics contend that arms races can lead to war, but others see arms races as stabilizing factors in the balance of power. U.S. President Dwight D. Eisenhower in an April 16, 1953, speech offered this poignant analysis of arms races: "The worst to be feared and the best to be expected can be simply stated. The worst is atomic war. The best would be this: a life of perpetual fear and tension; a burden of arms draining the wealth and labor of all peoples. Every gun that is made, every warship launched, every rocket fired, signifies, in the final sense, a theft from those who are cold and are not clothed. The world in arms is not spending money alone. It is spending the sweat of its laborers, the genius of its scientists, the hopes of its children." Eisenhower might well have agreed with Soviet President Mikhail Gorbachev, who wrote in *Perestroika* (1987) that: "The arms race, just like nuclear war, is unwinnable." There may well be an important difference between conventional arms races, which seem to culminate in ARMS STABILITY, and nuclear arms races, which are most dangerous in their early stages when the adversaries have vulnerable strategic forces that make very tempting targets for a preemptive strike.

arms sale   The transferral of weapons produced in one country to military forces or insurgent movements in another. The pattern of arms sales in recent times was from the advanced industrialized states of the West, especially the United States, Great Britain, and France, and from the Soviet Union to other states, especially in the Middle East. In this way a great deal of high-technology and advanced weapons systems have been made available to states that are unable to produce these systems themselves. Increasingly, indigenous arms suppliers, such as China and Argentina, have emerged in the Third World. As the domestic market for new weapons systems in the advanced industrialized world contracts, so competition for Third World markets is likely to become more intense. *See also* MERCHANT OF DEATH.

arms stability   1. An arms race pause during which both sides digest recent arms acquisitions and do not initiate major new procurement programs. 2. A point in an arms race at which neither side has a significant advantage over the other.

arms transfer   1. Any selling of armaments. 2. The movement of military supplies of all kinds from industrialized countries to the THIRD WORLD. *Compare to* MERCHANT OF DEATH.

Armstrong, Neil (1930–   )   The U.S. astronaut who, on July 20, 1969, was the first person to step (from his spacecraft) onto the surface of the moon. He then said: "That's one small step for a man, one giant leap for mankind."

army 1. A comprehensive term for all of the land military forces of a state. A "real" army is a permanent and bureaucratically structured standing force as opposed to a temporary and amateur militia force assembled only in an emergency. 2. The largest administrative and tactical unit of a nation's land forces. 3. All the armed forces of a nation. U.S. Secretary of War Elihu Root wrote in his *Annual Report* (1899) that "the real object of having an army is to provide for war." But as U.S. President Calvin Coolidge warned in a 1925 speech: "No nation ever had an army large enough to guarantee it against attack in time of peace or insure it victory in time of war." B. H. Liddell Hart, one of this century's preeminent military analysts, was forced to conclude regretfully in *Thoughts on War* (1944) that "the Army, for all its good points, is a cramping place for a *thinking* man. As I have seen too often, such a man chafes and goes—or else decays." Of course, he was talking about the British Army.

GENERAL MACARTHUR SAVES THE ARMY

Paralyzing nausea began to creep over me. In my emotional exhaustion I spoke recklessly [to President Franklin D. Roosevelt in 1933 about his plans to cut the army's budget] and said something to the general effect that when we lost the next war, and an American boy, lying in the mud with an enemy bayonet through his belly and an enemy foot on his dying throat, spat out his last curse, I wanted the name not to be MacArthur, but Roosevelt. The President grew livid. "You must not talk that way to the President!" he roared. He was, of course, right, and I knew it almost before the words had left my mouth. I said that I was sorry and apologized. But I felt my army career was at an end. I told him he had my resignation as Chief of Staff. As I reached the door his voice came with that cool detachment which so reflected his extraordinary self-control, "Don't be foolish, Douglas; you and the budget must get together on this."

[George] Dem [the secretary of war] had shortly reached my side and I could hear his gleeful tones, "You've saved the army." But I just vomited on the steps of the White House.

SOURCE: General Douglas MacArthur, *Reminiscences* (1964).

---

army, standing 1. A military force in time of peace. 2. A larger military force than is minimally necessary to maintain domestic order. Since ancient times free peoples have been warned of the dangers of a standing army. Plato in *The Republic* (370 B.C.) warned that "every care must be taken that our auxiliaries [soldiers], being stronger than our citizens, may not grow too much for them and become savage beasts." During the U.S. Constitutional Convention of 1787 Elbridge Gerry, a delegate from Massachusetts, is supposed to have advised: "A standing army may be likened to a standing member—an excellent assurance of domestic tranquillity, but a dangerous temptation to foreign adventure." Henry David Thoreau in his *On the Duty of Civil Disobedience* (1849) concluded that "the objections which have been brought against a standing army, and they are many and weighty, and deserve to prevail, may also at last be brought against a standing government." Even U.S. President Woodrow Wilson, in a speech in Pittsburgh, Pennsylvania (January 29, 1916), professed: "I am not one of those who believe that a great standing army is the means of maintaining peace, because if you build up a great profession those who form parts of it want to exercise their profession." Nevertheless, the United States only after World World II reluctantly accepted the necessity of maintaining a large military force in a time of relative peace—to be both a deterrent during the Cold War and as an instrument of national policy during limited wars.

army attaché The senior army officer in a diplomatic mission who serves in the dual capacity of the senior representative of her or his nation's ground forces and a member of the official staff of an ambassador or minister to a foreign country. He or she serves as a military observer and reports on the military personnel, plans, and developments of the country where stationed. In most countries he or she is referred to as the *military attaché*. There may also be parallel *air* and *naval attachés*. Some states have a *defense attaché*, who would have the broadest range of responsibilities.

Arnhem, Battle of The September 1944 battle in Holland during WORLD WAR II. Allied airborne forces futilely sought to secure a bridge over the Rhine River at Arnhem, which would have allowed for a rapid advance into Germany. But because German resistance was too strong and ground forces could not exploit the initial gains of the paratroopers, the Allies were forced to withdraw without gaining their objective.

A BRIDGE TOO FAR

On the narrow corridor that would carry the armored drive, there were five major bridges to take. They had to be seized intact by airborne assault. It was the fifth [for Operation Market Garden], the crucial bridge over the Lower Rhine at a place called Arnhem, sixty-four miles behind the German lines, that worried Lieutenant General Frederick Browning, Deputy Commander, First Allied Airborne Army [on September 10, 1944]. Pointing to the Arnhem bridge on the map he asked, "How long will it take the armor to reach us?" Field Marshal Montgomery replied briskly, "Two days." Still looking at the map, Browning said, "We can hold it for four." Then he added, "But, sir, I think we might be going a bridge too far."

SOURCE: General Roy E. Urquhart, *Arnhem* (1958). This last phrase of Browning's ("a bridge too far") would be used as the title of Cornelius Ryan's 1974 book on the battle and of a major film made from it.

Arnoldson, Klas P. (1844–1916)   The Swedish peace activist who helped further the dissolution of the union between Norway and Sweden in 1895. When he was awarded the Nobel Peace Prize in 1908 (along with FREDRIK BAJER), much of the Swedish public was outraged—because Arnoldson, a Swede, had favored Norway's claim to independence.

Aron, Raymond (1905–1983)   The French sociologist and political commentator who was the foremost European intellectual supporter of the American leadership of the Western world during the post–World War II period. His *The Imperial Republic: The United States and the World, 1945–1973* (1974) continues to serve as a response to critics of an American foreign policy that protected Western Europe from the Soviet Union. Aron's writings were an important counterpoint to the intellectual leftism epitomized by his onetime friend Jean-Paul Sartre (1905–1980), whose philosophy heavily influenced European youth and the

Third World. In *The Opium of the Intellectuals* (1962) Aron gives Marx and the French left an ironic twist. If, as Karl Marx (1818–1883) asserted, "Religion is the opium of the people," then Marxism was an equally stupefying drug specially designed, it seemed, for intellectuals, preventing them from believing the evidence of their senses— that communism as it evolved in the Soviet Union offered a far less desirable life for the masses than the capitalistic economics of the West. Aron also managed to be a philosopher, strategist, theoretician, and foreign policy analyst. He wrote extensively on problems of peace and war and national and international security. His most famous work was *Peace and War* (1962), which some critics suggested was the nearest contemporary writing had come to a work of the brilliance and insight of THUCYDIDES' *History of the Peloponnesian War* (5th century B.C.). Aron applied a ruthless French logic to his discussion of the evolution of the international system, the logic of superpower relations, which he described in terms of "enemy brothers," and to the problems of power and security. He was an expert on KARL VON CLAUSEWITZ, on the rise of TOTAL WAR in the nineteenth and twentieth centuries, and on the contemporary STATE SYSTEM. In *The Great Debate* (1965) Aron provided a major analysis of the strategic debates between the United States and its European allies. Though sometimes critical of American policy, he was balanced and judicious in his interpretations and in his writings. During the 1970s he argued that the United States had to find a middle way between isolationism and globalism.

arret de merchandise   French term for the confiscation and sale of enemy goods from ships of neutral states.

arret de prince   French term meaning "the verdict or decision of the state"; in practice, the temporary detention by a state of foreign ships ordered to prevent the dissemination of politically significant news, or in anticipation of a declaration of war (in which case the ships of belligerents would be interned—detained in place until the end of the war).

arrogance of power   A phrase often applied to the foreign policy of the United States during the mid-

1960s. It was mostly associated with former U.S. Senator J. William Fulbright (1905–   ) of Arkansas, democrat, chairman of the Senate Foreign Relations Committee (1959–1975), who was a major critic of U.S. intervention in Vietnam and the Dominican Republic. In 1966 Fulbright's book, *The Arrogance of Power,* helped fuel the debate on U.S. foreign policy. Colonel Harry G. Summers, Jr., would later write in his analysis of American strategy during the Vietnam War, *On Strategy* (1982): "Observers have faulted our intervention in Vietnam as evidence of American arrogance of power—attempts by the United States to be the World's Policeman. But there is another dimension to American arrogance, the international version of our domestic Great Society programs where we . . . saw it as our duty to force the world into the American mold—to act not so much the World's Policeman as the World's Nanny. It is difficult today to recall the depth of our arrogance."

arsenal   1. Any place where weapons and munitions are held.   2. A factory where military forces manufacture weapons.   3. All of the weapons belonging to a person or a state.   4. An armory.

arsenal of democracy   U.S. President Franklin D. Roosevelt's phrase, first uttered in a December 29, 1940, speech, to describe the U.S. policy of supplying weapons to the states opposing the fascist powers in World War II. When the United States went into the war a year later, the phrase became even more significant and literal. According to Walter Isaacson and Evan Thomas's *The Wise Men* (1986), "[John] McCloy was instrumental in the fight for [the LEND-LEASE ACT OF 1941] and even helped contribute its key slogan. In a conversation with [Felix] Frankfurter, he used the phrase 'arsenal of democracy,' which he had picked up from Jean Monnet. 'Don't use those words for a few weeks,' said Frankfurter, who then went to the White House and told Robert Sherwood to use the phrase in an address he was writing for Roosevelt."

Article 100A   The heart of the 1986 SINGLE EUROPEAN ACT that allows for decisions to be made by "qualified majority"—thus decisions of the EUROPEAN COUNCIL do not have to be unanimous.

Article 231   The "war guilt" clause in the TREATY OF VERSAILLES of 1919, which read: "The Allied and Associated Governments affirm and Germany accepts the responsibility of Germany and her allies for causing all the loss and damage to which the Allied and Associated Governments and their nationals have been subjected as a consequence of the war imposed upon them by the aggression of Germany and her allies." Responsibility for causing the war cannot be attributed to Germany and its allies alone, and this article quickly became a subject of controversy and resentment in Germany.

artificial boundary   *See* BOUNDARY, ARTIFICIAL.

art of war   1. A scientific attitude toward military operations implying that the application of specific techniques can solve almost any military problem.   2. A mystical approach to military strategy and tactics implying that all things being equal, an intangible aptitude for command will win the day. The debate over whether war is more of an art or a science is eternal. One famous analysis asserts that it is most like a trade. Frederick Engels wrote in a September 25, 1857, letter to Karl Marx (quoted in Edward Mead Earle, ed., *Makers of Modern Strategy,* 1945): "To the question whether war should be called an art or a science, the answer given is that war is most like a trade. Fighting is to war what cash payment is to trade, for however rarely it may be necessary for it actually to occur, everything is directed towards it, and eventually it must take place all the same and must be decisive."   3. The title of two separate classics on military strategy: the first written by SUN-TZU in ancient China and the second by the Italian NICCOLÒ MACHIAVELLI in the sixteenth century. The nineteenth-century Prussian general KARL VON CLAUSEWITZ is considered the preeminent philosopher of the art of war.

Arusha Convention   A 1969 trade agreement between the European Economic Community and Kenya, Tanzania, and Uganda that ended in 1975, when it was replaced by the LOMÉ CONVENTION.

Arusha Declaration   The formal policy issued in 1967 by Tanzania's President Julius Nyerere (1921–   ) announcing that his country will have

---

LEARNING THE ART OF WAR

[During the American Civil War Colonel Mosby captured a] young German lieutenant who . . . was on his way to join his regiment in Sheridan's army. . . . He was dressed in a fine beavercloth overcoat; high boots, and a new hat with gilt cord and tassel. After we were pretty well acquainted, I said to him, "We have done you no harm. Why did you come over here to fight us?" "Oh," he said, "I only come to learn de art of war." I then left him and rode to the head of the column, as the enemy were about, and there was a prospect of a fight. It was not long before the German came trotting up to join me. There had been such a metamorphosis that I scarcely recognized him. One of my men had exchanged his old clothes with him for his new ones, and he complained about it. I asked him if he had not told me that he came to Virginia to learn the art of war. "Yes," he replied. "Very well," I said, "this is your first lesson."

Source: John S. Mosby, *Memoirs* (1917).

---

a socialist state. Political rights would be denied to anyone "associated with the practices of capitalism."

Aryan 1. The ancient Indo-European people with Eastern European origins who migrated southeast as far as India. 2. The word adopted by NAZI Germany to describe "Nordic" origins of ancient Germans. The Germans considered themselves to be the "master race" and other Nordics—the Dutch, Norwegians, and Danes—were invited to join them. "Mixed races," such as the French, were problematic for Nazi racial theorists, but all other origins were deemed inferior according to this now-discredited, and always despicable, racist ideology.

Aryan Nations A loose organization of U.S. NEO-NAZI groups that share a common bond of racism and anti-Semitism. Founded in 1974, the Aryan Nations serves a coordinating function for its constituent organizations, which maintain contact through a computer network bulletin board and seek new recruits from alienated youths and imprisoned convicts. In recent years such American neo-Nazi groups have been successfully encouraging the development of similar groups in Germany.

ASA (Association of Southeast Asia) A group established in 1961 as an effort to improve cooperation among the Federation of Malaya, the Philippines, and Thailand. Disputes among its members doomed it to failure, and it was superseded first by another futile attempt at cooperation by Malaysia, the Philippines, and Indonesia (called Maphilindo) and subsequently by the more successful ASEAN.

ASAT *See* ANTI-SATELLITE WEAPON.

ASEAN (Association of Southeast Asian Nations) A regional group of non-Communist Southeast Asian countries. ASEAN was formed on August 8, 1967, when the member countries—Indonesia, Malaysia, the Philippines, Singapore, and Thailand—signed the Bangkok Declaration. Growing out of the colonial experiences of the members and formed against a backdrop of the intensifying war in Vietnam, the main purposes of ASEAN were to promote the economic, social, and cultural development of the members through cooperation; to safeguard the region against great power rivalry; and to act as a forum for the resolution of intraregional differences. Although there was considerable skepticism when ASEAN was formed, the organization has been remarkably successful. In 1984 Brunei became the sixth member. Its members have highly dynamic economies and are sometimes referred to as the "little dragons." This dynamism is reflected in the fact that ASEAN is the United States' fifth largest trading partner after the European Community; Canada, Japan, and Mexico. *See also* ZONE OF PEACE, FREEDOM AND NEUTRALITY.

Asia minor The West Asian peninsula that forms the largest part of the Republic of Turkey.

Asian Development Bank (ADB) A regional development bank created in 1966 and headquartered in Pasay City, the Philippines. It was designed to foster economic growth and contribute to the acceleration of economic development of the developing member countries in Asia. The bank has a membership of 47 countries, 32 of which are in the Asian region.

Asquith, Herbert H. (1852–1928)   The British Liberal prime minister (1908–1916) who abolished the right of the House of Lords to veto legislation and brought the British Empire into World War I. After the 1916 Battle of the Somme, in which Great Britain lost half a million men, he was forced to resign and was succeeded by DAVID LLOYD GEORGE. Asquith was the wit who first observed that the British War Office kept three sets of figures: "One to mislead the public, another to mislead the Cabinet, and a third to mislead itself" (quoted in Alistair Horne, *The Price of Glory,* 1962).

Assad, Hafez al- (1930–   )   President of Syria since November 13, 1970, when as minister of defense he seized power from Salah Jadid, who had himself grabbed power in 1966 with Assad's assistance. Assad is a member of an ethnic and religious minority, the Alawites. The overwhelming majority of Syrians are Sunni Muslims. Despite their minority status, Alawites have a disproportionate hold on power in both the Syrian government and the ruling Baath Party. Assad, though considered a radical Arab leader, has constructed a secular government and consequently has been confronted domestically by violent Islamic fundamentalist opposition. Chief among Syrian opposition forces has been the MUSLIM BROTHERHOOD. Assad demonstrated his ruthlessness in February 1982 when he directed Syrian military forces to crush the Brotherhood and its stronghold in the HAMAH MASSACRE. An estimated 25,000 of Hamah's citizens perished during nearly a month of carnage and destruction. Assad also has exported terrorist violence beyond his own country's borders: Syria is considered to be one of the principal nations involved in state-sponsored TERRORISM. Nevertheless, the United States courted Assad to join the coalition against Iraq during the PERSIAN GULF WAR. At the price of a token force sent to the gulf, Assad has gained an artificial respectability and opened economically advantageous ties to the West. In 1991 Assad joined the other Arab states in the region and started the ARAB-ISRAELI PEACE TALKS.

assassination   The murder of a politically prominent person. The original assassins were thirteenth-century Muslims whose main goal was the murder of Christian Crusaders and other political rivals. Assassination is a time-honored if not honorable way of removing people from public office. U.S. Presidents Lincoln, Garfield, McKinley, and Kennedy were assassinated. Presidents Theodore Roosevelt, Franklin Roosevelt, Truman, Ford, and Reagan all narrowly escaped death in various attempted assassinations. Since 1980 the president or prime ministers of Algeria, Bangladesh, India, Lebanon, Liberia, Pakistan, and Sweden have been assassinated. Other heads of state, such as Pope John Paul II and British Prime Minister Margaret Thatcher, have barely avoided death by assassination. The events leading to the start of World War I were put into motion by the assassination of Archduke Franz Ferdinand of Austria in 1914. Many of the major figures of the twentieth century have died at the hands of assassins: Leon Trotsky, Mohandas K. Gandhi, John F. Kennedy, Martin Luther King, Jr., Indira Gandhi. After the assassination of President Lincoln, Benjamin Disraeli told the British House of Commons on May 1, 1865, that "assassination has never changed the history of the world." He was perhaps wrong in the short term. To the extent that the political objectives of assassins are achieved by a murder, assassins can win. For example, the assassination of President Anwar Sadat of Egypt in 1981 certainly chilled Middle East peace efforts.

While some governments actively sponsor assassinations, it is specifically illegal for the United States to do so. Executive Order 12333, signed by President Ronald Reagan in 1981, states: "No person employed by or acting on behalf of the United States government shall engage in, or, conspire to engage in, assassination." However, this did not stop the Reagan Administration from bombing the home of Libya's MUAMMAR AL-QADDAFI in 1986 in the expectation that he would be killed.

MAJOR POLITICAL FIGURES ASSASSINATED IN THE TWENTIETH CENTURY

1900	King Humbert I of Italy
1901	President William McKinley of the United States
1908	King Carlos I of Portugal
1909	Prince Hirobumi Ito of Japan
1911	Prime Minister Piotr Stolypin of Russia

1913	Prime Minister Nazim Pasha of Turkey President Francisco Madero of Mexico King George I of Greece
1914	Archduke Franz Ferdinand of Austria
1918	Czar Nicholas II of Russia Prime Minister Stephen Tisza of Hungary
1922	Foreign Minister Walter Rathenau of Germany
1923	General Francisco "Pancho" Villa of Mexico
1928	President-elect Alvar Obregón of Mexico
1932	President Paul Doumer of France
1933	President Luis Sanchez Cerro of Peru King Nadir Shah of Afghanistan
1934	Chancellor Engelbert Dollfuss of Austria King Alexander I of Yugoslavia Foreign Minister Louis Barthou of France
1935	Senator Huey Long of Louisiana, U.S.
1939	Prime Minister Armand Calinescu of Romania
1940	Leon Trotsky, Russian revolutionary leader
1942	Admiral Jean Darlan of France
1945	Prime Minister Ahmed Maher Pasha of Egypt
1948	Independence leader Mohandas K. Gandhi of India Count Folke Bernadotte of Sweden
1951	King Abdullah I of Jordan Prime Minister Liaquat Ali Khan of Pakistan
1958	King Faisal II of Iraq
1959	Prime Minister S. W. R. D. Bandaranaike of Ceylon
1960	Prime Minister Hazza el-Majali of Jordan
1963	Prime Minister Abdul Karim Kassem of Iraq Prime Minister Ngo Dinh Diem of South Vietnam President John F. Kennedy of the United States
1965	Black Muslim leader Malcolm X of the United States
1966	Prime Minister Hendrik Verwoerd of South Africa
1967	Civil rights leader Martin Luther King, Jr., of the United States Senator Robert F. Kennedy of New York, U.S.
1971	Prime Minister Wasfi Tal of Jordan
1973	Ambassador Cleo Noel of the United States Governor Richard Staples of Bermuda Prime Minister Luis Carrero Blanco of Spain
1975	King Faisal of Saudi Arabia Prime Minister Sheikh Mujibur Rahman of Bangladesh Ambassador Ismail Erez of Turkey
1976	Ambassador Francis Meloy of the United States Ambassador Christopher Ewart-Biggs of the United Kingdom
1978	Former Prime Minister Aldo Moro of Italy
1979	Ambassador Adolph Dubs of the United States Ambassador Richard Sykes of the United Kingdom Admiral Louis Mountbatten of the United Kingdom President Park Chung Hee of South Korea
1980	Archbishop Oscar Romero of El Salvador President William Tolbert of Liberia Former President Anastasio Somoza of Nicaragua
1981	President Ziaur Rahman of Bangladesh President Anwar Sadat of Egypt President-elect Bashir Gemayel of Lebanon
1982	Opposition leader Benigno Aquino of the Philippines
1983	Prime Minister Maurice Bishop of Grenada
1984	Prime Minister Indira Gandhi of India
1986	Prime Minister Olaf Palme of Sweden
1987	Prime Minister Rashid Karami of Lebanon
1988	President Mohammed Zia ul-Haq of Pakistan
1991	Former Prime Minister Shahpur Bakhtiar of Iran
1991	Former Prime Minister Rajiv Gandhi of India
1992	President Mohammed Boudiaf of Algeria

Asser, Tobias (1838–1913)   The Dutch professor of law who shared the 1911 Nobel Peace Prize (with ALFRED FRIED) for his efforts at codifying and advancing international law.

assessment   **1.** Analysis of the security, effectiveness, and potential of an existing or planned intelligence activity.   **2.** Judgment of the motives, qualifications, and characteristics of current or prospective employees or AGENTs.   **3.** A financial contribution made by a government (such as the United States) to the regular budget of an international organization (such as the United Nations) to which it belongs.   **4.** A contribution to a political party that is determined according to a schedule of rates and made in order to retain a civil service or patronage appointment.   **5.** Analysis of a tactical or strategic problem by a military or intelligence staff.

assessments, scale of   The formula for setting membership dues used in an international organization. For example, Bolivia is charged 0.01 percent of the cost of running the United Nations, while Canada is charged 3.09 percent; Japan, 11.38 percent; and the United States, 25 percent.

asset   **1.** Any resource—person, group, relationship, instrument, installation, or supply—at the disposition of an intelligence organization for use in an operational or support role. Often used with a qualifying term, as in *agent asset* or *propaganda asset*.   **2.** A military capability or particular diplomatic advantage.

assimilation   The gradual incorporation of a state's recent immigrants into the dominant culture. Assimilation is often a matter of degree. It is complete when immigrant groups have accepted the language and values of their new state. When it is incomplete and immigrant groups retain the language and culture of their ethnic homelands, there is often the danger of political instability and the growth of separatist movements.

associated powers   All those states fighting against the AXIS powers in World War II. Shortly after the United States entered the war, U.S. President Franklin D. Roosevelt suggested that the name United Nations be used instead.

associated states   States that participate in an alliance effort (usually military) but that are not formally part of the alliance.

association   **1.** A loose reference to close relations between states that are not necessarily bound in a formal alliance.   **2.** A concept used in international law for a situation in which a state has responsibility for its domestic affairs but not for its foreign policy, which is in the responsibility of another state. This is very close to the idea of a PROTECTORATE, except that under rules established by the United Nations General Assembly the population must consent to the association with the principal state.

Association Agreements   EUROPEAN COMMUNITY arrangements with non-EC states or international organizations that create reciprocal rights or obligations.

Association of Southeast Asia   *See* ASA.

Association of Southeast Asian Nations   *See* ASEAN.

assured destruction   *See* MAD.

Aswan High Dam   A 360-foot electricity-generating dam on the Nile River in Egypt. In July 1956 both the United States and Great Britain withdrew their previous year's offers of $70 million to help finance the dam due in part to uncertainty as to the project's feasibility but more as a reaction to Egyptian President GAMAL ABDAL NASSER's display of anti-Western and anti-British attitudes during the SUEZ CRISIS, when he nationalized the Suez Canal. The Aswan High Dam was constructed in the 1960s with Soviet loan assistance at a cost of about $1 billion. It was completed in 1970. The dam, one of the largest in the world, increased Egypt's cultivable land by one-third and electric power by half.

asylum   **1.** A place of protection for those fleeing authority; forced removal from such places was traditionally a sacrilege. In ancient Greece, temples were inviolate, and those inside had the protection of the gods and could not be removed by force. Later, Christian churches became places of asylum.   **2.** A charitable refuge for people unable to care for themselves.   **3.** A place of protection for those fleeing political persecution. Many states, such as France, the United Kingdom, and the United States, have long traditions of granting *political asylum* for those fleeing foreign tyrannies—especially those who would be unjustly persecuted if forced to return. In recent years the question of asylum has been caught up in a controversy over whether "economic" refugees are as worthy of asylum as "political" refugees. Article 14 of the UNIVERSAL DECLARATION OF HUMAN RIGHTS states: "Everyone has the right to seek and to enjoy in other countries asylum from persecution." Since the declaration is not legally binding, the problem of finding a state that will grant asylum remains. Normal immigration is in effect a grant of asylum. *Compare to* SANCTUARY.

asylum, diplomatic   The right to offer asylum within the physical area of a diplomatic mission. Diplomatic asylum is not universally recognized as a legal right. It is usually a function of local custom, humanitarian practice, and diplomatic expediency. For example, the Diplomatic Asylum Convention of 1954 signed by more than a dozen Latin American states provides that: "Asylum granted in legations, war vessels, and military camps or aircraft, to persons being sought for political reasons or for political offenses shall be respected by the territorial State in accordance with the provisions of this Convention."

asymmetry   A condition of not having equivalent characteristics, similar strengths, or a close correspondence among parts of something. International relationships are often asymmetric when one state is more dependent—militarily or economically—on another than that other is on it.

ATA (Anti-Terrorism Assistance)   The U.S. State Department's antiterrorist program, which provides assistance to foreign governments that request it. ATA includes training for border guards and customs officials and improvements in airport security measures. More than 40 foreign governments have taken advantage of the program since it began in 1984.

Ataturk, Mustapha Kemel (1881–1938)   The founder of the republic of Turkey in 1923 following the collapse of the 600-year-old OTTOMAN EMPIRE. The empire, which at its peak controlled vast stretches of northern Africa, southeastern Europe, and western Asia, had failed to keep pace with European social and technological developments. Defeated in World War I, shorn of much of its former territory, and partially occupied by forces of the victorious European states, the Ottoman structure was repudiated by Turkish nationalists who rallied under the leadership of Ataturk, a military officer who had defeated the British at GALLIPOLI. After a bitter war against invading Greek forces, the nationalists expelled them from Anatolia. The sultanate and caliphate, the temporal and religious ruling institutions of the old empire, were abolished, and Turkey became a republic with Ataturk as president—a position he held for the rest of his life. Born Mustapha Kemel, he added the name Ataturk,

which means "father of the Turks," in 1933. Functioning as a benevolent dictator, he forced the new republic to concentrate on modernization and Westernization. The social, political, linguistic, and economic reforms and attitudes introduced by Ataturk formed the ideological base of modern Turkey. Ataturkism combines secularism with nationalism and looks toward the West for inspiration and support. The meaning, continued validity, and applicability of Ataturkism are the subject of frequent discussions and debates in Turkey's political life.

Atlantic, Battle of the   The name given in both world wars to the naval warfare in the Atlantic Ocean between German U-boat submarines and the naval and merchant forces of Great Britain and the United States. In both instances the German threat to Allied shipping was defeated—but only after enormous losses. In World War II about 2,800 Allied (mostly British) ships were sunk. But radar,

Kemal Ataturk (Library of Congress)

long-range aircraft, and escort carriers literally turned the tide of the battle.

Atlantic Alliance   The security alliance between the United States and Western Europe that was established by the Atlantic Treaty of 1949 and subsequently developed into a military organization—the NORTH ATLANTIC TREATY ORGANIZATION. In 1966 France withdrew from the integrated military organization, NATO, but remained a member of the alliance. With the French withdrawal, NATO headquarters shifted from Paris to Brussels.

Atlantic Charter   The statement of broad principles for the post–World War II era issued by U.S. President Franklin D. Roosevelt and British Prime Minister Winston Churchill after their first wartime meeting on shipboard, in Placentia Bay off Newfoundland on August 14, 1941. It was considered a press release so that Roosevelt would not have to submit it to the U.S. Congress for ratification. The charter declared that the United States and the United Kingdom sought no territorial aggrandizement, desired no territorial changes "not in accord with the freely expressed wishes of the peoples concerned," respected "the right of all peoples to choose the form of government under which they will live," and promised that NAZI tyranny would be replaced with a peace that would allow all nations to dwell in safety and have freedom of the seas. *Compare to* TEHRAN CONFERENCE.

Atlantic Community   **1.** The West in general. **2.** The NORTH ATLANTIC TREATY ORGANIZATION. **3.** The United States, Great Britain, and Canada. According to William Safire in the *New York Times Magazine* (January 5, 1992), WALTER LIPPMANN first used "Atlantic Community" in 1944 to describe the common interests of these three states.

Atlantic Council of the United States   An "establishment" nonpartisan private organization dedicated to furthering American foreign policy interests by generating public debate and policy recommendations on international issues; founded in 1961. It publishes the *Atlantic Community Quarterly*. The council contributes in several ways to the maintenance of the dialogue between the United States and Western Europe, something that is

becoming increasingly important as relationships across the Atlantic are loosened as a result of the end of the COLD WAR.

Atlanticist   An individual who believes that the U.S. commitment to the NORTH ATLANTIC TREATY ORGANIZATION is the nation's paramount military obligation because the defense of Western Europe is integral to the security of the United States itself.

Atlantic Wall   The German fortifications on the shorelines of Western Europe that were built during World War II to impede an anticipated Allied invasion. This defensive wall consisted variously of concrete fortifications for defenders, explosive mines at the shoreline, and waterline obstacles (such as railroad rails stuck vertically into the ground, known as asparagus beds) designed to frustrate a military assault from the sea. The portion of this so-called wall in Normandy, France, was breached by Allied forces on D-DAY.

atomic bomb   The popular misnomer for the fission bomb, which was used twice by the United States in August 1945, against the Japanese cities of Hiroshima and Nagasaki, in an effort to end World War II quickly. There were doubts about whether the bombs would explode, since the only one test had been conducted in the desert at ALAMOGORDO, New Mexico. But the bombs worked and the Japanese surrendered.

Controversy over the use of the bombs continues to this day. William Manchester wrote in his World War II memoir, *Goodbye, Darkness* (1980): "You think of the lives which would have been lost in an invasion of Japan's home islands—a staggering number of Americans but millions more of Japanese—and you thank God for the atomic bomb." But this judgment is not shared universally, and there has been much criticism of the United States for using the bomb without warning on a country that appeared to be on the verge of defeat. It also has been suggested that the United States used the atomic bombs on Japan to ensure that the war ended before the Soviet Union could establish a stronger position in the Far East. Whatever the case, the use of the bomb marked a new era of destructive power in warfare. THOMAS C. SCHELLING, in *Arms and Influence* (1966), argued that genocide in war had always been possible but only after defeating the enemy; with the advent of atomic weapons it became possible prior to the enemy's defeat. Until the early 1950s the atomic bomb was the only NUCLEAR WEAPON, but it has since been superseded by hydrogen or thermonuclear bombs. *See also* MANHATTAN PROJECT.

GALBRAITH AND THE BOMB

John Kenneth Galbraith . . . thinks the A-bombs were unnecessary and unjustified because the war was ending anyway. The A-bombs meant, he says, "a difference, at most, of two or three weeks." But at the time, with no indication that surrender was on the way . . . Allied casualties were running to over 7,000 per week. Two weeks more means 14,000 more killed and wounded, three weeks more, 21,000. Those weeks mean the world if you're one of those thousands or related to one of them. . . . What did he do in the war? He worked in the Office of Price Administration in Washington. I don't demand that he experience having his ass shot off. I merely note that he didn't.

SOURCE: Paul Fussell, *Thank God for the Atom Bomb* (1988). Fussell, a U.S. infantry veteran who saw considerable combat in World War II, has written extensively about what war means to the infantry. He is especially annoyed with policy analysts, of whom John Kenneth Galbraith is merely representative, who suggest that the atomic bombs should not have been used when they were. He feels that the bombs, which made a military assault on Japan unnecessary, literally saved tens of thousands of American lives. That is why he titled his book *Thank God.* . . .

---

atomic power **1.** Any state that acknowledges possessing nuclear weapons. **2.** The capability to destroy using atomic weapons.

atomic stalemate The strategic position of the two superpowers where neither could attack the other without receiving unacceptable damage in return. This notion was a major feature of the COLD WAR, but its characteristics could well be reproduced in regions such as South Asia, where India and Pakistan are engaged in a nuclear arms race.

atomic umbrella The Soviet Union's "Gromyko Plan" of 1962, which called for universal disarmament except for the retention of a modest "atomic umbrella" as a deterrent. *Compare to* NUCLEAR UMBRELLA.

atoms for peace A 1950s phrase for civilian use of nuclear power, as proposed by U.S. President Dwight D. Eisenhower to the United Nations General Assembly in December 1953. Eisenhower urged that the atomic powers contribute fissionable materials to an international agency that would maintain security over these materials and develop methods for peaceful use of atomic energy. Though the proposal was opposed by the Soviet Union, it led to the establishment of the INTERNATIONAL ATOMIC ENERGY AGENCY in 1957. The atoms for peace program provided for cooperative research and development not only with allies but with nonaligned countries as well. Unfortunately, it also gave those countries much of the technical capability they needed to make nuclear weapons.

attaché French word meaning "one assigned to." In practice, this is usually a technical specialist (such as military, economic, cultural) assigned to a diplomatic mission. *See also* ARMY ATTACHÉ.

attentat clause That portion of an EXTRADITION treaty or law which asserts that the murder of a head of state (or family member) is not to be considered a political crime for purposes of extradition. As mere criminal defendants, suspected perpetrators of such crimes are extraditable. Not all states agree with this practice because of the belief that violence against political leaders is a classic act of political protest. Because Belgium first enacted the attentat clause in 1856, it is sometimes called the *Belgium Clause.*

attentive public That relatively small portion of the public (usually estimated at around 5 to 10 percent) that has a sustained interest in and some knowledge of foreign affairs. Sometimes it is defined very roughly in terms of the readership of quality newspapers. The attentive public is usually contrasted with the mass public, which has little interest in or knowledge about foreign policy and tends to have swings of mood. It is sometimes argued that the attentive public provides a degree of stability that helps to offset these mood swings.

Attlee, Clement (1883–1967) The leader of the British Labour Party (1935–1955) who succeeded Winston Churchill as prime minister in 1945. Attlee's government granted independence to India and Pakistan, brought Great Britain into the North Atlantic Treaty Organization, decided that Britain should develop its own nuclear deterrent, created the National Health Service (a system of socialized medicine), and nationalized major industries. In the 1950 general election he retained power by such a narrow majority that another election was called in 1951. Labour lost, partly because it had not ended wartime rationing, and Atlee remained as opposition leader until his retirement in 1955. Compared to his ever-theatrical and witty predecessor, Attlee was a dull figure. Nevertheless, he was the first to observe that Soviet communism was "the illegitimate child of Karl Marx and Catherine the Great" (*The Times*, April 12, 1956).

attribution theory The tendency to explain the behavior of others in terms of their individual attributes rather than as a response to the situation in which they find themselves. In this perspective an adversary may be characterized, for example, as inherently expansionist. ROBERT JERVIS has been the major figure in applying attribution theory to analyses of relations between states.

attrition 1. A reduction of effectiveness by constant wear. 2. A policy of not replacing people who resign, die, or are fired, thus allowing an organization gradually to reduce its personnel. 3. A military tactic of gradually wearing down the enemy's forces. Every war is a WAR OF ATTRITION in that each side seeks to destroy soldiers of the other side. But the term *war of attrition* implies that one side is wearing down the enemy at roughly equal the rate that its own forces are diminishing. The stalemate on the Western Front during World War I before the United States went in and altered the military balance is the classic example of a war of attrition in this century. The Iran-Iraq war of the 1980s in a more recent example.

audience 1. Those who attend an event, such as an opera or a meeting, primarily to listen to others. 2. A formal meeting between a diplomatic envoy and the head (or his or her formal representative) of the state to which the envoy is accredited. 3. A meeting with the pope, even by nondiplomatic personnel. 4. A hearing in a formal court. 5. A pompous term for a meeting with an important person.

Aung San *See* SUU KYI.

Auschwitz The largest of Germany's World War II concentration (extermination) camp complexes; located in Poland, its name has become the symbol of the Nazi policy of GENOCIDE. An estimated 1.5 to 2 million innocent men, women, and children, mostly Jews, were worked to death or systematically executed there. Two thousand people at a time were murdered in its enormous gas chambers. Portions of Auschwitz are now a museum.

Auschwitz became controversial again in 1984 when Carmelite nuns established a convent on the grounds, specifically in a building that was used to store Zyklon B poison gas. This affronted many Jews around the world as well as many Polish Americans, who considered it an instance of Polish insensitivity to Jewish suffering and an example of the nation's refusal to deal with its history of anti-Semitism. In 1987 Jewish and Catholic leaders reached an agreement to move the convent. When it had not been moved by the deadline of February 1989, Jewish demonstrations at the site commenced, particularly after seemingly anti-Semitic remarks by the Polish cardinal, Józef Glemp, were publicized. Pope John Paul II intervened to defuse the volatile situation. A new convent, off the grounds, is now complete.

AUSCHWITZ IN ACTION

Prisoners, selected for gassing straight from the trains on the railway line, and others selected in the camp, were driven to the crematoria on foot, those who were unable to walk were taken in motor trucks. . . . In the middle of the road lorries were continually fetching the weak, old, sick, and children, from the railway. In the ditches at the road-sides lay SS men with machine guns ready to fire. And SS men addressed the crowd huddled in the yard telling them that they were going to the baths for disinfection as they were dirty and lousy, and in such a state they could not be admitted into the camp. The gassing was carried on under the personal supervision of the doctor SS-Hauptsturmführer Mengele. The prisoners who arrived in the yard of the crematorium were driven to the dressing-room over the door of which was the inscription "Wasch und Desinfektionsraum." In the dressing room . . . there were clothing pegs with numbers. The SS men advised the victims huddled in the cloak-room to remember the number of the peg [to] find them [their clothes] again easily afterwards. After undressing they were driven through a corridor to the actual gas chamber which had previously been heated with the aid of portable coke braziers. This heating was necessary for the better evaporation of the hydrogen cyanide. By beating them with rods and setting dogs on them about 2,000 victims were packed into a space of 210 sq. meters.

From the ceiling of this chamber, the better to deceive the victims, hung imitation shower-baths, from which water never poured. After the gas-tight doors had been closed the air was pumped out and through four special openings in the ceiling the contents of cans of cyclon, producing cyanide hydrogen gas, were poured in.

SOURCE: Central Commission for Investigation of German Crimes in Poland, *German Crimes in Poland* (1947).

Australia Group An informal organization of a group of nations that have joined together to establish voluntary export controls on about 40 chemicals that could be used in the production of chemical weapons. The group was established in response to an Australian initiative in 1984 and includes in its membership Australia, Austria, Canada, Japan, New Zealand, Norway, Switzerland, the United States, and the individual members of the European Community and the Commission of the European Communities. Although some members impose formal controls while others depend on voluntary notification by their private chemical-producing companies, all share a commitment to stemming the proliferation of chemical weapons. In September 1989 a conference on the issue was hosted by Australia and included officials from governments and chemical industries in 66 countries. The participants pledged to cooperate in stemming chemical weapons proliferation and called for a global treaty on chemical weapons.

Austrian State Treaty The 1955 agreement of the United States, the Soviet Union, Great Britain, and France that provided for the withdrawal of all occupying Allied troops, Austrian independence within its 1937 borders, a ban on any future ANSCHLUSS, and the permanent neutrality of Austria in foreign and military affairs. What is perhaps most surprising is not that the agreement took eight years to reach but that it was reached at the height of the Cold War. As Kurt Steiner has argued in the article "Negotiations for an Austrian State Treaty" (A. L. George, P. J. Farley, and A. Dallin, eds., *US-Soviet Security Cooperation*, 1988), because Austria was small and relatively unimportant it was easier to avoid partition as a solution. Moreover, "the fact that neither side had a preponderance of influence or power in the area was an additional factor. Given these circumstances, proposals to remove a neutral Austria from the competition between the two power blocs did not involve any costs that either side considered unacceptably high, including a loss of face or prestige."

Austro-Hungarian Empire The Central European power that first emerged in 1526 under the rule of the Hapsburg monarchy. In 1867 the Austrian and Hungarian domains merged under the Compromise of 1867 (or *Augsleich*, meaning "equalization"), which gave Hungary equal status with Austria. The multinational empire included many smaller subject peoples within its borders. World War I was sparked by nationalist tensions as the empire desired to expand into the Balkans. At the end of World War I, the Austro-Hungarian Empire was dissolved in the Versailles settlements, and a variety of new states emerged as a result: Austria, Czechoslovakia, Hungary, Poland, Romania, and Yugoslavia.

autarchy 1. An AUTOCRACY. 2. A policy of national (or regional) SELF-SUFFICIENCY designed to prevent a state from being dependent for critical materials from nondomestic sources. This meaning of autarchy is also spelled "autarky." The SOVIET UNION was generally held to be an autarchy as it had an abundance of many critical raw materials. In fact, it had difficulty in exploiting these materials, and Moscow, even before the 1991 breakup of the Soviet Union, increasingly moved away from autarchic policies. Autarchy was the elusive goal of the total national economic self-sufficiency programs that were pursued in the countries of Central Europe after World War I and involved an effort to obtain all basic goods and services domestically. The pursuit of autarchy proved folly and worse, as no Central European country had sufficient land for food production or the raw materials and markets to meet its nation's needs. Still, the Austro-Hungarian successor states and those carved out of western Russia attempted to nurture their own infant industries through import laws and government subsidies. This inhibited intra-European commerce after World War I and supported the economic disintegration that led to the GREAT DEPRESSION. *See also* ECONOMIC NATIONALISM.

authentication   1. A security measure designed to protect a communications system against acceptance of a fraudulent transmission or simulation by establishing the validity of each transmission, message, or originator. 2. A means of identifying individuals and verifying their eligibility to receive specific categories of information. 3. Evidence by proper signature or seal that a document is genuine and official.

authentication, agent   *See* AGENT AUTHENTICATION.

authenticator   A symbol or group of symbols, or a series of bits, selected or derived in a prearranged manner and usually inserted at a predetermined point within a message or transmission for the purpose of attesting to its validity.

authoritarianism   Government control by an individual or small group of individuals whose claim to power is maintained by subordinates, who sustain control of the governing apparatus by following orders from above, and by a public that is unwilling or unable to rebel against this control. Sometimes the ruler's personality, as with Adolf Hitler or Joseph Stalin, may be a significant element in maintaining the necessary balance of loyalty and fear. Authoritarianism differs from TOTALITARIANISM in that the latter may have a specific ideology that justifies it and involves greater state control over all aspects of society. Under some circumstances an authoritarian state could allow limited freedom of expression and political opposition so long as the regime does not feel threatened. *See also* DICTATOR; FASCISM.

authority   1. The idea of legitimate power or the right to exercise influence over others. Authority is something that is exercised within states by legitimate governments. In the international system authority is far less evident, which helps to explain why relations among states have so much to do with strict power relations rather than with notions of legitimacy and authority. 2. A government-owned corporation. 3. The power inherent in a specific government position that allows an incumbent to perform assigned tasks.

autocracy   A DICTATORSHIP by a single individual; STATISM in which one person has unlimited political power in a state. This differs from an absolute monarchy in that a monarch claims power through succession and may have institutional checks, such as noble councils, while an autocrat takes authority and strips away institutional limits. The classic example of an autocracy is NAZI Germany under ADOLF HITLER. *See also* AUTARCHY.

autogolpe   *See* PERU COUP.

autolimitation   The INTERNATIONAL LAW concept most associated with the German scholar George Jellinck (1851–1911). It holds that, just as sovereign states may create and abolish their own municipal (internal) laws at will, a parallel self or autolimitation is the only force that binds them in international affairs. Consequently, there can be no such thing as a truly binding international treaty, no such thing as a true international law.

autonomous risks   A category of risks in crises that stem from the inherent uncertainties, unpredictability, and the capacity of things to go wrong rather than from coercive bargaining between the participants. Although some analysts discuss the manipulation of such risks in actual crises, policymakers have always been eager to minimize them and prevent the situation from getting out of control.

autonomy   1. Political independence; a sovereign state is said to have autonomy. Because of the interdependent nature of the modern world economies, autonomy in a pure sense—that is, both political and economic—is no longer viable. It is always relative. *Compare to* AUTARCHY. 2. Less than full political independence; a situation in which a region within a larger sovereign state has a limited measure of authority in the conduct of its internal affairs. **3.** Local control over nonpolitical affairs; for example, a region could be granted cultural or religious autonomy. **4.** The ability of military leaders in a fascist regime to take actions regardless of the policies of a civilian government.

Avanguardia Nazionale (AN) "National Vanguard," an Italian right-wing terrorist organization founded by neo-fascists in 1959. In the 1960s the group established a working relationship with other European right-wing terrorist organizations in a loosely knit organization dubbed the Black Orchestra. On December 7, 1970, the AN failed in an attempt to take control of the Italian government by COUP D'ETAT. The group's most infamous incident was its reported involvement in the bombing of a Bologna train station in 1980, in which over 80 persons were killed. The AN is now thought to be defunct.

avulsion A rapidly occurring change in a riverbank or oceanfront caused by the force of a flood, hurricane, or other natural disaster. An avulsion, in contrast to an ACCRETION, does not affect an international boundary.

AWACS (Airborne Warning and Control Systems) The U.S.-manufactured flying radar and military communications stations that are critical for directing defenses and responses to attack in modern conventional wars. Long-range look-down radar and sophisticated computers allow for the identification of over-the-horizon threats and the coordination and direction of friendly interceptor aircraft. By circling at a great height over a safe area of the battlefield, AWACS radar can identify all aircraft for a range of 200 miles, a range denied to ground-based radar because of the curvature of the earth. AWACS consist of a radar antenna dish attached to a converted Boeing 707 airframe. The AWACS are operated by forces of the North Atlantic Treaty Organization and the United States. Sales of AWACS to Saudi Arabia in 1981 was achieved only after a bitter dispute in the U.S. Congress because of the concern that the Arabs might use them against Israel. During the PERSIAN GULF WAR the AWACS of both the United States and the Saudis were used to great effect to coordinate the air war against Iraq.

Axis **1.** The World War II coalition (also known as the Tripartite Pact of 1940) of Nazi Germany, Fascist Italy, and Japan. The name is short for Rome-Berlin Axis, the structure formed by the signing of the Anti-Comintern Pact in 1936. The word *axis* was used, rather than *alliance*, to imply that the Axis powers were pivotal to world politics and other states would revolve about them. The 1936 partners were also located along the north-south axis of Europe. Their pact initially was seen as a way to restrain Soviet expansion. Tokyo saw a congruity of interest with Berlin and joined in 1937. Hungary, Romania, Slovakia, Bulgaria, and Croatia (in that order) formally became members of the Axis in 1940 and 1941. Interestingly, the pact did not require Germany to declare war on the United States after the December 7, 1941, Japanese attack on Pearl Harbor. (It would have been

This 1936 Soviet cartoon showed Italy to be an unequal partner in the Axis. (Library of Congress)

required if the United States had attacked Japan.) Because Japan was clearly the aggressor, Hitler's declaration of war against the United States was both gratuitous and, as it turned out, stupid. It was Winston Churchill, speaking in the British House of Commons on November 11, 1942, who first referred to southern Europe as "the soft underbelly of the Axis" because he felt that an Allied invasion of the European continent through southern France or Italy would meet far less resistance than an assault on the ATLANTIC WALL. His arguments carried and the Allies invaded Sicily and Italy in 1943 before the 1944 D-DAY landing in northern France. **2.** Any political or military alliance between two powers.

THE AXIS AGREEMENT

The governments of Germany, Italy, and Japan have agreed as follows:

I   Japan recognizes and respects the leadership of Germany and Italy in the establishment of a new order in Europe.

II Germany and Italy recognize and respect the leadership of Japan in the establishment of a new order in Greater East Asia.

III Germany, Italy and Japan . . . undertake to assist one another with all political, economic and military means when one of the three contracting powers is attacked by a power at present not involved in the European war or the Chinese-Japanese conflict. . . .

SOURCE: The Axis pact of September 27, 1940, quoted in *Time*, October 7, 1940.

Ayala, Baltasar (1548–1584) The Spanish Netherlands jurist whose 1582 work (republished in 1912) *De Jure et Officiis Bellicis et Disciplina Militarii* (*On the Law and Duties of War and Military Discipline*) was a significant influence on the development of the precepts of modern international law by HUGO GROTIUS.

ayatollah A title of respect (from Persian into Arabic, meaning "giving divine signs") given to the most respected teachers and scholars by Shi'ite Muslims. Ruholla Khomeini (1901–1989), as the Ayatollah Khomeini, inspired and led the IRANIAN REVOLUTION of 1979. From the Iranian revolution that brought him to power until his death Khomeini was often known as The Ayatollah, as if he were the only ayatollah in Iran.

Aylwin Azocar, Patricio *See* PINOCHET, AUGUSTO.

Ayub Khan, Muhammad (1907–1974) The military dictator who ruled Pakistan as its president from 1958 to 1969.

Azaña, Manuel (1880–1940) The president of the Spanish Republic when civil war broke out in 1936. First elected president in 1931, his government curbed the power of the army, improved education, and granted autonomy to the Basque provinces and Catalonia. It failed to break up the large and powerful land estates. Azaña's Republican Party was defeated in the Cortes (parliament) election in 1933, but a POPULAR FRONT coalition favoring Azaña's reforms won in 1936. He returned to the presidency in May 1936, but the conservative reaction to his reforms caused the SPANISH CIVIL WAR to erupt ten weeks later. He remained president throughout the war and fled to France in February 1939, after concluding that the republican cause was lost.

Azania A black nationalist name for South Africa. There has long been speculation that a black majority government, should it ever gain complete power, might change the name of South Africa to Azania.

Azanian African People's Organization (AZAPO) A splinter group of the AFRICAN NATIONAL CONGRESS. Founded in 1978, AZAPO is a radical group with a blacks-only membership policy that has found a following in the black townships of South Africa.

Azerbaijani-Armenian Civil War The fighting between the former Soviet republics of Azerbaijan (largely Muslim) and Armenia (largely Christian) that began in 1988 over the status of the Armenian majority population in of the Nagorno-Karabakh enclave of Azerbaijan. The conflict intensified in 1992 after the Armenians of Nagorno-Karabakh (an area about the size of the U.S. state of Rhode Island), declared themselves to be an independent republic. By the end of 1992 the fighting had spread beyond the Nagorno-Karabakh enclave to the border between Armenia and Azerbaijan.

B

Baader-Meinhoff Gang   *See* RED ARMY FACTION

Baathism   An Arab political movement that advocates Pan-Arabism, the concept that there is only one Arab nation. Founded as a political party in Syria in 1910, it was not until the early 1950s, when it combined with the Syrian Socialist Party to form the present Baath Socialist Party, that it began to be influential. While Baathist governments in Syria and Iraq adhere to some of the party's original principles, such as using socialism as a vehicle of Arab revival (*baath* means "renaissance" in Arabic), other principles such as free elections and free speech are ignored. With its emphasis on Pan-Arabism, Baathism can encourage attempts by political leaders to become leaders of the Arab world—as was evident with Saddam Hussein's efforts to dominate the Persian Gulf in 1990.

Babi Yar   A ravine in Ukraine, near Kiev, where the Germans shot, clubbed, and buried alive an estimated 200,000 Jews, Gypsies, and Soviets during World War II.

back channel   An informal method for government-to-government and sensitive leadership communications, as opposed to normal or routine diplomatic methods. The use of a back channel can be very effective in making breakthroughs in negotiations or in implementing new departures in policy. At the same time, it can cause confusion as it creates a second level and undercuts more formal negotiations that may be taking place simultaneously. The back channel of the early 1970s between U.S. President Richard Nixon's National Security

Advisor, Henry Kissinger, and Soviet Ambassador to the United States Anatoly Dobrynin illustrated both the advantages and the dangers of this approach. The use of this channel facilitated a breakthrough in the SALT negotiations but at the expense of concessions by the United States, which the delegation then had to claw back. At the same time, without the channel, the superpower détente of the early 1970s would have been much more difficult to achieve.

backgrounder   In the United States, a journalist's interview with a government official in which the information obtained can be used but attributed only to an anonymous source. In Great Britain, such an interview is held under LOBBY TERMS.

backgrounder, deep   A journalist's interview of a government official that yields information that can be neither directly used nor attributed to any source.

back tell   The transfer of INTELLIGENCE from a higher to a lower echelon of an organization.

bacteriological weapons   Munitions that rely for their effects on incubation within human targets. Bacteriological (or biological) weapons are different from chemical weapons in that they employ living organisms to produce death or disease in humans, plants, or animals. A 1925 Geneva Protocol prohibits the use of chemical or biological offensive weapons. None of the major combatants used such weapons during World War II—even though all had the capacity to do so. The only major exception was

Germany's extensive use of poison gas to murder millions of innocent men, women, and children in CONCENTRATION CAMPS. *See also* BIOLOGICAL WARFARE; CHEMICAL WARFARE.

Badoglio, Pietro (1871–1956)   The Italian Army field marshal named by King Victor Emmanuel to replace BENITO MUSSOLINI on July 25, 1943. Badoglio dissolved the Fascist Party, then arranged an armistice with the Allies in September of that year and joined the Allied side. The Germans retaliated by occupying the northern two-thirds of Italy and installing Mussolini as ruler of a new "Italian Social Republic."

Baghdad Pact   *See* CENTRAL TREATY ORGANIZATION.

bagman   1. The go-between in a political payoff; one who, literally or figuratively, carries the money in a bag from the one offering the bribe to the one accepting it.   2. Someone who transports illegal campaign contributions, usually in cash, from one place to another.   3. In the United States, the military officer who constantly attends the president, carrying the secret codes by which the president could launch an immediate retaliatory nuclear strike. *Compare to* BLACK BAG JOB; FOOTBALL.

Bajer, Fredrik (1837–1922)   The Danish legislator and peace activist who founded the International Peace Bureau in 1891 (now located in Geneva). He shared the 1908 Nobel Peace Prize with KLAS P. ARNOLDSON.

Baker, James A., III (1930–   )   The U.S. Secretary of State from 1989 to 1992. After serving as White House chief of staff (1981–1985) and secretary of the treasury (1985–1988) in the Reagan Administration, he successfully managed the presidential election campaign of then–Vice President GEORGE BUSH in 1988. A skilled negotiator who deserves much credit for assembling and maintaining the PERSIAN GULF WAR coalition, he was often mentioned as a future presidential candidate. In the aftermath of the war against Saddam Hussein, Baker initiated a major peace conference on the Middle East. But while he got Israel and its neighboring Arab states (and the Palestinians) to begin a long, drawn-out "peace process," his GOOD OFFICES

were not sufficient to get them to reach any formal agreements. While he sought new relationships, based on mutual friendship, between the West and the states of the former Soviet Union, he was unable to prevent civil war from breaking out in the former Yugoslavia and in some former Soviet republics. Baker reluctantly resigned as Secretary of State in the summer of 1992 to manage President George Bush's ultimately unsuccessful reelection bid. *See also* MADRID CONFERENCE.

Baker Plan   A debt relief plan for 15 THIRD WORLD countries proposed by U.S. Secretary of the Treasury James Baker in 1985, in Seoul, South Korea, at the joint annual meeting of the WORLD BANK and the INTERNATIONAL MONETARY FUND. Baker recommended that the 15 countries adopt market-oriented policies aimed at creating more flexible and productive economies; that international institutions such as the World Bank and the Inter-American Development Bank lend them further billions; and that the world's commercial banks lend additional billions. Because these billions were not forthcoming, the plan died.

Bakhtiar, Shahpur (1914–1991)   The last prime minister of Iran under Shah MOHAMMED REZA PAHLEVI. After serving as prime minister for a few weeks in 1979, he fled to France when the revolutionary forces of the AYATOLLAH KHOMEINI took power. The revolutionary forces that had tried to kill him earlier finally succeeded in 1991, when two men using kitchen knives slit this throat at his home near Paris.

baksheesh   A Middle Eastern word for the tip or bribe that is an expected part of many normal business transactions in the THIRD WORLD.

Bakunin, Mikhail (1814–1876)   The Russian philosopher who was a founder of the modern anarchist movement. He appealed to emotion and mass instinct over reason. He wanted to destroy the Imperial Russian State and replace it with a federation of peasant communes. Bakunin had a small following of socialist youth in the 1870s. Later he was a major influence on the BOLSHEVIKS. His influence is still apparent today in terrorist organizations such as the West German RED ARMY FACTION and the Italian RED BRIGADES. "Bakunin" as a word has also been used to mean "madman." *See also* ANARCHY.

balance 1. A condition of equilibrium. 2. A condition in which the military forces and weapons of one state have neither an advantage nor a disadvantage over the parallel forces of another state. 3. The internal military adjustments that a state may make to cope with remaining threats to its national security after an arms control treaty is implemented.

balanced forces 1. Military force structures in which capabilities, roles, and missions are divided among ground, sea, and air forces in a relatively equivalent manner. Since the early 1950s the United States has maintained forces that were roughly balanced in this sense. The advantage of such a capability is that it provides more flexibility than an emphasis on one type of force. 2. A situation in which adversaries or actual enemies are roughly equal in military capability. The lack of a decisive advantage for one side or the other is characteristic of balanced forces in this sense of the term. 3. An equilibrium between tactical and strategic forces to create a well-rounded military capability. *See also* STRATEGIC WEAPON; TACTICAL WEAPONS.

balance of payments A tabulation of a nation's debit and credit transactions with foreign countries and international institutions. A favorable balance—more money coming in from other countries than is going out—is an economic advantage. An unfavorable balance over a significant time is one indication of problems within a nation's economy. The balance of payments is broader then the BALANCE OF TRADE as it also includes "invisible exports" such as insurance and shipping.

balance-of-payments deficit A balance-of-payments deficit occurs when international payments are greater than receipts. It can be eliminated by (1) increasing a country's international receipts (e.g., more exports or more tourism from abroad) or (2) reducing expenditures in other countries. The United States has run a major deficit with Japan largely because it imports so many Japanese cars and electronic goods. This deficit has caused considerable strain in the relationship between the two countries.

balance of power 1. The foreign policy stance taken by states to prevent any one state or alliance from gaining a preponderance of power in relation to its rivals; thus a military balance (and therefore peace) is maintained. Charles de Montesquieu (1689–1755) was one of the first to note the ARMS RACE implications of this policy. In *The Spirit of the Laws* (1748) he wrote: "A new disease is spreading over Europe; it has seized upon our princes and induces them to maintain an inordinate number of soldiers. The disease . . . inevitably becomes contagious; for, as soon as one state increases what it calls its forces, the others immediately increase theirs; so that nothing is gained except mutual ruination." Since the seventeenth century, European powers have pursued a balance-of-power policy. This may be seen in the opposition to Louis XIV in the late seventeenth century and to Napoleon in the early nineteenth. Great Britain has consistently attempted to throw its weight behind the weaker coalition on the European continent, so that no single power should dominate Europe. Since World War II European North Atlantic Treaty Organization members have sought to maintain the balance of power (or what might be called the "balance of terror" in the nuclear age) by ensuring that the United States provided a counterweight to Soviet expansionist tendencies during the COLD WAR. 2. A principle of international relations that asserts that when any nation seeks to increase its military potential, neighboring or rival nations will take similar actions to maintain the military equilibrium. This is why U.S. Secretary of State Henry Kissinger asserted that "the management of a balance of power is a permanent undertaking, not an exertion that has a foreseeable end" (*White House Years,* 1979). 3. A purely descriptive way to describe the actual distribution of power in the world—economic, political, and military—without implying that an equally "balanced" distribution exists. In this sense the term is sometimes used to describe an equilibrium of power that may be very stable; at other times, it is simply a synonym for the distribution of power, which may or may not be in equilibrium. Because this use of the term has multiple meanings, it is described by Inis Claude in *Power and International Relations* (1962) as "an ambiguous concept." Part of the reason is that it can be used to describe policies, situations, and international systems. In addition, it is sometimes loosely used as a synonym for the term *distribution of power*, sometimes as a synonym for a *power equilibrium*, and sometimes as an interchangeable term with *power politics*. **4.** The classic delicate balance of nineteenth-century Europe, starting from the CONGRESS OF VIENNA (1815), in which a relatively stable international system of powers was maintained until the 1853–1856 Crimean War pitted Great Britain and France against Russia and the national unifications of Italy (1861) and Germany (1871) disrupted the status quo. Balance-of-power strategy assumes that nations have no (or the same) ideological preference—that they will just as well oppose or support any member of the international system. Second, it assumes that each nation sees its self-interest as maintaining other member states as well as its own. Remnants of traditional balance-of-power politics can be found in the U.S. courtship of the People's Republic of China during the Nixon Administration, when U.S. attitudes shifted from seeing China as an unacceptable partner to trying to use its potential as a third superpower to alter the balance between the United States and the Soviet Union.

balance of terror WINSTON CHURCHILL's phrase for the COLD WAR standoff caused by the nuclear devastation that could be delivered by either the United States or the Soviet Union. This standoff essentially came into effect in 1953 after the Soviet Union announced it also had hydrogen bomb technology. This strategic nuclear balance deterred direct attacks on each other's territory or forces because of the prospect of devastating retaliations: Neither country, in theory, would risk nuclear war, because neither could win in any meaningful sense of the term. The element of terror or mutual fear distinguishes this balance of terror from the BALANCE OF POWER. While the classic balance of power involved occasional recourse to war to restore equilibrium and remove HEGEMONY by one state, the balance of terror makes war an irrational act because of the probability of the utter destruction of both sides. *Balance* has a different meaning here; with nuclear weapons two sides do not need to be equally powerful, as long as the weaker can still devastate the

stronger—that is, as long as it retains a SECOND-STRIKE CAPABILITY. Thus this "balance" calls for invulnerable retaliatory capabilities that enable the strategic forces of both sides to survive a first-strike attack and still retaliate. Once it became clear that both superpowers were in this position, a high degree of strategic stability was created because neither side had any incentive for a first strike. With the end of the Cold War, the balance of terror became less relevant but still viable—because both the United States and Russia, even after the dramatic reductions of the nuclear arsenals, retain ample nuclear weapons to devastate each other. *See also* MAD.

balance of trade The amount by which the value of merchandise exports exceeds or falls short of the value of merchandise imports. Such situations are said to create a *trade surplus* or a *trade deficit*, respectively. The balance of trade is the visible element of a nation's BALANCE OF PAYMENTS; it excludes payments for service and transfers of funds.

balancing behavior *See* BANDWAGONING.

Balch, Emily (1867–1961) The American economist, sociologist, and pacifist who shared the 1946 Nobel Peace Prize (with JOHN R. MOTT) for a lifetime of work furthering justice and peace. She was secretary general of the Women's International League for Peace and Freedom (1919–1922; 1934–1935), strongly supported the United Nations, and aided Nazi victims in Europe and the Japanese-Americans who were interned by the United States during World War II.

Baldwin, Stanley (1867–1947) The cautious, conservative prime minister of Great Britain (1923, 1924–1929, and 1936–1937) who smoothly handled a general strike of 2.5 million workers in 1926 and the ABDICATION CRISIS. He had a personal distaste for foreign affairs. Yet it was he who first stated in a July 30, 1934, speech in the House of Commons: "When you think about the defense of England, you no longer think of the chalk cliffs of Dover. You think of the Rhine. That is where our frontier lies today." And it was he who first prophesied in a November 10, 1932, speech in the House of Commons: "Any town which is within reach of an aero-

Balewa, Abubakar Tafawa (1912–1966)

Arthur James Balfour (Library of Congress)

drome can be bombed within the first five minutes of war from the air, to an extent that was inconceivable in the last war, and the question will be whose morale will be shattered quickest by the preliminary bombing? I think it is well for the man in the street to realize that there is no power on earth that can protect him from being bombed. Whatever people may tell him, the bomber will always get through." Baldwin was thoroughly criticized then and now for not responding properly to the dangers of German rearmament; but he did not believe the British public would support additional military expenditures. Moreover, his fatalism about the bomber always getting through provided great incentives for avoiding war and was one strand in the policy of APPEASEMENT.

Balewa, Abubakar Tafawa (1912–1966)   The first prime minister of independent Nigeria. He took office in 1960 and was deposed and murdered during a military coup six years later.

Balfour, Arthur James (1848–1930)   The conservative prime minister of Great Britain from 1902 to 1905. He served as foreign secretary during 1916 and 1917.

Balfour Declaration   The 1917 letter from British Foreign Secretary Arthur James Balfour to the British Zionist leader Edmond Rothschild, which declared that the British government viewed "with favor the establishment in Palestine of a National Home for the Jewish people." The declaration was significant because the British had just taken control of Palestine from the Ottoman Empire, so this policy allowed for limited Jewish migration to Palestine in the interwar period. In addition, the founders of the modern state of Israel used this "promise" of statehood to great effect in the years prior to independence. As for the British, A. J. P. Taylor wrote in *English History 1914–1945* that "one purpose of the Balfour Declaration was to put a barrier between the French in Syria and the Suez Canal. This was an aspect not aired in public." *Compare to* MCMAHON LETTERS.

THE BALFOUR DECLARATION

Foreign Office

November 2, 1917

Dear Lord Rothschild,

I have much pleasure in conveying to you, on behalf of His Majesty's Government, the following declaration of sympathy with Jewish Zionist aspirations which have been submitted to, and approved by, the Cabinet: "His Majesty's Government view with favour the establishment in Palestine of a National Home for the Jewish people, and will use their best endeavours to facilitate the achievement of this object, it being clearly understood that nothing shall be done which may prejudice the civil and religious rights of existing non-Jewish communities in Palestine, or the rights and political status enjoyed by Jews in any other country." I shall be grateful if you would bring this declaration to the knowledge of the Zionist Federation.

Yours sincerely,

(Signed) ARTHUR JAMES BALFOUR

SOURCE: *The Times,* London, November 9, 1917

Balkanization 1. The division of territory into small, politically unmanageable and mutually hostile parts, thus dispersing power. In the wake of the Soviet withdrawal from Eastern Europe at the close of the COLD WAR, Balkanization once again became a major issue just as it had prior to World War I. 2. A term used to characterize the intentional fragmentation of a region into several independent and mutually hostile centers of power by an imposing force. By dividing a region into smaller sections, the ruling power can prevent the development of a future, unified, concerted threat from the region. This term was first used to describe Russia's policy toward the Balkan nations in the late nineteenth century.

Balkan League The 1912 alliance of Bulgaria, Greece, Montenegro, and Serbia for military actions against the Turks in the BALKAN WARS.

Balkan question The pre–World War I dispute over the political fate and self-determination of the peoples of the Balkan peninsula (present-day Albania, Bosnia-Herzegovina, Bulgaria, Croatia, Greece, Romania, Slovenia, and Yugoslavia). Discontent over the resolution of these issues led to the assassination of Archduke Franz Ferdinand of Austria-Hungary by a Serb in Sarajevo, Bosnia, on June 28, 1914. This led to a declaration of war on Serbia by Austria-Hungary and the beginning of World War I as Europe's inflexible alliances and a public mood in favor of war took effect. Following the dissolution of the Austro-Hungarian Empire after World War I, successor states emerged but contention continued. During the four decades of Communist regimes in the Balkans that began after World War II, nationalist struggles were suppressed or used to set groups against each other. With the overthrow of most of the region's Communist regimes, this area has again emerged as a disputed region in Europe. In 1991 Bosnia-Herzogovina, Croatia, and Slovenia declared their independence from Yugoslavia. This brought civil war between Croatia and the Serbian-led former Yugoslav army and between Bosnia and its ethnic Serbs. Macedonia is again a disputed territory between Serbia and Greece. The Balkan question thus remains unanswered.

Balkan wars 1. The 1912 military efforts of the BALKAN LEAGUE, which forced the Turks out of Europe and obtained independence for Albania. 2. The 1913 armed conflict that began when Bulgaria attacked its former allies in the Balkan League. They then joined with Turkey to defeat Bulgaria and parceled out portions of its territory.

ballistic missile A pilotless projectile that does not rely on aerodynamic surfaces to produce lift and consequently follows a ballistic trajectory when thrust is terminated—meaning that when it runs out of "gas," it falls to earth. The course of a missile as well as its impact point are determined by its initial position, thrust, and angle, as with a bullet or shell. While the term is used for space rockets and even for terrestrial missiles, usually it is used to describe INTERMEDIATE-RANGE NUCLEAR FORCES and STRATEGIC NUCLEAR WEAPONS that leave the earth's atmosphere temporarily during flight and then return to strike their targets. Prior to the 1980s the accuracy of ballistic missiles was such that they were effective only on large targets such as cities. But refinements in the accuracy and new technology allowing several independently targetable bombs or warheads (known as MIRVs) to be placed on the front end of ballistic missiles raised the chilling possibility that they might be used for a first strike against COUNTERFORCE targets. Improvements in accuracy meant that they also could be used to deliver chemical weapons or improved conventional munitions. This, in turn, has encouraged a number of THIRD WORLD countries, such as Argentina, Egypt, India, Pakistan, and South Africa, to seek to develop this technology for use in possible regional conflicts.

ballistic missile defense (BMD) All measures designed to nullify or reduce the effectiveness of an attack by ballistic missiles after they are launched; usually conceived as a system with several independent layers. BMDs can be constructed to protect a large area, such as a city or region, or as a point defense protection around a missile silo. Naturally, the more precise the target to be defended, the more possible the task. But many analysts fear that any BMD system can be beaten because it will always be relatively easy and cheap for the opponent simply to build more offensive weapons that will saturate the defense. A powerful and vocal school of thought holds that the attempt to build a BMD shield is destabilizing and inevitably leads to an ARMS RACE. If international stability rests on mutual assured destruction, anything that lets one nation feel less vulnerable automatically makes the other more fearful and behave less predictably. But the end of the Cold War and the demise of the Soviet Union appear to have eased the arms race consequences of such a defense. This easing of fears, combined with concern over the continued spread of nuclear weapons and ballistic missiles to Third World nations, is likely to lead to a continued interest in the United States and other powers in the development and deployment of some ballistic missiles defenses. *See also* ABM; ALPS; SDI.

Baltic Conventions   The international rules for the use and protection of the marine environment of the Baltic Sea, first agreed in the Baltic Gdansk Convention of 1973 by the states that border on this sea. Also known as the Baltic Code, it was supplanted and expanded by the Baltic Helsinki Convention of 1974.

Baltic nations   The states of Estonia, Latvia, and Lithuania. Each was officially granted independence by the Soviet Union in September 1991 after being under Russian, German, and Soviet domination throughout most of the twentieth century. During World War I the Baltic provinces fought for their own independence, while German and Bolshevik troops fought for control of the area. The Baltic nations enjoyed independent status as republics after World War I until 1939, when the Soviet government occupied them, seeing them as important military bases. Germany occupied all three nations from 1941 until 1944, when the Soviet military defeated it on the eastern front. Estonia, Latvia, and Lithuania then were annexed to the Soviet Union. Independence movements in the three states began long before 1988, when the Soviet government confirmed the secret details of the NAZI-SOVIET NONAGGRESSION PACT that allowed the 1939 Soviet occupation. They were the first three republics of the former Soviet Union to be recognized, in 1991, as sovereign nations by the Soviet Union and the rest of the world.

bamboo curtain   A parallel to the term IRON CURTAIN, used in the 1950s to describe the physical and ideological barriers along the borders of the People's Republic of China.

banality of evil   *See* ARENDT, HANNAH.

banana   1. A fruit widely grown in Latin America for export.   2. By analogy, something having to do with Latin, especially Central, America. Thus a "banana republic" is an unstable government and "banana diplomacy" is concerned with Central American states. Because the use of "banana" as an adjective is considered disparaging, no diplomat would use the word in this sense.

Banda, Hastings (1902–   )   The American-educated medical doctor who became the first president of independent Malawi in 1964. The dictator of a one-party state, he named himself "president for life" in 1971 and outlawed public criticism of his administration.

Bandaranike, Sirimavo (1916–   )   The world's first female prime minister, she succeeded her assassinated husband as prime minister of Ceylon from 1960 to 1965. As prime minister again from 1970 to 1977, she thwarted a leftist coup, sponsored a new constitution, and changed the named of her country to the Republic of Sri Lanka. Noted for jailing political opponents without charges or trials, she was stripped of power, expelled from parliament, and barred from active politics for five years (1980–1985). Since then she has been a leading critic of the ruling regime. *See also* SRI LANKAN CIVIL WAR.

Bandaranike, Solomon (1899–1959)   The prime minister of Ceylon from 1956 until his assassination by a disgruntled Buddhist monk.

Bandung Conference   The 1955 meeting of delegations from 29 Asian and African countries held at Bandung on the island of Java in Indonesia under the sponsorship of Indonesian President ACHMED SUKARNO. It was significant for Sukarno both domestically and in terms of Indonesia's world standing. Notably the conference established a common outlook and identity for many THIRD WORLD states that wanted to be neutral or nonaligned in the COLD WAR—both of which concepts were enunciated as alternatives to siding with one or other of the superpowers. Although U.S. Secretary of State John Foster Dulles condemned these approaches, Third World states used them to attempt to contribute to the evolution of a peaceful international system and ease the existing polarization. The Bandung declaration of the principles on which relations among the newly independent states were to be conducted included mutual respect for territorial integrity and sovereignty; nonaggression; noninterference in others' internal affairs; equality and mutual benefit; and peaceful coexistence. In sum, the Bandung Conference helped coalesce the NONALIGNED MOVEMENT, sped up the DECOLONIZATION process, and established a sense of collective identity among the participants. This first Afro-Asian solidarity conference was instigated by the prime ministers of Burma, Ceylon, India, Indonesia, and Pakistan at a summit meeting in 1954.

THE BANDUNG CONFERENCE AND THE AMERICAN REVOLUTION

[Indian Prime Minister Jawaharlal] Nehru had a particularly high regard for America's revolutionary past. In preparing for the Bandung Conference on Afro-Asian unity in 1955, for which Nehru was in large measure responsible, the organizers deliberately selected the nineteenth of April, 1955, as the opening day. This was the 180th anniversary of the Battle of Lexington-Concord, where American farmers broke into armed rebellion against British colonial rule. The opening ceremony that night began with the reading of Longfellow's "The Midnight Ride of Paul Revere." The resolutions which were finally adopted by the Conference were phrased in the language of Jefferson and Lincoln.

SOURCE: Chester Bowles, *Promises to Keep* (1971). Bowles (1901–1986) was U.S. Ambassador to India (1951–1953; 1963–1969).

---

bandwagon effect 1. An increase in support for a candidate or a proposal because it seems to be winning. Before the era of television, a real bandwagon was popular in U.S. political campaigns. As the musically weighted wagons were pulled through the streets, supporters of the candidate (or the music) would literally climb on or march along with the bandwagon as a gesture of enthusiasm and support. 2. Any instance of the "herd instinct" in politics.

bandwagoning Alignment with a dominant state or coalition. Bandwagoning behavior consists of joining such a coalition and is often contrasted with *balancing behavior*, in which the weaker coalition is joined in an effort to counter either a dominant single power or a stronger coalition. Bandwagoning behavior can result either from the desire to appease the dominant power, especially if that power is aggressively pursuing further gains, or the hope of obtaining a share of the gains in the event that the dominant power is willing to distribute the benefits that accrue from its aggressive policies.

Bangkok Declaration *See* ASEAN.

Bangladesh War of Independence The Indo-Pakistani War of 1971 that separated East from West Pakistan and transformed East Pakistan into the separate nation of Bangladesh. When India was partitioned along religious lines and the independent states of India and Pakistan were created in 1947, Pakistan was made up of two widely separated Muslim areas: East Pakistan, which was carved from east Bengal and the Sylhet district of Assam, and West Bengal, created from western Bengal (the name was changed to West Pakistan in 1955). Almost from the advent of independent Pakistan, frictions developed between East and West Pakistan, which were separated by over 1,000 miles of Indian territory. The economic dislocation brought on by partition accentuated economic grievances, and, over time, these became a major cause of dissatisfaction in population-heavy East Pakistan, whose citizens felt exploited by the West Pakistan–dominated central government in Karachi. In 1971, following a Pakistan Army crackdown on dissidents, Bengali nationalists declared an independent People's Republic of Bangladesh. As open fighting grew between the army and the Bengali Mukti Bahini ("freedom fighters"), an estimated 10 million Bengalis, mainly members of the Hindu minority, sought refuge in India. The crisis put new strains in Pakistan's relations with India. The two had fought a war as recently as 1965, concentrated mainly in the west. The refugee pressure in India produced new tensions in 1971, and India intervened on the side of the Bangladeshis. The battle was over in less than a month. On December 16, 1971, Pakistani forces surrendered and the new nation of Bangladesh was born. Bangladesh now enjoys warm relations with Pakistan. A 1974 accord on mutual recognition was followed more than two years later by the establishment of formal diplomatic relations.

Banjul Charter   A term used to describe the African Charter of Peoples' and Human Rights, which was drafted at Banjul, Gambia, and adopted in 1981 by the ORGANIZATION OF AFRICAN UNITY in a meeting at Nairobi, Kenya. In the preamble to the charter, emphasis is placed on the right to development and on the fact that civil and political rights cannot be dissociated from economic, cultural, and social rights. The rights included in the charter include the rights to self-determination; to control of resources; to economic, cultural and social development; to peace and security; and to a decent environment.

Bank for International Settlements   The bank for CENTRAL BANKs based in Basel, Switzerland. It was created in 1930 to foster international financial cooperation. Today it seeks to simplify international financing, cooperates with the INTERNATIONAL MONETARY FUND, and purchases and sells gold, foreign currencies, and bonds for central banks.

Banna, Hassan al- (1903–1949)   Founder of the MUSLIM BROTHERHOOD in Egypt, an organization dedicated to returning Arab regimes to fundamental Islamic values with governments based on the Koran. Banna was a charismatic leader, and the early success of the Brotherhood is attributed to his personal popularity. He was assassinated by agents of the Egyptian government, who held his organization responsible for the 1945 assassination of Prime Minister Nokrashi Pasha and a number of other high government officials.

Banna, Sabri al-   *See* ABU NIDAL.

Bantustan   The overarching name for the 14 percent of South Africa's land area designated as "homelands" for the indigenous black peoples. Under APARTHEID, black political rights were limited to these areas. The Bantu Homelands Act of 1970 required that every black person in South Africa be

a citizen of one of these "homelands" even if she or he had never been to one. Shortly thereafter the United Nations General Assembly responded by condemning the establishment of Bantustan as a violation of black South Africans' inalienable rights. Now that the South African government has voted to end apartheid, the status of these homelands is in doubt. This issue is made all the more complicated by the fact that the Bantustans have become political power bases for regional black leaders who are resistant to efforts to end apartheid, which would curtail their power.

banzai   The World War II battle cry (meaning "ten thousand years," or "long live the emperor") of Japanese troops. A banzai charge was a final desperate assault designed to inflict maximum damage on the enemy at close range before an honorable death in battle. *Compare to* KAMIKAZE.

Bao Dai (1913–   )   The last emperor of Vietnam. He ascended the throne in 1932 and was generally subservient to the French colonial government prior to World War II. In 1945 he abdicated the throne under pressure from HO CHI MINH's Democratic Republic. Later, in 1949, France encouraged Bao Dai to become head of the as-yet unrecognized government of South Vietnam. In July 1954 he appointed Ngo Dinh Diem to the position of premier of Vietnam. When Vietnam was divided in accordance with the 1954 Geneva Agreements, Bao Dai assumed the role of head of state of South Vietnam. In 1955 he was deposed by a plebiscite that made South Vietnam a republic, was succeeded by Diem (as president), and retired to southern France.

Barbarossa   The CODE NAME for the June 22, 1941, German invasion of the Soviet Union. With his hatred of communism and desire for living space and food supplies to the east, German dictator Adolf Hitler, following his victory over France, was convinced that—while reducing war production and demobilizing forces, and without providing any winter equipment—he could conquer the Soviet Union in one quick campaign. Hitler told his generals prior to the invasion: "You have only to kick in the door, and the whole rotten structure will come crashing down" (quoted in Robert Payne, *The Life*

German troops in the Soviet Union in 1941. (National Archives)

and Death of Adolph Hitler, 1973). The attack, which was delayed six weeks while the Germans saved their Italian allies from defeat in Greece and Yugoslavia, occurred in three prongs toward Leningrad, Moscow, and Kiev along a 1,900-mile battlefront. Nine million men fought each other. Over 20 million Soviets and other Slavic peoples would eventually die in repulsing the Germans. But elsewhere, the invasion was not universally viewed as a bad thing. The totalitarianism of Hitler and Stalin so effectively competed for evil reputations that then–U.S. Senator HARRY S TRUMAN said on hearing of the invasion: "If we see that Germany is winning the war we ought to help Russia, and if Russia is winning we ought to help Germany, and in that way let them kill as many as possible" (*New York Times,* July 24, 1941).

Barbie, Klaus (1913–1991)   The German GESTAPO officer who, during World War II, earned the title "Butcher of Lyon" for his executions and deportations to death camps of thousands of Jewish French citizens and French resistance fighters. After the war the U.S. government knowingly employed him in counterintelligence operations (1947–1951), then helped him to escape to South America. In 1983 Bolivia extradited him to France where in 1987 he was convicted of crimes against humanity and sentenced to life in prison, where he died.

bargaining chip   1. Anything one might be willing to trade in a negotiation; a deliberately created element or condition designed to provide a negotiating

advantage.   2. Any military force, weapons system, or other resource, present or projected, that a nation is willing to downgrade or discard in return for a concession by a military rival. The phrase was first used in this context during the SALT talks (1969–1979) between the United States and the Soviet Union. Because the Nixon Administration and its successors believed that the Soviet Union signed SALT I only because the United States had approved the development of such weapons as the ABM, the Poseidon submarine, and the Minuteman III missile systems, it asked the Congress to approve, as a bargaining chip for SALT II, the development of the MX MISSILE, the B-1 bomber, and the cruise missile. The bargaining chip strategy has been attacked on several grounds: first, because developing weapons systems just to trade them away at the negotiating table is too expensive; second, developing weapons systems just as a hedge in negotiations is inflammatory to the arms race; and third, because frequently bargaining chips are not bargained away after all.

bargaining strength   The relative power each party holds during a negotiation. One government has great bargaining strength via-à-vis another if both sides know that it has the military power to impose its will regardless of the outcome of negotiations; management has great bargaining strength over labor if it has so much excess inventory that a short strike would be desirable. The final settlement often reflects the bargaining strength of each side. The most famous statement on a bargaining position backed by force comes from Mario Puzo's novel *The Godfather* (1969): "I'll make him an offer he can't refuse."

bargaining theory   Explanations about an outcome when two parties want to reach an agreement but have very different preferences about the content of that agreement. Bargaining theory developed during the COLD WAR around the concept of bargaining between states. It was applied to situations—usually crises—in which there was a mixture of common and conflicting interests. The common interest of the participants in reaching a bargain was accompanied by conflicting interests over the nature of the bargain. Much of the theory was concerned with the coercive elements of bargaining or what THOMAS C. SCHELLING in *Arms and Influence* (1966) called *coercive diplomacy.* Accommodation as an element of bargaining, however, also was discussed in GLENN H. SNYDER and Paul Diesing's *Conflict Among Nations* (1977), in which an emphasis was placed on the idea of "accommodating cheaply."

Barre Plan   A proposal approved by the European Economic Community's Council of Ministers in 1969 to further integrate EEC economic and monetary policy by automatically making limited cash reserves available for member states to borrow if necessary. The plan sponsor, Raymond Barre (1924–   ), was then the vice president of the Commission of the European Communities and later served as the prime minister of France from 1979 to 1981.

barter   Trade in which merchandise is exchanged directly for other merchandise without the use of money. Barter is an important means of trade for countries whose currency is not readily convertible. Before money was invented, it was the form of exchanges for early civilizations. *See also* CONVERTIBLE CURRENCY.

Baruch Plan   Bernard Baruch's (1870–1965) 1946 proposal to the United Nations Atomic Energy Commission that would have placed all atomic weapons under the control of a newly created international agency. Baruch, as the U.S. representative to the commission, called for the United States to destroy its existing atomic bombs. But the plan was rejected by the Soviet Union because it would have prevented the development of Soviet nuclear weapons and left the United States, even without actual bombs, in sole possession of the technology to create them.

base   1. A permanent concentration of military personnel or materiel. The location of such a base sometimes is a matter of historical accident but often is a function of the internal politics of a state. 2. The personnel or materiel of a state located in an allied state. For example, the United States has had bases on the territory of allies in Europe and the Far East since World War II. These bases were seen as a visible manifestation of the U.S. commitment to the security of its allies, but also became targets for protest when the United States was unpopular with the domestic public or a peace movement in the allied state.

base force   A concept that was the central element in the Bush administration's plan for downsizing the U.S. military establishment for the post–COLD WAR world. Under this concept the U.S. Army was to be reduced from 16 to 12 active divisions, the U.S. Navy from 530 to 450 ships and from 15 to 12 carrier battle groups, and the U.S. Air Force from 22 to 15 active fighter wing equivalents. The base force was designed to be adaptable, able to protect U.S. security interests and deal with contingencies across the spectrum of conflict from low-level crisis to global war-fighting. The base forces were to be organized into strategic forces, Atlantic forces, Pacific forces, and contingency forces with supporting capabilities, including transportation, reconstitution, and research and development. The size of the force was reduced even further by the Clinton administration in 1993.

bashing   Extreme and public criticism (often unwarranted and irrational) of a person, policy, or nation. Bashing can be international or domestic in focus. For example, in the United States in recent years, "Japan-bashing" has Americans berating Japan for its illegal selling of sensitive submarine technology to the Soviet Union (the Toshiba case), for what U.S. citizens perceive to be its unfair trade practices, and for its "hiding" behind the U.S. defense umbrella in the Pacific without paying its "fair share."

basic encyclopedia   A military compilation of identified installations and physical areas of potential tactical or strategic significance as objectives for attack.

basic human needs   The minimum requirements of food, shelter, and clothing that make up a decent standard of living. The United Nations since the mid-1960s, the International Bank for Reconstruction and Development since the early 1970s, and the United States since 1978 have supported a basic human needs approach to development—that foreign assistance programs should focus on critical problems in those functional sectors that affect the lives of the majority of the people in developing countries. Proponents of this development strategy claim that nurturing a country's human resources will cause employment opportunities to increase, worker productivity to grow, and income to be more equitably distributed, with little sacrifice to the rates of economic growth. Critics of this basic human needs approach contend that entrenched power elites oppose any redistribution of wealth or land and that this strategy sharply conflicts with the domestic development strategies in many of the less-developed countries. *See also* FOREIGN AID.

basic intelligence *See* INTELLIGENCE, BASIC.

basing mode The way in which ICBMs are deployed or stored; for example, in hardened underground silos, in submarines, on movable vehicles, and so on.

basket 1. A group of related issues scheduled for discussion at a political meeting or international conference. 2. A grouping of different currencies. *See also* BASKET OF CURRENCIES.

basket of currencies The means of determining the value of a unit of an INTERNATIONAL CURRENCY. In order to reduce as much as possible the fluctuations in the value of an international currency such as the SDR (SPECIAL DRAWING RIGHTS), the EUA (EUROPEAN UNIT OF ACCOUNT), or the ECU (EUROPEAN CURRENCY UNIT), the unit is pegged to the value of a combination, or basket, of several currencies rather than just one. Baskets are usually weighted; that is, a strong currency will represent a larger percentage of the value of the unit than a weak currency. The value of the international currency unit usually is computed and quoted on a daily basis in terms of U.S. dollars; as the value of each component part of the basket fluctuates against the dollar, the total value of the unit in terms of dollars varies.

basket I The first of three "baskets," or sections, into which the Final Act of the CONFERENCE ON SECURITY AND COOPERATION IN EUROPE was subdivided. It contains a declaration of ten principles relating to the conduct of relations among states as well as a series of CONFIDENCE-BUILDING MEASURES (CBMs) relating to European military security.

basket II The second of three "baskets," or sections, into which the Final Act of the Conference on Security and Cooperation in Europe was subdivided. It deals with economic, scientific, technical, and environmental cooperation, emphasizing the development of East-West trade, the planning of joint research projects, and increased tourism.

basket III The third of three "baskets," or sections, into which the Final Act of the Conference on Security and Cooperation in Europe was subdivided. It deals with cooperation in humanitarian and other fields, specifically advocating the freer movement of ideas, information, and people through family reunification, increased access to broadcast and printed information, and increased educational and cultural exchanges.

Basque Fatherland and Liberty *See* ETA.

Basque terrorism A campaign of violence by Basque separatists carried on in the hope of achieving independence for their ethnic homeland in northern Spain. The fascist regime of FRANCISCO FRANCO inadvertently stoked the nationalist fervor of a fiercely independent but repressed people who were intent on maintaining their cultural and linguistic identity. Because the Basques generally supported the losing side in the SPANISH CIVIL WAR, the victorious Nationalists sought to suppress Basque culture. The Basque nationalist organization, *Euzkadi ta Askatusna* (ETA), or "Basque Fatherland and Liberty," began in 1968 a series of anti-Spanish terrorist acts that continues today. In 1980 the four Basque provinces were granted regional political autonomy by the Spanish government. However, such measures did not appease Basque terrorists, who appear to be ready to settle for nothing less than total Basque sovereignty.

Bastogne *See* BULGE, BATTLE OF THE.

Bataan The peninsula in the Philippines to which General DOUGLAS MACARTHUR's forces retreated after the Japanese invasion of the Philippines in World War II. From January to April 1942 Allied forces fought off the advancing Japanese. After exhausting all food and ammunition, they were finally forced to surrender. Upon orders of President Franklin D. Roosevelt, General MacArthur, with his family and a small staff, retreated to safety in Australia. Because these were the only ground forces fighting the Japanese in the first months of the war, they received disproportionate publicity but none of the relief that was promised. Indeed, shortly after the fighting began American planners had realized that no relief was possible and "wrote off" the entire force.

THE SONG OF BATAAN

No mama, no papa, no Uncle Sam,
No aunts, no uncles, no nephews, no nieces,
We're the battling bastards of Bataan:
No rifles, no planes, or artillery pieces,
And nobody gives a damn.

SOURCE: Song of the U.S. soldiers during the 1942 defense of Bataan in the Philippines, quoted in *Time*, March 9, 1942.

Bataan Death March   The 1942 80-mile march to prisoner-of-war camps that 70,000 captured U.S. and Filipino troops were forced to make by their Japanese guards after the fall of Bataan in World War II. It is estimated that 10,000 died along the way.

Batista, Fulgencio (1901–1973)   The dictator and sometime president of Cuba (1940–1944; 1952–1959) who controlled Cuba from 1933 until he was overthrown by FIDEL CASTRO. Following "the sergeants' revolt" in 1933, which he organized, Batista ruled the island through puppet governments until he was elected president in 1940. Batista used a system of political patronage to gain the support of the army, government bureaucrats, and labor. He also initiated reform programs, including limited land redistribution. Following defeat in the 1944 elections, Batista retired. He returned to politics to overthrow President Carlos Soccors before the 1952 elections. A corrupt and brutal dictator, Batista provoked growing opposition. Forces led by Castro revolted unsuccessfully in July 1953. But by 1958, the island was gripped by civil war. As rebel forces prepared to take Havana on January 1, 1959, Batista went into exile. *See also* CUBAN REVOLUTION.

Japanese troops on Bataan in 1942. (National Archives)

Battenberg   The name of a family of German counts that caused considerable controversy at the beginning of World War I. Prince Louis of Battenberg (1854–1921), a naturalized British subject, was first sea lord (the highest-ranking officer) of Great Britain's Royal Navy when the war began. Prejudice against him because of his family origin forced his resignation two months into the war. He renounced the title of Battenberg in 1917 and took the surname Mountbatten. His son LOUIS MOUNT-BATTEN would rise to be an admiral in World War II and first sea lord in the postwar period.

Battle Act of 1951   The United States law known formally as the Mutual Defense Assistance Control Act of 1951, which calls for the automatic embargo of military and strategic materials to states that the U.S. government declares to be a threat. This law also forbids foreign aid to both designated "threat" states and to their military suppliers. All of the North Atlantic Treaty Organization states have similar laws, but they are inherently full of loopholes because so much that is militarily useful (such as computers and chemical production technology) has equally valid nonmilitary applications. Thus German companies in the 1980s were legally able to sell Libya and Iraq technology to create chemical weapons because it is essentially the same technology for legitimate civilian use. *See also* COCOM.

Battle of . . .   *See* location of battle. For example, for Battle of Britain see BRITAIN, BATTLE OF.

battlefield nuclear weapons   *See* TACTICAL NUCLEAR WEAPON.

battleship   The most powerful ships of the world's BLUE WATER NAVIES until World War II, when AIRCRAFT CARRIERS not only supplanted them as the most powerful CAPITAL SHIPS but showed that the battleship was strategically insignificant in comparison. The name comes from the premodern "line of battle ship." The first modern "big-gun" battleship was the British Royal Navy's *Dreadnought*, completed in 1906. It had ten 12-inch guns; the largest previous ship had only four 10-inch guns. As the battleship was essentially a platform for big guns,

all the major naval powers raced to build bigger ships that would carry even bigger guns. Observing this situation, future Prime Minister Winston Churchill said in the House of Commons on March 17, 1914: "The offensive power of modern battleships is out of all proportions to their defensive power. Never was the disproportion so marked. If you want to make a true picture in your mind of a battle between great modern ironclad ships you must not think of it as if it were two men in armour striking at each other with heavy swords. It is more like a battle between two egg-shells striking each other with hammers." Even the most powerful battleships ever built, the Japanese World War II–era *Yamoto* and *Musashi*, could, with their 18-inch guns, send only an automobile-size projectile 20 miles or so. An aircraft carrier could send its more versatile projectiles hundreds of miles. On December 7, 1941, the Japanese put out of service all of the American battleships at Pearl Harbor—using six aircraft carriers. But tactical success proved insignificant in the end. American aircraft carriers escaped attack because they were at sea at the time—and it was these same carriers that six months later at the 1942 BATTLE OF MIDWAY sank four Japanese carriers. Only the U.S. Navy still uses the classic big-gun battleship for such tasks as shore bombardment in Korea, Vietnam, Lebanon, and the Persian Gulf.

The USS Missouri *firing its big guns during the Korean War. (National Archives)*

bay According to the 1958 Geneva Convention on the Territorial Sea and the Contiguous Zone, which was accepted by the 1982 United Nations Convention on the Law of the Sea, "a bay is a well-marked indentation whose penetration is in such proportion to the width of its mouth as to contain landlocked waters and constitute more than a mere curvature of the coast." In addition, an "indentation shall not, however, be regarded as a bay unless its area is as large as, or larger than, that of the semi-circle whose diameter is a line drawn across the mouth of that indentation."

Bay of Pigs **1.** The southern Cuban inlet that was the landing site in 1961 of an ill-fated United States–sponsored invasion of Cuba by 1,500 expatriate Cubans trained by the U.S. Central Intelligence Agency to overthrow the government of FIDEL CASTRO. It was a total failure and a major embarrassment to the administration of JOHN F. KENNEDY. It was thought that the invasion would trigger a general uprising against the Castro regime; but this never happened and within two days all the invaders were either dead or captured. The United States was then forced by Castro to ransom the 1,179 survivors for $53 million worth of food and medical supplies. It has often been suggested that Kennedy's poor management of this operation encouraged the Soviets to place the missiles in Cuba that led to the CUBAN MISSILE CRISIS. **2.** Any fiasco or flop. Just as Napoleon had his Waterloo, Kennedy had his Bay of Pigs. But Napoleon nearly won while Kennedy's failure was an embarrassment because it was an incompetent effort, based on grossly wrong intelligence, that was poorly planned and led and lacked adequate air cover. So, in common parlance, if you have a Bay of Pigs you haven't merely lost—you've disgraced yourself as well.

Beagle Channel Dispute The disagreement between Chile and Argentina over which state had sovereignty over what areas and what islands in the waterway that divides the two countries at the southernmost part of South America. While the British arbitrated the dispute in favor of Chile in 1977 (it was the British ship HMS *Beagle* that discovered and named the channel in 1830 while conveying Charles Darwin on the voyage that would lead to his theory of evolution), Argentina rejected

---

DEFEAT IS AN ORPHAN

Before he left for the press conference in the State Department auditorium, Kennedy told the group there was only one way to cut off speculation about the Bay of Pigs decision—to tell the truth: while all senior officials who were consulted backed the expedition, the final responsibility was his alone.

Facing the reporters, Kennedy brushed aside the stories about who was to blame: "There's an old saying that victory has a hundred fathers and defeat is an orphan." What mattered was only one fact: "I am the responsible officer of the government."

SOURCE: Peter Wyden, *Bay of Pigs: The Untold Story* (1979). Wyden notes that "When historian [Arthur M.] Schlesinger later asked him about the source of that apt quotation, Kennedy said: "Oh, I don't know; it's just an old saying." In fact, it is attributed to *The Ciano Diaries* (1939–1943) of Count Galeazzo Ciano, Mussolini's foreign minister, who used it in a journal entry of September 9, 1942.

---

the decision. In 1979 both sides agreed that Pope John Paul II would arbitrate. In 1984 both sides accepted the pope's decision, which allowed Argentina to control the Atlantic waters of the channel and Chile to control the corresponding Pacific waters.

bear **1.** A term characterizing a decline in prices, particularly on a stock market, as opposed to *bull,* a term related to rising prices. **2.** The Soviet Union, whose national symbol was the bear. The bear as a symbol of danger to the United States was used to great effect by presidential candidates and advertising agencies during the COLD WAR.

Beatty, David (1871–1936) The British admiral who led the battlecruiser fleet at the 1916 BATTLE OF JUTLAND; later he was first sea lord (the uniformed head of the Royal Navy) from 1919 to 1927. At Jutland British ships tended to sink more readily than the opposition German ships. This occasioned Beatty's famous remark: "There's something wrong with our bloody ships today." What was "wrong" was that the British ships tended to lack watertight subdivisions and efficient damage-control systems. The British won the battle, but because of their better damage-control capabilities, some German battleships that sustained greater damage than some sunk British ships stayed afloat.

Beer Hall Putsch ADOLF HITLER's abortive effort to take control of the German state of Bavaria in November 1923. Angered by the French occupation of the Ruhr and runaway inflation, a National Socialist (NAZI) meeting in a vast beer hall in Munich ended in a street procession led by Hitler and World War I General ERICH LUDENDORFF. The Nazis intended it to be a prelude to a general revolution against the WEIMAR REPUBLIC, but local police stopped the demonstration with small-arms fire. Hitler fled but was found and arrested; he used his trial as a platform for Nazi propaganda. Sentenced to nine months in a comfortable prison at Landsberg, Hitler wrote a combination political manifesto and autobiography, *Mein Kampf* (*My Battle*) (1925), which contained his fanatical ideas on racism, anti-Semitism, and anti-Marxist politics.

THE BEER HALL PUTSCH
AND THE POPE

During my reunion with the Pope [in 1944], His Holiness took a few minutes to reminisce about the events in Germany when Hitler failed to seize power during the so-called beer hall putsch. All the foreign representatives at Munich, including Nuncio Pacelli [later to be Pope Pius XII] were convinced that Hitler's political career had ended ignominiously in 1924. When I ventured to remind His Holiness of this bit of history, he laughed and said, "I know what you mean—Papal infallibility. Don't forget I was only a monsignor then!"

SOURCE: Robert Murphy, *Diplomat Among Warriors* (1964).

Beernaert, Auguste (1829–1912) The Belgian representative at The Hague conferences of 1899 and 1907 whose advocacy of international law, compulsory international arbitration, and opposition to slavery—especially in his country's African colony of the Congo—earned him the Nobel Peace Prize in 1909 (which he shared with PAUL HENRI D'ESTOURNELLES DE CONSTANT).

beggar-thy-neighbor policy A state's efforts to reduce unemployment and increase domestic production by raising tariffs and instituting other measures that inhibit imports. States that pursued such policies in the early 1930s found that other states retaliated by raising barriers against the first state's exports, which tended to worsen the economic difficulties that precipitated the initial protectionist action. Such actions are the equivalent in the economic sphere of actions that trigger and fuel arms races in the security sphere. *Compare to* PROTECTIONISM.

Begin, Menachem (1913–1992) The Polish-born prime minister of Israel (1977–1983) who led the IRGUN terrorist organization of the 1940s. Irgun's violence was calculated to make the preservation of Great Britain's Palestine mandate too costly. Irgun was responsible for the bombing of the KING DAVID HOTEL in July 1946 and the massacre of an estimated 200 Arab villagers, including women and children, at DEIR YASSIN in 1948. Begin served in the Knesset, the Israeli parliament, from 1948 to 1967 and was a member of a national unity government (1967–1970). He became prime minister as head of the right-wing coalition led by the Likud Party in 1977. He opened negotiations with Egyptian President Anwar Sadat in 1977 when Sadat accepted his invitation to visit Jerusalem and begin a peace process between Israel and Egypt. U.S. President Jimmy Carter helped to mediate the CAMP DAVID ACCORDS, which resulted in the 1979 Egypt-Israeli peace treaty for which Begin shared with Sadat the 1978 Nobel Peace Prize. Begin's policy was to increase the number of Israeli settlements on the WEST BANK. But his invasion of Lebanon in 1982 to attack Palestinian guerrillas resulted in an unpopular, drawn-out war, which provoked unprecedented antigovernment demonstrations. This and the death of his wife influenced his decision to retire from public life in 1983.

behavioralism 1. A philosophic disposition toward the study of the behavior of people in political situations as opposed to studying the institutional structures of politics. Thus, for a behavioralist, the structure of a foreign ministry should not be studied, because what is really important is the behavior of its officials. 2. The study of politics that emphasizes the use of the scientific method for empirical investigations and the use of quantitative techniques. **3.** An approach to political science and international politics that developed in the 1950s, largely in the United States, through the influx of the natural scientists and other social scientists into the discipline. The behavioralists challenged the realist domination of the study of international politics on the grounds that realists such as HANS J. MORGENTHAU had failed to define their central concepts, were overly deterministic in their approach, and had not produced theories that were empirically testable (*See* REALISM.) The behavioralist movement was in large part a protest about what had gone before. The main objective of the behavioralists was to develop rigorous and systematic approaches and methods that would explain behavior and provide the basis for generalizations about political phenomena. In relation to foreign policy, one of the most important behavioral contributions was the decision-making approach established by RICHARD SNYDER and his associates. This replaced the abstraction of the state with the reality of decision makers who could be observed, understood, and explained. In this connection, Snyder introduced concepts and insights from psychology and sociology that were to be used to explain behavior that had hitherto been explained largely through the abstraction of the power maximizing state. Other analysts such as Morton Kaplan (1921–   ) approached the subject in different ways, focusing on the patterns of interaction in the international system. Here too, though, there was clearly an attempt to be scientific and to discern laws that could both explain and predict. The behavioralist approach was never as enthusiastically embraced in Great Britain and the rest of Europe as it was in the United States. Indeed, by the mid-1960s there was a reaction against it, led by HEDLEY BULL, whose case for the classical approach to international relations published in *World Politics* (1966) polarized the classical and scientific approaches to a greater extent than was warranted. Moreover, by the late 1960s there were claims that political science should move beyond behavioralism and reintroduce value judgments and the like. In spite of this reaction, many of the ideas and approaches generated by the behavioral revolution have become commonplace in the study of international politics and foreign policy.

behavioralism, cognitive A concept used by HAROLD and MARGARET SPROUT, which contends that people respond to their milieus through perception and in no other way.

behavioralism, post- The critical response to behavioralism which held that, as political science adopted a behavioral orientation, it became less relevant to the study of politics. An overemphasis on being empirical and quantitative caused too much attention to be devoted to easily studied trivial issues at the expense of important topics. Post-behavioralism as a movement within political science does not advocate the end of the scientific study of politics; it mainly suggests that there is more than one way of advancing knowledge and that methodologies should be appropriate to the issue under study.

behavioral sciences All of the academic disciplines that study human and animal behavior using empirical research. This term was first put into wide use in the early 1950s by the Ford Foundation to describe its funding for interdisciplinary research in the social sciences and by faculty at the University of Chicago seeking federal funding for research—and concerned, in an era of MCCARTHYISM, that their social science research might be confused with socialism. The behavioral approach led to an emphasis on explaining foreign policy and international relations in scientific terms. An effort was made to determine regularities and patterns of behavior and to provide generalizations about behavior that were sometimes based on quantification. Although this aroused criticism from those who saw international relations as a matter of wisdom or history rather than science, many analysts still attempt to enhance our understanding of international relations through a behavioral or scientific approach.

Belgian Congo The poorly administered central African colony that was unified by Belgium in the 1880s and became the state of Zaire in 1971. *See also* CONGO; CONGOLESE CIVIL WAR.

Belgian neutrality Traditional efforts by Belgium in the nineteenth and first part of the twentieth century to remain neutral in European wars. After two centuries of Spanish rule, the country passed to the Austrian Hapsburg family as a consequence of the Treaty of Utrecht (1713). It was annexed to France by Napoleon Bonaparte in 1794. After his defeat in 1815, Belgium was awarded to the Netherlands. A revolt by the inhabitants led to the independent state of Belgium in 1830. For 84 years, Belgium remained neutral in an era of intra-European wars until German troops overran it during their attack on France in 1914. In the interwar years Belgium reverted to its former policy of neutrality, trying not to provide Nazi Germany with an excuse to invade. As in 1914, this approach failed, and Belgium was occupied by the Germans in 1940. Thus before each of the world wars Belgium tried to follow a policy of neutrality. Recognizing the need for a better means of preserving its independence, however, Belgium abandoned its twice-unsuccessful neutrality policy in 1945 and became one of 12 founding members of the NORTH ATLANTIC TREATY ORGANIZATION in 1949. Brussels even became the host city for NATO headquarters when the organization left Paris in 1966.

Belgium Clause   *See* ATTENTAT CLAUSE.

Belgrano   The Argentinean naval cruiser (formally the *General Belgrano*) sunk by a British submarine, HMS *Conqueror,* during the 1982 FALKLANDS WAR. The sinking, which took 368 lives, proved controversial because while the British had declared a 200-mile EXCLUSION ZONE around the Falklands, the *Belgrano* was outside of the zone and was heading even farther away when it was sunk. The controversy was further inflamed when contradictory information emerged about who had made the decision to sink it. John Nott, the British defense minister, told the House of Commons on May 5, 1982: "The actual decision to launch a torpedo was clearly one taken by the submarine commander." While that was technically true, it also turned out, according to the *Sunday Mirror* (September, 11, 1984), that the British cabinet authorized the submarine commander to initiate the sinking. Some critics contend that the sinking of the *Belgrano* was deliberately intended to sabotage a Peruvian peace plan which otherwise might have succeeded in defusing the situation and in avoiding further hostilities. The military consequence, however, was

that the Argentinean navy remained in port and did not become a key element in the war. Interestingly, the *Belgrano* began life as the U.S. cruiser *Phoenix* and was a survivor of the Japanese attack on PEARL HARBOR in 1941.

bellicism   **1.** An approach to war that sees it in terms of honor, glory, and gain rather than something to be avoided.   **2.** An emphasis within a nation on the martial spirit.

belligerency   The legal condition of the parties involved in a war, either civil or international, as recognized by other states. International law on belligerency creates both rights and duties for the parties to the conflict as well as for those states declaring themselves neutral in regard to it. According to international law only existing states are qualified to become belligerents and make war. Consequently, the diplomatic recognition by neutral states of the parties in a civil war is extremely important in giving them legal status. The recognition that a state of belligerency exists within a state bestows legitimacy on the insurgent group; this allows the states that recognize it to provide all support short of actual intervention without being in violation of international law. For example, during the American Revolution, the recognition by France that a state of belligerency existed allowed the French to supply what were then Great Britain's colonies with material aid without committing a formal act of hostility against Britain. Of course, there is always the risk that the state engaged in fighting the insurgent forces may take punitive action against those supporting insurgents who, from its point of view, are nothing more than domestic criminals.

belligerent   **1.** The term of international law for a state at war with another.   **2.** The armed forces of a nation at war as opposed to its ordinary citizens. In the TOTAL WARs of the twentieth century, however, this distinction has increasingly been blurred. GIULIO DOUHET wrote in his 1921 *The Command of the Air:* "Any distinction between belligerents and nonbelligerents is no longer admissible today either in fact or theory. . . . When nations are at war, everyone takes part in it; the soldier carrying his gun, the woman loading shells at a factory, the farmer growing wheat, the scientist experimenting in his laboratory . . . It begins to look now as if the safest place may be the trenches."

Ben Bella, Ahmed (1918–   )   The Algerian revolutionary leader who became the first prime minister of independent Algeria in 1962. He was then elected as the first president of the Algerian Republic in 1963. By legally expropriating most foreign-owned land, he forced 800,000 colons (French settlers) to become refugees in France. In 1965 his one-party authoritarian rule fell to a military coup and he was imprisoned until 1980. *See also* ALGERIAN WAR OF INDEPENDENCE.

Benelux   *Bel*gium, the *Nether*lands, and *Lux*embourg. The Benelux Economic Union (BEU) customs union agreement among these three small European nations was agreed to during World War II and came into effect in 1948. The three countries, all founding members of the European Economic Community as well, formed an economic union in 1960.

Benes, Eduard (1884–1948)   The president of Czechoslovakia at two critical junctures in modern Czechoslovakian history; first from 1935 to 1938 and later from 1946 to 1948. In 1938 Adolf Hitler supported the Sudeten German minority in Czechoslovakia against its government by applying the principle of national SELF-DETERMINATION. After Great Britain and France agreed to Hitler's demands for redrawn German/Czech borders, Benes was forced by them to agree. Hitler then reneged on the agreement, attacked Czechoslovakia in September 1938, took control of the country, and forced Benes into exile.

Benes returned in 1945 and was elected president in 1946. He was president in 1948 when Stalinist Communists expelled the democratic members of the coalition Czechoslovakian government in Prague, possibly murdered Foreign Minister JAN MASARYK, and forced Benes to resign. He died shortly thereafter. *See also* MUNICH AGREEMENT.

Ben Gurion, David (1886–1973)   The Polish-born Israeli Zionist leader, the founder and leader of Israel's Labor (Mapai) Party, and the first prime minister and minister of defense of Israel from 1948

to 1953. Following a brief retirement, he again served as prime minister from 1955 to 1963.

benign neglect   A policy of allowing a situation to improve, or at least not get worse, by leaving it alone for a while. The phrase was first used by the earl of Durham in an 1839 report to the British Parliament, in which he observed: "Through many years of benign neglect by Britain, Canada had become a nation much more prosperous than England itself."

Bentham, Jeremy (1748–1832)   A British philosopher who held that self-interest was the prime motivator of human behavior and that a government should strive to do the greatest good for the greatest numbers. He wanted institutions to justify themselves on practical grounds of the level of useful welfare achieved. He was thereby the prophet of the movement of *utilitarianism*, which he preached from the 1770s but which first became prominent in the 1810s. Bentham held that governments were created because of people's desire for happiness, not by divine intervention. His beliefs, writings, and actions make Bentham the major social reformer of nineteenth-century England. Bentham is also credited with coining the word *international* and wrote extensively on the futility and irrationality of war; a severe rationalist, he called for international laws and institutions for the arbitration of disputes. His most influential work is *Principles of Morals and Political Philosophy* (1780).

Beria, Lavrenti Pavlovich (1899–1953)   The head of JOSEPH STALIN's Soviet secret police, the NKVD (see KGB), from 1938 until he was murdered in 1953. He controlled a vast internal empire of prison camps and security agencies. Following Stalin's death in 1953, when the principle of collective leadership was revived, Beria posed as a defender of socialist legality. In June his security forces apparently tried a coup, but it failed and Beria was arrested and shot in the Kremlin, perhaps by Marshal GEORGI ZHUKOV. Subscribers to the *Great Soviet Encyclopedia* were then told to remove his biography by pasting over it an article sent to them on the Bering Sea.

Berlaymont   The EUROPEAN COMMISSION headquarters building in Brussels.

Berlin, Battle of   1. The bombing of Berlin, Germany, by Allied air forces during WORLD WAR II. The objective of the battle was explained by Air Marshal Sir ARTHUR HARRIS, the head of British Bomber Command: "The Battle of Berlin will continue until the heart of Nazi Germany ceases to beat" (*Time*, December 6, 1943).   2. The last battle of World War II in Europe, from April 16 to May 2, 1945, when the Soviet RED ARMY captured the city of Berlin. There were an estimated 300,000 Soviet and 1 million German casualties (killed and wounded). Immediately thereafter the Soviet soldiers were encouraged literally to rape and plunder the city. This they did with great enthusiasm.

INSTRUCTIONS TO THE RED ARMY
AS IT ADVANCED ON BERLIN

Kill! There is nothing that is innocent in the German. Neither in the living nor in the unborn. Follow the directive of Comrade Stalin and trample into the ground forever the Fascist beast in his cave. Break by force the racial haughtiness of German women! Take them as your lawful prey! Kill, you brave advancing Red soldiers!

SOURCE: Ilya Ehrenburg, speaking to the Red Army as it advanced into Germany, quoted in Alfred Vagts, *A History of Militarism*, rev. ed. (1959).

Berlin, Treaty of   1. The 1921 treaty that formally ended hostilities between the United States and Germany. This was necessary because the U.S. Senate had refused to ratify the 1919 TREATY OF VERSAILLES.   2. The 1971 Quadripartite Agreement on Berlin by the Soviet Union, the United States, Great Britain, and France that accepted the then-status quo in Berlin with access to West Berlin guaranteed.

Berlin Blockade   The first of the Berlin crises during the COLD WAR. After World War II Berlin, as well as the rest of Germany, had been divided into four zones of occupation with sectors administered by France, Great Britain, the Soviet Union, and the United States. With Berlin 110 miles inside the Soviet occupation zone, the Soviets believed it vulnerable and exerted pressure. The blockade occurred from June 1948 to May 1949 when the Soviet authorities stopped all overland travel (by

---

HOW THE BERLIN AIRLIFT BEGAN

General Lucius D. Clay (1897–1978) of the United States Army, the military governor of U.S.-occupied Germany, has been called the "father of the Berlin airlift." In an interview with his biographer he explains how it began.

Q: What was the War Department's response when you began the airlift?

CLAY: I never asked.

Q: You never asked?

CLAY: No, I never asked permission or approval to begin the airlift. I asked permission to go in on the ground with the combat team, because if we were stopped we'd have to start shooting. This was where the Russians had an advantage in that we would have had to initiate the fighting to get through. But we didn't have to start fighting to get through in the air, so I never asked permission. I should add that by July, after the airlift had begun, I was convinced that if we moved a combat team along the autobahn the Russians would let it through. However, in contradistinction to the air, where I went ahead on my own—the only way the airlift could be stopped was by the Russians' using their fighter planes to bring our planes down. But they would have to commit an act of war. If we moved on the ground and they put obstacles in front of us, we had to open up the attack. And therefore I did not want to be put in the position where we opened the attack without approval. So with the ground movement I asked permission. I did not ask permission for the airlift.

SOURCE: Jean Edward Smith, *Lucius D. Clay: An American Life* (1990)

---

highway and railroad) to Berlin. The western sector of Berlin had 2.4 million inhabitants. With few foodstocks, they faced starvation. The Soviets' blockade was in retaliation to the introduction of a strong currency in the western zones but also to forestall the emergence of a West German state and, if possible, force the United States out of Europe. The United States and its allies responded to the ten-month blockade with a massive airlift of food, fuel, and other basic supplies to the city. With the blockade increasingly counterproductive, the Soviets announced that railroads and roads closed for nearly a year "for repairs" would be reopened to western traffic.

When the blockade started, West Berlin had only food for a month and coal for ten days. The "Berlin Airlift" consisted of over a quarter-million individual flights that supplied the city with 2.3 million tons of food and fuel. The crisis was especially important because of the care taken by the superpowers to prevent war from resulting. Although both made coercive moves, neither crossed the line between COERCION and violence. This was important to the development of CRISIS MANAGEMENT as a key element in keeping the Cold War from becoming a hot war.

Berlin crises The series of COLD WAR confrontations over the status of Berlin, Germany. West Berlin was an island of western influence within a Soviet region. The BERLIN BLOCKADE (1948–1949) increased U.S. involvement in the defense of Western Europe. The Soviets under NIKITA S. KHRUSHCHEV again made the "Berlin question" the focus of East-West tension in 1958. The growing military strength of West Germany in the NORTH ATLANTIC TREATY ORGANIZATION and the presence of U.S. ground forces with nuclear weapons alarmed Moscow. Khrushchev demanded that all Western forces be withdrawn from Berlin, or he would transfer control of the city to East Germany. He also warned Western European nations that their NATO military partnership with the United States would mean their destruction in a nuclear war. West German Chancellor Konrad Adenauer backed the tough line of U.S. Secretary of State John Foster Dulles toward Moscow. Former U.S. Secretary of State Dean Acheson explained what was at stake in this crisis: "If Khrushchev could split the western alliance over Berlin and force the Allies ignominiously to withdraw, abandoning the 2,500,000 citizens of West Berlin whom we had sworn to defend, Germany and all Europe would know that Khrushchev was master of Europe. And we Americans would have shown that we, too, knew that Khrushchev was master" (*Saturday Evening Post*, March 7, 1959). So the West unanimously rejected the Kremlin ultimatum. It reaffirmed its access rights to Berlin and rejected any transfer of authority over Berlin to East Germany. The Soviets backed down from their demands in march 1959. Later the BERLIN WALL had

the effect of stabilizing the situation in Berlin, especially by reducing the outflow of East German refugees.

Berlin document The final document (official title: "For Peace, Security, Co-operation and Social Progress in Europe") of the conference of European Communist parties held in East Berlin in 1976. This conference was attended by 29 delegations, representing all the European Communist parties except those of Albania and Iceland. The Berlin document was not signed, or endorsed by vote, but merely issued. It put emphasis "on the equality and independence of all communist parties and their right to decide their own policies without external interference." *See also* EUROCOMMUNISM.

Berlin Wall The concrete-and-barbed wire wall built by East Germany in 1961 to divide East and West Berlin. It was designed to prevent the flight of East Germans to the West. Just prior to the construction of the wall, the exodus had reached 2,000 per day. The United States accepted the wall because it recognized that the steady emigration was undermining the East German state and that this in turn could challenge the Soviet position in Eastern Europe. In other words, vital interests were at stake for the Soviet Union in a way that they were not for the United States. In fact, historian Michael R. Beschloss has argued in *The Crisis Years* (1991) that U.S. President John F. Kennedy encouraged the Soviets to erect the wall, at least tacitly, by not taking advantage of the advance opportunities they presented for him to warn against it. At the same time, Kennedy did reaffirm the U.S. commitment to protect West Berlin and responded vigorously to Soviet probes challenging Western rights in the city. Indeed, the wall became the occasion for one of the most dramatic speeches ever given by a U.S. president. To bolster the morale of the West Berliners, Kennedy visited the city on June 26, 1963, and before a crowd of cheering thousands said: "All free men, wherever they may live, are citizens of Berlin. And therefore, as a free man, I take pride in the words, 'Ich bin ein Berliner!' " This literally translates to "I am a doughnut," but everyone knew what he meant.

The wall became the symbol of the division of Eastern and Western Europe. It was a sign of

Berliners celebrate on top of the Berlin Wall on November 10, 1989, with the Brandenburg Gate in the background. (U.S. Naval Institute)

improving relations between the two Germanys when in 1987 East Germany told its guards along the wall *not* to shoot their own citizens attempting to escape to the West. Finally, when the collapse of communism in Eastern and Central Europe, especially in East Germany, allowed the wall to be dismantled in October of 1989, commentator George F. Will wrote that in 1989 "Voyager 2 discovered 1,500-mph winds on Neptune, but even more impressive winds blew down the Berlin wall" (*Newsweek*, January 1, 1990). *See also* GERMAN REUNIFICATION.

Bernadotte, Folke (1895–1948)   The Swedish count and United Nations mediator for Palestine who was assassinated on September 17, 1948, in Jerusalem by the STERN GANG (formally known as Lehi). Bernadotte was targeted by the militant Zionist organization for trying to consider the interests of all parties in Palestine. The newly emergent state of Israel failed to identify the count's assassins formally, though evidence was available to do so, in an effort not to provoke a confrontation with Lehi.

Berne International Copyright Convention   The 1886 agreement that holds that copyrighted works published in any signatory country automatically have copyright protection in the territories of all other signatories to the convention, which form the Berne Union. While it has been revised every few decades in other cities, the agreement, as amended, is still known as the Berne Convention. *See also* WORLD INTELLECTUAL PROPERTY ORGANIZATION.

Berne Treaty of 1874   The treaty that established the General Postal Union (now the UNIVERSAL POSTAL UNION) to integrate international mail services.

Bernhardi, Friedrich von (1849–1930)   The German general who advocated German military expansion in his book *Germany and the Next War* (1911). This caused some controversy elsewhere in Europe because he asserted that "war is a biological necessity." In many respects it was typical of the tradition of militarism that had developed in Germany that, combined with pan-German thinking, encouraged the assertive foreign policy of Kaiser

William's government before World War I. Although pacifism also was strong in Germany, it was unable to compete with the nationalist and militarist sentiments expressed by officers and publicists such as Bernhardi. *See also* MILITARISM; NATIONALISM.

Berri, Nabih (1939–   )   The secular leader of AMAL, one of the two primary SHI'ITE militias in Lebanon. His mediation efforts during the June 1985 TWA FLIGHT 847 hijacking established him as a major power broker in Lebanon.

Berrill Report   A 1977 review of British diplomatic representations that was occasioned by 1975 newspaper exposés of high living and extravagance in British embassies abroad. The report proposed a merger of the diplomatic service with the BRITISH COUNCIL and a severe reduction in the scale of overseas representation. Overall it offered a very unflattering portrait of current British diplomacy. Then it further outraged the diplomats when, after suggesting that economic work was the real heart of modern British diplomatic efforts, it recommended a "merger of the Home Civil Service and the Diplomatic Service and the creation within the combined Service of a Foreign Service Group (FSG) which would staff most of the jobs in the U.K. and overseas" dealing with international issues. Nothing much came of the report's recommendations. (For the full report, *see* Central Policy Review Staff, *Review of Overseas Representation* [London: HMSO, 1977].)

best and the brightest   Particularly in the United States, a description of the intellectual and managerial talent each new presidential administration claims it will bring to Washington to solve the nation's problems. The phrase is now used almost cynically since David Halberstam in his book *The Best and the Brightest* (1972) showed how all that talent still managed to lead the nation into the morass of Vietnam in the 1960s.

Bethmann-Hollweg, Theobald von (1856–1921)   The chancellor of Germany from 1909 to 1917. It was his international strategies that eventually helped start World War I. He told the Reichstag (German legislature) on August 4, 1914: "Our

invasion of Belgium is contrary to international law but the wrong—I speak openly—that we are committing we will make good as soon as our military goal is reached." Then he feigned surprise that Great Britain entered the war because of this action: "Just for a word—'neutrality,' a word which in wartime has so often been disregarded—just for a scrap of paper, Great Britain is going to make war on a kindred nation which desires nothing better than to be friends with her" (*New York Times,* August 19, 1914). He did delay unrestricted submarine warfare for more than two years, rightly fearing that it would help bring the United States into the war. In 1917 he was deposed by the German military.

BEU   *See* BENELUX.

Bevan, Aneurin (1897–1960)   The Welsh labor leader and member of the British Parliament (1929–1960) who, as minister of health in the postwar Labour government, established the National Health Service. He resigned from the cabinet in response to defense budget increases in 1951 and was subsequently a critic of his own party's proposals on unilateral disarmament. He told an October 2, 1957, Labour Party Conference on unilateral nuclear disarmament: "If you carry this resolution and follow out all its implications and do not run away from it, you will send a Foreign Secretary, whoever he may be, naked into the conference chamber."

Beveridge Plan   The 1942 report, *Social Insurance and Allied Services,* prepared under the direction of British economist William Beveridge (1879–1963), that proposed the "cradle-to-grave" social programs adopted by Great Britain shortly after World War II.

Bevin, Ernest (1881–1951)   The British Labour politician who was FOREIGN SECRETARY (1945–1951) in the postwar government of CLEMENT ATTLEE. He was known for his support of the MARSHALL PLAN and the NORTH ATLANTIC TREATY ORGANIZATION and for his opposition to the creation of the state of Israel. Bevin was a key figure in the process whereby the United States agreed to an "entangling alliance" with Western Europe through the

North Atlantic Treaty. His efforts toward this end were systematic and were sustained by an intense anticommunism and a realism about the role of power in international politics that was not always shared by members of the Labour Party. He is widely regarded, however, as the greatest British foreign secretary of the twentieth century.

Bhindranwale, Sant Jarnail Singh (1947–1984)   The militant Sikh religious and political leader who organized and inspired a wave of Sikh violence and terrorism in India in the early 1980s. Bhindranwale used the GOLDEN TEMPLE OF AMRITSAR as his base of terrorist operations, which led the Indian government to mount a massive assault on the Sikh shrine in June 1984. He and hundreds of his followers were killed during the assault, which had far-reaching implications for the government of INDIRA GANDHI. Bhindranwale's death at the Golden Temple made him a martyr in the eyes of many Sikhs.

Bhopal disaster   The 1984 leak of poison gas from the Union Carbide pesticide plant in Bhopal, India, which killed over 3,500 and additionally injured an estimated 200,000 people. In 1989 the company settled claims against it for $470 million. In 1991 the Indian Supreme Court approved this amount but said that company officials could still face criminal charges. The disaster brought attention to the disparity between industrial safety in the West and in the THIRD WORLD.

Bhutan-India Treaty   The 1949 agreement between Bhutan and India wherein Bhutan agreed to "be guided by the advice" of India in foreign affairs matters, while retaining control of its own internal affairs. The Bhutanese do not interpret the treaty as obligating them to act in strict accordance with India's advice. In 1971 Bhutan opened an office in New Delhi to handle diplomatic matters with other countries. In the same year, with Indian sponsorship, Bhutan became a member of the United Nations.

Bhutto, Benazir (1953–   )   Prime minister of Pakistan from 1988 to 1990. Harvard and Oxford educated, she is the daughter of Zulfikar Ali Bhutto. In 1990 she was deposed amid charges of corruption by her party and relatives—and a government

more acceptable to the military was installed. She remains a leader of the Pakistan People's Army.

Bhutto, Zulfikar Ali (1928–1979)   The Pakistani politician who became president of his country in the turmoil that followed the BANGLADESH WAR OF INDEPENDENCE. While his party won elections in 1977 the army, unhappy with a new constitution and failing economic programs, seized power in a coup, arrested Bhutto, and executed him in 1979. *See also* ZIA UL-HAQ, MOHAMMED.

Biafra   The 75,000-square-mile region of southeastern Nigeria that seceded from the national government and proclaimed its independence in 1967. After a civil war that ended in 1970, the outnumbered Biafran forces of the largely Christian Ibo ethnic group formally signed an act of surrender to the central government. Hundreds of thousands and perhaps millions died of starvation in Biafra during the civil war, which is known by the victors as the War for Nigerian Unity.

bias   **1.** One of two measurements of a missile's accuracy (the other being CIRCULAR ERROR PROBABLE [CEP]). Bias refers to the probable average distance a warhead will be from its actual aiming point, or designated ground zero, when it detonates. Clearly the degree of bias in a missile's flight path is crucial if the object is to destroy a hard target, but it is much more difficult to measure than CEP. **2.** Something that can distort the effect of a sample or undermine the integrity of research.

big brother   **1.** An artificial form of familial protection created to offer a substitute for a missing father figure. **2.** The symbol used by George Orwell (1903–1950) in his novel *1984* (1949) of a government so big and intrusive that it literally oversees and regulates every aspect of life. Orwell wrote: "On each landing, opposite the lift shaft, the poster with the enormous face gazed from the wall. It was one of those pictures which are so contrived that the eyes follow you about when you move. BIG BROTHER IS WATCHING YOU, the caption beneath it ran." The term has evolved to mean any potentially menacing power constantly looking over one's shoulder in judgment. *Compare to* ANIMAL FARM. **3.** During the COLD WAR this became a description of the hegemonic relationship that the Soviet Union had with the other European Communist governments.

Big Five **1.** The permanent members of the United Nations SECURITY COUNCIL: the United States, Russia (formerly the Soviet Union), the United Kingdom, China, and France. **2.** The victorious powers at the 1919 PARIS PEACE CONFERENCE: France, the United States, Great Britain, Italy, and Japan.

Big Four **1.** The states that occupied Germany after World War II: the United States, the United Kingdom, the Soviet Union, and France. **2.** The major states combatting fascism in World War II: the United States, Great Britain, the Soviet Union, and China. **3.** The major states at the Paris Peace Conference of 1919: the United States, France, Great Britain, and Italy. Their individual representatives—Woodrow Wilson, Georges Clemenceau, David Lloyd George, and Vittorio Orlando, respectively—were formally designated the Council of Four.

big lie **1.** An untruth so great or audacious that it is bound to have an effect on public opinion; a common tactic of PROPAGANDA. Both ADOLF HITLER

The Big Four at the Paris Peace Conference. From left to right: Lloyd George, Orlando, Clemenceau, and Wilson. (National Archives)

in Germany and Senator Joseph R. McCarthy (1908–1957) in the United States were skillful users of this dishonorable but long-practiced political tactic. As Hitler wrote in *Mein Kampf* (1927), "The great masses of the people will more easily fall victim to a great lie than to a small one." But in this he was echoing NICCOLÒ MACHIAVELLI, who wrote in *The Prince* (1532): "It is necessary that the prince should know how to color his nature well, and how to be a great hypocrite and dissembler. For men are so simple, and yield so much to immediate necessity, that the deceiver will never lack dupes." **2.** Greek philosopher Plato's (427–347 B.C.) concept of the royal lie, the noble lie, the golden lie from book 3 of *Republic* (370 B.C.), in which he asserts that the guardians of a society may put forth untruths necessary to maintain social order. Plato wrote: "The rulers of the States are the only ones who should have the privilege of lying, either at home or abroad; they may be allowed to lie for the good of the state." Plato's noble lie was simply a poetic or allegorical way of telling ordinary people difficult truths. It is absolutely incompatible with the big lie of propaganda. **3.** Criticisms from a political opponent. There is much truth in journalist Hunter S. Thompson's observation from *Fear and Loathing on the Campaign Trail* (1973): "Skilled professional liars are as much in demand in politics as they are in the advertising business."

bigot list The names of all those who have legitimate access to a very secret intelligence or military mission. History's most famous bigot (meaning "narrow") list consisted of all those who knew the exact date and place of the World War II D-Day invasion of France on June 6, 1944.

big stick The informal title for U.S. President Theodore Roosevelt's foreign policy; it came from the adage "Speak softly and carry a big stick." The most famous example of his "big stick" policy was the separation of the isthmus of Panama from the state of Colombia to create a new government that would be more cooperative in the U.S. effort to build a canal. When Roosevelt met with his cabinet to report on this event, he asked Attorney General Philander C. Knox (1853–1921) to construct a defense. The attorney general is reported to have remarked, "Oh, Mr. President, do not let so great

An atomic bomb test on Bikini, July 25, 1946. (National Archives)

an achievement suffer from any taint of legality." Later, when Roosevelt sought to defend his heavily criticized actions to the cabinet, he made a lengthy statement and then asked, "Have I defended myself?" Secretary of War Elihu Root (1845–1937) replied, "You certainly have. You have shown that you were accused of seduction, and you have conclusively proved that you were guilty of rape" (David McCullough, *The Path Between the Seas: The Creation of the Panama Canal: 1870–1914*, 1977). The term *big stick* still refers to a U.S. foreign policy backed by a threat of force. It is even today part of the everyday rhetoric of American politics. U.S. President Gerald Ford in a campaign speech of October 16, 1976, said: "Teddy Roosevelt . . . once said 'Speak softly and carry a big stick.' [My opponent] Jimmy Carter wants to speak loudly and carry a fly swatter." Former U.S. Secretary of State Alexander M. Haig, Jr., was quoted in *USA Today* (December 2, 1986) saying "We've tended to forget Teddy Roosevelt's advice. 'Speak softly and carry a big stick.' We've tended to speak too threateningly while we carried a feather."

Big Three   The World War II Allied leaders: Winston Churchill, Joseph Stalin, and Franklin D. Roosevelt; or the states they represented: Great Britain, the Soviet Union, and the United States. This term is also applied to the leaders of the victors in World War I, namely Woodrow Wilson of the United States, David Lloyd George of Great Britain, and Georges Clemenceau of France.

Bikini   **1.** An atoll in the Pacific Ocean. It was taken from the Japanese by U.S. forces during World War II and became the site of numerous U.S. atomic tests in the late 1940s and 1950s. The original population was forced to move to other islands prior to the tests and allowed to return in 1970, when the islands were considered safe. But 1978 studies showed that they were not safe from radioactivity after all and a new evacuation commenced. In 1985 the United States agreed to replace radioactive topsoil and make Bikini fit for human habitation.   **2.** The skimpy women's swimsuit that was named after the location of the atomic tests since it was so "explosive."

Biko, Stephen (1946–1977) South African black opposition leader and head of the Black Consciousness Movement, killed in September 1977 after prolonged interrogations and beatings by the South African security police. Biko emerged as a martyr of the South African antiapartheid movement, and his widely publicized death became a symbol of the international antiapartheid movement. A major motion picture, *Cry Freedom,* based on journalist Donald Woods' book *Biko* (1979), received wide attention in the West.

bilateral "Two party" or "two country," as in the 1951 U.S.-Japanese Security Treaty that provided for the U.S. defense of a disarmed Japan or the U.S.-Canada Free Trade Agreement of 1988 that seeks to eliminate tariffs between the two states by 1998.

bilateral infrastructure Permanent facilities or installations that concern only two NORTH ATLANTIC TREATY ORGANIZATION members and are financed by mutual agreement between them (e.g., facilities required for the use of forces of one NATO member in the territory of another). *See also* INFRASTRUCTURE.

bilateralism 1. Joint economic policies between two nations; specifically, the agreement to extend to each other privileges (usually relating to trade) that are not available to others. *Compare to* MOST FAVORED NATION. 2. Joint security policies between two nations; specifically, treaties of alliance in the event of war. Bilateralism in defense typically involves a pledge between two states to support each other militarily in the event of an attack from a third state. But in practice most bilateral agreements are guarantees by major powers to protect weaker states from possible aggression. Thus, if the territorial integrity of the weaker state is threatened, intervention of the stronger friend is supposedly assured. A famous example of this is the decision by Great Britain and France to declare war against Germany in 1939 in fulfillment of bilateral guarantees that each had given to Poland. 3. Joint diplomatic postures or actions by nations, whether or not in the form of a formal alliance. This is in contrast to UNILATERALISM, in which each state goes its own way without necessarily regarding the interests of the others.

Bilderberg Conferences Meetings of prominent business and political leaders of Western Europe and North America that are held annually by invitation and in great secrecy to discuss issues of mutual concern. The conferences are named for the Bilderberg Hotel in Oosterbeck, the Netherlands, at which the first conference was held in May 1954. Recurring issues at the conferences have been communism, European integration, and the developing countries.

billiard ball model A representation of international relations that focuses on their position in the international game and ignores the internal dynamics and influences that impinge on foreign policy behavior. This model is generally equated with a state-centric model of international relations, with the billiard balls representing the states. The behavior or movement of each ball is determined by the position and movement of the other balls on the table. Each ball is a self-contained unit. Linkages and economic interdependencies among states are excluded from this model of international politics. ARNOLD WOLFERS used the term *billiard ball model* in his *Discord and Collaboration* (1962) as something of a straw man. He suggested that in this model, "by definition, the stage is preempted by a set of states each in full control of all territory, men and resources within its boundaries. Every state represents a closed impermeable and sovereign unit, completely separated from all other states." He then went on to explain why this is an inaccurate picture of international relations.

bimultipolarity Several states loosely allied with a SUPERPOWER that acts to militarily constrain them. The superpower, in turn, disciplines its weaker allies so that they live in peace with their peer states. Thus the Soviet Union, for example, maintained the peace in Eastern Europe during the COLD WAR.

binary weapon A shell or bomb containing two substances that remain inert while kept separate but that mix in flight to form a new substance that is harmful in some way. Normally these are chemical weapons. The design is safer to store and transport than in systems in which the poisonous chemicals are already combined. *See also* CHEMICAL WARFARE.

binding   **1.** A term used to describe an agreement that involves a definite commitment.   **2.** A provision in a trade agreement that no tariff rate higher than the rate specified in the agreement will be imposed during the life of the agreement without payment or compensation. *Compare to* BOUND RATES.

biological warfare   Attacking an enemy with infectious disease-causing agents. The essence of biological warfare is simple. It involves developing a naturally occuring infectious agent so that its lethality is enormously increased. This would make it possible to infect large populations or large territorial areas with very small samples. Thus a war would be fought by deliberately infecting the enemy army's food and water supplies, or its civilian population, with deadly diseases. The ideal biological agent is one with a very fast infection and death rate but that also becomes inert very rapidly, allowing one's own troops to pass through or occupy the no-longer defended areas. Although such weapons have been developed by a number of states, including Iraq, they have not been used partly because they are difficult to control and use with discrimination. Great Britain's research effort in this area often has been justified in terms of the need to develop antidotes.

biopolitics   The use of ecological models and data in political analysis. Biopolitical analysts suggest that biological and environmental conditions have a significant impact on economic and political development.

bipartisan   **1.** Used to refer to a policy or initiative that has the support of both major political parties in a two-party–dominated state. Countries with governments based on a parliamentary majority do not need to develop bipartisan consensus in the same way as does the United States, where the party of the president does not necessarily control the Congress.   **2.** Sometimes used as a synonym for a lack of partisanship as, for example, when a bipartisan or nonpartisan commission is formed to deal with a particularly intractable problem.

bipartisanship   **1.** Cooperation by usually differing political parties and institutions on political issues.

Bipartisanship occurs when the leaders of interested political parties wish to assure that a given topic will not become the subject of partisan disputes. **2.** Consultation and cooperation between the U.S. president and the leaders of both parties in the U.S. Congress on major foreign policy issues. The high point of this occurred after World War II when the Republicans under the leadership of U.S. Senator ARTHUR H. VANDENBERG of Michigan supported the Truman Administration's efforts to rebuild Europe and contain Soviet expansionism. This bipartisan attitude—that politics ends "at the water's edge"—continued until the American foreign policy consensus broke down over the Vietnam War during the Johnson administration. According to U.S. Representative Lee H. Hamilton of Indiana: "As long as I've been in the Congress, the President, every President, calls for bipartisanship in foreign policy. But bipartisanship requires Congress' informed consent. It cannot merely be a call to support the President's policy" (*Los Angeles Times,* May 15, 1987). U.S. Secretary of State James A. Baker III sought to define bipartisanship during his confirmation hearings before the Senate Foreign Relations Committee on January 17, 1989: "Bipartisan is also a great deal more than Dean Acheson's holy waters sprinkled on political necessity. It's the lubricant that enables the branches of government to overcome their natural constitutionally designed friction, a

---

SENATOR VANDENBERG DEFINES BIPARTISANSHIP

To me "bipartisanship foreign policy" means a mutual effort, under our indispensable two-Party system, to unite our official voice at the water's edge so that America speaks with maximum authority against those who would divide and conquer us and the free world. It does not involve the remotest surrender of free debate in determining our position. On the contrary, frank cooperation and free debate are indispensable to ultimate unity. In a word, it simply seeks national security ahead of partisan advantage. Every foreign policy must be totally debated (and I think the record proves it has been) and the "loyal opposition" is under special obligation to see that this occurs.

SOURCE: Senator Arthur H. Vandenberg, *The Private Papers of Senator Vandenberg,* ed. Arthur H. Vandenberg, Jr., (1952).

---

friction that arises from our differing perspectives and our different responsibilities." Other nations generally regard bipartisanship as something particularly desirable in the United States because it contributes to consistency and continuity in foreign policy.

bipolar crisis A straightforward confrontation between the two major international actors. The Cuban Missile Crisis, for example, was essentially a bipolar crisis. This kind of crisis is less complicated than a multipolar crisis or a BIPOLYCENTRIC CRISIS.

bipolarity A structure of power in the international system in which only two powers really matter. The COLD WAR international system was characterized by bipolarity but was not unprecedented. Athens and Sparta and later Rome and Carthage are examples of bipolar situations in the ancient world. In most cases of bipolarity the two great powers are adversaries, as each one fears the other, and the SECURITY DILEMMA is particularly intense. Conversely, the decline of bipolarity and the end of the Cold War were inextricably related. Bipolarity does *not* mean the division of the international system into two rival alliance systems as with the North Atlantic Treaty Organization and the Warsaw Pact. The bloc system during the Cold War was a result of bipolarity, not a cause of it. *Compare to* MULTIPOLARITY; UNIPOLARITY.

bipolycentric crisis An unstable situation such as that of the October 1973 YOM KIPPUR WAR in the Middle East, in which major powers—in this case, the United States and the Soviet Union—are involved but are tied to local actors involved in hostilities and preoccupied with their own immediate interests rather than the impact on global stability. As analysts Christopher Shoemaker and John Spanier note in *Patron-Client State Relationships* (1984), in these bipolycentric crises, "The relationships involved are both greater in number and more complex: local state to local state, local state (or client) to each superpower (or patron), and patron to patron. In terms of this greater number of relationships than in a BIPOLAR CRISIS, it should be obvious that the number of opportunities for misperceptions, miscalculations, and miscommunications rise correspondingly." Thus "a

bipolycentric crisis is clearly more dangerous than a bipolar one."

bipolycentrism Term used by analysts Christopher Shoemaker and John Spanier in *Patron-Client State Relationships* (1984) that refers to the fact of BIPOLARITY combined with an emerging POLYCENTRIC world in which a large number of states are capable of going to war with their neighbors.

Birch, John (1918–1945) A U.S. Army officer who was killed by Chinese Communist troops while on an Office of Strategic Services mission in northern China. His name was later adopted by a far right U.S. political organization that claimed him as the first casualty in the war between the THIRD WORLD Communists and the free world.

Bismarck, Otto von (1815–1898) Known as the Iron Chancellor, Bismarck was the man responsible for the unification of Germany through the REALPOLITIK of "blood and iron." As he said in a September 30, 1862, speech in Berlin: "The great questions of the day will be decided not by speeches and majority votes, that was the mistake of 1848 and 1849, but by iron and blood" (quoted in Edward Crankshaw, *Bismarck*, 1981). He became chancellor of Prussia in 1862 and embarked on a course that produced German unification. In 1867 the North German Federation of more than three dozen states was organized with Bismarck as its chancellor. In 1870 efforts to remove impediments to German unification led to the Franco-Prussian war, which Prussia won because of French disorganization under Napoleon III and the superior organization of the German GENERAL STAFF system. This victory, which ended French domination in Europe, allowed the North German Federation to annex the formerly French region of Alsace-Lorraine (a move that became a source of resentment in France and bred the desire for revenge that encouraged the French to go to war in 1914) and the states of South Germany. Modern Germany was formally created under Prussian dominance January 18, 1871, at Versailles, France, when Bismarck arranged for the ruling princes of the federation member states to make Kaiser William I (1797–1888) the emperor of Germany. Bismarck later focused on consolidating German gains through the isolation of France, a reinsurance treaty with Russia, and the manipulation of the BALANCE OF POWER in ways that ensured that Germany was always in the superior coalition. In effect, he reaffirmed a cardinal rule for Germany: to avoid having enemies on two fronts at the same time. By the time he left office in 1890, Bismarck had strengthened the aggressive and militarist forces that continued to haunt Germany and Europe into the twentieth century. Winston Churchill's book *The World Crisis* (1928) quotes a prophetic Bismarck: "If there is ever another war in Europe, it will come out of some damned silly thing in the Balkans." (It did!)

Bitberg   The site of a military cemetery in Germany containing the graves of World War II–era German soldiers. It was the cause of an international controversy in 1985 when U.S. President Ronald Reagan announced he would place a wreath on the graves there as an act of reconciliation. Since many of the graves were those of SS soldiers who ran CONCENTRATION CAMPS and shot U.S. prisoners during the Battle of the Bulge, Reagan was severely criticized for honoring the memory of men who had not acted honorably in war.

Bizonia   The jointly administered United States and British occupation zones in post–World War II Germany from 1946 to 1948.

black   **1.** A popular metaphor meaning "bad"; for example, Black Friday was the day the stock market crashed in 1929, a BLACKLIST is one no one wants to be on, and BLACK MONEY is illegal income.   **2.** In intelligence operations, a term used in certain phrases (e.g., "living black," "black border crossing") to indicate reliance on illegal *concealment* (hiding or keeping out of sight) rather than on *cover* (phony identification). Sometimes an entire intelligence operation, from inception to conclusion, is "black."   **3.** Secret; for example, a black market is a hidden (from tax collectors) underground economy.   **4.** A reference to someone of African ancestry.

black and tans   The nickname, derived from a breed of Irish dog, of the British troops sent to repress rebellion in Ireland after World War I; so called because their khaki uniforms were worn with a distinctive dark green, almost black, cap. They were especially despised by the Irish because of their brutality.

black bag job   **1.** In the United States, a term used by the Federal Bureau of Investigation for illegal missions to gather intelligence or to plant communications intercept devices.   **2.** The bribing of someone to obtain information.   **3.** A U.S. Central Intelligence Agency term for a nonmilitary covert operation. *Compare to* BAGMAN.

black box approach   A means of analyzing international politics that ignores the personalities of the various political actors within a state and focuses solely on the state itself and its formal interactions with other states. It is very similar to the BILLIARD BALL MODEL. *See also* RICHARD SNYDER.

Black Brigades   A group of radical SHI'ITE extremists active in Kuwait and Iraq.

black budget   The classified (secret) portion of the U.S. budget that hides sensitive programs involving high-technology military and covert operations. According to Tim Weiner's *Blank Check* (1990): "The black budget is a challenge to the open government promised by the Constitution. Today close to a quarter of every dollar in the Pentagon's budget for new weapons is cloaked in blackness. . . . Every dollar spent in secret defies the Framers' intent that the balance sheet of government should be a public document."

Black Hand   The Serbian nationalist group that wanted to liberate all Serbs and include them in the kingdom of Serbia. The group used terrorism and propaganda and inspired such fear in the Hapsburg Empire that it was anxious to crush Serbia as soon as it had a pretext—as it did with the assassination of the Archduke FRANZ FERDINAND in 1914.

Black June   Terrorist organization founded by ABU NIDAL, named after the month in 1976 in which Syrian troops came to the aid of Lebanese Christians and helped them to win a temporary victory in that country's civil war. Black June stood in violent opposition to the PALESTINE LIBERATION ORGANIZATION's diplomatic and political approaches to the Palestinian problem, and in 1979 it assassinated three European PLO representatives. In 1982 members shot and critically wounded SLOMO ARGOV, the Israeli ambassador to Great Britain. This assassination attempt proved to be the catalyst for the ensuing Israeli invasion of Lebanon.

blacklist   **1.** A grouping of individuals or organizations that are banned, boycotted, or disapproved, usually by a government. Originally, they were lists prepared by merchants containing the names of people who had gone bankrupt. Later, employers used them to punish those who had joined labor unions. Blacklists generally carry no legal authority, though they have been issued by governments in an effort to silence or preclude opposition. While blacklists are not necessarily associated with terrorism, all blacklists are designed to intimidate. Most are clandestine. Artists, writers, and performers are frequently associated with blacklisting and have been the victims of blacklists in political environments as diverse as the United States during the McCarthy era of the 1950s and Argentina during the DIRTY WAR. Blacklisted persons often are unable to pursue their careers; many go into exile. Because of the undemocratic nature of blacklists, people are often added to them for frivolous reasons. This was illustrated in a successful 1962 libel suit against Aware, a U.S. organization that sought out and publicized the names of people in the entertainment industry who were supposedly sympathetic to communism. Entertainer John Henry Faulk was blacklisted in part because he attended a 1946 meeting that was also attended by a known Communist. The meeting was a tribute to the United Nations cosponsored by the American Bar Association. The Communist who attended "with" Faulk and hundreds of others was the Soviet representative to the United Nations.   **2.** A computer data base of criminal suspects wanted by INTERPOL.   **3.** People, agencies, ships, and so on that break a boycott or embargo and are subject to subsequent punishment. **4.** An official COUNTERINTELLIGENCE listing of actual or potential enemy collaborators, sympathizers, intelligence suspects, and other persons whose presence within the nation menaces its security.

black money   **1.** Illegal or secret political campaign contributions, usually in cash.   **2.** Money used to support BLACK OPS.

black ops   Also *black operations*; the most secret (and possibly illegal) covert operations of an intelligence agency or special operations military unit.

Black Order   A right-wing Italian terrorist organization that opposes Italy's parliamentary democracy. It has been implicated in many neofascist terrorist attacks that occurred in Italy during the 1970s, most notoriously the 1980 bombing of the Bologna railway station, in which more than 80 persons died. *See also* NEOFASCISM.

black propaganda   *See* PROPAGANDA.

Black September   **1.** September 1970, when civil war broke out in Jordan between the forces of King Hussein and the PALESTINE LIBERATION ORGANIZATION. The king prevailed and the remaining PLO elements were forced into neighboring Syria and Lebanon.   **2.** A PLO terrorist suborganization, named after the 1970 war between Jordan and the PLO, which was responsible for the murder of nine Israeli athletes at the 1972 Munich Olympics. Among the most violent of Palestinian terrorist groups, it also assassinated Jordanian Prime Minister Wasfi el-Tal in Cairo in 1971 and U.S. Ambassador Cleo Noel and Belgian chargé d'affaires Guy Eid at the Saudi Arabian embassy in Khartoum in 1973. It is often suggested that Black September is a clandestine wing of AL-FATAH and the PLO whose presence allows the mainstream organizations to remain blameless for terrorist acts. Some members of the group have been assimilated into what is now considered the ABU NIDAL Organization.

blackshirts   **1.** The paramilitary organization of the Italian fascists, created in 1921 by BENITO MUSSOLINI. Largely composed of disaffected veterans from World War I, they were used to break up strikes and threaten as well as harm political opponents. When some 50,000 of them traveled from Naples on to Rome in October 1922 in the so-called MARCH ON ROME, King Victor Emmanuel III named Mussolini the head of government, thus beginning the fascist dictatorship.   **2.** The SS of Nazi Germany.   **3.** The uniformed militia of any political (but usually fascist) party used to intimidate opponents. *Compare to* SA.

black terrorism   **1.** Violence of the far right committed to engender fear; fascist TERRORISM. Like terrorism of the left, or *red terrorism,* black terrorism often seeks to undermine existing political systems. Black terrorists often find allies in police, military, and the security forces of repressive regimes. Latin American DEATH SQUADS are examples of this. Liberals, leftists, and religious minorities (especially Jews) are their frequent targets.   **2.** Terrorism committed in the U.S. by African-American militants.

blitz   **1.** A fast, almost lightninglike military attack; short for the German term BLITZKREIG.   **2.** Intense aerial bombardment.   **3.** The German bombing of England during World War II, specifically the bombing during the BATTLE OF BRITAIN. In late August 1940 the German Luftwaffe shifted its attacks from airfields, which was a change in strategic policy, and launched almost nightly air raids against the cities of Coventry, London, and other industrial centers. The British sent many of their children to the countryside or overseas. When it was suggested that the two daughters (Princess Elizabeth and Princess Margaret) of King George VI and Queen Elizabeth be sent to Canada for safety, the queen responded: "The Princesses could never leave without me and I could not leave without the King—and, of course, the King will never leave" (quoted in David Sinclair, *Queen and Country,* 1979). This sharing in the common danger, especially when the royal residence, Buckingham Palace, was bombed, increased the popularity of the British monarchy. As the blitz continued, a system of shelters, largely underground train stations and cellars, saved many lives during attacks. Abnormal amounts of fog and rain from mid-August to late September prevented the Luftwaffe from operating with maximum effectiveness; even more so did the Royal Air Force and radar warnings. Overall an estimated 30,000 civilians died in the blitz. By October 12 Hitler's Operation Sea Lion, the invasion of England, was postponed. The bombing had not brought the British to beg for surrender.

blitzkreig   German for "lightning war," the tactical method used by the German Army in the invasion of Poland, France, and the Soviet Union during World War II. The classic blitzkreig campaign involves swift strikes with tanks and planes and a series of

St. Paul's Cathedral in London during air raid of December 29, 1940. (National Archives)

MURROW COVERS THE BLITZ

I'm standing on a rooftop looking out over London. At the moment everything is quiet. For reasons of national as well as personal security, I'm unable to tell you the exact location from which I'm speaking. Off to my left, far away in the distance, I can see just that faint red angry snap of antiaircraft bursts against the steel-blue sky. But the guns are so far away that it's impossible to hear them from this location.

About five minutes ago the guns in the immediate vicinity were working. I can look across just at a building not far away and see something that looks like a flash of white paint down the side, and I know from daylight observation that about a quarter of that building has disappeared, hit by a bomb the other night. I think probably in a minute we shall have the sound of guns in the immediate vicinity. The lights are swinging over in this general direction now. You'll hear two explosions. There they are! That was the explosion overhead, not the guns themselves. I should think in a few minutes there may be a bit of shrapnel around here. . . .

SOURCE: Edward R. Murrow, radio broadcast from London during the blitz. Quoted in Alexander Kendrick, *Prime Time* (1969); and Joseph E. Persico, *Edward R. Murrow* (1988).

---

army columns exploiting weak spots in the enemy line. Advance units pass behind the enemy, destroying its lines of communication and disrupting unit cohesion. The emphasis is on preventing the opposition from gathering strength and winning by paralyzing and unexpected attacks that destroy military coordination. Winston Churchill described the German blitzkreig in his 1948 history of World War II, *The Gathering Storm*, thus: "We had seen a perfect specimen of the modern Blitzkreig: the close interaction on the battlefield of army and air force; the violent bombardment of all communications and of any town that seemed an attractive target; the arming of an active FIFTH COLUMN; the free use of spies and parachutists: and above all, the irresistible forward thrust of great masses of armor." Ironically, while the Germans perfected the execution of the blitzkreig (and gave it its name), its creators were British armored warfare theorists JOHN F. C. FULLER, BASIL H. LIDDELL HART, and Gifford Le Quesne Martel (1889–1958). As the Nazi tank commander General Heinz Guderian (1888–1974) wrote in his memoir, *Panzer Leader* (1952): "It was principally the books and articles of the Englishmen, Fuller, Liddell Hart and Martel, that excited my interest and gave me food for thought. These far-sighted soldiers were even then trying to make of the tank something more than just an infantry support weapon."

bloc   **1.** Any group or coalition of groups organized to further an interest. For example, in the United States are interest groups such as a farm bloc, a civil rights bloc, and so on.   **2.** An ad hoc coalition of legislators that transcends party lines to further or obstruct a legislative proposal.   **3.** A combination of states that supports or opposes a given issue or interest. By their very nature all alliances are blocs. But the word also is used to describe voting coalitions in international organizations such as the United Nations and as a shorthand way of referring to segments of the world, such as the African bloc or the THIRD WORLD bloc.

blockade   A military action in which one state attempts, by force, to prevent another from importing by land or sea either some or all goods. Traditionally a blockade involves the exercise of sea power, wherein one navy patrols another nation's coastline, stopping ships from entering and preventing the enemy's merchant and naval vessels from leaving harbor. It can be directed against the resupply of enemy forces in the field, can be limited to the supply of specific goods to a state, or can be used to deprive the enemy population of food, raw materials, and munitions in order to force a surrender.

Because a blockade has historically been considered an ACT OF WAR, softer words are often substituted. For example, during the 1962 CUBAN MISSILE CRISIS the United States used a "quarantine" to prevent some Soviet missiles from getting to Cuba by sea; and in 1990 the United States "interdicted" ships going to Iraq. In each instance the softer word was used to indicate that the United States did not seek further military action—at that time. In peacetime a blockade can be used by one state against another to pursue a legal dispute. Such action is typically restricted to preventing the blockaded nation's vessels, but not others, from having access to designated ports. During formal wars, international law allows for the confiscation of the cargo of belligerent as well as neutral vessels attempting to run the blockade. For such action to be legal under international law, the blockading power must provide adequate warning time so that neutral states can allow their ships to pass out of harm's way.

Bloody Friday   July 21, 1972, when 11 civilians were killed in a spate of PROVISIONAL IRISH REPUBLICAN ARMY bombings in Belfast, Northern Ireland.

Bloody Sunday   **1.** January 9, 1905, when troops of the czarist government of Russia opened fire on a crowd of unarmed marchers in St. Petersburg who wanted to petition the Czar Nicholas II to end the war with Japan and grant civil rights and an eight-hour workday. Over 100 men, women, and children were killed and hundreds more wounded. More than any other single event, Bloody Sunday united the Russian people against the autocratic rule of the czar, who previously had largely been viewed as a kindly father figure. It led to the RUSSIAN REVOLUTION OF 1905.   **2.** January 30, 1972, when 13 Catholic demonstrators were shot and killed by a British Army unit in Londonderry, NORTHERN IRELAND. The incident led to violent IRISH REPUBLICAN ARMY reprisals, including an arson attack on the British embassy in Dublin and the shooting of 13 British soldiers. Bloody Sunday and its aftermath contributed to the imposition of direct rule over Northern Ireland by the British government.

blue berets or blue helmets   Any of the various United Nations PEACEKEEPING FORCES who wear pale-blue headgear with their national uniforms.

blue water navy   A naval force with the ability to patrol and fight effectively anywhere in the world. An oceangoing navy of this kind is often contrasted with COAST GUARDS, which many countries maintain rather than investing in long-range naval capabilities.

Blum, Léon (1872–1950)   The first socialist (and first Jewish) premier of France for the POPULAR FRONT from 1936 to 1937 and again in 1938. His government in 1936 produced the Matignon Agreements granting labor a 40-hour workweek, minimum wages, paid vacations, and collective bargaining. After France was overrun by the Germans in 1940 he was arrested; later he was sent to BUCHENWALD concentration camp. He survived the war to become the premier of France's postwar interim government in 1946.

Blunt, Anthony (1907–1983)   The art historian who was a Soviet spy while he served with the British intelligence agency MI5 during World War II and after. When he was discovered by the authorities to be a traitor in 1964, he cooperated with British intelligence and was secretly pardoned. But when in 1979 it became public that he was the "fourth man" in the CAMBRIDGE SPY RING, he was forced to give up his public positions and honors (including a knighthood). Only his reputation as an art historian remained unsullied.

BMD   *See* BALLISTIC MISSILE DEFENSE.

boat people   **1.** The more than 1 million REFUGEES who have fled Indochina since Communist governments came to power there in 1975; they usually used small boats to escape. The refugees, from Vietnam, Laos, and Kampuchea (Cambodia), include many Chinese families. Many boat people have been given refuge by hospitable countries, but the numbers grew so great in some places, such as Hong Kong, that in 1991 some boat people were forcibly repatriated, amid great controversy. **2.** Refugees from Haiti and Cuba who leave their homelands by boat and seek to land in the United States.

body count   **1.** The number of dead after a battle. This has been one measure of victory since ancient times. Such counts are often exaggerated. According to French diplomat and historian Philippe de

Commynes (1447–1511) in his *Memoires* (1524): "I have been in several actions, where for one man that was really slain, they reported a hundred, thinking by such an account to please their masters." **2.** The quantitative manner in which U.S. forces measured their success during the VIETNAM WAR: in terms of enemy dead. As soldiers naturally want to please their superiors, these counts became greatly exaggerated. Thus the progress of the war was grossly distorted and misled both military planners and the public. According to writer David H. Hackworth's *About Face* (1989): "Sometimes a body count was completely made up to mask a screwed-up mission. In just one instance, a battalion commander asked one of his company COs over the radio to tell him his college football jersey number to have something to report for a botched operation ('Eighty-six,' said the company commander; 'Eighty-six!' exclaimed the battalion commander. 'Great body count!')." Because body count mathematics were so discredited by the Vietnam War, the U.S. military made it a policy never to estimate the number of enemy dead during the PERSIAN GULF WAR.

MISLEADING INDICATORS

The only measure of the war the Americans were interested in was quantitative; and quantitatively, given the immense American fire power, helicopters, fighter-bombers and artillery pieces, it went very well. That the body count might be a misleading indicator did not penetrate the command; large stacks of dead Vietcong were taken as signs of success. That the French statistics had also been very good right up until 1954, when they gave up, made no impression.

SOURCE: David Halberstam, *The Best and the Brightest* (1972).

Boer War   The 1899–1902 armed conflict between the Dutch settlers of South Africa (the Boers) and the British, also known as the South African War. The independent Boer republics of Transvaal (later, the South African Republic) and the Orange Free State were created in 1852 and 1854. The diamond strike at Kimberley in 1870 and, 16 years later, the discovery of extensive gold deposits in the Witwatersrand region of the Transvaal resulted in an influx of European (mainly British) investment and immigrants. The Boer reaction to this flood and to British political intrigues against the two republics led to war in 1899. With the shrinking of the planet through the railroad and steamship, Great Britain had more massive and more mobile forces. Displaying an unprecedented projection of military power abroad, Britain sent 250,000 soldiers to southern Africa to defeat the army of the Boer republics. After a bitter guerrilla war, the Boer republics surrendered and became part of the British Empire; the two former republics and the two British colonies of the Cape and Natal were joined on May 31, 1910, to form the Union of South Africa, a dominion of the British Empire, with its white population controlling most domestic matters. Under the Statute of Westminster of 1934, the union achieved status as a sovereign state within the British Empire. Conflict between AFRIKANERS and English-speaking groups continued to influence political developments. *See also* VEREENIGING, TREATY OF.

Bokassa, Jean-Bedel (1921–   )   Self-styled emperor of the Central African Republic, whose reign was characterized by excesses of all kinds, including cannibalism and the terroristic repression of his people. Bokassa, a former captain in the French Army, ruled autocratically for more than 13 years before being overthrown by a French-backed coup in 1979. While in exile, he was sentenced to death for his crimes against the nation. He returned home in 1986 and was again sentenced to death, but the sentence was commuted to life in prison.

Boland Amendment   Any of a variety of legislative amendments beginning in 1982 that were attached to defense-related appropriations acts which prohibited U.S. funding of the CONTRAS in Nicaragua beyond levels that were specifically authorized by the U.S. Congress. The amendments, sponsored by Edward Boland, the chairman of the House Intelligence Committee, were designed to prevent the executive branch from covertly supporting contra operations. Much of the controversy over the IRAN-CONTRA AFFAIR was over the question of whether the Boland Amendment was violated when the Reagan Administration used the profits (or "residuals," as officials called them) from arms sales to Iran to fund contra activities.

Bolshevik   1. Member of the Russian revolutionary group that prevailed after the civil war that followed the RUSSIAN REVOLUTION OF 1917 and eventually became, under the leadership of V. I. LENIN, the Communist Party of the Soviet Union. The Bolsheviks neutralized their political opposition with mass arrests and the suppression of rival parties. Through the CHEKA secret police, a wave of "Red terror" was unleashed that did not even begin to abate until after the death of JOSEPH STALIN in 1953.   2. Any Communist.   3. A person with a decidedly leftward political orientation.   4. A nonconformist.

Bolshevism   The advocacy of violent revolution, especially to overthrow democratic or fascist regimes.

bolstering   A term developed by analysts Irving Janis and Leon Mann in *Decision Making: A Psychological Analysis of Conflict, Choice and Commitment* (1977) that is used to identify ways in which policymakers convince themselves that the action they choose will yield a favorable outcome. Bolstering tends to be used when policymakers do not have an ideal solution at hand—yet, for one reason or another, cannot avoid making a decision. Rather than admit that the benefits from this decision are likely to be limited and the costs rather higher than they would like, policymakers engage in bolstering by emphasizing the positive and downplaying the negative. Part of a broader process known as DEFENSIVE AVOIDANCE, bolstering is a way of coping with stress. The belief of British Prime Minister Anthony Eden during the Suez Crisis of 1956 that the United States would not oppose military intervention by Great Britain and France provides a good example of bolstering.

bomb in the basement   Term used to describe those states that are generally believed to possess nuclear weapons but have not publicly acknowledged this; for example, India, Israel, Pakistan, and South Africa (although the last of these has now signed the Non-Proliferation Treaty). It is their "unacknowledged" status that figuratively keeps their bombs in their basements.

Bonar Law, Andrew   *See* LAW, ANDREW BONAR.

bonded warehouse A warehouse authorized by customs authorities for storage of goods on which payment of duties is deferred until the goods are removed.

Bonn Conventions The 1952 agreements among France, Great Britain, the United States, and West Germany that recognized German sovereignty except in regard to the reunification of East and West Germany, the status of Berlin, and the presence of NORTH ATLANTIC TREATY ORGANIZATION forces.

Bonn Declaration The Joint Statement on International Terrorism issued by Canada, France, Great Britain, Italy, Japan, the United States, and West Germany at a 1978 meeting in Bonn, West Germany. It declared that it was the intention of the major Western powers to "intensify their joint efforts to combat international terrorism." The agreement specified that nations which do not cooperate in the "extradition and prosecution of those that have hijacked an aircraft" would be subject to an aviation boycott by the signatory parties to the declaration. *See also* HAGUE CONVENTION OF 1970.

Bonn-Moscow Treaty A key development in West Germany's policy of OSTPOLITIK, this 1970 treaty between the Federal Republic of Germany and the Soviet Union was a formal acceptance by Bonn of the territorial adjustments caused by World War II. The treaty provided for the mutual renunciation of force and the recognition that all borders in Europe, including the ODER-NEISSE LINE, were inviolable (i.e., they could not be changed by force—as opposed to "immutable," which means that they could not be changed by peaceful means either). Signed in 1970 in Moscow, the treaty was hailed in *Pravda* as an acknowledgment of postwar realities and was defended by West German Chancellor WILLY BRANDT on the grounds that it gave nothing up that had not been lost much earlier. Yet if Brandt accepted the division of Europe and Germany in the short term, his hope was that this would help to set in motion long-term processes that would help to transcend this division. From the perspective of the early 1990s and the newly reunified Germany, the policy looks very farsighted.

book burning The destruction of books for political and PROPAGANDA purposes. Although they were not the first, the NAZIS were famous for book burnings. They were major events accompanied by bands and, appropriately enough, torchlight parades. "Un-German" books by Albert Einstein, Sigmund Freud, and H. G. Wells, among others, were burned by the thousands. In partial response to this effort to destroy part of the cultural heritage of Europe, U.S. President Franklin D. Roosevelt said: "We all know that books burn—yet we have the greater knowledge that books cannot be killed by fire. People die, but books never die. No man and no force can abolish memory. No man and no force can put thought in a concentration camp forever. No man and no force can take from the world the books that embody man's eternal fight against tyranny of every kind" (*Publisher's Weekly*, May 9, 1942).

boost phase That portion of the flight of a BALLISTIC MISSILE or space vehicle during which the booster and sustainer engines operate. The boost phase lasts for the first few minutes of flight before the missile leaves the earth's atmosphere and starts to coast. The missile is easily visible to orbiting satellites during this phase, not only by radar but by infrared sensors, and is therefore highly vulnerable. The boost phase is the ideal time for a BALLISTIC MIS-

A 1933 book burning in Germany. (National Archives)

SILE DEFENSE system to operate against a missile. By destroying the missile at this stage, before the front end or "bus" has separated and the reentry vehicles have been released, the problems of decoys and the multitude of targets a MIRVed missile ultimately presents are avoided.

booty   Goods legally taken from an enemy during combat operations, or goods informally (and illegally) taken from the enemy or citizens of occupied territory.

Borden, Robert L. (1854–1937)   The prime minister of Canada from 1911 to 1920. He was a major influence in making the self-governing dominions of the British Empire equals in foreign affairs with Great Britain.

border   1. The imaginary line that separates one political jurisdiction from another. Borders can be international (between states) or internal (between provinces within a state).   2. A geographic area that lies close to a BOUNDARY of another state.

border tax adjustments   The remission of taxes on exported goods, including sales taxes and value added taxes, designed to ensure that national tax systems do not impede exports. The GATT permits such frontier adjustments on exports for indirect taxes, on the ground that these are passed on to consumers, but not for direct taxes (e.g., income taxes assessed on producing firms). The U.S. government makes little use of border tax adjustments, since it relies more heavily on income (or direct) taxes than do most other governments. But many other states, particularly the United Kingdom and Canada, use them extensively.

boring from within   One group secretly placing its agents in the middle of a competing group to weaken and ultimately destroy it. This is a long-standing technique of Communist infiltration into non-Communist organizations.

Borlaug, Norman (1914–   )   The U.S. plant biologist who developed the new strains of grain that led to the GREEN REVOLUTION. For this advance in feeding the hungry of the THIRD WORLD, he was awarded the Nobel Peace Prize in 1970.

Bormann, Martin (1900–1945?)   The top personal assistant to ADOLF HITLER who disappeared at the end of World War II. He has been widely reported to have survived the war and to be living in South America. At the NUREMBERG TRIALS he was found guilty in absentia and sentenced to death. After finding a skeleton in Berlin that was tentatively identified as his, the West German government in 1973 stated that Bormann died in 1945. Subsequent findings have cast considerable doubt on this conclusion.

Bosnia-Yugoslavia War   *See* YUGOSLAVIAN CIVIL WAR.

BOSS   Bureau of State Security: the South African secret police.

Botha, Louis (1862–1919)   The first prime minister of the Union of South Africa from 1910 until his death. While he fought the British as a general in the BOER WAR, he led the movement for reconciliation with the British after the war. During World War I he led the military campaign that forced the Germans out of Namibia, then known as South West Africa. South Africa would remain in power there until NAMIBIAN INDEPENDENCE was achieved in 1990. Botha was succeeded as prime minister by JAN CHRISTIAN SMUTS.

Botha, Pieter W. (1916–   )   The leader of South Africa as prime minister and later as state president from 1978 until poor health forced him to resign in 1989. His policies of modest racial reforms while maintaining the APARTHEID was not enough for anti-apartheid critics and cost him the support of the far right of his National Party (which split off in 1982 to form the Conservative Party). He successfully sponsored a new constitution that gave limited political powers to "Asian" and "coloured" citizens of South Africa, but he suppressed all efforts for greater political participation by blacks. The constitutional reforms also made him the last prime minister of South Africa and, after 1984 elections, the first state president. After suffering a stroke in January 1989, he resigned as leader of the National Party. He was succeeded as state president by F. W. DE KLERK in October 1989.

bottom-up development   The creation of new economic opportunities for the poor masses in a developing country in the expectation that their increasing prosperity eventually will offer economic benefits to the middle and upper classes. This is in contrast to *trickle-down development,* which primarily benefits the middle and upper classes in the expectation that their prosperity will in turn generate jobs and economic upward mobility for the poor.

Boulding, Kenneth (1910–1993) A U.S. leader in the field of PEACE RESEARCH. Author of *The Image: Knowledge in Life and Society* (1956) and *Conflict and Defense: A General Theory* (1962), Boulding sought to elucidate the key elements in what he described in the latter book as "a general theory of conflict that can be derived from many different sources and disciplines." Although interested in international conflict, he saw this as part of a larger set of social processes. He wanted to understand processes of conflict more fully and to devise ways in which they could be controlled. He believed that conflict is a process, and he built on the work of LEWIS F. RICHARDSON in this respect, noting the importance of perceptions in exacerbating conflicts. Boulding also argued that there was a diplomacy-war cycle and that the key to breaking it is to develop countercyclical instruments, ways of breaking out of the cycle to prevent war. Indeed, in his view, "one of the great organizational problems of mankind was the control of violence or, more generally, the control of conflict to the point where procedural institutions are adequate to handle it." In his specific concern with finding solutions to the problem of conflict, Boulding established an objective that has continued to provide one of the key rationales for peace research. *See also* CONFLICT THEORY; PEACE, STABLE; ZONE OF PEACE.

Boumedienne, Houari (1927–1978) The minister of defense in the first government of independent Algeria in 1962. In 1965 he led a coup against the government and ruled as a dictator until his death from natural causes. He nationalized what remained of foreign-owned enterprises and redistributed land from major Algerian landowners. His government did compromise via mixed companies, arrangements that gave the Algerian government a holding of 51 percent. This allowed for foreign investment, especially in energy, by such companies as Getty Petroleum.

boundary 1. An international border. 2. In the military, a control measure drawn along identifiable terrain features and used to delineate areas of tactical responsibility for subordinate units. Within their boundaries, units may fire and maneuver in accordance with the overall plan without close coordination with neighboring units unless otherwise restricted.

boundary, artificial A political division that follows lines of latitude or longitude rather than natural terrain features. For example, the 38th parallel of latitude that divides North and South Korea is an artificial boundary. *Compare to* BOUNDARY, NATURAL.

boundary, de facto An international or administrative boundary whose existence and legality is not recognized but that is a practical division between separate national or provincial administering authorities.

boundary, de jure An international or administrative boundary whose existence and legality is recognized in international law and by sovereign states.

boundary, natural A political division of area that follows the geographic features of terrain such as rivers, mountains, or oceans.

boundary disclaimer A statement on a map or chart that the status and/or alignment of international or administrative boundaries is not necessarily recognized by the government of the publishing nation.

bound rates MOST FAVORED NATION tariff rates resulting from GATT negotiations, and thereafter incorporated as integral provisions of a country's schedule of CONCESSIONS. The bound rate may represent either a reduced rate or a commitment not to raise the existing rate (known as a *ceiling binding*). If a GATT contracting party raises a tariff to a higher level than its bound rate, the beneficiaries of the binding have a right under the GATT to retaliate against an equivalent value of the offending county's exports, or to receive compensations, usually in the form of reduced tariffs on other products they export to the offending country.

Bourgeois, Leon V. A. (1851–1925) The French public official and diplomat who was awarded the 1920 Nobel Peace Prize for his work in establishing the LEAGUE OF NATIONS.

bourgeois 1. A middle-class citizen, as distinct from the aristocracy or the poor. 2. A negative reference by intellectuals to the cultural or political attitudes of the middle class. 3. In the context of MARXISM, a member of the ruling class in capitalistic societies; one who has a vested interest in the perpetuation of CAPITALISM. The class as a whole is the bourgeoisie. Karl Marx (1818–1883) distinguished between the haute bourgeoisie, the real leaders of industry, and the petit bourgeoisie, the owners of small businesses, whom he felt really belonged with the PROLETARIAT.

bourgeois revolution The Marxist concept of a political revolution that benefits only the middle and upper classes, not the poor PROLETARIAT.

bourgeois socialism The Marxist term for contempt for the nonrigorous SOCIALISM advocated by a middle class that is really just as happy never to see socialism implemented.

Bourguiba, Habib ibn Ali (1903–   ) The leader of Tunisia, first as premier and then as president, from the time of independence from France in 1956 until 1987. In that year his prime minister, General Ben Ali, deposed him by citing Bourguiba's senility.

bourse 1. The Paris stock exchange where securities are bought and sold. 2. A similar exchange in states that have been influenced by French culture and business practices.

Boutros Ghali, Boutros (1922–   ) The Egyptian diplomat who became secretary general of the United Nations in 1992. He is the first Arab and the first African to lead the United Nations. Prior to his election the African bloc mounted a major campaign to have one of their own as secretary general. Asserting that it was their turn to lead, they submitted a list of eight candidates (including Boutros Ghali) to the Security Council.

Boxer Rebellion The peasant uprising of 1898–1901 supported by the Chinese empress dowager, T'zu Hsi (1835–1908), to drive all foreigners from China. "Boxers" was the name that foreigners had given to a group of Chinese peasants, the Secret Order of the Harmonious Fists, who practiced Chinese martial arts and believed that their supernatural power made them impervious to bullets. The group originally aimed to overthrow the Qing (also spelled Ch'ing) dynasty. But the royal court cajoled them into an alliance to drive away foreigners and attack Christian converts who flouted Chinese traditions. Between 1898 and 1900 the Boxers controlled northern China. In August 1900 an international force crushed the rebellion. The empress dowager fled Beijing. A protocol was signed in September 1901 ending hostilities and providing for reparations to the foreign powers. The crushing of the rebellion intensified anti-imperialist attitudes and further reduced the ability of the ruling dynasty to control the country, which, in turn, led to the abolition of the dynasty and the proclamation of the republic of China in 1911 under SUN YAT-SEN. *Compare to* OPIUM WARS.

boycott 1. Ostracize. In nineteenth-century Ireland, Charles C. Boycott, a former British Army officer, ran the estate of an absentee owner. Because his methods were so oppressive, the local citizens as a group refused to deal with him and he was forced to flee home to England. Thus "boycott," or nonviolent intimidation through ostracism, got its name. 2. In the context of labor relations, a refusal to deal with or buy the products of a business, as a means of asserting pressure in a labor dispute. 3. A tactic in diplomacy wherein one nation or group of nations pointedly ignores the diplomatic efforts of another. 4. A state's deliberate policy of not buying the products of or doing business with another state—hostile or nonhostile—as a means of influencing the domestic or foreign policies of the state being boycotted. For example, the boycott of exports from South Africa and of companies with significant investments in that country has exerted so much pressure that the regime has begun to revise its racial policies. In international law there is no distinction between boycotts and similar actions such as SANCTIONS and EMBARGOes. 5. A national policy of refusing to do business with companies that also do business with a specified country. This is a kind of economic warfare. For example, the Arab states of the Middle East have long had a policy of boycotting companies that also did business with Israel. The Export Agreement Act of 1977 prohibits U.S. companies from "refusing, or requiring any other person to refuse, to do business with or in the boycotted country . . . pursuant to an agreement with, a requirement of, or a request from or on behalf of the boycotting country." **6.** A mass consumer tactic to force companies to change a particular policy. For example, a two-year boycott of canned tuna fish was successful in forcing the major producers to announce that they would only buy "dolphin-safe" tuna—tuna that was caught without inadvertently killing dolphins—in the future. **7.** A political tactic to change or influence a government policy. For example, in the United States, when the Idaho legislature in 1990 passed a bill severely restricting abortion, pro-choice groups threatened to boycott Idaho potatoes if the governor signed the bill. The governor then found "other" reasons to veto it.

boycott, cultural   Individual efforts by people in the entertainment industry to prevent their products, such as live performances, movies, or records, from being available in a particular regime as a protest against certain policies. For example, some film producers, such as Woody Allen, have announced that their pictures will not be released in South Africa due to its policy of apartheid.

boycott, sports   The prevention of athletes of one state from attending international competitions held in other states as a political protest. For example, when the 1980 Olympic Games were held in Moscow, the United States and most of its Western allies boycotted the games to protest the 1979 Soviet invasion of Afghanistan. Four years later the Olympic Games were held in Los Angeles. The Soviet Union and its Eastern European allies then retaliated by staying at home.

bracero program   In the United States, the legal importation of Mexican farm workers, or *braceros*, as seasonal workers. The practice started during World War II when the farm labor shortage was great. It was sanctioned by law in 1951 but was long opposed by organized labor and was terminated by the U.S. Congress in 1964. Since that time, however, an informal and unofficial bracero program has evolved, due to the large numbers of illegal aliens coming into the United States from Mexico.

brain drain   A reference to a perceived flow of human capital—talent—out of a country or an organization. While historically used to describe the exodus of physicians, scientists, and other professionals from a particular country, it is used colloquially to refer to the departure of any valued group of employees. Brain drains are especially acute problems for developing countries. Too often their nationals go abroad to get advanced training and degrees and refuse to return home because of the greater professional opportunities and more comfortable lifestyle offered by the developed world.

brainwashing   Altering a person's attitudes on social and political issues by severe physical and psychological conditioning. The phrase came into English to describe the way the North Koreans "reeducated" some U.S. prisoners during the Korean War of 1950 to 1953. (The term now is applied to the techniques used by religious cults to indoctrinate new converts.) Brainwashing is countered by *deprogramming,* an equally rigorous system of reinstating the victim's original views.

Brandt, Willy (1913–1992)   The mayor of West Berlin (1957–1966) when the BERLIN WALL was built in 1961. He later became West German foreign minister (1966–1969) and chancellor (1969–1974). Brandt was the first member of Germany's Social Democrat Party to become chancellor in the postwar period, thus displacing the Christian Democrat Party after its two decades in power. Brandt opened the way for Great Britain's entry into the European Community and decisively improved relations with the Soviet Union and other states of Communist Eastern Europe. A backlash to his policies had set in by 1973; critics claimed he was giving too much to the East and getting little in return. His kneeling at the location of the Warsaw ghetto and his reciting a psalm in Jerusalem also brought critics, who opposed his "emotional" approach to international politics. He revalued the German mark at a higher

Willy Brandt (Library of Congress)

rate to demonstrate the financial strength of West Germany and urged a comprehensive energy policy. Brandt was forced to resign as chancellor in 1974 when one of his aides proved to be an East German spy. For his efforts to achieve a rapprochement with East Germany and the Soviet bloc, for creating closer ties to Western Europe, and for encouraging nuclear disarmament, he was awarded the Nobel Peace Prize in 1971. *See also* OSTPOLITIK.

Brandt Commission An international study group (formally, the Independent Commission on International Development Issues) founded and headed by former West German Chancellor WILLY BRANDT, created in September 1977 and dissolved in December 1980. The commission gathered information on and proposed solutions to NORTH-SOUTH problems. Its first report, published in 1980, made the following recommendations to the United Nations and leaders of the world: 0.7 percent of the gross national product of the developed countries should

be committed to international development, this amount to be increased to 1 percent of the GNP by the end of the century; a new World Development Fund financed by international taxes on trade, ocean mining, and arms sales should be created and used for the general economic development of needy countries; international agreements on the supply, pricing, and conservation of energy resources should be negotiated; and a North-South summit meeting of approximately 25 nations representing the major world groupings should be convened to provide political backing for reforms in the international economic system.

The second Brandt Commission report, published in 1983, advocated the issue by the International Monetary Fund of an extra $40 billion of SPECIAL DRAWING RIGHTS (SDRs) to solve a world liquidity shortage; the doubling of the IMF national quotas by members; greater availability of low-conditionality financing by the IMF for low-income countries; increased borrowing authority for the World Bank; aid to the poorest countries to be doubled in real terms by 1985; a world conference on the future of the IMF and the World Bank; and removal of all remaining trade barriers in developed countries to the import of tropical products. While the Brandt Commission generated much publicity, it resulted in only minor actions. For example, in 1986 the IMF established a $3 billion pool of economic adjustment loans for the world's poorest states with 0.5 percent interest rates. *Compare to* CANCUN SUMMIT; COMMITTEE OF THE WHOLE; CONFERENCE ON INTERNATIONAL ECONOMIC COOPERATION; NORTH-SOUTH DIALOGUE; PALME COMMISSION.

Brandt Doctrine The 1969 declaration of West German Chancellor Willy Brandt that there existed "two states in Germany." This helped lead to the BONN-MOSCOW TREATY of 1970 and the West German policy of OSTPOLITIK, the ultimate aim of which was the removal of the division of Europe and of Germany.

Branting, Karl (1860–1925) The Swedish prime minister (1920, 1921–1923, 1924–1925) who is considered the father of modern Swedish socialism. He was awarded the 1921 Nobel Peace Prize (with CHRISTIAN L. LANGE) for his advocacy of disarmament in the LEAGUE OF NATIONS.

Braun, Eva (1912–1945)   ADOLF HITLER's mistress from 1932 on. She committed suicide with him in 1945. They had been married a day earlier.

Braun, Wernher von (1912–1977)   The German rocket scientist who led the development of the V-WEAPONS used in the terror bombing of Great Britain during World War II. He escaped prosecution as a Nazi war criminal (his rockets were built by thousands of slave laborers in concentration camp conditions) because he fled to the American line at the end of the war and developed missiles for the United States. He became a guiding force in the U.S. space program and a U.S. citizen in 1955. His sanitized 1960 film biography was entitled *I Aim at the Stars*. Critics responded: that may be, but he *hit* London.

breaking relations   A state's formal severance of diplomatic contact with another state to indicate strong disapproval of actions or policies. Because this is often a cut-off-your-nose-to-spite-your-face tactic, a more common tactic is to publicly recall the ambassador for CONSULTATIONS. This expresses disapproval but allows the diplomatic mission to remain.

Brecher, Michael (1925–   )   A Canadian-born political scientist who is interested in PERCEPTION and who has related this to academic studies on both India and Israel. However, Brecher is perhaps best known for a series of works on CRISIS. He has developed an elaborate but extremely useful framework for the study of crisis decision making that has been used by other scholars to study particular crises, such as the Berlin Crisis of 1948–1949 and the Czechoslovakian invasion crisis of 1968. Brecher himself used it in a study of Israel entitled *Decisions in Crises: Israel, 1967 and 1973* (1980). In 1988 he coauthored (with Jonathan Wilkenfeld) a massive two-volume handbook on crisis, one volume of which dealt with crises from a foreign policy perspective and the other with the perspective of the international system.

Brest-Litovsk Treaty   The harsh 1918 peace treaty between Germany and Soviet Russia that took Russia out of World War I. The German negotiators wanted to erect satellite states in all German-occupied areas. This meant that Russia was reduced to its early seventeenth-century boundaries and lost one-third of its population and chunks of its industry. LEON TROTSKY briefly opposed the treaty but V. I. LENIN saw it as a temporary expedient to gain breathing space for the BOLSHEVIKS. The treaty was annulled at the PARIS PEACE CONFERENCE in 1919.

Bretton Woods system   The international monetary system devised by a World War II conference of leading world economists at Bretton Woods, New Hampshire, United States. To abolish the economic ills believed to be responsible for the 1929 Great Depression and World War II, a new international monetary system was created that established rules for an EXCHANGE RATE system, BALANCE-OF-PAYMENTS adjustments, and supplies of RESERVE ASSETS; the conference also founded the INTERNATIONAL MONETARY FUND and the INTERNATIONAL BANK FOR RECONSTRUCTION AND DEVELOPMENT. The Bretton Woods system is generally perceived to have collapsed in August 1971, when the United States suspended the convertibility of dollars into gold. An attempt was made to salvage the system through the Smithsonian Agreement of December 1971. Although this included a multilateral realignment of exchange rates and a DEVALUATION of the dollar against gold, it did not succeed in its objective, and in April 1973 a system of floating exchange rates was instituted.

Brezhnev, Leonid Il'ich (1906–1982)   General secretary of the COMMUNIST PARTY OF THE SOVIET UNION from 1964 to 1982, the longest-ruling general secretary apart from JOSEPH STALIN. During World War II he rose to the rank of major-general as a political officer in the Red Army. In 1960, while NIKITA S. KHRUSHCHEV was still the party leader, Brezhnev became head of state when he was chosen as chairman of the Presidium of the U.S.S.R. Supreme Soviet. Brezhnev and ALEXEI N. KOSYGIN led the ouster of Khrushchev from the Soviet government in 1964. As the first secretary of the Soviet Communist Party from 1964 while Kosygin was premier, Brezhnev became the dominant figure in the government. By 1977 he had the Soviet constitution changed to combine the offices of first secretary and president. His program of "Goulash communism" continued a strong military emphasis but gave some attention to improving the availability of

Leonid Brezhnev (right) and Nikita Khrushchev review a parade in Moscow in November 1963. (Library of Congress)

consumer goods. (Goulash, a spicy Hungarian meat-based stew, came to mean "more" for the workers. But ultimately the Brezhnev regime could not provide enough goulash.) The continuing stress on military buildup led to the attainment of strategic parity with the United States but was catastrophic to the Soviet economy. Under Brezhnev the Soviet government became more repressive than it had been under Khrushchev. Nobel laureate ALEXANDER SOLZHENITSYN, whose books describe the GULAGS, was expelled. Jewish citizens were harassed and their emigration to Israel was temporarily blocked. The few Soviet citizens who criticized their government for violating human rights provisions of the 1975 HELSINKI ACCORDS, such as ANDREI SAKHAROV, were exiled. Although some CPSU loyalists viewed Brezhnev as one of the great Soviet leaders of the century, many others did not. His November 17, 1982, obituary in *The Times* (London) summed up his tenure in office: "Under Brezhnev's leadership the Soviet Union achieved its most prolonged period of internal stability even though many problems were pushed out of sight rather than solved."

In foreign policy Brezhnev had periods of success and some stark failures. U.S. Presidents Nixon, Ford, and Carter followed a policy of DÉTENTE based on supposed arms limitations despite the Soviet Union's crushing of Czechoslovakia in 1968 and Brezhnev's restrained support for North Vietnam. Détente led to increased commercial contacts with the West as well as arms control agreements. It also appeared to involve a recognition by the United States that the Soviet Union was now its equal. It was undermined, however, by the Soviets' failure to realize that their activities in the Third World eroded U.S. popular support for détente. Perhaps even more critical, however, was the 1979 intervention in Afghanistan, which was a disaster for the Soviet Union.

Attacks on the Brezhnev era started shortly after his death in 1982 and continued under MIKHAIL GORBACHEV, who exposed to the CPSU and to the entire country the stagnation, the postponed decisions, and the missed opportunities that occurred throughout the Brezhnev era. Brezhnev's faults and acts of corruption were further scrutinized after Gorbachev attained power in 1985. Family members and friends close to Brezhnev were found to be guilty of bribery and misuse of government funds. Many of Brezhnev's military medals (of which he had more than Stalin and Khrushchev combined—and more military distinctions than Marshal GEORGI ZHUKOV, who had saved Leningrad and liberated Berlin during World War II) had to be returned by his widow. In 1988 every city, street, factory, or institute that had been named after Brezhnev was renamed.

Brezhnev Doctrine   The term used to describe the justification offered by the Soviet Union for its CZECHOSLOVAKIAN INVASION in August 1968, which stated that the Soviet Union had the right to intervene with military force in the SOCIALIST COMMONWEALTH. The doctrine was promulgated in *Pravda* on September 25, 1968, and argued that Czechoslovakia was a member of the socialist commonwealth and, as such, could not exercise its sovereignty in ways inimical "to the interests of world socialism." It also argued that the socialist commonwealth could act jointly to deal with threats to it from subversive forces within a particular nation. Brezhnev himself argued much the same thing in a speech to the Polish Communist Party Congress in Warsaw on November 12, 1968. The Brezhnev Doctrine was also known as the doctrine of *limited sovereignty* since it placed the security of the socialist bloc above the sovereignty of particular members and put forward a concept of intervention in members' domestic affairs. Thomas Franck and Edward Weisband's *Word Politics* (1972) contend that many elements in the Brezhnev Doctrine were reminiscent of, and were probably echoes of, the justifications given by the U.S. Johnson Administration for its intervention in the DOMINICAN CIVIL WAR in 1965.

Although the West accepted the reality of Soviet power in Eastern Europe and did not attempt to prevent the Soviet action in Czechoslovakia on the grounds that vital Soviet interests were involved, the Brezhnev Doctrine continued to rankle. By 1989 the new leadership of the Soviet Union effectively renounced the Brezhnev Doctrine in favor of what Gennady Gerasimov, a GORBACHEV aide, called the "Sinatra Doctrine" (*Newsweek,* January 1, 1990). This meant that each East European country could say, as Frank Sinatra did in a famous song, "I did it my way."

Briand, Aristide (1862–1932)   The French political leader who, as minister of foreign affairs (1925–1932), helped create the KELLOGG-BRIAND PACT. He was 11 times premier of France between 1909 and 1929. For his efforts in seeking a rapprochement with Germany, through the LOCARNO PACTS, which guaranteed European borders, he shared the Nobel Peace Prize in 1926 with GUSTAV STRESEMANN.

Brighton bombing   The PROVISIONAL IRISH REPUBLICAN ARMY (PIRA) bombing of the Grand Hotel in Brighton, England, on October 12, 1984, during the annual conference of the Conservative Party. Prime Minister MARGARET THATCHER was unhurt, but five persons died of wounds received from the blast and the subsequent collapse of the rooms surrounding the sixth-floor bathroom in which the device was detonated. Several other members of the government, including Minister of Trade and Industry Norman Tebbit and his wife, were badly injured. The PIRA later expressed its regret over Thatcher's escape from injury. Patrick Joseph

Magee, a resident of Belfast, Northern Ireland, was convicted of the bombing in 1986.

brink   A crisis situation in which states are seen as being very close to war. The CUBAN MISSILE CRISIS is generally seen as the closest to the brink of war that the United States and the Soviet Union came during the COLD WAR.

brinkmanship   **1.** The deliberate taking of very large risks in a negotiation in an effort to force the opposition to make concessions. As a tactic this is inevitably reckless and sometimes a bluff. According to Thomas C. Schelling's *The Strategy of Conflict* (1963), brinkmanship is the "deliberate creation of a recognizable risk of war, a risk that one does not completely control. It is the tactic of deliberately letting the situation get somewhat out of hand, just because its being out of hand may be intolerable to the other party and force his accommodation." **2.** A description of the foreign policies of U.S. President Dwight D. Eisenhower's secretary of state, John Foster Dulles, who advocated going to the brink of war as a negotiating tactic. In a famous *Life* magazine interview (January 16, 1956), Dulles asserted that "the ability to get to the verge without getting into the war is the necessary art. If you cannot master it, you inevitably get into war. If you try to run away from it, if you are scared to go to the brink, you are lost." The clear implication of this is that the nuclear age simply requires the taking of risks. In such a context the fear of war and an unwillingness to take such risks would place the shy state at the mercy of other states that were less inhibited.   **3.** A tactic in trade negotiations: Major and seemingly disproportionate disruptions in international commerce are threatened unless one side gives way.   **4.** A tactic that some Third World countries, notably Brazil, have used to get more favorable terms for the repayment of debt to Western banks: a threat to default on substantial loans.

Brinton, Crane (1898–1968)   The professor of history at Harvard University who was the author of *Ideas and Men* (1950), *The Shaping of the Modern Mind* (1953), and perhaps his most famous work, *The Anatomy of Revolution* (first published in 1938 and revised in 1952). In his *Anatomy* Brinton compares four revolutions—the English (1640), American (1776), French (1789), and Russian (1917). Brinton identified common aspects of all revolutions: the problems with the old regimes, the first stages of revolution, types of revolutionaries, and the progress from the rule of the moderates to the rule of the extremists and their reigns of terror and virtue. He also discusses the *Thermidorean reaction*, described as "a period of convalescence from the fever of revolution." The book went beyond single case studies and attempted to discern patterns and uniformities, a key objective of contemporary social science.

Britain, Battle of   The air battle over southeastern England between the British (RAF) and German (Luftwaffe) air forces that began in August 1940 after the fall of France. Had Germany achieved AIR SUPERIORITY, it would have launched an invasion of England and the history of World War II might have been different. But even though it started the battle with more than three times the aircraft as Great Britain, Germany lost because the British had radar and ULTRA communications intercepts, superior fighters (Spitfires and Hurricanes), and the extremely tenacious Royal Air Force fighter pilots.

THEIR FINEST HOUR

What General Weygand called the Battle of France is over. I expect that the Battle of Britain is about to begin. Upon this battle depends the survival of Christian civilization. Upon it depends our own British life, and the long continuity of our institutions and our Empire. The whole fury and might of the enemy must very soon be turned on us. Hitler knows that he will have to break us in this island or lose the war. If we can stand up to him, all Europe may be free and the life of the world may move forward into broad, sunlit uplands. But if we fail, then the whole world, including all that we have known and cared for, will sink into the abyss of a new Dark Age, made more sinister, and perhaps more protracted, by the lights of perverted science. Let us therefore brace ourselves to our duties, and so bear ourselves that, if the British Empire and its Commonwealth last for a thousand years, men will say, "This was their finest hour."

SOURCE: Winston Churchill, speech in the House of Commons in anticipation of the Battle of Britain, June 18, 1940.

Winston Churchill's August 20, 1940, tribute to them in the House of Commons—"Never in the field of human conflict was so much owed by so many to so few"—was as heartfelt as it was accurate. From July 10 to October 31, 1940, the Germans lost an estimated 1,733 bombers and fighters to 915 British fighters (and 449 RAF pilots). Hitler made a major blunder in the air war when the Germans shifted their attacks from airfields to London (the BLITZ). *See also* HUGH C. T. DOWDING.

British Army of the Rhine   The British military forces stationed in Germany. Initially an army of occupation, it is now an element of the NORTH ATLANTIC TREATY ORGANIZATION.

British Asians   Indian or Pakistani residents of former British African colonies who are legally citizens of the United Kingdom.

British Commonwealth   1. A nineteenth-century euphemism for the British Empire. **2.** The COMMONWEALTH OF NATIONS formed by the United Kingdom and 48 of its former colonies.

British Council   An independent organization created in 1934 that functions as the cultural relations organization of the British foreign ministry.

British Empire   The overseas possessions of the British monarch, particularly in the nineteenth and early twentieth centuries. After the defeat of the Spanish Armada in 1588 firmly established Great Britain as a major sea power, its interests outside Europe grew steadily. Attracted by the spice trade, British mercantile interests spread first to the Far East, then to North America. The territorial foundation of the twentieth-century British Empire, minus parts of Africa and India, had already been laid by the time of the American Revolution in 1776. By the end of the Napoleonic wars in 1815, the United Kingdom was the foremost European power and its navy ruled the seas. Peace in Europe allowed the British to focus their interests on more remote parts of the world, and during this period the British Empire reached its zenith. By the early twentieth century it consisted of about one-quarter of the earth's land and population—thus the expression: "The sun never sets on the British Empire."

John Seeley, in his book *The Expansion of England* (1883), first observed: "[The British] seem, as it were, to have conquered and peopled half the world in a fit of absence of mind." William H. McNeil expanded on this thought in *The Pursuit of Power* (1982), writing that "from the 1840s onward, far more drastically than in any earlier age, Europe's near monopoly of strategic communication and transportation, together with a rapidly evolving weaponry that remained always far in advance of anything local fighting men could lay hands on, made imperial expansion cheap—so cheap that the famous phrase to the effect that Britain acquired its empire in a fit of absence of mind is a caricature rather than a falsehood." The losses and destruction of WORLD WAR I, the GREAT DEPRESSION of the 1930s, and decades of relatively slow growth made it difficult for the United Kingdom to maintain its preeminent international position. Control over the empire loosened during the interwar period. Ireland (with the exception of six northern counties) broke away from the United Kingdom in 1921. Nationalism became stronger in other parts of the empire, particularly in India and Egypt. In 1926 the United Kingdom, completing a process begun a century earlier, granted Australia, Canada, and New Zealand complete autonomy within the empire. After World War II, with the rise of nationalism in Africa and Asia, the remainder of the empire was dismantled. Almost all of Britain's former colonies now belong to the COMMONWEALTH OF NATIONS. Today all that is left of the empire are the odd bits of territory, still under direct rule by the United Kingdom, such as the Falkland Islands and Gibraltar. It was the British ambassador to the United States, David Ormsby Gore (1918–1985), who asserted that: "In the end it may well be that Britain will be honored by the historians more for the way she disposed of an empire than for the way in which she acquired it" (*New York Times,* October 28, 1962). *See also* COLONIALISM; IMPERIALISM.

British Expeditionary Force   The name given to the British troops that were sent to France at the beginning of each of the two world wars.

British Nationality Act of 1981   The United Kingdom law that held that all Commonwealth citizens residing in Britain prior to 1973 could become British subjects if they registered before the end of 1987. Thereafter they would have to undergo a more complicated naturalization procedure if they wished to become legal citizens of the United Kingdom.

British Union of Fascists   The BLACKSHIRTS, organized in 1938 by OSWALD MOSLEY. Many considered it a counterpart to the German and Italian fascist groups. During World War II its leader, Mosley, was imprisoned and the union disbanded. The union was widely considered to be a German FIFTH COLUMN in Britain—just waiting for a successful German invasion to collaborate.

Brodie, Bernard (1910–1978)   The American who was the first major academic theorist of NUCLEAR WARFARE. His 1946 book, *The Absolute Weapon,* contained all the fundamental ideas of nuclear strategy that others would refine and expand upon. According to Brodie, the ATOMIC BOMB and particularly the HYDROGEN BOMB placed the United States (and all other nuclear powers) in a dilemma—it could either preemptively strike an enemy before that enemy could develop its own atomic weapons or accept DETERRENCE and its implications as the only sane strategy. Brodie was the first analyst to recognize that nuclear weapons brought us "a long way from the subtleties of [the traditional strategists] a Clausewitz, a Jomini, or a Mahan. . . . It brings us, in short, to the end of strategy as we have known it" (*Harper's,* October 1955). One of the great strengths of Brodie's analyses was that he always recognized the relationship between war and strategy on the one hand and politics and history on the other. In this sense he differed signifi-

20TH-CENTURY MONARCHS OF THE BRITISH EMPIRE
(see individual entries for each)

Name	Reign
Edward VII	1901–1910
George V	1910–1936
Edward VIII	1936
George VI	1936–1952
Elizabeth II	1952 to present

cantly from many other strategic analysts of the nuclear era who were much more technologically or mathematically oriented and who produced analyses that were more rigorous than Brodie's but contained far less wisdom and insight about the relationship between war and politics. This relationship was explored in his other major books, which include *Strategy in the Missile Age* (1959), *Escalation and the Nuclear Option* (1966), and *War and Politics* (1973). In a chapter devoted to the work of Brodie, Ken Booth in John Baylis and John Garnett (eds.), *Makers of Nuclear Strategy* (1991), held, "He was a strategists' strategist, who insisted on thinking about first principles. Strategic history will acclaim Brodie as the Clausewitz of the age of nuclear deterrence."

Brookings Institution   A private research organization devoted to education and publication in economics, government, and foreign policy; located in Washington, D.C., United States. Brookings every year generates a vast amount of research in international relations and international economics—most of which it publishes itself through a publishing unit that rivals in size and prestige many of the best university presses. Brookings, one of the best known and most respected of the world's THINK TANKS, was founded in 1916 as the Institute for Government Research by Robert S. Brookings (1850–1932). In 1927 it was merged with the Institute of Economics (founded 1922) to form the current Brookings Institution.

brownshirts   *See* SA.

Brundtland Report   The United Nations–sponsored 1988 report of the World Commission on Environment and Development, *Our Common Future*. It is called the Brundtland Report after Gro Harlem Brundtland (1939–   ), prime minister of Norway, the chair of the commission that was established in 1983 to formulate innovative, concrete, and realistic action proposals with which the international community can confront critical issues of environment and development. The report offers a consensus of principles for the responsible management of the earth's resources. The concept of SUSTAINABLE DEVELOPMENT it advocated has been adopted by many subsequent publications. A

majority of world governments, all the major international institutions, and key nongovernmental organizations have since accepted and endorsed the findings of the report as the basis for future policymaking. The report also has had a profound influence on the world's public opinion as the issues it dealt with have been popularized and disseminated throughout the world by the mass media.

Brüning, Heinrich (1885–1970)   The chancellor and foreign minister of Germany from 1930 to 1932. Because of his stern economic measures he lost the support of the Reichstag (German legislature) and ruled by emergency decree until forced to resign by President PAUL LUDWIG VON HINDENBURG. He fled Germany after ADOLF HITLER came to power and spent the rest of his life in the United States, at Harvard University, teaching government.

Brussels   1. The capital of Belgium.   2. The city that, because it is where the bureaucracy of the EUROPEAN COMMISSION is located, has come to symbolize the administrative power of the EUROPEAN COMMUNITIES.

Brussels, Treaty of   *See* ACCESSION, TREATIES OF.

Brussels Conference   A 1937 meeting called by the LEAGUE OF NATIONS to seek action in the wake of Japan's invasion of China. It could only agree to verbally chastise Japan. The meeting was symptomatic of the ineffectiveness of the League.

Brussels Pact   A 1948 defense alliance of Belgium, France, Great Britain, Luxembourg, and the Netherlands. This 50-year defense alliance was broadened and expanded into the ATLANTIC ALLIANCE the following year. The pact also provided for economic and social committees to meet periodically and further the idea of a Western European union. The nonmilitary aspects of the pact were transferred to the COUNCIL OF EUROPE in 1960. What is left of the pact, which in 1955 after Germany and Italy joined became the WESTERN EUROPEAN UNION, has been concerned with defense policy. The main purpose of the pact was to demonstrate to the United States that Western Europe was capable of coordinated and effective action in security matters and was therefore worthy of a U.S. security guarantee.

Bryan, William Jennings (1860–1925) The U.S. Secretary of State under President Woodrow Wilson in 1913 who had been the unsuccessful Democratic candidate for president of the United States in 1896, 1900, and 1908. Bryan resigned in 1915 because he disputed policies that he thought would eventually bring the United States into World War I.

Brzezinski, Zbigniew (1928–   ) The scholar of the Soviet Union and Eastern Europe who became U.S. National Security Advisor (1977–1981) in the Carter Administration. A contemporary of HENRY A. KISSINGER and STANLEY HOFFMANN at Harvard University in the 1950s, Brzezinski established his reputation as an outstanding scholar with *Political Power USA/USSR* (1964), written with Samuel Huntington, and with a massive study of political processes in Eastern Europe entitled *The Soviet Bloc: Unity and Conflict* (1968), which remained one of the definitive studies of the bloc until the revolutions of 1989. His innovative thinking was evident in *Between Two Ages: America's Role in the Technetronic Era* (1970). Brzezinski was very much a realist in his approach to international politics, had a robustly negative view of the Soviet Union and a willingness to use force to protect American interests. He argued that the United States should not go ahead with arms control unless the Soviet Union exhibited restraint in its geopolitical behavior. This emphasis on LINKAGE was to haunt the Carter Administration during the debate over SALT II in 1979. After leaving government, Brzezinski returned to his career as a scholar and commentator on international security issues and wrote several books dealing with aspects of the U.S.-Soviet relationship, the fate of the Soviet bloc, and the future of the Soviet Union itself. These included *Game Plan* (1986), *In Quest of National Security* (1988), and *The Grand Failure: The Birth and Death of Communism in the Twentieth Century* (1989). It is clear from all these publications that Brzezinski's basic geopolitical approach to international politics continues to have considerable impact on his thinking.

BTN See CUSTOMS CLASSIFICATION.

Buchan, Alastair (1918–1976) The British national security analyst who was a major influence on the post–World War II development of STRATEGIC STUD-IES as an academic specialty, Buchan wrote widely on the causes, probabilities, and effects of wars. He founded the London-based Institute for Strategic Studies in 1958; its annual handbook, *The Military Balance,* quickly became required reading by both North Atlantic Treaty Organization and Warsaw Pact analysts and spawned many imitations. During the 1960s and 1970s Buchan wrote and edited many works on NATO, European security, and Atlantic relations, including *Europe's Futures, Europe's Choices* (1969).

Buchenwald One of the first German CONCENTRATION CAMPS, located near Weimar, Germany. Beginning in 1937 opponents of the Nazis, German Jews, and other political prisoners were forced to work long shifts in nearby armaments factories. While not an extermination camp as such, about 6,000 inmates a month were worked or beaten to death during World War II.

THE LIBERATION OF BUCHENWALD

There were two rows of bodies stacked up like cordwood. They were thin and very white. Some of the bodies were terribly bruised, though there seemed to be little flesh to bruise. Some had been shot through the head, but they bled but little. All except two were naked. I tried to count them as best I could and arrived at the conclusion that all that was mortal of more than five hundred men and boys lay there in two neat piles. . . . I pray you to believe what I have said about Buchenwald. I have reported what I saw and heard, but only part of it. For most of it I have no words.

SOURCE: Edward R. Murrow's radio broadcast on the liberation of Buchenwald (April 1945) quoted in Alexander Kendrick, *Prime Time* (1969).

---

buffer **1.** A small state between two more powerful neighbors that functions (or was expressly created) to reduce the possibility of conflict between them. Because buffer states create a physical distance between powers, they often reduce the possibility of direct confrontations. History presents many examples of small states or groups of states acting as buffers between larger ones. Among them are Afghanistan between India and Russia, Eastern Europe between the Soviet Union and Western

Europe, Uruguay between Brazil and Argentina, and Namibia between South Africa and Angola. **2.** Organizational procedures or structures that absorb disruptive inputs and thus protect the continuity or equilibrium of the core group. For example, people in job positions near the boundaries of organizations, such as receptionists, often absorb a wide variety of messages and demands. These inputs are filtered, processed, and passed to the technical core of the organization in a sequential and routine form. Because the inputs have been "buffered," the central work processes are not disrupted. **3.** Stocks of commodities of international significance that are purchased and sold at certain prices so as to stabilize market fluctuations. For example, goods from a stockpile may be sold when prices reach predetermined ceiling prices and purchased to add to the stocks when prices reach floor prices. **4.** A special zone, such as a DEMILITARIZED ZONE, separating two military forces. Sometimes these zones have United Nations troops (as in Lebanon) or third party troops (as in the Sinai) stationed within them.

build-down **1.** Reducing a nuclear arsenal by taking out of service more old warheads than new ones are put in. A build-down does not always change strategic relationships, because fewer new weapons can often be more accurate and more powerful than larger numbers of older ones. **2.** A gradual budget cutback in a government program. **3.** In common speech, the exact amount of a budget cut; for example, "There was a build-down of $2 million."

Buisson, Ferdinand (1841–1932)   The French educator who was awarded the 1927 Nobel Peace Prize (with LUDWIG QUIDDE) for his advocacy of pacifism, support of a RAPPROCHEMENT with Germany, and work on behalf of the LEAGUE OF NATIONS.

Bulganin, Nikolai A. (1895–1975)   The premier of the Soviet Union from 1955 to 1958. Along with Defense Minister GEORGI ZHUKOV and NIKITA S. KHRUSHCHEV, he was part of a collective leadership that Khrushchev came to dominate. After Khrushchev consolidated his power, Bulganin was forced out of the Communist Party's Central Committee and became chairman of the economic council of Stavropol, a decidedly minor post, until his retirement in 1960.

Bulge, Battle of the   The final German offensive on the Western Front in World War II. The attack came along the French-German border in the Ardennes during December 1944. Parts of the U.S. lines were pushed back as far as 50 miles. (This penetration of the front was the "bulge.") The U.S. troops besieged at the crossroads of Bastogne were hard-pressed to hold on until they were relieved by fresh U.S. forces, who finally broke through the German encirclement on December 26. As the Allied forces concentrated their forces on the "bulge," the Germans were killed, captured, or forced to withdraw. By late January 1945 the "bulge" was gone—and so were the last of the German Army's effective reserves in the West. During this battle at Malmèdy, Belgium, SS troops murdered more than 70 American prisoners of war in flagrant violation of international law. The Malmèdy incident caused extensive Allied reprisals until the end of the battle.

This last gasp of the Germans was futile from the beginning. Even before the battle, German Commander General Sepp Dietrich complained: "All Hitler wants me to do is to cross a river, capture Brussels, and then go on and take Antwerp! And all this in the worst time of the year through the Ardennes where the snow is waist deep and there isn't room to deploy four tanks abreast let alone armored divisions! Where it doesn't get light until eight and it's dark again at four and with re-formed divisions made up chiefly of kids and sick old men—and at Christmas!" (Quoted in Peter Elstob, *Hitler's Last Offensive*, 1971.)

NUTS!

On December 22, [1944, when] the Germans called on Major-General Anthony McAuliffe, the American commander besieged in Bastogne, to surrender, they received a single word answer: "Nuts!" Asked what this answer meant, they were told, with scarcely less brevity, that its meaning was: "Go to hell."

SOURCE: Martin Gilbert, *The Second World War*, rev. ed. (1989). "Nuts!" is the most famous single-word statement of World War II. There has been much speculation that McAuliffe really used another four-letter word much in use during World War II, but all historical accounts support the accuracy of "Nuts!"

Bull, Hedley (1932–1985)   A leading figure in the study of international relations in Great Britain and Australia. His *The Control of the Arms Race* (1961) was one of three almost simultaneous publications that helped to establish the theory or philosophy of ARMS CONTROL—as opposed to DIS-ARMAMENT—in the early 1960s. In the mid-1960s Bull wrote a polemic against what he described as the scientific or behavioral approach to international relations, which he regarded as the product of American social science. This polemic both reflected and exacerbated a division between those scholars who took a traditionalist or historical and wisdom-based approach and those who attempted to apply scientific techniques to the study of international politics.

Bull was perhaps most famous, however, for *The Anarchical Society* (1977) in which he identified three approaches to international relations. The first was an approach that he traced back to HUGO GROTIUS and the tradition of international law. In this approach, which Bull himself adhered to, the emphasis was placed on the notion that there was a society of states with certain rules, norms, and institutions. Diplomacy, the BALANCE OF POWER, and even war were the institutions of this society of states. An alternative approach, which Bull traced to IMMANUEL KANT, placed the emphasis not on the relations among states but on those among people. The main challenge to the Grotian approach, however, came from those who took a Hobbesian view and argued that international relations was rather like relations among individuals in the Hobbesian STATE OF NATURE. Without a Leviathan or government to keep order, insecurity and conflict were endemic. While Bull acknowledged the importance of this perspective, he contended that the forces of anarchy were mitigated by the elements of society. In some of his later work Bull traced the way in which the norms of international society in nineteenth-century Europe had provided the basis for the global international politics of the second half of the twentieth century. Bull blended analytical rigor with erudite scholarship; his contribution to thinking about international relations was immense.

Bulletin of the Atomic Scientists   A nontechnical journal on political and strategic issues of interest to atomic scientists and the general public, published since 1945 by the Education Foundation for Nuclear Science. Articles typically deal with United States–Russian relations, nuclear testing, regional conflicts, and the spread of nuclear power and weapons. It is famous for a clock on its cover, the *Doomsday Clock,* which is a symbol of the threat of nuclear war. When superpower tensions mounted the clock moved closer to midnight. Now that the COLD WAR is over and tensions over nuclear war have eased, the hands on the clock were moved farther back from midnight; but the clock remains as a symbol of the dangers still posed by the world's arsenals of nuclear weapons.

Bülow, Bernhard von (1849–1929)   The chancellor of Germany from 1900 to 1909. His pursuit of German imperialistic goals and his alienation of possible allies ensured that when WORLD WAR I came, as it finally did in 1914, Germany would have to fight on two fronts.

Bunche, Ralph J. (1904–1971)   The African-American who as director of the United Nations' Division of Trusteeship was a leading influence in the post–World War II DECOLONIZATION movement. For mediating the Arab-Israeli dispute in 1948–1949, he was awarded the Nobel Peace Prize in 1950.

Bundesbank   The CENTRAL BANK of Germany created in 1957 by Article 88 of the Basic Law (the German Constitution). Headquartered in a Frankfurt suburb, it is, because of the economic strength of the German mark, the most powerful central bank in the EUROPEAN COMMUNITY. Critics contend that its policy of high interest rates in the early 1990s (designed to forestall inflation) was a drag on the economies of the rest of Europe. Other EC states have not been able to lower interest rates as much as they want to stimulate their economies because such lowering would cause an increased outflow of funds to German banks—which in turn lowers the value of their currencies. This persistent problem is a major argument in favor of a single currency and a single central bank for the EC as envisioned by the MAASTRICHT TREATY.

Bundesrat   1. The Federal Council of Germany, the upper house of the legislature, which has limited veto powers over laws passed by the BUNDESTAG. 2. Austria's national senate.

Bundestag   The federal legislature of Germany, the lower house, which operates as the major legislative chamber.

Bundeswehr   The armed forces of Germany. Under Article 26 of the Basic Law (the German Constitution), the Bundeswehr cannot be used to wage aggressive war but only for defense.

Bundy, McGeorge (1919–   )   The U.S. National Security Advisor for Presidents John F. Kennedy and Lyndon B. Johnson (1961–1966). During the CUBAN MISSILE CRISIS Bundy was one of the leading proponents of a blockade as opposed to an air strike. He was subsequently one of the prime architects of the escalating U.S. involvement in the VIETNAM WAR. Later he was head of the Ford Foundation (1966–1979) and a prominent critic of the undesirability of nuclear war. His major study, *Danger and Survival* (1988), examined the impact and role of nuclear weapons during the Cold War. *See also* DETERRENCE, EXISTENTIAL.

Bundy, William P. (1917–   )   The U.S. assistant secretary of defense for international affairs in the Kennedy Administration, who became the assistant secretary of state for Far Eastern affairs in the Johnson Administration. Because he and his brother, McGeorge, were both actively involved at high levels on the same issues, such as Vietnam, the two men were often mistaken for one another.

burden-sharing   1. The issue of how the costs and benefits of a military alliance are equitably borne and divided. In the context of the NORTH ATLANTIC TREATY ORGANIZATION, this refers to the periodically asked question of which allies should bear what expenses for the alliance. It sometimes refers to the relative share of total NATO defense expenditures paid by Europeans compared to that paid by the United States. The concept of burden-sharing, though, presents many difficulties. The whole notion of "fair share" on which it is premised is necessarily imprecise; different statistical and financial indicators will present different conclusions on the manner in which the burden should be dis-

tributed. For example, single indicators, such as the percentage of gross national product devoted to defense, may be used to make a political point—and often a misleading one. Demands for greater burden-sharing often obscure other important differences among allies. In the United States those who demand that allies share a greater portion of the burden may want the United States to do less. Others traditionally have demanded that all NATO members, including the United States, should do more, especially at the conventional level, so that dependence on nuclear weapons can be reduced. One can only conclude that disputes about burden-sharing are inherent in collective security arrangements. This problem became evident during and after the confrontation with Iraq following its invasion of Kuwait in August 1990. Not only did the United States expect its European allies to participate militarily, but it also wanted Arab states such as Saudi Arabia and Kuwait to help with the costs of the military operations. The argument for burden-sharing was that the United States was protecting not only its own interests but also those of the regional states and its industrialized allies, especially Germany and Japan, states that are more dependent on imported oil than the United States. Although Japan argued that it had not been consulted prior to the U.S. commitment of forces and therefore should not be expected to send forces, great criticism arose in the United States that Japan was once again being a "FREE RIDER." In any event both Germany and Japan agreed to help pay the costs of the war that were incurred predominantly by the United States. 2. The self-imposed obligation on the part of the developed world to mutually help the underdeveloped world better itself. 3. In the context of the European Community, the way in which the burdens (or benefits) of imports from non-EC states are distributed.

Bureau 210   The intelligence organization of Iran, which fosters and sponsors Islamic revolutionary groups in many countries.

Burgess, Guy (1911–1963)   The British journalist who was discovered to have been a Soviet spy since his days as a youthful member of the CAMBRIDGE SPY RING. After exposure in 1951 he escaped to the Soviet Union, with the help of ANTHONY BLUNT.

burn **1.** In espionage, to deliberately expose the real status of a secret agent. **2.** The legally authorized destruction, by burning, of classified material. This is why some government agencies put their waste paper in "burn bags."

burned In espionage, a term used to indicate that a secret agent has been exposed (especially in a surveillance) or that his or her reliability as a source of intelligence has been compromised.

burn notice A formal statement by an intelligence agency to other agencies, domestic or foreign, that an individual or group has become unreliable for any of a variety of reasons.

Burton, John W. (1937–   ) An Australian scholar and former diplomat who became the key figure in the development of the WORLD SOCIETY approach to global affairs. Burton is stimulating, if idiosyncratic, in his thinking about international relations. His major books, *International Relations: A General Theory* (1965), *Systems, States, Diplomacy and Rules* (1968), *Conflict and Communication* (1969), and *World Society* (1972), develop his theories at length. Among the most controversial of his ideas is the emphasis he places on human needs rather than state interests and his argument that there is no such thing as an objective conflict of interests. His view is perhaps most succinctly expressed in his 1968 volume, in which he argued, "In an ideal situation of complete information and efficiency in decision making, states would avoid all dysfunctional conflict." This view has not been widely accepted and is vigorously and somewhat contemptuously rejected by the realist school of thought. It has, however, provided the basis for Burton's thinking, and his contributions to the field of CONFLICT RESOLUTION have taken this argument as the starting point. *Compare to* REALISM.

bus *See* FRONT END.

Bush, George Herbert Walker (1924–   ) The president of the United States from 1989 to 1993. After eight years as vice president under President RONALD W. REAGAN (1981–1989), Bush became the first serving vice president to be elected president since Martin van Buren in 1836. After combat duty

President George Bush (left) and his vice president, J. Danforth Quayle. (Office of the Vice President)

as a navy pilot in World War II, he earned a bachelor's degree in economics from Yale University in 1948, then moved to Texas and prospered in the oil industry. After two terms in the House of Representatives representing Texas (1967–1971), he was appointed ambassador to the United Nations (1971–1973) by President Richard M. Nixon. After serving as chairman of the Republican National Committee (1973–1974), he was appointed chief of the U.S. Liaison Office (effectively ambassador) in China (1974–1975). He returned to be director of the Central Intelligence Agency (1976–1977) for President Gerald Ford. Bush was Ronald Reagan's main competition for the Republican presidential nomination in 1980 but accepted Reagan's offer of the vice presidency.

As president, Bush continued to wind down the COLD WAR with the Soviet Union, used military force in 1989 to overthrow and arrest the Panamanian dictator Manuel Noriega, and after the Iraqi invasion of Kuwait in 1990 committed massive American forces to defend Saudi Arabia and liberate Kuwait. Domestically he was plagued by continuing large deficits and a lengthy recession. This, coupled with criticism that he seemed to lack a clear vision for the NEW WORLD ORDER he espoused, led to his defeat for reelection in 1992. *See also* PANAMA INTERVENTION; PERSIAN GULF WAR.

Buthelezi, Mangosuthu Gatsha (1928–   ) The leader of the Zulu tribe in South Africa and the head of the INKATHA FREEDOM PARTY, the traditional rival of the AFRICAN NATIONAL CONGRESS.

Butler, Nicholas Murray (1862–1947) The president of Columbia University in New York (1901–1945) who shared the 1931 Nobel Peace Prize with JANE ADDAMS for his work in establishing, and as president (1925–1945) of, the Carnegie Endowment for International Peace. Butler was a major advocate of the KELLOGG-BRIAND PACT.

Butterfield, Herbert (1900–1979) The British historian whose early writings, such as *Christianity and History* (1950), offered a Christian perspective on history that, in opposition to many social scientists, reasserted the critical role of individuals and individual choice in history. In 1958 Butterfield founded and then chaired the British Committee on the Theory of International Politics, which took a historical and religious perspective on the notions of war and peace, the nation-state system, and foreign policy. He wrote in *Christianity, Diplomacy and War* (1953), "The greatest menace to our civilization today is the conflict between giant organized systems of self-righteousness—each system only too delighted to find that the other is wicked—each only too glad that the other's sins give it the pretext for still deeper hatred and animosity." Butterfield had a real sense of the tragic in international politics and saw one of its key problems as our inability to see into the minds of others and thereby be reassured that they do not intend harm. As he wrote in "Morality and International Order" (in Brian Porter, ed., *The Aberystwyth Papers*, 1972): "In the realm of international politics . . . there is a fundamental human predicament which conditions both the men and their conduct, conditions even the virtuous, helping to generate their fears and to shape their policies." The nature of this predicament was that power provoked fear even when there was no intention of using it to inflict harm. This in turn led to countermeasures, which in turn produced counterfears. In essence Butterfield saw the nature of the SECURITY DILEMMA as one of the constantly recurring themes in international politics.

button, the The symbolic starting device for a nuclear war. Thus, "pushing the button" has become a metaphor for the end of the world.

buy national acts Laws, first passed in the 1930s, that require government agencies to give a preference to domestic-made goods when making purchases. "Buy national" practices are used by all major trading states.

Byrnes, James F. (1879–1972) U.S. Secretary of State from 1945 to 1947. A former U.S. Senator (1931–1941) from South Carolina and Supreme Court Associate Justice (1941–1942), he was an advisor to President Franklin D. Roosevelt at the YALTA CONFERENCE and, as secretary of state, accompanied President Harry S Truman to the POTSDAM CONFERENCE.

C

cabinet **1.** The leaders of the executive branch departments of a government who report to and advise its chief executive; for example, the president's cabinet, the prime minister's cabinet. **2.** The staff advisors to a EUROPEAN COMMUNITY commissioner, headed by a chef de cabinet. Liaisons among the various chefs de cabinet are a critical element in the EC administrative machinery. **3.** A group of legislators from the majority party in a parliament who are chosen by the head of their party (the prime minister) to administer the major departments of the government. They, led by the prime minister, are collectively responsible for all government policies.

cabinet government **1.** A PARLIAMENTARY SYSTEM in which the CABINET as a whole, rather than just the prime minister who heads it, is considered the executive. The cabinet is collectively responsible for its performance. In the United Kingdom, cabinet ministers are typically drawn from among the majority party's members in Parliament; in COALITION governments, the cabinet reflects the multiparty nature of the legislature. **2.** A concept informally applied to a new American president's assertion that cabinet members are going to work together as a team. Such team spirit usually does not last long.

Cable News Network *See* CNN.

cabotage **1.** Coastal trade or navigation. **2.** A state's requirement that passengers and goods being transported within the state be carried by local (not foreign) carriers. **3.** In the context of the EUROPEAN COMMUNITY, the right of all transport compa-nies of all member states to operate freely anywhere in the EC.

Cabral, Amilcar (1921–1973) The Guinean nationalist who led the political and military fight for the independence of the Portuguese colony of Guinea in Africa. By the late 1960s he was the de facto ruler of those parts of the colony not occupied by Portuguese troops. He was assassinated 20 months before Portugal recognized the independence of the republic of Guinea-Bissau in 1974.

cadre **1.** The most dedicated members of a political party. In countries where the Communist party is the ruling party, cadre usually refers to a party member who holds a responsible position in the party organization or the government (or both). If it is a high official position, such officeholders are often referred to as the high-ranking cadre. **2.** The founding members of a political organization who thereupon expand the organization by enlisting new members. **3.** A detachment from an existing organization capable of being the nucleus about which a new large organizational unit can be built. In a military context, cadres of commissioned as well as noncommissioned officers have always been a critical element in the rapid expansion of an army.

Cairo Conference The World War II meeting of U.S. President Franklin D. Roosevelt, British Prime Minister Winston Churchill, and China's General Chiang Kai-shek held in Cairo, Egypt, from November 22 to 26, 1943. The conference was designed to enhance the stature of Chiang and approve his war plans against Japan. Here it was decided that Taiwan was part of China and that Korea would be a free, united, and independent nation after the war. The Soviet Union accepted this last proposition at the YALTA CONFERENCE.

Cali cartel   A group of drug dealers based in the Colombian city of Cali. In the early 1990s, the Cali cartel surpassed the MEDELLIN CARTEL as the largest producer of cocaine and the most important force in the drug trade in Colombia. According to the U.S. Drug Enforcement Administration, as reported in *Time* (July 1, 1991), the Cali cartel produces about 70 percent of the cocaine entering the United States and about 90 percent of the cocaine entering Europe. The drug cartels have massively corrupted the government of Colombia. This fact has strained relations with the United States, which wants greater and more effective cooperation with Colombia to curb illicit drug traffic. Because the Cali is less violent than the Medellin cartel, it has attracted less attention and has consequently been more success- ful in its illegal activities.

Callaghan, (Leonard) James (1912–   )   The La- bour Party Foreign Secretary (1971–1976) who succeeded HAROLD WILSON as prime minister of Great Britain in 1976. After a series of disruptive labor strikes, he was defeated by Conservative MAR- GARET THATCHER in the 1979 general election. He then retired as leader of his party.

de Callieres, François (1645–1717)   The French diplomat whose classic *On the Manner of Negotiat- ing with Princes* (1716) offers the following advice that is still sound: "The government cannot exercise too great a care in its choice of men to serve abroad. In making such a choice the Foreign Minister must set his face like a flint against all family influence and private pressure, for nepotism is the damnation of diplomacy."

calling cards   The business identification cards of diplomatic agents on which are printed the diplo- mat's name, rank, and embassy. On arrival at a post (and depending on custom), the cards are delivered to other members of the diplomatic community as a means of introduction. Traditionally, a newly arrived foreign service officer sends (or the ambas- sador has sent on his or her behalf) two cards and one of his or her spouse's cards to all appropriate members of the DIPLOMATIC CORPS. The two cards are meant for each diplomat and her or his spouse.

Calvo clause   A provision customarily incorpo- rated into business contracts with foreign investors in South America: that foreign nationals party to the contract will rely exclusively on legal remedies of the Latin government to resolve disputes over the contract and not seek diplomatic intervention in disputes by their home states. While such clauses seek to operationalize the CALVO DOCTRINE, their validity has been disputed because a private con- tract cannot prevent a state from exercising its right under international law to offer diplomatic assis- tance to one of its citizens. The United States has refused to relinquish its right to intervene for its aggrieved citizens when the host country refuses to allow arbitration.

Calvo Doctrine   The principle first advanced in 1868 by Argentine jurist Carlos Calvo (1824–1906) of the immunity of a sovereign state from external intervention; that the final authority on internal matters must be the host state's judicial system. Consequently, diplomatic pressure or military force on behalf of the business interests of foreigners is improper. The doctrine was meant to prevent U.S. intervention on behalf of foreign investors in Argentina. The later DRAGO DOCTRINE is a restate- ment of the Calvo Doctrine.

Cambodian holocaust   The murder of an estimated 1.5 to 3 million Cambodians (out of a total popula- tion of less than 8 million) by the KHMER ROUGE, the Communist guerrilla force that took control of the country after U.S. support was withdrawn in 1975. The new regime, led by POL POT, ordered the evacu- ation of all cities and towns, sending the entire pop- ulation out into the countryside to till the land. Thousands starved or died of disease during the evacuation. Many of those forced to evacuate the cities were resettled in "new villages," which lacked all provision for food or medical care. Those who resisted or who questioned orders were executed immediately, as were most military and civil leaders of the former regime. The new government sought to restructure Cambodian society completely. The regime controlled every aspect of life and reduced everyone to the level of abject obedience through terror. Public executions of those considered unreliable or discovered to have links with the previous government were common. Torture centers were established where detailed records were kept of the thousands murdered there. Few succeeded in fleeing the country or escaping the military patrols. Agriculture was collectivized, and the surviving part of the industrial base was abandoned or placed under state control. Cambodia was left with neither a national currency nor a banking system. Although solid estimates of the number who died between 1975 and 1979 are not available, it is known that hundreds of thousands were executed by the regime, often most brutally. Hundreds of thousands more died of starvation and disease. The massive killing did not stop until the Vietnamese occupied most of the country and the Khmer Rouge fled to remote areas. This occupation began with border skirmishes in 1973, which intensified to full-scale battles by 1977. Deep ethnic hatreds between the Cambodians and the Vietnamese made a peaceful solution difficult. Then in 1978 a Vietnamese invasion force (backed by the Soviet Union) defeated the Khmer Rouge (backed by China) in what many analysts consider to have been a PROXY WAR. By 1979 the Vietnamese occupied the capital city of Phnom Penh. The Vietnamese would stay until a United Nations–sponsored peace plan in 1991 allowed Cambodia's former ruler NORODOM SIHANOUK to return and form a transitional government pending elections.

Cambodian incursion   The April-to-June 1970 invasion by U.S. and South Vietnamese forces of North Vietnamese and Vietcong staging areas and sanctuaries in neutral Cambodia. This action was defended as an attempt to buy the time needed to make the South Vietnamese army self-sufficient while U.S. troops in South Vietnam were increasingly reduced. The incursion, which came on top of a secret bombing campaign, set off violent demonstrations in the United States against the VIETNAM WAR. It was justified by U.S. President Richard Nixon as being necessary to prevent the United States from being seen as a helpless giant in the face of a real crisis. The incursion precipitated a civil war in Cambodia that led to the creation of the Communist state of Kampuchea in 1975.

NIXON'S RATIONALE

Tonight, American and South Vietnamese units will attack the headquarters for the entire Communist military operation in South Vietnam. This key control center [located in Cambodia] has been occupied by the North Vietnamese and Vietcong for five years in blatant violation of Cambodia's neutrality.

This is not an invasion of Cambodia. The areas in which these attacks will be launched are completely occupied and controlled by North Vietnamese forces. Our purpose is not to occupy the areas. Once enemy forces are driven out of these sanctuaries and once their military supplies are destroyed, we will withdraw.

SOURCE: U.S. President Richard M. Nixon, speech to the nation on the incursion into Cambodia, April 30, 1970. Nixon, according to author William Shawcross in *Sideshow* (1979), lied in this speech about attacking "the headquarters for the entire Communist military operation in South Vietnam," because he had been specifically told by his secretary of defense, Melvin Laird, that no such "key control center" existed. And it was supreme cynicism for Nixon to complain that the enemy was "in blatant violation of Cambodia's neutrality" when the United States also had been conducting military operations there, mainly bombing, for more than a year.

Cambridge Spy Ring   A group of upper-class British subjects who were recruited to spy for the Soviet Union while they were students at Cambridge University in the 1920s and 1930s. The most notorious were ANTHONY BLUNT, GUY BURGESS, DONALD MACLEAN, and KIM PHILBY. *See also* FIFTH MAN.

Cameroon plebiscite   The 1961 election in the British Cameroons in Africa, held under United Nations auspices to allow the citizens to practice self-determination in government. After World War I Cameroon, which had been under German control, was divided between France and the United Kingdom. In 1946 the French and British mandates were converted by the United Nations into trusteeships. In 1958 the UN General Assembly voted to end the French trusteeship, which became independent as the republic of Cameroon in 1960. Thus the 1961 plebiscite was conducted to determine whether the people there wished union with Nigeria or with the New Republic of Cameroon. The voters in the northern two sections chose to join Nigeria;

those in the southern section, Cameroon. The southern part was unified in 1961, and the new Federal Republic of Cameroon was born. From 1961 until the spring of 1972, Cameroon was governed as a federation, with East (formerly French) Cameroon and West (formerly British) Cameroon having individual governments, each with a parliament and ministries, in addition to the federal government structure. A 1972 referendum created a unitary government, the United Republic of Cameroon. In 1984 a constitutional amendment changed the official name to simply the Republic of Cameroon.

campaign 1. Continuous operations leading toward a known goal, a clearly defined single objective—such as selling a product, electing a candidate, or defeating an enemy. 2. Synchronized military operations conducted throughout a THEATER OF WAR employing all land, sea, and air forces to achieve national or alliance strategic objectives. Within a theater of war, "theaters of operations" may be established to better coordinate and focus combat efforts. In this case, campaigns are devised to achieve large-scale strategic objectives. The traditional military campaign began when the combatant force left its home base to engage the enemy and ended when it returned home—victorious or defeated.

Campaign for Nuclear Disarmament (CND) Founded in 1958 in the United Kingdom, this is the West's oldest major antinuclear protest movement. The activities of the CND provided an additional chapter in a long tradition of dissent from British foreign and defense policy. It was composed of a wide spectrum of British citizens and received mass support based on fear of nuclear war. It marked the breakdown of the all-party consensus on postwar British foreign policy that placed considerable emphasis on the North Atlantic Treaty Organization and on the development of Britain's own independent nuclear deterrent. The CND worked partly through mass demonstrations and partly by getting the left wing of the Labour Party to call for unilateral nuclear disarmament. In the early 1960s the Labour Party rejected UNILATERALISM, the CND's main goal. In the 1980s, however, the CND emerged as a force once again. This time, though, it was part of a broader European movement for nuclear disarmament. It was fueled initially by the neutron bomb debate of

the late 1970s and then by what was widely seen in Europe as the belligerent and frightening approach of the United States under the Reagan Administration. Once again, the movement had a major impact on the Labour Party. In two elections during the 1980s, the party presented a platform that included unilateral nuclear disarmament—and lost overwhelmingly. In the aftermath of these two electoral defeats, the party moved away from this position and embraced MULTILATERALISM. The DÉTENTE of the latter half of the 1980s and the subsequent end of the COLD WAR further defused the nuclear issue in Britain and elsewhere. *See also* BERTRAND RUSSELL.

Campbell-Bannerman, Henry (1836–1908) The Liberal Party prime minister of Great Britain from 1905 to 1908. His administration gave self-government to white South Africa and negotiated the ENTENTE CORDIALE with Russia in 1907.

Camp David The U.S. president's vacation home in the Catoctin Mountains in Maryland. Called Shangri-La by President Franklin D. Roosevelt (after the mystical place of enchantment in James Hilton's 1933 novel, *Lost Horizon*), its name was changed to Camp David by President Dwight D. Eisenhower in honor of his grandson. Camp David is no Spartan camp; it has a swimming pool, a bowling alley, tennis courts, and a movie theater, among other luxuries. Ever since the Eisenhower Administration of the 1950s, all presidents have used Camp David for diplomatic meetings with foreign officials. Indeed, since the camp is far more informal and private than the White House, an invitation is considered a special honor.

Camp David, Spirit of The temporary thaw in the COLD WAR brought about by the 1959 summit meeting at Camp David in the United States between U.S. President Dwight D. Eisenhower and Soviet Premier Nikita S. Khrushchev. The intention was to transform this conciliatory spirit into a comprehensive settlement of Cold War issues during the PARIS SUMMIT CONFERENCE OF 1960, but the U-2 INCIDENT prevented this.

Camp David Accords The international agreements negotiated and signed in September of 1978 by Egyptian President Anwar Sadat and Israeli

Prime Minister Menachem Begin at Camp David in the United States. President Jimmy Carter sequestered the two heads of state at Camp David while he and his staff mediated the agreements.

The first agreement, entitled "A Framework for Peace in the Middle East," provided for a five-year transitional period for the WEST BANK and the GAZA STRIP. During this phase the existing Israeli military government in these regions would be replaced by a Palestinian self-governing authority to be set up following negotiations among Egypt, Israel, and Jordan, with Palestinian representation. The document further provided for the withdrawal of some Israeli forces from the occupied territories and for the confinement of the remainder to specified locations. The final status of occupied Palestine was left for subsequent negotiation. Jordan, Lebanon, and Syria were invited to negotiate with Israel on the basis of this document. Because of Palestinian opposition, they never did.

The second agreement, entitled "Framework for the Conclusion of a Peace Treaty Between Egypt and Israel," provided for an Israeli-Egyptian peace treaty by December 17, 1978 (signed March 26, 1979). The second agreement also required an eventual Israeli military withdrawal to its 1967 Sinai frontier, the removal of Israeli settlements in the Sinai region, a largely demilitarized Sinai with United Nations forces on the border and at Sharm el Sheikh, and unrestricted passage for Israeli shipping through the Suez Canal in exchange for Egypt's diplomatic recognition of Israel and of Israel's right to exist as a nation. This second agreement was fully implemented. The Camp David Accords were a great achievement of the Carter Administration. Carter notes in *Keeping Faith: Memoirs of a President* (1982) that "Henry Kissinger telephoned to congratulate me, saying that I was working him out of his career of criticizing the government by not leaving him much to criticize." Given Kissinger's role in the DISENGAGEMENT negotiations after the Yom Kippur War of October 1973, this was perhaps the ultimate accolade.

Camus, Albert (1913–1960)   The French novelist and philosopher, winner of the 1957 Nobel Prize in literature, who also wrote influential essays on the nature of rebellion and the role of terrorism in political revolutions. While he wrote of the admirable and morally correct sacrifice of one's life in an act of violence directed against a repressive entity, he condemned mass revolutionary terror. His major works are *The Stranger* (1942), *The Myth of Sisyphus* (1942), and *The Plague* (1947).

U.S. President Jimmy Carter with Egyptian President Anwar Sadat (left) and Israeli Prime Minister Menachem Begin (right) after the signing of the Camp David Accords. (Jimmy Carter Library)

Canaris, Wilhelm   *See* ABWEHR.

Cancun Summit   The 1981 International Meeting on Cooperation and Development held in Cancun, Mexico, in response to the BRANDT COMMISSION recommendation for a North-South summit. The summit was attended by heads of state or government from 22 developing and developed countries. Its chief purposes were to discuss procedures for global economic negotiations and to consider how best to approach the economic problems of the developing world. The 14 developing countries represented were Algeria, Bangladesh, Brazil, China, Guyana, Ivory Coast, India, Mexico, Nigeria, the Philippines, Saudi Arabia, Tanzania, Venezuela, and Yugoslavia. Representing the developed world was Austria, Canada, France, West Germany, Japan, Sweden, the United Kingdom, and the United States. The talks failed to resolve the major differences between the groups, such as the developing nations' demand that the United Nations exercise authority over international agencies such as the World Bank. *Compare to* COMMITTEE OF THE WHOLE; CONFERENCE ON INTERNATIONAL ECONOMIC COOPERATION; NORTH-SOUTH DIALOGUE.

CAP   *See* COMMON AGRICULTURAL POLICY.

capability   **1.** The capacity to do something, which depends on having certain kinds of resources. Although it is often used in relation to military matters, the concept of capability is more general and may consist of various dimensions—economic and political as well as military. **2.** A measure that is used, albeit very roughly, to determine the position of states in the power hierarchy of international politics. **3.** The ability to do a particular kind of thing such as mount a military attack. Strategists analyze the capabilities as well as the intentions of a state to assess what degree of threat it represents.

capacity building   The development of a nation's physical and human INFRASTRUCTURE for economic advancement. The term is used in the context of the THIRD WORLD to refer to the needs for better ports, bridges, and roads as well as a better-trained and educated work force.

capital   The designation applied in economic theory to one of the three traditional factors of production, the others being land and labor. Capital can refer either to physical resources such as plant and equipment or to financial resources such as cash or credit.

capital account   In international finance, that part of the BALANCE OF PAYMENTS that comprises short- and long-term international financial flows, such as those associated with investment in government and private securities, direct investment abroad, and foreign bank deposits. *Compare to* CURRENT ACCOUNT.

capital flight   **1.** The removal of financial capital from a state to safer places where interest rates are higher and inflation is lower or to escape confiscation by a government. **2.** The illegal movement of stolen funds across international borders to escape taxation or other unpopular economic conditions.

capitalism   **1.** The private ownership of a state's productive capacities along with a largely unrestricted marketplace for goods and services. **2.** An economic system characterized by a combination of private property, a generally unrestricted marketplace of goods and services, and a general assumption that the bulk of the work force will be engaged in employment by private (nongovernmental) employers engaged in producing goods to sell at a profit. Scottish economist Adam Smith (1723–1790) provided the first systematic analysis of the economic phenomena of laissez-fare capitalism. In *The Wealth of Nations* (1776), Smith described an "invisible hand" that promotes the general welfare as long as individuals pursue their self-interest. To advocates of capitalism, this form of economic organization provides the greatest chance of maximizing economic performance and defending political liberty while securing something approaching equality of opportunity. However, unrestrained laissez-faire capitalism is today only a theory because all of the capitalist societies of the West have MIXED ECONOMIES that temper capitalism with government regulation and social welfare measures. *Compare to* MARXISM.

capitalist encirclement   The traditional fear of the Soviet Union that the capitalist world sought actively to bring about its downfall. From its inception in 1917 to its dissolution in 1991, the Soviet Union met with hostility from capitalist governments. Over a dozen states sent troops to support the White Russians against the Bolshevik revolutionaries in 1917. The new Soviet Union was forced to make large concessions to Germany in exchange for peace in 1918. Hitler's invasion in 1941 killed more than 20 million Soviet citizens. During the COLD WAR the U.S. policy of CONTAINMENT worked to place capitalistic military power around the Soviet periphery. Thus the Soviet Union's fears were not irrational. As the Cold War ebbed so did the historic fear of capitalist encirclement. Indeed beginning in the 1990s, many Russians and citizens of former Soviet republics were rushing to become capitalists themselves.

capital sector   The world economy as a whole wherein investment funds (capital) flow with relative ease across national borders.

capital ship   The biggest and most powerful class of warship of any given era. Until World War II traditional BATTLESHIPS were the capital ships of all major navies, but advancing tactics and technology saw them replaced by the AIRCRAFT CARRIER.

capitulary armistice   *See* ARMISTICE.

capitulation   1. The SURRENDER of an armed force, a town, or a fort.   2. A formal agreement between belligerents stating the terms of surrender of troops or places.

capitulations   Treaty provisions for EXTRATERRITORIALITY that exempted foreign nationals from the jurisdiction of local courts. Instead, foreign nationals charged with crimes were tried by their own courts, often by their local CONSUL. Capitulations date at least from 1536, when the sultans of the Ottoman Empire allowed France, through its consuls, to apply French law to French citizens in Turkey. Other European powers soon obtained similar powers in Turkey, and this practice spread to states such as China, Egypt, and Morocco. As such states were increasingly able to resist European pressures, they developed their own sophisticated legal systems and increasingly resented European interference; capitulations gradually faded away. Today the very suggestion would be considered a gross breach of SOVEREIGNTY.

captive nations   A COLD WAR term used by Westerners for the Soviet satellite states of Eastern Europe: the Baltic States, Bulgaria, Czechoslovakia, East Germany, Hungary, Poland, and Romania.

Caraballeda Declaration   The statement signed by the foreign ministers of the CONTADORA GROUP and the LIMA GROUP at their 1986 joint meeting in Caraballeda, Venezuela. It called for participation by Nicaragua and the United States in peace negotiations; an end to external support for irregular forces and insurgencies; reduction of arms acquisitions; reduction of foreign military advisors and installations; adoption of measures to achieve national reconciliation, pluralist democracy, and full respect for human rights; and creation of a Central American parliament. The statement was subsequently endorsed by Costa Rica, El Salvador, Guatemala, Honduras, and Nicaragua as well as by the European Community and Japan. *See also* CONTRAS; REAGAN DOCTRINE.

Cárdenas, Lázaro del Rio (1895–1970)   The Mexican President (1934–1940) who was known for his efforts to implement the social and economic goals of the MEXICAN REVOLUTION. During his administration, he implemented the provisions of the Constitution of 1917, expropriating unused land from private owners and nationalizing the subsoil, giving ownership of oil reserves to the state. In 1938 the Mexican government expropriated foreign oil companies, nationalized the petroleum industry, and created Petroleos Mexicanos (PEMEX) to manage the oil industry. Cárdenas also improved labor conditions, social welfare, and the educational system. For these actions, some have called Cárdenas the last "revolutionary" president of Mexico. He was succeeded by Manuel Ávila Camacho (1897–1955) who served as president from 1940 to 1946.

Caribbean Basin Initiative   An inter-American program of economic aid and trade preferences for 28 states of the Caribbean region. It was begun by U.S. President Ronald Reagan in an address to the Organization of American States meeting in Washington in 1982. The initiative provided for 12 years of duty-free access to the U.S. market for most Caribbean Basin products. The program was later extended by the Customs and Trade Act of 1990.

Caribbean Community and Common Market (Caricom) Established by a treaty signed at Chaguaramas, Trinidad, in 1973, Caricom's purposes are to promote regional economic integration and development and to coordinate the foreign policies of the member states. In May 1974 Caricom officially replaced the former Caribbean Free Trade Association (CARIFTA). Caricom has 13 members: Antigua and Barbuda, the Bahamas, Barbados, Belize, Dominica, Grenada, Guyana, Jamaica, Montserrat, St. Christopher and Nevis, St. Lucia, St. Vincent and the Grenadines, and Trinidad and Tobago. The Dominican Republic, Haiti, and Surinam are observers. Its headquarters are in Georgetown, Guyana. *See also:* OCHO RIOS DECLARATION; ORGANIZATION OF EASTERN CARIBBEAN STATES.

Caribbean Development Bank The regional DEVELOPMENT BANK created in 1970 to promote the economic cooperation and integration of the less-developed states of the Caribbean.

Carlos (1950–   ) Alias of Ilyich Ramirez Sanchez, the Venezuelan-born international terrorist popularly known as "Carlos the Jackal." Carlos, among the best known of modern terrorists, has been associated with many terrorist organizations, most notably the POPULAR FRONT FOR THE LIBERATION OF PALESTINE.

Carnegie Endowment for International Peace Founded and funded in 1910 by the American philanthropist Andrew Carnegie (1836–1919), this U.S. organization continues to operate programs of research and publications on foreign policy issues; it publishes the influential journal *Foreign Policy. See also* NICHOLAS MURRAY BUTLER.

carnet A customs document permitting the holder to carry or send merchandise temporarily into cer-

tain foreign countries (for display, demonstration, or similar purposes) without paying duties or posting bonds.

Carr, Edward Hallett (1892–1982) The British diplomat and scholar who was one of the first modern proponents of political REALISM in the analysis of international relations. Carr's *The Twenty Years' Crisis, 1919–1939: An Introduction to the Study of International Relations* (1939; 2d ed., 1946) was written "with the deliberate aim of counteracting the glaring and dangerous defect of nearly all thinking, both academic and popular, about international politics in English-speaking countries from 1919 to 1939—the almost total neglect of the factor of power." It was a landmark in the development of international relations theory. In it Carr argued that in the idealist or utopian vision of international relations, wishing had "prevailed over thinking." He also held that there is not a natural harmony of interest among states. Although his incisive indictment of idealism is often held up by realists as a seminal development, Carr's position on realism was not one of unadulterated support. As he wrote in *The Twenty Years' Crisis:*

> Realism itself, if we attack it with its own weapons, often turns out in practice to be just as much conditioned as any other mode of thought. In politics, the belief that certain facts are unalterable or certain trends irresistible commonly reflects a lack of desire or lack of interest to change or resist them. The impossibility of being a thorough-going realist is one of the most certain and most curious lessons of political science. Consistent realism excludes four things which appear to be essential ingredients of all effective political thinking: a finite goal, an emotional appeal, a right of moral judgment and a ground for action.

Carr's Marxist orientation colored both his works and subsequent analyses of them. His chief historical contribution is his ten-volume *A History of Soviet Russia* (1950–1977), which examines the social, economic, and political life of the Soviet Union but downplays crueler facets of the Soviet state. In this work, Carr shows events and decisions through the eyes of Lenin and other Soviet leaders.

cartel 1. A formal alliance or informal arrangement among industrial, commercial, or state-controlled enterprises in the same type of business designed to secure international control of a commodity. A cartel usually seeks to regulate production so as to raise prices and maximize profits. Cartels almost always fail in their goals if there are ample supplies of the commodity or available substitutes. In the end even temporarily successful cartels fail because they often drive up prices to such an extent that new sources enter the market. The only notable exception to universal cartel failure is the de Beers diamond cartel: as the single major buyer of all the world's diamonds, it has been able to control the market since the turn of the century. 2. An agreement between BELLIGERENT states to arrange for specified nonhostile relations, such as an exchange of wounded or postal communications.

cartel ship An unarmed ship in time of war sailing under a guarantee of freedom from attack or capture. A cartel ship usually carries prisoners to be exchanged.

Carter, James Earl "Jimmy" (1924–) The president of the United States from 1977 to 1981. He enunciated a foreign policy that placed considerable emphasis on human rights, nuclear nonproliferation, North-South relations, and other issues relating to international order. The Carter Administration was instrumental in investigating the state terror of Argentina's DIRTY WAR and pressuring that government to curb its abuses of human rights. Its policy of making human rights a cornerstone of U.S. foreign policy was considered exemplary by some and naive by others. In Carter's initial conception, CONTAINMENT of the Soviet Union was to be transcended. However, Soviet geopolitical gains in the Third World together with domestic pressures—including those from his own national security advisor, ZBIGNIEW BRZEZINSKI—compelled Carter to adopt a tougher line. With the Soviet invasion of Afghanistan in December 1979, Carter reluctantly reverted to Cold War policies. Yet the administration was never able to change the image that it was weak and confused. This was partly because of events over which the administration had little control.

The IRANIAN HOSTAGE CRISIS was a major frustration for President Carter and cast a dark shadow over his White House tenure. The seeming paralysis of the U.S. government that ensued from the November 4, 1979, seizure of the U.S. Embassy in Tehran and its 52 occupants was a serious blow to the Carter Administration and to the president's hopes for reelection. Carter's initial response to the crisis was an economic boycott and the severing of diplomatic relations. On April 24, 1980, the President approved, over the objections of Cyrus Vance, his secretary of state, an ill-fated military rescue attempt, in which eight U.S. servicemen died. Vance resigned in protest and the domestic situation grew worse. Carter was defeated in the November 1980 election by Ronald Reagan. On January 20, 1981, Reagan's inauguration day, Iran released the hostages. While Carter was disdained by many as president, he has since become widely respected for the way in which he conducts his "ex-presidency." Instead of seeking to generate personal wealth, he has sought a life of good works by, for example, building homes for the homeless or mediating Third World conflicts.

Carter Doctrine The policy put forth by U.S. President Jimmy Carter in his State of the Union address to Congress on January 23, 1980: "An attempt by any outside forces to gain control of the Persian Gulf region will be regarded as an assault on the vital interests of the United States of America, and such an assault will be repelled by any means necessary, including military force." The press called this statement the Carter Doctrine and characterized it as a reversal of the NIXON DOCTRINE. The policy was directed at the Soviet Union, since it represented the only "outside force" capable of gaining control of the Persian Gulf. The doctrine was a response to the 1979 Soviet AFGHANISTAN INTERVENTION, which was widely interpreted in the United States as a geopolitical move toward the gulf and as the culmination of the expansionist policy that the Soviet Union had followed throughout the 1970s. The promulgation of the Carter Doctrine was also the U.S. response to the failure of the Nixon Doctrine, as demonstrated by the fall of Iran's MOHAMMED REZA PAHLEVI, who had been the United States' surrogate gendarme in the Gulf. Without a surrogate, the United States had to revert to more direct involvement. This message was underlined by the creation of a Rapid Deployment Joint Task Force (or Rapid Deployment Force [RDF] for short) on March 1, 1980, to deal with contingencies in the Gulf. The Carter Doctrine and the RDF also reflected the abandonment of the DETENTE policy of the 1970s and the return to COLD WAR policies.

U.S. policy in the Gulf since the Carter Doctrine has been fully consistent with the notion that the United States has vital interests at stake there. The RE-FLAGGING policy during the IRAN-IRAQ WAR as well as the PERSIAN GULF WAR against Iraq were exercises in the implementation of the Carter Doctrine. Moreover, although the standard joke about the RDF was that it was not very rapid, not easily deployable, and not much of a force, its creation not only marked a change in U.S. thinking about military intervention but provided the command structure to facilitate future intervention. During the 1980s the RDF was transformed into U.S. Central Command, which provided the operational command structure for the war in the Persian Gulf in early 1991.

Casablanca Conference   The January 1943 meeting between U.S. President Franklin D. Roosevelt and British Prime Minister Winston Churchill following the successful Allied invasion of North Africa. There it was decided that the war would be continued until the "unconditional surrender" of Germany and Japan was obtained, that Sicily would be invaded next, that the cross-channel invasion of France would be delayed until spring 1944, and that the bombing of Germany would be increased.

Case Act   *See* EXECUTIVE AGREEMENT.

Casement, Roger D. (1864–1916)   The Irish leader who sought German support for an Irish revolt against Great Britain during World War I. He was executed by the British for treason.

Casey, William Joseph (1913–1987)   The director of the CENTRAL INTELLIGENCE AGENCY from 1981 to 1987. A World War II spymaster (working for the OFFICE OF STRATEGIC SERVICES, he sent agents behind NAZI lines), he became Ronald Reagan's presidential

campaign director in 1980 and was rewarded with the directorship of the CIA. During his tenure he backed extensive covert activities in Afghanistan, Angola, Cambodia, Nicaragua, and elsewhere. Various sources have asserted that he had major roles in the IRAN-CONTRA AFFAIR and the OCTOBER SURPRISE; he died of a brain tumor before he could be adequately questioned on these charges. But even had he lived, he probably would have shed little light on these matters because he was notorious for maintaining his DENIABILITY.

CASEY'S EVASION

[Casey] bears heavy responsibility [for the Iran-contra affair]. He was an early and enthusiastic convert to what even his loyal friend William F. Buckley described as "a hare-brained scheme." Casey's support was so unwavering at points when the enterprise looked dead that he deserves billing as co-architect. His greatest sin, however, was his willingness to leave Congress in the dark, a clear violation of his lawful responsibility as DCI [Director of Central Intelligence] regarding covert operations. Had Casey insisted, at any point, that he would not touch a finding that ordered him not to notify Congress, the whole idea would likely have collapsed on the spot. Instead, he embraced the evasion.

SOURCE: Joseph E. Persico, *Casey* (1990).

---

cash and carry   A retail policy of selling something without credit and without delivery included. This phrase was widely used in the context of U.S. neutrality prior to its entry into World War II. It was felt that if the United States sold goods to foreign states for cash and required the purchaser to transport the goods overseas, then the United States could stay out of the European war and still help France and Great Britain.

Cassin, René (1887–1976)   The French jurist who won the 1968 Nobel Peace Prize for his work in drafting the 1948 United Nations UNIVERSAL DECLARATION OF HUMAN RIGHTS.

Castro, Fidel (1926–   )   The revolutionary and Communist leader of Cuba who assumed power following the 1959 revolution. Beginning in the 1950s, Castro began to organize opposition to Cuban dicta-

Fidel Castro (seated) as a young guerrilla leader. (Library of Congress)

tor FULGENCIO BATISTA. He was jailed from 1953 to 1955 following a failed attack on a military barracks. Leading a revolutionary force called the 26th of July Movement, Castro initiated a three-year guerrilla war against Batista that culminated in the fall of Batista's government in 1959. As prime minister of Cuba, Castro purged the moderate elements of the anti-Batista forces by 1960 and sought alliances with the Soviet Union. His government nationalized industry, redistributed land, increased wages, and improved health care and education. Castro, a dynamic speaker, has retained power over the island's politics, serving as chief executive officer of the Communist Party of Cuba (Partido Comunista de Cuba) and president of the State Council of the Cuban National Assembly since 1976. In foreign affairs, Cuba has been a primary sponsor of revolutionary movements in Latin America and in Africa.

Though none of these groups has been able to duplicate the success of Castro's revolution, the lack of success has done little to inhibit him. In 1974–1975 Cuban forces intervened with decisive effect on the side of the MPLA in the ANGOLAN CIVIL WAR. Subsequently between 12,000 and 17,000 Cuban troops supported Ethiopia against Somalia during the war in the HORN OF AFRICA. There has been much speculation about Castro's motives for the African adventures, particularly as his forces suffered considerable casualties. The most likely reason, however, is that he believed Cuba to be fulfilling a revolutionary mission. Whatever the case, in the United States the Cuban forces were seen as proxies of the Soviet Union. This became another factor leading to the decline of superpower DETENTE in the 1970s.

In the 1960s the U.S. Central Intelligence Agency, unsettled by Castro's alliance with the Soviets and his attempts to export his revolution, made several attempts on his life (including poisoning his famous cigars), as documented by the CHURCH COMMITTEE. But Castro survived them all, and even in the days of PERESTROIKA, GLASNOST, and the fall of the Soviet Union, he remains an unrepentant Marxist.

casus belli   Latin for "cause or grounds of war"; acts of one state that become the reason or pretext for another state to formally declare war. According to Article 51 of the United Nations Charter, war is permissible for individual or collective self-defense on the part of states. Thus the only legitimate *casus belli,* other than those actions sanctioned by the UN Security Council or General Assembly, is that of self-defense. A famous example of a *casus belli* was the 1939 decision of Great Britain and France to live up to their treaty obligations as guarantors of the independence of Poland and declare war on Germany after Poland was invaded and dismembered by Germany and the Soviet Union.

casus foederis   Latin for "cause or grounds of alliance"; the hostile act of one state that entitles the injured state to call upon an allied state to fulfill the terms of an existing treaty of alliance.

catalytic attack   An offensive designed to bring about a war between major powers through the disguised machinations of a third power. In recent decades there has been some concern that a catalytic attack with nuclear weapons by a minor nuclear power could trigger a nuclear war between the major powers.

catalytic war   A military conflict that results from a CATALYTIC ATTACK. During the early days of the development of nuclear strategic theory, such a conflict was a topic of common concern. While fears tended to be exaggerated during the Cold War, as nuclear proliferation occurs and the international system becomes more complex, the possibility of catalytic war may increase rather than diminish.

cathedral   **1.** A major church. **2.** Authoritative: something that comes from a high office or authority. **3.** The "GATT cathedral," more properly called the multilateral agricultural framework of the General Agreement on Tariffs and Trade, a group of major agricultural trading countries (Argentina, Australia, Brazil, Canada, the European Community, India, Japan, New Zealand, and the United States) that meets periodically to discuss international agricultural trade issues. The meetings provide an opportunity for high-level domestic policymakers and agricultural trade policy officials to discuss the implications of domestic agricultural policies on international trade.

Catholic Bishops' letter   A declaration of the U.S. Catholic bishops, published as *The Challenge of Peace* (1983), which examined the moral issues of nuclear weapons. The letter said in part, "We are saying that the decisions about nuclear weapons are among the most pressing moral questions of our age. While these decisions have obvious military and political aspects, they involve fundamental moral choices. In simple terms, we are saying that good ends (defending one's country, protecting freedom, etc.) cannot justify immoral means (the use of weapons which kill indiscriminately and threaten whole societies)." The Catholic bishops were not alone in reaching this conclusion.

caudillismo   Dictatorial rule by a strong political or military personality, the *caudillo. Caudillismo* has long been a defining feature of Latin American politics of both the left and the right. For example, the right-wing Cuban caudillo, FULGENCIO BATISTA, in 1959 was deposed and replaced by the left-wing Cuban caudillo, FIDEL CASTRO.

caudillo   The Spanish word for "dictator." The most famous *caudillo* was Spain's FRANCISCO FRANCO; but the word has also been applied to various South American despots.

CCCN   *See* CUSTOMS CLASSIFICATION.

C cubed   *See* COMMAND, CONTROL AND COMMUNICATIONS.

CDI   *See* CONVENTIONAL DEFENSE INITIATIVE.

CE   The abbreviation for *Communauté Européenne,* "European Community," in French. This abbreviation is often used as a product mark to indicate that the manufacturer has conformed to EC regulations.

cease engagement   **1.** A command that weapons will disengage a particular target or targets and prepare to engage another target.   **2.** A truce between two warring parties.   **3.** An order indicating that the enemy has surrendered. When U.S. Admiral William F. Halsey learned of the Japanese intention to surrender on August 15, 1945, he issued the following order: "Cease firing, but if any enemy planes appear, shoot them down in a friendly fashion."

cease-fire   **1.** The general order to stop firing during an engagement of any military unit.   **2.** A command given to air defense artillery units to refrain from firing on, but to continue to track, an airborne object. Missiles already in flight are permitted to continue to intercept. With regular military units a cease-fire order goes down the chain of command and is implemented easily enough. Often, as in the Arab-Israeli War and the Iran-Iraq War, for example, cease-fires are brokered by third parties, such as the United States or the United Nations. But obtaining cease-fires is much more difficult in the midst of a civil war fought by irregular forces. For example, during the Lebanese Civil War and Yugoslavian Civil War, innumerable cease-fire agreements broke down (and fighting continued) because commanders did not have the ability or the inclination to control the forces on their side.

Ceauşescu, Nicolae (1918–1989)   The Communist dictator of Romania from 1967 to 1989. He was elected to another five-year term as president in 1989, but this term abruptly ended as he and his wife, amid the downfall of communism in East Central Europe, were executed on December 25, 1989, on orders of a revolutionary tribunal. Born to a peasant family, Ceauşescu joined the Communist Party at age 14. He was arrested a year later and spent the years 1936 to 1938 and 1939 to 1944 either in prison or in concentration camps. In 1948 he was appointed deputy minister of agriculture, and by 1950 he had assumed the leadership of the army's political section as deputy minister of the armed forces. Ceauşescu adhered to the "national" faction of the Romanian Communist Party (PCR) and became its first secretary in 1965. He moved to

the position of general secretary a few months later and became the head of state in 1967. Ceauşescu sought a more individual foreign policy, did not participate in the invasion of Czechoslovakia in 1968, and rejected Soviet proposals that Romania remain primarily agrarian. This gained him favor from Western governments. However, by 1989 he was one of the most despised leaders in Europe. He had filled numerous posts with his own family members, rejected all concepts of reform or GLASNOST, and created a large private security force that violently put down any type of protest against his government. As a result of over two decades of his leadership, Romania became the poorest country in East Central Europe.

Cecil, Robert (1864–1958)   The British aristocrat (he was Viscount Cecil of Chelwood) and public official who won the 1937 Nobel Peace Prize for his work in the formation and maintenance of the LEAGUE OF NATIONS. He originated the plan that the League should have social, economic, and humanitarian functions—and thus not be limited to traditional political issues.

ceiling binding   *See* BOUND RATES.

cell   An insular subdivision of a compartmentalized terrorist, intelligence, or guerrilla organization, comprised of perhaps three to five persons, designed to function more or less independently so as to reduce the risk of damage to the overarching organization in the event of infiltration, discovery, arrest, and the like. In a cellular structure, communication and interaction between cells is discouraged in the interest of protecting the integrity of the cell system; similarly, ideally the identity of organizational contacts is revealed to only one member of each cell.

CEN   *Comité Européen de Normalisation,* the EUROPEAN COMMUNITY's manufacturing standards organization, located in Brussels. CENLEC is a parallel organization for electrical products.

censorship   **1.** State control of publications and communications, personal and public. Censorship is one of the hallmarks of authoritarian regimes in Europe from the eighteenth century and of dictatorial regimes worldwide in the twentieth century.

Censorship is never completely effective. When newspapers are formally censored or controlled by the government, informal "underground" presses (such as SAMIZDAT in the Soviet Union) spring up. In Nazi Germany and the Soviet Union censorship extended to the state's reading private mail, jamming radio programs from outside the country, determining what books would be in libraries or bookstores, and mandating what subjects could be taught in schools. This kind of all-embracing censorship is a major distinguishing characteristic of TOTALITARIANISM. **2.** Wartime curtailment of freedom of news reporting and personal communications, undertaken so that the enemy not be given, even inadvertently, useful information. Pressure not to disclose military secrets sometimes results in *self-censorship* by the news media. For example, during the Persian Gulf War the major media reporters, for the most part, acceded to a pool system whereby a small number of reporters were allowed limited access to military events but then were obligated to share the fruits of these events (film footage or facts) with all other reporters.

CENSORING HISTORY

[World War II] correspondents had no quarrel with censors. They had a tough job. They didn't know what might be brought up against them. No one could discipline them for eliminating [deleting text from news reports], and so in self-preservation they eliminated pretty deeply. Navy censors were particularly sensitive to names of places, whether they had any military importance or not. It was the safest way. Once when I felt a little bruised by censorship I sent through Herodotus' account of the battle of Salamis fought between the Greeks and Persians in 480 B.C., and since there were place names involved, albeit classical ones, the Navy censors killed the whole story.

SOURCE: John Steinbeck, *Once There Was A War* (1958).

---

center   **1.** The middle.   **2.** The large central *core* of a political constituency whose support (or suppression) is essential to a government if it is to maintain itself in power. Used in this sense, it also implies a sense of moderation as opposed to extremism. In democratic elections parties some-times move their policies to the center to obtain more votes.   **3.** The elite or ruling class within a polity.   **4.** As used in DEPENDENCY THEORY, the center or core refers to the industrialized states of Europe, Japan, and North America.   **5.** During the COLD WAR, the collective term for the leadership of Soviet intelligence operations.

CENTO   *See* CENTRAL TREATY ORGANIZATION.

Central American Common Market   The result of the 1960 General Treaty of Common Customs Tariffs, which provided for the coordination of economic policies between Costa Rica, El Salvador, Guatemala, Honduras, and Nicaragua.

Central American Defense Council (CONDECA)   A military alliance against possible Communist aggression, established on December 14, 1963, with headquarters in Guatemala; the original members were El Salvador, Guatemala, Honduras, and Nicaragua. Honduras withdrew in 1973 and, after the overthrow of the Somoza regime in Nicaragua in 1979, only El Salvador and Guatemala were left as members. At a meeting on October 2, 1983, the defense ministers of El Salvador, Guatemala, and Honduras agreed to revive the council.

central bank   In most countries, the main monetary authority. Functions may include issuing a country's currency, carrying out a nation's monetary policy, and managing its FOREIGN EXCHANGE reserves and the external value of its currency. In the United States, the Federal Reserve System functions as the nation's central bank (although it is not formally a central bank and is subject to only limited influences by the executive and legislative branches). In the United Kingdom the central bank is the Bank of England. In France it is the *Banque de France*. In Germany it is the BUNDESBANK. At a 1991 meeting at MAASTRICHT, the Netherlands, the leaders of the European Community agreed to create a regional central bank by 1999.

Central Europe   The region generally understood to encompass the states of Austria, Czechoslovakia, Germany, Hungary, Poland, Romania, and Switzerland.

central front The border that once existed (1945–1990) between East and West Germany, along which were arrayed the NORTH ATLANTIC TREATY ORGANIZATION and WARSAW PACT armies. This area contained the highest concentration of modern weapons and combat troops in the world. During the COLD WAR it was often seen as the theater in which a third world war most likely would be fought. Consequently, security analysts were preoccupied with the balance of weapons and troops on this front.

Central Intelligence Agency (CIA) The agency created by the National Security Act in 1947 to coordinate intelligence activities for the United States. The director of Central Intelligence, a member of the president's cabinet, is the principal spokesperson for the U.S. INTELLIGENCE COMMUNITY. Both the director and the deputy director of the CIA are appointed by the president by and with the advice and consent of the Senate. Under the direction of the president or the NATIONAL SECURITY COUNCIL, the CIA collects, produces, and disseminates foreign intelligence and counterintelligence. (The collection of foreign intelligence or counterintelligence *within* the United States must be coordinated with the Federal Bureau of Investigation.) The CIA has no police, subpoena, or law enforcement powers, and has no internal security functions. The CIA has often been at the forefront of antiterrorist operations; however, at times some of its covert operations have supported activities that have been deemed illegal. These issues were addressed in the U.S. Senate CHURCH COMMITTEE report, issued in 1976. Instances of CIA activity of which the Senate committee was critical include organizing and/or supporting attempts to overthrow established foreign governments in Iran (1953), Guatemala (1954), and Indonesia (1958). The CIA was implicated in the overthrow of the Allende government in Chile in 1973, including the financing of right-wing Chilean terrorist organizations and the support of a violent military coup. The committee report also cited several CIA plots to assassinate foreign leaders and the CIA's involvement with instruments of state terrorism such as the Iranian secret police organization SAVAK. George Bush, speaking as director of the CIA in 1976, said: "I think the American people support the concept of a strong Central Intelligence Agency, and if they don't, they'd better . . ." (*New York Times,* May 9, 1976). *See also* COVERT OPERATIONS; FINDING; INTELLIGENCE; NATIONAL INTELLIGENCE DAILY.

centrally planned economy A socialist or Communist economic system wherein the government owns most means of production (factories and other businesses) and makes all significant economic decisions.

central nuclear war A war between military superpowers involving the use of nuclear weapons against each other's homelands. Although strategic analysts have discussed the idea of limited or strategic nuclear war, there are serious doubts about whether limitations could be maintained in a conflict of this kind—thus any war in which nuclear weapons were utilized would probably expand into a central nuclear war.

Central Powers The losing side in World War I: mainly Germany, Austria-Hungary, Turkey, and Bulgaria.

central strategic warfare A COLD WAR phrase for full-scale nuclear war—the exchange of long-range ballistic missiles between the United States and the Soviet Union. Even central strategic warfare can come in a variety of forms, given the endless distinctions between COUNTERFORCE and COUNTERVALUE strikes. Nevertheless, it is widely accepted in strategic thought that the transition to central strategic warfare, whatever precedes it, would be the biggest single step in any ESCALATION. To the extent that the only real purpose of U.S. and Russian possession of ballistic nuclear forces is to deter each other from attacking their respective homelands, the onset of central strategic warfare would coincide with the breakdown of DETERRENCE— although some analysts argue that intrawar deterrence would still operate.

Central Treaty Organization (CENTO) A United States–led alliance created in 1955 to deter Soviet expansion in the Middle East. Originally known as the Baghdad Pact, it changed its name to CENTO when Iraq withdrew in 1959. The original members were Britain, Iraq, Iran, Pakistan, and Turkey. The United States was only an associate member because it was not a land power in the region. Iran withdrew in 1979 after the fall of its shah; Pakistan and Turkey quickly followed. CENTO was then dissolved.

central war   The COLD WAR term for a war in Europe between the members of the NORTH ATLANTIC TREATY ORGANIZATION and the WARSAW PACT.

CEP   *See* CIRCULAR ERROR PROBABLE.

CERDS   *See* CHARTER OF ECONOMIC RIGHTS AND DUTIES OF STATES.

certificate of inspection   A document certifying that merchandise (such as perishable goods) was in good condition immediately prior to its shipment.

certificate of manufacture   A statement (often notarized) in which a producer of goods certifies that manufacture has been complete and that the goods are now at the disposal of the buyer.

certificate of origin   A document required by certain countries for tariff purposes, certifying the country of origin of specified goods.

cession   The transfer of SOVEREIGNTY over a territory from one state to another, usually by treaty. The people living in the transferred area automatically became citizens of the acquiring state.

CFE Treaty   *See* CONVENTIONAL FORCES EUROPE TREATY.

Chaco War   The 1932–1935 conflict between Bolivia and Paraguay over the 100,000-square mile Chaco Borcal region. The 1938 Chaco Peace Treaty established the current borders of the two states. Paraguay got most of the disputed land and Bolivia was given access to the Atlantic Ocean.

Chad Civil War   The 1975–1987 conflict in the central African state of Chad between the Muslims of the north and the largely Christian forces of the south. Libya sent troops in 1983 to help the north.

In response France and Zaire sent troops to help the south. In 1984 a mutual withdrawal of foreign forces was negotiated. France and Zaire withdrew; Libya reneged. In 1986 Chadian forces began an offensive that forced Libya out of most of the north. An uneasy truce began in 1987.

chain of command   The succession of commanders from a superior to a subordinate through which authority is exercised or policies implemented. Chains of command exist in both civilian and military organizations.

chain reaction   *See* ACTION-REACTION.

challenge inspection   The nonscheduled examination by one state of another's military stockpiles and facilities to ascertain whether arms control agreements have been followed. Such surprise inspections are generally considered a way of inhibiting temptations to cheat.

Chamberlain, (Joseph) Austen (1863–1937)   The Foreign Secretary of Great Britain (1924–1929) who helped to negotiate the LOCARNO PACTS of 1925 by which Germany and its neighbors recognized the inviolability of their borders. These pacts were an effort to reestablish stability in Europe after World War I. For this work Chamberlain shared the 1925 Nobel Peace Prize with CHARLES G. DAWES. Austen was the half brother of Neville Chamberlain.

Chamberlain, (Arthur) Neville (1869–1940)   The Conservative Party prime minister of Great Britain (1937–1940) at the beginning of World War II. His policy of APPEASEMENT with Nazi Germany brought not "peace for our time," as he told the world upon returning from the negotiation of the MUNICH AGREEMENT on September 30, 1938, to a hero's welcome, but the dismemberment of Czechoslovakia and World War II. According to Duff Cooper's *Old Men Forget* (1953), "For him, the dictators of Germany and Italy were like the Lord Mayors of Liverpool and Manchester, who might belong to different political parties and have different interests, but who must desire the welfare of humanity and be fundamentally reasonable, decent men like himself. This profound misconception lay at the root of his policy and explains all his mistakes." Chamberlain, once lord mayor of Birmingham, was the only British prime minister who based his career on municipal government. This is why Winston Churchill is credited with saying of Chamberlain as he was appeasing the dictators: "See that old town clerk looking at European affairs through the wrong end of a municipal drainpipe." When war finally came, Chamberlain told the House of Commons: "This is a sad day for all of us, and to none sadder than to me. Everything that I have worked for, everything that I have hoped for, everything that I have believed in during my public life has cracked into ruins" (*Time*, September 11, 1939). As Denmark and Norway were occupied by German forces in the spring of 1940, Chamberlain was forced to resign as prime minister. Churchill succeeded him. Ironically, it was the failure of the Royal Navy (which Churchill led as first lord of the admiralty in Chamberlain's cabinet) to stop the invasion of Norway that was the immediate cause of Chamberlain's downfall and Churchill's elevation.

LLOYD GEORGE URGES
CHAMBERLAIN TO RESIGN

It is not a question of who are the Prime Minister's friends. It is a far bigger issue. He has appealed for sacrifice. The nation is prepared for every sacrifice so long as the Government show clearly what they are aiming at, and so long as the nation is confident that those who are leading it are doing their best. I say solemnly that the Prime Minister should give an example of sacrifice, because there is nothing which can contribute more to victory in this war than that he should sacrifice the seals of office.

SOURCE: David Lloyd George, speech in the House of Commons on whether Neville Chamberlain should remain as prime minister, May 8, 1940. The day before in the House, Leo Amery, Chamberlain's longtime friend and colleague, spoke to Chamberlain Oliver Cromwell's stinging words to a parliament three centuries earlier: "You have sat too long for any good you have been doing. Depart, I say and let us have done with you. In the name of God, go!" Chamberlain resigned on May 10, 1940.

Chamizal Tract Dispute   The border disagreement between Mexico and the United States that occurred as a result of a change in the Rio Grande riverbed in 1864. The United States occupied the disputed land in spite of the fact that a 1911 International Arbitration Commission said that the land, known as Chamizal, belonged to Mexico. In 1962 U.S. President John F. Kennedy said that the United States should have accepted the arbitrators' decision. Consequently in 1967 the land was formally transferred to Mexico.

Chamorro, Violeta Barrios de (1929–   )   The owner of the most influential newspaper in Nicaragua who won election in 1990 as president of Nicaragua by leading a 14-party anti-SANDINISTA coalition. Nicaragua has had vast economic problems in converting from a Communist to a market system. By 1992 Chamorro's governing coalition was on the verge of disintegration, Chamorro was charged with being too much under the influence of the Sandinista Communists, and the countryside remained volatile because of economic hardships and lingering divisions from the NICARAGUAN CIVIL WAR.

chancellery   **1.** A nation's FOREIGN MINISTRY. **2.** The physical location of a state's FOREIGN OFFICE. The U.S. Department of State building is in effect the chancellery of the United States; the Quai d'Orsay is the chancellery of France.

chancellor   **1.** The PRIME MINISTER in some states, such as Germany and Austria.   **2.** A civil official in charge of the administrative aspects of a diplomatic mission.   **3.** Any of a variety of administrative, secretarial, or legal officials. The word comes from the *chancellarii* of ancient Rome, who were legal clerks. Over the centuries the word's meaning evolved from "lowly clerk" to "clerk of the highest rank." For example, the chancellor of the Exchequer in the United Kingdom is the minister in charge of that nation's public finances.   **4.** A high-ranking official in a university, usually directly under the university president.

chancery   **1.** The office of a chancellor. **2.** The bureaucratic offices of an embassy or other diplomatic mission where passports are issued, visas obtained, and so on. **3.** A place where public records and official archives are stored. **4.** A court of law in the United Kingdom.

chancery, head of The second in charge, after the ambassador, in a British embassy. (The U.S. equivalent is "deputy chief of mission.")

channel 1. The route of formal communications between central and field offices of a military or civilian bureaucracy. To "go through channels" is to follow the previously created means for getting things done. *See also* BACK CHANNEL; DIPLOMATIC CHANNELS. 2. The English Channel, the narrow body of water that separates Great Britain from the European mainland. *See also* ANGLO-FRENCH CHANNEL AGREEMENT.

Chapultepec, Act of The final act of the 1945 Inter-American Conference for Problems of War and Peace signed in the Chapultepec Palace in Mexico City, Mexico. The act, which declared that a military attack on any Western Hemisphere state was to be considered as an attack on all, was formalized by the INTER-AMERICAN TREATY OF RECIPROCAL ASSISTANCE of 1947.

chargé d'affaires 1. The embassy or legation official who is often the second in command to the chief of the mission; the individual formally in charge of the mission when the head is absent or not yet appointed. 2. The individual responsible for the property and documents of an inactive diplomatic mission.

chargé d'affaires ad interim The temporary head of a diplomatic mission after the final departure of the chief of mission, often an ambassador, and before the arrival of his or her replacement.

chargé d'affaires en titre The permanent head of a diplomatic mission of less than the highest level, usually accredited only to a minister for foreign affairs (rather than a head of state).

charisma Compelling personal magnetism of such strength that it alone may empower a leader. The word *charisma* is derived from the Greek word meaning "divine grace." The concept was first developed by German sociologist MAX WEBER, who separated charismatic authority from both the traditional authority of a monarch and the legal authority given to someone by constitutional provi-

sions. Charismatic leadership, if it is to be lasting, must ultimately be institutionalized or routinized. Thus the initial leader of a movement or organization may be a charismatic spellbinder such as Napoleon Bonaparte or Adolf Hitler, but his or her successors (if any) are often, of necessity, comparatively dull bureaucrats.

charter 1. The formal document issued by a monarch granting special privileges to groups or individuals, as in England's Magna Charta of 1215 or the Charter of Liberties, which preceded it. Some of the original U.S. colonies were created by such charters granted to trading companies or to other groups to establish governments in the New World. The charters themselves ultimately came to symbolize independent powers of self-government. 2. The government document that allows a group of people to create a business corporation. 3. A document that establishes the purposes and powers of a municipal corporation, a city. A municipal corporation must have a charter like any other corporation. The municipality can perform only those tasks and exercise only those powers that are stated in the charter. If the given state permits home rule, a city is allowed to implement its own charter. Otherwise, it is limited to statutory charters spelled out by the state legislature. 4. The constitution of an international body, such as the United Nations.

charter member A founding member of a formal organization. For example, France is a charter member of the United Nations.

Charter of Economic Rights and Duties of States (CERDS) A broad set of guidelines for the conduct of international economic relations, similar in its principles to the NEW INTERNATIONAL ECONOMIC ORDER. Originally proposed by Mexican President Luis Echeverria, CERDS was adopted in 1974 by the United Nations General Assembly. Many developed countries opposed the nonbinding charter. Its most controversial provisions are Article 2, the right of states to absolute sovereignty over their natural resources, with compensation for nationalization of foreign businesses only according to domestic laws; Article 5, the right of states to form primary resource CARTELs; Article 19, the right of developing states to preferential and nonreciprocal treatment (lower the normal tariff rates without having in return to give parallel low rates to FIRST WORLD trading partners); and Article 28, the right of developing states to peg their export prices to import costs. CERDS has been largely ignored by the developed world. However, many of the issues raised by CERDS are discussed through the GATT.

Charter of Paris for a New Europe The document signed at a meeting of heads of state or government in Paris in November 1990. The document, which reaffirmed human rights, pledged mutual friendship and cooperation, and encouraged conventional arms control efforts, was widely seen as marking an end to the Cold War in Europe and the beginning of a new Europe that was whole and free. The charter was signed by all European states (except Albania) plus Canada and the United States.

Charter 77 1. An informal association of Czech dissidents that first emerged in the 1970s. 2. A signed manifesto protesting the repression of human rights in Czechoslovakia published in Western newspapers on January 6, 1977. It was critical in developing the moral underpinning for CIVIC FORUM. The Charter 77 movement, which became formal with its 1977 manifesto, formally disbanded itself in 1992 because it had achieved its goals of returning Czechoslovakia to democracy. According to VACLAV HAVEL, one of Charter 77's founders, who spent almost five years in prison for activities on behalf of democracy: "One cannot help a certain nostalgia, but it is also a reason to rejoice. We never thought we would live to the moment that we could abolish Charter 77" (*New York Times,* November 5, 1992).

Chatham House The term sometimes used to describe the Royal Institute of International Affairs that is housed in Chatham House, 10 St. James's Square, London. It is the leading British think tank on international affairs. Its activities include hosting speeches, many of which are given by distinguished public officials; the publication of scholarly works; and the publication of two journals, *The World Today* and *International Affairs.*

chauvinism An excessive, unreasoning, and unreasonable patriotism. The word comes from Nicholas Chauvin, a fanatically uncritical supporter of France's Napoleon Bonaparte.

checkpoint 1. A predetermined spot on the surface of the earth used as a means of controlling movement, a registration target for fire adjustment, or reference for location. 2. Center of impact of an explosive weapon; a burst center. 3. Geographical location on land or water above which the position of an aircraft in flight may be determined by observation or by electrical means. 4. A place where military police stop, question, or search vehicular or pedestrian traffic in order to enforce circulation control measures and other laws, orders, and regulations.

CHEKA (Chrezvychaynaya Kommissiya) The acronym and popular term for the Commission for Fighting Counterrevolution and Sabotage, the BOLSHEVIK security police responsible for systematic purges and acts of terror during the early years of the Soviet Union. CHEKA, which operated from 1917 to 1922, was eventually succeeded by the KGB.

chemical warfare All aspects of military operations involving the employment of lethal and incapacitating chemical, generally gaseous, munitions or agents (and the warning and protective measures associated with such offensive operations). Chemical warfare is the modern way of referring to the use of gas as a weapon. The most infamous example is the use of poison gas in World War I, started by the Germans. Chemical warfare may be the one clear example of the use of a weapons system being deterred by two alliances possessing amounts of the weapon. This, at least, is the explanation for the nonuse of gas or chemical weapons in World War II. There were two major exceptions to this. The Germans extensively used poison gas to murder millions of civilians in their CONCENTRATION CAMPS; and according to William L. Shirer's *The Rise and Fall of the Third Reich* (1959): "The British had decided . . . as a last resort and if all other conventional methods of defense failed, to attack the German beachheads [if they invaded England] with mustard gas, sprayed from low-flying airplanes." The most recent extensive use of poison gas was by Iraq on its Kurdish minority and on its Iranian opponents during the IRAN-IRAQ WAR. The Western press and Western leaders expressed outrage at this, to which Tariq Aziz, foreign minister of Iraq, responded: "If Iraq or Iran or any other state is suddenly in a position to produce chemical weapons, the raw materials and facilities were obtained from industrial countries. Europe is the main source. For Europe to be outraged and shed crocodile tears is pure hypocrisy" (*U.S. News & World Report,* January 16, 1989). Riot control agents such as tear gas and herbicides generally are not considered to be chemical warfare agents. Chemical warfare, which was condemned by all civilized nations and is outlawed by the Geneva Protocol of 1925, appears to have been practiced by the Soviet Union in Afghanistan and was certainly practiced by Iraq in its war with Iran. At the outset of the Persian Gulf War against Iraq in 1991 there were worries that Iraq would use chemical weapons, but this did not occur.

Chernenko, Konstantin (1911–1985) The oldest general secretary to serve the Communist Party of the Soviet Union. He replaced YURI ANDROPOV in 1984 as the Soviet leader at the age of 75, but not without controversy. MIKHAIL GORBACHEV, then a member of the ruling POLITBURO as well as the protégé of the late Andropov, also was a strong candidate for the position. Those in the Politburo who were strong supporters of LEONID BREZHNEV advocated Chernenko to replace Andropov, whereas the others endorsed Gorbachev to carry on the reforms initiated by Andropov. Both factions were evenly represented within Chernenko's government. They thus prohibited either side from gaining a decisive advantage. Chernenko entered office a sick man. His health deteriorated quickly, causing his term as general secretary to end less than a year after it started. Gorbachev quickly replaced him.

Chernobyl 1. The site in Ukraine (80 miles north of Kiev) where a Soviet nuclear reactor in a power plant accidentally exploded on April 26, 1986, causing the world's worst nuclear accident. The explosion released more radioactive material into the atmosphere than all of the world's previous atmospheric nuclear explosions combined. Soviet officials belatedly warned the nearby populations of the radiation leak. Some communities in the surrounding areas were not notified of the imminent

danger until more than a week later. The immediate casualties were firefighters, soldiers, plant workers, and livestock. However, because warnings to neighboring communities were so delayed, estimates of related deaths from radiation have been predicted to be as high as 75,000. Infant mortality rates, incidents of deformities at birth, and cases of cancer today are alarmingly high in the region. In 1987 six of the plant's top officials were sentenced to up to ten years in prison. 2. By analogy, any major disaster. For example, French critics of EuroDisney, the theme park that opened near Paris in 1992, called it a "cultural Chernobyl."

Chetniks Serbo-Croation word for "partisans"; the traditional name of those Serbs who fought against the Turks in the nineteenth century. During World War II the Chetniks were the Serbian monarchist partisan forces that opposed the Serbian Communist partisans under JOSIF BROZ TITO, some going so far as to collaborate with the Germans to oppose them. Thus they were considered traitors, and dealt with accordingly, by the Tito forces in the postwar period. *See also* PARTISAN WARFARE.

Chequers The Tudor mansion that is the official country retreat of Great Britain's prime minister, located about 35 miles from London.

Chiang Kai-shek (1887–1975) President of the Nationalist government in mainland China from 1928 to 1949 and president of the Republic of China in TAIWAN from 1950 until his death. In his youth Chiang joined the revolutionary activities that overthrew the Manchu dynasty. In the early 1920s he was an organizer for the KUOMINTANG, or Nationalist Party. During the next ten years Chiang tried to neutralize the regional warlords, eliminate the CHINESE COMMUNIST PARTY (CCP), and stay out of war with Japan. In 1928 Chiang established and headed a new central government in Nanking. Nevertheless, the Sino-Japanese war broke out in 1937, and China fought alone until 1941 when the Allies in World War II declared war on Japan after the attack on PEARL HARBOR. Following the Japanese surrender in 1945, Chiang Kai-shek resumed civil war against the CCP until he lost control of the mainland in 1949 and fled to the island of Taiwan,

Chiang Kai-shek (National Archives)

where he remained head of an exile government. According to historian Barbara W. Tuchman in *Stilwell and the American Experience in China* (1970), Chiang's "great talent was not military but political, exercised through a mastery of balance among factions and plots so that he came to be called the 'Billiken' after the weighted doll that cannot be knocked over." Before his death, he saw the rapprochement between his ally, the United States, and his Communist rival on the mainland. In Taiwan after 1949, Chiang had adopted land reform and fostered favorable conditions for rapid economic development. Thanks to his policies, which were continued by his son, Chiang Ching-Kuo (1910–1988), Taiwan has emerged as a highly prosperous newly industrialized nation. Today Taiwan is governed by an elected National Assembly that elects the president and vice president and can amend the constitution. While originally a one-party state, since the late 1980s a multiparty and more democratic system has emerged. *See also* SOONG MEI-LING.

chief executive **1.** The individual in a corporation who is personally accountable to the board of directors for the performance of the organization; the top manager. **2.** The elected leader of a government, such as a president or prime minister. All political chief executives are ultimately accountable to the voters. *Compare to* CHIEF OF STATE.

chief of mission The ambassador or other diplomat who has been placed in charge of a DIPLOMATIC MISSION.

chief of protocol The staff officer of a DIPLOMATIC MISSION who decides questions of diplomatic etiquette and ceremony.

chief of state The ceremonial head of a government, such as a king, queen, or president; synonymous with *head of state*. This differs from the CHIEF EXECUTIVE of a government, such as a prime minister, chancellor, or president. A president may be a ceremonial head of government, a chief executive, or both, as with the President of the United States. Jimmy Breslin in *How the Good Guys Finally Won* (1975) analyzed the U.S. president's confusing mixture of roles thus: "The Office of President is such a bastardized thing, half royalty and half democracy, that nobody knows whether to genuflect or spit." *Compare to* COMMANDER IN CHIEF.

Chilean coup *See* SALVADOR ALLENDE; AUGUSTO PINOCHET.

China card A U.S. policy of expanding the political ties between the United States and the People's Republic of China to influence Soviet policy and the development of U.S.-Soviet relations. The China card was "played" by the United States in the early 1970s as a means of putting pressure on the Soviet Union to move toward DETENTE. Moreover, whenever U.S. Secretary of State Henry Kissinger was angry with Moscow, the number of favorable references to China in his speeches increased dramatically. In the late 1970s the Carter Administration was also keen on playing the China card against the Soviet Union. The difficulty was that China was playing its own game, as shown by the fact that DENG XIAOPING's visit to Washington in January 1979 was followed by the Chinese invasion of Vietnam.

China-Japan Peace Treaty of 1952

U.S. Ambassador Patrick J. Hurley (center) seeks to mediate the Chinese Civil War on August 27, 1945. Seated far left is Mao Zedong; on far right is Zhou Enlai. (National Archives)

China-Japan Peace Treaty of 1952 The post–World War II peace agreement between the Republic of China (Taiwan) and Japan.

China-Japan Peace Treaty of 1978 The post–World War II peace agreement between the People's Republic of China and Japan.

China lobby Those people and organizations that urged the United States to support CHIANG KAI-SHEK in his civil war against the Chinese Communist Party, especially during the late 1940s and 1950s.

Chinese Civil War The more than two-decade-long (1927–1949) struggle between the Communists led by MAO ZEDONG and the Nationalists (the KUOMINTANG) led by CHIANG KAI-SHEK for control of China. The Communists prevailed on the mainland in 1949 and the remnants of the Nationalist forces fled to Taiwan, where they formed the Republic of China.

THE CHINESE CIVIL WAR
A Chronology

1912 China proclaimed a republic. Last Manchu emperor abdicates. KUOMINTANG (the Nationalist Party) founded.

1921 Chinese Communist Party founded.

1926 Chiang Kai-shek, as commander in chief of the National Revolutionary Army, mounts a campaign against the northern warlords.

1927 Chiang Kai-shek destroys the Communist apparatus in Shanghai and establishes anti-Communist government in Nanking. Nationalist-Communist split becomes formal.

1928 All of China nominally under Chiang Kai-shek's control; Nationalist government receives prompt international recognition.

1930 Chiang Kai-shek launches "Bandit Extermination Campaign" against the Communists.

1931 Mao Zedong proclaims the establishment of the

Chinese Soviet Republic under his chairmanship. Japan seizes Manchuria and establishes puppet regime.

1934 Communists, under military pressure from Chiang Kai-shek, evacuate their bases in the south and begin the LONG MARCH.

1935 Mao Zedong gains unchallenged command of the Communist Party and establishes new headquarters in Yenan, Shanxi province.

1937 Chinese and Japanese troops clash near Marco Polo Bridge outside Beijing; the beginning of the second Sino-Japanese War. A Nationalist-Communist united front is created to fight Japan.

1945 Japan surrenders.

1946 The United States sponsors a military truce between Nationalist and Communist forces.

1947 U.S. General George C. Marshall's mediating mission fails; full-scale civil war resumes.

1949 Beijing taken by Communist forces without a fight. Mao Zedong proclaims the founding of the People's Republic of China.

Chiang Kai-shek and his remaining Nationalist forces flee to Taiwan.

Chinese Communist Party (CCP)   The ruling party of mainland China since 1949. The CCP was founded in 1921 in Shanghai, China. Although MAO ZEDONG was one of its founders, the party in its early years was dominated by leaders who had close relationships with the Soviet Union. In the 1920s SUN YAT-SEN with Soviet assistance organized a new political party, the KUOMINTANG (KMT, or "Chinese Nationalist Party"), along Leninist lines, and entered into a close alliance with the fledgling CCP. After Sun's death in 1925, one of his protégés, CHIANG KAI-SHEK, seized control of the KMT and succeeded in bringing most of central China under his rule. In 1927 Chiang destroyed the CCP's party organization and executed many of its leaders. The survivors fled into the mountains of eastern China where they began their two-decade-long effort to seize China from the KMT. Instead of depending on the urban proletariat to achieve success of revolution, as advocated by orthodox Marxist-Leninist theoreticians, Mao insisted on establishing revolutionary bases in rural areas where enemy forces

were the weakest and then seizing cities from the countryside. Mao's style of guerrilla warfare was not accepted until the 1935 LONG MARCH—after the party had suffered repeated failures of city uprisings and formal warfare against the much better armed Nationalist forces. Under Mao's leadership the CCP survived the Long March, expanded during the Sino-Japanese war, and eventually drove CHIANG KAI-SHEK and his Nationalist forces to the island of TAIWAN. The CCP established its rule over mainland China in 1949. Mao's economic policy, however, was disastrous, and by the early 1960s he was sidelined by other party leaders. To recapture his dominance of the party, Mao started the CULTURAL REVOLUTION that toppled most of his opponents. His control of and vision for the CCP was not to be questioned again until after his death in 1976. The post-Mao CCP adopted economic reform policies within China and an OPEN DOOR policy to the outside world under the leadership of DENG XIAOPING. China became more prosperous and power was gradually decentralized. Afraid of losing their power and privileges, the hard-liners asserted control of the CCP after they crushed a pro-democracy movement in TIANANMEN SQUARE in June 1989. Unwilling to return to Mao's policy but uncertain about the future of reform, the current leadership of the CCP is pursuing a hybrid policy of limited economic reform and tight political control.

Chinese-Taiwanese Conflict   The legacy of the CHINESE CIVIL WAR. The island of TAIWAN had historically been controlled by China. After World War II control reverted from Japanese occupation back to China and its Nationalist government. When this government was defeated by the Chinese Communists, the Nationalists, headed by CHIANG KAI-SHEK, fled to Taiwan in December 1949. About 1.5 million people (half of them military personnel) left the mainland. The government on Taiwan then disputed the claim of the People's Republic of China, established on October 1, 1949, to be the legitimate government of the mainland. In addition to Taiwan, the Nationalists retained control of several smaller islands: the Pescadores, Quemoy, Matsu, the Nanchi Islands, and the Tachen Islands.

This internal Chinese dispute became a major international issue because of the Korean War. On June 27, 1950, a few days after the North Korean attack on the South, the United States interposed the Seventh Fleet between the combatants. Then in February 1953 President Dwight D. Eisenhower, in an effort to encourage the Communists to settle the Korean War, announced that the Seventh Fleet would no longer shield Communist China. This was popularly described as "the unleashing of Chiang Kai-shek," but it was more propaganda than military effort. As part of its global strategy of containing communism, the United States committed itself to the security and independence of Taiwan. When in 1954 the People's Republic of China began to bombard the island of Quemoy, the United States and Taiwan signed a mutual security treaty in which the United States agreed to defend Taiwan, the Pescadores, and "such other territories as may be determined by mutual agreement." For its part, the Taiwan government agreed not to attack the mainland without prior consultation with the United States.

While both governments threatened an attempt at "liberation" of the mainland, the likelihood of major confrontation diminished considerably after another confrontation over Quemoy in 1958. This was especially the case after 1971 when there was a dramatic breakthrough in Sino-American relations. The United States supported the admission of the People's Republic of China to the United Nations, although, much to its chagrin, Taiwan was expelled. In 1972, at the end of U.S. President Richard Nixon's visit to China, Beijing reiterated that it was unwilling to accept the idea of "one China, two governments," "two Chinas," or an "independent Taiwan." For its part, the United States acknowledged that the Taiwan issue should be settled by the Chinese themselves. This process of NORMALIZATION continued throughout the 1970s. It was announced on December 15, 1978, that the United States had agreed to recognize the People's Republic of China as the sole legal government and that full diplomatic relations were to be established on January 1, 1979. Unofficial links were to be maintained with the people of Taiwan. In effect, the China-Taiwan conflict had reached the stage of ritualization—more ceremony than reality. Although neither side had formally accepted the status quo, the practicalities of the situation made war unlikely in spite of a significant imbalance in the military power of the two states. In many areas of armament the People's

Republic of China has a ten-to-one numerical superiority over Taiwan, but the prospects of this superiority being used have greatly receded since the mid-1950s. Taiwan, eager to deter any military adventurism by Beijing, ensures that its armed forces are sufficiently modern and effective to inflict enormous costs on any aggressor. As China has moved toward developing a market economy in the 1980s, military tensions with Taiwan have declined. At least a million Taiwan residents have visited China since 1987. Indirect trade and indirect investment is booming. The indirect trade runs heavily in Taiwan's favor. A lure for indirect investment by Taiwan business in the mainland is the cheaper labor costs, an advantage Taiwan itself is losing as economic success drives up wages. Ideologically, the Taiwanese authorities hope that private contacts will rekindle the sense of "one China" after almost 40 years of separation. They also hope that the message of Taiwan's political and economic success will influence the pace and character of change occurring in China and hasten the day when the unification of China will take place.

Chinese–United States rapprochement   The renewal of Chinese diplomatic and cultural ties with the United States. The defeat of the nationalist forces on China's mainland in 1949 marked the beginning of almost a quarter century of hostility between Communist China and the United States. Such hostility was reinforced by the KOREAN WAR and later the VIETNAM WAR, which found the two countries on opposing sides. Not until the early 1970s did U.S. and Chinese political leaders act on the realization that good bilateral relations were in their common interest, thanks to the common international threat posed by the Soviet Union. Secret negotiations led to U.S. President Richard Nixon's 1972 state visit to China, where both governments issued the SHANGHAI COMMUNIQUE that paved the way for the normalization of diplomatic relations in 1979. In the meantime, under the leadership of DENG XIAOPING, China embarked on economic reforms and political liberalization. Between 1978 and 1989 China's efforts were well received in the West. This positive reception was reversed in June 1989 when a prodemocracy student movement was crushed by China's hard-line leaders in TIANANMEN SQUARE. China's relations with the United States and other Western nations have since remained strained because of China's violation of human rights (by Western standards) and its unfair trade practices (by using prison labor to produce exports).

choke points　1. Places such as bridges, tunnels, or railroad junctions through which military personnel and supplies must pass; thus, among the most important potential military targets in the event of war.　2. Those points on vital sea lanes that can be controlled or closed easily to merchant and naval shipping. A characteristic of a maritime choke point is extreme narrowness, thereby allowing contiguous powers or others to exert control. The Strait of Gibraltar, between the Mediterranean Sea and the Atlantic Ocean, and the Strait of Hormuz, between the Persian Gulf and the Indian Ocean, are examples.

chop　1. The authority to CLEAR or approve a bureaucratic or political decision; the right to participate in a policy's development.　2. To sign off on a policy or document, thus indicating approval. 3. Colloquialism used in the NORTH ATLANTIC TREATY ORGANIZATION for the process of handing over operational control of forces from nations to the Supreme Allied Commander Europe (SACEUR). National governments have full responsibility for their troops to the point at which they are prepared to "chop" their forces—something that was of major concern to NATO military commanders during the Cold War.

Chou En-lai　See ZHOU ENLAI.

Christian Democrats　Moderately conservative, center right political parties that have heavily influenced post–World War II politics in Italy, Germany, the Netherlands, and Sweden. While they espouse traditional Christian values, they are not religious parties as such. They tend to stand for mixed economies with a moderate welfare state. The Christian Democrats have been major political opponents to left-wing or Communist parties.

Christian Phalange　The Christian militia of Lebanon, formed in the 1930s in reaction to perceptions of growing Muslim influence and power in the country. The Phalange represents the traditional landowning and commercial powers of Lebanon, where Christians have held a disproportionate share of political power. The Phalange has been an integral participant in the Lebanese civil wars and internal conflicts and has battled the PALESTINE LIBERATION ORGANIZATION and Muslim militias AMAL and HEZBOLLAH. The group has received the support of Israel and the United States. Phalangists were responsible for the massacres at SABRA AND SHATILA.

Christopher, Warren (1925–　)　The Los Angeles lawyer who in 1993 became U.S. Secretary of State in the administration of President WILLIAM J. CLINTON. Previously he was an assistant attorney general (1967–1969) in the Johnson Administration and the deputy secretary of state (1977–1981) in the Carter Administration. In this last position he bore the primary responsibility for negotiating an end to the IRANIAN HOSTAGE CRISIS.

Chukaku-Ha　"Nucleus" or "Middle-Core Faction," an ultra-leftist Japanese group that is the largest militant organization in Japan, with an estimated 3,000 members. It is dedicated to the abolition of the monarchy and constitutional democracy and the severance of U.S.-Japanese ties.

Chunnel　See ANGLO-FRENCH CHANNEL AGREEMENT.

Church Committee　The 1975–1976 U.S. Senate Select Committee to Study Governmental Operations with Regard to Intelligence, chaired by Senator Frank Church (1924–1984) of Idaho. It was established to investigate allegations that the CENTRAL INTELLIGENCE AGENCY played a major role in destabilizing the leftist government of SALVADOR ALLENDE in Chile, which was then replaced by a military regime. The committee found the allegations to be valid and delved into a far-reaching investigation of the U.S. intelligence community, where it uncovered numerous instances of illegal and ethically questionable activity. Other illegal covert actions included assassination plots against foreign political figures and involvement with state terrorist organizations. Overall the committee exposed some of the excesses of the CIA, asserted that COVERT OPERATIONS should be considered an exception to normal U.S. overseas operations, and created the conditions that encouraged President Ronald Reagan to issue in 1981 Executive Order 12333, which prohibits the U.S. government from using ASSASSINATION as a tool of foreign policy.

Churchill, Winston (1874–1965)   The prime minister of Great Britain (1940–1945; 1951–1955) during most of World War II. After an adventurous career as a soldier, war correspondent, and author, Churchill entered Parliament in 1900. During World War I he was first lord of the Admiralty (head of the Royal Navy) but was forced out of the office in 1915 following the unsuccessful Allied campaign in GALLIPOLI. He resumed his commission in the army and commanded a battalion in the trenches in France. After about a year of combat his old political ally DAVID LLOYD GEORGE appointed him minister of munitions (1917–1918) in a new coalition government. During the interim between world wars he was war secretary (1918–1921), colonial secretary (1921–1922), and chancellor of the Exchequer (1924–1929). For most of the 1930s he was a politically isolated backbencher. But his constant warning both in speeches and print about the danger of a rearmed Germany, his eloquent denunciation of APPEASEMENT, and his unmatched rhetorical skill made him an obvious choice as a war leader. When NEVILLE CHAMBERLAIN resigned as prime minister in May 1940 after early German successes in the war, Churchill succeeded him.

He first became prime minister as the Germans overran Western Europe, as the defeated British and French armies had to be evacuated from DUNKIRK, and as Great Britain stood alone against a seemingly unstoppable German military. Then, as U.S. President John F. Kennedy would say in a April 9, 1963, speech conferring honorary American citizenship on Churchill: "In the dark days and darker nights when England stood alone—and most men save Englishmen despaired of England's life—he mobilized the English language and sent it into battle. The incandescent quality of his words illuminated the courage of his countrymen." Churchill and the British Empire alone led the world's resistance to Nazi tyranny until the United States entered the war. Just prior to the BLITZ and the BATTLE OF BRITAIN, Churchill told the House of Commons on June 18, 1940: "Let us therefore brace ourselves to our duties, and so bear ourselves that, if the British Empire and its Commonwealth last for

Winston Churchill (Library of Congress)

a thousand years, men will say, 'This was their finest hour.'" As George Orwell would later write: "Whether or not 1940 was anyone else's finest hour, it was certainly Churchill's" (*New Leader,* May 14, 1949). But once the United States entered the war, the British leadership role diminished as the U.S. role increased. Churchill's policy then and in the postwar period was to keep as closely allied to the United States as possible.

Forced to resign after the Conservative defeat in the election of 1945, he retained the leadership of his party and thus served again as prime minister from 1951 until his retirement in 1955. After a November 30, 1954, tribute to him by both houses of Parliament on his eightieth birthday, he responded: "Mr. Attlee described my speeches in the war as expressing the will not only of Parliament but of the whole nation. It fell to me to express it, and if I found the right words you must remember that I have always earned my living by my pen and by my tongue. It was a nation and race dwelling all around the globe that had the lion's heart. I had the luck to be called upon to give the roar. I also hope that I sometimes suggested to the lion the right place to use his claws."

BLOOD, TOIL, TEARS, AND SWEAT

I would say to the House, as I said to those who have joined this Government: "I have nothing to offer but blood, toil, tears and sweat."

We have before us an ordeal of the most grievous kind. We have before us many, many long months of struggle and of suffering. You ask what is our policy? I will say: It is to wage war, by sea, land and air, with all our might and with all the strength that God can give us: to wage war against a monstrous tyranny, never surpassed in the dark, lamentable catalogue of human crime. That is our policy. You ask, What is our aim? I can answer in one word: Victory—victory at all costs, victory in spite of all terror, victory, however long and hard the road may be; for without victory, there is no survival.

SOURCE: Winston Churchill, speech to the House of Commons on becoming prime minister, May 13, 1940.

CIA   *See* CENTRAL INTELLIGENCE AGENCY.

Ciano, Caleazzo (1903–1944)   The Italian foreign minister (1936–1943) during much of World War II. His rise to political prominence was predictable after he married BENITO MUSSOLINI's daughter in 1930. But he turned against his father-in-law in 1943. Mussolini was deposed and imprisoned but rescued by Adolf Hitler and put back into power—albeit temporarily; but long enough to agree to have Ciano, his son-in-law, executed for treason in January 1944.

CIEC   *See* CONFERENCE ON INTERNATIONAL ECONOMIC COOPERATION.

CILSS (Comité Inter-états pour la Lutte contre la Secheresse au Sahel)   An organization formed in 1973 of seven contiguous African states in the Sahel region to coordinate relief, rehabilitation, and developmental activities that combat the effects of drought. The name of the organization is officially translated as the "Permanent Interstate Committee for Drought Control in the Sahel." The Arabic

word *Sahel* means "shore"; thus the shore of the Sahara is called the Sahel. The seven original member states are Burkina Faso (formerly Upper Volta), Chad, Gambia, Mali, Mauritania, Niger, and Senegal. Cape Verde Islands joined CILSS in 1975; Guinea-Bissau joined in 1984 and became the ninth member. In order to coordinate the activities of CILSS with technical and capital assistance from the donor countries of the ORGANIZATION FOR ECONOMIC COOPERATION AND DEVELOPMENT and other multinational aid agencies, the CLUB DU SAHEL was formed in 1976.

circular error probable (CEP)   An indicator of the accuracy of a weapons delivery system, used as a factor in determining probable damage to a target. It is the radius of the circle within which half of all warheads fired at the same target will fall. This measure is used to gauge the suitability of a missile for a particular task. Against a city, for example, high CEPs can be accepted because the force of a nuclear explosion will cause enough damage, even if the missile lands some distance from its actual target. *Compare to* BIAS.

circumvention   A way of getting around a treaty, commitment, or obligation; a polite term for cheating on an international agreement.

CIS   *See* COMMONWEALTH OF INDEPENDENT STATES.

citadel   1. A major fortress in a strategic location. 2. A small fort constructed within a larger one intended as a last refuge for the GARRISON. This is where the battle can be prolonged after the larger fort has fallen.   3. The central, most heavily protected part of a warship.

citizen   1. An individual who owes allegiance to, and in turn should receive protection from, a state. Citizens are usually born in or naturalized into the state.   2. A person with special privileges. Roman citizens in their ancient empire had special legal rights. That is why U.S. President John F. Kennedy, in his speech in Berlin on June 26, 1963, said: "Two thousand years ago the proudest boast was *civis Romanus sum* [I am a Roman citizen]."   3. A person who is a normal resident of a country in which sovereignty is supposed to belong to the people. In

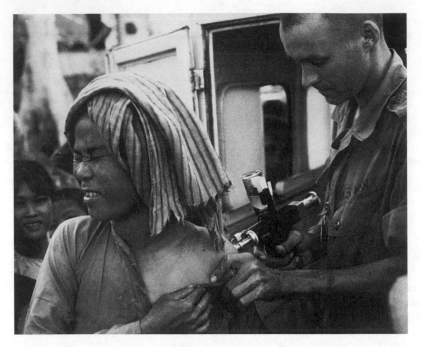

A U.S. Navy hospital corpsman practices civil action when he inoculates a refugee against cholera in South Vietnam in 1966. (National Archives)

contrast, in a monarchy a normal resident is a SUBJECT and owes allegiance to a king or queen.

citizen of the world   **1.** An individual who is well traveled and at home in many cultures.   **2.** An individual who does not claim allegiance to only one state but to all states—to the world. This is impractical in modern times when being stateless means not having a place to live and work. The phrase dates back to the philosopher Socrates (470–399 B.C.), who is supposed to have said, upon being asked to name his country, "I am not an Athenian nor a Greek, but of the world."

citizenship   The dynamic relation between an individual and his or her state. This involves rules of what a citizen might do (such as vote), must do (pay taxes), and can refuse to do (pledge allegiance). The concept has been increasingly associated with benefits or entitlements that a citizen can demand from government. In many states citizenship is required for public employment.

citizenship, dual   **1.** Being a citizen of two governments at the same time. For example, all citizens of the United States are citizens of both the United States and the state (such as Utah or Ohio) in which they reside.   **2.** Having citizenship in two separate nations at the same time. This is not uncommon. For example, the children of some American citizens born in Israel are immediately considered citizens of both Israel and the United States. But children born in France of foreign parents must reside in France for five years before they are eligible for citizenship.

City of Poros   A Greek passenger liner hijacked in 1988 by members of the ABU NIDAL organization. Nine people were killed and more than 100 injured. A second attack, apparently intended to take place after the ship docked, went awry when a car bomb detonated prematurely, killing only the vehicle's two occupants.

civic action   **1.** The use of military units to undertake projects useful to a local population. Also known as *military civil action,* this has the dual effect of (1) providing needed services in areas such as education, transportation, public health, sanitation, and so on, and (2) improving the standing of the military forces with the population.   **2.** The use of organized civilian volunteers to provide specific community services.

Civic Forum (Občanké) A Czech political organization that became prominent after the Prague street demonstrations of November 17, 1989, that began the VELVET REVOLUTION. Leaders of various opposition groups coordinated the campaign to topple the country's Communist leadership and afterward to begin political and economic reforms.

civil affairs **1.** Military government; the administrative process by which an occupying army exercises executive, legislative, and judicial authority over foreign territory. **2.** A vague term for all those matters concerning the relations between military forces and the surrounding nonmilitary authorities; in effect, military public relations.

civil affairs agreement An agreement that governs the relationship between allied armed forces located in a friendly country and the civil authorities and people of that country.

civil defense **1.** The efforts of a civilian population, to minimize, by passive measures, the effects of enemy action against all aspects of civilian life. This ranges from the creation of air raid shelters to emergency plans to ration food and fuel. Arms control expert Paul C. Warnke was not optimistic about the effectiveness of civil defense in a nuclear war: "What kind of civil-defense program is going to protect you against 6,000 nuclear warheads? It depends upon whether you want to die in the field or die in a hole. Would you rather be roasted or boiled? It doesn't make any real difference. There *is* no civil defense against the number of warheads that we and the Soviet Union have deployed against one another" (*Los Angles Times,* September 29, 1981). **2.** The emergency repairs to utilities and other essential facilities destroyed or damaged by enemy action.

civil disobedience U.S. philosopher Henry David Thoreau's (1817–1862) belief from his essay *On the Duty of Civil Disobedience* (1849) that an individual should not support a government if it sanctions policies with which one disagrees. Thoreau's idea of civil disobedience implied a willingness to stand up publicly and accept the consequences of one's

action—in his case, by going to jail. Today the phrase is used to refer to acts of lawbreaking designed to bring public attention to laws of questionable morality and legitimacy. The most famous practitioners of civil disobedience in this century were MOHANDAS K. GANDHI in India and MARTIN LUTHER KING, JR., in the United States.

civilian control The placement of a state's military forces under the command of its civil authorities. The U.S. Constitution (Article II, Section 2) by making the president "commander in chief of the army and the navy" mandates civilian control in the United States. Many other states have similar provisions in their constitutions. But this has not stopped the military in many states from taking control of them via a COUP D'ETAT when political or economic conditions become unstable. Often, after stability is restored, elections are held and civilian control is reinstated. This has happened in recent decades in Argentina, Chile, Greece, and Thailand.

CLAUSEWITZ ON CIVILIAN CONTROL

The subordination of the political point of view to the military would be contrary to common sense, for policy has declared the war; it is the intelligent faculty. War is only the instrument, and not the reverse. The subordination of the military point of view to the political is, therefore, the only thing which is possible.

SOURCE: Karl von Clausewitz, *On War* (1832).

---

civilian internee **1.** A nonmilitary person who is detained or imprisoned during armed conflict or occupation for security reasons, for protection, or because she or he has committed an offense against the detaining power. **2.** A term used to refer to persons interned and protected in accordance with the 1949 GENEVA CONVENTION relative to the Protection of Civilian Persons in Time of War. *See also* PRISONERS OF WAR.

civilized states An old-fashioned term for the West; not appropriate to use because it implies that Western society is intrinsically better than those found among other nations—especially those once subjugated by COLONIALISM.

civil-military relations   The dynamics between a nation's armed forces and its civilian society or civilian political leadership.

civil war   A fratricidal conflict between military forces of the same state or political entity, sometimes termed an *internal war*. Most of organized warfare since World War II—such as the conflicts in Greece, Korea, Nicaragua, Northern Ireland, and Vietnam—has pitted citizens of the same nation against one another. Civil war usually occurs when a government, for one reason or another, has lost legitimacy or when divisions in a state (for example, between rival ethnic groups) can no longer be worked out through the normal political process.

clandestine operations   *See* COVERT OPERATIONS.

Clark Air Force Base   The U.S. Air Force Base in the Philippines whose lease renewal was under discussion until the eruption of Mount Pinatubo in 1991 destroyed it and stopped the discussions.

Clark Amendment   A 1976-to-1985 amendment prohibiting the United States from supplying any insurgent force in Angola. This legislative amendment was sponsored by Senator Dick Clark of Iowa, who was the Senate's leading expert on Africa. The Clark Amendment was one manifestation of the VIETNAM SYNDROME and was eventually overturned by the Reagan Administration, which wanted to pursue the REAGAN DOCTRINE of support for forces struggling against Marxist-Leninist governments. *See also* ANGOLAN CIVIL WAR.

classified information   **1.** Secrets, usually military. **2.** Any matter in any form that requires protection in the interests of NATIONAL SECURITY. There is constant discussion, sometimes classified, that too much information is classified for too long a period of time. During World War II, B. H. Liddell Hart in *Thoughts on War* (1944) wrote: " 'Secret' and 'confidential' are the most abused words in the official vocabulary, the refuge of the clerkly-minded staff officer whose sense of discrimination has long since been submerged by his sense of regulations, and this very abuse of the words defeats its own end, for when minutes relating to a change of soldiers' underwear are labeled 'secret' it is little wonder that the word becomes meaningless in use." Thomas B. Allen and Norman Polmar in *Merchants of Treason* (1988) noted that the U.S. Air Force extended the concept of classified information when it "asked its civilian employees with security clearances to sign an agreement calling on them not to discuss or publish classified information *and information that could be classified in the future.* Thus to the concept of 'classified' information was added the bizarre idea of 'classifiable' information—ordinary data that someday might undergo a transformation into secret data."

classify   **1.** The arrangement of bureaucratic positions into groups based upon their specific tasks and responsibilities.   **2.** To make secret; to ascertain that official information requires, in the interests of NATIONAL SECURITY, a specified level of protection against unauthorized disclosure.   **3.** To categorize as an analytical technique.

class struggle   The continuous conflict between social classes over resources and power in a capitalist society. Karl Marx and Friedrich Engels wrote in their 1848 *Communist Manifesto*: "The history of all hitherto existing society is the history of class struggles." Marxists believe that the tension between the exploiting bourgeoisie and the exploited working-class proletariat eventually leads to revolution. When it happened in 1917 in Russia, it came somewhat as a surprise because this was not the highly industrialized society in which Marxists predicted the revolution would come.

Claude, Inis L., Jr. (1922–   )   One of the leading American analysts of the United Nations and also of many of the concepts and ideas relating to collective management of the international system. One of his most famous works, *Swords into Ploughshares* (4th ed., 1971), provided a comprehensive introduction to the role of global international organizations such as the League of Nations and the United Nations. More interesting is *Power and International Relations* (1962), which is concerned with different approaches to the management of power in international relations.

Clausewitz, Karl Maria von (1780–1831)   The Prussian general who wrote *On War* (1832), the

Karl von Clausewitz (Library of Congress)

most famous book on Western military strategy and tactics; the father of modern strategic thought. In fact, Clausewitz has been quoted much more than he has been read and his reputation has undergone a series of ups and downs. Because of his emphasis on the decisive battle (one that ends war) and TOTAL WAR, he was criticized in the interwar period for the kind of thinking that led to the slaughter on the Western Front. This is not surprising, partly because *On War* was never properly finished and partly because Clausewitz argued on several levels. At times he wrote about the philosophy of war. It was in this connection, where he regarded war as a duel on an extensive scale, that Clausewitz developed the concept of total war (a war fought for the total defeat of the enemy and having no limits). Yet for Clausewitz this was a theoretical abstraction; he saw real war as differing from the absolute in several ways. Not only was real war full of FRICTION, but it was also determined by its political context—

the fact that it was a continuation of politics by other means. At the same time Clausewitz was fully aware of the changes in war that had been initiated under France's Napoleon Bonaparte and recognized that democracy and nationalism would have a profound impact on future wars. He was concerned that in the future real war would come closer to the absolute conception, and that even if the stakes were relatively small the war would become large and powerful. It is against this background that his notion of war being a continuation of politics moves from being an observation to being an imperative or an injunction. This notion of the political control of military actions endeared Clausewitz to strategic analysts in the nuclear age, who were often described as neo-Clausewitzians. Clearly each age looks to Clausewitz for different things and his work is constantly reinterpreted. *See also* FOG OF WAR.

PATTON ON CLAUSEWITZ

Upon meeting General George Patton during the Second World War, [U.S. Assistant Secretary of War John] McCloy had asked the celebrated military hero if he had ever read the leather-bound volumes of Clausewitz and Jomini that were conspicuously displayed in his command tent.

"Hell, no," Patton had answered. "But it impresses the hell out of the war correspondents."

SOURCE: Gregg Herken, *Counsels of War* (1987).

---

clausula rebus sic stantibus   *See* REBUS SIC STANTIBUS.

clear   1. To approve or authorize (or obtain approval or authorization) for something. For example, a proposed law may clear one house of a legislature; thus it has been approved by that house. 2. To be no longer suspected of committing a crime. 3. To pass a security check.   4. The text of a signal that has not been encoded.   5. To authorize an aircraft to take off, land, and so on. *Compare to* CHOP.

Clemenceau, Georges (1841–1929)   The radical premier of France (1906–1909; 1917–1920) famous for his quip, "War is too important to be left to the generals." From the beginning of WORLD

WAR I he complained of and drew attention to military incompetence. In November 1917 French President RAYMOND POINCARE asked Clemenceau to become premier for a second term when France was in the last year of the war. Clemenceau appointed himself minister of war as well. He had the Allies accept Marshal Ferdinand Foch as overall commander in chief of the Allied forces and rallied his nation for the END GAME. His famous speech to his chamber of deputies on March 8, 1918, was: "My home policy? I wage war. My foreign policy? I wage war. Always, everywhere, I wage war." Known as "the tiger" even before the war for his aggressive political views, he earned his nickname again for his aggressiveness at the PARIS PEACE CONFERENCE, where he fought for harsh conditions for Germany and scoffed at the idealism of U.S. President Woodrow Wilson. Clemenceau complained of Wilson: "How can I talk to a fellow who thinks himself the first man in two thousand years to know anything about peace on earth?" (quoted in Thomas A. Bailey, *Woodrow Wilson and the Lost Peace*, 1944). Nevertheless, because the French public felt that he had been too lenient with Germany, he lost his office in the elections of 1920.

KEYNES ON CLEMENCEAU

He felt about France what Pericles felt of Athens—unique value in her, nothing else mattering. . . . He had one illusion—France: and one disillusion—mankind, including Frenchmen, and his colleagues not least. . . . Nations are real things, of whom you love one and feel for the rest indifference—or hatred. The glory of the nation you love is a desirable end—but generally to be obtained at your neighbor's expense. Prudence required some measure of lip-service to the "deals" of foolish Americans and hypocritical Englishmen, but it would be stupid to believe that there is much room in the world, as it really is, for such affairs as the League of Nations, or any sense in the principle of self-determination except as an ingenious formula for rearranging the balance of power in one's own interests.

SOURCE: John Maynard Keynes, *The Economic Consequences of the Peace* (1920).

---

client state **1.** A state whose interests are subordinated to another state's foreign or domestic policies.

For example, during the Cold War many of the states of Eastern Europe were client states of the Soviet Union. **2.** A state involved in a relationship with a stronger power, or PATRON. Although client states are often crucially dependent on their patrons, they are still able to exercise what is sometimes described as REVERSE INFLUENCE on occasion. Some of this influence comes from the fact that patrons often come to have a stake in the continued existence or success of their client and do not want it to collapse. *See also* PATRON-CLIENT RELATIONS.

clientitis A common malady of administrators and diplomats whereby they grow to identify more with the interests of their clients (the people who are served by the agency or live in the country in which a diplomatic mission is located) than with the interests of the political figure or nation that appointed them in the first place. Diplomats may call the malaise *localitis*.

CURING CLIENTITIS

So strongly is this danger [of clientitis] anticipated by the British Foreign Office that it is their habit, when a man has been too long in the Far East, to appoint him somewhere in Latin America. Such mutations are often resented by the official himself and cause surprise to the public. "How odd," people exclaim, "to send to Montevideo a man who has lived for years in Indonesia! How like the Foreign Office." It is not so odd or irrational as all that. The business of a diplomatist is to represent his own government in a foreign country; if he lives too long in a foreign country, he may lose touch with his own home opinion and his representative value will be diminished. Expert knowledge is essential to judgment; but such knowledge can be obtained from experts whose business it is to advise and inform, not to judge or decide.

SOURCE: Harold Nicolson, "Diplomacy Then and Now" (*Foreign Affairs,* October 1961).

Clinton, William Jefferson "Bill" (1946–   ) The President of the United States since 1993. As the Governor of Arkansas (1979–1981; 1983–1993), he gained a reputation as an innovator in domestic policy. After winning the nomination of the Democratic Party he conducted a campaign that stressed the comparatively poor performance of the American economy under incumbent President GEORGE BUSH. After decisively defeating Bush, he asserted that the domestic economy would be his first priority. But on assuming office he was faced with continuing international crises in Somalia, the Middle East, the former Yugoslavia, and the former Soviet Union.

cloak and dagger A theatrical phrase for the COVERT OPERATIONS of intelligence services. U.S. Senator Frank Church of Idaho, when he was chairman of the Senate Select Committee on Intelligence Activities, told an interviewer that "95 percent or 98 percent of the information that is gathered [by the Central Intelligence Agency] comes from either overt sources or through the technical facilities that are available to the agency. The old cloak-and-dagger work which is connected romantically with the espionage methods of the past accounts for precious little" (*Parade*, September 21, 1975). All of the major intelligence services of the world, such as the CIA, the KGB, the Mossad, and so on, use cloak-and-dagger efforts to supplement their open methods of gathering data. *Compare to* CHURCH COMMITTEE.

Club du Sahel An informal association of the nine members of CILSS and other governments and multilateral development agencies. Its purpose is to coordinate international resources for Sahelian development. The first meeting of the club was held in Dakar, Senegal, in March 1976 when representatives from CILSS and 28 other countries and international agencies attended.

Club of Rome A private organization of influential scholars, industrialists, and scientists founded in 1968 to analyze what it termed "the world problematique," or how population, food supply, and natural resources can be put in balance. *See* LIMITS TO GROWTH.

Clubb, Oliver Edmund (1901–1989) The U.S. Foreign Service officer (1928–1952) whose accurate reporting of the CHINESE CIVIL WAR led to false charges of a pro-Communist bias during the height of MCCARTHYISM. Forced out of the U.S. State Department, he then began a distinguished academic career as an East Asian scholar.

CMEA *See* COMECON.

CNI *See* DINA.

CNN (Cable News Network) The worldwide 24-hour-a-day news service that has become a DIPLOMATIC CHANNEL through which governments communicate with each other. Ironically, it also can complicate communications. During the PERSIAN GULF WAR, for example, CNN conveyed to Iraqi leader Saddam Hussein the nervousness of the American debate at a time when the Bush Administration was trying to convey its toughness and willingness to go to war if necessary.

coalition **1.** The ad hoc uniting of political forces to support legislation or elect candidates. Actors in a coalition are often wide apart on many issues but are able to put their differences aside in the interests of the issue at hand. **2.** In a PARLIAMENTARY SYSTEM, an agreement between political parties to form a government. **3.** A group of international actors who temporarily combine to further a common interest such as the waging of war against a common enemy or the passing of a proposal in an international conference. **4.** A loose synonym for an ALLIANCE.

coast guard The small navy that patrols a state's shoreline. As the primary maritime law enforcement agency of the government, it has a major role in suppressing smuggling and illicit drugs, but in wartime it may operate under the state's BLUE WATER NAVY.

Cobden, Richard (1804–1865) A pamphleteer and politician in nineteenth-century England who became one of the leading figures on the more liberal and radical side of British political life as a member of the MANCHESTER SCHOOL. Cobden was extremely critical of the BALANCE OF POWER and argued that principle should count for more than expediency in international relations. According to A. J. P. Taylor's *The Troublemakers* (1957), "Cobden was the most original and profound of the radical dissenters; the one who most clearly passed from opposition to the formulation of an alternative foreign policy." He saw the maintenance of peace as crucial to the progress of freedom and thought this was best achieved by minimizing relations between governments and maximizing the connections between peoples. Taylor describes Cobden as the real British foreign secretary of the early 1860s: "He negotiated the commercial treaty with France, preached international arbitration, and was the first to propose an agreed limitation of armaments." Some observers also have suggested that it was a sign of Cobden's influence and impact that no British government seriously considered military intervention in Europe between 1864 and 1906.

cobweb model   A model of international relations which emphasizes that there are many different kinds of actors and that there are many linkages and interdependencies among them. This idea is developed fully by Richard Mansbach, Yale Ferguson, and Donald Lampert in *The Web of World Politics* (1976). With its emphasis on the multiplicity of actors and the interdependencies among states, it challenges the state-centric or BILLIARD BALL MODEL. *See also* COMPLEX INTERDEPENDENCE.

Coca-Cola   A nonalcoholic American beverage that became the symbol of U.S. business interests abroad. Both the left and the right have framed American international trade policies in terms of "making the world safe for Coca-Cola."

Cochin China   The term applied to that part of the colony of French Indochina that became Vietnam in 1954.

COCOM (Coordinating Committee on Export Controls)   The COLD WAR–era group of those representatives from all North Atlantic Treaty Organization countries (except Iceland and Spain), plus Japan, that was responsible for compiling lists of strategic goods not to be sold by NATO states and Japan to the Soviet bloc. Each state through EXPORT CONTROLS was responsible for seeing that its citizens respected the embargo. COCOM, created in 1949, still meets regularly in Paris to review a strategic EMBARGO list. It reviews militarily relevant technology transfers for possible embargo and also tries to anticipate strategic end uses of items manufactured for civilian purposes. With the movement toward Western-style democracy in Eastern Europe and the former Soviet Union and lessening of Cold War tensions beginning in 1989, the rationale and utility of

COCOM has increasingly been questioned. In 1991 COCOM reduced by one-half the number of high-technology items (such as personal computers) that were embargoed; and in 1992 COCOM was considering an end to all restrictions on civilian telecommunications equipment. Although the issue of TECHNOLOGY TRANSFER remains a delicate one, especially given the number of DUAL USE TECHNOLOGIES now available, there is broad agreement that COCOM needs to establish what are often described as "higher fences around fewer products or targets." *Compare to* BATTLE ACT OF 1951.

code name   A word used to refer to a military, intelligence, or diplomatic initiative that must be kept secret until the operational aspects of the event can be announced. Many code names are used well after the operation is over. For example, "Overlord" is still used by historians to refer to the Allied preparations for the June 6, 1944, D-Day invasion of France.

CHURCHILL ON CHOOSING CODE NAMES

Operations in which large numbers of men may lose their lives ought not to be described by code-words which imply a boastful and overconfident sentiment, such as "Triumphant," or conversely, which are calculated to invest the plan with an air of despondency, such as "Woebetide," "Massacre," "Jumble," "Trouble," "Fidget," "Flimsy," "Pathetic," "Jaundice" . . .

    After all, the world is wide, and intelligent thought will readily supply an unlimited number of well-sounding names which do not suggest the character of the operation or disparage it in any way and do not enable some widow or mother to say that her son was killed in an operation called "Bunnyhug" or "Ballyhoo."

SOURCE: Winston Churchill, August 8, 1943, note to General Ismay, reprinted in *The Second World War: Closing the Ring* (1951).

---

code of conduct   1. The rules on how a captured soldier should conduct her- or himself as a prisoner of war. These vary among states but usually imply a duty to try to escape, a refusal to make disloyal statements, and a refusal to give information beyond personal identification.   2. An international instrument that specifies acceptable international behavior by nation-states or multinational corporations. For example, in multilateral trade negotiations, several codes of conduct designed to "harmonize" the use of nontariff trade measures were negotiated in the Tokyo round. GATT Articles III through XXIII contain commercial policy provisions that have sometimes been described as its code of good conduct in trade matters. **3.** A compendium of ethical norms promulgated by an organization to guide the behavior of its members. Many government agencies have formal codes of conduct for their employees. **4.** Rules of behavior that may be tacit rather than explicit, that tend to be based on prudence rather than on law or morality, and that help to avoid war between great powers. For example, states may tolerate a minor degree of smuggling (as has historically existed between France and Spain over the Pyrenees Mountains on their border) because it is not worthwhile for either side to totally suppress such activities.

codetermination Labor participation in all aspects of management, even to the extent of having union representatives share equal membership on an organization's board of directors. In Germany, where codetermination has been legally required since 1951, the process is called *Mitbestimmungsrecht,* literally meaning "the right of codetermination." This was an important factor in the post–World War II West German "economic miracle."

code word **1.** A word or phrase whose political use changes its meaning. Code words are often used when it is not politic or respectable to address an issue directly—and to create semantic confusion. For example, U.S. President Dwight D. Eisenhower said in his State of the Union Address of January 7, 1960: "We live . . . in a sea of semantic disorder in which old labels no longer faithfully describe. Police states are called 'people's democracies.' Armed conquest of free people is called 'liberation.'" **2.** A foreign word or phrase that means one thing literally, but has an idiomatic meaning to native speakers. For example, in Japanese *zensho shimasu* literally means "I will do my best." This could be considered an accommodating answer during diplomatic negotiations. But the phrase also means "no way," which is quite a different answer. **3.** A CODE NAME.

Cod Wars The 1972-to-1976 confrontations between Iceland and Great Britain over deep-sea fishing rights. There was no shooting, but many ships purposely bumped or sideswiped each other on the high seas. Iceland finally broke diplomatic relations with Great Britain in 1976 after British fishing trawlers continued to violate the 200-mile radius restricted fishing zone declared by Iceland in 1975. Later that year diplomats met in Oslo, Norway, and an accord was reached by which the British agreed to limit the time its trawlers spent in Icelandic waters. Diplomatic relations were then restored.

coercion **1.** The exertion of influence through threats to inflict harm or costs unless the target behaves in the desired fashion. Coercion is often contrasted with brute FORCE; it is generally agreed that coercion is far more cost effective. Thomas Schelling in *Arms and Influence* (1966) describes the difference as that between taking something and making someone give it to you. **2.** The use of threats by a government in order to intimidate the population and maintain its position.

coercive diplomacy *See* BARGAINING THEORY.

coexistence **1.** An international situation whereby states with different social systems and conflicting ideologies refrain from actual war. Coexistence is less than peace but preferable to war. It was often used to refer to strained relations between the Soviet Union and the West. As Indian Prime Minister Jawaharlal Nehru often asserted: "The only alternative to coexistence is codestruction" (*Observer,* August 29, 1954). The Soviet concept of peaceful coexistence that prevailed during the COLD WAR is generally traced back to V. I. Lenin and his statement that it was the desire of the Soviet Union to live in peace with all nations and to concentrate on building socialism in one country. The notion was reiterated by Nikita Khrushchev at the Twentieth Party Congress in 1956 when he rejected the thesis that war between capitalist and socialist powers was inevitable. This was an attempt to bring Marxist-Leninist doctrine into line with the realities of the nuclear age. While peaceful coexistence was concerned with the avoidance of war, it never implied an end to competition. It could even be understood as an effort to ensure that the world was safe for the competition that was inherent between the two systems. To the Soviets the notion of peaceful coexistence was both competitive and dynamic; it certainly did not imply acceptance of the status quo. 2. Any contentious relation in which genuine rivals (political, organizational, etc.) purposely refrain from a direct confrontation, which might otherwise logically be expected of them.

cognitive dissonance   Developed by Leon Festinger in *A Theory of Cognitive Dissonance* (1957), this concept is based on the assumption that people like balance or consistency between their beliefs and their perceptions. A disconnection between these two things is highly disconcerting for an individual, with the result that efforts are generally made to keep the two things in accord. Since belief systems tend to have an overall cohesion and information comes in discrete bits, it is often easier to downgrade or ignore new information than change one's beliefs—thereby seeing simply what one expects to see. When it is no longer possible to ignore information that contradicts beliefs, a major shift occurs in belief systems. Too often, however, such a transformation comes only after traumatic events have highlighted the gap between the beliefs and reality. The desire for cognitive consistency is a factor in intelligence failures. A good example comes from Norway. In 1940 the Norwegian government believed that Nazi Germany would not violate its neutrality. As a result it ignored information indicating that an invasion was likely. When the invasion came in April, Norway was less prepared than it might otherwise have been, and after two months it was forced to surrender.

Colby, Bainbridge (1869–1950)   The U.S. Secretary of State (1920–1921) during the last year of the Wilson Administration.

cold war   1. War with no traditional combat (in contrast to a *hot war*) that emphasizes instead ideological conflict, BRINKMANSHIP, and constant international tension. This concept is not new. Philosopher Thomas Hobbes wrote in *Leviathan* (1651) that: "War consists not in battle only, or the act of fighting; but in a tract of time, wherein the will to contend by battle is sufficiently known: and therefore the notion of time, is to be considered in the nature

of war; as it is in the nature of weather. For as the nature of foul weather, lyeth not in a shower or two of rain; but in an inclination thereto of many days together; so the nature of war, consists not in actual fighting; but in the known disposition thereto, during all the time there is no assurance to the contrary. All other time is peace." 2. In particular, the hostile but nonlethal relations between the Western democracies and the Soviet Union that began in 1945 after World War II and ended in 1989. Herbert Bayard Swope (1882–1958) first used this phrase as a speechwriter for financier Bernard Baruch (1870–1965). When Baruch told the Senate War Investigating Committee on October 24, 1948, "Let us not be deceived—today we are in the midst of a cold war," the phrase became part of everyday speech. The Cold War originated from differences over Eastern Europe and the then-divided Germany. Its basic characteristic was an intense international competition between the United States and its Western European allies (with the NORTH ATLANTIC TREATY ORGANIZATION as its military alliance) and the Soviet Union and its Eastern European allies (with the WARSAW PACT as its military alliance) that never led to direct hostilities. The competition extended to both LIMITED and PROXY WARs. However, because neither superpower wanted it to end in war between them, the rivalry was conducted within a framework of tacit rules or CODES OF CONDUCT. Because both sides wanted to avoid the danger of nuclear war, they avoided direct confrontations but actively sought indirect confrontation, especially in the THIRD WORLD. Thus each supported insurgencies against the other's CLIENT STATES. For example, the Soviets supported North Korea and North Vietnam in their war against the United States. In turn the United States supported the Afghan guerrillas in their war against Soviet occupation.

Initially war weariness in the wake of World War II and then fear that nuclear war would be disastrous forced both sides to keep this rivalry under control. But by the late 1980s the Cold War had thawed to the point of almost disappearing. The Soviet Union under the leadership of MIKHAIL GORBACHEV simply decided, out of its own self-interest, to end the war so that it could devote more resources to its domestic needs. The end of the Cold War saw the Soviets retreat from their domination of Eastern Europe and open a new era of international cooperation, especially through the United Nations. *Compare to* CONTAINMENT; END OF HISTORY. **3.** Any behind-the-scenes tension between two parties who cannot openly confront each other.

Cold War, Second   A term popularized by Fred Halliday in *The Making of the Second Cold War* (1983), which argued that the superpower relationship had gone from DETENTE into a second period of Cold War in the late 1970s. Although Halliday makes a good case that the demise of détente marked another fundamental change in the relationship, many historians find it more persuasive to see the period from 1947 to 1989 as all part of one Cold War in which periods of relaxation were followed by increased tension within an overall superpower relationship that was a mix of cooperation and conflict.

Cold War critics   Those who took issue with the development of U.S. policy toward the Soviet Union in the latter half of the 1940s and the early 1950s. They included former Vice President Henry Wallace (1888–1965), journalist WALTER LIPPMANN (1889–1974), Senator Robert Taft (1889–1953), and journalist I. F. Stone (1907–1989). They dissented from the emerging thrust of U.S. foreign policy for different reasons, and all articulated alternative approaches. Wallace (vice president during President Franklin D. Roosevelt's third term from 1941 to 1945) advocated a much more conciliatory approach to the Soviet Union and attacked Truman's foreign policy from a liberal perspective. Stone too was critical of many aspects of U.S. foreign policy, attributing responsibility for the Cold War to Washington as well as Moscow. Lippmann was primarily concerned that the policy of CONTAINMENT would lead to a gap between commitments and capabilities. Taft, a conservative Republican from Ohio, saw the main danger as being the possibility that containment would place a great strain on the domestic economy and undermine democratic institutions.

Cold War revisionists   U.S. analysts who argue that the United States rather than the Soviet Union was responsible for the Cold War. Their ideas and interpretations are in direct opposition to those of the Cold War traditionalists, who believe that the United States in the late 1940s was simply reacting to Soviet aggression; the traditionalists dominated the study of Cold War origins until the mid-1960s. Revisionists tend to emphasize U.S. strength and assertiveness—particularly the monopoly of the atomic bomb—and Soviet weakness and defensiveness because of its losses in World War II. Many also adopt a neo-Marxist position and contend that the main determinant of U.S. foreign policy is the desire for markets and raw materials. In line with this revisionists argue that U.S. ambitions in Eastern Europe, the desire for an open door and access to markets, were the main reasons Washington reacted so strongly to the Soviet domination of the region. There are, of course, moderate revisionists and radical revisionists. Radical revisionist interpretations include William Appleman Williams's *The Tragedy of American Diplomacy* (1962) and Gabriel Kolko's *The Roots of American Foreign Policy* (1969). Much more sophisticated, however, are the postrevisionists, those scholars who acknowledge some of the insights that revisionist analyses have yielded yet see the problem in much more balanced ways than those who place all the responsibility on either the Soviet Union or the United States. The postrevisionist literature sees the origins of the Cold War in terms of interaction processes and acknowledges the role of misperception and misunderstanding as well as conflicts of interests in fueling the Cold War.

collaboration   **1.** Cooperation.   **2.** An act of TREASON that involves actively aiding an enemy who has occupied one's country. This is always a matter of degree. For example, most citizens of Nazi-occupied Europe in World War II passively cooperated with their masters in minor ways. Only those who actively worked to make the occupation a success were considered traitors. Famous examples include VIDKUN QUISLING in Norway and PIERRE LAVAL and PHILIPPE PÉTAIN in France.

collateral damage   The unintended or incidental destruction that occurs during a military attack. For example, a school or hospital that is bombed by an air raid directed against a nearby enemy airfield can be said to have suffered collateral damage. Such excuses are usually not much consolation to the victims and their families. *See also* SELECTIVE STRIKE; SURGICAL STRIKE.

collective defense   A formal or ad hoc military alliance created in anticipation of a specific threat, as opposed to a general COLLECTIVE SECURITY arrangement. Frontier militia units that band together to meet a common enemy have created a collective defense. It differs only in size with what states do when confronted with a common enemy.

collective engagement   The Bush Administration's term for its post–Cold War diplomatic strategy: While reserving the right to take unilateral action, it would for the most part engage in international efforts in association with the other major players (both states and international organizations such as the United Nations) on the international scene.

collective security   1. A formal arrangement whereby protection against aggression in the international system is maintained by the action of an international community or alliance. It is the practical manifestation of a theoretical system of WORLD ORDER in which an aggressor has to face the combined weight of allied peace-loving states. It was intended as an alternative to the BALANCE OF POWER system for ensuring international stability. This approach seeks to go beyond balance of power politics and develop a global arrangement whereby the strength of all nations (meaning the totality of their military forces) would be employed against any aggressor. The principle of collective security, as it evolved after World War I, was based on faith in rationality and international organization, on the assumption that aggression could be clearly recognized, and on the belief that collective action would either deter or defeat any state attempting to disrupt the peace of the international system. The original institutional form of collective security in modern times was the post–World War I LEAGUE OF NATIONS. But neither the League nor the whole idea of collective security worked. When the League was put to the test over Japanese and Italian aggression in the 1930s, both it and its members failed to either act with conviction or intervene militarily. Members of its successor organization, the United Nations, are officially bound to this same doctrine of collective security. It is the guiding principle behind the UN SECURITY COUNCIL. The ability of any of the five permanent members to veto proposals for collective action denied the UN a major role in thwarting aggression during the COLD WAR. But the PERSIAN GULF WAR showed that collective security envisioned by the UN founders was still possible.   2. A synonym for COLLECTIVE DEFENSE. Strictly speaking, this is an incorrect usage. Collective security is directed against any aggressor whereas a collective defense arrangement traditionally has been directed against a specific enemy.

collectivization   The Soviet Union's forced consolidation of peasant village lands into large *collective farms* controlled by the state. This movement began in 1929 when Joseph Stalin and the Communist Party decided that the existence of individual and village farms was an un-Marxist capitalistic relic. This Communist effort to extend economic and political control into the countryside was met by great resistance. Through military reprisals, banishment to forced labor camps, and a contrived famine in which millions perished, by 1938 over 93 percent of the peasant holdings were collectivized—a process that, with the dissolution of the Soviet Union in 1991, now is being reversed.

collegial model   An image of U.S. foreign policy decision making discussed by ALEXANDER L. GEORGE in *Presidential Decisionmaking in Foreign Policy* (1980); it posits cooperation among the U.S. president's advisors in solving problems even though they bring divergent perspectives to bear on the problems. *Compare to* COMPETITIVE MODEL.

Collins, Michael (1890–1922)   The Irish revolutionary leader whose negotiations with Great Britain resulted in the ANGLO-IRISH TREATY OF 1921, which gave Ireland (less the six northern counties) dominion status as the Irish Free State in 1922. Collins became its first prime minister, but because he agreed to this partition, he was killed in the fighting that ensued between his Free State Army and the group he had once led, the IRISH REPUBLICAN ARMY.

Colombo Plan   An economic development program for South and Southeast Asia that first came about as a result of a meeting of British Commonwealth foreign ministers held in Colombo, Ceylon (now Sri Lanka), in January 1950. The plan started with six-year development programs for Ceylon, India, Malaya, North Borneo, Pakistan, Sarawak, and Singapore that Australia, Canada, New Zealand, and the United Kingdom agreed to fund. The United States joined as a donor country in 1951; Japan in 1954. The program has since been expanded to include most countries of the region.

colonialism 1. The effective political control of a dependent territory and its people by a foreign military power. The essence of colonialism as a concept, and especially in modern pejorative usage, is the idea of deliberate exploitation of another country and its inhabitants. 2. The treating of another state as if it were in fact a colony, usually by means of economic exploitation. 3. Internal colonialism, where an economically dominant part of a country treats a distant region just as it might a genuinely foreign colony.

For true colonialism to exist two conditions are necessary: (1) the land held as a colony must have no real political independence and (2) the relationship must be one of forthright exploitation. Countries maintain colonies to increase their own wealth and welfare—either by extracting resources, material, or labor from the colony more cheaply than could be bought on a free market or by ensuring a market for their own goods at advantageous rates. In practice there have been few examples of true colonialism because colonies were usually given some degree of self-government, and their exploitation also often functioned as a sort of economic development. Colonial government frequently has been justified, sincerely or otherwise, as an attempt to spread "civilization" to socially underdeveloped societies (the WHITE MAN'S BURDEN), and few empires have not benefited from the economic advantage to its producers and merchants of captive colonial markets. The heyday of colonialism was the late nineteenth century when Europe was clearly "the world's overlord" and the major European countries had colonies throughout Asia and Africa. Europeans grabbed colonies in Africa and Asia in part for economic considerations but also to provide a safety valve for their conflicts at home. In the competition of the great powers, colonies were seen as adding to national power. The obverse was that if other states had colonies, it was also necessary to have them oneself to compete effectively. Yet such IMPERIALISM contained within itself the seeds of its own decay: It was the ideas of democracy and national SELF-DETERMINATION, transported from Europe to the colonies, that provided the impetus for the DECOLONIZATION movement.

colonial wars The use of military force by the states of Europe, Japan, and the United States both to conquer large areas of Africa and Asia and subsequently to maintain domination over these areas against efforts by the local population to achieve national SELF-DETERMINATION. In the period after World War II the term began to carry pejorative connotations; many critics argued that in Vietnam the United States had stumbled into what was, in effect, a colonial war.

combatant 1. In international law, all of the individual members of BELLIGERENT forces subject to the laws, rights, and duties of war. 2. A soldier or unit assigned to duty as an active fighter or fighting unit, as distinguished from duty in a service capacity, such as the administrative, supply, or medical services.

combined operation 1. A mission conducted by forces of two or more allied nations acting together for the accomplishment of a single goal. 2. A mission conducted by forces of two or more armed services of the same nation. *Joint operation* is a synonomous term. A typical example of a combined operation is the invasion of a hostile country by seaborne landing of army units. Combined operations are notoriously difficult for a host of technical reasons: Different communications methods, probably different and possibly incompatible communications machinery, rival traditions, ambiguity about relative rank structures and authority relations—all which interact to maximize the chance of failure. Apart from technical difficulties, serious tensions often arise between the commanders of the different services because of contradictory priorities. The naval commander knows that ships are most vulnerable while near to land and wants to get them away quickly, while the army commander wants time to ensure that the troops are safely on the beachhead and that all equipment has been transferred. Most countries make some effort to prepare for these problems by establishing peacetime joint planning staffs to accustom officers from the different services to working together. Part of the difficulty is that interservice rivalry often means that the route to top positions is via experience with a single service, and time spent on combined operations staff training is time taken away from the pursuit of career advancement.

come-as-you-are war   **1.** A war that leaves no time for the resupply (or augmentation) of personnel or materiel. Examples include the first weeks of World War II in the Pacific from the point of view of the Americans, Australians, and the British; and the first weeks of the Korean War, when the North Koreans overran most of South Korea and nearly pushed U.S. forces off the Korean peninsula.   **2.** A contingency of sufficient gravity to require regular and reserve units to deploy in a peacetime configuration without the benefit of additional training, personnel, and equipment.

COMECON   The Western term for the Council for Mutual Economic Assistance (CMEA), which was formed in 1949 to coordinate the economic development of the Soviet bloc in Eastern Europe. The Russian name is *Soviet Ekonomicheskoy Vzaymopomoshchi*. This was roughly the Soviet Union's and Eastern Europe's equivalent to the EUROPEAN COMMUNITY or alternatively the economic equivalent to the WARSAW PACT. The dominance the Soviet Union had over COMECON made this latter analogy perhaps more appropriate. The original members were Albania, Bulgaria, Czechoslovakia, Hungary, Poland, Romania, and the Soviet Union. East Germany joined in 1950. Albania was expelled in 1961 as punishment for forming too close a link with China when the SINO-SOVIET SPLIT began to emerge. Mongolia joined in 1962, Cuba in 1972, and Vietnam in 1978. Yugoslavia was an associate member.

COMECON was used by the Soviet Union to counter the increasing integration of the Western European economy following Stalin's refusal to permit East European countries to participate in the MARSHALL PLAN. Above all, it was a way of enforcing supranational planning in the interest of the Soviet Union. In Eastern Europe it was widely believed that COMECON functioned to skim off the best results of its industrial production, especially that of East Germany, for export to the Soviet Union. In addition, it was used partly as a tool of

Soviet propaganda and as a technical support structure for THIRD WORLD countries whose membership in an international Communist movement was of less interest to East Europe than to the Soviet Union. COMECON dissolved in the wake of the 1991 breakup of the Soviet Union.

Cominform (Communist Information Bureau)   A Soviet-dominated political and propaganda organization created in 1947 that reestablished COMINTERN. It adopted the new name to suggest that it exchanged only information, but it did far more: It coordinated the work of Communist parties in East Central and Eastern European states. It never achieved the importance of THE INTERNATIONAL and was disbanded in 1956.

COMINT   *See* COMMUNICATIONS INTELLIGENCE.

Comintern   Communist International. The organization created by the COMMUNIST PARTY OF THE SOVIET UNION in 1919 to lead the worldwide movement toward communism. It also suggested the idea of POPULAR FRONT coalitions with socialists in the late 1930s to oppose the fascists. It was disbanded by Stalin in 1943 in an effort to show solidarity with the Soviet Union's wartime Western allies.

comity   **1.** A reciprocal courtesy by which one state, court, house of a legislature, and so on defers the exercise of some authority to some other state, court, or house.   **2.** The provision of the U.S. Constitution that "the citizens of each state shall be entitled to all privileges and immunities of citizens in the several states." With the adoption of the 1986 SINGLE EUROPEAN ACT and the increasing economic integration of Europe, a parallel kind of comity gradually is being developed for the citizens of the EUROPEAN COMMUNITY.

command   **1.** The power given a military officer for the direction of a significant element of an armed force. While one officer may be said to have command, it is inherently a team effort.   **2.** An ORDER given by one in authority.

command and control   The exercise of authority and direction by a military commander over his or her assigned forces in the accomplishment of a mission. Since antiquity command and control (which is often abbreviated to C² and pronounced "C squared") was exercised by a leader on the battlefield. Only in the twentieth century has it become possible to exercise command and control from a considerable distance. German Field Marshal Alfred von Schlieffen in *Cannae* (1936) offers this World War I–era description of the now-familiar WAR ROOM:

> [The 'Modern Alexander' would direct the battle] from a house with roomy offices where telegraph, telephone and wireless signaling apparatus are at hand, while a fleet of autos and motorcycles ready to depart, wait for orders. Here in a comfortable chair by a large table the modern commander overlooks the whole battlefield on a map. From here he telephones inspiring words and here he receives the reports from army and corps commanders and from balloons and dirigibles which observe the enemy's movements.

commandant   The functional title, not a rank, of the officer in charge of a significant military installation or function. For example, the head of the U.S. Marine Corps is a commandant even though his rank is that of a four-star general. The word is derived from a French term meaning "the officer in command." The title is widely used in French-, Spanish-, and Portuguese-speaking states. Heads of military schools are often called commandants. However, at West Point and the Air Force Academy in the United States, the commandant is in charge only of training and discipline; a dean of faculty is in charge of academic subjects. In both cases they report to a superintendent.

command, control, and communications   The expansion of traditional COMMAND AND CONTROL functions to include modern communications. As concepts they are synonymous because one really is not possible without the other. Also known as C³ and pronounced "C cubed."

command, control, and communications countermeasures   The integrated use of operations security, military deception, jamming, and physical destruction, supported by intelligence, to deny information to, influence, degrade, or destroy the enemy's command, control, and communications (C³) capabilities and to protect friendly C³ against such actions. Also known as C³CM and pronounced "C cubed CM."

command, control, communications, and intelligence   Usually referred to by the acronym C³I, pronounced "C cubed I": The combined capacity to deliver orders to military units; to continually monitor and control their presence, movements, and status; to be well informed of enemy movements and intentions; and to be able to relay and receive messages reliably, quickly, and secretly. Sometimes C³I can offer too much of a good thing. As Arthur T. Hadley describes in *The Straw Giant* (1986): "In Vietnam, overcontrol led to disasters large and small. On the last day of the American involvement there, the White House was requesting the tail numbers of the helicopters being used to lift the Americans off the embassy roof in Saigon. Mired in such gnat-sized details, those at the command summit had lost control over the strategic direction of American policy, while those at the bottom were robbed of initiative and lost flexibility and confidence in themselves." Nevertheless, C³I is a crucial if somewhat neglected dimension of the strategic nuclear force posture. During the late 1970s the vulnerability of U.S. C³I assets became a major concern of U.S. defense planners in relation to a possible DECAPITATION STRIKE by the Soviet Union, and considerable resources were devoted to upgrading these capabilities to ensure CONNECTIVITY between the NATIONAL COMMAND AUTHORITIES and the strategic retaliatory forces.

command decision   1. An order given by a military leader that is especially consequential because of the dangers it implies or its indication of a new policy direction.   2. A pompous description of any decision by an appropriate military authority.   3. A president's, prime minister's, or monarch's decision involving the use of military force.

command economy   The economic ideal of modern communist states wherein industry is controlled by the central government, which makes all decisions, appoints all managers, and sets prices and production levels.

commander in chief   1. The military or naval officer in charge of all forces in a THEATER OF WAR. 2. In the United States, the term used to refer to the president as the ultimate authority over the armed forces of the United States. This authority is granted under Article III, Section 2, of the U.S. Constitution, which states "the president shall be commander in chief of the army and the navy of the United States and of the militia of the several states when called into the actual service of the United States." The last president to exercise his authority as commander in chief to command troops in the field was James Madison during the War of 1812. At Bladensburg, Maryland, U.S. troops under their president met the British and were soundly defeated. The British then marched on Washington, D.C., to burn the White House and all other public buildings. No subsequent president, while in office, has sought to lead in battle. 3. The officer in charge of a branch of a military service, or of all services in a given area. For example, CINCPAC is the commander in chief, Pacific, commanding all U.S. military and naval units in the Pacific Region. 4. The leader of the armed forces of any state. In a democracy this is always a civilian, such as a PRIME MINISTER. In a military dictatorship it is the DICTATOR. However, outside of the United States this term in seldom used for a civilian CHIEF OF STATE. *Compare to* CIVILIAN CONTROL.

commander's estimate of the situation   *See* ESTIMATE OF THE SITUATION.

command net   A communications network that connects a military unit with its subordinate echelons for the purpose of COMMAND AND CONTROL.

command of the air   GIULIO DOUHET's concept, from his book *The Command of the Air* (1921), of having sufficient air forces "to be in a position to prevent the enemy from flying while retaining the ability to fly oneself." The more common phrase for command of the air is AIR SUPERIORITY. This latter phrase does not imply total dominance of the air—only enough dominance that an enemy cannot seriously interfere with continuing operations against it.

command of the sea   The traditional object of a military strategy based on a BLUE WATER NAVY: the free use of the sea and the denial of its free use to any enemy. This concept has been important ever since the age of discovery in the sixteenth century. As Sir Walter Raleigh wrote in his *History of the World* (1614): "Whosoever commands the sea commands the trade; whosoever commands the trade of the world commands the riches of the world, and consequently the world itself." Yet it remained for Alfred Thayer Mahan's *The Influence of Sea Power Upon History* (1890) to provide the definitive rationale for seeking to command the seas: "It is not the taking of individual ships or convoys, be they few or many, that strikes down the money power of a nation; it is the possession of that overbearing power on the sea which drives the enemy's flag from it, or allows it to appear only as the fugitive; and by controlling the great common, closes the highways by which commerce moves to and from the enemy's shores. This overbearing power can only be exercised by great navies." British Prime Minister Winston Churchill, in an October 11, 1940, speech in the House of Commons, elaborated: "When we speak of command of the seas, it does not mean command of every part of the sea at the same moment, or at every moment. It only means that we can make our will prevail ultimately in any part of seas which may be selected for operations, and thus indirectly make our will prevail in every part of the seas." Increasingly, however, the term *command of the sea* has given way to the idea of a sea control, which is more localized and more in keeping with Churchill's assessment than with Mahan's.

commercial attaché   The commerce expert on the diplomatic staff of her or his country's embassy or large consulate.

commission   1. To put in or make ready for service or use, as to commission an aircraft or a ship. 2. A written order giving a person rank and authority as an officer in the armed forces. 3. The rank and the authority given by such an order. 4. A group responsible for a government activity, whether on an ad hoc or a permanent basis. Commissions tend to be used when (1) it is desirable to have bipartisan leadership, (2) their functions are of a quasi-judicial nature, or (3) it is deemed important to have wide representation of ethnic groups, regions of the country, differing skills, and so on. 5. Internationally, a

United Nations group, numbering from 28 to 36 members, that meets once a year or every two years and is charged with investigating a particular subject area, such as human rights.

commissioned officer   A military officer who holds a grade and office under a commission issued by the head of state. In the U.S. Army, Air Force, and Marine Corps, a person who has been appointed to the grade of second lieutenant or higher is a commissioned officer; currently four-star general is the highest commissioned grade. In the navy, ensign is the lowest commissioned rank; four-star admiral is the highest.

Commission of the European Communities   *See* EUROPEAN COMMISSION.

commitment   A pledge to behave in a particular way in the future even though it will restrict one's freedom of action. Commitments are the basis for ALLIANCES and for security guarantees. They are an important feature of international politics as they help to structure international order by creating expectations about future behavior. Reneging on commitments damages one's CREDIBILITY and so is discouraged.

Committee of Ministers   *See* COUNCIL OF EUROPE.

Committee of Permanent Representatives   *See* COUNCIL OF MINISTERS.

Committee of the Whole   **1.** The complete membership of a legislature when it considers an issue en masse.   **2.** In the United States the working title of what is formally the Committee of the Whole House on the State of the Union. Composed of all members of the U.S. House of Representatives, it is used to debate measures that the leadership wants to expedite.   **3.** An entity created by the United Nations General Assembly in December 1977 to monitor implementation of decisions reached in the UN regarding the NEW INTERNATIONAL ECONOMIC ORDER and to serve as a forum on global economic problems. The committee is open to all UN members. *Compare to* BRANDT COMMISSION; CANCUN SUMMIT; CONFERENCE ON INTERNATIONAL ECONOMIC COOPERATION; NORTH-SOUTH DIALOGUE.

Committee of Twenty-Four   A committee created by the United Nations General Assembly in 1961 to monitor the implementation of the General Assembly's 1960 "Declaration on the Granting of Independence to Colonial Countries and Peoples." Sometimes referred to as the Committee on Decolonization. The formal name of the committee is "The Special Committee on the Situation with Regard to the Implementation of the Declaration on Decolonization." In carrying out its mandate, the committee sends missions to territories and prepares reports on colonial problems, liberation movements, and territorial disputes. Sixty former colonial territories with over 80 million people have achieved independence since 1960. The committee continues its work because there are still more than a dozen colonies left—mostly small islands in the Pacific Ocean and Caribbean Sea.

Committee on Decolonization   *See* COMMITTEE OF TWENTY-FOUR.

Committee on the Present Danger   A nonprofit citizens' group founded in the United States in 1976 that considered the main threat to U.S. national security to be "the Soviet drive for dominance based upon an unparalleled military buildup." The committee advocated a stronger U.S. military position and more defense spending to counter the Soviet buildup and to close the WINDOW OF VULNERABILITY. The committee was very effective in lobbying against SALT II and in favor of enhancing U.S. military capabilities. It helped to produce a climate in which restoring U.S. military strength was seen as both urgent and vital—an atmosphere that contributed to RONALD W. REAGAN's victory in the 1980 presidential elections. Some members of the committee later became prominent in the Reagan Administration, including WILLIAM CASEY, JEANE KIRKPATRICK, and PAUL H. NITZE. The committee became inactive with the ending of the COLD WAR.

commodity   The unprocessed products of mining and agriculture, for example, coffee beans (but not ground coffee) and wheat (but not flour). An exception is sugar, which is considered a commodity although it is shipped after processing. Because commodities are traded on futures market and sold at auction, they are very vulnerable to price changes.

This vulnerability is of particular international significance because many THIRD WORLD states achieve an overwhelming percentage of their foreign earnings from the sale of just a few commodities.

commodity agreement An international understanding, formally accepted by the principal exporters and importers, regarding international trading of a raw material and usually intended to affect its price. Commodity agreements may involve decisions to accumulate stockpiles in times of high production and low prices and to draw on those stockpiles when production declines and prices increase. In this way, commodity producers' foreign exchange earnings, which are vital for their development, and the quantity and price of goods available to consumers can be more stable from year to year. Some countries would like to use commodity agreements to raise prices for the commodities they produce. Consuming countries generally are willing to agree to only those commodity agreements that seek to moderate extreme price fluctuations.

common agricultural policy (CAP) The farm policies of the EUROPEAN COMMUNITY. Its goals are stated in Article 39 of the Treaty of Rome: to improve productivity, to create stable markets and regular supplies, and to provide reasonable prices to consumers as well as a fair return for farmers. The CAP, although successful in increasing food production and rural living standards, has been a source of conflict within the EC, because it involves a complicated set of price supports and subsidies that seem to benefit the food-producing members at the expense of the food-importing members.

common European house An oft-used phrase of former Soviet President MIKHAIL GORBACHEV that implied that all European states were members of one big family. This phrase downplayed the very real economic, military, and political divisions of Eastern and Western Europe during the COLD WAR. It also implied that the United States was not part of the family. While the phrase is linked to Gorbachev, he was not the first Soviet leader to use it. Soviet President LEONID BREZHNEV said in a speech in Bonn, Germany, on November 23, 1981: "Whatever may divide us, Europe is our common home; a common fate has linked us through the centuries

and it continues to link us today." Because the phrase was so associated with the leaders of the former Soviet Union, it has not been used widely by Western leaders—even though the point it makes is perfectly obvious and true.

common external tariff A tax rate on certain imported goods uniformly applied within a regional grouping of countries, such as the European Community. For example, the EC permits free internal trade, but applies common external tariffs against many products imported from nonmember countries. *See also* CUSTOMS UNION.

common good 1. Something that benefits an organized society as a whole. All states have an inherent obligation to promote the common good. Common goods such as clean air or safe streets are identified by the fact that they cannot be denied to any citizen. Common good is a far broader concept than PUBLIC GOOD. 2. Property (land and/or buildings) held in common by an entire political community. *See also* TRAGEDY OF THE COMMONS.

common heritage of mankind A designation of the seabed in international waters, as established under international law by the 1982 United Nations Conference on the LAW OF THE SEA.

common market 1. A politically defined area in which all trade in goods and services is conducted on the same terms: a CUSTOMS UNION. 2. A popular term for the European Economic Community (EEC), the economic arm of the EUROPEAN COMMUNITY; the world's largest customs union with 265 million people. The EEC was established in 1958 by the TREATY OF ROME. The original members (Belgium, France, Italy, Luxembourg, the Netherlands, and West Germany) were referred to as "The Six"; in 1973 "The Six" became "The Nine" when Denmark, Ireland, and the United Kingdom joined through a TREATY OF ACCESSION. The United Kingdom initially had declined to join and then had been blocked from entering by Charles de Gaulle of France in the 1960s. When Greece became a member in 1981, "The Nine" became "The Ten." In 1986 Spain and Portugal became the eleventh and twelfth members. Some of the purposes and activities of the EEC are the elimination of tariffs and other restrictions on trade between member states; the maintenance of a common tariff toward other countries; the free movement of citizens and capital within the EC; the establishment of a COMMON AGRICULTURAL POLICY; and the association of overseas countries with the Common Market to increase trade and to promote development. The Treaty of Rome explicitly envisioned an eventual political union. The term *common market* is being used rather less often as the European Community moves toward the creation of a single market and as Western Europe moves toward political union. The success of the EEC in the 1980s was another factor that weakened the Communists of Eastern Europe with their poor economies. *See also* EURATOM; EUROPEAN COAL AND STEEL COMMUNITY; EUROPEAN MONETARY SYSTEM; EUROPEAN PARLIAMENT.

common security   *See* MUTUAL SECURITY.

commonwealth   The belief of Thomas Hobbes (1588–1679) and other European philosophers of his era that the members of a social order have a "common weal," or good, which is in their collective interest to preserve and protect. They considered anarchy and chaos to be the greatest threat to civilized society. "Common weal" evolved into "commonwealth," which came to mean the modern, centralized federal state. Thus the republic established in Great Britain under Oliver Cromwell from 1649 to 1660 was called the Commonwealth. Four American states are, formally, commonwealths rather than states: Pennsylvania, Virginia, Massachusetts, and Kentucky.

Commonwealth of Independent States (CIS)   A term used to describe the institutional successor to the Soviet Union. The CIS was created on December 21, 1991, when leaders of 11 former Soviet republics met in Alma-Ata, Kazakhstan. The republics that became members of the commonwealth are Armenia, Azerbaijan, Belarus, Kazakhstan, Kyrgyzstan, Moldova, Russia, Tajikistan, Turkmenistan, Ukraine, and Uzbekistan. Three of the four remaining former republics of the Soviet Union (Estonia, Latvia, and Lithuania) refused to join the CIS. And the last of the 15 previous Soviet republics, Georgia, chose to be represented in the CIS only by "observers." Azerbaijan subsequently

withdrew. The CIS is not a state in that it provides no common citizenship and no officials elected by the entire population of the CIS. Its function is to regulate only those common concerns that the constituent states through a Council of Heads of States agrees to. The CIS has been given the authority to provide unitary control over the strategic nuclear weapons of the former Soviet Union and to create an economic union for its members.

Commonwealth of Nations   The formal association of the states that were once colonies of the BRITISH EMPIRE. It is an entirely voluntary association for the purpose of international cooperation and consultation. The members have no treaty obligations or binding commitments. Fifty states were members of the Commonwealth in 1992, but not all former colonies are members. Some, such as Egypt and Iraq, were never members. Others, such as Fiji, Ireland, Pakistan, and South Africa, were once members but left because of various disagreements. In the immediate post–World War II period Commonwealth members were given trade preferences and other economic assistance, but when the United Kingdom joined the EUROPEAN COMMUNITY those preferences dissipated. The British monarch is the ceremonial leader of the Commonwealth. The British Empire was transformed into the British Commonwealth in the interwar period. This was seen as a way for Great Britain to maintain its position as an international actor and avoid the kind of disintegration that characterized the empires of the other European powers. The idea of the Commonwealth came partly from Jan Smuts of South Africa, who in 1917 described it to the leaders of the other dominions. After stating that the term *British Empire* was a misnomer, Smuts suggested that the British Empire was different from others that had been concerned with assimilation: "You do not want to standardize the nations of the British Empire; you want to develop them to fuller, greater nationality . . . this is the fundamental fact that we have to bear in mind—that the British Commonwealth of Nations does not stand for standardization or denationalization but for the fuller, richer and more varied life of all the nations that are comprised in it." Smuts also was responsible for the crucial resolution adopted by the Imperial War Conference on March 16, 1917, which acknowledged that readjustment had to be based on "a full recognition of the dominions as autonomous nations of an Imperial Commonwealth, and of India as an important portion of the same." This resolution led the way to the Statute of Westminster of December 1931, which set out to remove the remaining restrictions on the independence of Commonwealth countries. At this time the Commonwealth was a "white man's club" of those states ruled by white settlers—Australia, Canada, New Zealand, South Africa—and accompanied rather than superseded the empire. Nevertheless, it provided the basis for the complete transformation of the British Empire into the British Commonwealth. The word *British* was dropped in 1949 to emphasize the equality of member states. The Commonwealth has had a secretariat in London since 1965.

communal conflict   Tensions between different ethnic or religious groups within a state that can lead to terrorist attacks or civil war. Examples include the conflicts between Serbs and Croats in Yugoslavia, Protestants and Catholics in Northern Ireland, and Hindus and Muslims in India.

communications   1. Routes and means of transportation for troops and supplies, especially in a THEATER OF WAR. 2. The means of giving and receiving military orders and intelligence. The classic comment on what to do if there is a communications foul up, as is often the case in war, is credited to the British Admiral Horatio Nelson, who said before his great victory at the 1805 Battle of Trafalgar against the French: "But, in case signals can neither be seen or perfectly understood, no captain can do very wrong if he places his ship alongside that of an enemy." 3. An activity that takes place among states as they attempt to influence each other's behavior. Communication involves both a transmitter of a signal or message and a recipient. Clearer communication sometimes is seen as a way of enhancing understanding. 4. A term used to refer to transactions among states. In the 1950s KARL DEUTSCH and other scholars focused on communication flows as a key development in the INTEGRATION process in Western Europe.

communications intelligence   Technical, military, and political information derived from foreign communications by someone other than the intended recipient. Also called COMINT. *See also* CRYPTOLOGY.

communiqué   1. A formal statement by a government to the press or public. 2. Joint statements made by parties during or after diplomatic sessions. They were especially popular during U.S.-Soviet SUMMIT meetings when the world's press hungered for news of any kind. Seldom was it reported that these statements were usually drafted and negotiated in advance by staff members so that they could be blessed by the leaders and dispensed at the appropriate time. According to Helmut Sonnenfeldt in "Summit Speak" (*The New Republic*, May 30, 1988), "As the art of the communiqué evolved, the language became ritualistic, and often the documents discussed matters that had not come up at all. The most you could say of their accuracy as historical record is that they were not inconsistent with what was or might have been said. Indeed, by including a matter in the communiqué, reference to it in the actual meetings could become superfluous."

THE COMMUNIQUE AS EXIT VISA

Humphrey had written a final communiqué before the meeting. I told him he couldn't possibly do that.

"On the contrary, Minister, you can't write the communiqué after the meeting. We have had to get agreement from half a dozen other departments, from the EEC Commission, from Washington, from the Qumrani Embassy—you can't do that in a few hours in the middle of the desert."

So I glanced at it. Then I pointed out that it was useless, hypothetical, sheer guesswork—it may bear no relation to what we actually say.

Sir Humphrey smiled calmly. "No communiqué ever bears any relation to what you actually say."

"So why do we have one?"

"It's just a sort of exit visa. Gets you past the press corps."

SOURCE: Jonathan Lynn and Antony Jay, *The Complete Yes Minister* (1984).

---

communism   An idealized stateless and classless social system with common ownership of land and capital in which each member would contribute according to capabilities and take according to needs. Communism is not SOCIALISM; in socialism, the structures of the state are still in place. Communists consider socialism to be just a transitional stage from the despised system of CAPITALISM to the idealized communism. All of the twentieth-century's "Communist" states have been socialist states because they never got beyond their transitional stage. Communism is intellectually derived from Karl Marx's doctrine of social and economic development known as MARXISM. It is based on ECONOMIC DETERMINISM, which interprets history in terms of the CLASS STRUGGLE. In Marxist thinking, the eventual triumph of the PROLETARIAT is inevitable. A DICTATORSHIP OF THE PROLETARIAT will establish a new political order and eventually the state will wither away. V. I. LENIN expanded on the ideas of Marx to form MARXISM-LENINISM, the doctrine by which he temporarily unified a diverse group of republics with different ethnic and nationalist bases to form the Soviet Union. As an international movement during the COLD WAR, the Soviet version of communism was seen as a threat to the FREE WORLD. Communism, because it directly threatened capitalism, was an ideology that the Western powers found anathema. Western nations, rightly suspecting that the Soviet Union was trying to subvert their governments, developed anti-Communist policies such as CONTAINMENT. The term *communism* was used in the 1950s to describe the bloc of states led by the Soviet Union that included China and the states of Eastern Europe. As the Chinese and Yugoslav experiences showed, however, Communist movements that came to power through their own efforts, as opposed to those that came to power with the help of the RED ARMY, were unwilling to subordinate themselves to Moscow. With the demise of the Soviet Union, communism as a doctrine has become discredited in Europe and the former Soviet Union, but it is still the official ideology in the People's Republic of China, Cuba, and North Korea.

Communism, Goulash   A mid-1980s term for the economic reforms in Hungary and other Eastern European states, including the Soviet Union, which emphasized more consumer goods, more "goulash" (a Hungarian meat stew) for the people. Goulash communism became obsolete when the Communist governments of Eastern Europe were deposed in 1989.

Communist International   *See* COMINTERN.

Communist Manifesto, The   The ideological declaration of MARXISM, written by Karl Marx (1818–1883) and Frederick Engels (1820–1895) at the request of the 1847 Second Congress of the Communist League in London. It was first published in 1848.

FAMOUS THOUGHTS FROM
THE COMMUNIST MANIFESTO

A spectre is haunting Europe—the spectre of Communism.

•

The history of all hitherto existing society is the history of class struggles.

•

Political Power, properly so called, is merely the organised power of one class for oppressing another.

•

Let the ruling classes tremble at a Communistic revolution. The proletarians have nothing to lose but their chains. They have a world to win. WORKING MEN OF ALL COUNTRIES, UNITE!

Communist Party of the Soviet Union (CPSU)   The political party that controlled the UNION OF SOVIET SOCIALIST REPUBLICS (U.S.S.R.) from 1917 until 1991. The CPSU was created from the Russian workers' movement. It was organized by V. I. LENIN and other Russian Marxists. Lenin integrated the concepts of MARXISM with his own. Thus the main doctrine of the party under Lenin recognized the CPSU as the leading organization of the proletariat, because without the power of the proletariat, the building of socialism and communism would be impossible. The CPSU led the struggle of the workers and peasants in three revolutions: the 1905–1907 bourgeois-democratic revolution in Russia, the February 1917 bourgeois-democratic revolution, and the Great October Socialist Revolution of 1917. U.S. journalist John Reed wrote in *Ten Days That Shook the World* (1926) of the moment in Petrograd when Lenin assumed power in 1917: "Now Lenin, gripping the edge of the reading stand, letting his little winking eyes travel over the crowd as he stood there waiting, apparently oblivious to the long-rolling ovation, which lasted several minutes. When it finished he said simply, 'We shall now proceed to construct the Socialist order!' "

Until 1990 the CPSU was the Soviet people's only legal political party. About 10 percent of the population were members. The party exercised control through the nomenklatura, a list of senior positions that had to be filled by select party members. As a result nearly all of the most important managerial, administrative, and intellectual jobs were filled by party loyalists. In addition the party organized most social life, controlled the trade unions, and had the sole right to put up candidates in elections (none of which were contested). Senior party members received many privileges, such as access to imported goods and better educational opportunities for their children, providing yet another incentive to membership. The party, which holds the distinction of ruling longer than any other party in the world, began suffering in the late 1980s from nonrecruitment and significant resignations. The final blow to this once-powerful and important organization of the Soviet Union came from the resignation of the secretary of the CPSU, MIKHAIL GORBACHEV, and his decision to dissolve the party's governing powers in August 1991, following an abortive coup attempt in which top party leaders were implicated.

community   **1.** A group of people or nations who share the same basic values and outlook and who cooperate in the pursuit of common objectives. The term *community of states* is sometimes used to refer to the idea of an international society.   **2.** A political arrangement in which members expect that conflicts which arise will be settled without the use of force. Closely related is the notion of SECURITY COMMUNITY.   **3.** The EUROPEAN COMMUNITY.

community law   The totality of the binding treaty provisions, legislation, regulations, directions, and so on of the EUROPEAN COMMUNITY.

Compact of Free Association   A 1981 agreement by the United States with the Marshall Islands and the Federated States of Micronesia, two island groups in the North Pacific for which the United States has been the United Nations Trustee since 1947. The compact provides for a change in the status of the islands from trustee territories to freely associated states that are to have self-government in domestic and foreign affairs, with the United States remaining responsible for their defense and external security for 15 years. It was endorsed by UN-observed plebiscites in the territories in 1983 and approved by the U.S. Congress in 1985; it was signed by President Ronald Reagan on January 14, 1986.

Company, the   An informal term for the CENTRAL INTELLIGENCE AGENCY.

comparative advantage   What a state or region has when it makes those goods it can make relatively more efficiently than other goods. Modern trade theory holds that, regardless of a state's productivity or labor costs relative to those of other states, it should produce for export those goods in which it has the greatest comparative advantage and import those in which it has the greatest comparative disadvantage. The state that has few economic strengths will find it advantageous to devote its productive energies to those lines in which its disadvantage is least marked, provided it has the opportunity to trade with other areas. The comparative advantage theory was first proposed by the English economist David Ricardo (1772–1823) in 1817. *Compare to* ABSOLUTE ADVANTAGE.

comparative foreign policy   The systematic study of the international behavior of states in order to ascertain patterns of behavior and their underlying determinants. The idea of the comparative study of foreign policy was promoted as part of a scientific approach to international politics. The argument was that comparison would make it possible to achieve better generalizations about state behavior. JAMES ROSENAU, one of the leading figures in this field, posed the question in his *The Scientific Study of Foreign Policy* (1971) as to whether comparative foreign policy was "fad, fantasy or field?" Although there has been no definitive answer to this question, it is clear that comparative foreign policy has not yielded the generalizations about state behavior that its proponents hoped for. Nevertheless, it continues to be a field of study.

comparative politics The study of the ways in which different societies cope with the problems of political structures and government. It seeks to develop an understanding of how different institutional mechanisms work within their contexts and, more ambitiously, to develop general hypotheses concerning government. Perhaps the main problem for comparative politics as a science is that it lacks a generally agreed upon theoretical framework that would identify what the principal tasks of a political system are and thereby locate the institutions or structures that should be compared. Thus it is difficult to know which comparisons are useful. As a result researchers have tended to stick to obvious comparisons within a limited range.

compartmentation **1.** Establishment and management of an intelligence organization so that information about the personnel, organization, or activities of one component (or CELL) is made available to any other component only on a NEED TO KNOW basis. The term is derived from the naval practice of dividing ships' hulls into watertight compartments. **2.** In UNCONVENTIONAL WARFARE, the division of an organization or activity into functional segments or cells to restrict communication between them and prevent knowledge of the identity or activities of other segments except on a need-to-know basis.

compellence A method by which one international actor can force another to do something it would not otherwise do. Compellence is a variation on the idea of DETERRENCE. While deterrence is intended to inhibit an adversary from taking inimical actions, compellence involves threatening the other party to force it to do something that it does not want to do. With deterrence, threats are implemented only if prohibited actions are taken. Compellence, in contrast, typically involves initiating an action (often an act of war) and desisting only when the opponent responds in the way that one desires. Bombing an adversary to force it to sue for peace fits into this concept of compellence. Compellence is achieved by changing an adversary's cost-gain calculus (an assessment of whether a possible gain is worth the cost of achieving it). Being offensive in nature, it is used to alter the status quo rather than uphold it. *Compare to* FORCE MAJEURE.

competitive model A model of foreign policy decision making discussed by ALEXANDER L. GEORGE in *Presidential Decisionmaking in Foreign Policy* (1980); it refers to arrangements that allow for open and uninhibited expressions of diverse opinions, analyses, and advice. Such a system tends to have overlapping jurisdictions and be based on the notion that competition among advisors is creative and constructive. The danger is that it also can cause policy paralysis and confusion. *Compare to* COLLEGIAL MODEL.

competitiveness The ability of a state to achieve economic success in comparison to other states. In the United States in the late 1980s, the term became an abbreviated way of referring to the need for a comprehensive national INDUSTRIAL POLICY, to the persistent problem of the lagging productivity of U.S. workers, and to an increasingly unfavorable U.S. BALANCE OF TRADE. Competitiveness goes beyond the concerns of international trade to a concern for, indeed a reevaluation of, a state's entire business structure.

complex conglomerate system An analytical construct in international relations in which there are many autonomous actors of different types that tend to make ALIGNMENTS which are diffuse, flexible, and related to specific situations. These alignments often arise in relation to a specific issue and may exist only in relation to that issue. The concept was developed by Richard Mansbach, Yale Ferguson, and Donald Lampert in *The Web of World Politics* (1976).

complex interdependence The notion that international relations can no longer be understood in terms simply of the interactions between states. The BILLIARD BALL MODEL has been replaced by a different conception based on economic, social, and political interdependencies among nations, the rise of nonstate actors, and the emergence of transnational linkages among societies that, in part at least, are independent of government. This system has been described in terms of the COBWEB MODEL or the COMPLEX CONGLOMERATE SYSTEM.

compound duty *See* DUTY, COMPOUND.

comprador 1. Portuguese for "buyer"; a term for a native agent used by foreign (originally colonial) businesses as an intermediary. 2. Business interests in the Third World that have close ties to First World counterparts. Marxists use this term in a critical way to suggest the continued exploitation of Third World workers by compradors who represent the old colonial powers.

Comprehensive Test Ban Treaty (CTBT) A treaty that would prohibit all test explosions of nuclear devices. Such an agreement does not exist. However, partial measures have been undertaken. The PARTIAL TEST BAN TREATY (PTBT) of 1963 prohibited nuclear tests in the atmosphere; thereafter Great Britain, the Soviet Union, and the United States conducted their tests underground. China and France remained outside this agreement and have continued to conduct atmospheric tests. At the conclusion of the first SALT talks, agreement was reached on the Threshold Test Ban Treaty of 1974. This limited the size of nuclear devices that could be tested to 150 kilotons but does not impose real limitations on the superpowers. After all, the devices they typically test are nuclear-trigger mechanisms that create relatively small explosions. Those who favor a CTBT argue that the inability to test new or existing nuclear weapons would reduce the confidence of the military in such weapons, forcing them to be more cautious in their estimation of their capabilities. This in turn would reduce the military's faith in prospects for a successful first strike. The argument against this position is that the ability to test new nuclear devices results in safer, tamperproof, more accurate, and smaller weapons. With the end of the COLD WAR the prospects for a CTBT may well be enhanced.

compromis d'arbitrage A French term for the agreement of two or more states to submit a dispute to arbitration.

compromise 1. In intelligence terminology, the known or suspected exposure of clandestine personnel, installations, or other assets or of classified information or material to an unauthorized person. After such exposure or possible exposure, the material is said to be *compromised*. 2. In diplomatic terminology, the end state of a negotiation or bargaining process that reflects the fact that none of the parties has achieved all it wanted, but that all have achieved some of what they wanted.

CONADEP (Comisión Nacional Sobre la Desaparición de Personas) Argentina's "National Commission on Disappeared Persons." CONADEP was established by the democratic, civilian government of Raul Alfonsin Foulkes to investigate the state terrorism of the military regime that ruled Argentina from March 1976 until December 1983. The report of CONADEP, issued on September 21, 1984, was unable to account for 8,960 people who disappeared in the Argentine DIRTY WAR. The CONADEP report extends over 50,000 pages and documents a system of terror that included 340 clandestine jails and a regimen of torture, rape, and murder. In 1985 high-ranking military officers were found guilty by a civilian court of crimes (documented by CONADEP) committed during this period. *See also* ARGENTINE FASCISM.

concealment *See* BLACK.

concentration camps A prison system used by a nation to detain or exterminate political opponents, dissidents, members of ethnic or religious minority groups, or other individuals deemed dangerous or undesirable by the regime. While the term dates from the BOER WAR, concentration camps became infamous as an integral part of the NAZI repression and extermination of Jews, Gypsies, Poles, Communists, homosexuals, and others. More than 6 million Jews and a like number of others were killed in the Nazi concentration camps, most in poison gas chambers; others died from the inhumane conditions in the camps and maltreatment. During World War II many outsiders refused to believe the level of atrocities in these camps until the prisoners were liberated by U.S. and Soviet forces. Concentration camps have been used as forced labor camps; the Soviet system of GULAGS has been categorized in this way. *See also* HOLOCAUST.

Conceptual Military Framework *See* CONVENTIONAL DEFENSE INITIATIVE.

Concert of Europe The system of managing relations among the great powers of Europe that was

Slave laborers in the Buchenwald concentration camp freed by U.S. troops on April 16, 1945. The face on the second level from bottom, closest to the third post from left, is that of sixteen-year-old Elie Wiesel, who was awarded the Nobel Peace Prize in 1986. (National Archives)

established by the Congress of Vienna in 1815. Historians and international relations analysts differ about how long the concert lasted, with some seeing it as lasting only until 1822, others as enduring until the 1850s, and still others seeing it as prevailing throughout the nineteenth and even into the early twentieth century. The differences depend in part on the degree of cooperation that is deemed necessary for a CONCERT SYSTEM to exist and operate. The system was based on a willingness of the five great powers in Europe—Austria, Great Britain, France, Prussia, and Russia—to restrain diplomacy and the use of force, to limit their objectives, and to manage the BALANCE OF POWER through periodic conferences. Underlying the system were shared goals and values among the great powers, at least as far as their foreign policies were concerned; the ability of governments to act relatively free of domestic constraints and pressures; and a common desire to preserve the key elements of the system. In practice the great powers tended to meet in the aftermath of wars or crises and agree on the distribution of the spoils in ways that were generally held to be satisfactory. The system demanded a certain flexibility of alignment in an effort to maintain a

balance of power and has been described by Michael Mandelbaum in *The Fate of Nations* (1988) as a "managed balance of power system." Richard Langhorne, a historian who believes that the Concert of Europe did not finally break down until 1914, argues in *The Collapse of the Concert of Europe* (1981) that the area of restraint also covered a carefully defined region—although disputes over this added to the demise of the system. He contends that the concert system broke down for a variety of reasons, including the rise of Germany, which challenged fundamentally the balance of power; the growing rigidity of the alliance system in Europe; increased democratization, which made it very difficult to make the kinds of territorial arrangements that did not lead to grievances and to demands for revenge; and the extension of European rivalry to Africa and the Far East.

concert system   A term used to describe a system in which the great powers cooperate to manage the BALANCE OF POWER and to impose both restraint and constraint on the use of force. Some analysts, including Charles Kupchan and Clifford Kupchan in "A New Concert for Europe" (in G. Allison and

G. Treverton, eds., *Rethinking America's Security,* 1992), contend that such a system should be used to manage security in Europe in the post–COLD WAR era. They argue:

> Concert represents the most attenuated form of collective security . . . a small group of major powers agrees to work together to resist aggression; they meet on a regular basis to monitor events and, if necessary, to orchestrate collective initiatives. A concert's geographic scope is flexible. . . . Decisions are taken through informal negotiations, through the emergence of a consensus. The flexibility and informality of a concert system allow the structure to retain an ongoing current of balancing behavior among the major powers.

While this is a thoughtful approach to the new agenda of European security problems, the kinds of ethnic and nationalist acts that seem most likely to occur in Europe are not readily amenable to great power direction. Nevertheless, it is not impossible that elements of the old concert system may reappear in the management of international security problems in Europe and elsewhere in the years ahead.

concessional terms Special lower-than-market-interest loans to THIRD WORLD borrowers.

concessions In GATT trade negotiations, those reductions a country offers to make in its own tariff and nontariff import barriers to induce other countries to make reductions in barriers to its exports. *See also* RECIPROCITY.

conciliation 1. The bringing together of two disputing sides to agree on a voluntary compromise. 2. An international dispute-settling technique whereby a disagreement is submitted to a standing or ad hoc independent commission that examines the facts of the case and makes a recommendation for settlement. However, this recommendation is only advisory and the parties, unlike the similar process of ARBITRATION, are under no formal obligation to accept it. *See also* MEDIATION.

conclusum 1. A diplomatic note that sums up international negotiations. 2. A joint memoran-

dum by two or more parties to a negotiation that summarizes agreements to date.

concordat 1. A formal agreement between a state and a church. 2. Formal agreements between governments and the papacy. For example, in 1933 the government of Nazi Germany negotiated with the papacy an agreement whereby the status and property of the Catholic church in Germany was assured in exchange for the church's agreeing that priests would take no part in politics. Thus the church was officially silent about German atrocities throughout the Nazi era.

Concordat of 1905 The agreement that separated the Catholic church from the state in France. The state no longer paid Catholic clergy, and congregations had to maintain their own churches and schools. The French Catholic church became a private religious organization. This agreement followed the French national trauma of the DREYFUS AFFAIR, in which Catholic military leaders scapegoated a Jewish officer to cover up their own dishonorable duplicity in treason.

Concorde The Anglo-French supersonic passenger plane that was built in the 1970s by Great Britain and France. Although the project was very costly it was highly prestigious, especially because the United States had decided not to build its own supersonic passenger aircraft. The Concorde began regular air service in 1976. Because of claims of its excessive noise and ecological damage, there was great opposition to the plane in the United States. After extended negotiations it was given permission to use only a few U.S. airports. That, coupled with the fact that it could carry only 100 passengers at a time, meant that the plane was not economically viable. Even though the plane flies scheduled service to airports on most continents, it has created an overall net loss to date of about $4 billion to Britain and France. Their taxpaying citizens still wonder if the prestige was worth it.

CONDECA *See* CENTRAL AMERICAN DEFENSE COUNCIL.

conditionality An economic policy demanded of a THIRD WORLD borrower by the International Monetary Fund or other lender as a condition of a loan. Typical conditionalities are austerity measures to reduce inflation, currency devaluations, reduced food subsidies, and so on. Some Third World analysts consider conditionalities to be a new form of colonialism—another means by which the West seeks to continue domination of its former colonies.

condominium **1.** Joint rule by two or more states over the same territory, each of which exercises sovereignty. For example, there was a Franco-British condominium over the New Hebrides islands from 1914 to 1980. **2.** Private property that is jointly owned. **3.** The idea of two-power domination of the international system. During the Cold War fears were expressed that the United States and the Soviet Union might attempt to establish a condominium over the international system.

Condor Legion The German armed forces that aided the fascist side during the SPANISH CIVIL WAR. While the legion totaled less than 10,000 men at any one time, its rotation policies gave over 16,000 German soldiers combat experience in what was widely considered a "rehearsal" for WORLD WAR II. The legion, which included air elements, was notorious for the killing of many civilians in the northern Spanish town of Guernica in 1937. One of artist Pablo Picasso's most famous paintings commemorates the destruction of this Basque town.

confederation **1.** A group of independent states that delegates powers on limited issues to a central government. In a confederation, the central government is decidedly limited and thus may be inherently weak as it has few powers of it own. The United States was a confederation from 1781 to 1789. **2.** A military alliance. **3.** An alliance of private interests that combine to exert pressure on a government or advance the welfare of its members. The Confederation of British Industry is an example. *Compare to* FEDERATION.

Conference on Disarmament The United Nations forum on world disarmament. Since 1959 the UN has sponsored a variety of groups dedicated to furthering disarmament. This conference, which consists of 40 states, including the five major nuclear powers, is its latest manifestation. Prior to 1983 it

was known as the Committee on Disarmament. The UN, since its founding, has been concerned with general and complete disarmament as an ultimate goal. The conference meets annually in Geneva and reports to the UN General Assembly.

Conference on Disarmament in Europe *See* CONFERENCE ON SECURITY AND CONFIDENCE-BUILDING MEASURES AND DISARMAMENT IN EUROPE.

Conference on International Economic Cooperation (CIEC) A 27-state consultation group of developing and developed countries, familiarly called the NORTH-SOUTH DIALOGUE, convened in response to a suggestion by French President Valery Giscard d'Estaing in 1974. In an effort to create a permanent forum to discuss North-South issues, the World Bank in 1977 created the BRANDT COMMISSION to continue the work of CIEC. *Compare to* CANCUN SUMMIT; COMMITTEE OF THE WHOLE.

Conference on Security and Confidence-Building Measures and Disarmament in Europe (CDE) A conference that grew out of the Madrid follow-up meeting to the CONFERENCE ON SECURITY AND COOPERATION IN EUROPE (CSCE) and convened in Stockholm in 1984. The main objective of CDE has been to seek agreements that limit the size of military exercises taking place in Europe without the participating countries informing the other members of the CDE. The purpose is to remove the fear that traditionally attends unannounced major exercises: that they are really a cover for troop mobilization prior to war. To this end the CDE talks have had to face up to the problem of VERIFICATION. In a proposal made in September 1986 and signed by all members, a plan was accepted to allow air inspection by teams of observers, as long as the aircraft are flown by pilots from the countries carrying out the exercises. Although this is only a modest achievement, it is a valuable first step that, until the 1987 INF TREATY, marked the first time that the Soviet Union had agreed to such "intrusive" on-site inspections. *Compare to* CONFIDENCE-BUILDING MEASURES.

Conference on Security and Cooperation in Europe (CSCE) The international meeting attended by the United States, Canada, and 33 countries of

Europe to discuss East-West issues of mutual concern. The notion of a pan-European security conference was a Soviet idea but was eventually used by the West to press the HUMAN RIGHTS issue. Meetings of the 35 were held in Helsinki, Finland, and Geneva, Switzerland, beginning in July 1973 and culminating in the HELSINKI ACCORDS of 1975. Follow-up sessions of the conference were held in Belgrade, Yugoslavia, during 1977 and 1978; in Madrid, Spain, from 1980 to 1983; and in Vienna, Austria, beginning in 1986. The CSCE process also provided the framework within which the CONVENTIONAL FORCES EUROPE TREATY (CFE) talks took place. Although the CFE talks were limited to the 23 North Atlantic Treaty Organization and Warsaw Pact nations, the CFE participants reported to the Conference on Security and Cooperation in Europe. Moreover the CFE agreement was signed at a CSCE Summit in Paris, France, in November 1990. It appeared at this meeting that with the end of the Cold War, the Conference on Security and Cooperation in Europe could provide a basis for a COLLECTIVE SECURITY system in Europe. As the membership has expanded to include the new nations of the former Soviet Union, however, the CSCE has become even more unwieldy and did not prove very effective in dealing with the YUGOSLAVIAN CIVIL WAR.

Conference on the Law of the Sea　*See* LAW OF THE SEA.

confidence-building measures (CBMs)　**1.** An extension of diplomacy whereby states take small initiatives designed to create modest trust with adversaries that lead to larger initiatives that can lead to greater trust, and so on.　**2.** A form of ARMS CONTROL that seeks to reduce the fear of a surprise attack; they build trust between adversaries by putting limitations on acts that may be interpreted as militarily threatening. Thus international tensions are less likely to develop into war because neither side would feel the compulsion to make a preemptive strike. CBMs typically require notice of large-scale military exercises. Traditionally there has been a fear that major military exercises were masks for troop concentrations intended to launch an attack. By letting potential enemies know that an exercise is planned and

inviting them to send military observers to check that it really is an exercise, this fear is alleviated. CBMs, or confidence- and security-building measures (CSBMs) as they are also known, were pioneered through Basket 1 of the 1975 HELSINKI ACCORDS. Through the CONFERENCE ON SECURITY AND COOPERATION IN EUROPE (CSCE), they have been improved upon by further agreements in Stockholm, Sweden.

confirmation　**1.** The affirmation of a previously existing TREATY by a new regime.　**2.** The required approval of a legislature to high-level appointments of the executive.　**3.** A characteristic of an intelligence information item that is reported for a second time, preferably by a source independent of the original one.

conflict management　An approach to violence that emphasizes the need to control it and prevent it from escalating to higher levels. As such it is often differentiated from conflict resolution, which is seen as finding a way of resolving the conflict. Managerial approaches to conflict are often criticized for focusing on the symptoms of the underlying problems and simply trying to mitigate consequences rather than dealing with fundamental causes. Nevertheless, it is arguable that in many cases, resolution is impossible and conflict management is the only realistic alternative.

conflict of laws　**1.** A situation in which the laws of more than one government apply to a legal situation. A judge may then have to choose which jurisdiction's laws are most applicable. The situation is particularly thorny when a subnational law precedes national legislation; the conflict comes after the national legislation takes effect.　**2.** A situation in which the laws of more than one state apply to a case involving private parties (as opposed to the states themselves); the problem then becomes one of INTERNATIONAL LAW.

conflict resolution　**1.** Ending disputes by nonviolent and usually nonjudicial methods.　**2.** The generic professional practice of negotiation.　**3.** Efforts to deal with organizational disagreements in a constructive sense, as opposed to viewing conflict as a deviancy to be crushed.

conflict theory   An approach to disputes—military, diplomatic, and interpersonal—that is explicitly methodological in its orientation, that sets out to develop hypotheses about the causes of conflict and then systematically examines empirical evidence that either verifies or refutes these hypotheses. Conflict theorists are interested in all manifestations of conflict whether at the domestic or international level and tend to see similar dynamic processes at work in all conflicts.

confrontation   1. An extended conflict between states that does not use overt warfare but depends on political, economic, psychological, and covert warfare to achieve objectives.   2. In particular, the early 1960s hostilities of this kind between Malaysia and Indonesia. These hostilities started with the expansionist foreign policies of Indonesia's ACHMED SUKARNO, who wanted to take over the northern parts of the island of Borneo, controlled by Malaysia. Minor border clashes ended when in 1965 the Indonesian military, discovering that confrontation was more "Communist plot" than nationalistic fever, launched a domestic killing spree that saw an estimated 600,000 Indonesians murdered (mainly ethnic Chinese but including some Communists) and deposed Sukarno.

confrontation politics   Political action that is premised on the notion that individuals can best achieve change by dramatic acts such as sit-ins, demonstrations, and obstructionism. The ultimate reason is to alert a larger political community to a problem situation in order to generate a consensus for change.

confrontation states   Originally, those Arab countries that border on Israel and "confront" Israel militarily. The term has grown to include other hostile Arab states as well. By 1977 this term became a synonym for the REJECTION FRONT.

confusion agent   An individual who is dispatched by a sponsor state or organization for the primary purpose of confounding the intelligence or counter-intelligence apparatus of another country rather than for the purpose of collecting and transmitting information.

Congo   The name of the current Republic of Zaire in Africa from its independence from Belgium in 1960 to 1971. Before 1960 it was known as the colony of the Belgian Congo.

Congolese Civil War   The secessionist movements and military rebellions that followed Zaire's independence from Belgium in 1960. Parliamentary elections were held in April 1960. The Congolese National Movement (MNC) won a majority of the seats, and Patrice Lumumba (1925–1961) was named prime minister. After much maneuvering, the leader of the Alliance of the Bakong (ABAKO) Party, Joseph Kasavubu (1910–1969), was named president. On July 5 the army mutinied and political authority broke down. Belgian troops intervened on July 10 to protect Belgian nationals. On July 11 Moise Tshombe (1919–1969), governor of Katanga (now Shaba), declared his province an independent country, and the central government requested United Nations assistance to maintain order and restore the country's territorial integrity. The UN sent a peacekeeping force, but when it refused to place this force under the central government's orders, Prime Minister Lumumba requested and received direct Soviet aid. Lumumba's relations with the United Nations and President Kasavubu deteriorated rapidly. On September 5, 1960, Kasavubu dismissed Lumumba. Lumumba rejected this dismissal and in turn dismissed Kasavubu. Colonel Joseph Mobutu (1930–   ), now known as Mobutu Sese Seko, took over the government, expelled Soviet and Communist-bloc diplomats and technicians, and imprisoned Lumumba, who attempted to escape and died in Katanga under mysterious circumstances. Mobutu returned the reins of government to Kasavubu in 1961. Tshombe, however, continued to hold out in Katanga against central government and UN military forces. UN Secretary General U Thant devised a plan in 1962 to reintegrate Katanga, and Tshombe and the central government finally reached an agreement in mid-January 1963. UN troops remained in the country until the end of June 1964. Shortly after the end of the Katanga secession, rebellion against the central government broke out again. Through the exploitation of tribal hatreds and unhappiness over the fruits of independence, leftist rebel leaders extended the rebellion over much of the northern and eastern part of the country by June 1964. In July former Katangan leader Tshombe was named prime minister of the central government. Rebel fortunes soon waned as central government forces began to recapture rebel-held cities. On November 24 Belgian airborne troops, transported in U.S. Air Force planes, parachuted into Stanleyville and liberated it from the rebels. Central government forces gradually reclaimed control over more rebel-held areas until, by mid-1966, only a few isolated bands of rebels were still holding out. Lieutenant General Mobutu, commander in chief of the national army, seized control of the government on November 24, 1965, and cancelled scheduled elections. By 1967 he had consolidated power and began a quarter century of dictatorial rule. In 1971 he changed the name of the Congo to Zaire. His rule has kept his country one of the poorest in the world, but by creative corruption he has made himself one of the richest men in the world.

congress   1. A state's legislature, such as the U.S. Congress.   2. A national or international meeting of political leaders, scientists, or other individuals with common interests.   3. A political party in India, formally known as the INDIAN NATIONAL CONGRESS.

Congress of Vienna   The meeting held by the victorious powers at the end of the Napoleonic Wars in 1815 to redraw the map of Europe and establish an approach to security based on the principles of legitimacy, compensation, restoration, and BALANCE OF POWER. The Napoleonic Wars showed the dangers that could arise when one power tried to dominate the continent and when the democratic ideas from the French Revolution spread. The Congress of Vienna initiated a period in which five powers (Austria, France, Great Britain, Prussia, and Russia) accepted the mainly conservative CONCERT OF EUROPE to oppose revolutionary movements. The congress also established the rules of modern diplomatic procedure and classified diplomatic representatives into their current categories. The terms great power and small power originated here. *See also* AMBASSADOR.

connectivity   The linkage between NATIONAL COMMAND AUTHORITIES and strategic forces that needs to be maintained to ensure strategic retaliation after a

nuclear attack. Maintaining connectivity became a major concern for U.S. defense planners and policymakers in the late 1970s and early 1980s.

conquer   To defeat militarily an army and its nation so that the entire society is in the control of the victors. As Genghis Khan was pleased to say: "The greatest pleasure is to vanquish your enemies and chase them before you, to rob them of their wealth and see those dear to them bathed in tears, to ride their horses and clasp to your bosom their wives and daughters" (quoted in James Chamgers, *The Devil's Horsemen,* 1979). Julius Caesar would have agreed. He wrote in *The Gallic War* (51 B.C.), "War gives the right to the conquerors to impose any condition they please upon the vanquished." This is, in effect, still true today—except that it not considered polite or politic to say so.

Consensus of Cartagena   A declaration signed at Cartagena, Colombia, on June 22, 1984, following a meeting of the foreign and finance ministers of 11 Latin American countries: Argentina, Bolivia, Brazil, Chile, Colombia, the Dominican Republic, Ecuador, Mexico, Peru, Uruguay, and Venezuela. The ministers met to discuss their external debt problems and to seek easier repayment terms from their creditors for their combined $350 billion debt. Among the declaration's demands were an immediate, drastic reduction in interest rates; the establishment of a special fund by the INTERNATIONAL MONETARY FUND for the relief of the existing high interest rates; permission for specially hard-pressed governments to postpone interest payments; and more assistance from the IMF with fewer conditions attached. While there was no immediate action, the debt problem was taken out of the hands of banks alone and dealt with by GROUP OF SEVEN governments at the highest levels, some loan adjustments were made, and interest rates eventually came down. *See also* BAKER PLAN; DEBT RELIEF.

constitution   The basic political and legal structure of a government. Constitutions can be written (which are based on a specific document supplemented by judicial interpretations and traditional practices), unwritten (where there is no specific document but many laws, judicial decisions, and accepted practices that in their totality establish the principles of governance), or autocratic (where all power is in the hands of a dictator or elite, which defines governance in its interests—even though the state may have a formal legal document that calls for democratic government).

constitutional convention   A group of individuals chosen either by popular vote or legislative appointment to draft or revise a constitution. After a new or revised constitution has been produced by the group, it must be ratified either by a direct vote of the people or by their legislature.

constitutional monarch   A king, queen, or emperor who is the CHIEF OF STATE in a state whose constitution limits his or her powers. For example, the queen of the United Kingdom and the emperor of Japan are both constitutional monarchs.

constructive engagement   The continuation of political and economic ties with regimes with which a state has severe disagreements in the expectation that the ties will eventually lead to changes in the objectionable policies and practices. Constructive engagement was often used to describe the relations of the United States with South Africa. In September 1985, in response to bipartisan congressional pressure, President Ronald Reagan was forced to modify the constructive engagement policy, and by executive order he imposed limited economic sanctions on South Africa. The order prohibited U.S. banks from making loans to most agencies of the South African government and urged U.S. corporations engaged in business in South Africa to comply with the SULLIVAN PRINCIPLES. The sanctions were lifted by President George Bush when his administration perceived that South Africa had started making real progress toward ending APARTHEID in 1991.

consul   1. An individual who represents the commercial (as opposed to the diplomatic and political) interests of his or her government and its citizens in a foreign state. According to *Satow's Guide to Diplomatic Practice* (1986): "So various are the functions of a consul that there can be no precise and at the same time universally acceptable definition of the term." A consul is always under the administrative and political supervision of an AMBASSADOR.   2. Ambrose Bierce in *The Devil's Dictionary* (1911) defines a consul: "In American politics, a person who having failed to secure an office from the people is given one by the Administration on condition that he leave the country."

consul, honorary   A resident of her or his own country who represents, usually on a part-time and limited basis, the business interests of a foreign country; used only when the foreign country has no other consular representation.

consular agent   1. A part-time consul for a government that does not maintain a regular consulate.   2. Any official whose work is formally directed by a consul.

consular body   All of the foreign consular officers in a city or state, also called the *consular corps*.

consular commission   The document by which a state designates an individual to act as a consul in a foreign state.

consular corps   *See* CONSULAR BODY.

consular declaration   A formal statement (usually written), made to the consul of a foreign state, describing goods to be shipped.

consular district   The geographic area assigned to a particular consul.

consular formalities and documentation   Certain procedures that many countries—especially developing countries—require in connection with the importation of goods, such as special invoices that must be approved by an official of the importing country. These procedures, which are often in place because of bureaucratic inertia and to encourage bribes, can impede trade, particularly since fees are often charged for the required authorizations. The U.S. government is continuing to encourage some developing countries to reduce requirements for consular formalities and documentation as part of their concessions in the TOKYO ROUND of multilateral trade negotiations.

consular functions   All efforts to help the citizens of both the state represented as well as the state in which the consulate is located with business matters in either country. This varies from issuing passports and visas to conducting trade negotiations.

consular invoice   A document required by some foreign states that describes a shipment of goods and shows information such as the consignor, consignee, and value of the shipment. Certified by a consular official of the foreign state, it is used by CUSTOMS officials to verify the value, quantity, and nature of the shipment.

consular officer   Any individual at a consulate, from the consul on down, who performs consular functions.

consular section   That part of a larger diplomatic post, such as an embassy, that deals with consular matters.

consulate   The physical office of a consul.

consulate general   The main consulate (when there is more than one), supervised by a consul general.

consul general   A consul of the highest rank; one who supervises other consuls. A consul general typically is assigned to a large foreign city and often supervises several consulates in a consular district.

consultation   A term that covers a spectrum from informing another party about a policy decision or action after it has been taken to advance discussions in which the views of another party are taken into account in making the decision. Consultation is important both domestically, in executive legislative relations, and internationally in alliances such as the North Atlantic Treaty Organization, where during the 1980s the European allies complained that the administration of U.S. President Ronald Reagan did not consult them and instead made unilateral initiatives. Full consultation is a prerequisite for MULTILATERALISM as an approach to world affairs.

consultations   1. The seeking of advice from administrative superiors. In diplomatic usage, ambassadors may be called back to their home countries for consultations in order to show displeasure to the country to which they are assigned. This is less

of a sign of displeasure than formally BREAKING RELATIONS but nevertheless sends a strong symbolic message.   2. The solicitation of the advice of other states in an international organization.   3. A thoroughgoing review by interested states of trade policy actions by signatories to GATT that may "impair," or adversely affect, the trade interests of other signatory states. Consultations may be requested under Articles XXII and XXIII of the GATT by any signatory that feels its trade has been "impaired."

Consultative Assembly   *See* COUNCIL OF EUROPE.

Contadora Group   The foreign ministers of Colombia, Mexico, Panama, and Venezuela, who met in 1983 on the Panamanian island of Contadora to seek diplomatic methods for reducing political tensions and military conflict in Central America. They generally viewed the problems of the region in terms of economic, social, and political inequalities rather than in terms of East-West conflict and favored the provision of outside economic aid and the termination of foreign military assistance. The overall effort to achieve peace through negotiated settlements was called the Contadora process.

containment   The underlying basis of U.S. foreign and military policy from the end of World War II until 1990: a limitation of the expansion of Communist influence. It was first espoused by GEORGE F. KENNAN in a July 1947 *Foreign Affairs* article, "The Sources of Soviet Conduct," in which he asserted that "Soviet pressure against the free institutions of the Western World is something that can be contained by the adroit and vigilant application of counterforce." (Officially the article was credited to X because Kennan wrote it while serving as a U.S. foreign service officer, but it was never a secret who the actual author was.) Importantly, Kennan noted that the source of Soviet behavior was not a feeling of recent injustice by others but was a long-term push to expand, dating back centuries.

While there was broad agreement on the objective of containment (at least until the reaction against U.S. involvement in Vietnam in the late 1960s), different strategies have been used to implement this objective. From 1947 until 1950 the emphasis was on rebuilding U.S. allies in Western Europe and on implementation of the TRUMAN DOCTRINE; for a few years after the outbreak of the Korean War it moved to what John Lewis Gaddis in *Strategies of Containment* (1982) termed *perimeter defense* (the use of conventional ground forces to defend the boundaries of the FREE WORLD and its allies); with the Eisenhower Administration's "New Look" it was more asymmetrical and emphasized MASSIVE RETALIATION; the Kennedy and Johnson administrations reverted to the idea of perimeter defense and limited war and ended up escalating the war in Vietnam. The Nixon Administration did not abandon containment but tried instead to uphold it through greater reliance on allies and regional proxies, exploiting the Sino-Soviet split, and using DETENTE to encourage Soviet restraint. The Carter Administration initially tried to transcend or ignore containment, but embraced it after the Soviet invasion of Afghanistan in 1979. The Reagan Administration not only pursued a highly military containment policy but tried to go beyond it and roll back some of the Soviet gains of the 1970s in the Third World through support for anti-Communist revolutionary movements. The Bush Administration saw containment come to an end with the demise of the Soviet Union—a development that vindicated the logic of the policy's initial architect.

containment, economic **1.** The idea that developed in the U.S. 1947 and 1948 policy of restraining the Soviet Union in part through rebuilding the European economies to meet domestic needs, to erode support for Communist parties and Communist-controlled labor unions in Western Europe, and to minimize chances of subversion. Implemented through the MARSHALL PLAN, this phase in the evolution of U.S. containment policy was intended in large part to limit direct U.S. involvement in maintaining the balance of power in Europe though reestablishing an indigenous balance. **2.** An attempt to isolate and weaken the Soviet Union through the maintenance of strict restrictions on trade with and technology transfer to the Soviet bloc. This was to be done through the Coordinating Committee on expert Controls (COCOM). **3.** More generally, an attempt to minimize or constrain the power of a state through restrictions on trade. Such sanctions are sometimes punitive but also may be designed as part of a strategy of economic containment.

containment, extended The attempt by the United States to contain not only the Soviet Union but other Communist states, such as China. The extension of containment from Europe to Asia was done with insufficient attention to regional differences, which made it a successful policy in Europe and a disastrous one in Indochina's VIETNAM WAR.

content analysis A methodology that examines the frequency of particular words and phrases in the statements of a person or government and draws certain conclusions from this. Content analysis has been used, particularly by analyst OLE R. HOLSTI, to examine the decisions and actions of Germany's Kaiser WILLIAM II in July 1914, just before World War I and has been used as the basis for major studies of such postwar foreign policy decision makers as John Foster Dulles and Henry Kissinger.

contiguous zone **1.** An area that lies next to either a state in or an area of conflict. Contiguity is an important factor in interstate relations because states are more likely to be involved in conflicts with their neighbors than with states that are far away. **2.** That part of the international waters adjacent to the TERRITORIAL WATERS of a state in which the state exercises control for immigration or customs purposes.

continental shelf **1.** Land adjacent to the mainland that is submerged in relatively shallow water. An area called the continental slope separates the shallow shelf from the deep ocean. **2.** An international law reference for the seabed and subsoil of the submarine areas that extend beyond a state's TERRITORIAL WATERS to the outer edge of the geographical continental shelf. The 1982 United Nations convention on the LAW OF THE SEA placed limits on areas a state can claim as its continental shelf. Within those limits states can exercise sovereignty and exploit mineral or other natural resources.

continental strategy The United Kingdom policy of making a firm commitment to help a continental European ally fight a land war in Europe by the dispatch of a British force, as happened at the beginning of both world wars. The continental strategy is even more entrenched now that Great Britain's membership in the North Atlantic Treaty Organization involves keeping a major part of the British army and air force permanently based in Europe—although whether this will long survive the end of the Cold War remains uncertain.

continuous voyage doctrine   *See* CONTRABAND OF WAR.

contraband   1. Products that are formally declared by governments to be illegal to import or export. 2. Smuggled items; illegal trade.

contraband of war   Items that a neutral state cannot supply to a belligerent state without risking seizure and confiscation of the items by an opposing belligerent state. Contraband can be anything from food to munitions; it is whatever a belligerent defines as useful to an enemy. Under the international law doctrine of continuous voyage (or continuous transportation), goods carried on neutral ships bound for neutral ports have been seized if their ultimate destination was an enemy port.

contracting party   A country that has signed a treaty such as the GATT and thereby accepts the specified obligations and benefits contained therein.

contras   Members of the United States–backed "democratic resistance movement" in Nicaragua (1979–1990). The contras opposed the Communist SANDINISTA government, so called because they were *contra* (in Spanish, "counter") revolutionaries (that is, against the revolution). The contras were founded, and armed, largely by former members of the Nicaraguan National Guard originally established by then-President ANASTASIO SOMOZA, the right-wing dictator deposed by the Sandinistas in 1979. Once in power, the Sandinistas established a repressive regime and popular support declined; the Guardsmen, who had fled the country after the revolution, operated their armed resistance movement out of jungle bases just over the border in Honduras.

Their cause was greatly aided by the election of Ronald Reagan as president of the United States in 1980. Reagan called the contras "freedom fighters" and said (in a March 1, 1985, speech) that they "are

the moral equal of our Founding Fathers and the brave men and women of the French Resistance." Reagan approved a covert CENTRAL INTELLIGENCE AGENCY aid program in December 1981. During the first Reagan Administration the CIA poured millions of dollars of financial aid, medical supplies, and arms into contra coffers in accord with what was termed the REAGAN DOCTRINE and in defiance of congressional limits. However, the contras failed to score any significant military successes, and as the seamier details of the CIA's involvement began to leak out, congressional support for the contras weakened; in 1985 and 1986 contra funding was limited to nonlethal humanitarian aid. Though the administration was successful in the latter part of 1986 in securing another $100 million aid package, the exposure of the IRAN-CONTRA AFFAIR all but destroyed congressional support for Reagan's "freedom fighters."

In the summer of 1989 Central American leaders reached an agreement that called for the disarming of the guerrillas, free and open Nicaraguan elections, and a general amnesty for contras who wished to return home. The administration of U.S. President George Bush then endeavored to keep enough nonlethal American aid flowing to the contras to sustain them in their Honduran base camps, as an insurance policy until after the promised 1990 Nicaraguan elections took place. The contras disbanded in 1990 after a democratically elected government replaced the Sandinista regime.

controlled goods   Products restricted by domestic or international law from being sold to certain designated states. For example, in most nations it is illegal (without specific government permission) to export nuclear weapons technology.

controlled response   In military terminology, the selection from a wide variety of feasible options of the one that will provide the specific military response most advantageous in the circumstances. It also implies the availability of more violent options that are deliberately held in abeyance.

controlled source   *See* SOURCE.

Control of Arms on the Seabed Treaty   The agreement on the "Prohibition of the Employment of

Nuclear Weapons and other Weapons of Mass Destruction on the Seabed and the Ocean Floor and in the Subsoil Thereof," which was proposed by the United Nations General Assembly in 1971. The United States, the Soviet Union, and 76 other states were signatories. They are now obligated not to place on the seabed "any nuclear weapons or any other types of weapons of mass destruction as well as structures, launching installations, or any other facilities specially designed for storing, testing or using such weapons." This treaty is often criticized as spurious because it deals only with actions that none of the nuclear weapons–holding states wish to take anyway. Additionally, there is no provision for preventing submarines with nuclear missiles from resting temporarily on the bottom of the sea. Furthermore, the placing of nuclear weapons on the ocean floor of a state's own territorial waters is not prohibited. Nevertheless, it is still a constraint and to many is worth having in place. *Compare to* OUTER SPACE TREATY.

convention   1. A meeting of the members of a single political party.   2. A CONSTITUTIONAL CONVENTION.   3. An international agreement on matters that are not as significant as those that are regulated by treaty.   4. An accord resulting from an international conference. The most famous conventions are probably the Geneva conventions of 1864, 1906, and 1949, which concern the treatment of various persons during war.   5. A synonym for TREATY.

conventional arms transfer   The transfer of nonnuclear weapons, aircraft, equipment, and military services from a supplier to a recipient state. The developed states of the world often bemoan the fact that the THIRD WORLD spends so much of its wealth on conventional arms—and that those arms are used in civil wars and by oppressive regimes. At the same time, these developed states (the United States, Great Britain, and France, among others) compete with each other to sell weapons to the Third World. In the interests of their domestic economies they all increase the potential for violence elsewhere, using the excuse that "If we don't do it, someone else will."

Conventional Arms Transfer Talks   Negotiations held between the United States and the Soviet Union

between 1977 and 1979 to discuss the possibility of imposing limits on the weapons supplied to Third World states by both states. The talks were initiated by the Carter Administration, which gave arms transfer restrictions a high priority. They took place, however, within the context of a deteriorating superpower relationship, and this together with divergent objectives and perspective doomed them to failure.

Conventional Defense Initiative (CDI)   An initiative to identify the main deficiencies of the North Atlantic Treaty Organization (NATO) and provide a plan of action to eliminate them, adopted by NATO in May 1985 (along with the *Conceptual Military Framework,* designed to address NATO's military deficiencies). Priorities included greater cooperation in research, development, and armaments production, and improved infrastructure planning. Largely a response to pressures from U.S. Senator Sam Nunn of Georgia for greater BURDEN-SHARING and emphasis on strengthening conventional forces by NATO, CDI attempted to reduce NATO's reliance on nuclear weapons and move more toward reliance on conventional defense.

conventional forces   *See* CONVENTIONAL WARFARE.

Conventional Forces Europe Treaty (CFE Treaty)   The 1990 North Atlantic Treaty Organization–Warsaw Pact arms control agreement that grew out of the CONFERENCE ON SECURITY AND COOPERATION IN EUROPE. The talks formally opened in 1989 in a climate of optimism largely because the Soviet leader, Mikhail Gorbachev, had in 1988 announced large unilateral reductions in Soviet forces in Europe. The CFE Treaty limited the number of weapons in Europe from the Atlantic Ocean to the Ural Mountains. A ceiling of 20,000 per alliance was imposed on tanks and 30,000 on armored combat vehicles—figures that meant NATO had only to make marginal cuts while the Warsaw Pact states had to implement much greater reductions. The treaty also included ceilings of 20,000 artillery pieces, 2,000 helicopters, and 6,800 combat aircraft. Although the treaty achieved parity on conventional weapons in Europe—something that NATO had never been able to accomplish through its own efforts—its primary importance was as a symbol of the end of the Cold War in Europe. The CFE Treaty negotiations benefited considerably from the new atmosphere in East-West relations. They were overtaken somewhat by political events in Europe and the effective disintegration of the Warsaw Pact. Nevertheless, these events provided added impetus for an orderly dismantling of the military confrontation in Europe. The CFE Treaty, signed in Paris on November 19, 1990, still awaits ratification by all signatory states. The collapse of the Warsaw Pact and the Soviet Union has left successor governments to sort out the details of how armaments will be reduced in Central Europe.

conventional tariff A tax on imported goods established through the "conventions" (agreements) that result from tariff negotiations under GATT auspices.

conventional warfare All aspects of military operations involving regular (and sometimes irregular) military forces using any weapons short of nuclear weapons. Thus *conventional forces* are military units capable of undertaking operations using only nonnuclear weapons. A *conventional weapon* is anything capable of inflicting damage to an enemy, so long as that weapon is not nuclear, biological, or chemical; modern conventional weapons include projectiles (such as bullets) and explosives (such as mines). But this distinction between ways of killing people has more political than military import. For example, low-yield battlefield nuclear weapons might be less destructive to life and property than a conventional heavy air raid. Yet the use of nuclear weapons would be considered a major ESCALATION because of the political significance of their first use in a conflict. But even a conventional war could be a disaster comparable to nuclear war. According to Mikhail Gorbachev's *Perestroika* (1987): "This is not only because conventional weapons are many times more destructive than they were during the Second World War, but also because there are nuclear power plants consisting of a total of some 200 reactor units and a large number of major chemical works. The destruction of those facilities in the course of conventional hostilities would make the [European] continent uninhabitable." *Compare to* BIOLOGICAL WARFARE; CHEMICAL WARFARE; NUCLEAR WARFARE.

conventional weapons *See* CONVENTIONAL WARFARE.

conventional wisdom Something that is generally believed to be true. Those who use the phrase are often establishing straw men to be knocked down; in such instances, conventional "wisdom" really means "that which most people believe to be true, but really isn't." The phrase first gained currency after economist John Kenneth Galbraith used it in his book *The Affluent Society* (1958), in which he observed: "Only posterity is unkind to the man of conventional wisdom, and all posterity does is bury him in a blanket of neglect."

Convention on the Law of the Sea *See* LAW OF THE SEA.

convergence The belief that socialist and capitalist societies will continue to grow more alike in response to parallel bureaucratic and technological developments. However, this thesis generally ignores the crucial difference between bureaucracies that are and those that are not subject to electoral power. In one sense, however, the model could be regarded as correct: the convergence that has developed since 1990 has been a convergence of opinion on the importance of capitalism and a free market.

conversion *See* ARMS CONVERSION.

conversion capability The ability of a country to transform its potential military or economic power into actual power as reflected in the willingness of other nations to accord with its preferences. Put differently, this can be seen as the ability to turn power from capability into influence.

convertibility The characteristic of a CURRENCY that is freely exchangeable into the currency of any other nation. A country's currency is convertible if the government of that country allows the completely free use of that currency for the purchase of currencies of other nations. Currency becomes unconvertible when a government orders that neither its citizens nor foreigners possessing domestic currency shall buy foreign exchange except for approved purposes or in limited amounts. Convertible currency also may mean currency that may be redeemed in gold or other precious metal.

convertible currency   A monetary unit that can be bought and sold for other currencies at will. This is also known as a HARD CURRENCY (in contrast to SOFT CURRENCY, which is not valued on world markets).

cookie pushers   A derogatory reference to professional diplomats; it implies that they spend too much time at social functions (and presumably eating cookies)—and thus are (1) overly concerned with diplomatic niceties and (2) overweight.

Coolidge, Calvin (1872–1933)   The vice president of the United States who became president (1923–1929) after the death of WARREN G. HARDING. The Coolidge Administration occupied Nicaragua to protect American business interests; supported the KELLOGG-BRIAND PACT, which outlawed war; and approved the Rogers Act of 1924, which consolidated the U.S. diplomatic and consular services and created a merit selection system for the U.S. Foreign Service.

Cooperation Council for the Arab States of the Gulf   *See* GULF COOPERATION COUNCIL.

cooptation   Bringing possibly dissident group members into an organization's or government's policymaking process to prevent such individuals from posing a threat to the ultimate goals of the organization or government. The classic analysis of cooptation is to be found in Philip Selznick's *TVA and the Grass Roots* (1949).

co-optive power   A concept developed by Joseph Nye in *Bound to Lead* (1990), which refers to the ability of a state to structure a situation to lead other states to define their own interests or preferences in ways that are compatible with the co-optive state's interests. Sources of co-optive power are culture and ideology. The ability to structure a regime in ways that bring about desired domestic behavior also can be understood as a form of co-optive power. The liberal trading regime that has predominated since World War II is a good example of the ability of the United States to structure a situation in ways that other states see as also being advantageous to them. The emphasis on the transition to democratic regimes in Eastern Europe also reflects the attraction of U.S. institutions and ideals as models to be emulated. *See also* SOFT POWER.

Coordinating Committee on Export Controls   *See* COCOM.

Coral Sea, Battle of the   The May 1942 Pacific Ocean naval engagement between Japan and the United States. While the battle was inconclusive (each side sank one of the other's AIRCRAFT CARRIERS), it forced the Japanese to cancel an invasion of Port Moresby, New Guinea. The battle's historical significance lies in the fact that it was the first time in World War II that a Japanese advance was turned back and the first time ever that a major sea battle was fought without the opposing ships ever sighting each other—it was a battle of aircraft carriers. A month later at the BATTLE OF MIDWAY the tide of war turned permanently against the Japanese.

cordon   A military force placed to deny the enemy access to an area.

cordon sanitaire   Literally translated from the French to mean "sanitary cordon"; a phrase once used to describe the line of sentries posted around a city or other area to restrict passage in an effort to control the spread of a contagious disease. In this century it has come to mean a BUFFER state between two rivals. Technically, it is the term that French officials applied to the chain of successor states in East Central and Eastern Europe after World War I. These states were meant to shield Western Europe from the spread of Soviet Bolshevism and to keep Germany and the Soviet Union apart. In the aftermath of World War II the Soviet Union used Eastern Europe as a *cordon sanitaire* to inhibit influence from Western Europe. The Soviets consolidated their position by imposing Communist governments on the people of Eastern Europe. Soviet President MIKHAIL GORBACHEV, however, adopted a much more permissive attitude toward Eastern Europe. Thus after 1989 a massive rejection of communism occurred in most of Eastern Europe with the tacit encouragement of the Soviets. With the demise of the Soviet Union itself in 1991, the Russians no longer feel a compelling need for a *cordon sanitaire* to protect them from what the Communist government once considered to be the contagion of Western capitalism.

core   *See* CENTER.

COREPER   *See* COUNCIL OF MINISTERS.

corporatism   1. A social structure in which corporations, nongovernmental entities with great power over the lives and professional activities of their members, play an intermediary role between the public and state. The practice goes back to medieval times when trade guilds or corporations controlled the work lives of craftsmen and traders. At the height of their power the guilds represented a third force in society along with the Roman Catholic Church and the nobility.   2. A theoretical concept originated by the French sociologist Emile Durkheim (1858–1917) that found political expression in the FASCISM of the 1930s and 1940s. Fascist corporatism suggested that people engaged in a particular trade—employers as well as workers—had more in common with one another than with people of the same class or status in other trades. Thus in Spain and Italy legislative assemblies and councils of state were organized around trade corporations rather than around geographic constituencies. Corporatist theory appealed to the fascists because it bypassed both class conflict and democratic elections.   3. In modern usage, the increasing tendency for states to work closely with major business corporations and trade unions to enhance international competitiveness. This is sometimes called *neocorporatism*.

Correlates of War Project   A project that was begun in 1963 by J. David Singer and Melvin Small at the University of Michigan that set out to identify the variables most frequently associated with the onset of war in the period since 1815. The aim, as described by the authors in *Resort to Arms* (1982), was to "ascertain which factors characterize those conflicts that terminate in war and which accompany those that find a less violent resolution." Accordingly, they set out to identify trends and fluctuations in "the frequency, magnitude, severity and intensity of war" during that period. The initial results of the study, which went up to 1965, were published as *The Wages of War, 1816–1965*; the data base was subsequently extended to 1980, and the results were published in *Resort to Arms*. The research examined 118 international wars and 106 civil wars, focusing on such questions as the war-proneness of nations. Among the conclusions was the fact that in the period studied there were 67 interstate wars and 51 imperial and colonial wars; there was no evidence that international war was on the increase; that the Europeans were the most war-prone, with France (22 wars) and Great Britain and the Soviet Union (19 each) at the top of the list; that the initiators of war "win" in almost 70 percent of the wars, but that in terms of battle deaths the victors lose as many men as the vanquished, and sometimes more; that while international wars do not begin in a cyclical fashion, "there is some suggestion of a 15- to 20-year periodicity between peaks in the amount of war under way at any given time." The main findings on civil wars were that 1860, 1963, and 1972 led the years in which the most civil wars were under way; that civil war has not been on the increase; that the countries which led the list in terms of civil war experience were China (11), followed by Colombia and Spain (7 each). The authors also suggest that there are interesting although not yet fully explored parallels between civil and international wars in terms of their numbers and patterns over time.

correlation of forces   The Soviet Union's concept of its comparative capacity to compete with the West in all important ways—the combined economic, military, diplomatic, and ideological strength of one country against another. The Soviets saw military force as just one component of an essentially political conflict between Soviet communism and the capitalist world, whereas Western attitudes tended to separate the various forms of power and influence a nation has. It was often noted by Western analysts that all Soviet theorists since Lenin have recorded their agreement with KARL VON CLAUSEWITZ's dictum that war is "nothing but the continuation of politics by other means." To the Soviet military thinker this was axiomatic, and therefore any particular piece of military hardware also was considered to be an ideological and diplomatic weapon.

Corrigan, Mairead (1944–   )   The cofounder of the Northern Ireland Peace Movement who shared the 1976 Nobel Peace Prize with the group's other cofounder, Betty Williams (1943–   ), for their community based effort to end the Protestant-Catholic bloodletting. The Nobel Committee said that these two "have shown us what ordinary people can do to promote the cause of peace . . . They never heeded the difficulty of their task, they merely tackled it because they were so convinced that this was precisely what was needed." *See also* NORTHERN IRELAND.

cosmopolitanism   **1.** Understanding a variety of cultures outside one's own; the opposite of PAROCHIALISM. It became a term of abuse in the Soviet Union for any expressions of admiration for bourgeois capitalistic culture.   **2.** The belief in the ancient ideal of a world state, to which all people would belong. *See* CITIZEN OF THE WORLD.

Council for Mutual Economic Assistance (CMEA) *See* COMECON.

Council of Europe   An organization of European countries founded in 1949 to promote European unity, protect human rights, and promote social and economic progress. Headquartered in Strasbourg, France, it consists of two organs: the Committee of Ministers, consisting of the foreign ministers of the member states; and the Parliamentary Assembly, sometimes called the Consultative Assembly, comprised of parliamentarians either elected or appointed by their national parliaments. The Committee of Ministers makes recommendations to individual governments and also may draw up conventions and agreements. The assembly, a deliberative body without legislative authority, adopts resolutions that are then presented to the Committee of Ministers. Note that the Council of Europe is not a EUROPEAN COMMUNITY institution but an independent organization responsible only to its members (most of the states of Western Europe, including all of the EC states). While it was initially organized by the International Committee of the Movements for European Unity, the council has been overshadowed by the EC with whom it has an annual joint meeting. The council is supported by proportional assessments of member states. Since 1989 representatives of Eastern and Central European states have attended council meetings as nonvoting members.

Council of Four   The formal name for the BIG FOUR at the 1919 Paris Peace Conference.

Council of Ministers   The principal decision-making body for the EUROPEAN COMMUNITY. Each member government has one representative on the council. It can act only on proposals submitted by the EUROPEAN COMMISSION. While the commission can attend council meetings, it has no vote. Each council member serves as council president for rotating six-month terms. The president represents the council at meetings of the EUROPEAN PARLIAMENT and also frequently represents the EC in dealings with third countries. Most issues before the council are discussed in advance by the Committee of Permanent Representatives (*Comité des Représentants Permanents*, or COREPER), the group that prepares the council's work. COREPER consists of the senior ambassadors who head each member state's delegation to the European Commission. Although the council and the commission share the policy-making role, the council has become dominant since the LUXEMBOURG AGREEMENT of 1966. *See also* COMMON MARKET; EURATOM; EUROPEAN COAL AND STEEL COMMUNITY.

council of war   An assemblage of the most senior officers of a military force, initiated by the commander, to seek advice or consensus on how to deal with an emergency or combat problem. Councils of war have a long history. Roman military commander Vegetius wrote in his *De Re Militari* (A.D. 378), "It is the duty and interest of the general frequently to assemble the most prudent and experienced officers of the different corps of the army and consult with them on the state both of his own and the enemy's forces." But in recent centuries these councils have been disdained as the refuge of a poor commander. Napoleon Bonaparte (1769–1821) said: "Councils of war will be what the effect of these things has been in every age: they will end in the adoption of the most pusillanimous or (if the expression be preferred) the most prudent measures, which in war are almost uniformly the worst that can be adopted" (*Military Maxims,* 1827). U.S. General Halleck advised General Mead after the 1863 Battle of Gettysburg: "Call no council of war. It is proverbial that councils of war never fight" (quoted in Shelby Foote, *The Civil War,*

1963). U.S. President Theodore Roosevelt agreed. He wrote in his *Autobiography* (1913): "A council of war never fights, and in a crisis the duty of the leader is to lead and not to take refuge behind the generally timid wisdom of a multitude of councilors."

Council on Foreign Relations An influential private organization that since 1921 has functioned as a U.S. foreign policy establishment. One cannot simply join the council; one must be nominated and then elected to membership. Its 1990 *Annual Report* states that "election to the council is based on an estimate of a candidate's special intellectual pursuits, experience, and involvement in American foreign policy; active interest in the council and its programs; and standing in his or her own professional community." In this way the organization limits its membership to the 2,670 (in 1990) movers and shakers of American foreign policy. While headquartered in New York, it holds meetings throughout the United States. Its major journal is *Foreign Affairs.*

counselor/counsellor 1. A lawyer. 2. A formal advisor to a high-level official. 3. A diplomatic official: the second in command of an embassy or legation who functions as the deputy to the CHIEF OF MISSION. (In the U.S. Foreign Service the formal title is DCM, Deputy Chief of Mission.) While ATTACHES are often given the rank of counselor, they rank below the regular counselor in a diplomatic hierarchy.

counterfactual 1. Untrue; description of a statement contrary to the facts of a situation. 2. Of or related to a statement about a hypothetical event; what might have occurred if something else had not happened instead.

counterforce 1. A weapon or military unit specifically designed to parallel an enemy weapon or unit. As such, counterforce has been used throughout history. Only since the 1960s has the concept been applied, primarily by U.S. strategic analysts, to nuclear weapons strategy. 2. Using nuclear weapons to destroy, or damage, the military installations of an enemy as opposed to its population centers. Counterforce policy was first proclaimed by U.S. Secretary of Defense Robert S. McNamara (*Department of State Bulletin,* July 9, 1962): "The United States has come to the conclusion that . . . basic military strategy in a general nuclear war should be approached in much the same way that more conventional military operations have been regarded in the past. That is to say, principal military objectives, in the event of a nuclear war . . . should be the destruction of the enemy's military forces, not of its civilian population." Subsequent U.S. secretaries of defense at times seemed more concerned with keeping a potential enemy guessing about U.S. intentions. Thus Secretary James Schlesinger, for example, testified before the Senate Armed Services Committee on February 5, 1974: "We have no announced counterforce strategy, if by counterforce one infers that one is going to attempt to destroy [missile] silos. We have a new targeting doctrine that emphasizes selectivity and flexibility." Yet Schlesinger placed great emphasis on hard target kill capabilities (that is, the use of accurate missiles capable of destroying Soviet silos), which made sense only in terms of the continuation of counterforce strategies. *Compare to* COUNTERVALUE.

counterinsurgency Descriptive of those military, paramilitary, political, economic, psychological, and civic efforts undertaken by a government to defeat revolutionaries using GUERRILLA WARFARE. The basic tactics are (1) to gain intelligence that allows for the location and destruction of insurgent hiding places; and (2) to convince citizens to trust the government sufficiently to report guerrilla activities. *Compare to* INSURGENCY.

counterintelligence Those activities that seek to identify and thwart espionage and sabotage by hostile INTELLIGENCE AGENCIES. *Compare to* INTELLIGENCE.

counterpart funds Local currency available to a foreign state as the result of its aid programs to the local state. For example, a foreign state may "sell" aid goods to a local state for local SOFT CURRENCY that can be spent only locally.

counterrevolution Something that opposes a REVOLUTION, such as the forces that have been overthrown and now seek to regain power.

counterterrorism Efforts to prevent TERRORISM and, if necessary, to punish terrorists in the expectation that retaliation will discourage further terrorist acts. Counterterrorist policy relies heavily on INTELLIGENCE gathering and analysis and is most successful when terrorist actions are prevented. It includes a wide variety of economic, political, social, psychological, and military approaches. COUNTERINSURGENCY and LOW-INTENSITY WARFARE are among the military means employed as counterterrorism weapons against guerrilla forces. PARAMILITARY ORGANIZATIONS such as DEATH SQUADS often have been utilized, especially by Latin American nations. However, history has shown that counterterrorism can be very difficult to carry out in a democratic society that attempts to uphold traditional civil freedoms.

countertrade An international transaction whereby the exporting state arranges to purchase goods or services from the importing state so that the latter can offset some or all of the foreign exchange costs of the imports. In countertrade the exporting party is usually an industrialized state and the purchaser either a Communist state or a developing country. In the 1980s countertrade accounted for 25 percent of world trade. *Compare to* MANAGED TRADE.

countervailing duty A retaliatory extra charge that a state places on imported goods to offset the subsidies or bounties granted to the exporters of the goods by their home governments, thus limiting the imports' ability to undercut the prices of domestic goods.

countervailing strategy The strategic retaliatory policy first adopted by the United States in 1974 when it was put forth by Secretary of Defense James Schlesinger and known at that time as the Schlesinger Doctrine. It called for the United States always to have the ability to match any Soviet threat at any particular level. It was a more subtle alternative to the previous policy of mutual assured destruction (MAD). The phrase was developed to avoid arguments about whether a nuclear war could be "won"; "countervailing" implied that it at least would not be "lost." This doctrine later became part of U.S. President Jimmy Carter's PRESIDENTIAL DIRECTIVE 59. *See also* LIMITED NUCLEAR OPTIONS.

countervailing theory The concept that when one group obtains too much influence in a pluralist society, another group or coalition will spring up to counter or oppose its power. This concept, while widely applicable and obviously indebted to the theory of BALANCE OF POWER, is usually credited to economist John Kenneth Galbraith. In his *American Capitalism* (1956), he held that large industries have an inherent tendency to generate the development of large buyers and unions that seek to countervail their power; in effect both buyers and sellers are prevented from abusing power by the development of countervailing powers in the economy.

countervalue 1. In the context of nuclear weapons, any nonmilitary target, such as a city. A countervalue target is anything that is not of military use. Potential countervalue attacks, the threatened destruction of industrial and population centers, are the essence of DETERRENCE. 2. A euphemism for civilian targets themselves. *Compare to* COUNTERFORCE.

country desk The office within a FOREIGN MINISTRY that has the daily duty of monitoring and analyzing the activities of a given foreign country. The person in charge of a country desk is the *desk officer.* Langhorne A. Motley, former U.S. Assistant Secretary of State for Inter-American Affairs, describes what it is like running a regional bureau to which country desks report: "[It's] like being given 1,000 pounds of canaries and a box that will only hold 500 pounds. Right away, you begin banging on the sides of the box, trying to keep enough canaries in the air so that the box won't burst open. After a while, your arms get tired" (*New York Times,* May 10, 1985).

country team A coordinating and supervisory body of embassy officials headed by the chief of the diplomatic mission, usually an ambassador, and composed of the senior member of each represented department or agency. Its purpose is to advise the chief of the mission on social, economic, political, and military problems, so that all of the resources in the country could be coordinated through her or him.

coup de grace 1. French term meaning "stroke of mercy," a final and decisive end to a battle.

2. The pistol shot to the head of a firing squad's target delivered if the victim is not yet dead after the squad has fired.

coup de main French term meaning "stroke of the hand," a sudden and vigorous attack that successfully obtains an objective. But as Napoleon Bonaparte warned, "The success of a coup-de-main depends absolutely upon luck rather than judgment" (*Military Maxims,* 1827).

coup d'état French term meaning "a stroke or sharp blow to the state"; a sudden and often violent change in the leadership of a government brought about by those who already hold some power. This differs from a REVOLUTION in that revolutions are usually brought about from below by those not then in power and involves a major social and economic change. A coup d'état tends to occur during a time of social instability and political uncertainty and is usually the work of "right-wing" elements determined to impose social discipline and political order. A coup need not be a major military undertaking. Typically small units take over government buildings, communications and media facilities, transportation hubs, and the like, then capture or kill all those high government officials who would be a threat to the coup organizers. Frequently the makers of a coup d'état return power to the politicians after a fairly short time, when they believe that their aims of stabilizing and ordering the political system have been achieved. For example, in both Argentina and Chile military governments that took power in coups during the 1970s returned power to civilian control in the 1980s. Then again sometimes the military takes power and keeps it. For example, Colonel Muammar al-Qaddafi took power in Libya in a 1969 coup and has stayed in power ever since. The tendency of the military to be involved in coups d'état stems from its virtual monopoly of coercive means and the way in which it is usually, at least in the context of any particular social system, seen as apolitical or even "above politics."

coup d'oeil **1.** French term meaning "stroke of the eye," the art of rapidly distinguishing the weak points of an enemy's position and of discerning the military advantages and disadvantages of the terrain; the ability to quickly make an accurate esti-mate of a combat (or sometimes a diplomatic) problem. Jean-Charles de Folard (1669–1752) wrote in his 1724 work *Nouvelles découvertes sur la guerre:* "The coup d'oeil is a gift of God and cannot be acquired: but if professional knowledge does not perfect it, one only sees things imperfectly and in a fog, which is not enough in these matters where it is so important to have a clear eye . . . To look over a battlefield, to take in at the first instance the advantages and disadvantages is the great quality of a general." **2.** According to the 1747 *Instructions of Frederick the Great for His Generals,* the coup d'oeil is also the "judgment that is exercised about the capacity of the enemy at the commencement of a battle."

courier, diplomatic *See* DIPLOMATIC COURIER.

courtesy call **1.** A diplomatic meeting scheduled only because not to do so might seem insulting to one of the parties. **2.** A meeting someone is obligated to attend because of the office he or she holds, or because it is appropriate to do so.

COURTESY CALL DIALOGUE

[In 1959 U.S. Vice President Richard] Nixon went to the Kremlin for a courtesy call on [the Soviet General Secretary Nikita] Khrushchev. . . .

[Khrushchev] opened up by telling Nixon that he knew all about him—he was the enemy of the Soviet Union, the enemy of Communism, the white knight of Capitalism.

Nixon conceded that he didn't like Communism but as for Capitalism, well, he had grown up a poor boy, working in a small orchard, doing all the chores. Khrushchev snorted. He, Khrushchev, had grown up the poorest of the poor. He had walked barefoot. He had had no shoes. He had shoveled shit to earn a few kopeks. Nixon shot back that he'd been poor and barefoot, too—and had shoveled shit.

What kind of shit? Khrushchev demanded. Horseshit, Nixon said. That's nothing, Khrushchev replied. He had shoveled cow shit—loose, runny, stinking cow dung. It got between your toes. I too shoveled cow shit, Nixon said tightly.

Well, Khrushchev grumbled, maybe Nixon had shoveled cow shit once or twice, but he, Khrushchev, has shoveled human shit. That was the worst. Nixon couldn't top that.

Source: Harrison E. Salisbury, *A Time of Change* (1988).

Court of St. James's The royal court of the government of Great Britain; thus ambassadors to that state are formally accredited to the Court of St. James's. St. James's was the London palace where formal receptions were once held.

covenant 1. The belief of some religions that God has promised salvation to humanity. 2. The biblical concept of a promise sanctioned by an oath with an appeal to God to punish any violation of the agreement. 3. Something that is legally binding, such as a restriction in a property deed. 4. An international treaty, such as the Covenant of the League of Nations, the first part of the Treaty of Versailles of 1919, which formally ended World War I. 5. A political compact.

cover *See* BLACK.

covert operations The secret activities of intelligence agencies that are planned and executed to hide the identity of, or permit plausible denial by, the sponsor. These actions are different from *clandestine operations* in that emphasis is placed on concealment of the identity of the sponsor rather than on concealment of the operation itself. Since World War II covert operations have become an inherent part of the foreign policy of all major military powers. U.S. President Gerald R. Ford said: "I don't know how a President could conduct foreign policy without a degree of covert operations" (*Time*, January 26, 1976). Nevertheless, many citizens feel uncomfortable about the lack of accountability inherent in covert activities. Some even feel that it is dishonorable for a democracy to engage in them at all. But responding to the perceived necessity of such work, U.S. Secretary of State George P. Shultz once advocated: "We have to get over the idea that covert is a dirty word" (*Washington Post*, May 16, 1986). Covert operations are usually conducted by a state's intelligence agencies, such as the Central Intelligence Agency (United States), KGB (Soviet Union), and Mossad (Israel). *Compare to* OVERT OPERATIONS.

CPSU *See* COMMUNIST PARTY OF THE SOVIET UNION.

credentials 1. Official certifications. 2. The LETTRES DE CRÉANCE that accredit diplomats to a foreign government. 3. Eligibility for joining an international organization; the previously established criteria for participation in a formal meeting.

credibility 1. The belief of foreign governments that a threat or promise will be fulfilled in the event of specific contingencies. In a negotiation one side has credibility if the other side believes it is not bluffing—even when it is bluffing. 2. The military capability that allows a state to do unacceptable damage to an enemy even after absorbing a FIRST STRIKE. Thus military credibility works as a deterrent.

credibility gap The difference between official accounts of events by a government and the public's understanding of those events from other sources such as the news media and political critics. A credibility gap encourages increasing public mistrust and disbelief of government officials. In the United States, credibility was an especially acute problem for the administrations of Lyndon B. Johnson and Richard M. Nixon: the first for lies about the Vietnam War, the second for lies over the Watergate scandal. Public trust in government tended to increase during the Reagan Administration, at least until the exposure of the Iran-Contra Affair.

Creditanstalt Austria's largest commercial bank in the early twentieth century, which collapsed in the spring of 1931. After the 1929 New York Stock Market crash, the world economy had begun to move into depression. The traditional deflationary medicine—maintaining the gold standard and changing to a system of fixed exchange rates in trade—was not working. The failure of the Creditanstalt plunged Europe into financial panic and deepened the worldwide depression.

Cremer, William R. (1828–1908) The British trade union organizer who received the 1903 Nobel Peace Prize for his work in founding the International Arbitration League, which evolved into the HAGUE TRIBUNAL.

crescent of crisis *See* ARC OF CRISIS.

Cresson, Edith (1934–) The Socialist Party politician who became France's first female prime minister (1991–1992). She inadvertently caused controversy when she accused Japan of seeking the economic domination of the world and asserted (via a four-year-old interview publicized after she took office) that one-quarter of all English, American, and German men were homosexual. The protests that followed included that of Anthony Marlow, a Tory member of the British House of Commons, who stated: "Mrs. Cresson has sought to insult the virility of the British male because the last time she was in London she did not get enough admiring glances. I wanted to put down a motion saying, 'This House does not fancy elderly Frenchwomen,' but I was told this was out of order" (*Newsweek,* July 1, 1991). But it was not her controversial remarks about foreigners that led to her downfall. A lagging economy and socialist losses in national elections led to her forced resignation in 1992 after less than a year in office.

crimes against humanity A post–World War II phrase for the ill treatment of civilians. According to the 1945 charter of the International Military Tribunal (the legal framework for the NUREMBERG TRIALS), crimes against humanity consist of "murder, extermination, enslavement, deportation and other inhumane acts against any civilian population before or during war; or persecution on political, racial or religious grounds in execution of or in connection with any crime within the jurisdiction of the domestic law of the country where perpetrated." See also NUREMBERG PRINCIPLES.

crimes against peace WAR CRIMES; planning, provoking, and waging an aggressive war; any war in violation of international treaties or agreements. *See also* NUREMBERG PRINCIPLES.

crimes against the law of nations 1. Violations of INTERNATIONAL LAW. 2. TERRORISM. 3. CRIMES AGAINST HUMANITY.

crisis 1. An inherently unstable situation ready for major change. As then–U.S. Senator John F. Kennedy said in a 1959 speech, "When written in Chinese, the word 'crisis' is composed of two characters—one represents danger and the other represents opportunity." 2. A foreign policy problem that threatens the security of the state and must be dealt with by the highest levels of a government, which are forced to make critical decisions within a brief time span. Charles Hermann, in *International Crises* (1972), provided the classic definition of a foreign policy crisis in terms of three conditions: a high threat to values and interests, a short time to respond, and the element of surprise. (There has subsequently been considerable discussion by Hermann and others about whether surprise is a necessary condition for a foreign policy crisis.) This definition approaches crisis from a rational or a decision-making perspective. 3. Any situation involving a perceived increase in the probability of war. 4. Any period of heightened tension in international politics. 5. Any situation in which problems seem to have reached the point at which they may burst or become uncontrollable. Fortunately, as historian Arthur M. Schlesinger, Jr., has observed: "History, by putting crisis in perspective, supplies the antidote to every generation's illusion that its own problems are uniquely oppressive" (*New York Times Magazine,* July 27, 1986). Unfortunately, as analyst Herman Kahn has said: "If you have a crisis, both sides say something like this: 'Look, nothing at issue is worth the serious risk of nuclear war. It's just crazy for us to continue this terrible crisis. One of us has to be reasonable *and it isn't going to be me*' " (*Newsweek,* April 22, 1974). *See also* STRESS.

crisis management Controlling reactions in an unstable situation to maximize one's own interests and limit an opponent's options into an ACTION-REACTION mode. There are two aspects to crisis management: (1) regulating a crisis so that it does not get out of hand and lead to war and (2) using COERCION to force an adversary to back down. The difficulty lies in striking a balance between the need to coerce and the need to control.

Crisis management is often crafty diplomacy in contrast to BRINKMANSHIP—taking a tough line and calling the opponent's bluff. Effective crisis management will maintain communications with the adversary, avoid overt violence, not demand too much from the adversary, and leave a graceful line of retreat open. While threatening behavior may be essential to give a clear signal of resolve, it must be used cautiously. Absolute clarity of international expression is vital to avoid causing panic in an opponent. The essence of this careful approach is summed up by U.S. President John F. Kennedy's remark (reported by his brother Robert in *Thirteen Days: A Memoir of the Cuban Missile Crisis,* 1969): "If anybody is around to write after this, they are going to understand that we made every effort to find peace and every effort to give our adversary room to move."

crisis of capitalism The Marxist idea that the capitalist system is so full of internal contradictions that it will eventually collapse.

crisis slide A concept developed by Coral Bell in *The Conventions of Crisis* (1971) to describe a situation in which a series of crises involving the same powers gradually becomes more dangerous because the decision makers see fewer and fewer options in each one. The result is a slide into war.

crisis stability A concept closely related to STRATEGIC STABILITY and that depends on the lack of any incentive (particularly in a nuclear crisis) for either side to initiate a FIRST STRIKE, either because it fears its own forces will be destroyed or because it has an opportunity to destroy those of the adversary.

critical defense zone A territory or region whose protection is regarded as vitally important to the national security of a state. The state generally will be prepared to use force to prevent a hostile or potentially hostile power from moving into this area.

critical intelligence Information that is crucial and requires the immediate attention of a commander or head of state. It is required to enable the commander to make decisions that will provide a timely and appropriate response to actions by a potential or actual enemy.

critical international studies 1. Also known as *critical theory,* this approach to INTERNATIONAL RELATIONS is a reaction to structural REALISM and is based on the assumption that all politics, including that between states, is both open-ended and rooted in ethics. In many respects this approach can be understood as the successor to both IDEALISM and MARXISM. 2. Any approach to the study of international relations that is critical of its own assumptions.

critical point 1. A key geographical position important to the success of an operation. 2. In terms of time, a crisis or a turning point in an operation. 3. A selected spot along a line of march used for reference in giving instructions. 4. A place where there is a change of direction or change in slope in a ridge or stream. 5. Any place along a route of march where interference with a troop movement may occur. 6. That point between two bases from which it will take the same time to fly to either base.

critical risk A concept developed by Glenn Snyder and Paul Diesing, in *Conflict Among Nations* (1977), which refers to the degree of war risk that a protagonist in a CRISIS situation is prepared to accept. This will be determined in part by the payoffs attached to different outcomes as well as by the tolerance for risk and the estimate of the adversary's resolve.

critical technologies 1. Scientific or industrial processes that are deemed to be of major importance to the national security of the United States and its military allies. 2. Areas of advanced technology where the United States has been challenged or overtaken by other states. 3. Technologies that the United States is unwilling to transfer to others.

critical theory *See* CRITICAL INTERNATIONAL STUDIES.

cruise missile A pilotless aircraft that flies, using radar guidance and preset computer control, hundreds or thousands of miles to a target. There are three basic types of cruise missiles: the GROUND-LAUNCHED CRUISE MISSILE (GLCM), fired from a mobile launcher; the AIR-LAUNCHED CRUISE MISSILE (ALCM); and the SEA-LAUNCHED CRUISE MISSILE (SLCM). They can be armed with either nuclear or conventional warheads and are considered very accurate.

crypto-Communist During the COLD WAR, a secret Communist sympathizer; a FELLOW TRAVELLER.

cryptography 1. The science of the principles, means, and methods for rendering plain information unintelligible by putting it into secret codes; alternatively, the breaking or reconverting of encrypted information into intelligible form.   **2.** The designing and use of cryptosystems. *See also* ULTRA.

cryptology   The science that treats hidden, disguised, or encrypted communications. It embraces communications security and COMMUNICATIONS INTELLIGENCE.

Crystal Night   *See* KRISTALLNACHT.

CSCE   *See* CONFERENCE ON SECURITY AND COOPERATION IN EUROPE.

C squared   *See* COMMAND AND CONTROL.

C³CM   *See* COMMAND, CONTROL, AND COMMUNICATIONS COUNTERMEASURES.

C³I   *See* COMMAND, CONTROL, COMMUNICATIONS AND INTELLIGENCE.

C-20 (Committee of 20)   *See* GROUP OF 20.

C²   *See* COMMAND AND CONTROL.

Cuban Boatlift   *See* MARIEL BOATLIFT.

Cuban missile crisis   The 1962 showdown between the United States and the Soviet Union over the Soviet stationing of nuclear missiles in Cuba. The missiles would have threatened the U.S. mainland only 90 miles away and therefore constituted an escalation in international tension. U.S. President John F. Kennedy demanded the removal of the missiles, imposed a naval quarantine on Cuba, and waited for the Soviet response. For about a week there was intense fear that neither side would give way and that nuclear war was imminent. Although Soviet ships did not seriously challenge the quarantine, it took a threat of invasion by the United States before the Soviet Union agreed to remove the missiles. This was sweetened by a U.S. promise not to invade Cuba and an informal understanding that the United States would remove its nuclear missiles in Turkey. Because the Soviet Union gave in to the U.S. threat, the Soviet military moved against Nikita Khrushchev (who led the Soviet Union at the time), enabling his enemies on the Politburo to oust him from power a year later. U.S. Secretary of State Dean Rusk offered his now-famous summary of the point in the crisis at which Soviet ships stopped rather than challenge the quarantine: "We were eyeball-to-eyeball and the other fellow just

A U.S. Defense Department photo that helped prove that the Soviet Union was assembling missiles in Cuba. (John Fitzgerald Kennedy Library)

blinked" (*Saturday Evening Post,* December 8, 1962). But the Soviet perspective was quite different. Khrushchev wrote in his memoirs, *Khrushchev Remembers* (1971): "[In] bringing the world to the brink of atomic war, we won a Socialist Cuba. It's very consoling for me personally to know that our side acted correctly and that we did a great revolutionary deed by not letting American imperialism intimidate us. The Caribbean crisis was a triumph of Soviet foreign policy and a personal triumph in my own career as a statesman. . . . We achieved, I would say, a spectacular success without having to fire a single shot!" In recent years there have been more disclosures about the crisis not only by the participants on the U.S. side but also by the Soviet Union. There is still disagreement, however, about how dangerous the crisis was. Those who emphasize U.S. nuclear superiority in 1962 generally believe that the Soviet Union would never have gone to war. (Their corollary is that the United States could have been much tougher.) Others believe, however, that the possibility of nuclear war was very real, not least because there was great potential for the crisis to get out of control and lead to inadvertent war.

Cuban National Liberation Front   A   U.S.-based anti-CASTRO organization made up primarily of Cuban exiles who live in Florida. In the late 1960s and early 1970s, the group staged a series of bombings and assaults against targets in the United States associated with or perceived to be sympathetic to the Castro government.

Cuban Revolution   The six-year struggle (1953–1959) led by FIDEL CASTRO to overthrow Cuban dictator FULGENCIO BATISTA. Batista, who came to power through a military coup in 1952, jailed opponents, controlled the press, and embezzled funds. Although Batista promised presidential elections for 1954, Castro led an unsuccessful attack against the Moncada military barracks on July 26, 1953. Upon his release from prison in 1955, Castro went to Mexico where he organized a force called the 26th of July Movement. After landing a small yacht in Cuba on December 2, 1956, Castro and his followers began a three-year guerrilla campaign. Damaged by unfavorable propaganda, a corrupt bureaucracy, and an ineffective military, Batista's

government continued to decline in popularity at home and abroad. On January 1, 1959, Castro's revolutionary forces entered Havana.

Fidel Castro's Cuban Revolution and the Communist regime he subsequently founded has been a role model and a source of support and training for Third World revolutionary movements around the globe. At the First Conference for Afro-Asian-Latin American People's Solidarity, held in Havana in 1966, and later known as the Trilateral Conference, Castro outlined a grand revolutionary strategy to combat "American imperialism" through armed revolutionary groups. Since that time, the Cuban government has been a conspicuous supporter of left-wing guerrilla movements, particularly in Latin America and Africa. This support has included supplies of arms, weapons and tactical training, ideological indoctrination, and the use of military advisors and troops. During the late 1960s and early 1970s, Havana became internationally infamous as a haven for terrorist hijackers, most notably Palestinian extremists. More recently, Cuba has been a sponsor of the Salvadoran FMLN and the Colombian M-19. Cuba has seemed willing to provide some degree of support to almost any organization espousing an anti-U.S. and anti-Israel ideology and is considered by the U.S. Department of State to be one of the foremost state sponsors of TERRORISM. Since the end of the COLD WAR and the demise of the Soviet Union, the Cuban Revolution has lost its once-considerable Soviet economic subsidy. As Cuban economic conditions continued to deteriorate in the early 1990s, many political analysts believed that it was only a matter of time before Cuba followed most of the rest of the Communist world and took a capitalistic turn.

cultivation   Growing things; in the contexts of social advancement and of spying, this is a deliberate and calculated association with a person for the purpose of obtaining information or gaining control.

cult of personality   A placing of political power and authority in a single individual rather than in the office she or he holds. The phrase came from the 1956 meeting of the Communist Party of the Soviet Union, where JOSEPH STALIN, the Soviet dictator from 1924 until his death, was denounced for his excesses in office. Stalin's successor, Nikita

Khrushchev, told the Twentieth Congress of the Communist Party on February 25, 1956: "The cult of the individual acquired such monstrous size chiefly because Stalin himself, using all conceivable methods, supported the glorification of his own person. . . . Comrades! We must abolish the cult of the individual decisively, once and for all."

cultural aggression   The intrusion of one culture on another, usually through the mass media, popular entertainment, or commerce. Thus Third World states sometimes complain that Western ideas, music, and clothing are polluting their native culture. And the French are notorious for complaining about American cultural aggression in Europe.

cultural boycott   *See* BOYCOTT, CULTURAL.

cultural exchange model   Michael Haas's conception, from his book *International Conflict* (1974), that violent decisions are the outcome of insufficient knowledge of and interaction between parties to a dispute.

cultural relations   Ties between states that are predominantly cultural (having to do with the arts or education) in character. Such ties can be a preliminary to the development of fuller relationships. Maintaining cultural links also is one way of keeping communication channels open when the relationship between the states is tense.

cultural revolution   1. A significant change in the thought, ideology, or mindset of a society. This is an important concept in the post–Karl Marx development of MARXISM. A cultural revolution is seen as a corrective to Marx's assumption that only physical and legal restraints have to be changed to liberate the proletariat. The totality of the attitudes, expectations, and intellectual orientations of bourgeois society have to be changed as well.   2. The Great Proletarian Cultural Revolution launched by the CHINESE COMMUNIST PARTY's Chairman MAO ZEDONG during his last decade in power (1966–1976). It was designed to remove his political opponents within the party and renew the spirit of the LONG MARCH. In the late 1950s Mao's mismanagement brought disaster to China's economy and starvation to millions of Chinese. As a result, political

power began to shift to more moderate leaders such as LIU SHAOQI, DENG XIAOPING, and others. Claiming that the country was becoming increasingly capitalist, Mao encouraged high school and university students to organize themselves into RED GUARDS to overthrow the "the capitalist roaders within the party." Soon the moderate leaders were purged, the party organizations were paralyzed, and the country became increasingly chaotic. The military then sided with Mao and stabilized the situation. The cultural revolution encouraged a cult of Chairman Mao; it emphasized Maoist thought as the only guiding principle for all revolutionary undertakings in China. Maoist thought was summarized in his LITTLE RED BOOK of quotations that became the symbol of the cultural revolution. The activist phase of the cultural revolution came to an end in 1969 when the CCP's Ninth National Congress decided to rebuild the party, stabilize the economy, and reconstruct international relations. However, radicals such as the GANG OF FOUR continued to exhort "politics in command" internally and unremitting struggle against both the Soviet Union and the United States externally. A moderate group led by Premier ZHOU ENLAI promoted economic growth, stability, and a pragmatic policy. Mao tried unsuccessfully to maintain a balance between these two forces while he struggled to find a successor who would embody his preferred combination of each. The infighting between the radical Gang of Four and the moderate faction continued until Mao's death in September 1976. The Gang of Four was purged by a coalition of political, police, and military leaders in October 1976. This paved the way for Deng Xiaoping's political reemergence in 1977. The cultural revolution was officially ended by CCP's Eleventh Party Congress in August 1977.

cumul   The accrediting of a single individual diplomat as an envoy to more than one foreign government. This has often been the practice of small governments.

Curie, Marie Sklodowska (1867–1934)   The Polish-born physicist who was the first to win two Nobel prizes. With Henri Becquerel and her husband, Pierre Curie, she shared the prize in physics in 1903 for their discovery of radioactivity that was central to the revolutionary work in nuclear physics. In 1911 she received the prize for work related to the advance of chemistry for her discovery of radium and polonium (named for her homeland). She was also the first woman to teach at the Sorbonne in Paris, beginning in 1906. Seeing World War I as a battle for civilization, Curie set aside her laboratory research, equipped ambulances through private gifts, got a driver's license, and went to the front to teach military doctors and medical orderlies accelerated courses on the use of radiological instruments, which they had previously ignored. She was made head of the Radiological Service of the French Red Cross. The radiology courses she taught for U.S. army doctors saved many lives during the war and thousands more when these physicians returned home. After World War I she was vice president of the International Commission for Intellectual Cooperation of the League of Nations. Beginning in 1920 she worked at the new Curie Foundation to develop "curietherapy" and to establish safety standards for those who work around radioactivity.

currency Money issued by the monetary authorities (usually the CENTRAL BANK) of a state. Its value vis-à-vis other currencies is determined by international currency traders including the central banks themselves. While the term *currency* is used interchangeably with "cash," there is a big difference. Because of modern checking accounts, there is always vastly more currency in existence than a state's physical cash monies represent. However, a state's overall money supply often is defined as the totality of existing cash plus bank deposits. *See also* HARD CURRENCY; SOFT CURRENCY.

currency basket *See* BASKET OF CURRENCIES.

current account In international finance, the part of the overall BALANCE OF PAYMENTS that records short-term transactions (trade, tourism, services, dividends, interest) while excluding long-term transactions (investment, loans, government grants). *Compare to* CAPITAL ACCOUNT.

current intelligence 1. INTELLIGENCE of all types and forms of immediate interest that is usually disseminated without the delays necessary to complete evaluation or interpretation. 2. Intelligence that reflects the current situation at either the strategic or tactical level.

***Curtiss-Wright* case** *See* UNITED STATES V CURTISS-WRIGHT EXPORT CORPORATION.

Curzon line The border between Poland and Soviet Russia proposed in 1920 by George Curzon (1859–1925), the British foreign secretary, which attempted to divide Polish and Ukranian areas. Poland claimed areas hundreds of miles to its east and attacked the Soviet Union. After initial victories the Poles were driven back almost to Warsaw. Stubborn resistance and French aid saved them. By the 1921 Treaty of Riga the two sides divided the disputed area along the final line of military operations. Neither side was satisfied. Only after World War II was the Curzon line accepted by both sides as the definitive eastern frontier of Poland.

customary international law *See* INTERNATIONAL LAW, CUSTOMARY.

customhouse broker A person or organization licensed to enter and clear things through CUSTOMS.

customs 1. The officials authorized to collect the DUTY levied by a state on imports and exports. 2. The procedures involved in such collection. 3. The duties themselves.

customs and administrative entry procedures Bureaucratic formalities at ports of entry that can result in procedural delays and increased imports costs that may inhibit trade, even when that is not the intent. Among the more common procedures are the issuance of health and sanitary certificates, CERTIFICATES OF ORIGIN disclosing such information as the place and name of the manufacturer, and CONSULAR INVOICES.

customs area The jurisdiction(s) covered by common customs regulations. This could be a single state or the multiple states of a CUSTOMS UNION *Compare to* FREE TRADE ZONE.

customs barrier Any protectionist measure that inhibits FREE TRADE. *See also* PROTECTIONISM.

customs classification A detailed coding system and description of goods that enter into international trade, used by customs officials as a guide in determining which TARIFF rate applies to a particular item. Most major trading nations—except for the United States and Canada—today classify imported goods in conformity with the Customs Cooperation Council Nomenclature (CCCN) (formerly the Brussels tariff nomenclature, or BTN). The council is headquartered in Brussels, Belgium.

customs clearance Administrative and security units at an international BORDER crossing that collect customs duties and approve imports or exports.

customs conditional clearance The duty-free importation of an item for a limited period (such as a personal automobile) or because it is in transit to a final destination in another state. This is also called *customs temporary admission.*

customs union A group of states that has eliminated barriers to trade among themselves and imposed a common TARIFF on all goods imported from other states. The European COMMON MARKET is a customs union, as are the United States in themselves. A customs union also can be described as a *free trade bloc.* The United States' recent agreement with Canada and Mexico, the 1992 NORTH AMERICAN FREE TRADE AGREEMENT, should lead to a North American customs union or free trade bloc. In fact, some commentators predict that the world will divide into rival trading blocs, with the North American bloc competing with a European bloc and a North/East Asian bloc led by Japan. *Compare to* FREE TRADE AREA.

customs war Active trade competition between two states or groups of states in a common market, indicated by the aggressive raising or lowering of tariff rates and other international trade barriers.

cybernetics The science or systematic study of communication and control in organizations of all kinds, according to Karl Deutsch in *The Nerves of Government* (1966). The emphasis is on information and its transmission through the organization and the responses that are made to it. The organization will try to stop communication breakdowns and adapt to its environment through the process of feedback of information, which leads to adjustments of performance. The basic cybernetic model was used by John Steinbruner to develop a theory of foreign policy decision making in *The Cybernetic Theory of Decision* (1974). Steinbruner rejects the rational decision-making model (which he terms the analytic paradigm) in favor of one that suggests that governments monitor a few critical variables and modify their behavior accordingly to maintain an equilibrium.

Cyprus Civil War The ethnic conflict between the Greek and Turkish populations on the Mediterranean island nation of Cyprus that flared up so badly in 1963 and 1964 that United Nations peacekeeping forces were sent in to maintain a cease-fire. The UN forces have been there ever since. *See also* GRIVAS, GEORGE T.

Cyprus conflict The conflict between Greece and Turkey over the Mediterranean island of Cyprus, which has a majority Greek-Cypriot population (463,000) but a large minority of Turkish Cypriots (108,000). Although the majority of the population looks toward Greece, Cyprus is actually closer to Turkey. In 1974 a coup in Cyprus by Nicos Sampson and supported by the military junta in Greece sparked Turkish fears that Cyprus would form a union with Greece. The subsequent large-scale intervention by Turkish forces in 1974 was widely condemned by its North Atlantic Treaty Organization allies and led to an arms embargo by the United States. In its aftermath, the island was partitioned between its Greek majority and Turkish minority.

czar 1. The title (also spelled "tzar" or "tsar") of the autocratic rulers of Imperial Russia. It stems from the Roman word *caesar.* NICHOLAS II, who was murdered by Communists in 1918, was the last Russian czar. When the Communist regime in the Soviet Union started to fall apart in 1991, the PRETENDER to the Russian monarchy, Grand Duke Vladimir Kirillovich Romanov (cousin to the murdered Nicholas), told the press that "monarchy could offer a good solution" (*New York Times,* August 30, 1991). When the grand duke died suddenly in 1992, the pretender hat (or crown) passed to his daughter, the Grand Duchess Maria, an

Oxford University graduate who lives in Madrid, Spain. **2.** In the United States, a slang term for any high-ranking administrator who is given extraordinary power over something; for example, a drug czar.

Czechoslovakian coup of 1948 The bloodless Communist takeover of the Czechoslovakian government that forced the resignation of President EDUARD BENES, instigated the probable murder of Foreign Minister JAN MASARYK, and began four decades of oppressive rule. Czechoslovakia had offered the last glimmer of democracy in East Central Europe at the time. The Communist takeover had proceeded in three stages from 1946—authentic leaders of democratic parties were forced out, pliant new leaders became mere façades, and finally monolithic Communist control was established. *Compare to* VELVET REVOLUTION.

Czechoslovakian dissolution The 1992 peaceful agreement by the two halves of Czechoslovakia to break up into the independent Czech Republic and the independent Slovakia effective January 1, 1993. The two ethnic groups, which were forged into one community in 1918 after the fall of the Austro-Hungarian Empire in the wake of World War I, have had continual (though peaceful) civil conflicts since the end of Communist rule in 1989.

Czechoslovakian-German Treaty The treaty of friendship signed in February 1992 by Czech President VACLAV HAVEL and German Chancellor HELMUT KOHL. The treaty was criticized in Czechoslovakia because it did not contain any provisions for reparations for German actions during World War II and allowed German capital too great a role in the Czech economy. Nevertheless, it was ratified by the Czech parliament in April 1992.

Czechoslovakian invasion The 1968 occupation of Czechoslovakia by Soviet and Warsaw Pact forces. This ended the PRAGUE SPRING effort headed by ALEXANDER DUBCEK to introduce greater freedoms to Czechoslovak society and set up the hardline government of GUSTAV HUSAK.

DAC *See* DEVELOPMENT ASSISTANCE COMMITTEE.

Daladier, Edouard (1884–1970) The socialist premier of France for ten months in 1933, two months in 1934, and from 1938 to 1940, who appeased the Nazis in 1938 and signed the MUNICH AGREEMENT. Daladier followed Great Britain's NEVILLE CHAMBERLAIN in forcing Czechoslovakia to cede the Sudetenland to Adolf Hitler in 1938 at Munich. As both prime minister and minister of war and defense (1936–1940) in the period leading up to World War II, he bears considerable responsibility for France's lack of preparedness for, and performance in, the war. After France surrendered to the Germans in 1940, he sought to establish a French government in exile in North Africa but was arrested and tried for taking France into war. He remained in prison until 1945. While he served again in the National Assembly (1945–1958), he never again gained ministerial rank.

Dalai Lama (1935–   ) The religious and political leader of Tibet, considered by his followers to be the fourteenth reincarnation of a previous Dalai Lama. In 1959 he and 9,000 subjects fled to exile in India following the Chinese occupation of Tibet. In 1989 he was awarded the Nobel Peace Prize for his nonviolent struggle against Chinese rule and his efforts to obtain Tibet's independence through peaceful means.

Dal Khalsa A SIKH separatist group, founded in 1978 in India with the purpose of demanding an independent and sovereign Sikh state. The Dal Khalsa was officially banned by the Indian govern-

ment after allegedly participating in 1982 riots in northern India.

damage control 1. A naval term for measures taken aboard a ship after it has been damaged from enemy action or accident to keep the ship afloat and retain its ability to function. 2. When applied to politics, efforts to contain the effects of a mistake or scandal so that the individuals involved will once again find themselves in a stable situation with an ability to continue fighting the political wars. U.S. Secretary of State Henry Kissinger once offered this theory of damage control: "One iron rule in situations like this is, whatever must happen ultimately should happen immediately. Anybody who eventually has to go should be fired now. Any fact that needs to be disclosed should be put out now, or as quickly as possible, because otherwise . . . the bleeding will not end" (*Time*, December 8, 1986). According to David R. Gergen, a White House director of communications under President Ronald Reagan: "The single most important rule of damage control is to know all the damage before the rest of the world does. When you're in a running story and you don't know where the bottom is, more often than not it will fall out from under you" (*New York Times*, September 28, 1987).

damage limitation A nuclear strategy that seeks to minimize the amount of COUNTERVALUE damage; that is, to prevent enemy nuclear attacks against industrial and population centers. This can be accomplished, in theory, by not attacking the enemy's cities but keeping in reserve a second strike capacity that could do so. Thus an incentive is given to the enemy to avoid attacking your cities in order to save its own. Another way of limiting damage is to attempt to reduce the adversary's ability to retaliate, whether through a counterforce first strike, through defensive measures, or through some combination of the two. The difficulty is that one side's efforts to promote damage limitation undermines the other's assured destruction capability. Damage limitation was first enunciated as an objective of U.S. military strategy in 1963 but was superseded fairly quickly, at least at the declaratory level, by an emphasis on assured destruction.

Danilof, Nicholas (1934–)   The American *U.S. News & World Report* reporter who was arrested in Moscow on trumped-up spy charges in 1986. After a few weeks he was exchanged for Gennadi F. Zakharov, a United Nations employee who had been arrested earlier in the United States as a spy. The diplomacy that led to this exchange took on its own momentum and led to the "nonsummit" between Ronald Reagan of the United States and Mikhail Gorbachev of the Soviet Union at REYKJAVIK.

Danube-Adria Group   *See* HEXAGONAL GROUP.

Danube Dam   A joint Austrian-Czechoslovak-Hungarian project that was designed to provide hydroelectric power for these three countries. The officially titled Gabcikovo-Nagymaros Dam project, planned in 1986, was scheduled to be completed in 1993. Austria committed $400 million in funding. However, environmental protests and lawsuits were lodged to stop the building of this complex. The Hungarian government adamantly opposed the dam because of potential environmental damage to Hungary and abandoned the project in 1991. The project was in abeyance until 1992 when Slovakia decided to separate from the Czech part of the former Czechoslovakia. Slovakia, ignoring the protests of its neighbors, completed the dam by the end of 1992, maintaining that it needed the power for its own economic development. Critics continue to assert that the billion-dollar dam will destroy wildlife, damage underground aquifers, and otherwise cause irreparable environmental damage.

Danzig   A port city in northern Poland, now called Gdansk. In the TREATY OF VERSAILLES Germany lost this Baltic port as well as the strip of land known as the POLISH CORRIDOR, which was designed to give Poland an outlet to the sea. Designated an INTERNATIONAL CITY in 1919, it was then supervised by a League of Nations commission. As Adolf Hitler's power increased in the 1930s with Germany's occupation of Austria and Czechoslovakia, he demanded reparations to Germany for Danzig and the Polish corridor. Just prior to World War II Hitler pushed German nationality claims to the city. The day after the Nazi-Soviet Nonaggression Pact of August 23, 1939, was signed, local Nazis assumed control in Danzig. A week later, on the day Germany invaded Poland (September 1, 1939), local Nazis also annexed Danzig. Because Great Britain and France were pledged to defend Poland, they declared war on Germany. The German invasion of Poland, ostensibly over Danzig, thus began World War II. After the war Danzig was returned to Poland. Renamed Gdansk, its shipyards gave birth to the SOLIDARITY movement in 1980.

Dardenelles, the   The waters that connect the Black Sea with the Mediterranean Sea. Along with the Sea of Marmara and the Bosporus, they are collectively called "the Straits." Turkish control of the Straits has historically deprived Russia of a reliable outlet for foreign trade and naval power in the Mediterranean. For centuries the Russians and the Soviet Union applied pressure to get greater access to them. *See also* GALLIPOLI.

Darlen, François (1881–1942)   The admiral in charge of the French Navy at the beginning of World War II. After holding various high offices in the German-controlled VICHY government, he ordered French forces not to oppose the November 1942 Allied invasion of North Africa. Later that month the United States made him head of government in French North Africa. But the next month, on Christmas Eve, he was murdered by an anti-Vichy assassin.

Dartmouth Conferences   Meetings between Soviet and U.S. scholars and citizens that began with the visit of a small group of Soviets to Dartmouth College, in New Hampshire, in October of 1960. This developed into an institutionalized set of linkages that generally met in plenary session every two years and that formed smaller working groups and task forces to work on specific issues such as regional conflicts or arms control. The U.S. government provided the funding for the initial sessions; after 1970 funding was provided by private sources. The sessions, many of which were held in Moscow, brought together influential citizens and scholars from both countries and proved particularly helpful during periods of tension during the COLD WAR when more formal and official channels of communication seemed very limited. Many participants were prominent citizens or had formerly held high office in the two countries. Norman Cousins (1912–1990), former editor of the *Saturday Review,* was the founder of the Dartmouth Conferences, although the idea is said to have come from U.S. President Dwight D. Eisenhower.

Dashmesh Regiment   A SIKH terrorist organization dedicated to the establishment of an autonomous state in the Khalistan region of India. Organized in 1982, the group was named after the Sikhs' revered tenth and last guru, Gobind Singh, who in the eighteenth century greatly influenced the Sikh religion and forged the Sikhs into a warrior class. Following the 1984 assault on the GOLDEN TEMPLE OF AMRITSAR, Dashmesh gained increased converts and popular support. It has assassinated many prominent Indian political, religious, and media figures, including a Hindu newspaper editor and the president of the Amritsar branch of the Bharatiya Janata Party.

date that will live in infamy   December 7, 1941, the day the Japanese attacked PEARL HARBOR. U.S. President Franklin D. Roosevelt first used this phrase in his December 8, 1941, request for a DECLARATION OF WAR to the U.S. Congress.

Dawes, Charles G. (1865–1951)   The first U.S. Director of the Budget in the Harding Administration who as chairman of the Committee of Experts of the Allied Reparations Commission was the major impetus behind the DAWES PLAN of 1924—a scaling-down of World War I REPARATIONS and a reorganization of Germany's financial system. For this he shared the Nobel Peace Prize in 1925 with AUSTEN CHAMBERLAIN of Great Britain. Dawes later served as vice president of the United States

(1925–1929) under President Calvin Coolidge. President Herbert Hoover appointed him ambassador to Great Britain (1929–1932). It was in that post that he made the now-famous observation that American diplomacy is "easy on the brain but hell on the feet" (*New York Times,* June 3, 1931).

Dawes Plan   The 1924 arrangements brokered by U.S. financier CHARLES G. DAWES that allowed Germany to continue paying its World War I REPARATIONS after the WEIMAR REPUBLIC was unable to pay. Dawes chaired a "Committee of Experts," which designed a plan that called for the end of the RUHR occupation, a sliding scale of payments that avoided the question of a grand total, and a reorganization of the *Reichsbank* (the German CENTRAL BANK). The plan stabilized the currency and credit markets but collapsed in 1929. When Germany failed to meet scheduled payments a new plan, the YOUNG PLAN, was implemented.

Dawson's Field   A former British Royal Air Force airfield located north of Amman, Jordan. During September 6–10, 1970, three Western airliners, with more than 400 passengers aboard, were taken to Dawson's Field by POPULAR FRONT FOR THE LIBERATION OF PALESTINE skyjackers, who demanded the release of imprisoned fellow PFLP terrorists. The PFLP held the hostages and the three aircraft until Great Britain, Switzerland, and West Germany bowed to their demands and exchanged seven PFLP members for the hostages on September 29–30. After the exchange, the PFLP blew up the three airliners before news cameras. Because of the Dawson's Field incident, King Hussein of Jordan, viewing it as the final straw in his long-simmering dissatisfaction with the Palestinian guerrillas then based in Jordan, ordered his military to expel the Palestinians, most of whom fled to Lebanon. *See also* BLACK SEPTEMBER.

Dayan, Moshe (1915–1981)   The Israeli general whose bald head and eye patch came to personify Israel's military prowess. He lost his left eye fighting with the British Army in Syria during World War II. As Israeli chief of staff during the SUEZ CRISIS of 1956, he directed the conquest of the Sinai. During the 1967 SIX-DAY WAR he was minister of defense, a post he held until after the 1973 YOM KIPPUR WAR.

After two years as foreign minister (1977–1979) in MENACHEM BEGIN's government, he resigned in protest over policies on the WEST BANK. Dayan argued against some Israeli West Bank settlements, opposed the government seizure of uncultivated Arab lands, and supported movements toward Palestinian self-rule in the OCCUPIED TERRITORIES. Dayan's reputation has fluctuated. After 1967 it was very high, but the initial gains made by Egypt and Syria during the Yom Kippur War damaged it. Chaim Herzog's *The War of Atonement* (1975) not only suggests that Dayan was responsible for some of Israel's weaknesses but contends that "the initial Arab onslaught and success threw him into a fit of pessimism which colored his evaluations right through the war. He spent a considerable amount of time in the front line, away from the nerve center, frequently creating an air of pessimism around him and giving advice which, had it been heeded, could have changed the course of the war and would have left Israel without the trump cards that proved to be so valuable in the disengagement negotiations."

DCM (deputy chief of mission) The second in command at an important embassy. Sometimes the DCM will hold the rank of ambassador but will not be "the" ambassador. The DCM is the CHARGÉ D'AFFAIRES AD INTERIM when the chief of mission is away.

D-Day **1.** The unnamed day on which a particular military operation commences. Such a designation could also mark a commencement of hostilities. **2.** The time reference system used in military plans, involving a letter that shows the unit of time employed and figures, with a minus or plus sign, to indicate the amount of time before or after the referenced event; for example, "D" is for a particular day, "H" for an hour. Similarly, D + 7 means 7 days after D-day; H + 2 means 2 hours after H-hour. **3.** In WORLD WAR II, June 6, 1944, the day the Allies crossed the English Channel and landed on the beaches of Normandy, France, and began the SECOND FRONT against Adolf Hitler's FORTRESS EUROPE. Code named Operation Overlord, this campaign and the growing Soviet counteroffensive in the east ended World War II in Europe. On the eve of D-Day the Allied commander, U.S. General Dwight D. Eisenhower, told his forces: "You are about to embark upon the Great Crusade toward which we have striven these many months. The eyes of the world are upon you. The hopes and prayers of lib-

U.S. troops land in Normandy on D-Day. (National Archives)

erty-loving people everywhere march with you. In company with our brave allies you will bring about the destruction of the German war machine, the elimination of Nazi tyranny over the oppressed peoples of Europe, and security for ourselves in a free world." But he also prepared this message if the invasion failed: "Our landings in the Cherbourg-Havre area have failed to gain a satisfactory foothold and I have withdrawn the troops. My decision to attack at this time and place was based upon the best information available. The troops, the air, and the Navy did all that bravery and devotion to duty could do. If any blame or fault attaches to the attempt it is mine alone" (quoted in Harry C. Butcher, *My Three Years With Eisenhower,* 1946). Fortunately for the Allies the D-Day invasion was an overwhelming success with far fewer casualties than were estimated.

DDR   *See* GERMAN DEMOCRATIC REPUBLIC.

dealers   In the United States, soft-liners in the Reagan Administration (1981–1989) who wanted to negotiate with the Soviet Union on arms control and regarded the pressure strategy advocated by the SQUEEZERS as being counterproductive and too expensive.

dean of the diplomatic corps   *See* DOYEN.

death camps   The German CONCENTRATION CAMPS of World War II.

death squads   Right-wing thugs who have terrorized the citizens of several Latin American states with their torturings and murders of actual and perceived leftists and sympathizers. The term probably first appeared in Brazil in the 1960s with the *Escuadros da Morte,* groups consisting of off-duty police officers who acted as brutal vigilantes against criminals. However, after the coup of 1964, the groups were used to silence dissidents. In Argentina, vigilante paramilitary groups preyed on leftists, liberals, and their families and friends. Argentinean military officers were often integral members of the squads. El Salvador's death squads were active up to 1991. Often paramilitary in nature, their attacks have been seen as both a cause and a product of the civil war that was formally ended in January 1992.

It has been estimated that 40,000 Salvadoran noncombatants were slain by government security forces and underground death squads. *See also* CONADEP; DISAPPEARED.

Debray, Regis (1940–   )   French left-wing revolutionary theorist and intellectual. Debray was a disciple of ERNESTO "CHE" GUEVARA and helped to popularize both Guevara's legend and his brand of rural guerrilla warfare. Debray was arrested in Bolivia while a member of Guevara's final expedition but was released after serving three years of a 30-year sentence. In recent years Debray has softened his violent rhetoric and has served as a Third World advisor to French President François Mitterrand.

debriefing   **1.** Questioning someone (a spy, a soldier, a diplomat, etc.) after he or she has returned from a mission.   **2.** Formally instructing an individual about her or his responsibilities regarding government secrets as the person leaves a position in which he or she dealt with classified information.

debt crisis   A situation that arose in the early 1980s regarding the continued inability of THIRD WORLD states, especially those of Latin America, to continue to repay the loans that they had received for development. The origins of the debt crisis are generally traced back to the 1970s and the two oil price increases. After the Arab OIL EMBARGO of 1973, oil producers transferred most of their money to private banks, which provided large-scale loans to developing nations. The increase in interest rates as the result of the oil price increases in 1979 imposed greater costs on the borrowers. A collapse in commodity prices in the early 1980s that followed had significant implications for the export earnings of Latin American countries. The result, according to Robert Pastor in *Latin America's Debt Crisis* (1987), was a vast increase in the external debt of all developing countries, from $400 billion in 1978 to $900 billion in 1985. Latin America was responsible for a large share of this debt; by the end of 1986 the total debt of Latin American nations was $382 billion—with Argentina, Brazil, Mexico, and Venezuela accounting for three-quarters of this. This figure was around 50 percent of the region's annual gross domestic product. Close to 90 percent of this debt was owed to commercial banks. Moreover, around one-third of the exports of the debtor countries was taken up in interest payments. The crisis began in August 1982 when the Mexican minister of finance announced that Mexico could no longer service its debt. The possibility of large-scale defaults on repayments and interest was seen as a major threat to the international financial community. Consequently, a rescheduling of the debt was agreed on, part of which required the Latin America countries to begin domestic austerity measures. Although this succeeded in easing fears and avoiding large-scale defaults, it did not solve the problem. In 1985, then-U.S. Treasury Secretary James A. Baker III, in a speech to the International Monetary Fund and World Bank, proposed a "program for sustained growth" and a shift from austerity programs to attempts to stimulate growth. Additional loans were to be provided by both commercial banks and the World Bank. By 1987, however, Third World debt had increased to over $1 trillion. By 1987 U.S. banks such as Citicorp and Chase Manhattan decided to write down their Latin American loans by 25 percent. No overall strategy for dealing with the debt crisis has been devised, but a series of palliatives, such as providing new credit for old loans, has at least kept it within manageable bounds. It does, however, cast a long shadow over the future of the international economy.

debt-for-equity swap   A financial arrangement whereby a THIRD WORLD state pays off a substantial portion of its debt to a foreign bank with the proviso that the funds are to be reinvested in the local economy, thereby generating economic development.

debt-for-nature swap   A financial arrangement whereby a conservation group buys a deeply discounted THIRD WORLD state's debt, then donates the debt obligation to that state in return for specific conservation measures, such as preserving a specific portion of a tropical rain forest.

debtor nation   1. A state that borrows more from all other states than it loans them.   2. A state that receives more investments from all foreign sources than from its own internal sources.

debt relief   Any means of releasing developing countries from their obligations to repay loans from commercial banks of the developed world and international institutions. The 1976 Manila Declaration, drafted by the GROUP OF 77, called for debt relief in the following forms: cancellation of debts owed by the poorest countries; a moratorium on debts owed by those countries most seriously affected by the increase in the price of oil; and consolidation of the debts of other developing countries with an international financial institution and a rescheduling of payments over at least 25 years. Debt relief has been discussed in the CONFERENCE ON INTERNATIONAL ECONOMIC COOPERATION (CIEC) as well as at the UNITED NATIONS CONFERENCE ON TRADE AND DEVELOPMENT (UNCTAD), and is an integral part of the demands of the NEW INTERNATIONAL ECONOMIC ORDER. *See also* BAKER PLAN.

debt restructuring   The reworking of the payment schedule of international debts of a state so that the carrying charges (interest and principal) are easier to bear. This may or may not include provisions for forgoing past-due interest or reducing principal.

decade of neglect   In the United States, the Reagan Administration's reference to the 1970s as a period when, in its view, United States military and security needs had been ignored. The argument was applied to strategic forces and obtained some credence from the fact that the air force was still flying 1950s-era B-52 bombers. In other respects, however—such as the deployment of MIRVed missiles and the development of cruise missiles—U.S. strategic forces were significantly augmented during the period of "neglect." The term was a very subtle one as it implicitly blamed the limits of U.S. power on poor decisions rather than on long-term trends in the international system.

decapitation strike   A nuclear strike that destroys an adversary's NATIONAL COMMAND AUTHORITIES and reduces the likelihood of RETALIATION.

deception   Those measures designed to mislead enemies by manipulation, distortion, or falsification of evidence to induce them to react in a manner prejudicial to their interests. Deception is inherent in warfare. SUN-TZU wrote that all warfare was based on it. NICCOLÒ MACHIAVELLI found that "Though fraud in other activities be detestable, in the management of war it is laudable and glorious, and he who overcomes an enemy by fraud is as much to be praised as he who does so by force" (*The Discourses,* 1517).

deceptive basing   Concealing the location of critical pieces of equipment, such as radar or missiles, by constantly moving them from one shelter to another to make it more difficult for the enemy to pinpoint and destroy them. Some of the deployment plans for the MX MISSILE focused on deceptive basing.

decision regime   A concept developed by Charles Kegley in "Decision Regimes" (in Charles Hermann et al., eds., *New Directions in Foreign Policy,* 1987) that is composed of cognitive beliefs emerging from a political process. "Decision regimes may emerge when there is leadership consensus regarding the substance of policy as well as the process by which it is made. The former are termed substantive decision regimes, the latter, procedural decision regimes." They are really consensus-based rules for action based on shared appraisals of the state's position in the world.

declaration   1. A formal document that states a course of action (usually accompanied by justifying reasons for it) to which the signatories (either individuals or states) bind themselves. The American Declaration of Independence of 1776 is probably the most famous of all political declarations. 2. An announcement of war (or neutrality), which expresses to the world a state's intentions on a matter. 3. A statement of intention by a political leader. The leader can be either in power, speaking for the government, or out of power, speaking for an opposition party. For example, in 1986 the British Labour Party declared that it would dismantle all British nuclear weapons should it regain power. It has since backed away from this point. 4. A customs form on which, upon entering a country, one must declare items for which DUTY should be paid. 5. In the context of the United Nations, a unanimous statement (as opposed to a RESOLUTION, which is adopted only by a majority of the members). Such declarations lack the full force of a TREATY because they are often general statements of principle that are not specifically binding

on any party. For example, the UNIVERSAL DECLARATION OF HUMAN RIGHTS was adopted by the United Nations in 1948 and ignored, without penalty, by all dictatorial and oppressive regimes.

declaration of war   1. Any announcement of war. 2. The formal obligation (under INTERNATIONAL LAW) on the part of a state formally to notify another sovereign state that a STATE OF WAR exists between them if the first state intends to commence hostilities. Declarations of war first came about when states felt it necessary to separate their military actions from the activities of privateers. Therefore, before the beginning of hostilities, a formal statement of intention, a declaration, to make war on another state was promulgated. This announcement also was necessary to inform neutral countries of forthcoming war. In 1907 this practice was formalized by The Hague Convention Relative to the Opening of Hostilities, which established an international obligation on the part of signatories to announce that a legal state of hostilities existed with another state by making a formal declaration to this effect.

Several factors have worked to reduce the use of formal declarations of war in the period since the convention was agreed. As the idea of COLLECTIVE SECURITY developed, states sought to avoid using a formal declaration for fear of being called aggressors; a preference developed to justify their actions in terms of self-defense. The growth in wars of national liberation and civil wars in the twentieth century has meant that states specifically avoid declaring war on insurgents to prevent rebels from gaining the status of a BELLIGERENT. Formal declarations of war before the start of a conflict prevent the use of surprise as an initial strategic advantage. Since World War II, no formal declarations of war were made in the case of Korea, Vietnam, the Arab-Israeli conflicts, the Iran-Iraq war, Afghanistan, and the Falkland Islands. Formal declarations of war seem to be rapidly becoming quaint relics of diplomatic history.

declaratory policy   1. The stated FOREIGN POLICY positions of a nation.   2. The publicly announced DOCTRINE about when, and how, a state will use its nuclear weapons. Declaratory policy does not tell what tactics and strategy might be used in a nuclear war; it just highlights the conditions under which

President Franklin D. Roosevelt reading the joint resolutions of Congress declaring that a state of war exists with Germany and Italy, December 11, 1941. (Library of Congress)

THE DECLARATION OF WAR THAT STARTED WORLD WAR I

The Royal Serbian Government not having answered in a satisfactory manner the note of July 23, 1914, presented by the Austro-Hungarian Minister at Belgrade, the Imperial and Royal Government are themselves compelled to see to the safeguarding of their right and interests, and, with this object, to have recourse to force of arms. Austria-Hungary consequently considers herself henceforward in state of war with Serbia.

SOURCE: The Austro-Hungarian Declaration of War on Serbia, July 28, 1914, reprinted in Great Britain, *Collected Documents Relating to the Outbreak of the European War* (1915). This declaration came a month after the assassination of the Austrian heir Franz Ferdinand by Serbian terrorists in Sarajevo. These courtly words then initiated the greatest mass slaughter the world had seen to date. When British Prime Minister Winston Churchill had to justify why the declaration of war against Japan on December 8, 1941, was made in similar diplomatic language, he responded: "When you have to kill a man it costs nothing to be polite."

---

nuclear weapons might be used and presents a justification for such use. It is distinct from operational policy, which sets the guidelines for the detailed planning of a military mission (how many aircraft, from which base, etc.), or targeting policy, which establishes which military targets will be attacked under what conditions.

declaratory strategy *See* STRATEGIC DOCTRINE.

declassification The decision that in the interests of national security, CLASSIFIED INFORMATION no longer needs protection against unauthorized disclosure, coupled with removal or cancellation of the "classified" designation.

Decline of the West The title of a book by German historian Oswald Spengler (1880–1936), *Der Untergang des Abendlands*. It appeared in 1918 with the German defeat in World War I and fit the German mood with its prognosis of an inevitable decline for Western civilization. While it gained journalistic notoriety, the general hostility to things German and its ponderous style inhibited its reception in the English-speaking world. It essentially held that civilizations developed, foundered, and declined on a mechanistic timetable.

decolonization The post–World War II process by which the major practitioners of COLONIALISM in Europe (Belgium, France, Great Britain, Holland, and Portugal) and the United States granted independence to the majority of states that now make up the THIRD WORLD. This process was fostered by ideals of democracy and nationalism and by the devastation Europe had sustained in World War II: problems at home forced attention away from colonial upkeep. The decolonization process varied according to how much resistance colonial powers put up. Often the countries went through three stages: indigenous elite opposition to the foreign colonial power; foreign-educated local leaders' opposition to colonial rule; and finally a mass movement against the colonial power. In some cases, as in India and Pakistan, the transition to nationhood was relatively smooth, except for local fratricidal fighting. In other areas, such as French Algeria and Indochina extensive fighting preceded independence. Decolonization has taken place in southeast Asia, including the Philippines and Indonesia, and most of north and sub-Saharan Africa. It will be largely completed when majority rule is obtained in South Africa. Yet the process has left a legacy of unsettled boundaries as well as ethnic and nationalist tensions.

Decolonization Committee *See* COMMITTEE OF TWENTY-FOUR.

DeConcini reservation A TREATY RESERVATION sponsored by Dennis DeConcini, U.S. Democratic Senator from Arizona, and attached to the Panama Canal Neutrality Treaty, which was ratified by the U.S. Senate on March 16, 1978. The DeConcini reservation specifies that both United States and the Republic of Panama have the independent right to take military action if necessary to stop the canal from being closed or otherwise interfered with. According to the treaty, if a future government of Panama or any other power tries to interfere with the normal operations of the Panama Canal, the United States has the right to intervene militarily. The passage of this reservation by the Senate led to widespread protests in Panama. *See also* PANAMA CANAL TREATIES.

decoupling In the context of the NORTH ATLANTIC TREATY ORGANIZATION, this refers to the separating of the U.S. NUCLEAR UMBRELLA from Western Europe. The question here is whether U.S. nuclear forces are coupled to the conventional defense of Europe or serve merely for SANCTUARIZATION of the United States.

decredentialization *See* CREDENTIALS.

deepening *See* EUROPEAN COMMUNITY DEEPENING.

deep strike strategy The prevention of an enemy's advance by disrupting the forward movement of its forces, especially by extending hostilities to its rear areas. This strategy was adopted by the NORTH ATLANTIC TREATY ORGANIZATION during the COLD WAR to respond to a possible WARSAW PACT attack. It was argued that NATO could hold the first wave of a Warsaw Pact conventional offensive but, given the numerical superiority of the enemy, the second echelon (reinforcements) was likely to break through. The deep strike approach sought to make sure that the second echelon never reached the forward edge of the battle area because NATO air and armored forces attacking behind enemy lines would destroy or disrupt it before it ever got a chance to reinforce its front-line forces.

deescalation A reversal of the process of ESCALATION in a crisis or during hostilities designed to ensure that the situation is defused. Little attention has actually been given to how the participants in a crisis can move away from the BRINK of war in a way that leaves neither side with disadvantages or vulnerabilities. This is unfortunate as the process of deescalation in a crisis or war is of vital importance because it is the only means of retreating from a building momentum toward war. Deescalation is often concerned with allowing a graceful and face-saving way out of the situation for an opponent and smoothing mutual suspicions.

de facto 1. Latin term for "in fact or actual." The reality of de facto is often contrasted with the legality of DE JURE (which means "by law"). Thus a de facto government may or may not be the legal government. 2. Diplomatic recognition that implies acceptance but falls short of formal legal (de jure) recognition.

de facto boundary *See* BOUNDARY, DE FACTO.

defection 1. The transfer of loyalties from one side to another. The Cold War was peppered with instances of high-level intelligence agency officials defecting from one side to another. But individuals not formally associated with a government also could defect just by moving away—if they could get away. Such an action can be taken by individuals or by entire groups, families, or military units. States also can defect from alliances. In the international relations literature, there has been growing interest on the circumstances under which this is most likely to occur. **2.** Actions that depart from tenets of international cooperation or that violate the norms of a REGIME. Defection can offer advantages if the adversary assumes that there will be further cooperation. Consequently, the notion of defection has been discussed in GAME THEORY.

defense **1.** The act of protecting one's side rather than attacking another side in a dispute. **2.** Used very strictly to refer to actions taken simply to protect oneself rather than inflict harm on others. **3.** A euphemism for "military." For example, most states refer to their military policies as defense policies, even though these policies usually contain offensive as well as defensive capabilities. Similarly, the armed forces of a state are generally referred to as defense forces, even though they may be used not only for protection but also to extend influence or power over others. The elasticity of the term is perhaps best expressed in the familiar adage, "The best defense is a good offense." **4.** Used in conjunction with the term *strategic* to cover the notion of protecting oneself against nuclear weapons, especially those that are likely to arrive on ICBMs. *Compare to* STRATEGIC DEFENSE INITIATIVE.

defense, active **1.** Seeking to defeat forces that initiated hostilities rather than merely to hold the line against them. **2.** An attempt to defend against a nuclear attack through active measures (such as ABMs) rather than through passive protective measures (such as civil defense).

defense, area **1.** The protection of a specific geographic area against an enemy. **2.** The protection of a major population center or a nuclear missile site using antimissile weapons. The ABM TREATY of 1972 severely restricts this kind of area defense.

defense, point The protection of a specific and relatively small place, such as a nuclear missile silo complex, a military air base, or a command bunker. A point defense is considered a major element of DETERRENCE because its whole purpose is to allow the target to survive a FIRST STRIKE from the enemy and retaliate.

Defense, U.S. Department of (DOD) The United States federal agency, created in 1949, that is responsible for providing the military forces needed to both deter war and protect U.S. national security interests. These uniformed forces consist of the army, navy, marine corps, and air force, which comprise approximately one million men and women on active duty. They are backed, in case of emergency, by members of the reserve components. In addition, the DOD employs almost a million civilians. The creation of a single Department of Defense to replace the separate departments of the War and Navy was a major effort to consolidate and integrate the military services and to avoid interservice rivalry. Critics of the DOD argue that interservice consolidation has not been achieved in any meaningful way because the department tends to function as a holding company for the individual services. One illustration of this is the fact that the individual service secretaries (army, navy, air force) are still retained. Interservice rivalry remains a major problem and is likely to be intensified as the DOD attempts to come to terms with the end of the Cold War. Initial efforts at downsizing the military have involved equal misery for all the services rather than a clear sense of priorities.

defense attaché *See* ARMY ATTACHÉ.

defense conversion *See* ARMS CONVERSION.

Defense Intelligence Agency (DIA) A unit within the U.S. Department of Defense created in 1961 to gather and coordinate military intelligence apart from signals intelligence (which is the concern of the NATIONAL SECURITY AGENCY). It was designed to avoid the duplication that had previously characterized the military intelligence-gathering processes of the individual services. The DIA manages the defense attaché system and other foreign intelligence resources and helps formulate the National Intelligence Estimates. It also helps to provide the list of strategic targets that are embodied in the SINGLE INTEGRATED OPERATIONS PLAN. It employs a large staff of mainly civilian analysts, who report on all aspects of foreign countries (including U.S. allies) that might affect their military posture.

Defense Security Assistance Agency   The unit of the U.S. Department of Defense that administers arms sales to foreign governments.

defense support   That element of foreign assistance that provides economic aid to some of the states to which the United States gives military assistance. Its purpose is to enable them to maintain a desired level of forces for the common defense that they could not otherwise provide from their own resources.

defensive avoidance   Term used by foreign policy analysts to describe ways in which decision makers deal with situations in which they expect to incur high costs or risks and in which they are not satisfied with the available alternatives. These include wishful thinking, attempts to shift responsibility to others, and procrastination—which is often based on the conviction of Charles Dickens's character, Mr. Micawber, "that something will turn up."

definition of the situation   **1.** The way policymakers perceive the situation facing them. This phrase, coined by Richard Snyder and others in *Foreign Policy Decision-Making* (1962), also implies that the perceptions of policymakers are dynamic rather than static. This was recognized in the successive, overlapping definitions of any one situation. This concept prepared the way for fuller and deeper efforts to examine the role of perceptions and to assess their influence on foreign policy.   **2.** A term that is sometimes used more generally to refer to the way policymakers perceive and make sense of a situation or problems with which they are confronted.

De Gasperi, Alcide (1881–1954)   The prime minister of Italy from 1945 to 1953. He led the underground resistance to fascism in World War II and helped organize the Christian Democrat Party, which dominated Italian postwar politics. He advocated close ties to the United States, Italian participation in the North Atlantic Treaty Organization, and European integration.

de Gaulle, Charles (1890–1970)   The leader of the French government in exile during World War II

who became the symbol of French resistance to Nazi occupation. A career army officer, he entered the French government as undersecretary of state for defense and war in 1940. After Germany conquered France in 1940, he fled to Great Britain and proclaimed: "France has lost a battle but France has not lost the war." In a broadcast from London on June 18, 1940, he said: "I, General de Gaulle, now in London, call on all French officers and men who are at present on British soil, or who may be in the future . . . to get in touch with me. Whatever happens the flame of French resistance must not and shall not be extinguished." He led the French overseas resistance to Germany (the "Free French" forces) from England and then from Algiers. When the Allies liberated France in 1944, de Gaulle became head of the French government, but his ideas for a strong president system were rejected, and he retired from political life in 1946. In 1958 crises in the FOURTH REPUBLIC, especially those connected with the Algerian war and a possible military

Charles de Gaulle (Library of Congress)

attack on Paris by rebellious French military units, led to his becoming the last premier of the Fourth Republic. He insisted that a constitution be drawn up for a new FIFTH REPUBLIC and became its first president. He resolved the Algerian crisis by granting independence to Algeria in 1962. At about this time he complained: "How can you expect to govern a country [France] that has two hundred and forty-six kinds of cheese?" (*Newsweek*, October 1, 1962). In modern French politics GAULLISM resembles other brands of modern European conservatism, though it places an unusual emphasis on national independence. For example, de Gaulle strived for a foreign policy that was independent of both the United States and the Soviet Union. In foreign affairs he opposed British entry into the Common Market and felt that excessive reliance on the North Atlantic Treaty Organization would restrict France's pursuit of its rightful objectives in Europe. After de Gaulle returned to power in 1958, he reduced France's participation in NATO and required NATO to move its headquarters and other installations outside of France. A highly authoritarian—some said monarchical—leader, he resigned after a referendum defeat in 1969.

Deir Yassin An Arab village outside the city of Jerusalem where on April 9, 1948, more than 200 villagers were massacred by Jewish terrorists. Men, women, and children died in the attack by IRGUN and Lehi, militant Zionist organizations that claimed that Deir Yassin was a hotbed of anti-Jewish activity. The Deir Yassin massacre was one of the key events cited as a reason for the exodus of Palestinians from present-day Israel.

de jure Latin for "in law," descriptive of something that has a formal legal foundation based on a legislative statute or executive action. Often contrasted with DE FACTO, especially but not exclusively in relation to diplomatic recognition.

de jure boundary *See* BOUNDARY, DE JURE.

De Klerk, F. W. [Frederik Willem] (1936–   ) The president of South Africa since 1989 (when he succeeded PIETER W. BOTHA), who in 1990 released NELSON MANDELA from prison, legalized the AFRICAN NATIONAL CONGRESS, and started to dismantle APARTHEID. In 1992 he boldly called for a national referendum on negotiations that would create a new constitution that would share political power among the races. Despite opposition from the far right, it (and he) won overwhelmingly. In the spring of 1993 talks were continuing between De Klerk's government and representatives of the ANC, the INKATHA FREEDOM PARTY, and other groups on a new constitution for South Africa.

delegation 1. A small group of individuals sent to represent a larger group. For example, each member state sends a delegation to the United Nations. 2. The official party sent to an international meeting. 3. The formal authority assigned to an agency or individual. For example, a diplomat's authority in a given situation is her "delegation."

delictum juris gentium Latin for "a crime against the law of nations." This phrase is often used when an international law is broken.

delivery system The means by which a weapon's destructive mechanisms are carried to its target; included are the propulsion system, its means of guidance, and any other components (such as penetration aids and decoys) that enable the weapon's kill mechanism to reach its target. For an artillery round, the delivery system is the gun that fires it.

CHURCHILL ON DE GAULLE

[In 1941] Churchill was finding de Gaulle a sore trial. A resolute trencherman, he bitterly resented the French leader's habit of interrupting his meal-times with long impassioned phone calls. On one such occasion, at Chequers, Churchill refused the call, but de Gaulle persisted so assiduously that Sawyers, the valet, begged the [prime minister] to yield. Cheeks crimson, his napkin crumpled, Churchill strode from the dining room. Ten minutes later, returning to rapidly cooling soup, Churchill, still crimson, was enveloped in mulish silence. Suddenly he burst out: "Bloody de Gaulle! He had the impertinence to tell me that the French regard him as the reincarnation of Joan of Arc." As always, Churchill had had the last word. "I found it very necessary to remind him that we had to burn the first!"

SOURCE: Richard Collier, *The Road to Pearl Harbor: 1941* (1981).

For a gravity bomb dropped from the air, the aircraft is the delivery system. With a missile the delivery system is more complicated. In addition to the weapons platform from which it fired (such as a mobile launcher, aircraft, or launching tube), the rocket or turbojet itself is regarded as a delivery system, as are the radar guidance systems, even if this radar is on the ground and only remotely directs the missile to its target.

delivery vehicles The means of sending ("delivering") nuclear weapons to an enemy target. They can be ICBMS, bomber aircraft, CRUISE MISSILES, or whatever is capable of doing the job. This concept is used in many ARMS CONTROL negotiations, when an agreement may be possible on a quantity of warheads and the total number of delivery vehicles they can have.

Delors, Jacques (1925–   ) The French politician who, as president of the EUROPEAN COMMISSION (1985–   ), has been one of the guiding forces for European economic and political integration. As the architect of a "United States of Europe," Delors is credited with creating the conditions for the passage of the SINGLE EUROPEAN ACT and the MAASTRICHT TREATY. Delors himself claims that he subscribes "to Gramsci's dictum: always have a pessimism of the intellect but always hold on to an optimism of the will" (*Guardian Weekly*, April 5, 1992). This makes him well suited to be one of the architects of European integration.

Delta Force The U.S. military's antiterrorist strike force. Created in 1977, it is best known for its unsuccessful 1980 rescue attempt during the IRANIAN HOSTAGE CRISIS. Eight men died and several more were injured in the Iranian desert when a helicopter crashed into a fixed-wing aircraft during the operation. The aborted mission has been severely criticized for both its planning and implementation. In October 1985 the Delta Force was involved in the interception of the Egyptian airliner transporting the hijackers of the ACHILLE LAURO.

demarche A general-purpose diplomatic term for a new initiative to a problem. It often follows a stalemate in negotiations and can be a specific request for action, a demand that something be done, a threat or warning, and so on.

demilitarization 1. The process or policy of excluding military forces from a designated area. This can be achieved either by negotiations or by force of arms. Demilitarization can be provided for as part of a treaty or imposed by a victor. 2. The act of destroying military equipment and material to prevent its being used for the originally intended military or lethal purpose.

demilitarized zone (DMZ) A BUFFER zone in which the locating or concentrating of military units, or the retention or establishment of military installations of any kind, is prohibited. DMZs are often used to separate contentious states. For example, there is a DMZ between North and South Korea.

democracy The Greek word for "rule by the ordinary people, the plebeian public." In the nineteenth century new revolutionary conceptions of democracy called for the placement of all power in the hands of the people. The problem of constructing a state that could exercise that power resulted in debates over the definition of the truly democratic state. Theories ranged from ANARCHY, or total absence of a governing mechanism, through SOCIALISM and various other forms of state control of industrial production and public welfare, to TOTALITARIANISM, or control by an all-powerful state acting on behalf of all the people. Thus the term *democracy* is often used by totalitarian regimes, which may call themselves "people's democracies"; one person's democratic regime is another's totalitarian despotism. Democracy, like beauty, is in the eye of the beholder.

Because it is used to describe so broad a range of institutional possibilities, the term *democracy* often loses its meaning in political discussion. But it continues to serve as an ideal in political debate. The founders of the United States were suspicious of the pure democracy available only to the free male citizens of ancient Athens. As Aristotle had warned, pure democracies tend to degenerate into dictatorial tyrannies. This fear of the mob led the American founders to create a REPUBLIC, a form of government one step removed from democracy, that is meant to protect the people from their own passions by allowing them to elect representatives that rule for them. The frustration of coming to grips with the concept and the reality of democracy is illustrated by Winston Churchill's remark in the British House of Commons in 1947: "No one pretends that democracy is perfect or all wise. Indeed, it has been said that democracy is the worst form of government except all those other forms that have been tried from time to time."

PRESIDENT WILSON ON MAKING THE WORLD SAFE FOR DEMOCRACY

The world must be made safe for democracy. Its peace must be planted upon the tested foundations of political liberty. We have no selfish ends to serve. We desire no conquest, no domination. We seek no indemnities for ourselves, no material compensation for the sacrifices we shall freely make. We are but one of the champions of the rights of mankind. . . .

It is a fearful thing to lead this great peaceful people into war, into the most terrible and disastrous of all wars, civilization itself seeming to be in the balance. But the right is more precious than peace.

SOURCE: President Woodrow Wilson, speech before a Joint Session of Congress requesting a Declaration of War against Germany, April 2, 1917. According to William Safire in *Safire's Political Dictionary* (1978): "Had it not been for one man . . . Wilson's phrase might never have caught on. Senator John Sharp Williams of Mississippi . . . was leaning forward, concentrating intently on the speech. When Wilson said, 'The world must be made safe for democracy,' he began slowly—and alone—to clap, continuing until others joined him. This underlined for the reporters in the press gallery that a phrase had been turned."

---

democracy, bourgeois In MARXISM, a phrase of contempt for Western representative government because it only truly represents the middle and upper classes at the expense of the poor PROLETARIAT.

democracy, consociational Governance by elite leaders representing the pluralistic elements in a multicultural state that gradually guides a fragmented polity into a stable and representative government. The Netherlands and Switzerland are examples of onetime consociational democracies. Many developing countries with severe tribal divisions are sometimes described as current consociational democracies.

democracy, constitutional Any democratic government that has formal limits, by means of a CONSTI-TUTION, on what it can do. The United States, while a REPUBLIC in structure, is a constitutional democracy in concept. Thomas Jefferson wrote in 1798: "In questions of power, then, let no more be heard of confidence in man, but bind him down from mischief by the chains of the Constitution."

democracy, direct Any governing arrangement in which decisions are made by the people themselves, as opposed to being made only by their elected representatives. Examples include the political meetings of male citizens in the ancient Greek city-states and the New England town meeting. Modern forms of direct democracy include the initiative, the referendum, and the recall, which allow citizens to directly enact laws or to remove officials by voting.

democracy, directed Guided democracy; a phrase that is often used to justify the absence of anything even remotely resembling Western representative democracy in DEVELOPING COUNTRIES. It rests on the argument that THIRD WORLD peoples cannot be allowed full participation in electoral politics because they are in no position to make rational political choices due to their nations' low level of general education (if not mass illiteracy) and poor communications. Additional justification is that they might demand more in social benefits than their government can afford. The stated goal of most directed democracies is that as barriers to rational participation diminish and economic conditions improve, the people will be "guided" into a modern democracy.

democracy, economic Equality in economic areas, which parallels the more traditional equality in political areas. In an economic democracy, all citizens would have a right to a job, decent housing, adequate food, and so on.

democracy, guided The term used to refer to the period in Indonesian politics (1959–1965) in which President ACHMED SUKARNO firmly established a system of presidential rule based on a revival of the constitution that had been developed immediately after Indonesia's Declaration of Independence in 1945. The parliamentary system had effectively collapsed in 1957. During the period of guided democracy Sukarno tried to balance the competing forces of the army and the Indonesian Communist Party.

democracy, pluralistic A governing arrangement in which real power is possessed by an assortment of groups and institutions that, from time to time, unite to advance the interests and people they represent. A major problem with this kind of system is that the groups and institutions often do not unite but work against each other, thereby making the system incapable of dealing with new challenges. *Compare to* PLURALISM.

democracy, representative A government in which citizens rule through elective representatives, who must be periodically reelected in order to keep them accountable. All genuine REPUBLICS are representative democracies.

democratic accountability The principle that in a democracy the government should be responsible to the people (through elections) and to its representative institutions (through oversight).

democratic centralism The Communist Party doctrine, espoused by V. I. LENIN, which held that conflicting views should be freely expressed at all levels of the Communist Party hierarchy; that the party central committee should listen to them before making decisions; but after a decision has been made, the policy must be unquestioningly accepted and implemented by all party members.

Democratic Front for the Liberation of Palestine (DFLP) A Marxist/Leninist Palestinian nationalist group founded in 1968. It has often opposed what it considers the "moderate" policies of YASIR ARAFAT and the PALESTINE LIBERATION ORGANIZATION. The group's terrorist acts have usually taken place within Israel or the occupied territories. The most infamous DFLP incident occurred in May 1974, when DFLP terrorists disguised as Israeli Defense Force members killed 27 Israelis and wounded 134 in the MA'ALOT MASSACRE.

democratic government Any form of government that is effectively able to transform citizen preferences into government policies.

democratic socialism SOCIALISM achieved through honest elections, as opposed to socialism imposed by force.

demonstration 1. A political meeting to show support for or opposition to a policy. 2. A military attack or show of force made with the aim of deceiving the enemy; no contact is sought. *Compare to* SHOT ACROSS THE BOW.

demontage The dismantling of a defeated state's munitions factories so that they can be destroyed or transferred to a victor's state. The 1945 POTSDAM CONFERENCE agreed to the demontage of Germany's war-making capabilities.

denaturalization The formal revocation of the citizenship of someone who became a naturalized citizen under false pretenses. For example, Nazi war criminals who lied about their background upon entering the United States have had their citizenship revoked and have been deported back to Germany.

Deng Xiaoping (1904–   ) China's paramount leader since the death of MAO ZEDONG in 1976. Deng Xiaoping was one of the early organizers of the Red Army in southern China after the Communist Party split with KUOMINTANG (the Nationalist Party) in 1927. He participated in the LONG MARCH and was a political officer in the army in the 1940s. After the Communists took power in the mainland, Deng became secretary general of the party in 1954 and a member of the ruling POLITBURO in 1955. Deng was purged during the CULTURAL REVOLUTION but was reinstated in 1973 and made vice premier, vice chair of central committee, and chief of general staff. After the death of ZHOU ENLAI in 1976, however, he was again stripped of all power. With the fall of the GANG OF FOUR, Deng returned to power in 1977. He quickly consolidated his control of the party and the military and embarked on economic reform policies inside China and the OPEN DOOR policy to the outside world. He intensified the developing RAPPROCHEMENT with the United States begun under President Richard M. Nixon and visited Washington, D.C., in 1979 to cement the friendship. By mid-1979 he had resigned from most official posts in the party and government but has nevertheless retained actual control of most state affairs. His reform policies suffered a setback in 1989 when a student prodemocracy movement in TIANANMEN SQUARE was crushed by the military with Deng's consent.

deniability   The previously prepared insulation of a political leader from a decision that he or she actually made but is later able to plausibly deny it because no paper or other trail leads to the top. Plans for deniability are important parts of covert actions and diplomacy. In effect deniability allows political leaders to lie about their actions. Nevertheless, if they lie under oath before a legislative committee or at a trial, they may be subject to prosecution for perjury.

denial measure   An action to hinder or deny the enemy the use of space, personnel, or facilities. It may include destruction, removal, contamination, or erection of obstacles.

denoncer un traite   French for the formal notice of the intention of terminating a treaty that one state gives to the others who have also signed it. Such notice may be within the provisions of the treaty and thus perfectly legal, or it may be a unilateral act of repudiation that might entail reprisals, diplomatic or otherwise, by the other states.

denuclearization   1. Moving away, in whole or in part, from reliance on nuclear weapons. This can be the result of unilateral or multilateral actions of alliances or of individual governments. In 1991 both the United States and the Soviet Union each unilaterally announced major programs of denuclearization when they "independently" volunteered to remove whole categories of nuclear weapons (such as nuclear artillery shells and land mines) from Europe. 2. International bans on placing nuclear weapons in certain areas, such as the seabed or outer space. *See also* NUCLEAR-FREE ZONE.

Department of State   *See* STATE, U.S. DEPARTMENT OF.

dependence   1. The notion of one state's reliance on another for something of value, whether security or economic well-being, which cannot be achieved without help from another state. 2. The opposite of INDEPENDENCE. 3. A condition of reliance on others that, when it is mutual or reciprocal, is described in terms of INTERDEPENDENCE. *Compare to* SELF-SUFFICIENCY.

dependency theory   A radical view of the relations that Western capitalist states actually have with the THIRD WORLD. The basic belief is that major capitalist powers such as the United States and the members of the European Community have not really given up their colonial powers but in fact exercise enormous political control over Latin American, African, and Asian countries. However, they do this now by the use of economic pressure and by exploiting their superior market position to extract unfair advantages in international trade. According to the theory, as most of the finance for industrial and agricultural development in the Third World has to come from the money markets in the developed capitalist states (the *center* or *core*), the development of the Third World is tied to the economic interests of the West. By pointing out how irrelevant formal political control may be, the theory does help to show how long-lasting are the chains of empire that were cast during the nineteenth century. Combined with the spread of multinational companies outside the control of any Western governments—companies that frequently do control the raw resources of poor countries—the general notion of economic dependency cannot be ignored.

dependent state   1. A PROTECTORATE. 2. A state that relies on another state for protection or economic viability.

dependent territory   A modern-day colony; an overseas possession (such as the Falkland Islands or Gibraltar in the case of the United Kingdom) that wishes to remain dependent on the traditional colonial power even though it could be independent.

deployment   1. The positioning of troops and equipment in preparation for a possible battle. 2. The act of extending battalions and smaller units in width, in depth, or in both width and depth to increase their readiness for contemplated action. 3. In naval usage, the change from a cruising approach

or contact disposition to a disposition for battle.
4. In a strategic sense, the relocation of forces to desired areas of operation. 5. The designated location of troops and troop units as indicated in a troop schedule. 6. The series of functions that transpire from the time a packed parachute is placed in operation until it is fully opened and is supporting its load.

deportation The expulsion from a state of someone who is not a citizen of the state and who, for one reason or another, has become PERSONA NON GRATA there. The reason may be illegal entry or the inability of the person to meet requirements for residence.

depository 1. In economics, a bank. 2. The state that has undertaken the responsibility for safekeeping the original documents of a multilateral treaty.

deprogramming *See* BRAINWASHING.

deputy chief of mission *See* DCM.

Desert Fox The nickname of World War II German General ERWIN ROMMEL.

Desert One The code name for the April 1980 aborted U.S. DELTA FORCE attempt to rescue Americans during the IRANIAN HOSTAGE CRISIS.

Desert Rats The nickname of the British and Commonwealth soldiers who defeated the forces of ERWIN ROMMEL in the North African campaigns of World War II.

Desert Storm *See* PERSIAN GULF WAR.

destabilization 1. Outside but covert interference with a country's political and economic system to cause such turmoil that the government falls and the economy collapses. For example, in the 1970s the United States used COVERT OPERATIONS to destabilize the government of SALVADOR ALLENDE of Chile. 2. Measures that undermine the stability of the strategic balance.

de-Stalinization 1. The mid-1950s policy of the Soviet Union to reverse some of the harshest aspects of JOSEPH STALIN's rule and to undermine Stalin's previous status as infallible. It is generally agreed

that de-Stalinization began in 1956 when NIKITA KHRUSHCHEV denounced Stalin's CULT OF PERSONALITY. 2. By analogy, any lessening of the restrictions of a harsh governing regime.

D'Estournelles de Constant, Paul Henri (1852–1924) The French baron and diplomat who shared the 1909 Nobel Peace Prize (with AUGUSTE BEERNAERT) for his long-term efforts to form a European Union and his short-term efforts toward a Franco-German rapprochement.

destroyers-for-bases The 1940 agreement between Great Britain (which was then fighting the BATTLE OF THE ATLANTIC) and the United States. In exchange for 50 World War I–vintage destroyers, the United States was given 99-year leases for naval and air bases on British possessions in the Atlantic Ocean and the Caribbean Sea.

desuetude No longer in use; characteristic of a treaty that no longer has force because of obsolescence. For example, the ANTI-COMINTERN PACT of 1936 between Germany and Japan became obsolete when those governments lost World War II and subsequent governments under new constitutions renounced aggressive wars.

detection 1. The discovery by any means of the presence of a person, object, or phenomenon of potential military significance. 2. In tactical operations, the perception of an object of possible military interest but unconfirmed by recognition. 3. In surveillance, the determination and transmission by a surveillance system that an event has occurred. 4. In arms control, the first step in the process of ascertaining the occurrence of a violation of an arms control agreement.

détente 1. French term meaning "the easing of strained relations." In international politics the term describes a lessening of tensions and an improvement in a relationship between adversaries. There are major problems with the term in that it can be used variously to describe a condition, a climate, a process, or a policy. *Compare to* ENTENTE. 2. The process of Soviet-American relations in the 1970s, which included political summit conferences, economic agreements leading to increased trade, and strategic arms limitations (SALT) agreements. The term *détente* was used to differentiate the relationship from the COLD WAR, which had predominated since the late 1940s. The superpower détente was controversial. Critics charged that the Soviet Union was using it to advance its own interests at the expense of the United States. It is generally conceded that this era of détente ended with the Soviet AFGHANISTAN INTERVENTION in December 1979. The United States responded with retaliatory sanctions against the Soviet Union in 1980 (notably the grain embargo and the boycott of the Moscow Olympic Games), the shelving by the U.S. Senate of the SALT II treaty, and the election of the conservative Ronald Reagan as president in November 1980. President Reagan repudiated détente in favor of more assertive American policy toward the Soviets. Détente emerged again in the mid-1980s as a result of the initiatives of Soviet leader Mikhail Gorbachev, and this time it led not to renewed Cold War but to the end of the Cold War. *Compare to* CONTAINMENT.

determinism   The belief that the social, geographical, and political environments of an individual or a state are the most important factors in deciding what directions an individual or state will take. Thus individual choice becomes a secondary factor. *See also* SPROUT, HAROLD AND MARGARET.

deterrence   Dissuasion of a person or a state from an action by instilling within that person or state fear of the consequences. Deterrence is a state of mind brought about by the existence of a credible threat of unacceptable counteraction; it is the foundation of U.S. defense policy. The underlying notion is that, as long as a possible enemy believes that an attack upon a state will result in a massive counterattack, there will be no war. Consequently large survivable forces are essential to maintain peace. In its broadest use, deterrence encompasses any strategy, force deployment, or policy intended to persuade a potential enemy not to attack. Although it has a general applicability, the concept of deterrence has become inextricably connected to nuclear weapons, in large part because deterrence has been their only role since World War II. Proponents of deterrence argue that during the Cold War both superpowers were deterred from attacks against

each other by the costs that would be incurred. This is known as *mutual deterrence. Compare to* COMPELLENCE.

deterrence, discriminate   Term used as the title of the report of the 1988 U.S. President's Commission on Integrated Long Term Strategy cochaired by FRED IKLE and ALBERT WOHLSTETTER. The commission argued that U.S. reliance on punitive conceptions of nuclear deterrence should be superseded by a more discriminate approach in which greater emphasis would be placed on new conventional technologies and on the use of nuclear weapons to defeat aggression in ways that would avoid apocalyptic outcomes. The emphasis would be on controlled and selective operations, whether at the nuclear or conventional level, as part of a more flexible approach to global contingencies. This has become the basic defense policy of the United States in the early 1990s.

deterrence, existential   A concept developed by MCGEORGE BUNDY in "Existential Deterrence and its Consequences" (in D. Maclean, ed., *The Security Gamble*, 1984), which argues that nuclear weapons per se, rather than particular nuclear strategies, have a great impact in terms of deterrence. The argument is essentially that existential deterrence operated in the U.S.-Soviet relationship and had a profoundly inhibiting effect on the willingness of either superpower to take risky actions. Central to the thesis is the idea that nuclear weapons themselves deter much more than the use of these weapons by the adversary. Their impact is pervasive and deeply affects any idea of initiating the use of force, even at the conventional level, against the other superpower.

deterrence, extended   A strategy wherein one nuclear power seeks to deter another not only from attack on itself but also from attack on its allies. NORTH ATLANTIC TREATY ORGANIZATION strategy has relied on extended deterrence: that the United States, by threatening to use nuclear weapons, has deterred not only a Soviet nuclear attack but also conventional aggression in Western Europe. While the credibility of this policy has been debated interminably, in practice extended deterrence seems to have worked.

deterrence, graduated   A strategic policy that emphasizes the need for multiple options between doing nothing and MASSIVE RETALIATION. It was developed in an article in *World Politics* (January 1956) by British Rear Admiral Anthony Buzzard. As a critique of the Eisenhower Administration's massive retaliation strategy, the notion of graduated deterrence was one of the forerunners of the FLEXI-BLE RESPONSE strategy enunciated by the Kennedy Administration in the 1960s. The essence of Buzzard's proposal was that greater emphasis should be placed on COUNTERFORCE targeting and on limiting hostilities through more restrained policies.

deterrence, intrawar   The idea that deterrence can be continued into war itself and prevent ESCALATION by convincing the adversary that such an action would be pointless and suicidal.

deterrence, minimum   Preventing a nuclear attack by possessing a relatively small number of weapons—just enough to inflict unacceptable levels of damage on the attacker. Critics of minimum deterrence contend that its advocates are insensitive to the requirements of stability in a deterrence relationship and ignore the need to ensure that even after absorbing a FIRST STRIKE there are sufficient systems available for retaliation.

deterrence, nuclear   Preventing an attack upon oneself or one's allies through the threat to inflict unacceptable costs on the adversary with nuclear weapons in retaliation. The three requirements for effective deterrence are: capabilities that can ride out an enemy FIRST STRIKE, credibility that relates to one's willingness to retaliate, and communication that makes clear to the adversary what actions are censured and what the likely costs of taking them would be.

deterrence by denial   The traditional role of military defense. The argument is that one can prevent war by having such strong defenses that a potential enemy knows an aggressive war cannot be won. Thus the enemy is being "denied" victory, or the territory that might be gained, and is in some general sense being "deterred" from trying.

deterrent, independent   A traditional description of the British, and sometimes the French, strategic nuclear forces. But the term also is applicable to any other state that possesses nuclear forces—especially those that are self-designed and built entirely from the state's own resources. The main reason for the acquisition and maintenance of these forces is a desire to have national control over the means to threaten the use of or employ nuclear weapons. For example, French and British nuclear forces are based on a recognition that a community of interests between allies cannot be assured at all times, especially when the states are separated by large geographic distances. They also are based on doubts about the viability of extended deterrence in situations where it would be suicidal for the United States to implement its nuclear threat. The usefulness of independent nuclear forces remains controversial. Their credibility is questioned on the grounds that their use might lead to national annihilation.

deterrent effect   Discouraging individuals or states from taking a certain action by means of policies, laws, or retaliatory capabilities designed to prevent the unwanted behavior because of fear of the consequences. DETERRENCE, which seems to have worked well as a matter of defense policy, has had a poorer record of success in the domestic arena. Some people will violate the law no matter how severe the penalties.

Deutsch, Karl Wolfgang (1912–1992)   The Czechoslovakian-born U.S. political scientist who advanced the application of the social sciences (and its quantitative techniques in particular) to the study of international relations. Deutsch also was a principal theoretician for modern analyses of nationalism and the determinants of POLITICAL INTEGRATION. His focus on communication flows among states was innovative, and his analyses of Western Europe and the Atlantic region were extremely important in enhancing the understanding of political and economic integration. His major works include: *Nationalism and Social Communication* (1953); *The Nerves of Government* (1963); *The Analysis of International Relations* (1968); *Nationalism and Its Alternatives* (1969); *Politics and Government: How People Decide Their Fate* (1970).

Deuxième Bureau   The French Department of Military Intelligence, parallel to the British MI6.

De Valera, Eamon (1882–1975) The Irish revolutionary leader who was prime minister of Ireland (1932–1948, 1951–1954, 1957–1959) and president (1959–1973). In 1921 he was part of the irreconcilable minority in the Dáil (the Irish legislature) that refused to recognize the ANGLO-IRISH TREATY that gave independence to the Irish Free State but granted Ulster (NORTHERN IRELAND) special status.

devaluation **1.** Reducing the value of a nation's CURRENCY in relation to gold, or to the currency of other countries, when this value is set by government intervention in the exchange market. Devaluation normally refers to fixed EXCHANGE RATES. (In a system of flexible rates, if the value of the currency falls, it is referred to as depreciation; if the value of the currency rises, it is referred to as appreciation.) British Prime Minister Harold Wilson is credited with the most famous piece of double talk on devaluation when in a broadcast to his nation in 1967 he announced the devaluation of the pound: "From now on the pound abroad is worth 14 percent or so less in terms of other currencies. It does not mean, of course, that the pound here in Britain, in your pocket or purse or in your bank, has been devalued." Wilson's statement was misleading because a devalued currency means that imports cost more. Thus if an economy is heavily dependent on imports, as Great Britain is, then the overall standard of living must fall. However, devaluation has the beneficial effect of increasing exports because a state that devalues its currency makes its products less expensive to foreign buyers. **2.** A diplomatic stratagem whereby something once considered of great value in negotiations is deliberately, as a matter of policy, considered less important than it was before. For example, in the United States after the Iran-Contra scandal broke, the Reagan Administration "devalued" the American hostages held in Lebanon.

developed countries Industrialized states with per capita incomes of over $3,000 U.S. dollars a year and with higher standards of living than in the non-industrialized world. Whether a country is termed developed or developing is determined by such factors as GROSS NATIONAL PRODUCT, education, level of industrial development and production, health and welfare, and agricultural productivity. In general, the developed market economies of the FIRST WORLD together with the developed, centrally planned economies of what used to be known as the SECOND WORLD are considered the developed countries—even though there is a world of difference between the two. *Compare to* MORE-DEVELOPED COUNTRIES.

developing countries Used with the terms THIRD WORLD, *less-developed countries*, *underdeveloped countries*, and *the South* to refer to those states with comparatively low per capita incomes and standards of living. The lowest-income developing countries are often referred to as the FOURTH WORLD.

development The gradual process of increasing economic growth so that the benefits of increased production and a more equitable distribution of income improve social and political conditions. The word is usually used in the context of the THIRD WORLD, but the differences are only a matter of degree; after all, the comparatively rich industrialized states are still developing too. The ultimate goals of development are higher standards of living, better health and nutrition, more widespread educational opportunity, and increased personal freedoms. *Compare to* SUSTAINABLE DEVELOPMENT.

development administration The management of THIRD WORLD political and economic assistance programs. This is usually a joint effort between donor and recipient states, often with the additional involvement of international organizations.

development assistance *See* FOREIGN AID.

Development Assistance Committee (DAC) The 19-member committee of the ORGANIZATION FOR ECONOMIC COOPERATION AND DEVELOPMENT established to coordinate, monitor, and evaluate OFFICIAL DEVELOPMENT ASSISTANCE from member countries to developing countries. The DAC includes 19 countries—Australia, Austria, Belgium, Canada, Denmark, Finland, France, Germany, Ireland, Italy, Japan, The Netherlands, New Zealand, Norway, Sweden, Switzerland, the United Kingdom, and the United States—and the Commission of the European Communities. *See also* FOREIGN AID.

development banks **1.** Regional banks of the THIRD WORLD that focus on economic development programs; for example, the AFRICAN DEVELOPMENT BANK. **2.** Lending faculties of international organizations that focus on economic development programs.

development cooperation   A term synonomous with "development assistance" that has a less charitable implication and therefore is preferred by some THIRD WORLD states that wish to emphasize the interdependent nature of the development process and play down its charitable aspects.

development decades   The United Nations' ten-year plans for international economic development aimed at furthering the self-sufficiency of DEVELOPING COUNTRIES. The first development decade, proclaimed by U.S. President John F. Kennedy in an address to the UN General Assembly on September 25, 1961, set as its goal a minimum rate of growth in national income of 5 percent in developing countries by the end of the decade. DEVELOPED COUNTRIES were asked to provide 1 percent of their national incomes as financial aid to developing countries. Subsequent development decades have been proclaimed every ten years since. The only goal that has been met has been the proclaiming of a new development decade every ten years. While the developing states generally had sustained growth in the 1960s and 1970s, they never achieved their 5 percent goal. Then in the 1980s incomes in many states of Africa and Asia actually declined. Of course, the picture is not all gloomy. Some states during this same period (such as Malaysia, Singapore, and Taiwan) have become major economic success stories.

development finance companies (DFCs)   Independent financial institutions in DEVELOPING COUNTRIES that are run technically and managerially by the INTERNATIONAL FINANCE CORPORATION and supported financially by the INTERNATIONAL BANK FOR RECONSTRUCTION AND DEVELOPMENT. DFCs are central to DEVELOPMENT because they are the principal lenders to medium- and small-scale development projects, they act as a channel for foreign capital, they can mobilize domestic private savings for investment purposes, and they can identify and promote new investment opportunities.

development indicators   Economic and social statistical time series that demonstrate the extent to which development programs have been effectual. Development indicators are produced by Third World governments, by various United Nations' agencies such as the WORLD HEALTH ORGANIZATION and the INTERNATIONAL LABOR ORGANIZATION, and by other international agencies such as the ORGANIZATION FOR ECONOMIC COOPERATION AND DEVELOPMENT. These statistics are widely used by scholars and governments to assess economic and social progress and by aid donors to determine where to focus economic assistance.

devil's advocate   A member of a decision-making group who argues a case contrary to the other members. The presence of a devil's advocate is often regarded as a way of ensuring that GROUPTHINK does not occur. The difficulty, however, is that if a devil's advocate is too vigorous she or he will be excluded from the group. The other danger is that this dissent will simply be used to legitimize the decision-making process on the grounds that all aspects of the issue and various alternatives have been explored.

devil theories of war   The belief that certain inherently evil groups, such as munitions makers or capitalists, cause wars for their benefit at the general expense of humankind. Believers in devil theories feel that wars are caused by evil individuals or groups more so than by accidents or national policies.

devolution   The transfer of power from a central to a local authority. For example, the decolonization movement can be seen as the gradual devolution of political authority from the occupying power to local governments.

Dev-Sol   A left-wing Turkish terrorist group whose plot to assassinate U.S. President George Bush during his 1991 visit to Turkey was thwarted by Turkish police. According to *Time* (August 5, 1991), whose report relied on a Turkish newspaper account: "The group was planning to assassinate Bush in Ankara with a remote-controlled bomb that was to be planted either in Ataturk's Mausoleum, which he visited, or in a parked car that would explode as the President's limousine left the mausoleum." The plot was foiled the night before when Turkish police raided three Dev-Sol SAFE HOUSEs and killed 12 alleged conspirators. Started in the 1970s, Dev-Sol, which supports itself by armed robberies and drug trafficking, espouses a hazy leftist ideology and purportedly seeks to overthrow the Turkish government.

DFCs   *See* DEVELOPMENT FINANCE COMPANIES.

diaspora   A movement of national or religious groups from their homelands to scattered areas throughout the world. Generally the people are driven from their homes by persecution, invasion, or some other historical event. The word was first used with regard to the dispersal of the Jews from ancient Israel in A.D. 135. But it has also been applied to Africans, Palestinians, and others.

Diaz, Porfirio   *See* MEXICAN REVOLUTION.

dictator   Ancient Rome's word for the leader to whom extraordinary powers were given in times of crisis. Under the Roman republic, the office was inherently temporary, but Julius Caesar and the caesars who followed him gave "dictatorship" its modern definition as a government in which one person or party controls all political power. In this century, ADOLF HITLER of Germany and BENITO MUSSOLINI of Italy were dictators who came to power as the leaders of mass movements. Others, such as JOSEPH STALIN of the Soviet Union, rose by taking over a party that was already in control of a government. The dictators just mentioned, whose power was based on their personalities and control of force, must be differentiated from many modern dictators, such as the current leaders of China, who tend to be just the "first among equals" within a ruling elite. Then there are the small state dictators, such as IDI AMIN DADA or the DUVALIER FAMILY, who are not so much dictators as leaders of criminal gangs that have taken over a state.

dictator, tinhorn   A THIRD WORLD tyrant who acts more important than he or she really is (thus "tinhorn," which means phony) because the regime is artificially propped up by foreign sponsors. Tin-

horn dictators are known by the fact that they cannot stay in power on their own. For example, in a speech in the U.S. Senate on September 9, 1969, Senator Stephen M. Young of Ohio denounced the United States–supported "tinhorn dictators" in South Vietnam: "The fact is that these tinhorn dictators could not remain in power for more than three days without the support of our armed forces. They are well aware of the fact that, once there is peace in Vietnam, they will be forced to flee and to join their unlisted bank accounts in Hong Kong and Switzerland." What Young predicted in 1969 was essentially what happened in 1975. Nguyen Van Thieu (1923–   ), the last president of South Vietnam, fled to exile in Europe when he saw his army and government collapse as soon as the United States forces withdrew from South Vietnam.

dictatorship   **1.** A form of government in which all real power is held by a single individual or a small group. In this sense an absolute monarch is a dictator. **2.** The practice dating from ancient Rome of temporarily giving all power to a single leader in time of emergency. **3.** The specific formal office held by a dictator.

Dictatorship of the Proletariat   The concept of MARXISM used to justify the critical role of the Communist Party after a capitalistic system was overthrown. The theory holds that until the people are educated enough to understand the true meaning of Communist ideology, entrusting political and social decisions to them is pointless. Thus the party must have total control of power, at least until the state withers away. The fact that such a withering never happened reduced enthusiasm for this concept and led to the overthrow of many "dictatorships of the proletariat" in 1990 and 1991.

Diego Garcia   An island in the Indian Ocean about 1,000 miles south of India that has been a British possession since 1794. The United States has maintained naval and air bases there since the 1960s and has pre-positioned forces on these bases for contingencies in the Persian Gulf.

Diem, Ngho Dinh (1901–1963)   The American-educated Vietnamese political leader of the Catholic ruling elite who led South Vietnam following the partition of Vietnam into North and South in 1954. This division, done at the GENEVA CONFERENCE OF 1954, ended French involvement in the area. Diem became president of South Vietnam in 1955. His regime, supported by the United States, instituted harsh repressive measures against dissenters. He was murdered eight years later during a military coup d'etat carried out with tacit U.S. support.

Dien Bien Phu   A French stronghold in northern Vietnam (about 150 miles northwest of Hanoi) during the INDOCHINA WAR. This was the scene in spring 1954 of a decisive French defeat, which led to France's withdrawal from the war and the settlement of the Vietnam question, for the time, at the GENEVA CONFERENCE OF 1954. According to the French commander in Vietnam, General Henri Navarre, "There is no doubt that if the American air force had been heavily involved, as was proposed to me by the Pentagon, and as [U.S.] President [Dwight D.] Eisenhower had not dared to do, Dien Bien Phu would certainly have been saved. The U.S. would not have had to become involved later as it was obliged to do" (quoted in Michael Macclear, *Vietnam: The Ten Thousand Day War,* 1981). Nevertheless, the planning of French officers was inept to say the least. Dien Bien Phu, located in a valley, was a self-made trap. The fortress city fell to the Communists after a 55-day siege with artillery shelling from surrounding hills.

diet   A legislature; most notably the Japanese parliament.

diffusion of power   The spread of strength and influence to more actors in the international system, a change that has resulted in the erosion of the dominance of the United States and the former Soviet Union. The diffusion of power is often related to the issue of U.S. decline and the end of the bipolar international system. JOSEPH NYE has written very effectively on this and has identified five trends that have contributed to power diffusion: the growth of economic interdependence; the rise of transnational actors; the emergence of strong nationalist sentiments even in weak states, thereby making them much more difficult to control, influence, or subju-

gate; the spread of technology, including the technology of weapons of mass destruction; and a changing political agenda in which states have to cope with transnational organizations.

diktat   German for a diplomatic or military settlement imposed by force. German conservatives and ultra rightists in the 1930s often used this word to refer to the TREATY OF VERSAILLES and thus built up pressure to break it. The word came into English when it was often used to refer to German diplomacy just before and during the first part of World War II.

Dillon Round   Multilateral trade negotiations held in Geneva in the early 1960s under the auspices of GATT; named in honor of C. Douglas Dillon, then U.S. Secretary of the Treasury. The developed world agreed to a 20 percent reduction in tariffs on 20 percent of dutiable imports.

dimensionality of nations   *See* RUMMEL, RUDOLF J.

Dimona   The site of Israel's nuclear weapons research and development facility.

DINA   *Direccion de Intelligencia Nacional* (National Intelligence Directorate), the secret police organization of the AUGUSTO PINOCHET regime in Chile, established in June 1974. DINA was a major instrument of state terror, using mass detention, torture, and murder to squelch existing or potential criticism of the military government. DINA agents were active in right-wing DEATH SQUADS and also operated abroad. They were implicated in the September 1976 assassination in Washington, D.C., of Orlando Letelier, former foreign minister of Chile under SALVADOR ALLENDE. DINA was disbanded in 1978, and the *Central Nacional de Informationes* (National Center for Information, or CNI) was established as its replacement.

diplomacy   1. The formal relations that sovereign states maintain with each other; in effect, all of the regular and idiosyncratic intentional communications that states have with each other except for war. It is frequently said that diplomacy has failed when war begins. However, many states throughout history have taken KARL VON CLAUSEWITZ's attitude that war is only "the continuation of diplomacy by other means." **2.** The art, science, and practice of maintaining and conducting international relations and negotiations. The vast bulk of the communications necessary for this are conducted at relatively low levels. According to American diplomat LAWRENCE EAGLEBURGER, "The essence of diplomacy is how you manage the day-to-day business, the confidence you build, the atmosphere you create, so that when the tough times come you can do business" (*New York Times*, June 23, 1986). **3.** According to Ambrose Bierce's *The Devil's Dictionary* (1911), "The patriotic art of lying for one's country." *Compare to* AMBASSADOR. **5.** Skillful negotiations in any area. **6.** Adlai E. Stevenson, when he was U.S. Ambassador to the United Nations, defined diplomacy as "Protocol, alcohol, and Geritol" (Herbert J. Muller, *Adlai E. Stevenson*, 1967).

BISMARCK'S CIGAR DIPLOMACY

When you enter on a discussion which may lead to vehement remarks, you should smoke. When one smokes, the cigar is held between the fingers; one must handle it, not allow it to fall, and thereby violent movements of the body are avoided or weakened. With regard to the mental condition, it does not deprive us of our intellectual capacity, but it produces a state of kindly repose. The cigar is a diversion, and this blue smoke which rises in curves and which the eye involuntarily follows, pleases and renders us more flexible. The eye is occupied; the hand is engaged; the organ of smell is gratified;—one is happy. In this state one is very disposed to make concessions; and our business—that of diplomatists—continually consists in the making of mutual concessions.

SOURCE: Otto von Bismarck, quoted in Charles Lowe, *Bismarck's Table Talk* (1895).

---

diplomacy, atomic   The POWER POLITICS of a state with nuclear weapons; any foreign policy position that relies for its effect on the implicit or explicit threat of nuclear force.

diplomacy, bilateral   Diplomatic negotiations between only two states. *Compare to* DIPLOMACY, MULTILATERAL.

diplomacy, checkbook   Using money, either openly or as secret bribes, to influence diplomatic events.

diplomacy, classic   The diplomatic practices of the European monarchies that evolved after the medieval period and lasted until the age of revolution in the late eighteenth century. According to war scholar Quincy Wright, classic diplomacy

> assumed the coexistence of many sovereign states each respecting the territorial integrity and political independence of the others. These states dealt bilaterally with controversies . . . by means of the exchange of diplomatic representatives. Diplomats . . . conclude[d] treaties under the sole instruction of the prince they represented. Through these treaties, a network of obligations arose which confirmed the sovereignty of states, the immunity of diplomats, the freedom of the seas, the sanctity of treaties, and the rights of belligerents and neutrals in time of war. The system recognized that the rights of princes to initiate war . . . was implicit in their sovereignty, as was their right to keep out of the wars of others so long as they observed an impartial neutrality. (*Journal of International Affairs* 17, no. 1, 1963)

While elements of classic diplomacy are still evident in modern practices, its essential bilateral character first began to dissipate when the Napoleonic Wars created an ever-expanding multilateral diplomatic world.

diplomacy, coercive   The use of various political, economic, or military threats to induce acquiescence to diplomatic demands.

diplomacy, conference   Multilateral talks and negotiations undertaken at international meetings—whether ad hoc, such as a conference held by the triumphant allies at the end of a war (such as the Potsdam Conference after World War II), or continuously, through longstanding international organizations (such as the United Nations).

diplomacy, crisis   Formal international communications under conditions of high tension, when war seems imminent unless last-minute diplomatic efforts can stop it. See also CRISIS.

diplomacy, cultural   The exchange of artistic or educational programs to encourage greater mutual understanding between two states.

diplomacy, dollar   1. The extension of U.S. business into foreign states.   2. A pejorative term for diplomatic and military efforts that help U.S. businesses penetrate into the markets of other states. 3. The foreign policy of the administration of U.S. President William Howard Taft (1909–1913), which actively sought to expand U.S. trade in Latin America. As Taft stated in his annual message to Congress in 1912: "The diplomacy of the present administration has sought to respond to modern ideas of commercial intercourse. This policy has been characterized as substituting dollars for bullets."   4. Diplomatic efforts to stabilize the U.S. dollar in international currency markets.

diplomacy, gunboat   *See* GUNBOAT.

diplomacy, measured   Well-planned, systemic diplomatic efforts as opposed to sudden dramatic initiatives by political leaders.

diplomacy, media   Diplomatic communications that avoid established DIPLOMATIC CHANNELS in favor of statements made through the mass media. Press releases and television news interviews, inherent parts of propaganda and misinformation campaigns, can also yield positive diplomatic results. For example, in 1977 when President Anwar Sadat of Egypt used the news media to announce that he would go anywhere for peace, President Menachem Begin of Israel used this statement as the "excuse" to invite Sadat to Jerusalem, a visit that eventually led to a peace treaty between the two nations. *See also* CNN.

diplomacy, multilateral   Diplomatic activities among more than two states. *Compare to* DIPLOMACY, BILATERAL.

diplomacy, open   International negotiations conducted in public. This was the essence of the first of U.S. President Woodrow Wilson's famous FOURTEEN POINTS—that there should be "open covenants of peace openly arrived at, after which there shall be no private international understandings of any kind." Of course, many analysts argue that open diplomacy is an impossibility because if it is open, it cannot be diplomacy—an inherently secret endeavor. Many critics, however, accept the proposition that the results of negotiations should be open.

diplomacy, parliamentary   1. A type of CONFERENCE DIPLOMACY in which representatives of states at international meetings form coalitions, majorities, and minorities in much the same way that legislators behave in a parliament or legislature. 2. Diplomatic activities involving the legislatures of national governments.

diplomacy, personal   1. International negotiations undertaken by a major political actor, such as a head of government or foreign minister, as opposed to the regular negotiations of professional diplomats. U.S. President Theodore Roosevelt's personal diplomacy earned him the Nobel Peace Prize when he brokered the end of war between Russia and Japan in 1905, and U.S. President Jimmy Carter's personal diplomacy led eventually to a peace treaty between Egypt and Israel.   2. International negotiations undertaken by private citizens without the approval of their governments. Some states, such as Israel and the United States (via the Logan Act of 1909), have laws that make it illegal for unauthorized private citizens to interfere with the conduct of diplomacy.

diplomacy, ping pong   The first internationally visible sign of the RAPPROCHEMENT between the United States and China. In order to signal a willingness for further public contacts between the two countries, the Chinese in 1971 invited a U.S. Ping-Pong team that had been playing in Asian countries to visit China. This visit was accompanied by massive publicity and speculation that higher-level relations would soon develop.

diplomacy, private   1. A term used during the Cold War to refer to private exchanges between citizens of the Soviet Union and the United States. According to David Newsom's *Private Diplomacy with the Soviet Union* (1987), there were at least 216 nongovernmental organizations in the United States involved in exchanges, conferences, and dialogues with Soviet counterparts. **2.** Any exchanges between citizens of one state with those of another on issues involved in the relationship between the two states. Note that the difference between private and personal diplomacy is that personal diplomacy involves political negotiations of some kind while private does not.

diplomacy, preventive **1.** Efforts to anticipate major international problems and resolve them while they are still relatively small. **2.** The role of United Nations PEACEKEEPING FORCES—to keep regional conflicts from escalating into larger conflagrations.

diplomacy, public **1.** Programs designed to inform or influence public opinion in foreign countries. The chief means of public diplomacy are publications, motion pictures, cultural exchanges, and radio and television. The United States has, for instance, used short-wave radio to provide information to closed societies. **2.** The public relations efforts of diplomats and heads of states. *Compare to* DIPLOMACY, MEDIA. **3.** Formal discussions and negotiations undertaken at open forums such as ad hoc international meetings or sessions of permanently established international organizations such as the United Nations; in effect, CONFERENCE DIPLOMACY.

THE PERILS OF PUBLIC DIPLOMACY

The Prince and Princess of Wales were on a highly publicized goodwill visit to Australia in 1983. The Princess, while on a walk attended by the press, sought to show British affection toward Australian children by wading into a group of them. She "patted one tousle-headed mite on the head. 'And why aren't you in school today?' she inquired. 'I was sent home, miss,' the urchin replied, 'because I've got head lice.' "

SOURCE: *The Times* (London), April 13, 1983.

diplomacy, quiet **1.** Low-key diplomatic contacts, hidden from the public eye, that may eventually yield important results. **2.** The role of the Secretary-General of the United Nations in using GOOD OFFICES to help resolve problems among the various member states.

diplomacy, sauna In Finland, the government's tradition of inviting visitors to continue discussions (necessarily informal ones), literally in a sauna.

diplomacy, secret **1.** Confidential negotiations that lead to publicly stated foreign policies. **2.** Confidential negotiations that lead to equally confidential, *not* publicly proclaimed agreements between states. Article 18 of the Covenant of the LEAGUE OF NATIONS created an obligation of member states to register international agreements with the Secretariat of the League. This has since been continued by the United Nations Secretariat. **3.** A practice believed by many liberal and radical thinkers after World War I to have been a cause of that war.

diplomacy, shuttle International negotiations dependent on the work of a third-party neutral who travels back and forth between the capitals of the states involved. HENRY A. KISSINGER, U.S. Secretary of State (1973–1977) under Presidents Richard M. Nixon and Gerald R. Ford, became a famous shuttle diplomat when he flew between Middle Eastern capitals during the 1970s. *Compare to* PROXIMITY TALKS.

diplomacy, tacit Informal, often indirect, diplomatic communications that signal a state's intentions or receptivity to new proposals from others. For example, PING PONG DIPLOMACY was tacit diplomacy in action.

diplomacy, tin cup Requesting other states to pay for one's own diplomatic or military adventures. For example, during the Reagan Administration various U.S. friends and allies were invited to contribute funds to the CONTRAS in Nicaragua because Congress curtailed the president's ability to use U.S. funds legally. Again in the wake of the invasion of Kuwait by Iraq in 1990, U.S. representatives solicited allies to help pay for the U.S. military buildup and actions in the Persian Gulf.

diplomat **1.** A very polite individual; one who has both skill and good manners in interpersonal relations. **2.** A professional expert in negotiation and information transmission in an international context. It is often held that particular diplomatic techniques and training are necessary to ensure that no personal emotion or style should color formal international communications. Career diplomats of differing states may have more in common and are better able to treat the matters they discuss objectively and unemotionally, than may ordinary politicians. But as foreign policy is increasingly made, in all countries, directly by the heads of the executive branch of government, and as international meetings increasingly depend on direct confrontations between leading politicians, it is often suggested that diplomacy as a special technique (and the diplomatic corps as professional experts both in the making and execution of foreign policy) is becoming old-fashioned.

diplomat, amateur   An appointee to a diplomatic post who is not a career diplomat but the beneficiary of political patronage. Over a third of all United States ambassadors stationed abroad are such amateurs—usually substantial contributors to the political party in power. All of the developed states have professional FOREIGN SERVICES; only the United States and some Third World states use large numbers of amateur diplomats.

diplomat, career   A professional, as opposed to an amateur, diplomat; an individual who has had formal training as a member of a diplomatic service (such as the United States Foreign Service).

diplomat, citizen   Any person who makes an effort to improve international relations by building interpersonal links between two contentious states. Such persons usually have no legal or formal diplomatic standing.

diplomat de carriere   The French phrase for "career diplomat."

diplomatic agent   A formal representative sent by one state to another. Four categories of diplomatic rank for these agents were established at the Congress of Vienna in 1815. Ranks are important, because diplomatic precedence is based on rank and seniority. The ranks in order are (1) AMBASSADORS, papal LEGATES and NUNCIOS; (2) ENVOYS extraordinary and MINISTERS plenipotentiary; (3) MINISTERS RESIDENT; and (4) CHARGÉS D'AFFAIRES.

diplomatic asylum   *See* ASYLUM, DIPLOMATIC.

diplomatic channels   The normal means by which governments collect and exchange information. A state's most formal diplomatic channel to another state is its diplomatic mission located in that nation, but often informal channels exist as well. *See also* CNN.

diplomatic community   1. All those individuals engaged worldwide in the professional practice of maintaining international relations; all those formally associated with a DIPLOMATIC MISSION, from the ambassador down to the lowest clerk.   2. The heads of mission and their staffs in a given locality. Thus there are separate diplomatic communities in London, Madrid, Moscow, and so on.

diplomatic conference   1. Any formal international meeting.   2. An international meeting called for the specific purpose of codifying or amending international law.

diplomatic corps   1. All of the foreign diplomats who live in a capital city. *Dean of the diplomatic corps* is an honorary title given to the senior foreign ambassador, the one who has been in residence the longest.   2. The career agents who represent the interests of their state abroad by gathering and evaluating information on the politics of the host state, by protecting the legal interests of fellow nationals who have problems in the host country, and by handling international negotiations and the delivery of special messages (including threats and bribes) to the host government.

diplomatic courier   One who transports documents and diplomatic pouches to and from a foreign ministry and its agents abroad. The inviolability of a courier's person and baggage is one of the most accepted tenets of INTERNATIONAL LAW. Great Britain's diplomatic couriers are called Queen's (or King's) messengers.

diplomatic deafness   A technique often used by diplomats; they claim not to hear what they do not want to hear.

diplomatic franchise   *See* FRANCHISE DIPLOMATIC.

diplomatic history   1. The background to international relations; all that went before on any given international issue.   2. The academic study of past diplomatic events. As George Malcolm Young wrote in *Victorian England* (1936), "The greater part of what passes for diplomatic history is little more than the record of what one clerk said to another clerk."

diplomatic illness   Feigning illness to avoid having to attend a diplomatic event when an outright refusal to go might cause offense.

diplomatic language   1. Polite talk.   2. The one language that most of those in a diplomatic community would be expected to know. This was Latin from the Middle Ages until the mid-eighteenth century, when French took over. Since World War II English has been the effective language of international diplomacy—even though there is no formal recognition of this fact.

diplomatic law   That branch of INTERNATIONAL LAW that sets the rules and norms by which diplomatic agents function. Modern diplomatic law was codified by the 1961 VIENNA CONVENTION ON DIPLOMATIC RELATIONS.

diplomatic lever   Something that a first party can use to encourage a second party to take an action that the first party desires. For example, in the United States the Carter Administration tried to use a grain embargo to encourage the Soviet Union to withdraw from Afghanistan after the 1979 invasion. It did not work. But in 1990 the Bush Administration successfully used the forgiveness of billions in debts to encourage the Egyptian government to send ground troops to Saudi Arabia and participate in the Persian Gulf War.

diplomatic lists   The periodically published catalogs of the names and ranks of all of the diplomatic personnel accredited to a state.

diplomatic mail   1. The sealed containers (*diplomatic pouches*) transported by DIPLOMATIC COURIERS. They are exempt from customs inspection.   2. Any object of any size that diplomatic personnel may send or receive without interference from the host government. Some states have abused their diplomatic mail privilege by using their pouches to smuggle illegal drugs or materials for terrorists.

diplomatic mission   1. An official representation, permanent or ad hoc, of one state to another or to an international organization, such as the United Nations. It can be a single individual or the entire staff of a large embassy, usually headed by a chief of mission.   2. The physical building that houses a diplomatic mission.   3. The goal(s) that the members of a diplomatic mission seek to achieve.

diplomatic note   *See* NOTE.

diplomatic pouch   *See* DIPLOMATIC MAIL.

diplomatic privileges and immunities   The special rights given to formally accredited diplomatic officials that make them immune from the civil and criminal laws of the nation to which they are assigned. This immunity also applies to the grounds of an embassy, which under international law is considered territory of the foreign government. Abuses of diplomatic immunity have received widespread publicity. They range from excessive parking tickets received—and ignored—by United Nations diplomats in New York City to using diplomatic offices as centers for terrorism against the host country. The most famous violation of diplomatic immunity by a host government in recent decades was the IRANIAN HOSTAGE CRISIS.

diplomatic recognition   The creation of formal diplomatic ties between states. The creating or breaking of such recognition is a major tool of foreign policy. The new state of Israel achieved immediate international legitimacy because of United States recognition in 1948. Whether to recognize Communist China was a major issue of American politics from the late 1940s to the Nixon Administration's rapprochement in the 1970s. Winston Churchill, in a November 17, 1949, speech in the House of Commons on the issue of recognizing Communist China, said: "Recognizing a person is not necessarily an act of approval. . . . One has to recognize lots of things and people in this world of sin and woe that one does not like. The reason for having diplomatic relations is not to confer a compliment, but to secure a convenience." More recently the breakup of the Soviet Union was, in effect, certified by the international community when the component states were granted diplomatic recognition and admitted to the United Nations. And the YUGOSLAVIAN CIVIL WAR became an international war in 1991 when Germany encouraged the rest of the European Community (belatedly followed by the United States) to recognize the breakaway states of Slovenia, Bosnia, and Croatia.

diplomatic relations   1. All of the formal interactions of states after they have recognized each other. To facilitate these interactions (or relations), they exchange ambassadors (and other diplomatic personnel) who establish embassies (or other missions) from which they conduct their business.   2. The CHANNELS of diplomacy.   3. Normal relations between states. These can be cut off, often as a prelude to the opening of hostilities.

diplomatic service   That branch of a state's civil service that recruits and trains the individuals who staff its foreign missions. In the United States the employees who represent their government overseas are often members of the Department of State's Foreign Service and are known as Foreign Service Officers.

diplomatic summit   See SUMMIT.

diplomat in chief   The political leader of a government, such as a president or chief of state, for whom a state's diplomats work.

diplomatist   1. One who is a practitioner of diplomacy.   2. Any government employee engaged in international relations whether located at home or abroad in a diplomatic mission.   3. A synonym for "diplomat."

THE IDEAL DIPLOMATIST

These, then, are the qualities of my ideal diplomatist. Truth, accuracy, calm, patience, good temper, modesty and loyalty. They are also the qualities of an ideal diplomacy. "But," the reader may object, "you have forgotten intelligence, knowledge, discernment, prudence, hospitality, charm, industry, courage and even tact." I have not forgotten them. I have taken them for granted.

SOURCE: Harold Nicolson, *Diplomacy* (1939).

---

direct action   1. Political violence, such as the assassination of a political rival.   2. Obstruction of the political process to just within the limits of the law, as with general strikes or mass protest demonstrations.   3. A French terrorist organization, better known as ACTION DIRECTE.

direct action mission   A military term for an act involving operations of an overt, covert, clandestine, or low-visibility nature conducted primarily by special operations armed forces in hostile or denied areas.

direct investment   See FOREIGN INVESTMENT.

directive   1. An order by a government official demanding action from lower-rank officials.   2. An order from an international organization that is binding on member states. For example, the European Community Council of Ministers issues directives that member states are obligated to obey even if it means amending national laws.

dirty nuclear weapon   See NUCLEAR WEAPON, DIRTY.

dirty tricks   1. COVERT OPERATIONS undertaken by an INTELLIGENCE AGENCY.   2. Dishonorable acts committed during a political campaign by the opposition or by pranksters, usually to discredit a candidate. Examples include starting false rumors, creating phoney scandals with forged evidence, and disrupting campaign schedules.

dirty war   Officially known as the "Process of National Reorganization," the military junta's brutal program for stamping out political opposition, leftist guerrillas, labor organizers, and the intelligentsia of Argentina, 1976–1983. It was conducted by the military forces and by right-wing DEATH SQUADS that operated with the approval and sometimes the participation of the military. Tens of thousands of Argentines were arrested and tortured in hundreds of secret government jails. At least 9,000 are known to have been killed; their bodies were placed in unmarked graves or dumped at sea. The basis of the dirty war lay in its clandestine approach, as the government seized its victims with no formal or legal basis or controls. No documentation was made so as to preclude any "paper trail" of the atrocities. The victims of the dirty war, which number perhaps 20,000 to 30,000, simply "disappeared." The ruling junta declared any inquiries into the conduct of the security forces and into the whereabouts of the DISAPPEARED to be illegal. The dirty war did not end until the government that condoned it was toppled after its defeat in the FALKLANDS WAR with Great Britain and until its economic policies brought Argentina's economy to the brink of ruin.

disappeared, the Latin Americans who have fallen victim to the government-sponsored or condoned murder of liberals, leftists, labor unionists, and the intelligensia, often through right-wing DEATH SQUAD violence. In Spanish the disappeared are called *desparecidos,* or the "disappeared ones." The problem of disappearing citizens has been endemic in much of Latin America, including Mexico. The worst examples, with tens of thousands of victims, occurred under the military regimes in Argentina and Chile during the 1970s and early 1980s.

disarm 1. To remove the detonating device or fuse of a bomb, mine, missile, or other piece of explosive ordnance; or to render an explosive device incapable of exploding in its usual manner. 2. To remove weapons from captured troops. 3. To abolish the military forces of a defeated power. 4. To reduce the number of—or more technically correct but less frequently used—to eliminate one's armaments.

disarmament A process whereby states seek to negotiate limits on their war-making capabilities. General and complete disarmament has never been within realistic reach, even though the United Nations has made it an official policy goal. Disarmament differs from ARMS CONTROL in that the former involves reductions in the types or levels of armaments, whereas the latter consists of measures designed to improve the security of states and may or may not involve an actual reduction of weapons. Disarmament has roots in the mid-nineteenth-century view that the very existence of weapons and military preparations cause wars. Modern condemnations of MERCHANTS OF DEATH and the MILITARY-INDUSTRIAL COMPLEX follow this tradition. The most famous statement on disarmament comes from the Bible: "They shall beat their swords into plowshares, and their spears into pruning-hooks; nation shall not lift up sword against nation, neither shall they learn war any more" (Isaiah 11:4). But Niccolo Machiavelli, in *The Prince* (1513), warned: "Among other evils which being unarmed brings you, it causes you to be despised." And Winston Churchill, in a July 13, 1934, speech in the House of Commons, said, "It is the greatest possible mistake to mix up disarmament with peace. When you have peace you will have disarmament."

A DISARMAMENT FABLE

Once upon a time all the animals in the zoo decided that they would disarm, and they arranged to have a conference to arrange the matter. So the Rhinoceros said when he opened the proceedings that the use of teeth was barbarous and horrible and ought to be strictly prohibited by general consent. Horns, which were mainly defensive weapons, would, of course, have to be allowed. The Buffalo, the Stag, the Porcupine, and even the little Hedgehog all said they would vote with the Rhino, but the Lion and the Tiger took a different view. They defended teeth and even claws, which they described as honorable weapons of immemorial antiquity. . . . Then the Bear spoke. He proposed that both teeth and horns should be banned and never used again for fighting by any animal. It would be quite enough if animals were allowed to give each other a good hug when they quarreled.

SOURCE: Winston Churchill, speech of October 24, 1928, reprinted in *Winston S. Churchill: His Complete Speeches,* ed. R. R. James, vol. 5 (1974).

---

discrimination 1. Bigotry; intolerance toward those of differing groups or beliefs. 2. Inequity of trading terms accorded one or more exporting states by an importing state. This may take the form of preferential tariff rates for imports from particular states or trade restrictions that apply to the exports of some states but not to similar goods from other states. *Compare to* MOST FAVORED NATION.

disengagement 1. A break in contact with an enemy and a subsequent move to a place of safety. This is used to describe warring forces that cease engaging in direct combat (e.g., the disengagement of Israeli and Egyptian forces at the end of the

1973 Yom Kippur War) or to describe the withdrawal of a commitment of forces in a specific situation (e.g., the potential disengagement of the United States from Western Europe). **2.** In ARMS CONTROL, a general term for proposals that would result in greater geographic separation of opposing forces. **3.** A general easing of tensions between two adversaries.

disengagement zone   A region in which there is a mutual pullback of forces. This can come at the end of a conflict, or it can be the result of a peacetime agreement to ease military confrontation.

disinformation   **1.** An INTELLIGENCE term for the purposeful lies that a government overtly or covertly releases to the international mass media in order to mislead or embarrass adversary states. For example, a Soviet disinformation campaign spread a rumor in 1985 that the deadly AIDS virus was created in a U.S. military laboratory and was being spread around the world by U.S. servicemen. The United States uses disinformation too. After the 1986 air raid on Libya the Reagan Administration purposely planted news stories that top aides of Libyan leader Colonel Muammar al-Qaddafi were plotting a coup and that the United States was planning another raid, all in an effort to destabilize the Libyan government. Certainly the most elaborate disinformation campaign in history was the bodyguard of lies that protected the Allied invasion by misdirecting the Germans about the time and place of the D-Day landing during World War II. **2.** The secret transmission of false information to rival intelligence agencies. **3.** The lies that a government tells its own people in order to hide actions that would be considered unacceptable and would possibly be "checked" by another branch of government if known. As Niccolo Machiavelli advised in *The Prince* (1513), "Men are so simple and so ready to obey present necessities, that one who deceives will always find those who allow themselves to be deceived." *Compare to* PROPAGANDA.

dispersal   **1.** In the context of nuclear war, the moving of people from high-density population areas to low-density population areas. The procedure is designed to increase the percentage of the population that survives nuclear explosions, as it will be covering a larger geographical area. This concept can be compared to the process of diffusion on a microscopic scale, one example of the similarity of both humans and germs at war. **2.** Deliberately moving troops, vehicles, or weapons systems (such as missiles) into widely spread positions to present a less compact and therefore a less rewarding target.

displaced person   **1.** A civilian who is outside the national boundaries of his or her country because of war or natural disasters; a REFUGEE. **2.** The World War II–era term for citizens of countries occupied by Nazi Germany who found themselves outside their homelands and wanted either to be repatriated or to emigrate further. An estimated 10 million people were processed through displaced persons camps monitored by Great Britain and the United States between 1945 and 1949.

dissident   **1.** A COLD WAR term for people in the Soviet Union and Eastern Europe who defied the authority of the state and demanded greater respect

Displaced Jewish teenagers on their way to Palestine in June 1945. (National Archives)

for human rights. Many dissidents were imprisoned as enemies of the state, although under MIKHAIL GORBACHEV this eased greatly. **2.** By analogy, any activist for greater human and political rights in any oppressive regime. Dissidents often risk imprisonment and murder. For example, in 1989 when dissident students and workers demonstrated for greater political rights in TIANANMEN SQUARE in Beijing, China, the military attacked the unarmed crowd, killing more than 2,000 protestors.

divide and conquer **1.** The ancient Roman military concept of gaining victory by splitting up the forces of an enemy; in a political context, winning control by keeping the opposition divided and at odds with itself. **2.** To gain victory because the enemy experiences internal quarrels and divides its forces. This has often happened with allies who fall out and are thus more easily conquered by a common enemy.

divided nations Historically accepted nations that, because of wars or international tensions, have split into two or more differing regimes. Germany and Vietnam are examples of divided nations that have since reunited. Korea and Ireland are still divided between northern and southern components.

divine right of kings The seventeenth-century notion that monarchs rule by the will of God and are subject to God alone. Thus any effort to change or replace a monarch would not—indeed could not—be justified. It was Alexander Pope (1688–1744) who wrote in *The Dunciad* (1728) that it was "the right divine of Kings to govern wrong."

division The smallest unit in an army that can operate independently. Although a division may consist predominantly of one arm of the service, such as infantry, most divisions are mixed. Thus the difference between an infantry division and an armored division is not that one has only foot soldiers and the other only tanks but rather that each has proportionally more of one or the other. Divisions are the "building blocks" of armies, and assessments of one's own forces and the enemy's are often presented in terms of the number of divisions in the order of battle. A full-strength division will contain as many as 20,000 soldiers.

Djilas, Milovan (1911–   ) The onetime Yugoslavian Communist who wrote the now-classic indictment of European communism, *The New Class* (1957), which argues that instead of producing a classless society, the Communists had instead developed a new class system consisting of party officials, managers of the nationalized industries, and bureaucrats. According to Djilas, these people, especially those near the top, were the only ones in the Communist states to have any power. They used the repressive forces of the state, especially the secret police, to ensure total obedience, and their control over education and media to secure greater acquiescence to their version of a ruling ideology. This enabled them to enjoy a standard of living vastly higher than ordinary members of society. And they were able to pass on this privilege to their children. Even though they could not legally own much more than ordinary citizens, access to high-quality education and easy entrance to prestige jobs guaranteed their children the same status that they themselves possessed. Thus they constituted an upper social class, albeit a nontraditional one.

Djilas affair The controversy that arose in 1954 when Yugoslavia's vice president, Milovan Djilas, published an article in the official newspaper *Borba* calling for liberalization of strict party discipline. In 1955 Djilas went on trial for attempting to undermine the party structure and was ousted from his position and from the Yugoslav Communist Party.

D Notice A request to a media source by the British Ministry of Defence that certain information not be published because dissemination would damage state security. In Great Britain, the media invariably complies with D Notices, mainly because the issuing committee, itself an unofficial body, is trusted not to abuse its responsibility. Although ignoring a D Notice is not in itself an offense, publication of sensitive information might well leave an editor or a journalist liable to prosecution under the Official Secrets Act.

doctrine **1.** A legal principle or rule. **2.** A foreign policy, such as the BREZHNEV DOCTRINE, CARTER DOCTRINE, EISENHOWER DOCTRINE, MONROE DOCTRINE, NIXON DOCTRINE, REAGAN DOCTRINE, or TRUMAN DOCTRINE. **3.** The principles by which military leaders guide their actions in support of their goals. Morris Janowitz wrote in *The Professional Soldier* (1960): "Generals and admirals stress the central importance of 'doctrine.' Military doctrine is the 'logic' of their professional behavior. As such, it is a synthesis of scientific knowledge and expertise on the one hand, and of traditions and political assumptions on the other." A military doctrine consists of "correct" answers or ready-constructed solutions to anticipated problems.

Doctrine, Calvo　*See* CALVO DOCTRINE.

Doctrine, Drago　*See* DRAGO DOCTRINE.

Doctrine, no cities　*See* NO CITIES DOCTRINE.

Doctrine, Schlesinger　*See* SCHLESINGER DOCTRINE.

DOD　*See* DEFENSE, U.S. DEPARTMENT OF.

Doenitz, Karl (1891–1980)　The German admiral who commanded the U-boats (submarines) during World War II. As ADOLF HITLER's formal successor in 1945, Doenitz agreed to authorize UNCONDITIONAL SURRENDER to the Allies. At the NUREMBERG TRIALS he was sentenced to ten years' imprisonment for war crimes. According to Telford Taylor in *Nuremberg and Vietnam* (1971): "At Nuremberg [German] Admirals Erich Raeder and Karl Doenitz, successively commanders in chief of the German navy, were charged with war crimes in that they were responsible for U-boat operations. . . . But the evidence at the trial, which included testimony by the U.S. naval commander in the Pacific, Admiral Chester W. Nimitz, established that in this regard the Germans had done nothing that the British and Americans had not done."

dogs of war　William Shakespeare's phrase for unrestrained military destruction. It comes from the play *Julius Caesar* (Act III, Scene 1) when Mark Antony plans military action to revenge Caesar's death:

And Caesar's spirit ranging for revenge,
With Ate by his side come hot from hell,
Shall in these confines with a monarch's voice
Cry "Havoc," and let slip the dogs of
　war;

That this foul deed shall smell above the
　earth,
With carrion men, groaning for burial.

Dollard hypothesis　A concept of aggression developed from the work of social psychologist John Dollard and his colleagues in the book *Frustration and Aggression* (1939). They argued that aggressive behavior generally stemmed from frustration over the inability to achieve goals. The greater the frustration, the greater the likelihood that it would lead to destructive behavior. The Dollard hypothesis has been modified and applied to international relations. One of its most telling criticisms comes from James Dougherty and Robert Pfaltzgraff in *Contending Theories of International Relations* (1981) in which they argue that Dollard moved too easily from the level of the individuals to that of collectivities without acknowledging the dangers in such a shift.

dollar diplomacy　*See* DIPLOMACY, DOLLAR.

Dollfuss, Engelbert (1892–1934)　The Austrian chancellor from 1931 until his death who was a Christian Social Party "strongman" and who was a determined foe of ANSCHLUSS. He was assassinated by Austrian Nazis in 1934. The German embassy in Vienna helped hatch this murder plot.

domain　A term used to refer to the area in which an ACTOR can exert influence in international relations.

domestic analogy　A comparison between relations within states and those among states. This is used by some analysts to explain why international politics can never be like domestic politics and by more reformist thinkers who argue that the institutions of domestic society should be reproduced in international society.

domestic-content protection　Laws that require products to contain a specified percentage of parts that are locally produced. For example, Canada requires that 50 percent of Canadian television broadcasts must be Canadian made. France has a similar law. The European Community considers a product to be domestically produced if it has 40 percent EC-made content. And the United States requires domestic automobiles to contain 75 percent locally produced parts. But there are many loopholes to this. Ford Motor Company, for example, sends U.S.-made parts to Mexico for assembly of complete cars, then legally claims that the cars, assembled in Mexico, are made in the United States because they have 80 percent U.S. parts. All domestic-content laws are inherently protectionist as they are designed to protect local jobs.

domestic intelligence   *See* INTELLIGENCE, DOMESTIC.

domestic jurisdiction   A concept closely related to SOVEREIGNTY and that denies the impact of international law within states.

dominant powers   Those great powers that tried and in some cases succeeded—at least temporarily—to dominate their regions. Their dominance was usually ended by the creation of a coalition of other great powers. This usage derives from Martin Wight's book *Power Politics* (1979). While usually discussed in the context of Europe (where France, Germany, and the Soviet Union were once, in turn, dominant powers), the concept also can be applied historically to the United States in the Western Hemisphere and Japan in East Asia.

Dominican Civil War   The 1965–1966 conflict in the Dominican Republic, a Caribbean island nation, in which U.S. intervention defeated Cuban-backed Communist insurgents and restored a constitutionally elected government. Following free elections in 1962, Juan Bosch (1909–   ) was inaugurated as president in 1963. Bosch was then overthrown by a military coup, and the government was turned over to a provisional civilian regime headed by a three-member JUNTA. Another military coup in 1965 led to an outbreak of violence between military elements favoring the return to government of Juan Bosch (the "Constitutionalists") and those who proposed a military junta committed to early general elections (the "Loyalists"). On April 28 U.S. military forces landed to protect U.S. citizens and to evacuate U.S. and other foreign nationals. The situation in Santo Domingo continued to deteriorate into near anarchy. Communist leaders, many of whom were trained in Cuba, took an increasingly important role in the

U.S. GIs in Santo Domingo, the Dominican Republic, in 1965. (National Archives)

revolutionary movement. More U.S. forces landed on April 30 to prevent what was feared to be a real possibility—a complete Communist takeover. As President Lyndon B. Johnson explained in a May 3, 1965, speech: "We don't propose to sit here in our rocking chair with our hands folded and let the Communists set up any government in the Western Hemisphere." On May 6 the Organization of American States formed an Inter-American Peace Force to cooperate in establishing peace and conciliation. The peace force included the U.S. troops in the Dominican Republic and military elements from Brazil, Costa Rica, Honduras, Paraguay, and El Salvador. Negotiations with both sides by an OAS ad hoc committee resulted in the installation of an interim government headed by Provision President Hector Garcia-Godoy. This government held elections in June 1966, witnessed by OAS observers, in which Joaquin Balaguer (1907–   ) defeated Juan Bosch for the presidency and assumed office on July 1, 1966. The Inter-American Peace Force was withdrawn completely by the end of the summer. *See also* JOHNSON DOCTRINE.

dominion   **1.** Political control over a specific territory.   **2.** A state such as Canada or Australia that as part of the British Empire was completely autonomous in domestic and foreign matters but united by a common allegiance to the British monarch. Once there were more than two dozen dominions, but the term has become obsolete since World War II.

domino theory   The COLD WAR notion, held in particular by U.S. strategists, that if a critically situated country falls to communism, its neighbors will soon fall as well. This was a major reason for U.S. involvement in the VIETNAM WAR. Doris Kearns quotes U.S. President Lyndon B. Johnson in *Lyndon Johnson and the American Dream* (1976): "I knew that if the aggression succeeded in South Vietnam, then the aggressors would simply keep on going until all of Southeast Asia fell into their hands, slowly or quickly." President Richard M. Nixon would later say, "Now I know there are those that say, 'Well, the domino theory is obsolete.' They haven't talked to the dominoes" (*New York Times*, July 3, 1970). The domino metaphor was part of the rationale for U.S. military aid in the 1950s to Greece and Turkey, provided in accord with the TRUMAN DOCTRINE. It was popularly explained by President Dwight D. Eisenhower in a press conference on April 7, 1954, with reference to the strategic importance of Indochina. He said: "You have a row of dominoes set up. You knock over the first one, and what will happen to the last one is a certainty that it will go over very quickly."

The domino theory has not proved very useful as a predictor of Communist expansion because states cannot simply be equated with dominoes. Nevertheless, the Reagan Administration analyzed the dangers presented by the left-wing government in Nicaragua in the same way: If Nicaragua stayed Communist, the administration believed the rest of Central America would follow, and eventually Mexico as well, leaving the United States with an enemy at its southern border. The domino theory is a way of inflating threats and providing justification for taking action in a given instance, on the grounds that failure to do so would produce effects on neighboring nations. Although a domino theory exaggerates the stakes, domino effects do occur—as was evident in the wave of revolution and reform that swept Eastern Europe in 1989.

donner la main   The seat of honor; the place at the right hand of the host in a diplomatic reception.

Donovan, William Joseph (1883–1959)   The World War I hero (wherein he acquired the nickname of "Wild Bill") who later became attorney general of the United States (1925–1929). After several diplomatic missions for President Franklin D. Roosevelt, he became head of the OFFICE OF STRATEGIC SERVICES (OSS) in 1942 with the rank of major general. The OSS was the predecessor organization to the Central Intelligence Agency. He left the OSS in 1945. In 1953 he became ambassador to Thailand; he retired the following year.

Doolittle Raid   In WORLD WAR II, the April 18, 1942, bombing of several Japanese cities by 16 U.S. Army B-25 bombers, led by Lieutenant Colonel James Doolittle (1896–   ), which took off from the U.S. Navy aircraft carrier *Hornet* and landed in China. The raid itself was militarily insignificant; the planes only carried a one-ton bomb load. But it was a tremendous boost to U.S. morale and it forced Japan to devote resources to home defense. While it seemed to be a suicide mission, 73 of the 80 aircrew members survived. Three who were captured by the Japanese were executed. Overall, the Doolittle raid was a portent of the U.S. bombing of Japan that would end only with the ATOMIC BOMB.

doomsday briefcase   *See* FOOTBALL.

Doomsday clock   *See* BULLETIN OF THE ATOMIC SCIENTISTS.

doomsday machine   HERMAN KAHN's concept, from the book *On Thermonuclear War* (1961), of a theoretical device that would automatically set off enough hydrogen bombs to destroy the entire world if the state that built it suffered severe damage from an aggressor's nuclear weapons. Thus the doomsday machine, with its ability to kill virtually everyone on earth, would function as a deterrent. The crucial element of this concept is that once the machine is activated, even its creators cannot deactivate it. This automatic nature of the device would provide CREDIBILITY.

Kahn's theory had impact because it took the logic of the U.S. Air Force's war plans to their ultimate conclusion to illustrate their absurdity. In the event of an attack from the Soviet Union, the Strategic Air Command (SAC) planned to unleash all its nuclear weapons against the Soviets. Kahn used the doomsday machine theory to argue for a more flexible range of responses to a nuclear attack. According to Gregg Herken's *Counsels of War* (1987), Kahn "had actually borrowed the idea from physicist Leo Szilard in order to burlesque the concept of deterrence. Critics, however, mistook Kahn's subtle satire for advocacy." Fred Kaplan, in *The Wizards of Armageddon* (1983), recounts: "As Kahn half expected, not a single military officer liked the idea. Yet the Doomsday Machine was only a slightly absurd extension of existing American and [North Atlantic Treaty Organization] policy: the Soviets do something provocative, and we blow up most of their citizens, which provokes them to blow up most of ours."

double agent   A person in contact with two opposing intelligence agencies, only one of which is aware of the double contact. Thus a double agent is a spy whom the enemy thinks is working for them when he or she is really loyal to the other side. As a spy a double agent has the often unique ability of physically moving back and forth between the opposing sides.

double-column tariff   *See* TARIFF, DOUBLE-COLUMN.

double standard   A judgment of similar people or events according to unequal measures. This is part of the inherent hypocrisy of diplomacy and international relations in which states criticize the behavior of their enemies but often ignore similar actions taken by their friends.

double taxation   Taxation of the same money twice. One form of double taxation is taxing a corporation on its profits, then taxing its stockholders on dividends from the corporation. Another is the taxation of the income of foreign nationals who will be taxed on the same income when they return home. Most of the world's developed states allow taxes paid on foreign income to be credited against domestic tax liability. The individual or corporation then winds up paying, in total, only the higher of the two rates.

doublethink   The term coined by George Orwell in *1984* (1949) that "means the power of holding two contradictory beliefs in one's mind simultaneously, and accepting both of them." A slogan from the novel illustrates doublethink: "War is Peace, Freedom is Slavery, and Ignorance is Strength."

double zero option   The nuclear arms reduction proposal that eventually became the essence of the INF TREATY: that both intermediate- and short-range intermediate (thus the double) be removed (thus the zero) from Europe by both the United States and Soviet Union.

Douglas-Home, Alexander (1903–   )   The Conservative Party British Foreign Secretary (1960–1963) who became prime minister (1963–1964) upon the retirement of HAROLD MACMILLAN after the PROFUMO AFFAIR. While he led his party to defeat in the 1964 general election, he again served as foreign secretary (1970–1974).

Douhet, Giulio (1869–1930)   Italian army officer who became one of the great theorists of AIR POWER. Sometimes seen as playing as critical a role in relation to air power as ALFRED THAYER MAHAN did in relation to sea power, Guilio Douhet's most famous work was *Command of the Air* (first published in 1921 and reissued in a revised edition in 1927). Douhet's main thesis was that aircraft had immense potential for offensive military operations, that there was no effective defense against them, and that therefore they could and should be used for attacks against population centers. He believed that such attacks would have a devastating effect on civilian morale. During WORLD WAR II some of Douhet's ideas were proved wrong: the BATTLE OF BRITAIN demonstrated that there were defenses against offensive aircraft and that morale was not necessarily destroyed by bombing of civilians. Nevertheless, Douhet's ideas were used after World War II in states such as the United States to justify the creation of air forces that were independent of the other military services. Controversy over the effectiveness of strategic bombing continued, however, and the issue became contentious during the VIETNAM WAR with United States' bombing of North Vietnam. In the PERSIAN GULF WAR waged by the United States and its coalition partners against Iraq

dove

in 1991, the United States had almost uncontested control of the air space over Iraq. Air power proved to be a very effective weapon against both Iraqi armed forces and the infrastructure of the Iraqi state. Even so, critics took issue over lack of discrimination and the destruction of civilian targets. If Douhet's theory was uncertain in relation to conventional bombing, there was little argument that the advent of nuclear weapons had brought with it the potential for putting Douhet's theories into practice in a manner that was uncontestable. *See also* AIR WARFARE.

BRODIE ON DOUHET

Douhet possessed the largest and most original mind that has thus far addressed itself to the theory of air power. The few basic ideas which he elaborated were not altogether his own creations—the general merits of strategic bombing were being advanced in British and American official circles more than a year before World War I ended—but he was the first to weave them into a coherent and relatively comprehensive philosophy. That philosophy is fairly completely presented in his first book-length publication, *The Command of the Air,* published originally in 1921.

SOURCE: Bernard Brodie, *Strategy in the Missile Age* (1959). According to Brodie, "When American Air Force officers have talked about 'understanding air power' they have usually meant what is actually the Douhet thesis on air power, practically *in toto.*"

---

dove *See* HAWK.

Dowding, Hugh C. T. (1882–1970) The victorious commander in chief of the Royal Air Force's Fighter Command during the BATTLE OF BRITAIN. Although he is almost unknown among major World War II commanders, he won one of the most decisive battles in history. According to Gavin Lyall in the article "Air Chief Marshal Lord Dowding" (*The War Lords,* Sir Michael Carver, ed., 1976): "A straightforward defensive battle can never end in an instantly recognized victory; the Battle of Britain came to be seen as a triumph only later. For the moment, invasion had been merely postponed. . . . Dowding—who had never been publicized as the commander—was finally and quietly relieved of command."

downgrade To reduce the security classification of a piece of CLASSIFIED INFORMATION.

Downing Street *See* NUMBER 10 DOWNING STREET.

doyen The *dean of the diplomatic corps,* the most senior diplomat in a given capital. The doyen, whose duties are largely ceremonial, takes precedence over all other members of the diplomatic corps and functions as their representative to the host government. In many Catholic countries the doyen is ex-officio the papal NUNCIO. The wife of a male doyen is called a doyenne (but a female doyen is a doyen).

Dozier, James (1931–   ) The U.S. Army Brigadier General who was abducted by the Italian RED BRIGADES in Verona on December 17, 1981. He was freed in Padua on January 28, 1981, as ten members of an Italian rescue team stormed the apartment in which he was being held.

Drago Doctrine The policy that states should not use their military forces in foreign states to force the payments of debts owed by the citizens of the second (foreign) country to citizens of the first. This doctrine, now widely endorsed, was first formulated by Luis M. Drago (1859–1921) when he was the foreign minister of Argentina in 1902. *Compare to* CALVO DOCTRINE.

dragoman 1. A native interpreter employed by Western diplomatic missions in the Middle East. 2. A tourist guide in the Middle East.

Drang Nach Osten German term meaning "drive toward the East." This referred to Germany's desires from 1870 to 1945 to conquer parts of Eastern Europe to provide more living space, or LEBENSRAUM, for the German people.

drawback 1. The repayment by a government, in whole or in part, of customs duties assessed on imported merchandise that is subsequently manufactured into a different article or reexported. 2. The refund upon the exportation of an article of the domestic tax to which it has been subjected; a refund of DUTY.

dreadnought *See* BATTLESHIP.

Dresden The German city that was the target of intensive bombing by British and U.S. forces on February 13 and 14, 1945, near the end of WORLD WAR II. The resulting firestorm killed at least 60,000 people, more than the number killed in the explosion of the first atomic bomb at Hiroshima. (Some estimates suggest 120,000 deaths because Dresden was full of refugees.) The bombing has been criticized by some for being purely vindictive and of no strategic value. Others have asserted that it was a valid military target whose destruction helped to shorten the war.

Dreyfus Affair The greatest trauma of France's THIRD REPUBLIC. Alfred Dreyfus (1859–1935), the first Jewish member of the French GENERAL STAFF, was falsely convicted of treason for selling military secrets to the Germans and imprisoned on Devil's Island in 1894. A military investigator and the Dreyfus family later found that the evidence against him was a forgery. In 1898 novelist Emile Zola wrote "J'Accuse," an open letter to the French president charging army leaders one by one of sacrificing an innocent man to save the army's reputation. After the forger confessed in 1898, a new trial was held the next year. Dreyfus was again found guilty, but his sentence was reduced. At this point the president of the republic pardoned him. France was then divided into Dreyfusards and anti-Dreyfusards. The Dreyfusards demanded complete exoneration and saw their enemies as conservatives, army leaders, anti-Semites, and the Catholic church. Antimilitarism and anticlericalism became powerful forces in French politics. In the CONCORDAT OF 1905, the republic moved left and restricted the power of the Catholic church. The next year Dreyfus was acquitted and reinstated in the army. The Dreyfus Affair was a great spur to ZIONISM because it convinced many Jewish leaders that complete assimilation would never be possible; the only alternative was an independent Jewish state.

drôle de guerre French term for "funny (peculiar) war." *See* PHONY WAR.

dual agent One who is simultaneously and independently employed by two or more INTELLIGENCE AGENCIES covering targets for both.

dual basing A means by which U.S. troops could quickly reinforce North Atlantic Treaty Organization forces in an emergency. The idea is to retain Americans forces at their bases in the United States but to establish a base for their supplies and equipment in Europe. In a crisis the U.S. troops can quickly fly to their prepositioned stores and deploy for action.

dual citizenship *See* CITIZENSHIP, DUAL.

dual function (*Dwifungsi*) A term first used to describe the role of the army in Indonesia in the mid-1960s. The army had been critically important not only in obtaining Indonesian independence but also in maintaining the integrity of the Indonesian state against separatist movements: it had defeated an attempted coup by Communists in 1965. Under *Dwifungsi* the army has become both a military force and a "social political force" engaged in national development to implement the principles of PANCASILA on which the state is founded. This notion continues to describe the role of the army in Indonesia, even though considerable progress has been made in terms of modernization.

dual key 1. Requiring at least two military officers, each with a separate key, to activate or launch nuclear weapons. 2. An arrangement by which the United States shares control of a nuclear weapons system with the allied state in which it is based. These weapons cannot be launched without the consent of both governments. To ensure this, officers from both states are required to carry out part of the launch sequence together, in this case literally by turning their individual keys. Many of the North Atlantic Treaty Organization's battlefield nuclear weapons are held under a version of this system.

dual (multi)-capable weapons 1. Military offensive devices, systems, or vehicles capable of selective equipage with different types or mixes of armament or firepower. 2. Sometimes restricted to mean weapons capable of handling either nuclear or nonnuclear munitions. For example, certain standard cannons used by most North Atlantic Treaty Organization member armies are also capable of firing nuclear shells. Dual-capable weapons pose particular problems in ARMS CONTROL negotiations because it is virtually impossible to verify that such weapons are not, in fact, being prepared for a nuclear role.

dual pricing   The practice of selling an identical product for different amounts in different markets. The practice of dual pricing may often relate to EXPORT SUBSIDIES or DUMPING.

Dual Use Initiative   A 1991 United States diplomatic proposal, supported by Germany and Japan, to limit the export of DUAL USE (especially nuclear) TECHNOLOGIES unless the recipients accepted full-scope safeguards that would ensure that there was no diversion of the technologies into military purposes.

dual use technologies   Equipment or techniques that have predominantly civilian applications but also can be used for military purposes. By the early 1980s dual use technologies had become a major problem in relation to TECHNOLOGY TRANSFER as civilian technologies were at the leading edge of technological development. As a result the United States tried to get its European allies to accept more restrictive policies on the transfer to the Soviet Union and Eastern Europe of civilian technologies with dual uses. Technology related to nuclear power is inherently dual use, as it has peaceful and nonmilitary purposes but also can be diverted into military purposes.

Dubcek, Alexander (1921–1992)   The Slovak leader of Czechoslovakia during the PRAGUE SPRING of 1968. As a result of a languishing economy, a demand for Slovak equality with Czechs, and a longing for freedom, Dubcek tried to develop a liberal Communist regime based on "socialism with a human face" and independent of the Soviet Union. Soviet chairman LEONID BREZHNEV claimed the right of the Soviet Union to interfere in domestic affairs of faltering Communist regimes and invaded Czechoslovakia. Thus Dubcek's reform movement was crushed by 175,000 predominantly Soviet troops. Dubcek, who had run the only popularly supported Communist regime in Eastern Europe, was imprisoned briefly by the Soviets in 1968 and forced to retire from politics in 1969. As a national hero, he reemerged in government after the 1989 VELVET REVOLUTION in Czechoslovakia and was elected chairman of the Federal Assembly.

Ducommun, Elie (1833–1906)   The Swiss journalist, public official, and railroad manager who won the 1902 Nobel Peace Prize (with CHARLES A. GOBAT) for his voluntary work in the European peace movement—specifically with the Berne-based Permanent International Bureau of Peace, a clearinghouse for information on national peace societies.

Dulles, Allen Welsh (1893–1969)   The director of the Central Intelligence Agency of the United States from 1953 to 1961. He played a key role in planning the BAY OF PIGS operation and was forced to resign after its failure. He was the younger brother of John Foster Dulles.

Dulles, John Foster (1888–1959)   The U.S. Secretary of State for most of the Eisenhower Administration (1953–1959). As secretary of state, he became associated with the doctrine of MASSIVE RETALIATION by the United States to deter Soviet aggression. Dulles was also instrumental in building up a network of security treaties (primarily SEATO and the ANZUS PACT) as preventive means in the U.S. struggle against expansionist communism. Dulles believed that the COLD WAR was a conflict of good versus evil and could not tolerate the idea that states could be both moral and neutral. He said: "The principle of neutrality pretends that a nation can best gain safety for itself by being indifferent to the fate of others. This has increasingly become an obsolete conception, and, except under very special circumstances, it is an immoral and shortsighted conception" (*Department of State Bulletin,* June 18, 1956). Dulles was seen by many as pompous and self-righteous; his opponents hated him as much for himself as for his policies. According to Townsend Hoopes's *The Devil and John Foster Dulles* (1973), "He lacked in large measure the statesman's dispassionate vision and the courage to peer across the perilous divide to the bristling trenches of alien ideology, to identify there, and then to build on, the hidden elements of possible reconciliation." William Manchester in *The Last Lion* (1983) credits Winston Churchill with coining the progression that succinctly summarized the feelings of so many people for this monomaniacal cold warrior: "Dull, duller, Dulles." *See also* AGONIZING REAPPRAISAL; BRINKMANSHIP; HOLSTI, OLE R.

WAS DULLES EVER WRONG?

When John Foster Dulles was Secretary of State, he was asked whether he had ever been wrong. Mr. Dulles thought long and hard. "Yes," he finally said, "once—many, many years ago. I *thought* I had made a wrong decision. Of course, it turned out that I had been right all along. But I was *wrong* to have *thought* that I was wrong."

SOURCE: Henri Temianka, *Facing the Music* (1973).

Duma The national elected legislature of Imperial Russia established in 1906 by Czar NICHOLAS II and abolished by the Russian Revolution of 1917. It had had only limited powers.

Dumbarton Oaks The Georgetown estate in Washington, D.C., that was the site for an August–October 1944 meeting attended by representatives of Great Britain, the Soviet Union, and the United States to discuss the details of the postwar collective security organization, the UNITED NATIONS. The meeting was a major step in the movement toward the creation of the UN and prepared the way for the subsequent conference in San Francisco at which the UN Charter was signed.

dum dum bullet A projectile that expands when it hits an animal target. Because these bullets create a more severe wound than normal bullets would, the Hague Declaration of July 29, 1899 (signed by 15 states) prohibits their use in war. They were named for Dum Dum, a town in India where they were notoriously made.

dumping 1. Abandoning a political candidate or supporter who has become useless, unpopular, or embarrassing. 2. Selling a product in export markets below that product's selling price in domestic markets. States seek to protect themselves from this practice by enacting *antidumping laws*. Additional tariffs imposed on imports that have been dumped are called *dumping duties*. An international antidumping code was negotiated under the auspices of GATT; it established both substantive and procedural standards for national antidumping proceedings. Sometimes antidumping lawsuits are

British and French prisoners at Dunkirk. (National Archives)

used to inhibit foreign competition even when there are no strong legal grounds for a legal challenge. Such suits, or the threat of them, become in effect nontariff barriers to trade.

Dunant, Henri *See* INTERNATIONAL RED CROSS.

Dunkirk The port in France near the Belgian border where French and British troops were trapped by advancing German forces in May 1940. The Germans withheld their assault on these forces because they expected to destroy them with aerial attacks. But rearguard actions and the Royal Air Force provided eight days for a hectic British evacuation effort in a flotilla of vessels that ferried 200,000 British and 130,000 French soldiers across the English Channel to safety. Before the Germans realized that their air power alone was inadequate, the Allies had rescued the core of the army that, five years later, with the help of the United States and the Soviet Union, would conquer Germany.

Dunkirk, Treaty of   The 1947 Anglo-French treaty for joint military action in the event of future German aggression; superceded first by the Brussels Treaty and then by the NORTH ATLANTIC TREATY, which created the North Atlantic Treaty Organization.

Durand line   The boundary between Afghanistan and British India created in 1893 by British diplomat Mortimer Durand (1850–1924). It has been the subject of constant border disputes between Pakistan (once part of British India) and Afghanistan.

duty   1. A tax placed on imported goods. A duty is different from a TARIFF in that the duty is the actual tax imposed or collected, while the tariff, formally speaking, is the schedule of such duties. However, the terms tend to be used interchangeably.   2. A legal or moral obligation to do something because of one's official position, one's profession, and so on. But as George Bernard Shaw warns in *Caesar and Cleopatra* (Act III, 1899): "When a stupid man is doing something he is ashamed of, he always declares that it is his duty."   3. The traditional obligation of those in military service to die for his or her country if circumstances warrant. According to Richard A. Gabriel and Paul L. Savage's *Crisis in Command* (1978): "Military life . . . is unique in that it clearly levels upon the officer . . . responsibilities which transcend his career or material self-interest. . . . at some point an officer may be called upon to do his duty and 'be faithful unto death.' " Or as U.S. General George S. Patton, Jr., put it in *War as I Knew It* (1947): "Any commander who fails to attain his objective, and who is not dead or severely wounded, has not done his full duty."

duty, ad valorem   A tax placed on products on the basis of value (*ad valorem* is Latin for "according to value"). The advantage of an ad valorem duty is that it fluctuates with economic conditions—that is, the duty rises and falls with prices. The disadvantages of the ad valorem system are that valuation is often problematic, it is an expensive system to maintain, and it opens the doors to possible corruption. *Compare to* DUTY, SPECIFIC.

duty, antidumping   A tax created to offset the price advantage gained by exporters when they sell goods in a foreign state at a price lower than that at which the same items sells at home or at a price even lower than the cost of production. *See also* DUMPING.

duty, compound   A tax that combines attributes of ad valorem and specific duties. "Two cents per pound plus 5 percent ad valorem" is an example of a combined duty.

duty, countervailing   A tax imposed in addition to the regular duty for the purpose of counteracting the effect of a bounty or subsidy in another country. *Compare to* EXPORT SUBSIDY.

duty, export   A tax placed on products leaving a state. Export duties are specifically forbidden in the United States by the U.S. Constitution, which provides that "no tax or duty shall be laid on articles exported from any state." Other states, however, lay export duties even on their chief exports—to raise taxes, to bolster domestic production of some items, or to encourage the retension of scarce raw materials within the state for domestic purposes.

duty, specific An import tax imposed on the basis of a unit of measurement—so much per pound, per bushel, per dozen. Specific duties avoid the problems of appraisal associated with ad valorem taxes. The disadvantages of specific duties are that they require a minute detailing of rates for the many imported products and that they do not automatically reflect changes in the value of goods. *Compare to* DUTY, AD VALOREM.

duty, transit A tax imposed by a state for simply allowing items to pass through its borders en route from one state to another. Neither the United States nor the European Community imposes transit duties. Generally they are found only in isolated instances in the THIRD WORLD.

duty officer An official assigned to be available constantly for call in emergencies during a given time period. This is often equivalent to "officer of the day" or "officer of the deck" in the military.

duty suspension A temporary unilateral reduction in TARIFFS.

Duvalier family The family that dominated politics in Haiti from 1957 to 1986. François "Papa Doc" Duvalier (1907–1971), a physician, held a series of steadily more important positions in the government of President Dumarsais Estimé (1900–1953). When Estimé was overthrown in 1950, Duvalier became the central opposition figure to President Paul E. Magloire (1907–   ), who resigned in 1956. In September 1957 Duvalier, running on a program of popular reform and black nationalism, won the presidential election. He reduced the army and formed the TONTON MACOUTE ("Uncle Knapsack"), a ruthless force that terrorized Duvalier's enemies. Upon his death in 1971, his son Jean Claude (1951–   ) succeeded him as president for life. Then the youngest president in the world, Duvalier continued his father's repressive measures, and in 1986, amid increasing violence aimed at the regime, he was forced into exile to France. *See also* HAITIAN COUP.

Dwifungsi *See* DUAL FUNCTION.

dynasty **1.** The transfer of political power through a succession of rulers directly related by blood, such as the Hanovers in Great Britain, the Hapsburgs in Imperial Austria, or the Romanovs in Russia. Dynastic succession typically occurs by primogeniture, a system in which the eldest male heir inherits the crown. **2.** A political family, such as the Kennedys in the United States or the Gandhis in India, whose various members seek and gain political office over a long period of time.

Eagleburger, Lawrence (1930–) The career U.S. foreign service officer and ambassador to Yugoslavia (1977–1980) who in 1989 became the deputy secretary of state until Secretary of State JAMES A. BAKER III resigned to become White House Chief of Staff in August 1992. Thereupon Eagleburger was promoted to acting secretary of state. After his 1992 defeat for reelection, President George Bush formally appointed Eagleburger secretary of state for the remaining weeks of his Administration. He was able to do this unilaterally (without Senate confirmation) because the U.S. Congress was then in recess. Eagleburger then served as secretary until the new WILLIAM J. CLINTON Administration was installed on January 20, 1993.

Earth Summit The United Nations Conference on Environment and Development (UNCED), which was held in Rio de Janeiro, Brazil, in 1992. Most member states were represented by heads of state or government. The relationship between economic development and environmental impact had been recognized at the UN Conference on the Human Environment, held in Stockholm, Sweden, in 1972. It was the focus of *Our Common Future,* the 1987 report of the UN World Commission on Environment and Development. However, between 1972 and 1987 little was done to integrate, in practical terms, concerns for development and the environment in economic planning and decision making. Progress was made in specific instances but overall the environment of the planet deteriorated. OZONE LAYER depletion, GLOBAL WARMING, ACID RAIN, deforestation, and other major environmental problems grew more serious. In December 1989 the United

Nations decided to hold UNCED in 1992, which produced the Earth Charter, a list of basic principles to govern the economic and environmental behavior of nations; Agenda 21, a blueprint for action in major areas affecting the relationship between the environment and the economy; an international framework for environmentally sound TECHNOLOGY TRANSFER to developing countries; and conventions on issues such as global warming, biological diversity, and deforestation.

Eastern Bloc A COLD WAR term for the Soviet Union and its satellite states in Eastern Europe: Bulgaria, Czechoslovakia, East Germany, Hungary, Poland, and Romania.

Eastern Front *See* WESTERN FRONT.

Eastern Question The pre–World War I tension over the fate of the failing OTTOMAN EMPIRE.

Easter Rising The April 1916 revolt against British rule in Dublin, Ireland, by about 2,000 Irish partisans. After a week of heavy street fighting, which began on Easter Monday, the rebels were all killed or captured. Twelve of their leaders were then executed. Because the incident occurred during the middle of World War I, the insurgents expected German support, but this never materialized because of the British naval blockade. The Easter Rising led to the ANGLO-IRISH WAR OF 1919–1921, which ended with Irish independence.

East of Suez That part of the former BRITISH EMPIRE to the east of Egypt's Suez Canal. British military forces were located there to provide for the defense of India while it was part of the empire. After Indian independence in 1947, successive British governments did not withdraw forces from the area despite the high cost and the loss of their original rationale. In the late 1960s Great Britain ended its military roles east of Suez because it could no longer afford them financially, not because of a policy decision to reject the role itself. With the removal of British forces as a stabilizing influence in the Persian Gulf region, the United States subsequently gave strong support to the shah of Iran. He became America's "surrogate gendarme" in the gulf. But the fall of the shah in 1979 forced the United States to become more directly involved in the area. *See also* IRANIAN REVOLUTION; PERSIAN GULF CRISIS.

East Timor occupation   The 1975 takeover of the Portuguese colony of East Timor, an island north of Australia, by Indonesia just as it was about to be granted independence. The brutal suppression of the local independence movement, the killing of more than 100,000 people of the island's total population of less than 700,000, and the gross illegality of the occupation has been widely condemned. Indonesia has rejected Portugal's offer to hold a referendum in the former colony, has refused to allow the United Nations to send observers, and has generally prohibited foreign press from visiting East Timor. Condemnations continued through 1992 but there was no talk of using force. According to Brent Scowcroft, the National Security Advisor to U.S. Presidents Gerald Ford and George Bush: "It made no sense to antagonize the Indonesians. . . . East Timor was not a viable entity" (*New York Times,* December 6, 1991).

East-West   **1.** A term used to symbolize the COLD WAR–era division of Europe. The East consisted of the Soviet Union and its Eastern European satellites; the West consisted of the United States and its Western European allies (plus Japan). **2.** A metaphorical symbol of the difference between European and Asian cultures. The most famous statement of this is that part of Rudyard Kipling's (1865–1936) poem *The Ballad of East and West* (1889), which says: "Oh, East is East, and West is West, and never the twain shall meet."

Eban, Abba (1915–   )   The South African–born, British-educated Israeli diplomat who figured prominently in the 1949 negotiations that led to the creation of the State of Israel. He served as Israel's first representative to the United Nations (1948–1959), ambassador to the United States (1950–1959), deputy prime minister (1963–1966), and foreign minister (1966–1974). Noted for his eloquence, he said after the SIX-DAY WAR: "I think that this is the first war in history that on the morrow the victors sued for peace and the vanquished called for unconditional surrender" (*New York Times,* July 9, 1967).

EBAN ON ISRAELI NUCLEAR WEAPONS

When next he [Dean Rusk] saw Abba Eban after the 1967 war, the two men had a testy exchange. Rusk called on Eban to formulate a plan for the return of occupied Arab territories. When Eban demurred, Rusk reminded him that for twenty years the United States had assured the Arabs that Israel had no territorial ambitions and that, on the first day of the Six-Day War, Israeli Prime Minister Levi Eshkol had announced in a radio address that Israel had no expansionist designs. Eban merely shrugged his shoulders and said simply, "We have changed our minds." As Eban went out the door of his office Rusk called after him, "And don't you be the first power to introduce nuclear weapons into the Middle East." "No," Eban replied, and then he smiled thinly. "But we won't be the second."

SOURCE: Thomas J. Schoenbaum, *Waging Peace and War* (1988).

Ebert, Friedrich (1871–1925)   The German Social Democrat who was the WEIMAR REPUBLIC's first president until his death in 1925. He was succeeded by Field Marshal PAUL HINDENBERG.

EC   *See* EUROPEAN COMMUNITY.

ECE   *See* ECONOMIC COMMISSION FOR EUROPE.

ECJ   *See* EUROPEAN COURT OF JUSTICE.

economic action   The use of monetary or trade measures (as opposed to political or military ones) to influence the policies or actions of another state, either to hurt the economy of a real or potential enemy, as with a trade embargo, or to help the economy of a friendly power, as with loans or favorable terms of trade.

Economic and Monetary Union   The EUROPEAN COMMUNITY goal of a common central bank, a common currency, and a common monetary policy, agreed to in the 1991 MAASTRICHT TREATY.

Economic and Social Council (ECOSOC)   The principal organ that coordinates the economic and social affairs of the UNITED NATIONS among its SPECIALIZED AGENCIES and institutions. The council has 54 members, with 18 elected each year for a three-year term. Each member has one vote and resolutions are adopted by simple majority. The council discusses international economic and social issues and formulates policy recommendations on these issues; it also interacts with other nongovernmental organizations regarding matters of mutual concern. The council has six functional commissions, six standing committees, and five regional UNITED NATIONS ECONOMIC COMMISSIONS, one each for Africa, Asia and the Pacific, Europe, Latin America and the Caribbean, and Western Asia.

Economic Commission for Europe (ECE)   A United Nations forum for economic cooperation by the European Community, other European states, and North America. Created in 1947, it was the only European organization during the Cold War where the states of Eastern and Western Europe met on a regular basis. Its focus in recent years has been on achieving greater European cooperation on environmental issues.

Economic Community of West African States (ECOWAS)   An organization created in 1975 by the Treaty of Lagos, signed by 15 African states. The community's chief purposes are the elimination of restrictions on trade between members; the establishment of a common tariff toward other countries; the free movement of people, services, and capital within the community; the integration of regional transport and communications systems; the reduction of disparities in the level of development between member states; and mutual defense assistance. The community's executive secretariat is headquartered in Lagos, Nigeria.

economic containment   *See* CONTAINMENT, ECONOMIC.

economic determinism   The doctrine that economic concerns are the most important motivating factors of individual behavior and historical development and that all moral, political, or social justifications for action can be ultimately traced to economic motives. This is an important facet of COMMUNISM.

economic growth   Any increase in a state's productive capacity, leading to an increase in the production of goods and services. Economic growth usually is expressed by the yearly rate of increase in real GROSS NATIONAL PRODUCT.

economic mobilization   The restructuring of a peacetime economy in response to a wartime emergency.

economic nationalism   **1.** A desire to make a state self-sufficient in terms of trade, so that it needs neither imports nor exports for its economic health; also known as AUTARCHY or national self-sufficiency. **2.** Economic policies based on a state's self-interest alone, as opposed to those more concerned with the economic viability of a larger sphere such as a region, a political grouping of states (e.g., the FREE WORLD, the THIRD WORLD, etc.), or the world economy in general. Economic nationalism often encompasses trade restrictions and other policies of PROTECTIONISM.

economic potential   The total capacity of a state to produce goods and services as opposed to what it is actually (or currently) producing. To assess economic potential, analysts add to current economic activity all those assets that are at rest, such as the unemployed and unused factory capacity, and other factors, such as the educational level of the population and ease of obtaining raw materials. Measures of economic potential are an important means of measuring an adversary's ability to respond to crises.

economic potential for war   That share of the total production capacity of a nation that can be used for military purposes.

economic summit   *See* SUMMIT, ECONOMIC.

economic warfare **1.** An aggressive use of the means of production and trade to achieve national objectives. Economic warfare has many levels of intensity, ranging from freezing an enemy's assets and confiscating its property during a formally declared war to using secret methods to destabilize an opponent's economy during a cold war. **2.** The normal peacetime competition between nations for markets and trade advantages.

economic zone, exclusive *See* EXCLUSIVE ECONOMIC ZONE.

economy The prosperity of a state relative to previous levels of individual income or GROSS NATIONAL PRODUCT. Thus an economy is healthy and growing if such economic indicators are rising; unhealthy or declining if such indicators are descending.

economy, interlinked The concept from Kenichi Ohmae's 1990 book, *The Borderless World,* that the economies of Europe, Japan, and the United States are thoroughly dependent on one another and that further integration is both beneficial and inevitable.

ECOSOC *See* ECONOMIC AND SOCIAL COUNCIL.

ECOWAS *See* ECONOMIC COMMUNITY OF WEST AFRICAN STATES.

ECSC *See* EUROPEAN COAL AND STEEL COMMUNITY.

ECU *See* EUROPEAN CURRENCY UNIT.

EDC *See* EUROPEAN DEFENSE COMMUNITY.

Eden, Anthony (1897–1977) The Conservative Party foreign secretary (1935–1938, 1940–1945, and 1951–1955) who succeeded Winston Churchill as prime minister of Great Britain in 1955. According to Robert Rhodes James's biography, *Anthony Eden* (1986), "The greatest single service rendered to his country by Anthony Eden" was his 1940 work as secretary of state for war in the months after DUNKIRK when he helped to rebuild the British Army. But his tenure as prime minister was not successful. Suddenly in power after 15 years in the very large shadow of Churchill, he promptly destroyed his political career with his misjudgments in the SUEZ CRISIS of 1956; he was forced to resign early in 1957. Eden's obituary summed up the problem: "He was the last Prime Minister to believe that Britain was a great power and the first to confront a crisis which proved she was not" (*Times* [London], January 16, 1977). During his life people noted Eden's handsome demeanor and elegant clothes but did not find him brilliant. British journalist Malcolm Muggeridge (1903–1990) truculently asserted: "[Eden] was just empty of content like his television appearances in which a flow of banalities were presented in the persuasive manner of an ex-officer trying to sell one a fire-extinguisher at the front door. . . . as an active politician, he was not only a bore; he bored for England" (*Tread Softly,* 1966).

EDI *See* EUROPEAN DEFENSE INITIATIVE.

Edward VII (1841–1910) Queen Victoria's eldest son who succeeded her as the British monarch (1901–1910). He enjoyed great personal popularity, improved relations with France, promoted approval of the ENTENTE CORDIALE, agreed to reforms of the House of Lords, and was succeeded by his second son, GEORGE V.

Anthony Eden (left) with U.S. Secretary of State John Foster Dulles. (Library of Congress)

Edward VIII (1894–1972) The grandson of EDWARD VII who succeeded his father, GEORGE V, as the British monarch in 1936. Within a few months he gave up his throne to marry a commoner, the twice-divorced American socialite Wallis Simpson. In his abdication speech of December 11, 1936 (largely written by Winston Churchill), he said: "You must believe me when I tell you that I have found it impossible to carry the heavy burden of responsibility and to discharge my duties as King as I would wish to do without the help and support of the woman I love." British journalist Alistair Cooke in *Six Men* (1977) assessed the abdicator: "The most damning epitaph you can compose about Edward—as a Prince, as a King, as a man—is one that all comfortable people should cower from deserving: he was at his best only when the going was good." After his ABDICATION he was known as the duke of Windsor. Edward VIII was succeeded by his brother, GEORGE VI. *See also* ABDICATION CRISIS.

EEC *See* COMMON MARKET.

Eelam People's Revolutionary Liberation Front (EPRLF) A Marxist-Leninist Tamil separatist organization, originally dedicated to the establishment of a Communist Eelam (the name given by Tamil separatists to their envisioned sovereign nation-state in the northern and eastern sections of Sri Lanka). India supports the EPRLF, viewing it as a viable alternative to even more hostile Tamil organizations, such as the LIBERATION TIGERS OF TAMIL EELAM. *See also* SRI LANKAN CIVIL WAR.

EEZ *See* EXCLUSIVE ECONOMIC ZONE.

EFA *See* EUROPEAN FIGHTER AIRCRAFT AGREEMENT.

effectiveness, doctrine of *See* ESTRADA DOCTRINE.

EFTA *See* EUROPEAN FREE TRADE ASSOCIATION.

Eichmann, Adolf *See* ARENDT, HANNAH.

Einstein, Albert (1879–1955) The German-born physicist whose special theory of relativity postulated that space and time are relative, not absolute. From 1912 through 1916, at the University of Berlin, Einstein developed his general theory of rela-

tivity, the first new theory of gravity since Isaac Newton's in the late seventeenth century. After winning the Nobel Prize for physics in 1922, Einstein was for the rest of his life one of the world's most influential theoretical physicists. As a famous Jewish scientist, he fled Nazi Germany when Hitler came to power in 1933 and from then to the end of his life was associated with the Institute for Advanced Study at Princeton University in New Jersey. During World War II he called for the development of the atomic bomb. According to British novelist C. P. Snow's *Variety of Men* (1967), Einstein's "public life . . . was unlike that which any other scientist is likely to experience again. No one knows quite why, but he sprang into the public consciousness, all over the world, as the symbol of science, the master of the twentieth-century intellect, to a large extent the spokesman for human hope." In 1952 Einstein was offered the presidency of Israel. In his November 18, 1952, letter declining the offer, he stated: "Since all my life I have been dealing with the world of objects I have neither the natural ability nor the experience necessary to deal with human beings and to carry out official functions" (quoted in Abba Eban, *An Autobiography*, 1977).

EINSTEIN URGES FDR TO BUILD A-BOMB

. . . it may become possible to set up a nuclear chain reaction in a large mass of uranium, by which vast amounts of power and large quantities of new radium-like elements would be generated . . . This new phenomenon would also lead to the construction of bombs, and it is conceivable—though much less certain—that extremely powerful bombs of a new type may thus be constructed. A single bomb of this type, carried by boat and exploded in a port, might very well destroy the whole port together with some of the surrounding territory. However, such bombs might very well prove to be too heavy for transportation by air.

SOURCE: Albert Einstein, letter to U.S. President Franklin D. Roosevelt, August 2, 1939. Years later Einstein would say of his role in the development of the atom bomb: "If only I had known, I should have become a watchmaker" (*New Statesman*, April 16, 1965).

Eisenhower, Dwight David "Ike" (1890–1969) The president of the United States (1953–1961) who, while commander of Allied forces in Western

Europe, orchestrated the Anglo-American efforts to defeat Germany in WORLD WAR II. As returning war hero, "Ike" won the 1952 presidential election overwhelmingly. In the midst of the frustrating LIMITED WAR of Korea, Americans flocked to support a winning general who pledged: "I will go to Korea." Eisenhower wrote in his memoirs that the end of the war was achieved only after he threatened to use atomic weapons. "The lack of progress . . . demanded, in my opinion, definite measures on our part to put an end to these intolerable conditions. One possibility was to let the Communist authorities understand that, in the absence of satisfactory progress, we intended to move decisively without inhibition in our use of weapons. . . . We dropped the word, discreetly, of our intention. . . . Soon the prospects for armistice negotiations seemed to improve" (*The White House Years*, vol. 1, 1963). With the war over within six months through a negotiated armistice, the rest of the Eisenhower years were noted for COLD WAR diplomacy and the lack of domestic initiatives. Yet this belies the fact that the Eisenhower Administration was basically one of peace abroad and prosperity at home. Eisenhower actually began to engage in a serious dialogue with the Soviet Union's NIKITA S. KHRUSHCHEV, which was the harbinger of the subsequent superpower DÉTENTE. Perhaps most important of all, although Eisenhower did not exercise detailed control over day-to-day foreign policy, when it came to major issues of war and peace he was the key decision maker—and invariably weighed in on the side of prudence and restraint, keeping his secretary of state, JOHN FOSTER DULLES, on a very tight rein. In recent years Eisenhower's reputation as a president has risen sharply, as his decade of the 1950s is compared to what followed. Analysts, such as Fred Greenstein in *The Hidden-Hand Presidency: Eisenhower as Leader* (1982), have looked anew at Eisenhower's "hidden hand" style of leadership, which entailed deft behind-the-scenes maneuvering with a public posture of a leader who was above the political fray. *See also* KOREAN WAR.

Eisenhower Doctrine   The 1957 statement of U.S. policy in the Middle East that originated in an address given by President Dwight D. Eisenhower to a joint session of Congress. Eisenhower requested

General Dwight D. Eisenhower talks to paratroopers in England just before they take off for the invasion of France on the eve of D-Day, June 6, 1944. (National Archives)

authority to provide military and economic aid to countries in the Middle East who requested such aid and, at their request, to use U.S. armed forces in the area, consistent with the United Nations Charter and formal UN actions, in order "to secure and protect the territorial integrity and political independence of such nations, requesting such aid, against overt armed aggression from any nations controlled by international Communism." The Eisenhower Doctrine later was used as the legal basis for the U.S. intervention in Lebanon during the 1958 crisis in that country. It differs from all other presidential doctrines in that it was formally adopted as a joint resolution of the U.S. Congress.

Eksund   A ship carrying 150 tons of munitions (including antiaircraft missiles) from Libya to the Irish Republican Army, captured by French authorities in October 1987 when it inadvertently strayed into French waters in transit to Ireland. While those munitions were intercepted, it was determined that at least four other shipments of similar size got through. This smuggling of arms to Northern Ireland was a gross violation of international law and further strained relations between the United Kingdom and Libya.

El Alamein, Battle of   1. The decisive October 23–November 4, 1942, North African desert battle of World War II between German and Italian troops (led by ERWIN ROMMEL) and British Commonwealth forces (led by BERNARD MONTGOMERY). El Alamein is only 70 miles from Alexandria. The Germans were seeking to capture Egypt and the Suez Canal—thus depriving Britain of its oil lifeline. The stunning British victory in which Rommel lost 59,000 men to Montgomery's 13,000 was a turning point of the war. British Prime Minister Winston Churchill said in a November 10, 1942, speech: "This is not the end. It is not even the beginning of the end. But it is, perhaps, the end of the beginning." After the war, in his history of that conflict, *The Second World War* (*vol. 4, 1954*), he wrote: "Before Alamein we never had a victory. After Alamein we never had a defeat." After this victory, Montgomery methodically drove Rommel back to Tripoli. There U.S. forces joined to form a pincer movement to liquidate the Axis position in North Africa. **2.** A July 1942 battle in the same place when British forces under General Claude Auchinleck repulsed an attack by Rommel but were unable to successfully counterattack.

DESPERATE ORDERS FOR A DESPERATE SITUATION

The defense of Egypt lies here at Alamein. . . . [I]f we lose this position we lose Egypt; all the fighting troops now in the Delta must come here at once, and will. Here we will stand and fight; there will be no further withdrawal. I have ordered that all plans and instructions dealing with further withdrawal are to be burnt, and at once. We will stand and fight here.

If we can't stay here alive, then let us stay here dead.

SOURCE: General B. L. Montgomery, to his officers on taking command of the British Eighth Army, August 13, 1942, quoted in Nigel Hamilton, *Monty* (1981).

---

electronic intelligence (ELINT)   All forms of information gathering based on radio and radar. It can be passive and simply involve the monitoring of already existing activities; it also can involve the use of electronic means to generate new information, as with radar, which identifies the location, course, and nature of moving objects. All major powers carry out ELINT-gathering operations, often by sending their ships or submarines close to a possible opponent's shores; sometimes by deliberately triggering an alert in order to record the signals activities that follow. The largest volume of ELINT is gathered by ground stations. A major difficulty with ELINT is managing the sheer volume of information that it generates. To determine what ELINT is useful and what is only "noise," the U.S. National Security Agency uses the largest computer complex in the world. With the end of the Cold War and the new emphasis given to regional security and to the economic dimensions of national security, it seems likely that ELINT will decline in importance compared to HUMAN INTELLIGENCE (HUMINT) in the future. *See also* SIGNALS INTELLIGENCE.

ELINT BANALITY

Sometimes the [World War II British] cryptographers would labor for hours over a message, only to discover it was of mind-numbing banality, as in the following case. The Abwehr [German intelligence] sent a message to its head of station in Algeciras, Spain, an officer code named "Cesar." The decoded message said: "Be careful of Axel. He bites." Was this a code within a code? It turned out to refer to the arrival of a guard dog for the station compound, a theory confirmed a few days later with the decrypting of an Enigma reply which read: "Cesar is in hospital. Axel bit him."

SOURCE: Phillip Knightley, *The Second Oldest Profession* (1986).

---

elements of national power   All the means (military, economic, political, etc.) that are available for employment in the pursuit of national objectives. Some analysts distinguish between the tangible elements of national power, such as economic and military capabilities, and the intangibles, such as national morale and the level of education of the population. Over time, the importance of such elements as military capabilities or economic resources may change very considerably. With the end of the Cold War and the rise of Japan and Western Europe, it seems that the world has entered an era in which the economic elements of national power are more important than the traditional military elements.

ELINT   *See* ELECTRONIC INTELLIGENCE.

elite theory   **1.** The belief that only those with special talents or belonging to a particular group should govern society. This theory has been widely criticized for being undemocratic and ultimately oppressive. All monarchical and fascist regimes are founded on this meaning of elite theory.   **2.** Empirical political analyses which conclude that the real controlling power in democratic societies are the small groups that come to dominate the various interests, such as the military, business, politics, religion, labor, and so on. *See also* PARETO, VILFREDO; PLURALISM.

elite troops   **1.** Military units that have been given special training or weapons that might make them more effective than regular units under certain conditions.   **2.** Military units that think they are better than others of the same nation because of the unit's distinguished history, fancy emblems, or conceited attitudes.

Elizabeth II (1926–   )   The queen of the United Kingdom and head of the COMMONWEALTH OF NATIONS since 1952 when she succeeded to the throne upon the death of her father, GEORGE VI. She is married to Philip, duke of Edinburgh. Their son Charles, Prince of Wales, is her heir apparent. As a constitutional monarch, her powers are largely ceremonial and informal. She is widely reported to be the single richest woman in the world.

El Salvador Civil War   The 12-year (1980–1992) Marxist insurrection of the Farabundo Marti National Liberation Front (FMLN) guerrilla coalition to overthrow the United States–backed rightist Salvadoran regime and establish a Communist state. After an estimated 75,000 deaths, many by DEATH SQUADS from both sides, a formal peace was negotiated at the United Nations. The 1992 agreement, signed in Mexico City by all major parties, calls for a radically reduced national army, the insurgents' transformation into a political party, and a new police force that is to include elements of the former guerrilla forces.

Elysée Palace   The official Paris residence of the president of France.

embargo   The formal prohibition of the import or export of commodities from the vessels of specific nations. An embargo is a mildly hostile act, more related to foreign policy than to trade policy. For example, shortly after the Communists came to power in Cuba, the United States embargoed sugar from Cuba in an effort to disrupt that state's economy. (The Cuban sugar embargo is still in effect.) And during the COLD WAR the members of the North Atlantic Treaty Organization prohibited the export of strategic materials to Warsaw Pact states. *See also* COCOM.

embargoed   Information given to reporters that may not be made public until a preset time; thus the information is "embargoed" until, for example, 5:00 P.M. or when an official takes a specified action. Typically major reports or budget proposals are embargoed so that the media can have time to analyze the material and to allow all media sources

A Salvadoran guerrilla poster. (U.S. Naval Institute)

time to obtain the items. Often one media outlet violates the embargo; at that point the others are free to use the material—and the violator may have trouble getting similar materials next time.

embassy **1.** The highest category of diplomatic mission that represents one state in the capital of another, headed by an AMBASSADOR. In this context, the embassy refers to all of the diplomatic staff as well as to all of the support personnel. **2.** The actual building or buildings (also called the mission) used to house the office (the chancery) and personal quarters of the embassy staff, including the ambassador. **3.** The job (also called the mission) of an ambassador. Thus an ambassador's mission (the job) might be to negotiate a treaty, which might be signed in the mission (a building), which is also known as the embassy.

embassy row A street in a capital upon which many foreign embassies are situated. In Washington, D.C., this term is often applied to that portion of Massachusetts Avenue on which the Australian, Austrian, Brazilian, British, Chilean, Irish, and Greek embassies, among others, are located.

EMC *See* EXPORT MANAGEMENT COMPANY.

EMCF *See* EUROPEAN MONETARY COOPERATION FUND.

emergency powers The authority given to a government or executive agency that allows normal legislative procedures and/or judicial remedies to be suspended. In Western democracies such emergency powers are usually strictly controlled by the legislature and permitted only for a limited period. In nondemocratic countries emergency powers are frequently invoked during "states of siege" (which may be declared for almost any reason), when all civil liberties are suspended.

eminence The title used to address cardinals of the Roman Catholic Church since the seventeenth century.

Eminent Persons Group (EPG) A group established by the British Commonwealth of Nations' heads of government during a 1985 meeting in Nassau, the Bahamas, to promote dialogue between the South African white minority government and leaders of South Africa's black majority population, to review that state's progress toward ending APARTHEID, and to consider the imposition of economic sanctions by commonwealth and Western countries to encourage white South Africans to press their government for democratic reforms and an end to apartheid. While the group failed to generate a dialogue between blacks and whites in South Africa, this effort helped to create the political climate that made possible the imposition of economic SANCTIONs in the late 1980s. These sanctions, many believe, helped convince the South Africans to reconsider apartheid.

empathy The quality of being able to understand the perspective of another government or set of decision makers and how a particular situation might look from its vantage point. Empathy is not the same as sympathy but does require a willingness to overcome ETHNOCENTRISM and other psychological tendencies, such as that of seeing oneself as acting from outside pressures and seeing others as acting from innate characteristics.

EMS *See* EUROPEAN MONETARY SYSTEM.

EMU *See* ECONOMIC AND MONETARY UNION; EUROPEAN MONETARY UNION.

EMUA European Monetary Unit of Account; *see* EUROPEAN UNIT OF ACCOUNT.

en clair French for "in clear"; a message sent in plain text—not in code.

END *See* EUROPEAN NUCLEAR DISARMAMENT.

end game **1.** In chess, the final moves made when only a few pieces are left on the playing board. **2.** In world politics, the last part (the final events) of a policy line that is coming to a conclusion or a natural finish. For example, once the United States decided to take all its troops out of Vietnam as the South Vietnamese government began to collapse in 1975, the "end game" began. In arms control the end game sometimes proves to be the most difficult part of the negotiation, as even minor concessions take on major political importance. For example, during the SALT II negotiations, the last 10 percent of the agreement took almost as long to negotiate as the first 90 percent.

end of history Policy analyst Francis Fukuyama's theme first put forth in his article "The End of History?" (*The National Interest,* Summer 1989), in which he wrote, "What we may be witnessing is not just the end of the cold war, or the passing of a particular period of postwar history, but the end of history as such; that is, the end point of mankind's ideological evolution and the universalization of Western liberal democracy as the final form of human government." The Fukuyama thesis sometimes is referred to as "endism" and frequently has been dismissed as a nonsensical argument. For many of his critics the end of the COLD WAR simply has ushered in a new and in some respects more interesting phase of history.

end use The final task to which a technology is put. There is concern in the United States that the end use of many DUAL USE (both commercial and military) TECHNOLOGIES, ostensibly sold for peaceful purposes, will be military.

enemy alien A person who is outside the boundaries of his or her country and is in territory of, or territory occupied by, a belligerent power.

enemy capabilities Those particular qualities and abilities of another state that one sees as threatening or able to do harm. During the Cold War far more emphasis was placed on capabilities rather than intentions, an emphasis that resulted in a great deal of WORST CASE ANALYSIS.

enforcement terrorism *See* TERRORISM, ENFORCEMENT.

English School An approach to INTERNATIONAL RELATIONS most often associated with British writers. It emphasizes traditional or classical analyses and is not enthusiastic about more scientific and quantitative approaches. Among the main proponents of the English School are such figures as HERBERT BUTTERFIELD and HEDLEY BULL. Members of this school have been concerned with elucidating the key concepts and ideas of international politics, and much of their work has revolved around the idea of INTERNATIONAL ORDER.

enhanced radiation weapon The *neutron bomb.* Most nuclear weapons engineering has striven to maximize immediate effect of the blast and to cut down on energy release through radiation. Enhanced radiation weapons seek to minimize the blast and its heat, which causes physical destruction, and to boost the emission of high-energy radiation in the form of neutron particles. The usual objective for a nuclear weapon is to destroy physical structures—bridges and factories, buildings, concrete silos and bunkers, and so on. The human death rate associated with an ordinary nuclear explosion is usually regarded as collateral damage. Enhanced radiation weapons, in contrast, are intended not for strategic operations against fixed enemy physical plants but for tactical strikes against its armies.

The neutron bomb was designed in the United States to be used against the massive tank forces of the WARSAW PACT. It has never been used in combat and is not deployed in Europe. The neutron bomb was a controversial issue in the late 1970s as the Carter Administration first mobilized European support for U.S. development and deployment and then backed away from the plan when the Europeans had been brought on board. Nevertheless, the issue helped sensitize the European public to the nuclear issue and was a key factor in the reemergence of strong antinuclear movements throughout many Western European states.

Enigma The World War II German code machine that was obtained secretly by the British and duplicated. This most important INTELLIGENCE breakthrough of the war was obtained by Poland's intelligence service two weeks before the outbreak of war in 1939—and was simply given to the British. This allowed the Allies to read many of the German encoded messages throughout the war. The intelligence was known as ULTRA.

Eniwetok The Pacific atoll in the Marshall Islands where the United States successfully tested the first HYDROGEN BOMB in 1952.

U.S. Colonel Paul W. Tibbets, Jr., pilot of the Enola Gay, about to drop the atomic bomb on Hiroshima, waves from his cockpit before takeoff, August 6, 1945. (National Archives)

Enola Gay   The name (it was that of the pilot's mother) painted on the fuselage of the United States B-29 bomber that dropped the ATOMIC BOMB on HIROSHIMA on August 6, 1945.

enosis   Union with Greece; the political goal of the Greek majority population on Cyprus and the occurrence that Turkey has tried to prevent throughout the CYPRUS CONFLICT.

en poste   The status of a diplomat who has assumed his or her official duties at a designated diplomatic or consular post.

Entebbe Raid   The 1976 rescue by the Israeli military of 103 passengers from the hijacked Air France Flight 139 who were being held captive at the Entebbe airport in Uganda by terrorists of the POPU-LAR FRONT FOR THE LIBERATION OF PALESTINE. Because most of the hostages were Jewish, because all of the non-Jewish passengers were released, and because the hijackers had the cooperation of Ugandan dictator IDI AMIN DADA, the Israeli government took the substantial risk of a rescue attempt 3,000 miles from home. The rescue was an astounding success. Israeli soldiers stormed the airport, killed seven hijackers and 20 Ugandan soldiers, and saved all but four of the hostages at the loss of only one Israeli soldier (the commander, Johnathan Netanyahu).

entente   French for "an understanding." In diplomatic usage, an entente is more than a DETENTE but less than a formal treaty; however, it may imply a tacit ALLIANCE.

entente, triple   *See* TRIPLE ENTENTE.

Entente Cordiale   The 1904 "friendly understanding" between France and Great Britain in the face of the naval race by Germany and the TRIPLE ALLIANCE of Germany, Austria, and Italy. It settled several territorial disputes, including France's recognition of British control of Egypt, and asserted that France would be in charge of the naval defense of the Mediterranean. After Russia joined in 1907, this alliance became the TRIPLE ENTENTE, one of the two great alliances whose later inflexibility helped lead to WORLD WAR I.

environmental possibilism   *See* SPROUT, HAROLD AND MARGARET.

envoy   1. A messenger or representative.   2. Any DIPLOMATIC AGENT.   3. A diplomat who ranks just below an AMBASSADOR. Historically, the full title is *envoy extraordinary* so that such individuals might be distinguished from low-level messengers.

EPG   *See* EMINENT PERSONS GROUP.

EPLF   *See* ETHIOPIAN-ERITREAN WAR.

Erhard, Ludwig (1897–1977)   The German economist and Christian Democratic chancellor (1963–1966) whose laissez-faire policies as minister of economics for postwar reconstruction are credited with what became known as the West German "economic miracle." A resolute ATLANTICIST, he worked to maintain close ties with the United States.

Eritrean People's Liberation Front   *See* ETHIOPIAN-ERITREAN WAR.

Eritrean War   *See* ETHIOPIAN-ERITREAN WAR.

ERP   1. *Ejercito Revolucionario de Pueblo* (People's Revolutionary Army), an Argentine left-wing organization founded in 1970. Influenced by the TUPAMAROS of Uruguay, ERP adopted a TROTSKYITE philosophy and recruited from the lower economic classes of Argentine society. The group used "Robin Hood" tactics to win popular support and carried out a campaign of kidnappings, assassinations, and assaults on military targets. The ERP was largely undone by the military government's DIRTY WAR in the middle and late 1970s.   2. One of the left-wing guerrilla groups of El Salvador encompassed under the umbrella organization FMLN.

ESA   1. *Ejercito Secreto Anticomunista* (Secret Anti-Communist Army), a Guatemalan right-wing DEATH SQUAD that played a major role in that state's extremist violence since the 1960s. As a paramilitary organization, the ESA had strong ties to the government and carried on a government-condoned, extralegal, antileftist campaign with impunity.   2. A Salvadoran right-wing death squad.

escalation   An intensification or increase in the level of violence of a military clash; it can be deliberate or unpremeditated. Escalation can take many forms. It can be an increase in the number of belligerents involved, an extension of the geographical scope of the conflict, or an increase in the numbers or types of weapons that one or both sides use. Introducing chemical or nuclear weapons into a conflict that had been confined to conventional forces would be an obvious escalation. Using the analogy of a ladder, strategists think of potential conflict arrayed as a series of steps from minimum to maximum violence. Indeed, the official doctrine of the North Atlantic Treaty Organization, that of FLEXIBLE RESPONSE, assumes a ranking of possible military reactions rather than a predetermined strategic plan. U.S. Admiral Carlisle A. H. Trost, Chief of Naval Operations, boasted that: "Our ships are built to fight . . . on every rung in the ladder of escalatory violence" (*New York Times,* October 8, 1988). Although the ESCALATION LADDER metaphor, developed most fully by HERMAN KAHN, has been widely used, many critics believe that a more appropriate analogy is that of a slide. In this second view, escalation is not a controlled, deliberate process but a process that can get out of control all too easily. On a ladder it is possible to go down as well as up; on a slide it is very difficult to stop or get off.

   Escalation became particularly associated with U.S. policy during the Vietnam War because of the constant debate over whether that war should be expanded. As U.S. President Lyndon B. Johnson said, "Our numbers have increased in Vietnam because the aggression of others has increased in Vietnam. There is not, and there will not be, a mindless escalation" (*Time,* March 4, 1966). He may not have thought that his subsequent escalation of the war was mindless, but many others certainly did and said so.

escalation, horizontal   A strategic option particularly advocated by the U.S. Navy during the early 1980s, which held that the United States would not necessarily respond to Soviet aggression only in the location at which it occurred; instead, Washington might decide to extend the conflict to other regions where the prospects of success were much greater and where it might be able to hurt the Soviet Union more. Such a strategy necessarily involved major FORCE PROJECTION capacity that justified the huge 600-ship navy then planned by the Reagan Administration. Critics argued that horizontal escalation would make it impossible to bring about a peaceful end to any superpower conflict and that it ran counter to principles of CRISIS MANAGEMENT and ESCALATION CONTROL.

escalation control   **1.** The key concept in NORTH ATLANTIC TREATY ORGANIZATION strategy, developed for a possible war with the former WARSAW PACT: that levels and types of force could be arrayed along a continuum of violence and undesirability. All combatants would prefer, other things being equal, to fight at a lower rather than a higher level of escalation. For the sake of simplicity it was possible to think in terms of four successive levels of violence in a NATO-Warsaw Pact conflict. The first was a purely conventional war, the second involved the use of battlefield nuclear weapons, and the third and fourth respectively saw the use of INTERMEDIATE-RANGE NUCLEAR FORCES and finally CENTRAL STRATEGIC WARFARE. The essence of NATO's strategy of flexible response was to match the Warsaw Pact at each level of escalation. The aim was to deprive pact forces of the option of being able to move up a level of violence if they were not winning at the existing one. A power takes control of an escalation ladder when it can increase the violence of its actions without the enemy being able to counter at that level. NATO was generally thought not to have sufficient forces at either the conventional or the short-range nuclear levels to be able to claim to exert escalation control at those stages on the ladder. This presented serious problems in that NATO might have been faced with the choice of either escalating to a very advanced level of nuclear confrontation or admitting defeat. In any event, of course, the Soviet Union was reluctant to take any action that might start hostilities in Europe, partly because there were very serious doubts about the ability of the belligerents to control escalation. During the COLD WAR, then, the most important threshold in Europe was not that between conventional and nuclear weapons but between peace and anything else. The reason for this can be explained in terms of EXISTENTIAL DETERRENCE.   **2.** The limitations or restrictions placed on nuclear exchanges that would allow a nuclear war to be fought on such a limited scope that it would not destroy the whole human race—only most of it.

escalation dominance   The quality of one side in a war that has superior force capacity not only at the current level of escalation but at successive levels. It is in control in the sense that the enemy cannot escape from a weak position in one phase by moving on to the next step in the ESCALATION LADDER, because it would be at a disadvantage at that stage as well. Furthermore, the dominating side does have that choice. So if it is suffering more casualties than it thinks acceptable, it can try to terminate conflict by increasing the intensity level to a point at which its relative advantage may be even greater. The key to escalation domination is that the dominating side must have superiority at every level. Although U.S. defense planners have seemed to be obsessed with this notion at times, it is arguable that it has had little practical relevance.

escalation ladder   HERMAN KAHN's model from his book *On Escalation* (1965) of the gradations of military ESCALATION as a ladder of 44 rungs. Because Kahn's model first used nuclear weapons at rung 15, this meant that there were 30 rungs on the ladder involving nuclear war. This 30-different-varieties approach to nuclear war gave Kahn's escalation ladder model great notoriety. Kahn said he attempted "to describe the way stations of ascending conflict so that the elements can be recognized, and the distance from all-out war estimated."

escalation matching   A military strategy that intimidates a foe by assuring it that its every move will be matched and overpowered. When used correctly, this technique can cause a small but more aggressive nation to "back down," thereby limiting the escalation of a war.

escalation slide   *See* ESCALATION.

Eshkol, Levi (1895–1969)   The prime minister of Israel from 1963 until his death. He led his nation during the 1967 SIX-DAY WAR.

espionage   Actions designed to obtain a government's secrets, usually diplomatic or military, through clandestine operations. The case is often made that mutual espionage is a stabilizing factor in international relations. For if each side knows that the other is not preparing a surprise attack, then they both are able to remain calm. But if such information is not available, some analysts always are ready to believe the worst about the opposition and argue for a preemptive attack—thus initiating a war that could have been avoided with more effective espionage. *Compare to* INTELLIGENCE.

THE HOOVER COMMISSION ON ESPIONAGE

There are no rules in such a game. Hitherto acceptable norms of human conduct do not apply. If the U.S. is to survive, longstanding American Concepts of "fair play" must be reconsidered. We must develop effective espionage and counterespionage services and must learn to subvert, sabotage and destroy our enemies by more clever, more sophisticated, and more effective methods than those used against us. It may become necessary that the American people be made acquainted with, understand and support this fundamentally repugnant philosophy.

SOURCE: Commission on the Organization of the Executive Branch, *Report on the Intelligence Community,* July 4, 1954. This commission was chaired by former U.S. President Herbert Hoover.

---

esprit de corps   1. The sense of spirit or morale of a group, especially the pride that individual members take in their military units. Frederick the Great in 1768 said it existed when a soldier had "a higher opinion of his own regiment than all the other troops in the country" (quoted in E. M. Lloyd, *A Review of the History of the Infantry,* 1908).   2. The soldier's

belief that her or his own army and fellow citizens are really better than those of another nation. The earl of Chesterfield wrote in a letter of February 7, 1749, that the "silly, sanguine notion, which is firmly entertained here, that one Englishman can beat three Frenchmen, encourages, and has sometimes enabled, one Englishman, in reality, to beat two."

TOLSTOY'S EQUATION: X = ESPRIT DE CORPS

Force (the volume of motion) is the product of the mass into the velocity. In warfare the force of armies is the product of the mass multiplied by something else, an unknown X.

Military science, seeing in history an immense number of examples in which the mass of an army does not correspond with its force, and in which small numbers conquer large ones, vaguely recognize the existence of this unknown factor. . . .

X is the spirit of the army, the greater or less desire to fight and to face dangers on the part of all the men composing the army, which is quite apart from the question whether they are fighting under leaders of genius or not, with cudgels or with guns that fire thirty times a minute. . . . The Spirit of the army is the factor which multiplied by the mass gives the product of the force. To define and express the significance of this unknown factor, the spirit of the army, is the problem of science.

SOURCE: Leo Tolstoy, *War and Peace* (1865–1869).

---

essential equivalence   1. The condition of two or more states having roughly the same number of nuclear weapons, although the kinds and sizes may differ greatly. This notion was promulgated by James Schelsinger (1929–   ) in the first half of the 1970s. Although it was most often spelled out in terms of CAPABILITY—and especially that for destroying hard targets—the requirement for essential equivalence was partly about options; anything the Soviet Union could do to the United States, the United States also had to be able to do back. This was necessary to ensure that the Soviet Union did not believe it had ESCALATION DOMINANCE, as this might have given Moscow the psychological edge in a crisis.   2. A definition of nuclear PARITY.

establishment   1. The people who have the real power in any society; an inherently conservative and often secretive ruling class. The term first surfaced in Great Britain during the 1950s and is often traced to an article written by Henry Fairlie in the *Spectator* (September 1955). It soon crossed the Atlantic, and by the 1960s there was much talk of an "Eastern Establishment" and a "Protestant Establishment." Now the word has become so trite and overused that "establishments" are to be found all over; or not found because secretiveness is part of their essence. **2.** The collective holders of power in a segment of society: political, military, social, academic, religious, or literary. It is always the establishment that revolutionaries—whether political, intellectual, organizational, or other—wish to overthrow, so they can become the new establishment. **3.** A government installation, together with its personnel and equipment, organized as an operating entity. **4.** A table setting out the authorized numbers of personnel and equipment in a military unit; sometimes called a *table of organization* or *table of organization and equipment*.

estimate **1.** An analysis of a foreign situation, development, or trend that identifies its major elements, interprets its significance, and appraises future possibilities and the prospective results of the various actions that might be taken. **2.** An appraisal of the capabilities, vulnerabilities, and potential courses of action of a foreign nation or combination of nations in consequence of a specific national plan, policy, decision, or contemplated course of action. William Shakespeare in *Henry V* (1598) offered the classic advice on estimating: "'Tis best to weigh the enemy more mighty than he seems." Today this is called a WORST CASE ANALYSIS. **3.** An analysis of an actual or contemplated clandestine operation in relation to the situation in which it would be conducted in order to identify and appraise such factors as available and needed assets and potential obstacles, accomplishments, and consequences. *See also* INTELLIGENCE ESTIMATE.

estimate of the situation A logical process of reasoning by which a commander considers all the circumstances affecting a military situation and arrives at a decision as to the best course of action to be taken. While this is a logical process, it is also to some extent an art. U.S. General George S. Patton, Jr., wrote in *War As I Know It* (1947): "It is sad to remember that, when anyone has fairly mastered the art of command, the necessity for that art usually expires—either through the termination of war or through the advanced age of the commander." T. E. Lawrence (of Arabia), in a letter reprinted in B. H. Liddell Hart's *Memoirs* (1965), observed: "With two thousand years of examples behind us, we have no excuse when fighting, for not fighting well." To paraphrase, with 2,000 years of examples of estimating situations behind us, there is no excuse when estimating for not estimating well. *Compare to* DEFINITION OF THE SITUATION.

Estimé, Dumarsais *See* DUVALIER FAMILY.

Estonia *See* BALTIC NATIONS.

Estrada Doctrine The 1930 assertion by the minister of foreign affairs of Mexico, Genaro Estrada (1887–1957), that all governments should be granted DIPLOMATIC RECOGNITION if they are in effective control of their states. This also is known as the *doctrine of effectiveness*.

ETA *Euzkadi ta Askatasuna* ("Basque Fatherland and Liberty"), a violent Basque separatist movement. Founded in 1959 as an organization dedicated to democratic ideals and the preservation of Basque heritage and language in northern Spain and southern France, by the 1960s ETA had evolved into a group using violence to secure Basque independence from Spain. The group has become one of the most active terrorist organizations in the world. ETA's most infamous terrorist attack was the 1973 assassination of Luis Carrero Blanco, the prime minister of Spain. The ETA also has a long history of kidnappings for ransom, from which it has obtained the equivalent of many millions of U.S. dollars. The ETA has received training in Lebanon, Libya, and Nicaragua, and has close ties with the PROVISIONAL IRISH REPUBLICAN ARMY (PIRA). Although many ETA members have been arrested by Spanish and French police in recent years, the ETA seems able to rebound easily because of the large size of the group's support base and the high level of nationalist sentiment among Basques. *See also* BASQUE TERRORISM.

ETC *See* EXPORT TRADING COMPANY.

Ethiopian Civil War   The revolt against the dictatorial Marxist regime of Mengistu Haile Mariam (1937–   ) that began soon after he, as part of a military junta, overthrew Emperor HAILE SELASSIE in 1974. Despite massive Soviet aid, the Mengistu regime's policies destroyed the economy, caused millions to die by famine in the 1980s, and encouraged a resurgence of separatist guerrilla movements. Mengistu, who consolidated his personal power in 1977 by executing the previous head of state, General Teferi Benti, continuously fought off increasingly strong insurgents until he was forced to flee into exile in Zimbabwe as rebel forces advanced on the capital of Addis Ababa in 1991. The leader of the insurgency, Meles Zenawi (1955–   ), convened a national conference of the fighting factions in July 1991. Out of this emerged a new coalition government with Zenawi as president.

Ethiopian-Eritrean War   The conflict between Eritrea, the northern province of Ethiopia, and the central government of Ethiopia. Eritrea, an Italian colony since 1890 that came under British control in 1941, expected independence after World War II. Instead, in 1952 the United Nations recommended that it be federated with Ethiopia. Guerrilla separatists have been active ever since. The war intensified after 1974 when the Soviet-backed Marxist government sought unsuccessfully to destroy the insurgents. Instead, after several million deaths from war, famine, and disease, insurgents led by the Eritrean People's Liberation Front (EPLF) defeated the central government and declared independence in 1991. In 1991 the new coalition government of Meles Zenawi gave Eritrea the right to seek independence in a May 1993 national referendum. Though essentially independent, Eritrean government policy has been not to seek UN membership or formal diplomatic recognition until after the 1993 referendum.

Ethiopian-Italian War   *See* ABYSSINIAN-ITALIAN WAR.

Ethiopian-Somalian Conflict   *See* SOMALIAN CIVIL WAR.

ethnic cleansing   The dispossession or murder of one socially distinct group by another. While practiced on a large scale by Germany in World War II (against Jews and Gypsies among others), the term itself as well as the large-scale reappearance of the practice in Europe dates from the YUGOSLAVIAN CIVIL WAR of the early 1990s when the Serbs, who controlled most of the former Yugoslavian army, began killing or forcing into exile (or refugee camps) massive numbers of Muslim Slavs, Croats, and other minorities. This pattern increased as the Serbs occupied portions of Bosnia and Croatia, states that had seceded from Yugoslavia. Allegations of atrocities by Serbs were given greater credence when in 1992 mass graves were uncovered and CONCENTRATION CAMPS reminiscent of Nazi Germany were exposed. While the Serbs' ethnic cleansing campaign has been turned against them in areas controlled by non-Serbs, there is overwhelming evidence that the Serbs have been both the major initiators and by far the greater practitioners of these atrocities. By spring 1993 overall deaths from ethnic cleansing approached a hundred thousand—and an estimated two million people had been made homeless.

ethnocentrism   1. The idea that governments and peoples in a particular nation view other cultures or nations through their own particular cultural or national lens and as a result often fail to understand them. In this sense, to be ethnocentric is to be limited in one's approach and perspective and to fail to understand the differences of value and perspective that might inform the behavior of other groups or nations. Ethnocentrism makes empathy very difficult as it prevents one from placing oneself in the shoes of others and understanding how they see the world and the ways in which their perceptions differ from one's own. 2. A tendency to see one's own group or nation not only as the center of everything but also as superior. Chinese notions of China as the Middle Kingdom and of other nations as barbarians is a good example of ethnocentric thinking. 3. The national equivalent of egocentrism. 4. According to Ken Booth in *Strategy and Ethnocentrism* (1979), ethnocentrism also is used as a synonym for being culture bound, limited by the attitudes of or the learning available from a single society.

ethno-nationalism   Nationalistic feelings that are limited to one's particular ethnic group; feelings that do not extend to all of the citizens of the state. Ethno-nationalism is one of the prime causes of civil wars and breakups of political unions. Recent examples include Yugoslavia that, during the YUGOSLAVIAN CIVIL WAR, broke up into factions dedicated to a murderous ETHNIC CLEANSING. Similar but less deadly ethnic antagonism led to the dissolution of the Soviet Union into 15 different republics and the 1992 division of Czechoslovakia into two separate states—one Czech and one Slovak.

Etzioni, Amitai (1929–   ) The German-born U.S. sociologist who wrote a major analysis of the dynamics of international political integration, *Political Unification* (1965). Exploring several examples of efforts at political integration, including the European Economic Community and the West Indies Federation, Etzioni attempted to define the conditions for success in unification efforts. Etzioni also has worked extensively on decision-making processes and on complex organizations, and some of his ideas, such as the notion of MIXED SCANNING, are discussed in relation to foreign policy decision making. He also wrote *The Kennedy Experiment* (1967), an analysis of the evolving U.S.-Soviet relationship in the aftermath of the Cuban Missile Crisis, in which Etzioni demonstrated how unilateral gestures of restraint by one side were reciprocated by the other. *See also* INTEGRATION, POLITICAL.

EUA *See* EUROPEAN UNIT OF ACCOUNT.

EURATOM (European Atomic Energy Community) One of the three units of the European Community. It was created at the same time as were the other communities by its own separate TREATY OF ROME. Its membership is the same as the rest of the EC. Its purpose is to promote the development of nuclear energy for peaceful purposes, to develop common health and safety standards for the nuclear industry, and to maintain a common market in nuclear materials. However, the monitoring of specific nuclear installations is a responsibility of member states.

EUREKA The European Research Coordination Agency created in 1985 by 17 West European countries (the then ten Common Market countries, plus Austria, Finland, Norway, Portugal, Spain, Sweden, and Switzerland) to pool research in such advanced technological fields as artificial intelligence, lasers and particle beams, microelectronics, new materials, optronics, and supercomputers. EUREKA has a nonmilitary emphasis and is directed at the commercial exploitation of civilian research.

Euro-Atlantic system What some observers see as the successor to the NORTH ATLANTIC TREATY ORGANIZATION security system, which predominated during the Cold War. The essence of the Euro-Atlantic system idea is that it involves the United States as an active participant while extending the European elements of the alliance system into Eastern Europe and into at least some of the states of the former WARSAW PACT.

Eurocommunism A version of COMMUNISM espoused by some Communist parties in Western European democracies in response to their need to compete electorally with socialist and conservative parties. As a term, *Eurocommunism* refers to the independent and diverse policies of West European Communist leaders and their conflict with the Soviet Communist Party. The Eurocommunist leaders in France, Italy, and Spain strongly resisted any claim by the Soviet Communist Party of a right to interfere or require international Communist unity. In addition, they emphasized their evolutionary and democratic intentions, rejected the doctrine of the DICTATORSHIP OF THE PROLETARIAT, and committed their parties to civil liberties and pluralist democracy. Because the term *Eurocommunism* lumped together the considerably different national Communist parties, many analysts were skeptical of its utility when it first emerged in the late 1960s. Now the term is obsolete—especially because many of the "Eurocommunist" parties have dropped the word *Communist* from their names in the wake of the democratization of Eastern Europe beginning in 1989. *See also* HISTORIC COMPROMISE.

Eurocurrencies Deposits denominated in U.S. dollars and other major currencies held in commercial banks outside their state of origin. Such deposits, originally held only in European banks, now exist all over the world. The international trade in Eurocurrencies functions as a source of international short-term capital that tends to flow to countries offering the highest interest rates. *See also* PETROCURRENCIES.

Eurogroup An informal grouping of the European members of the NORTH ATLANTIC TREATY ORGANIZATION (except France) whose goals are to ensure a "more cohesive European contribution to the common defense" and to coordinate European political and strategic efforts in terms of the alliance. The Eurogroup was formed in 1968 partly in response to pressure from the U.S. Congress for U.S. troop cuts in Europe and for greater BURDEN-SHARING. Eurogroup, in an effort to make better use of existing resources, fostered the creation of a series of subgroups to deal with specific areas: for example, Eurolog to deal with logistics and Euroco to deal with communications systems. Although Eurogroup continues its coordinating activities, it has been less important than other European groupings such as the Western European Union. The members of Eurogroup are: Belgium, Denmark, Germany, Greece, Italy, Luxembourg, the Netherlands, Norway, Portugal, Turkey, and the United Kingdom.

Euromissile 1. The Tomahawk cruise missiles and the Pershing II ballistic missiles that the United States deployed in North Atlantic Treaty Organization countries in the 1980s in order to offset a new generation of short- and intermediate-range Soviet missiles. Both the Soviet and the U.S. missiles were later removed as a result of the INF TREATY of 1987. 2. Any nuclear weapons above the tactical or battlefield nuclear weapon level located in Europe and intended for use on targets in Eastern or Western Europe. *See also* GRAY AREA WEAPONS.

European Assembly The former name of the EUROPEAN PARLIAMENT.

European Atomic Energy Commission *See* EURATOM.

European Bank for Reconstruction and Development The entity created in 1990 to help finance the industrial and economic development of the newly emerging democracies of Eastern Europe. Created by the EUROPEAN COMMUNITY, its formally stated goals are "to promote, in consultation with the IMF

(International Monetary Fund) and the World Bank, productive and competitive investment in the states of central and eastern Europe, to reduce, where appropriate, any risks related to the financing of their economies, to assist the transition to a more market-oriented economy and to speed up the necessary structural adjustments."

European Coal and Steel Community (ECSC) One of the three units of the EUROPEAN COMMUNITY, the ECSC was established by the 1951 Treaty of Paris by Belgium, France, Italy, Luxembourg, the Netherlands, and West Germany. It arose from the plan proposed by Foreign Minister Robert Schuman of France the previous year for pooling the coal and steel production of France and West Germany to be supervised by a supranational authority. His goal was to enmesh Germany within a network of European economic integration and to prevent an untrammeled German rearmament. Great Britain was invited to join the ECSC discussions but declined. The ECSC has an executive body, parliamentary assembly, and court of justice headquartered in Luxembourg. It has worked to remove all obstacles to open trade within its community.

European Commission The bureaucracy of the EUROPEAN COMMUNITY that functions as a common executive and policy-developing arm for the European Coal and Steel Community (ECSC), the European Economic Community (EEC), and the European Atomic Energy Community (EURATOM). The commission from its headquarters in Brussels supervises over 16,000 "Eurocrats." Seventeen commissioners are appointed by the member governments for four-year terms. There are two commissioners each from France, Italy, Germany, Spain, and the United Kingdom, and one each from Belgium, Denmark, Greece, Ireland, Luxembourg, the Netherlands, and Portugal. The commission, which adopts measures by simple majority, acts in the interests of the community as a whole. The commission can be dismissed only by a vote of censure in the European Parliament. The commission is responsible for ensuring the implementation of the Treaty of Rome and community rules and obligations; submission of proposals to the Council of Ministers; execution of the council's decisions; reconciliation of disagreements among

The poster that won first prize in a 1950 U.S. government—sponsored competition on the theme "Intra-European Cooperation for a Better Standard of Living." (Library of Congress)

PEAN COURT OF JUSTICE. The three communities are regarded increasingly as a single entity, the European Community. However, they also are referred to in the plural as the European Communities.

THE EUROPEAN COMMUNITY
A Chronology

1946	Former Prime Minister Winston Churchill of Great Britain declares: "We must create a sort of United States of Europe."
1947	Benelux creates the economic union of Belgium, Luxembourg, and the Netherlands.
1949	Council of Europe created.
1951	European Coal and Steel Community created.
1957	European Economic Community and European Atomic Energy Community (EURATOM) are created by treaties in Rome—considered the birth of the Common Market.
1958	European Parliament meets for the first time.
1959	European Free Trade Association (EFTA) created.
1963	President Charles de Gaulle of France prevents Denmark, Great Britain, Ireland, and Norway from joining the EC.
1973	Denmark, Great Britain, Ireland, and Norway join the EC when new French President Georges Pompidou ends France's opposition.
1974	European Council created.
1981	Greece joins EC.
1986	Spain and Portugal join EC. Single European Act passed.
1991	EFTA agrees to merge with EC by 1993. Maastricht Treaty calls for single currency and central bank by 1999.

---

council members; administration of EC policies, such as the Common Agricultural Policy (CAP) and coal and steel policies; taking necessary legal action against firms or member governments; and representing the community in trade negotiations with nonmember countries.

European Community (EC)   The collective term for three distinct European Communities: the European Economic Community (the COMMON MARKET or EEC), the European Coal and Steel Community, and the European Atomic Energy Community (usually referred to as EURATOM). Since 1967 the community has shared five major institutions: the EUROPEAN COMMISSION, the EUROPEAN COUNCIL, the COUNCIL OF MINISTERS, the EUROPEAN PARLIAMENT, and the EURO-

European Community deepening   The idea that the POLITICAL INTEGRATION process should be made stronger among the existing members of the EC before the EC is opened up to new members—especially those from Eastern Europe.

European Community widening   The process of adding new members to the European Community. Critics of this argue that it will dilute the union and set back the POLITICAL INTEGRATION process and that the emphasis should be on deepening cooperation among the existing members. The argument for widening, however, is that it is necessary for the economic development of Eastern Europe.

European Corps   *See* FRANCO-GERMAN CORPS.

European Council   A forum for meetings of heads of state and government of the member countries of the EUROPEAN COMMUNITY. The president of France, the heads of government of the other member states, the president of the European Commission, the EC foreign ministers, and one of the vice presidents of the commission participate in European Council sessions. The SINGLE EUROPEAN ACT was the first document to recognize the European Council's existence. It requires that the European Council "shall meet at least twice a year" but does not provide a statement of its functions. These have evolved over time to include providing policy direction and political momentum to greater European economic and political integration. Note that this European Council is a totally separate entity from the COUNCIL OF EUROPE.

European Council of Human Rights   An institution of the COUNCIL OF EUROPE established in 1959 to enforce the 1950 European Convention on Human Rights.

European Court of Justice (ECJ)   The supreme judicial authority of the EUROPEAN COMMUNITY. The ECJ is the final arbiter on the legality of acts of the EUROPEAN COMMISSION and the Council of Ministers. It decides on the compatibility of national and EC laws. Some of its decisions have advanced integration by means of judicial review.

European Currency Unit (ECU)   The international unit of account created for the EUROPEAN MONETARY SYSTEM (EMS), used as the denominator of EMS debts and credits and as a reserve credit in the EUROPEAN MONETARY COOPERATION FUND. Initially the ECU was valued at the March 12, 1979, quotation for the Common Market's EUROPEAN UNIT OF ACCOUNT and was composed of a weighed BASKET OF CURRENCIES of members of the European Economic Community. ECU credit cards and traveler's checks are already in use. ECU currency eventually may be the common money of the EC. But many feel, as an *Economist* editorial (March 5, 1988) noted, "If the ecu is to win the hearts and minds of tomorrow's Europeans, it needs more than governmental prods. It should have a new name. . . . The best name would be . . . the 'monnet,' which intellectuals will like because of the link to Jean Monnet and almost everybody else will understand because it sounds like cash."

European Defense Community (EDC)   The common European military force (1950–1954) whose formation was a key theme in Atlantic relations. In 1950 French Premier René Pleven, fearful of German rearmament, proposed an integrated continental military force through the Pleven Plan. A treaty creating this force was signed in 1952 by Belgium, France, Italy, Luxembourg, the Netherlands, and West Germany. Great Britain, however, refused to join, while many French critics became concerned about the possible loss of French sovereignty through the union. When the French National Assembly refused ratification of the EDC Pact in 1954, the EDC dissipated. Since the EDC was intended to provide a framework for German rearmament and entry into the NORTH ATLANTIC TREATY ORGANIZATION, the United States was dismayed by this outcome. Britain suggested an alternative framework, however, using the WESTERN EUROPEAN UNION as the framework for German rearmament. This was achieved through the Treaties of London and Paris, and in 1955 West Germany was admitted to NATO with restrictions imposed through the WEU.

European Defense Identity   The idea of a Western European defense independent of the United States that would enhance West European self-reliance in defense and security matters. The idea has been around since the early 1950s, but because of differences among the major European powers, the ambivalence of the United States, the comfortable framework provided by the NORTH ATLANTIC TREATY ORGANIZATION, and the overwhelming nature of the Soviet threat, there was great concern in Europe not to do anything that would either push the United States out of Europe or encourage it to leave. With the end of the COLD WAR, however, greater independence from the United States is conceivable, while greater cooperation and independence on security matters seems to be a natural consequence of European economic and political integration. There is still debate, however, about the relationships between a European Defense Identity and the ATLANTIC ALLIANCE. During 1991 this debate centered around the role of the WESTERN EUROPEAN UNION, which seems the most likely institutional vehicle for such an identity. The United States and Great Britain, supported by the Netherlands and Portugal, wanted the WEU to be a European pillar in NATO, whereas France and Germany wanted it to be responsible primarily to the EUROPEAN COMMUNITY. Even after the MAASTRICHT TREATY meeting the issue remained unresolved, but it is likely to continue to be a source of friction both in Atlantic relations and among the West European powers themselves.

European Defense Initiative (EDI)   A proposal for a system of strategic defense against missile attack for the European members of the NORTH ATLANTIC TREATY ORGANIZATION. Manfred Woerner, then the West German defense minister, made the proposal during a meeting of NATO defense ministers in Brussels in December 1985. The proposed EDI system seeks to improve European defenses against all airborne threats, including aircraft and intermediate-range and tactical nuclear missiles. As such, it would supplement the U.S. STRATEGIC DEFENSE INITIATIVE. Now that the Cold War is over and NATO is redefining its role and mission, this initiative is undergoing reevaluation—especially now that funding for SDI research in the United States is being drastically curtailed.

European Development Fund   A EUROPEAN COMMUNITY institution that provides grants and loans to associated and THIRD WORLD states.

European Economic Area   The single regional common market formed by the EUROPEAN COMMUNITY and the EUROPEAN FREE TRADE ASSOCIATION. This pact, agreed to in 1991 and set to take effect in 1993, effectively incorporates the EFTA into the EC. This plan will increase the land area of the EC by more than 50 percent, but the additional gross national product represented by the EFTA is only a 14 percent increase. Nonetheless, this will be the world's biggest free trade area, with 380 million consumers and 46 percent of world trade.

European Economic Community (EEC)   *See* COMMON MARKET.

European Fighter Aircraft Agreement   The 1988 arrangement among Great Britain, Italy, Spain, and West Germany for the jointly manufactured European Fighter Aircraft (EFA) to meet Western European needs in the 1990s. The cost for each country of the EFA's production has been set at the same percentage of the 800 scheduled aircraft that each country will take. Therefore, Great Britain and Germany will each pay 33 percent, Italy will pay 21 percent, and Spain will pay 13 percent. While each will build parts of the airframe or engine, there will be four assembly plants, one in each participating country. However, in early 1992 Germany, pressed for cash because of the costs of unification, withdrew from the agreement—thus throwing the whole project in doubt. The remaining states in the group (Britain, Italy, and Spain) then had to decide if it was economically possible to continue with the EFA without Germany. When a less-expensive version of the fighter was agreed upon, Germany returned to the consortium in late 1992.

European Free Trade Association (EFTA)   A regional organization established in 1959 as an alternative to the COMMON MARKET. The EFTA provides a free trade area for industrial products among member countries. Unlike the European Economic Community, EFTA members did not set a common external tariff and did not include agricultural trade. The original members (Austria, Denmark, Great Britain, Norway, Portugal, Sweden, and Switzerland) were referred to as "The Seven" (or "The Outer Seven"), in contrast to "The Six" original members of the Common Market. By 1990 the EFTA had seven members (Austria, Finland, Iceland, Liechtenstein, Norway, Sweden, and Switzerland). In January 1984 free trade in industrial goods was established between the EUROPEAN COMMUNITY and the EFTA states. In 1991 the EFTA agreed to merge with the EC by 1993.

European Monetary Cooperation Fund (EMCF)   A fund for the settlement of claims by the central banks of COMMON MARKET countries on each other resulting from intervention under the EUROPEAN MONETARY SYSTEM. The EMCF, originally created in 1973, is intended eventually to become a European Monetary Fund analogous to the International Monetary Fund. The EMCF is also known by its French acronym FECOM (*Fonds Europèen de Cooperation Monetaire*).

European Monetary System (EMS) The monetary system adopted in 1979 by the EUROPEAN COMMUNITY to establish closer financial cooperation and create stable exchange rates in the EC. The EUROPEAN CURRENCY UNIT (ECU) is used as the denominator of the EMS exchange rate mechanism; each national currency was related to the ECU and to the other EMS currencies in a parity grid, an arrangement that fixed the relative values of each currency vis-à-vis each other. Each nation's CENTRAL BANK had to maintain its place on the grid by being in effect the buyer of last resort, by buying its currency at the parity rate on demand. In 1992 Italy and the United Kingdom found it too expensive to maintain their currencies at parity with the German mark. So, in September 1992, complaining about high German interest rates, they withdrew from the EMS, leaving its future in doubt. *Compare to* SNAKE, THE.

European Monetary Union (EMU) The EUROPEAN COMMUNITY's long-range goal for a common currency managed by a single central bank. The EMU was first endorsed at a summit meeting at The Hague in 1969 but was not formally agreed to until the 1991 MAASTRICHT TREATY.

European NATO All members of the NORTH ATLANTIC TREATY ORGANIZATION except for the United States and Canada. Although European NATO is not, as such, a formal subgrouping within NATO, certain institutions, such as the WESTERN EUROPEAN UNION, serve to express and coordinate specifically European interests.

European Nuclear Disarmament (END) A movement created in response to public concern over deployment of new nuclear weapons in Western Europe during the late 1970s. Founded in 1980, and based in the United Kingdom, END has more wide-ranging aims than the older CAMPAIGN FOR NUCLEAR DISARMAMENT. END has called for a nuclear-free Europe and made contacts with peace movements in Eastern Europe.

Considerable suspicion fell on END because these activities coincided with a period when the Soviet Union was trying to play up Western European antinuclear sentiment to bolster its position in the INF negotiations with the United States. In fact, the movement owed more to Ronald Reagan than it did to the KGB, but the coincidence of END's activities with Soviet propaganda damaged its credibility. Nevertheless, END's goals were substantially achieved with the end of the COLD WAR and the announcements by the United States and the Soviet Union that they would be withdrawing all their European-based nuclear weapons. Of course, those withdrawals still leave in place the independent nuclear deterrents located in France, Great Britain, and the former Soviet Union.

European Parliament One of the five major institutions of the EUROPEAN COMMUNITY. Although chiefly a deliberative body that meets in both Luxembourg and Strasbourg, France, it has the right to question the EUROPEAN COMMISSION and the COUNCIL OF MINISTERS, to dismiss the commission, and to reject the community budget. Before June 1979 the parliament consisted of 198 members appointed by the national parliaments of their respective countries. Direct elections were held in 1979, and the size of the parliament was more than doubled. In 1982 the parliament passed legislation for a community-wide uniform system of proportional representation. The SINGLE EUROPEAN ACT creates a true legislative role for the European Parliament.

European Recovery Program *See* MARSHALL PLAN.

European Regional Development Fund A fund established by the Council of Ministers on March 18, 1975, to support development projects in backward areas and thereby reduce regional economic imbalances in the EUROPEAN COMMUNITY. The EUROPEAN COMMISSION, which administers the fund, is empowered to give fund money to member governments, chiefly on the basis of fixed national quotas for specific investment projects. In 1979 a nonquota system was also introduced, providing for the financing of specific EC measures to aid areas in more than one country affected by the same problem.

European Security Conference   *See* HELSINKI ACCORDS.

European Security Identity   *See* EUROPEAN DEFENSE IDENTITY.

European Social Charter   *See* SOCIAL CHARTER.

European Strategy Group (ESG)   A nongovernmental group founded in 1985 and funded by private sources that brings together senior European research specialists on security issues. These are drawn mainly from European research institutes such as CHATHAM HOUSE and similar "think tanks" in France, Germany, Great Britain, and Italy. The purpose of the ESG is to provide a framework for collaborative European research on European, Atlantic, and East-West security issues. It provides a collaborative counterpart to a similar group in the United States known as the Aspen Strategy Group.

European Unit of Account (EUA)   A common accounting measure adopted by the COMMON MARKET in 1971. The EUA was originally established as equivalent to the U.S. dollar; subsequently its value fluctuated daily in terms of a basket of currencies of the members of the European Economic Community. In 1979, with the creation of the EUROPEAN MONETARY SYSTEM, the EUA was replaced by the ECU (EUROPEAN CURRENCY UNIT).

Eurospeck   A tiny part of one European state located within the borders of a different state. According to *The Economist* (July 16, 1988), "Baarle-Hertog, for example, is a patch of Belgium in Holland; Campion d'Italia is an Italian enclave in Switzerland, Büsingen a West German one; Kleinwalsertal is a bit of Austria accessible only from West Germany. And there is Llivia, a totally Spanish (sorry, Catalan) town three miles inside France, which has been an enclave for 328 years and has every intention of staying one." Citizens of Eurospecks have the same rights as the citizens of the larger states that exercise sovereignty in them. While once significant causes of quarrels between states, Eurospecks are now historical anomalies

that will become less important as Europe becomes more integrated.

Eurostat   The statistical agency of the EUROPEAN COMMUNITY, located in Luxembourg.

Eurostrategic   A concept applied to short- and intermediate-range nuclear weapons designed or deployed to be used in a European theater of war. Eurostrategic as a term came into circulation with the Euromissile debate in the late 1970s. It demonstrates the highly relative, even subjective aspect of some strategic thinking. The problem is that, for a long time, strategic weapons were defined as the ICBMs and bombers in the arsenals of the United States and the Soviet Union. These new weapons had the range to hit targets in the Soviet Union as far east as Moscow. Nor surprisingly, the Soviet Union then argued that these are therefore just as much strategic weapons as ICBMs in the U.S. silos. As the Soviet Union's European-deployed SS-20 missiles could not reach the United States, the imbalance does indeed raise problems of fairness in arms control negotiations. Thus from the viewpoint of a European, including a Soviet, all nuclear ballistic and cruise missiles with ranges over a few hundred kilometers are "strategic." What may be a "theater weapon" to one or both superpowers is, in its effect, indistinguishable from a strategic missile to the inhabitants of Europe. Thus Eurostrategic missiles are those than can hit only Western and Eastern Europe.

Euroterrorism   The efforts of usually left-wing terrorists to launch attacks against mainly military, governmental, and corporate targets in Europe. The Euroterrorists include ACTION DIRECTE in France, the RED ARMY FACTION in Germany, and the RED BRIGADES in Italy.

Euzkadi   The Basque name for "homeland," given to the independent Basque nation envisioned by separatists. *See also* ETA.

evaluation   In INTELLIGENCE usage, appraisal of an item of information in terms of its credibility, pertinence, and accuracy. Appraisal is accomplished at several stages within the intelligence cycle with progressively different contexts. Initial evaluations, made by case officers and report officers, focus on the reliability of the source and the accuracy of the information as judged by data available at or close to their operational levels. Later evaluations, by intelligence analysts, are concerned primarily with verifying accuracy of information and may, in effect, convert information into intelligence.

Évian Agreements The 1962 negotiations at Évian, a town on the French side of Lake Geneva, that led to independence for Algeria.

evil empire U.S. President Ronald Reagan's view of the Soviet Union. On March 8, 1983, he told a meeting of the National Association of Evangelists, "While they preach the supremacy of the state, declare its omnipotence over individual man, and predict its eventual domination of all peoples of the earth—they [the Soviet Union] are the focus of evil in the modern world." This became known as the "Evil Empire Speech." Later, as Soviet leader Mikhail Gorbachev began to end the COLD WAR, Reagan diplomatically ceased to describe the Soviet Union as evil. Of course the empire of the Soviet Union, evil or not, ceased to exist altogether by the end of 1991.

Excellency, Your A title used for ambassadors, presidents of republics (except the president of the United States, who is "Mr. President"), cabinet ministers (except for members of the United States cabinet, who are "Mr. or Madame Secretary"), and wives of ambassadors. When Henry A. Kissinger was first designated U.S. Secretary of State on August 23, 1973, reporters asked whether he should be called "Dr. Kissinger" or "Mr. Secretary." He joked: "I don't stand on protocol. If you just call me 'Excellency,' that will be sufficient."

exchange control The regulation by governments of the buying and selling of foreign currencies. This is usually invoked to prohibit the flight abroad of capital.

exchange of notes The most common means of formally recording agreements among states; diplomatic NOTES (letters) are exchanged between an ambassador and a foreign minister. Such correspondence typically summarizes something already agreed to by the parties.

exchange permit A government permit sometimes required by the importer's government to enable the importer to convert his or her own country's currency into foreign currency with which to pay a seller in another country.

exchange rate 1. The cost of one CURRENCY in terms of another, that is, the number of units of one currency that may be exchanged for one unit of another currency. With a fixed exchange rate system, the rates are relatively constant and are adjusted only periodically. Such a system is possible only when governments through their CENTRAL BANKS guarantee the rates and become, in effect, the buyers of last resort. This happens only in times of great economic stability. In recent decades the more common practice is to have floating exchange rates where the price of one currency vis-à-vis another fluctuates on a daily basis in response to market conditions. 2. The value of a state's currency in terms of a specified amount of precious metal, usually gold. This GOLD STANDARD was widely used during the nineteenth century but was abandoned prior to World War II.

exclusion zone An area of the ocean that a belligerent state in a war declares to be off limits to all shipping; thus ships discovered to be in such an exclusion zone will be deemed operating in the interests of the enemy and subject to attack. Nonbelligerent nations may not recognize the legitimacy of any such zones that violate their rights as neutrals. These zones were an especially contentious issue in the Persian Gulf during the 1980s, when Iran unilaterally declared a wide area of water to be an "exclusion zone." The United States did not recognize the zone and indeed sent warships to protect neutral shipping. *See also* REFLAGGING.

exclusive economic zone (EEZ) An INTERNATIONAL LAW concept that has evolved since World War II meaning that a state has unilaterally extended its sovereignty to include its adjacent waters. The zone is declared to control the economic resources of the area, generally fishing and mining. The 1982 United Nations Convention on the LAW OF THE SEA formally codified the EEZ concept to allow coastal nations to have exclusive jurisdiction to the seabed and waters up to 200 miles from their shores. However, some nations, most notably the United States, may not accept the UN Convention or recognize the EEZs of other nations.

executive action 1. The last stage of the policy-making process. 2. An intelligence community term for assassination.

executive agreement 1. An international accord that is not embodied in a formal treaty. 2. A device that permits a U.S. president or other head of state to enter into open or secret arrangements with foreign governments without obtaining the approval of their legislature. In the United States there are two broad categories of executive agreements: presidential agreements and congressional-executive agreements. The first are those made solely on the basis of the constitutional authority of the president; the second cover all international agreements entered into under the combined authority of the president and the Congress. The vast majority of executive agreements are entered into in pursuit of specific congressional authority. By the Case Act of 1972, Congress required that the U.S. Secretary of State transmit to the Congress all executive agreements to which the United States is a party no later than 60 days after such agreements have entered into force. The president must report secret agreements only to the foreign relations committees of the two houses. The act did not give Congress the authority to disapprove an executive agreement. Because there is often a thin line between what constitutes an executive agreement a president can make independently and a treaty that must be ratified by the Senate, there is often considerable concern that a president might use executive agreements to avoid the Senate's constitutional role in the foreign relations process. Executive agreement procedures on the U.S. model are not necessary in most states since in a PARLIAMENTARY SYSTEM the executive, the prime minister, automatically speaks with the authority of the legislature.

executive document In the United States a document, usually a treaty, sent to the Senate by the president of the United States for consideration or approval. These are identified for each session of Congress as Executive A, 97th Congress, 1st Session; Executive B, and so on. They are referred to committee in the same manner as other measures. Unlike legislative documents, however, treaties do not die at the end of a Congress but remain live proposals until acted on by the Senate or withdrawn by the president.

executive officer The military term commonly, if informally, used in government offices, for the individual who is just under the boss in the hierarchy and runs the day-to-day operations of the agency.

exequatur A foreign ministry document that authorizes a CONSUL of another state to perform his or her duties. The host state may revoke it at any time. According to Article 12 of the VIENNA CONVENTION ON CONSULAR RELATIONS: "The head of a consular post is admitted to the exercise of his functions by an authorization from the receiving State termed an exequatur, whatever the form of this authorization."

ex gratia An INTERNATIONAL LAW term meaning voluntarily and without admitting legal responsibility. It is used when a government wants to compensate people for an incident but not accept blame. For example, on July 11, 1988, after 290 people were killed on Iran Air Flight 655 when a U.S. warship accidentally shot it down over the Persian Gulf, the United States announced that "ex gratia" compensation would be made to the families of the deceased.

existential deterrence *See* DETERRENCE, EXISTENTIAL.

expatriation 1. The voluntary renunciation of citizenship. 2. The deprivation of citizenship by due process of law. 3. Involuntary exile from one's homeland. 4. Residing abroad.

experts *See* ADVISORS.

export A product sent to a foreign country for sale there. *Compare to* IMPORT.

Export Agreement Act of 1977 *See* BOYCOTT.

export broker A person or organization that brings together buyers and sellers for a fee but does not take part in actual sales transactions.

export commission house   An organization that, for a percentage of the sale, acts as a purchasing agent for a foreign buyer.

export controls   Laws and regulations that limit the type or amount of a product that can be sent out of a country for overseas sale.

export credits   Loans, or loan guarantees, that allow foreign states or corporations to buy the lender's domestic products for overseas sale.

export duty   *See* DUTY, EXPORT.

export guarantee   Insurance against bad debts from foreign buyers of products. To encourage exports, many governments have agencies that, under appropriate conditions, guarantee that exports eventually will be paid for by either the foreign buyer or the guaranteeing agency.

Export-Import Bank (Eximbank)   An independent agency of the U.S. government to facilitate export-import trade. It provides export credits and direct loans to foreign buyers and sells insurance and export guarantees to U.S. manufacturers. The bank's funds are derived from stock subscribed by the U.S. Treasury in 1945 (the year the bank was established), the repayment of loans, interest earnings, and loans from the U.S. Treasury and from private banks; it receives no budgetary appropriations. Reversing its initial intention to abolish the bank, the Reagan Administration used this agency as an instrument in its efforts to promote international rescue packages for Latin American debtor nations. Many other states have organizations that perform similar functions but are not necessarily called banks. For example, in the United Kingdom the Ministry of Trade and Industry has an Export Credits Guarantee Department that encourages British exports by offering similar export guarantees.

export license   A document issued by a government that permits the "licensee" to engage in the shipping of designated goods to certain foreign destinations.

export management company (EMC)   A private company that functions as the export department for several manufacturers, soliciting and transacting export business on behalf of its clients in return for a commission, salary, or retainer plus commission. Also known as an *export trading company*.

export processing zone   An area within a state wherein corporations are given major tax concessions to encourage foreign companies to locate there and produce or assemble goods for domestic and foreign consumption.

export quota   A specific restriction or target objective on the value or volume of exports of specified goods imposed by a government on domestic producers. Such restraints may be designed to protect domestic producers and moderate world prices of specified commodities. Commodity agreements sometimes contain explicit provisions to indicate when export quotas should go into effect among producers. Export quotas also are used in connection with ORDERLY MARKETING AGREEMENTs and VOLUNTARY RESTRAINT AGREEMENTs.

exports, visible   Tangible items such as consumer goods, industrial machinery, and so on, that are physically shipped to a foreign market for sale. These are in contrast to "invisible exports" such as bank, insurance, tourism, and other services that cannot be seen as they cross borders.

export subsidy   A special government incentive to encourage increased foreign sales. It is usually a direct government payment or other economic benefit given to domestic producers of goods that are sold in foreign markets. The GATT recognizes that export subsidies may distort trade, unduly disturb normal commercial interests, and hinder the achievement of GATT objectives, but it does not clearly define what practices constitute export subsidies. *Compare to* DUTY, COUNTERVAILING.

export trading company (ETC)   *See* EXPORT MANAGEMENT COMPANY.

expropriation   The taking of private property by a government, which may or may not pay a portion of its value in return. For example, when a revolutionary Communist government comes to power (as has happened in 1917 in Russia, 1949 in China, and 1959 in Cuba), it may take over, in the name of the people, the property of the previous ruling classes. *Compare to* NATIONALIZATION.

extended deterrence   *See* DETERRENCE, EXTENDED.

external delegation   EUROPEAN COMMUNITY representatives to international organizations and non-EC states. These are permanent offices that operate as EC embassies.

Extraditables   The MEDELLIN CARTEL'S shadow organization for conducting NARCO-TERRORISM. The group was spawned as a response to the Colombian government's crackdown on cocaine smuggling operations. By 1990 the Extraditables had killed several hundred and wounded several thousand people in more than 200 separate bombings and shootings. Its most heinous crimes were the November bombing of an Avianca jetliner that killed 107 passengers and the truck bombing of a Bogotá police headquarters that killed over 60 persons. In January 1990 the Extraditables approached Colombia's government in search of a deal, declaring that the government had won the drug war. Bogotá rejected the offer.

A new government came to power in August of 1990. When the new president of Colombia, César Gaviria Trujillo (1947–   ), chose to cut back on the war on drug traffickers and scuttle a pending treaty with the United States that would have made it easier to extradite them, narco-terrorism declined sharply. In effect, the new government made a deal with the Extraditables.

extradition   The surrender by one state to another of a person accused or convicted of an offense in the receiving state. Even among long-standing Western allies, requests for the extradition of suspected or even convicted terrorists have proven to be problematic and have led to strained diplomatic relations between nations. For example, in the 1980s Germany refused to extradite to the United States terrorists of Middle Eastern origin because of fears of reprisals against German citizens. Many states, such as Canada, will not extradite someone already serving a life sentence in that state to another country, such as the United States, if the death penalty is at issue. Generally, extradition of criminals from one state to another is not possible unless there exists a preexisting treaty. Even so, most extradition treaties prohibit extraditing people for political crimes. For example, in 1980 Joe Doherty was convicted by the United Kingdom in absentia (without being present at the trial) of killing a British soldier in 1980. After his 1983 arrest in New York, Doherty fought extradition, arguing that since he was a member of the IRISH REPUBLICAN ARMY, the killing was a political crime and therefore exempt from the United States–United Kingdom extradition treaty. Finally the United States in 1992 returned Doherty to the United Kingdom. But the United States did not extradite him. Instead it avoided the whole issue of political crimes and deported Doherty after his request for ASYLUM was refused.

extraterritorial apprehension   A proactive response to TERRORISM by apprehending terrorists outside one's own state and bringing them back for trial. This response raises some difficult issues of domestic and international law. If it is not done within the bounds of extradition laws and treaties, it may amount—legally speaking—to an illegal kidnapping.

extraterritoriality   A state's exercise of its authority and laws outside of its physical limits, such as on its ships at sea, over its own soldiers in foreign countries, and in the residences of its diplomats stationed abroad. There have been occasions when the United States has attempted to apply its export control regulations to firms in other countries to ensure that certain technology is not supplied to a third party. Such claims for extraterritorial jurisdiction, however, do not receive a very enthusiastic response. *Compare to* TERRITORIALITY PRINCIPLE.

F

Fabian Society   An influential group of British socialists at the turn of the twentieth century. It took its name from the ancient Roman general Fabius Maximus, who defeated Hannibal of Carthage by patiently waiting before attacking. The Fabians, many of whom were civil servants, wanted a gradual and democratic approach to major social reform. They were especially interested in collective municipal ownership, which was called gas-and-water socialism. Their better-known members included Sidney and Beatrice Webb, H. G. Wells, and George Bernard Shaw. The Fabian Society still exists but does not enjoy the prominence of influence it had in the early years of the twentieth century.

factor analysis   The practice of understanding events mathematically through labeling them and subjecting them to statistical analysis. Bruce Russett, in *Trends in World Politics* (1965), explained this in terms of using a computer to record United Nations votes, which are then analyzed through factor analysis. The process would tag all votes with a similar underlying pattern of voting, such as that which occurred during the Cold War when Communist nations, NORTH ATLANTIC TREATY ORGANIZATION nations, and the nonaligned nations tended to vote in blocs.

Each of these basic alignments would be identified as representing a different 'factor' or underlying "superissue." This technique allows us to discover both how many such different alignments there actually are and to find the frequency of each. It provides a statistic . . . that expresses the percentage of variation on roll calls in the Assembly that is accounted for by a particular factor or superissue. Also, after identifying the factors we can locate particular nations on these factors by deriving "factor" scores. The factor scores tell us how pro-West, or pro-East, any given country is.

The virtue of this approach is that it goes beyond impressionistic judgments to give an objective view of the subject.

Fahd ibn Abdul Aziz (1922–   )   The current king of Saudi Arabia who succeeded KHALID IBN ABDUL AZIZ in 1982. It was his government that in 1990 asked U.S. and coalition forces to defend the oil-rich kingdom after the Iraqi conquest of Kuwait. After the Iraqis were expelled from neighboring Kuwait during the PERSIAN GULF WAR, his administration helped to get the Arab-Israeli peace process moving at the MADRID CONFERENCE.

fail-deadly   A launch system that allows nuclear weapons to be fired without authoritative consent. If the central government of a state should fail (lose radio contact, be destroyed, etc.), the individual bases containing missiles would be allowed to launch in spite of the absence of specific consent. The decision about whether to have fail-safe or fail-deadly procedures is related to broader issues about centralization versus delegation and to issues of political control and operational autonomy.

fail-safe   **1.** The military procedure by which forces moving to engage an enemy would abort their mission and return to base unless they received formal confirmation of their orders. The main feature of a fail-safe arrangement is the automatic nature of mission cancellation. With the advent of intercontinental bomber forces, fail-safe procedures prevented planes from flying beyond a given geographical point unless the crews received specific orders confirming that they should continue with the attack. **2.** In the context of nuclear weapons, security procedures that attempt to prevent the unintentional launching of a nuclear attack. The logic behind the systems, and hence the term, is that they are all set up so that any failure in the correct procedures makes launch impossible. Additionally, design features ensure that the malfunction of one component cannot result in an unintentional detonation. If the central government of a nation should fail (lose radio contact, be destroyed, etc.), the individual bases containing missiles would be safe because they could not launch in the absence of specific orders. Theoretically the danger with this procedure is that it could encourage an adversary to attempt to destroy the NATIONAL COMMAND AUTHORITY and thereby decapitate its strategic forces. Yet even with a fail-safe system it is possible to have procedures to ensure retaliation.

fair trade **1.** Preferential trade for the products of developing states in the markets of developed states. This is what THIRD WORLD states would like to see as a replacement for FREE TRADE, which they see as having inherent biases against them. The case for the replacement of free trade by fair trade has been argued by the GROUP OF 77 through the UNITED NATIONS CONFERENCE ON TRADE AND DEVELOPMENT (UNCTAD). In essence the argument of Third World states is that the inherent biases of the system must be eliminated through a series of changes including preferential treatment, the stabilization of prices for their exports, and the deliberate expansion of markets for their manufactured goods. **2.** An argument for reciprocity in terms of access to markets. The idea of fair trade is used in this way most often in relation to the lack of access of foreign firms to the Japanese market—although even if greater access is provided, it is not clear how successful the efforts to sell foreign products would be in Japan.

Faisal ibn Abdul Aziz (1906–1975) The king of Saudi Arabia from 1964 until he was murdered by

a nephew in 1975. He was succeeded by KHALID IBN ABDUL AZIZ.

Faisal I (1885–1933) Faisal ibn Hussein, the commander of the ARAB REVOLT against the Turks during World War I, who in 1920 was installed as king of Syria by the British, then was expelled when the French seized control of Syria later in that same year. Again with British assistance, he became king of Iraq in 1921 and ruled until his death. He was succeeded by his son Ghazi, who ruled from 1933 until he was killed in a 1939 automobile accident. Ghazi's son, FAISAL II, then succeeded him.

Faisal II (1936–1958) The grandson of FAISAL I who gained the throne of Iraq when his father was killed in an automobile accident. Only four years old at the time, Faisal II's powers were placed in the hands of a regent. He was not officially crowned until he became 18 years old in 1953. He was assassinated in 1958 and Iraq was proclaimed a republic. *See also* IRAQI COUP.

fait accompli **1.** Something that has already happened, is in place, and is unchangeable without extraordinary effort. A fait accompli places the onus for subsequent action on others. **2.** A one-sided act that suddenly creates a new political and diplomatic situation. The surprising nature of faits accompli can bring surprises of their own. For example, when the Soviet Union deployed nuclear missiles in Cuba, it precipitated the Cuban Missile Crisis of 1962; when the Argentines occupied islands in the South Atlantic that they called the Malvinas, it precipitated the Falklands War of 1982.

FAL *(Fuerzas Amadas de Liberacion)* "Armed Forces of Liberation," a left-wing guerrilla group that during the EL SALVADOR CIVIL WAR was affiliated with the Communist Party of El Salvador; one of the constituent groups in the umbrella organization FMLN.

Falange The Spanish party of FASCISM founded by José Antonio Primo de Rivera (1903–1936). It refused to accept defeat at the polls in 1936, precipitating the Spanish Civil War, and was the only legal political party during the regime of FRANCISCO FRANCO.

Falasha *See* OPERATION MOSES.

Falk, Richard (1938–)   One of the leading figures in the development of the WORLD ORDER approach to international politics, as well as a prolific and critical commentator on the policies of the United States and other governments on such issues as human rights. Among his best-known books are *The Status of Law in International Society* (1970), *Human Rights and State Sovereignty* (1981), and *The End of World Order* (1983). *See also* WORLD ORDER MODELS PROJECT.

Falklands War   The 1982 conflict between Great Britain and Argentina over the sovereignty of a group of islands called the Falklands by the British (the Malvinas by the Argentines) that dates back to the early 1800s when Spain had control of the

A British paratrooper escorts an Argentine prisoner of war. (U.S. Naval Institute)

THATCHER ON THE FALKLANDS WAR
Before and After

BEFORE

The eyes of the world are now focused on the Falkland Islands; others are watching anxiously to see whether brute force or the rule of law will triumph. Wherever naked aggression occurs it must be overcome. The cost now, however high, must be set against the cost we would one day have to pay if this principle went by default. And that is why, through diplomatic, economic and if necessary through military means, we shall persevere until freedom and democracy are restored to the people of the Falkland Islands.

SOURCE: Prime Minister Margaret Thatcher, speech in the House of Commons, April 14, 1982.

AFTER

Early this morning in Port Stanley, 74 days after the Falkland Islands were invaded, General Moore accepted from General Menendez the surrender of all the Argentine forces in East and West Falkland together with their arms and equipment. In a message to the Commander-in-Chief Fleet, General Moore reported: "The Falkland Islands are once more under the Government desired by their inhabitants. God Save the Queen."

SOURCE: Margaret Thatcher, speech in the House of Commons, June 15, 1982.

---

islands. In 1833 British forces occupied the islands and deported the Argentines living there. But Argentina, as the sovereign successor to Spain, continued to claim the islands in spite of the fact that the postdeportation island inhabitants insisted on remaining a British dependency. On April 2, 1982, Argentina's military forces invaded and occupied the Falklands, claiming that they were recapturing them from a colonial power. The British government, taken by surprise, was outraged, especially because Argentina was then ruled by an oppressive military dictatorship. For its part, the junta, led by General Leopoldo Galtieri, did not believe that Great Britain would fight over this issue. But British Prime Minister Margaret Thatcher greatly enhanced her personal popularity by sending an armada to retake the islands, then occupied by about 20,000 Argentine soldiers. The largest naval engagements since World War II were then fought. While the Argentine Air Force, using French Exocet missiles, inflicted severe damage to the British fleet (sinking some destroyers and frigates), the land battle was over quickly; the Argentines formally surrendered on June 14, 1982. About 750 Argentines and 256 British were killed during the war.

The Argentine populace, shocked by the defeat, began to call for the removal of the military government, which had promoted the military action in order to stir national sentiment and draw attention away from the worsening domestic economic crisis. Argentines who had been silenced by the military government also began to agitate for an investigation into those who had DISAPPEARED during the military regime's DIRTY WAR and to call for a return to democracy. Even though the dictatorial regime of General Galtieri was toppled by the war, the subsequent democratically elected government has not dropped its claim to sovereignty over the islands.

fallback position   1. The defensive ground that a military unit takes up after an initial defensive area has been overrun.   **2.** By analogy, in negotiations, a position taken up after one retreats from an earlier stand.   **3.** A contingency plan in the event that things go wrong.

fallout   1. The precipitation to earth of radioactive particle matter from a nuclear cloud.   **2.** The particulate matter itself. Fallout is the secondary consequence of a nuclear explosion, consisting of dust particles and water droplets thrown up into the atmosphere that have been made radioactive by the initial explosion. Some studies of possible fallout in a nuclear war suggest that the amount of fallout particles will cause a devastating NUCLEAR WINTER.

FALN   1. *Fuerzas Amadas de Liberacion Nacional,* "Armed Forces of National Liberation": a Puerto Rican separatist organization, first noticed in 1974 when it bombed five New York City banks. Many of the FALN's operations have been staged against perceived symbols of capitalism and imperialism both in the continental United States and on the island of Puerto Rico itself. The group is believed responsible for more than 100 bombings in Chicago, New York, and Washington. **2.** A Venezuelan Marxist guerrilla group active in the 1960s and early 1970s. By the late 1960s the group had disrupted Venezuelan society to the point where

the government declared a state of siege. Government security forces then focused on halting the FALN and by the mid-1970s rendered it inactive.

Fanon, Frantz Omar (1925–1961)   The French West Indian–born psychiatrist who became a leading ideologist of the FLN during the Algerian revolution. His most important book (which has been very influential in the THIRD WORLD), *The Wretched of the Earth* (1961), argued that only a violent socialist revolution by nonwhite colonial peoples could break the psychological, political, and economic oppression of Europeans: "Violence is a cleansing force. It frees the native from his inferiority complex and from his despair and inaction; it makes him fearless and restores his self-respect."

FAO   *See* FOOD AND AGRICULTURE ORGANIZATION OF THE UNITED NATIONS.

FAR   *See* FORCE D'ACTION RAPIDE.

FARC   *Fuerzas Amadas Revolutionarias de Colombia,* "Revolutionary Armed Forces of Colombia": the largest of the leftist guerrilla movements in Colombia, created in 1966 as the military wing of the Colombian Communist Party. Its primary goal is to overthrow the government and the ruling class. It is pro-Soviet, pro-Cuban, and vehemently anti–United States. Run as a military organization, with an estimated 5,000 members, the FARC is considered the most effective insurgent organization in South America. *See also* M-19; NARCO-TERRORISM.

FARL   *Factions Armees Revolutionaires Libanaises,* "Lebanese Armed Revolutionary Faction," sometimes also called the LARF: a Lebanese left-wing, anti-Zionist terrorist group, created in the late 1970s and dedicated to the establishment of a Marxist-Leninist state in Lebanon. With its roots in the POPULAR FRONT FOR THE LIBERATION OF PALESTINE, the group consists mostly of Lebanese Christians who established the organization's terrorist reputation with a series of killings of U.S. and Israeli diplomats in France. The group has conducted most of its terrorist operations in Western Europe.

FARN   *Fuerzas Amadas de la Resistencia Nacional,* "Armed Forces of National Resistance": a left-wing

Salvadoran guerrilla group (one of the constituent groups in the umbrella organization FMLN) during the EL SALVADOR CIVIL WAR.

Farouk I (1920–1965)   The king of Egypt (1936–1952) whose inept military campaign against Israel in 1948 and internal corruption led to a military coup (led by GAMAL ABDAL NASSER) that forced Farouk's abdication and exile. He then became, in the eyes of the media, the archetypal degenerate playboy ex-king. The only memorable thing he ever said was this supposed analysis of the state of modern monarchy: "There will soon be only five kings left—the Kings of England, diamonds, hearts, spades and clubs."

fascism   **1.** An antidemocratic, antiparliamentary political philosophy that advocates governance by a DICTATOR, assisted by a hierarchically organized, strongly ideological party, to maintain a totalitarian and regimented society through violence, intimidation, and the arbitrary use of power. Often the word is applied broadly to any authoritarian non-Communist regime. In the 1920s and 1930s in Europe, fascist movements justified themselves in part as a means to stop the spread of Bolshevism.   **2.** A mass-based REACTIONARY political movement in an industrialized nation that, through the means of a charismatic leader, espouses nationalism in the extreme. The main difference between totalitarian fascism and totalitarian communism is that fascism professes sympathy toward many aspects of private capitalism and would resolve the conflict between capital and labor by using the government to enforce their relations to one another in the interest of full employment and high productivity. Charismatic leadership is believed to appeal to the irrational and cements the loyalty of the mass public to the nation through its emotional commitment to an individual. Italy's Benito Mussolini (1883–1945) created the prototype of the modern fascist state in the 1920s. The word *fascism* is derived from the official symbol of power and justice of ancient Roman magistrates: a bundle of sticks (fascis) with an ax protruding. Mussolini used this ancient symbol of justice to represent his modern style of tyranny.   **3.** A variant of TOTALITARIANISM. According to Mussolini, in *The Doctrine of Fascism* (1931), "The fascist conception of the state is all-embracing,

A 1937 Soviet cartoon mocks the oppression of Benito Mussolini's fascism. (Library of Congress)

and outside the state no human or spiritual values can exist, let alone be desirable. In this sense Fascism is totalitarian." *See also* AUTHORITARIANISM.

Fatah, al-   The largest organization in the PALESTINE LIBERATION ORGANIZATION, founded in 1957 in Kuwait as an anti-Israeli guerrilla force independent of the control of any Arab state. Led by YASIR ARAFAT since 1964, Fatah emerged as the preeminent PLO group in 1969, allowing Arafat to become chairman of the PLO Executive Committee. Fatah's long-standing goal is to liberate the whole of Palestine and to create in its place a democratic Palestinian state. It holds that liberation can be achieved only by armed struggle with Israel. During the 1960s the organization became known for its small but violent forays into Israeli territory from bases in Jordan. In September of 1970 King Hussein of Jordan responded to confrontations between his troops and Fatah forces by expelling Fatah from Jordanian soil; the vanquished forces retreated to

Syria and Lebanon. BLACK SEPTEMBER, the violent Fatah splinter group that carried out the MUNICH MASSACRE at the 1972 Olympic Games, was born of, and named after, the month of this expulsion. It has sought to function as a separate terrorist wing of the organization in order to give Arafat and the larger PLO a fig leaf of DENIABILITY. Fatah itself carried out terrorist activities in Western Europe and the Middle East in the 1970s and made its training facilities available to a wide array of international terrorists. However, Fatah has never been a true military threat to Israel. The organization was forced to flee its bases in southern Lebanon in 1982, when the Israeli army launched an offensive across the Lebanese border, dispersing Fatah and other PLO groups to Tunisia, South Yemen, Algeria, and a number of other countries throughout the Middle East. The group has been reinfiltrating Lebanon for several years. Its headquarters are currently in Tunis, Tunisia.

Fatah Revolutionary Council (FRC) The terrorist organizations of ABU NIDAL. Nidal and his operatives operate under a variety of organizational guises, which the U.S. Department of State groups together under the umbrella term Abu Nidal Organization, or ANO. The Nidal group typically does not use the FRC name when claiming responsibility for a terrorist attack but instead uses one of its many aliases.

fatwa *See* RUSHDIE, SALMAN.

FECOM *See* EUROPEAN MONETARY COOPORATION FUND.

fedayeen *See* LEBANESE CIVIL WAR.

Federal Bureau of Investigation (FBI) The main investigative arm of the United States Department of Justice. It is responsible for gathering and reporting facts, locating witnesses, and compiling evidence in matters in which the federal government is, or may be, a party in interest. With regard to espionage the FBI is the domestic counterpart of the CENTRAL INTELLIGENCE AGENCY. Only the FBI has the legal authority to engage in counterespionage within the United States. The FBI also directs a Terrorist Research and Analytical Center (TRAC) that gath-

ers intelligence on domestic terrorism, conducts criminal investigations, and makes arrests. The FBI "HURT" (Hostage Response Team) is the primary national antiterrorist hostage rescue unit. Other nations have similar organizations; in the United Kingdom, for example, the parallel agency is MI5.

federalism 1. A governing structure in which a central, overarching government shares power with subnational provincial or state governments. The principal historical reason for the formation of federal systems of government has been a common external threat. Tribes, cities, colonies, or states have joined together in voluntary unions to defend themselves. However, not all systems so formed have been federal. A federal system has the following features: (1) a written CONSTITUTION that divides governing powers between the central government and the constituent governments, giving substantial powers and sovereignty to each; (2) levels of government, through their own instrumentalities, that exercise power directly over citizens (unlike a CONFEDERATION, in which only subnational units act directly on citizens while the central government acts only on the subnational governments); and (3) a constitutional distribution of powers that cannot be changed unilaterally by any level of government or by the ordinary process of legislation. 2. An approach to integration that attempts to link states which are still acknowledged as separate entities through the establishment of some form of power sharing at the center of the federation.

federalism, world An overarching government encompassing all states. The term implies that a worldwide organization, such as the UNITED NATIONS, would someday have enough authority to cope with the inherent anarchy of the international system. World federalism is an idealist concept that has no hope of realization until all states are willing to give up elements of their traditional sovereignty for the general good.

Federal Republic of Germany West Germany; the self-governing state created after World War II in 1949 out of the British, French, and United States zones of occupied Germany. Led by KONRAD ADENAUER, it increasingly allied itself with the West and gained full sovereignty in 1955. Its East German parallel state, created out of the Soviet zone of occupation, was the German Democratic Republic. Both states merged in the GERMAN REUNIFICATION of 1990.

federation **1.** A union of states in which power is shared between the states and a central authority. Generally, the central authority handles such issues as foreign policy security and overall economic policies, and the separate units have authority over other issues. *Compare to* FEDERALISM. **2.** The goal that efforts at regional integration attempt to achieve through constitutional or power-sharing arrangements, as opposed to those of FUNCTIONALISM. A federation differs from a CONFEDERATION in that the latter places much more emphasis on the independence of its members.

feedback A concept derived from SYSTEMS ANALYSIS that refers to the process whereby information about the effect of an action on the environment comes back into the organism (i.e., the group or government), thereby allowing modification of behavior to take place if necessary. This is more likely if there is negative feedback, which suggests that a policy or action is not having the desired effect. If the feedback is positive then the action or policy is more likely to be continued without modification.

fellow traveler **1.** During the COLD WAR, a person sympathetic to Communist ideology but not formally a Communist Party member. **2.** An individual passively in agreement with any cause or group.

FFP *See* FOOD FOR PEACE.

field theory A theory that developed in physics, was then taken over into psychology, and from there was introduced into the analysis of international relations by QUINCY WRIGHT. The essence of this approach was an exploration of the behavior of states in terms of their national attributes within the context of a geographical-social field defined by time and space coordinates.

fifth column A secret band of traitors within a state that commits subversion or sabotage while waiting to join the forces of an invading enemy. The term comes from the Spanish Civil War when General Emilio Mola advanced on Madrid in 1936 with four columns of troops and boasted that a fifth column awaited him within the city. But Peter Wyden's *The Passionate War* (1983) notes: "Mola made the phrase famous but did not coin it. . . . It was first applied to Russian sympathizers within the besieged fortress of Ismail in 1790." During World War II the term came to be used in the United States and Great Britain for anyone secretly sympathetic with the Germans. *Compare to* QUISLING, VIDKUN.

A FAMOUS FIFTH COLUMNIST

The U.S. ambassador in London—Joseph Kennedy, the father of the man who became President—had little faith in Britain's ability to survive, and he didn't mind who knew it. As early as 1 July [1940] the British Prime Minister had written in his diary, "Saw Joe Kennedy who says everyone in the USA thinks we shall be beaten before the end of the month." Now there was only a week of it left. The British Foreign Office heard that Kennedy had summoned neutral journalists to a press conference in order to tell them that Hitler would be in London by 15 August. Such behavior infuriated Foreign Office officials—one wrote, "He is the biggest Fifth Columnist in the country"—but there was little they could do about him.

SOURCE: Len Deighton, *Fighter* (1978).

---

fifth man The last member of the CAMBRIDGE SPY RING. It was long speculated that such a person existed but no one knew for sure until 1991, when John Cairncross admitted that he had been recruited to spy for the Soviet Union at Cambridge University in the 1930s. Later, as a British intelligence agent, he gave secrets to the Soviets. He had been granted immunity from prosecution after secretly admitting his guilt to British authorities many years earlier. When he was 78 years old and living in the south of France he admitted his crimes, stating: "I hope this will finally put an end to the 'fifth man' mystery" (*New York Times*, September 23, 1991).

Fifth Republic The current political system of France that dates from 1958, when a revolutionary authoritarian group seized control of the Algerian administration and threatened mutinies by most of the French Army in Algeria. This proved too much for the FOURTH REPUBLIC, whose premier invited World War II hero General CHARLES DE GAULLE to become prime minister. De Gaulle insisted that a new constitution be drawn up in six months and submitted to a referendum. He and his loyal followers, who were a determined minority in France, felt that the troubles of the previous governments stemmed from undisciplined National Assemblies and a cumbersome multiparty system. The new constitution mandated a hybrid organization with strong presidential powers, a weakened legislature, and a prime minister responsible to the National Assembly. It had the essentials of a democracy—free speech and free elections. When it was approved in a popular referendum by 80 percent of the voters, the Fifth Republic was born.

PRESIDENTS OF THE FIFTH FRENCH REPUBLIC

Name	Term of Office
Charles de Gaulle	1959–1969
Georges Pompidou	1969–1974
Valéry Giscard d'Estaing	1974–1981
François Mitterrand	1981–

---

final act   1. A document that summarizes the binding agreements and obligations of an international conference.   2. The HELSINKI ACCORDS of 1975.   3. The SINGLE EUROPEAN ACT of 1986.

final solution   The term used by Nazi Germany for the murder of all of the Jews of Europe during the HOLOCAUST of World War II. They succeeded in killing 6 million, mostly in CONCENTRATION CAMPS.

finding   1. A decision by a judge or a jury on a question of fact or law.   2. A formal, written, signed-off-on determination of a U.S. president that a COVERT OPERATION of the CENTRAL INTELLIGENCE AGENCY is legal, important to national security, and (according to law) will be reported to the appropriate congressional committee in a timely fashion. Title XXII of the Intelligence Oversight Act of 1980 mandates "a report to the Congress concerning any finding or determination under any section of this chapter. That finding shall be reduced to writing and signed by the president." This law was an effort

---

GOERING'S DIRECTIVE

I herewith commission you to carry out all preparations with regard to . . . a total solution of the Jewish question in those territories of Europe which are under German influence. . . . I furthermore charge you to submit to me as soon as possible a draft showing the . . . measures already taken for the execution of the intended final solution of the Jewish question.

SOURCE: Hermann Goering's July 31, 1941, directive to Reinhard Heydrich, quoted in William L. Shirer's *The Rise and Fall of the Third Reich* (1959). According to Shirer, "Heydrich knew very well what Goering meant by the term [final solution] for he had used it himself nearly a year before at a secret meeting after the fall of Poland, in which he had outlined the first step in the final solution, which consisted of concentrating all the Jews in the ghettos of the large cities, where it would be easy to dispatch them to their final fate."

---

by the U.S. Congress to curb what it considered to be excesses by the CIA around the world.

Finlandization   The restriction of a smaller state's sovereignty by the practical consequences of establishing a MODUS VIVENDI with a larger and stronger neighboring state. The term originated in the relation between Finland and the Soviet Union, in which Finland retained its independence but was tied to the Soviet Union by a 1948 treaty that required Finnish neutrality, limited Finnish foreign policy initiatives, and inhibited domestic political behavior. The potential Finlandization of other close neighbors of the Soviet Union was frequently the subject of international speculation—until the disintegration of the Soviet Union in 1991. While *Finlandization* as a word will have a future as long as strong states seek to inhibit the actions of their weaker neighbors, it is history as far as Finland is concerned. In 1992 Finland signed a treaty with Russia that provided that their future relations will be premised on equality. Most specifically it ends Finland's formal obligation, forced upon it in 1948, to defend the Soviet Union if a third state sought to attack through Finland. Finland is now committed to joining the EUROPEAN COMMUNITY.

Finnish-Russian War   The "winter war" of 1939–1940 that started when JOSEPH STALIN demanded the cession of Finnish territory to the

Soviet Union. When the Finns refused, the RED ARMY invaded on November 30, 1939. The small Finnish army put up an effective resistance, holding off the million-man Soviet force at first; but they were worn down by the effort and forced to accept Soviet demands for bases and territory by early March of 1940. Finland retained its independence and later joined Germany in the 1941 invasion of the Soviet Union. The Red Army's difficulties in Finland in 1939–1940 may have encouraged Adolf Hitler in planning his 1941 invasion. By September 1944 a Soviet-Finnish armistice took Finland out of the war.

Finnish War of Independence   The post–World War I (1918–1920) revolt of the Finnish people against Russian rule, which had begun in 1809. During the upheaval of the civil war that followed the RUSSIAN REVOLUTION OF 1917, the Finns, aided by German troops, defeated the Red Army that was sent against them. The 1920 Treaty of Dorpat recognized their independence.

firebreak   A term taken from forest fire-fighting in which a gap is made in a stand of trees in an effort to limit the spread of fire. A firebreak in the context of war has much the same function and can be understood as something that helps to demarcate and limit the level of hostilities. For example, there is a conceptual firebreak between the use of conventional and nuclear weapons.

First International   *See* INTERNATIONAL, THE.

first strike   1. An attack on an enemy before it can attack, an offensive taken to gain the initial advantage in a battle or war. Famous first strikes at the beginning of a war include the 1941 Japanese attack on Pearl Harbor and the Israeli attack on the Egyptian air force at the start of the Six-Day War. 2. The surprise launching of a nuclear attack against another nuclear power to inhibit its ability to respond in kind.

first-strike capability   The ability of a nuclear armed state to destroy so much of another's retaliatory forces (usually with a surprise nuclear attack) that the other side cannot retaliate effectively. This phrase has been used primarily with reference to the strategic relationship between the United States and

the former Soviet Union. The strategic nuclear policy of the United States is to maintain a SECOND-STRIKE CAPABILITY to encourage DETERRENCE; that is, to maintain nuclear forces in such numbers and variety that no first strike by another side could prevent the United States from then inflicting unacceptable damage on the other side. During the late 1970s nuclear analysts became concerned that the Soviet Union was developing a first-strike capability, thus creating a "window of vulnerability" that Moscow was likely to exploit. Then in the early 1980s it was argued that it was the United States which was closest to acquiring a first-strike capability with the deployment of the MX missile and the Trident submarine. Arguments were greatly exaggerated in both instances. All claims of a first-strike disarming capability rest on outrageously optimistic assumptions and tend to ignore the strong probability of retaliation. What Herman Kahn wrote in *On Escalation* (1965) is still valid: "Almost every analyst is now agreed that the first use of nuclear weapons—even if against military targets—is likely to be less for the purpose of destroying the other's military forces or handicapping its operations, than for redress, warning, bargaining, punitive, fining or deterrence purposes."

first use   A reference to the first use of nuclear weapons in a war. It was usually discussed in the context of a war between the two superpowers or the two COLD WAR blocs in Europe. The North Atlantic Treaty Organization strategy of FLEXIBLE RESPONSE acknowledged that if NATO was unable to resist a Soviet conventional attack, it would then have been forced to introduce nuclear weapons into the conflict. This introduction could either be through some kind of demonstration, intended to persuade the Soviets to desist from further aggression, or it could be designed to influence tactical developments on the battlefield. "First use" is often confused with "first strike," which generally refers to surprise attacks designed to destroy an enemy's strategic retaliatory forces. First use, in contrast, is a much more limited notion as it is only a possible response to aggression. Winston Churchill, in a December 14, 1950, speech in the British House of Commons, offered this counterargument to those who said the West should automatically forgo future first use: "The argument is now put forward that we must never use the atomic bomb until, or unless it has been used against us first. In other words, you must never fire until you have been shot dead. That seems to me a silly thing to say and a still more imprudent position to adopt."

First World The wealthy, industrialized, and largely Western democracies: the United States, Canada, Western Europe, Australia, New Zealand, and Japan. These countries also are referred to as "the North," the OECD countries, or the DEVELOPED COUNTRIES. *See also* FOURTH WORLD; SECOND WORLD; THIRD WORLD.

First World War *See* WORLD WAR I.

Five Power Defense Arrangements The formal understanding among Australia, Great Britain, Malaysia, New Zealand, and Singapore that they will "consult" with one another if Malaysia or Singapore is militarily attacked. The five states conduct joint military exercises each year. The arrangement is less than a treaty or alliance, but it offers Malaysia and Singapore a measure of defense that is definitely psychologically and possibly militarily significant.

Five Power Treaty The WASHINGTON NAVAL CONFERENCE (1921–1922) agreement to limit the naval arms race overall and particularly to reduce Pacific Ocean tensions. Its principal achievement was in limiting the size of capital ships (over 10,000 tons with larger than 8-inch guns) of the major naval powers: the United Kingdom, the United States, Japan, France, and Italy.

five-year plans 1. Economic development plans of the Soviet Union that began under JOSEPH STALIN and emphasized the rapid development of heavy industry. Soviet economists wrote the first five-year plan in 1927 and the Sixteenth Congress of the Soviet Union approved it in 1929. The first plan mandated a doubling in oil production and coal output and a trebling of steel production and electricity. Stalin's collectivization policy in agriculture was meant to supply adequate food supplies to support this rapid industrialization. While the early five-year plans were successful in that they met their goals, successive five-year plans did not stop the Soviet economy from crumbling in ways that

showed that central planning could never substitute for the play of the market. 2. The current economic plans of China that prioritize different sectors of the economy on a medium-term basis.

flag A cloth with distinguishing color or design that has a unique meaning or functions as a signal—traditionally of the nationality of a ship or a military unit. Flags have been used since ancient times for identification. In the twentieth century they have become less important as identifiers and more important as national icons—the most important symbol of the state. Nations adopt flags that reflect their history or culture. Often flags are purposely designed to reflect unity. For example, the flag of the United Kingdom was created in 1606 shortly after England and Scotland were united. The combination of the two national flags created today's Union Flag (or "Union Jack"). The original United States flag designed in 1777 had 13 alternating red and white stripes to represent the unity of the 13 former colonies. With the addition of white stars (to represent each state) in a blue field, the "stars and stripes" has remained the national symbol of the United States.

flag, showing the 1. A state's efforts to make its presence known by sending military units or ships flying its flag, in order to participate in an action or show of fire. 2. High-profile involvement in something by a state, a government agency, or a private company.

flag, striking the The traditional signal of a desire to surrender by lowering one's flag.

flag of convenience The flag of the country in which a merchant ship is registered—rather than in the country where it is owned or does business—to avoid certain fees, safety requirements, and so on; the ship then must legally fly the foreign country's flag. This is different from REFLAGGING, which is a diplomatic undertaking designed to qualify previously ineligible merchant ships for naval protection from friendly powers—whose flag they then fly.

flag officer A traditional military designation for an admiral, because naval ships fly a special flag to indicate an admiral is on board. In this century some states have expanded the meaning to include any officer above the lowest levels of admiral or general.

flag of truce   A white flag carried by a military messenger with an important message, usually having to do with the surrender of one side or the other. Sometimes a flag of truce and an accompanying offer to negotiate are used as a stratagem to gain time. Combatants who carry a flag of truce are traditionally protected from attack or capture.

flexible response   1. The ability of military units to effectively respond to an enemy threat or attack on any scale; to meet an enemy threat with a parallel level of counterthreat. This implies that there is an option to use a variety of conventional forces as well as nuclear weapons as the circumstances warrant. The concept, also known as *graduated response,* is usually credited to U.S. General Maxwell D. Taylor. In his book *The Uncertain Trumpet* (1960) he wrote: "Flexible response should contain at the outset an unqualified renunciation of reliance on the strategy of massive retaliation. It should be made clear that the United States will prepare itself to respond anywhere, any time, with weapons and forces appropriate to the situation." This concept heavily influenced U.S. President John F. Kennedy, who said in his Inaugural Address of January 20, 1961, "We intend to have a wider choice than humiliation or all-out war." **2.** The strategic doctrine of the Kennedy Administration that emphasized the need to be able to match the Soviet Union at any level of capability and options. The idea was that the United States should not have to escalate hostilities because of a lack of options at any particular level of conflict. Implicit in this notion was the possibility that the superpowers could fight a limited war whether at the conventional or the nuclear level. The implication for force posture was that the United States and its allies should augment their conventional forces so that the North Atlantic Treaty Organization would be able to hold Soviet aggression at the conventional level and would not have to use nuclear weapons. This was not welcomed by many Europeans, who saw it as an attempt at DECOUPLING the United States from Europe and at using Europe as a battleground in a superpower conflict.   **3.** The official NATO doctrine adopted in 1967 as a way around the contradictions of maintaining the credibility of the MASSIVE RETALIATION doctrine and of building up an adequate conventional defense against the Warsaw Pact. The argument for this strategy was that it was crucial to present the Soviet Union with risks it would be psychologically unwilling to run. This doctrine also asserted that NATO strategy must be based on the force actually available. Sustained conventional resistance to a Warsaw Pact attack was not a true option, especially after France left the integrated military structure in 1966. NATO's strategy of flexible response was different from the flexible response strategy of the United States as articulated by U.S. Secretary of Defense ROBERT S. MCNAMARA in the early 1960s. Whereas McNamara had advocated sustained conventional resistance as a way of reducing reliance on nuclear weapons, NATO agreed to a strategy that placed more emphasis than in the past on conventional resistance but that also continued to emphasize the possibility of nuclear ESCALATION. The strategy was sometimes described as a mixture of assured response and flexible escalation. Critics argued that NATO was still too dependent on nuclear weapons. Frank Barnaby in *The Automated Battlefield* (1986) quotes Morton Halperin, when he was U.S. Deputy Assistant Secretary of Defense, describing NATO's policy of flexible response: "The NATO doctrine is that we will fight with conventional forces until we are losing, then we will fight with tactical nuclear weapons until we are losing, and then we will blow up the world."

FLN *(Front de Liberation Nationale)*   "National Liberation Front," the Algerian nationalist party created in 1954 to fight for Algeria's independence from France. In response to widespread FLN terrorism, the French took repressive measures against the native population. The FLN's military wing fought a guerrilla war against the French. Algeria's European settlers, through the OAS, responded with mass terrorism of their own. After the eight-year ALGERIAN WAR OF INDEPENDENCE, the FLN won and the new state of Algeria was established in 1962.

FLNC *(Front de Liberation Nationale Corse)*   "Corsican National Liberation Front," a separatist, anti-French organization founded on the Mediterranean island of Corsica in 1976, which has carried out bombings and assassinations in France. *Compare to* FRANCIA.

Florence Agreement   The agreement sponsored by the United Nations Educational, Scientific and Cultural Organization (UNESCO) to facilitate international exchanges of publications, objects of artistic and scientific interest and other materials, and to recommend international agreements that promote the free flow of ideas. The text of the Florence Agreement was adopted unanimously in July 1950 but entered into force in various countries at later dates. The agreement provides for the duty-free entry, under specified conditions, of various categories of intellectual and artistic materials listed in the annexes to the agreement.

FLQ   *See* QUEBEC LIBERATION FRONT.

FMLN (*Frente Farabundo Marti de Liberacion Nacional*)   "Farabundo Marti National Liberation Front," the umbrella organization for five Salvadoran left-wing guerrilla groups formed in 1980 to create a more effective INSURGENCY and as a prerequisite for Cuban military aid and materiel. The FMLN received external support from Communist countries (such as Cuba, the Soviet Union, and Vietnam), which sent arms and supplies primarily through Nicaragua during the EL SALVADOR CIVIL WAR. FMLN members were routinely trained at camps in Nicaragua and Cuba. The primary safe havens for the FMLN were Nicaragua and the ill-defined border region between El Salvador and Honduras. The FMLN regularly conducted guerrilla warfare and actively sought through TERRORISM to prevent the establishment of a legitimate political process in El Salvador. The 1992 peace accord that ended the civil war called for the FMLN to transform itself from an insurgency to a political party.

FNLA   *See* ANGOLAN CIVIL WAR.

Foch, Ferdinand (1851–1927)   The French Army general who, as coordinator and then "supreme generalisimo," led the Allies to final victory over Germany in World War I. This began with the French victory in the 1918 Second Battle of the Marne. Foch kept the initiative afterward, helped in large measure by the newly arrived U.S. Army and masses of newly invented tanks. Foch accurately predicted, upon reviewing the 1919 Treaty of Versailles, "This is not peace. This is an armistice for twenty years" (quoted in Paul Seabury and Angelo Codevilla, *War*, 1989).

foco   Spanish for a small rural group that both lives together and conducts military operations as a single guerrilla unit. The foco, which is a concept that came from FIDEL CASTRO and his 1950s Cuban revolution, is asserted to be the necessary basis of a successful guerrilla movement. The small group, because it acts as a focal point for discontent, is supposed to help create the conditions for a successful revolution. ERNESTO "CHE" GUEVARA, Castro's revolutionary colleague, tried to expand the concept to Bolivia in the early 1960s but failed. *See also* GUERRILLA WARFARE, RURAL.

FOFA   *See* FOLLOW ON FORCES ATTACK.

foggy bottom   A irreverent phrase for the U.S. State Department, because its current building is located on a site known locally as "Foggy Bottom" that was once a swamp. (It is now drained.) The term lives on, because "foggy" aptly describes the kinds of pronouncements so often necessitated by diplomacy.

fog of war   The descriptive phrase for the confusion and uncertainty that is an inherent factor of combat. It is as if a literal fog descends upon the battlefield and blinds the combatants to what the enemy and even other elements of their own forces are doing. In the days of black gunpowder, the fog was almost as literal as it was proverbial. Battlefields were so covered in smoke from cannon and rifle fire that the air became too thick for visibility. This accounts for British Admiral Horatio Nelson's famous instructions to his captains that in the event of signals being invisible through the smoke of battle, "No captain can do very wrong if he places his ship alongside that of an enemy."

Prussian General Karl von Clausewitz is often credited with coining the phrase "fog of war." In *On War* (1832) he wrote: "War is the province of uncertainty; three-fourths of the things on which action in war is based lie hidden in the fog of a greater or less certainty." But the idea was found in print more than 100 years earlier. For example, Chevalier Folard in *Nouvelles Découvertes sur la Guerre* (1724) wrote that in war "one only sees things imperfectly and in a fog."

The fog of war is no less important a concept today. The black powder is gone but battlefields have so expanded that it is even more difficult for individual unit and overall commanders to assess what is going on. Enhanced electronic communications make it ever easier for the highest ranks to talk to the lowest. But new technology will never completely dissipate the fog because it thrives in uncertainty. And as French Marshal Ferdinand Foch was so fond of saying: "The unknown is the governing condition of war." *Compare to* FRICTION.

follow on forces attack (FOFA)   The official NORTH ATLANTIC TREATY ORGANIZATION doctrine during the COLD WAR for repelling a conventional Soviet attack on Western Europe. It was based on the assumption that NATO forces would be able to hold the first wave of a Soviet attack but not the second echelon. Therefore, it was important to prevent Soviet reinforcements from arriving by interdicting the concentrated Soviet forces and by disrupting key Soviet CHOKE POINTS. Advances in the technologies of target acquisition, precision guidance and discrimination, it was argued, would make it possible to destroy both static and mobile targets at considerable distances from the forward edge of the battle area. FOFA was essentially a plan to attack the second and subsequent Soviet echelons by air power and missiles before they reached the main land battle. Then NATO armies would have to deal only with the first-echelon troops.

Food and Agriculture Organization of the United Nations (FAO)   One of 16 SPECIALIZED AGENCIES of the United Nations, the FAO was founded at a conference in Quebec, Canada, on October 16, 1945. Since 1979 that date has been observed annually as World Food Day. The FAO works to raise levels of nutrition and standards of living; to improve the production, processing, marketing, and distribution of food and agricultural products from farms, forests, and fisheries; to promote rural development and improve the living conditions of rural populations; and, through these means, to eliminate hunger. To achieve these goals, the FAO undertakes programs to promote investment in agriculture; better soil and water management; improved yields of crops and livestock; the transfer of technology to, and development of agricultural research in, developing countries. With its headquarters in Rome, Italy, the General Conference of the FAO, composed of all UN member nations, meets every other year while its council, consisting of 49 member nations elected by the conference, serves as the governing body between conference sessions.

Food for Peace (FFP)   The United States government's overseas food donation program launched in 1954. Under this program, U.S. agricultural surpluses are donated to "friendly governments" through nonprofit relief organizations or voluntary agencies, such as CARE or the Catholic Relief Services. The program is administered jointly by the Agency for International Development and the U.S. Department of Agriculture.

food weapon   The use of food by states with an agricultural abundance to influence the foreign policy of states needing to import food to feed its population. The United States was able to use the supply of grain to the Soviet Union as an incentive for Moscow to enter into a more regularized détente relationship. It has been argued that the United States and Europe should use its food resources more aggressively to obtain additional influence in the Third World. But food is a weapon that must be used with great subtlety. Famine relief may not bring immediate gratitude, but it can be the start of a long-range constructive relationship for both the giver and receiver. Thus food becomes not so much a weapon as a diplomatic tool.

football   A slang term for the briefcase, carried by a military officer, that follows the president of the United States at all times. It contains the secret launch codes needed to initiate a nuclear attack and is also known as the *doomsday briefcase*.

Football War   The brief war between El Salvador and Honduras that erupted after the Honduran national soccer team beat the El Salvador team in a 1969 World Cup preliminary game. But the under-

---

PRESIDENT REAGAN'S FOOTBALL

As President, I carried no wallet, no money, no driver's license, no keys. But wherever I went, I carried a small plastic-coated card, and a military aide was always close by carrying a small bag referred to as "the football." It contained directives for launching our nuclear weapons, and the plastic card listed codes confirming that it was actually the President of the United States who was ordering the unleashing of these weapons. The decision to launch was mine alone to make.

SOURCE: Ronald Reagan, *An American Life* (1990).

---

lying cause was a boundary dispute and the destabilization created by several hundred thousand workers from El Salvador living illegally in Honduras. In response to the riots, the El Salvadoran Army crossed its border into Honduras on July 14. After 3,000 people died, the ORGANIZATION OF AMERICAN STATES arranged a cease-fire on July 16 and branded El Salvador as the aggressor. El Salvador did not withdraw all its forces from Honduras until August. In 1980 the two states finally signed a peace treaty ending the formal state of war that had existed since 1969.

force   Organized violence or use of military instruments by states to achieve their foreign policy and security objectives. Ironically, states resort to force both as a continuation of their policy and as a reflection of the fact that they have failed to attain these objectives by nonforcible means. As well as being used directly to take things, force also can be threatened. Indeed, as Thomas Schelling noted in *Arms and Influence* (1966), it is cheaper and easier to make someone give you what you want rather than to have to take it for yourself.

Force d'Action Rapide (FAR)   The French army's "Rapid Action Force," about 40,000 troops organized in the early 1980s by the socialist government of President François Mitterand so that France would have the capability for rapid intervention in Europe or elsewhere. France's allies viewed the force as demonstrating a willingness to come rapidly to the aid of North Atlantic Treaty Organization forces in an emergency. It also represents France's increased interest in having a force projection capacity to intervene out of the European theater.

force de frappe   The original name for France's strategic nuclear force. Created by CHARLES DE GAULLE to build on a program initiated under the FOURTH REPUBLIC, it was an expression of French independence from U.S. and Soviet superpower influence in Europe and the rest of the world. French nuclear capability was justified by the argument that the U.S. nuclear umbrella over North Atlantic Treaty Organization states lacked credibility because of the growing Soviet nuclear arsenal. The political rationale for the *force de frappe* was the same that led de Gaulle to withdraw from NATO's integrated military structure in 1966: the greater independence of France in world affairs. France's strategic forces are now more often described as a *force de dissuasion,* a "deterrent force." In 1992 French President François Mitterrand offered a reappraisal of French nuclear defense policy and suggested for the first time that French nuclear weapons might be integrated—at some unspecified time in the future—with those of other European Community states. Mitterrand said that it is well known that Great Britain and France have a clear nuclear doctrine for their national defense. Then he asked: "Is it possible to imagine a European doctrine? That question will very quickly become one of the major issues in the construction of a European defense" (*The Economist,* January 18, 1992).

force majeure   1. French for "superior or irresistible force"; compelling circumstances. Force majeure describes the brutal reality by which things are often accomplished in international relations; it is an underlying influence in all negotiations when one state has the obvious force to impose its will. 2. The title of a standard clause in some contracts exempting the parties for nonfulfillment of their obligations as a result of conditions beyond their control, such as earthquakes, floods, or war.

force multiplier   Any piece of technology that allows a smaller body of soldiers or set of tanks, artillery, fighter aircraft, and so on to defeat a larger force of similar type. While the concept is new, the phenomenon is as old as warfare itself, particularly if innovations in tactics also are classed as force multipliers. The development of the phalanx formation by ancient Greek soldiers, which allowed them to overcome larger numbers of less well-organized enemies, is an early example. At a technological level, the most obvious examples are the small units of European soldiers, with rifles and machine guns, that could often defeat large numbers of primitively armed natives in colonial battles. Force multipliers were much in evidence during the Persian Gulf War when the high-technology weapons and tactics of the United Nations coalition offset the local numerical superiority of Iraqi troops.

force projection The ability to send military forces to distant locations and, if necessary, land them under fire in order to engage the local enemy. Such capacity is the classic requirement of a state that wishes to be able to exert influence on a worldwide scale. The whole concept of force (or *power*) projection was well summed up at the beginning of this century when British diplomat Edward Grey (1862–1933) asserted that the British army should be "a projectile to be fired by the Navy" (quoted in Keith Robbins, *Sir Edward Grey,* 1971).

force ratio The numerical comparison of troops or equivalent pieces of equipment between two sides. Force ratios are a common way to measure the relative strength of opposing forces. The conventional superiority of the Warsaw Pact over the North Atlantic Treaty Organization was often expressed in terms of such simplistic ratios. But force ratios can be deceptive. As analyst Ardant du Picq wrote

---

KHRUSHCHEV ON FORCE RATIOS

You can no longer calculate the alignment of forces on the basis of who has the most men. Back in the days when a dispute was settled with fists or bayonets, it made a difference who had the most men and the most bayonets on each side. Then when the machine gun appeared, the side with more troops no longer necessarily had the advantage. And now with the atomic bomb, the number of troops on each side makes practically no difference to the alignment of real power and the outcome of a war. The more troops on a side, the more bomb fodder.

SOURCE: Nikita Khruschev, *Khruschev Remembers* (vol. 1, 1971).

---

in *Battle Studies* (1868): "What good is an army of two hundred thousand men of whom only one-half really fight, while the other one hundred thousand disappear in a hundred ways? Better to have one hundred thousand who can be counted upon."

Force 17 A PALESTINE LIBERATION ORGANIZATION group created in the early 1970s as a personal security force for YASIR ARAFAT. In 1985 it began to launch attacks against targets in Israel. In September of that year the organization killed three Israelis in Cyprus. This prompted an Israeli air raid on PLO bases in Tunisia.

Ford, Gerald R. (1913–   ) The president of the United States (1974–1977) after RICHARD M. NIXON resigned in disgrace because of the Watergate scandals. Ford was appointed vice president by Nixon in 1973, with the consent of the Congress, to replace Spiro Agnew, who had earlier resigned in disgrace. Ford was narrowly defeated for election in his own right when he ran against JIMMY CARTER in 1976. Ford is the only person to have served as U.S. president without election to that office by the people. In foreign policy Ford continued the policies of the Nixon Administration, a continuity that was symbolized by the continued role of HENRY A. KISSINGER as secretary of state. The Ford DÉTENTE policy, however, ran into trouble domestically because of Soviet involvement in the ANGOLAN CIVIL WAR. In the 1976 presidential campaign Ford, who was being attacked from the Republican right as well as from some Democrats for being soft on the Soviet Union, banned the word *détente* from his political vocabulary.

foreign 1. Concerning other states. 2. Strange; external to one's native land.

foreign affairs 1. International relations; the activities of states with one another. 2. Sexual liaisons between individuals from different states.

Foreign Affairs A U.S. journal published by the Council on Foreign Relations since 1922. It has traditionally been the most prestigious of all international relations journals, wherein foreign ministers and even heads of state publish their analyses of current issues. Critics sometimes complain that the

Vice President and Mrs. Gerald R. Ford escort President and Mrs. Richard M. Nixon from the White House on the day of Nixon's resignation, August 9, 1974. (Copyright The Washington Post; reprinted by the permission of the D.C. Public Library)

contributors are often more distinguished than the contributions. This is somewhat unfair as *Foreign Affairs* continues to provide an excellent sense of the key issues facing the United States and the international community.

foreign aid All government grants and concessional loans (i.e., loans made with terms lower than commercial rates), in currency or in kind, broadly aimed at transferring resources from developed to less-developed countries for the purposes of economic development or income distribution. Foreign aid may be bilateral (from one country to another) or multilateral (distributed through international financial institutions, such as the World Bank or the International Monetary Fund). Foreign economic assistance may be given as project aid (wherein the donor provides money for a specific project, such as a dam or a school) or as program aid (wherein the donor does not know what projects the money will be spent on). Economic assistance consists of both hard loans (at commercial bank interest rates) and soft loans (concessional, or at low interest rates).

Aid may be tied to multilateral aid agencies (the loans may be partially financed by the recipient country), or aid may be tied in bilateral arrangements (the money must be spent on procurement in the donor country or must be transported by the donor country's shipping).

Countries give foreign aid for various reasons: to give humanitarian assistance after wars or natural disasters; to strengthen allies militarily against external or internal threats; to promote the economic development of the recipient country (this type of aid is often called development assistance); or simply to meet the basic needs of the poor citizens of the recipient country. The first significant instance of foreign aid was that given by the United States to its allies during and right after World War I. But this was ad hoc. Not until the Truman Administration did foreign aid, in the form of the MARSHALL PLAN, become institutionalized and a continuous part of American foreign policy.

foreign aid, prestige Aid that is not meant for economic or social development but for political payoffs or diplomatic bribery. For example, it could take the form of a helicopter fleet for the personal use of a Third World dictator.

foreign exchange 1. The CURRENCY or credit instruments of a foreign state; cash in foreign currencies. 2. Transactions involving the purchase and/or sale of currencies. *See also* DEVALUATION; EXCHANGE RATE.

foreign exchange controls Governmental restrictions on the use of specified types of currency, bank drafts, or other means of payment in order to regulate imports, exports, and the balance of payments.

foreign investment The purchasing of corporations and properties in a state by individuals or corporations from another state. Historically, this has been a major avenue of economic development. Many states have laws that limit foreign direct investment, the practice of multinational corporations creating subsidiaries in other than their home states. The main advantage of foreign investment is that it creates jobs and economic growth—both highly desirable from the point of view of the host country. But many states, especially those in the THIRD WORLD, are very sensitive to the exploitative possibilities of foreign investment. They often resent large profits sent out of their state instead of being reinvested there and dislike the loss of control over local industry implied by foreign ownership.

foreign legion 1. A military unit serving outside its homeland. 2. A military unit consisting of foreign nationals, not of the citizens of the nation it serves. 3. The French Foreign Legion, which both served outside its homeland and was made up of foreign nationals. However, since the end of the French colonial wars in the 1960s, the legion has been headquartered in France.

foreign ministry A governmental department that is charged with the management of international affairs; the agency in most governments that corresponds to the U.S. Department of State and the British Foreign Office.

foreign office 1. The British foreign ministry (formally the Foreign and Commonwealth Office). It is equivalent to the U.S. Department of State. 2. Any nation's foreign ministry. A foreign office is the department of government that has the primary responsibility for the conduct of foreign policy. Foreign offices vary greatly in size and shape but are generally organized along both geographic and functional lines. They cover the whole network of information and advice that starts with cables and other reports from one's embassies in other countries and is enshrined in analyses and recommendations for the government official in charge of foreign policy as well as the prime minister or president.

foreign policy All of a state's relations with and policies toward other states. Often this is a matter of bargaining. That is why Italian dictator BENITO MUSSOLINI once told British Foreign Secretary George Curzon (1859–1925) that "my foreign policy is 'nothing for nothing' " (quoted in George Seldes, *Sawdust Caesar,* 1938). Mussolini knew, even though he did not turn out to be an astute practitioner of the art, that the essence of foreign policy was gaining an advantage for one's own state while giving as little as possible in return. Of course, what political leaders often rationalize as a deliberate, well-thought-out foreign policy is in reality what British diplomatic historian Harold Nicolson (1886–1968) has called a fortuitous "chain of circumstances" (*The Congress of Vienna,* 1946).

According to George F. Kennan's *Realities of American Foreign Policy* (1954): "A political society does not live to conduct foreign policy; it would be more correct to say that it conducts foreign policy in order to live." A nation's foreign policy, even though it may be largely the prerogative of an executive branch, is always grounded in its domestic policy. Two-time U.S. presidential candidate Adlai E. Stevenson wrote in *What I Think* (1956): "We cannot be any stronger in our foreign policy—for all the bombs and guns we may heap up in our arsenals—than we are in the spirit which rules inside the country. Foreign policy, like a river, cannot rise above its source." And U.S. Secretary of State Henry Kissinger has said essentially the same thing: "No foreign policy—no matter how ingenious—has any chance of success if it is born in the minds of a few and carried in the hearts of none" (*Washington Post,* August 4, 1973). The other major tenet of foreign policy on which there is general agree-

MAYBE IT'S A CASE OF TOO MANY COOKS.

A contemporary cartoon shows U.S. President Franklin D. Roosevelt brewing the foreign policy soup. (Library of Congress)

international relations focuses on foreign policy. It is commonly known as foreign policy analysis.

THE CHAIN OF CIRCUMSTANCE IN FOREIGN POLICY

Nobody who has not watched "policy" expressing itself in day-to-day action can realize how seldom is the course of events determined by deliberately planned purpose, or how often what in retrospect appears to have been a fully conscious intention was at the time governed and directed by that most potent of all factors—"the chain of circumstance." Few indeed are the occasions on which any statesman sees his objective clearly before him and marches towards it with undeviating stride; numerous indeed are the occasions when a decision or an event, which at the time seemed wholly unimportant, leads almost fortuitously to another decision which is no less incidental, until, little link by link, the chain of circumstance is forged.

SOURCE: Harold Nicolson, *The Congress of Vienna* (1946).

ment is Hans J. Morgenthau's assertion (from *Politics Among Nations*, 5th ed., 1978), "The objectives of foreign policy must be defined in terms of national interest."

To understand foreign policy in more fundamental ways, however, it is necessary to go beyond bland appraisals and generalities. In this connection, there are various ways in which foreign policy can be approached and understood. One way is to see it in terms of several levels, ranging from broad aspirations and the general orientation of the state toward its international environment to specific actions designed to deal with particular problems or achieve specific goals. K. J. Holsti's *International Politics: A Framework for Analysis* (1972) divides foreign policy into four elements: foreign policy orientations, national roles, objectives, and actions. Foreign policies can differ in the mix of active and reactive elements, in the extent to which states support the status quo or pursue revisionist or even revolutionary objectives, and in the impact that policies have on the international system or on other states. As for the making of foreign policy, this is generally discussed in terms of formulation and implementation. In view of all this, it is not surprising that a field of study in

Foreign Policy   The journal, published quarterly, of the Carnegie Endowment for International Peace; published since 1970. Considered essential reading by many government officials, foreign policy analysts, and members of the press, particularly in the United States, where it originates.

foreign policy oversight   The total process by which a national legislature, through its various committees, continuously monitors the administration of its state's foreign policies. The information gained from hearings and investigations presumably leads to remedial legislation.

foreign relations   1. The relationship and dealings between independent states. 2. The academic study of foreign policies. *See also* FOREIGN POLICY.

foreign secretary   A state's senior foreign policy official or minister, who reports to the head of government. The SECRETARY OF STATE is the foreign secretary of the United States. Harold Macmillan, during his tenure as the British foreign secretary, once summed up the continuing dilemma of all foreign secretaries in a speech in the House of Commons on July 27, 1955: "A Foreign Secretary . . . is always faced with this cruel dilemma. Nothing he can say can do very much good, and almost anything he may say may do a great deal of harm. Anything he says that is not obvious is dangerous; whatever is not trite is risky. He is forever poised between the cliché and the indiscretion."

foreign service 1. A corps of professional diplomats; all of the diplomats of a state stationed both home and abroad. They may be organized as a separate diplomatic or foreign service, or simply integrated with the regular civil service of a nation. Merit-based (as opposed to political patronage) systems for selecting diplomats based on competitive examinations are relatively new. The Rogers Act of 1924 combined U.S. diplomatic and consular services into the present U.S. Foreign Service, the diplomatic corps, known as Foreign Service Officers (FSOs), responsible for administering U.S. foreign policies. While most U.S. ambassadors gain their positions through a long career in the Foreign Service, historically a significant number of them are patronage appointees whose only outward qualification for the job is a demonstrated ability to make large campaign contributions to the party in power. While many distinguished outsiders have been appointed to ambassadorships, the de facto selling of these offices is a continuous, if quiet, bipartisan national scandal. In 1943 the United Kingdom combined its Foreign Office and Diplomatic Service, its Consular Service, and its Commercial Diplomatic Service into the British Diplomatic Service. In 1965 the Commonwealth Service and the Trade Commissioner Service were also brought into the Diplomatic Service. 2. Military or civilian service in foreign locations.

foreign sovereign immunity The principle that the judicial processes of one state cannot be imposed on other states. This leads to the effective immunity of states—as well as their agents and property—from the judicial process of others. As governments have become more involved in regulation, however, the notion of absolute immunity has given way, in some instances, to more restrictive notions of immunity. For example, the United States Congress, in 1976, passed the Foreign Sovereign Immunities Act which reaffirmed that only public official acts and not commercial or private acts could be regarded as immune. It also established procedures for lawsuits against foreign sovereigns.

foreign tax credit The principal means by which states cope with the problem of international double taxation. The foreign tax credit is a dollar-for-dollar credit against domestic income tax liability for income taxes paid to foreign countries.

foreign trade zone *See* FREE TRADE ZONE.

formalistic model A model of foreign policy decision making discussed by ALEXANDER L. GEORGE in *Presidential Decisionmaking in Foreign Policy* (1980); it refers to the very orderly policymaking structure headed by the U.S. President with well-defined procedures, clear lines of communication, and a structured staff system. The process discourages conflict among a president's advisors. The danger is that this system militates against a full and frank exploration of policy alternatives.

Formosa The colonial Portuguese name for the island of TAIWAN; the physical location of the Republic of China.

Forrestal, James V. (1892–1949) The secretary of the U.S. Navy during the latter part of World War II who became the first secretary of the new Department of Defense from 1947 to 1949. Although personally opposing service unification, he was a major player in the development of the National Security Act of 1947 (which combined the armed services into one agency) and subsequently attempted to strengthen the office of the secretary of defense at a time when it was considered weak vis-à-vis the military. The armed services, however, were very reluctant to cooperate, and the frustrations and pressures associated with a position that carried great responsibility but little power contributed to Forrestal's suicide in 1949. Nevertheless, he has to be considered part of the group including GEORGE F. KENNAN and DEAN ACHESON that reshaped United States foreign policy to counter Soviet expansion after World War II.

Fortress America A vague term for the concepts of ISOLATIONISM that have been prevalent often in the United States since World War I. Under some interpretations of the term, Fortress America would consist of the Western Hemisphere; in other interpretations, it would be confined to North America and adjoining islands. Sometimes Hawaii is included. The underlying idea was that the United States should build strong defenses for the area encompassed by the term and refrain from military involvement in the rest of the world. In the period after World War II, proponents also argued that the United States should emphasize air and sea power to prevent any threats to the U.S. homeland.

Fortress Europe   **1.** *Festung Europa,* the German propaganda term from WORLD WAR II which implied that AXIS fortifications were so strong that a successful Allied invasion of the continent would be impossible. **2.** By analogy, the term applied the post–1992 EUROPEAN COMMUNITY because economically it will be so strong that other states will have difficulty penetrating it, economically speaking. Indeed, one reason why the United States has been eager to retain the North Atlantic Treaty Organization in spite of the end of the Cold War is that it is a symbol of cooperation between the United States and Western Europe. It is hoped in Washington that continued security cooperation will make Western Europe less likely to adopt exclusive economic policies.

Forty Committee   The committee of the U.S. NATIONAL SECURITY COUNCIL that was set up to authorize and oversee COVERT OPERATIONS. The Forty Committee orchestrated the covert aid the United States provided to the anti-Soviet factions in the ANGOLAN CIVIL WAR in 1975.

forward basing   The permanent stationing of military units in or near the area they are expected to have to fight in should a confrontation occur. Thus the British army of the Rhine and the U.S. Seventh Army were forward based in West Germany, rather than in their home countries, during the COLD WAR. Forward basing is sometimes politically controversial within the country providing the troops because it is believed to be more expensive than home basing (largely because of foreign exchange costs). From time to time, therefore, critics wanting to cut defense budgets, yet unwilling to accept an actual reduction in military preparedness, call for home basing rather than forward basing. This has intermittently been a particularly strong demand in the United States and also has occurred in Great Britain. In fact, because of the costs of relocation, in the short term it would be more expensive to have these forces based at home than overseas. Nevertheless, with the end of the Cold War, the United States is reducing (but not eliminating) its forward-based forces in both Western Europe and northeast Asia.

forward defense   An outmoded NORTH ATLANTIC TREATY ORGANIZATION defense policy of stopping any Soviet invasion of West Germany at the border. Trying to win a war without surrendering any territory runs contrary to many military doctrines which hold that a fixed linear forward defense, that is, a commitment to stay in place along the whole front, is disastrous and yields far too much initiative to the enemy. However, West Germany insisted on the forward defense strategy as a precondition for its contribution to NATO. The West German Defense White Paper of 1969 enunciated the reasons why this has remained a continuing preoccupation:

> The federal Government considers forward defense to be an inalienable prerequisite of the German defense contribution. Any aggression in the central region will affect German soil and the German population directly and would soon threaten the heart of our territory. Any abandonment of even a small part of the Federal German territory without defense is unacceptable for political, economic and military reasons. Preparations for defense must therefore be designed to guarantee an immediate and effective military response to instill in our people the necessary feeling of security and confidence.

The Germans also were favorably disposed to the escalatory elements of FLEXIBLE RESPONSE to ensure that West Germany did not become a battlefield for sustained conventional hostilities. The end of the Cold War and the reunification of Germany, however, meant the end of forward defense as it had traditionally been understood in NATO.

forward presence   The presence of U.S. military forces in forward deployed areas such as Japan, South Korea, and Western Europe. This is regarded as an important feature of U.S. military posture in the post–Cold War world even though the North Atlantic Treaty Organization, for example, has abandoned its FORWARD DEFENSE in Germany. Forward presence is intended in large part to make clear that the United States still has interests overseas that it is prepared to use force to protect.

four freedoms U.S. President Franklin D. Roosevelt's vision for the post–World War II world, which he stated in his January 6, 1941, State of the Union Address to Congress:

In the future days, which we seek to make secure, we look forward to a world founded upon four essential human freedoms.

The first is freedom of speech and expression everywhere in the world.

The second is freedom of every person to worship God in his own way everywhere in the world.

The third is freedom from want, which, translated into world terms, means economic understandings which will secure to every nation a healthy peacetime life for its inhabitants everywhere in the world.

The fourth is freedom from fear—which, translated into world terms, means a worldwide reduction of armaments to such a point and in such a thorough fashion that no nation will be in a position to commit an act of physical aggression against any neighbor—anywhere in the world.

Four Policemen The United States, the United Kingdom, the Soviet Union, and China. In the neo-Metternichean concept advanced at the TEHRAN CONFERENCE by U.S. President Franklin D. Roosevelt in 1943, these four powers were to maintain order in the world after the defeat of the AXIS powers.

Four Powers Agreement **1.** The 1945 agreement of the United States, the United Kingdom, the Soviet Union, and France for the prosecution and punishment of Nazi war criminals. This led to the NUREMBURG TRIALS. **2.** The 1971 TREATY OF BERLIN.

Fourteen Points U.S. President Woodrow Wilson's idealistic statement of aims as a proposed basis for ending World War I with a "just and generous" peace, made in an address to the U.S. Congress on January 8, 1918. It called for freedom of the seas; disarmament; removal of trade barriers; ways to settle the nationalities question, especially in central Europe; and an international organization to guarantee peace, namely the LEAGUE OF NATIONS. French Premier Georges Clemenceau supposedly complained at the 1919 PARIS PEACE CONFERENCE: "Mr. Wilson bores me with his Fourteen Points; why, God Almighty only has ten." Wilson's idealistic call for "open covenants of peace openly arrived at" was widely derided then and now; for example, U.S. President Richard M. Nixon once said: "You cannot in today's world have successful diplomacy without secrecy. It is impossible. I used to say that I believe in the Wilsonian doctrine of open covenants openly arrived at. But that was Wilson at his idealistic best and his pragmatic worst" (*Los Angeles Times,* May 17, 1974).

Fourth International *See* INTERNATIONAL, THE.

Fourth Republic The government of France (1946–1958). In 1946 a new constitution renamed the Chamber of Deputies the National Assembly and added a second chamber called the Council of the Republic (not unlike the old Senate). This constitution attempted to make selection of prime ministers more straightforward, but in practice their appointment was harder and their tenure was precarious. The Fourth Republic suffered from instability; during its 12-year life there were 20 cabinets. This meant that there was little continuity in foreign policy. In 1958 the Fourth Republic was effectively destroyed by the issue of Algerian independence, which brought France to the brink of civil war. A new constitution was adopted that provided an opportunity to replace the weak government of the Fourth Republic with a much stronger, more centralized, and more decisive system known as the FIFTH REPUBLIC. *See also* ALGERIAN WAR OF INDEPENDENCE.

Fourth World Those DEVELOPING COUNTRIES with extremely low per capita annual incomes, no financial reserves, slight expectation of economic growth, and limited natural resources—in effect, the poorest of the poor. Also known as the LEAST-DEVELOPED COUNTRIES. *Compare to* FIRST WORLD; SECOND WORLD; THIRD WORLD.

Four Tigers Hong Kong, Singapore, South Korea, and Taiwan; so named because their economies have shown such aggressive growth in recent times. Also known as the *Little Dragons*.

FP-25 *(Forces Populares 25 de Abril)* "Popular Forces—[April] 25," a Portuguese left-wing terrorist organization, named for the date in 1974 when the right-wing dictatorship that had led Portugal since 1926 was overthrown. The group seeks the violent overthrow of the Portuguese government and the establishment of a Marxist state in its place. Its stated goals are to "use armed force against imperialism" and to lead a "workers' assault on bourgeois power." It is strongly against the NORTH ATLANTIC TREATY ORGANIZATION and the United States. The group has committed a series of assassinations, bombings, and rocket attacks against Portuguese government and economic targets as well as against U.S. and NATO interests in Portugal.

frais de representation French phrase meaning "expense account"; a diplomatic agent's allowance for official entertainment.

France, Battle of The May–June 1940 conquest of France by Germany. The two states had technically been at war since the previous September, when France and Great Britain declared war on Germany after its conquest of Poland. In the Battle of France Germany accomplished in six weeks what it could not do in the four years of World War I, because of the advent of armored forces and BLITZKREIG tactics. While the German troops were about equal in number to the defenders, the German Army actually had fewer tanks (2,500 to 3,250) than the French. What the Germans had that made the difference was a superior tactical doctrine on how to use tanks and aircraft. The French MAGINOT LINE with its fixed guns proved useless, and French and British forces near the English Channel were surrounded at DUNKIRK and evacuated in June.

As the battle for France ended and the Germans marched victoriously into Paris, General CHARLES DE GAULLE defiantly fled to England to continue the fight as leader of the FREE FRENCH. On June 18, 1940, he made a BBC radio broadcast to his defeated nation: "This war has not been decided by the Battle of France. This war is a world war. All our mistakes, all our delays, all our suffering, do not alter the fact that there is in the universe all the means needed to crush our enemies one day." Only when it became certain that Germany would prevail in the north of France did Fascist Italy attack in the south. This led U.S. President Franklin D. Roosevelt to state in a June 10, 1940, speech: "On this tenth day of June 1940, the hand [Italy] that held the dagger has struck it into the back of its neighbor. . . . Neither those who sprang from that ancient stock nor those who have come hither in later years can be indifferent to the destruction of freedom in their ancestral lands across the seas." News of the fall of France was met with both incredulity and anger in the United States and Great Britain.

franchise d'hotel French phrase meaning "local residence immunity," a diplomat's immunity from civil and criminal legal actions in the host state.

franchise diplomatic **1.** French phrase meaning "diplomatic immunity," the privileges and immunities traditionally granted to diplomats. **2.** A diplomat's freedom from taxation by the host state. *See also* DIPLOMATIC PRIVILEGES AND IMMUNITIES.

franchise douaniere French phrase meaning "customs immunity," a diplomat's freedom from customs duties on personal and household belongings.

FRANCIA *(Front d'Action Nouvelle Contre l'indépendence et l'autonomie)* "New Action Front Against Independence and Autonomy for Corsica," a militant organization that violently opposes the Corsican separatist movement, especially the FLNC. Comprised primarily of French settlers on the Mediterranean island of Corsica, it seeks to counter the activities of the FLNC and all other Corsican separatist groups.

Franco, Francisco (1892–1975) The general who led an army from Spanish Morocco against the elected government and defeated it in the SPANISH CIVIL WAR (1936–1939). Most of his followers were members of the FALANGE, various monarchists, and landowners loyal to the Roman Catholic Church. Franco then ruled Spain as dictator, as head of the only legal political party and commander of the armed forces until his death. While supported by Nazi Germany and Fascist Italy in the civil war, he was skeptical of ideologies and remained neutral in World War II. Largely because of his own preparations, Spain moved easily into a constitutional liberal monarchy after his death.

Franco- An obsolete term for France—and all things French—because in the early Middle Ages the "Franks," a Germanic group, invaded and conquered Gaul, the area of modern France. Now the word is properly used only in combination with another. Thus the Franco-Prussian War of 1870 was the war between France and Prussia. (France lost and the victorious William I was crowned emperor of Germany at Versailles near Paris, which the French took as further insult.) Today the term is often used in the context of "Franco-German cooperation" in the building of Europe.

Franco-German brigade The joint military unit of France and Germany. There is much talk that these

Francisco Franco (right) meets Adolf Hitler (left) in October 1940. Presumably the man in the middle is the translator. (U.S. Naval Institute)

5,000 troops could be expanded into a true European military force—one that would allow the EUROPEAN COMMUNITY to project force outside of the framework of the NORTH ATLANTIC TREATY ORGANIZATION.

Franco-German corps A military organization proposed in October 1991 by President François Mitterrand of France and Chancellor Helmut Kohl of Germany whose scope and function would go well beyond the brigade that had been established some years earlier. (As proposed, the corps would be about ten times bigger than the brigade currently is.) In 1993, to allay fears that this new joint European corps would undermine NATO, France and Germany asserted that the corps would be put under NATO command during emergencies. Although other West European nations were invited to join, Great Britain and the United States saw the proposal as a challenge to the existing security arrangements within the NORTH ATLANTIC TREATY ORGANIZATION. The Franco-German initiative was related to the MAASTRICHT TREATY meeting and the moves toward the establishment of a EUROPEAN DEFENSE IDENTITY as part of the progress toward the POLITICAL INTEGRATION in Western Europe.

Francophone 1. Any person who speaks French. 2. A term that is used to refer to those parts of Africa that look primarily to France as the postimperial patron and in which French is a key language. French culture also continues to have a major influence in these states. Some 35 states in all, located especially but not exclusively in North Africa, view France in this way. France encourages such sentiment, seeing it as a means of maintaining its influence outside Europe.

frank and candid exchange of views A phrase typically used to indicate diplomatic negotiations that have reached an impasse over differences neither side is prepared to publicize in the hope that future negotiations may resolve some of them. In short, negotiations that go nowhere. According to U.S. economist John Kenneth Galbraith, "There are few ironclad rules of diplomacy but to one there is no exception. When an official reports that talks were useful, it can safely be concluded that nothing was accomplished" (*Foreign Service Journal,* June 1969).

Franz Ferdinand (1863–1914)

Franz Ferdinand (1863–1914) Archduke of Austria and heir-apparent to the throne of Austria-Hungary who was assassinated, along with his wife Sofia, in Sarejevo, Bosnia-Herzegovina, on June 28, 1914. His assassin, Gavrilo Princip, was a member of "Young Bosnia," a group with ties to the Serbian BLACK HAND organization. The murder of Franz Ferdinand led to Austria's ultimatum to Serbia. Serbia's refusal to meet a few of the demands in the ultimatum, which infringed on its sovereignty, led in July 1914 to the start of World War I.

THE ASSASSINATION OF FRANZ FERDINAND TOLD BY ONE OF THE CONSPIRATORS

Before Franz Ferdinand arrived in Sarajevo all the twenty-two conspirators were in their allotted positions, armed and ready. They were distributed 500 yards apart over the whole route along which the Archduke must travel. . . .

When the car passed Gabrinovic . . . , he threw his grenade. It hit the side of the car, but Franz Ferdinand with presence of mind threw himself back and was uninjured. . . . The cars sped to the Town Hall and the rest of the conspirators did not interfere with them. After the reception . . . the Archduke was persuaded to drive the shortest way out of the city. . . . The road . . . was shaped like the letter V, making a sharp turn at the bridge over the River Nilgacka. Franz Ferdinand's car could go fast enough until it reached this spot but here it was forced to slow down for the turn. Here Princip had taken his stand. As the car came abreast he stepped forward from the curb, drew his automatic pistol from his coat and fired two shots. The first struck the wife of the Archduke, the Archduchess Sofia, in the abdomen. She was an expectant mother. She died instantly. The second bullet struck the Archduke close to the heart. He uttered only one word; "Sofia"—a call to his stricken wife. Then his head fell back and he collapsed. He died almost instantly. The officers seized Princip . . . [and] all but killed him.

SOURCE: Borijove Jevtic, *New York World,* June 29, 1924.

Franz Joseph (1830–1916) The Hapsburg ruler of the multinational Austrian monarchy from 1848, when his feeble uncle, Ferdinand, abdicated in his favor during the revolution of that year. He ruled through the *Ausgleisch,* or compromise, of 1867 that transformed the Austrian empire into the dual monarchy of Austria-Hungary, where the two states were separate except for defense and foreign affairs.

fratricide 1. Brother murdering brother; thus a CIVIL WAR is often called a fratricide. 2. The concept that subsequent nuclear warheads may be less effective than the first one on the same target. The debris left in the air after initial explosions may damage the guidance systems of immediately following missiles. Also, the electromagnetic pulse of one nuclear explosion may burn out the arming circuits of closely following warheads.

free city *See* INTERNATIONAL CITY.

freedom fighter A revolutionary fighting for a cause that one supports. Otherwise, a terrorist.

freedom flotilla *See* MARIEL BOATLIFT.

freedom of the seas The traditional belief that, with the exception of TERRITORIAL WATERS, all seas are open to all; that no sovereign or other authority can restrict travel on or usage of the high seas.

free enterprise A political and economic system in which most of the society's goods and services are provided by the private sector. *See also* CAPITALISM.

Free French The World War II French government in exile led by CHARLES DE GAULLE. In 1942 they renamed themselves the "fighting French."

free list A list of goods that do not require an IMPORT LICENSE to be shipped to a particular country. For example, books are on the free list on most of the world's democratic states because books published overseas, especially in foreign languages, do not face competing domestic products—after all, every new book also is a new product.

free port A port of entry and its surrounding locality into which foreign merchandise may be brought without being subject to the payment of any customs DUTY. Free ports are relatively rare today but include Aden, the Canary Islands, Gibraltar, and Manaus, Brazil. *See also* FREE TRADE ZONE.

free rider One who consumes PUBLIC GOODS but does not contribute to their production. Washington has long complained that the United States has produced security in the Pacific and that Japan has been a free rider, accepting the benefits without any effort or contribution of its own. In practice, of course, such situations are rarely absolute—which is why there are arguments over BURDEN-SHARING.

free trade International commerce unhampered by government restrictions or tariffs. Since World War II, U.S. policy has favored free trade—with a variety of politically expedient limitations. The argument for free trade is that it leads to greater competition and specialization as nations focus production on those goods that they can produce most efficiently. The rationale is that all nations will benefit by being able to obtain better products at lower prices. Free trade, however, also means that inefficient industries are very vulnerable to competition from overseas—as the U.S. automobile industry discovered in relation to Japan. Third World states also argue that free trade has a structural bias in the terms of trade, in that imports from the advanced industrialized nations may increase while raw material and commodity exports from the Third World cannot—at least to anything like the same extent. Accordingly, Third World states demand that free trade be replaced by FAIR TRADE. In 1824 English historian Lord Macaulay (1800–1859) wrote, "Free trade, one of the greatest blessings which a government can confer on a people, is in almost every country unpopular." This is still true today. *Compare to* PROTECTIONISM.

free trade area A cooperative arrangement by a group of states that agree to remove barriers to commerce with each other, while each maintains its own differing schedule of TARIFFs applying to all other nations. The best example is the European Free Trade Association. *Compare to* CUSTOMS UNION.

free trade bloc *See* CUSTOMS UNION.

free trade zone An enclosed, policed area in a seaport or at an airport or other inland point that is treated, for CUSTOMS purposes, as lying outside the territory of the country. Goods of foreign origin may be brought into this area without payment of a customs DUTY, pending eventual transhipment or reexportation. Duties are imposed on the merchandise (or items manufactured from the merchandise) only when the goods pass from the zone into an area of the country subject to its customs authority. In the United States, these areas are called *foreign trade zones*.

free world **1.** The COLD WAR term for the Western European and North American representative democracies plus Japan. **2.** Those portions of the world without Communist or dictatorial regimes.

FRELIMO (*Frente da Liberataçāo de Moçambique*) "Front for the Liberation of Mozambique," the coalition of anti-Portuguese political groups formed in 1964 to conduct a guerrilla war against Portuguese colonial rule. After ten years of sporadic warfare and major political changes in Portugal, Mozambique became independent in 1975. Mozambique then became a Marxist state with FRELIMO as the only party allowed. But by the late 1980s FRELIMO began to retreat from its dogmatic MARXISM. In 1990 Mozambique's constitution was revised to permit a multiparty system. Major economic and political reforms may now be possible since a negotiated settlement was reached with the RENAMO guerrilla insurgency in 1992.

French Associated States Modern-day Cambodia, Laos, and Vietnam, or colonial French Indochina. Prior to their gaining independence in the aftermath of the French defeat at DIEN BIEN PHU and the subsequent 1954 Geneva Conference on Indochina, these French colonies were referred to as the French Associated States and collectively as French Indochina.

French Equatorial Africa The federation of French colonies in West Central Africa that lasted from 1908 to 1958. It included what are now the states of Cameroon, Central Africa, Chad, Congo, and Gabon.

French West Africa The federation of French colonies in West Africa that lasted from 1895 to 1958. It included what are now the states of Benin, Burkina Faso, Guinea, Ivory Coast, Mali, Mauritania, Niger, and Senegal.

Freud, Sigmund (1856–1939) The Austrian founder of psychoanalysis with his books *The Interpreta-*

tion of Dreams (1900) and *Three Essays on the Theory of Sexuality* (1905). Although not usually linked to international politics, in 1915 he wrote the essay "Thoughts for the Times on War and Death" and in 1932 exchanged letters with ALBERT EINSTEIN outlining his views about war and peace. In essence, Freud saw war as a consequence of *thanatos,* the death instinct, which he believed was inherent in humans and sometimes overpowered *eros,* the self-preservation instinct. Freud revised his schema in his classic *Civilization and Its Discontents* (1930), postulating the two instincts, libido and aggression, with the latter dominant. He argued that the way to prevent war was to establish a central authority as supreme arbiter in all conflicts among states. While theoretically attractive, it has not been possible to establish such an international authority. In this sense, Freud's thinking about international politics was not particularly innovative and suffered from a failure to appreciate fully the difficulties of transcending international divisions in the interwar period.

FREUD ON WAR

A belligerent state permits itself every such misdeed, every such act of violence as would disgrace the individual. It makes use against the enemy not only of the accepted *ruses de guerre,* but of deliberate lying and deception as well—and to a degree which seems to exceed the usage of former wars. The state exacts the utmost degree of obedience and sacrifice from its citizens, but at the same time it treats them like children by an excess of secrecy and a censorship upon news and expressions of opinion which leaves the spirits of those whose intellects it thus suppresses defenceless against every unfavorable turn of events and sinister rumor.

SOURCE: Sigmund Freud, *Reflections on War and Death* (1915).

FRG   *See* FEDERAL REPUBLIC OF GERMANY.

friction   KARL VON CLAUSEWITZ's concept from *On War* (1832) that no matter how well designed a military operation may be, the reality of delays, misunderstandings, and so on will make its inevitable execution less than ideal. While originating with the military, friction has become a generally recognized phenomenon in all aspects of the administration of public and international affairs. It is related to Clausewitz's idea of the FOG OF WAR.

CLAUSEWITZ ON FRICTION

Arrange maneuvers in peacetime to include . . . causes of friction, in order that the judgment, circumspection, even resolution, of the separate leaders may be exercised. . . . It is of immense importance that the soldier . . . whatever be his rank, should not see for the first time in war those phenomena of war which, when seen for the first time, astonish and perplex him.

SOURCE: Karl von Clausewitz, *On War* (1832).

Fried, Alfred (1864–1921)   The Austrian journalist who shared the 1911 Nobel Peace Prize (with TOBIAS ASSER) for his contribution to the writing, development, and editing of pacifist literature.

front   **1.** The most forward line of battle in a war. **2.** A group (or a group of organizations) that joins to oppose a regime. For example, the National Liberation Front (FLN) successfully opposed French colonial rule in Algeria.   **3.** A dummy organization established to work clandestinely for a cause. **4.** An individual who represents himself or herself as another with that other's permission.

Front de Liberation du Quebec, Le   *See* QUEBEC LIBERATION FRONT.

front end   The section of a ballistic missile that remains after the propellant stages have been disengaged. It is this section that leaves the earth's atmosphere and continues the ballistic flight through the midcourse phase and the terminal phase. The front end of a more advanced missile would consist of components such as warheads, guidance computers, and decoys. The unit that houses all of these constituents is known as the *bus.*

frontier   **1.** Geographically, a border region, the area that functions as a transition zone between political units.   **2.** Historically, the place, state, or group "out in front" of civilization. Thus certain regions were said to be at the frontier of the civilized world.

front line states   **1.** From 1974 to 1980, an ad hoc caucus supported by the ORGANIZATION OF AFRICAN UNITY consisting of Angola, Botswana, Mozambique, Tanzania, and Zambia, the five countries bordering the "front line" of the southern African states of Zimbabwe and Namibia, which at the time were ruled by white minorities. Their goal as a caucus was to achieve black majority rule throughout southern Africa by means of peaceful negotiations, if possible.   **2.** In June 1980, following the independence of Zimbabwe, the OAU recognized a new group of front line states (Angola, Botswana, Mozambique, Zambia, and Zimbabwe) thought to be in conflict with South Africa and called for outside states to assist them in their "struggle against the racist Pretoria regime."

FRUS (Foreign Relations of the United States)   Sets of historical documents released and published by the State Department that are intended to constitute the official record of the foreign policy of the United States. They are an invaluable source to researchers of U.S. foreign policy as they contain memoranda, minutes of meetings, telegrams, and other material relevant to the development and implementation of U.S. foreign and security policy. The only problem is that they tend to be published decades after the fact.

FSO   *See* FOREIGN SERVICE.

Fuchs, Klaus (1911–1988)   The German-born physicist who worked at British and U.S. atomic research installations in the late 1940s and was also a spy for the Soviet Union. Caught in 1950, he spent nine years in prison, then went to East Germany and the Soviet Union to resume his career in nuclear physics. It is estimated that the atomic secrets Fuchs passed on may have saved the Soviet Union a year in the development of its atomic bomb.

Fujimori, Alberto (1938–   )   The president of Peru who succeeded Alan Garcia Perez (1949–   ) in 1990. Organizing a "Cambio [change] 90" grassroots political movement, Fujimori, a relatively unknown agronomist, won the election with promises of economic reforms to cure recession and hyperinflation. But plagued by the murderous disruptions of the SENDERO LUMINOSO insurgency, in

---

A SPY'S MOTIVATION

At this time I had a complete confidence in Russian policy and I believed that the Western Allies deliberately allowed Russia and Germany to fight each other to the death. I had, therefore, no hesitation in giving all the information I had. . . . At first I thought that all I would do would be to inform the Russian authorities that work upon the atom bomb was going on. They wished to have more details and I agreed to supply them. I concentrated at first mainly on the products of my own work, but in particular at Los Alamos I did what I consider to be the worst I have done, namely to give information about the principles of the design of the plutonium bomb.

SOURCE: Klaus Fuchs, from his formal confession of January 27, 1950, reprinted in Norman Moss, *Klaus Fuchs: The Man Who Stole the Atom Bomb* (1987).

1992 he suspended the constitution and assumed emergency powers. *See also* PERU COUP.

Fukuda Doctrine   The unofficial name for Japan's policy toward the five ASEAN states, put forth by Japanese Prime Minister Takeo Fukuda (1905–   ) at a 1977 ASEAN summit meeting in Kuala Lampur. The doctrine consists of three principles: that Japan will not seek to become a regional military power; that Japan will seek to increase its economic, social, political, and cultural ties with ASEAN; and that Japan will try to act as an intermediary between ASEAN and the nations of Indochina in seeking the long-term goal of regional peaceful coexistence.

Fulbright, J. William (1905–   )   The U.S. Senator from Arkansas from 1945 to 1975 who as chairman of the Senate Foreign Relations Committee (1959–1975) was a leader of congressional opposition to the Vietnam War. He prophetically said in an April 21, 1966, speech in the Senate: "Past experience provides little basis for confidence that reason can prevail in an atmosphere of mounting war fever. In a contest between a hawk and a dove the hawk has a great advantage, not because it is a better bird, but because it is a bigger bird with lethal talons and a highly developed will to use them." In 1946 he sponsored the Fulbright Act for international scholarly exchanges. At first it was financed by the sale of U.S. materiel left in foreign nations after World War II. Later it was supported by U.S. appropriations. This was expanded by the Fulbright-Hays Act of 1961. *See also* ARROGANCE OF POWER.

full command The military authority and responsibility of a superior officer to issue orders to subordinates. The concept covers every aspect of military operations and administration and exists only within national services. The term COMMAND, as used internationally, implies a lesser degree of authority than when it is used in a purely national sense. It follows that no North Atlantic Treaty Organization commander would have full command over the forces that are assigned to him or her. This is because nations, in assigning forces to NATO, assign only operational command or operational control in wartime. In peacetime the forces remain under national command. *See also* CHOP.

Fuller, John Frederick Charles (1878–1966) The chief of staff of the British Tank Corps in World War I who in the interwar years published many of the theoretical analyses on tank warfare that would be adopted by Germany as the BLITZKRIEG. Fuller asserted that there is a science of war guided by principles or laws that can be studied as an art, and that the key to success lies in the application of these principles to changing conditions. To Fuller, the aim of all strategy should be the dislocation and paralysis of the enemy's COMMAND AND CONTROL system. Fuller, who retired as a major general in the early 1930s, was never trusted with a significant role in World War II because of his open support for British Fascists in the late 1930s.

full power The rights of a diplomatic representative who has complete authority to act for her or his government, subject only to constitutional restraints (such as a requirement for treaty ratification by a legislature) that cannot be waived.

functionalism International cooperation in areas in which there are common needs and that are essen-tially technical and nonpolitical in nature. Function-alism has been both an approach to peace and an approach to INTEGRATION, as the assumption was that areas of functional cooperation would gradu-ally be expanded. As James Dougherty and Robert Pfaltzgraff note in *Contending Theories of Interna-tional Relations* (1981), "Functionalism is based upon the hypothesis that national loyalties can be diffused and redirected into a framework for inter-national cooperation in place of national competi-tion and war." Carried to its ultimate conclusion, functionalism contains a form of FABIAN SOCIETY–style socialism on an international scale, for it posits the growing importance of welfare demands on the state. Because the state is inadequate for solving many problems due to the interdependent nature of the modern world, the obvious answer is said to lie in international organizations. The classic statement of functionalism was presented in David Mitrany's *A Working Peace System* (1943). Mitrany expected "ramification" to occur in which cooperation in one area would produce a need for cooperation in other sectors and would lead eventu-ally to political agreement. There are many prob-lems with functionalist theory, however, including the fact that it downplays power considerations and ignores the difficulty of separating the technical and the political. Nevertheless, it provided the basis for much theorizing about integraion and for the development of NEOFUNCTIONALISM.

functionalist school Those analysts who focus on functional cooperation as an effective approach to regional and global integration and to the problem of conflict in the international system. The func-tionalist school has increasingly given way to the neofunctionalist.

fungibility Transferability; a term taken from law and sometime used in relation to power. Power is fungible when it can be transferred from one func-tion to another. The term sometimes is used in rela-tion to particular types of military capabilities. Cruise missiles, for example, are fungible weapons since they can be adapted to a variety of platforms and can be launched from land, sea, or air.

G

Gagarin, Yuri (1934–1968)   The Soviet cosmonaut who was the first human in space. On April 12, 1961, his spacecraft, *Vostok I,* orbited the earth. The official Soviet government announcement said this "flight was a triumph of socialism." It was the Soviet way of gloating that it had beaten the United States in the race to put a man in space. Less than a month later, on May 5, Alan B. Shepard, Jr. (1923–   ) would become the first American in space.

Gaither Report   The 1957 report of a U.S. committee chaired by H. Rowan Gaither of the Ford Foundation that was set up by President Dwight D. Eisenhower to examine weaknesses in United States security policy. The report, which was submitted to the White House shortly after SPUTNIK, emphasized the need for the United States to take measures to make its strategic nuclear forces less vulnerable to an enemy attack—a recommendation that the administration acted upon. The report also advocated the construction of FALLOUT shelters for the population. Although a few modest steps were taken to do so, this recommendation had far less impact on the development of national policy. The Gaither Report was part of a much wider attempt in the late 1950s to pressure the Eisenhower Administration into a stronger defense effort, especially at the strategic nuclear level.

Gaitskell, Hugh (1906–1963)   The leader of the British Labour Party from 1955 to 1963. He succeeded CLEMENT ATTLEE as party leader and most likely would have become prime minister (instead of HAROLD WILSON) in 1964 had he not died. Gaitskell was a moderating force in his party, often in conflict with those on the far left. For example, he opposed unilateral nuclear disarmament and reduced his party's emphasis on nationalization of industry and other socialist measures.

GAITSKELL IN "BAD ODOUR"

In 1947 Gaitskell was Minister of Fuel and Power in the Labour government. Winston Churchill, as leader of the Conservative Party then in opposition, disagreed with Gaitskell's announced policy of fewer baths to conserve fuel. In an October 28, 1947, speech in the House of Commons, Churchill denounced what he called a "lousy" policy:

> [Gaitskell has] advocated a policy of fewer baths. I really must read the words which he is reported to have used, as I think they constitute almost a record. "Personally, I have never had a great many baths myself, and I can assure those who are in the habit of having a great many, that it does not make a great difference to their health if they have less. As to their appearance, most of that is underneath, and nobody sees it." When Ministers of the Crown speak like this on behalf of His Majesty's Government, the Prime Minister and his friends have no need to wonder why they are getting increasingly into bad odour. I had even asked myself, when meditating upon these points, whether you, Mr. Speaker, would admit the word "lousy" as a Parliamentary expression in referring to the Administration, provided, of course, it was not intended in a contemptuous sense, but purely as one of actual narration!

Gallipoli   The peninsula on the European part of Turkey at the southern end of the Dardanelles. From April 1915 to January 1916, a British and French amphibious force, which was joined by troops from Australia and New Zealand, sought to take Turkey (an ally of Germany) out of WORLD WAR I. They sought to dominate the straits joining the Black and Mediterranean seas and thus give Russian ships free access to the latter. WINSTON CHURCHILL, then the civilian head of the British navy, is generally credited with conceiving the plan, which the British and French high commands grudgingly accepted. Its botched execution in the field led to half a million casualties on both sides, and the Allies had to evacuate their exhausted troops from Gallipoli. Churchill was made a scapegoat and forced to resign as first lord of the Admiralty. Gallipoli, as the great amphibious failure of World War I, haunted Allied planners during World War II.

Galtung, Johan (1930–   )   The Norwegian theorist who, though not a Marxist, has developed structural theories of imperialism, violence, and integration. Galtung uses many concepts of MARXISM or neo-Marxism in his work and has been one of the major analysts to develop the distinction between the CENTER (the rich and powerful states) and the periphery (outlying areas where the states have little share in the wealth or power enjoyed by those at the center or core of the international system) in world politics. Galtung also is an important figure in PEACE RESEARCH, where his notion of *structural violence* has been particularly influential. The essence of this idea is that the coercion built into oppressive political systems (such as that of South Africa under APARTHEID) that deprives citizens of political, economic, and social rights is itself a form of violence, even though the government may resort to overt violence fairly infrequently. He also has been influential in other areas. In "A Structural Theory of Integration" (*Journal of Peace Research* 5, no. 4, 1968), he developed important ideas on INTEGRATION. Galtung has worked in the area of futurology and in 1973 wrote *The European Community: A Superpower in the Making*. His ideas, however, have been most influential in peace research and in the conceptualization of relations between the advanced industrialized states and the Third World.

game of nations   INTERNATIONAL RELATIONS; DIPLOMACY; a sporting description for the pastime of sovereign states. Many analysts agree that because there is a great deal of GAME THEORY and game playing in international affairs, the "game of nations" is an accurate description of the strategy and tactics in play.

GAMES NATIONS PLAY

The Game of nations . . . differs from other games . . . in several important respects. First, each player has his own aims, different from those of the others, which constitute "winning"; second, every player is forced by his own domestic circumstances to make moves in the Game which have nothing to do with winning and which, indeed, might impair chances of winning; third, in the Game of nations there are no winners, only losers. The objective of each player is not so much to win as to avoid loss.

The common objective of players in the game of nations is merely to keep the Game going. The alternative to the Game is war.

SOURCE: Egyptian Vice President Zakaria Mohieddin, speaking before the Egyptian War College in 1962; quoted in Miles Copeland, *The Game of Nations* (1969).

---

game theory   A quantitative approach to decision making related to problems of conflict and collaboration between rational actors in an uncertain world. Game theory is based on the essentially logical features of competitive games. Given assumptions about preferences, psychological tendencies to take risks, and sets of rules defining actions with possible gains and losses from these actions, it is possible to determine how people are most likely to react to possible actions of others. Game theory was first developed in the 1920s by Hungarian-born U.S. mathematician John von Neumann (1903–1957) and expanded during the 1940s by him and German-born U.S. economist Oskar Morgenstern (1902–1977). Game theory is excellent for classes of games where winners take all by optimizing strategy but can go awry for games where parties gain by collaboration. Game theory is often illustrated by the "prisoners' dilemma" paradigm. It supposes that two people have been arrested on suspicion of having committed a crime together and are being held in separate cells. There is not enough evidence to prosecute unless one confesses and implicates the other. Both of them know this they but they cannot talk to each other. The dilemma is that the best outcome, not being convicted, is available only if they trust each other. So if X decides to trust Y, but Y fears X may not be trustworthy, Y may confess to get a lesser sentence; X then gets a worse one. This dilemma calls for both to cooperate, to minimize the worst that can happen, rather than trying for the outcome that is maximum. This is called the MINIMAX strategy; game theorists consider it to be the most probable outcome.

Prisoner's dilemma and other game structures such as "zero sum" and "chicken" are sometimes used to describe or explain relations among states. Particularly noteworthy is Robert Axelrod's *Evolution of Cooperation* (1984), which demonstrates that when iterative or "tit-for-tat" strategies are followed in prisoner's dilemma, the long-term benefits of cooperative strategies become very clear. This tendency can be seen in relation to the arms race or to the strategy of escalation. When both states strive to achieve superiority in armaments, especially at the nuclear level, the most likely outcome is that they will simply achieve stalemate at a higher level of arms and at great cost. If they have a degree of trust and neither tries to maximize gains at the expense of the adversary, then they can find less costly solutions. Similarly, escalatory strategies can lead both sides in a crisis to a worse level of security than if they had cooperated to keep things under control.

While game theory is useful for highlighting some of the dilemmas in foreign policy decision making and for illuminating the range of outcomes in situations of strategic interdependence, it also has its limitations. It is excessively formal and its assumptions about rational choice are, in many respects, very artificial. *See also* DEFECTION.

Gamsakhurdia, Zviad (1939–   ) The first president of the Georgian Republic in the former Soviet Union in 1991. A non-Communist nationalist leader, he was overwhelmingly elected president in May 1991 but was soon being accused of creating a dictatorship. He banned exports of food and industrial goods from Georgia to other republics, maintained control of television, radio and newspapers, and ordered troops to repress minorities as well as Geor-

Indira Gandhi (Library of Congress)

gians who opposed him. Gamsukhurdia's autocratic leadership pushed Georgia into a brief civil war toward the end of 1991 and beginning of 1992, which ended only temporarily when he was forced to flee to Armenia on January 6, 1992. He retreated to the Chechenya region inside neighboring Russia, where he continued to direct small-scale guerrilla operations in Georgia. *See also* GEORGIAN CIVIL WAR.

Gandhi, Indira (1917–1984) Prime minister of India from 1966 to 1977 and 1980 to 1984, she was the only child of JAWAHARLAL NEHRU. The head of the Congress Party, she subverted parliamentary democracy in 1975 by jailing political opponents,

Gandhi, Mohandas Karamchand (1869–1948)

assuming dictatorial powers, and implementing a semitotalitarian campaign of mass sterilization of Indian males by irreversible vasectomy. In 1976 over 7 million men were sterilized. Under the threat of civil war Gandhi called for an election in 1977 and was soundly defeated. In 1980 she returned to power with a stunning electoral victory. As prime minister, she attempted to steer a course of neutralism during the COLD WAR. India is a diverse country, and its 15 million-person Sikh religious minority in the Punjab region demanded greater autonomy. During the Indian army's assault on the Sikhs' sacred GOLDEN TEMPLE OF AMRITSAR shrine, 600 died. Gandhi's Sikh bodyguards assassinated her by machine gun fire in her garden a few months later on October 21, 1984. Her son RAJIV GANDHI succeeded her as prime minister.

Gandhi, Mohandas Karamchand (1869–1948) The nationalist leader in India, known as the Mahatma (great soul), who utilized Hindu methods of passive or nonviolent resistance (AHIMSA) in heading the movement to achieve independence from British colonial rule. The son of a well-to-do merchant (*gandhi* means "grocer"), he grew up north of Bombay. He earned a law degree in Great Britain and was a lawyer in South Africa from 1893 to 1915. He pursued social justice there through intense nonviolence (*Satyagraha*). He returned to India and became head of the Congress Party after the AMRITSAR MASSACRE in 1919. He led a march to the sea to protest the hated British salt tax in 1929 and later pursued near-starvation fasts to gain publicity for the cause of Indian independence. In 1942, during World War II, he called on Great Britain simply to "quit India." Although he wanted only one India, there was a split within India between Muslims and Hindus. Thus both India and Pakistan (the mainly Muslim areas of British India) gained independence in 1947. Gandhi strongly advocated NEUTRALITY (nonalignment in international affairs), a theme that was taken up by his followers, including India's first prime minister, JAWAHARLAL NEHRU. Gandhi was assassinated in 1948 by a Hindu fanatic. *See also* CIVIL DISOBEDIENCE.

Mohandas K. Gandhi strolls with family members. (Library of Congress)

GANDHI ON PASSIVE RESISTANCE

Passive resistance is a method of securing rights by personal suffering; it is the reverse of resistance by arms. When I refuse to do a thing that is repugnant to my conscience, I use soul-force. For instance, the government of the day has passed a law which is applicable to me. I do not like it. If by using violence I force the government to repeal the law, I am employing what may be termed body-force. If I do not obey the law and accept the penalty for its breach, I use soul-force. It involves sacrifice of self.

Everybody admits that sacrifice of self is infinitely superior to sacrifice of others. Moreover, if this kind of force is used in a cause that is unjust, only the person using it suffers. He does not make others suffer for his mistakes. . . . Passive resistance is an all-sided sword, it can be used anyhow; it blesses him who uses it and him against whom it is used. Without drawing a drop of blood it produces far-reaching results.

SOURCE: M. K. Gandhi, *The Collected Works 10* (1963)

Gandhi, Rajiv (1944–1991) The oldest son of INDIRA GANDHI. After a career as a commercial airline pilot, pressure from his mother and the Congress Party made him reluctantly but successfully stand for election in 1981. One of his mother's major political advisors, he was chosen by the party as her successor when she was assassinated in 1984. He was prime minister of India from 1984 to 1989. In 1991, while campaigning for a return to that post, he also was assassinated.

Gandhi, Sanjay (1947–1980) The younger son of Indira Gandhi who was being groomed as her political heir until his death in a plane crash.

Gang of Four **1.** Any political faction made up of four members. **2.** The most powerful radical faction inside the Chinese Communist Party during the second phase of the CULTURAL REVOLUTION from 1969 to 1976. The group, led by JIANG QING, MAO ZEDONG's wife, came into prominence in 1965 when Mao used their radicalization of the arts to purge political opponents. As the Cultural Revolution intensified, the Gang of Four advanced to high positions in the government and the party. At the peak of their power, they controlled education, arts and sciences, media, and propaganda outlets. Upon Mao's death in 1976, the Gang of Four were arrested by orders from DENG XIAOPING and later convicted of treason for their activities during the Cultural Revolution. Deng, who had twice been purged for rightist tendencies, became the central leader in Chinese politics and rehabilitated many of his colleagues purged during the Cultural Revolution. **3.** A reference to the FOUR TIGERS of East Asia: Hong Kong, Singapore, South Korea, and Taiwan. **4.** Term used to describe McGeorge Bundy, George Kennan, Robert McNamara, and Gerard Smith, who wrote "Nuclear Weapons and the Atlantic Alliance" (*Foreign Affairs* 60, no. 4, 1982), in which they argued that the North Atlantic Treaty Organization should adopt a strategy of no first use of nuclear weapons.

Garcia Robles, Alfonso (1911–1991) The Mexican career diplomat who shared the 1982 Nobel Peace Prize (with ALVA REIMER MYRDAL) for his work on banning nuclear weapons from Latin America.

GARI *See* ACTION DIRECTE.

garrison **1.** A permanent military base. **2.** The forces assigned to a permanent base. **3.** Descriptive of a soldier who is ignorant of the "real" army. **4.** Descriptive of peacetime equipment or items not taken into combat. **5.** To assign troops to a place.

garrison state Policy analyst HAROLD D. LASSWELL's concept of a society organized primarily for violence as opposed to other purposes. The notion of the garrison state encompasses military states as well as police states. Lasswell wrote that "the master challenge of modern politics . . . is to civilianize a garrisoning world, thereby cultivating the conditions for its eventual dissolution" ("The Garrison State Hypothesis Today," *Changing Patterns of Military Politics,* ed. Samuel P. Huntington, 1962).

GATT (General Agreement on Tariffs and Trade) The multilateral trade agreement that since 1947 has been the basis for international commerce. It is premised on three basic principles: (1) nondiscriminatory treatment of all signatories in trade matters; (2) the reduction and eventual elimination of an array of tariff and nontariff barriers to trade, generated mostly through periodic GATT negotiations; and (3) resolution of conflicts or damages arising from trade actions of another signatory through consultation. The agreement contains many practical exceptions to these principles and no international sanctions for their violation. Since 1947 the GATT has served as a forum for multilateral trade negotiations, called "rounds." After each round tariffs have been reduced. The GATT stipulates that all agreements under its auspices include the most-favored nation clause and that all bilateral concessions be extended to all members. The GATT dismantled many Great Depression–era trade barriers and fostered a sharp upsurge in the international exchange of goods. However, upholding the GATT has become particularly difficult with the rise of protectionist sentiment in various nations including the United States. *See also* DILLON ROUND; KENNEDY ROUND; TOKYO ROUND; URUGUAY ROUND.

Gaullism The approach to foreign policy associated with French President CHARLES DE GAULLE. Several key elements in de Gaulle's thinking had a major impact on French foreign policy. These included the desire for French independence and grandeur, which resulted in the development and deployment of an independent deterrent and the decision to leave the NORTH ATLANTIC TREATY ORGANIZATION's integrated military structure; the desire to create a more independent Western Europe that would eventually form the basis for a Europe "from the Atlantic to the Urals"; the desire for Europe to be a third force in international relations capable of balancing the superpowers; and the demand for France to be treated as a great power. The problem for de Gaulle was that he started from a limited power base and had to contend with a bloc structure that in the 1960s still appeared very robust. Yet much of his approach to foreign policy survived him. Gaullism, however, has had to be modified in important ways, not the least of which is the willingness of France to submerge its sovereignty in European Community structures that would also constrain its more powerful neighbor—a united Germany.

Gaza Strip   The territory that, along with the WEST BANK, has been occupied by Israel since the 1967 SIX-DAY WAR. The Gaza Strip is a narrow area bordered by Egypt on the southwest, the Mediterranean Sea on the west, and Israel on the north and east. Its 140 square miles of territory supports a mostly Arab population of over half a million. In November 1988 Gaza was declared part of the independent Palestinian state by the PALESTINIAN NATIONAL COUNCIL. Since December 1987 Gaza and the West Bank have been the scene of the INTIFADA.

GCD   *See* GENERAL AND COMPLETE DISARMAMENT.

Gdansk   *See* DANZIG.

GDR   *See* GERMAN DEMOCRATIC REPUBLIC.

General Agreement on Tariffs and Trade   *See* GATT.

general and complete disarmament (GCD)   The utopian notion that all states will someday divest themselves of all military capabilities. It is "general" in that it would apply to all military forces in all countries; it is "complete" in that it would provide for the elimination of all but basic domestic police forces. Calls for GCD became fashionable between the two world wars. The League of Nations debated proposals on GCD in 1927 and 1934. It also was made a founding goal of the United Nations. Support for GCD is based on the belief that weapons and armed forces themselves are responsible for war; eliminating the means will result in the elimination of the practice. This thinking is rooted in the tradition of PACIFISM and in the view that armaments themselves produce both fear and insecurity.

General Assembly   The largest element of the UNITED NATIONS, in which all member states are represented and each has a single vote. It is the main deliberative body of the United Nations. Decisions on important questions, such as recommendations on peace and security, admission of new members, and budgetary matters, require a two-thirds majority. Decisions on other questions are reached by a simple majority. Each year the regular session of the General Assembly starts on the third Tuesday in September and continues usually until mid-December. Most issues are allocated to its seven main committees for consideration. The First Committee and Special Political Committee deal with disarmament and international security. The Second Committee handles economic and financial matters. The Third Committee is concerned with social, humanitarian, and cultural matters. The Fourth Committee takes care of decolonization matters. The Fifth Committee considers administrative and budgetary matters. The Sixth Committee is in charge of legal matters. Draft resolutions are then submitted to the General Assembly for adoption. Special or emergency sessions may be called by the SECURITY COUNCIL, by a majority of member states, or by one member if the majority concurs. While the decisions of the assembly have no legally binding force for governments, they carry the weight of world opinion on major international issues as well as the moral authority of the world community.

general defense   A variant of armed NEUTRALITY most associated with Switzerland. The Swiss deter aggression against themselves by being prepared to rise up as one nation against any invader; they publicly proclaim that any invader would meet massive resistance by a thoroughly trained and armed citizen militia.

The General Assembly of the United Nations (Library of Congress)

generalized system of preferences (GSP)   A system approved by GATT in 1971 that authorized developed countries to give preferential TARIFF treatment to developing countries; this in effect waives the MOST-FAVORED NATION principle. GSP, considered an effective method for stimulating economic growth in developing countries, grew out of United Nations Conference on Trade and Development sessions in the mid-1960s. The EUROPEAN COMMUNITY has included GSP in both the Yaounde and Lomé Conventions. In 1976 the United States became the last developed country to adopt the system. *Compare to* REVERSE PREFERENCES.

general-purpose forces   The vast bulk of the forces in a large nation's military; those units that are available for deployment or redeployment at any time for any mission, as opposed to those units that are dedicated to a particular mission and consequently cannot be redeployed readily. General-purpose forces are usually conventional, not nuclear.

general staff   The planning unit of a military organization. These are the officers in the headquarters of divisions or similar large units that assist their commanders in planning, coordinating, and supervising operations. A general staff often consists of four or more principal functional sections: personnel (G-1), military intelligence (G-2), operations and training (G-3), logistics (G-4), and civil affairs/military government (G-5). (A particular section may be added or eliminated by the commander, depending on demonstrated need.) In brigades and smaller units, staff sections are designated S-1, S-2, and so on, with corresponding duties. The idea of a general staff principally originates from the Prussian military reforms of the mid-nineteenth century, which transformed an inefficient army into the foremost military machine in Europe. The Prussian (later German) General Staff has been admired, though seldom fully imitated, by military thinkers in most countries. It consisted of an elite group of intellectually inclined officers, selected early in their careers, who then spent the rest of their professional lives as staff officers. The General Staff had the full-time job of designing plans for the wars that Germany might have to fight. They were not allowed to be line commanders and saw little combat; their professional loyalties were to the General Staff and to the state. Because they worked and planned together over a long period of time, they were able, once war began, to communicate easily, to trust one another, and to avoid confusion and disagreements over appropriate strategies and tactics. In World Wars I and II the ability of the German military to coordinate its efforts and to put its plans into effect was, in consequence, often better than that of the Allied armies opposing them. But the German model has had few complete imitators. In most of the North Atlantic Treaty Organization, for example, staff posts are held for a few years at a time by officers who rotate through a variety of military occupations. Therefore, real expertise and, even more crucially, the communal loyalty of a general staff never develops. Nevertheless, all of the military general staffs of today are modeled to one degree or another, directly or indirectly, on the German model—even if their officers and citizens do not realize it.

WILSON SEEKS TO FIRE THE GENERAL STAFF

When [in 1914 U.S. President] Wilson read in the Baltimore *Sun* that the General Staff was working on a war plan which was based on hostilities between Germany and the United States, he directed the Secretary of War to launch "an immediate investigation, and if it proved true, to relieve at once every officer of the General Staff and order him out of Washington," claimed General Bliss, the acting chief of staff at the time. . . . Once Bliss explained to Wilson that preparation of theoretical war plans had been a primary function of the war college division since 1903, the President dropped the matter.

SOURCE: D. Clayton James, *The Years of MacArthur* 1 (1970).

---

general strike   A work stoppage by a major portion of the entire work force of a locality or state. General strikes have tended to be more political and ideological than pragmatic and economically oriented in their goals, and historically have been more often staged in Europe than in the United States. European labor unions have often acted in unison against their governments, while U.S. unions have been more interested in bread-and-butter issues than in political confrontation. General strikes have been decidedly infrequent since World War II.

general theories   A term that is used to describe theories that are ambitious in scope and attempt to explain at a very general and widely applicable level either the actions taken by states or the patterns of interaction among states. Hans J. Morgenthau's notion of POWER POLITICS is a good example of a general theory and is one that focuses on a single organizing device for understanding the complexity of international politics.

Geneva   The Swiss city that, because of Switzerland's traditional neutrality, has been the site of numerous international conferences. After World War I the League of Nations headquarters was located there. Today it contains the European Office of the United Nations and the main offices of many international, and international nongovernmental, organizations.

Geneva Conference of 1954   The meeting of the Big Four (the United States, the Soviet Union, Great Britain, and France) in which the Geneva Armistice Agreements were drafted and signed. China and the three states of French Indochina were invited to participate in the meetings in Geneva, Switzerland. Talks began the day after the French defeat at DIEN BIEN PHU. It was in this context that U.S. President Dwight D. Eisenhower first outlined the DOMINO THEORY, which compared the situation in Indochina to a line of dominoes ready to fall under Communist pressure. Independence was granted to the three former French colonies in Indochina: Cambodia, Laos, and Vietnam. These accords also provided for the temporary partitioning of Vietnam along the seventeenth parallel into a Communist North Vietnam and a non-Communist South Vietnam. The agreement ended France's colonial hold on Indochina, which had begun in the 1860s. After World War II France had neither the military and financial resources nor the political will to continue dominating Indochina. *See also* NGHO DINH DIEM.

Geneva Conventions   Agreements between nations made in Geneva, Switzerland, that established rules for the humane treatment during wartime of the sick, the wounded, prisoners of war, civilians, and other persons. When reference is made to the Geneva Convention currently in effect, it generally connotes the Geneva Convention of 1949. However, these were revisions of similar 1906 and 1929 humanitarian CONVENTIONS.

genocide   Acting with intent to destroy a national, ethnic, racial, or religious group; an attempt at wholesale extermination of any category of people by a political authority controlling them. The word combines the Greek *genos*, meaning "family or clan," with the Latin *occidio*, which means "extermination." The term was coined by Raphael

Lemkin (1900–1960), a Polish-born legal scholar who lost 49 members of his family in the HOLO-CAUST. He devoted the remainder of his life to lobbying for international laws against genocide. The United Nations Convention on the Prevention and Punishment of the Crime of Genocide, first passed by the General Assembly in 1948, was a result of tireless lobbying by Lemkin. It has since been ratified by almost 100 states.

GENOCIDE EXPANSIVELY DEFINED

In the present Convention, genocide means any of the following acts committed with intent to destroy, in whole or in part, a national, ethnical, racial or religious group, as such:

(a) Killing members of the group;

(b) Causing serious bodily or mental harm to members of the group;

(c) Deliberately inflicting on the group conditions of life calculated to bring about its physical destruction in whole or in part;

(d) Imposing measures intended to prevent births within the group;

(e) Forcibly transferring children of the group to another group.

SOURCE: Article II of the 1948 Convention on the Prevention and Punishment of the Crime of Genocide

---

gentlemen's agreement   An oral agreement that is not legally binding. A traditional anonymous legal maxim defines it as "an agreement which is not an agreement, made between two persons, neither of whom is a gentleman, whereby each expects the other to be strictly bound without himself being bound at all." Informal international agreements have been called gentlemen's agreements. (In a sense, of course, all international agreements are gentlemen's agreements because, short of war, they are not enforceable.) They are very useful in international relations when formal treaties are inappropriate or when governments want essentially secret agreements that are not binding on their successor governments.

geographical determinism   The belief that a state's physical location is one of the greatest influences on the manner in which it conducts itself in the inter-

national system. For example, during the Cold War, Finland's physical location near to the Soviet Union determined that its best course of action would be to become a neutral BUFFER state, albeit one that was deferential toward Moscow.

geographically disadvantaged state   A state in a poor physical location, such as one that is landlocked; or a state with few natural resources, severe weather patterns, and so on.

geopolitics   1. A term coined by Swedish political scientist Johan Rudolph Kjellen (1864–1922) in his attempt to describe the state not only as a legal entity but as a power. According to G. R. Sloan's *Geopolitics in United States Strategic Policy 1890–1987* (1988), Kjellen used "geopolitik" to describe those conditions and problems of a state that originate in its geographical characteristics. 2. A method of conducting international relations that emphasizes the political or strategic importance of geographical factors such as terrain, distance, or physical location. The Middle East, for example, because of its location and its energy resources, is regarded as geopolitically significant. 3. Loosely used, a virtual synonym for POWER POLITICS because the term implies a close association between geographical characteristics and considerations of national power.   4. A term used to describe an approach to explaining international politics in terms of geographical factors. One of the most important proponents of this school of thought was HALFORD J. MACKINDER, who saw Eastern Europe and Eastern Siberia as crucial pivotal areas in the rise and fall of nations and civilizations and developed the HEARTLAND THEORY to describe this. Another important writer on geopolitics was NICHOLAS J. SPYKMAN, who emphasized the importance of the Eurasian RIMLAND, an emphasis that provided much of the basis for U.S. attempts to contain Soviet power after World War II. Spykman wrote in *America's Strategy and World Politics* (1942): "Who controls the Rimland rules Eurasia; who rules Eurasia controls the destinies of the world."

George, Alexander L. (1920–   )   As a ground-breaking U.S. analyst who brought insights from psychology to international relations and foreign policy, George has had a major impact on the development of international relations as an academic discipline. Several key themes stand out in his work. The first is the importance of psychological variables, something that he emphasized in a study he coauthored with his wife, Juliette, entitled *Woodrow Wilson and Colonel House* (1956). Subsequent works on political decision making and on the importance of policymakers' OPERATIONAL CODES provided frameworks that other scholars used for their own case studies. Perhaps the greatest element in George's contribution, however, was the emphasis he placed on comparative case studies, what he called the method of "focused comparison" (which asked the same questions in each case), which he used intuitively in *The Limits of Coercive Diplomacy* (1971) and more explicitly in *Deterrence in American Foreign Policy* (1975). In both these works George set out to discover the conditions under which certain kinds of strategy failed and the conditions under which they succeeded. A similar theme was evident in work he did on superpower cooperation in CRISIS prevention and management. He authored, coauthored, or coedited several works in this area, including *Managing U.S.-Soviet Rivalry* (1983) and *U.S.-Soviet Security Cooperation* (1988). In *Presidential Decision Making in Foreign Policy* (1980) he dealt with the way U.S. presidents use information and advice. In this study George identified several models of decision making, including the COLLEGIAL MODEL and the COMPETITIVE MODEL. He also developed the notion of multiple advocacy, which he saw as a way of ensuring that the policymakers were sensitive to different arguments and avoided the premature closure of discussion. In this as in his other works, George displayed erudite scholarship and a concern with policy relevance that has led a whole generation of younger scholars to follow his lead.

George, David Lloyd *See* LLOYD GEORGE, DAVID.

George V (1865–1936)   The British monarch from 1910 until his death. The son of EDWARD VII, he led his country through World War I and much of the Great Depression. He was unusually popular in an era when other European monarchs (such as his relatives Kaiser William and Czar Nicholas) were deposed. Nevertheless, he left as a successor a son, EDWARD VIII (later the Duke of Windsor), who was shallowly trained and incapable of assuming his full responsibilities as king. Fortunately, a second son, GEORGE VI, salvaged the family honor when he became king upon his brother's abdication.

George VI (1895–1952)   The British monarch from 1936 until his death. As the second son of George V, he was trained for a career in the Royal Navy, but the unexpected ABDICATION of his brother EDWARD VIII in 1936 made him king. The manner in which he and his family conducted themselves during World War II won them almost universal praise. He was succeeded by his daughter, ELIZABETH II.

Georgian Civil War (1991–1992)   The fighting that began in the fall of 1991 after ZVIAD GAMSAKHURDIA was voted into power during the first elections of the Soviet Republic of Georgia. After getting 87 percent of the vote for president, Gamsakhurdia's government soon became divided as he assumed an increasingly authoritarian style, censored the press, and sought to silence the parliamentary opposition. In addition, he failed to address or negotiate the growing nationalism problems that his republic faced with the armed South Ossetian and Abkhasian minorities. In August 1991 the National Guard, which he had created, turned against him. After a series of shooting incidents, the confrontation turned to open warfare on December 22. Following two weeks of heavy fighting, Gamsakhurdia fled, but small-scale fighting has continued; EDUARD SHEVARDNADZE then stepped in as the temporary head of state, pending new elections.

geostrategic region   An area or region that is particularly significant either because of its location or because it has rich natural resources that states would like to control. Examples include the Ruhr Valley with its coal and the Persian Gulf with its oil.

geritocracy   A description of the Soviet Union's leadership in the late 1970s and early 1980s—the leaders were very old and very sick.

German Democratic Republic (GDR or DDR)   The formal name of East Germany (the Soviet zone of occupied Germany) after World War II. It was an independent Communist state and a member of the WARSAW PACT until GERMAN REUNIFICATION.

German question   1. The concern in the immediate aftermath of World War II over the division of Germany; in particular, whether it should be unified. 2. After West Germany was integrated into the NORTH ATLANTIC TREATY ORGANIZATION in 1955 and the division of Germany seemed settled temporarily, the German question concerned the status of the city of Berlin—half of which was a Western enclave deep within Communist East Germany.   3. In general, a reference to concern about Germany's boundaries and its relations to its neighbors.

German Reich   The name for the union of German states first applied by historians to the Holy Roman Empire (962–1806), which was abolished by Napoleon I. The second or Prussian Reich was created by OTTO VON BISMARCK in 1871 under the Hohenzollern dynasty. This lasted until the last KAISER was overthrown in 1918. When the Nazis came to power in 1933, they proclaimed a Third Reich (1933–1945), which they boasted would last 1,000 years—but actually lasted only for 12.

German reunification   The 1990 political merger of East Germany, the GERMAN DEMOCRATIC REPUBLIC (GDR), with West Germany, the FEDERAL REPUBLIC OF GERMANY (FRG). During the summer and autumn of 1989, rapid change began in the GDR; this led to German unification. Growing numbers of East Germans emigrated to the FRG via Hungary after the Hungarians decided not to use force to stop them. Thousands of East Germans also tried to reach the West by staging sit-ins at FRG diplomatic facilities in other East European capitals. The exodus generated demands within the GDR for political change. On October 7 Soviet leader Mikhail Gorbachev visited Berlin to celebrate the fortieth anniversary of the establishment of the GDR and urged the East German leadership to pursue reform. On October 18 ERICH HONECKER resigned as head of state amid a split in the Communist Party and was replaced by EGON KRENZ. The exodus continued as did pressure for political reform. On November 9 the hated BERLIN WALL was opened, and East Ger-

mans poured through the wall into the western sectors of Berlin. On November 12 the GDR began dismantling the wall. On November 28 FRG Chancellor HELMUT KOHL outlined a ten-point plan for the peaceful unification of the two Germanys based on free elections in the GDR and a unification of their two economies. In December the GDR legislature eliminated the Communist Party's monopoly on power. The entire Politburo and Central Committee, including Krenz, resigned. The formation and growth of numerous political groups and parties marked the end of the former Communist system. Prime Minister Hans Modrow headed a caretaker government that shared power with the new democratically oriented parties. In early February 1990 the Modrow government's proposal for a unified, neutral German state was rejected by Chancellor Kohl, who affirmed that a unified Germany must be a member of the North Atlantic Treaty Organization. On March 18 the first free elections were held in the GDR, and a government was formed that called for a policy of expeditious unification with the FRG. On July 1 the two Germanys entered officially into an economic and monetary union.

During 1990, in parallel with internal German developments, the post–World War II Four Powers—the United States, Great Britain, France, and the Soviet Union—negotiated to end their reserved rights over Berlin and Germany as a whole. Of key importance was overcoming Soviet objections to a united Germany's membership in NATO. This was accomplished in July when the alliance issued the London Declaration on NATO's goals in the post–Cold War era that made NATO (even with all of Germany included) seem less threatening to the Soviet Union. On July 16 President Gorbachev and Chancellor Kohl announced agreement in principle on a united Germany in NATO. This cleared the way for signing the Treaty on the Final Settlement With Respect to Germany in Moscow on September 12. In addition to terminating Four Power rights, the treaty mandates the withdrawal of all Russian forces from Germany by the end of 1994, makes clear that the current borders of Germany are final and definitive, and specifies the right of a united Germany to belong to NATO. It also provides for the continued presence of British, French, and U.S.

troops in Berlin during the interim period of the Soviet withdrawal. In the treaty, the Germans renounced nuclear, biological, and chemical weapons and stated their intention to reduce Germany's armed forces. The conclusion of this final settlement cleared the way for unification of the FRG and GDR. Formal political union occurred on October 3, 1990, with the accession (in accordance with Article 23 of the FRG's Basic Law) of the five *Laender* (internal German states), which had been reestablished in the GDR. On December 2, 1990, all-German elections were held for the first time since 1937.

POSTWAR LEADERS OF DIVIDED GERMANY*

West	*East*
Konrad Adenauer (1949–1963)	Walter Ulbricht (1950–1971)
Ludwig Erhard (1963–1966)	
Kurt Kiesinger (1966–1969)	Eric Honecker (1971–1989)
Willy Brandt (1969–1974)	
Helmut Schmidt (1974–1982)	Egon Krenz (1989–1990)
Helmut Kohl (1982–1990)	

*See individual entries for each.

Gestapo 1. The secret police organization of NAZI Germany and of Nazi-occupied Europe that, under the direction of Heinrich Mueller in the period between 1936 and 1945, became notorious for physical torture and psychological terror in dealing with its victims. The police-state character of Nazi Germany created by the Gestapo was pervasive. The Gestapo was notorious for sending people to CONCENTRATION CAMPS. At the NUREMBERG TRIALS the Gestapo as an organization, along with the SS and the Nazi Party, was indicted for crimes against humanity. Mueller vanished toward the end of the war and his fate remains a mystery. 2. By analogy, a "gestapo" is any oppressive and brutal police force.

Ghazi *See* FAISAL I.

Giap, Vo Nguyen (1912–) The Vietnamese Communist politician and soldier who defeated the French at DIEN BIEN PHU in 1954 and, as the North Vietnamese Defense minister, played a leading role in defeating South Vietnam and the United States during the VIETNAM WAR. He then became the defense minister of a unified Vietnam (1976–1980).

Gibraltar question The dispute between Spain and Great Britain over the status of the Gibraltar peninsula, the self-governing British crown colony that Spain had ceded to Great Britain in the eighteenth century. Because "the rock," as it is known, lost its strategic importance as the gateway to the Mediterranean with the advent of air travel, the British were willing to consider Spain's demands that it be returned. But in a 1967 referendum the citizens of Gibraltar voted 12,138 to 44 to remain British. In 1969 the Spanish restricted land access to Gibraltar. But after the death of Spanish dictator FRANCISCO FRANCO in 1975 and the subsequent reemergence of democracy in Spain, that state's increased interaction with the United Kingdom, because of its desire to enter the NORTH ATLANTIC TREATY ORGANIZATION (accomplished in 1982) and the EUROPEAN COMMUNITY (accomplished in 1986), created better relations. Thus negotiations on Gibraltar resumed in 1980 and the border was reopened in 1982.

Gierek, Edward (1913–) The Polish Communist leader who succeeded WLADYSLAW GOMULKA as first secretary amid widespread rioting in 1970. Ten years later in 1980 amid widespread civil unrest encouraged by the SOLIDARITY movement, he too was forced to resign. Gierek was succeeded briefly by Stanislaw Kania (from September 1980 to October 1981) who, in turn, was replaced by WOJCIECH JARUZELSKI.

Giscard d'Estaing, Valéry (1926–) The Conservative Independent Party president of France (1974–1981). A financial expert with aristocratic origins, he was defeated for reelection by Socialist FRANÇOIS MITTERRAND. He remains active with the renamed Conservative Party, the Union for French Democracy, and the European Parliament.

glasnost The Russian word that literally means "publicity" but has been taken to connote "transparency" or "openness." It is closely connected with PERESTROIKA. At first, under MIKHAIL GOR-

BACHEV, glasnost entailed encouraging the media to point out deficiencies of officials carried over from the "stagnation" period of LEONID BREZHNEV. In 1986 the scope of this word broadened in the wake of the Chernobyl nuclear-plant accident. Glasnost began to encompass the publication of previously banned works, permitting greater criticism in Soviet society, and the percolation to the surface of diverse political, cultural, and national movements. The new era of glasnost allowed radio, television, and all creative arts to express their genuine views and interpretations of events openly. Access to Western radio and television broadcasts was not only permitted but encouraged.

Glassboro   A town in New Jersey that is the home of Glassboro State College. Shortly after the 1967 SIX-DAY WAR, Soviet Premier Alexei Kosygin and U.S. President Lyndon B. Johnson met there for a summit meeting (June 23–25, 1967) to discuss the war and issues of nuclear strategy and nonproliferation. Glassboro was chosen for this impromptu summit because Kosygin was in New York at a United Nations meeting and both sides wanted a site halfway between Washington and New York.

global integration   In theory, the gradual process through which the states of the earth will evolve into a single economic, social, and political unit. To achieve this idea, NATIONALISM and international ANARCHY have to be overcome.

global interdependence   The idea that all of the states of the modern world are interlinked economically, environmentally, and militarily; therefore, it is often argued that new national and international policies leading to greater economic and environmental cooperation are needed to achieve lasting peace and social justice. In recent decades all of the leaders of the developed world have advocated greater global interdependence mainly because all their economies need to continue to grow. The most important theorist emphasizing the impact of new interdependencies on international relations has been ROBERT O. KEOHANE.

globalism   1. A United States foreign policy of active involvement, both politically and militarily,

in all parts of the world; the polar opposite of ISOLATIONISM. The notion of globalism is inherent in the crusading tradition in U.S. foreign policy but became particularly important during the Cold War when the United States saw itself as locked in a global Manichean struggle with the Soviet Union. Moscow was seen as attempting to achieve global domination; preventing this required that the United States be willing to intervene almost anywhere there appeared to be a Soviet challenge. The problem was that this policy did not distinguish between areas that were of vital interest to the United States and those that were peripheral. Globalism was encouraged by the DOMINO THEORY and by a failure to discriminate between challenges that were masterminded by the Soviet Union and those that stemmed from local and regional aspirations and were primarily expressions of NATIONALISM. The United States' involvement in the Vietnam War was simultaneously an expression and a result of globalism. The cost of the war, however, and the divisive impact it had on the U.S. populace helped to curb the impulse toward indiscriminate globalism of the kind that had prevailed through much of the Cold War. In the aftermath of Vietnam, the United States was much more careful about overseas commitments, acknowledging that they had to be based on interests rather than the other way around.   2. A more expansive approach to solving international problems than REGIONALISM. Globalism in this sense recognizes that there are certain problems (such as global warming and the depletion of the ozone layer) that are best dealt with on a worldwide basis.

global office   1. An office whose work is done by various units located in different states.   2. The ability to transfer office jobs abroad to take advantage of lower wages and other reduced costs, made possible by electronic communications and rapid air freight services.

globaloney   Nonsense related to international affairs. The word is usually credited to a speech by Representative Clare Boothe Luce in the U.S. House of Representatives on February 9, 1943: "Much of what Mr. [Henry A.] Wallace calls his global thinking is, no matter how you slice it, still globaloney."

Wallace was then vice president of the United States.

global rivalry   International competition between major powers. It can take many forms. Early in the twentieth century the great powers competed for colonies; later there were arms races and space races. Of course the ultimate global rivalry is war.

Global 2000 Report   A study commissioned by U.S. President Jimmy Carter that comprises the coordinated findings, statistics, and analyses of 13 U.S. government agencies concerning the projected state of the world in the year 2000; the report is formally entitled *The Global 2000 Report to the President: Entering the Twenty-First Century*. The document concludes that "if present trends continue, the world in 2000 will be more crowded, more polluted, less stable ecologically, and more vulnerable to disruption than the world we live in now." The global model, or set of projections, prepared for the study represents the first full-scale demographic and ecological model published by a government. The report concludes that the Global 2000 Model, although gloomy, is a more optimistic model than previous projections prepared by the CLUB OF ROME and various commissions of the United Nations.

global village   The notion that through modern electronic communications the people of the whole world may become as closely linked as people in a premodern archetypical village. The Canadian communications theorist Marshall McLuhan (1911–1980) first wrote that "the new electronic interdependence recreates the world in the image of a global village" (*The Gutenberg Galaxy*, 1962).

global warming   A gradual change in the earth's climate believed to be brought about by the consequences of burning fossil fuels, the large-scale clearing of rain forests, and the use of chemicals not found widely in nature. This is one of the most important issues for environmental policy and protection. It is contended that if global warming is not halted, many coastal regions and port cities will be in danger of flooding as the polar ice caps gradually melt and raise the level of the sea; additional changes will occur in agricultural regions. However,

not all scientists believe that there is a real danger or that a real change exists. Some analysts assert that what is perceived as global warming is merely a normal cyclical change that will eventually and naturally reverse. *See also* GREENHOUSE EFFECT; MONTREAL PROTOCOL.

Gnomes of Zurich   A derogatory designation for the secretive financial and banking personnel and institutions of Zurich, Switzerland, long a world financial center.

Gobat, Charles A. (1843–1914)   The Swiss lawyer and educator who was awarded the 1902 Nobel Peace Prize (with ELIE DUCOMMUN) for his work with the INTERPARLIAMENTARY UNION and the Permanent International Bureau of Peace.

Goebbels, (Paul) Joseph (1897–1945)   NAZI Germany's minister for PROPAGANDA who manipulated the German press, radio, and culture to further ADOLF HITLER's goals. His book-burnings and rabble-rousing through constant lies and misrepresentation in his totally controlled mass media mobilized support for Nazi despotism among many German citizens—at least until Allied bombs started falling on them as World War II progressed. In 1945, as the Soviet Red Army advanced on

A contemporary cartoon depicting Goebbels' intentions. (Library of Congress)

Berlin, Goebbels (and his wife), alone among Nazi leaders, chose to join Hitler in committing suicide—after first poisoning all six of his children.

Goering, Hermann   *See* GÖRING, HERMANN.

Golan Heights   The hills on the Israeli-Syrian border that were first occupied by Israel during the SIX-DAY WAR of 1967. This area was expanded during the YOM KIPPUR WAR of 1973 (but decreased after the creation of United Nations buffer zones in 1974). Since 1974 a United Nations Disengagement and Observer Force in the Golan Heights has separated the two sides. The ARAB-ISRAELI PEACE TALKS were given new impetus when the newly elected Israeli government of YITZHAK RABIN in 1992 indicated some willingness to exchange land in the Golan Heights for a comprehensive peace with Syria.

Golden Crescent   A term used to describe the three countries of Southwest Asia—Afghanistan, Iran, and Pakistan—that produce the drug heroin for worldwide distribution. Around 20 percent of the heroin that enters the United States, for example, originates here.

Golden Temple of Amritsar   The holiest of SIKH shrines, located in Amritsar in the northern state of Punjab in India. On June 5–6, 1984, the Indian military attacked the Golden Temple in an assault on Sikh separatists led by Jarnail Singh Bhindranwale (1947–1984). More than 600 Sikhs died in the bloody onslaught, including Bhindranwale, and the shrine itself sustained structural damage from artillery fire. Indian army casualties also numbered in the hundreds. The assault on the temple was a response to Sikh demands for autonomy in the Punjab. It signaled the beginning of a new wave of Sikh violence, which culminated in the assassination of Prime Minister INDIRA GANDHI by her Sikh bodyguards in October 1984.

Golden Triangle   **1.** The opium-producing areas of Burma, Laos, and Thailand in Southeast Asia. Illegal narcotics are smuggled from there to the rest of the world, but mostly to Europe. The Golden Triangle is the source of about 20 percent of the illegal heroin that enters the United States.   **2.** The most economically developed part of western continental Europe—the area bounded by Paris, France; the Ruhr River; and Milan, Italy. *Compare to* SILVER TRIANGLE.

gold-plating   A critical term for military procurement policies that call for the purchase of all possible bells and whistles for a weapons system or other needed item instead of less expensive, more basic equipment.

gold standard   A monetary system in which the currency is held at a parity with a coined monetary unit defined by its gold content and is convertible into this gold coin on demand. Under this system coins are minted freely, without an appreciable charge for the process; gold coins circulate freely and may be freely exported, imported, or melted down; gold is unlimited legal tender; and gold constitutes a large part of the state's monetary reserve. Because of the first two conditions, the term is sometimes referred to as the *gold coin standard*. A close cousin is the *gold bullion standard,* which differs only in that a special condition of convertibility is imposed: a stipulated minimum of bullion must be purchased with paper money for redemption to take place.

The gold standard was refined and developed mainly by bankers in Great Britain in the nineteenth century to remove impediments to the free movement of jobs, markets, and foreign investment. It was part of an evolution toward FREE TRADE. The gold standard was supposed to provide an automatic adjustment mechanism to help eliminate BALANCE OF PAYMENTS imbalances between states. Deficits were paid for by outright gold transfers. This reduced the domestic money supply and made imports relatively more expensive while exports became less expensive. Because the gold standard prevented a state from manipulating its currency to influence the health of its economy, it was abandoned by all major states prior to World War II. The United Kingdom, which was the first state to adopt a gold standard in 1821, was the last major state to abandon it in 1936.

Golkar   A term used to describe the Joint Secretariat of Functional Groups, a party established in Indonesia in 1964 to coordinate the political activities of the army. In the elections held in 1971 the

Golkar, using heavy patronage, won an overwhelming victory against the nationalist and Muslim parties. The Golkar has been the dominant electoral party ever since and has consistently supported General Suharto (1921–   ), who has been president since 1967.

Gomulka, Wladyslaw (1905–1982)   The Polish nationalist who emerged as the Communist leader of Poland during the civil unrest and strikes of 1956. He allayed Soviet fears that Poland would leave the WARSAW PACT, halted collectivization of Polish agriculture, slightly improved relations between the Communist government and the Catholic church, and encouraged ANTI-SEMITISM as an excuse for the shortcomings of his administration. He was deposed as first secretary in 1970 amid rioting over government reforms that increased food prices; his successor was EDWARD GIEREK.

good neighbor policy   A phrase first used by U.S. President Herbert Hoover, but more famous as a description of U.S. President Franklin D. Roosevelt's policies toward Central and South America. Roosevelt stated in his inaugural address of March 4, 1933: "I would dedicate this nation to the policy of the good neighbor—the neighbor who resolutely respects himself and, because he does so, respects the rights of others—the neighbor who respects his obligations and respects the sanctity of his agreements in and with a world of neighbors." Roosevelt's policy called for noninterference in the internal affairs of Latin American and Caribbean nations. Roosevelt decided that the United States had to devote its resources to combating the effects of the Great Depression rather than financing interventions as had previous administrations.

good offices   The unbiased use of one's formal position, one's office, to help others settle their differences; often used in context of an offer to mediate a conflict.

Gorbachev, Mikhail Sergeyevich (1931–   )   The last leader of the Soviet Union (1985–1991), whose administration ended the Cold War, freed Eastern Europe from Soviet domination, withdrew Soviet support for Third World conflicts in Afghanistan, Angola, and Nicaragua, and so reformed Soviet

politics that a 1991 coup by Communist hard-liners failed and the Soviet Union itself was dissolved peacefully. In power only six years, Gorbachev was one of the most influential individuals in the twentieth century. He was awarded the Nobel Peace Prize in 1990 and is generally revered in the West. Yet at home he grew so unpopular that no role was available to him in the new COMMONWEALTH OF INDEPENDENT STATES.

Gorbachev was born to a peasant family in the Stavropol territory in southern Russia and graduated with a law degree from Moscow State University in 1955. He joined the Communist Party of the Soviet Union in 1952 and worked his way up to become the first secretary of the Stavropol city party committee in 1966. By 1970 he was head of the territorial party organization and became a full member of the Central Committee of the Communist Party a year later. From 1978 to 1985 he was the party secretary of agriculture. When he was made a full member of the ruling POLITBURO in 1980, he was its youngest member. In March 1985, following the death of KONSTANTIN CHERNENKO, Gorbachev was appointed to the top job, general secretary of the CPSU. Before he took the position of president in 1990, he served as chairman of the U.S.S.R. Supreme Soviet Presidium (1988–1989) and as chairman of the U.S.S.R. Supreme Soviet from May 1989. His differing titles are indicative of the tinkering that was going on with the structural arrangements of the Soviet government.

Gorbachev sought to implement GLASNOST and PERESTROIKA in all aspects of Soviet society. His basic domestic problem was that he wanted to reform the Communist Party while too many others wanted to replace it. Notably younger than his immediate predecessors, Gorbachev arranged for a summit with U.S. President Ronald Reagan almost immediately upon gaining office. According to Reagan's press secretary Larry Speakes's book *Speaking Out* (1988): "Gorbachev's three predecessors, Leonid Brezhnev, Yuri Andropov, and Konstantin Chernenko, had all died during Reagan's first four years in office. Whenever Reagan was asked why he waited so long for a summit with the Soviets, his answer was, 'They kept dying on me.' " There's much truth to this flippant remark. Throughout the early 1980s none of the Soviet leaders was strong enough, either physically or politically, to initiate

Mikhail Gorbachev (right) meets with U.S. President Ronald Reagan (center) and President-elect George Bush (left) in December 1988. (U.S. Naval Institute)

the kind of reform proposals that came from Gorbachev. At first the West was skeptical of Gorbachev's intentions. But his very real reforms at home gave increasing credence to policies for ending the Cold War abroad. He established his credentials as a newfound friend for the West by withdrawing all Soviet forces from Afghanistan, allowing Eastern Europe to pursue a political future free of Soviet dominance, stopping Soviet subsidies to Third World Communist regimes, cooperating with the West during the Persian Gulf War, and developing warm relations with Western leaders. Following an attempted coup in August 1991 during which Gorbachev was held captive for a few days, he returned to the presidency to watch helplessly as his country dissolved. He helped the Soviet Union to evolve peacefully into the Commonwealth of Independent States and then, with the New Year, retired from public office. Ironically, Gorbachev can be credited with being most responsible for the dissolution of the Soviet Union. Because of his domestic reforms, the hard-line coup failed and reformers, who were always willing to go farther than Gorbachev, went so far as to reform the Soviet Union out of existence.

Gorbachev doctrine   Not a doctrine but a term applied in popular journalism to Soviet "new thinking" about foreign policy, which was associated with MIKHAIL GORBACHEV and had as a main theme the benefits for the Soviet Union of cooperation with Western Europe and the United States. The key

---

ASSESSING GORBACHEV

Political obituaries published since Gorbachev left office differ greatly. Western commentators tend to agree, and rightly, that his role in international affairs has earned him a great and positive place in history. More than anyone else, he deserves credit for ending the Cold War, liberating Eastern Europe, reuniting Germany and ending Russia's long isolation from the West. On the other hand, many people, particularly in Russia, insist that no leader who presided over the disintegration of his own country, the crisis of its economy and the collapse of his own party can be called successful. Others try to strike a balance: Gorbachev brought freedom but eliminated sausage.

SOURCE: Stephen F. Cohen, "What's Really Happening in Russia?" *The Nation,* March 2, 1992.

---

to this thinking was Gorbachev's acknowledgment that actions taken by the Soviet Union, even though they had defensive purposes, could legitimately be construed by others as threatening. In essence, Gorbachev was acknowledging that the United States and the Soviet Union were locked in a SECURITY DILEMMA. Recognition that the problem was inherent in the relationship of the two superpowers was the first step toward mitigating the effects of the security dilemma. Although there was a tendency by conservative critics in Europe and the United States to dismiss Gorbachev's new approach as a trick, it was in fact the foreign policy dimension of GLASNOST and PERESTROIKA. Moreover, many concrete steps followed this new thinking, including agreements on reducing conventional and nuclear armaments in Europe and a more permissive attitude toward change in Eastern Europe. Arguably it also was part of a way of thinking that got out of control and contributed to the ultimate disintegration of the Soviet Union and its replacement by the COMMONWEALTH OF INDEPENDENT STATES.

Gorbymania   The word coined to describe the great enthusiasm with which MIKHAIL GORBACHEV was received in the West. This is contrasted with "Gorbyphobia"—the decided lack of enthusiasm for him in the Soviet Union. He is a politician with no natural constituency in his native land. The former Communists blame him for the dissolution of the

Soviet Union and their power. The new democrats do not trust him because he stood up for the Communists too long.

Göring (Goering), Hermann (1893–1946)   ADOLF HITLER's corpulent second in command in NAZI Germany. After distinguished service as a World War I fighter pilot, he joined the Nazi Party in its earliest days and aided Hitler's rise to power. He amassed a vast private fortune by corruption and taking assets of Jews forced into exile or CONCENTRATION CAMPS. His possession of these ill-gotten assets is the only justification for some historians' description of him as an "industrialist." As head of the Luftwaffe (German air force) he effectively lost the BATTLE OF BRITAIN for Germany. Convicted of war crimes at the NUREMBERG TRIALS, he would have been hanged by the Allies had he not committed suicide hours before his scheduled execution.

LOUSY GÖRING

[Goering] would send signals to his commanders advising them which units he proposed to visit on the following day. These signals shed an interesting light on the absence of spit and polish in the German squadrons [during the Battle of Britain]. Goering was fastidious and he had obviously found some of the pilots, to whom he was lavishly handing out decorations, not quite to his liking. As a result his signals now instructed the commanding officers to make quite sure that the men whom he was going to decorate were properly deloused; he had obviously had an unfortunate experience.

SOURCE: F. W. Winterbotham, *The Ultra Secret* (1974).

Gorshkov, Sergei G. (1910–1988)   The admiral who transformed the fleet of the Soviet Union from a collection of small coastal ships in the 1950s to a BLUE WATER NAVY that would rival the United States Navy in the 1980s.

Gottwald, Klement (1896–1953)   A founder of the Czech Communist Party in 1921. After spending World War II in the Soviet Union, he became the first Communist president of Czechoslovakia in 1948 by means of a coup. A hard-line Stalinist, he continued his dictatorial regime until his death—presumably (and fittingly) caused by pneumonia caught while attending JOSEPH STALIN's funeral in March 1953.

Government Communication Headquarters The headquarters of British SIGNALS INTELLIGENCE located in Cheltenham, England. The British government discloses very little information about this, but it is clearly tied very closely with similar establishments such as the United States NATIONAL SECURITY AGENCY.

government in exile The legal representatives of a state whose territory is under foreign occupation; they reside in a friendly state while attempting to regain control from the occupiers. Many European governments in exile were established in Great Britain during World War II.

governor-general The representative of the British monarch to a state that still owes allegiance to the British crown. A governor-general performs parallel functions in his or her state as the monarch does in Great Britain. This includes summoning and dissolving parliaments, assenting to bills, and appointing ministers. These functions are mostly ceremonial. After all, since 1930 many members of the COMMONWEALTH OF NATIONS, such as Australia, have effectively told the crown whom to appoint as their governor-general.

Gowon, Yakubu (1934–) The Nigerian military officer who took power in a bloody 1966 coup and then led his country during a civil war with secessionist BIAFRA (1967–1970) in which almost 2 million Nigerians died. Gowon was overthrown by another coup in 1975 while abroad.

GPALS (Global Protection Against Limited Strikes) A scheme for a much more modest version of U.S. President Ronald Reagan's STRATEGIC DEFENSE INITIATIVE that reflected the Bush Administration's desire to keep ballistic missile defense alive but on a less ambitious scale than that envisioned by President Reagan. The plan for refocusing the program was announced on January 29, 1991. The new scheme envisages 750 ground-based defensive missiles as well as 1,000 space-based interceptors. The rationale is that the system would be able to destroy incoming missiles whether they were launched accidentally or deliberately by a small nuclear power. The war in the Persian Gulf together with the concerns about the command and control of nuclear forces in the former Soviet Union have intensified interest in GPALS. Moreover, the big constraint on the implementation of the scheme—the ABM TREATY—may be amended in ways that permit some deployment. On October 5, 1991, Mikhail Gorbachev announced that Moscow was prepared to consider proposals from the United States on nonnuclear antimissile defense systems, a move that reflected a major shift from earlier opposition to any attempt to amend the ABM Treaty. There is still an argument, however, about whether the threats to the United States are sufficiently serious to deploy a system that could cost anywhere between $40 billion and $120 billion. Moreover, the idea of space-based defenses still has less support than the idea of ground-based interceptors. In June 1992 the Bush Administration announced that it was prepared to cooperate with Russia in the development of GPALS defenses. Russian and United States officials subsequently engaged in discussions about this possibility. The U.S. administration sought over $5 billion for the continuation of the GPALS program, but Congress allotted only about $1 billion. Nevertheless, this program has continued at a significant level of funding.

graduated deterrence *See* DETERRENCE, GRADUATED.

graduated response *See* FLEXIBLE RESPONSE.

graduation A concept pertaining to developing countries, whereby as they advance economically and become more developed, they assume greater responsibilities and obligations within the GATT. This term also applies to the GENERALIZED SYSTEM OF PREFERENCES (GSP), whereby certain more advanced developing countries may be removed or "graduated" from eligibility on all or only some GSP-eligible products.

grain embargo *See* EMBARGO.

Gramsci, Antonio (1891–1937) An Italian revolutionary socialist who helped found the Italian Communist Party and became its general secretary in 1924. While under arrest by the Italian government, he developed some of his major ideas in *Prison*

Notebooks (1929–1935). Many of his arguments criticized orthodox Marxism, especially the elements of determinism that it contained. Gramsci's work emphasized that the hegemony of dominant social and economic groups stemmed in large part from the ability to impose their values, beliefs, and culture on those they subordinated. Consequently, it was necessary to engage in a "battle of ideas" in order to transform the consciousness of the masses. Such a transformation was essential if revolution was to take place. Gramsci's ideas regarding the establishment and maintenance of hegemony have increasingly been incorporated into writings on international relations in which theorists have argued hegemonic powers retain their dominance partly because of the attractiveness of their ideas.

Grand Alliance The popular term for the British, Soviet, and United States coalition against Nazi Germany in WORLD WAR II.

grand bargain The notion put forth in the West just prior to the demise of the Soviet Union that Moscow be promised huge amounts of Western economic assistance in exchange for fundamental political reforms. But the failed coup by Communist hard-liners in August 1991 precipitated the reforms before the aid was committed. Nevertheless, substantial aid has flowed in from the West since 1991.

grandeur The idea of status or prestige as one of the key objectives of foreign policy. It is a notion associated particularly with President CHARLES DE GAULLE of France.

Grand Mosque Also known as the Great Mosque, it is the holiest of all Islamic shrines. Located in Mecca, Saudi Arabia, it houses the Kaaba, the Muslim holy of holies, toward which all Muslims around the world face in prayer each day. On November 20, 1979, on a day when it was filled with religious pilgrims, the Grand Mosque was seized by a large band of armed Sunni fundamentalist fanatics. The attack shocked the Islamic world. After a five-day siege several thousand Saudi troops and police assaulted the massive structure, retaking it after a bloody room-to-room battle with the well-armed terrorists. In the end, 127 people were killed and 451 injured.

grand strategy 1. The overall strategic policies of a state or alliance. All aspects of military strategy logically follow from this overall strategy. 2. Strategy at a higher level than that used for one theater of war or one campaign.

GRAPO (*Grupo de Resistencia Antifascista, Primero de Octubre*) "October 1st Anti-fascist Resistance Group," a Maoist, Spanish urban terrorist group dedicated to the removal of U.S. and North Atlantic Treaty Organization military installations from Spain and the establishment of a revolutionary regime. Formed in 1975, GRAPO has committed numerous assassinations, bombings, and kidnappings against Spanish military personnel and facilities.

gray area weapons 1. Nuclear weapons that are neither strategic and of intercontinental range nor tactical and useful on the battlefield; in effect, INTERMEDIATE-RANGE NUCLEAR FORCES. 2. Weapons so difficult to classify that they have to be specifically addressed during arms control negotiations—they cannot be grouped with other systems.

graymail Implied or explicit threats by criminal defendants in national security–related cases to reveal classified information during their trials if the charges are not dropped or reduced. The word is a variation of the common term *blackmail*.

gray propaganda *See* PROPAGANDA.

great debate The controversy that took place from January to early April 1951 in the United States Senate and in the country at large about the wisdom of the Truman Administration's decision to send U.S. troops to Europe as part of the U.S. commitment to the NORTH ATLANTIC TREATY ORGANIZATION. The main critics of the decision were Senators Kenneth Wherry of Nebraska and Robert Taft of Ohio. When it was discovered that only four divisions were to be deployed, the debate lost some of its intensity. Even then, though, disagreement continued over some major issues about the U.S. role in the world, the relationship between the United States and its allies, the most appropriate strategy for dealing with the Soviet Union, and the balance of authority between the president and

Congress. Consequently, when there is a debate over the fundamentals of foreign policy in the United States—as is occurring in the aftermath of the Cold War—it is often referred to as "another great debate."

Great Depression The time between the United States' stock market crash of October 29, 1929, and World War II, when the Western world suffered the worst economic decline of the century. The Great Depression had massive international implications. It created the political conditions that furthered the spread of FASCISM and also made it more difficult for democratic governments to respond effectively to political extremists such as Adolf Hitler in Germany. It was the economic dislocation caused by massive unemployment in Germany that allowed Hitler to gain power.

Greater East Asia Co-Prosperity Sphere The Japanese scheme for economic control over the Asian territories it conquered during WORLD WAR II. The Imperial Council of Japan in July 1941 proclaimed this as part of its plan to expel European powers from Asia and establish an Asian confederation under Japanese economic and military control. The United States responded with a trade embargo against Japan and increased support for China. Because of the economic and military reverses suffered by Japan and its puppet governments in occupied lands as the war wore on, the term developed a cynical overtone. It became such an object of ridicule that it was known internationally as the "sphere of co-poverty and co-suffering."

great game 1. International ESPIONAGE in general. 2. British author Rudyard Kipling's term for the competition over the Indian subcontinent between Russia and Great Britain in the eighteenth and nineteenth centuries; more specifically, the rivalry over Afghanistan. According to analyst Steven R. Weisman, the objective of the great game "in three bloody Anglo-Afghan wars was to block the Russian bear's reach south to the warm waters of the Persian Gulf and the India Ocean. Today [1987] the game has drawn the United States into its greatest covert military operation since the Vietnam War" (*The New Republic,* August 10, 17, 1987). While the United States won the latest round with the

withdrawal of Soviet forces in 1989, the "game" in Afghanistan continues.

great leap forward A military approach toward economic development practiced in China (1958–1960). Believing that the economic and technical development of China could be accomplished at a vastly faster pace and with greater results if the people were aroused ideologically, MAO ZEDONG, the CHINESE COMMUNIST PARTY chairman, mobilized the peasantry and mass organizations and stepped up ideological guidance and indoctrination of technical experts. The rural areas were organized into people's communes, self-supporting communities for agriculture, small-scale industry, schooling, administration, and local security. The Great Leap Forward was an economic disaster. Among its economic consequences were a shortage of food and raw materials for industry, overproduction of poor-quality goods, and demoralization of the peasantry, workers, intellectuals, and even the party and government CADRE. As a result Mao was sidelined for a time by other party leaders.

Great Man Theory of History The belief that important individuals, rather than broad historical trends, have the most impact on events. Traditional political history has long been biased in favor of interpreting the past in light of the Great Man Theory. But Russian novelist Leo Tolstoy in *War and Peace* (1865) offered a famous debunking of the theory. He asserted that national leaders are really "history's slaves" as opposed to its masters; that "the actions of Napoleon and Alexander were as little voluntary as the action of any soldier who was drawn into the campaign by lot or by conscription. . . . It was necessary that millions of men in whose hands lay the real power . . . should consent to carry out the will of these weak individuals. . . . To elicit the laws of history we must leave aside kings, ministers and generals, and select for study the homogeneous, infinitesimal elements which influence the masses."

Great Mosque *See* GRAND MOSQUE.

Great Pacific War WORLD WAR II in the Pacific theater.

Great Patriotic War   1. The war of 1812 in which Imperial Russia and winter weather defeated Napoleon's France. 2. The Soviet phrase for WORLD WAR II.

great powers   The somewhat elusive and loose term for those states that most help to shape the international system. In addressing the question of what is a great power, Martin Wight in *Power Politics* (1979) notes, "It is easier to answer it historically, by enumerating the great powers at any date than by giving a definition." There is always agreement, after the fact, about which states were the great powers. During the Cold War the term tended to be used far less, with emphasis being placed instead on SUPERPOWERS and REGIONAL POWERS. With the end of the Cold War, however, and the growing diffusion of power in the international system, the term great powers may well come back into vogue.

Great Purge   The mass terror that JOSEPH STALIN used to impose his personal rule on the Communist Party and the general population of the Soviet Union from 1935 through 1938. An estimated 8 million victims were sent to labor camps, known as GULAGS,

A 1937 German cartoon depicting the Soviet purges. (Library of Congress)

where at least 2 million died. At least a million others were simply executed. While the Communist Party in particular was "purged" of those individuals perceived to be competitors of Stalin, the purge spanned all social and political divisions, encompassing common Soviet citizens as well as most of the Central Committee of the Communist Party (the Soviet parliament). The Soviet military was especially hard hit, losing most of its senior officers. The Great Purge was implemented by Stalin's secret police, the NKVD. "Show trials" were utilized to discredit public figures. By the beginning of World War II Stalin had eliminated all potential opposition within the Soviet Union. While Stalin purged people before and after, the period of intensive purging (1935–1938) came to be known as the *Great Terror*.

Great Russia   The central and northeastern parts of European Russia.

Great Terror   *See* GREAT PURGE.

Great War, the   What *World War I* was called before World War II necessitated giving it a number.

Great White Fleet   That portion of the United States Navy sent on a world cruise by President Theodore Roosevelt during 1907–1908. It literally flew the flag to demonstrate U.S. strength as a naval power. Since camouflage was not a consideration, the ships were painted white.

Greece, invasion of   The October 28, 1940, Italian attack that brought Greece into WORLD WAR II. The date is celebrated in Greece by the remembrance of the one-word reply—*ochi* (no)—given by Prime Minister Ioannis Metaxas (1871–1941) to a series of demands made by Italian leader Benito Mussolini. Despite Italian superiority in numbers and equipment, the Greeks drove the invaders back into Albania. Adolf Hitler was forced to divert German troops to protect his southern flank and attacked Greece in early April 1941. By the end of May the Germans had overrun most of the country, although Greek resistance was never suppressed entirely. German forces withdrew in October 1944.

Greek Civil War   The first armed conflict of the COLD WAR. When the occupying Germans withdrew in late 1944, the principal Greek resistance movement, which was controlled by Communists, sought to take control of the country and undertook a siege of the British forces in Athens during the winter of 1944–1945. When the siege was defeated, an unstable coalition government was formed. Continuing tensions led to the dissolution of that government and the outbreak of civil war in 1946. First the United Kingdom and later the United States (through the TRUMAN DOCTRINE) gave extensive military and economic aid to the Greek government. Communist successes in 1947–1948 enabled them to move freely over much of mainland Greece, but with extensive reorganization and U.S. material support, the Greek national army eventually defeated the Communist guerrillas. Yugoslavia, which had given more aid to the Greek Communists than had the Soviet Union, closed its borders to the insurgent forces in 1949 after Marshal JOSIP BROZ TITO broke with Stalin and the Soviet Union. Hostilities ceased in the fall of 1949 after some 80,000 Greeks were killed in the war.

Greek Colonels' Coup   The 1967 military coup in Greece by a group of army colonels. Civil liberties were suppressed, special military courts were established, and political parties were dissolved. Several thousand opponents were imprisoned or exiled to remote Greek islands. The junta's July 1974 attempt to overthrow Archbishop Makarios, the president of Cyprus, in order to install a client regime on the island brought Greece to the brink of war with Turkey in the CYPRUS CONFLICT. Senior Greek military officers then withdrew their support from the junta. A government of national unity was installed until elections were held in November 1974.

green   **1.** Young or inexperienced; an individual who has much to learn.   **2.** Concerning the environment. Thus "green politics" are environmental politics. A "green party" is mainly concerned with environmental issues. It does not necessarily have to have the word "green" in its name. "Green taxes" tax things that are considered environmentally undesirable in order to discourage their use. The "greens" are having a significant effect on politics in Europe and North America. For example, France, Germany, and the United Kingdom all have Green parties that field candidates for state and national legislatures and lobby for greater environmental protection efforts. However, the greens have yet to break out of the minor or fringe party category.

Green Book   The volume of political philosophy that Libya's MUAMMAR AL-QADDAFI purportedly wrote to justify his ruling style, a combination of Islamic zeal and traditional socialism that he calls the "third universal way." *Compare to* LITTLE RED BOOK.

green card   **1.** A wallet-size document identifying an alien as a permanent resident of the United States legally entitled to find work.   **2.** A European automotive insurance document indicating that a driver is insured in multiple states.

Greenham Common   The site of a Royal Air Force base in Berkshire, England, also used by the U.S. Air Force. During the 1980s it became the focal point for the antinuclear protest movement. Because the base was partly on common ground (hence the name Greenham Common), the peace protesters had a legal right to camp there. The "Peace Camps" that sprang up all around the perimeter fence of the base were famous for being populated entirely by women, whose activities included sit-down protests outside the main gates of the base.

greenhouse effect   The warming of the planet earth because of accumulating gases produced by the firing of fossil fuels in the atmosphere, notably carbon dioxide, trap infrared radiation. Eventually this may affect weather patterns. This was a major topic for the EARTH SUMMIT meeting on the environment. *See also* GLOBAL WARMING.

green line   **1.** The line in Nicosia, Cyprus, dividing the Greek Cypriot and Turkish Cypriot quarters; the line was established in 1963 following an outbreak of fighting between the two communities known as the CYPRUS CIVIL WAR.   **2.** The line separating Christian and Muslim areas in Beirut, Lebanon. **3.** Israel's borders before the 1967 SIX-DAY WAR.

green paper   A British term for a widely available government document containing policy alternatives on an issue. Green papers are designed to generate public debate on important questions facing the state.

Greenpeace

A Greenpeace vessel follows the USS Kittware *just prior to a 1989 Trident II missile test. (U.S. Naval Institute)*

Greenpeace An international lobby that seeks to protect whales, dolphins, seals, and other aspects of the marine environment from fishing fleets and nuclear testing. It also monitors the world's environment for radioactive and toxic waste pollution. Greenpeace International, founded in 1971 and headquartered in England, has 1.2 million members. Some Greenpeace members are environmental activists who engage in nonviolent interference with what they consider to be environmental abuse. Thus members have put themselves in physical danger to protect whales and stop atmospheric nuclear testing. The Greenpeace flagship, the RAINBOW WARRIOR, was bombed by France in 1985 to prevent it from interfering with French nuclear testing in the South Pacific. One crew member was killed, the French government apologized, and two French agents were convicted of the crime and each sentenced to ten years in prison.

green revolution The phrase that refers to the development of new hybrid grain seeds and the application of scientific methods to agriculture in DEVELOPING COUNTRIES to achieve higher crop production. The introduction of new seed varieties (highly responsive to fertilizer, hardy, and able to produce a grain that matures early) in the mid-1960s saw many developing countries approach self-sufficiency for the first time. However, the green revolution also requires fertilizers and other chemicals that are difficult for Third World farmers

to acquire or are harmful to the environment with repeated use.

Greenwich Mean Time (GMT) Solar time at the meridian of Greenwich, England, used as a basis for standard time throughout the world. It is normally expressed in four numerals (0001 through 2400) and is also called *Zulu Time*.

Grenada, invasion of The U.S.-led military action (with token support from several Caribbean states) of October 25, 1983, that took control of the Caribbean island nation of Grenada away from a Marxist military government, which had seized power six days earlier.

After obtaining independence in 1974, Grenada adopted a parliamentary system based on the British model. On March 13, 1979, the New Joint Endeavor for Welfare, Education, and Liberation (New JEWEL) Movement ousted the prime minister in a nearly bloodless coup d'etat and established a People's Revolutionary Government headed by Prime Minister Maurice Bishop (1944–1983). The new government, strongly Marxist-Leninist in orientation, moved to establish close ties to Cuba, the Soviet Union, and other Communist bloc countries. In October 1983 a power struggle within the government resulted in the arrest and subsequent execution of Bishop and several members of his cabinet by elements of the People's Revolutionary Army. Following the breakdown of civil order, the U.S.

Soldiers of the Caribbean Multinational Force on Grenada. (Department of Defense)

Reagan Administration acted in response to requests for military intervention from the GOVERNOR-GENERAL of Grenada and from the Organization of Eastern Caribbean States; and to guarantee the safety of the approximately 1,000 American citizens (mostly medical students) on the island. Within 60 days, all U.S. combat units were gone and the island was left in the control of a civilian council, which would govern pending elections.

President Ronald Reagan said in a speech on Lebanon and Grenada, October 27, 1983: "Grenada, we were told, was a friendly island paradise for tourism. Well it wasn't. It was a Soviet-Cuban colony being readied as a major military bastion to export terror and undermine democracy." Critics of the intervention argued that the students were never in danger and that the Cuban threat was greatly exaggerated. Some also suggested that the invasion would not have taken place had it not been for the bombing of a U.S. Marine base in Lebanon a few days earlier, which required that the Reagan Administration take strong action to restore its reputation in foreign policy.

gringo 1. A pejorative Mexican term for U.S. troops first used during the Mexican War of 1846–1848. The Spanish word *gringo* had long meant a foreigner (originally Greek) who spoke

unintelligibly. 2. Now a pejorative Latin American term for all YANKEES.

GRIT (graduated reciprocation in tension reduction) A concept developed by Charles Osgood in *An Alternative to War or Surrender* (1962). Osgood, a professor of psychology and communications research, proposed that the United States should reverse the arms race by taking initiatives that would decrease the tension in its relationship with the Soviet Union. Osgood described the scheme as a "flexible, self-regulating procedure in which the participants carefully monitor their own initiatives on the basis of their own evaluation of the reciprocating actions taken by the other side." The basic principle is that conciliatory or tension-reducing measures by one side will encourage the adversary to do the same and thereby gradually create an atmosphere of trust in which both sides will be able to take more far-reaching measures. Osgood, however, emphasized that in the early stages of the process, the unilateral initiatives should undermine neither nuclear deterrence nor U.S. conventional capabilities. He also argued that the unilateral initiatives should be public and should be accompanied by an invitation for the adversary to reciprocate. It is sometimes claimed that the moves by U.S. President John F. Kennedy and Soviet leader Nikita Khrushchev to move from the crises over Berlin and Cuba in 1961 and 1962 and agree on the partial Test Ban Treaty of 1963 were achieved through a series of unilateral and reciprocated initiatives. Some of Soviet President Mikhail Gorbachev's arms reduction measures of the late 1980s had the same quality, as did the initiative taken by U.S. President George Bush in September 1991 to reduce U.S. nuclear weapons.

Grivas, George T. (1898–1974) The Greek Cypriot World War II resistance leader who from 1955 to 1959 led the guerrilla forces on Cyprus in their successful fight for independence from Great Britain. He then spent the rest of his life fighting, both politically and militarily, for ENOSIS—union of Cyprus with Greece. *See also* CYPRUS CIVIL WAR.

Gromyko, Andrei Andreevich (1909–1989) The foreign minister of the Soviet Union from 1957 to 1985. He was also Soviet Ambassador to the United

Andrei Gromyko (far left) meets with U.S. President John F. Kennedy in the White House in 1963. (Library of Congress)

gross national product (GNP) The monetary value of all of the goods and services produced in a state in a given year. This is one of the most important measures of the health of a nation's economy. The real GNP expresses the gross national product in terms of constant dollars, meaning that the figures have been adjusted to take inflation into account.

Grotius, Hugo (1583–1645) The Dutch jurist and theologian (born Huig van Groot) who is considered to be the founder of INTERNATIONAL LAW, at least in its modern sense. A child prodigy, he was a jurist by age 17. In 1621, after being sentenced to life imprisonment in Holland for his political and religious views, he escaped (in a chest supposedly carrying books) to France where he published *De jure belli et pacis* (*The Rights of War and Peace*) in 1625. Although Grotius also wrote several religious tracts, his work on international law is his most important intellectual contribution. Contemporary analysts refer to this work as the Grotian tradition of thinking about international politics. Starting from the precepts of natural law, Grotius wrote on the JUST WAR THEORY while codifying existing practices and customs into a system of international jurisprudence.

ground-launched cruise missile (GLCM) Politically the most controversial, but militarily the least

Hugo Grotius (Library of Congress)

States (1943–1946), Soviet representative to the United Nations (1946–1948), Soviet Ambassador to Great Britain (1952–1953), and first deputy foreign minister (1946–1947). Gromyko was a Stalinist whose policies hinged on military security rather than political forms of security. While an unrepentant cold warrior, he was responsible for a program of DÉTENTE with the West. He was named to the Soviet Politburo in 1973, helping to consolidate Leonid Brezhnev's power. Gromyko proposed to the Central Committee that Mikhail Gorbachev become the general secretary of the CPSU in 1985. That same year Gromyko became chairman of the Presidium of the U.S.S.R. Supreme Soviet. He held this largely ceremonial post until his retirement in 1988, when Gorbachev succeeded him.

important, of the general family of CRUISE MISSILES. Although they can be equipped with conventional warheads, the GLCMs in operation with North Atlantic Treaty Organization forces were deployed in a theater nuclear force role. They are intermediate-range weapons capable of traveling several thousands of miles, but are very slow compared with ballistic missiles and are vulnerable to surface-to-air missiles and other defenses. The advantage of GLCMs is that they are highly mobile, being fired from self-powered launch vehicles, and can thus be driven around a region and hidden relatively easily. The U.S.-owned GLCMs deployed in Europe were at the center of the EUROMISSILE debate; it was agreed in the INF TREATY of 1987 that they would be removed from Europe. This removal was known as the ZERO OPTION.

Group of 18 The committee of management experts who in 1986 issued a stinging report on United Nations administrative and financial management; it was formally called the Group of High-level Intergovernmental Experts to Review the Efficiency of the Administrative and Financial Functioning of the United Nations.

Group of Five The five major non-Communist economic powers: the United States, Germany, Great Britain, Japan, and France. The heads of state of this group have met at formal summits since 1975. When Italy and Canada are included, the countries have been referred to as the GROUP OF SEVEN.

Group of Seven **1.** The seven major industrialized states whose leaders attend an annual economic summit: the United States, France, Britain, Germany, Canada, Italy, and Japan. Because of the totality of their economic power, they have been called a global board of directors and are often referred to as "the G-7." **2.** The M7 or Megadiversity 7; a conservationist classification for the states that contain more than half of all of the animal species of the earth: Australia, Brazil, Colombia, Indonesia, Madagascar, Mexico, and Zaire.

Group of 77 An organization of DEVELOPING COUNTRIES that has its origins in the "Caucus of 75" developing countries organized preparatory to the first UNITED NATIONS CONFERENCE ON TRADE AND DEVELOPMENT in Geneva in 1964. By the time UNCTAD I had completed its deliberations, the group had expanded by two members and issued a "Joint Declaration of the 77 Developing Countries" appraising the work of the conference. This numerical designation for the group has persisted, although by 1985 membership had increased to more than 120 countries. The Group of 77, or G-77, has continued to function as a caucus for the developing countries on economic matters in many forums including the United Nations. In contrast, the NONALIGNED MOVEMENT (whose members and concerns overlap to some extent those of the Group of 77) functions as a major political voice of the developing countries.

Group of Six An organization of nonnuclear countries seeking to achieve nuclear disarmament. The group came into being in 1984 when the leaders of the six countries (Prime Minister Indira Gandhi of India; President Miguel de la Madrid of Mexico; President Julius Nyerere of Tanzania; Prime Minister Olof Palme of Sweden; Prime Minister Andreas Papandreou of Greece; and President Raul Alfonsin of Argentina) issued a joint appeal called the Five Continents Peace Initiative. This statement called on the five major nuclear powers (United States, Soviet Union, United Kingdom, France, and China) to halt testing, production, and deployment of nuclear weapons. In 1985, following a summit meeting in New Delhi, the six leaders issued the Delhi Declaration reiterating the call for a nuclear freeze and calling, in addition, for a comprehensive test ban treaty, a ban on the militarization of outer space, and eventual nuclear disarmament.

Group of Ten The finance ministers of Belgium, Canada, France, Germany, Italy, Japan, the Netherlands, Sweden, the United Kingdom, and the United States (with Switzerland as an observer), who informally oversee the activities of the INTERNATIONAL MONETARY FUND.

Group of 20 **1.** The Interim Committee of Finance Ministers of the INTERNATIONAL MONETARY FUND composed of the finance ministers of the five wealthiest IMF members (the GROUP OF FIVE) plus 15 elected from the rest of the fund's members.

2. Representatives of 20 countries who constitute the Joint World Bank-IMF Ministerial Committee (or the Development Committee). These committees, representing both developed and developing countries, advise the fund and the World Bank on the structure of the international financial system.

Group of 24   An organization of finance ministers from 24 developing members of the INTERNATIONAL MONETARY FUND. The group, representing eight countries from each of the African, Asian, and Latin American country groupings in the GROUP OF 77, was formed in 1971 to counterbalance the influence of the GROUP OF TEN (which represents the developed countries in the IMF). The group continues to meet at regular intervals, usually in conjunction with formal IMF ministerial meetings.

Group of Two   The United States and Japan, the two largest economic powers; used in reference to bilateral economic cooperation.

groupthink   The psychological striving for consensus, which tends to stifle both healthy dissent and the analysis of viable alternatives in small decision-making groups. Groupthink tends to occur when individuals value membership in the group and identify strongly with their colleagues. It also may occur because the group leader does not encourage dissent or because of stressful situations that make the group more cohesive. Its essence, though, is that members suppress doubts and criticisms about proposed courses of action, with the result that the group chooses riskier and more ill-advised policies than would otherwise have been the case. Groupthink, because it refers to a deterioration of mental efficiency and moral judgment due to in-group pressures, has an insidious connotation. The term derives from Irving L. Janis's *Victims of Groupthink: A Psychological Study of Foreign Policy Decisions and Fiascoes* (1972; 2d ed., 1982).

Groves, Leslie Richard   (1896–1970)   The U.S. Army general who headed the Manhattan Project, the massive World War II research and development effort that produced the ATOMIC BOMB.

GSG-9   *Grenzschutzgruppe 9*, the German antiterrorist force established following the MUNICH MAS-SACRE at the 1972 Olympics. It is a national hostage rescue unit also trained to guard high-ranking officials in high-risk situations. It also provides security for German embassies around the world when they seem threatened. Its best-known operation was the October 17, 1977, rescue of 91 hostages aboard a hijacked Lufthansa airliner in Mogadishu, Somalia.

GSP   *See* GENERALIZED SYSTEM OF PREFERENCES.

Guadalcanal, Battle of   The first major U.S. land victory against Japan during World War II. When the Japanese built an air base on the island of Guadalcanal in the Solomon Islands in 1942, the United States responded in August of that year with a major invasion. Air, naval, and fierce jungle fighting continued for six months until, in February 1943, the Japanese evacuated the island, leaving behind about 25,000 dead. U.S. losses were about 1,500 dead and 5,000 wounded. Guadalcanal was strategically significant because it could have served as an air base for Japanese attacks on Australia, the chief base for Anglo-American operations in the South Pacific at that time. This victory and the naval victory at MIDWAY were the major turning points of World War II in the Pacific.

Guantanamo Bay   The site of a U.S. naval base in Cuba. It dates from a 1903 treaty between the United States and Cuba. Since the Castro regime came to power in 1959, the Cuban government has pressed for the land's return and has refused to accept the rent that the United States is obligated to pay. In 1992 the Bush Administration was heavily criticized for detaining at Guantanamo thousands of Haitian refugees picked up at sea instead of allowing them entry to the United States. Most of the refugees were returned to Haiti; only a few were allowed to move to the United States.

guarantee   Some kind of SECURITY UMBRELLA that one state extends over another. The purpose of the guarantee is to protect the other state from attack by a third party. The idea of a guarantee is also related to the concept of COMMITMENT. The United States' nuclear guarantee to Western Europe during the Cold War was a matter of some controversy, as some critics suggested that it lacked credibility. *See also* ALLIANCE.

Entrance to the United States' Guantanamo Bay naval base in Cuba. (U.S. Naval Institute)

Guatemalan Coup   The 1954 U.S. Central Intelligence Agency–managed overthrow of the elected government of President JACOBO ARBENZ GUZMÁN (1913–1971) in Guatemala. When the Guatemalan government in 1952 expropriated almost a quarter million acres of land belonging to the U.S.-based United Fruit Company, the company complained of inadequate compensation. The United States denounced the compensation offer and declared the Guatemalan government to be dominated by Communists. A 1954 CIA-sponsored invasion from Honduras led by Colonel Carlos Castillo Armas (1914–1957) took over the government, forced Arbenz into exile, and returned most of the United Fruit Company's land. This, in part because it repeated the success of the 1953 coup in Iran that regained the throne for MOHAMMED REZA PAHLEVI, seemed to confirm the effectiveness of U.S. covert actions as a way of combating Communist expansionism. This 1954 success in Guatemala is often cited as one of the main reasons the CIA thought it could later repeat its performance at the BAY OF PIGS in Cuba.

Guatemalan National Revolutionary Unity   *Unidad Revolucionaria Nacional Guatemalteca* (or URNG), a loose coalition of four of the major Guatemalan insurgent groups using terrorist tactics: the *Organización Revolucionaria del Pueblo en Armas* ("Revolutionary Organization of the People in Arms"), the *Ejército Guerrillero de los Pobres* ("Guerrilla

Army of the Poor"), the *Fuerzas Armadas Rebeldes* ("Rebel Armed Forces"), and the *Partido Guatemaltero del Trabajo* ("Guatemalan Party of Labor"). The groups signed a unity agreement that was a precondition for increased Cuban support in 1980, and the URNG was formalized in Havana in 1982. Cooperation and coordination among the groups is incomplete and irregular. Cuba in the past has made significant arms supplies to the coalition, but in recent years Cuban support is thought to have been limited to minor financial aid for black market arms purchases. All of the member groups are strongly anti–United States, though most of their activities have been directed against the Guatemalan Army. Their original goal was to overthrow the right-wing military governments that have dominated Guatemala since the 1950s, and end massive human rights abuses. International organizations such as Amnesty International and the United Nations Human Rights Commission have often complained about these human rights abuses of the Guatemalan governments, especially toward the Maya Indians. International attention was given to these abuses in 1992 when RIGOBERTA MENCHÚ was awarded the Nobel Peace Prize for her efforts to publicize them. One hopeful sign is that the new democratically elected civilian government of President Jorge Serrano, inaugurated in 1991, has promised to prosecute human rights abusers and has started negotiations with URNG.

Guernica   *See* CONDOR LEGION.

Guerrilla Forces of Liberation (GFL)   A Puerto Rican separatist organization, unknown prior to its claim of responsibility for a 1987 series of bombings in Puerto Rico.

guerrilla warfare   Military actions by irregular forces in enemy-controlled territory. The term was first used to refer to the Spanish partisans who fought against Napoleon Bonaparte's French troops in the early 1800s, but today any armed uprising by the people of a nation against their rulers may be considered guerrilla warfare. Since guerrilla troops do not follow normal battle tactics or use standard weapons in open combat, they are much more difficult for traditional troops to control. Because they never form into large units nor allow themselves to be trapped into fighting pitched battles, guerrillas are able to avoid the damage that the massed firepower and superior numbers of a regular army could inflict. Very large armies find their effective personnel substantially reduced when forced to garrison hundreds of villages and towns and to send guard detachments with every supply convoy. It is widely believed that a drawn-out guerrilla war will prove the undoing of and eventually defeat an orthodox army, but history provides little evidence for this. In 1812 the Napoleonic armies were defeated only by Wellington's traditional British army, and in World War II the French resistance was of use only in support of the 1944 Allied invasion. In Vietnam the U.S. Army was almost invariably successful in actual operations against the Vietcong, who were almost completely destroyed in the 1968 Tet Offensive; thereafter the United States fought the regular army of North Vietnam, an army that had already shown its worth in the entirely orthodox campaign against the French in 1954. The reason for the apparent success of guerrilla warfare is that it is usually practiced in countries where a foreign "army of occupation" has no support among the indigenous population. While the guerrillas generally achieve no significant military success, the costs of continuing to garrison troops and maintain a presence by force is often too much for the political will of the occupying power, which may decide to withdraw or to accommodate the guerrilla leaders, though remaining militarily undefeated. According to Robert Taber's *The War of the Flea* (1965): "The guerrilla fights the war of the flea, and his military enemy suffers the dog's disadvantages; too much to defend; too small, ubiquitous, and agile an enemy to come to grips with." Mao Zedong, leader of the People's Republic of China (1949–1976), summed up the essence of guerrilla strategy: "The enemy advances, we retreat; the enemy camps, we harass; the enemy tires, we attack; the enemy retreats, we pursue" (quoted in H. E. Salisbury, *The Long March*, 1985). U.S. Secretary of State Henry Kissinger summed up its result: "The conventional army loses if it does not win. The guerrilla wins if he does not lose" (*Foreign Affairs,* January 1969).

GEORGE BERNARD SHAW ON GUERRILLA WARFARE

Soldiering is the coward's art of attacking mercilessly when you are strong, and keeping out of harm's way when you are weak. That is the whole secret of successful fighting. Get your enemy at a disadvantage, and never, on any account, fight him on equal terms.

SOURCE: George Bernard Shaw, *Arms and the Man,* Act II (1894).

---

guerrilla warfare, rural   Tactics and strategy of GUERRILLA WARFARE designed to foment popular rebellion in the rural areas of underdeveloped nations in the interest of overthrowing the political status quo and establishing a revolutionary government. Rural guerrilla theory looks to the countryside as the vanguard of the revolution and has as its model the Cuban revolution of FIDEL CASTRO and ERNESTO "CHE" GUEVARA. Guevara and REGIS DEBRAY stand as the two foremost theorists of revolution through rural uprising. The FOCO, the concept of a revolutionary guerrilla group living as a community, living and raiding as a united entity, forms the basis of rural guerrilla theory and is the essence of the Latin American guerrilla movements of the 1960s. Rural guerrilla insurgency theory finds value in urban insurgencies, but only as complements to the primary revolutionary thrust of rural guerrilla warfare.

guerrilla warfare, urban Tactics and strategy of GUERRILLA WARFARE practiced in urban and metropolitan settings, utilizing armed attacks, assassinations, kidnappings, and robberies as means of upsetting the political status quo and establishing a revolutionary state. The evolution of modern urban guerrilla practice and theory is in large part a function of the decline and defeat of many of the rural-based Latin American insurgencies of the 1960s. By the late 1960s, rural guerrilla movements in Bolivia, Colombia, and Guatemala, among others, were displaying symptoms of collapse and strategic failure. Leftist revolutionaries in Argentina, Brazil, and Uruguay found that urban strategies offered many improvements over the rural insurgencies advocated by ERNESTO "CHE" GUEVARA, REGIS DEBRAY, and other more traditional theorists. Urban warfare seemed to offer more accessible targets, improved sources of supplies and funds, and an expanded recruiting pool. Besides, in these countries urban areas contained the most students and intelligentsia, who comprised the greatest percentage of Marxist devotees sympathetic to the guerrillas' aims. The Uruguayan TUPAMAROS were the first guerrilla group to recognize the potential of the urban area as a focus of revolutionary activity rather than simply a complement to the rural struggle. They found the urban strategy to be an ideal method of provoking the government into repressive counterinsurgency measures. The Tupamaros' goal—and one of today's urban guerrilla—was to provoke the authorities into actions that would incite the general population into mass rebellion. The Tupamaros' goal was only partially met, for though they succeeded in provocation, their urban guerrilla strategy so weakened Uruguay's civilian government that the military assumed control of the country and destroyed the Tupamaros through an intense campaign of repression.

guestworkers Foreign nationals who are employed in another nation. The term is used in Western Europe, especially Germany, to refer primarily to Turkish workers. The guestworkers generally do menial jobs and are not eligible for the kinds of benefits available to citizens. They also are the target of considerable hostility. Their presence, however, reflects the fact that they can earn much more in Western Europe than they can in their own country. Guestworkers also exist in large numbers in the oil-rich Persian Gulf states. However, unlike in Europe, they are a mix of menial THIRD WORLD workers and highly trained Western technicians. While the Westerners tend eventually to return home, the Third World guestworkers often remain for generations. Denied citizenship even if locally born, many of them become, in effect, stateless alien residents in their native land.

Guevara, Ernesto "Che" (1928–1967) The legendary guerrilla leader, born in Argentina, who fought with FIDEL CASTRO in the Cuban revolution. He was highly influential as a revolutionary theorist; his treatise *Guerrilla Warfare* (1960) has become a standard text for Latin American revolutionaries. Guevara became one of the leaders of Castro's Cuba after the successful overthrow of FULGENCIO BATISTA, but in 1965 he left Cuba to foment and lead revolutionary guerrilla movements. In October 1967 he was captured by Bolivian government forces and executed.

guidance 1. Policy, direction, decision, or instruction having the effect of an order when promulgated by a higher echelon. 2. In weaponry, the entire process by which target intelligence information perceived by a guided missile is used to effect proper flight control to cause timely direction changes for successful target interception.

gulags 1. The prison and forced labor camps of the Soviet Union. Author ALEXANDER SOLZHENITSYN traces the gulag back to V. I. Lenin, but it was under Joseph Stalin that the brutal gulag system reached its terrifying zenith. Solzhenitsyn himself was sent to a gulag for referring to Stalin as "the man with the mustache" in personal correspondence. *Gulag* is the Russian acronym for *Glavnoye Upravleniye Ispravitelno-Trudovykh Lagerey* ("Chief Administration of Corrective Labor Camps"). The term came into English with the publication of Solzhenitsyn's *Gulag Archipelago* (1974), the first major account of Soviet prison labor camps. According to Solzhenitsyn, an estimated 13 to 25 million died because of the harsh conditions in the gulag system. These included peasants during Stalin's COLLECTIVIZATION drive; millions more sentenced during the GREAT PURGE of the late 1930s; and returning Soviet prisoners of war from World War II deemed "traitors to the fatherland" for not having died in battle. As part of the Soviet plan for economic development, gulag labor built up Siberia, Central Asia, and the Far North. Prisoners were often taken and sentenced just to fulfill labor quotas. **2.** By analogy, "gulag" now applies to any state's system of forced labor camps for political prisoners, such as those in China.

Gulf Cooperation Council   The economic cooperation and integration entity created by six Persian Gulf states (Bahrain, Kuwait, Oman, Qatar, Saudi Arabia, and the United Arab Emirates) in 1981 to deal with financial, economic, and social planning; financial, economic, and trade cooperation; industrial cooperation; oil; and social and cultural services. The council, formally the Cooperation Council for the Arab States of the Gulf, has its headquarters in Riyadh, Saudi Arabia.

Gulf of Sidra incident   **1.** The August 1981 aerial dogfight between U.S. and Libyan fighter planes over international waters in the Gulf of Sidra. The United States shot down two Libyan jets after one of them fired on the U.S. Navy planes. The United States purposely scheduled naval maneuvers in the gulf to challenge Libyan leader MUAMMAR AL-QADDAFI's assertion that the gulf, which is that part of the Mediterranean Sea that dips slightly into Libya, is in Libyan territorial (and not international) waters. The U.S. position was that Libya's claim that the gulf was its territorial waters was absurd, and its maneuvers were designed to defend the principle of freedom of the seas.   **2.** The March 1986 encounter between U.S. naval units operating in international waters in the Gulf of Sidra and Libyan gunboats. When Libyan patrol boats fired surface-to-air missiles at aircraft from U.S. aircraft carriers, the United States responded by attacking the boats. The United States estimated that at least two of the boats were sunk and 150 Libyan sailors were killed. Again, the U.S. naval maneuvers were scheduled to defy Libya's assertion that the gulf waters were territorial.

Gulf of Tonkin Resolution   The 1964 joint resolution of the U.S. Congress that sanctioned the Johnson Administration's use of large numbers of U.S. forces in an escalation of the VIETNAM WAR. It was premised on a presumed attack on U.S. ships in Vietnam's Gulf of Tonkin by North Vietnamese naval units. It stated that Congress "approves and supports the determination of the President, as Commander in Chief, to take all necessary measures to repel any armed attack against the forces of the United States and to prevent further aggression." The Johnson Administration considered this resolution as the moral and legal equivalent of a declaration of war. Later those who opposed the war would denounce the resolution as a fraud because there was little evidence that there ever was an attack on American ships in the Tonkin Gulf. Indeed, historian Barbara W. Tuchman in *The March of Folly* (1984) would write: "With evidence accumulating of confusion by radar and sonar technicians in the second clash, [President] Johnson said privately, 'Well, those dumb stupid sailors were just shooting at flying fish.' So much for casus belli." But there was little initial opposition. The House of Representatives passed it unanimously. In the Senate there were only two dissenting votes. Senator Jacob K. Javits, who voted for the resolution, would later write in *Who Makes War* (1973): "In voting unlimited presidential power most members of Congress thought they were providing for retaliation for an attack on our forces; and preventing a large-scale war in Asia, rather than authorizing its inception."

Gulf states   The oil-rich states surrounding the Persian Gulf: Bahrain, Iran, Iraq, Kuwait, Oman, Qatar, Saudi Arabia, and the United Arab Emirates.

Gulf War   **1.** The IRAN-IRAQ WAR of 1980–1988. **2.** The PERSIAN GULF WAR of 1990–1991.

gunboat   A small naval vessel. The use of gunboat diplomacy in the context of international politics implies that a great power is seeking to have its way with a small power through the threat of force. Traditional *gunboat diplomacy* follows the recommendation of Oliver Cromwell (1599–1658) who said that: "A Man-of-war is the best ambassador." One of the most famous cases of gunboat diplomacy occurred in 1904 when U.S. Secretary of State John Hay sent a telegram to U.S. foreign officers with a message for the Sultan of Morocco: "This Government wants Perdicaris alive or Raisuli dead." This incident concerned the kidnapping of Ion H. Perdicaris by Raisuli, a Moroccan outlaw. U.S. warships were sent to Morocco, even though the telegram, according to historian Barbara W. Tuchman's "Perdicaris Alive or Raisuli Dead" (*American Heritage,* August 1959), "was not an ultimatum, because Hay deliberately deprived it of meaningfulness by [ordering the Navy], 'Do not land marines or seize customs without Department's specific instructions.' But this sentence was not allowed to spoil the effect: It was withheld from the press." In the end Perdicaris was released and Raisuli became a local governor. (Ironically, this whole incident over the protection of a U.S. citizen was misguided because Perdicaris was *not* a U.S. citizen; but people thought he was at the time.)

guns and butter   A phrase that since the 1930s has succinctly summed up a state's policy alternatives between military spending (the guns) or domestic spending (the butter). For example, U.S. Senator William Proxmire said in a speech in the Senate on September 3, 1969, "Not too long ago it was commonplace to hear that this nation could afford both guns and butter—that we could provide for our defense, meet our world commitments and take care of pressing national problems. Now it has become fashionable to take the opposite view—we can have either guns or butter, but not both."

Gush Emunim   Hebrew for "the Bloc of the Faithful," an Israeli right-wing, strictly orthodox organization, founded in 1974 and dedicated to the permanent and formal annexation of the OCCUPIED TERRITORIES. This organization was responsible for much of the WEST BANK Jewish terrorism of the early 1980s, including bombings that injured the Arab mayors of Nablus and Ramallah.

Guzmán, Jacobo Arbenz   *See* ARBENZ GUZMÁN, JACOBO.

H

Haas, Ernst (1924–) One of the leading analysts in the study of political INTEGRATION. Haas wrote *The Uniting of Europe* (1958) and *Beyond the Nation-State: Functionalism and International Organization* (1964), in which many ideas of NEO-FUNCTIONALISM were developed and enunciated. Central to his thinking was the notion that integration stems from the beliefs and actions of elites who see the process as having certain specific advantages. He emphasized functionally specific international programs, which he saw as means of maximizing national welfare and the integration process—a task that was facilitated by the learning which took place in government and by the processes of "spillover," as those who had benefited from SUPRANATIONAL organizations in one sector extended their cooperation to other sectors. By the 1970s, however, Haas had identified certain conditions under which the integration process was likely to be reversed. Actors could change their views about the advantages of regional cooperation or could decide that the problems they were trying to solve through regional integration were not in fact regional problems. If Haas has always been self-critical in his views, however, he also has been a scholar who has consistently pushed at the frontiers of knowledge and understanding and who has developed an eclectic approach to international relations. In a book published in 1990 entitled *When Knowledge Is Power: Three Models of Change in International Organizations,* for example, he dealt with the theme of organizational learning, adding new insights and understanding in this area.

Habash, George (1925–) The medical doctor who leads the POPULAR FRONT FOR THE LIBERATION OF PALESTINE (PFLP), one of the most radical terrorist groups within the Palestine Liberation Organization. The PFLP, under Habash's direction, conducted some of the most infamous of Palestinian terrorist acts, including the DAWSON'S FIELD incident that led to the BLACK SEPTEMBER ouster of the Palestinian guerrilla groups from Jordan. He has often been considered to be a rival to YASIR ARAFAT, whom he finds too prone to compromise. The hard-line Habash is motivated by a leftist ideology in a way that Arafat is not. Habash caused a major embarrassment to the French government in 1992 when he was secretly allowed into France for medical treatment. When Habash's presence was revealed, the French government equivocated: Habash, whose group was linked to the hijacking of an Air France jet to ENTEBBE in 1976 and the murder of two French policemen at Orly Airport in 1978, was allowed to leave hastily. President François Mitterand of France denied that he had prior knowledge of Habash's admission. In a television interview on February 4, 1992, Mitterand announced the dismissal of a few rather low-level officials who had been linked to the decision, but stated that none of his ministers would resign because the affair was "not serious enough," involving as it did only an "error of judgment" about a "retired terrorist" (*The Economist,* February 8, 1992). Presumably, some noted, those guilty of terrorist acts all over the world would now announce their "retirements" and move to safe haven in France.

habit-driven actor A concept developed by rational analyst James Rosenau in *Turbulence in World*

Politics (1990) to describe ideal types of ACTORs "whose behavior derives from a habit function developed over time out of memories, traits, beliefs, expectations, scenarios, and prior experiences that lead them to make the same choices that they made previously in the same context." They are different from actors who make rational calculations in that they tend to act according to cultural norms and bureaucratic inertia.

Hagana   Hebrew for "defense"; the underground army of Jewish Palestine before Israeli statehood was declared in May 1948. It was then incorporated into the official Israel Defense Forces.

Hague, The   The capital of the Netherlands. Many elements of international law begin with "the Hague" because conferences that created them were held at The Hague.

Hague Convention of 1970   The Convention for the Suppression of Unlawful Seizure of Aircraft of the United Nations International Civil Aviation Organization, which deals with the unlawful seizure of aircraft and establishes an extradite or prosecute requirement for terrorist offenses. It obliges each signatory state to make offenses punishable by "severe penalties." Thus each state must make aircraft hijacking a part of its domestic criminal law. While 130 countries have signed this convention, none of them is obliged to extradite a hijacker except under the terms of a separate EXTRADITION treaty. This means that extradition of hijackers may still be refused on the basis of provisions in a treaty that exclude extradition for political offenses or deny the extradition of a state's own citizens. *See also* BONN DECLARATION; MONTREAL CONVENTION.

Hague Peace Conferences   International conferences held in the capital of the Netherlands in 1899 and 1907. The 1899 conference, convened at the invitation of Russia, focused on arms limitations and laws of war. German resistance stopped any real disarmament. Conventions adopted there defined certain practices relating to war on land and sea, and there were declarations (not renewed in 1907) prohibiting the use of DUM DUM BULLETs and asphyxiating gases. The conference also set up the Convention for the

Peaceful Settlement of International Disputes with a panel of judges known as the Permanent Court of Arbitration.

The 1907 conference achieved even less than the 1899 meeting. Convened at the urging of the United States, it adopted several conventions relating to the rights and duties of neutral states, the laying of mines, and the status of enemy merchant ships in wartime. The conference accepted the principle of compulsory arbitration. Another meeting was to be held in 1915, but this was impossible because of the outbreak of World War I, which showed the limits of the Hague Conference arbitration approach to international conflict. Even so, some underlying assumptions were retained and influenced the approach of the LEAGUE OF NATIONS during the interwar period.

Hague Tribunal   The WORLD COURT located in The Hague.

Haig, Alexander M., Jr. (1924–   )   The career U.S. Army officer who, after serving as a staff assistant to National Security Advisor Henry A. Kissinger in the first Nixon Administration, then became White House Chief of Staff (1973–1974). He was made Supreme Allied Commander Europe (SACEUR) from 1975 to 1979. He became President Ronald Reagan's first secretary of state in 1981. He

---

HAIG CONVINCES KISSINGER

The prospect of [General Alexander] Haig as SACEUR, a potentially important foreign-policy proconsul in Europe, had initially enraged the other indispensable figure of the infant [Ford] administration, Secretary Kissinger. When Kissinger threatened to veto the posting . . . Haig then "stormed into Henry's office and had a little talk about what could come out" in a Senate hearing or a series of leaks. Looming over that conversation with his old boss were all the shadows they had cast together, yet so far publicly escaped—the truth of the wiretaps . . . [and] the long trail of sordid policies not yet exposed. "It took about a half an hour," said one Kissinger confidante of the talk that September, "and Henry saw what a great NATO supreme commander Al would make."

SOURCE: Roger Morris, *Haig: The General's Progress* (1982).

was forced to resign in 1982 over policy differences with the president and the White House staff. Haig's short tenure as secretary of state was a tempestuous one. He was the most pro-European member of the Reagan Administration at a time when the European allies and the United States were at odds over policy toward the Soviet Union. He also differed with other members of the administration over the role of the secretary of state. From the outset, he demanded that he be regarded as the "vicar" of foreign policy. His one attempt at shuttle diplomacy was in the Falklands crisis, but despite his best efforts he was unable to prevent Great Britain and Argentina from going to war.

Haig, Douglas (1861–1928)   The British field marshal who commanded British forces in World War I on the Western Front from 1915 to 1917. His strategy of trench warfare attrition was unimaginative and criticized for its high casualties, but it eventually won—with the help of U.S. reinforcements. Haig lacked the common touch. Field Marshal Bernard Montgomery in *A History of Warfare* (1968) tells the story that Haig would inspect troops in total silence. "One of his staff suggested it would create a good impression if he would occasionally stop and speak to one or two men. He took the advice and asked one man: 'Where did you start this war?' The astonished soldier replied: 'I didn't start this war, sir; I think the Kaiser did.' I understand that Haig give it up after this encounter!" British Prime Minister David Lloyd George supposedly once described Haig as being "brilliant up to the top of his army boots."

Haile Selassie (1892–1975)   The ruler of Ethiopia as regent (1916–1928), king (1928–1930), and emperor (1930–1974), whose program for modernization was interrupted by the ABYSSINIAN-ITALIAN WAR, which temporarily forced him into exile. Italy annexed Ethiopia in 1936, and Selassie returned to Ethiopia in 1941 after Allied forces chased out the Italians. Thereafter he continued reform efforts and functioned on the international scene as an elder statesman to newly independent African states. He gradually lost touch with his domestic situation and was deposed by a military coup in 1974, dying as a captive of the military. His deposition led to the ETHIOPIAN CIVIL WAR.

Emperor Haile Selassie in 1969. (Library of Congress)

HAILE SELASSIE'S UNHEEDED PLEA TO THE LEAGUE OF NATIONS, JUNE 30, 1936

I assert that the problem . . . today . . . is the very existence of the League. It is the confidence that each State is to place in international treaties. . . . In a word, it is international morality that is at stake. . . . Should it happen that a strong government finds that it may, with impunity, destroy a small people, then the hour strikes for that weak people to appeal to the League. . . . God and history will remember your judgment. . . . What reply have I to take back to my people?

SOURCE: Haile Selassie's address to the League of Nations at Geneva, Switzerland. He charged the Italians with using poison gas on civilians and with poisoning fields and wells. The League responded by condemning Italian aggression but did nothing effective to help. The League's inability to cope with even this small war highlighted its international impotence.

Haitian boat people   Refugees from Haiti who seek asylum in the United States by leaving their Caribbean island in small boats in an attempt to land 600 miles to the north in Florida. No one knows how many have drowned in the attempt, but during 1991 and 1992 tens of thousands were intercepted by the U.S. Coast Guard and Navy and interned at the U.S. GUANTANAMO BAY naval base in Cuba pending repatriation. This policy has been widely criticized in the United States as racist because similar refugees from Cuba (who are mostly white) are routinely granted asylum while the Haitians (who are all black) are not.

Haitian Coup   The 1991 military coup that overthrew the government of Jean-Bertrand Aristide (1953–   ). Aristide, a Catholic priest, in 1990 became Haiti's first democratically elected leader, winning 67 percent of the vote in national elections. But when he sought to curb the power of the military and fired 8,000 unnecessary public employees, the military, in September 1991, took over the government, rehired almost all of the fired employees, and installed Marc L. Bazin (1932–   ) as prime minister. A team of French, American, and Venezuelan diplomats negotiated with the new government to gain Aristide's release (from prison) into exile. In October 1991 the ORGANIZATION OF AMERICAN STATES called for an economic boycott of Haiti to protest the coup. This international boycott, supported by the United States, has been only partially effective. But it has so hurt the Haitian economy that large numbers of HAITIAN BOAT PEOPLE have been seeking refuge in the United States. Meanwhile, in exile Aristide seeks international help to restore his regime. In a September 1992 address to the United Nations General Assembly, he denounced the Vatican for being the only state to grant diplomatic recognition to the military regime: "Rejected by all the states of the world, these criminals are still recognized by the Vatican, the only state to bless the crimes it should have condemned in the name of the God of Justice and Peace. What would have been the Vatican's attitude if Haiti was inhabited by whites? What would have been Pope John Paul II's attitude if Haiti had been Polish?" (*New York Times,* September 30, 1992).

Halifax, Lord (1881–1959)   Born Edward F. L. Wood, the British Ambassador to the United States during most of World War II (1941–1946). He was the viceroy of India (1925–1931) and became foreign minister after Anthony Eden resigned to

protest NEVILLE CHAMBERLAIN's policy of APPEASEMENT. In 1941 he was Chamberlain's favorite to be prime minister but was passed over in favor of Winston Churchill.

Hallstein doctrine   The position of the KONRAD ADENAUER government of the Federal Republic of Germany, enunciated by Foreign Minister Walter Hallstein (1901–1982) in 1955, that the FRG was the only German state. This was an important COLD WAR issue: Adenauer refused to give up his dream of German reunification, which was anathema to the Soviet Union. The FRG did not recognize the sovereignty of the German Democratic Republic (East Germany) and regarded diplomatic recognition of it an unfriendly act, because it implied that Germany was permanently divided. This doctrine became increasingly irrelevant as tensions eased in Europe in the 1960s and was abandoned in favor of OSTPOLITIK, in which the Federal Republic established diplomatic relations with members of the WARSAW PACT.

Halperin, Morton H. (1938–   )   One of the younger U.S. nuclear weapons strategists who came to prominence in the late 1950s and early 1960s and whose book *Limited War in the Nuclear Age* (1963) was widely regarded as a classic treatment of its subject. Although Halperin wrote on other aspects of nuclear strategy, his other famous work is *Bureaucratic Politics and Foreign Policy* (1974), which provided an illuminating and helpful account of the ways in which bureaucratic politics can influence foreign and security policy. In the early 1970s Halperin worked for U.S. National Security Advisor Henry Kissinger but became one of the targets of Kissinger's wiretapping—a development that led him to initiate legal action against his boss. He has subsequently become a high-ranking figure in the American Civil Liberties Union.

Halt in Belgrade proposal   A proposal that was made on July 28, 1914, by Kaiser WILLIAM II of Germany in an effort to stop the SARAJEVO crisis from escalating into a war between the rival alliances in Europe. In essence he proposed that Austrian military action against Serbia result only in a temporary occupation of the northern portion of Serbia (as far south as Belgrade) rather than the complete subjugation of that state. This temporary action would provide a guarantee that Serbia would meet Austrian demands without the Austrian victory being a direct challenge to Russia. Unfortunately German pressure for its Austrian ally to halt in Belgrade was neither sufficiently strong nor sustained enough to reverse the momentum of the 1914 crisis toward WORLD WAR I.

Hamah Massacre   The Syrian government's response to political opposition. Because the city of Hamah in Syria was a hotbed of antigovernment activity in 1982, President HAFEZ AL-ASSAD ordered the Syrian Army to level it in order to destroy the MUSLIM BROTHERHOOD, the opposition group that used Hamah as its base. Over a two-week period much of the city was destroyed along with an estimated 25,000 civilians killed, including several thousand members of the Muslim Brotherhood. The Hamah incident also caused Syria to break diplomatic relations with Iraq later in 1982. Syria accused Iraq of supporting the Brotherhood's efforts to destabilize the Syrian regime.

Hamas   The Palestinian Islamic fundamentalist political movement in the Israeli-occupied territories and neighboring Jordan. By the early 1990s, Hamas, with its goal of destroying, as opposed to negotiating with Israel, had grown to be a serious rival to the PALESTINE LIBERATION ORGANIZATION for leadership of the Palestinian cause.

Hammarskjöld, Dag (1905–1961)   The Swedish diplomat and economist who was the second secretary general of the United Nations, from 1951 until he died in 1961 in a plane crash while on a peace mission in the Congo.

Soon after the Belgian Congo gained its national independence in 1960, conditions became chaotic and an international police force under the United Nations was sent in to reestablish order and to supervise Belgian withdrawal. After accusing Hammarskjöld of being prejudiced against the leftist regime of Patrice Lumumba, Soviet Premier Nikita Khrushchev sent Soviet military equipment, technicians, and advisors to assist Lumumba and even threatened to dispatch Soviet "volunteers." Khrushchev urged the removal of Hammarskjöld and the replacement of the secretary general's office with a TROIKA. For his pursuit of peace in the

Congo, Hammarskjöld was posthumously awarded the Nobel Peace Prize in 1961. *See also* CONGOLESE CIVIL WAR.

hammer and sickle   The Communist emblem displayed on the flag of the former Soviet Union. The crossed tools represented the union of industrial workers (symbolized by the hammer) and agricultural workers (symbolized by the sickle).

Hapsburg Empire   *See* AUSTRO-HUNGARIAN EMPIRE.

hard currency   Money that can be exchanged easily for the currency of another state, also known as CONVERTIBLE CURRENCY. Hard currencies are widely used in international trade because they are readily acceptable as payments for goods and debts. Generally speaking, the currencies of the industrialized states of the West are considered "hard." In contrast, because the currencies of many developing countries are not convertible, they are considered to be SOFT CURRENCY.

Dag Hammarskjöld (Library of Congress)

Harding, Warren Gamaliel (1865–1923)   The U.S. President who won election in 1920 with a call to a "return to normalcy" after the excitement of World War I. He accomplished little in office and is usually scorned by historians, who have consistently rated him to be one of the worst presidents ever. He died suddenly in 1923, leaving his successor, CALVIN COOLIDGE, a variety of government scandals for which Harding was not personally responsible but that gave his administration its well-deserved reputation for corruption. In foreign policy, Harding's achievements were at much the same level as in domestic policy. This was hardly surprising given the ISOLATIONISM that dominated the United States at the time and which resulted in the U.S. Senate's rejection of the Treaty of Versailles and of U.S. participation in the League of Nations. It was Alice Roosevelt Longworth, in her book *Crowded Hours* (1933), who made the most famous assessment of Harding: "I think everyone must feel that the brevity of his tenure of office was a mercy to him and to the country. Harding was not a bad man. He was just a slob."

hard kill   Totally destroying a target as opposed to merely disabling it; striking a target in such a way as to produce unambiguous visible evidence of its destruction. A target that is only disabled and not destroyed is a *soft kill*.

hard target   **1.** Something protected against a nuclear blast, such as a missile SILO or a command bunker. Often buried deep underground, hard targets have walls of steel-reinforced concrete several feet thick. They can be destroyed only by enormous blast power, requiring a combination of extreme accuracy and very high yield from ground-burst nuclear warheads. Because both the United States and Russia are concerned with minimizing the vulnerability of their retaliatory missiles, they have dispersed these weapons in submarines and hardened silos. But during the 1970s and 1980s there was doubt about the survivability of missiles emplaced in silos because of possible counterforce strikes by increasingly accurate multiple-warhead missiles. **2.** In the context of conventional warfare, an armored vehicle immune to an ordinary high-explosive shell, in contrast to a "thin-skin" or *soft target* such as a truck or a human body.

Harmel Report   The document approved by North Atlantic Treaty Organization members in 1967 that defined the future tasks of the alliance in terms of DÉTENTE as well as defense. The Harmel Report, the result of a study directed by Belgium's Foreign Minister Pierre Harmel, is credited with initiating NATO support for détente in Europe to accompany the continued emphasis on DETERRENCE.

harmonization   **1.** A method of cutting tariffs to make such taxes on most items more nearly uniform within each individual country's tariff schedule. Most proposals for harmonization involve formulas that would produce relatively large cuts in high tariffs and smaller cuts in lower tariffs.   **2.** The creation of common laws and standards for all member states in an economic union, such as the European Community.

Harriman, William Averell (1891–1986)   Born to wealth as the son of railroad magnate Edward H. Harriman (1848–1909), young Harriman spent the second half of his life at the forefront of U.S. diplo-

---

HARRIMAN VERSUS RUSK

In late 1962 and 1963 [Averell Harriman] clearly emerged as a figure in the Department [of State] openly challenging [Secretary of State Dean] Rusk for leadership, obviously a candidate for Secretary of State, a job which he, a man so private about his own feelings, would once admit wistfully was the only job he had ever wanted. . . . Although he had not been a particular fan of Rusk's from the start, he had begun by being extremely correct with him. But Rusk's style soon irritated him, and those who were around him detected a very subtle patronizing of the Secretary. (It showed at one staff meeting. . . . Rusk addressed his team, saying that [British Labour leader] Harold Wilson was in town and that it looked as if he was going to win the election and become Prime Minister, and perhaps they had better do something for him. Did anyone know where he was staying? No one knew, so Rusk dispatched [George] Ball to call the British embassy and find out. Ball left, came back white-faced a few minutes later, and whispered to Rusk, "He's Averell's house guest." Harriman, sitting there, never moved a muscle.)

SOURCE: David Halberstam, *The Best and the Brightest* (1972).

matic efforts to win WORLD WAR II and the COLD WAR. He was President Franklin D. Roosevelt's Ambassador to the Soviet Union (1943–1946); President Harry Truman's Ambassador to Great Britain (1946); secretary of commerce (1946–1948); and European administrator of the MARSHALL PLAN (1948–1950). From 1955 to 1958 he was the Democratic governor of New York. For President John F. Kennedy he negotiated the 1963 PARTIAL TEST-BAN TREATY and as undersecretary of state for political affairs played a major role in formulating VIETNAM WAR policy. In 1965 President Lyndon B. Johnson appointed him ambassador at large. He then became the chief U.S. negotiator at the Paris Peace Talks with North Vietnam until he was relieved by representatives of the new Nixon Administration in 1969.

Harris, Arthur (1892–1984)   The Royal Air Force Marshal in charge of the British Bomber Command during World War II. Because losses were too heavy when British bombers sought to attack specific German targets in daylight, he became the strongest advocate of the nighttime area bombing of cities. His policies, which were embraced by the United States when it joined the war, caused massive death and destruction in German cities. Critics contended that such random devastation of both civilian and military targets was militarily indefensible. Defenders maintained that he was only doing to the Germans what they sought to do first to England. "Bomber Harris" was especially criticized for the DRESDEN raid of 1945. It is estimated that Harris's Bomber Command lost 50,000 men; but they also killed approximately 500,000 Germans.

HARRIS AND THE CONSTABLE

[Air Marshall Arthur Harris, head of Bomber Command in World War II] spent much of the war racing his Bentley [automobile] at breakneck speed between High Wycombe and the Air Ministry, and was the bane of motor-cycle policemen on the London road. "You might have killed somebody, sir," said a reproachful constable who stopped him late one night.

"Young man, I kill thousands of people every night!" snapped Harris.

SOURCE: Max Hastings, *Bomber Command* (1979).

Hart, Basil H. Liddell   *See* LIDDELL HART, BASIL H.

Haughey, Charles (1925–   )   The prime minister (or *Taoiseach*) of Ireland (1979–1981, 1982, 1987–1992) who was last forced out of office by allegations that he lied about wiretapping the telephones of Irish journalists. The Haughey administrations were noted for their strained relations with Great Britain over the issue of Northern Ireland.

Haushofer, Karl (1869–1946)   The father of German geopolitical theory, which placed emphasis on the primacy of geography over all other factors. After leaving the Bavarian Army, where he had attained the rank of major general, Haushofer developed his theories of geopolitics. He was influenced by the ideas of a political geographer, F. Ratzel, who argued in "The Territorial Growth of States" (*Scottish Geographical Magazine*, 1896) that "the territory of a state has no definite area fixed for all time—for a state is a living organism and therefore cannot be contained within rigid limits." Ratzel also developed the notion of LEBENSRAUM, or "living space." Haushofer was also influenced by HALFORD J. MACKINDER and his ideas about the future ascendancy of land power. As G. Sloan pointed out in *Geopolitics in United States Strategic Policy 1890–1987* (1988), Haushofer continued the nineteenth-century idea that Germany was incomplete and had a unique and separate destiny from the other European states, which was to create unity from the diversity of Central Europe. His importance was enhanced in Germany by his close ties with key members of the NAZI party, especially Rudolph Hess. Moreover, it is sometimes suggested that Adolf Hitler derived some of the ideas expressed in *Mein Kampf* from Haushofer.

One of the most important of Haushofer's ideas was that Germany had a natural affinity of interest with Japan and with Russia, and that an alliance of the three nations would create an "inner line" that would be globally dominant. This idea is sometimes seen as the basis for the NAZI-SOVIET NONAGGRESSION PACT, which was abandoned when Hitler decided to invade the Soviet Union—an act that Sloan describes as "the antithesis of Haushofer's geopolitical doctrine."

Havel, Vaclav (1936–   )   The president of Czechoslovakia since 1989. A leader of CIVIC FORUM, he had been a dissident playwright whose plays included views on the necessity of a multiparty system to prevent a government from initiating human rights abuses. His opposition to the oppressive Communist government was further publicized in CHARTER 77 documents, of which he was a founder, spokesman, and initial signatory. Several prison sentences were not enough to deter the playwright from organizing and leading demonstrations against the government in 1988 and 1989. On December 29, 1989, Havel succeeded GUSTAV HUSAK as president. He was officially elected to a two-year term as president by the people in a general election in June 1990. But in July 1992, in the wake of the breakup of Czechoslovakia into independent states, Havel resigned so that he would not have to preside over the dissolution. However, in January 1993 Havel was elected the first president of the new Czech Republic. *See also* VELVET REVOLUTION.

haves and have-nots   The rich and the poor; the industrialized states and the THIRD WORLD. The phrase dates back at least to Spanish novelist Miguel de Cervantes (1547–1616), who wrote in *Don Quixote,* "There are in the world two families only, the Haves and the Have-Nots."

hawk   A metaphorical description of one inclined toward military action. A *dove,* a far more peaceful bird in metaphor and a traditional symbol of peace, is not. The terms were widely used in the United States during the VIETNAM WAR as a quick way of describing someone's attitude toward participation in the war. These terms were first used in a Cold War context during the Kennedy Administration of the early 1960s. "Dovish" described those presidential advisors who supported a policy of accommodation with the Soviet Union. The hard-liners, in contrast, were "hawkish." An early use came from Charles Bartlett, writing on the Cuban Missile Crisis for the *Saturday Evening Post* (December 8, 1962): "The hawks favored an air strike to eliminate the Cuban missile bases. . . . The doves opposed the air strike and favored a blockade." U.S. Senator Henry M. Jackson stretched this bird

metaphor just about as far as it can go: "I'm not a hawk or a dove. I just don't want my country to be a pigeon" (*Time,* March 22, 1971). The hawk/dove dichotomy spread after it gained wide usage in the United States. Defense analysts began to describe the Soviet hard-liners on arms control issues as hawks; and Middle East experts saw hawks and doves competing in Israeli politics.

Hay, John (1838–1905)   The private secretary to U.S. President Abraham Lincoln throughout the U.S. Civil War (1861–1865) who, after a varied career as a diplomat and author, became secretary of state in 1898 and served Presidents William McKinley and Theodore Roosevelt in that post until his death.

Hayek, Friedrich August von (1899–1992)   The Austrian-born 1974 Nobel Prize winner in economics who advocated LAISSEZ-FAIRE capitalism. His book *The Road to Serfdom* (1944) was a bestseller that warned of the dangers of central planning and big government. After World War II, he taught in the United States at the University of Chicago. When in 1991 the 91-year-old Hayek was awarded the U.S. Presidential Medal of Freedom, Austin Furse, the White House Director of Policy Planning, said: "More than almost anyone else in the twentieth century, this guy was vindicated by the events in Eastern Europe" (*New York Times,* November 19, 1991).

Hay-Herbert Treaty of 1903   The treaty between the United States and Great Britain that established the precise location of the boundary between Canada and Alaska.

Hay-Pauncefort Treaty of 1901   The Anglo-American treaty that ended an earlier agreement (the Clayton-Bulver Treaty of 1850) stipulating British and American joint construction and operation of a PANAMA CANAL. This treaty removed the last obstacle to U.S. construction of the canal and mastery of the Caribbean.

Hay-Varilla Treaty of 1903   The agreement between the United States and Panama that guaranteed the independence of Panama and established the area of a PANAMA CANAL zone granted in perpetuity to the United States. This treaty, since revised by the PANAMA CANAL TREATIES, allowed canal construction to begin.

head of state   *See* CHIEF OF STATE.

heartland theory   An important concept in GEOPOLITICS developed by HALFORD J. MACKINDER. While it had several different variants, its most developed form emphasized the strategic importance of controlling the heartland—the eternal geographical pivot of history. This idea was closely related to Mackinder's belief that one of the most enduring features of international politics was the struggle between land and sea powers. The heartland itself gradually developed as Mackinder refined his ideas. In "The Geographical Pivot of History" (*Geographical Journal*, No. 23, 1904) it was central Asia; by 1919 it was extended to include eastern Siberia and parts of Eastern Europe; by 1943 the heartland had become synonymous with the Soviet Union. In Mackinder's thinking, control of the heartland was the key to doing well in the international struggle for power and domination. Mackinder's *Democratic Ideals and Reality* (1919), was famous for this statement: "Who rules East Europe commands the Heartland: Who rules the Heartland commands the World-Island: Who rules the World-Island commands the World." According to Michael Howard, in "The Influence of Geopolitics . . ." (*Parameters,* September 1988), this "is self-evident nonsense. There are few areas of less importance to the hegemony of the world than East Europe, however defined." *Compare to* RIMLAND.

Heath, Edward (1916–   )   The conservative British prime minister (1970–1974) who took the United Kingdom into the European Community. His attempts at establishing "stabilization" in regulating labor relations failed and, amid a struggle with mine workers, his government lost power in the 1974 elections. In 1975 he was ousted as Conservative Party leader by MARGARET THATCHER. He resurfaced on the world scene in the fall of 1990, when he went to Iraq to entreat Saddam Hussein to release Western hostages. Later, when he complained to Queen Elizabeth that U.S. Secretary of State James A. Baker III had not gone to Baghdad,

this dialogue ensued (reported in *Guardian Weekly,* February 16, 1992):

> THE QUEEN: He couldn't go to Baghdad like you.
>
> MR. HEATH: Why not? I went.
>
> THE QUEEN: Well, I know you did but you're expendable now.

It is thus the queenly ordained fate of all former British prime ministers to be "expendable."

heavy   1. In military usage, the largest and most powerful of a series of bombers, tanks, or other weapons. While all tanks are heavy, the heavy tank is the heaviest.   2. An enemy. Because motion picture villains were often portrayed by large actors, they were and are called "heavies."   3. A military unit with greater firepower capability than another of comparable size but less "heavy" equipment.

Hegel, George Wilhelm Friedrich (1770–1831)   The German philosopher who greatly influenced figures as diverse as Karl von Clausewitz and Karl Marx. Hegel's chief works include *The Science of Logic* (1812), which outlines his dialectic method: thesis plus antithesis leads to synthesis. His most fully developed ideas appeared in *Philosophy of Right* (1821). Hegel's work focuses on the notion of the state. His argument that the state has an objective reality is sometimes identified as one of the antecedents of contemporary REALISM. He posited three main phases in history: the Asiatic, with absolute monarchy; the Greco-Roman, with individual freedom; and the Germanic-European, with the synthesis of freedom within a strong state. Another key element in Hegel's thinking was the idea that what was rational had the potential to become actual—and that historical development had a rational structure. Hegel's ideas about historical progress leading to fuller freedom and the Absolute, or God, continued to be influential and were a key element in informing the argument of Francis Fukuyama in the late 1980s that the demise of communism and the triumph of liberal democracy meant the END OF HISTORY.

hegemonic stability theory   The notion that international order is a consequence of the dominance of a single power and that for the order to be maintained, this dominance must be perpetuated. This theory has been applied primarily in relation to political economics, where the hegemonic power of the United States was seen as the basis for the postwar liberal regime of economic cooperation. In this context, HEGEMONY is seen as a prerequisite for cooperation among states. Although a hegemonic leader is crucial in the establishment of a regime, the regime can continue even if that leadership disappears.

hegemonic war   A war caused by major changes of power in the international system. The notion of hegemonic war has been developed most fully by Robert Gilpin in "The Theory of Hegemonic War" (*Journal of Interdisciplinary History,* Spring 1988). There he traces the idea back to THUCYDIDES. Gilpin argued that a hegemonic war is caused by broad changes in the international system, involves the basic hierarchy of power in the system, and generally threatens or transforms this hierarchy. Implicit in the theory is the notion that a hegemonic state always will be challenged by a subordinate state or states. The outcome of the war will be either the perpetuation of its position by the existing hegemony or its replacement by the challenger who now becomes the new hegemonic power, and the cycle begins once again.

hegemony   1. Effective political control, whether formal or informal, by one over a variety of others. 2. A term used to describe the notion of a state in a position of primacy in the international system. It is a softer term than "domination"; it generally implies that the hegemonic state exerts influence because it possesses, according to Robert Keohane in *After Hegemony* (1984), "superiority of economic and military resources" that enables it to implement "a plan for international order based on its interests and its vision of the world. A hegemonic power is one which is able to establish the rules or values on which the international system operates."

heir apparent   1. The next individual in line for a hereditary position such as that of king.   2. By analogy, an administrative or political figure who, it is assumed, will achieve the office or power of a current leader on that leader's death or retirement. Many an heir apparent of this type has turned out to be less apparent than it was believed.

Helsinki Accords   The final act of the Conference on Security and Cooperation in Europe, signed on August 1, 1975, by Canada, the United States, and 33 European countries (including the Soviet Union) in Helsinki, Finland. The negotiations had been pressed by the Soviet Union in the hope that it might be able to use the conference to enhance the legitimacy of its control over Eastern Europe. But it became a device that the West was able to use to pressure the Soviet Union and the Communist governments of Eastern Europe to give greater respect to human rights.

The Helsinki Accords had several elements. The first was a "Declaration on Principles Guiding Relations between Participating States." These included respect for sovereign authority, refraining from the threat or use of force, the inviolability of borders (a term that was chosen instead of "immutability" to allow for peaceful changes), respect for the territorial integrity of states, the peaceful settlement of disputes, nonintervention in internal affairs, respect for human rights and fundamental freedoms, and equal rights and self-determination of peoples.

The Helsinki Accords also contained several "baskets" of specific measures. The first basket dealt with security and disarmament and included provisions for prior notification of military maneuvers, exchanges of observers, and other confidence-building measures. A second basket focused on cooperation in economics, science, technology, and the environment and identified ways of promoting increased commercial exchanges between East and West. Basket 3 focused on cooperation in humanitarian and other fields and emphasized the free

---

HEGEL ON THE BENEFITS OF WAR

War has the higher meaning that through it . . . the ethical health of nations is maintained, since such health does not require the stabilizing of finite arrangements; just as the motion of the winds keeps the sea from the foulness which a constant calm would produce, so war prevents a corruption of nations which a perpetual, let alone an eternal peace would produce.

SOURCE: George W. F. Hegel, *The Philosphy of Right* (1821).

---

movement of information, peoples, and ideas. It included cultural and educational exchanges.

The Helsinki Accords also noted that periodic review meetings would be held to continue the multilateral exchanges on European cooperation. Consequently, the CONFERENCE ON SECURITY AND COOPERATION IN EUROPE became a continuing process of dialogue about implementation of the Helsinki Accords. It also provided a framework for consolidating détente, for enhancing confidence-building measures, and in the late 1980s and early 1990s for helping to manage the far-reaching political and strategic changes in Europe.

Henderson, Arthur (1863–1935)   The British Labour Party leader and foreign secretary (1929–1931) who won the 1934 Nobel Peace Prize for his work in chairing the 1932–1935 International Disarmament Conference of the LEAGUE OF NATIONS.

Herter, Christian A. (1895–1966)   The governor of Massachusetts (1953–1957) who became, during the Eisenhower Administration, U.S. Under Secretary of State (1957–1959) and then Secretary of State (1959–1961) upon the death of JOHN FOSTER DULLES.

Herz, John (1908–   )   The German-born U.S. international relations analyst who is perhaps best known for his work on the rise and demise of the territorial state. In 1957 Herz wrote an influential article, "The Rise and Demise of the Territorial States" (*World Politics* 9), in which he argued that the territorial state was in decline because of the development of weapons of mass destruction, which made borders permeable and made it impossible for the state to fulfill its traditional role of protecting its citizens. In a subsequent article entitled "The Territorial State Revisited: Reflections on the Future of the Nation State" (*Polity* 1, no. 1, Fall 1968), Herz reappraised his earlier argument and suggested that territoriality was not necessarily at an end. Herz's other major contribution was his elucidation of the notion of the SECURITY DILEMMA, one of the major dynamics of an anarchic international system. This idea appeared in his *International Politics in the Atomic Age* (1959).

Herzl, Theodore (1860–1904)   The Austrian journalist who, in the 1890s, founded modern ZIONISM

by calling for a Jewish national homeland in Palestine. This action came as Europe and Russia experienced a resurgence of anti-Semitism at the end of the nineteenth century. The DREYFUS AFFAIR in France convinced Herzl and many of the followers of Zionism that it was not possible for Jews to be truly assimilated in European society. In *The Jewish State* (1896) he proposed plans for the creation of a Jewish commonwealth in Palestine: "The Jewish question," he wrote, "is a national question which can be solved only by making it a political world-question to be discussed and settled by the civilized nations of the world in council."

hexagonal group   A loose-knit grouping of the states of Austria, Czechoslovakia, Hungary, Italy, Poland, and Yugoslavia. It developed out of the Danube-Adria Group founded in the late 1970s and focused on the common border issues of Austria, Hungary, Italy, and Yugoslavia. Czechoslovakia joined in May 1990 and the organization became known as the pentagonal group. Poland joined in June 1991. The breakup of Yugoslavia and Czechoslovakia has hindered the development of the group.

Hezbollah   "The Party of God" or "The Party of Allah," a radical SHI'ITE Muslim organization that is largely influenced by the Islamic revolution in Iran, devoted to the establishment of a fundamentalist Islamic state in Lebanon. By Western standards, Hezbollah is an amorphous organization, loose-knit and quite informal. Formed in 1982, the group is vehemently anti–United States and anti-Israel. Much of Hezbollah's terrorist activities have been directed against U.S. and Israeli targets. By 1984 Hezbollah had effectively absorbed all the other Lebanese extremist Shi'ite factions. Hezbollah has been the kidnapper of most if not all of the Western hostages taken in Lebanon from the 1980s to the early 1990s.

Higgins, William R. (1945–1989)   The U.S. Marine Corps lieutenant colonel, detached to the United Nations' multinational PEACEKEEPING FORCE in Lebanon, who was taken hostage in February 1988. Higgins was murdered in 1989 by his terrorist captors in supposed retaliation for the Israeli kidnapping on July 27, 1989, of HEZBOLLAH leader Sheikh Abdel

Karim Obeid. The killers provided graphic proof that they had carried out their death threat in the form of a videotape released to the world media which showed Higgins's lifeless body slowly twisting at the end of a rope. His remains were returned to the United States for proper burial in December 1991.

high commissioner 1. The leader of a diplomatic mission from one British Commonwealth state to another. She or he has the same rank and enjoys the same privileges and immunities an ambassador does. 2. The highest-level civilian administrative official appointed to manage a dependent or occupied territory. For example, the United States used a high commissioner to run its portion of occupied Germany after World War II. 3. The head of an international commission.

higher law The notion that no matter what the laws of a state are, there remains a loftier code of behavior to which individuals have an even greater obligation. Those who wish to attack an existing law or practice that courts or legislators are unlikely or unwilling to change often appeal to this higher law. Martyrs have often asserted a higher law in defiance of the state, thus earning their martyrdom. The classic presentation of this concept is in Sophocles' (496–406 B.C.) play *Antigone* in which the heroine defies the king, asserts a higher law as her justification, and "forces" the king to have her killed. Because the courts of any state may enforce only the law of the land, appealing to a higher law is always chancy business. People who practice CIVIL DISOBEDIENCE to protest colonial rule, military intervention, or unfair practices in society have often cited higher law as their justification.

High Level Group A formal body of military and civilian officials within the NORTH ATLANTIC TREATY ORGANIZATION that does policy planning for the Nuclear Planning Group of NATO-member defense ministers.

high politics The traditional focus of statecraft; the issues of power and national security. Foreign policy analysis was initially concerned almost exclusively with issues of high politics—the major decisions of peace and war. Increasingly, though, there has been a move away from this exclusive pre-

occupation and a recognition that the study of high politics has to be accompanied by a focus on LOW POLITICS (i.e., issues relating to more mundane but extremely important matters such as economic well-being). Ironically, the initial focus regarding the integration of Western Europe was very much on low politics, which was deemed to be much easier to settle than issues of foreign and security policy; but increasingly the process is moving into the area of high politics as an attempt is made to encompass security and defense.

high seas Those parts of the world's oceans that are not part of any state's territorial waters. *See also* LAW OF THE SEA.

hijacking Stealing goods (or goods plus a vehicle) while they are in transit. When terrorists hijack a vehicle with people they also are guilty of kidnapping—holding a person against his or her will. The hijacking of aircraft is now usually called SKYJACKING.

Himmler, Heinrich (1900–1945) The Bavarian chicken farmer who rose from Adolf Hitler's personal bodyguard in the early 1920s to head of the SS in 1929. Himmler's SS, which murdered the leader of the rival SA in 1934, by 1936 also controlled the GESTAPO, and operated the system of CONCENTRATION CAMPS. Himmler, who directed Nazi Germany's reign of terror throughout occupied Europe, committed suicide after being captured by British forces in 1945.

Hindenburg, Paul Ludwig von (1847–1934) The World War I German field marshal and hero of the Russian front who became president of the WEIMAR REPUBLIC from 1925 to his death. It was Hindenburg who made ADOLF HITLER chancellor in 1933 despite his personal disdain for the "Austrian corporal." Hitler then became president upon Hindenburg's death. While Hindenburg has been reviled by many for helping Hitler to gain power legally in Germany, others have defended him—on the grounds of senility. Even Winston Churchill asserted that while Hindenburg "betrayed all the Germans who had re-elected him to power. . . . There is a defense for all this. . . . He had become senile. He did not understand what he was doing. He could not be held physically, mentally or morally responsible for opening the floodgates of evil upon . . . civilization" (Winston Churchill, *Great Contemporaries,* 1937).

Hindenburg disaster   The explosion of the hydrogen-filled German dirigible (named in Hindenburg's honor) in Lakehurst, New Jersey, on May 6, 1937. This accident killed 36 people and the trans-Atlantic dirigible business.

Hirohito (1901–1989)   Emperor of Japan from 1926 until his death. There is considerable disagreement over his role in Japan's military aggression in the 1930s in Manchuria and China, his role in bringing Japan into the AXIS, and his role in the sneak attack on the United States at PEARL HARBOR in 1941. However, in August 1945 before the dropping of two atomic bombs on Japan, with defeat certain, he personally intervened to urge the Supreme Council of the Japanese government to sue the Allied governments for peace. At the POTSDAM CONFERENCE the Allies had threatened "prompt and utter destruction" if the Japanese refused to surrender. The devastating atomic blasts followed and the emperor broke the deadlock in the Supreme Council to accept the Potsdam ultimatum as a basis for surrender. At the time of surrender the emperor's status was left ambiguous. While many (including the governments of Australia, China, and New Zealand) thought he should have been tried (and if found guilty, executed) as a war criminal, the United States allowed him to renounce the traditional divinity of Japanese emperors and become a constitutional monarch. The emperor, however, remains extremely important in Japan as a figure of national unity and historical continuity. Hirohito was succeeded as emperor by his son AKIHITO.

Hiroshima   The Japanese city that was destroyed on August 6, 1945, by the first nonexperimental ATOMIC BOMB dropped from the U.S. B-29 bomber ENOLA GAY. More than 70,000 of its 200,000 residents were killed by the blast and firestorm. Thousands more died later from wounds and radiation poisoning. Eighty percent of the city's structures were destroyed when the bomb was exploded 1,000 feet in the air for maximum effect. The strength of the explosion was equivalent to 14,000 tons of TNT, or 14 kilotons. Three days after the destruc-

---

HIROHITO ACCEPTS SURRENDER

Despite the best that has been done by everyone . . . the war situation has developed not necessarily to Japan's advantage. . . . Moreover, the enemy has begun to employ a new and most cruel bomb, the power of which to do damage is indeed incalculable, taking the toll of many innocent lives. Should we continue to fight, it would not only result in an ultimate collapse and obliteration of the Japanese nation, but it would also lead to the total extinction of human civilization. . . . We have resolved to pave the way for a grand peace for all the generations to come by enduring the unendurable and suffering what is insufferable.

SOURCE: Emperor Hirohito's radio address to his nation at the close of World War II on August 15, 1945. The Japanese were astounded not only because he announced Japan's surrender to the Allies, but because this was the first time that most of them heard his voice.

---

tion of Hiroshima, a second atomic bomb was dropped on Nagasaki. Devices of this size are considered small in comparison to modern nuclear weapons.

The decision to drop atomic bombs on Hiroshima and Nagasaki was controversial at the time and has remained so. Even the scientists who developed the bombs disagreed over whether a weapon developed to use against Germany should be used against a country that had shown no inclination to build nuclear weapons. There also was disagreement on whether these bombs should be used against targets of slight military value, as well as on the need for the second attack on Nagasaki. But this first use of nuclear weapons was justified on the basis of the estimates of likely U.S. and Japanese casualties during an invasion of Japan. Some critics have suggested that the bombing was not so much one of the final acts of World War II as it was one of the first acts of the COLD WAR against the Soviet Union. But one thing is absolutely certain: Hiroshima and Nagasaki have become symbols of the destructiveness of atomic weapons—and a constant warning to the rest of the world. According to B. Bruce-Briggs in *The Shield of Faith* (1989), "Hiroshima, which was not much of a city to begin with, sort of a Japanese Toledo, made the best of a horrid situation, and generated a respectable tourist trade from being flattened in an innovative manner. Nagasaki, at the wrong end of Japan and lacking an airport, just went back to work—nobody cares about who is second."

THE OFFICIAL U.S. STATEMENT ON HIROSHIMA

Sixteen hours ago an American airplane dropped one bomb on Hiroshima, an important Japanese Army base. The bomb has more power than 20,000 tons of T.N.T. It had more than two thousand times the blast power of the British "Grand Slam" which is the largest bomb ever yet used in the history of warfare.

The Japanese began the war from the air at Pearl Harbor. They have been repaid many fold. And the end is not yet. With this bomb we have now added a new and revolutionary increase in destruction to supplement the growing power of our armed forces. In their present form these bombs are now in production and even more powerful forms are in development.

It is an atomic bomb. It is a harnessing of the basic power of the universe. The force from which the sun draws its power has been loosed against those who brought war to the Far East.

SOURCE: Statement by the President of the United States (Harry S Truman), White House Press Release on Hiroshima, August 6, 1945. Truman said the bomb had the power of "20,000 tons of T.N.T." Later estimates reduced that figure to 14,000 tons.

---

historic compromise A phrase invented by Enrico Berlinguer (1922–1984), secretary-general of the Italian Communist Party (1972–1984), to describe his goal of a coalition government for Italy based on an equal balance between the democratic parties of the left and the right. Berlinguer argued that only a coalition government of Christian Democrats, Communists, and Socialists would reflect Italy's political and social realities. His call for a coequal role for the Communists was based on the fact that his party got 34 percent of the vote in the national parliamentary elections of 1976 and controlled many of Italy's largest city governments, such as those of Bologna, Florence, Milan, Rome, and Venice. The Italian Communist Party was never trusted enough to be invited to join a coalition government. Consequently in 1991, seeking to change

its image since the Cold War was over, it renamed itself the Democratic Party of the Left.

Hitler, Adolf (1889–1945) The leader of NAZI Germany who personified evil in the twentieth century because he started World War II by invading Poland, conquered and brutally occupied most of Europe, kidnapped and enslaved millions of innocent people, spread a pernicious racist ideology, and systematically murdered over 12 million civilians (including 6 million Jews) in CONCENTRATION CAMPS.

In pre–World War I Vienna Hitler was an unsuccessful artist and acquired his racist nationalism, anti-Semitism, and anti-Marxism. At the outbreak of World War I Hitler so identified with German nationalism that he, although Austrian, moved to Munich and joined the German Army. After his discharge as a corporal, he joined the German Workers' Party, which in 1920 became the National Socialist German Workers' (Nazi) Party. A demagogic speaker, he stressed the alleged betrayal of Germany—what he called the STAB IN THE BACK—by liberals on the home front, and blamed many of Germany's ills on imagined Jewish conspiracies. He soon controlled the Nazi Party and led its unsuccessful BEER HALL PUTSCH in Munich in 1923. While the Nazi electorate expanded rapidly after the onset of the GREAT DEPRESSION, the party never achieved a majority prior to coming to power. Only after months of deadlock among German political parties was Hitler asked to form a government as chancellor in January 1933. After President PAUL VON HINDENBURG died in 1934, Hitler assumed that office as well. Once in power, Hitler and his party first undermined and then, using the excuse of the REICHSTAG FIRE, abolished democratic institutions and opposition parties. Hitler consolidated his power through terror and intimidation, the main vehicles of which were the SA, SS, and the GESTAPO. He also installed a program of racism that resulted in the deliberate, widespread extermination of Jews and other minority groups during WORLD WAR II. In the mid-1930s Hitler also began to restore Germany's economy and military strength. He pursued a ruthless foreign policy in which he brilliantly used the fear of war that existed in other European states, especially Great Britain and France, to make territorial gains and establish the domination of the THIRD REICH in Europe. There has been considerable

The conquering tourist: Adolf Hitler visits the Eiffel Tower in Paris, June 23, 1940. (National Archives)

debate among historians about whether Hitler had an overall strategy. A. J. P. Taylor in *The Origins of the Second World War* (1961) suggests that Hitler was a master of improvisation rather than a policymaker with a long-range vision. Taylor believes that Hitler, like most other foreign policy makers, was too absorbed by events to follow preconceived plans. Other historians, however, disagree. Alan Bullock, whose *Hitler: A Study in Tyranny* (1952) remains one of the definitive analyses of the Nazi leader, suggests that Hitler was brilliant at improvisation precisely because he had a clear sense of what he wanted to achieve—German domination over Europe. At the tactical level, Hitler was brilliant as well, at least until he overplayed his hand with the invasion of Poland in 1939 and subsequently imitated Napoleon Bonaparte by invading the Soviet Union. Prior to 1939, however, he was able to get virtually everything he wanted in Europe through the FAIT ACCOMPLI, as in the reoccupation of the Rhineland, and through a strategy of BRINKMANSHIP and blackmail that played on the existing fear of war. In Nazi Germany, in contrast, war was glorified. This gave Hitler an immense advantage in situations such as the MUNICH AGREEMENT, when the threat of war led Britain and France to capitulate to German demands. Hitler overreached himself, however, and led Germany to war and defeat. As the Soviet Red Army marched into Berlin, Hitler committed suicide in his underground bunker. See MEIN KAMPF.

Hitler-Stalin Pact *See* NAZI-SOVIET NON-AGGRESSION PACT.

Hoare-Laval Pact The 1935 proposal by the British and French governments to settle the Abyssinian-Italian war with substantial concessions to Italy. Negotiated by British Foreign Secretary Samuel Hoare (1880–1959) and French Premier PIERRE

LAVAL, its abject APPEASEMENT so enraged British public opinion that the pact was rejected by the government and Hoare was forced to resign. Nevertheless, the rejection of the pact made it that much easier for Italy to take over all of Abyssinia (Ethiopia).

Hobbes, Thomas (1588–1679)   The English SOCIAL CONTRACT theorist whose *Leviathan* (1651), a highly influential book of political philosophy, asserted that, in a state of nature, humanity is in a chaotic condition "of war of everyone against everyone." For safety's sake, people formed governments to which they surrendered their freedom but from which they got security and order. Hobbes's government is an absolute monarchy. While Hobbes preferred kings who were not tyrants, his theorizing offered no recourse to individuals finding themselves under one. As the first of the major social contract theorists (the others were JOHN LOCKE and JEAN-JACQUES ROUSSEAU), he provided the foundation upon which the others would build and ultimately influence the American and French revolutions. Although in *Leviathan* he referred only in passing to relations among sovereigns, his comments provided the basis for what has subsequently been termed the Hobbesian tradition in thinking about international politics. Hobbes argued that "in all times, Kings and Persons of Sovereign authority, because of their Independency, are in continuall jealousies, and in the state and posture of Gladiators; having their weapons pointing, and their eyes fixed on one another; that is their Forts, Garrisons and Guns upon the Frontiers of their Kingdomes; and continuall Spyes upon their neighbours; which is a posture of War." Because there was no Leviathan to control and regulate the relations among sovereign entities, they were closer to the state of nature than people under a common power and law. Subsequent commentators such as HEDLEY BULL, in *The Anarchical Society* (1977), pointed out that sovereign entities such as states were very different from individuals in what Hobbes termed a state of nature, in that they could engage in war and other activities simultaneously. Nevertheless, Hobbes clearly captured the suspicion and insecurities that exist in a system in which there is no central overriding authority. This, in part, explains why he is widely regarded as one of the key figures in REALISM.

Hobson, John A. (1858–1940)   The English economist who went to the BOER WAR in South Africa as a correspondent for the Manchester *Guardian* and whose work, *Imperialism: A Study* (1902) was crucial in changing the prevailing view of IMPERIALISM from a matter of national pride to a phenomenon that was generally regarded as exploitative. This book also influenced the subsequent development of Soviet revolutionary V. I. Lenin's theory of imperialism. Hobson argued that in the capitalist system, those with surplus capital prefer to invest it abroad rather than redistribute it at home. Those who controlled industry sought to "broaden the channel for the flow of their surplus wealth by seeking foreign markets and foreign investments to take off the goods and capital they cannot sell or use at home." In Hobson's view, financial interests were the dynamic force in imperial expansion and manipulated the other forces of society for their economic ends.

Ho Chi Minh (1892–1969)   The French- and Soviet-educated founder of the Vietnamese Communist Party in 1930 and the VIET MINH in 1941. He was the dominant figure in North Vietnamese affairs from World War II until his death. After World War II, supported by Communist and left-wing elements in Indochina, Ho campaigned against the French and concluded an armistice agreement at Geneva, Switzerland, in 1954. This agreement divided Vietnam into a Communist North and a non-Communist South. Ho became president of North Vietnam and began an active guerrilla campaign and then open warfare against South Vietnam. The United States supported the South, seeing this as a way to stem the spread of communism. Following a sharp decline in U.S. support for the corrupt South Vietnamese government during the Nixon and Ford administrations, North Vietnamese forces occupied South Vietnam and consolidated it with the North in 1975. Vietnam became an ally of the Soviet Union and an enemy of China in the Communist world. While Ho never lived to see the victory he fathered, the South Vietnamese capital of Saigon was renamed Ho Chi Minh City in his honor. *See also* BAO DAI; VIETNAM WAR.

Ho Chi Minh (left) meets Mao Zedong of China. (Library of Congress)

Ho Chi Minh trail   The network of supply routes from North to South Vietnam during the VIETNAM WAR. Much of U.S. strategy during the war focused on cutting the trail and stopping the constant flow of men and supplies. The trail, which took advantage of mountain terrain, reached into the neighboring states of Laos and Cambodia. Thus the United States expanded the war into these "neutral" states. Despite extensive air and ground attacks, the United States and South Vietnam were never able to block the trail for long. *See also* LAOTIAN INCURSION.

Hoffmann, Stanley (1935–   )   The prolific U.S. analyst and commentator on international relations whose work is characterized by great incisiveness, enormous subtlety and complexity in argument, and enormous range. Hoffmann's expertise ranges from French politics and foreign policy, through such topics as the North Atlantic Treaty Organization, European integration, and international law, to United States foreign policy. He also is an international relations theorist of some distinction, and in such works as *Gulliver's Troubles, or the Setting of American Foreign Policy* (1968) he offers a complex yet compelling analysis of the international system, its various levels, and the relationship among them. In *The State of War* (1965) Hoffmann outlines the basis of his philosophy, which he traces back in many respects to JEAN-JACQUES ROUSSEAU. Perhaps most impressive of all about Hoffmann's writings on international relations is the way in which he is able to move with great ease from theoretical and conceptual issues to policy issues; his commentaries, whether critical or supportive of U.S. policy, are always relevant, incisive, and compelling.

Holocaust   NAZI Germany's systematic persecution and murder of the Jews of Europe from 1933 to 1945. Europe had a long tradition of ANTI-SEMITISM encouraged by the Christian churches. At the beginning of the century Germany was not even considered to be the most anti-Semitic state in Europe. (Russia was.) Prior to World War I Austria, where German leader Adolf Hitler grew up, was far more outwardly hostile to Jews than Germany. After the war, however, Hitler used the Jews as a scapegoat for every German misfortune. And his racist ideology espoused the BIG LIE that Jews were less than human, inferior to other Germans and deserving of less-than-human treatment. State-condoned and -directed persecution of Jews began soon after Hitler's rise to power in 1933. Many authorities date the Holocaust from the infamous 1935 NUREMBURG LAWS (which classified as Jewish anyone who had at least one Jewish grandparent, and which deprived Jews of full citizenship in Germany) and from the 1938 KRISTALLNACHT. After Kristallnacht, Jews were arrested and forced to pay for the Nazi wave of violence that had destroyed their homes, synagogues, and businesses. Roughly one-quarter of the half-million German Jews fled the country by 1939; almost all who remained were interned in CONCENTRATION CAMPS. Hitler's FINAL SOLUTION to the Nazis' so-called Jewish problem was the wholesale extermination or GENOCIDE of European Jews. By the end of World War II, an estimated 6 million Jews had been killed in the Holocaust. *See also* AUSCHWITZ; WANNSEE CONFERENCE.

Holocaust revisionists   1. Those who would reevaluate the history of the Holocaust.   2. Anti-Semitic or NEO-NAZI groups that issue propaganda denying that the Holocaust ever took place. In paid editorials and privately published books, they, without historical evidence, insist that there were no mass executions of Jews in NAZI-controlled Europe. Those who are already disposed to anti-Semitism, who are igno-

The crematoria of the Buchenwald concentration camp at Weimar, Germany. (National Archives)

rant of history, and who are simply ignorant sometimes believe this effort to deny history and belittle Jewish suffering. Anticipating future denials of the horrendous nature of the Holocaust, U.S. General Dwight D. Eisenhower wrote in an April 15, 1945, letter to General George C. Marshall that: "The things I saw beggar description . . . I made a visit deliberately in order to be in a position to give *firsthand* evidence of these things if ever, in the future, there develops a tendency to charge these allegations merely to 'propaganda' " (quoted in Stephen D. Ambrose, *Eisenhower*, 1983).

SHOULD REVISIONISM BE BANNED?

But should one fight against such [Holocaust revisionist] journals? Should one sue them? Should one ban them? I believe one should. The youngsters who have these rags thrust into their hands are often very ignorant about the Third Reich. If they are served up such a concoction of lies and alleged evidence some of them, at least, may be impressed. What must impress them even more is that nobody is taking any action against these articles, from which they are bound to conclude that if these statements are not stopped then they must probably be true. We should not allow this kind of conclusion. . . .

The survivors of the Holocaust, just like the members of any religious community, are entitled not to have their martyrdom mocked. The claim of the "Auschwitz lie" is a slap in the face of all those who have gone through the martyrdom of Auschwitz, and indeed a slap in the face of their children. On the soil of Germany, which bears the responsibility for Auschwitz, it seems to me entirely legitimate to protect the survivors and their children against such slaps by penal legislation.

SOURCE: Simon Wiesenthal, *Justice Not Vengeance* (1989). Wiesenthal (1908–   ), a Holocaust survivor, has become the world's best-known Nazi hunter. The Jewish Documentation Center, which he directs in Vienna, Austria, is a clearinghouse for information on World War II Nazi criminals.

Holsti, Kalevi J. (1935–   ) A Swiss-born Canadian scholar of international relations whose *International Politics: A Framework for Analysis* (4th ed., 1983) is one of the most widely used textbooks in the field. Holsti has made important contributions in several areas, including that of ROLE THEORY. He also has written on the nature of the study of international relations in *The Dividing Discipline: Hegemony and Diversity in International Theory* (1985) and has published a major study of the evolution of international order and its relationship to the use of force, *Peace and War: Armed Conflicts and International Order, 1648–1989* (1991), which examines 177 international wars. (He is the brother of OLE R. HOLSTI.)

Holsti, Ole R. (1933–   ) A Swiss-born U.S. international relations analyst and pioneering scholar on CRISIS. Using both quantitative and qualitative approaches, he has analyzed crisis decision making and the interactions among the participants in crises. His *Crisis, Escalation, War* (1972) added considerably to the understanding of the dynamics of ESCALATION both in the period before World War I and more generally. Holsti also was author of a famous study of JOHN FOSTER DULLES entitled "The Belief System and National Images: A Case Study" (in James Rosenau, ed., *International Politics and Foreign Policy,* 1969) in which he demonstrated how Dulles's closed belief system about the Soviet Union made him treat any Soviet conciliatory move as either a sign of Soviet weakness or as a trick. This study, which used CONTENT ANALYSIS, became the model for similar studies of other decision makers. (He is the brother of KALEVI J. HOLSTI.)

Holy Loch The site on the west coast of Scotland that in 1960 became a U.S. naval base for nuclear submarines. This base, together with its counterpart in Rota, Spain, was constructed to operate Polaris and later Poseidon submarines closer to the Soviet Union. Closer bases allowed the submarines to stay out on patrol for longer periods and extend the time their missiles were within range of Soviet targets. Following the introduction of the longer-range Trident C-4 as a replacement for the Poseidon missile, the submarines based in Spain were redeployed to the United States. Thus Holy Loch was the only European base for the operation of U.S. strategic nuclear submarines. As more Trident II missile-carrying submarines came into service in the 1990s, Holy Loch was no longer needed as a forward base. It was closed down as a U.S. base in 1991.

Holy See The office and jurisdiction of the pope of the Roman Catholic Church; the Vatican Court.

Home, Alexander Douglas *See* DOUGLAS-HOME, ALEXANDER.

home rule Self-government by local political entities. Thus a city within a province can be granted the right of home rule by its provincial or national government; so too a colony from its imperial ruler. Indeed the first phase of DECOLONIZATION was often the granting of limited home rule in a colony.

Honecker, Erich (1912–   ) The hard-line Communist leader of the German Democratic Republic (East Germany) from 1971 to 1989. He supervised the construction of the BERLIN WALL and became not only WALTER ULBRICHT's choice as his successor, but Moscow's choice as well. Despite progress in matters of international recognition as well as intermittent domestic reform, 1989 proved to be the year that the Communist façade of prosperity could no longer endure in East Germany. Mikhail Gorbachev's Soviet reform policies in the late 1980s caused the economy of the GDR to deteriorate. When the mass exodus of East Germans began in 1989, Honecker was in Bucharest seeking medical attention for a gall bladder problem. Upon his return, he was forced out of power by the other POLITBURO members and replaced by EGON KRENZ. Initially his departure from the leadership was considered respectable. Then Honecker was arrested and expelled from the party. He fled in 1991 to the Soviet Union for asylum. Under Gorbachev, Honecker was assured safety from German authorities. With the dissolution of the Soviet Union and the resignation of Gorbachev, Honecker in July 1992 was extradited to Germany where he faced trial on charges of corruption (for stealing millions in state funds) and manslaughter (for the 49 East Germans killed while trying to flee to the West). However, in January 1993, citing the fact that Honecker was dying of liver cancer, the German government released him from prison. He immediately flew into exile in Chile.

honest broker An impartial third party who seeks to mediate international disputes. The first use of the phrase is usually credited to German Chancellor Otto Von Bismarck, who said in a speech to the Reichstag on February 19, 1878: "If we are to negotiate peace . . . I imagine an essentially modest role . . . that of an honest broker, who really intends to do business." Since then the phrase has been used by political leaders often. For example, in the context of Mideast peace talks, U.S. Secretary of

State James A. Baker III said, "The U.S. is and will be an honest broker" (*Newsweek*, November 11, 1991). *Compare to* POWER BROKER.

Hong Kong The series of islands off the southeast coast of China. On June 9, 1898, after the Chinese had suffered five decades of repeated military defeat at the hands of the British Navy, a convention was signed in Beijing to lease China's Hong Kong, its adjacent New Territories, and other islands to Britain for 99 years. On December 19, 1984, British Prime Minister Margaret Thatcher and Chinese Prime Minister Zhao Ziyang, acting on behalf of their respective governments, signed a Joint Declaration on the Question of Hong Kong, which states that British sovereignty and jurisdiction over Hong Kong will continue until June 30, 1997; Hong Kong will from July 1, 1997, become a Special Administrative Region of the People's Republic of China.

From a small cluster of fishing villages in the 1840s with a population of 3,650, Hong Kong has developed into a modern industrial and financial trading center inhabited by a population of almost 6 million. Under the terms of the Sino-British Joint Declaration, Hong Kong's lifestyle will remain unchanged for 50 years after the Chinese take over the jurisdiction, and China's socialist system will not be practiced in the SAR. The SAR will have its own government and legislature composed of local inhabitants and will enjoy a high degree of autonomy. However, the central government in Beijing will be responsible for Hong Kong's foreign affairs and defense. Some Hong Kong residents are doubtful about this promise of the Chinese government; as 1997 nears, these doubts may lead to increased capital outflow and emigration of the affluent population.

honors **1.** Battle or campaign streamers attached to the standard or colors of a military unit to indicate some special distinction, such as participation in a major victory. **2.** Formal military ceremonies for visiting dignitaries.

honors of war Allowing a defeated force, in testimony of its valor and honorable actions during combat, a measure of dignity by allowing it to surrender while still armed or with colors flying.

Hoover, Herbert (1874–1964) The president of the United States from 1929 to 1933. Hoover had the great misfortune to become president just when the GREAT DEPRESSION almost destroyed the U.S. and world economies. He believed that the depression was the result of the international consequences of the Versailles Treaty, rather than of any fundamental internal economic condition of the United States. A whole generation of Americans grew up holding him personally responsible for economic events that no president of the time could have controlled. Ironically, Hoover, who made a fortune early in life as an engineer, headed allied relief operations during and after World War I, and served as secretary of commerce under Presidents Warren G. Harding and Calvin Coolidge, had a worldwide reputation as a preeminent administrator. While he is remembered as a conservative president, Hoover first entered government service during the Democratic administration of Woodrow Wilson. In 1920 he was even mentioned as a possible candidate for the Democratic presidential nomination. His roots were much more in the progressive rather than the conservative tradition. Yet he was not an innovator, and there were few important developments in United States foreign policy during the Hoover Administration. Policies of ISOLATIONISM and noninvolvement in European affairs were continued even though the international order that had been established after World War I was just beginning to crack—and might have been more robust with stronger U.S. support. In later life Hoover was respected as an "elder statesman." His speeches in late 1950 and early 1951 criticizing the Truman Administration's decision to send U.S. troops to Europe helped to precipitate the GREAT DEBATE of 1951.

horizontal escalation *See* ESCALATION, HORIZONTAL.

Horn of Africa The easternmost point of the African continent, where the Gulf of Aden meets the Indian Ocean, forming a "horn" of Somalia and Ethiopia. Ras Asir (formerly Cape Guardafui) juts at this point forming the top of the horn. The easternmost part is Ras Hafun in Somalia. The horn acquired strategic importance during the 1970s because of its proximity to the routes used by oil tankers operating between the Persian Gulf and those states that import large amounts of gulf oil. It took on added importance in 1977–1978 when it became an arena for superpower competition. The crisis was sparked by Somali IRREDENTISM and Ethiopian weakness. Somalia, which had been a CLIENT STATE of the Soviet Union, attacked Ethiopia, which had been a client state of the United States until Washington had distanced itself from Ethiopia because of human rights abuses. When Somalian troops occupied the contested region of Ogaden, Moscow stepped in to fill the breach, and Soviet and Cuban forces intervened decisively to eject the Somali forces. Critics in the United States saw Soviet actions as Machiavellian in the extreme, but the U.S. response was low key, demanding simply that Somalia's territorial integrity be respected. The Soviets agreed to this and the superpower dimension of the crisis was defused. Although this incident had revealed the ability of small states to manipulate the superpowers and, in this case, actually to bring about a reversal of alliances, the main lesson drawn in Washington was that the Soviet Union was not behaving with restraint in the Third World. This lack of restraint undermined support for DÉTENTE and for SALT II.

Horthy, Nikolaus (1868–1957)   The chief of the Austro-Hungarian Navy in World War I who afterward defeated Communist revolutionary forces in Hungary. He controlled Hungary as REGENT but, because he never allowed the actual heir to the Hungarian throne to return, he was effectively dictator from 1920 to 1944. Admiral Horthy took Hungary into World War II as an ally to Adolf Hitler; when he tried to negotiate a separate peace with the Allies in 1944, the Germans occupied Hungary. He was forced to resign and was taken prisoner by the Germans. Horthy was freed at the end of the war and lived most of the rest of his life in Portugal. Because Hungarian troops helped the Germans to occupy Yugoslavia during the war, the Yugoslavs wanted to try Horthy as a war criminal, but the U.S. liberators of Hungary refused to deport him.

hostage   **1.** An individual held to guarantee that certain agreements will be honored. The taking of hostages is forbidden under Article 34 of the Geneva Convention of 1949. But in one sense, according to some analysts, we are all hostages. Fred Ikle, writing in *Foreign Affairs* (January 1973), observes: "The jargon of American strategic analysis . . . dulls our sense of moral outrage about the tragic confrontation of nuclear arsenals. . . . It fosters the current smug complacency regarding the soundness and stability of mutual deterrence. It blinds us to the fact that our methods for preventing nuclear war rests on a form of warfare universally condemned since the Dark Ages—the mass killing of hostages." **2.** Kidnapping victims of terrorist groups that hope to use these innocent individuals as bargaining chips; in recent years, a tactic used often in the Middle East. In the United States, "the hostages" refers to the various U.S. and European citizens who were held in Lebanon for varying times from the mid-1980s to 1991 by an assortment of terrorist groups.

hostage, nuclear   *See* NUCLEAR HOSTAGE.

host nation   A state that willingly allows the forces and/or supplies of allied states (or alliances such as the North Atlantic Treaty Organization) to be located on, to operate in, or to transit through its territory.

host nation support   Civil and military assistance rendered in peace and war by a HOST NATION to allied forces that are located on or in transit through the host nation's territory. Such assistance is premised on bilateral or multilateral agreements concluded between the host nation, an alliance, and states that have military units operating on the host nation's territory. In the context of the North Atlantic Treaty Organization, host nation support is part of European efforts at greater BURDEN-SHARING.

hot line   **1.** The communications links between the WHITE HOUSE and the KREMLIN established for instant contact in the event of a crisis. The creation of this direct telecommunications link in the aftermath of the 1962 Cuban Missile Crisis reflected a desire to ensure that rapid communications would be available in any future crises. The Hot Line Agreement of 1963 provided for radio telegraph and wire telegraph communications circuits. In 1971 the superpowers agreed to modernize the system with satellite circuits, which became operational in 1978. The radio telegraph was then terminated but the wire telegraph was kept as a backup. In 1984 there was another agreement to provide for facsimile transmissions, making it possible to transmit more rapidly and to send items such as maps and charts. **2.** Any communications system that links chief executives of governments with each other. **3.** The communications that link a chief executive with his or her military commanders.

hot pursuit **1.** The legal doctrine that may allow a law enforcement officer to arrest a fleeing suspect who has been chased into another jurisdiction. **2.** The doctrine of international maritime law that allows a state to seize a foreign vessel that has initiated an act of war on the territory of the invaded state and is pursued into international waters. **3.** Pursuit of an enemy while in sight of, or in contact with, it. **4.** The pursuit of an enemy across international borders.

The Washington terminal of the Washington–Moscow Direct Communications Links in 1988. (U.S. Naval Institute)

hot war *See* COLD WAR.

Hoxha, Enver (1908–1985) The World War II resistance leader who was the Communist dictator of Albania from 1946 until his death. *See also* ALBANIAN ISOLATIONISM.

HRU (Hostage Rescue Unit) A specially trained and equipped antiterrorist strike force, with particular expertise in the safe rescue of HOSTAGES. Well known HRUs include the U.S. Delta Force, the French GIGN, and the West German GSG-9.

Hughes, Charles Evans (1862–1948) The U.S. lawyer who was governor of New York (1907–1910); associate justice of the United States Supreme Court (1910–1916); Republican candidate for the presidency in 1916; the U.S. Secretary of State (1921–1925) who presided over the WASHINGTON NAVAL CONFERENCE (1921–1922); member of the PERMANENT COURT OF ARBITRATION (1926–1930); judge of the PERMANENT COURT OF INTERNATIONAL JUSTICE (1928–1930); and chief justice of the United States Supreme Court (1930–1941).

Huks The Hukbalahap guerrilla organization in the Philippines during the 1940s and early 1950s. Originally formed to oppose the occupying Japanese Army, following the end of World War II the Huks fought the Army of the Philippines, then the corrupt instrument of the unpopular oligarchic regime of President Manuel Roxas y Acuna (1892–1948). The Huk insurgency is credited with forcing many governmental and social reforms of the early 1950s. The Huks were dissolved in the mid-1950s. However, many of the guerrillas, unhappy that there was no meaningful land reform and redistribution of wealth, joined the Communist insurgency that began in the 1960s and still continues through the activities of the NEW PEOPLE'S ARMY.

Hull, Cordell (1871–1955) The U.S. Senator from Tennessee (1931–1933) who was U.S. Secretary of State for most of the administration of President Franklin D. Roosevelt (1933–1944). He was a delegate to the United Nations Conference at San Francisco in 1945 and has often been called its founder.

He was awarded the Nobel Peace Prize in 1945, largely for the Roosevelt Administration's GOOD NEIGHBOR POLICY toward Latin America.

CORDELL HULL'S ART OF SAYING NOTHING ELABORATELY

[Cordell Hull's] caution in refusing to commit himself sometimes reaches fantastic lengths. At his press conference he has developed to a fine point the art of saying nothing elaborately: "That situation is complicated by the interplay of many phases which are receiving our most careful analysis. However, each phase is made up of so many individual circumstances and conditions that we are attempting to investigate each phase of the circumstances and conditions so that we will have a true comprehension of the entire development. . . ." And then the Secretary is apt to add a touch of irony to the confusion he has created: "We always want to be helpful to you gentl'men." When not provoked into extreme caution, his answers are likely to be direct, dry, witty, but always skillfully meaningless.

SOURCE: Benjamin Stolberg, "Cordell Hull: The Vanishing American" (*The American Mercury,* April 1940).

---

human intelligence (HUMINT)   A category of INTELLIGENCE derived from information collected and provided by human sources.

human rights   **1.** Those rights to life, health, and freedom to which all people are entitled simply because they are human beings. The notion of human rights does not depend on the rights or privileges allowed to people by governments. Much of the concern over human rights comes because of the fact that they are not universally observed by governments. Among the rights included in the 1948 UNIVERSAL DECLARATION OF HUMAN RIGHTS are respect for the integrity of persons, which includes freedom from political killing, disappearance, or torture; respect for civil liberties including freedom of speech, peaceful assembly, religion, movement, and emigration; and the right of citizens to change their government. There also has been considerable debate about whether rights include economic and social rights. While the United States government has seen these as lacking the same fundamental status as political rights, other countries, especially those of the Third World, disagree. In this broader view of human rights, emphasis is placed on the right to work, to social security, and to adequate food, health, and housing. For the people in many Third World states, these rights are more important than political rights, as they are essential to their survival.   **2.** A term sometimes used in the United States to describe the Carter Administration's foreign policy, which emphasized the promotion of human rights and called for all people to be free from government-sponsored political violence and to enjoy civil and political liberties. The Carter Administration found it difficult to implement a human rights policy consistently and effectively, given the other considerations that also played a part in its decision-making process.

HUMAN RIGHTS AS SELF-INTEREST

One of the most moving statements ever made on human rights as self-interest was that of Martin Niemöller (1892–1984), the World War I German U-boat commander who became a Protestant minister. For speaking out against Nazi rule he spent World War II in the Dachau concentration camp.

"First they came for the Jews and I did not speak out—because I was not a Jew. Then they came for the Communists and I did not speak out—because I was not a Communist. Then they came for the trade unionists and I did not speak out—because I was not a trade unionist. Then they came for me—and there was no one left to speak out for me."

SOURCE: James Bentley, *Martin Niemöller* (1984).

Human Rights Watch   A U.S. organization that monitors and reports on human rights around the globe. Founded in 1878, Human Rights Watch operates through a network of approximately 3,000 citizens who monitor events in their homelands. The degree of personal danger that many monitors assume is demonstrated by the fact that dozens have been killed, many more beaten or imprisoned.

Hume, David (1711–1776)   The Scottish philosopher, historian, and political economist whose most famous work was *A Treatise of Human Nature*

(1739–1740), which was revised and republished as an *Enquiry Concerning Human Understanding* (1752). Although Hume in some of his writings discussed the BALANCE OF POWER and its operation, his main contribution to the study of politics and international relations lay in his theory of knowledge. Hume distinguished between two types of reasoning—formal deductive or abstract reasoning, as found in mathematics; and empirical knowledge, which comes from observation as well as beliefs and value judgments. After attempting to develop a science of politics, he placed politics and morals in the province of value judgments.

HUMINT   *See* HUMAN INTELLIGENCE.

Hungarian Uprising   The anti-Communist revolt in Hungary that began on October 23, 1956. This protest against Stalinism and Soviet control began when demonstrators, demanding the resignation of the Communist government and the withdrawal of Soviet troops from Hungary, were fired upon. The momentum of dissent continued as a spontaneous workers' council was formed and pre–World War II democratic parties were revived. Hungarian reformist leader IMRE NAGY overthrew the hard-line Communist government and announced the country's departure from the WARSAW PACT so that the Hungarian government would become independent from the Soviet Union. The revolt ended quickly after Soviet troops reentered the capital of Budapest on November 1. Nagy was replaced by JANOS KADAR, who declared Hungary's commitment to the Soviet government. The uprising cost about 27,000 Hungarian and 7,000 Soviet casualties.

Huns   The German people in general. Ever since the Huns, an Asian tribe, descended from the north and ravaged Roman provinces in the fifth century, this has been a term of invective in the Western world. During both world wars the Germans were often called Huns in literature, speeches, and propaganda. If the Germans had invaded England in 1941, when such an action seemed imminent, Prime Minister Winston Churchill "had already decided upon the final sentence of his call to eternal resistance: 'The hour has come; kill the Hun' " (according to William K. Klingaman, *1941*, 1988).

THE KAISER ADDRESSES HIS HUNS

You must know, my men, that you are about to meet a crafty, well-armed cruel foe. Meet him and beat him! Give no quarter! Take no prisoners! Kill him, when he falls into your hands! Even as, a thousand years ago, the Huns under their King Attila made such a name for themselves as still resounds in terror . . . so may the name of Germany resound through Chinese history a thousand years from now.

SOURCE: Kaiser William II in a speech to his troops at the time of the 1900 Boxer Rebellion in China, quoted in Emil Ludwig, *Wilhelm Hohenzollern* (1926). It was thus the kaiser himself who first created the modern image of "the Hun."

Hurley, Patrick J. (1883–1963)   The former U.S. Secretary of War (1929–1933) who was sent to China in 1944 by President Franklin D. Roosevelt as an ambassador. His mission was to achieve peace between the Chinese Communists and the Chinese Nationalists. He gave up the effort in 1945 and sharply criticized U.S. State Department policies in China.

Husak, Gustav (1913–1991)   The World War II resistance fighter who, as ALEXANDER DUBCEK's deputy premier during the PRAGUE SPRING, succeeded Dubcek in 1969 as head of the Czech Communist Party. Once in power, he dismantled Dubcek's reforms and presided over a hard-line Stalinist regime until forced to resign in 1989 in the VELVET REVOLUTION.

Hussein, Saddam (1937–   )   The dictator of Iraq since 1979. As a leader of the Ba'ath Party coup that overthrew the previous dictator in 1968, he became the de facto leader of Iraq by 1979 after murdering all opponents. In 1979 he formally became president. He has ruthlessly suppressed all opposition and nurtured a CULT OF PERSONALITY that is reminiscent of the Stalinist Soviet Union. In 1980 he sought to take advantage of the turmoil caused by the IRANIAN REVOLUTION by invading some border areas. The ensuing IRAN-IRAQ WAR lasted eight years and ended in a draw. Once again Hussein miscalculated when he invaded Kuwait in 1990 and found most of the world in a military alliance against him. Pushed out of Kuwait by the

PERSIAN GULF WAR (though he continues to claim it as Iraq's own), he remains in power but has had to suppress revolts in the north by the Kurds and in the south by Shi'ites.

Hussein Ibn Talal (1935–   )   The king of Jordan since 1952. He succeeded to the throne when his father, King Talal, was deposed and institutionalized for mental incompetence. Hussein has long been considered a moderate in the Arab world who, until the PERSIAN GULF WAR, had excellent relations with the West. Because of Jordan's proximity to Israel, the impact of Mideast wars and Palestinian refugees threatens the kingdom's stability almost constantly. During the 1967 SIX-DAY WAR Jordan lost the WEST BANK to Israel and gained massive numbers of new refugees. The Palestinian guerrillas became such a problem that in 1970 a civil war, known as BLACK SEPTEMBER, broke out between the Palestine Liberation Organization (PLO) and Jordan who, with the indirect help of Israel, forced the PLO rebels to retreat into neighboring Syria and Lebanon. Hussein healed his rift with the PLO gradually as he supported their effort for an independent state on the West Bank. After Iraq invaded Kuwait in 1990, Hussein futilely tried to broker an Arab solution to the conflict. But his seeming tilt toward Iraq angered both the West and the Arab states allied against Iraq. The end result of the war was that Jordan had even more Palestinian refugees—this time from Iraq, Kuwait, and the gulf states—with less aid from the West and the oil-rich Arab states to support them. For this reason Hussein's crown and the stability of his state are effectively held hostage to the Palestinian question. Thus Jordan was the Arab state most eager to begin formal peace talks with the Israelis in 1991.

Hu Yaobang (1915–1989)   General secretary and chairman of the Chinese Communist Party from 1981 to 1987. A veteran of the LONG MARCH, Hu worked closely with DENG XIAOPING in both the Communist party and the army throughout his political life. After the Communist Party took over control of China, Hu became the head of the Communist Youth League in 1952. Like Deng, Hu was twice purged and rehabilitated during the CULTURAL REVOLUTION. As a pro-reform leader, Hu was pro-

moted in the early 1980s to general secretary and then to chairman of the party. Hu became a scapegoat and lost his job in 1987 when Deng's reform policy was under siege by the party hard-liners. When he died students in Beijing used the occasion of Hu's funeral to protest against the Communist government. The protest soon evolved into a pro-democracy movement, which ended in military suppression by the army in TIANANMEN SQUARE on June 4, 1989.

hydrogen bomb   A thermonuclear bomb; the second major development (after the atomic bomb) in the field of nuclear weapons. Although there had been earlier discussion, the public debate in the United States about the development of the hydrogen bomb became much more intense after President Harry S Truman announced on January 31, 1950, that he had ordered the Atomic Energy Agency to work on what was commonly called the "superbomb" or "super." Whereas the atomic bomb was based on fission, the hydrogen bomb was based on fusion—although it used a fission bomb as a detonator—and was many times more powerful. From the start of the debate there were questions about the possible utility of the hydrogen bomb as a military weapon. Although it gave the United States a short-term arms edge over the Soviet Union, the result of long-term nuclear plenty on both sides was that policymakers concluded that nuclear weapons were useful only to deter their use by others. It was BERNARD BRODIE in "Strategy Hits a Dead End" (*Harper's*, October 1955) who first recognized that the hydrogen bomb "brings us, in short, to the end of strategy as we have known it." Military planners and some strategic thinkers such as HERMAN KAHN took a different approach and developed plans for the military use of these weapons as part of a strategy of limited strategic war. In the final analysis, however, Brodie was right. Plans for the limited use of nuclear weapons were designed primarily to give credibility to DETERRENCE strategies, but the political leadership in both Moscow and Washington recognized that if deterrence failed, the use of these weapons would be mutually disastrous. *See also* DOOMSDAY MACHINE.

hyperinflation   *See* INFLATION.

IAEA *See* INTERNATIONAL ATOMIC ENERGY AGENCY.

Ibarruri, Dolores (1895–1989)   The most famous speaker of the republican cause of the SPANISH CIVIL WAR, known as "La Pasionaria." This Spanish Communist leader encouraged the troops by saying: "Better to die on one's feet than to live on one's knees." Then she told their wives: "We prefer to be widows of heroes rather than wives of cowards" (*Speeches and Articles*, 1938). After the fascist triumph she fled to the Soviet Union but returned to Spain in 1977.

Ibn Saud (1880–1953)   The Arab sheikh who by politics and war created the modern Kingdom of Saudi Arabia out of various feuding sheikhdoms of the Arabian peninsula. He then ruled as the first king of this new state from 1932 until his death. In 1933 he invited United States oil interests to develop the oil wealth of his kingdom. Since he owned the kingdom, which he had named after himself, this soon made him the richest man in the world.

IBRD *See* INTERNATIONAL BANK FOR RECONSTRUCTION AND DEVELOPMENT.

ICA *See* INTERNATIONAL COMMODITY AGREEMENT.

ICBM (intercontinental ballistic missile)   A land-based long-range rocket, armed with one or more nuclear warheads. ICBMs are intercontinental because they literally can be fired from territory on one continent into territory on the other side of the world. The SALT II negotiations in 1979 established that the shortest distance, or definitional range for an ICBM, was 5,500 kilometers. U.S. ICBMs, part of the U.S. strategic nuclear TRIAD, were first developed in the late 1950s and deployed from the early 1960s. They gave the Cold War superpowers the ability to deliver nuclear weapons over long distances at great speed. Because these weapons could not be defended against, the United States and the Soviet Union had to come to terms with constant vulnerability to nuclear attack. At first ICBMs had only a single warhead each. Because they were initially highly inaccurate, they could be targeted only on large cities. By the mid-1960s they became more accurate and could carry multiple independently targeted reentry vehicles (MIRVs). The MX missile, the United States' third generation of ICBM, is extremely accurate. *See also* MISSILE GAP; PEENEMÜNDE.

ICSC *See* INTERNATIONAL CIVIL SERVICE COMMISSION.

IDA *See* INTERNATIONAL DEVELOPMENT ASSOCIATION.

IDCA *See* INTERNATIONAL DEVELOPMENT COOPERATION AGENCY.

idealism   The use of high moral principles as a guide to foreign policy. This is in contrast to REALISM, which is more pragmatic and concerned with immediate NATIONAL INTEREST. However, proponents of idealism maintain that moral force is ultimately more effective and more enduring than physical power. U.S. President Woodrow Wilson's futile advocacy that the United States join the League of Nations after World War I is considered one of the century's great examples of idealism in INTERNATIONAL RELATIONS.

Idris I (1890–1983)   The king of Libya (1951–1969) who was deposed in a coup led by Colonel MUAMMAR AL-QADDAFI. Idris then lived out the rest of his life in Egypt.

IFC   *See* INTERNATIONAL FINANCE CORPORATION.

IFAD   *See* INTERNATIONAL FUND FOR AGRICULTURAL DEVELOPMENT.

Ikle, Fred (1924–   )   The U.S. strategic analyst who, as an official in the Reagan Administration, helped produce the controversial 1988 study DISCRIMINATE DETERRENCE. Ikle's earlier work did not focus exclusively on strategic issues. His *How Nations Negotiate* (1964) was the first attempt to treat negotiation in a systematic and scholarly manner. He also wrote one of the first and surprisingly few attempts to think through what happens after detection of cheating on arms control agreements in "After Detection What?" (*Foreign Affairs,* January 1961). Ikle subsequently was a leading critic of the idea of mutual assured destruction (MAD).

illegal alien   An individual from one state who is unlawfully living or working in another state. The U.S. Department of Labor prefers to refer to such people as "undocumented workers," a term that retains the presumption of innocence and sounds less criminal.

ILO   *See* INTERNATIONAL LABOR ORGANIZATION.

IMF   *See* INTERNATIONAL MONETARY FUND.

immigration   **1.** Going to a new state with the intention of permanently remaining.   **2.** A government's policies that regulate the circumstances under which aliens may enter and remain. Historically governments have encouraged immigration when there was a labor shortage or new lands to settle. For example, earlier in this century Australia, Canada, and the United States sought immigrants of European origin for these reasons. In the post–World War II era West Germany sought foreign GUESTWORKERS to cope with a labor shortage. But once an economy turns down, nativist sentiment goes up and hostility is often directed toward immigrants who appear to take jobs from longer-term residents. For example, the 1992 resurgence of neo-nazis in Germany and the far right in France is directed at curtailing or reversing immigration.

immigration, illegal   The unlawful entry of an individual into a state; the entry of noncitizens into a state without gaining a VISA and submitting to customs inspection. There are two basic attitudes toward illegal immigration: (1) It is desirable because the immigrants perform low-paying jobs citizens do not want and effectively subsidize the economy; and (2) the immigrants are a drain on the economy because they tend not to pay taxes while using government services.

immutability   Changelessness; a characteristic of something that cannot be revised, such as a permanent border between two states. *Compare to* INVIOLABILITY.

imperialism   The political control of one state by another, usually for exploitative reasons. COLONIALISM, the result of wars of conquest, was supplemented in the late nineteenth century by a new economic and cultural imperialism.

The traditional rationale for an imperialism advocated by capitalistic interests was provided by Adam Smith in *The Wealth of Nations* (1776): "To found a great empire for the sole purpose of raising up a people of customers, may at first sight appear a project fit only for a nation of shopkeepers. It is, however, a project altogether unfit for a nation of shopkeepers; but extremely fit for a nation whose government is influenced by shopkeepers." Imperialism is associated with the creation of empires and the domination through the use or threat of force in areas outside the territory of the imperial power itself. The Roman Empire was an early example of imperialism. After the colonialism of the seventeenth and eighteenth centuries, a "new imperialism" emerged in the late nineteenth century as the European powers engaged in the SCRAMBLE FOR AFRICA, Asia, and Pacific Islands.

There has been much discussion of the causes of imperialism. British economist JOHN A. HOBSON, in *Imperialism* (1902), argued that the "new imperialism" involved the search for profits. It arose from the search to control markets and specific raw materials. These economic motivations provided the basis for the Leninist critique of imperialism as the highest form of capitalism and the argument that war between imperialist powers was inevitable. Imperialist powers tended to explain imperialism in terms of honor, duty, and a social Darwinism of racial superiority—ideas enshrined in Rudyard Kipling's poem about the WHITE MAN'S BURDEN. One of the most explicit examples of this kind of thinking can be found in Lord Curzon's Address at the Town Hall of Birmingham (December 11, 1907), in which he stated:

> Wherever this [British] empire has extended its borders . . . there misery and oppression, anarchy and destitution, superstition and bigotry, have tended to disappear and been replaced by peace, justice, prosperity, humanity, and freedom of thought, speech and action. . . . Imperialism is . . . animated by the sense of sacrifice and the idea of duty. Empire can only be achieved with satisfaction or maintained with advantage provided it has a moral basis. To the people of the mother state it must be a discipline, an inspiration and a faith. To the people of the circumference, it must be more than a flag or a name, it must be the sense of partnership in a great idea, the consecrating influence of a lofty purpose.

In fact, the great European empires of the late nineteenth and early twentieth century were characterized not only by exploitation and oppression but also, at least in some cases (such as that of Belgium in the Congo), by incredible harshness, brutality, and misrule. Other colonial administrations sought to improve life in the colonies and eventually prepare their territories for independence. The disintegration of the colonial empires, however, came not from reaction against the excesses of imperialism but from the dissemination of ideas of democracy and nationalism, which the Europeans had largely introduced to the areas they dominated. In this sense imperialism contained the seeds of its own destruction. In the second half of the twentieth century the DECOLONIZATION process was completed and the last remaining empire, the Soviet Union, disintegrated rapidly between 1989 and the end of 1991. Nevertheless, Third World rhetoric still frequently complains of NEOCOLONIALISM and CULTURAL IMPERIALISM.

imperialism, cultural 1. The notion that one state might dominate others not through territorial conquest and explicit subordination but through the more insidious imposition of its values and culture. During the 1960s, for example, there was concern in European states, especially in France, about the imposition of U.S. cultural values upon their societies. 2. Modernization. When THIRD WORLD leaders denounce Western cultural imperialism, they are often concerned with what they perceive to be threats to traditional values—values that they contend are every bit as valid as those of the West. Thus the Iranian Revolution of 1979, for example, rejected those aspects of modernization that were contradicted by traditional religious teachings.

imperial overstretch Paul Kennedy's concept from his book *The Rise and Fall of the Great Powers* (1987) that global powers often find themselves stuck with military and economic obligations far greater than they can provide or pay for. Kennedy sees this as a major cause of the decline of great powers and cites Spain under Philip II as an example. His argument is that the United States is suffering from a similar overstretch. Critics have challenged this concept on several grounds, however. One is that the United States is not an imperial power. A second is that when Kennedy was writing, the United States had less extensive and less onerous military commitments than at the height of the Cold War, when it was also at the height of its power. As JOSEPH NYE pointed out in *Bound to Lead* (1990), even after President Ronald Reagan's defense buildup the United States devoted only 6 percent of its gross national product to defense, compared with almost 10 percent in the early 1960s. Moreover, the United States devotes a far smaller share of governmental spending to the military than did earlier powers that suffered from imperial overstretch. While imperial overstretch might have had some validity in these earlier cases, its application to the United States was one of Kennedy's most vulnerable arguments.

imperial presidency *See* PRESIDENCY, IMPERIAL.

imperium   **1.** Supreme power or authority.   **2.** A state that is a great power.   **3.** The physical area of an empire.

import   A product brought into a country from abroad. *Compare to* EXPORT.

import duty   *See* DUTY.

import license   A document required and issued by some national governments authorizing the importation of goods into their individual countries. *Compare to* FREE LIST.

import quota   A means of restricting imports by the issue of licenses to importers, assigning to each a specific limit, after determination of the amount of any commodity that is to be imported during a period. Such licenses also may specify the country from which the importer must purchase the goods. The device works against FREE TRADE and the maximization of international trade generally but may be adopted by a government because of internal pressures from traders and workers suffering from foreign competition that they cannot match.

Inchon invasion   The September 15, 1950, amphibious landing of U.S. forces during the KOREAN WAR at Inchon on the east coast of Korea near Seoul. This was a hastily improvised but brilliantly executed flanking maneuver that caught the North Korean Communist invaders completely by surprise and allowed United Nations forces under U.S. General Douglas MacArthur to retake South Korea and advance beyond the THIRTY-EIGHTH PARALLEL to the Yalu River. According to historian Max Hastings, Inchon "summons a vision of military genius undulled by time, undiminished by more recent memories of Asian defeat. Inchon remains a monument to 'can do,' to improvisation and risk-taking on a magnificent scale, above all to the spirit of Douglas MacArthur. . . . The amphibious landings . . . were MacArthur's masterstroke" (*The Korean War*, 1987).

incidents   Brief clashes or other military disturbances of a transitory nature and not involving pro-tracted hostilities. Examples include the GULF OF SIDRA INCIDENT, the PUEBLO INCIDENT, and the U-2 INCIDENT.

incorporation, doctrine of   *See* ADOPTION, DOCTRINE OF.

incrementalism   An approach to decision making and to foreign policy that emphasizes small steps. This can be an intellectual response to uncertainty or a political response to pressures against bolder moves or more fundamental initiatives. The danger with incremental decision making of either kind is that the policymakers rarely stand back and ask whether the overall direction is appropriate. By its very nature incrementalism militates against a fundamental reappraisal of policy and therefore can lead to gradual commitments or gradual escalation.

incursion   **1.** A more politic word for a military INVASION of another state's territory, as in the CAMBODIAN INCURSION during the Vietnam War.   **2.** A sudden hostile but short-lived RAID, as in the frequent incursions into Israel by Palestinian terrorists.

independence   **1.** A term used to describe a situation in which a state is not controlled by or subordinate to other states. States that are subordinated to or dominated by other states often seek to achieve independence; former colonies that have achieved it usually celebrate an annual *independence day* to commemorate the removal of external rule.   **2.** A word that is often used synonymously with or consecutive with SOVEREIGNTY (as in the term *sovereign independence*) even though independence is essentially a political concept and sovereignty is a legal concept. The implication is that a state may be formally sovereign but not really independent.   **3.** A notion that is manifested in state behavior which does not accord with the preferences of others. For example, most of the members of the North Atlantic Treaty Organization would have preferred that France not withdraw from NATO's military structure in 1966. And the United States would have preferred that its European allies not offer diplomatic recognition to Communist China in the 1950s. In each instance a state did what it had an independent right to do—even though this action was not in accord with the preferences of one or more allies.

independent deterrent   *See* DETERRENT, INDEPENDENT.

independent variables   Those factors that shape international actors' behavior and determine the variations in it. JAMES ROSENAU, in *The Scientific Study of Foreign Policy* (1971), identified five main variables that have an impact on foreign policy behavior: individual, role, governmental, societal, and systemic. Rosenau saw the nature and strength of these variables as crucial to foreign policy behavior.

Indian-Chinese War   *See* SINO-INDIAN CONFLICT.

Indian National Congress   The formal name of the Congress political party in India. The parent of independence movements in India, it began in 1885. Its first leaders accepted British cononial rule but asked for more educated native Indian officials. A second stage of leaders rejected piecemeal British reforms from about 1905. In 1919 they demanded self-government. In a third stage, beginning in 1920, MOHANDAS GANDHI transformed the party into a mass movement and used it to mount a popular campaign against British rule. After independence in 1947 the Congress Party became and has mostly remained the leading party in India; leaders JAWAHARLAL NEHRU, INDIRA GANDHI, and RAJIV GANDHI all belonged to the Congress Party.

Indian partition   The 1947 division of the Indian subcontinent into Pakistan (principally populated with Muslims) and the Republic of India (chiefly Hindu). In 1946 Great Britain offered independence to India, but Hindu-Muslim difference forced partitioning. The Muslim League (which had been pressing for a separate Muslim state) and the All-Indian Conference approved the plan, and on August 15, 1947, India, divided into the two countries of Pakistan and India, became independent. While the transfer of power itself was peaceful enough, Hindu-Muslim communal riots and the migration of about 18 million people from one side to another cost an estimated 1 million lives.

India-Pakistan War   1. The 1965 border conflict also called the KASHMIR DISPUTE.   2. The 1971 bor-

der fighting that accompanied the BANGLADESH WAR OF INDEPENDENCE.

indicator   In INTELLIGENCE usage, an item of information that reflects the intention or capability of a potential enemy to adopt or reject a course of action. *Compare to* SOCIAL INDICATOR.

indigenous personnel   The local people employed at an overseas military base, diplomatic installation, or factory.

indirect approach   A flanking maneuver that seeks to force the enemy to move from a strong position by threatening its rear. Sometimes called a *strategic envelopment* or *end run,* this is as applicable to politics as to war. The best-known modern advocate of the indirect approach is BASIL H. LIDDELL HART. However, the essence of his analyses built on the works of SUN-TZU, who wrote in his *Art of War* (fourth century B.C.): "In all fighting, the direct method may be used for joining battle, but indirect methods will be needed in order to secure victory."

Indochina   The name of the former colonies and protectorates of France on the Indochinese peninsula: Cambodia, Laos, and Vietnam. They were under the direct or indirect rule of France from 1884 to 1954. Neighboring Thailand, in contrast, managed to remain independent.

Indochina War   France's military efforts to retain its Southeast Asian mainland colonies after World War II. Nationalist guerrillas led by HO CHI MINH began fighting in 1946 after negotiations on a future relationship with France broke down. After a major defeat at DIEN BIEN PHU in 1954, the French agreed to a cease-fire and withdrawal of troops. The GENEVA CONFERENCE OF 1954 then granted independence to France's Indochinese colonies. *See also* VIETNAM WAR.

Indonesian Massacres   The 1965–1967 politically organized murder of an estimated half-million local Chinese and other dissidents, said to be Communists, by the Indonesian military and local militia. The killings were instigated in response to a failed coup attempt by the Indonesian Communists. In connection with the massacres, it is often pointed out that the word "amok"—as in "run amok"—is an Indonesian word. It is certainly descriptive of this incident.

Indonesian War of Independence　The post–World War II guerrilla insurgency that forced the Dutch colonial power to agree to Indonesian sovereignty in 1949. The Indonesian independence movement began during the first decade of the twentieth century and expanded rapidly between the two world wars. Its leaders came from a small group of young professional men and students, some of whom had been educated in the Netherlands. Some, including ACHMED SUKARNO, Indonesia's first president, were imprisoned for their political activities. The Japanese occupied Indonesia for three years during World War II and, for their own purposes, encouraged a nationalist movement. Many Indonesians were appointed to positions in the civil administrations, which had been closed to all but ruling nobles under the Dutch. On August 17, 1945, three days after the Japanese surrender, a small group of Indonesians led by Sukarno proclaimed independence and established the Republic of Indonesia. The new republic resisted Dutch efforts to reestablish complete control; after four years of warfare and negotiations, sovereignty was transferred on December 27, 1949. The next year Indonesia became the sixtieth member of the United Nations.

industrial defense　All nonmilitary measures to assure the uninterrupted productive capability of vital facilities and attendant resources essential to MOBILIZATION.

industrial mobilization　The transformation of industry from its peacetime activity to the industrial program necessary to support national military objectives. It includes the MOBILIZATION of materials, labor, capital, production facilities, and contributory programs.

industrial policy　Government regulation of the planning and production of manufactured goods through law, tax incentives, and cash subsidies. The United States does not have a comprehensive industrial policy as compared to other nations, especially Japan, whose government exercises considerable control over industrial planning and decision making. This is because of the traditional American abhorrence of central planning, which is associated with COMMUNISM and considered the antithesis of the free enterprise system. But because of increasing economic competition from states in which government and business work cooperatively to advance industrial interests, there is now a considerable debate in the United States over whether the national government should develop a more cohesive and comprehensive industrial policy. *Compare to* COMPETITIVENESS.

industrial preparedness　The state of readiness of industry to produce essential materiel to support national military objectives.

industrial security　That portion of INTERNAL SECURITY that is concerned with the protection of classified information in the hands of private industry.

infant industry argument　The trade stance calling for a policy of temporary protection (generally in the form of a high TARIFF) for an industry that has the potential to be competitive in the world market. Often a new industry realizes declining costs as output expands and production experience is acquired. In the initial phase of production startup, infant domestic industry may not be competitive with existing world producers. Thus it is often argued that temporary nurturance is required on the part of the domestic government.

infiltration　**1.** The movement through or into an area or territory occupied by either friendly or enemy troops or organizations. This movement is made by small groups or by individuals at extended or irregular intervals. When used in connection with the enemy, it infers that contact is avoided.　**2.** In INTELLIGENCE usage, placing an agent or other person in a target area in hostile territory. This usually involves crossing a frontier or other guarded line. The methods of infiltration are known as black (clandestine), gray (through legal crossing points but under false documentation), and white (legal).

inflation　A rise in the costs of goods and services equated to a fall in the value of a state's currency.

Hyperinflation is an inflation so extreme that it destroys the value of paper money. The most famous example of this occurred in Germany in the 1920s. Economist John Maynard Keynes was correct when he wrote: "There is no subtler, no surer means of overturning the existing basis of society than to debauch the currency. The process engages all the hidden forces of economic law on the side of destruction, and does it in a manner which not one man in a million is able to diagnose" (*Economic Consequences of the Peace*, 1919). V. I. Lenin is often credited with being the first to say that "the best way to destroy the capitalist system is to debauch the currency," but this statement has not been found in his published writings.

influence   **1.** The capacity of one actor to persuade another to behave in ways that it would otherwise not behave, a central concept in political science and the study of relations whether personal or international. Influence usually requires some kinds of resources that can be translated into either threats of deprivation or inducements. Used in this sense, influence is an all-embracing term, and POWER (which generally involves threats or sanctions) is subsumed within it as simply one form of influence.   **2.** An ability to change the behavior of others that is akin to power but clearly differentiated from it by the fact that influence, in this more restricted sense, is noncoercive whereas power rests on coercion.   **3.** Something that actors are said to possess when they are able to persuade another to act in ways that accord with their preferences.   **4.** Someone or something that has an impact on a policy choice or a policy outcome.

infrastructure   **1.** A political party's or a government's administrative "skeleton"; the individuals and processes that make it work.   **2.** The institutional framework of a society that supports its educational, religious, and social ideology, which in turn supports the political order.   **3.** Permanent installations and facilities for the support, maintenance and control of air, land, or naval forces. A military organization such as the North Atlantic Treaty Organization, with large forward-based strength and even larger reinforcement needs during mobilization, is necessarily deeply concerned with infrastructure provisions.

INF Treaty   The 1987 Intermediate Nuclear Forces Treaty (ratified in 1988) between the United States and the Soviet Union that eliminated their intermediate-range and short-range intermediate nuclear missiles. It covered U.S. and Soviet land-based nuclear missiles with ranges from about 300 to 3,400 miles (500 to 5,500 kilometers), banned the production and flight testing of INF missiles, eliminated all U.S. and Soviet INF missile systems (within three years), and eliminated all facilities to deploy, store, repair, and produce INF missile systems once all U.S. and Soviet INF missile systems were destroyed. For the first time, an entire class of missiles on both sides were eliminated. The treaty embodied the principle of unequal reductions; the Soviets eliminated deployed systems capable of carrying about four times as many warheads as those eliminated by the United States. The treaty also established the most stringent and comprehensive verification system in the history of arms control, including several kinds of on-site inspections.

inherent bad faith model   A term used by analysts to describe a situation in which there is such suspicion about another state that even if that state makes conciliatory overtures, they will be dismissed as either some kind of trick or as simply a result of temporary weakness rather than as representing a real desire to improve relations. Inherent bad faith models on both sides bedeviled U.S.-Soviet relations until MIKHAIL GORBACHEV was able to convince the United States that he was genuine in his efforts for a new more cooperative relationship. *Compare to* SECURITY DILEMMA.

Inkatha Freedom Party   The political movement of the Zulu tribe of South Africa. Led by MANGOWUTHU GATSHA BUTHELEZI, this is the principal rival to the AFRICAN NATIONAL CONGRESS for leadership of the black majority population. Indeed the tribal antagonism is so great that COMMUNAL CONFLICT has been a frequent occurrence, especially because of the Inkatha Freedom Party's insistence that their political demonstrators carry "cultural weapons"—spears, shields, and clubs.

U.S. President Ronald Reagan (right) and Soviet leader Mikhail Gorbachev exchange pens after signing the INF Treaty in December 1987. (U.S. Naval Institute)

innocent passage   The right of ships belonging to one state to pass through the territorial waters of another state so long as they are not threatening the security of the latter. This right was embodied in the 1982 United Nations Convention on the Law of the Sea, which established innocent passage for a zone of 12 miles from any coast. The right of innocent passage conflicts to some extent with the desire of coastal states to extend the area of seas that they control but is an important element in facilitating naval transit.

in-place force   A North Atlantic Treaty Organization–assigned force that in peacetime, is stationed principally in the designated combat zone of the NATO command to which it is committed. The Soviet Union had similar in-place forces in WARSAW PACT states throughout the COLD WAR. The Soviet (now Russian) forces are now all in the process of being withdrawn; the U.S. forces are being reduced.

inspector general   A job description (of military origin) for the administrative head of an inspection or investigative unit of a larger agency.

instability   The lack of equilibrium. An international system is regarded as unstable or suffers from instability if it is prone to large-scale war or other disruptive changes. In a political system instability refers to the possibility that the system will break down, either through revolution or through civil war.

Institute for International Finance A private organization of bankers that does country RISK ANALYSES for the benefit of commercial banks that lend to developing nations. Its objectives are to provide lending banks with more complete and pertinent information regarding economic conditions in those countries and to encourage borrowing nations to deal in a more timely fashion with their economic problems. Based in the United States in Washington, D.C., it was established in 1983 by officials of 35 Western and Japanese banks.

Institute for International Law A private Geneva, Switzerland–based organization of legal scholars from many states that promotes the progressive codification of INTERNATIONAL LAW. It was awarded the Nobel Peace Prize in 1904 for its efforts in creating general principles of international jurisprudence.

institutional memory The collective traditional practices and general recollections of government organizations. This can be achieved through continuity of personnel and through written records.

Institutional Revolutionary Party (PRI) *Partido Revolucionario Institucional,* the leading Mexican political party founded by Plutarco Elías Calles (1877–1945) in 1929 as the National Revolutionary Party, renamed the Party of the Mexican Revolution in 1938, and renamed PRI in 1946. Calles used the party to pacify the country and institutionalize the rule of military leaders and politicians who had led Mexico since the end of the Mexican Revolution in 1920. The party, organized in a corporatist fashion with workers, government officials, and peasants incorporated, also represents business interests. Although the PRI's popularity has declined in recent years, PRI candidate Carlos Salinas de Gortari (1948–   ) won 50.36 percent of the vote in the 1988 presidential election.

insurgency 1. An armed attempt to foster a revolution through attacks against governmental or societal targets. Modern insurgencies usually take the form of GUERRILLA WARFARE. Insurgencies often rely on terrorist acts to (a) publicize their cause, both domestically and internationally; (b) attract popular support and participation; (c) seek retribution; (d) spark governmental repression so as to incite popular insurrection and antigovernment sentiment; (e) make strategic gains against a far stronger adversary with the use of limited resources. 2. An organization or political movement designed to overthrow a legally constituted government through use of subversion and armed conflict. Bernard B. Fall, in "The Theory and Practice of Insurgency . . ." (*Naval War College Review,* April 1965), warned that governments "will seek a military solution to the insurgency problem, whereas by its very nature, the insurgency problem is militarily only in a secondary sense, and politically, ideologically, and administratively in a primary sense." *Compare to* COUNTERINSURGENCY. *See also* WAR OF NATIONAL LIBERATION.

insurrection An uprising against the government, whether the government is indigenous or imposed from outside by a foreign power. Insurrection is a term that is closely related to REVOLUTION and to INSURGENCY but generally refers to the initial stages of these events. Insurrections may be put down fairly easily or may grow into more serious challenges to the government. The forces carrying out insurrections are generally weak and therefore try to avoid direct military confrontation, at least at the outset, with government forces.

MAZZINI ON INSURRECTION

Insurrection—by means of guerrilla bands—is the true method of warfare for all nations desirous of emancipating themselves from a foreign yoke. This method of warfare supplies the want—inevitable at the commencement of the insurrection—of a regular army; it calls the greatest number of elements into the field, and yet may be sustained by the smallest number. It forms the military education of the people, and consecrates every foot of the native soil by the memory of some warlike deed.

SOURCE: Giuseppe Mazzini, *General Instructions for Members of Young Italy* (1831). Mazzini (1805–1872) was the Italian revolutionary who led the fight for a united Italy under a republican form of government.

---

integration 1. A stage in the INTELLIGENCE CYCLE in which a pattern is formed through the selection and combination of evaluated information. 2. The process of making differing military units or services more compatible so that they may better operate as an integrated force in time of war.

integration, political 1. A voluntary process of joining together to create a new political community—one that is generally regarded as larger than the traditional nation state. Ernst Haas in *The Uniting of Europe* (1958) sees integration as a process "whereby political actors in several distinct national settings are persuaded to shift their loyalties, expectations and political activities toward a new center, whose institutions possess or demand jurisdiction over the preexisting national states." This process has been at work in the European Community and is still going on as the EC moves toward political union. It can be achieved in a variety of ways but is discussed most often in relation to FUNCTIONALISM and NEOFUNCTIONALISM. 2. The result of a process of joining together to build a new political community. To be viable the new community will evoke loyalty from the populations of the smaller units that joined together. If it does not, then a process of disintegration will take place.

intelligence 1. An individual's ability to cope with his or her environment and to deal with mental abstractions. 2. Information. The military and other organizations concerned with national security use the word thus in its original Latin sense. Intelligence in this context also implies secret or protected information, even though some of the best sources are open rather than covert. Courtney Whitney in *MacArthur: His Rendezvous* (1956) quotes U.S. General Douglas MacArthur as saying: "Expect only five per cent of an intelligence report to be accurate. The trick of a good commander is to isolate the five percent." General William C. Westmoreland, the commander of all U.S. forces during most of the Vietnam War, says, "Intelligence is at best an imprecise science. It is not like counting beans; it is more like estimating cockroaches" (*Christian Science Monitor,* January 27, 1982). 3. The product of organizations engaged in such intelligence-gathering activities. This is particularly apposite given that so much

information has to be concerned with estimating not simply the capabilities of others but also their intentions—which they might not yet fully know themselves. Another objective of much intelligence activity is to estimate the degree of stability of a regime or a political system. This requires both understanding and forecasting of complicated social political and economic processes. Sherman Kent in a famous study of intelligence, *Strategic Intelligence for American World Policy* (1965), observed that one of the key elements in intelligence was the "speculative-evaluative" component. In a sense, therefore, intelligence assessments are designed to know the unknowable, discover the undiscoverable, and predict the unpredictable. *Compare to* COUNTERINTELLIGENCE; ELECTRONIC INTELLIGENCE; ESPIONAGE.

intelligence, basic The relatively stable information or slowly changing data about a state or region such as its population, government, culture, leaders, highways, railways, and so on. This information may be used as reference material in the planning of operations at any level and in evaluating subsequently gathered intelligence material.

intelligence, domestic Information relating to activities or conditions within a state that threaten internal security and that might require the employment of troops. The Federal Bureau of Investigation is the U.S. domestic intelligence agency; MI5 is that of Great Britain. In the Soviet Union the KGB handled both domestic and foreign intelligence.

intelligence, strategic 1. Information collected by an intelligence agency that can be used for formulating a state's diplomatic and military policies; it is long range and widely focused, as opposed to TACTICAL INTELLIGENCE. 2. Information relating to an adversary's strategic forces.

intelligence, tactical 1. Information required for a specific localized diplomatic or military mission; it tends to be short range and narrowly focused, as opposed to strategic intelligence. 2. Information relating to an adversary's tactical forces.

intelligence agency A government unit responsible for collecting and interpreting information about the military potential and political intentions of rival states. As Phillip Knightley writes in *The Second Oldest Profession* (1986), "It was not until 1909, in Britain, that the first intelligence agency came into being, a government department, financed from government funds, its employees largely civilians, created to steal secrets from other countries and to protect its own, empowered to operate in peace as well as in war." In 1929 U.S. Secretary of State Henry L. Stimson ordered the dismantling of the U.S. government's only secret intelligence (code-breaking) capabilities because he was dealing as a gentleman with the gentlemen sent as ambassadors and ministers from friendly nations, and "Gentlemen do not read each other's mail" (*On Active Service in Peace and War*, 1948). Allen Dulles, former director of the U.S. Central Intelligence Agency, disagreed. He wrote in *The Craft of Intelligence* (1963): "When the fate of a nation and the lives of its soldiers are at stake, gentlemen do read each other's mail—if they can get their hands on it." Intelligence agencies have always had a certain mystical quality, perhaps because they are so associated with fictional exploits. This even affects heads of state. Arthur M. Schlesinger, Jr., in *A Thousand Days* (1965), quotes U.S. President John F. Kennedy: "If someone comes in to tell me this or that about the minimum wage bill, I have no hesitation in overruling them. But you always assume that the military and intelligence people have some secret skill not available to ordinary mortals." For examples of intelligence agencies, *see* CENTRAL INTELLIGENCE AGENCY, KGB, MI5, MI6, MOSSAD.

intelligence community 1. All spies; the employees of the world's civilian and military intelligence agencies. 2. All of a single nation's military and civilian intelligence-gathering agencies. For example, the leading members of the U.S. intelligence community include the Central Intelligence Agency, the National Security Agency, the Defense Intelligence Agency, the Department of State, and the Federal Bureau of Investigation.

intelligence cycle The steps by which information is converted into INTELLIGENCE and made available to users: planning and directing, collection, processing, integration and analysis, and dissemination.

intelligence estimate The appraisal of available information relating to a specific situation or condition with a view to determining the courses of action open to the enemy or potential enemy and the order of probability of their adoption. *See also* ESTIMATE.

intelligence failure The faulty collection, assimilation, evaluation, or dissemination of intelligence, which allows one to be caught by surprise by an international development such as a surprise attack or the collapse of a regime. Although there are often arguments about the extent of the failure, famous intelligence failures include the United States failure to foresee the Japanese attack on Pearl Harbor, the Israeli and U.S. failure to foresee the Arab attacks that led to the Yom Kippur War, and the Soviet Union's failure to anticipate Operation Barbarosa (the German invasion) during World War II. Intelligence failures have many causes, including the difficulty of differentiating between what Roberta Wohlstetter in *Pearl Harbor: Warning and Decision* (1962) termed the "signals" predicting an event and the surrounding "noise"; MISPERCEPTION, COGNITIVE DISSONANCE, and other psychological factors, organizational obstacles such as hierarchy; and cultural factors such as ETHNOCENTRISM. In fact, what is most surprising is not that intelligence failures occur, but that they are relatively rare.

intelligence oversight The review of the policies and activities of intelligence agencies by appropriate legislative review committees. This was not formally done by the U.S. Congress until the 1970s, when reports of Federal Bureau of Investigation and Central Intelligency Agency abuses of their operating mandates encouraged both houses of the Congress to create committees that would systematically and formally watch over the intelligence operations of the executive branch. Parliamentary systems, which are used in most of the world, have far less opportunity for comparable oversight because PRIME MINISTERs, who ultimately direct intelligence agencies, lead both the executive and the legislative branches of government.

intelligence signals The gathering of political and military intelligence through the monitoring of electronic communications. In the United States, for example, the NATIONAL SECURITY AGENCY coordinates and analyzes the signals intelligence gathered by satellites in space and strategically located "listening posts" around the world.

Inter-American Defense Board   A permanently constituted international organization, established in 1942, composed of army, navy, and air force officers appointed by each of the governments of the American republics. (All of the governments of the Western Hemisphere, except colonies, are formally republics even when they have in fact been ruled as dictatorships.) The board studies and recommends to the governments of the republics measures necessary for closer military collaboration in preparation for the collective self-defense of the American continent against aggression.

Inter-American Treaty of Reciprocal Assistance   Popularly known as the Rio Treaty because it was the result of a conference in Rio de Janeiro, Brazil, this 1947 treaty established a permanent defense alliance among all American states. Each nation agreed to meet armed aggression or threat of aggression; no distinction was made, however, between American and non-American aggressor states—the provisions applied to all aggression regardless of source. In the event of attack, the foreign ministers of signatory nations were to meet immediately and decide whether to respond by severing diplomatic relations, imposing economic sanctions, or using armed force, but no state would be required to use force without its consent. The Rio Treaty served as a model for the later North Atlantic Treaty that established the ATLANTIC ALLIANCE.

intercontinental ballistic missile   *See* ICBM.

interdependence   **1.** A relationship of mutual dependence of states on each other. Interdependence can exist along several different dimensions, although the one that is emphasized in the literature most often is economic. The term itself, according to Edward Morse in "Interdependence in World Affairs" (in James Rosenau and others, eds., *World Politics,* 1976), was introduced in the eighteenth century by the physiocrats in France and by critics of the British

government's mercantilist economic policies. Morse himself emphasized that the outcome of the actions of two or more interdependent parties are mutually contingent. He also distinguished between "generalized levels of interdependence and interdependence in specific activities."   **2.** Systemic interdependence; a relatively new characteristic of the international system. Morse, in the above article, defines it as something that can be measured by "the extent to which events occurring in any given part or within any given component unit of a world system affect (either physically or perceptually) events taking place in each of the other parts or component units of a system." The advantage of this definition is that it highlights the sensitivity of actors in an interdependent situation to each other's policies. It also is neutral in that it does not assume that such sensitivity leads to cooperation. There is a tendency among some analysts of interdependence to suggest that the idea has fundamentally transformed the nature of international politics and provided far greater incentives for cooperative behavior. In fact, interdependence also can be a source of tension and conflict where states resent the impact of the actions of others on their own agendas. *See also* GLOBAL INTERDEPENDENCE.

interdiction   **1.** Stopping something before it becomes a major problem.   **2.** Military action to divert, disrupt, delay, or destroy enemy forces before they can be used against friendly forces. While a traditional ambush would be an interdiction, so would the use of air power to destroy bridges, railway junctions, or other CHOKE POINTS inside enemy territory.

interests section   A quasi-embassy that one state maintains in another when diplomatic relations have been severed or never existed. The "section" may be located in the "old" embassy or as an office within another state's physical facilities. For example, the United States has an interests section within the Swiss embassy in Havana; Cuba has a parallel unit in the Czech embassy in Washington. As Glenn Simpson wrote in *Insight* (August 29, 1988): "[In the] surreal world of interests sections . . . embassies that are not embassies [are] staffed by diplomats who are not diplomats [to] manage relations that do not exist."

intergovernmental organization An international group through which nations cooperate on a government-to-government level. Examples include the Asian Development Bank, the International Monetary Fund, and the Organization of American States. Such organizations are usually contrasted with SUPRANATIONAL organizations.

intermediate-range nuclear forces (INF) Nuclear weapons with ranges between 500 and 5,500 kilometers. The term emerged from 1981 negotiations between the United States and the Soviet Union that resulted in the INF TREATY. Previously these weapons systems were known as THEATER NUCLEAR FORCES. This term had become unacceptable within the North Atlantic Treaty Organization because "theater" implied that these weapons might be used separately from other U.S. strategic systems instead of together. The term is not applied to weapons in the tactical battlefield or short-range categories.

internal security 1. The condition of law and order prevailing within a state. 2. The prevention of action against resources, industries, and institutions; and the protection of life and property in the event of a domestic emergency by the employment of all measures, in peace or war, other than military defense. 3. Condition resulting from measures taken within a command to safeguard defense information coming under its cognizance, including physical security of documents and materials.

internal tariff *See* TARIFF, INTERNAL.

international 1. Anything that relates to the relationship of two or more nations. The word was coined by political theorist JEREMY BENTHAM in *Principles of Morals and Legislation* (1780) to differentiate internal or domestic law from that which came into play in relations among nations. He said it was "calculated to express, in a more significant way, the branch of law which goes under the name of the law of nations." Bentham also was the first to use the term INTERNATIONAL LAW. 2. An attitude, approach, or orientation that goes beyond thinking in terms of domestic matters of a particular nation.

International, The A term used to describe the International Working Men's Association—also known as the First International—which was formed in London in 1864 and which developed rapidly before collapsing as a result of divisions between the socialists and anarchists within its membership. The Second (Socialist) International was formed in 1889. After becoming preoccupied by the issues of war and peace in the period leading up to 1914, the Second International held several congresses in the interwar period, which illustrated the growing importance of socialist ideas in major European states. It was overtaken in importance, however, by the Third (Communist) International established in 1919, which enunciated the idea of world revolution as its objective. The Third International became the main link between the Soviet government in Moscow and Communist parties in capitalist states. It was dissolved in 1943 as a gesture of wartime solidarity with the Soviet Union's newfound capitalist allies. Soviet leader Joseph Stalin could hardly continue to advocate revolution in the states, mainly the United States and Great Britain, that were helping him to defeat Nazi Germany. A Fourth International was established by exiled Russian revolutionary Leon Trotsky in 1938, but it was an abortive effort to take over the world Communist movement from Stalin. In 1951 a new Socialist International was organized in West Germany to further the cause of democratic socialism. This last and current international represented the social democratic parties of Western Europe and was not in any real way allied with the Soviet Union. Indeed, during the Cold War it favored an ever stronger North Atlantic Treaty Organization to halt and deter Soviet aggression.

international affairs 1. A loosely used term that is used as a synonym for INTERNATIONAL POLITICS. It can include almost anything that is not exclusively domestic in nature. 2. The name of a journal published by the Royal Institute for International Affairs, or Chatham House, in London. 3. The name of a journal that was published in Moscow beginning in 1954 and gave the Soviet interpretation of world events. It ceased publication in 1991.

international agreement A treaty, an accord, a convention, a protocol, or a pact; any understanding between states that is regulated by INTERNATIONAL LAW.

International Atomic Energy Agency (IAEA) The
United Nations agency, created in 1957, to facilitate
the peaceful uses of atomic power. It grew out of
U.S. President Dwight D. Eisenhower's ATOMS FOR
PEACE proposals. It administers the international
safeguards on atomic power created by the 1968
NUCLEAR NON-PROLIFERATION TREATY. The IAEA's
two main objectives are to seek to accelerate and
enlarge the contribution of atomic energy to peace,
health, and prosperity throughout the world and to
ensure, so far as it is able, that assistance provided
by it is not used in such a way as to further any military purpose. The IAEA safeguards system is primarily based on nuclear material accountancy,
verified on the spot by IAEA inspectors. Committed
non–nuclear weapon states must submit their entire
nuclear fuel cycle activities to IAEA safeguards.
The IAEA also facilitates emergency assistance to
member states in the event of a radiation accident.
Two IAEA-prepared international conventions—
the Convention on Early Notification of a Nuclear
Accident and the Convention on Assistance in the
Case of a Nuclear Accident or Radiological Emergency—came into force respectively in 1986 and
1987 after the CHERNOBYL accident in the Soviet
Union. The IAEA's policies and programs are
directed by the General Conference composed of all
IAEA member states, which meets annually, and by
a 35-member board of governors.

**International Bank for Reconstruction and Develop-
ment (IBRD) or World Bank** A sister organization to the INTERNATIONAL MONETARY FUND, located
in the United States in Washington, D.C. Created as
a part of the 1944 BRETTON WOODS SYSTEM, the
World Bank started operations in 1946. Its purpose,
after initially dealing the reconstruction of Europe
after World War II, has been both to lend funds at
commercial rates and to provide technical assistance to facilitate economic development in the
developing countries.

International Brigades **1.** Military units made up
of citizens from various states. **2.** The antifascist
volunteers from abroad who fought in the SPANISH
CIVIL WAR of 1936 to 1939. There were Anglo-
American, French, Italian, and Polish brigades,
among others. Many of these men were recruited by
their local Communist parties. Others served in an
idealistic effort to defeat fascism and further
democracy.

international city An urban area placed under the
sovereignty of a group of powers so that no one of
them or any others can gain political control. Also
known as a *free city*. This concept often has been
used as a compromise in territorial disputes. For
example, after World War I DANZIG was made an
international city so that neither Germany nor
Poland could control it.

International Civil Aviation Organization (ICAO)
One of the United Nations' SPECIALIZED AGENCIES
established in April 1947 to ensure the safe and
orderly growth of international civil aviation
throughout the world. It also encourages the arts of
aircraft design and operation for peaceful purposes
and the development of airways, airports, and air
navigation facilities for international civil aviation,
and promotes safe, regular, efficient, and economi-
cal air transport for the people of the world. The
ICAO has adopted international standards and recommended practices that govern the performance of
airline pilots, flight crews, air traffic controllers, and
ground maintenance crews. Aircraft telecommunications systems—radio frequencies and security
procedures—also are specified by the ICAO. Headquartered in Montreal, Quebec, Canada, the
ICAO's policy is set by an assembly of representatives of all member states, which meets once every
three years. The assembly elects its council, its executive body, composed of representatives from 33
nations, which carries out the ICAO's daily business.
The council may act, if requested by the member
states concerned, as a tribunal for the settlement of
any dispute relating to international civil aviation.

international civil service A term that does not
refer to any particular government entity but to any
bureaucratic organization that is by legal mandate
composed of differing citizenships and nationalities. Examples include the the Commission of the
European Communities, the International Labor
Organization, and the United Nations Secretariat.
Sometimes the term is used to collectively refer to
the employees of all international bureaucracies.

International Civil Service Commission (ICSC) A 15-member commission created by the United Nations in 1974 to make recommendations concerning the personnel policies of the various United Nations secretariats.

International Commodity Agreement (ICA) A multilateral trade arrangement between producer and consumer countries to stabilize commodity prices and/or supplies. It typically contains economic provisions such as buffer stocks, controls, or long-term contracts and is administered by a central body representing the members. CARTELS such as OPEC are not ICAs because they lack consumer participation.

International Court of Justice *See* WORLD COURT.

International Criminal Police Organization *See* INTERPPOL.

international currency 1. The money of a major economic power that is widely accepted throughout the world. Examples include the German mark, the Japanese yen, and the United States dollar. 2. Artificial financial assets, such as SPECIAL DRAWING RIGHTS, used by banks. 3. Money that is equally acceptable in more than one state. For example, the French franc is also the official currency of Monaco. *See also* EUROPEAN CURRENCY UNIT.

International Development Association (IDA) An affiliate of the INTERNATIONAL BANK FOR RECONSTRUCTION AND DEVELOPMENT established in 1959 to lend money to developing countries at low interest for long repayment periods. Because many developing countries cannot afford development loans at ordinary rates of interest and in the time span of conventional loans, the IDA provides development assistance through SOFT LOANS. The IDA's funds are furnished by regular "replenishments" from member countries and by loans from the IBRD.

International Development Cooperation Agency (IDCA) The U.S. agency created in 1979 to coordinate the activities of and provide policy direction to the Agency for International Development, the Overseas Private Investment Corporation, and other trade and development programs. The agency's director reports both to the U.S. president and the secretary of state and is charged with ensuring that development goals are considered in executive branch decisions affecting the developing countries. She or he is responsible for U.S. participation in international aid organizations such as the United Nations Development Program and the World Food Program and for advising the president on the selection of U.S. representatives to executive boards of directors for multilateral development banks such as the Inter-American Development Bank.

international division of labor The specialization of a state's productive capacities depending on the availability of natural resources, skilled labor, and other factors. All such specializations are a matter of degree depending on local conditions.

international economy The ECONOMY of the entire world, as opposed to the economy of a single state or region. As the world becomes increasingly integrated economically, economic policies and analysis will be increasingly international in scope.

International Finance Corporation (IFC) An offshoot of the INTERNATIONAL BANK FOR RECONSTRUCTION AND DEVELOPMENT, established in 1956 to provide capital for private enterprise projects in developing countries. Generally the IFC will invest directly in private enterprise projects that meet the following criteria: They must be expected to generate a profit; they must benefit the host country; and local investors must provide a share of the required capital.

International Fund for Agricultural Development (IFAD) One of the SPECIALIZED AGENCIES of the United Nations, created in 1976 to help developing countries increase their food production with low-interest loans. Its main goal is to help end the chronic hunger and malnutrition suffered by at least 20 percent of the population of the developing world. The IFAD hopes to achieve this goal by providing loans on favorable terms to finance projects that will bring small farmers and the landless into the development process, thus benefiting the poorest sections of the rural population. In addition to the food production objectives, the IFAD also is concerned with the impact each project may have on employment, nutrition, and income distribution. Some of the IFAD's projects are cofinanced by other financial and development institutions such as the International Bank for Reconstruction and Development and various regional development banks. The governments concerned usually contribute a share to the IFAD's projects. The IFAD's supreme authority is its governing council, on which all member states are represented. The council is categorized into three groups—developed nations, oil-exporting developing nations, and other developing nations—each having the same number of votes. Under this arrangement, the donor nations as well as the developing nations simultaneously hold two-thirds of the votes. Daily operations are conducted by the executive board, composed of 18 executive directors (six from each group) and 18 alternates, and chaired by the president of IFAD. Its headquarters is in Rome, Italy.

internationalism   **1.** Cooperation among states to further the common good; an attitude or approach that is oriented toward the international role of the state and that transcends a narrow self-interested nationalism.   **2.** In the United States, an approach to international politics that is contrasted with that of ISOLATIONISM. This sense of internationalism should not be equated with GLOBALISM: It is much more discriminate about international involvement, seeing this as crucial only where significant national interests are at stake.   **3.** A now-dated term for working class solidarity across national lines. This was strongly advocated by the early BOLSHEVIKS, especially LEON TROTSKY, who called for socialist revolutions in all states. This policy so contrasted with JOSEPH STALIN's policy of SOCIALISM IN ONE COUNTRY that it was a major factor in the rift between Trotsky and Stalin.

internationalist   **1.** One who advocates any form of INTERNATIONALISM.   **2.** A technical expert or scholar in INTERNATIONAL LAW or INTERNATIONAL RELATIONS.

internationalization   The multilateral protection of a specified part of the land or sea; often used in the

context of rivers or straits that come under international agreements.

International Labor Organization (ILO)   One of 16 SPECIALIZED AGENCIES of the United Nations, the ILO was established in 1919 under the Treaty of Versailles as an autonomous agency associated with the LEAGUE OF NATIONS. In 1946 the ILO became the first specialized agency associated with the United Nations. The ILO works to promote social justice for working people everywhere. It formulates policies and programs to help improve working and living conditions; creates labor standards to serve as guidelines for national authorities; carries out an extensive program of technical cooperation to help governments in making these policies effective in practice; and engages in training, education, and research to help advance these efforts. The International Labor Conference, the ILO's annual policy-making convention, is composed of delegates from each member country—two from the government and one each representing workers and employers. One of its most important functions is the adoption of conventions and recommendations that set international labor standards in such areas as employment services, freedom of association, hours and conditions of work, industrial safety, labor inspection, social insurance, vacation with pay, wages, and worker's compensation. Since the founding of the ILO, more than 300 conventions and recommendations have been adopted. Conventions are binding only if members ratify them. Headquartered in Geneva, Switzerland, the ILO holds an annual session of all its member states. The work of ILO is guided by the governing body, consisting of 28 government members, 14 worker members, and 14 employer members. In 1969 the ILO was awarded the Nobel Peace Prize for its efforts in improving working conditions throughout the world.

international law   All of the treaties, customs, and agreements between states. Political philosopher JEREMY BENTHAM coined the phrase in 1780 in *Principles of Morals and Legislation,* but many others before and since have tried to give substance and theoretical cohesiveness to practices that are often chaotic and frequently break down into war. When the international concern at issue applies to individuals, it becomes a matter of CONFLICT OF LAWS. HUGO GROTIUS is often called the father of international law because of his 1625 *De jure belli et pacis* (*The Rights of War and Peace*). Grotius asserted that it was possible to create a code of international law suitable for every time and place. However, many still believe what Stewart L. Murray wrote in *The Future Peace of the Anglo-Saxons* (1905): "There is no such thing as international law, for the thing so miscalled is merely international custom." Others, such as Lewis Henkin in *How Nations Behave* (1971), assert: "In relations between nations, the progress of civilization may be seen as movement from force to diplomacy, from diplomacy to law."

international law, conventional   Those aspects of INTERNATIONAL LAW that are derived from formal agreements, treaties, or conventions.

international law, customary   The main source of INTERNATIONAL LAW after treaties and other agreements that establish formal rules of behavior after repeated usage by many states over long periods of time. Customary law is generally found in the actual behavior of states and in their statements. Many of the "rules" of custom are eventually codified in treaties, partly because this provides greater precision and partly because it provides greater legitimacy. Article 38 of the Statute of the International Court of Justice lists "international custom, as evidence of a general practice accepted as law" as one of the bases on which it will make its rulings. The concept is the same as that of the Latin term *lex non scripta*.

international law, positive   The precepts to which a state binds itself in the treaties and other agreements that it signs.

international law, private   1. CONFLICT OF LAWS. 2. Business law in an international context. 3. The set of legal principles that determine which state's courts will decide a dispute and which state's law will be applied.

International Law Commission   Established by the United Nations General Assembly in 1947, the International Law Commission's main purpose is to promote the progressive development of INTERNATIONAL LAW and its codification. The commission meets annually and is composed of 34 members who are elected by the General Assembly for five-year terms. Members serve in their individual capacity, not as representatives of their governments. The main task of the International Law Commission is to prepare drafts on topics of international law, recommended by the General Assembly or the Economic and Social Council, or of the commission's own choice. When the commission completes draft articles on a particular topic, the General Assembly usually convenes an international conference that presents the articles as a convention for adoption and then opens it to states to become parties. Two examples are the 1961 and 1963 Vienna Conventions on Diplomatic and Consular Relations.

international legislation   1. Treaties or conventions with such a large number of signatories that these documents effectively create rules or laws of almost universal application.   2. Legal concepts, promulgations, or directives put forth by international organizations such as the United Nations or the European Community. They may (as with EC directives) or may not (as with UN declarations) be binding on member states.

International Meeting on Cooperation and Development   *See* CANCUN SUMMIT.

international military post   Any international post authorized to be filled by a military official whose pay and allowances remain the responsibility of the parent state.

International Monetary Fund (IMF)   A multinational banking organization created after World War II in 1947 as a SPECIALIZED AGENCY of the United Nations to maintain international monetary stability. The IMF lends funds to member states to finance their temporary balance-of-payments problems, facilitates the expansion and growth of world trade, and promotes international monetary cooperation. It is based in the United States in Washington, D.C.

international morality   1. The notion that universal moral norms provide prescriptions and proscriptions for states both in their external and their internal policies. **2.** An idea that is invoked by states to condemn actions that they do not like. This invocation of the idea of international morality can be either genuine or cynical. **3.** A source of contention between realists, who see morality as irrelevant to state behavior, and those espousing other approaches to international relations, who regard it as important in moving beyond a Hobbesian world and establishing a greater degree of international order. *Compare to* REALISM.

international order **1.** Loosely used to refer to the existing distribution of power or, more vaguely, the existing state of affairs in the INTERNATIONAL SYSTEM. **2.** The idea that there is a sense of regulation in the international system based on respect for the rules of international society such as sovereignty, nonintervention, international law, and international morality. **3.** A term that is sometimes used prescriptively rather than as a description of the existing state of affairs; that is, there should be more order as opposed to the relative ANARCHY that now exists. Those who call for greater international order in this context tend to favor stronger INTERNATIONAL ORGANIZATIONS and a concomitant lessening of the SOVEREIGNTY of states.

international organization **1.** Any group whose members are nation-states. They can be universal in scope, such as the United Nations; or regional, such as the Organization for African Unity or the Organization of American States. The essential point is that they involve some degree of formalized structure and procedure, as well as rights and obligations that go along with membership. States can use such organizations as an instrument of policy when it is expedient for their governments to do so. The United States worked through the United Nations, for example, in responding to Iraq's 1990 invasion of Kuwait. **2.** A term that includes functional organizations whose task is to regulate a particular specialized activity that crosses national boundaries, such as telecommunications. **3.** NONGOVERNMENTAL ORGANIZATIONS (NGOs) that deal with particular international issues such as humanitarian assistance or human rights. Amnesty International is an example of this kind of international organization.

International Peace Bureau *See* PERMANENT INTERNATIONAL PEACE BUREAU.

international peace force An appropriately constituted PEACEKEEPING FORCE established for the purpose of preserving peace between hostile parties. An example is the multinational United Nations force in Cyprus, which is stationed between the Greek and Turkish sectors.

International Physicians for the Prevention of Nuclear War The organization of medical doctors founded in 1980 in Geneva, Switzerland, by American and Soviet physicians, which won the 1985 Nobel Peace Prize for spreading authoritative information on the catastrophic effects of nuclear war.

international political economy (IPE) That part of the discipline of INTERNATIONAL RELATIONS that focuses on the intersection of political and economic considerations. IPE focuses on issues such as international trade and finance and has generally been concerned with the development of cooperation among states. The contributions made by scholars within this area have had an important impact on the way in which international relations more broadly have been approached. This is evident, for example, in the concept of regimes, which was developed initially in the field of IPE but also has been used in the study of international security.

international political system **1.** The term used to describe the way in which STATES interact on a regularized basis. **2.** A meaning derived from SYSTEMS ANALYSIS in which international politics are seen as a system that is either stable or unstable. Considerable emphasis is placed on those factors that lead to stability and those that lead to instability. **3.** The global system of relations among states or within a state system.

international politics **1.** The totality of the principles, personalities, and processes that determine who gets what, when, and how at the international level. **2.** The study of the relations among states. This is a narrower term than INTERNATIONAL RELATIONS as it generally focuses on government-to-government interactions and on relations among states rather than among peoples. It often is distinguished from the study of domestic politics by the lack of a central overriding authority that is able to provide the kind of law and order that characterizes domestic politics—at least in stable states. Although history provides the basis for much of this study, the focus is on the general rather than the unique aspects. As K. J. Holsti, in *International Politics: A Framework for Analysis* (1972), put it: "Students of international politics try to understand and explain the causes and nature of war, imperialism, escalation, crisis, or alliance without having to describe every war, imperialist, escalation, crisis or alliance in history." *See also* STRATEGIC STUDIES.

International Red Cross   The worldwide charitable organization created in 1864 as the agency of the First International Convention for the Amelioration of the Condition of Soldiers Wounded in Armies in the Field. It was founded by Jean Henri Dunant (1828–1910), a Swiss philanthropist, after he saw that there was no organized way to aid the thousands of wounded from the 1859 Battle of Solferino in northern Italy. The modern Red Cross has three parts: (1) the International Conference, a policymaking body that meets every four years (a permanent nine-member International Commission deals with policy problems between meetings); (2) the League of Societies, which coordinates the work of the more than 100 separate national societies; and (3) the International Committee of the Red Cross, composed of Swiss citizens who, because of their traditional neutrality, can act as intermediaries between warring parties. This last committee is the one that visits prisoner-of-war camps to ensure proper treatment, distributes relief supplies, and traces missing persons. Because of its Swiss origins, the symbol and flag of the Red Cross, a red cross on a white field, is the reverse in color of the national flag of Switzerland. Some national members of the League of Red Cross Societies do not use the name or symbol of the cross because of its Christian associations. Therefore, Muslim states operate Red Crescent societies, Iran the Red Lion, Israel the Red Star, and so on. This is why the 1986 meeting of the International Conference of the Red Cross formally changed its name to the International Red Cross and Red Crescent Movement. The Red Cross has been awarded Nobel Peace Prizes on four occasions. Dunant shared the first Nobel Peace Prize

with FRÉDÉRIC PASSY in 1901. The Red Cross as an organization won the Nobel Peace Prize in 1917, 1944, and 1963.

international refugee   *See* REFUGEE.

international relations   **1.** All interactions among states and other actors. It includes international economic relations and international law as well as international politics. This is the academic field of study that examines the political, military, and economic interactions among nation-states and other nongovernmental actors. It is a broader term than international politics as it includes nongovernmental relations and can encompass the actions of private individuals and groups, and activities such as cultural exchanges that are not necessarily political in character.   **2.** A term that is sometimes deliberately used instead of INTERNATIONAL POLITICS by those who want to emphasize new developments such as growing interdependence among states. **3.** Loosely—and strictly speaking, wrongly—used as a synonym for world politics or international politics. International politics is more exclusive than international relations, even though the two terms are often used interchangeably. Some scholars believe that as the focus of attention has changed from HIGH POLITICS, involving such issues as war, peace, and security, to LOW POLITICS, involving international trade and regulation, economic interdependence and integration, so the term international relations is a much more appropriate one to describe the discipline.   **4.** The totality of private interactions among citizens of differing countries.   **5.** The practice of DIPLOMACY.

As an academic discipline, international relations focuses on contacts and dealings among states and other actors in the international system. International relations did not really develop as an academic discipline until the twentieth century, partly because political philosophy focused on the principles and practices of governance within political units rather than on the relations between them. However, important political thinkers such as HUGO GROTIUS, THOMAS HOBBES, JEAN-JACQUES ROUSSEAU, EMERICH DE VATTEL, KARL VON CLAUSEWITZ, and IMMANUEL KANT had immense insight into various aspects of international relations. Their observations helped to establish a variety of intellectual traditions that underpin the contemporary study of international relations. Although there are several traditions within the field—including the Marxist, the neo-Marxist, and the Kantian—probably the two most important are the Grotian tradition, which emphasizes that there is a society of states bound by common rules, customs, and shared norms, and Hobbesian realism, which focuses on the anarchical nature of the international system and sees international relations as dominated by the political struggle for power.

During the period between World Wars I and II, the Grotian tradition with its emphasis on the norms of international society was not only dominant but became closely bound up with an idealism based on the desire fundamentally to transform international relations in ways that would ensure that the horror of World War I would never be repeated. Consequently, the studies of international relations done during this period were predominantly prescriptive in tone and aim. The starting point of many of these idealists was the belief that flawed political arrangements, especially international anarchy and secret diplomacy, led to war—and had done so in 1914. The concomitant assumption was that once the problems were correctly identified, they then could be eradicated, so long as governments listened to the prescriptions. The problem with the idealist approach, as E. H. CARR noted in *The Twenty Years' Crisis* (1939), was that "wishing prevailed over thinking." Carr himself is seen along with HANS MORGENTHAU as one of the main architects of the approach of REALISM in international relations. Although the development of realism grew out of the reaction against idealism, its roots can be traced back to THUCYDIDES, NICCOLÒ MACHIAVELLI, Hobbes, and Rousseau. Morgenthau's *Politics Among Nations* (1948) was immensely influential. He started from the assumption that international politics, like all politics, was a struggle for power and that states defined their national interest in terms of power. Although critics focused on the shortcomings of Morgenthau's writings, his idea of international politics as a struggle for power provided the basis for much later theorizing. Indeed, much of the contemporary debate has been dominated by what is generally described as NEO-REALISM. This is best exemplified in the analysis of

KENNETH WALTZ, who argued that the structure of the international system—a term that covered both anarchy and the distribution of power within the system—was the key to understanding international relations.

Critics have focused on the fact that Waltz, like Morgenthau, not only disregards the internal attributes of states but overlooks crucial aspects of the subject such as economic processes, international political institutions, and growing interdependence. In essence, they argue that neo-realism construes international relations too narrowly. Although the debate between neo-realists and their critics has been one of the most important elements in contemporary theorizing about international relations, the academic study of international relations has become much more broadly based. It not only has several distinct components—including international security studies, international political economy, world order perspectives, analysis of world systems, the study of international institutions and political integration, and foreign policy analysis—but also it uses a variety of methodologies ranging from quantification to more traditional historical case studies. Although the contemporary discipline of international relations is highly diverse, this diversity is itself a symptom of the rich complexity of the subject matter and the exciting nature of the discipline.

international studies 1. A term loosely used to describe the study of INTERNATIONAL POLITICS or INTERNATIONAL RELATIONS. 2. A broad focus of study that encompasses anything outside a given state. This can include studies of a particular foreign region or area of the world even if it focuses on the domestic politics, economics, culture, society, and history of that state rather than its interactions with others. This is an all-embracing use of the term international.

international system 1. Any group of independent political units that interact with one another in a regularized manner. As K. J. Holsti in *International Politics: A Framework for Analysis* (1972) has pointed out, these units can be tribes, city-states, nations, or empires, but whatever the case, the analyst "is concerned with describing the typical or characteristic behavior of these political units towards each other and explaining major changes in these patterns of interaction." International systems are generally held to be anarchic, not in the sense that they are chaotic but in that they lack a central overriding authority. Much discussion has focused around the extent to which the interactions are determined by the structure of power in the system. There has been much debate, for example, about whether bipolar or multipolar systems are most stable. There also has been a great deal of discussion about the impact of the structure of the system (in terms of the distribution of power among the major political units) on the behavior of particular units within it. **2.** A major part of the external environment for any state. The structure of power, norms of behavior, and patterns of alignment and enmity that operate at the system level have an important influence on the foreign policies of individual states which have to adapt to the pressures, demands, and opportunities that arise at the level of the international system.

International Telecommunication Union (ITU) The United Nations SPECIALIZED AGENCY (since 1947) that seeks to maintain and expand international cooperation in telecommunications of all kinds. Founded in Paris, France, in 1865 as the International Telegraph Union, it changed to its current name in 1934. Basic policy is decided on by a plenipotentiary conference, which meets once every five years. An administrative council, composed of 41 members and elected by the plenipotentiary conference with due regard for equitable geographical representation, meets annually and coordinates the work of the four permanent organs at ITU headquarters in Geneva, Switzerland: the General Secretariat, the International Frequency Registration Board, the International Radio Consultative Committee, and the International Telegraph and Telephone Consultative Committee.

international trade **1.** Commerce between states. **2.** Commerce between private parties who are citizens of different states. **3.** Commerce between a state and a private party in another state. **4.** That branch of economics concerned with all of the above. *See also* FREE TRADE; PROTECTIONISM.

International Tribunal of the Law of the Sea One of the two major institutions to be set up under the United Nations Law of the Sea Convention signed in 1982, the tribunal is to be located in Hamburg, Germany. A Preparatory Commission, beginning in 1983 and meeting twice a year, has been working on, among other things, rules for the International Tribunal for the Law of the Sea. *See also* LAW OF THE SEA.

International Tribunal on War Crimes in Vietnam The mock trial of the United States and its allies in the VIETNAM WAR held in Sweden in 1967. This forum, sponsored by BERTRAND RUSSELL, other European intellectuals, and THIRD WORLD representatives, publicized U.S. violation of the Kellogg-Briand Pact, the United Nations Charter, and the Geneva Indochina Agreements. In 1974 a parallel trial was held to publicize "Crimes Against Human Rights in Latin America." Meeting in Rome, Italy, it focused on the issue of political prisoners in Bolivia, Brazil, Chile, Paraguay, and Uruguay.

international war A military conflict between independent states as opposed to a CIVIL WAR, which occurs within a state.

internee A person who, during war, is kept within a particular state or is forced to stay in a certain place. Protected persons, as defined in the Geneva Conventions of 1949, may be made internees only in accordance with the requirements therein stated.

internment camp A prison, often operated by the military, for the confinement of enemy ALIENS during wartime. During World War II the United States forced 120,000 citizens of Japanese ancestry into such camps. While this was a gross violation of civil liberties for which the United States formally apologized and offered reparations (through the Civil Liberties Act of 1988), this internment was quite different from that which Germany forced on its Jewish citizens, who were systematically murdered in CONCENTRATION CAMPS. However, neither of these famous examples were technically internment, because only noncitizens who are enemy aliens can be interned.

interoperability The interchangeability of spare parts and equipment. In this context interoperability has traditionally been a major concern for the North Atlantic Treaty Organization because it is not one unified military force but separate forces, each with its own procurement policies and own armaments industries to support. Thus there have been incompatibilities between equipment that seriously reduced the efficiency of the overall NATO force. The lack of interoperability was seen in radio sets that cannot be intertuned, too many different calibers of ammunition for weapons of the same generic type, and incompatible radar identification systems. Interoperability was a much more realistic objective for NATO than the goal of standardization. Interoperability also can be a problem within a state if it has multiple military forces. For example, the United States has experienced interoperability problems between its marine and army forces.

SOLVING INTEROPERABILITY PROBLEMS WITH A CREDIT CARD

All four services [in the United States] continue to purchase independent, incompatible communications equipment.

The first Army assault waves [during the 1983 Grenada invasion] were unable to speak with Navy ships offshore to request and coordinate naval gunfire. One Army officer reportedly was so frustrated in trying to communicate with the offshore ships that he went to a civilian phone on the island and used his AT&T credit card to call buddies at Fort Bragg so they could get to the navy and coordinate fire support. The Joint Chiefs of Staff pooh-poohed the story, but some troops privately insist it's true.

SOURCE: Barry Goldwater, *Goldwater* (1988).

Interparliamentary Union An international organization made up of delegates from the legislative branches (parliaments, congresses, etc.) of representative governments, created in 1889 by FRÉDÉRIC PASSY to further world peace. Almost all states with freely elected legislatures are members.

Interpol The International Criminal Police Organization. Since 1923 this intergovernmental organiza-

tion has promoted cooperation and mutual assistance with criminal investigations. It is headquartered in Paris, France.

interposition forces *See* PEACEKEEPING.

interpretation 1. The explanation of the true intentions of parties that concluded an international agreement; how each side understands the words of the document. 2. A stage in the intelligence cycle in which the significance of information is judged in relation to the current body of knowledge.

interregnum 1. The time period of a temporary vacancy on a throne due to the death or abdication of a ruler, lasting until the new ruler is elected or enthroned. 2. By analogy, any time period during which the rule of one person or party has ended and until the new ruling person or party is in power.

interservice rivalry The angling for advantage between the military services (such as the army or navy) of a single state. Unfortunately, this is not competition for glory that might have beneficial consequences; modern interservice rivalry is mainly about procurement funds. The costs of weapons systems are so high that success by one service to buy a major new weapon inevitably will cut back what is available to the others. In this connection it was sometimes suggested during the Cold War—and not entirely in jest—that the main enemy of the U.S. Navy was not the Soviet Navy but the U.S. Air Force. From the navy point of view, x number of new bombers for the air force effectively costs the

---

NAVAL BIAS

The President [Franklin D. Roosevelt]—who was an old Navy man—continually made it plain that in an even argument he would be inclined to favor the Navy's case against that of the Army. This nettled [General George C.] Marshall, but he kept his mouth shut until one day Roosevelt's naval bias was so obvious that he blurted out, "At least, Mr. President, stop speaking of the Army as 'they' and the Navy as 'us.' "

SOURCE: Leonard Mosley, *Marshall* (1982).

---

navy *y* number of new ships. Interservice rivalry is a universal phenomenon whenever a state has separate military services. The most commonly suggested solution to the problem is the unification of a state's armed forces.

interstate organization   An institution created by only two states. If three or more states are involved, it becomes an INTERGOVERNMENTAL ORGANIZATION.

intervention   **1.** Action taken by a state, group of states, or an international organization that "interferes coercively in the domestic affairs of another state" (John Vincent, *Nonintervention and International Order,* 1974). Such action can be overt or covert (and since World War II there has been a great deal of covert intervention) but generally involves a change in the level of external involvement in the target state. Although most states are subject to some level of penetration, an intervention (particularly a MILITARY INTERVENTION) generally goes well beyond the norm to involve the use of military force to influence outcomes or arrangements in the domestic affairs of the target state. Once the influence has been exercised, the intervening power withdraws its forces.   **2.** An action that breaches state sovereignty and therefore runs against the norms of international society. At the same time, some commentators argue that there are circumstances under which intervention is justified: that where there are flagrant human rights violations, for example, justice should prevail over order. This kind of issue was raised by the Vietnamese invasion of Kampuchea (Cambodia), which was condemned by the West but which stopped the atrocities of the Khmer Rouge against its own people. Intervention, however, can sometimes have disappointing results. Former U.S. Secretary of State Dean Acheson wrote (in the introduction to Louis J. Halle's *Civilization and Foreign Policy,* 1955): "It is our role to intervene in world affairs with sporadic and violent bursts of energy and with decisive and definitive effect—to appear on the scene in the nick of time like a knight errant, rescue the lady, and ride away. But the experience brought its disillusionment. The lady did not remain as glamorous; she did not even seem particularly grateful; she became demanding. And then, too, there was no secure and serene place to ride to."

intifada   Arabic for "uprising"; the term applied to the unrest in the Israeli-occupied GAZA STRIP and the WEST BANK that began in early December 1987. Initially the movement was a reaction to an automobile accident in which several Gaza Arabs were killed when their vehicle collided with an Israeli vehicle; rumors spread that the collision was not an accident. Riots and civil disobedience mounted after another Palestinian was killed during Israeli attempts to quell the protests. The demonstrations were staged primarily by young Palestinians, most of whom had grown up under Israeli occupation and seemed unafraid to meet Israel's military in the streets. The *intifada* manifests itself primarily in the throwing of stones and Molotov cocktails, the writing of anti-Israeli graffiti, and the taunting of the Israeli forces of occupation. Commercial strikes occur with regularity, and there are routine demonstrations against the continued Israeli presence.

Israel's response has been the object of criticism from many quarters. Israeli troops have answered stones with bullets; many residents have been jailed or deported by the Israeli government. In late 1988 the Israeli government began to destroy the homes of Palestinian activists. In its February 1989 annual report on human rights, the U.S. Department of State charged Israel with substantial human rights violations as a result of its response to the *intifada,* asserting that troops had caused "many avoidable deaths and injuries." Many participants in the *intifada,* as well as many analysts, cite the uprisings as a major impetus of the November 1988 PALESTINIAN NATIONAL COUNCIL declaration of Palestinian statehood. By the end of 1992 more than 1,000 Palestinians and over 100 Israelis had been killed in the ongoing *intifada.*

intrawar bargaining   Negotiations during gaps or firebreaks between rounds of nuclear exchange. It is thought that sophisticated strategic options and targeting policies would allow for bargaining and negotiation during such times to end a nuclear war before it reached MAD (mutual assured destruction) levels. Intrawar bargaining, and the allied concept of INTRAWAR DETERRENCE, hinges on the idea that each side initially would refrain from destroying targets of special value to the enemy. The argument is that if one side does not hit major civilian targets in the first round of nuclear warfare, it can hope to deter its opponent from retaliating; then persuade it to end the war because of the threat to launch COUNTERVALUE strikes in a further escalation if the bargaining fails.

intrawar deterrence   *See* DETERRENCE, INTRAWAR.

invasion   1. An attack by one state on another. 2. One aspect of a larger military campaign. For example, D-Day was the 1944 Allied invasion of France in World War II.

inverted U-curve   A term used to summarize the impact of STRESS on cognitive performance and the quality of decision making. It refers to the fact that low to moderate levels of stress generally lead to enhanced levels of performance whereas high levels of stress degrade performance and reduce the quality of decision making. High levels of stress result in greater cognitive rigidity and a less serious or productive search for information, and can lead to premature closure of the search for options.

inviolability   A characteristic of an existing international border implying that it should not be changed by force. This term was used in the 1975 Helsinki Accord rather than IMMUTABILITY, which the East German government wanted. By referring only to change through the use of force, the notion of inviolability left the way open for peaceful border changes.

invisible government   1. Any organization, whether public or private, that exercises secret and unaccountable power. Both the U.S. Central Intelligence Agency and the Soviet Union's KGB have been called invisible governments. 2. In representative democracies, rule by political party bosses—the real, although unseen, powers behind the elected representatives of the people.

Iranamok   In the United States, the term some journalists (most notably those associated with the magazine *The New Republic*) used to refer to the IRAN-CONTRA AFFAIR because "I ran amok" sounded so much like what really happened: Certain people in the White House ran amok.

Iran-contra affair   The U.S. scandal arising in the fall of 1986, when it was revealed that the Reagan Administration had secretly sold arms to the government of Iran to convince the regime to use its GOOD OFFICES to gain the release of U.S. hostages in Lebanon, and had used the profits to fund the CONTRAS in Nicaragua. At the time it was illegal to sell arms to Iran, illegal to fund the contras beyond limits set by the Congress (through the BOLAND AMENDMENT), and against the expressed policy of the United States to negotiate for, let alone trade arms for, the release of hostages. Because the Iran-contra operation was undertaken primarily by the National Security Council without the formal approval of the departments of defense and state, the affair called into question the coherence of the Reagan Administration's foreign policy.

Iranian hostage crisis   The massive violation of DIPLOMATIC PRIVILEGES AND IMMUNITIES that occurred in Iran when government-backed "students" took over the American embassy complex of buildings in Tehran on November 4, 1979, and held 53 Americans hostage for 444 days, until January 20, 1981. The crisis so dominated the last year of U.S. President Jimmy Carter's administration that it badly damaged Carter's reelection prospects, especially after an unsuccessful rescue effort on April 24, 1980. The Iranians agreed to free the hostages only after the Carter Administration agreed to some of the Iranian demands "in principle." As one last insult, the hostages were freed on the day Ronald Reagan succeeded Carter as president. More than a decade later Rosalynn Carter, the former First Lady, assessed the political damage of this crisis to the Carter Administration: "People want a country to be tough. If we had bombed Tehran, I think Jimmy would have been re-elected, even though the hostages would have died. But our country is stronger when we stand for peace and human rights" (*New York Times*, November 19, 1990). *See also* OCTOBER SURPRISE.

Iranian Revolution　The 1978–1979 strikes and demonstrations that led to the overthrow of the monarchy of MOHAMMED REZA SHAH PAHLEVI and its replacement by an Islamic fundamentalist state under the autocratic rule of the AYATOLLAH KHOMEINI.

Iranian terrorism　State-sponsored violence by one of the world's states most active in supporting TERRORISM and subversion against other states. The SHI'ITE Muslim fundamentalist government of the AYATOLLAH KHOMEINI demonstrated an exceptional readiness to use terrorism and subversion as a policy tool, in the name of spreading its Islamic revolution to other nations and ridding the Middle East of Western influence. While Iranian government personnel have been used directly in terrorist operations, particularly those against Iranian dissidents, the government preferred to support (directly or indirectly) extremist groups such as the Lebanese HEZBOLLAH; Iran also used terrorism during the IRAN-IRAQ WAR as part of a broader strategy to deter Kuwait, Saudi Arabia, and other Arab states from more actively supporting the Iraqi cause. To do this, Iran recruits disgruntled Shi'ites from the gulf states and elsewhere, gives them paramilitary and terrorist training, and returns them home. Most of the Iranian-backed terrorist acts that have been perpetrated in the gulf area are conducted by Iranian-inspired and sponsored Shi'ite radicals. But Iranian terrorist-related activities have reached well beyond the gulf. Egyptian officials announced in 1987 that they had apprehended members of what they described as a new Iranian-backed terrorist ring. Also in 1987, Tunisia broke relations with Iran, charging that it was supporting fundamentalist groups trying to undermine the government. Iran has shown a disregard for internationally accepted conventions and norms, including those applying to diplomats. In addition to the IRANIAN HOSTAGE CRISIS, British and French diplomats also have been the victims of Iranian violations of diplomatic standards; and Anglo-Indian author SALMAN RUSHDIE has been threatened with death by the regime.

Iran-Iraq War　The dispute over borders started by Iraq's leader SADDAM HUSSEIN when he invaded Iran in 1980. After an estimated 2 million casualties (including half a million dead) on both sides during an eight-year long war of attrition, a United Nations–arranged cease-fire became effective in 1988.

Iraqi coup　The 1958 military takeover of the Kingdom of Iraq that abolished the monarchy and murdered King FAISAL II. The coup was led by General Abdul Karim Kassem (1914–1963), who declared Iraq a republic with himself as both prime minister and defense minister. Kassem was killed in a subsequent 1963 military coup when the Arab Socialist Renaissance Party took power. While this Ba'ath Party was ousted in another military coup in less than a year, it regained power, again by a coup, in 1968. This Ba'ath regime is the government that SADDAM HUSSEIN has led since 1979.

Irgun　The popular name for *Irgun Zvai Leumi,* or National Military Organization, an Israeli terrorist group founded in 1937 that directed a broad campaign of terror against Palestinian and British targets. On July 22, 1946, Irgun bombed the King David Hotel in Jerusalem, the British headquarters in Palestine. More than 90 died in the attack. The group's most infamous act was the April 9, 1948, DEIR YASSIN massacre of Arab villagers. Irgun was led by MENACHEM BEGIN, who later became the prime minister of Israel. Irgun was disbanded in September 1948 when most of its members joined the armed forces of the new State of Israel.

Irish Peace Treaty　*See* ANGLO-IRISH TREATY OF 1921.

Irish Republican Army　The militant organization dedicated to forcing the withdrawal of Great

Britain from NORTHERN IRELAND and the reunification of the Irish nation. The IRA has its roots in the National Volunteer Force, an early-twentieth-century anti-British, republican organization, and was born out of the EASTER RISING of 1916. IRA guerrilla tactics were a major contributing factor in the creation in 1921 of the Irish Free State. A split developed in the republican movement between those opposed to a divided Ireland (under the leadership of EAMON DE VALERA) and those who favored acceptance of an Irish Free State as the most favorable of feasible political realities. The IRA battled the Free State Army during the Irish Civil War in 1921–1923 but was defeated by former IRA leader MICHAEL COLLINS (who was killed in the fighting) and his Free State forces. The IRA mounted a campaign of violence to drive Britain out of Northern Ireland in the 1930s. In 1939 the group was banned by the Free State of Ireland. After the declaration of the Republic of Ireland in 1949, the IRA focused its energies on Northern Ireland. During the late 1950s and early 1960s the IRA maintained a military presence at the Northern Ireland border and was responsible for the deaths of many British and Northern Irish security men. This border strategy was effectively terminated in 1961 through the successful Northern Irish policy of internment of IRA suspects, which was tacitly supported by the southern republic. Following the failure of the border violence, the IRA turned to a nonviolent approach and supported civil disobedience campaigns organized to further civil rights causes. However, this approach did not satisfy the more radical members of the IRA who, partly in response to a wave of Protestant violence against Irish Catholics, split from what became known as the Official IRA and formed the PROVISIONAL IRISH REPUBLICAN ARMY (PIRA) in 1970. The Official IRA has pressed for a socialist, unified Irish state primarily through nonviolent means. The Provos, as PIRA members are called, stress nationalistic and Catholic goals to be obtained by force. As the conflict in Northern Ireland became more bitter and violent, the Official IRA became less visible and popular, and the PIRA became the predominant organization. The political wing of the IRA is SINN FEIN, which on occasion has supported the PIRA in its campaign of violence. *Compare to* ULSTER DEFENSE ASSOCIATION.

iron curtain   During the COLD WAR, the political, social, and economic schism between the states of Eastern and Western Europe. The phrase was made famous by Winston Churchill in a March 5, 1946, speech at Westminster College in Fulton, Missouri, in which he said: "From Stettin in the Baltic to Trieste in the Adriatic, an iron curtain has descended across the continent. Behind that line lie all capitals of the ancient states of central and Eastern Europe: Warsaw, Berlin, Prague, Vienna, Budapest, Belgrade, Bucharest and Sofia, all these famous cities and the population around them lie in what I must call the Soviet sphere, and all are subject in one form or another, not only to Soviet influence but to a very high and in many cases increasing measure of control from Moscow." Now the phrase also is used to refer to any hostile and seemingly permanent political division. However, Churchill was not the first to use the term. George W. Creel, in *A Mechanistic View of War and Peace* (1915), said that France is "a nation of 40 millions with a deep rooted grievance and an iron curtain at its frontier." Ethel Viscountess Snowden, in *Through Bolshevik Russia* (1920), wrote: "We were behind the 'iron curtain' at last." Even Nazi propaganda chief Joseph Goebbels said: "If the German people lay down their arms, the whole of Eastern and Southern Europe, together with the Reich, will come under Russian occupation. Behind an iron curtain mass butcheries of people would begin" (*Manchester Guardian,* February 23, 1945). In 1992 Mikhail Gorbachev, the last president of the Soviet Union, would also speak at Westminster College. Standing at the same lectern from which Churchill had spoken, he said that the 1946 "speech was singled out as the formal declaration of the Cold War"—and that he was glad it was over.

Iron Guard   An Eastern European fascist organization that was active, particularly in Romania, between the two world wars. The Iron Guard assassinated Romanian Prime Minister Ion Duca in 1933 and Prime Minister Armand Calinescu in 1939.

Iron Lady   *See* THATCHER, MARGARET.

iron law of negotiation   "The side in a hurry makes the concessions." This concept was developed by Richard N. Perle in his article "The Iron Law of Arms Control" (*New York Times,* August 1, 1988).

iron law of oligarchy "Who says organization says oligarchy." Robert Michels (1876–1936), a German sociologist, wrote in *Political Parties* (1915) that organizations are by their nature oligarchic because majorities within an organization are not capable of ruling themselves:

> Organization implies the tendency to oligarchy. In every organization, whether it be a political party, a professional union, or any other association of the kind, the aristocratic tendency manifests itself very clearly. The mechanism of the organization, while conferring a solidity of structure, induces serious changes in the organized mass, completely inverting the respective position of the leaders and the led. As a result of organization, every party or professional union becomes divided into a minority of directors and a majority of the directed.

Iron Triangle During the VIETNAM WAR, a major VIET CONG–controlled area to the north of Saigon. This 125-square-mile area, laced with tunnels and fortification, was a staging base for attacks on the capital and the site of many United States military actions.

irredentism The long-standing and frustrated efforts to incorporate into a state land areas over which it has no legal claim but that nevertheless are considered part of the state's natural political unit because of a common language or previous political affiliation. Irredentism emerged in Italy in the 1870s. *Italia irredenta* (Italy unredeemed) is the phrase that described the desire to "liberate" or annex areas under foreign control that were considered Italian because of their language and culture. Irredentism is a form of nationalism that can occur wherever ethnic or cultural allegiance is not adequately accounted for by political boundaries. It is an ideological element of many terrorist organizations and was a major factor leading to conflict in the HORN OF AFRICA and the former Yugoslavia.

irregular forces Armed individuals or groups who are not members of the regular armed forces, police, or other internal security forces. They can be revolutionaries seeking to overthrow their governments (such as the VIET CONG), informal groups seeking to resist occupation (such as UNDERGROUND forces), or a group of terrorists.

Islam The religion based on the teachings of the seventh-century prophet Muhammad, which are contained in the Koran, a book that is a counterpart to the Judeo-Christian Bible. The followers of Islam are called Muslims. Located mainly in North Africa, the Middle East, and South Asia, they make up about one-fifth (three-quarters of a billion) of the world's population. *See also* ARAB; SHI'ITE; SUNNI.

Islamic fundamentalism Past and present Islamic revival movements. In the twentieth century such movements (the IRANIAN REVOLUTION, e.g.) were often a reaction to increased Western political and social penetration of the Middle East. Islamic fundamentalists believe that all aspects of human and social life should be based on Islamic doctrine. Moreover, these groups tend to oppose secular ideologies that, in their eyes, have failed to bring about greater economic and social justice.

Islamic Jihad A radical and violent SHI'ITE group that has claimed responsibility for many of the bloodiest terrorist acts in Lebanon. The group is shadowy, and some experts suspect that Islamic Jihad is simply an umbrella cover name used by various pro-Iranian Lebanese Shi'ite organizations, including HEZBOLLAH. Acts for which the group has claimed responsibility include the April 1983 bombing of the U.S. embassy in Beirut that killed 63 persons; the October 1983 Beirut suicide bombing at the U.S. Marines barracks that killed 241; the November 1983 attack against an Israeli army post in Tyre, Lebanon, that killed 61 persons; and the September 1984 bombing of the U.S. embassy annex in East Beirut. The group also has been responsible for the kidnapping of various American hostages in Lebanon.

Islamic Jihad in Hejaz A Saudi SHI'ITE extremist organization linked to Iran, the Lebanese ISLAMIC JIHAD, and HEZBOLLAH, that undertakes terrorist missions against the SUNNI Muslim government of Saudi Arabia. Hejaz, sometimes spelled "Hasa," is a Saudi province with a large Shi'ite population that has long complained of discrimination by the ruling majority Sunnis. Thus the Islamic Jihad in Hejaz

A contemporary cartoon of U.S. isolationism at the beginning of World War II. (Library of Congress)

ALMOST THE LAST NEUTRAL.

seeks to destabilize the Sunni regime through terrorist attacks. It has claimed responsibility for the shootings of Saudi diplomats in Turkey in 1988; in Pakistan in 1988; and in Thailand in 1989. The Saudi government, in turn, has sought to contain the growing Shi'ite unrest and violence by instituting harsh reprisals against suspected Shi'ite extremists.

Islamic republic   A Muslim theocracy; a state that seeks to combine the religious dogma of Islam with representative government.

Islamic states   Those states of North Africa (such as Algeria and Libya), the Middle East (such as Saudi Arabia and Iraq), and South Asia (such as Pakistan and Indonesia), whose populations are mostly Muslim.

isolationism   **1.** The policy of inhibiting as much as possible a state's international relations so that state can exist in peace by itself in the world. Isolationism was the dominant mood in U.S. foreign policy for many periods in its history, particularly during most of the nineteenth century and the two decades between the world wars. Isolationism is often confused with NEUTRALITY (a policy of staying out of the wars of other states) or NONALIGNMENT (not joining any of several competing military alliances). Because of the increasingly interdependent nature of world trade, communications, and politics, isolationism—which inevitably inhibits economic growth—is viable today only in dictatorial states. For example, Albanian isolationism, caused by its Communist government in the post–World War II era, made Albania the poorest state in Europe. **2.** MULTILATERALISM. According to U.S. commentator George Will (*The New Season,* 1988), "Isolationism is a sin that dare not speak its name, so today it comes cloaked in the language of multilateralism. A reluctance to act other than in concert with allies achieves the traditional goal of isolationism: It immobilizes America, by making America hostage to the most hesitant member of the alliance." **3.** A national introspection and turning inward so that foreign policy activities are reduced to the minimum. *Compare to* GLOBALISM; INTERNATIONALISM.

isolationist **1.** One who advocates ISOLATIONISM or RETRENCHMENT as a main theme in foreign policy. **2.** A term used in derogatory fashion against those who advocate retrenchment even though they are not isolationist but simply want a reordering of national priorities to give more attention to domestic needs. By using this term critics seek to undermine the legitimacy of the argument for retrenchment. **3.** Individuals or groups that have an aversion to military involvement overseas.

Israeli War of Independence   The 1947–1948 war between Israel and the Arab world. The creation of the State of Israel in 1948 followed more than a half century of efforts by Zionist leaders to establish a sovereign nation as a homeland for Jews. Attachment to the land of Israel is a recurrent theme in Jewish life since the destruction of Jerusalem by the Romans in the year 70 and the dispersal of the Jews that followed. Not until the founding of ZIONISM by Theodore Herzl at the end of the nineteenth century were practical steps taken toward securing international sanction for Jewish settlement in Palestine, then a part of the OTTOMAN EMPIRE. The BALFOUR DECLARATION in 1917 asserted the British government's support for the creation of a Jewish homeland in Palestine. This declaration was supported by a number of other countries and took on added importance following World War I, when the United Kingdom was assigned the Palestine Mandate by the League of Nations. Jewish immigration grew slowly in the 1920s, but NAZI persecution during the 1930s and World War II greatly increased the tide. With the end of World War II and the revelation of the near extermination of European Jewry by the Nazis, international support for Jews wishing to settle in Palestine overcame British efforts to restrict immigration.

International support for establishing a Jewish state led to the adoption in November 1947 of the United Nations Partition Plan, which called for dividing Palestine into a Jewish and an Arab state and for establishing Jerusalem separately as an international city under UN administration. Violence between the Arab and Jewish communities erupted almost immediately. Toward the end of the British mandate, the Jews planned to declare a separate state, a development the Arabs were determined to prevent. On May 14, 1948, the State of Israel was proclaimed. The following day, armies from neighboring Arab nations engaged in open warfare with Israeli defense forces. Subsequently, a truce was brought about under UN auspices, and, in 1949, four armistice agreements were negotiated and signed at Rhodes, Greece, between Israel and its neighbors, Egypt, Jordan, Lebanon, and Syria. As a result of the 1947–1948 battles and these agreements, the Jewish state encompassed almost 50 percent more territory than the total allotted to it under the Partition Plan, and included within its boundaries the western sector of Jerusalem. *See also* ARAB-ISRAELI WARS.

Istanbul Synagogue Massacre   The September 6, 1986, attack at Neve Shalom, Istanbul, Turkey's oldest Jewish temple, during which terrorists brandishing automatic weapons interrupted a Saturday worship service and fired on the congregation, leaving 22 dead. The terrorists then poured gasoline on the bodies and set them afire. The terrorists are thought to have been ABU NIDAL Organization operatives acting with Syrian, Iranian, Libyan, and Syrian governmental assistance.

item-by-item negotiations   A method of international trade bargaining in which negotiators separately consider the probable trade effects of each TARIFF cut proposed. The intent is to ensure that at the end of the negotiations, the total effect of cuts offered and received by each participating country will be in approximate balance. Early GATT negotiations followed this approach, which eventually became quite cumbersome, leading to the LINEAR REDUCTION OF TARIFFS formula.

Iwo Jima   The small Pacific Ocean island that was the site of one of the most costly battles of WORLD WAR II. During February and March of 1945 U.S. Marines assaulted this heavily fortified Japanese-held island fortress. Almost all of the approximately 25,000 Japanese defenders were killed. The Americans suffered almost the same number of casualties, which included 7,000 dead. Iwo Jima was of strategic importance only because it could function as an air base for U.S. B-29 bombers and their fighter escorts, which then attacked the Japanese home islands. Control of Iwo Jima was returned to Japan in 1968.

Iwo Jima

The flag raising by the U.S. Marines on Iwo Jima, February 23, 1945, is one of the most famous battlefield pictures of World War II. (National Archives)

AN INSTANT SYMBOL

Darkroom technicians knew immediately that the Suribachi photo was something very special. It didn't fit the pattern of a conventional news picture; the face of only one man was clearly visible, the rest were either hidden by hands and arms raising the flag, or their heads were turned.

But it was a masterpiece of instantaneous composition and lighting that captured the mood of the unfolding drama on Iwo Jima. Its stage-like setting and the powerful position of the men gave it the graven look of a posed statue; so much so, in fact, that cynics and critics of the Marine Corps later suggested the photo was staged. . . .

When the photo appeared on front pages of virtually every newspaper in the States, it became an instant symbol for millions on the homefront—an indelible portrait of patriotism and determination.

SOURCE: Bill D. Ross, *Iwo Jima* (1983).

Jackson, Henry M. "Scoop" (1912–1983) The U.S. Representative and subsequently Senator from Washington state who served in Congress from 1941 until his death in 1983. Jackson became an influential senator on national security issues, partly because he combined domestic liberalism with a hard-line stance toward the Soviet Union and an emphasis on U.S. military strength. Jackson chaired a subcommittee of the committee on government operations, and the staff report from the hearings he held influenced the subsequent evolution of the National Security Council. He also was a vocal supporter of the North Atlantic Treaty Organization in the late 1960s and early 1970s when there was strong congressional pressure for reducing United States forces in Europe. He was perhaps most influential, however, during the 1970s when, supported by a strong staff—which included Richard Perle, who would later play a key role in the Reagan Administration—he challenged key elements of the Nixon-Kissinger DÉTENTE policy toward the Soviet Union. He placed great pressure on the Soviet Union to respect human rights and was very critical of arms control negotiations, introducing the Jackson Amendment to SALT I and then complaining that SALT II did not meet the injunctions for equal ceilings. The demise of détente in the late 1970s was partly a result of the pressure exerted by Jackson against policies that he believed were soft on Moscow and dangerous for the United States. Yet it would be too simplistic to regard him as an unreconstructed HAWK. In the 1980s, for example, he was a strong advocate of steps to lessen the risk of inadvertent nuclear war. His combination of domestic liberalism and robustness on national security issues has been regarded by other Democrats as an excellent combination, and they sometimes refer to themselves as Jackson Democrats.

Jackson Amendment The amendment attached to the U.S. Senate Resolution that ratified the Interim Agreement on Offensive Arms in 1972, introduced by Senator HENRY M. JACKSON, which held that (1) Congress would consider any Soviet actions that endangered the survivability of U.S. deterrent forces to be grounds for abrogating the treaty; (2) the Congress urged the president to seek a future treaty that "would not limit the U.S. to levels of intercontinental strategic forces inferior to the limits provided for the Soviet Union"; and (3) the United States should pursue "vigorous research and development and modernization programs as required by prudent strategic posture." This amendment was an expression of Senate insistence on equality in any long-term strategic agreements with the Soviet Union.

Jackson-Nunn Amendment An amendment introduced into the Senate in 1973 that stipulated that the president should seek from the European allies funds to offset the balance-of-payments deficit resulting from the deployment of United States forces in Europe. In the event that the United States failed to obtain the total offset, the number of U.S. troops in Europe would be reduced by a percentage equal to the percentage shortfall in offsets. The Jackson-Nunn Amendment passed the Senate on September 25, 1973, by 84 votes to 5. Although it seemed to be directed at the Europeans, it was largely a defensive measure designed to reduce support for more drastic legislation to reduce troops in Europe largely by dealing with the balance-of-payments and burden-sharing aspects of the problem. It did not have an immediate effect on BURDEN-SHARING, but it did help to erode support for troop cut legislation.

Jackson-Vanik Amendment   An amendment to the Trade Act of 1974 that prohibited extending U.S. government credits and most favored nation trade status to any Communist country that restricted free emigration of its citizens. The amendment was prompted by congressional concern over the Soviet Union's treatment of its Jewish minority. With the opening of emigration between the Soviet Union and Eastern Europe, this amendment was being re-examined.

Jakes, Milos (1922–   )   The last general secretary of the Communist Party in Czechoslovakia. His term began in December 1987 and ended during the VELVET REVOLUTION of November 1989. Although he initiated some reform throughout his career in government, progressive results were not visible, leaving the people of Czechoslovakia to contend with a dilapidated infrastructure and a ravaged economy.

Japan bashing   *See* BASHING.

Japanese Peace Treaty   The 1951 agreement that ended the state of war between the United States (and its allies) and Japan, re-established Japanese sovereignty, and provided for the withdrawal of occupation forces. By this treaty Japan also recognized Korean independence and renounced all claims to former Pacific Island possessions. The U.S.-Japanese Security Treaty, which provided for the U.S. defense of a disarmed Japan, was signed on the same day.

Japanese Red Army (JRA)   A small left-wing revolutionary group formed in Japan in 1971. Many JRA members have been university educated and are products of the prosperous Japanese middle class. The group's primary source of funds has been Palestinian factions and Libya. The stated ultimate goal of the JRA is the overthrow of the Japanese government and monarchy, and the establishment of a left-wing people's republic in Japan. The JRA has conducted terrorist acts on behalf of the POPULAR FRONT FOR THE LIBERATION OF PALESTINE, most notably the 1972 LOD AIRPORT MASSACRE in Israel. *See also* ANTI-IMPERIALIST INTERNATIONAL BRIGADE.

Jaruzelski, Wojciech (1923–   )   The Polish Army general who became his country's prime minister in 1981 and introduced MARTIAL LAW to cope with the disorder caused by the SOLIDARITY movement. He later said that martial law was necessary because Solidarity was so belligerent and because the Soviet Union planned to intervene militarily if he acceded to the reforms demanded by the union movement (*New York Times,* May 20, 1992). In 1985 he resigned as prime minister but continued in power as head of the Communist Party. After the 1988 strikes he supported negotiations with Solidarity. Ironically it was with the support of Solidarity that he was elected president of Poland in 1989. His short term ended in 1990 when he resigned in order to allow the first general presidential election to take place in November 1990, which resulted in the election of LECH WALESA as president.

Jellicoe, John (1859–1935)   The admiral who commanded the British forces at the 1916 Battle of JUTLAND. He has often been criticized for fighting a conservative battle and for not pursuing the German fleet more aggressively. But he knew that to "win" he needed only to tie—to force the Germans to withdraw. This he did. What he could not afford to do was to allow the Germans to destroy his fleet and take command of the sea. Jellicoe knew, as Winston Churchill wrote in *The World Crisis* (1923), that he "was the only man on either side who could lose the war in an afternoon." *See also* BEATTY, DAVID.

Jervis, Robert (1940–   )   The American who is the leading analyst of international affairs in applying concepts from psychology to the study of international relations and foreign policy. Jervis's most famous work, *Perception and Misperception in International Politics* (1976), shows how certain common kinds of misperception frequently occur in decision making with major impact on interstate relations. In an earlier work, *The Logic of Images*

(1970), Jervis had examined ways in which states try to manipulate the images others have of them. He had drawn an important distinction between signals and indices and highlighted the ways in which governments attempted to manipulate both of these to create desired images, whether of resolve, determination, or firmness. More recently Jervis has turned his attention to problems of nuclear strategy. Aware of the dangers of what in his earlier work he had termed spiral models of international conflict, Jervis offered an incisive critique of U.S. strategic policy. He was critical of certain aspects of deterrence strategy, especially the emphasis on "countervailing" developed under the Carter Administration and the idea of "prevailing" enunciated by the Reagan Administration. His ideas on nuclear strategy are developed in *The Illogic of American Nuclear Strategy* (1984) and *The Meaning of the Nuclear Revolution* (1989). Clearly one of the leading figures in the field, Jervis has managed to develop both theoretical insights and policy relevant ideas on a wide variety of issues. *See also* ATTRIBUTION THEORY; PERCEPTION.

Jiang Qing (also spelled Chiang Ch'ing) (1914–1991)   Third wife of Chinese Communist Party Chairman MAO ZEDONG and the most influential woman in China during the CULTURAL REVOLUTION. In the 1930s Jiang was an actress with the stage name Lang Ping. She had played minor roles for some left-wing movie companies in Shanghai and Chungking before she joined the Communist forces in Yen-an. There she met Mao and soon they married. As a prenuptial agreement (to soothe criticism of their marriage by many of Mao's colleagues), Jiang pledged to maintain a low profile and stay out of politics. In the early years of the People's Republic of China, Jiang kept her pledge and remained out of public view except to serve as Mao's hostess to visiting foreign dignitaries or to participate in some cultural events. In 1963, however, she started an art reform movement to infuse the traditional Beijing opera and ballet with revolutionary themes. At the time Mao was struggling under the attack by his party colleagues for his failed economic policies. He endorsed the reform movement, which evolved into the Great Proletarian Cultural Revolution in which Mao was able to PURGE all his political opponents. Mao rewarded Jiang by naming her the first

deputy head of the Cultural Revolution. As the senile Mao grew detached from running day-to-day affairs, Jiang formed an alliance with three other radical party members (later known as the GANG OF FOUR) in a struggle for control of party and state affairs against a more moderate group headed by ZHOU ENLAI and DENG XIAOPING. Shortly after Mao's death in 1976, Jiang and her group were arrested. The Gang of Four were tried in 1980–1981 for treason and convicted. Jiang received a suspended death sentence but it was commuted two years later to life imprisonment. Jiang refused to confess to her charged crimes. She died in prison in 1991.

jihad   Arabic term usually translated as "holy war" and characterized by the SHI'ITE conviction to spread the Islamic revolution. The concept of jihad grants divine approval to the Islamic battle against infidels; hence, Shi'ite revolutionaries view terrorist acts as justifiable efforts to overthrow the corrupt institutions and states that are the enemies of Islam.

jingoism   Strong nationalist sentiment characterized by a proclivity for a belligerent foreign policy. The term first came into use in England in the mid-1870s, when the British seemed on the verge of war with Russia. A popular song went:

> *We don't want to fight,*
> *But by Jingo, if we do,*
> *We've got the ships, we've got the men,*
> *We've got the money too.*

"By Jingo" was a euphemism for "by God" or "by Jesus." The song soon crossed the Atlantic and became increasingly popular in the United States. According to William Ralph Inge, in *Christian Ethics and Modern Problems* (1932): "In the earlier part of the modern period, men massacred each other in the name of what they called religion; in the latter part the chief appeal has been chauvinism or jingoism, miscalled patriotism."

Jinnah, Mohammed Ali (1876–1948)   The first leader (formally the GOVERNOR-GENERAL) of Pakistan. Jinnah organized India's Muslim population to demand a separate state, and this movement culminated in the creation of an independent Pakistan in 1947. He died after only one year in office and was succeeded by Khwaja Naximuddin in

1948. While his tenure as head of state was brief, he is revered as the founder of his nation.

Jodl, Alfred (1890–1946)   The chief of the German Army's operations staff (1939–1945) during World War II. He was hanged as a war criminal after being convicted at the NUREMBERG TRIALS.

John Bull   **1.** A character used as a personification of England or Great Britain in general.   **2.** A typical Englishman. This usage dates from the 1727 satire, *The History of John Bull,* by John Arbuthnot (1667–1735). *Compare to* MARIANNE, UNCLE SAM.

John Paul II (1920–   )   The first non-Italian pope since the sixteenth century and the youngest in over a century. Born in Poland, as Karol Wojtyla he rose to be archbishop of Cracow in 1963. In 1967 he was elevated to cardinal and in 1978 was elected pope to succeed Pope John Paul I, whose papacy had lasted only a month. As Pope John Paul II, he both actively and covertly supported the transition to democracy in Poland and the rest of Eastern Europe despite his wounding in a 1981 assassination attempt by MEHMET ALI AGCA. He has asserted conservative, traditional views on abortion, clerical celibacy, and papal authority in doctrinal matters. He has also attempted to limit liturgical experiment. His 1988 encyclical, "The Social Concerns of the Church," points out that international trade and finance operates to the disadvantage of poorer nations. Without any concessions to population control, he urges the pursuit of social justice in the Third World. John Paul II, with the active cooperation of the Reagan Administration, was extremely supportive of the 1980s anti-Communist movements in Eastern Europe—especially SOLIDARITY in Poland.

Johnson, Lyndon B. (1908–1973)   The U.S. vice president who became president when President JOHN F. KENNEDY was assassinated on November 22, 1963, and was elected in his own right in 1964. Johnson's questionable and ineffective tactics in pursuing the VIETNAM WAR divided the country and marked his presidency as a tragic one. The irony was that Johnson felt that losing Indochina—which was not his to lose—would lead to a conservative backlash that would have undercut his widely

Lyndon B. Johnson visits troops in Vietnam in 1966. (National Archives)

respected domestic programs of civil rights expansion and poverty eradication. By escalating United States involvement, however, he lost the more liberal Democrats who were alienated by the war. In part, this problem reflected Johnson's lack of experience in foreign policy as well as his decision-making style. As president he did not welcome criticism or dissent and was shielded from some of the more realistic appraisals of the Vietnam policy by aides such as National Security Advisor Walt Rostow. After Johnson declined to run for a second full term, the Republicans and RICHARD M. NIXON won the presidency in 1968.

Johnson Doctrine   The rationale enunciated by the Johnson Administration to justify U.S. military intervention in the DOMINICAN CIVIL WAR in 1965. The justification initially was cast in terms of saving U.S. citizens whose lives were endangered by the growing disorder and was buttressed by the argument that it was necessary to restore law and order. Increasingly, however, the emphasis was placed on the danger from "Communist conspirators" trained in Cuba who had hijacked what had started as a popular democratic revolution. Finally President Johnson claimed the "unilateral right of the United States to intervene militarily in any sovereign state of the hemisphere if, in the opinion of the U.S. that state were in danger of falling to the communists." Thomas Franck and Edward Weisband (*Word Poli-*

tics, 1971) claim that the Johnson Doctrine provided a model that the Soviet Union imitated in the development of the BREZHNEV DOCTRINE. It also reflected the specific application of the doctrine of intervention to counterrevolution that was first enunciated in the TRUMAN DOCTRINE and that became a recurring theme in U.S. foreign policy throughout the COLD WAR.

Joint Chiefs of Staff The military advisory body to the secretary of defense and to the president of the United States. It consists of the chiefs of staff of the U.S. Army and Air Force, the chief of naval operations, the commandant of the marine corps (but only when marine corps matters are at issue), and a chairperson, who is generally considered the spokesperson for the nation's military establishment. The group has been heavily criticized because it does not operate as a unified command but works mainly to perpetuate interservice rivalries and identities. While an organization known as the Joint Chiefs of Staff operated during World War II, the current organization was created by the National Security Act of 1947.

In 1986 the role of the chairman of the Joint Chiefs of Staff was strengthened by making the position that of the president's "principal military advisor" instead of, as before, the representative of the collective opinion of all of the service chiefs. General John W. Vessey, Jr., then chairman, Joint Chiefs of Staff, said that the job was "to give the president and secretary of defense military advice before they know they need it" (*New York Times*, July 15, 1984).

joint operation *See* COMBINED OPERATION.

joint staff **1.** A staff formed of two or more of the services of the same country. **2.** In the United States, the staff of the JOINT CHIEFS OF STAFF as provided for under the National Security Act of 1947.

joint venture An international business undertaking. There are four major kinds of joint ventures: between two or more interests from the same foreign country; between foreign partners from different countries; between foreign interests and private parties from the host country; and between foreign interests and the host government. The last two types have been the most prevalent forms of joint ventures since the end of World War II. The new states in Eastern Europe and the former Soviet Union see joint ventures as one of the most promising ways of moving toward market economies and becoming integrated into the international economic system. *See also* MULTINATIONAL CORPORATIONS.

Jomini, Antoine Henri (1779–1869) A general and military critic of the Napoleonic era whose systematic efforts to develop principles of warfare made him a founder of modern military thought. He was the first to delineate the significant differences between STRATEGY and TACTICS in his greatest work, *Precis on the Art of War* (1836). While Jomini and KARL VON CLAUSEWITZ were contemporaries, it was Jomini who dominated later nineteenth-century thinking about the art of war. Clausewitz, in turn, has been far more influential in the twentieth century. To Jomini war was a game to be played by the generals, not politicians. He divorced the concept of war from national survival, confining it instead to a theory of operations where universal conceptions and doctrines would provide the framework of victory regardless of the type of weapon or geography. In this approach he failed to take into account the irrational aspect of nations at war and the unpredictable acts of desperate men. He diverged from Clausewitz by holding that the fundamental objective of military operations was to occupy enemy territory rather than to annihilate the enemy's military system.

Jones Act **1.** The 1916 law of the United States that authorized independence to the Philippines "as soon as a stable government can be established therein." It was superseded by the Tydings-McDuffie Act of 1934, which promised absolute independence (granted in 1946). **2.** The 1917 law that granted political autonomy to Puerto Rico and U.S. citizenship to all its people.

Jouhaux, Léon (1879–1954) The French labor leader who won the 1951 Nobel Peace Prize for his life's work toward removing social and economic inequalities both within and between nations.

Juan Carlos (1938–   ) The king of Spain since 1975. He is the grandson of Alfonso XIII

Juan Carlos of Spain (Embassy of Spain)

(1886–1941), the previous king of Spain (1902–1931). Since his youth Juan Carlos was groomed for the monarchy by the Spanish dictator FRANCISCO FRANCO. Formally designated as Franco's successor in 1969, he came to power in 1975 as an authoritarian monarch. But instead of continuing the fascist traditions of his predecessor, he facilitated the transition of his country from dictatorship to liberal democracy. During a 1981 attempted military coup, he boldly and publicly ensured the coup's failure, thereby solidifying his position as a popular CONSTITUTIONAL MONARCH.

junta **1.** A collective military dictatorship of a group of senior officers, such as the one that existed in Argentina in the early 1980s and took the decision to invade the Falklands or retrieve the Malvinas (depending on one's point of view). **2.** A ruling board that has taken control of a country after a COUP D'ÉTAT. **3.** A Spanish word for an assembly of people with administrative or legislative functions.

jus sanguinis Latin for "right of blood"; the legal principle that one's nationality or citizenship at birth is the same as that of one's parents.

jus soli Latin for "right of land"; the legal principle that one's nationality or citizenship at birth is determined by where one's birth occurred. This is the case, for example, in the United States: anyone born there is instantly a citizen.

Just Defense A British organization that believes and argues that both international security and stable peace would be best achieved through an emphasis on nonoffensive defense. The term was intended as a play on the JUST WAR THEORY and also to emphasize what was being advocated—exclusively defense. In the early and mid-1980s the group was particularly active in setting out a series of principles based around the notion of defensive or nonprovocative defense (i.e., defensive forces that are not configured in ways that enable them easily to engage in offensive actions) and less reliance on nuclear weapons, which it was hoped would provide the basis for the reestablishment of a national consensus on defense. The end of the Cold War has made its concerns less pressing.

Justice Commandos of the Armenian Genocide (JCAG) A terrorist group that seeks Armenian autonomy by attacking Turkish diplomats around the world. Its goal is to reestablish the Independent Republic of Armenia that existed briefly in eastern Turkey after World War I. *See also* ARMENIAN TERRORISM.

justiciable **1.** Descriptive of a dispute that may be appropriately decided by a particular court. An international dispute is said to be justiciable if the parties involved are willing to submit it to an international court or to ARBITRATION. **2.** An international dispute that can be decided on some grounds recognized by INTERNATIONAL LAW, as opposed to disputes that are considered nonjusticiable or political in nature.

just war theory A set of propositions on the proper use of military force. The theory, which dates from the Middle Ages, deals with when it is morally acceptable or just to go to war, and what forms of war are permissible if the war is just. According to St. Thomas Aquinas, "For a war to be just, three conditions are necessary—public authority, just cause, right motive" (*Summa Theologica*, 1267–73). A major tenet of just war theory is the doctrine of *proportionality:* that the damage of a military action had to be justified in terms of its relation to the original justification for going to war. A distinction is usually made between *jus ad bellum* (justification for going to war) and *jus in bello* (justification for acts in war). Just war theory sets two main restrictions on the use of force that pose acute difficulties with regard to modern warfare. The requirement that discrimination should be maintained between those who are actively and willingly engaged in the combat and those who are innocent noncombatants is particularly difficult to observe in an age of total war and weapons of mass destruction. The second requirement, that of proportionality, which teaches that to be just means ought to be appropriate to the ends that they hope to achieve, seems equally difficult to maintain in a world in which the dominant security regime is based on the threat to annihilate the population of the adversary.

U.S. President Theodore Roosevelt in a message to Congress on December 4, 1906, said: "A just war is in the long run far better for a nation's soul than the most prosperous peace obtained by acquiescence in wrong or injustice." That may be so, but as author Mark Twain warned in *A Pen Warmed Up in Hell* (F. Anderson, ed., 1972): "Statesmen will invent cheap lies, putting blame upon the nation that is attacked, and every man will be glad of those conscience-smoothing falsities . . . and thus he will by and by convince himself that the war *is* just, and will thank God for the better sleep he enjoys after this process of grotesque self-deception." Nevertheless, it is generally conceded that World War II, for example, was a just war from the point of view of the ALLIES, even though some supporters of that war would argue that the bombings of DRESDEN and HIROSHIMA lacked proportionality. *See also* CATHOLIC BISHOPS' LETTER.

Jutland, Battle of   The most significant naval engagement of WORLD WAR I, fought in 1916 by the British and German fleets in the North Sea. The British, who outnumbered the Germans, lost more ships and men; but they forced the Germans to retreat back to port. Because the Germans never again challenged British command of the high seas during the war, the battle was considered a British victory. *See also* BEATTY, DAVID; JELLICOE, JOHN.

K

Kadar, Janos (1912–1989) The Hungarian Communist who came to power after the Soviet invasion of Hungary during the HUNGARIAN UPRISING of 1956. He then became first secretary of the Hungarian Communist Party and premier. Clearly a sympathizer of Soviet leader NIKITA S. KHRUSCHEV's reformism, but a member of the multiparty coalition government under Prime Minister IMRE NAGY, Kadar emerged as the Hungarian leader responsible for restoration of Soviet control in Hungary. Under Kadar, Nagy was executed and the Soviet Union took an active role in defining terms of "normalization" in Hungary. However, Kadar deviated from strict Communist rule and in 1961 declared that "whoever is not against us is with us." He then pursued economic reform that allowed both Communists and non-Communists to prosper. Political and economic disputes materialized in the 1980s and Kadar could no longer govern. He was relieved from power in 1988 and died the following year—coincidentally, on the same day that the Hungarian Supreme Court annulled the verdict of treason passed on Imre Nagy in 1958.

kaffiyeh A cloth headcovering worn by Arabs as protection against the elements. The *kaffiyeh* has been frequently worn by and identified with Palestinian terrorists, who have worn the headdress over their faces to conceal their identities. The *kaffiyeh* worn in this fashion has become a symbol of the INTIFADA. YASIR ARAFAT's ubiquitous *kaffiyeh* is worn in the more traditional fashion, draped on top of the head.

Kahn, Herman (1922–1983) The nuclear theorist and futurologist whose analyses of defense strategy in a nuclear age helped the United States move away from its 1950s policy of MASSIVE RETALIATION to the current one of FLEXIBLE RESPONSE. Kahn argued that it was necessary to think about ways of fighting limited, as opposed to unlimited or spasm, nuclear wars. Indeed, any chance of imposing some kind of restraint in warfare was possible only if there had been prior thinking as to how it might be achieved. He distinguished among different kinds of nuclear DETERRENCE but saw it as operating even at very high levels of violence as both the United States and the Soviet Union would be deterred from inflicting ultimate strikes against each other's cities. In works such as *On Thermonuclear War* (1960), *Thinking about the Unthinkable* (1962), and *On Escalation: Metaphors and Scenarios*

Herman Kahn (Library of Congress)

(1965) he not only wrote about millions of deaths from nuclear war and suggested that the survivors might envy the dead, but did it in a way that seemed detached and totally amoral. As John Garnett wrote in a chapter on Kahn in John Baylis and John Garnett (eds.), *Makers of Nuclear Strategy* (1991), "Kahn, quite uncompromisingly, stared right down the throat of thermonuclear war without flinching. What is more he was the first person to do it, and when a totally unprepared public was suddenly confronted by his findings they reacted with a mixture of fear, horror and amazement." Critical opinion too was often unfavorable. James Newman, for example, writing in *Scientific American* (204, no. 3, 1961), described *On Thermonuclear War* as "an insane, pornographic book, a moral tract of mass murder: how to plan it, how to commit it, how to get away with it, how to justify it." Kahn's willingness to think through some of the "what if" questions, however, helped to highlight some of the dangers involved in deterrence. Moreover, it was clear that although Kahn focused in large part on surviving nuclear war, his main concern was how to avoid it. He believed this could be discerned best through analysis rather than emotion. *See also* DOOMSDAY MACHINE; ESCALATION.

KAHN ON NUCLEAR WAR

When one examines the possible effects of thermonuclear war carefully, one notices that there are indeed many postwar states that should be distinguished. If most people do not or cannot distinguish among these states it is because the gradations occur as a result of a totally bizarre circumstance—a thermonuclear war. The mind recoils from thinking hard about that; one prefers to believe it will never happen. If asked, "How does a country look on the day of the war?" the only answer a reasonable person can give is "awful." It takes an act of iron will or an unpleasant degree of detachment or callousness to go about the task of distinguishing among the possible degrees of awfulness.

SOURCE: Herman Kahn, *On Thermonuclear War* (1961).

---

kaiser **1.** A variant of *caesar*, the ancient Roman term for "emperor." **2.** The title of the rulers of Austria from 1804 to 1918. **3.** The title of the rulers of Germany from 1871 to 1918. In twentieth-century political history, "*the* Kaiser" usually refers to the leader of Germany during World War I, WILLIAM II.

kamikaze **1.** The Japanese suicide pilots (or their aircraft) who sought to crash into U.S. ships during World War II. The word means "divine wind" in Japanese, a reference to the storm that destroyed a Chinese invasion fleet centuries before. **2.** By analogy, any suicide mission.

Kampuchea The name given to Cambodia in 1976 when the KHMER ROUGE established Democratic Kampuchea. In 1979 the occupying Vietnamese renamed the state the People's Republic of Kampuchea. In 1989, as Vietnamese forces withdrew, the country returned to its former name of Cambodia. *See also* NORODOM SIHANOUK.

Kant, Immanuel (1724–1804) The German philosopher who, at the time of the French Revolution, produced works such as *Toward Eternal Peace* (1795) and *Metaphysical Elements of Justice* (1797) that argued against monarchy. For Kant, sovereigns acting for their own purposes treated citizens as the means to achieve territorial conquest in wars. But this was unacceptable, because citizens had a right to be treated with respect. In republics where the citizen had a say it was more difficult to go to war than in a monarchy. Consequently, for perpetual peace to be achieved, Kant believed that it was essential for all states to be republican. Ideas emphasizing the nature of the state as the key determinant of war or peace provided the basis for much subsequent thinking, including the argument of U.S. President WOODROW WILSON that peace could be achieved when there was openness of government. The contemporary argument that democracies do not fight each other is heir to the ideas of Kant.

Kashmir dispute The disagreement between India and Pakistan over Kashmir, a mountainous area west of Tibet. Following division of the subcontinent in 1947 to form India with a Hindu majority and Pakistan with a Muslim majority, India got Kashmir when its maharaja (ruling prince) chose to join India, although three-quarters of his subjects were Muslim. India has maintained that this decision and subsequent elections in Kashmir have made the province an integral part of India. Pakistan has asserted Kashmir's right to self-determination in accordance with an earlier Indian pledge and a United Nations resolution. The dispute triggered open warfare between the two countries in 1947–1948 and in 1965. Although the Kashmir issue was to be settled by a plebiscite to be held under the auspices of the UN, India continued its armed occupation of the area, thus reinforcing tensions between it and Pakistan that remain today.

Kashmir Liberation Army (KLA)   A terrorist group that seeks the independence of Kashmir from India. In 1984 it kidnapped Indian diplomat Ravindra Mhartre in Birmingham, England, and demanded the release of Magbool Boot, the KLA leader who was awaiting execution for the murder of a policeman in India. After the KLA murdered the diplomat, the Indian government executed its prisoner. Later that same year the KLA took credit for the AIR INDIA EXPLOSION: the bombing of an Air India 747 aircraft that, en route from Toronto to London, exploded over the Atlantic Ocean killing 329 people on board.

Katyn Forest   The site in western Russia where the Soviet military systematically executed 15,000 Polish prisoners (including 4,000 military officers) in 1940. The Germans uncovered the graves in 1943 and publicized the fact that the victims had been murdered by the Soviets. The Soviets continued to deny their guilt in this atrocity until 1990 when MIKHAIL GORBACHEV's government admitted that this was one World War II crime for which the Germans were not guilty.

Keitel, Wilhelm (1882–1946)   The German Army officer who was second only to ADOLF HITLER in directing Germany's aggression in WORLD WAR II. He was convicted of war crimes at the NUREMBURG TRIALS and sentenced to hang.

Kellogg, Frank B. (1856–1937)   The U.S. Senator from Minnesota (1917–1923) and ambassador to Great Britain (1923–1925) who was secretary of state (1925–1929) under President Calvin Coolidge. His most notable achievement was the KELLOGG-BRIAND PACT of 1928, which earned him the Nobel Peace Prize for 1929.

Kellogg-Briand Pact   The 1928 treaty that "outlawed" war. The multilateral treaty, also known as the Pact of Paris, renouncing war as an instrument of national policy, was cosponsored by FRANK B. KELLOGG, U.S. Secretary of State, and ARISTIDE BRIAND, the French foreign minister. Briand had wanted a bilateral security treaty between Washington and Paris but failed to get it. Instead he got an innocuous pact condemning war. It was initially signed in Paris by 15 major military powers; eventually 62 acceded to its fine sentiments. It read in part: "The high contracting parties solemnly declare in the names of their respective peoples that they condemn recourse to war for the solution of international controversies, and renounce it as an instrument of national policy in their relations with one another." Unfortunately this did nothing to inhibit WORLD WAR II. As U.S. Senator Carter Glass said of it: "I am unwilling to have anybody in Virginia suppose that I am simple enough to imagine that this treaty is worth a postage stamp in bringing about peace . . . but it would be psychologically bad to defeat it" (*Time*, January 28, 1929).

Kennan, George F. (1904–   )   The United States foreign service officer and ambassador to Yugo-

---

KEITEL HANGS

Field Marshal Keitel, who was immediately behind von Ribbentrop in the order of executions, was the first military leader to be executed under the new concept of international law—the principle that professional soldiers cannot escape punishment for waging aggressive wars and permitting crimes against humanity with the claim they were dutifully carrying out orders of superiors.

Keitel entered the chamber two minutes after the trap had dropped beneath von Ribbentrop, while the latter still was at the end of his rope. . . .

After his black-booted, uniformed body plunged through the trap, witnesses agreed Keitel had showed more courage on the scaffold than in the courtroom, where he had tried to shift his guilt upon the ghost of Hitler, claiming that all was the Fuhrer's fault and that he merely carried out orders and had no responsibility.

SOURCE: Kingsbury Smith, on the October 16, 1946, hanging of Nazi war criminals, *It Happened in 1946*, ed. Clark Kinnaird (1947).

Frank Kellogg poses for photographers across the street from the White House in 1925. (Library of Congress)

slavia (1961–1963) and the Soviet Union (1952) who authored the United States policy of CONTAINMENT in the post–World War II period. Kennan's famous "long telegram" from Moscow to the State Department in 1946 outlined what he regarded as Soviet objectives as well as the need for a U.S. response. The ideas in the telegram subsequently provided the basis for Kennan's article "The Sources of Soviet Conduct," which appeared under the pseudonym X in *Foreign Affairs* (25, no. 4, 1947) and provided the public rationale for the U.S. policy of containment. Although Kennan used military analogies in this article, he saw containment as essentially political in character and believed that it was crucial that the United States rebuild Western Europe economically so that it could provide an indigenous countervailing power to that of the Soviet Union. Kennan believed that Soviet expansionist probes were not the result of feelings about recent injustices from the West, but of long-term Russian expansionist tendencies that must be opposed. Kennan did not like the subsequent militarization of containment—a process that developed largely in response to the Korean War but was consistent with the thinking and recommendations of NSC-68 and PAUL H. NITZE, who replaced Kennan as director (from 1947 to 1949) of the POLICY PLANNING STAFF at the State Department and who saw the competition between the totalitarian Soviet Union and the Western democ-

racies largely in military terms. Indeed, much of Kennan's subsequent career as a scholar consisted of successive critiques of American policy and recommendations for moving beyond the military stalemate that the COLD WAR had degenerated into by the early 1950s. This was evident in his proposals for military disengagement in Europe, which appeared in the mid-1950s, and his subsequent criticisms of American military strategy and the reliance on the first use of nuclear weapons. In a sense the divergences between Kennan and Nitze over the nature of the Soviet threat and the appropriate U.S. response defined the main parameters of the American debate over foreign and security policy throughout the Cold War. Kennan was always scrupulous both in his efforts to understand the Soviet Union and in his willingness to criticize the United States, as he did in *American Diplomacy 1900–1950* (1951), in which he provided a trenchant critique of what he termed the legalist and moralist approach to foreign policy.

Upon leaving government, Kennan became a prolific scholar and lively critic. His works on the Soviet Union included *Russia Leaves the War* (1956) and *Russia and the West under Lenin and Stalin* (1961). Among his later works are *The Nuclear Delusion* (1982) and *Sketches from a Life* (1989). His two volumes of *Memoirs* (1967 and 1972) are fascinating and reveal a man who regarded himself as a foreign policy specialist and who disliked having to deal with amateurs in Congress. His contributions to the debate could never be ignored, even though it is ironic that the initial author of the main organizing theme of postwar U.S. foreign policy had become one of the major critics of containment's implemention. However, it is for his contribution to containment that Kennan will most be remembered—in particular for his prediction that a long term and vigilant policy by the United States would cause a mellowing of Soviet power. As he put it in the X article:

> . . . the United States has it in its power to increase enormously the strains under which Soviet policy must operate, to force upon the Kremlin a far greater degree of moderation and circumspection than it has had to observe in recent years, and in this way to promote tendencies which must eventually find their outlet in either the break-up or the gradual mellowing of Soviet power. For no mystical, Messianic movement—and particularly not that of the Kremlin—can face frustration indefinitely without eventually adjusting itself in one way or another to the logic of that state of affairs.

The developments in the Soviet Union in the latter half of the 1980s and its demise in 1991 can be seen as the ultimate vindication of the containment strategy conceived by George Kennan.

Kennedy, John Fitzgerald (1917–1963) President of the United States (1961–1963) whose administration is now more noted for its style than its substance. His charming and charismatic personality tended to overshadow his failure to get any major legislation through a conservative-dominated Congress, and his foreign policy was marked by frustration with Cuba over the BAY OF PIGS, the Soviet Union over the CUBAN MISSILE CRISIS, and Vietnam, where he placed 16,000 American military ADVISORS. But in spite of all this, Kennedy will always be remembered as the president who brought a sense of youthful vigor to the White House and launched the SPACE RACE with his decision to put U.S. astronauts on the moon within a decade. Just as President Franklin D. Roosevelt used radio to create a personal relationship with the American public, Kennedy became the first president effectively to use live television on a regular basis. Perhaps Kennedy's most significant decision for the future of

John F. Kennedy (John Fitzgerald Kennedy Library)

the nation was his selection of LYNDON B. JOHNSON to be his vice president—with all the good and ill that implied for the 1960s. Kennedy was assassinated in Dallas, Texas, on November 22, 1963.

Kennedy, Joseph Patrick (1888–1969) The multimillionaire father of U.S. President John F. Kennedy who was the United States Ambassador to Great Britain from 1938 to 1940. His support of APPEASEMENT toward Nazi Germany and U.S. isolationism brought him into conflict with the British and with U.S. President Franklin D. Roosevelt. His resignation was warmly received.

Kennedy Round The sixth series of tariff negotiations (Geneva, 1964–1967) under GATT. Named in honor of the late President John F. Kennedy, during whose administration the U.S. Congress passed the Trade Expansion Act of 1962. The talks are credited with having reduced the average level of world tariffs by one-third.

Kenyatta, Jomo *See* MAU MAU.

Keohane, Robert O. (1940–   )   One of the major American theorists in international relations in general and international political economy in particular. Keohane, along with JOSEPH NYE, was one of the earliest U.S. analysts to provide a serious and systematic discussion of the implications of TRANSNATIONALISM and INTERDEPENDENCE for the operation of the international system. Their two books, *Transnational Relations and World Politics* (1972) and *Power and Interdependence: World Politics in Transition* (1977), were important analyses of the changes brought about by new forces in world politics. Keohane also has been one of the leading figures in the development of REGIME theory though his book *After Hegemony: Cooperation and Discord in the World Political Economy* (1984). One of the most interesting aspects of Keohane's work is that besides being very innovative in his thinking, he stands at the juncture of NEOREALISM and NEOLIBERALISM, combining elements of both approaches in distinctive ways.

Kerensky, Aleksandr (1881–1970)   The prime minister of the RUSSIAN PROVISIONAL GOVERNMENT from July to October during the RUSSIAN REVOLUTION OF 1917. Kerensky looked on World War I as a chance to overthrow the czarist regime and create a liberal government with enlightened leaders at the helm. With the abdication of Czar Nicholas II, the Provisional Government was formed with the Ministry of Justice assigned to Kerensky. He helped promulgate many civil liberties but agreed to meet treaty obligations to the Allies rather than conclude hostilities with Germany. Nor did he pursue land reform for the peasantry. After becoming minister of war and navy in April, Kerensky unsuccessfully conducted a major military offensive in June. Antiwar demonstrations ensued in July. Kerensky then became prime minister, but despite many concessions the already tenuous support of the Provisional Government melted away, especially with soldiers deserting en masse. The BOLSHEVIKS garnered more popular support and controlled the military forces in St. Petersburg. Kerensky's attempt to check them precipitated his fall along with the Provisional Government in the October 1917 coup. After unsuccessfully seeking to rally opposition forces, Kerensky fled Russia, eventually settled in New York, and spent the rest of his life in exile.

Keynes, John Maynard (1883–1946)   The English economist who, as the chief representative of the British treasury, was attached to the British delegation to the PARIS PEACE CONFERENCE after World War I. He was critical of the heavy punitive reparations on Germany and divisions in Central Europe. He resigned from the delegation and wrote a scathing attack on the economic aspects of the peace and the negotiations. Keynes's book, *The Economic Consequences of the Peace* (1920), became a best-seller and shaped British attitudes toward the peace. Several years later he wrote the most influential book on economics of this century, *The General Theory of Employment, Interest and Money* (1936). Keynes founded a school of thought known as Keynesian economics, which called for using a government's fiscal and monetary policies to positively influence a capitalistic economy. He was a strong

John Maynard Keynes (Library of Congress)

advocate of pump priming (the use of government spending on public works and welfare to jump start an economy out of recession) and one of the developers of modern macroeconomics (the theory linking relationships among broad economic trends such as national income, consumer savings, employment levels, etc.). Most governments of modern industrial states now use Keynes's theories, admittedly or unadmittedly, to justify deficit spending to stimulate their economies. Keynes also is credited with providing the definitive economic forecast: "In the long run we are all dead."

KEYNES ON THE DANGER OF IDEAS

The ideas of economists and political philosophers, both when they are right and when they are wrong, are more powerful than is commonly understood. Indeed the world is ruled by little else. Practical men, who believe themselves to be quite exempt from any intellectual influences, are usually the slaves of some defunct economist. Madmen in authority, who hear voices in the air, are distilling their frenzy from some academic scribbler of a few years back. I am sure that the power of vested interests is vastly exaggerated compared with the gradual encroachment of ideas. Not, indeed, immediately, but after a certain interval; for in the field of economic and political philosophy there are not many who are influenced by new theories after they are twenty-five or thirty years of age, so that the ideas which civil servants and politicians and even agitators apply to current events are not likely to be the newest. But soon or late, it is ideas, not vested interests, which are dangerous for good or evil.

SOURCE: John Maynard Keynes, *General Theory of Employment, Interest and Money* (1936).

KGB *(Komitet Gosudarstvennoy Bezopasnosti)* "Committee for State Security," the internal security police and international espionage organization of the Soviet Union that was the primary instrument of JOSEPH STALIN's terror. Begun as the CHEKA, it quickly became the arm of repression for the BOLSHEVIKS against dissidents and enemies in the RUSSIAN CIVIL WAR that followed the revolution in 1917. It was given wide powers, including arrest, torture, control of concentration camps, and execution, and in time was the instrument of the RED TERROR, characterized by mass

reprisals. In 1922 the Cheka was transformed into the GPU, an abbreviation for the *Gosudarstvennoye Politicheskoye Upravlenie* ("State Political Administration"), with much the same functions, but different targets—kulaks (wealthy peasants), recalcitrant party members, and private entrepreneurs, among others. In 1934, the GPU became the NKVD, an abbreviation for *Narodny Komissariat Vnutrennikh Del* ("People's Commissariat of Internal Affairs"). The newly named internal police basically retained the same characteristics as its predecessors, but its powers were expanded. Beginning in the 1930s it supervised a vast system of labor camps. The NKVD became the most powerful organ in Soviet Russia, above party control and directly under Stalin. In 1943 it was split in two. Besides the NKVD, the NKGB (*Narodnyi Komissariat Gosudarstvennoy Bezopasnozti*, or "People's Commissariat of State Security") came into existence and was largely responsible for the arrest of millions of Soviet soldiers imprisoned by the Nazis during the war and "socially undesirable elements" that had lived in occupied Nazi territory. In 1946 the NKGB was dubbed the MGB, which in 1953 was renamed the KGB. Its authority and jurisdiction, however, was circumscribed. The KGB has employed force more sparingly, and to curb possible usurpation of power it was subordinated to tighter party and government control. After its leadership participated in the abortive RUSSIAN COUP OF 1991, the KGB was given new leadership, lost many of its functions and personnel, and began opening up its files to the media. Since the demise of the Soviet Union at the end of 1991, it has become the intelligence service of Russia and has started cooperating with the U.S. CENTRAL INTELLIGENCE AGENCY to fight TERRORISM, drug smuggling, and organized crime. It has been formally renamed the Ministry of Security (or MB for *Ministerstvo Bezopasnosti*), but the world press still calls it the KGB.

Khalid ibn Abdul Aziz (1913–1982)   The king of Saudi Arabia from 1975 to 1982. After becoming crown prince in 1965, he succeeded to the throne when King FAISAL IBN ABDUL AZIZ was assassinated. When King Khalid died of a heart attack, he was succeeded by FAHD IBN ABDUL AZIZ.

Kharg Island   An island in the Persian Gulf close to the coast of Iran, which is one of the main facilities for Iran's oil exports. Kharg Island, which is about 40 miles long and 20 miles wide, houses a 60-square-mile tank farm; it receives oil from the Iranian mainland through underwater pipelines. During the IRAN-IRAQ WAR, the oil facilities on Kharg Island were one of Iraq's major targets. As a result the amount of oil that Iran was able to export was seriously reduced.

Khmer Rouge   A Communist Guerrilla organization that rose to power in the Southeast Asian country of Cambodia (Kampuchea) in the 1970s. *Khmer* means "a native of Cambodia." *Rouge* is French for "red," meaning Communist. They were originally formed in the early 1970s to resist the U.S. installed government of LON NOL. The Khmer Rouge overthrew his regime in 1975. POL POT, the Khmer Rouge commander, then instituted a reign of terror that resulted in more than 1 million deaths by torture, starvation, disease, overwork, and outright murder. The organization currently operates out of heavily populated refugee camps on the Thai-Cambodian border, and is amassing manpower and firepower for a future attempt to retake control of Cambodia, which was occupied from 1978 to 1989 by the Vietnamese military. The Khmer Rouge has received vast amounts of arms, supplies, and funding from the People's Republic of China. Extortion has proven to be a primary source of funds for the group; for instance, the organization has earned tens of thousands of U.S. dollars a week by selling mining passes to prospective ruby miners in the areas it controls in Cambodia. Despite criticism, the Khmer Rouge was allowed to participate in the United Nations–brokered coalition government under NORODOM SIHANOUK set up in 1991 to end the civil war. But the Khmer Rouge's refusal to lay down its arms and permit UN troops to deploy in large areas threatens the peace.

Khomeini, Ayatollah Ruhollah (1901–1989)   SHI'ITE Muslim spiritual leader of the IRANIAN REVOLUTION and political leader of the Islamic Republic of Iran when that nation was at the forefront of state-sponsored TERRORISM. Largely unknown in the West before his unseating of the SHAH in 1979, Khomeini had been an active Iranian dissent leader since the 1940s. He despised all things Western and referred to

the United States as the "Great Satan." Through his charismatic leadership he inflamed the Iranian people. Almost as soon as he gained control of Iran he began to export Islamic fundamentalism to Arab states throughout the Persian Gulf. During the IRAN-IRAQ WAR, many of the gulf states as well as the United States aided Iraq because they feared that a victorious Iranian army would not stop at Iraq's borders.

Khrushchev, Nikita S. (1894–1971)   The general secretary of the Communist Party of the Soviet Union from 1954 to 1964. Khrushchev, a miner, joined the BOLSHEVIKS in 1918 and fought in the Russian Civil War. Very active in the ranks of the party, he moved up its ladder over the years, holding diverse local positions. Khrushchev became a Stalinist par excellence and was one of JOSEPH STALIN's most rabid followers and executors of drastic policies. In 1934 he was elected to the Central Committee of the CPSU. In 1939 he obtained membership in the POLITBURO. During World War II Khrushchev was Stalin's special emissary on a number of fronts. After Stalin's death a major power struggle ensued. Khrushchev, through adroit maneuvering, became all-powerful in 1955. In order to garner support for himself, Khrushchev engineered the beginnings of a de-Stalinization program, which became known in a then secret but now famous speech in February 1956 at the Twentieth Congress of the CPSU. The speech aired Stalin's crimes and self-deification (the CULT OF PERSONALITY), told of the rehabilitation of many of his victims, and promised some relaxation in censorship, but the party monopoly of political power remained inviolate. He was the first Soviet leader to denounce Stalin's crimes, to allow a relatively moderate policy in the arts and literature, and to raise the living standards of the Soviet people. The Khrushchev years were also known for continuing problems in agriculture, the launching of SPUTNIK I and the SPACE RACE, repression during the HUNGARIAN UPRISING of 1956, a growing rift with China that was known as the SINO-SOVIET SPLIT, advocacy of peaceful COEXISTENCE, and an increased rapprochement with Third World countries. Also noteworthy were the shooting down of a U.S. spy plane in the U-2 INCIDENT, the CUBAN MISSILE CRISIS in 1962, and a nuclear test ban treaty in 1963. His division of the

Nikita Khrushchev at the United Nations in September 1960. (Library of Congress)

party structure into industrial and agricultural groupings (which rankled the apparatchiks), his failures in agriculture (which led to the necessity of buying wheat from the United States), and his many grandiose unrealized promises caused Khrushchev to be deposed on October 15, 1964. He died quietly in Moscow as a "pensioner of all-union significance" during his forced retirement seven years later. He was not buried with full honors in the Kremlin wall (the traditional site of interment for high-ranking Communists).

Khyber Pass   The most northerly and important of the mountain passes leading from Afghanistan to Pakistan; the historic commercial and military route from Russia to India.

Kiesinger, Kurt-Georg (1904–1988)   The first World War II–era Nazi Party member to become chancellor of West Germany (1966–1969) after World War II. His economic policies helped achieve a recovery from the recession of the mid-1960s. Internationally he sought RAPPROCHEMENT with the Communist states of Eastern Europe while at the same time seeking greater integration with Western Europe and the North Atlantic Treaty Organization.

killing fields   The descriptive name often used for Cambodia when it was under the control of the murderous KHMER ROUGE. *See* also CAMBODIAN HOLOCAUST.

Kim Il-Sung (1912–   )   Chairman of the ruling Korean Workers Party and president of Democratic People's Republic of Korea (North Korea). Kim was a leading organizer of armed resistance to the Japanese occupation of Korea in the 1930s. During World War II he led a Korean contingent in the Soviet army and returned to establish a Communist government under Soviet auspices in North Korea (the land on the Korean peninsula above the THIRTY-EIGHTH PARALLEL) in 1945. In 1950 he started the KOREAN WAR with an attempt to expand his rule over South Korea. Only with aid from Chinese military "volunteers" was he able to repel a subsequent invasion of North Korea by United Nations forces under the command of U.S. General DOUGLAS MACARTHUR. As the president of North Korea, he also has encouraged and enjoyed his personal cult. After the dismantling of Communist governments in Eastern Europe and the Soviet Union, Kim's North Korea became one of the few remaining nations that maintain authoritarian rule.

King, Martin Luther, Jr. (1929–1968)   The African-American southern Baptist minister who became the leader of the civil rights movement in the United States. His tactics of nonviolent confrontation with southern segregationist policies aroused so much sympathy and support in the rest of the nation that they led to landmark civil rights legislation. In 1957 King journeyed to India to study MOHANDAS K. GANDHI's technique of nonviolence. For his mobilization of peaceful support for civil rights, he was awarded the 1964 Nobel Peace Prize. King was assassinated in Memphis, Tennessee, on April 4, 1968. His impact on the civil rights of all Americans was so strong that his birthday was made a national holiday in 1983. *See also* CIVIL DISOBEDIENCE.

king can do no wrong   The concept of SOVEREIGN IMMUNITY derived from a principle of feudal law which held that since the king was at the top of the legal structure of the state, he could not be sued in court by anyone under him—meaning everybody else. In most CONSTITUTIONAL MONARCHIES today specific legislation makes the king (or queen) liable for some contracts and certain classes of torts.

King David Hotel incident   The July 22, 1946, bombing of the King David Hotel, the British headquarters in Jerusalem, by a Jewish terrorist organization (the IRGUN) led by MENACHEM BEGIN. Over 90 people died in the attack that, although directed against the British military, killed many civilians.

kings, divine right of   *See* DIVINE RIGHT OF KINGS.

King's shilling   In Great Britain, the coin given to new army recruits at one time as a token of their enrollment in "the King's service." Those who have "taken the King's shilling" have legally signed on and have an obligation to be loyal.

Kinnock, Neil (1942–   )   The leader of the British Labour Party from 1983 to 1992. He refocused his party to make it more moderate in approach, especially on foreign policy, and divested it of its radical left elements. Nevertheless, after leading Labour to its fourth general election defeat in a row (the last two with Kinnock as party leader), he stepped down as Britain's opposition leader.

THE TRANS-ATLANTIC ALL PURPOSE POLITICAL SPEECH

Why am I the first Kinnock in a thousand generations to be able to get to a university? Why is Glenys the first woman in her family in a thousand generations to be able to get to a university? Was it because all our predecessors were thick? Did they lack talent? Those people who could sing and play and write poetry? Those people who could make wonderful beautiful things with their hands? Those people who could dream dreams, see visions? Was it because they were weak, those people who could work eight hours underground and then come up and play football, weak? Does anybody really think that they didn't get what we had because they didn't have the talent or the strength or the endurance or the commitment? Of course not.

SOURCE: Neil Kinnock speech broadcast May 21, 1987; reported in *The New York Times* (September 12, 1987). U.S. Senator Joseph R. Biden, Jr. (1942–   ) from Delaware was forced to withdraw from the 1988 race for the Democratic presidential nomination when opponents released a videotape showing him repeating almost word for word this Kinnock speech.

Kirkpatrick, Jeane (1926–   )   The United States Ambassador to the United Nations during the first Reagan Administration (1981–1985). In a 1979 *Commentary* article she stated what became known as the Kirkpatrick Doctrine: that right-wing authoritarian dictatorships are preferable to left-wing totalitarian dictatorships because right-wing dictatorships could be reformed and left-wing ones could not. When critics complained about her support for despicable regimes, she responded: "We must make it perfectly clear that we are revolted by torture and can never feel spiritual kinship with a government that engages in torture. But the central goal of our foreign policy should be not the moral elevation of other nations, but the preservation of a civilized conception of our own national self-interest" (*U.S. News & World Report,* March 2, 1981). The 1989–1990 events in Eastern Europe seem to have discredited a major portion of her doctrine.

Kirov, Sergei (1886–1934)   BOLSHEVIK revolutionary and Soviet party official who became an ally of JOSEPH STALIN and supported him in his rise to power. In 1926 Kirov became head of the Communist Party in Leningrad and was known for his aggressive economic modernization. He was made a member of the POLITBURO in 1930. In 1934 Kirov was murdered in an assassination secretly engineered by Stalin. Kirov, although a loyal Stalinist, was getting to be too popular, which did not fare well with Stalin. Stalin used his murder as an excuse to initiate the purges of the 1930s, which came to be known as the GREAT PURGE.

Kissinger, Henry A. (1923–   )   The German-born Harvard University political scientist who became U.S. President Richard M. Nixon's National Security Advisor (1969–1973); then secretary of state under Presidents Nixon and Gerald Ford (1973–1977). While he shared the Nobel Peace Prize in 1973 (with LE DUC THO) for his efforts to bring peace to Vietnam, he was also widely criticized for the United States' Vietnam War policies—especially for his involvement in the CAMBODIAN INCURSION.

Kissinger first came to prominence with his book *A World Restored* (1957), which dealt with the impact of revolutionary change on the nineteenth-century international order. While this work established him as very clearly within the realist tradition of thought about international relations, he also wrote several books that made him one of the leading strategic analysts in the United States. These included *Nuclear Weapons and Foreign Policy* (1957), in which Kissinger seemed to embrace the possibility of limited nuclear war, and *The Necessity for Choice* (1960), in which he backed away from some of his ideas on limited nuclear war and argued, like many other nuclear strategists of the period, for more emphasis on conventional forces, especially in Europe. Kissinger's main concern as a strategist was with devising ways to make U.S. COLD WAR policies more effective. Even as an academic he saw his role as one of policy advisor. He had an opportunity actually to make policy, however, when he was chosen by Nixon as his National Security Advisor. In this position, Kissinger eclipsed Secretary of State William Rogers, and eventually replaced him. He also presided over major changes in U.S. foreign policy, including the opening to China and the development of DÉTENTE and arms control with the Soviet Union. His style was one of secret diplomacy based on a shrewd appreciation for power considerations. One of his most effective

policies was in the Middle East, where he skillfully disengaged Egypt from its close relationship with the Soviet Union. Yet because he did not really understand U.S. domestic politics, he never succeeded in legitimizing his policies domestically or establishing a base for them that was essentially independent of him. After he left office, the détente he had cultivated with the Soviet Union fell apart. Nevertheless, Kissinger's two volumes of memoirs, *White House Years* (1979) and *Years of Upheaval* (1982), provide fascinating accounts of his period in office and are one of the best sources for a close-up view of foreign policymaking in the late 1960s and the first half of the 1970s.

Kissinger *Report*   The findings of the National Bipartisan Commission on Central America, a 12-member commission established by U.S. President Ronald Reagan in 1983 to make long-term recommendations for U.S. policy in Central America. Henry Kissinger was its chair. The commission's 1984 *Report* asserted that Central America is an area of vital interest to the United States, and rec-

Henry Kissinger as National Security Advisor in 1969. (Library of Congress)

ommended that the U.S. Congress fund a five-year economic program of $8 billion for the region, that military aid to El Salvador be sharply increased, and that U.S. covert action on behalf of Nicaraguan CONTRAS be continued as an incentive to negotiations. The report also recommended that aid to El Salvador be made contingent on periodic reports to Congress of progress toward free elections, democratic procedures, an effective judicial system, and an end to DEATH SQUAD activity. The report's recommendations essentially became the policy of the United States and eventually helped end the EL SALVADOR CIVIL WAR and the NICARAGUAN CIVIL WAR.

Kitchener, Horatio Herbert (1859–1916)   The British general who became a national hero after he defeated the Sudanese at the 1898 Battle of Omdurman. He later commanded the British forces in South Africa during the BOER WAR. As secretary of state for war when WORLD WAR I began in 1914, he was in charge of transforming Great Britain's small peacetime army into a massive wartime organization. It is Kitchener's face that appears on the famous 1914 recruiting poster with the pointing finger over the slogan "Your Country Needs You." This led Margot Asquith, the wife of the British Prime Minister Herbert Asquith, to remark: "If Kitchener was not a great man, he was, at least, a great poster" (quoted in Philip Magnus, *Kitchener*, 1958). Many analysts then and now thought that Kitchener's unexpected death in 1916 was his greatest contribution to an eventual Allied victory.

PROVIDENCE AND KITCHENER

On 5 June the *Hampshire*, with [Minister of War] Kitchener on board, struck a mine within two hours of leaving Scapa Flow. Kitchener and most of the crew were drowned. So perished the only British military idol of the First World War. The next morning [Lord] Northcliffe burst into his sister's drawing-room with the words: "Providence is on the side of the British Empire after all." This reflected a common view that the secretary for war still held the key to victory, and that Kitchener had been incapable of turning it.

SOURCE: A. J. P. Taylor, *English History 1914–1945* (1965). According to Sir Arthur Conan Doyle, Kitchener "had flashes of genius but was usually stupid."

Kjellen, Johan Rudolf   *See* GEOPOLITICS.

Klinghoffer, Leon   *See ACHILLE LAURO.*

Knesset   The unicameral parliament of Israel.

Knorr, Klaus (1911–   )   The German-born American who became one of the leading figures in the STRATEGIC ANALYSIS community of the 1950s and the 1960s and author or editor of a number of publications dealing with the utility and limitations of military power, the Atlantic Alliance, intelligence assessments, and U.S. national security. One of his most important contributions to the strategic debate was a volume he coedited with Thornton Read entitled *Limited Strategic War* (1962), which provided a comprehensive and balanced set of analyses of an extremely controversial subject. Other important books include *On the Uses of Military Power in the Nuclear Age* (1966), in which he explored the changing utility of military power. Knorr's work, however, has not been restricted to strategic analysis, as is evident in *The Power of Nations: the Political Economy of International Relations* (1975), his writings on science and defense, and his analyses of the potential and problems of nuclear energy.

Knox, Philander Chase (1853–1921)   The U.S. Secretary of State throughout the administration of President William H. Taft (1909–1913). Knox was a leading proponent of DOLLAR DIPLOMACY.

Kohl, Helmut (1930–   )   The Christian Democrat chancellor of West Germany (since 1982) whose administration achieved the reunification of East and West Germany in 1989. As chancellor of a united Germany, Kohl also has been a strong advocate of German integration with Western Europe through the European Community and has worked with President François Mitterrand of France to form a joint military force, the FRANCO-GERMAN BRIGADE.

Kola Peninsula   An area of major military activity, the location of the Russian Navy's principal submarine base at Murmansk. This is one of only two places (the other being Turkey) where the Commonwealth of Independent States borders a North Atlantic Treaty Organization member country—in this case, Norway. Control of the land adjacent to the Kola Peninsula in northern Norway would be vitally important for the control of the Norwegian and Barent seas in the event of war.

Kondratieff cycle   *See* LONG WAVE.

Koreagate   A late 1970s scandal involving a Korean businessman, Tong Sun Park, who bribed various members of the U.S. Congress. Over several years he gave at least $850,000 in bribes to encourage United States aid to South Korea.

Korean Airlines Flight 007   The civilian Korean airliner that was shot down by Soviet fighter aircraft on August 30, 1983, when it strayed into Soviet territory near the Sea of Japan. All 269 people on board were killed, including a U.S. congressman. This severely strained U.S.-Soviet relations at the time. Many theories have arisen as to why the plane went off course and flew over a piece of Soviet territory that housed many military installations. The theories can be grouped under two main headings: conspiracy theories in which the flyover was deliberate as part of some intelligence mission, and Murphy's law theories that postulated it was simply a pilot or navigational error. There also have been continued questions about whether the Soviets knew it was a civilian airliner or might have mistaken it for a U.S. reconnaissance plane that was also in the vicinity. It seems unlikely that there will ever be definitive answers about the incident.

Korean War   The war between Communist North Korea and non-Communist South Korea that began on June 25, 1950, when the North invaded the South. At the end of World War II, the Soviet Union accepted the Japanese surrender north of the THIRTY-EIGHTH PARALLEL in Korea and established a Communist state, while the United States accepted the Japanese surrender south of that line and established a pro-Western state. Negotiations to unify the two states failed and the issue was turned over to the United Nations. By 1949 both the United States and the Soviet Union had withdrawn the majority of their troops from the Korean Peninsula. The decision on the part of U.S. President Harry S Truman and his advisors to promote intervention was a reversal of a policy previously announced by U.S. Secretary of State Dean Acheson that Korea lay outside the "defense perimeter" of the United States. The decision was based on the belief that the actions of North Korea reflected larger policy interests promoted by the Soviet Union and Communist China and therefore required a strong U.S. response. The U.S. intervention was a symbolic signal to the Soviets that the United States was determined to halt the spread of communism. With the encouragement of the United States, the United Nations Security Council (with the Soviet Union temporarily absent) asked member nations to aid South Korea in resisting the invasion. Thus the war, called a "police action," was fought under the UN flag by U.S. forces with small contingents from over a dozen other nations.

The war initially went very badly for South Korean and UN forces, but with the landing of U.S. forces in the INCHON INVASION, North Korean forces were forced to retreat. In spite of reassurances that the United States was interested only in restoring the STATUS QUO ANTE BELLUM, U.S. General Douglas MacArthur continued to advance into North Korea. Assurances were given to Communist China that the United States was not interested in going beyond the Yalu, the river border between North Korea and China. MacArthur, however, made threatening statements. The Chinese attempted to make clear to Washington how seriously it viewed the attempt to unify Korea under United Nations auspices. But this concern was not fully appreciated in Washington and MacArthur was allowed to continue to advance toward the Yalu. When his actions finally provoked Chinese intervention, the United States was taken by surprise both politically and operationally. The UN forces were compelled to retreat in the face of the North Korean and Chinese "volunteer" offensive. Fighting eventualy stabilized along the thirty-eighth parallel. But the war continued until 1953 when newly elected U.S. President Dwight D. Eisenhower let it be known that unless there was a cessation of hostilities, the United States was prepared to use nuclear weapons. U.S. Secretary of State John Foster Dulles said at the time: "The principal reason we were able to obtain the armistice was because we were prepared for a much more intensive scale of warfare. . . . we had already sent the means to the theater for delivering atomic weapons. This became known to the Chinese Communists through their good intelligence sources and in fact we were not unwilling that they should find out" (quoted in McGeorge Bundy, *Danger and Survival,* 1988). After three years, an armistice was signed (July 27, 1953) that maintained the division of the Koreas almost exactly where it was before the war started. No peace treaty has ever been signed. The Korean War is an example of a LIMITED WAR with ambiguous objectives.

PRESIDENT TRUMAN EXPLAINS U.S. INVOLVEMENT IN THE KOREAN WAR

In Korea the Government forces, which were armed to prevent border raids and to preserve internal security, were attacked by invading forces from North Korea. The Security Council of the United Nations called upon the invading troops to cease hostilities and to withdraw to the thirty-eighth parallel. This they have not done, but on the contrary have pressed the attack. The Security Council called upon all members of the United Nations to render every assistance to the United Nations in the Execution of this resolution. In these circumstances I have ordered United States air and sea forces to give the Korean Government troops cover and support.

The attack upon Korea makes it plain beyond all doubt that Communism has passed beyond the use of subversion to conquer independent nations and will now use armed invasion and war.

SOURCE: President Harry S Truman, statement of June 27, 1950

Kosygin, Alexei N. (1904–1980)   Soviet premier after the ouster of NIKITA S. KHRUSHCHEV in 1964. He was gradually eclipsed by LEONID BREZHNEV.

Krasnoyarsk   The site of a large radar installation built by the Soviet Union that was regarded by the Ronald Reagan Administration as a violation of the ABM TREATY, which limits radars to the periphery of the country. There were also allegations that the radar had a capacity for battle management. Even though the Krasnoyarsk radar was used by the Reagan Administration to justify its own strategic defense initiative (SDI) program, it was never made operational. Indeed, the Soviet Union eventually accepted the U.S. charge that it was a violation and agreed to dismantle it.

Kreisky, Bruno (1911–1990)   The chancellor of Austria from 1970 to 1983. A Social Democrat, he fled the Nazi occupation of Austria in 1938, going to Sweden as a journalist, and returned in 1946 as a foreign policy counselor. He was instrumental in negotiating the Austrian State Treaty in 1955, which formulated his nation's policy of permanent neutrality. Kreisky was Austria's foreign minister from 1959 to 1966 and chairman of the Socialist Party (1967–1970) before being elected chancellor. Domestically his government supported the effective social partnership program with balanced labor-management relationships. Internationally it belonged to the European Free Trade Association (EFTA). Mainly through the Socialist International, Kreisky initially supported the Sandinista revolution in Nicaragua and led two missions to the Middle East seeking to bring peace between Israel and the Palestinians. His peace efforts failed, in part because they were premised on Western diplomatic recognition of the Palestine Liberation Organization.

Kremlin, the   **1.** The historic seat of power in Russia.   **2.** The Moscow citadel in which are located the main offices of the Russian government.   **3.** A Cold War–era cognomen for the Soviet Union, Soviet government, or Soviet Communist Party.

Kremlinology   The study of public policy making in the former Soviet Union through inferences and guesses about who was doing what to whom among the Soviet leadership.

Krenz, Egon (1937–   )   The East German politician who was briefly the leader of the German Democratic Republic (East Germany), succeeding ERICH HONECKER as the first general secretary of the Socialist Unity Party of Germany (SED) and then as chairman of the State Council in 1989. However, his term as head of state was short-lived because he could not establish the people's trust in his new position. He is currently being investigated for an act of election fraud that occurred in 1989.

Kristallnacht   "The Night of Broken Glass," November 9, 1938. Many consider this to be the night when the HOLOCAUST began. On that night mobs in Germany and Austria, inspired and led by

		KOREAN WAR: A Chronology
1950	June 25	North Korea invades South Korea.
	June 26	U.S. President Harry S Truman authorizes U.S. air and naval forces to assist South Koreans.
	June 27	United Nations Security Council calls for cease-fire; asks member states to assist South Koreans.
	June 30	President Truman commits U.S. ground troops to South Korea.
	July 8	General Douglas MacArthur placed in command of all UN forces in Korea.
	August 6	North Korean offensive stopped near Pusan.
	September 15	Amphibious assault at Inchon allows UN forces to retake Seoul and move toward thirty-eighth parallel, the border between North and South Korea.
	October 7	UN forces invade North Korea.
	October 20	UN forces capture North Korean capital of Pyongyang and advance toward Yalu River, the border with China.
	November 1	Chinese troops ("volunteers") cross Yalu into North Korea and start pushing back UN and South Korean forces.
	December	General MacArthur announces that the United States should attack China with nuclear weapons.
1951	January 4	Chinese troops capture Seoul.
	March 14	UN forces retake Seoul.
	April 11	General MacArthur relieved of command by President Truman; General Matthew Ridgway made new commander.
	October	Peace talks begin in Panmunjon.
1952	April 28	General Mark Clark succeeds Ridgway as UN commander.
	November 4	General Dwight D. Eisenhower elected president of the United States after pledging "I will go to Korea."
	December 5	President Eisenhower visits Korea.
1953	July 27	Armistice signed at Panmunjon; prewar border, the thirty-eighth parallel, reestablished.

NAZI authorities and troops, attacked Jews and Jewish homes and places of business. Stores were looted, windows were broken; more than 20,000 Jews were arrested; and many were murdered as authorities stood by. Synagogues were sacked and burned to the ground as fire departments watched. The Nazis then confiscated insurance money and did not allow Jewish business owners to obtain any compensation for their losses.

Kronstadt   A Russian naval base on Kotlin Island in the Baltic Sea that protects the waterway entrance to St. Petersburg. The sailors stationed there played an important role in early Soviet history. Mutinies in 1905 and 1906 in favor of greater liberties were repressed by the Russian government. During July 1917 the sailors demanded that the Soviets seize power. The BOLSHEVIKS used the highly radicalized Kronstadters in many important capacities during the actual seizure of power in October's RUSSIAN REVOLUTION OF 1917. The cruiser *Aurora*, which aimed its guns at the Winter Palace of the czar, has since become a symbol of the coup. The sailors subsequently became loyal supporters of the Bolshevik regime and served on many fronts during the Russian

Civil War. With the onerous policies connected with WAR COMMUNISM, the peasant revolts due to forced requisitions, and labor disturbances, the Kronstadt sailors became disenchanted with a Bolshevik regime that was increasingly terroristic, monopolistic, and authoritarian. In February 1921 they demanded a Soviet democracy of left-wing groups, the end of one-party rule, and greater civil and personal liberties. The Bolsheviks regarded these demands as a threat and branded the sailors counterrevolutionaries. Refusing to surrender to the Bolsheviks, they were attacked by Red Army forces and their mutiny was ruthlessly suppressed by March 18. The Bolsheviks feared that the Kronstadters could possibly represent the aspirations of the proletariat and that this mutiny would initiate the beginning of another revolution that would engulf their fledgling government. To counter such tendencies V.I. Lenin soon instituted his NEW ECONOMIC POLICY.

Kropotkin, Peter (1842–1921)   The Russian aristocrat and theoretician who was the doyen of the international ANARCHISM movement prior to World War I. After decades of exile he returned to Russia in 1917 and became a vociferous opponent of the BOLSHEVIKS. But he was ignored by many anarchists who opted to aid the new regime. Many consider Kropotkin to be the chief theoretician of anarchist ideology. He coined the phrase communist-anarchism, believing that the needs of the individual and the collectivity should be equally balanced. He believed that humans are essentially perfectable and are characterized by mutually cooperative instincts rather than by the Darwinian concept of struggle. As an anarchist, he believed that the state was evil and that a decentralization of society, entailing a loose federation of communes, would be the basis of a future world.

Kubitscheck, Juscelino (1902–1976)   The president of Brazil (1956–1961) who proposed a joint program for hemispheric development in 1958 following U.S. Vice President Richard M. Nixon's tour of Latin America, which met with hostile demonstrations. In 1961 U.S. President John F. Kennedy proposed his ALLIANCE FOR PROGRESS along the lines of the Kubitscheck proposal.

Kulaks   *See* STALIN, JOSEPH.

Kuomintang (KMT)   Also known as the Nationalist Party, a political party that ruled all or part of mainland China between 1928 and 1949 and subsequently ruled Taiwan (the REPUBLIC OF CHINA) under CHIANG KAI-SHEK and his successors. Founded by SUN YAT-SEN in 1912 and later controlled by Chiang, the KMT became the ruling party in China, having limited the autonomy of the regional warlords. The party's program rested on Sun Yat-sen's three principles of the people: nationalism, democracy, and people's livelihood. However, preoccupied with fighting the Japanese externally and the Communists internally, Chiang's KMT failed to carry out the party's program. Following the victory of the Chinese Communists on the mainland in 1949, the KMT and its followers moved to the island of Taiwan, where the Republic of China has since existed and prospered.

Kurdish nationalism   The desire for an independent state on the part of the people who inhabit Kurdistan, an area consisting of mountains and an extensive plateau that covers portions of northeastern Iran, northern Iraq, eastern Turkey, and Armenia. Since the breakup of the OTTOMAN EMPIRE after World War I, the Kurds have been seeking greater autonomy. While their nationalistic ambitions have been repressed in Iran, Turkey, and Armenia, the most brutal oppression has been in Iraq, where reports of mass murder (using poison gas among other techniques) and extensive torture led the United Nations in 1991 to impose a de facto partition of northern Iraq as a safe haven for the approximately 3 million Iraqi Kurds.

Kurdish Worker's Party   *Partiya Karkeren Kurdistan* (PKK), a Turkish terrorist group organized in the 1970s, which seeks to establish a Marxist state in the Kurdish region of southeastern Turkey. Its primary targets have been in southeastern Turkey, but it also has struck against Turkish targets in Western Europe.

Kursk, Battle of   The greatest tank battle of WORLD WAR II. In July 1943 the Germans attempted a massive offensive on the south-central plain of Russia.

They were met by a Soviet counterattack so massive that the Germans not only never again launched a major offensive, but they continued to retreat until they were back in Germany—with the Soviet Red Army at their heels. This battle of 6,000 tanks and several million men marked the beginning of the Soviet Union's domination of Eastern Europe.

Kuwaiti 17   Seventeen pro-Iranian SHI'ITE Islamic fundamentalists convicted of terrorist bombings and imprisoned in jails in Kuwait in 1984. Fellow Shi'ites committed many other terrorist acts, including the abduction of Western hostages, in the hope of obtaining their release. But the Kuwaiti government was steadfast in its refusal to bow to demands for their release. In 1989 two of the 17 were released after serving complete five-year terms. The remaining 15 were thought to have been sent to Iran by Iraq after its conquest of Kuwait in August 1990.

La Belle Disco The West Berlin nightclub frequented by off-duty U.S. soldiers that was bombed in 1986, killing two U.S. soldiers and a Turkish woman, and wounding more than 200 others. The Reagan Administration, asserting that Libya was involved in the attack, launched a retaliatory air strike against the Libyan cities of Tripoli and Benghazi on April 15, 1986. *See also* MUAMMAR AL-QADDAFI.

Lafontaine, Henri (1854–1943) The Belgian legislator and professor of international law who won the 1913 Nobel Peace Prize for his leadership in the European peace movement.

Lagos, Treaty of *See* ECONOMIC COMMUNITY OF WEST AFRICAN STATES.

Lagos Plan of Action The goals that came out of a 1980 meeting of the ORGANIZATION OF AFRICAN UNITY in Lagos, Nigeria, that all African states should be self-sufficient in food and self-sustaining in economic growth by the year 2000.

laissez-faire 1. French for "allow to do"; a hands-off style of governance that emphasizes economic freedom so that the capitalist "invisible hand" can work its will. The concept is most associated with Scottish economist Adam Smith (1723–1790) and his book, *The Wealth of Nations* (1776). 2. An executive style of decision making that can mean either that the leader is above the battle or remote from the details, allowing staff members and advisors to make many decisions.

laissez-passer 1. French for "allow to pass"; a permit, in lieu of a passport, that allows someone to travel in a particular area. 2. A document that allows someone, usually a diplomatic agent, to pass through a given state's customs without the normally required baggage inspection.

Lake Success The Long Island, New York, city that in 1946 and 1947 was the temporary headquarters of the United Nations.

landlocked and geographically disadvantaged states (LLGDS) A phrase used to describe a bloc of developing countries that allied themselves to improve their bargaining position at the various sessions of the Third United Nations Conference on the LAW OF THE SEA (UNCLOS). The LLGDS, first organized at Caracas, Venezuela, in 1974, had enough power by the time of the New York UNCLOS sessions in 1976 to insist that subsequent bargaining texts include some guarantees of free transit to and from the seas for LLGDS and also provisions for an equitable share for them of the living and nonliving resources of the seas.

Lange, Christian L. (1869–1938) The Norwegian historian who was awarded the 1921 Nobel Peace Prize (with KARL BRANTING) for his work as secretary-general of the INTERPARLIAMENTARY UNION (1909–1933) and for his advocacy of disarmament as Norway's representative to the LEAGUE OF NATIONS.

Lansing, Robert (1864–1928) The U.S. Secretary of State from 1915 to 1920. In 1916 he negotiated the purchase of the Danish West Indies (now the U.S. Virgin Islands). During World War I he worked largely in the shadow of President Woodrow Wilson; but after the war he publicly broke with the president at the 1919 Paris Peace Conference over the issue of combining a peace treaty with the Covenant of the League of Nations. In 1920 he was asked to resign.

Lansing-Ishii Agreement The 1917 agreement between U.S. Secretary of State Robert Lansing and Japanese Ambassador to the United States Kikujiro Ishii (1866–1945), which affirmed China's territorial integrity and the OPEN DOOR principle while recognizing Japan's "special interests" in China but not in Manchuria. It was abrogated by an exchange of notes in 1923. This was an executive agreement, not sent for legislative ratification, that allowed the United States and Japan to cooperate in the war against Germany but only postponed tensions between the two countries in the Pacific.

Laos Accords Agreements reached in 1962 after a year of diplomatic wrangling at Geneva, Switzerland, over what U.S. President Dwight D. Eisenhower had called "the Laos mess" (more formally known as the LAOTIAN CIVIL WAR). While the agreement supposedly guaranteed the neutrality of Laos by forbidding it from joining alliances, providing bases to others, or accepting military aid, both the United States and North Vietnam resumed armed shipments to the various sides in violation of the neutralization agreement. At the same time, the accords helped the United States to avoid direct intervention.

Laotian Civil War The Communist-led insurrection in Laos that began in 1950 to gain independence from the French. The North Vietnamese supported Communist guerrillas, known as the PATHET LAO, in their resistance to the Laotian monarchy. While a coalition government, including Communists, was established in the wake of the 1962 LAOS ACCORDS, fighting continued and expanded as the neighboring VIETNAM WAR intensified. Following the North Vietnamese victory over South Vietnam in 1975, there was a parallel total Communist takeover of Laos.

Laotian incursion A 1971 military invasion of Laos by South Vietnamese troops with U.S. air and logistical support. Its objective was to cut off North Vietnamese supplies coming into the south from the Laotian portion of the HO CHI MINH TRAIL. The South Vietnamese faced greater opposition from the Communists than they had anticipated and were forced to withdraw within five weeks, defeated.

Larf *See* FARL.

Lasswell, Harold D. (1902–1978) A highly influential and prolific U.S. social scientist who made major contributions to the fields of communications, psychology (he pioneered the application of Freudian theory to politics), political science, sociology, and law. His most lasting legacy is probably his pioneering work in developing the concept and methodology of the policy sciences (a problem-solving orientation that encompasses policy formulation and execution). Lasswell's major works include *Propaganda Technique in World War I* (1927); *Psychopathology and Politics* (1930); *Politics: Who Gets What, When, How* (1936); *Power and Society,* with Abraham Kaplan (1950); *The Policy Sciences,* ed. with David Lerner (1951); *Preview of Policy Sciences* (1971).

Lateran Treaty The 1929 agreements between Benito Mussolini's Italy and Pope Pius XI's Holy See that settled issues that had set Church against state in Italy for nearly 60 years. The Lateran Treaty and accompanying Concordat established VATICAN CITY, the few acres around St. Peter's Basilica, as an independent state, made Catholicism the state religion of Italy, and promised to make Italian marriage law conform with Catholic teachings. A 1984 revision ended Catholicism as Italy's formal state religion.

Latin American Free Trade Association The regional economic alliance created by the 1960 Treaty of Montevideo. After modest success at reducing tariffs, it was replaced by the Latin American Integration Association in 1980 created by a second Treaty of Montevideo. The ultimate goal of the association is a free trade region. Members include Argentina, Bolivia, Brazil, Chile, Colombia, Ecuador, Mexico, Paraguay, Peru, Uruguay, and Venezuela. *See also* ANDEAN GROUP.

Latvia   *See* BALTIC NATIONS.

launch on warning   A theoretical strategic policy of beginning a nuclear retaliatory attack when it is believed that an enemy has launched a first-strike attack but before its missiles have exploded on their targets. However, it is assumed that no country would ever fire a retaliatory strike before it had actually received at least one nuclear detonation on its soil. It is not believed that launch on warning could ever be a safe policy because no nuclear power would risk firing a nuclear retaliatory strike before certain confirmation that it had been attacked. On the other hand, an adversary could never be sure that this would not take place and is unlikely to gamble on the possibility that it will not—something that suggests that DETERRENCE may be more robust than is sometimes argued.

launch under attack   A policy of waiting until enemy nuclear missiles detonate on one's territory before retaliating. A launch under attack policy is creditable only if a country has a secure SECOND-STRIKE CAPABILITY. Concepts such as LAUNCH ON WARNING and launch under attack refer only to nuclear missiles, which, because they cannot be recalled, cannot be committed without absolute certainty.

Laval, Pierre (1883–1945)   The premier of France (1931; 1935–1936) who, during WORLD WAR II, collaborated with the occupying Germans by helping to create and lead the VICHY government. Because he actively supported the Nazis, drafted French labor for Germany, and authorized a regime of terror, he was tried after the war, convicted, and executed for treason.

La Violencia   *See* VIOLENCIA, LA.

Law, Andrew Bonar (1858–1923)   The Canadian-born leader of Great Britain's Conservative Party from 1911 until ill health forced his resignation in 1921. He was chancellor of the Exchequer (1915–1918) in the World War I Liberal-led coalition government of DAVID LLOYD GEORGE. When he became party leader again in 1922 he took his party out of the coalition and became prime minister (1922–1923). He resigned after seven months, and was succeeded by STANLEY BALDWIN.

Law of Nations   A now-archaic term for INTERNATIONAL LAW. It was most associated with EMERICH DE VATTEL.

law of the sea   A general term covering the body of INTERNATIONAL LAW that has developed over the centuries and attempts to codify, to the extent possible, use of ocean waters for shipping and for other purposes. It covers such topics as the "rules of the road" for ships passing at sea, passage through international straits, and the sovereignty a nation has over the portion of the sea adjoining it. For centuries this sovereignty was considered to extend three miles from the coastline. In the period since World War II, more and more interest has focused on that aspect of the law of the sea governing resources of the sea and the seabed such as fishing rights and mining of minerals on the seabed.

The First United Nations Conference on the Law of the Sea, held at Geneva, Switzerland, in 1958, adopted four conventions—on the high seas, on the territorial sea and the contiguous zone, on the continental shelf, and on fishing and conservation of the living resources of the high seas. The second conference, held two years later, made an unsuccessful effort to reach agreement on certain aspects of the territorial sea and fishing zones. In 1969 the UN General Assembly adopted a declaration which stated that "the sea-bed and ocean floor, and the subsoil thereof, beyond the limits of national jurisdiction . . . as well as the resources of the area are the common heritage of mankind." The Convention on the Law of the Sea, a product of nine years of negotiation during the Third UN Conference on the Law of the Sea, was signed in Montego Bay, Jamaica, on December 10, 1982. The law represents a major overhaul of one branch of the international law. It established a seabed authority, headquartered in Kingston, Jamaica, that is responsible for working out acceptable procedures for exploiting the mineral resources of the seabed and ocean floor while waiting for two-thirds of the member nations to ratify the convention necessary for the law to enter into force. But the major industrial nations are not likely to ratify it because of disagreements with provisions regarding mining.

law of war   That part of INTERNATIONAL LAW that regulates the conduct of armed hostilities. It is often termed the law of armed conflict. Although wars between states are a consequence of international ANARCHY, they are not devoid of rules or laws, many of which can be traced back to medieval times. Laws of war developed considerably during the eighteenth and nineteenth centuries. With the major exception of the Napoleonic Wars, conflicts of this time were generally limited wars fought for specific purposes, not designed to overthrow other governments or destroy their states. In the context of the times laws meant to prevent "unnecessary suffering" (meaning suffering that would not affect the war's outcome) seemed eminently sensible. Thus laws of war developed both to protect civilians or noncombatants and to deal with soldiers who were wounded or captured. From the latter half of the nineteenth century onward, the laws of war were codified in treaties and conventions such as the Geneva Conventions of 1864, 1906, 1909, 1929, and 1949; and the Hague Conventions of 1899, 1907, and 1923. Further accords, such as the Geneva Protocol of 1925, prohibited the use of gas and bacteriological warfare. But as the laws of war were being codified, respect for them diminished. This occurred in part because of the development of TOTAL WAR, as it became increasingly difficult to separate combatants from noncombatants. Such separation is particularly difficult when conflicts are ideologically based, as during civil wars or revolutions, and in situations where the survival of the nation or cause is considered to be at stake. *See also* RULES OF ENGAGEMENT.

STALIN FINDS A LOOPHOLE IN THE LAW OF WAR

[During a World War II meeting between Joseph Stalin and Winston Churchill] when [Stalin] made one of his typical remarks, "I know sixty thousand German officers I'm going to shoot," Churchill became so agitated he paced the floor for several minutes, preaching about Christianity and civilization. It was against the laws of civilized warfare, he insisted, to shoot sixty thousand officers. Stalin waited patiently until he finished, then said again through his interpreter, "I know sixty thousand German officers I'm going to shoot when the war is over."

SOURCE: General Henry H. Arnold, *Global Mission* (1949).

Lawrence, Thomas Edward (1881–1935)   The World War I British military officer, better known as "Lawrence of Arabia," who was assigned to aid the ARAB REVOLT (1916–1918) against the OTTOMAN EMPIRE. The British government had promised to support independence for most Arab provinces in exchange for their rebellion against Turkish rule in an effort to pin down Turkish forces during the war and keep the Red Sea open to Allied shipping. Lawrence was a brilliant improviser of desert guerrilla tactics. He compared his unusual approach to naval warfare. He and his Arab raiders would "cruise" just out of sight of Turkish installations, then raid and retreat into such a vast expanse of desert that the Turks dared not follow. These attacks reduced the Ottoman Empire's ability to meet obligations made to its German ally. In his postwar memoir, Lawrence complained that the British Army "staff knew so much more of war than I did that they refused to learn from me of the strange conditions in which Arab irregulars had to act; and I could not be bothered to set up a kindergarten of the imagination for their benefit" (*Seven Pillars of Wisdom,* 1926). After the war Lawrence futilely worked for Arab self-determination, then sought to withdraw completely from public life by serving as an enlisted man, first in the Tank Corps, later in the Royal Air Force (1923–1935).

THE DEATH OF LAWRENCE

The manner of his death was such that almost inevitably a series of legends have grown up about it. There are people who believe to this day that Lawrence was not killed, that the accident was faked so as to allow him to undertake, incognito, important work in the Middle East during World War II. . . . Others believe that Lawrence committed suicide because life no longer held any appeal for him. . . . Other people are certain that Lawrence was killed by agents of a foreign power; some say French, some say German, some Arab. A more fanciful version is that he was killed by British agents because his next book would have exposed government secrets. A legend that has lingered longer than most is that Lawrence was a victim of his love of speed and of a death-wish. . . .

The facts are very different. They establish that Lawrence died after a road accident while trying to avoid a boy on a bike.

SOURCE: Phillip Knightley and Colin Simpson, *The Secret Lives of Lawrence of Arabia* (1969).

LDC **1.** Less-developed country. No single list of less-developed countries is accepted by all nations and international organizations, but the term generally applies to all states that are not members of the ORGANIZATION FOR ECONOMIC COOPERATION AND DEVELOPMENT (OECD). **2.** Sometimes LEAST-DEVELOPED COUNTRIES; the poorest of the less-developed countries—also known as the FOURTH WORLD.

League of Nations The international world order organization that preceded the UNITED NATIONS. Created by the Treaty of Versailles of 1919, it formally came into effect in 1920. While its last meeting was in 1939, it was not officially dissolved until 1946. U.S. President Woodrow Wilson first called for the League in an address to Congress (this was the last of his FOURTEEN POINTS), January 8, 1918: "A general association of nations must be formed under specific covenants for the purpose of affording mutual guarantees of political independence and territorial integrity to great and small states alike." Its covenant bound members to "respect and preserve" each member state's territorial integrity. Wilson viewed the League as an effective instrument for peace and justice. Sovereign member states promised to submit disagreements to arbitration or an international court, or to the League Council. Economic and even military sanctions were to be taken against those that did not abide by agreements. Article 16 of the League Covenant provided for what has become known as COLLECTIVE SECURITY: "Should any Member of the League resort to war . . . it shall ipso facto be deemed to have committed an act of war against all other Members of the League, which hereby undertake immediately to subject it to the severance of all trade or financial relations . . . and the prevention of all financial, commercial or personal intercourse between the nationals of the Covenant-breaking State and the nationals of any other State, whether a Member of the League or not." But when Germany, Italy, and Japan committed such acts of war in the 1930s, the League as a collectivity was unable to make a meaningful response—and therefore became increasingly irrelevant. Despite Wilson's best efforts, the United States Senate refused to join the League as Americans called for a return to diplomatic ISOLATIONISM after World War I. Nevertheless, the experience of the League was very important in providing at least some lessons for the United Nations. If it was an experiment that failed, it was still an important step forward in the effort to mitigate some of the consequences of international anarchy. *See also* MANDATES SYSTEM.

LEAGUE OF NATIONS: A Chronology

1918	U.S. President Woodrow Wilson in his FOURTEEN POINTS suggests that "a general association of nations must be formed under specific covenants for the purpose of affording mutual guarantees of political independence and territorial integrity to great and small states alike."
1919	At PARIS PEACE CONFERENCE 27 states agree to create a League of Nations. Covenant establishing the League is incorporated into Treaty of Versailles. League creates MANDATES SYSTEM.
1920	U.S. Senate refuses to allow U.S. participation in League.
1926	Germany joins League.
1931	China appeals to League because of Japanese aggression in Manchuria.
1932	LYTTON COMMISSION AND REPORT condemns Japanese aggression.
1933	Japan leaves League.
1934	Soviet Union joins League.
1935	Abyssinia appeals to League because of Italian aggression. League supervises SAAR plebiscite. League condemns Italian aggression in Abyssinia. Germany leaves League.
1937	League condemns Japanese aggression in China. Italy leaves League.
1939	Spain leaves League. Soviet Union expelled from League for invasion of Finland. League unable to prevent World War II.
1945	UNITED NATIONS created as successor organization to League.
1946	League formally ends.

leak   1. The disclosure of confidential or secret information by an individual in a government who wants to advance the public interest, embarrass a bureaucratic rival, or help a reporter disclose incompetence or skulduggery to the public. All governments use leaks as a means of influencing public policy. This is especially true at international conferences, when delegations attempt to influence domestic public opinion through the news media. 2. The inadvertent disclosure of secret information.

least-developed countries (LLDC)   Those states identified by the United Nations General Assembly in 1971 as without significant economic growth, with very low per capita incomes, and with low literacy rates. These countries are also known as the FOURTH WORLD. Although it is occasionally abbreviated to "LDC," usually an extra "L" is added to the acronym to differentiate it from that of the term "less-developed country," LDC.

Lebanese Civil War   The communal conflict that exploded into war in 1975 after a succession of religiously motivated assassinations by both Muslim and Christian factions in Lebanon. Prior to 1975, difficulties had arisen over the large number of Palestinian refugees in Lebanon and the presence of Palestinian fedayeen (commandos). Frequent clashes involving Israeli forces and the fedayeen endangered civilians in south Lebanon and unsettled the country. Coupled with the Palestinian problem, Muslim and Christian differences within the native population grew more intense, in large part because the Christian minority in control of the government was dominating an increasingly larger Muslim majority. The Muslims were dissatisfied with what they considered to be an inequitable distribution of political power and social benefits. In April 1975 a busload of Palestinians was ambushed by gunmen in the Christian sector of Beirut, an incident widely regarded as the spark that touched off the civil strife. Palestinian forces joined the predominantly leftist-Muslim side as the fighting persisted. In October of 1976 Arab summits in Riyadh, Saudi Arabia, and Cairo, Egypt, set forth a plan to end the war. The resulting Arab Deterrent Force, composed largely of Syrian troops, moved in at the Lebanese government's invitation to separate the combatants, and most fighting ended soon thereafter. But in mid-1978 clashes between the ADF and the Christian militias began again. A string of incidents—an assassination attempt against the Israeli ambassador in London, Israeli retaliatory air strikes against Palestinian positions in Lebanon, and responding Palestine Liberation Organization rocket attacks into northern Israel—led to the 1982 Israeli ground attack in Lebanon. Israeli forces encircled West Beirut by mid-June, beginning a two and one-half–month siege of Palestinian and Syrian forces in the city. U.S. diplomatic efforts led to an agreement for the evacuation of Syrian troops and PLO fighters from Beirut. The agreement also provided for the deployment of a three-nation Multinational Force during the period of the evacuation, and by late August U.S., French, and Italian units had arrived in Beirut. Following the conclusion of the evacuation, these units departed. Subsequently, Israeli troops entered West Beirut and Lebanese Christian militiamen massacred hundreds of Palestinian civilians in the SABRA AND SHATILA refugee camps in West Beirut.

Since then Lebanon has had only a nominal national government. The warring factions each have their enclaves and their militias are variously funded by Syria, Iran, Iraq, the PLO, and Israel, among others. At various times foreign forces were invited by the nominal central government to help restore order. During 1983 and 1984 British, French, Italian, and U.S. troops came and went to no avail. Lebanon descended into a state of medieval ANARCHY, where the only law was the local warlord and his militia. The civil war ended in late 1990 when Syria, because the world's attention was focused on the buildup to the PERSIAN GULF WAR, was able simply to send in sufficient troops to take over all but an Israeli-occupied security zone in the south. Since then Lebanon, with its Christian minority subdued or in exile and its Muslim majority ostensibly in control of the government, has been a political satellite of Syria.

Lebanese Insurrection   The 1958 Communist attempt to destabilize and take over the government of President Camille Chamoun (1900–1987) of Lebanon. In July 1958 Chamoun appealed to the United States for help. Citing the EISENHOWER DOCTRINE, the United States sent 15,000 marines. While they never engaged in combat and had no casualties, the marines so stabilized the regime that they were all withdrawn in October 1958.

Lebanonization A process whereby a state disintegrates as a result of feuds among various factions and a lack of governmental legitimacy. This, in essence, is what happened during the LEBANESE CIVIL WAR. Such conditions may encourage military intervention by external powers either to take advantage of the situation or in an effort to restore order.

Lebensraum German for "living space." This was the basis for Germany's expansionist policies toward Eastern Europe and western Russia during the first half of the twentieth century. Germany sought the fertile agricultural lands and mineral resources there for its own use. During World War II the Germans sought to exterminate whole populations of Jews and Slavs in Eastern Europe to create more Lebensraum for themselves. *Compare to* DRANG NACH OSTEN.

Lee Kuan Yew (1923–   ) The leader of Singapore since 1959, when it ceased being a British colony, until 1990 when he gave up formal power. Under Lee's often authoritarian leadership Singapore became a model of economic development.

legalistic-moralistic approach A term that was used by U.S. diplomat and Cold War theorist George Kennan in *American Diplomacy 1900–1950* (1951) to describe a central element in the U.S. approach to foreign policy. According to Kennan, the United States does not think in hard-headed terms about foreign policy; instead it adopts an approach that places excessive faith in both morality and in legalistic approaches to international problems. This he found very disturbing, since it leads the United States to move from periods of isolation in world affairs to indiscriminate global involvement to deal with enemies that it sees as the incarnation of evil.

legate 1. A diplomatic agent during the Middle Ages. 2. A diplomatic representative of the pope.

legation 1. A diplomatic agent or envoy (as well as his or her staff) in a second-class diplomatic establishment, one whose status is less than that of an EMBASSY. 2. The physical offices of such an establishment.

legation, right of The authority of a state to send and receive diplomatic agents. *Active legation* involves the sending of diplomats; *passive legation* involves receiving them.

legitimacy 1. A descriptive aspect of a social institution, a government or a family for example, that has both a legal and a perceived right to make binding decisions for its members. Only a public can grant legitimacy to an institution. Legitimacy is both a specific legal concept, meaning that something is lawful, and at the same time an amorphous psychosociological concept referring to an important element in the social glue that holds institutions together. The German sociologist Max Weber (1864–1920) is the foremost analyst of the legitimacy of governing structures. He asserted that there were three pure types of legitimate authority: charismatic (in which the personal qualities of a leader command obedience); traditional (in which custom and culture yield acquiescence); and legal (in which people obey laws enacted by what they perceive to be appropriate authorities). 2. The quality of an administration that has come to power through free elections or established constitutional procedures. Thus a government imposed by military force may lack legitimacy. As U.S. Ambassador to the United Nations Jeane J. Kirkpatrick has said: "A government is not legitimate merely because it exists" (*Time,* June 17, 1985). *Compare to* POLICE STATE.

Lehi *See* STERN GANG.

Lend-Lease Act of 1941 The U.S. law that empowered President Franklin D. Roosevelt to lend and lease military equipment, materials, farm commodities, machinery, and other goods for defense purposes to countries whose defense was deemed vital to U.S. security. Under the broad guidelines of the Lend-Lease Act, the United States was able to aid Great Britain prior to America's official entry into World War II in December 1941.

Lenin, Vladimir Ilyich (1870–1924)

V. I. Lenin (Library of Congress)

Lenin, Vladimir Ilyich (1870–1924)   Leader of the Communist phase of the RUSSIAN REVOLUTION OF 1917 and head of the BOLSHEVIK government there until his death in 1924. Born into a middle-class family, young Lenin was influenced by an elder brother, who was hanged in 1887 for revolutionary activity. For his involvement with the St. Petersburg Union of Struggle for the Emancipation of the Working Class, Lenin was arrested in 1895 and exiled to Siberia in 1897. After serving his term, Lenin emigrated to Switzerland in 1900 and founded the newspaper *Iskra* (*Spark*) to hammer out a common socialist ideology among disparate Russian Marxist groups. His ideas, expressed in *What Is to Be Done?* (1902), condemned accommodations with existing governments and the formation of mass parties. Lenin wanted the creation of a professional group of clandestine revolutionaries acting in the name of the proletariat. This was a new addition to the ideology of MARXISM. In 1903 his intransigence split Russia's Social Democrats between the moderate Mensheviks and his group, the Bolsheviks. Despite setbacks, Lenin devoted all his energies toward the formation of an elite party that he would lead. He returned to Russia during the unsuccessful revolution of 1905 but was back in exile the following year. During World War I Lenin maintained an internationalist stance, condemning both sides and calling on workers everywhere to rise up against their governments. He returned to Russia in October 1917 after the overthrow of Czar Nicholas II thanks to the largess of the German government. It allowed Lenin to travel from Switzerland to Russia in a sealed train in the hope that he would help take Russia out of the war. The Germans were not disappointed. According to Winston Churchill (speaking in the House of Commons, November 5, 1919): "Lenin was sent into Russia by the Germans in the same way that you might send a phial containing a culture of typhoid or of cholera to be poured into the water supply of a great city, and it worked with amazing accuracy."

Lenin, upon his arrival, condemned the new Provisional Government, called for immediate peace, and demanded land for the peasants and "All Power to the Soviets." Through his indomitable will, Lenin quickly forced the Bolsheviks, some of whom accepted the liberal provisional government, to his way of thinking, which culminated in their coup on November 7. American journalist John Reed reported that after the coup succeeded, Lenin was "gripping the edge of the reading stand, letting his little winking eyes travel over the crowd as he stood there waiting, apparently oblivious to the long-rolling ovation, which lasted several minutes. When it finished he said simply, 'We shall now proceed to construct the Socialist order!' " (*Ten Days That Shook the World*, 1926). Lenin became the first chairman of the Soviet of People's Commissars. He then consolidated the power of the Bolsheviks, formed the Soviet state, ended Russia's involvement in World War I, defeated all opposition parties during the RUSSIAN CIVIL WAR, and created the Third INTERNATIONAL. He attained these goals through a combination of peace with Germany (in the BREST-LITOVSK TREATY), stringent policies during the civil war (WAR COMMUNISM) and their subsequent relaxation (the NEW ECONOMIC POLICY), astute interparty maneuvering and control, political flexibility, PROPAGANDA, the suppression of democracy, and sheer ruthlessness. After suffering three strokes, Lenin died in January of 1924. In death he became the preeminent cultural icon of Soviet communism. His body was preserved and kept on public view in a tomb that became a place of pilgrimage for devout followers. With the demise of the Soviet Union in 1991, Lenin continued to help the Russian economy—as an attraction for foreign tourists.

Leninism   The theoretical interpretations and practical applications of MARXISM as defined by V. I. LENIN. The Russian revolutionary leader and first leader of the Soviet state attempted to adjust the doctrine of communism to include the political and economic changes of the early twentieth century. His contributions were so significant to the basic ideology of Soviet communism that the ideology became known as Marxism-Leninism. Its main ideological contributions to communism are (1) the theory that the high and final stage of monopoly capitalism, that of overseas colonialism and imperialism, results from the actions of trusts and cartels as the capitalist states seek investment outlets for surplus capital, markets for surplus production, and sources of cheap resources; (2) the belief that, as a result of imperial competition for investment and market opportunities, wars among capitalist states were inevitable; (3) the theory of "combined development," which holds that underdeveloped, colonial societies that include a mixture of slaveholding, feudalism, and capitalism may be susceptible to a Communist-inspired revolution immediately rather than, as Marx predicted, after capitalism had matured; (4) the theory that the Communist Party, guided by a small dedicated elite, can provide leadership for revolution and in implementing Marx's prescribed "dictatorship of the proletariat" during a period of SOCIALISM; and (5) the method for making decisions in the party that permits the presentation of individual views during the process but requires full support of all decisions after they have been made by the leadership. Lenin therefore not only added to the theory of Marxism, he challenged it on many points.

Letelier, Orlando (1932–1976)   Former foreign minister of Chile (1970–1973) under SALVADOR ALLENDE who was assassinated by a car bomb in 1976 on Embassy Row in Washington, D.C. In 1980 a U.S. Federal District Court concluded that the two assassins (both sentenced to prison in the United States) were agents of the right-wing regime of Chilean General AUGUSTO PINOCHET. In October 1988 the Reagan Administration demanded that the Chilean government pay $12 million in compensation for the victims' families and for costs incurred in the criminal investigation. In 1991 the Chilean Supreme Court upheld indictments against the military officers who ordered the assassination. In 1992 a five-member panel of arbitrators, meeting under the auspices of the Organization of American States, ordered Chile to pay $2.6 million to families of Letelier and the U.S. citizen who was also killed in the bombing.

Letitia conflict   Dispute between Colombia and Peru in which the LEAGUE OF NATIONS successfully intervened to end hostilities. The problem began in 1932 when Peru's troops under orders from President Luis Sanchez Cerro (1889–1934) seized Letitia, a territory that had been ceded to Colombia in

1922. While the League used its GOOD OFFICES to resolve the dispute, resolution was greatly helped by the 1934 death of President Sanchez Cerro. His successor, Oscar Benavides (1876–1945), quickly returned the territory to Colombia via a 1935 treaty.

lettres de cabinet French meaning "letters of the cabinet," formal communications, such as the CREDENTIALS of diplomats, from one foreign ministry to another.

lettres de chancellerie French meaning "letters of the chancellor's office," formal communications from an embassy to another embassy or government.

lettres de créance French meaning "letters of credence," the formal documents that newly appointed ambassadors present to the head of state of the foreign state to which they are accredited; the letters attest to the legitimacy of the ambassadors' mission.

level of analysis One of the classic issues in the study and analysis of international politics: the focusing of analysis on individual decision makers, on the state, or on the international system as a whole. The level of analysis chosen can lead to very different kinds of questions and answers about foreign policy behavior and other international phenomena. Some of the more interesting questions, however, are about the linkages between the levels, linkages that are still not fully understood.

levy 1. Tax assessment. 2. Military conscription. 3. The mandatory reassignment of enlisted personnel in military occupational specialties.

lex non scripta Latin for "unwritten law"; a reference to CUSTOMARY INTERNATIONAL LAW.

liberal 1. A supporter of political and social reform, increased government control of the economy, more government spending on behalf of the poor, and more laws protecting consumers, the environment, and criminal defendants. 2. In the context of trade policy, relatively free of government controls or restraints. The most liberal trade is FREE TRADE. 3. One who espouses the ideas of LIBERALISM.

liberalism 1. A political doctrine that advocated freedom from interference by the state, toleration by the state in matters of morality and religion, LAISSEZ-FAIRE economic policies, and a belief in natural rights that exist independently of government. Often known as classical liberalism, these concepts can be traced back to the English Magna Charta of 1215. By the nineteenth century liberalism had come to mean limited government with policies favorable to individual liberty and political equality. 2. The use of government to achieve social reform; the advocacy of government programs for the welfare of individuals. The rationale for this twentieth-century usage is that without such welfare state advantages, the masses have little chance to enjoy the traditional freedoms long espoused by the political theorists. So a term that once meant small government and low taxation has come to mean big government and high taxation. 3. In economics, an emphasis on the operation of the market rather than on government intervention and control. 4. A tradition in international affairs that places an emphasis on international institutions and the rule of law rather than on power and the use of force. Liberals of this school generally attempt to apply key elements in domestic politics to international politics, where their applicability is far less certain. One variant of liberalism prevalent in the United States assumes that there is a natural harmony of interests in international politics and that states which disturb it are, by definition, evil. Although liberalism probably represents the strongest challenge to REALISM as the dominant paradigm for understanding international relations, Robert Keohane in "International Liberalism Reconsidered" (in John Dunn, ed., *The Economic Limits to Modern Politics,* 1990) emphasizes its limitations "both as a framework for analysis and as a guide for policy. It is incomplete as an explanation, it can become normatively myopic, and it can backfire as a policy prescription."

liberalization A policy of reducing tariffs and other measures that restrict world trade, either unilaterally or multilaterally. Trade liberalization has been the objective of all GATT trade negotiations.

liberated territory Any area—domestic, neutral, or friendly—that, having been occupied by an enemy, is retaken by friendly forces.

liberation theology A type of Christian theology that proposes that corrupt political and social systems be overthrown, by violent means if necessary, to permit the formation of a political and social order closer to the ideals expressed and implicit in the teachings of Jesus Christ. Liberation theology is most clearly identified with the Roman Catholic Church in Latin America, where activist priests and lay Catholics have found in it a justification for armed revolution against repressive conditions. The Vatican of Pope John Paul II, however, has been very critical of armed insurrection under the banner of Catholic theology.

Liberation Tigers of Tamil Eelam (LTTE) A Sri Lankan TAMIL separatist guerrilla organization created in 1972 in reaction to the repression of government security forces. The Tigers, as the strongest of the Tamil militant organizations, were the only major group to fight the Indian Peacekeeping Forces that the Sri Lankan government requested in 1987. Their goal is an autonomous state in the northern and eastern portions of the island nation of Sri Lanka. The Tamils are a primarily Hindu minority, accounting for about 22 percent of the Sri Lankan population (the rest of which is largely Buddhist). *See also* SRI LANKAN CIVIL WAR.

Liberty The U.S. Navy ship attacked by Israeli fighter planes on June 8, 1967, during the SIX-DAY WAR. The ship, which was gathering electronic intelligence off the Egyptian coast, suffered 34 dead and 171 wounded in an attack that Israel maintained was an accidental case of mistaken identity. The incident almost provoked a superpower clash at sea, as the initial assumption in Washington was that the Soviet Union was responsible for the attack. Instead it provided the first occasion for the serious use of the HOT LINE for clarification and reassurance.

Libya coup The 1969 military coup that deposed King Idris (1890–1983) of Libya and sent him into exile in Egypt. The new regime, headed by a Revolutionary Command Council, abolished the monarchy and subsequently proclaimed the new Libyan Arab Republic. MUAMMAR AL-QADDAFI emerged as leader of the RCC and eventually as de facto chief of state, a position he retains today. An early objective of the new government was the withdrawal of all foreign military installations from Libya. Following negotiations, British military installations at Tobruk and U.S. facilities at Wheelus Air Force Base near

Tripoli were closed in 1970. By 1971 libraries and cultural centers operated by foreign governments were ordered closed, and since then the Libyan government has taken severe measures to restrict citizen contact with non-Arabic, non-Islamic influences. In the late 1970s Libyan embassies were redesignated as "Peoples Bureaus," as Qaddafi sought to portray Libya's foreign policy as an expression of the popular will. The Peoples Bureaus, aided by Libyan religious, political, student, and business institutions overseas, have transformed the traditional bounds of diplomacy, exporting Qaddafi's revolutionary philosophy abroad, taking direct action to control Libyans overseas, and often, it is suspected, serving as bases for TERRORISM.

Liddell Hart, Basil H. (1895–1970) The English military historian and journalist who wrote some of this century's most insightful critiques of strategy and tactics. He began his career as an army officer but was forced out of the military because of wounds received during World War I. Liddell Hart believed that military strategy should be based on the principle that one pursues war to create a future state of peace. He reintroduced the idea (from KARL VON CLAUSEWITZ) that destruction of the enemy's will to fight provides the basis for true victory. A strong advocate of the INDIRECT APPROACH in fighting a war, he maintained that the objective of battle is to create a situation so disadvantageous to the enemy that it will not fight—or if it does fight, it will lose quickly and decisively. His ideas on tank warfare were readily adopted by the German military before World War II and formed the basis for the BLITZKREIG.

THE CAPTAIN WHO TEACHES GENERALS

The walls of his study . . . are adorned with photographs of readers who found something of value in what the controversial Captain had to say. Heads of state are represented by Mussolini, Lloyd George, and John F. Kennedy; the British tank pioneers are there to a man; so, too, are many of the leading generals of the Second World War. But the photograph with the most appropriate inscription comes from the youthful commander of Israeli forces on the southern front against Egypt in 1948. General Yigal Allon wrote simply: "To Basil, the Captain who teaches Generals."

SOURCE: Jay Luvaas, *The Education of an Army* (1964).

Lidice   A village in western Czechoslovakia that the Germans destroyed in 1942 as a reprisal for the assassination of Reinhard Heydrick (1904–1942), the NAZI "protector" of Bohemia and Moravia. By murdering the entire male population of several hundred and deporting all the women and children to concentration camps, the Nazis sought to give a warning to German-occupied Europe and the world. Lidice became an international symbol of the barbarity of the German people under Adolf Hitler during WORLD WAR II.

Lie, Trygve (1896–1968)   The Norwegian statesman who was the first secretary general of the United Nations (1946–1953).

lifeboat ethics   A framework for the discussion of NORTH-SOUTH issues put forth by U.S. policy analyst Garrett Hardin (1915–   ) that holds that "each rich nation can be seen as a lifeboat full of comparatively rich people. In the ocean outside each lifeboat swim the poor of the world, who would like to get in, or at least share some of the wealth" (*Psychology Today*, September 1974).

light at the end of the tunnel   The description of a soon-to-emerge safe exit from a desperate situation that became the standard response of many U.S. officials in the 1960s about when the VIETNAM WAR would be successfully concluded. They were so often and embarrassingly wrong that the phrase is now associated with any stupid or false prediction of military or administrative success. The TET OFFENSIVE revealed definitively that there was no light at the end of this particular tunnel.

Likud   The Israeli political party that was formed in 1973 and came to power under MENACHEM BEGIN in 1977. The party continued in power or in a coalition government until 1992. In 1983 YITZHAK SHAMIR succeeded Begin as leader. In 1992 Likud was voted out of power and YITZHAK RABIN succeeded Shamir as prime minister.

Lima group   A group that came into being in 1985 with the signature of the Declaration of Lima by Argentina, Brazil, Peru, and Uruguay. The group

---

LIGHTS SEEN AT THE END OF THE TUNNEL: VIETNAM, 1953–1969

A year ago none of us could see victory. There wasn't a prayer. Now we can see it clearly—like light at the end of a tunnel.

SOURCE: General Henri Navarre, commander of French troops in Indochina, *Time,* September 28, 1953.

■

We don't see the end of the tunnel, but I must say I don't think it is darker than it was a year ago, and in some ways lighter.

SOURCE: U.S. President John F. Kennedy, press conference, December 12, 1962.

■

I urge you to remember that Americans often grow impatient when they cannot see light at the end of the tunnel.

SOURCE: U.S. President Lyndon B. Johnson, *Time,* June 17, 1966.

■

Their casualties are going up at a rate they cannot sustain. . . . I see light at the end of the tunnel.

SOURCE: Walt W. Rostow, head of the Policy Planning Council of the U.S. Department of State, quoted in *Look,* December 12, 1967.

■

We are running out of time in Vietnam. The light at the end of the tunnel has gone out. The corner around which victory was supposed to appear has turned into an abyss.

SOURCE: U.S. Representative Abner J. Mikva, speech in the House, October 14, 1969.

---

was established to promote support throughout Latin America for the Central American peace efforts of the CONTADORA GROUP, and to participate with them in peace negotiations. At a 1985 joint meeting in Cartagena, Colombia, the two groups agreed that any Central American peace agreement must be accepted by all parties, and to this end they urged private talks between Cuba and the United States. In 1986 the two groups met in Caraballeda, Venezuela, where they issued the CARABALLEDA DECLARATION calling on all parties involved in the Central American conflict to resume peace negotiations.

Lima Third World Indebtedness Conference A 1986 meeting in Lima, Peru, of 35 states that represented 70 percent of Third World indebtedness. The states demanded a solution to the DEBT CRISIS and political dialogue between the debtors and creditors.

limited nuclear options (LNOs) A variety of targeting plans for the limited use of strategic nuclear forces. The essential idea is to have a whole range of carefully prepared FLEXIBLE RESPONSES to any form of enemy nuclear use. LNOs first came to public knowledge in 1974, when U.S. President Richard M. Nixon's secretary of defense, James Schlesinger, announced a new COUNTERVAILING STRATEGY known as the Schlesinger Doctrine that moved the United States away from the emphasis on assured destruction (MAD). In fact, limited nuclear options supplemented rather than replaced the capability for assured destruction.

limited sovereignty *See* BREZHNEV DOCTRINE.

limited war 1. An armed conflict wherein at least one side refrains from using all of its resources to defeat the enemy, in contrast to an all-out, no-holds-barred, TOTAL WAR. Limits are put on wars by the fear of the intervention of the opposition's nonbelligerent allies or by domestic opposition in one's own country. From the point of view of the United States, the Korean and Vietnam wars are examples of limited wars of this kind. 2. A war in which a government does not impose burdensome demands on its society and economy to further a maximum war effort. This too is in contrast to a total war, in which all of the resources of the nation are put at the disposal of the military. 3. Any war involving a superpower that does not use its nuclear or other weapons of mass destruction. As George F. Kennan wrote in *The Realities of American Foreign Policy* (1954): "The day of total war has passed. . . . From now on limited military operations are the only ones which could conceivably serve any coherent purpose." 4. According to U.S. General Maxwell D. Taylor in *Swords and Plowshares* (1972): "A proper concept of limited war is one in which the objectives are limited to something less than the total destruction of the enemy but which carries no implication of curtailed resources or restricted tactics." 5. Any war that does not involve one's own country. U.S. Secretary of State Henry Kissinger once wrote, "The secret dream of every European was . . . if there had to be nuclear war, to have it conducted over their heads by the strategic forces of the United States and the Soviet Union" (*Survival*, November–December 1979). The secret dream of every American, of course, was that it be fought in Europe.

Limits to Growth The title of the 1972 report by researcher Donella H. Meadows and others to the Club of Rome which was based on a Massachusetts Institute of Technology computer model projecting that the interaction of inadequate food supply, continued population growth, dwindling natural resources, industrial growth, and increased pollution over the next 60 years would lead to a planetary doomsday. The book stimulated a debate between advocates of "growth" and of "no growth." While it was a major spur to the worldwide environmental movement, many of its predictions proved wrong.

linear reduction of tariffs A reduction in all taxes on imports maintained by all countries participating in a given round of trade negotiations by a given percentage, unless there are explicit "exceptions." Exceptions usually are confined to products so "sensitive" that increased imports might cause severe political and economic difficulties. This approach to negotiating tariff reductions was used in the GATT's Kennedy round to avoid the difficulties involved in item-by-item negotiations. *See also* HARMONIZATION; ITEM-BY-ITEM NEGOTIATIONS.

line in the sand The international boundary between Iraq and Saudi Arabia; U.S. President George Bush's phrase for the United States' commitment to the defense of Saudi Arabia after the August 2, 1990, Iraqi conquest of Kuwait and in the subsequent PERSIAN GULF WAR. He said "a line has been drawn in the sand," and effectively dared the Iraqis to cross it.

Liner Code　The United Nations Convention on a Code of Conduct for Liner Conferences (also known as the UNCTAD Liner Code Convention) signed in 1974. In addition to constraints on freight rates and limits on the open registry of ships, the code calls for a scheme to allocate more equitably the world's shipping. The code's cargo-sharing ratio reserves 40 percent of the shipping involved in any bilateral trade for the importing country, 40 percent for the exporting country, and 20 percent for cross-traders (i.e., third parties to the trading). The cargo-sharing provisions were the primary reason for rejection of the convention by some major maritime nations such as Denmark, Norway, Sweden, the United Kingdom, and the United States.

lingua franca　An auxiliary language for international communications. For example, Latin in the Middle Ages, French in the nineteenth century, and English in the twentieth century have served as linguae francae in the west. The original lingua franca was a variant of French widely used in the Eastern Mediterranean during the seventeenth century. To the Arab merchants in port cities, all Europeans were "Franks," or Frenchmen.

linkage　A tactic used in international negotiations where two or more otherwise unrelated issues are used as trade-offs or pressure points. The concept of linkage became important in the 1970s in U.S.-Soviet relations and in United States policy toward the North Atlantic Treaty Organization. In 1973 U.S. Secretary of State Henry Kissinger linked security and economic issues with his argument that the NATO allies could not confront the United States on economic policies and still expect to reap the benefits of security cooperation. In U.S.-Soviet relations, the United States offered economic concessions in return for concessions on arms control and support for a negotiated end to the Vietnam War. U.S. President Richard M. Nixon explained: "Kissinger and I developed a new policy for dealing with the Soviets . . . we decided to link progress in such areas of Soviet concern as strategic arms limitation and increased trade with progress in areas that were important to us—Vietnam, the Mideast, and Berlin. This concept became known as linkage" (*RN: Memoirs*, 1978). Later, linkage became a stick rather than a carrot. For example, U.S. Senator Henry Jackson succeeded in linking expanded U.S. trade with the Soviet Union to Jewish emigration. This Moscow rejected. U.S. Senator Abraham A. Ribicoff elaborated: "[The Soviets] may not want to address the problem of linkage, but any strategic-arms-limitation treaty requires 67 affirmative [Senate] votes. And any Senator considers all the factors affecting Soviet-American relations" (*Los Angeles Times*, November 19, 1978). Linkage became a major issue in the Carter Administration when National Security Advisor Zbigniew Brzezinski asserted that the United States should not continue with arms control negotiations with the Soviets so long as they were pursuing expansionist polices in the Third World. Even though this idea was rejected by Secretary of State Cyrus Vance, linkage had become a political fact of life; the United States was not going to compartmentalize arms control from other issues between the superpowers. Linkage is a concept that has been developed and used predominantly by the United States. It has not figured largely in the foreign policy of other states.　**2.** The links between a state's domestic and foreign policies.

Lippmann, Walter (1889–1974)　The U.S. journalist who was not only the preeminent political pundit of his time but a political philosopher who wrote pioneering analyses of public opinion and foreign policy. Lippmann is perhaps most famous, however, for his injunction that one of the key requirements of successful foreign policy is to keep commitments and capabilities in harmony. He was critical of the CONTAINMENT policy on the grounds that it was likely to lead to an overextension of U.S. capabilities. He was right. His major works include *A Preface to Politics* (1913), *Drift and Mastery* (1914), *Public Opinion* (1922), *A Preface to Morals* (1929), *The Cold War* (1947), *Isolation and Alliances* (1952), and *The Public Philosophy* (1955).

Lithuania *See* BALTIC NATIONS.

Little Dragons *See* FOUR TIGERS.

Little Entente Refers to bilateral alliances between three Danubian nations—Czechoslovakia, Romania, and Yugoslavia—after World War I. The agreements were directed mainly against Hungary in the 1920s. However, after ADOLF HITLER came to power in Germany in 1933, new agreements were created that were directed against Germany and the Soviet Union. France actively encouraged what became known as the "Little Entente System" and signed bilateral treaties of friendship with each of the three Little Entente states. None of these treaties was a military alliance; each merely required consultation with the other nations on questions of foreign policy. The Little Entente system first broke down when Yugoslavia signed a bilateral treaty of friendship with Bulgaria, which was pro-German and anti-Romanian. The final destruction of the system came when France betrayed Czechoslovakia by signing the MUNICH AGREEMENT of 1938.

Little Red Book A red-covered book of quotations from the works of CHINESE COMMUNIST PARTY chairman MAO ZEDONG. Virtually every Chinese citizen carried a copy of the red book during the CULTURAL REVOLUTION as a symbol of loyalty to Mao and his ideas. *Compare to* GREEN BOOK.

Litvinov, Maksim (1876–1951) The Soviet diplomat who signed the KELLOGG-BRAND PACT in 1928, was foreign minister from 1930 to 1939, and served as ambassador to the United States from 1941 to 1943. During the 1930s his diplomatic efforts were directed at the military isolation of Germany and Japan; he also achieved U.S. recognition of the Soviet Union through the LITVINOV AGREEMENT. He

was removed as foreign minister in 1939 just before the NAZI-SOVIET NONAGGRESSION PACT was signed; this may have been in part because he was Jewish. But as soon as the Germans violated the pact and invaded the Soviet Union in 1941, Litvinov was rehabilitated.

Litvinov Agreement An exchange of diplomatic NOTES between the United States and the Soviet Union in 1933. The United States had not recognized the Communist regime established in Russia in 1918. The Communists refused to confirm the validity of agreements made by previous Russian governments, would give no assurances as to the financial obligations to other nations incurred by them, and were carrying on an active propaganda campaign against capitalism in the rest of the world. At the invitation of U.S. President Franklin D. Roosevelt, Soviet Foreign Minister MAKSIM LITVINOV went to Washington, D.C., and subsequently formal notes were exchanged. On November 16, 1933, the United States officially recognized the government of the Soviet Union. Litvinov informally assured the United States government that the Soviet Union would halt its propaganda campaign in the United States. Once the United States accorded recognition, however, the Soviet Union paid no attention to this promise.

Liu Shaoqi (also spelled Liu Shao-ch'i) (1898–1969) Chairman of the People's Republic of China (1959–1968) who was considered MAO ZEDONG's heir apparent until he was purged and died during the CULTURAL REVOLUTION. One of the earliest Communist organizers in China, Liu became the predominant leader of China's labor movement and the urban component of the Chinese Communist Party, which worked underground after the Nationalist-Communist split in 1927. After the CCP achieved power on the mainland, Liu's cosmopolitan experience gained him increasingly important positions in the state and party. As head of state, he played a prominent role in both domestic economic planning and foreign affairs. Fearing that he was being sidelined, Mao Zedong started the Cultural Revolution in which Liu and other leaders who associated with him, such as DENG XIAOPING, were purged. The news of Liu's death was not revealed until 1980.

LLDC   *See* LEAST-DEVELOPED COUNTRIES.

Lloyd George, David (1863–1945)   The Welsh Liberal Party member of the British Parliament who served continuously from 1890 to 1945 and who, as prime minister (1916–1920), led the Allies to victory in WORLD WAR I. As chancellor of the Exchequer (1908–1915) in 1909 he proposed a budget that was rejected by the House of Lords. This precipitated a constitutional crisis that led to the Parliament Act of 1911, which took away the power of the House of Lords to veto legislation of the House of Commons. While originally opposed to British involvement in World War I, Lloyd George reversed his position after the 1914 German invasion of neutral Belgium. Made minister of munitions in 1915, he is credited with ending the shortage of artillery shells on the Western Front. In 1916 he served briefly as war minister, then replaced HERBERT H. ASQUITH as prime minister in a coalition government. As a war leader he introduced a shipping convoy system to defeat the German U-boat menace in the Atlantic, demanded a unified Allied command, and brought a general sense of determination toward winning the war. After the war he was one of the principal drafters of the Treaty of VERSAILLES, which also created the LEAGUE OF NATIONS. Following the Anglo-Irish War of 1919 to 1921, his government partitioned Ireland to create the Catholic Irish Free State in the south and Protestant Ulster in the north. This was unpopular with the Conservative Party members of his coalition government; they withdrew from the coalition in 1922. While he remained in Parliament until his death, he never again had a leadership position.

David Lloyd George (Library of Congress)

LLOYD GEORGE ON ALLIED STRATEGY IN WORLD WAR I

The real weakness of Allied strategy was that it never existed. Instead of one great war with a united front, there were at least six separate and distinct wars with a separate, distinct and independent strategy for each. There was some pretence at timing the desperate blows with a rough approach to simultaneity. . . . There was no real unity of conception, coordination of effort or pooling of resources in such a way as to deal the enemy the hardest knocks at his weakest point.

SOURCE: David Lloyd George, *The War Memoirs,* IV (1937).

---

loan guarantee   A contractual arrangement by which a government pledges to pay part or all of a debt's principal and interest to a lender or holder of a security in the event of default by a third-party borrower. The purpose of a guaranteed loan is to reduce the risk borne by a private lender by shifting all or part of the risk to the government. This makes the borrower eligible for lower interest rates.

lobby   A person or organization that seeks to influence government policy through legislation or administrative action. Lobbies can be trade associations, individual corporations, public interest groups, or other levels of government. The term arose from the use of lobbies and corridors in legislative halls as places to meet with and persuade legislators to vote a certain way. Since World War II many governments that have been or hope to be the beneficiaries of other governments' legislation or executive action have joined the traditional array of lobbyists in various national capitals.

lobby terms   In Great Britain, an agreement between politicians and journalists that information given may be published but not attributed as to source. Most journalists in the United States call such an interview a BACKGROUNDER.

localitis   *See* CLIENTITIS.

local war   1. A synonym for LIMITED WAR. 2. A war that is geographically localized, fought in a limited region. 3. From a superpower perspective during the Cold War, any war that did not involve attacks on each other's homelands.

Locarno Pacts   The 1925 reconciliation between Weimar Germany and its enemies of World War I: France, Great Britain, and Italy. Germany, led by GUSTAV STRESEMANN, accepted its western boundaries (established under the Treaty of VERSAILLES) as legitimate. Significantly no similar agreement was made on Germany's eastern frontiers, though the Germans agreed to arbitration with Poland and Czechoslovakia. These treaties, signed in Locarno, Switzerland, led to a feeling of security in Western Europe and respectability for Germany, which was admitted to the League of Nations the following year. The "spirit of Locarno" has often been cited as an element in the resurgence of German power in the 1930s. Germany under Adolf Hitler denounced the Locarno agreements in 1936. Nevertheless, for these agreements ARISTIDE BRIAND, AUSTEN CHAMBERLAIN, and Stresemann received Nobel Peace Prizes in 1925 and 1926.

Locke, John (1632–1704)   The English political philosopher and SOCIAL CONTRACT theorist whose writings on the nature of government have been a major influence on revolutionary movements. It is often said that the first part of the American Declaration of Independence, which established the essential philosophic rationale for the break with England, is Thomas Jefferson's restatement of John Locke's most basic themes. Locke's most influential works by far were his *Two Treatises of Government* (1690), in which he rejected the notion that kings had a divine right to rule, made the case for a constitutional democracy, and provided a justification for Enlightenment criticisms of absolutism and for REVOLUTION later used by the Americans. Locke wrote that humans, who are "by nature free, equal, and independent," chose to live with others—to give up their STATE OF NATURE to enter into a SOCIAL CONTRACT to gain the security that is impossible in nature. They consent to live by the will of the majority, and it is for this purpose that governments are created. And a government formed by the people with their consent can be dissolved by the people if their trust is betrayed. According to Locke: "Whenever the legislators endeavor to take away and destroy the property of the people, or to reduce them to slavery under arbitrary power, they put themselves into a state of war with the people, who are thereupon absolved from any further obedience, and are left to the common refuge which God hath provided for all men against force and violence."

Lockerbie bombing   *See* PAN AM FLIGHT 103.

Lod Airport Massacre   The 1972 attack on Tel Aviv's Lod Airport by three members of the JAPANESE RED ARMY. The terrorists fired on the crowds with

John Locke (Library of Congress)

automatic weapons, killing 27 persons and injuring many more before security officers killed two of the terrorists and subdued the third.

Lodge, Henry Cabot (1850–1924) The Republican U.S. Senator from Massachusetts (1893–1924) who successfully opposed Democratic President Woodrow Wilson's effort to have the United States join the LEAGUE OF NATIONS. As he said in the Senate on August 12, 1919: "I have loved but one flag and I can not share that devotion and give affection to the mongrel banner invented for a league."

Lodge, Henry Cabot, Jr. (1902–1985) The grandson of Henry Cabot Lodge and also the Republican U.S. Senator from Massachusetts (1937–1943; 1947–1953). After serving as the U.S. ambassador to the United Nations (1953–1960), he was the unsuccessful 1960 Republican candidate for vice president on a ticket headed by Richard M. Nixon. As the U.S. ambassador to South Vietnam (1963–1964; 1965–1967), he sanctioned the military coup that deposed the government of NGO DINH DIEM. He later served as ambassador to West Germany (1968–1969), head of the U.S. delegation to the Paris Peace Talks between the United States and North Vietnam (1969–1970), and U.S. special envoy to the Vatican (1970–1975).

Logan Act of 1909 See DIPLOMACY, PERSONAL.

Lomé conventions A series of agreements between the EUROPEAN COMMUNITY and 69 "associated" states of Africa, the Caribbean, and the Pacific, first signed in 1975 (at Lomé, Togo), through which the EC provides these states with financial and technical aid as well as duty-free entry of many of their products into European markets. The associated states no longer have to grant REVERSE PREFERENCES, as they did under the earlier YAOUNDE CONVENTIONS, to qualify for duty-free entry. In addition, the convention created a mechanism known as STABEX, which was designed to stabilize the export earnings of the associated states from selected primary products. Compensatory payments from the EC under STABEX are based on the amount by which the actual export earnings of a particular state's exports of the designated commodities to the EC in a given year fall below export

trends, and are extended only when such shortfalls attain a specified magnitude.

London Conference 1. The 1924 conference at which the French government accepted the DAWES PLAN, which fundamentally modified the reparations section of the Treaty of VERSAILLES by abolishing France's authority to compel German payments unilaterally. See also YOUNG PLAN. 2. The 1992 meeting of the foreign ministers of all the world's major powers, the states of the former Yugoslavia, and the former Yugoslavia's neighbors, in an effort to end the YUGOSLAVIAN CIVIL WAR.

London Debt Accord of 1953 The international agreement that settled West Germany's foreign debts after World War II. This agreement is considered the beginning of West Germany's postwar economic miracle. It meant that huge debts would not hold back the German economy, as had happened after World War I.

London Declaration See GERMAN REUNIFICATION.

London Naval Conference 1. The 1930 conference convened to reduce naval competition in ship categories that were not covered by the WASHINGTON NAVAL CONFERENCE—namely cruisers, destroyers, and submarines. When the Japanese delegation accepted a compromise that threatened their regional superiority in the Western Pacific, it was denounced at home as a "sellout." 2. The 1935–1936 meeting of Great Britain, Japan, and the United States at which Japan's demand for an upper limit on naval growth was rejected. The only agreement reached concerned limitations on the tonnage and gun size of battleships.

London Treaty of 1915 The secret agreement among France, Great Britain, and Italy that promised Italy specific territorial spoils if it entered World War I on the Allied side. It did. After the war, even though it violated the principle of SELF-DETERMINATION, the Allies (later including the United States) basically kept the deal but gave Italy less than it was promised by the treaty.

long cycle A concept used by those who analyze world systems and attempt to explain historical change. The idea of a long cycle involves what Joshua Goldstein, in *Long Cycles: Prosperity and War in the Modern Age* (1988), terms "a repetition of themes, processes and relationships along the path of an evolving social system." Goldstein uses the term to refer to the "HEGEMONY cycle." Such cycles are demarcated by HEGEMONIC WARS that "mark the end of a long period of hegemonic decline and rivalry and the rise of a new hegemony in the world system. This is followed by the weakening of the hegemonic power, by increasing competition as this power is challenged, and, ultimately, by another large scale war." Hegemony cycles take around 150 years to complete. Historically Goldstein identifies three hegemony cycles marked by major wars. The first wave is marked by the 1648 Treaty of Westphalia, which brought to an end the Thirty Years' War and the power of the Hapsburgs. The second cycle began with Dutch hegemony, and as this declined was characterized by Franco-British competition. In 1815 Great Britain emerged out of this as the new hegemonic power. There followed another period of competition in which Germany challenged for hegemony. This ended in 1945 with the United States as the new dominant power. Although these ideas have many critics, they nevertheless provide a useful way to explain patterns of continuity and change in international politics. They are closely linked in certain respects to STRUCTURALISM and to the theory of hegemonic war.

Long March   A 10,000-kilometer (6,000-mile) historic march by the Chinese Communists who crossed 18 mountain ranges and 24 rivers along their trek from southeast China to northwest China to break away from the military campaigns of the Nationalist forces in 1930s. About 100,000 Communist troops and other personnel started the march in 1934. Only 8,000 survived in 1935. MAO ZEDONG established his dominance of the party during the Long March and persuaded his colleagues to accept his guerrilla war strategies. The heroism attributed to the Long March inspired many young Chinese to join the CHINESE COMMUNIST PARTY in the late 1930s and early 1940s.

long-range theater nuclear forces   Missiles with a range greater than 1,000 kilometers (600 miles), but that clearly lacked the ability for intercontinen-

tal strikes. Included in this category were the Soviet SS-20 and the North Atlantic Treaty Organization/United States Cruise and Pershing II. The NATO systems were based in the European theater but were still capable of striking targets within Eastern Europe and the Soviet Union. These missiles were subsequently called long-range intermediate nuclear forces (INF) in order to avoid the implication that these systems could be used for a nuclear war that was confined only to the European theater. The INF TREATY of December 1987 eliminated all missiles with a range between 500 and 5,500 kilometers.

long telegram   *See* GEORGE F. KENNAN.

Long-Term Defense Program   The NORTH ATLANTIC TREATY ORGANIZATION's long-range plan to coordinate the defense plans and weapons production of its members. Unanimously approved at the 1978 NATO summit conference, this was NATO's response to the increased size and capabilities of the WARSAW PACT forces in Eastern Europe. It consisted of specific recommendations made by ten task forces in such areas as air defense, electronic warfare, reinforcements, and reserve mobilization.

long wave   The cycling of an economic phase from a period of expansion, topped by a peak, to a period of stagnation or trough; also known as a *Kondratieff cycle* after Nikolai Kondratieff (1892–   ), a Russian economist who developed the notion in his 1925 book, *Long Waves in Economic Life*. (Soviet officials were not pleased at his attempt to analyze economic conditions objectively. Consequently, he was arrested in 1930 and presumedly died in prison some time later because he was never heard from again.) Long waves, usually five or six decades in length, are explained by major innovations (such as railroads or computers) that occur at their start. These innovations account for economic (and political) activity long after their initial impact. JOSEPH A. SCHUMPTETER used long waves in his theories of economic development.

Lon Nol (1913–1985)   The president of Cambodia from 1970 to 1975. He was the prime minister (1966–1967; 1969–1970) who with U.S. support overthrew Prince NORODOM SIHANOUK and established a republic in 1970. But despite massive U.S. military aid, including extensive B-52 bombing raids on Communist opponents, he was in turn overthrown by the KHMER ROUGE guerrillas in 1975 and fled to the United States.

loose bipolarity　**1.** An international system in which there are two main powers with relatively cohesive blocs clustered around them as well as nations outside the blocs. This was the system that emerged after World War II. **2.** A term sometimes used to describe the Cold War international system as it had evolved by the 1960s when the blocs clustered around the two superpowers had lost some of their tightness or cohesiveness.

loose cannon　Someone who is so unpredictable in administrative or political matters that he or she is liable to cause great damage to someone else. The concept comes from the long recognized danger of having an untethered cannon rolling about the deck of a ship. A political loose cannon might be a politician's relative or an overzealous staffer.

Lorenz, Konrad Z. (1903–1989)　An Austrian behavioral psychologist whose book *On Aggression* (1967) deals with animals but also contributes to understanding the nature of aggression among humans. Lorenz's argument, in essence, is that aggression is a natural instinct and one that helps to ensure survival not only of the individual animal but also of its species. Apart from killing for prey, which is outside his definition of aggression, Lorenz found that most aggressive behavior occurs among members of the same species. Intraspecific aggression, as it was termed, was seen by Lorenz as being related to territory, and he noted that an animal was generally more willing to fight at the center of its territory than at the periphery. He also identified ritual forms of aggression in which animals, by making certain aggressive gestures, were sometimes able to avoid fighting—a development that sometimes has been very important to species survival. The implication of all this for international politics is that Lorenz saw humans as sharing the characteristic of innate aggression but as lacking the ritualistic qualities that characterize much aggression in the animal world. The idea that there is an aggressive instinct in humans has been criticized by anthropologists, psychologists, and others who have argued that it is dangerous to take lessons from the world of animals and simply apply them to humans. Nevertheless, Lorenz's ideas provide at least some insight into the importance of the TERRITORIAL IMPERATIVE in international politics.

Los Alamos　The U.S. town in the state of New Mexico that was the site of the first atomic bomb laboratory in 1942. It remains the location of U.S. nuclear research facilities.

low countries　A traditional name for Belgium, the Netherlands, and Luxembourg because they are situated so close to sea level. They are also known as BENELUX.

low-intensity conflict　**1.** A minor war that does not directly engage military SUPERPOWERS. **2.** A PROXY WAR. **3.** INSURGENCY or COUNTERINSURGENCY operations limited to relatively cheap conventional weapons. **4.** A show of force whereby military units are dispatched with no real intention to use them in combat; this is as much a diplomatic as it is a military action. *Compare to* LIMITED WAR.

low-intensity warfare　A type of conflict in which one actor generally unrestrained by rules and conventions of war wages a struggle against an actor who is constrained by institutional and legal restraints. Many conflict theorists argue that the Western powers face a greater threat from guerrilla insurgencies and terrorism than from conventional major-power conflicts, and that the democracies must be prepared to engage in low-intensity warfare to battle nontraditional foes.

low politics　Politics and policies that are concerned with economic and social issues rather than the traditional themes of statecraft, war, peace, and security. Some analysts argue that foreign policy in advanced industrialized states has become much more concerned with low politics than with HIGH POLITICS. In fact, it is not a matter of either/or. Foreign policy is concerned with both high and low politics.

Ludendorff, Erich (1865–1937)　The WORLD WAR I German general who led his troops to victory on the Eastern Front (at TANNENBERG) and defeat on the Western Front in 1918. He was an early supporter of ADOLF HITLER. In 1923 he was involved with Hitler's abortive BEER HALL PUTSCH, and in 1925 he was the unsuccessful Nazi candidate for president of Germany.

Luminous Path   An English translation for the name of the SENDERO LUMINOSO guerrilla group.

lumpenproletariat   The Marxist term for the underclass of the industrial world; those below the working class in economic status. The large numbers of marginally employed squatters who pervade most of the cities of the THIRD WORLD are sometimes referred to as the lumpenproletariat. *Compare to* PROLETARIAT.

Lumumba, Patrice (1925–1961)   The founder of the Congolese Nationalist movement in 1958 who became the first prime minister of an independent Congo (now Zaire) in 1960. He alienated the West when he asked the Soviet Union for help in suppressing a secessionist insurgency in Katanga province. After a military coup deposed him, he fled to the secessionists and was murdered by them. *See also* CONGOLESE CIVIL WAR.

Lusitania   The British passenger liner that was sunk by a German submarine on May 7, 1915, in Irish waters. About 1,200 civilians drowned, including 128 U.S. citizens. Germany's policy of unrestricted submarine warfare, which included the sinking of passenger ships such as the *Lusitania,* eventually helped bring the United States into World War I on the side of Great Britain and France.

Luthuli, Albert John (1898–1967)   The South African Zulu leader who was president of the AFRICAN NATIONAL CONGRESS from 1952 to 1967. For his nonviolent efforts to end APARTHEID, he was awarded the Nobel Peace Prize in 1960.

Luxembourg Agreement   **1.** The 1952 agreement by which West Germany agreed to pay $882,000,000 to Israel over the following decade as reparations for the loss of lives and property by the Jews of Germany during World War II. **2.** The 1971 agreement between the EUROPEAN COMMUNITY and the United Kingdom that detailed the terms of the United Kingdom's accession to the EC in 1973.   **3.** A 1986 declaration of the European Community. Following a dispute over the future method by which the community budget should be financed in 1965, France withdrew its representatives from both the EUROPEAN COMMISSION and the COUNCIL OF MINISTERS. The compromise, arranged when the French returned to the council, was an agreement by the council to differ. Under the Treaty of ROME, the council could make decisions by majority vote to resolve a deadlock. This was unacceptable to France. The Luxembourg Agreement (or Compromise) allowed member nations to retain the right to veto council decisions on issues of vital national importance. While the agreement enabled the EC's work to resume and strengthened the authority of the council within the EC, it ended hopes that the EC could move speedily toward a supranational authority.   **4.** The 1991 agreement by which the EUROPEAN FREE TRADE ASSOCIATION merged with the EC.

Lytton Commission   The League of Nations commission headed by Great Britain's Lord Lytton that in 1932 mildly condemned the Japanese aggression during the MANCHURIAN CRISIS in 1931. The Lytton Report offered only symbolic disapproval of Japan's aggression. It recommended that League member states refuse to recognize passports or postage of Manchukuo, Japan's puppet state.

M

Ma'alot massacre   The 1974 killing of 22 Israeli schoolchildren during a Palestinian terrorist attack. In an attempt to force Israel to release imprisoned Palestinians, three terrorists seized a northern Israel school with more than 100 students and teachers. In the rescue operation by Israeli forces, the terrorists had time to open fire on the children. While the three terrorists were killed, there was no way of knowing for sure how many children were victims of friendly fire from Israeli forces. In addition to the 22 dead, another 60 were wounded. The Israeli public criticized this seemingly botched rescue operation by the Israeli government, but reinforced the government's expressed policy of not giving in to terrorist demands no matter what the cost.

Maastricht Treaty   The 1991 agreement in which the leaders of the 12-nation EUROPEAN COMMUNITY decided on eventual political union. A single currency and a regional central bank were to be created by 1999. Only Great Britain reserved the right to later "opt out" of the monetary union. The Maastricht Treaty provided the framework for dozens of European-wide initiatives, from a common police force (to be called Europol) to coordinated social policies. Perhaps most significant, it also established "Provisions on a Common Foreign and Security Policy." The member states agreed to "inform and consult one another" on any matter of foreign and security policy of general interest and to coordinate their actions in international organizations and at international conferences. The COUNCIL OF MINISTERS was charged with the task of defining the common position to which the member states would then conform. In addition, the leaders of the EC agreed to strengthen the WESTERN EUROPEAN UNION, which would become the "defense component" of European union. Some critics saw this as a challenge to the continued predominance of the North Atlantic Treaty Organization in European security matters. But these new arrangements had to be approved individually by each member state. When Denmark, in a national referendum in June 1992, rejected the Maastricht Treaty, the seemingly unstoppable momentum toward European political integration was slowed. Later that year when France, in a September national REFERENDUM, barely approved the treaty and Italy and the United Kingdom were forced to pull out of the EUROPEAN MONETARY SYSTEM and devalue their currencies, the Maastricht Treaty began to be reevaluated throughout Europe.

MacArthur, Douglas (1880–1964)   The U.S. general who commanded the U.S. 42nd (Rainbow) division in France in World War I and subsequently became chief of staff of the U.S. Army. On his retirement in 1937, he was appointed a field marshal in the Philippine Army. In 1941 he was recalled to active duty as commander of the U.S. forces—and soon after, of all Allied forces—in a major portion of the Pacific theater during WORLD WAR II. As such, he accepted the surrender of the Japanese on September 2, 1945. During the following five years he served as Supreme Commander of Allied Powers and oversaw the reconstruction of Japan. According to U.S. General Bruce Palmer, "[MacArthur] could be called the

Douglas MacArthur in 1944, biting on his characteristic corncob pipe. (National Archives)

father of modern Japan. It was MacArthur the statesman, MacArthur the humanitarian, MacArthur the educator—not MacArthur the conqueror—who transformed a feudalistic military state, ravaged by war, into what is now a true democracy" (*Washington Post*, April 19, 1970). When war broke out between North and South Korea in 1950, MacArthur was placed in charge of the United Nations forces. After the brilliant INCHON INVASION, which outflanked North Korean forces, MacArthur advanced his army into North Korea and failed to foresee—or prepare for—the intervention by China that this provoked. He was relieved of his command by U.S. President Harry S Truman in April 1951 for his outspoken views regarding more aggressive U.S. military action against Communist China. Thereafter he retired to private life. *See also* PHILIPPINE INVASION.

TRUMAN FIRES MACARTHUR

With deep regret I have concluded that General of the Army Douglas MacArthur is unable to give his wholehearted support to the policies of the United States Government and of the United Nations in matters pertaining to his official duties. In view of the specific responsibilities imposed upon me by the Constitution of the United States and the added responsibility which has been entrusted to me by the United Nations, I have decided that I must make a change of command in the Far East. I have, therefore, relieved General MacArthur of his commands and have designated Lt. Gen. Matthew B. Ridgway as his successor.

Full and vigorous debate on matters of national policy is a vital element in the constitutional system of our free democracy. It is fundamental, however, that military commanders must be governed by the policies and directives issued to them in the manner provided by our laws and Constitution.

Source: President Harry S Truman, Statement of the President Relative to the Relief of General MacArthur, April 10, 1951.

MacArthur, Douglas (1909–   )   The nephew of U.S. General Douglas MacArthur who, as a career U.S. Foreign Service officer, helped establish the North Atlantic Treaty Organization and served as U.S. Ambassador to Japan (1956–1961), Belgium (1961–1965), Austria (1967–1969), and Iran (1969–1972).

MacBride, Sean (1904–1988)   An IRISH REPUBLICAN ARMY guerrilla fighter until 1937 who became, after a career in Irish politics, the secretary general of the International Commission of Jurists (1963–1970) and chairman of AMNESTY INTERNATIONAL (1970–1973). For his work on human rights and disarmament he shared the 1974 Nobel Peace Prize (with EISAKU SATO). In 1977 he was also awarded the Lenin Peace Prize by the Soviet Union.

McCarthyism   A U.S. phenomenon of extreme and irresponsible anticommunism. U.S. Senator Joseph R. McCarthy (1908–1957) of Wisconsin rose to fame and influence during the early 1950s by recklessly charging that individuals or organizations were Communist or influenced by Communists. McCarthy grew so reckless with his accusations that in 1954 he became one of the few senators in American history to be formally censured by the U.S. Senate for the fact that he "tended to bring the Senate into dishonor and disrepute." (The word McCarthyism is generally credited to *Washington Post* cartoonist Herbert Block, who first used it in March 1950 as the label for a barrel of mud that a Republican elephant was hesitant to use as a platform.) The practice of McCarthyism is not limited to McCarthy himself. The classic tactic of McCarthyism is the use of an unproven association with any individual, organization, or policy, which the accuser perceives as liberal or leftist and, as a result, un-American or even treasonous. Today any actions by public officials that flout individual rights and imply guilt by association would be considered—by anyone sensitive to the concept of due process of law—to be examples of McCarthyism. *See also* BIG LIE.

COMMUNISTS IN THE STATE DEPARTMENT?

While I cannot take the time to name all of the men in the State Department who have been named as members of the Communist Party and members of a spy ring, I have here in my hand a list of 205 that were known to the Secretary of State as being members of the Communist Party and who nevertheless are still working and shaping the policy of the State Department.

SOURCE: Joseph R. McCarthy, speech at Wheeling, West Virginia, making unfounded accusations that marked the era of McCarthyism, quoted in Richard H. Rovere, *Senator Joe McCarthy* (1959).

MacDonald, (James) Ramsay (1866–1937)   The first British prime minister from the Labour Party in 1924; he served as prime minister again from 1929 to 1935. In 1931 MacDonald's government faced losing power amid the economic problems of the Great Depression, so he formed a coalition government that was dominated by Conservatives. This infuriated many members of his Labour Party, who from then on considered him a traitor to their cause.

Macheteros   A Puerto Rican separatist group (in English, "Machete-wielders") that has attacked U.S. military personnel and local police; its members have "declared war" on the United States and want total independence for Puerto Rico, a Caribbean island commonwealth associated with the United States.

Machiavelli, Niccolò (1469–1527)   Italian Renaissance political philosopher whose major works, *The Prince* (1532) and *The Discourses* (1531), were important contributions to political analysis and led to the use of the term Machiavellianism to refer to cunning, cynical, and ruthless behavior based on the notion of the end justifying the use of almost any means. What Machiavelli actually noted in *The Prince* was that a prince would be judged by results: "So let a prince set about the task of conquering and maintaining his state; his methods will always be judged honorable and universally praised." Machiavelli, as one of the first policy advisors, developed a set of prescriptions and proscriptions for his prince that were designed to ensure that the prince would flourish politically. He disregarded the issue of morality—apart from those circumstances where it was prudent or necessary for the prince to appear to be moral. The conflicts between the city states of Renaissance Italy and the intrigues of the Borgia papacy provided fertile ground for Machiavelli's development of a set of axioms and ideas about obtaining, holding on to, and using power to advantage. As he wrote in *The Prince*: "Contemporary experience shows that princes who have achieved great things have been those who have given their word lightly, who have known how to trick men with their cunning, and who, in the end, have overcome those abiding by honest principles." In other words, princes should act like the centaur, half man and half beast. In view of this it was not surprising that Machiavelli took conflict and war for granted and argued in *The Prince* that "the first way to lose your state is to neglect the art of war; the first way to win a state is to be skilled in the art of war." Machiavelli's importance lies in several things: his emphasis on lessons from experience rather than moral principle, his emphasis on results, and his acknowledgment of the importance of power and conflict. Contemporary analysts regard Machiavelli as one of the intellectual forerunners of political REALISM.

Machtpolitik   *See* POWER POLITICS.

Mackinder, Halford J. (1861–1947)   The most famous theorist of GEOPOLITICS and the one who developed the HEARTLAND THEORY. Mackinder started from the proposition that ideas of political geography had to be built on ideas of physical geography, especially location. His main concern was to explain how geographical factors had influenced world history. In his attempts to do this he focused partly on the constant struggle between land powers and maritime powers and partly on a geographical region (broadly encompassing the area roughly synonymous with the post–World War II boundaries of the Soviet Union), which he described in *Geographical Journal* (1904) as "the geographical

pivot of history." In 1919 the area was broadened to include parts of Siberia and parts of Eastern Europe, and was termed the *heartland*. Surrounding the heartland was the "world island," which consisted of the landmasses of Africa, Asia, and Europe. The crucial strategic area, however, was the heartland, an idea that was summed up in the three lines that appeared in his *Democratic Ideals and Reality* (1919):

> *Who rules East Europe rules the Heartland*
> *who rules the heartland commands the World Island*
> *who rules the World Island commands the world.*

In an article entitled "The Round World and the Winning of the Peace" (*Foreign Affairs*, 21, July 1943), Mackinder developed a third version of the heartland theory. In this version the heartland and the territory of the Soviet Union were equivalent. More important than this refinement, however, was the fact that Mackinder acknowledged another area—the Midland Ocean—that he felt could balance the heartland. The Midland Ocean or North Atlantic was seen as having three elements: "A bridgehead in France, a moated aerodome in Britain, and a reserve of trained manpower, agriculture and industries in the eastern United States and Canada." Although there were obvious flaws in Mackinder's theories, they were in some respects very prophetic of the situation that developed after World War II.

Maclean, Donald (1913–1983)   The British diplomat who was a member of the CAMBRIDGE SPY RING. He supplied extensive data on the North Atlantic Treaty Organization, the Korean War, and nuclear weapons development to the KGB. After his exposure in 1951 he fled to the Soviet Union and remained there the rest of his life, working for Soviet intelligence.

McMahon letters   Correspondence from 1915 to 1916 between Henry McMahon (1862–1949), the British high commissioner in Cairo, and Hussein Ibn Ali (1852–1931), the sharif of Mecca, which promised support for an Arab state if the Arabs supported the British in their fight against the Turks during World War I. While Palestine was not mentioned by name in the letters, the Arabs claimed that the British implied that it would be included in an Arab state; thus their sense of betrayal by the BALFOUR DECLARATION of 1917, which promised a Jewish homeland there.

Macmillan, Harold (1894–1986) The Conservative Party prime minister of Great Britain from 1957 to 1963. He restored British confidence after the SUEZ CRISIS, did all he could to restore the SPECIAL RELATIONSHIP with the United States that had been strained by the crisis, supported the MULTILATERAL NUCLEAR FORCE concept in the North Atlantic Treaty Organization, and accelerated British efforts at decolonization. In a famous speech to the South African parliament on February 3, 1960, he said: "The wind of change is blowing through this [African] continent, and whether we like it or not, this growth of national consciousness is a political fact." In ill health and faced with a stagnant national economy, he resigned shortly after the PROFUMO AFFAIR scandal in 1963.

MACMILLAN THE GREEK

In 1942 during World War II Macmillan was the chief civilian representative of the British government at [U.S.] General Dwight D. Eisenhower's headquarters in Algiers. In a famous briefing to the British military staff assigned there, he summarized what he saw as the essence of the Anglo-American alliance: "[We] are Greeks in the American empire. You will find the Americans much as the Greeks found the Romans— great, big, vulgar, bustling people, more vigorous than we are, and also more idle, with more unspoiled virtues but also more corrupt. We must run [this HQ] as the Greek slaves ran the operations of the Emperor Claudius."

SOURCE: Alistair Horne, *Macmillan: 1894–1956* (1988).

McNamara, Robert S. (1916–   ) The U.S. Secretary of Defense under Presidents John F. Kennedy and Lyndon B. Johnson from 1961 to 1968. McNamara was the prime advocate of accepting the policy of mutual assured destruction (MAD), in which nuclear superiority was abandoned in favor of a

secure second-strike capacity. He also worked to shift the North Atlantic Treaty Organization's doctrine from reliance on MASSIVE RETALIATION to FLEXIBLE RESPONSE. But by far his greatest historical importance was his strong advocacy of the VIETNAM WAR. He deserves much of the responsibility for the ultimately ineffective strategies and tactics used by U.S. forces. As he once boasted: "I don't object to its being called 'McNamara's war.' I think it is a very important war and I am pleased to be identified with it and do whatever I can to win it" (*New York Times,* April 25, 1964). Yet according to Neil Sheehan's *A Bright Shining Lie* (1988), by the end of November of 1967 President Johnson would complain that McNamara had deteriorated into "an emotional basket case" because of the burdens of the war. Thus "McNamara learned through a press leak of his appointment as the new president of the World Bank."

In the 1980s McNamara came to the fore in nuclear debate once again by joining with other leading strategists of the 1960s in calling for NATO to abandon its doctrine of first use of nuclear weapons. This caused writers such as Michael Kinsley (*The New Republic,* November 28, 1983) to note that it is a cause for wonder how "anti-nuclear politics has served as a reentry vehicle into liberal respectability for dubious characters like Robert S. McNamara. . . . A decade ago they were widely regarded as war criminals; now a couple of high-minded pronunciamentos about how awful a nuclear war would be, and they start winning peace awards." Such a judgment is extremely harsh. After initially embracing the COUNTERFORCE strategy enunciated by the U.S. Air Force, McNamara was consistent in advocating reduced reliance on nuclear weapons. Moreover, during the Cuban Missile Crisis his advice to opt for a blockade rather than an air strike was very important in keeping things under control. His hawkishness on Vietnam, however, did highlight the fact that he did not fully understand the kind of conflict that the United States was becoming engaged in. This proved to be both a personal tragedy and a national one.

MAD (mutual assured destruction) The strategy of destroying an enemy with nuclear weapons as it destroys you as well; this was the reality of the SUPERPOWER nuclear weapons standoff that had developed by the mid-1960s. In 1965 U.S. defense officials realized that it would be impossible to retain a measure of strategic superiority capable of preventing tremendous damage to the United States in the event of nuclear war with the Soviet Union. Therefore, the United States would place the main emphasis in strategic planning on maintaining a "convincing capability to inflict unacceptable damage on an attacker." Since the Soviet Union had increasingly similarly equipped forces, it could do the same to the United States—hence the mutuality of the assured destruction. One complaint about the strategy was that it was immoral. Strategic analyst Fred C. Ikle, for example, argued that assured destruction "fails to indicate what is to be destroyed; but then, 'assured genocide' would reveal the truth too starkly" (*Foreign Policy,* January 1973). National security analyst Donald Brennan (*National Review,* June 23, 1972) argued that the "concept of mutual assured destruction provides one of the few instances in which the obvious acronym for something yields at once the appropriate description for it; that is, a Mutual Assured Destruction posture as a goal is, almost literally, mad." Ironically, the editor of *National Review,* William F. Buckley, Jr., believed MAD was essentially rational: "If the Soviet Union opted for a massive nuclear war, our option must be to return that hell in kind. And this option we would need to choose for so simple a reason as that we would not then have died for nothing, because it is better than nothing to rid the world of such monsters as would unleash such a war" (*Wall Street Journal,* May 21, 1982). Assured destruction, however, did not provide the basis for the United States' targeting strategy. Nevertheless, it was particularly appropriate as a description of the consequences of strategic nuclear war.

Madero, Francisco   *See* MEXICAN REVOLUTION.

madman theory   U.S. President Richard M. Nixon's concept that if a national leader seems to be a little bit crazy or irrational, the other side will be more responsive and pliable in international negotiations. Nixon's White House chief of staff, H. R. Haldeman, in his book *The Ends of Power* (1978), quotes Nixon: "I call it the Madman Theory . . . I want the North Vietnamese to believe that I've reached the point where I might do anything to stop the war. We'll just slip the word to them that, 'for God's sake, you know Nixon is obsessed about Communists. We can't restrain him when he's angry—and he has his hand on the nuclear button'—and Ho Chi Minh himself will be in Paris in two days begging for peace."

Madrid Conference   **1.** The first in a series of peace-seeking meetings between Israel, its Arab neighbors (Egypt, Jordan, Lebanon, and Syria), and Palestinians from the OCCUPIED TERRITORIES. This October 1991 conference sponsored by the United States and the Soviet Union accomplished little but for the fact that all sides sat down together to talk. But that in itself was a great deal.   **2.** The CONFERENCE ON SECURITY AND COOPERATION IN EUROPE held in Madrid from 1980 to 1983.

Maghreb   Arabic for "west"; a name given to the region comprised of Algeria, Libya, Morocco, and Tunisia—Arab states on the southern coast of the Mediterranean. These areas are to the west of the traditional heart of the Arab world.

Maghreb Agreements   Cooperative agreements on trade with the EUROPEAN COMMUNITY signed by Algeria, Morocco, and Tunisia in 1976.

Maginot Line   The continuous stationary fortifications that covered the Franco-German frontier, named after André Maginot (1877–1932), French war minister during various times in the 1920s and 1930s. Mostly built in the 1930s, it was the essence of French strategy to repulse possible German aggression. Unfortunately, it did not extend to Belgium or the Ardennes and had its guns fixed in one direction. Thus during World War II when the Germans invaded France, they easily flanked these stationary fortifications using BLITZKRIEG techniques. Because the French were so confident of the line's defensive capability and because it was so easily overcome, a "maginot line" has come to mean any defensive barrier that is fated to fail. *See also* FRANCE, BATTLE OF.

Magloire, Paul E.   *See* DUVALIER FAMILY.

Mahan, Alfred Thayer (1840–1914)   The U.S. naval officer whose writings have been a major influence on world history. Mahan, who rose to the position

Alfred Thayer Mahan (Library of Congress)

of admiral over a 30-year career, used history to show the relationship between the development of sea power and the relative success of European nations. He used this historical evidence to synthesize general principles of naval development regarding geography, territorial configurations, and nature of government which can be applied regardless of technical changes in weaponry. His major works, *The Influence of Sea Power Upon History 1660–1763* (1890) and *The Influence of Sea Power Upon the French Revolution and Empire, 1793–1812* (1892) became global classics and greatly influenced the worldwide naval buildup prior to World War I. His theories also were a major influence on U.S. desires to fight the 1898 Spanish-American War and to build the Panama Canal. Although his focus was historical, he derived from this history a number of lessons and generalizations that gave his work its distinctiveness and impor-

tance. Margaret Sprout (in Edward Mead Earle, ed., *Makers of Modern Strategy,* 1941) describes Mahan as an "evangelist of Sea Power" and argues that his contribution to the development of modern strategy was threefold: He developed a philosophy of sea power that achieved widespread recognition among politicians and statesmen as well as professional naval circles; he formulated a new theory of naval strategy; and he was an acute critic of naval tactics.

Mahan emphasized the need for expanding commerce and saw control of the seas as being necessary to ensure that this could take place. He highlighted the inadequacies of the existing United States naval policy, which emphasized coastal defense and protection of ships from raids, and provided a rationale for the United States to develop a large navy built around battleships to achieve the necessary degree of control. He also provided a rationale for the acquisition of overseas bases as without these, Mahan contended, ships were like "land birds unable to fly far from their shores." Mahan's emphasis on the importance of superiority in naval power also contributed to the intensity of the naval race between Great Britain and Germany in the decade leading up to World War I.

In addition to his general observations on the importance of sea power, Mahan contributed to thinking about how such power could best be used. In this connection, he focused on the need for large capital ships that could provide a concentration of force—a feature he regarded as one of the great principles of naval warfare—and achieve command of the sea. Although the development of both the submarine and the aircraft have had important implications for the relevance of some of Mahan's arguments about naval strategy, many of the ideas to which he gave birth have continued to have attraction for successive generations of naval officers in many countries.

Major, John (1943–   ) The United Kingdom's chancellor of the Exchequer who suddenly became prime minister in 1990 when MARGARET THATCHER was forced out of office by her own Conservative Party. The party was fearful that her personal unpopularity would cause it to lose the next general election. Major, who was Thatcher's own choice to succeed her, has continued some of her policies (in

John Major (British Information Services)

a far less acidic manner) and has departed from others, most notably her anti-Europeanism. This allowed him to lead the Conservatives to a narrow victory in the 1992 general election.

major nuclear power   Any state that possesses a nuclear striking force capable of posing a serious threat to any other state. This is in contrast to a minor nuclear power, which has a nuclear weapon but not a sophisticated means of delivering it and therefore poses only a local threat.

major player   A slang phrase for a person, an organization, or a sovereign state that is so powerful or influential regarding a particular policy issue that its views must be taken into account. To ignore views of a major player is to risk failure.

Malayan emergency   The 1948 to 1960 civil war in the Malayan archipelago in which Communist-led guerrillas known as the Malayan Races Liberation

Army (mainly ethnic Chinese Malayans) were eventually defeated by British and Malayan troops. These were many of the same guerrillas who had fought the Japanese during the World War II occupation. They resented the political dominance (under the British) of the Malays and Indians. The British colonial government was able to win the support of the majority Malay and Indian population, thus cutting the guerrillas off from their source of supply, with the acceleration of plans for independence, which came in 1963. This experience was widely cited as the example of how to win a guerrilla war against a Communist insurgency. (The military tactics used were therefore adopted during the VIETNAM WAR, but were ultimately ineffective because conditions in the two countries were radically different: The situation in Malaya [now Malaysia] was relatively favorable to counterinsurgency efforts, whereas in Vietnam the fundamental lack of legitimacy of the South Vietnamese government was a problem that could not be overcome.)

Malenkov, Georgi (1902–   )   The deputy premier of the Soviet Union (1946–1953) who succeeded JOSEPH STALIN in 1953 as both premier and first secretary of the Communist Party of the Soviet Union. But within a year NIKITA S. KHRUSHCHEV replaced him as first secretary, and by 1955, under attack for agricultural failures, he was deposed as premier and replaced by NIKOLAI A. BULGANIN.

Malthus, Thomas Robert (1766–1834)   The British economist, trained in mathematics and classics, who contributed to the study of population and to the development of economics as a discipline. His *Essay on the Principle of Population* (1798) held that the world's population must eventually outstrip its available food because, left unchecked, population increases geometrically, while food production increases arithmetically. Malthus wrote: "Almost everything that has been hitherto done for the poor has tended, as if with solicitous care, to throw a veil of obscurity over this subject and to hide from them the true cause of their poverty. When the wages of labour are hardly sufficient to maintain two children, a man marries and has five or six." Yet Malthus did not advocate zero population growth, arguing that growth should be limited through late marriage, chastity, and contraception to keep the increase in line with the growth in food supplies. He initially argued against raising workers' wages, because they would simply have more children and put greater pressure on food supplies. Malthus was the first person in Great Britain to have the title of professor of political economy. His *Principles of Political Economy* was published in 1820; a second edition appeared posthumously in 1836. Evident in most of his work was a relevance to public policy issues and a concern with empirical evidence. Although very controversial in many of his writings, Malthus was a key figure in the development of systematic analysis of population growth, an issue that has great significance for international relations. The term Malthusian has since come to refer to any solution to the problem of population growth and famine that suggests the inevitability or even the utility of their relation to each other as the only effective way of controlling overpopulation.

managed trade   **1.** A reference to policies and devices other than TARIFFs that governments, especially those in the West, have adopted since the late 1970s to limit the flow of imports from Japan and the new industrializing countries of the Third World (or else to regulate trade between the United States and the European Community). Managed trade instruments include voluntary quotas, special levies, orderly marketing agreements, and government subsidies to domestic producers.   **2.** A trade policy that depends more heavily on negotiations with international trading partners, as opposed to solely market forces, to improve a BALANCE OF TRADE.   **3.** A euphemism for traditional trade PROTECTIONISM. *Compare to* COUNTERTRADE.

Manchester School   A term used to refer to the British liberals and radicals of the nineteenth century who were often critical of Great Britain's foreign policy. The members of this school were in favor of noninterference or nonintervention in the affairs of other states and as a result came to be seen as ISOLATIONISTS. The key figures in the school were RICHARD COBDEN and John Bright (1811–1889).

Manchukuo   *See* MANCHURIAN CRISIS.

Manchurian Crisis   The Japanese conquest of the Chinese province of Manchuria in 1931, beginning

with the MUKDEN INCIDENT. While the puppet government of Manchukuo was created in 1932 by the Japanese as a diplomatic ploy, it was recognized only by Japan's AXIS partners, Germany and Italy (and the states they dominated). This crisis precipitated the STIMSON DOCTRINE, which called for a general refusal to diplomatically recognize governments created by aggression. After a LEAGUE OF NATIONS special commission (the LYTTON COMMISSION) reported that Manchuria was rightfully Chinese territory in 1933, the Japanese responded by withdrawing from the League. The Japanese would continue to occupy Manchuria until their 1945 defeat in World War II.

Mandates System   An arrangement established by the LEAGUE OF NATIONS after World War I that placed the colonies of Turkey and Germany under the control of some of the victor nations, which were established as "mandatory powers." Three types of mandates were created: Class A mandates (such as Iraq and Syria), which were almost ready for self-government; class B mandates (such as Tanganyika and Togoland), which were regarded as colonies although with certain rights; and class C mandates (such as the Marshall Islands and Namibia), which were given no promise of independence. Most of those mandates that did not achieve early independence were placed under the TRUSTEESHIP system of the United Nations.

Mandela, Nelson (1918–   )   The symbol of the South African antiAPARTHEID movement and president of the AFRICAN NATIONAL CONGRESS. Mandela, a lawyer, joined the ANC in 1944. In 1951–1952 he led a "defiance campaign" against apartheid laws. Named deputy national president of the ANC in 1952, he advocated nonviolent resistance and the creation of a nonracial state in South Africa. After the SHARPEVILLE INCIDENT in 1960, in which 69 unarmed black protesters were killed by the police, Mandela created a paramilitary group to carry out sabotage. Arrested in 1963, he was later convicted of sabotage and sentenced to life imprisonment. Mandela was imprisoned from 1963 to 1990. He consistently refused to accede to government demands that he renounce antiapartheid violence as a precondition to his release. Since his release he has been actively seeking to help a recently more sympathetic South African government move toward a democratic multiracial system of governance. By late 1992 his negotiations were stalled over the reluctance of the white population to accept constitutional reforms that would give controlling political power to the black majority population. This was complicated by the fact that the black population has become increasingly split with the Zulu-based INKATHA FREEDOM PARTY refusing to acknowledge the leadership of Mandela and the ANC.

maneuverable reentry vehicle   *See* MARV.

Manhattan Project   The WORLD WAR II United States research effort that resulted in the development of the ATOMIC BOMB. The Manhattan Project cost about $2 billion then—about $10 billion in today's money. U.S. President Harry S Truman said of the Manhattan Project, "We have spent $2 billion on the greatest scientific gamble in history—and won" (*Time,* August 13, 1945). With nuclear weapons, there was a shift from a BALANCE OF POWER to a BALANCE OF TERROR concept.

Manila Declaration   The DEVELOPING COUNTRIES' "blueprint" for UNITED NATIONS CONFERENCE ON TRADE AND DEVELOPMENT negotiations issued by the third ministerial meeting of the GROUP OF 77 held in 1976, just prior to UNCTAD IV. The declaration and its program of action contained coordinated positions for the developing countries on such issues as debt relief, an integrated program for commodities, technology transfer, controls on multinational corporations, international trade, and the world food crisis.

Manila Pact   *See* SEATO.

man on horseback   **1.** A military officer who is a potential dictator if a civilian regime falters. **2.** Any former military figure (usually a general) ambitious for civilian leadership.   **3.** Any dictator.

Mansfield, Michael J. "Mike" (1903–   )   The United States Senator from Montana (1953–1977) and the Democratic majority leader (1961–1977). He was a key figure in the attempt to restore congressional prerogatives in foreign policy that took place during the first half of the 1970s. After leaving the Senate he served as ambassador to Japan during both the Carter and Reagan administrations.

Mansfield Amendment   A term used to describe a series of amendments to legislation that were introduced in the U.S. Senate in May 1971, November 1971, September 1973, and June 1974 and that, had they passed, would have mandated a significant reduction in the U.S. military presence in Western Europe. They were named after their primary sponsor, Senate Majority Leader Mike Mansfield of Montana, and came after he introduced a long series of congressional resolutions (1966–1970) on the same matter. The pressure from the Senate pushed the Nixon Administration into negotiations with the Soviet Union on the possibility of mutual force reductions. Although these talks did not make much progress, they helped defuse the pressure—unilateral cuts seemed inappropriate when there was a possibility of reciprocal reductions. The changing international climate also helped to contain the congressional pressure: As the United States and the Soviet Union moved from the détente of the early 1970s to a period of renewed tension, the idea of cutting the number of U.S. troops in Europe seemed far less attractive. By 1974 support for the Mansfield Amendment had declined, and in 1975, after the end of the Vietnam War, Mansfield decided not to reintroduce the amendment. Nevertheless, the pressure had made West Europeans realize that they were expected to bear a greater share of the burden of the common defense.

Mansfieldism   A term sometimes used in Europe to describe congressional pressure in the United States for a reduction in the U.S. military presence in Western Europe. It was most used during the early 1970s MANSFIELD AMENDMENT controversy and in the early 1980s, as an upsurge of pressure for cutting U.S. troops in Europe swept the United States as a means of punishing the Europeans for adopting a softer line toward the Soviet Union than the United States wanted.

Mao Zedong (also spelled as Mao Tse-tung) (1893–1976)   The principal revolutionary thinker and supreme leader of the Chinese Communist Party from its founding in 1921 until his death. The son of

Mao Zedong (1893–1976)

an affluent farmer, Mao's first real revolutionary experience occurred in 1911 when he participated in the overthrow of the Manchu dynasty. While working as a librarian's assistant at Peking University in 1919, he became involved with the May Fourth Movement (student demonstrations protesting against the PARIS PEACE CONFERENCE's decision to hand over former German concessions in China to Japan instead of returning them to China). Committed to MARXISM, Mao returned to his native province of Hunan in 1920 as the principal of a primary school. He organized a small Communist group there. The next year he became one of the founders of the Chinese Communist Party. In 1923, when the Communists formed an alliance with SUN YAT-SEN's KUOMINTANG (Nationalist Party), Mao abandoned his job as principal and became a professional revolutionary. Mao soon concluded that a Chinese Communist revolution would succeed only by relying on the peasants, hundreds of millions strong, to encircle the cities from the countryside and thus defeat CHIANG KAI-SHEK, the Nationalist leader who sought to militarily wipe out the Communists. This tactic was a major departure from the traditional Communist route to power of urban uprisings by industrial

Mao Zedong (Library of Congress)

workers. Beginning in 1927, Mao expanded his Communist army, developed its rural bases, and perfected tactics of GUERRILLA WARFARE. After frustrating the first four military campaigns against them by Chiang's forces, in 1934 Mao and his troops were forced to abandon their base in Kiangsi province and set out for the northwest of China on what is known as the LONG MARCH. It was during this strategic retreat that Mao secured the unchallenged role of leader of the party. Between 1936 and 1945 Mao formed a loose alliance with Chiang in their mutual war against the Japanese invaders. By the time of the Japanese surrender in 1945, Mao's armed forces had grown to over a million; he was in control of over 90 million people. Despite Soviet leader Joseph Stalin's disapproval and U.S. efforts at mediation, after World War II Mao led the Communist forces to military victory over Chiang's Nationalist forces and established a new state, the People's Republic of China, in 1949.

In the early years of the People's Republic, Mao patterned his economic policy after the Soviet model. In 1956 after the Soviet Communist Party criticized the deceased Stalin for his PURGES, Mao initiated a policy of "letting a hundred flowers bloom," which allowed intellectuals to speak their minds, in the hope that a less repressive environment would win the commitment of the intellectuals to his policies of modernization. However, the intellectuals did not confine their criticism to mere defects of certain policies but raised fundamental questions about the repressive nature of the Communist system. Mao then gave up on the intellectuals and sought to inspire the rank and file of the workers and peasants to continue his Chinese socialist revolution. Mao's central planning policy of the GREAT LEAP FORWARD ended in economic disaster; he was forced into semiretirement when he was replaced as the chairman of the People's Republic. By 1965 Mao, realizing that the traditional methods of dislodging his opponents within the party was no longer working, initiated the CULTURAL REVOLUTION by which he remolded the whole party organization. Many of his longtime colleagues were purged, and violence took a heavy toll of civilian lives. China's economy came to a standstill for years.

Mao's influence on China's resurgence in modern history is indisputable. His theory of revolution, which departed from orthodox Marxism, led the Chinese Communists to power in a backward agricultural country. His efforts to build a new China that the rest of the world would have to reckon with, and his obsession with continuous revolution, brought China almost to economic bankruptcy. Mao's historic legacy is mainly that he created a unified modern China using innovative guerrilla warfare tactics. Under Mao, China not only developed nuclear weapons but also split with the Soviet Union. As a leader who had come to power through his own efforts, he was unwilling to subordinate Chinese interests to those of the international Communist movement as defined by Moscow.

Mao's final years were marked by declining health. He lived in virtual seclusion and left no heir apparent when he died in September 1976. Thereupon a power struggle ensued marked by the arrest of the GANG OF FOUR and the emergence of DENG XIAOPING as China's leader in August 1977.

Maoism   1. The ideas and ideology developed by MAO ZEDONG, especially those related to revolution. Mao integrated familiar ideas about GUERRILLA WARFARE into a more comprehensive approach to revolution based on the idea of what he termed people's war. He saw widespread popular support for the guerrilla as crucial to the success of the revolution and as something that could provide sustenance for the efforts of the insurgents; these ideas have influenced guerrilla movements worldwide, particularly the SENDERO LUMINOSO in Peru.   2. An approach to foreign policy that emphasized the lessons of the Chinese model of development for other THIRD WORLD states and that was part of the more general challenge posed by Mao to Soviet leadership of the international Communist movement. *See also* SINO-SOVIET SPLIT.

Maphilindo   *See* ASA.

march on Rome   An episode in BENITO MUSSOLINI's seizure of power in Italy in October 1922. Supposedly Mussolini and 25,000 of his private army, dressed in their BLACKSHIRTS, marched from Milan on Rome, as Italy was on the verge of anarchy and civil war. King VICTOR EMMANUEL III refused to use the army against the marchers and asked Mussolini to become prime minister, form a fascist government, and restore order. But there never was a serious march; only a ceremonial parade after the blackshirts arrived by train—and after Mussolini had power. The fascists had gained power not from a great march but from prior terrorism and intimidation. The "march on Rome" myth (created by Mussolini's fascist propaganda) is now used to refer to any mass demonstration of people assembled in a capital to make demands of a government.

Marcos, Ferdinand E. (1917–1989)   The president of the Philippines from 1965 until 1986, when he was forced into exile by a popular uprising led by CORAZON AQUINO. Initially his administration supported economic and social reforms. Then in 1972 Marcos declared martial law, citing anarchy, lawlessness, urban terrorism, and open rebellion by the New People's Army, the military wing of the Communist Party of the Philippines, as justification. Effectively a dictator during the eight years of martial law, Marcos introduced a political program called the New Society and a political party called the New Society Movement. During martial law Marcos suppressed democratic institutions and restricted civil liberties, ruling largely by decree and popular referenda. Nevertheless, the New Society program resulted in improved law and order and the introduction of some reforms. The government began a process of political normalization in 1978. Elections were held that year for an interim national assembly, in 1980 for local officials, and in 1981 for president. The New Society Movement won these elections with 80 to 90 percent of the vote. Marcos was reelected to a six-year term in 1981. Despite the end of martial law in 1981, Marcos retained his wide arrest and detention powers. The 1983 assassination of the leader of the opposition, BENIGNO AQUINO, as he returned from exile, coalesced popular dissatisfaction with Marcos, with the deteriorating economy, and with corrupt government. Marcos called a snap presidential election in December 1985 for February 1986. The opposition united under a ticket headed by Aquino's widow, Corazon. The election was marred by electoral fraud on the part of Marcos and his supporters. Because it became widely known that Aquino had actually won more votes than Marcos, Marcos was forced to flee the Philippines by a peaceful civilian-military uprising that ousted him and declared

From right, Imelda Marcos, Lyndon B. Johnson, Ferdinand Marcos, and Lady Bird Johnson at the White House in 1966. (Library of Congress)

Aquino winner of the election. Marcos, at the invitation of the United States, flew to luxurious exile in Hawaii and spent the rest of his life dealing with lawsuits from the Aquino government seeking to get back the billions he corruptly obtained during his years of public service.

Marianne   **1.** A classically dressed female character who personifies France in general. **2.** The French Republic. This usage dates from the revolutions of 1848. *Compare to* JOHN BULL; UNCLE SAM.

Mariel boatlift   The departure of people from the Cuban port of Mariel to Florida in the United States, occasioned when Cuban dictator FIDEL CASTRO announced on April 19, 1980, that Cubans living in the United States could come and get their relations. A makeshift "freedom flotilla" brought out 125,000 refugees over the next few months.

Almost all of these refugees remained in South Florida and are now working productively. But because Castro purposely sent out criminals and psychiatric patients, about 2,500 remain in U.S. prisons or mental institutions. Another 400 were deported back to Cuba.

Marighella, Carlos (1912–1969)   The Brazilian guerrilla leader who has been a major influence on leftist guerrilla organizations around the globe. His book, *The Mini-manual of the Urban Guerrilla* (1971), translated into many languages, was adopted as a "how-to" instruction book by the TUPAMAROS, who, in turn, were a major influence on urban guerrilla movements. The *Mini-manual* included techniques for raising funds (through ransoms and thefts), liquidating the opposition, forging documents, and performing surgery on wounded comrades. Marighella was killed by Brazilian police in 1969.

maritime strategy   **1.** A force projection capability based on naval power and sea-lift capability. A maritime strategy is necessarily adopted by any power that has a substantial navy and widely scattered military and commercial interests.   **2.** A master plan for the use of sea power in peace and war.   **3.** The strategy developed by the United States Navy in the 1980s to use U.S. maritime supremacy against the Soviet Union in the event of a crisis or war. The Maritime Strategy included forward deployment of forces early in a crisis and power projections into the Soviet submarine bastions.

marker   **1.** An I.O.U. (I owe you); a written indication of a debt, often a gambling debt.   **2.** A border indicator. In this context the word is used in the phrase "lay down a marker" to send a signal not to cross a line, whether figurative or literal.   **3.** A political obligation to someone. For example, if a political supporter contributed $250,000 to a candidate's campaign for election, that candidate, once elected, would be expected to give a sympathetic hearing to the supporter's request for an appointment to office or recommendations for new legislation.

market access   Availability of a national market to exporting countries, reflecting a government's willingness to permit imports to compete, relatively unimpeded, with similar domestically produced goods.

Marne, Battle of   **1.** The first major battle of WORLD WAR I when, in September 1914, the German Army advanced toward Paris and was stopped when French reserves were rushed to confront them. All possible vehicles (including the taxis of Paris) were used to bring reinforcements. The armies met and, after 250,000 casualties on each side, a relatively stable line of trenches was created that stalemated the war on the WESTERN FRONT for the next four years.   **2.** The last German offensive of World War I when, during July 1918, the Germans sought to advance but after initial successes were counterattacked and driven back; this turned into a general advance by the Allies that forced Germany to ask for the ARMISTICE.

Marshall, George Catlett, Jr. (1880–1959)   The chief of staff of the U.S. Army during WORLD WAR II, gen-

erally considered the American soldier most responsible for the ultimate victory. Marshall selected all the major commanders, allocated resources, and determined overall strategy. As a man of unstinting honor and integrity, he was revered by practically all who worked for or with him. According to Forrest C. Pogue (*George C. Marshall: Organizer of Victory*, 1973), Marshall would have commanded the D-Day invasion of Europe instead of Dwight D. Eisenhower, except for the fact that his civilian superior, U.S. President Franklin D. Roosevelt, decided Marshall would remain as chief of staff because, in Roosevelt's words: "Well I didn't feel I could sleep at ease if you were out of Washington." After his retirement from the army he was U.S. Ambassador to China (1945–1947), secretary of state (1947–1949), head of the American Red Cross (1949–1950), and secretary of defense during the first part of the Korean War (1950–1951). In 1953 he was awarded the Nobel Peace Prize for his work on the MARSHALL PLAN. In a November 16, 1945, speech U.S. President Harry S Truman said: "In a war unparalleled in magnitude and horror, millions of Americans gave their country outstanding service. General of the Army George C. Marshall gave it victory." It was because of Truman's admiration for Marshall that the European Recovery Program was named in Marshall's honor.

Marshall Plan   The economic recovery program for post–World War II Europe proposed by U.S. Secretary of State George C. Marshall, Jr., on June 5, 1947, at a graduation speech at Harvard University. Marshall there announced the European Recovery Program, the massive economic aid effort that became known as the Marshall Plan: "Our policy is directed not against any country or doctrine but against hunger, poverty, desperation and chaos. Its purpose should be the revival of a working economy in the world so as to permit the emergence of political and social conditions in which free institutions can exist." It directly addressed the policy of CONTAINMENT by attempting to end postwar financial problems in Western Europe and thus reduce vulnerability to communism while limiting U.S. involvement in Europe.

The Marshall Plan was the first large-scale foreign assistance program of the post–World War II period. Carefully constructed by the U.S. Congress in conjunction with the executive branch, it became part of the Foreign Assistance Act of 1948. Although scheduled to run for four years, the European Recovery Program actually operated as a separate program for only three years. Between 1947 and 1950, it supplied grants and credits of $13.2 billion U.S., as Western European industrial production rose 45 percent and reached a level 25 percent over that of 1938, the last prewar year. Such an increase had originally had a target date of 1952–1953. Most of the funds went to Great Britain ($3.2 billion), France ($2.7 billion), Italy ($1.5 billion), and West Germany ($1.4 billion). Funds also were offered to Eastern Europe, but Soviet leader Joseph Stalin refused to allow the Soviet satellite states to participate. After 1950 the program was merged with other defense and economic programs. From that time on, although economic aid to Europe continued on a diminished scale, it was linked so inextricably to other forms of aid that it is difficult to assess as part of the original European Recovery Program.

The plan worked so well and became so well known that the term Marshall Plan entered the language and means any massive use of federal funds to solve a major social problem. U.S. President Harry S Truman wrote in volume 2 of his *Memoirs* (1956): "I had referred to the idea [European Recovery Program] as the 'Marshall Plan' when it was discussed in staff meetings, because I wanted General Marshall to get full credit for his brilliant contributions. . . . He had perceived the inspirational as well as the economic value of the proposal. History, rightly, will always associate his name with this program, which helped save Europe from economic disaster and lifted it from the shadow of enslavement by Russian Communism." The Marshall Plan was significant historically as a major step on the road to a United States security commitment to Western Europe. The Atlantic Alliance was created in large part to provide a security shield behind which the Economic Recovery Program could come to fruition. This is somewhat ironic, given that the plan as initially conceived was intended to limit U.S. involvement in European security issues by reinvigorating the states of Western Europe in the hope that they would then be able to contain Soviet power by themselves. Equally ironic is the fact that in the aftermath of the collapse

of the Soviet Union, there has been much discussion of the need for a new Marshall Plan for Russia.

martial law   1. The military control over a state's internal territory in time of emergency because of public necessity. For example, martial law was declared in Los Angeles, California, in the United States, for a few days in 1992 to quell domestic rioting.   2. Arbitrary military rule imposed not by constitutional means, but by force. Typically after a military COUP D'ÉTAT martial law is declared until conditions stabilize.

MARV (maneuverable reentry vehicle)   The next stage in sophisticated warhead design after multiple independently targeted reentry vehicles (MIRVs). While a MIRVed missile can deliver several warheads against separate targets, once ejected from the missile's bus (or front end) they follow predetermined and predictable courses. A MARVed missile, on the other hand, would eject as many warheads, each also destined for a separate preselected target, but the warheads would then follow variable courses, making them much harder for ballistic missile defenses to destroy.

Marxism   1. The revolutionary doctrine developed by Karl Marx (1818–1883) and Friedrich Engels (1820–1895) that was based on the belief that human history is a history of struggle between exploiting and exploited classes. Their COMMUNIST MANIFESTO (1848) was written "to do for history what Darwin's theory has done for biology." Marxism maintains that the proletariat (working class) will suffer so from alienation that they will eventually revolt against the bourgeoisie, those who own the means of production, and overthrow the capitalist system. After a temporary period of rule by "the dictatorship of the proletariat," the classless society of communism would evolve. While Marxism had a strong influence on the economies of the Second, Third, and Fourth worlds, its full intent was never achieved. Marx's magnum opus, *Das Kapital* (1867), is frequently referred to as the bible of socialism. But with the collapse of the Soviet Union, Marxism as an economic, political, and social force in world politics has suffered an immense and probably irreversible blow. Although it may have some residual attraction in parts of the

Karl Marx (Library of Congress)

Third World, it is unlikely to be anything like the force it was during the Cold War. **2.** "The opium of the intellectuals," according to Edmund Wilson, in *Letters on Literature and Politics 1912–1972* (1977)—a play on Marx's assertion that religion was the opium of the suffering masses. *See also* COMMUNISM.

Marxism-Leninism Marxist theory filtered through the ideological slants given to it by V. I. LENIN and other leaders of the Soviet Union. While MARXISM is a general theory of economics and society, Marxism-Leninism presents practical approaches for revolutionaries seeking to overthrow capitalistic societies and install governments based on the precepts of Karl Marx. In essence, Marxism-Leninism is the theory on how to implement Marxism.

Masaryk, Jan (1886–1948) The Czechoslovakian ambassador to Great Britain from 1925 until 1938, when he resigned in protest over the MUNICH AGREEMENT. During World War II he was the foreign minister of the Czechoslovakian government in exile. After his country was liberated in 1945 by the Allies, he returned as foreign minister but fell to his death from a high window during the 1948 Communist coup. Whether he was pushed or jumped has never been fully determined. He was the son of Tomés Masaryk.

Masaryk, Tomés G. (1850–1937) The first president of Czechoslovakia from 1918 until ill health forced him to retire in 1935. As president he strongly supported the LEAGUE OF NATIONS. After seeking friendly relations with Germany, he realized that the increasing threat represented by Nazi Germany demanded more energy than he could bring to his office. Consequently, he resigned, knowing that his foreign minister, EDUARD BENES, would succeed him.

Mashraq Arabic term meaning "east"; the Arab states of the eastern Mediterranean seaboard: Egypt, Jordan, Lebanon, and Syria.

Mashraq Agreements Cooperative agreements on trade with the European Community signed by the MASHRAQ states.

massive retaliation The policy of the Eisenhower Administration, enunciated by U.S. Secretary of State JOHN FOSTER DULLES in 1954, that it would respond with the greatest possible force (implying nuclear weapons) to Communist aggression. The policy was motivated both by a desire to reduce defense spending and by a desire to avoid future involvement in LIMITED WARS such as the Korean War. Dulles explained his policy in a 1954 speech: "Local defense will always be important. But there is no local defense which alone will contain the mighty land power of the Communist world. Local defense must be reinforced by the further deterrent of massive retaliatory power. A potential aggressor must know that he cannot always prescribe battle conditions that suit him. . . . The basic decision was to depend primarily upon a great capacity to retaliate, instantly, by means and at times of our own choosing" (quoted in Henry L. Trewhitt, *McNamara*, 1971). Eisenhower's secretary of defense, Charles E. Wilson, called this policy the "new look" and emphasized its desirability by asserting that it would offer "a bigger bang for a buck." Massive retaliation was criticized on the grounds that, in too many circumstances, the response would be out of all proportion to the provocation; therefore it lacked credibility. And once the Soviet Union developed nuclear weapons of its own sufficient to retaliate against any possible U.S. nuclear strike against it, whether these weapons could do anything but deter the use of nuclear weapons by the other side was not clear. Soon after the Kennedy Administration took office in 1961, its secretary of defense, Robert S. McNamara, proclaimed that the U.S. policy of massive nuclear retaliation was "believed by few of our friends and none of our enemies." The policy of FLEXIBLE RESPONSE was then developed.

Mata Hari (1876–1917)   The Dutchwoman, born Margaretha G. Zelle, who was executed during World War I by the French as a German spy. Because she was sexually involved with a variety of high-ranking officers on both sides, her trial by a military court generated enormous publicity. Ever since, her name has personified the seductive female spy.

Mau Mau   The Kenyan anticolonial guerrillas who conducted violent anti-British operations during the 1950s. Primarily a nativist cult made up of the Kikuyu tribe of Kenya, the Mau Mau uprising (1952–1956) was supposedly led by Jomo Kenyatta (1893–1978), an anthropologist who later became prime minister of an independent Kenya in 1963. While imprisoned for leading the Mau Mau rebellion, Kenyatta always denied the charges. Despite imprisonment by the British from 1952 to 1961, Kenyatta, as the leader of Kenya from 1963 until his death in 1978, was one of the most pro-British of African leaders. His policies made Kenya a prosperous and stable state that attracted significant foreign investment and tourism.

Maximiliano Hernandez Martinez Anti-Communist Alliance   A Salvadoran right-wing DEATH SQUAD, with strong ties to that country's military and police forces. This group is generally believed to be responsible for the 1980 assassination of Archbishop OSCAR ROMERO as well as for a wide-ranging campaign of violence and repression against leftists, moderates, university students, and labor union members.

Mayaguez **incident**   The May 1975 seizure of a U.S. merchant ship, the *Mayaguez,* by a Cambodian gunboat. The ship, which was in international waters, was confiscated by Cambodia, which claimed it was in territorial waters. The 39 crew members were released on a fishing boat shortly before an ill-fated U.S. Marine rescue mission found the ship but not the crew. Several dozen of the marines died in a helicopter crash over the South China Sea. The rapid response of the FORD Administration showed that despite the Communist takeover of South Vietnam the month before (in April 1975), the United States was still prepared to use force if provoked.

Mazowiecki, Tadeusz (1927–   )   Poland's first non-Communist prime minister since before World War II. Mazowiecki was nominated to the position in 1989 by the Citizens' Committee because he had worked closely with LECH WALESA and SOLIDARITY through the 1980s. As prime minister from 1989 to the end of 1990, Mazowiecki initiated tough economic reforms to begin Poland's transition toward a market-oriented economy. These difficult reforms caused the committee to turn against him as well as his defeat in the first presidential elections in Poland. Mazowiecki lost to both Walesa and STANISLAW TYMINSKI in the first round of presidential elections held in November 1990.

measures short of war   Actions by one state against another without a formal declaration of war or the use of force. Measures short of war, accepted practices in customary INTERNATIONAL LAW, range in severity from breaking off diplomatic relations to embargoes, boycotts, and the freezing of a country's investments. While the phrase also covers the use of economic blockades or the occupation of disputed territory, such activities run the risk of escalating the dispute into war. The United Nations Charter requires the renunciation of those kinds of unilateral measures for solving international disputes. Instead, disputes should be taken to the International Court of Justice, the Security Council, the United Nations General Assembly, or similar regional agencies.

Medellin Cartel   The term used to describe the drug gangs in Colombia that controlled most South

American cocaine trafficking during much of the 1980s. The Colombian city of Medellin has been the base of operations for these criminal organizations, which were responsible, at one time, for 80 percent of the cocaine smuggled into the United States. The cartel's conflict with the Colombian government, however, not only caused immense violence in Colombia but also damaged the cartel, which lost its preeminent position to the rival CALI CARTEL.

mediation   The effort by an impartial third party to help resolve disputes. Unlike in ARBITRATION, a mediator has no power but that of persuasion. The mediator's suggestions are advisory in nature and may be rejected by both parties. The terms mediation and CONCILIATION tend to be used interchangeably. However, there is a difference. Conciliation is a less active word. It essentially refers to efforts to bring the parties together so that they can resolve their problems themselves. Mediation, in contrast, is a more active term. It implies that an active effort will be made to help the parties reach agreement by clarifying issues, asking questions, and making specific proposals. However, the usage of the two terms has been so blurred that the only place where it is really necessary to distinguish between them is in a dictionary. Much diplomatic activity is mediation of one conflict or another.

megaton   The explosive power of a nuclear weapon expressed in terms of the amount of a conventional explosive that would have to be detonated to produce the same energy release; 1 megaton is equivalent to exploding 1 million tons of TNT. A kiloton is equivalent to 1,000 tons.

Meinhof, Ulrike (1934–1976)   One of the founding members of the RED ARMY FACTION, or the Baader-Meinhof Gang. Imprisoned beginning in 1972, she hanged herself in her cell in 1976.

Mein Kampf   German for "my struggle," the book ADOLF HITLER wrote while in prison in 1923–1924 and published in 1925. It explained his fanatical anti-Semitism, racism, and anti-Marxist mass politics. It also played on the German hatred of the Treaty of VERSAILLES. This anarchic rightist memoir became the manifesto of the German National Socialist (NAZI) Party.

Meir, Golda (1898–1978)   The prime minister of Israel from 1969 to 1974. Born in Russia, she grew up in the United States and emigrated to Palestine in 1921. After Israeli independence she was appointed ambassador to the Soviet Union in 1948. Elected to the Knesset (the Israeli parliament) in 1949, she was minister of labor (1949–1956) and foreign minister (1956–1966). She became prime minister in 1969. After the 1973 YOM KIPPUR WAR her government was heavily criticized for its lack of preparedness and she resigned in 1974.

Melian Dialogue or **Debate**   Refers to the account by THUCYDIDES in his *History of the Peloponnesian*

Golda Meir with U.S. President Richard M. Nixon on the White House lawn. (Library of Congress)

War (fifth century B.C.) of the debate between the ancient Athenians and the Melians about whether the island of Melos should surrender to Athenian forces or fight. Melos was a colony of Sparta and had refused to join the Athenian empire. Before attacking Melos, the Athenians decided to offer the Melians the choice between war and surrender. The arguments and rejoinders provide a rich debate for students of international politics. They are full of ideas about relations between great and small powers and the role of power in international politics.

During the debate, the Athenians made no pretense that their arguments were couched in terms of justice, contending instead that "when these matters are discussed by practical people, the standard of justice depends on the equality of power to compel and in fact the strong do what they have the power to do and the weak accept what they have to accept." The reason they put forward for the conquest of Melos was one of self-interest and credibility. The Athenian argument was that if Athens was on friendly terms with Melos and failed to attack, Athenian subjects would see this as a sign of weakness. Against this the Melians contended that military actions would be counterproductive for Athens, as an attack on Melos would frighten other neutral states, which would fear for their own safety in the future and would consequently ally against a power they saw as a potential threat to themselves. In this argument, it is possible to discern a sophisticated and subtle kind of BALANCE OF POWER thinking. The same kind of thinking also was evident in the Melian argument that, although Melos had little power, its inferiority would be offset by its alliance with Sparta. Against Athenian arguments that this alliance meant very little, the Melians claimed that it was not in Sparta's self-interest to betray them, as this would result in Sparta losing the confidence of its friends and benefiting its enemies. The Athenians were not convinced, however, and presented the Melians with a choice between war and safety. The Athenian delegation argued that the safe rule was to "stand up to one's equals, behave with deference towards one's superiors and to treat one's inferiors with moderation." Although this can be understood as an attempt to use coercion rather than resort to brute military force, it failed. The final outcome was that the Melians decided to fight. When reinforcements came from Athens, however, the Melians were forced to surrender unconditionally. The Athenians then killed all the men and sold the women and children into slavery.

Menchú, Rigoberta (1959–   ) The Guatemalan exile (living in Mexico) who won the 1992 Nobel Peace Prize for her efforts to publicize the human rights abuses of the Guatemalan government over the past three decades. While the Nobel Committee in making the award said that her speaking and writing made her stand out "as a vivid symbol of peace and reconciliation across ethnic, cultural and social dividing lines," the foreign minister of Guatemala, Gonzalo Menédez Park, said she did not deserve the prize because she "is tied to certain groups that have endangered Guatemala" (*New York Times,* October 17, 1992). While Menchú has denied that she ever belonged to any of the guerrilla insurgent groups in Guatemala, she has been the most eloquent international publicizer of the social justice for which they purportedly fight. *See also* GUATEMALAN NATIONAL REVOLUTIONARY UNITY.

Mendes-France, Pierre (1907–1982) The French lawyer who was finance minister of France's Provisional Government (1943–1944), then minister of national economy (1944–1945) and prime minister and minister of foreign affairs between June 1954 and February 1955. He proposed that France, Great Britain, and the United States jointly control the North Atlantic Treaty Organization's nuclear force. A longtime critic of his nation's imperial war in Southeast Asia, he fulfilled an electoral promise by overseeing the French withdrawal from Indochina.

Mendoza, Declaration of A 1991 declaration signed by Argentina, Brazil, and Chile banning the development, production, acquisition, and stockpiling of biological and chemical weapons on their territory.

Mengistu Haile Mariam *See* ETHIOPIAN CIVIL WAR.

Mensheviks One of the two major factions (the BOLSHEVIK group was the other) of the pre–World War I Russian Social Democratic Labor Party. At its Second Congress in London in 1903, the beginnings of a break between the Bolsheviks (the majority) and the Mensheviks (the minority) occurred. The Bolsheviks, headed by V. I. LENIN, wanted only professional revolutionaries in the party, while the Mensheviks, such as Pavel Axelrod (1850–1928), believed that anyone who supported the party should be a member. Although attempts were made to breach the differences, the rift widened over the years, primarily due to Lenin's intransigence. The Mensheviks believed in Marxist determinism, which included the acceptance of a bourgeois phase before a proletariat revolution, and could not countenance Bolshevik methods such as expropriations, their avowal of themselves as the only Russian Marxist group, and their immediate desire for a proletariat revolution at any cost. With the fall of the Romanov dynasty in 1917, some Mensheviks cooperated with the Provisional Government. After the coup in October (the RUSSIAN REVOLUTION OF 1917), the Mensheviks refused to cooperate with the Bolsheviks. The Bolsheviks eventually suppressed the faction in 1922, and during the purges of the 1930s "Menshevism" was called treason.

mercantilism The seventeenth- and eighteenth-century economic philosophy that equated a state's power with its possession of gold and silver bullion, gained through a favorable BALANCE OF TRADE and domestic monopolies. Although this economic philosophy has few followers among modern economists and twentieth-century trade policy experts, some political leaders still favor policies that promote exports and protect domestic industries competing with imports, on the theory that a trade surplus—which results in the accumulation of monetary assets in exchange for real goods—is equated with economic strength and moral virtue. The problem with mercantilism, however, is that it downgrades cooperation. It is the economic equivalent of arms racing, in which efforts to achieve gains for one country at the expense of others can lead to all those involved being worse off.

mercenary A soldier for hire; one who will fight for whoever pays him or her without any particular regard to ideological concerns. Twentieth-century mercenaries range from hired killers, who call themselves mercenaries because it makes what they do sound more legitimate, to former members of some of the world's best armies who tend to work for the revolutionary or the counterrevolutionary movements of the THIRD WORLD.

MACHIAVELLI ON MERCENARIES

If any one supports his state by the arms of mercenaries, he will never stand firm or sure, as they are disunited, ambitious, without discipline, faithless, bold amongst friends, cowardly amongst enemies, they have no fear of God, and keep no faith with men. Ruin is only deferred as long as the assault is postponed; in peace you are despoiled by them, and in war by the enemy. The cause of this is that they have no love or other motive to keep them in the field beyond a trifling wage, which is not enough to make them ready to die for you. They are quite willing to be your soldiers so long as you do not make war.

SOURCE: Niccolò Machiavelli, *The Prince* (1513).

---

merchant of death **1.** A private business that sells arms and munitions in quantities suitable for military use. The term was widely used in U.S. congressional investigations after World War I. **2.** A government that sells arms and munitions to other governments; this traffic is usually one way—from the FIRST WORLD to the THIRD WORLD.

Merger Treaty The 1965 agreement, signed in Brussels, that brought three European Communities (the European Coal and Steel Community, the European Economic Community, and the Euratom) under the control of a single EUROPEAN COMMISSION guided by a council of ministers, the European Parliament, and the European Court of Justice.

Mexican Border Campaign The 1916–1917 expedition of the U.S. Army into Mexico to punish bandit leader PANCHO VILLA for murderous raids in the U.S. state of New Mexico. Fifteen thousand men under U.S. General John J. Pershing crossed the border into Mexico in 1916 and penetrated 300 miles into the interior. They generated great anti-U.S. feeling and never found Villa; they withdrew after almost a year.

Mexican Revolution The Mexican civil war that began as a revolt against dictator Porfirio Diaz (1830–1915) but transformed the country into a "revolutionary" society. Diaz, president for 35 years, was opposed in the 1910 elections by Francisco Madero (1873–1913), a wealthy landowner advo-

"The Dough Boy," a 1930s cartoon of a merchant of death. (Library of Congress)

cating liberal reforms, including a free press and an open political system. Diaz arrested Madero, who escaped and became a popular figure supported by bandit revolutionaries PANCHO VILLA and EMILIANO ZAPATA. Unable to quell dissent by landless and starving peasants and Indians as well as by a middle class unable to participate in the political system and unhappy over foreign investment in Mexico, Diaz resigned. Upon assuming the presidency in 1911, Madero could not mediate among radical revolutionaries, landowners, and Diaz supporters, who continued to fight against his government. General Victoriano Huerta (1854–1916) deposed and murdered Madero in 1913, touching off a bloody struggle for the presidency among Villa, Zapata, and Huerta. By 1917 Huerta was dead and Venustiano Carranza (1859–1920) defeated Villa and Zapata as president of a new Mexican republic.

MICE   An acronym for the classic means of forcing an otherwise unwilling person to spy against his or her country: Money, Ideology, Compromise, and Ego. *See also* SMICE.

microstate   Any state with an extremely small land area relative to other states; examples include Andorra, Liechtenstein, Monaco, and San Marino.

Middle East   **1.** The Arab states and Israel.   **2.** All of the Muslim states of North Africa and West Asia plus Israel.   **3.** Those states that directly bear on the Arab-Israeli conflict and the security of the Persian Gulf: Bahrain, Egypt, Iran, Iraq, Israel, Jordan, Kuwait, Lebanon, Libya, Oman, Qatar, Saudi Arabia, Syria, the United Arab Emirates, and North and South Yemen.   **4.** The NEAR EAST.

Also known as the Mideast. This is a geographical expression upon which there is no common agreement as to meaning. Whichever meaning of Middle East is used, however, it is clearly a region of considerable turbulence and competition for power and influence among the indigenous states, exacerbated by outside competition. Its location, its significance for some of the great religions of the world, and the fact that it is an immense source of energy resources (particularly oil and natural gas) make it very difficult for GREAT POWERS to ignore the region.

middle power   Powers that are not quite GREAT POWERS but that are not SMALL POWERS either. Those states that fit into this category tend to have regional rather than global interests and impact. According to Martin Wight in *Power Politics* (1979), middle powers have limited interests and limited means of defending them. He also contends that "middle powers appear when the qualifications for great-power status are being revised. The number of middle powers varies inversely with the number of great." Even acknowledging the point about revision, the difficulty with this category of powers is that it is static and, without further elucidation, conveys little sense of the dynamics of international politics. The term can refer to those states that are likely to become great powers and are clearly on their way up as well as to former great powers that are clearly on the way down. Moreover, it is not always clear at what point a middle power ceases to belong in this category and becomes a great or a small power. Because of these difficulties, some analysts try to find alternative terms, such as REGIONAL POWER.

Midgetman   A small intercontinental ballistic missile (SICBM), a mobile single-warhead missile developed but not deployed by the United States. Midgetman missiles were supposed to be small enough that they could be carried on trucks; thus they could be so widely dispersed that they would not be a good target for an enemy FIRST STRIKE. The small size of the missile gave it its nickname. In 1992 U.S. President George Bush, citing the end of the COLD WAR, announced the cancellation of the Midgetman program.

Midway, Battle of   The first major defeat of the Japanese Navy by the United States in WORLD WAR II. In June 1942 the Japanese attempted to seize Midway Island, 1,500 miles to the west of Hawaii in the mid-Pacific. The invasion fleet was detected when the United States broke Japan's secret radio codes. Three U.S. carriers were sent to attack a massive Japanese fleet, which included nine battleships and four carriers. In the carrier battle that ensued, the Japanese lost all four of their carriers; the United States lost one. This battle was important because it meant that six months after PEARL HARBOR, the United States had gained the offensive and had sunk four of the six carriers that had attacked the Hawaiian base.

MI5   The British intelligence agency responsible for internal security and counterespionage. Its duties are similar to those of the U.S. FEDERAL BUREAU OF INVESTIGATION. *Compare to* MI6.

MiG   A designation for Soviet fighter aircraft designed and developed by General Artem Mikoyan and General Mikhail Gurevich. The MiG-15 was the version of this aircraft used in air combat against U.S. fighters during the Korean War; the MiG-21 was the type used by North Vietnamese (and possibly other) forces during the Vietnam War.

militarism   1. A state's policy of seeking to gain its ends by the overt or threatened use of military force. U.S. President Woodrow Wilson defined militarism in a speech to the 1916 graduating class at West Point: "Militarism does not consist in the existence of any army, nor even in the existence of a very great army. Militarism is a spirit. It is a point of view. It is system. It is a purpose. The purpose of militarism is to use armies for aggression."   2. A

political culture and ideology that supports or extols military values, patriotism, and associated group behaviors or symbols. Obviously states that are in fact militaristic are likely to exhibit militarism in much of their social symbolism, for example, as with a general love of elaborate military uniforms.

military   1. Having to do with war, or the affairs of war, whether on land, sea, or in the air.   2. All of a state's defensive and offensive armed forces.   3. Land-based forces, as opposed to naval or air forces.

military advice   Recommendations given to civilian policymakers by leaders of armed forces. It is especially important in situations of crisis or war. After studying such advice in a series of Cold War crises, Richard Betts in *Soldiers, Statesmen and Cold War Crises* (1977) concluded that, on balance, military advisors of the United States have not been notably more belligerent than civilian advisors when it comes to considering the possible use of force.

military assistance   *See* SECURITY ASSISTANCE.

military attaché   *See* ARMY ATTACHÉ.

military bloc   A mutual ALLIANCE to prepare for war, usually by a group of states in a common geographical area. Examples include the NORTH ATLANTIC TREATY ORGANIZATION and the WARSAW PACT.

military civil action   *See* CIVIC ACTION.

military commission   A court convened by an authority within the armed forces for the trial of persons not usually subject to military law who are charged with violations of the laws of war; and, in places subject to military government or MARTIAL LAW, for the trial of such persons when charged with violations of ordinances, proclamations, and valid domestic civil and criminal laws of the territory concerned.

military deception   *See* STRATEGIC DECEPTION.

military diplomacy   1. International negotiations conducted by military officers on each side.   2. Specifically, negotiations conducted by the military leadership of the United States and the Soviet Union in an effort to establish a regime or set of rules designed to reduce the dangers of their relationship. The irony is that this relationship reached its peak shortly before the collapse of the Soviet Union in 1991.

military doctrine   *See* DOCTRINE.

military exercise   **1.** Any training by armed forces. **2.** A WAR GAME. **3.** Tactical maneuvers carried out in imitation of war. These efforts to simulate real war situations are critical if a military unit is to be ready for combat. When such exercises are large scale and near borders, it is common that neighboring states are notified so that they will not be alarmed. Often, as in South Korea and Europe, military exercises of the United States are conducted with allies so that the various national units can learn to coordinate their activities.

WAR GAME TACTICS

An umpire [in a military exercise] decided that a bridge had been destroyed by an enemy attack and flagged it accordingly. From then on, it was not to be used by men or vehicles. Shortly, a corporal brought his squad up to the bridge, looked at the flag, and hesitated for a moment; then resolutely marched his men across it. The umpire yelled at him:

"Hey, don't you see that that bridge is destroyed?"

The corporal answered, "Of course I can see it's destroyed. Can't you see we're swimming?"

SOURCE: President Dwight D. Eisenhower, *At Ease* (1967).

---

military government   *See* CIVIL AFFAIRS.

military governor   The army commander or other designated person who, in an OCCUPIED TERRITORY, exercises supreme authority over the civil population subject to the laws and usages of war and to any directive received from his or her government or superior.

military-industrial complex   A state's armed forces and their suppliers of technology and products. During his January 17, 1961, farewell address, U.S. President Dwight D. Eisenhower warned, "In the councils of government we must guard against the acquisition of unwarranted influence, whether sought or unsought, by the military-industrial complex. The potential for the disastrous rise of misplaced power exists and will persist." Malcolm C. Moos (1916–1982), Eisenhower's chief speechwriter during his second term, is usually credited with coining the phrase, which has become Eisenhower's single most memorable rhetorical contribution to world politics.

During the Cold War, the military-industrial complex of both SUPERPOWERS was widely seen as having an influence that was both pervasive and malignant—pervasive in that it had an impact on so many aspects of life and malignant in that this influence was generally seen as negative. It was believed that the military-industrial complex on both sides was against DÉTENTE or mutual accommodation and was against ARMS CONTROL. While there was something to such arguments, and to the belief that there were close linkages among the leaders of the military and U.S. industry (with many officers working for companies in the defense field after their retirement from the military), the idea that some kind of conspiracy existed, orchestrated by a monolithic group of military officers and industrialists, was less compelling. With the end of the Cold War, the military-industrial complex in the United States and Russia is being greatly cut back although not dismantled.

military intelligence   *See* INTELLIGENCE.

military intervention   The introduction of armed forces into another nation, against its will, in an attempt to determine political arrangements or outcomes within this nation. The term INTERVENTION has a similar, though less specific, meaning.

military law   **1.** MARTIAL LAW. **2.** The laws prevailing within military organizations.

military leader   **1.** An officer in a state's armed forces. **2.** A gentler way of referring to a DICTATOR.

military mind   A term that implies that professional officers are either less intellectually gifted than those who enter other professions, or have such a mind that they see the use of force as the universal solution to problems that may also lend themselves to diplomatic solutions.

SHEEP AND THE MILITARY MIND

[During World War I] the General said to me [J. F. C. Fuller]: "The [British] War Office is very nervous about an invasion, there are five million . . . sheep in Sussex, Kent and Surrey [in England]. When the enemy land, [the sheep] will at once be moved by route march to Salisbury Plain." I knew that this was an impossible task. . . . But there was no arguing over it, so I spent days and days working out march tables for sheep. One day I said to him: "Do you realize, sir, that should all these sheep be set in movement, every road will be blocked?" "Of course," he answered; "at once arrange to have a number of signposts ready and marked, 'Sheep are not to use this road.' " "But," I replied, "what if the less well-educated sheep are unable to read them?" This brought our conversation to an end.

SOURCE: J. F. C. Fuller, *Memoirs of an Unconventional Soldier* (1936). J. F. C. FULLER, who would rise to be the head of the British Tank Corps in World War I, mercifully did not identify the British general who thought that sheep could read.

---

military mission   Units of armed forces sent by invitation from one state to another. They can be as small as several individuals or as large as a division. By their nature they have strictly defined and limited tasks, typically having to do with training or other assistance. *Compare to* DIPLOMATIC MISSION.

military necessity   **1.** The principle whereby a BELLIGERENT has the right to apply any measures that are required to bring about the successful conclusion of an armed operation and that are not forbidden by the LAW OF WAR. **2.** A justification for actions that violate the laws of war. **3.** A military commander's obligation to conduct operations in such a manner that enemy leaders can consider the option of a negotiated settlement.

military occupation   *See* OCCUPATION.

military policy   A broad principle or course of action in respect to the affairs of armed forces adopted by an appropriate level within the military organization and made applicable to actions that fall under such authority. Military policy is derived from, and is an integral part of, general national policy in either war or peace. *Compare to* DOCTRINE.

military posture   An armed force's disposition, strength, and condition of READINESS as it affects capabilities.

military reform movement   A loosely organized body of U.S. defense analysts that since the mid-1970s have, in general, been asserting that the U.S. military establishment has been woefully inadequate and unsuccessful since 1945; that the overbureaucratic nature of the military establishment and the careerist and managerial ambitions of the officer corps has replaced a "service and leadership" attitude to soldiering; that the defense procurement has gone on the wrong track, focusing on buying more and more technologically advanced weapons systems, in smaller and smaller quantities but at greater and greater prices, so that the defense budget, although ever-increasing, actually buys less and less real security. Consequently, the whole U.S. strategy has outgrown existing military capacity. In particular, the North Atlantic Treaty Organization commitment is both wrongly handled in tactical terms, and distorting the overall defense posture so that other vital U.S. interests cannot be protected. Military reformers tend to focus on three levels. The first is that of "superstructure." Problems at this level include badly designed weapons that do not work well in combat; insufficient training time; inadequate ammunition and supplies of spare parts; lack of unit cohesion; and an outdated force structure. The second level that the reform movement focuses on is education and decision making within the armed services. The third level highlights problems within the "corporate culture" of the armed services. The reform movement has focused its efforts on bringing about changes in all three areas. Although the military reform movement has not disappeared completely, the success of the United States in the Persian Gulf War, together with the reduction in forces following the disintegration of the Soviet Union, has taken much of the impetus out of the movement.

military regime   A DICTATORSHIP; an AUTOCRACY in which the military controls its state's political system. Power is often obtained by a COUP D'ÉTAT. Typically, civil liberties and normal political and constitutional arrangements are suspended. While military regimes are frequently dictatorial, they are not necessarily totalitarian. Such regimes may even have a degree of political legitimacy, especially if they take over in an emergency and intend to restore the democratic government in the future. Military regimes are usually associated with Third World states, although both Spain and Greece in contemporary Europe have had them.

military situation room   *See* WAR ROOM.

military staff committee   *See* UNITED NATIONS MILITARY STAFF COMMITTEE.

military strategy   The art and science of employing the armed forces of a nation to secure the objectives of national policy by the application of force or the threat of force. *See also* STRATEGY.

military strongman   A critical description of a military DICTATOR in control of a state.

militia   *See* REGULAR ARMY.

Mill, John Stuart (1806–1873)   The British reformer and political philosopher best known for his arguments in favor of civil liberties for those with differing political opinions. In *On Liberty* (1859) he stated: "Though the silenced opinion be in error, it may, and very commonly does, contain a portion of truth; and since the general or prevailing opinion on any subject is rarely or never the whole truth, it is only by the collision of adverse opinions that the remainder of the truth has any chance of being supplied."

MILL ON INTERNATIONAL TRADE

It is commerce which is rapidly rendering war obsolete, by strengthening and multiplying the personal interests which act in natural opposition to it. And it may be said without exaggeration that the great extent and rapid increase of international trade, in being the principal guarantee of the peace of the world, is the great permanent security for the uninterrupted progress of the ideas, the institutions, and the character of the human race.

SOURCE: John Stuart Mill, *Considerations on Representative Government* (1861).

Mindzenty, Jozsef Cardinal (1892–1975)   The Roman Catholic primate of Hungary who was arrested for treason by the Communist government of Hungary in 1948 as part of the Soviet-led policy to suppress all opposition in Eastern Europe. During the HUNGARIAN UPRISING of 1956 against the Communist regime, he was freed by Hungarian insurgents. When Soviet forces repressed the revolt, Cardinal Mindzenty took refuge in the U.S. embassy in Budapest and remained there until he was allowed to move to Vienna in 1971.

minimax   A term from GAME THEORY, the quantitative analysis of conflict situations. In a minimax strategy, attempts are made to minimize the worst possible outcome rather than to maximize the best possible outcome. Minimax is the strategy most likely to be used, independently, by opposing sides, when they are unable to trust each other.

minimum deterrence   *See* DETERRENCE, MINIMUM.

minimum valuation   The assessment for TARIFF purposes of all items below a certain value in an import category as if they were of a given higher value.

minister   **1.** A cabinet-level government official; the head of a major agency in a parliamentary government.   **2.** The second-ranking diplomat (after the AMBASSADOR) at a permanent diplomatic mission. A minister plenipotentiary has full, as opposed to limited, powers to represent his or her state.   **3.** The head of a diplomatic mission when a state chooses not to send someone with the rank of ambassador. Such heads of missions are outranked by ambassadors from other states for social purposes but are the highest-ranking person in their own mission.

minister counselor   The title used by some states for the second in command of a diplomatic mission, ranking below an AMBASSADOR or MINISTER.

minister resident   A representative who may be the head of a DIPLOMATIC MISSION but who ranks below an AMBASSADOR.

Ministry of Foreign Affairs   *See* FOREIGN MINISTRY.

minor nuclear power   *See* MAJOR NUCLEAR POWER.

Minuteman   A class of U.S. nuclear missiles, deployed since 1960, named after the eighteenth-century colonists who fought against the British in the American War of Independence. One thousand Minuteman missiles have been deployed in deep underground hardened silos. This number was considered the force size sufficient to provide an assured destruction capability against both the Soviet Union and China. The single warhead Minuteman I was the first solid-fueled missile with intercontinental range. In 1966 it was replaced by the longer, heavier, and more accurate Minuteman II. This in turn was replaced in 1977 with the Minuteman III, which exchanged the single warhead for three independently targetable reentry vehicles (MIRVs). As a result of the June 1992 accord between U.S. President George Bush and Russian President Boris Yeltsin, the Minuteman missiles with three warheads are scheduled to be "downloaded" to a single warhead. *See* START II.

mirror image   A view of the adversary as having totally the opposite characteristics from oneself. There is a common tendency for states to see themselves as the repository of virtue and their adversaries as the repository of evil. Ironically, in a conflict situation each side tends to view the other in the same way.

MIRV   (multiple independently targetable reentry vehicle) A nuclear missile that divides in flight into as many as a dozen separate missiles, to hit as many separate targets. *Compare to* MARV.

MI6   The British intelligence agency responsible for foreign intelligence and espionage. It is what is usually meant when people refer to the British Secret Service. Its duties are similar to those of the U.S. CENTRAL INTELLIGENCE AGENCY. *Compare to* MI5.

misperception   An incorrect understanding of the nature of another actor, or the meaning of the policies or actions of other actors. Robert Jervis in *Perception and Misperception in International Politics* (1976) develops and identifies patterns of misperception, such as the tendency to regard another state as being much more centralized than it really is. In this context Alexander George, in *US-Soviet Security Cooperation* (1988), has pointed out that in any conflict between two states there at least six actors involved: each one as it sees the other, each one as it sees itself, and each one as it really is.

missile   1. Any projectile, such as a bullet or a rocket. 2. An unmanned weapon to which propulsive energy is applied after its initial launching. Rockets, which have been widely used in warfare since the eighteenth century, actually date back to ancient China. But modern missiles that could be guided to their targets by internal navigation systems, so-called guided missiles, were first used by Germany during World War II. *See also* V-WEAPONS.

missile gap   1. The Soviet lead over the United States in ICBMs, which was believed to exist in the late 1950s after the *Sputnik I* launch. Although based on erroneous intelligence estimates, the expectation was that the Soviet Union would deploy ICBMs more quickly and in greater numbers than the United States and was attempting to gain STRATEGIC SUPERIORITY in this area. Thus in 1960 presidential candidate John F. Kennedy asserted that the United States was behind the Soviet Union in nuclear missile deployment. However, after gaining office, the Kennedy Administration discovered that there was no such gap after all: Intelligence material from Soviet defectors revealed that the feared "gap" was illusory. Nevertheless, President Kennedy accelerated the deployment of the land-based MINUTEMAN program in order to allay concerns over the "gap." According to Henry L. Trewhitt: "The gap was chiefly the product of Air Force intelligence. The Air Force was riding the crest of its own missile-building program, and a higher assessment of Soviet capability naturally reinforced its position. . . . The missile gap, it turned out, had been calculated largely by anticipating all the weapons Soviet technology could produce. There had been little allowance for physical evidence" (*McNamara*, 1971). 2. Because Kennedy's missile gap evaporated, the term is sometimes used to deride a nonexistent issue.

Missile Technology Control Regime An attempt to prevent or contain the proliferation of ballistic missiles through an agreement among seven industrialized states: the United States, Great Britain, France, the Federal Republic of Germany, Italy, Canada, and Japan. The negotiations about prohibiting the transfer to Third World states of ballistic missiles capable of carrying nuclear weapons began in 1983 and were made public in 1987. The MTCR is a REGIME that sets out to establish common patterns of restraint and to ensure that all the major suppliers observe this. The big problem at the outset was that the regime did not include the Soviet Union. Although Moscow did become a de facto (if not an entirely reliable) supporter, China still remains outside the regime. Nor does it do anything about the rise of indigenous Third World capabilities for missile development. While the number of states that have agreed to join the regime has increased, its overall success remains in considerable doubt.

mission *See* DIPLOMATIC MISSION; MILITARY MISSION.

Mitbestimmungsrecht *See* CODETERMINATION.

Mitchell, William "Billy" (1879–1936) The World War I United States Air Corps general who was so insistent that the United States develop viable AIR POWER that he was court-martialed for his persistent and insubordinate criticism in 1925. Mitchell was the first to demonstrate that airplanes could sink a battleship. This notion seemed so outlandish at the time that U.S. Secretary of War Newton D. Baker, responding to Mitchell's 1921 offer to sink a battleship using bombs dropped from airplanes, said: "That idea is so damned nonsensical and impossible that I'm willing to stand on the bridge of a battleship while that nitwit tries to hit it from the air" (quoted in Emile Gauvreau and Lester Cohen, *Billy Mitchell,* 1942). In 1924 Mitchell predicted the exact time of day and location where Japanese air power would one day attack Pearl Harbor. In 1942 he was posthumously promoted to major general. In 1946 he was awarded a special medal by Congress, and in 1947 his dream of an independent air force became a reality.

THE VERDICT ON MITCHELL

The Court, upon secret written ballot, two-thirds of the members present at the time the vote was taken concurring in each finding of guilty, finds the accused guilty of all specifications and of the charge. Upon secret written ballot the Court sentences the accused to be suspended from rank, command and duty, with forfeiture of all pay and allowances, for five years. The Court is thus lenient because of the military record of the accused during the World War.

SOURCE: Verdict in the court-martial of Colonel William "Billy" Mitchell read by Major General Robert L. Howze, president of the court, quoted in *Time*, December 28, 1925.

Mitteleuropa German for "Central Europe"; an area that is traditionally seen by Germany as the natural focus for German foreign policy and as a place in which German influence can be very substantial.

Mitteleuropa plan The project advanced by German bankers after 1900 for continental economic domination through a CUSTOMS UNION between Germany and the Austro-Hungarian Empire. This never happened before World War I. Afterward the Treaty of VERSAILLES prohibited any ANSCHLUSS, or union between Germany and Austria. However, if Austria joins the EUROPEAN COMMUNITY as is expected by the end of the century, then the Mitteleuropa plan will have been effectively realized.

Mitterrand, François (1916–   ) The president of France since 1981. After fighting with the French RESISTANCE during World War II, he entered politics and directed various ministries in the 1950s. He was the socialist opposition leader during the presidencies of CHARLES DE GAULLE and VALÉRY GISCARD D'ESTAING. As president he has pursued a moderate socialistic program and has been a strong supporter of the European Community and of increasing European unity.

mixed actor model A model of the international system that recognizes the multiplicity of players. The mixed actor model does not denigrate the role of the state but acknowledges that nongovernmental or intergovernmental organizations also play an important role in the international system.

François Mitterrand (Embassy of France)

mixed economy   An economic system that incorporates elements of both laissez-faire CAPITALISM and SOCIALISM. All of the industrialized states of the west have mixed economies in that aspects of socialism lie side by side with free market capitalism. For example, the United Kingdom has a comprehensive system of socialized medicine within a basically capitalistic economy.

mixed scanning   A decision-making model put forth by AMITAI ETZIONI in *Public Administration Review* (December 1967) that calls for seeking short-term solutions to problems by using both INCREMENTALISM and comprehensive approaches to problem solving. For example, a foreign policy analyst responsible for reviewing political developments in Europe might superficially scan all recent developments (the comprehensive approach) but focus only on those political problems that have

changed since the last scanning (the incremental approach). In this way the analyst saves time by dealing in detail only with those situations that truly demand attention.

MNC or MNE   *See* MULTINATIONAL CORPORATION.

M-19 (*Movimiento 19 de Abril*)   "April 19th Movement," a Colombian urban guerrilla group whose rhetoric focuses on the liberation of Colombia from its ruling oligarchy. Its most infamous operation was the 1985 siege of the Palace of Justice in Bogotá, in which more than 100 people died (including 24 of the terrorists). The group used the international drug trade to raise funds and has received support and training from Cuba. In the early 1990s M-19 made peace with the Colombian government and entered the mainstream political process. The movement named itself after the date in 1970 when Colombia's dictatorial president from 1953 to 1957, Gustavo Rojas Pinilla (1900–1975), was defeated in a reelection bid.

MNR   Mozambique National Resistance, commonly known as RENAMO.

mobilization   1. Assembling and organizing national resources for war or other emergencies. It includes the assembly and deployment of supplies and personnel to key locations. Various actions, such as calling up reservists, closing frontiers, controlling or expelling aliens, and introducing emergency powers, are taken by the mobilizing government. If the danger is the threat of a nuclear attack, then increasing the alert status of strategic forces and protecting against sabotage may be the only elements of mobilization worth undertaking. Mobilization itself may be considered a provocative act: the mobilization race of the great powers in July 1914 helped to precipitate World War I. According to A. J. P. Taylor's *The First World War* (1963): "[Field Marshal Alfred von] Schlieffen, Chief of the German General Staff from 1892 to 1906, though dead, was the real maker of the First World War. 'Mobilization means war' was his idea. In 1914 his dead hand automatically pulled the trigger." On the other hand, the signals that mobilization sends to an adversary can be used for diplomatic effect as part of crisis bargaining (last-minute negotiations conducted under the threat of war). For example, the call-up of reserve forces by U.S. President John F. Kennedy was a key element in the Berlin Crisis of 1961. **2.** The process by which armed forces are brought to a state of immediate readiness for war or other national emergency. **3.** The process by which electoral support is generated for a candidate or issue; in effect, a marshaling of all the human, monetary, organizational, and political resources on behalf of a cause.

MOBILIZATION AS A ONE-WAY TRAIN

Your Majesty, it cannot be done. The deployment of millions cannot be improvised. If Your Majesty insists on leading the whole army to the East it will not be an army ready for battle but a disorganized mob of armed men with no arrangement for supply. Those arrangements took a whole year of intricate labor to complete and once settled, it cannot be altered.

SOURCE: General Helmuth von Moltke, explaining to Kaiser William II in 1914 why Germany could not redeploy its army to attack Russia instead of Belgium and France, quoted in Barbara Tuchman, *The Guns of August* (1962). According to Tuchman: "One army corps alone—out of the total of 40 in the German forces—required 170 railway cars for officers, 965 for infantry, 2960 for cavalry, 1915 for artillery and supply wagons, 6010 in all, grouped in 140 trains and an equal number again for their supplies. From the moment the order was given, everything was to move at fixed times according to a schedule precise down to the number of train axles that would pass over a given bridge within a given time."

Mobutu Sese Seko *See* CONGOLESE CIVIL WAR.

Modelski, George A. (1926–   )   The Polish-born American foreign policy analyst who, in his *Theory of Foreign Policy* (1962), looked at the foreign policymaking process of states in terms of traditional SYSTEMS ANALYSIS. Subsequently, in *Long Cycles in World Politics* (1987) he focused on patterns and causes of change in the global political system. Like other proponents of this approach, his focus was on the rise and fall of world powers and world empires. *See also* LONG CYCLE.

modernist school   An approach to the study of international relations that holds that examinations of struggles for power and security must be supplemented by the inclusion in field examinations of the role of nonstate actors, economic issues, and other nonsecurity-related issues in a world increasingly marked by INTERDEPENDENCE.

modernization   Economic and political DEVELOPMENT in THIRD WORLD states.

modus vivendi   Latin for "a way of living"; a temporary understanding pending a final agreement. It is a diplomatic term for the acceptance of a continuing working relationship despite fundamental disagreements that can be either ignored or held in abeyance for an indefinite period of time.

mole   A secret agent who has "burrowed" her- or himself into a sensitive position in one organization who then reports its secrets to an opposing organization or state. There are eternal rumors that the major intelligence services (the U.S. Central Intelligence Agency, KGB, MI5, etc.) have moles planted in the services of the others. Sometimes these rumors have proven to be true, as in the case of the CAMBRIDGE SPY RING.

Molotov, Vyacheslav M. (1890–1986)   The Russian revolutionary who helped V. I. LENIN plot the 1917 November coup and who later became JOSEPH STALIN's most loyal and highest-ranking ally. He was a member of the POLITBURO (1921–1957), chairman of the Council of People's Commissars, equivalent to prime minister (1930–1941); and foreign minister (1939–1949; 1953–1956). He negotiated the NAZI-SOVIET NONAGGRESSION PACT in 1939 and attended the TEHRAN, YALTA, POTSDAM, and SAN FRANCISCO CONFERENCES. British Prime Minister Winston Churchill wrote in *The Gathering Storm* (1948) that Molotov was "a man of outstanding ability and cold-blooded ruthlessness . . . I have never seen a human being who more perfectly represented the modern conception of a robot." After participating in an abortive coup against the leadership of NIKITA S. KHRUSHCHEV in 1956, he was demoted, then expelled from all Communist Party offices and sent to serve as ambassador to the Mongolian People's Republic (1957–1960). In 1984, at the age of 94, he was reinstated into the party. This was considered a sign of nostalgia for the good old days under Stalin.

Soviet Foreign Minister Vyacheslav Molotov signs the Nazi-Soviet nonaggression pact in Moscow on August 23, 1939; Joachim von Ribbentrop and Josef Stalin stand behind him. (National Archives)

Molotov-Ribbentrop Pact *See* NAZI-SOVIET NONAGGRESSION PACT.

Moluccans An East Asian people fighting to resist the absorption of their archipelago into Indonesia. During the 1970s they resorted to terrorism, primarily conducted in Europe, in an attempt to force the Dutch government, the island's former colonial master, to assist them in gaining independence. Among their violent activities of 1975 to 1977 were an attempt to kidnap Queen Juliana of the Netherlands, a bombing at the Indonesian consulate in The Hague, and two passenger train hijackings in the Dutch countryside.

monarch A king (or queen), a dynastic dictator, a despot (benevolent or malevolent) with established blood lines. When monarchs have limits put on their powers, they are known as CONSTITUTIONAL MONARCHS. Many republicans believe, as Mark Twain wrote in his *Notebooks* (1935): "The kingly office is entitled to no respect. It was originally procured by the highwayman's methods; it remains a perpetuated crime, can never be anything but the symbol of a crime. It is no more entitled to respect than is the flag of a pirate." *See also* DIVINE RIGHT OF KINGS; KING CAN DO NO WRONG.

monarchism **1.** A belief in rule by hereditary leaders. **2.** The advocacy of rule by a single all-powerful leader. Modern monarchist movements such as those in France and Russia today tend to be far right in political attitudes and seek the restoration of previously deposed monarchies.

Moneta, Ernesto T. (1833–1918) The Italian journalist and pacifist who shared the 1907 Nobel Peace Prize (with LOUIS RENAULT) for his advocacy of the peace movement and especially for his presiding over the 1907 International Peace Conference in Milan.

Monnet, Jean (1888–1979) The French economist who was a leading proponent of European unity. After World War II, Monnet drafted a successful plan for French economic revival and drafted the SCHUMAN PLAN, which established the EUROPEAN COAL AND STEEL COMMUNITY. Monnet became its first president. In the 1950s he became a strong proponent of a United States of Europe. The European COMMON MARKET is based to a large extent on Monnet's ideas. Historians often say that only three men ever united Europe: Napoleon, Hitler, and Monnet. (Monnet was by far the nicest.) From 1956 to 1975 he was president of the Action Committee for the United States of Europe.

Monroe Doctrine The statement by U.S. President James Monroe in his 1823 State of the Union message that the Western Hemisphere was no longer open to colonization and aggressive actions by European powers. The United States promised in return not "to interfere in the internal concerns" of Europe. The doctrine was actually formulated by Monroe's secretary of state, John Quincy Adams (who would succeed Monroe as president). The Monroe Doctrine had strong rhetorical and political usage up to the 1920s, on the eves of World Wars I and II, and in the debates that led up to the Cuban Missile Crisis in 1962; but its relevance is declining. After all, the United States "interfered" extensively in Europe during the world wars, and the Soviet Union was not deterred from seeking to "colonize" such Western Hemisphere countries as Cuba and Nicaragua. The Soviet attitude toward it was summarized by Communist Party leader Nikita Khrushchev: "We consider that the Monroe Doctrine has outlived its time, has outlived itself, has died, so to say, a natural death. Now the remains of this doctrine should best be buried as every dead body is so that it should not poison the air by its decay" (*New York Times,* July 13, 1960). In fact, the Soviet Union remained very cautious about involvement in Latin America, recognizing that it was in the U.S. sphere of interest and that Soviet intrusions would be seen as provocative. This fact did not stop Cuba from trying to exert its influence in the region in opposition to the United States.

THE MONROE DOCTRINE

The American continents, by the free and independent condition which they have assumed and maintain, are henceforth not to be considered as subjects for future colonization by any European powers.

We owe it, therefore, to candor, and to the amicable relations existing between the United States and those powers to declare that we should consider any attempt on their part to extend their system to any portion of this hemisphere as dangerous to our peace and safety. With the existing colonies or dependencies of any European power we . . . shall not interfere. But with the governments . . . whose independence we have . . . acknowledged, we could not view any interposition for the purpose of oppressing them, or controlling, in any other manner, their destiny, by any European power, in any other light than as a manifestation of an unfriendly disposition towards the United States.

SOURCE: U.S. President James Monroe, message to Congress, December 2, 1823.

Monroe Doctrine, Roosevelt Corollary to U.S. President Theodore Roosevelt's statement in his message to Congress of December 6, 1904, that: "In the Western hemisphere the adherence of the United States to the Monroe Doctrine may force the United States, however reluctantly, in flagrant cases of wrongdoing or impotence, to the exercise of an international police power." Roosevelt thus redefined Monroe's original prohibition against European intervention in Latin America to an assertion that the United States as a civilized nation had the right to intervene in internal matters to end "chronic wrongdoing" in a Latin American or Caribbean nation. Using this corollary, every

U.S. president from Roosevelt to Calvin Coolidge dispatched U.S. Marines to Latin American or Caribbean nations. U.S. occupying forces took control of the governments of Cuba (1904–1909, 1912, 1917–1922), the Dominican Republic (1916–1924), Haiti (1915–1934), Nicaragua (1912–1925, 1926–1933), and Panama (1903–1914) in order to protect U.S. commerce and investment. *Compare to* POLICEMAN OF THE WORLD.

Montgomery, Bernard Law (1887–1976) The leading British general of WORLD WAR II. His 1942 victory at EL ALAMEIN was the turning point of the North African campaign. After the United States entered the war, there was constant tension between him and the U.S. commanders. He led the British forces in the Allied invasion of France in 1944 and was shortly thereafter made field marshal. After the war he commanded the British occupied zone in Germany (1945–1946), served as chief of the Imperial General Staff (1946–1948), and was deputy commander of the North Atlantic Treaty Organization from 1951–1958. *See also* ARNHEM.

Montreal Convention The 1971 Convention for the Suppression of Unlawful Acts Against the Safety of Civil Aviation under the United Nations International Civil Aviation Organization. This agreement built on the work of the HAGUE CONVENTION by expanding the agreement to outlaw all acts that "endanger the safety of an aircraft in flight," not only hijacking; it also followed the 1963 TOKYO CONVENTION on the safety of hijacked passengers.

Montreal Protocol An international agreement on substances that deplete the ozone layer reached at a 1987 conference held in Montreal, Canada. Its purpose is gradually to phase out the use of chlorofluorocarbons (CFCs) and halons. The Montreal Protocol came into force on January 1, 1989, and has been ratified by 31 countries, which represent over 90 percent of world production of these chemicals. As a result of this agreement, the very high growth rates in atmospheric CFC concentrations that had been projected are not likely to occur. Nevertheless, because of the long atmospheric lifetimes of CFCs, their concentrations could continue to increase for several decades, which may lead to ozone depletion and GLOBAL WARMING.

Bernard Montgomery with U.S. General Dwight Eisenhower and Soviet Marshal Georgi Zhukov (l. to r.) in June 1945. (National Archives)

Montreux Convention The 1936 multilateral agreement on international use of the Turkish straits of the Bosporus and the Dardanelles, which provided that "in time of peace merchant vessels shall enjoy complete freedom of transit and navigation in the Straits, by day and by night, under any flag and with any kind of cargo without any formalities" except for sanitation requirements. The convention imposes some limitations on the size and length of stay of warships. The agreement recognized Turkish sovereignty in the straits and allowed Turkey to fortify the passages. If Turkey is neutral in time of war, the straits will be closed to all belligerents.

mood *See* ALMOND, GABRIEL.

Moon Treaty The international treaty governing utilization of the moon, approved by the United Nations General Assembly in 1979; formally known as the Agreement Governing the Activities of States on the Moon and Other Celestial Bodies. Article XI of the treaty declares the moon and its resources to be the "common heritage of mankind." While the treaty entered into force in 1984 after its ratification by five nations, neither the United States nor the Soviet Union (or Russia) has ratified it. And only the United States has ever been to the moon—where it planted the U.S., not the United Nations, flag.

more-developed countries A euphemism for the comparatively rich states of the West that is preferred by many in the THIRD WORLD to the term DEVELOPED COUNTRIES. It implies a sense of cultural equality and avoids opposites such as rich and poor, or advanced and backward.

Morgenthau, Hans J. (1904–1980) German-born American who became the key figure in the development of political REALISM as an approach to international politics—an approach that he explored most fully in *Politics Among Nations* (1948). Although he shared many of the basic assumptions of realism with REINHOLD NIEBUHR, he applied them to an analysis and understanding of international relations in a way that went far beyond any other scholar. Morgenthau started from the premise that human nature was basically selfish and involved a struggle or a quest for power. The most notable manifestation of this struggle was in relations among nations, where the problems stemming from the inherent nature of human beings are compounded by the dynamics of a competitive environment in which there are few mechanisms of control—apart from the power of others.

The concept of power was central to Morgenthau's analysis, and he contended that the basic starting point for understanding international relations was the assumption that "the statesmen think

Morgenthau, Hans J. (1904–1980)

and act in terms of interest defined as power," an assumption that he believed was borne out by "the evidence of history." As he put it in the fifth edition of *Politics Among Nations* (1973):

> The concept of interest defined as power imposes intellectual discipline upon the observer, infuses rational order into the subject matter of politics, and thus makes the theoretical understanding of politics possible. On the side of the actor, it provides for rational discipline in action and creates that astounding continuity in foreign policy which makes American, British or Russian foreign policy appear as an intelligible, rational continuum, by and large consistent within itself, regardless of the different motives, preferences, and intellectual and moral qualities of successive statesmen. A realist theory of international politics, then, will guard against two popular fallacies, the concern with motives and the concern with ideological preferences.

Although Morgenthau acknowledges that, in practice, statesmen do not always conform to such a rational and objective course, there is still at least tension between what is presented in *Politics Among Nations* as a fundamental explanation for—if not an iron law of—state behavior and in his other works, such as *A New Foreign Policy for the United States* (1969), in which he berates U.S. policymakers for allowing ideological considerations to determine U.S. foreign policy. Lack of consistency about whether the pursuit of interest in terms of power is descriptive or prescriptive is not the only shortcoming in Morgenthau's writings. Critics have pointed to his failure to explain fully how his concept of power actually works, and to his portrayal of the NATIONAL INTEREST as objective when in fact it is subjective. Nevertheless, few would deny Morgenthau's immense contribution to the development of international relations. Moreover, it became clear that for Morgenthau realism meant a passion for pragmatism and a contempt for excess in foreign policy whether stemming from ideological ambition or moral self-righteousness. These qualities gave his critique of United States involvement in Vietnam and his commentaries on nuclear strategy—especially "The Four Paradoxes of Nuclear Strategy" (*American Political Science Review*, 1964)—an incisiveness and persuasiveness that are rarely surpassed.

Morgenthau Plan   The plan for the deindustrialization of Germany after World War II that was proposed by Henry Morgenthau, Jr. (1891–1967), the U.S. Secretary of the Treasury (1934–1945). The plan, which was premised on the belief that a Germany with heavy industry would always be a threat to world peace, called for dismantling German industry, closing all mines, and reducing the society to an agricultural state. It was initially approved on September 15, 1944, by U.S. President Franklin D. Roosevelt and British Prime Minister Winston Churchill at the QUEBEC CONFERENCE; however, they later rejected the plan when news of it seemed to strengthen German resistance. It was officially killed when the United States realized that it needed to build up Germany as a BUFFER to Soviet expansion. This decision prompted Morgenthau's resignation from President Harry S Truman's cabinet.

Moro, Aldo (1916–1978)   The prime minister of Italy (1963–1968; 1974–1976) and leader of the Christian Democratic Party, abducted by the RED BRIGADES in Rome on March 16, 1978. The terrorists killed five bodyguards during the ambush of Moro's escort. Moro was subjected to a Red Brigades "people's court" and tried for his supposed crimes while in office. The Italian government refused to make any concessions to the terrorists, who demanded the release of imprisoned fellow members of their organization. On May 9 the Red Brigades directed police to a car in downtown Rome the trunk of which contained Moro's bullet-riddled body. During 1982 and 1983, 63 Red Brigade defendants were tried for the kidnapping and killing of Moro and other crimes. Life sentences were given to 32 of them, including Moro's murderers.

Moro Liberation Front (MLF)   A Philippine Muslim guerrilla organization that is the primary non-Communist separatist organization in the Pacific archipelago of the Philippines; also known as the Moro National Liberation Front (MNLF). The Moros seek Islamic rule on Mindanao and other southern islands of the Philippines and has battled the government since 1972. The MLF was born in response to rampant anti-Muslim violence of the 1960s; its name is derived from *Bangsa Moro*, the native term for "Islamic self-rule." Since the 1980s the MLF has been linked to the revolutionary government in Iran, which has provided support and training. Philippine President Corazon Aquino signed a truce with the MLF in 1986, and MLF violence has subsided substantially since that time.

Mosley, Oswald (1896–1980)   The British politician who founded the BRITISH UNION OF FASCISTS in 1932. He sought to imitate Adolf Hitler's brownshirt tactics of violent anti-Semitism by a uniformed private army. But the provocative marches he led in the East End Jewish neighborhoods of London spurred the passage of the Public Order Act of 1936 by which Parliament banned political uniforms and private militias. During much of World War II Mosley was imprisoned by the British.

Mossad   Israel's foreign intelligence-gathering and covert action agency, similar to the United States Central Intelligence Agency. Created in 1951, it has earned a reputation as one of the world's best electronic and human intelligence-gathering agencies. It was the Mossad which kidnapped Nazi war criminal ADOLF EICHMANN in Argentina in 1961 and returned him to Israel for trial and execution. The Mossad is also well known for its wide use of assassination against, for example, the PALESTINE LIBERATION ORGANIZATION, terrorists who perpetrated the MUNICH MASSACRE, and scientists working to build nuclear weapons for Iraq.

Mossadegh, Muhammad (1880–1967)   The Iranian prime minister (1951–1953) who precipitated a major crisis by nationalizing Iran's mainly British-owned oil industry. Relations between Mossadegh and the shah, MOHAMMED REZA PAHLEVI (which had never been good), then broke down completely; with the help of Iran's military and the U.S. Central Intelligence Agency, the shah staged a coup known as OPERATION AJAX, which had Mossadegh removed from office in 1953. Imprisoned for three years, Mossadegh then spent the rest of his life under house arrest. This U.S.-sponsored coup, which removed from office a popular nationalist leader and installed a dictator who ruled for the next quarter century with constant U.S. support, was the underlying reason for the hatred of the United States that burst forth in the IRANIAN REVOLUTION of 1979.

most favored nation   An international trade policy whereby states agree to grant each other the most favorable of their trade concessions available to any other state. States often use the granting or withholding of most favored nation status as a way of signaling approval or disapproval of a particular government or of certain kinds of behavior by a particular government. *Compare to* DISCRIMINATION.

mothball fleet   Navy ships placed in storage, usually anchored in bodies of water close to shipyards where they could be refurbished if needed in a national emergency.

mother of all battles   What Iraqi dictator SADDAM HUSSEIN predicted in 1990 would result if the United States–led coalition tried to take Kuwait away from his occupying forces. After Hussein's forces suffered the mother of all defeats in the 1991 PERSIAN GULF WAR, the "mother of all . . ." usage became especially useful for its mocking connotation.

Mother Theresa (1910–   )   Born of Albanian parents in Yugoslavia as Agnes Gonxha Bojaxhiv, this Roman Catholic nun has spent her life since 1928 working with the poor in India and in inner cities around the world. In 1979 she was awarded the Nobel Peace Prize.

Mott, John R. (1865–1955)   The U.S. Christian missionary who shared the 1946 Nobel Peace Prize (with EMILY BALCH) for leadership of the International YMCA (Young Men's Christian Association) movement.

Mountbatten, Lord Louis (1900–1979)   The member of the British royal family (a great-grandson of Queen Victoria) who, as a career naval officer, rose during World War II to be chief of Combined Operations (1942–1943) and Supreme Allied Commander in South-East Asia (1943–1946). In this last role he led the Allied forces that pushed the Japanese out of Burma. After the war he was made the last viceroy of India with a mandate to dissolve British rule as peacefully as possible. His plan for partitioning the subcontinent into the new states of India and Pakistan was implemented in 1947. He fulfilled his life's ambition of becoming first sea lord in 1955 (a position he held until 1959), the job his father, Prince Louis of BATTENBERG, was forced out of at the beginning of World War I. He was assassinated by PROVISIONAL IRISH REPUBLICAN ARMY terrorists off the coast of Ireland on August 27, 1979. Mountbatten's fishing boat was destroyed by a 50-pound bomb shortly after leaving the Irish shore, killing him, his 15-year-old grandson, and a young Irish companion. The assassination of the popular Mountbatten even outraged many IRA supporters.

Mozambique Civil War   *See* RENAMO.

Mozambique War of Independence   The ten-year (1964–1974) guerrilla war against the Portuguese colonial rulers of Mozambique. It ended only after a 1974 coup overthrew ANTONIO SALAZAR's dictatorial regime in Portugal and the new government quickly granted independence to FRELIMO (the Front for the Liberation of Mozambique).

MPLA   *See* ANGOLAN CIVIL WAR.

M-7   *See* GROUP OF SEVEN.

MTN   Multilateral trade negotiations; a descriptive term that could be applied to any of the seven rounds of negotiations held under the auspices of the GATT since 1947.

Mubarak, Hosni (1928–   )   The president of Egypt since 1981. As commander of the Egyptian armed forces during the 1973 YOM KIPPUR WAR with Israel, he emerged as a national hero because of the initial successes his forces had against the Israelis. This led to his appointment as vice president under ANWAR SADAT. After Sadat's assassination in 1981, Mubarak assumed the presidency and has continued with Sadat's policy of peace with Israel while rebuilding Egypt's ties to the Arab world, which were strained by the 1979 CAMP DAVID ACCORDS with Israel. Mubarak was successful in winning Egypt's readmission to the ARAB LEAGUE in 1982. (Egypt was expelled in 1979 after Sadat signed a peace treaty with Israel.) During the PERSIAN GULF CRISIS of 1990 he was a key figure in assembling the multinational coalition that fought in the PERSIAN GULF WAR.

Mugabe, Robert G. (1924–   ) The first prime minister of the Republic of Zimbabwe. As the founder of the Zimbabwe African National Union (ZANU) in 1963, he was imprisoned from 1964 to 1975 by the ruling white Rhodesian government. Once freed, he led a guerrilla civil war (1975–1979) that ended only when Great Britain (the former colonial power) sponsored elections in 1980. His ZANU party won a majority in the elections, which made him prime minister of a renamed country (from Rhodesia to Zimbabwe). The government of Mugabe, who is known as a Marxist, implemented moderate socialist policies that encouraged the white middle class to stay. Even though Mugabe, who became executive president in 1987, rules a one-party state, Zimbabwe is considered an African model of black-white cooperation. Mugabe's main black political rival during and since the ZIMBABWE CIVIL WAR has been Joshua Nkomo (1917–   ). But in 1987 Nkomo merged his party (the Zimbabwe African People's Union, or ZAPU) with ZANU and became part of Mugabe's government.

Mujahedin   **1.** Islamic fighters in a holy war; the name commonly applied to the disparate guerrilla groups that fought against the Soviet-backed regime that had been installed after the AFGHANISTAN INTERVENTION.   **2.** Iranian guerrillas who, because they consider themselves to be "Muslim democrats," oppose the Islamic fundamentalist government regime in power; formally the People's Mujahedin of Iran.

Mukden Incident   The 1931 seizure of the Manchurian city of Mukden by Japanese troops. The incident was a prelude to Japan's invasion and occupation of the whole of Manchuria. On the night of September 18, 1931, the Japanese Army used the pretext of an explosion along the Japanese-controlled railway to occupy Mukden. Within three months the whole of Manchuria was under Japanese control. CHIANG KAI-SHEK ordered his troops to pursue a policy of nonresistance and withdrawal. *See also* MANCHURIAN CRISIS.

Mulroney, Brian (1939–   ) The leader of Canada's Progressive Conservative Party who became prime minister in 1984. Domestically he has struggled against questions of Canadian unity with the 1992 electoral defeat of the new constitution he brokered to derail the efforts of Quebec separatists. Internationally he strongly supported the 1989 U.S.-CANADIAN FREE TRADE AGREEMENT and the 1992 NORTH AMERICAN FREE TRADE AGREEMENT. In early 1993 he announced that he would resign later in the year so that his party could select someone more personally popular to lead it in the next general election.

multicentric world   The concept developed by JAMES ROSENAU in *Turbulence in World Politics* (1990) to describe the contemporary international system that exists alongside the state system but that includes many more actors of many different types who are sovereign-free and evade many of the constraints and rules of the traditional state-centric world. Bureaucratic agencies, ethnic groups, drug cartels, fundamentalist religious groups, multinational organizations, and terrorist groups, as well as states make up this world.

multilateral   Many sided; an adjective that means that more than a single state is involved with an action or agreement.

multilateral agencies   International organizations such as the United Nations or the World Bank that have many independent states as members.

multilateral agreement   An agreement among three or more states. The GATT is an example because more than 100 states are signatories.

multilateralism   **1.** Actions or policies that are taken in cooperation with others as part of a concerted approach to problems or challenges in the international system.   **2.** The opposite of UNILATERALISM. It is often used in this way in relation to United States foreign policy to describe a policy involving CONSULTATION before decision making rather than a case in which the United States acts by itself and then coerces others to fall into line.

Multilateral Nuclear Force (MLF)   The 1963 Kennedy Administration proposal for the North Atlantic

Treaty Organization that called for a mixed-man fleet of Polaris-armed surface ships (with crews from different NATO nations) and jointly supervised by NATO states. Great Britain accepted this proposal, but it was rejected by France and never implemented. The MLF was an effort by the United States to share some of its nuclear missiles with NATO allies so that France and Great Britain would be discouraged from expanding their own nuclear forces. But France was determined to create its own FORCE DE FRAPPE.

multinational corporation (MNC)   A business with headquarters in one country and affiliates in others. MNCs (also known as TNCs, for transnational corporations, or MNEs, for multinational enterprises) have been credited with benefits for both home and host countries: They create wealth and jobs, pay taxes, help to generate and transfer technology, provide management skills, and generally contribute to the development of foreign economies. MNCs also have been the subject of international concern: They are large and have the potential power to manipulate prices and profits and the uses of new technology; intracompany transactions constitute a large part of world trade; MNCs tend to be centrally controlled by parent companies whose foreign activities are beyond the control of the home governments; and they have been accused of illegally interfering in the internal politics of both home and host governments. Codes of conduct for the activities of MNCs have been drafted by the United Nations Commission on Transnational Corporations, the Organization for Economic Cooperation and Development, the non-aligned countries, and the International Labor Organization, among others. But many nations (including the United States) support codes of conduct for MNCs only if they are voluntary and if they apply to both multinational and domestic enterprises in host countries.

multiple advocacy   An approach to decision making in which participants represent different points of view and participate fully and freely. The concept was developed by Alexander George in "The Case for Multiple Advocacy in Making Foreign Policy" (*American Political Science Review* 66, 1972), and represents a form of intellectual PLURALISM that contributes to high-quality decision making.

multiple independently targeted re-entry vehicle   *See* MIRV.

multipolarity   A situation in which there are more than two major powers. A multipolar system can center around three main powers (tripolarity) but is more generally made up of about five major powers with roughly equal capabilities. Nineteenth-century Europe was a classic multipolar system in which the BALANCE OF POWER among the major actors became an important consideration. In a five-power system, one power will often play the role of balancer, joining the weaker coalition to prevent the dominance of the stronger. This is why multipolarity is the basis of classic balance-of-power theories, in which individual states are protected by an automatic tendency for alliances to be created against any one state that seems to be getting more powerful relative to its partners in a multipolar system.

There has been much debate about the relative stability of multipolar as opposed to bipolar international systems. It is arguable that in a multipolar system, the SECURITY DILEMMA is less intense and less dangerous than in a bipolar world and that conflict also is likely to be more diffuse and less intense. On the other hand, a multipolar system is more complex, and therefore there are greater opportunities for conflict or war arising through miscalculation of the interests of others. The difficulty with such comparisons is that we have experience of a multipolar nonnuclear system and of a bipolar nuclear system but not yet of a multipolar nuclear system— which is, however, a very disturbing possibility. *Compare to* BIPOLARITY; UNIPOLARITY.

Munich Agreement   The deal that has become the metaphor for APPEASEMENT because it was in the south German city of Munich in 1938 that British Prime Minister Neville Chamberlain made a highly publicized but futile effort to appease German dictator Adolf Hitler. Following the ANSCHLUSS of Austria to Germany in 1938, Hitler, calling for self-determination, sought to incorporate into Germany those Germans living in Czechoslovakia (known as Sudeten Germans). In September 1938 Chamberlain along with EDOUARD DALADIER of France, BENITO MUSSOLINI of Italy, and Hitler met in Munich. At the time, the situation seemed strikingly similar to the beginning of World War I. Germany massed troops on the Czechoslovakian border and issued an ultimatum: yield the disputed territory or be invaded. France was bound by treaty to aid Czechoslovakia. Great Britain was bound to aid France. The only thing that stopped this train rushing toward war was the Anglo-French deal reached at Munich to sell out the Czechs. So Hitler got his demand for the SUDETENLAND. But within six months of gaining the Sudetenland, which he publicly announced was the "last territorial claim which I have to make in Europe," Hitler ordered the brutal occupation of all Czechoslovakia, proving that appeasement had failed and that he was a liar.

CHURCHILL DENOUNCES MUNICH AGREEMENT

I do not begrudge our loyal, brave people . . . the natural spontaneous outburst of joy and relief when they learned that the hard ordeal would no longer be required of them at the moment; but they should know the truth. They should know that there has been gross neglect and deficiency in our defences; they should know that we have sustained a defeat without a war, the consequences of which will travel far with us along our road; they should know that we have passed an awful milestone in our history when the whole equilibrium of Europe has been deranged, and that the terrible words have for the time being been pronounced against the Western democracies: "Thou art weighted in the balance and found wanting." And do not suppose that this is the end. This is only the beginning of the reckoning. This is only the first sip, the first foretaste of a bitter cup which will be proffered to us year by year unless by a supreme recovery of moral health and martial vigour, we arise again and take our stand for freedom as in the olden time.

SOURCE: Winston Churchill, speech in the House of Commons, October 5, 1938. This was a foretaste of the soaring rhetoric that Churchill would use to sustain his nation during World War II when he was prime minister.

Munich Massacre   The BLACK SEPTEMBER attack on Israeli athletes and coaches, reportedly sponsored by Libya, during the 1972 Olympic Games in Munich, West Germany. Eight terrorists entered the Israeli athletes' quarters, murdered two of them, and took nine hostages. During an unsuccessful rescue attempt, the terrorists killed the remaining hostages. Five of the terrorists died in a shootout with police. The other three were imprisoned, only to be freed by the Germans in response to terrorist demands made during a 1972 hijacking of a Lufthansa jetliner.

municipal   Internal as opposed to international. Thus municipal law operates within a state. In Latin, *municipium* refers to a self-governing governmental unit within the ancient Roman Empire.

murder board   An INTELLIGENCE review group that reexamines intelligence estimates (and estimators) after the fact—after sufficient time has passed to assess their initial accuracy.

Muslim Brotherhood   An organization founded in Egypt in 1928 to foster a regeneration of Islamic fundamentalism throughout the Arab world. The Brotherhood favors the abolition of most Western-style institutions, including parliamentary government. It calls for sweeping and, if necessary, violent economic, political, and social reforms in conformity with fundamentalist Islamic principles. It has drawn considerable support from across the social spectrum, and has continuously played an important role in Egyptian politics. In 1981 many Brotherhood members were expelled from the Egyptian armed forces after the assassination of ANWAR SADAT, but in recent years Egyptian President HOSNI MUBARAK has looked on the Brotherhood as a favorable alternative to even more radical groups such as those that were responsible for Sadat's death. The Brotherhood also has opposed the ASSAD regime in Syria, which ruthlessly responded in 1982 with an attack against the city of Hamah, whose population formed the core of the Brotherhood's support. An estimated 25,000 of Hamah's 180,000 citizens (and several thousand Brotherhood members) died as the Syrian army sought to wipe out the Brotherhood in the HAMAH MASSACRE.

Mussolini, Benito (1883–1945)   The Italian dictator who came to power after the MARCH ON ROME in 1922 and then dominated Italian politics until his execution by Italian partisans toward the end of WORLD WAR II. Mussolini, who started out as a teacher, journalist, and socialist, created the model of European FASCISM that was followed by ADOLF HITLER in Germany and FRANCISCO FRANCO in Spain.

Mussolini, Benito (1883–1945)

Benito Mussolini (left) and Adolf Hitler in Munich in 1940. (National Archives)

Mussolini pioneered many terrorist political tactics that were later imitated by Hitler. For example, from 1919 through 1922 Mussolini sought power with the help of a private militia of paramilitary thugs called the BLACKSHIRTS; Hitler had his BROWNSHIRTS. Mussolini had his supporters call him *Il Duce* (the leader); Hitler made his official title *Der Führer* (the same appellation in German). Mussolini's political movement was extremely nationalistic, with an ideology that mixed ideas from both right and left; so was Hitler's. Both were histrionic speakers who gained power in coalition governments, then consolidated power by outlawing other parties and making themselves dictator. Mussolini accomplished this by 1928; Hitler by 1933. Once

World War II began, Mussolini became very much the junior partner to Hitler, allowing Italian troops to be used essentially as auxiliaries to the Germans. In 1943, after the Allies invaded Sicily, he was voted out of office by his own Grand Council of Fascism. He was imprisoned but rescued by a German commando raid, then installed in a German puppet government in the north (the Italian Social Republic, which lasted from September 1943 to April 1945), only to be captured and executed on April 28, 1945. His body was then hung by its heels in a Milan public square and defiled by those Italians who had learned to despise him for the destruction he brought upon his country. *See also* ABYSSINIAN-ITALIAN WAR; LATERAN TREATY.

mutual aid   Arrangements made at government level between a state and one or more other states to assist each other.

Mutual and Balanced Force Reductions (MBFR) Negotiations on reducing Soviet and U.S. conventional forces in Central Europe that began in 1973 and were wound up in 1989 without coming to fruition. From the perspective of the United States and its European allies, the main purpose of the negotiations was not to bring about arms control but to stave off one-sided cuts being proposed in the U.S. Congress (the MANSFIELD AMENDMENT). The Soviet Union may have agreed to the talks for much the same reason: It saw U.S. troops in Europe as a guarantor of stability. In addition, it went ahead with the force reduction talks in order to get the North Atlantic Treaty Organization nations to agree to convene a Conference on Security and Cooperation in Europe, a process that led to the HELSINKI ACCORDS. There has been much discussion of why the MBFR talks failed. Part of the reason can be found in a lack of will. Yet the lack of progress also reflected differences of perspective, with the Soviet Union starting from the proposition that PARITY already existed and the West taking the view that asymmetrical reductions were necessary in order to bring about parity—a difference of view that was manifested in a data dispute that bedeviled the negotiations from the mid-1970s. Serious thinking about conventional arms control in Europe began again in the aftermath of the INF Treaty of 1987 and was given added impetus by Soviet leader Mikhail Gorbachev's decision to cut Soviet forces unilaterally. After a period of preliminary negotiation about the mandate, the CONVENTIONAL FORCES EUROPE talks began in 1989. They covered a broader geographical area—from the Atlantic Ocean to the Ural Mountains—and came to fruition in 1990 with an agreement that established parity between NATO and the Warsaw Pact. The irony was that by this time the pact itself was in the process of disintegration, and many commentators observed that political change had overtaken the arms control process in Europe. If this was so, it was largely because the MBFR negotiations were so protracted and had so little result.

mutual assured destruction   *See* MAD.

mutual deterrence   *See* DETERRENCE.

mutual hostage relationship   A term that was used to describe the relationship between the United States and the Soviet Union in which both were vulnerable to the strategic nuclear retaliatory forces of the other. In a sense each held the population of the other as hostage to deter an attack. The mutual hostage relationship was very closely related to the idea of mutual assured destruction (MAD).

mutual security   Achieving greater safety for oneself by taking actions that make opponents feel more secure. This mutual security is based on the assumption that unilateral attempts to achieve security by raising one's own military strength may simply increase the insecurity of others and are likely to lead to responses by other states that increase one's own insecurity. Thus states become entangled in a spiral of insecurity even if each state's actions are essentially defensive. But such actions, whatever their motive, can very easily be regarded as threatening by others. This phenomenon is known as the SECURITY DILEMMA. Mutual security seeks to mitigate the security dilemma by recognizing that both sides may be more secure with mutual restraints. Attempts to achieve unilateral increments of security ultimately may prove to be counterproductive. Also known as *common security*, this notion was developed by the PALME COMMISSION in the early 1980s and became a major theme of Soviet President MIKHAIL GORBACHEV's new thinking on international relations.

mutual support   1. That help that military units render each other against an enemy, because of their assigned tasks, their position relative to each other and to the enemy, and their inherent capabilities. Support often takes the form of an attack on the enemy from a different position. This takes pressure off those being helped by forcing the enemy to redeploy to meet the new threat.   2. A condition that exists when military or diplomatic efforts are able to directly help each other, thus preventing an adversary from attacking one position without being subjected to attack from several others.

MX Missile   The U.S. intercontinental ballistic missile, formally entitled the Peacekeeper, which contains ten individually targeted warheads. (Its name comes from a preliminary monicker, "missile experimental.") It was originally intended to be mobile and to have a significant COUNTERFORCE capability. President

Jimmy Carter proposed deploying the MX on an underground railway system with multiple firing points. While this system probably would have survived a nuclear attack on it, it had massive environmental effects and was abandoned by the Reagan Administration. Finally it was decided to base the MX in existing MINUTEMAN silos. Congress limited the number to 50 MXs that could be placed in existing silos. Authorization for additional MXs depended on congressional support for a new basing mode. It never came. Critics such as Senator Alan Cranston contended that the MX is an "unnecessary piece of goldplated military junk that serves no useful military purpose and is intended solely to serve political perceptions" (*New York Times*, March 20, 1985). Others asserted that it was essential to maintaining the land-based leg of the strategic TRIAD. Nevertheless, after the Cold War ended President George Bush announced in his January 28, 1992, State of the Union message, "We will eliminate all Peacekeeper missiles." As a result of the June 1992 accord between President Bush and Russian President Boris Yeltsin, the United States plans to withdraw from service the 50 MX missiles it has deployed. *See* START II.

THE SEXY MX

I recently watched a filmed launching of an MX missile. It rose slowly out of the ground, surrounded by smoke and flames and elongated into the air—it was indeed a very sexual sight, and when armed with the ten warheads it will explode with the most almighty orgasm. The names that the military uses are laden with psychosexual overtones: missile erector, thrust-to-weight ratio, soft lay down, deep penetration, hard line and soft line. A McDonnell-Douglas advertisement for a new weapons system proudly proclaims that it can "shoot down whatever's up, and blow up whatever's down."

SOURCE: Antinuclear activist Dr. Helen Caldicott, *Missile Envy* (1984).

Myanmar   The new name of Burma, given to it in 1989 by the military junta that seized power in 1988. After N Ne Win (1911–   ), Burma's dictatorial president since 1962, was forced out of office in 1988 by a GENERAL STRIKE and student rioting, the military seized power and promised elections. When May 1990 elections were decisively won by candidates opposed to the military, the military (first under General Than Shwe and since 1992 under General Saw Maung) simply continued its repressive regime. In 1992 MARTIAL LAW was lifted after three years. However, emergency decrees, such as the prohibition against more than five people meeting in public, remain in place. *See also* AUNG SAN SUU KYI.

My Lai   The South Vietnamese village wherein several hundred old men, women, and children were murdered in 1968 by a U.S. Army unit commanded by Lieutenant William Calley, Jr. (1943–   ). Despite complaints by several soldiers, the U.S. Army sought to ignore or cover up this atrocity until congressional inquiries and press reports forced a comprehensive investigation that led to Calley's court-martial in 1971. According to author Neil Sheehan's *A Bright Shining Lie* (1988): "What Calley and others who participated in the massacre did that was different was to kill hundreds of unarmed Vietnamese . . . point-blank with rifles, pistols, and machine guns. Had they killed just as many over a larger area in a longer period of time and killed impersonally with bombs. . . . and napalm, they would have been following the normal pattern of American military conduct." Sentenced to life imprisonment, Calley was nevertheless pardoned by President Richard M. Nixon in 1974.

Myrdal, Alva Reimer (1902–1986)   The Swedish public official, diplomat, and peace activist who shared the 1982 Nobel Peace Prize (with ALFONSO GARCIA ROBLES) for her work on population control and disarmament. Her book, *The Game of Disarmament: How the United States and Russia Run the Arms Race* (1977), was a widely read denunciation of both superpowers. She was the wife of GUNNAR MYRDAL.

Myrdal, Gunnar (1898–1987)   The Swedish economist whose 1944 book, *An American Dilemma: The Negro Problem and Modern Democracy*, sought to be "a comprehensive study of the Negro in the United States to be undertaken in a wholly objective way as a social phenomenon." It is considered the classic analysis of race relations in the United States. His other major work, *Asian Drama: An Inquiry into the Poverty of Nations* (1968), argued that land reform would go far to wipe out Third World poverty. He was awarded the Nobel Prize for economics in 1974. Myrdal was the husband of ALVA REIMER MYRDAL.

Nagasaki   *See* HIROSHIMA.

Nagy, Imre (1896–1958)   The premier of Hungary from 1953 to 1955 and again during the anti-Soviet revolt, the HUNGARIAN UPRISING, of October 1956. Lowered living standards had generated resentment among the population and the de-Stalinization movement in the Soviet Union undercut the pro-Soviet hard-liners in Budapest. All this inspired the 1956 uprising that temporarily brought Nagy back to power. Nagy attempted to negotiate with the Soviet government to allow Hungary to establish a multiparty coalition government with general elections to follow. When the Soviets reneged on a promise to withdraw troops, Nagy announced Hungary's departure from the WARSAW PACT, proclaimed Hungarian neutrality, and asked the United Nations for protection. The Soviets sent in more troops to crush the revolt. Nagy was captured, taken to Romania, and executed after a secret trial.

Namibian Independence   The movement that began in 1966 when the United Nations General Assembly declared that South Africa, then the administrative power of Namibia (formerly known as South West Africa) had failed its mandate and decided to take over the administration of the territory until its independence. A year later the General Assembly established the United Nations Council for Namibia. But South Africa defied the UN decision and continued to occupy Namibia. In 1976 the General Assembly recognized the South West African People's Organization (SWAPO) as the sole and authentic representative of the Namibian people. In 1978 the UN Security Council adopted Resolution 435 in which it endorsed the UN plan for the early independence of Namibia through free elections under UN supervision and control. In 1983 South Africa maintained that Namibian independence must be linked to withdrawal of Cuban forces from Angola. This was realized with the ending of the ANGOLAN CIVIL WAR. Thus in 1990 Namibia was declared independent. This ended 70 years of South African control. Sam Nujoma (1929–   ), a former SWAPO guerrilla who spent 23 years in exile, was elected first president of Namibia. See also TURNHALLE CONFERENCE.

Nanking, Rape of   The barbaric sacking and looting of the Chinese city of Nanking and the raping and killing of many of its residents by Japanese troops in 1937. Situated on the southeastern bank of the Yangtze River, Nanking was made capital of the Republic of China by CHIANG KAI-SHEK in accordance with the wish of SUN YAT-SEN, the founding father of KUOMINTANG (the Nationalist Party), in 1928. As a symbol of unified China under Chiang, Nanking was one of the earliest targets of the Japanese attack during the 1937–1945 SINO-JAPANESE WAR. In the days that followed Japanese occupation, the city was pillaged and the residents were rounded up for retribution. More than 50,000 civilians were slaughtered, many of them women and children. The Japanese atrocity in Nanking was one of the factors that the Communists highlighted to mobilize the people in their war against the Japanese.

Nansen, Fridtjof (1861–1930)   The Norwegian Arctic explorer and diplomat who won the 1922 Nobel Peace Prize for his work in Europe after World War

---

MOST JAPANESE HAVE NO IDEA . . .

The government still refuses to recognize the extent of Japanese wartime aggression in Asia, the crimes carried out by people like me. Most Japanese have no idea what happened. . . . Few know that soldiers impaled babies on bayonets and tossed them still alive into pots of boiling water. They gang-raped women from the ages of 12 to 80 and then killed them when they could no longer satisfy sexual requirements. I beheaded people, starved them to death, burned them, and buried them alive. . . . It is terrible that I could turn into an animal and do these things. There are really no words to explain what I was doing. I was truly a devil.

SOURCE: Hakudo Nagatomi (at age seventy-nine) telling of his actions in Nanking in 1937 as Japanese soldier, quoted in Joanna Pitman, "Repentance" (*The New Republic,* February 10, 1992).

I in repatriating prisoners of war, helping refugees, and aiding famine victims.

Nansen International Office for Refugees   The organization created by FRIDTJOF NANSEN to institutionalize his efforts to aid those displaced by World War I. It was awarded the Nobel Peace Prize in 1938 and dissolved by the end of that year when its work was taken over by the League of Nations Office of the High Commissioner for Refugees. A United Nations agency, the UNITED NATIONS HIGH COMMISSIONER FOR REFUGEES, continues this work.

NAPAP   *See ACTION DIRECTE.*

narco-terrorism   1. International TERRORISM linked to drug trafficking. Terrorist groups such as the PALESTINE LIBERATION ORGANIZATION and SENDERO LUMINOSO are active in the drug trade because they can fund their operations with its enormous profits, because they already have secret networks in place, and because it is a means of destabilizing Western societies. In their point of view, this last factor is just a bonus.   **2.** Terrorism perpetrated by drug kingpins and dealers to intimidate and neutralize governmental antidrug efforts. Colombian drug cartels, most notably the infamous MEDELLIN CARTEL, have been the most active practitioners of narco-terrorism through the assassinations of pros-

ecutors, judges, police, and other government officials. *See also* EXTRADITABLES.

Nassau Conference   The 1962 meeting in the Bahamas between President John F. Kennedy of the United States and Prime Minister Harold Macmillan of Great Britain, in which the United States agreed to supply Polaris missiles for British submarines. This meeting, which followed the British abandonment of its own missile program, Blue Streak, and the U.S. cancellation of the Skybolt missile (which had been promised to Great Britain), allowed Britain to retain an independent nuclear deterrent. President Charles de Gaulle of France in 1963 would cite this agreement as one of the reasons to keep Great Britain out of the European Community. He stated that it indicated an unacceptable lack of orientation toward Europe and too much dependence on the United States.

Nasser, Gamal Abdal (1918–1970)   The Egyptian Army colonel who, in 1953, led the coup that overthrew King FAROUK I, whom the military blamed for Egypt's poor performance in the 1948 ISRAELI WAR OF INDEPENDENCE. Initially minister of the interior, Nasser in 1954 ousted Muhammad Naguib (1900–1984), the leader of the ruling military junta. That year Nasser became prime minister; in 1956 he became president and remained so until his death. Nasser and his "Free Officer" movement enjoyed almost instant legitimacy as liberators who had ended 2,500 years of foreign rule. They were motivated by numerous grievances and goals but wanted especially to break the economic and political power of the landowning elite, to remove all vestiges of British control, and to improve the lot of the masses. A secular nationalist, Nasser developed a foreign policy characterized by advocacy of PAN-ARAB SOCIALISM, leadership of the nonaligned or Third World, and close ties with the Soviet Union. Nasser evolved into a charismatic leader, not only of Egypt but of the Arab world as a whole. When the United States held up military sales in reaction to Egyptian neutrality vis-à-vis Moscow, Nasser concluded an arms deal with Czechoslovakia in 1955. When the United States and the World Bank withdrew their offer to help finance the ASWAN HIGH DAM in mid-1956, he nationalized the privately owned Suez Canal Company. The SUEZ CRISIS that followed, exacerbated by growing tensions with Israel over guerrilla attacks from Gaza and Israeli reprisals, resulted in the invasion of Egypt that October by Britain, France, and Israel. While Egypt was defeated, the invasion forces were quickly withdrawn under heavy U.S. pressure. The Suez war (or, as the Egyptians call it, the tripartite aggression) instantly transformed Nasser into an Egyptian and Arab hero. Nasser soon after came to terms with Moscow for the financing of the Aswan High Dam—a step that enormously increased Soviet involvement in Egypt and set Nasser's government on a policy of close ties with the Soviet Union. In 1958, pursuant to his policy of pan-Arab socialism, Nasser succeeded in uniting Egypt and Syria into the United Arab Republic. Although this union failed by 1961, it was not officially dissolved until 1984. Nasser's domestic policies were arbitrary, frequently oppressive, yet generally popular. All opposition was stamped out, and opponents of the regime frequently were imprisoned without trial. Nasser's foreign policies, among other things, helped provoke the Israeli attack that began the SIX-DAY WAR of June 1967. This virtually destroyed the armed forces of Egypt, Jordan, and Syria and led to Israel's occupation of the Sinai Peninsula, the Gaza Strip, the West Bank, and the Golan Heights. Nasser, nonetheless, was revered by the masses in Egypt and elsewhere in the Arab world until his death from a heart attack in 1970. He was succeeded by his vice president, ANWAR AL-SADAT.

nation   1. A people united by a common language, culture, religion, and historical experience who regard themselves as separate and distinct from other groups. The sense of identity (we) and of exclusiveness (they) is crucial to the sense of nationhood. Although many nations are also states to form neat NATION-STATES, there is not always a perfect correspondence between the nation and the STATE. There was a Jewish nation, for example, even before the formation of the Jewish State of Israel. In the territory of the Soviet Union, many nations were under the domination of a single state—a situation that has now changed.   2. Sometimes used synonymously (and loosely) with the term state, even if it includes citizens of many historically distinct nations. *Compare to* NATIONALITY.

national   1. Having to do with an independent political entity.   2. A central as opposed to a lower level government.   3. A citizen of a given state.   4. A resident who, though not a citizen of a state, still owes permanent allegiance to that state.   5. Nationwide in scope such as a national program that impacts every region.

National Aeronautics and Space Administration (NASA)   The U.S. federal agency, created in 1958 after the launch of the Soviet satellite *SPUTNIK I*, whose principal statutory functions are to find solutions to problems of flight within and outside the earth's atmosphere; to develop and operate aeronautical and space vehicles; and to undertake the exploration of space with both manned and unmanned vehicles. During the early part of the SPACE RACE, NASA mesmerized the U.S. public and press. It scored major successes with the Apollo missions, which landed humans on the moon in the late 1960s and early 1970s. But squeezed budgets and an unwieldy combination of public bureaucracy and private contractors gave NASA programs great difficulties following the spectacular moon voyages. Its space shuttle program exposed more than a decade of poor leadership when, in January 1986, the shuttle *Challenger* exploded moments after launching. As NASA struggled to salvage the shuttle program and rebuild public confidence, the U.S. civilian space program seemed to fall behind that of the Soviet Union and ARIANESPACE, a consortium of European nations. On May 11, 1990, in a speech at Texas A&I University, U.S. President George Bush asserted that the United States should send astronauts to Mars as part of a "new age of exploration." This suggestion was immediately applauded by those who supported an expanded space program; but the goal's sincerity was questioned by those who noted that the president did not request additional funding for NASA. *Compare to* SOVIET SPACE PROGRAM.

national attributes   Characteristics of a nation— such as size, power, the nature of its political system—that are important in explaining its foreign policy.

national character   The common personal characteristics, life-styles, and cultural attitudes of the citizens of a nation-state. When people say the French are obsessive about food, the Japanese are workaholics, or the Americans are boorish, they are talking about what they perceive to be aspects of national character. It was English poet Samuel Taylor Coleridge who wrote in *Essays on His Own Times* (1850), "There is an invisible spirit that breathes through a whole people, and is participated by all, though not by all alike; a spirit which gives a color and character both to their virtues and vices, so that the same actions are expressed by the same words, are yet not the same in a Spaniard as they would be in a Frenchman." With the advent of modern social science, the notion of national character has been somewhat discredited. Yet there clearly are national habits, traditions, and patterns of behavior that are important and make it difficult to abandon completely the idea of national character.

National Command Authorities   The chief executive of a state, usually a president or prime minister, and their duly designated alternates or successors who have the legal right to give orders to the state's armed forces. A major problem in designing a strategic nuclear system, especially one based on the FAIL-SAFE concept of protection against accidental war, is that of establishing who can give the order to launch a nuclear attack and under what conditions. Ideally the authority to order nuclear weapons release is restricted to the highest political level possible, in all states. However, a surprise attack could easily kill such individuals, or cut them off from communication, regardless of any precautions that might be taken. The phrase National Command Authorities thus becomes the inevitably vague way of describing the list of those on whom such authority might devolve in the event of nuclear war.

national ensign   The flag of a state flown from the staff at the stern of its ships.

National Front for the Liberation of Corsica   *See* FLNC.

National Intelligence Daily   The morning summary of world events prepared by the U.S. Central Intelligence Agency for the president of the United States. This "newspaper" has a circulation of about 200 civilian, federal, and military officials.

national interest   **1.** Policy goals that are the special concern of a given state. Violation of them, either in the setting of domestic policy or in international negotiations, would be perceived as damaging to the state's future, both in domestic development and in international competition. The classic statement on this was made by British Lord Palmerston in a House of Commons speech, March 1, 1848: "We have no eternal allies, and we have no perpetual enemies. Our interests are eternal, and those interests it is our duty to follow." U.S. President John F. Kennedy in a speech at Salt Lake City, Utah, on September 26, 1963, confirmed this approach: "We must recognize that every nation determines its policies in terms of its own interests." President Charles de Gaulle of France was even more succinct when he said "No nation has friends—only interests" (*U.S. News & World Report,* September 19, 1966).   **2.** In the context of foreign policy, the security of the state. Theorizing about the national interest is often traced back to NICCOLÓ MACHIAVELLI, who held that national advantage ought to be the goal of foreign policy. U.S. Secretary of State Charles E. Hughes is quoted in Charles A. Beard's *The Idea of National Interest* (1934), as saying, "Foreign policies are not built upon abstractions. They are the result of practical conceptions of national interest arising from some immediate exigency." More recently, the national interest has been held to have two aspects: (1) minimum requirements involving a country's physical, political, and cultural integrity; and (2) variables within the total context of foreign policy. HANS J. MORGENTHAU is the international relations scholar most associated with the notion that a nation's foreign policy must further a national interest based on REALISM and be divested of a crusading idealistic spirit. Consequently, he became one of the severest critics of U.S. involvement in the VIETNAM WAR.   **3.** Whatever the policymakers say it is. In practice, national interest is a very elusive concept. Policymakers use it to justify their actions, while critics may argue that these same actions are inimical to the national interest. The difficulty is that, Morgenthau notwithstanding, unequivocal criteria for determining whether action is in the national interest are often difficult to find.

nationalism   A national consciousness; the totality of the cultural, historical, linguistic, psychological, and social forces that pull a nation together with a sense of belonging and shared values. The development of this feeling tends to lead to the political belief that this national community of people and interests should have its own political order, independent from and equal to that of all the other political communities in the world. The modern NATION-STATE was forged from such nationalistic sentiment. Nationalism has been a potent force in Western history since the French Revolution and around the world in the post–World War II DECOLONIZATION movement. Most of the wars of the last two centuries have been efforts to find relief for a frustrated sense of nationalism.

Political nationalism has often been compared to patriotism. For example, President Charles de Gaulle of France said: "Patriotism is when love of your own people comes first; nationalism, when hate for people other than your own comes first" (*Life,* May 9, 1969). Albert Einstein may have best summed up the phenomenon when he wrote in *The World As I See It* (1934): "Nationalism is an infantile disease. It is the measles of mankind." Much of the TERRORISM in the world is justified by the perpetrators in terms of nationalist sentiment. In the aftermath of the Cold War in Europe, there has been great concern about the reemergence of nationalism, or what is sometimes termed "hypernationalism," which is widely seen as the main potential source of instability in Europe. Analyst Jack Snyder has suggested in "Nationalism and Instability in the Former Soviet Empire" (*Arms Control and Contemporary Security Policy* 12, December 1991) that there are two forms of nationalism: (1) the intermingling type of nationalism, where multiple nationalities hold claims over statehood that are mutually exclusive (e.g., Serbs and Croats, Armenians and Izaris); (2) the great power form of nationalism in which one ethnic group, already ruling in a powerful state, believes that it has the right, obligation, or need to conquer other nationalities, which are seen as inferior, regardless of state's rights (e.g., Germany, Italy, and Japan in the 1930s). So far there seems to be little of this second type in post–Cold War Europe. Snyder also discussed the notion that much nationalism has a primordial source in which group consciousness and togetherness is reinforced by myths about the common past. Primordial myths have been a key element in shaping national consciousness in Eastern Europe, especially where ethnic boundaries did not conform to state boundaries. Primordial nationalism, with its obsessions with past wrongs and sacred lands, can cause intractable problems. It seems probable that one of the main tasks in post–Cold War Europe will be to contain and mitigate the effects of nationalism. *Compare to* PAN-NATIONALISM.

A SONG OF ENGLISH NATIONALISM

He is an Englishman!
For he himself has said it,
And it's greatly to his credit,
That he is an Englishman!
For he might have been a Roosian,
A French, or Turk, or Proosian,
Or perhaps, I-tal-i-an!
But in spite of all temptations
To belong to other nations,
He remains an Englishman!

SOURCE: William S. Gilbert, "He Is an Englishman!" *H. M. S. Pinafore* (1878).

---

nationality 1. The legal relation between a person and a state, which implies a duty of allegiance on the part of the person and an obligation for protection on the part of the state. At the same time a strong sense of nationality is a key element in NATIONALISM, especially as related to the idea of togetherness and exclusiveness. Nationality is not necessarily related to national origin. A person gains nationality via CITIZENSHIP. The concept is not restricted to people; thus corporations or ships have the nationality of the states that charter or register them. 2. That which constitutes a NATION. For example, as political philosopher John Stuart Mill wrote in *Considerations on Representative Government* (1861): "A portion of mankind may be said to constitute a Nationality if they are united among themselves by common sympathies, which do not exist between them and any others—which make them co-operate with each other more willingly than with other people, desire to be under the same government, and desire that it should be government by themselves, or a portion of themselves, exclusively."

nationalization The government takeover of a significant element of a state's private sector industry, land, transportation, and so on, usually with compensation to the former owners. Socialist governments tend to favor extensive nationalization as a matter of ideology, because they believe that they can manage industries or land in a more equitable and efficient manner than can the private sector. Indeed, the level of nationalization is an accurate measure of the degree of a nation's socialism. Ironically, even conservative and nonsocialist governments have resorted to nationalization, but in an effort to save a collapsing firm or service, rather than in ideological fervor. For example, in the early 1970s the conservative government of the United Kingdom nationalized the part of Rolls-Royce that made aircraft engines to keep the company in business. *Compare to* EXPROPRIATION.

national liberation The process of DECOLONIZATION, whether achieved peacefully through negotiations or forcefully through military action such as a WAR OF NATIONAL LIBERATION.

National Liberation Front *See* ALBANIAN ISOLATIONISM; ALGERIAN WAR OF INDEPENDENCE.

national objective Those fundamental aims, goals, or purposes of a nation—as opposed to the means for seeking those ends—toward which a policy is directed and resources are applied.

national refugee *See* REFUGEE.

national resilience The central security concept in Indonesia espoused by GOLKAR, the dominant political party. The Doctrine of National Resilience, as it is sometimes called by Indonesian dictator SUHARTO, has three main elements: "total people's defense," or *Hankamrata,* in which the role of the people is foremost in both peacetime security and in war; the need to uphold the territorial integrity of the Indonesian archipelago; and the recognition that the armed forces are both military and sociopolitical forces. Domestically national resilience is a doctrine for carrying out national development. Internationally it has helped create the conditions by which Indonesia could carry out the EAST TIMOR OCCUPATION despite worldwide protests.

national salute The traditional firing of 21 guns to honor a state's flag or the ruler of that state.

national security **1.** The physical integrity and value system of a state, particularly in regard to threats from other states. Threats to security are endemic in an international system that remains anarchic in character and has at least some of the characteristics of Thomas Hobbes's STATE OF NATURE. Life in the international system is not necessarily "nasty, brutish and short," but it is frequently nasty and brutish. Consequently, governments have to take prudent precautions against the possibility of AGGRESSION. But actions that are defensive in nature may appear to others as threatening, thereby provoking hostility and confirming the original sense of threat. Because states can never be sure that the precautionary measures of others are simply that, the result may be a spiral of fear and mistrust known as the SECURITY DILEMMA. **2.** A phrase used as justification to hide embarrassing or illegal activities on the part of a national government. *Compare to* CREDIBILITY GAP. **3.** The military capacity to successfully resist hostile action from within or without, overt or covert. In this latter context U.S. Admiral Thomas Moorer's warning is apt: "The Xerox machine is one of the biggest threats to national security ever devised" (*Time,* June 17, 1985). *Compare to* SECURITY.

National Security Advisor The assistant to the U.S. President for NATIONAL SECURITY affairs, who directs the staff of the NATIONAL SECURITY COUNCIL within the executive office of the president. Since the 1960s there has been a large degree of institutional competitiveness between the national security advisor and the secretary of state over control of foreign policymaking.

National Security Agency (NSA) The agency of the United States government that handles the interception, decoding, and analysis of virtually all signals intelligence, and indeed most of the other forms of electronic intelligence for the United States. Unlike the Central Intelligence Agency, it is not fully independent, but comes loosely under the control of the Department of Defense, although most of its employees are civilians. Established in 1952, it has a range of facilities worldwide to mon-

U.S. PRESIDENTS AND THEIR NATIONAL SECURITY ADVISORS

President	Term in Office	National Security Advisor
Dwight D. Eisenhower	1953–1961	Robert Cutler (1953–1955; 1957–1958) Dillon Anderson (1955–1956) William H. Jackson (1956) Gordon Gray (1958–1961)
John F. Kennedy	1961–1963	McGeorge Bundy (1961–1963)
Lyndon B. Johnson	1963–1969	McGeorge Bundy (1963–1966) Walt W. Rostow (1966–1969)
Richard M. Nixon	1969–1974	Henry A. Kissinger (1969–1974)
Gerald R. Ford	1974–1977	Henry A. Kissinger (1974–1976) Brent Scowcroft (1976–1977)
Jimmy Carter	1977–1981	Zbigniew Brzezinski (1977–1981)
Ronald Reagan	1981–1989	Richard Allen (1981) William P. Clark, Jr. (1981–1983) Robert McFarlane (1983–1987) Frank Carlucci (1987) Colin Powell (1987–1989)
George Bush	1989–1993	Brent Scowcroft (1989–1993)
William J. Clinton	1993–	Anthony Lake (1993–)

itor communications of other governments. The NSA is one of the most secret and secretive agencies in the U.S. government, with little or no congressional or public scrutiny. It relies heavily on highly advanced computer technologies and is reputed to have the largest staff (over 60,000) and to be the best funded of all U.S. intelligence agencies.

National Security Archive   A library of United States government documents focusing on foreign policy and national security, located in Washington, D.C. It was organized by investigative reporters to serve as a depository of information obtained under the Freedom of Information Act.

National Security Council (NSC)   The U.S. government organization within the executive office of the president whose statutory function is to advise the president on all those domestic, foreign, and military policies which bear on national security. The statutory members of the council are the president, the vice president, and the secretaries of state and

defense. The council's staff is directed by the president's NATIONAL SECURITY ADVISOR. Unlike the Department of Defense or the Department of State, which are independent government departments represented by cabinet secretaries fighting for their own departmental interests, the NSC is directly under presidential control. As a source of INTELLIGENCE evaluation, as well as representing the president's own think tank for developing policy in all military, strategic, and foreign affairs matters, the NSC is a natural rival to the Departments of State and Defense. In late 1986 revelations that the NSC was heavily involved with COVERT OPERATIONS and functioning like a "little" Central Intelligence Agency suggested that some NSC staff members went beyond their statutory authority in what came to be known as the IRAN-CONTRA AFFAIR. The ensuing scandal forced the Reagan Administration to reorganize the NSC internally and substantially change its staff.

National Security Organization   The formal structures for national security in the United States under the president as commander in chief. It consists of the National Security Council, the Central Intelligence Agency, the Department of Defense, and the Office of Emergency Planning.

national self-determination *See* SELF-DETERMINATION.

national self-sufficiency *See* AUTARCHY; ECONOMIC NATIONALISM.

national service A government's policy that a nation's youth should serve the state for a period of time in a military or civilian capacity before completing higher education and starting a career. For example, in France all men must serve a year in military or public service at home or abroad; and in Spain all men must serve 18 months in the military.

National Socialism The doctrine of the National Socialist German Workers' Party. This was the NAZI Party that, under ADOLF HITLER, held power in Germany from 1933 to 1945. The word Nazi comes from an abbreviation of the first word in the name of the party—*Nationalsozialistiche.*

national strategy Using all of the political, economic, and psychological powers of a state, together with its military forces, during peace and war, to secure national objectives. *See also* STRATEGY.

national technical means Methods of VERIFICATION in ARMS CONTROL agreements; principally satellites in earth orbit that can relay sufficiently detailed photographs to ascertain whether a state is building missile silos, concentrating forces, or engaging in any other activity in contravention of an arms control agreement. *Compare to* ON-SITE INSPECTION.

national will The collective desire of the people of a state to obtain a goal. The term has been used most often in the context of war to describe the ability of a state to endure the pain and sacrifice needed to ensure victory. The reaction of U.S. citizens to the Japanese sneak attack on Pearl Harbor in 1941 is a prime example of how a nation's will was aroused and focused on total victory in World War II. The Vietnam War offers an opposite example from U.S. history. According to Harry G. Sum-

mers, Jr., *On Strategy* (1982): "The failure to invoke the national will was one of the major strategic failures of the Vietnam War. It produced a strategic vulnerability that our enemy was able to exploit."

MISREADING THE NATIONAL WILL

Political leaders often believe that national will is merely a reflection of their personal will. Russian novelist Leo Tolstoy (1828–1910) debunked that notion in his novel *War and Peace* (1865–1869) when he described the 1812 Battle of Borodino between the French and the Russians:

> At the battle of Borodino Napoleon did not fire at any one, nor kill any one. All that was done by his soldiers. Therefore it was not he who killed those men. The soldiers of the French army went out to slay their fellow-men at Borodino, not owing to Napoleon's commands, but through their own desire to do so. The manner in which these men slaughtered one another did not depend on Napoleon's will, but proceeded independently of him, from the wills of the hundreds of thousands of men who took part in the affair. It only seemed to Napoleon that all this was due to his will.

---

nation-building Conscious efforts to create a sense of belonging and cohesiveness among a disparate group of people within a common state. This was one of the goals of the political, social, and economic development efforts of the United States in South Vietnam and other THIRD WORLD states during the 1950s and 1960s. Since the failure of the U.S. effort in Vietnam, the term has been used sparingly in the United States. Even so, for many Third World states that emerged from the decolonization process in the aftermath of World War II, building a sense of national identity among the various groups that make up their population has been a matter not simply of importance but of survival. This is why nation-building is sometimes regarded as a key element in the security policies of Third World states such as India, Indonesia, and Singapore.

nation-state **1.** A sovereign political unit with defined and internationally recognized boundaries whose citizens have common characteristics, such as race, religion, customs, and language; for example,

Japan. **2.** A country with defined and recognized boundaries and a diverse ethnic population but whose citizens share political ideals and practices to such an extent that unity and internal peace prevail; for example, the United States. **3.** A condition that many new states aim to achieve. As Caroline Thomas notes in *In Search of Security: The Third World in International Relations* (1987): "Most Third World states are artificial creations of the European colonial powers. Their territorial boundaries pay insufficient attention to ethnicity, indigenous historical divisions or even at times geography. They are the result of colonial scramble and divisions." She then concludes that "these youthful states must undertake the process of nation-building. They have to work to forge a domestic political and social consensus, to create a nation, so that state and nation become conterminous."

NATO   *See* NORTH ATLANTIC TREATY ORGANIZATION.

natural boundary   *See* BOUNDARY, NATURAL.

naturalization   Making a citizen of someone who was previously an alien. Most states have the following general requirements for naturalization: a period of residency (from two to 15 years), good character, physical and mental health, ability to earn a living, and proof that the applicant has renounced her or his former citizenship. But one or more of these requirements may be waived, and every state has its own set of specific requirements.

natural law   A set of moral principles that reflects human rationality and is not dependent on particular legal systems, whether at the national or international level. The philosophy of natural law has had immense impact and has been enshrined in Western thinking on war, providing much of the rationale for the JUST WAR THEORY. It was also the basis for much INTERNATIONAL LAW thinking in the sixteenth and seventeenth centuries. More recently, natural law theory and just war theory have been the basis for critiques of nuclear deterrence on the grounds that a nuclear attack could never be proportionate and would invariably kill the innocent. *Compare to* POSITIVISM.

naval attaché   *See* ARMY ATTACHÉ.

navicert   A document issued by a belligerent state to a ship of a neutral state asserting that no prohibited cargo is aboard. Its purpose is to ease the passage of the ship through waters controlled by belligerents. While such documents may avoid a search if the ship is stopped by a belligerent warship, they do not guarantee that the ship will be free from seizure or danger.

Nazi   The abbreviation for *Nationalsozialistische,* "National Socialist" in German. *Nazi* was short for the full name of the National Socialist German Workers' Party. Founded in 1919, this fiercely racist political party redefined socialism to include nationalism (a doctrine known as NATIONAL SOCIALISM) and evolved into the mechanism of the police-state totalitarianism of ADOLF HITLER's THIRD REICH. While the Nazis were eventually found guilty of massive crimes against humanity, they came to power quite legitimately as part of a coalition government during the last days of the WEIMAR REPUBLIC. Using the REICHSTAG FIRE as an excuse, Hitler suspended civil liberties shortly after he became chancellor in 1933. Thereafter he ruled with dictatorial powers and the implied consent of the military, the business community, and the civil service. These groups as well as the German aristocracy saw the Nazis as a bulwark against MARXISM. The Nazi terror that ensued was both physical and psychological, and included widespread persecution of minorities (such as Communists, Gypsies, homosexuals, Jews, and Slavs) as well as political dissidents and disabled persons. Nazi Germany's attempted extermination of Europe's Jewish population, which was rounded up and interned in CONCENTRATION CAMPS, has been estimated to have taken 6 million lives. Hitler and the Nazi rule engulfed most of Europe before Germany's defeat in WORLD WAR II. The term Nazi, and more recently NEO-NAZI, is now used to characterize white supremacist, militant right-wing movements in the United States and in Europe. *See also* FASCISM; HOLOCAUST.

Nazi-Soviet Nonaggression Pact   The August 23, 1939, agreement signed by German Foreign Minister JOACHIM VON RIBBENTROP and Soviet Foreign Minister VYACHESLAV M. MOLOTOV (and therefore also known as the Molotov-Ribbentrop Pact) that

WONDER HOW LONG THE HONEYMOON WILL LAST?

A contemporary cartoon lampooned the Nazi-Soviet Nonaggression Pact. (Library of Congress)

publicly stated that Germany and the Soviet Union would observe strict neutrality toward each other should either become involved in a war with others. This pact removed the danger of a two-front war for Germany and encouraged Adolf Hitler to start WORLD WAR II one week later with the invasion of Poland. Secret protocols promised that the Soviet Union could occupy the BALTIC NATIONS and half of Poland once war began. The Germans reneged on this cynical pact when they invaded the Soviet Union on July 22, 1941.

NBC warfare   Nuclear, biological, and chemical warfare; collectively, the three forms of war that fall outside the definition of CONVENTIONAL WARFARE. *Compare to* ABC WARFARE.

NCA   *See* NATIONAL COMMAND AUTHORITIES.

Near East   A vague geographical term for the former territories of the OTTOMAN EMPIRE in Asia and Africa. *Compare to* MIDDLE EAST.

necklace   A South African slang term for a gasoline-soaked automobile tire that is put around the neck of a victim and ignited. The necklace has been a common tool of "the children" in the townships of South Africa, used to execute black collaborators and informers and to discourage future black col-

laboration with the white regime. The act of burning persons alive through the use of the necklace is called a "Kentucky," after the fast food restaurant, Kentucky Fried Chicken.

need to know   A criterion used in national security procedures which requires that those who receive classified materials have to establish that they must have access to such information to perform their official duties. This system often fails because secret items often are moved bureaucratically by those who have no need to know at all. Thus many espionage successes come from corrupting the messengers and clerks who, in their departments, have access to the kind of information that would be denied to senior officers in other departments on a "need to know" basis. *Compare to* COMPARTMENTATION.

WHO NEEDS TO KNOW?

Humphrey disagreed. "The matter at issue concerns the defence of the realm and the stability of government."

"But you only need to know things on a 'need to know' basis" [said Bernard].

Humphrey became impatient. "Bernard, I need to know everything. How else can I judge whether or not I need to know it?" . . .

"So that means that you need to know things even when you don't need to know them. You need to know them not because you need to know them but because you need to know whether or not you need to know. And if you don't need to know you still need to know so that you know that there was no need to know."

"Yes," said Humphrey.

SOURCE: Jonathan Lynn and Antony Jay, *The Complete Yes Prime Minister* (1987).

---

negotiations   A process whereby two or more parties attempt to reach agreement on an issue on which they have differences and have divergent conceptions of the best outcome. Negotiation is akin to bargaining and is a process that helps to determine who gets what on a particular issue. Linda Brady in *The Politics of Negotiation* (1991) describes international negotiation as "a political process in which nations pursue their security interests and objectives while attempting to reconcile those interests with their negotiating partners." This definition could legitimately be broadened from security interests and applies equally well to economic interests. Indeed, negotiation may have a wide variety of purposes, including the cessation of hostilities, the creation of alliances, the reaching of an agreement on particular kinds of procedures that will be of common benefit, and the distribution or redistribution of resources. On occasion states may negotiate less with a view to the actual substance than with the objective of obtaining what Fred Ikle in *How Nations Negotiate* (1964) called "side benefits," such as propaganda gains. *Compare to* BARGAINING THEORY.

Nehru, Jawaharlal (1889–1964)   A close associate of MOHANDAS K. GANDHI during India's movement to gain independence from Great Britain who, as the chief figure in the Congress Party, became India's first prime minister in 1947 and stayed in that position until his death in 1964. Nehru initiated India's NONALIGNMENT policy in international affairs that largely stemmed from Gandhi's abhorrence of war. Still, he did not hesitate to take advantage of the United States–Soviet Union COLD WAR competition. In 1952 he signed a five-year Point Four pact with the United States for aid in the development of the Indian subcontinent; then in 1955 he signed a five-year trade pact with Moscow to bring Soviet economic and technical assistance to India. His policy of nonalignment allowed him to take aid from both sides. He became prominent as both a leader of the underdeveloped world and as an anticolonialist. To this end in 1961 he used Indian troops to expel the Portuguese forcibly from Goa, a small colonial enclave on the west coast of India. INDIRA GANDHI, Nehru's daughter, and her son RAJIV GANDHI would both serve as prime ministers of India as well. This is why Nehru is said to have founded a political dynasty.

neocolonialism   A word usually used as an accusation, to assert the fact that, in spite of the DECOLONIZATION process, many of the exploitative features and inequalities associated with COLONIALISM remain in relations between THIRD WORLD states and advanced industrialized states. For example, a common inequality occurs when raw materials are extracted from Third World states by multinational

Jawaharlal Nehru (Library of Congress)

corporations to be used in FIRST WORLD factories; the Third World state gets the low-wage mining jobs associated with the extracted minerals while the First World gets sophisticated high-wage manufacturing jobs.

neocorporatism   *See* CORPORATISM.

neofascism   "New" FASCISM that has many of the elements of the fascism practiced by Germany and Italy prior to and during World War II. The term is usually associated with post–World War II dictatorial regimes in South America. Argentina, Brazil, Chile, and Uruguay have all had extended periods of authoritarian rule that were labeled neofascist because the military took control, then suspended and massively violated traditional civil liberties. Neofascism is often defined as state terror by right-wing military governments.

neofunctionalism A variant of the functionalist thesis that political INTEGRATION is best achieved through limited cooperation in particular sectors that are expanded gradually. It has a regional rather than a global focus, places more emphasis on institution building than did the original theories of FUNCTIONALISM, and assumes that there will be a spillover effect from one area of activity to others.

neoinstitutionalist A foreign policy analyst or practitioner who stresses the building of organizational structures, REGIMEs, and habits of cooperation in international relations. *See also* ABSOLUTE GAIN.

neoisolationism A recurrent theme in U.S. politics, particularly when domestic concerns or unpopular wars make the public desire a reduction in military and other commitments to other parts of the world. Neoisolationist impulses were strong after defeat in the Vietnam War as well as after victory in the Cold War. *Compare to* ISOLATIONISM.

neoliberalism 1. The resurgence of international interest in freer trade in the post–World War II era—especially since the beginning of GATT in 1947. 2. The post–COLD WAR emphasis on the use of international institutions, such as the United Nations, and the international law as opposed to traditional power and force, to solve international problems. *See also* LIBERALISM.

neomercantilism The contemporary version of that element in mercantilism that emphasized that success in manufacturing could best be achieved through high tariffs on imported goods. Those who want to reestablish PROTECTIONISM in order to assist domestic industries are described as neomercantilists.

neo-Nazi Description of those who accept the racist ideology of World War II–era NAZI Germany. They advocate white supremacy, support far-right fascist politics, often call for the overthrow of established governments, and criminally attack non-whites and non-Christians. In 1992 Germany experienced a major resurgence of neo-Nazism when mostly unemployed East German youths rioted against recent Eastern European and THIRD WORLD immigrants. *See also* SKINHEADS.

neorealism The successor to REALISM as an approach to international politics; sometimes also described as *structural realism*. The essence of this approach, which is most commonly associated with KENNETH WALTZ in *Theory of International Politics* (1979), is that international anarchy and the distribution of power within the international system (both of which are encompassed by Waltz under the heading of structure) are the major determinants of state behavior. Like realism, neorealism gives little attention to domestic influences on state behavior. It does, however, go some way toward replacing the realist focus on the search for power with a new focus on the desire for security. Nevertheless, it has been severely criticized as an oversimplified approach to contemporary international relations.

net assessment 1. An overall evaluation of something, taking all factors into consideration. 2. The bottom line after bringing together all other evaluations. 3. An office in the Pentagon that prepares net assessments and military plans for the U.S. Secretary of Defense.

Neuilly, Treaty of The 1919 treaty between Bulgaria and the Allies at the end of WORLD WAR I. It was signed in the Parisian suburb of Neuilly-sur-Seine as part of the PARIS PEACE CONFERENCE.

neutralism 1. A political ideology that manifests itself in a rejection of commitment to the political ideology or foreign policies of other states or alliances. The term indicates a state's intention to remain uninvolved in any conflicts that may occur and to act with impartiality toward any belligerents, but not necessarily a state's intention to adopt the legal status of NEUTRALITY. Neutralism in the post–World War II period was practiced mainly by THIRD WORLD states that did not wish to be associated with either of the superpowers. The term was largely superseded by the concept of NONALIGNMENT, which is both a more accurate and a more positive expression of the position adopted by these states. 2. A term sometimes used to connote a state's willingness to help reduce tension between groups of states and to prevent the outbreak of war or broker a peace. This is what the United States sought to do throughout the first part of World War I; and this has been in essence the West European and U.S. position on the Middle East since the start of the ARAB-ISRAELI WARS.

neutrality   The international legal status of impartiality, during periods of war, adopted by states toward the warring countries and recognized by the belligerents. States declaring themselves neutral expect to be accorded rights of access to the belligerent countries for purposes of travel and trade, although in practice when that trade has included materials necessary to the survival or the military effectiveness of the belligerent state, such access has led to frequent debates. Thus declarations of neutrality have not been always successful in preventing the ultimate involvement of neutral nations in the conflicts among belligerents.

Neutrality first became a recognized position in international law in the eighteenth century. But legal recognition of the concept has not prevented its violation. Neutral Belgium, for example, was invaded by Germany in both world wars. And as wars became less limited in the twentieth century, the chances of a state maintaining a viable position of neutrality were greatly reduced. The only effective neutrality is "armed neutrality." This involves not just the determination to be neutral in a neighboring war, but a practical ability to defend one's borders. During World War II both Sweden and Switzerland had policies of armed neutrality premised on their ability to mount a credible defense. Traditional neutrality is an easy option in limited and small wars that do not involve superpowers, but it is a neutrality of those who do not care to be involved as opposed to that of a small state that fears involvement. During the Cold War traditional neutrality was severely criticized by the United States. For example, U.S. Secretary of State John Foster Dulles said: "The principle of neutrality pretends that a nation can best gain safety for itself by being indifferent to the fate of others. This has increasingly become an obsolete conception, and, except under very special circumstances, it is an immoral and short-sighted conception" (*Department of State Bulletin,* June 18, 1956). Or as U.S. Marine Corps General Lewis W. Walt put it: "Neutrality is a great thing; but who is going to enforce neutrality?" (*Washington Post,* January 5, 1971).

MACHIAVELLI ON NEUTRALITY

A prince is further esteemed when he is a true friend or a true enemy, when, that is, he declares himself without reserve in favor of some one or against another. This policy is always more useful than remaining neutral. For if two neighboring powers come to blows, they are either such that if one wins, you will have to fear the victor, or else not. In either of these two cases it will be better for you to declare yourself openly and make war, because in the first case if you do not declare yourself, you will fall prey to the victor, to the pleasure and satisfaction of the one who has been defeated, and you will have no reason nor anything to defend you and nobody to receive you.

Source: Niccolò Machiavelli, *The Prince* (1513).

---

neutrality, treaty of   An agreement between two states that if either is attacked by a third state, the other will remain neutral. *Compare to* NONAGGRESSION PACT.

neutral state   In international law, any state that follows a policy of NEUTRALITY (noninvolvement) during a war.

neutral zones   An area sometimes created during war to ensure the safety and protection of civilians and the wounded and sick, whether combatants or not. Neutral zones have often been created through the good offices of the INTERNATIONAL RED CROSS. They were established, for example, in Madrid in 1936 during the Spanish Civil War and in Jerusalem in 1948 during the first Arab-Israeli War.

neutron bomb   *See* ENHANCED RADIATION WEAPON.

ne varietur   Latin term meaning "no variation"; a disallowance of any departures from the text of a proposed document or agreement.

new class   **1.** MILOVAN DJILAS's description from his 1957 book, *The New Class,* for the bureaucrats in Communist states whose privileged posts allow them to live so much better than the mass of people that they are supposed to serve.   **2.** By analogy, any identifiable newly emerging class of highly educated technical or professional workers.

New Economic Policy (NEP) **1.** The basic economic system and policy of the Soviet Union from 1921 to 1928. The BOLSHEVIKS were jolted by the KRONSTADT uprising, in which sailors called for greater freedoms. Soviet President V. I. Lenin saw the uprising as a threat to the survival of his regime. He felt that a bond had to be forged between the city and the village and that drastic socioeconomic changes were necessary. The New Economic Policy was therefore born at the Tenth Party Congress in 1921. The Soviet regime relaxed its control over internal trade, industry, and agriculture. Forced requisitions were ended in favor of a tax in kind, and peasants were given greater security of land tenure and economic incentives to increase surpluses. Labor in the factories was demilitarized. Unions were given wider freedoms. Money was reissued and stabilized. Some private enterprise was allowed to emerge in light industry, internal distribution, and retail trade, thus creating the "Nepmen" (small-scale capitalists allowed to operate within the largely socialist economy). However, state monopolistic control of heavy industry, finances, and foreign trade remained in force. Despite the relaxations of NEP, the Bolsheviks maintained their party monopoly. Overall, NEP was successful; much of the nation's prewar economic production was restored. The Bolsheviks' suspicion of any forms of capitalism, fear of any loss of centralized power, and desire to collectivize the lands contributed to NEP's downfall. NEP was followed by the first of the FIVE-YEAR PLANS. **2.** The 1970s economic reforms of Malaysia, designed to encourage industrialization and ethnic equality. **3.** A commonly used phrase for any major innovation in a state's economic policies.

New International Economic Order (NIEO) A THIRD WORLD plan to increase the prosperity of the less developed states—at the expense of the more developed FIRST WORLD states. The phrase originated in "The Declaration on the Establishment of a New International Economic Order" and "The Programme of Action on the Establishment of a New International Economic Order" adopted by the United Nations General Assembly at its Sixth Special Session on May 1, 1974. The declaration specified certain principles upon which the new economic order should be founded in order to eliminate the widening economic gap between developing and developed countries. NIEO has become a convenient label for the "demands" of the developing countries. These demands, which have been negotiated primarily, although not exclusively, through UNCTAD by the Group of 77, include fairer trade, greater access to emergency funds, increased aid, reduced debt burden, and efforts to stabilize commodity prices. The New International Economic Order, however, remains a long way from being achieved.

New International Information Order *See* NEW WORLD INFORMATION AND COMMUNICATIONS ORDER.

new look *See* MASSIVE RETALIATION.

newly industrialized country (NIC) A state such as Singapore, South Korea, or Taiwan that has created a modern industrialized society during the last few decades. Physically located in the less-developed South, they are no longer part of the THIRD WORLD, in the sense that they are no longer poor or in need of development assistance.

new order **1.** The replacement of an international status quo with a new situation. Because the phrase was widely used by Japan and Germany during World War II in reference to their rule in the countries they occupied, it took on the connotation of change by force from aggressors. **2.** The term used to describe the political system in Indonesia as it developed under General SUHARTO, who replaced Achmed Sukarno as president in 1967. The "new order" was relatively successful in avoiding the instability of the years of pluralism and the excesses of the Sukarno period in both domestic and foreign policy.

New People's Army (NPA) The military arm of the Communist Party of the Philippines, formed about 1969 to overthrow the government of the Philippines through guerrilla warfare. The NPA caused constant problems of LOW-INTENSITY WARFARE for the regimes of FERDINAND E. MARCOS and CORAZON AQUINO during the 1970s and 1980s. However, with the achievement of one of their main political objectives, the withdrawal of U.S. forces from CLARK AIR

FORCE BASE in 1991 and from SUBIC BAY NAVAL STATION in 1992, the NPA has become less active.

New World Information and Communications Order (NWICO) A controversial proposal from UNESCO that first surfaced in 1974 as the New International Information Order. A UNESCO Commission for the Study of Communication Problems proposed in 1980 "effective legal measures designed to circumscribe the action of transnationals by requiring them to comply with specific criteria and conditions defined by national development policies." This legal doubletalk meant that Western news agencies (the "transnationals") should be censored by Third World states that feel threatened by a free flow of news and information. While representatives of Third World dictators advocate NWICO as an effort to fight cultural IMPERIALISM, this proposal has gotten nowhere because Great Britain and the United States, among others, are totally opposed to any proposal that would limit freedom of the press.

new world order The international political alignments that developed in the wake of the COLD WAR. This phrase, which has long been used in many contexts, gained considerable usage in 1990 as one Eastern European state after another broke away from the Soviet bloc. Then U.S. President George Bush, particularly during the Persian Gulf War of 1991, made the phrase his own. In an address to the nation as he announced the beginning of the war to liberate Kuwait on January 16, 1991, he said: "We have in this past year made great progress in ending the long era of conflict and cold war. We have before us the opportunity to forge for ourselves and for future generations a new world order, a world where the rule of law, not the law of the jungle, governs the conduct of nations." While the phrase was denounced by the *New York Times* in an editorial (January 26, 1991) as "an unfortunate phrase, reminiscent of Nazi sloganeering," it seemed to have become the very definition of the Bush Administration's foreign policy goals. Apart from notions involving cooperation between Washington and Moscow and a greater role for the United Nations, however, the concept of the new world order remains elusive. If anything, the Bush Administration seemed anxious to maintain the familiar United States leadership role in the world rather than move toward a more multilateral approach.

NGO *See* NONGOVERNMENTAL ORGANIZATION.

NIC *See* NEWLY INDUSTRIALIZED COUNTRY.

Nicaraguan Civil War **1.** The insurrection that intensified in 1972 when an earthquake devastated the capital city of Managua, killing or injuring an estimated 10,000 people and leaving 300,000 homeless. Many key businesses and government offices were destroyed, along with most of the downtown area. The government proved unable to cope with the emergency. The Marxist *Frente Sandinista de Liberación Nacional* (Sandinista National Liberation Front, or FSLN) had been fighting a sporadic guerrilla war since 1962 to overthrow the SOMOZA regime. (The FSLN took its name from Augusto Sandino, a Liberal Party general who opposed U.S. intervention and was assassinated in 1934.) Indications that Nicaraguan dictator Anastasio Somoza had embezzled aid donated after the 1972 disaster raised popular discontent with his government. By 1977 increasing reports of the government's torture and murder of opponents led to organized resistance by businesses, professional groups, and the Roman Catholic Church. The assassination of the *La Prensa* newspaper's editor, Pedro Joaquin Chamorro, in 1978 ignited a massive anti-Somoza uprising, which the FSLN quickly dominated as the opposition's only organized military force. After a few weeks of heavy fighting, pressure from the ORGANIZATION OF AMERICAN STATES and U.S. withdrawal of all support for Somoza led to his departure from the country and the transition of power to a SANDINISTA-dominated coalition on July 19, 1979. **2.** The 1980s conflict between the Sandinista government and the CONTRAS, which ended in 1990 when a democratically elected government replaced the Sandinista regime.

Nicholas II (1868–1918) Last czar and emperor of the Russia Empire, from 1894 to 1917. Although fluent in several languages, Nicholas was never considered bright. As he was also weak-willed and superstitious, his wife, Alexandra, tended to dominate him. As czar, he was intransigent and reactionary, believing his mandate was from God and his powers should be total. Nicholas, an autocratic ruler, was an anachronism in the early twentieth century. He was oblivious to growing societal problems, such as industrialization and the growing proletariat, the impoverishment of the countryside, and the disenchantment of a rising bourgeosie. He insisted on policies of Russification, which led to widespread anti-Semitic POGROMS. Inept at foreign affairs yet personally ambitious, Nicholas inopportunely got involved in a war with Japan in 1904, which ended in a humiliating defeat in 1905. This RUSSO-JAPANESE WAR was the catalyst for internal disturbances and the RUSSIAN REVOLUTION OF 1905. He was then forced to grant a limited constitution, form the DUMA (legislature), and agree to some curtailment of his authority. With the repression of this revolution, Russia achieved a certain amount of stability and peace for almost a decade. But as a member of the TRIPLE ENTENTE and guarantor of Serbia, Nicholas committed his empire to war in 1914. Inept policies, military losses, and his taking personal com-

Nicholas II of Russia (Library of Congress)

mand of his armed forces and placing the administration of his country in his wife's hands (who was dominated by the monk RASPUTIN) brought an almost total loss of support for his regime along with a general collapse of society. With the RUSSIAN REVOLUTION OF 1917 he was forced to abdicate in February of that year. Protection of himself and his family eroded with the fall of the RUSSIAN PROVISIONAL GOVERNMENT and the coming to power of the BOLSHEVIKS. Nicholas, his wife, their four daughters, and their hemophiliac son and heir, Alexis, were all reportedly shot by the Bolsheviks on July 17, 1918. Thus ended three centuries of rule by the ROMANOV DYNASTY, which had begun in 1613.

Nidal   *See* ABU NIDAL.

Niebuhr, Reinhold (1892–1971)   The primarily theological American scholar who wrote on a wide range of moral, political, and social issues. He has been described by Michael Joseph Smith in *Realist Thought from Weber to Kissinger* (1986) as "without question the most profound thinker of the modern realist school." The key to much of Niebuhr's thinking is his vision of human nature, which he sees as involving both a spiritual capacity for self-transcendence and an inevitable capacity for sin that stems in part from anxiety and manifests itself in the sin of pride. This sin leads in turn to an insatiable quest for security and for power. The sins that are evident at the individual level are even more apparent at the group and especially the state level. While all nations are guilty of the sin of pride, some are more guilty than others. Niebuhr tended to see democracies as less guilty and the Soviet Union, which had a pretentious ideology, as much more guilty. Although Niebuhr was critical of the United States because of its rather naive expectations about the possibility that world government might succeed in putting an end to POWER POLITICS, he believed that the U.S. policy of containing Soviet power was justified. Nevertheless, he became a strong critic of the United States' involvement in the Vietnam War, seeing the war as pointless. Niebuhr's great contribution was not so much in developing ideas about international politics as in applying ideas drawn from religion and theology to the analysis of relations among states. In this sense he provided a rather different basis for political REALISM than did most of its other proponents. Niebuhr's major works were *Moral Man and Immoral Society* (1932), *Human Nature and Destiny* (1942), *The Children of Light and the Children of Darkness* (1944), *The Irony of American History* (1952), and *Man's Nature and His Communities* (1965).

NIEO   *See* NEW INTERNATIONAL ECONOMIC ORDER.

nihilism   1. A philosophy and worldview that proposes that nothing is of value. 2. A late nineteenth-century movement in Russia that supported destruction of all institutions and political structures and advocated terrorism and violence. Nihilism differs from ANARCHISM in that nihilism is more of a state of mind than a political doctrine.

Nitze, Paul H. (1907–   )   One of the major architects of United States national security policy throughout the Cold War period. Nitze played a key role in the STRATEGIC BOMBING SURVEY during and after World War II. His major impact on postwar United States policy, however, came when he replaced GEORGE F. KENNAN as head of the POLICY PLANNING STAFF (from 1950 to 1953) in the State Department. Nitze believed that the Soviet threat was military rather than political in nature. His views were enshrined in NSC-68, which provided the basis for the militarization of the strategy of CONTAINMENT and an overall framework for the rearmament program sparked by the outbreak of the Korean War. Nitze became a leading critic of the Eisenhower Administration's strategy of MASSIVE RETALIATION, arguing that greater flexibility was needed. After helping to produce the GAITHER REPORT, he reentered government in the Kennedy Administration. In the Cuban Missile Crisis, he argued for an air strike rather than a quarantine, believing that the Soviet Union would not escalate because it knew the United States had strategic superiority. After serving as secretary of the navy under Kennedy and Lyndon B. Johnson, Nitze became deputy secretary of defense in 1967 and soon concluded that the United States should withdraw from the Vietnam War, though not simply abandon South Vietnam.

Under the Nixon Administration, Nitze became a member of the SALT delegation; although a sup-

porter of arms control, he felt that it had to complement military preparedness rather than be a substitute for it. Nitze became critical of what he regarded as the uncritical pursuit of agreement with the Soviet Union during the latter half of the 1970s. He once again reentered government to become the Reagan Administration's chief negotiator on INTERMEDIATE-RANGE NUCLEAR FORCES. His attempt to get an agreement during his famous WALK IN THE WOODS in July 1982 upset other members of the administration who were fundamentally opposed to arms control and was decisively rejected in both Washington and Moscow. With the breakdown of the talks in 1984, Nitze helped to design the Reagan Administration's responses to the more flexible policies initiated by Soviet President MIKHAIL GORBACHEV.

In many respects, Nitze symbolized the two-track approach of the United States to the Soviet Union during the Cold War—strength and resolve on the one side, negotiation and arms control on the other. As his biographer, David Callahan, pointed out in *Dangerous Capabilities* (1990), this made him vulnerable to attacks from both the left and the right: "When he pressed for military buildups his critics came from the left. Soviet experts charged that he distorted and overstated the threat of Russian aggression. . . . When Nitze's crusade was for arms control, it was the right that attacked him. These critics saw Nitze as an incurable problem solver . . . an arms controller out of control." Despite the criticism, Nitze was one of the most influential figures of the Cold War and one of the few who was not only there at the outset but remained until virtually the final stages.

Nixon, Richard M. (1913–   )   The only president of the United States (1969–1974) ever to be forced to resign from office in the face of almost certain impeachment by the U.S. Congress on charges of "high crimes and misdemeanors." In response to the scandals of WATERGATE, the House of Representatives' Committee on the Judiciary voted on July 27, 1974, to approve articles of impeachment. Nixon resigned before the full house could act on the committee's recommendation, so technically he was never impeached.

Nixon was elected to the U.S. House of Representatives from California in 1946 and 1948. As a member of the House Un-American Activities Com-

Richard M. Nixon answers questions at a February 1974 news conference. (Copyright The Washington Post; reprinted by permission of the D.C. Public Library)

nam, opening diplomatic relations with Communist China, and accomplishing détente with the Soviet Union; and in domestic policy, by signing initiatives from the Democratically controlled Congress on environmental policy, public service jobs, and workplace safety. He also maintained the United States' role in the world in a period when there was considerable pressure for disengagement. But his political duplicity will mark his place in history. Nixon was able to avoid being tried for his Watergate crimes because his successor, GERALD R. FORD, granted him a pardon for any crimes he may have committed while in office.

Nixon Doctrine   The U.S. foreign policy, stated by President Richard M. Nixon at a press conference on July 25, 1969, that sought to limit the role of the United States as POLICEMAN OF THE WORLD. The central thesis of the doctrine was that "America cannot—and will not—conceive all the plans, design all the programs, execute all the decisions and undertake all the defense of the free nations of the world. We will help where it makes a real difference and is considered in our interest." Former Secretary of State Dean Acheson said: "The 'Nixon Doctrine' is not a great contribution to the enlightenment of the world. It was a polite way of saying, 'Some of my predecessors made stupid mistakes, and I am trying to right them' " (*Washington Post,* December 10, 1970). Acheson's assessment is far too caustic. The Nixon Administration was faced with powerful domestic pressures for military retrenchment and even some kind of reversion to ISOLATIONISM. Under the influence of Henry Kissinger, Nixon's National Security Advisor, the administration responded in an innovative and sophisticated way. As well as the VIETNAMIZATION of the VIETNAM WAR, the administration attempted to maintain the CONTAINMENT policy through co-option of the Soviet Union into a more regulated DÉTENTE relationship in which Moscow would act with restraint, co-option of China into a system of "triangular diplomacy" whereby it could be used to balance the Soviet Union, and co-option of allies to uphold regional components of containment. In the North Atlantic Treaty Organization, for example, the emphasis was on greater BURDEN-SHARING by the European allies, while the shah of Iran became a surrogate gendarme in the Persian Gulf. The Nixon Doctrine

mittee, he developed a reputation as a virulent anti-Communist. In 1950 California sent him to the Senate. After being elected vice president twice (with Dwight D. Eisenhower in 1952 and 1956), he ran as the Republican nominee for president in 1960 against the Democratic candidate, John F. Kennedy, and lost by a narrow margin. He returned to California and ran for governor in 1962. Soundly defeated, he announced his retirement from politics. But in the wake of public dissatisfaction with the Vietnam War, he won the Republican nomination and the presidency in 1968.

Nixon had positive achievements in foreign policy, such as winding down U.S. involvement in Viet-is best understood as an attempt to come to terms with the limits of U.S. power while avoiding a retreat into isolationism. Robert Osgood encapsulated this idea in his comment in *Retreat From Empire?* (1973) that the doctrine involved "military retrenchment without political disengagement."

BREACHING THE DOCTRINE

[Henry] Kissinger was asked at a [White House Staff] meeting whether the [Cambodia] invasion did not expand the war. "Look," he replied, "we're not interested in Cambodia. We're only interested in it not being used as a base." The wider justifications he cited dealt with superpower relations. "We're trying to shock the Soviets into calling a conference," he said, "and we can't do this by appearing weak." William Safire asked if it did not breach the Nixon Doctrine, and Kissinger replied, "We wrote the goddam doctrine, we can change it."

SOURCE: William Shawcross, *Sideshow* (1979).

Kwame Nkrumah (Library of Congress)

Nixon in China Syndrome The ability of an individual who seemingly has a great stake in a policy to change or reform it more effectively than another individual who might have been in favor of the reform all along. Because it was U.S. President Richard M. Nixon, the vehement anti-Communist—a man who had fought all his political career to deny diplomatic recognition of "Red" China—who initiated the rapprochement with China, there was much less criticism than if the initiative had been taken by someone else.

Nkrumah, Kwame (1909–1972) The first prime minister of the Gold Coast (now Ghana) when it gained independence from Great Britain in 1957. When Ghana became a republic in 1960, Nkrumah became its first president. As the first postcolonial black ruler in Africa, he became the model for a whole generation of would-be nationalist leaders there. After creating a repressive one-party state, he was deposed by a military coup in 1966 and spent the rest of his life in exile.

NKVD Russian acronym for *Narodny Komissariat Vnutrennikh Del* (People's Commissariat of Internal Affairs), Soviet leader Joseph Stalin's secret police organization (1934–1943) during the period of the GREAT PURGE. The NKVD had sweeping authority, operating through a massive informer network, and conducted its own trials and executions. It inspired terror through ruthless tactics devised to preclude any perceived threat to Stalin's preeminence. Millions were exiled to Siberian GULAGS and to prisons, and at least a million others were executed. The NKVD was Stalin's primary tool for political intimidation and elimination of enemies, real or imaginary. In 1953, after a decade of bureaucratic name changes, it became the KGB.

Nobel Prize A group of the world's most prestigious awards, given each year to individuals or institutions for outstanding contributions in the fields of chemistry, economics, literature, peace, physics, and physiology and medicine. They were established by the will of Swedish scientist Alfred Nobel (1833–1896), the inventor of dynamite, who made a fortune in munitions. The story goes that after he read his own obituary in a newspaper when his death was mistakenly reported, he decided to use his wealth to change his reputation. Nobel wrote in an 1892 letter: "Perhaps my [dynamite] factories will put an end to war even sooner than your [Peace] congresses. On the day when two army camps may mutually annihilate each other in a second, all civilized nations will probably recoil with horror and disband their troops" (quoted in Nichola Halasz, *Nobel,* 1959). The Nobel Peace Prize winner is selected by a committee of five, elected by the Norwegian parliament. The Peace Prize is awarded in Oslo; all others are awarded in Stockholm. The Peace Prize has often been shared and is not awarded in years when the committee cannot find a suitable candidate.

NOBEL PEACE PRIZE WINNERS*

Year	Winner
1901	Jean H. Dunant, Frédéric Passy
1902	Elie Ducommun, Charles A. Gobat
1903	William R. Cremer
1904	Institute of International Law
1905	Bertha von Suttner
1906	Theodore Roosevelt
1907	Ernesto T. Moneta, Louis Renault
1908	Klas P. Arnoldson, Fredrik Bajer
1909	Auguste M. F. Beernaert, Paul H. Benjamin, D'Estournelles de Constant
1910	International Peace Bureau
1911	Tobias M. C. Asser, Alfred H. Fried
1912	Elihu Root
1913	Henri Lafontaine
1917	International Red Cross
1919	Woodrow Wilson
1920	Léon Bourgeois
1921	Karl Branting, Christian L. Lange
1922	Fridtjof Nansen
1925	J. Austen Chamberlain, Charles G. Dawes
1926	Aristide Briand, Gustav Stresemann
1927	Ferdinand E. Buisson, Ludwig Quidde
1929	Frank B. Kellogg
1930	Nathan Söderblom
1931	Jane Addams, Nicholas Murray Butler
1933	Norman Angell
1934	Arthur Henderson
1935	Carol von Ossietzky
1936	Carlos Saavedra Lamas
1937	E. A. R. Cecil
1938	Nansen International Office for Refugees
1944	International Red Cross
1945	Cordell Hull
1946	John R. Mott, Emily Balch
1947	The Quakers
1949	John Boyd-Orr
1950	Ralph J. Bunche
1951	Léon Jouhaux
1952	Albert Schweitzer
1953	George C. Marshall
1954	UN High Commissioner for Refugees
1957	Lester B. Pearson
1958	Father George H. Pire
1959	Philip J. Noel-Baker
1960	Albert J. Luthuli
1961	Dag Hammarskjöld
1962	Linus C. Pauling
1963	International Red Cross, League of Red Cross Societies
1964	Martin Luther King, Jr.
1965	UNICEF (UN Children's Fund)
1968	René Cassin
1969	International Labor Organization
1970	Norman E. Borlaug
1971	Willy Brandt
1973	Henry A. Kissinger, Le Duc Tho
1974	Sean MacBride, Eisaku Sato
1975	Andrei D. Sakharov
1976	Mairead Corrigan, Betty Williams

*See individual entries for each.

---

no cities doctrine　A nuclear policy of attacking military as opposed to civilian targets. Robert McNamara, U.S. Secretary of Defense (1961–1968), promulgated this idea at a commencement address at the University of Michigan on June 16, 1962 (reprinted in the *Department of State Bulletin,* July 9, 1962), as follows: "[The] principal military objectives in the event of a nuclear war stemming from a major attack on the [Atlantic] Alliance should be the destruction of the enemy's military forces, not his civilian population." This was essentially a statement that nuclear weapons would be used, as far as possible, in the traditional way of all military power. In effect, McNamara was abandoning the United States' standing threat to destroy the civilian population of the Soviet Union, for what would now be called a COUNTERFORCE strategy. (Indeed, the no cities doctrine was the first major public statement relating to the nuclear counterforce policy.) The idea was that the United States also would keep enough forces in reserve to deter Soviet retaliation against U.S. cities. These ideas of limited nuclear war seemed very attractive in a period when the United States still had strategic superiority. By the mid-1960s, however, McNamara had abandoned them in recognition of the fact that even strategic nuclear war also would involve mutual assured destruction (MAD). Compare to MASSIVE RETALIATION.

Noel-Baker, Philip J. (1889–1982)　The British international relations scholar and diplomat who won the 1959 Nobel Peace Prize for a lifetime of support for the League of Nations, the United Nations, and disarmament efforts.

no first use　A strategic policy, publicly proclaimed, of not being the first to use nuclear weapons in any conflict. The United States and the North Atlantic Treaty Organization have never advocated this as a policy, although the Soviet Union did. Indeed, the strategy of FLEXIBLE RESPONSE adopted in 1967 emphasized both an initial conventional resistance and the real possibility of nuclear escalation. While it was never officially stated, the only way the United States and NATO could have stopped a full-scale Warsaw Pact attack on Western Europe was through the use of nuclear weapons. According to U.S. critic George F. Kennan, "First use became irrational when the Russians developed the ability to respond in kind. . . . They have already renounced first use in every way they conceivably could. They've done so unilaterally. They've done so publicly, and with every indication of meaning it. We are the ones who are dragging our feet. If there is no first use of these weapons, there will never be any use of them" (*Esquire,* January 1985). The European allies, however, were reluctant to abandon the first use threat on the grounds that the threat posed unacceptable risks of escalation for the Soviet Union and thereby upheld the peace in Europe in a way that reliance on conventional forces to deter conventional aggression could not. With the end of the Cold War, the debate became moot.

no-man's land　1. The area between two opposing armies or between two fortified frontiers. 2. The World War I term for the area between opposing trenches.

nom de guerre　French term meaning "pseudonym assumed during a war." Noms de guerre are common among Palestinian terrorists, many of whom have adopted names linked to the term Abu, meaning "father of." For example, "Abu Nidal" means "father of the struggle."

nomenklatura   The ruling elite in a Communist system. Literally, it means just a list of names; but these are the names of the people who occupy the key positions in every sphere of society.

nonaggression pact   An agreement between two or more states not to take military action against each other. It is essentially a formal declaration of mutual restraint that can be disregarded easily if one of the parties to the agreement decides that it is no longer in its interests to exercise restraint. The best-known nonaggression pact is the one between Germany and the Soviet Union in 1939, which, many historians argue, prepared the way for World War II. This agreement did not prevent Nazi Germany from invading the Soviet Union, but it did encourage the Soviets to disregard warnings that an attack was imminent.

nonaligned countries   A COLD WAR term for states that deliberately chose not to be politically or militarily associated with either the West or the Soviet bloc. The word lost some of its meaning when many self-professed nonaligned states (such as Cuba and Libya) in practice aligned themselves with the Soviet Union. Others such as Egypt and Ethiopia were at different times during the Cold War aligned with one side and then the other. Still, for some states, such as India, nonalignment remains an important principle of foreign policy.

Nonaligned Movement   A formal grouping of THIRD WORLD states created to promote the political and economic interests of developing and dependent states. It supports efforts to remove colonial rule and stands behind the United Nations General Assembly's 1974 declaration on the NEW INTERNATIONAL ECONOMIC ORDER, calling for transfer of economic resources to the Third World. The Nonaligned Movement has its roots in the 1955 BANDUNG CONFERENCE. It began formal meetings using the name "nonaligned countries" in Belgrade, Yugoslavia, in 1961, reflecting the influence of Yugoslav President JOSIP BROZ TITO. At a Cairo, Egypt, meeting preparatory to the Belgrade conference, the following defini-

tion of nonalignment was adopted: a country must "(1) pursue an independent policy based on peaceful coexistence; (2) not participate in any multilateral military alliance such as the North Atlantic Treaty Organization, SEATO, CENTO, or the Warsaw Pact; (3) support liberation and independence movements; and (4) not participate in bilateral military alliances with the Great Powers."

nonalignment   A state's foreign policy of not entering into political or military ALLIANCES with any of several competing world powers. Nonalignment implies that a state will practice NEUTRALISM in its international relations.

nonbinding agreement   Agreements that do not have legal force but that come from oral understandings or promises which create obligations and expectations that they will be observed.

nongovernmental organization (NGO)   **1.** Any private organization.   **2.** A TRANSNATIONAL organization of private citizens that is actively concerned with the United Nations or other aspects of foreign relations. NGOs can be professional organizations, multinational businesses, or groups that lobby for a particular policy. Amnesty International and Greenpeace are examples.   **3.** An INTERNATIONAL ORGANIZATION that has not been created by an intergovernmental agreement. Many NGOs have consultative status at the United Nations. The League of Red Cross Societies and the World Federation of Trade Unions are examples.

nonintervention   The policy that one state should not intervene in the internal affairs of another. This is an especially sensitive international issue when the stronger of two states (such as the United States) has had a history of interfering in the domestic policies of states in a particular region (such as Latin America). The principle of nonintervention is closely related to the notion of SOVEREIGNTY. States have a right to sovereignty protected by international law, and other states have an obligation to respect this sovereignty—specifically by refraining from intervening in their internal affairs. The importance of this notion was underlined by the United Nations General Assembly, which, in December 1965, declared that "no state has the right to intervene, directly or indirectly, for any reason whatever, in the internal or external affairs of any other state" and "no state shall organize, assist, foment, incite or tolerate subversive, terrorist or armed activities directed towards the violent overthrow of another state, or interfere in civil strife in another state." But the sovereign equality of states is, in reality, only a theory. In practice, the international system is hierarchical; the strong, through a variety of means, dominate the weak. The classic element of domination is military intervention. Both the United States and the former Soviet Union have intervened within their respective spheres of interest in Latin America and Eastern Europe, and both developed rationales to justify such intervention. The BREZHNEV DOCTRINE was an obvious example of such a rationale, as was the Roosevelt corollary to the MONROE DOCTRINE.

nonmarket economy   An economic system in which economic activity is controlled by central planning, as opposed to market forces such as supply and demand. Economic factors, such as costs, inputs, investment allocations, prices, production targets, and most other aspects of economic decision making are executed in accordance with a national economic plan drawn up by the planning authority of a central government. The former Soviet Union (and most other Communist countries) had a nonmarket economic system.

nonproliferation   An attempt to prevent the spread of weapons or certain kinds of technologies. Initially the term was applied specifically to nuclear weapons, but increasingly it has focused more broadly on conventional technologies. An example of this is the MISSILE TECHNOLOGY CONTROL REGIME. *See also* NUCLEAR NONPROLIFERATION.

nontariff barriers   Government restrictions, other than taxes on imports, that distort the flow of international trade. All countries impose some nontariff barriers. Those that are legal under GATT include: antidumping regulations, border taxes, domestic subsidies, methods of classifying and placing values on imports, restrictions on the quality of goods that may enter a country, and sanitary and health requirements. Nontariff barriers tend to gain importance as import duties are lowered.

NORAID   A PROVISIONAL IRISH REPUBLICAN ARMY North American fund-raising organization founded in New York City in 1970. With about 100 chapters located throughout the United States, most scattered along the East Coast, NORAID has served as a financial conduit to supply millions of dollars for arms and other support.

Nordic Council   A Scandinavian advisory parliament made up of representation from the national legislatures of Denmark, Finland, Iceland, Norway, and Sweden. First proposed by Denmark in 1939, it was not formally established until 1953. The council provides funds for joint Nordic cultural, educational, and social welfare programs. It also furthers common legislation among the member states and encourages the free movement of citizens across their common borders.

Noriega, Manuel Antonio (1938–   )   The former dictator of Panama who is now in a United States prison after being convicted in 1992 of drug trafficking. As a general in the Panamanian Defense Forces, he came to power in Panama in 1981 as part of a military triumvirate that succeeded General OMAR TORRIJOS, who was killed in a plane crash. Effectively becoming sole leader in 1983, he installed figurehead presidents in 1984 and 1989 through rigged elections. Because for many years he was a covert agent of the U.S. CENTRAL INTELLIGENCE AGENCY who used his GOOD OFFICES to facilitate COVERT OPERATIONS throughout Latin America, the United States was willing to ignore his many corrupt activities. But Noriega's greed eventually led him into the drug trade as an associate of the MEDELLIN CARTEL. In February 1988 he was indicted in Miami, Florida, by a federal grand jury on charges of drug trafficking. After diplomatic efforts failed to remove him from power in Panama, he began to challenge the United States openly. Noriega escalated tensions between his state and the United States throughout the latter part of 1989. On December 15 he declared that Panama was in a state of war with the United States. The following day his troops murdered a U.S. Marine, and four days after that U.S. President George Bush ordered in U.S. troops, who forcibly removed the Noriega regime from power in the PANAMA INTERVENTION. Noriega escaped immediate capture and managed to reach the Vatican embassy

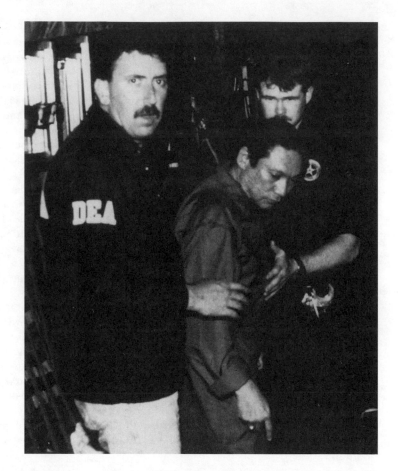

Manuel Noriega after his surrender to U.S.
Drug Enforcement Agency agents in 1989.
(U.S. Naval Institute)

in Panama City, where he requested protection. After ten days in the embassy he surrendered to U.S. Drug Enforcement Agency personnel and was immediately transported to the United States to face the criminal charges of which he was later found guilty.

normalization The process of establishing (or reestablishing) DIPLOMATIC RELATIONS that were previously severed or severely strained.

Normandy Landings *See* D-DAY.

North, Robert C. (1914–   ) One of the pioneering American figures in the application of quantitative techniques to understanding state interactions. North used econometric techniques to examine long-range trends from 1870 to 1914 in such matters as demographics, economics, and other aggregate data. He argues, particularly in *Nations in Conflict: National Growth and International Violence* (1975) with Nazli Choucri, that the growth of population within a state leads to greater demand for resources, which in turn leads to lateral pressures, which in turn impinge on other states. Collaborating with other scholars, including OLE R. HOLSTI, North used CONTENT ANALYSIS and a stimulus-response model to examine decision making in the SARAJEVO crisis of 1914 and the CUBAN MISSILE CRISIS and to explore the reasons for escalation on the one hand and peaceful resolution on the other. Not only has North been successful in applying quantitative techniques, he has done so in a way that has provided original insights and arguments.

North American Air Defense Command (NORAD) The combined U.S. and Canadian headquarters responsible for aerospace surveillance and the defense of North America against air and ballistic missile attack. With the end of the Cold War NORAD has increasingly been involved in drug interdiction activities.

North American Free Trade Agreement (NAFTA) The treaty that would create a common market among the United States, Canada, and Mexico. After the United States and Canada first signed a free trade agreement in 1989, the United States and Mexico started intensive discussions on the desirability of including Mexico. Impetus was given to this idea when the SINGLE EUROPEAN ACT of 1986 made Western Europe as a whole a more effective economic competitor. Because a North American trading bloc seemed a natural counterweight to Europe, the administrations of U.S. President GEORGE BUSH, Canadian Prime Minister BRIAN MULRONEY, and Mexican President CARLOS SALINAS DE GORTARI made the creation of a North American common market a priority. The treaty, which will gradually eliminate all trade barriers in North America, was approved by the three executives in 1992 and now awaits ratification by the respective legislatures.

North Atlantic Assembly The consultative parliamentary organization for the ATLANTIC ALLIANCE. It is a body made up of 188 parliamentarians chosen by their national legislatures and who generally have an interest in NORTH ATLANTIC TREATY ORGANIZATION matters. The assembly stemmed from a 1955 meeting of 158 parliamentarians at NATO headquarters, which were then in Paris, France; it was so successful that annual meetings were decided upon. From 1957 to 1965 it was called the NATO Parliamentarians Conference. In 1966 the renamed North Atlantic Assembly followed NATO, moved from Paris, France, to Brussels, Belgium, and began to establish closer working links with the alliance. The assembly meets twice a year in plenary session, and has a number of committees and its own secretariat that engage in various studies on key issues facing NATO. The assembly has advisory, consultative, and educational roles and regularly publishes committee reports that are invariably well informed and indicative of the knowledge, skill, and expertise of the people who make up the secretariat.

North Atlantic Cooperation Council An institutional structure that was announced at the North Atlantic Treaty Organization Summit in Rome, Italy, in November 1991 and that is intended as a forum for consultations and cooperation with NATO's former adversaries in Eastern Europe and the former Soviet Union. NATO also identified the key areas where it would try to help East Europeans: defense planning, democratic concepts of civil-military relations, civil/military coordination of air traffic management, and the conversion of defense industries to civilian production. The states of Eastern Europe, along with the Soviet Union, were invited to Brussels, Belgium, for a December meeting to begin the process of institutionalizing the links between the two parts of Europe. The inaugural session of the North Atlantic Cooperation Council was held on December 20, 1991, when foreign ministers from all the NATO members met with the foreign ministers of Bulgaria, the Czech and Slovak Federal Republic, Estonia, Hungary, Latvia, Lithuania, Poland, and Romania. (The representative of the Soviet Union also was present but received instructions from Moscow that all references to the Soviet Union were to be excluded from the text of the statement issued by the meeting.) The statement itself focused on "dialogue, partnership and cooperation," reiterated the importance of the agenda identified in the Rome declaration, and emphasized that the informal liaison procedures established since the revolutions of 1989 would be consolidated and regularized in annual meetings of the North Atlantic Cooperation Council, and in additional meetings as circumstances warranted.

North Atlantic Council The most important political body within the ATLANTIC ALLIANCE. The council was established by Article 9 of the North Atlantic Treaty, which stated: "The parties hereby establish a Council on which each of them should be represented, to consider matters concerning the implementation of this treaty. The Council shall be so organized as to be able to meet promptly at any time." Originally the council was to meet at the foreign minister level once a year, but in 1950 it created a semipermanent body consisting of "council deputies." In 1952, as part of the process of increasing institutionalization, the council was turned into a permanent body with a permanent representative from each nation who had the rank of ambassador and headed the national delegation. When the permanent representatives meet it is known as the council in permanent session. But the council also meets twice a year at the level of foreign ministers. In addition, the council occasionally meets at the level of heads of state or government. While less frequent, such meetings have become increasingly important. Such North Atlantic Treaty Organization summits are normally used to announce major initiatives. According to Bruce George and Jonathan Roberts in *Jane's NATO Handbook 1989–90* (1989), "The Council is the supreme authority of the Atlantic Alliance, the principal political organ and the primary consultative body of the Alliance. It is the chief policy making organ of the Alliance responsible for general questions on policy, the budgeting and administration, and for formulating broad political directives from which the military commands can develop the strategic plans of the Alliance. It also notifies the Allied governments of the military effort required of them."

THE NATO GUARANTEE

The Parties agree that an armed attack against one or more of them in Europe or North America shall be considered an attack against them all; and consequently they agree that, if such an armed attack occurs, each of them, in exercise of the right of individual or collective self-defense recognized by Article 51 of the Charter of the United Nations, will assist the Party or Parties so attacked by taking forthwith, individually and in concert with the other Parties, such action as it deems necessary, including the use of armed force, to restore and maintain the security of the North Atlantic area.

SOURCE: Article V of the North Atlantic Treaty of April 4, 1949.

North Atlantic Treaty Organization (NATO) 1. Another term for the ATLANTIC ALLIANCE, which was established in 1949 through the North Atlantic Treaty and which tied the United States and Western Europe together with a pledge, through Article V, that an attack on one of the signatories would be regarded as an attack on all and that any action deemed necessary, including the use of armed force, would be taken in response. Initially there were 12 signatories: the United States, Canada, Great Britain, France, Belgium, Luxembourg, the Netherlands, Italy, Portugal, Iceland, Norway, and Denmark. Greece and Turkey joined in 1952 and the Federal Republic of Germany joined in 1955, after a long and acrimonious debate. Spain joined in 1982 after the fall of Francisco Franco and the transition to democracy, thereby bringing the membership to 16 nations. When the Atlantic Alliance was created in 1949, it was widely seen, particularly in the United States, as a political guarantee pact. The organization was not really established until 1950, when the KOREAN WAR led to a more alarmist threat assessment and prompted the United States to send troops to Europe, initiate the process of West German rearmament (even though Germany was not yet a member and other European nations were unhappy about this), and appoint U.S. General Dwight D. Eisenhower as the first Supreme Allied Commander Europe (SACEUR). In a sense Korea put the "O" in NATO and changed it from a political guarantee into a collective defense organization. The distinction between the alliance and the integrated military organization was accentuated in the 1960s when France decided to opt out of the military organization (on the grounds that it subordinated France to Anglo-Saxons) while remaining a member of the alliance.

The history of NATO has been turbulent. There have been arguments over strategy and BURDEN-SHARING, with the United States demanding European increases in conventional forces and the Europeans preferring to rely instead on the protection of the U.S. nuclear guarantee—something that became increasingly uncertain as the Soviet Union developed nuclear forces capable of retaliating against the United States. There have also been arguments about whether NATO as a body should respond to contingencies outside the formal area of its responsibility as defined in Article VI of the treaty, which restricted the obligations to contingencies involving armed attacks on the territory of any of the parties in Europe or North America, and attacks on their vessels or aircraft north of the Tropic of Cancer. In other words, it excluded areas such as the Persian Gulf and the Indian Ocean, which in the 1980s became vital for NATO's security. The alliance has never had a consensus on amending Article VI. When out-of-area contingencies came within its purview, the United States in the

1980s made clear that it expected "compensation, facilitation, and where possible participation" from and by its allies when it used military force outside the NATO area. The problem was that there were considerable differences of perspective on these contingencies. Even so, the alliance provided a useful forum for informal discussions among the members on out-of-area contingencies.

For all its problems, NATO proved to be resilient. Not surprisingly, however, there is considerable uncertainty about the future of the alliance in post–Cold War Europe. Critics argue that NATO was a creation of the Cold War and that, with the end of the Cold War, it is moribund. Proponents argue that although there is no longer a Soviet threat (or even a Soviet Union), there is much potential for instability in Europe and NATO is an important hedge against this. At the very least, though, it is clear NATO no longer has a monopoly on dealing with security problems in Europe and will increasingly share the tasks with the CONFERENCE ON SECURITY AND COOPERATION IN EUROPE and the WESTERN EUROPEAN UNION. *Compare to* MANSFIELDISM; TRIPWIRE; WARSAW PACT.

NATO CHRONOLOGY

1949   North Atlantic Treaty, signed by Belgium, Canada, Denmark, France, Iceland, Italy, Luxembourg, the Netherlands, Norway, Portugal, the United Kingdom, and the United States, creates NATO.

1951   Allied Command Europe becomes operational with Supreme Headquarters Allied Powers Europe (SHAPE) located at Rocquencourt, near Paris, France.

1952   Greece and Turkey join NATO.

1955   West Germany joins NATO.
Soviet Union creates WARSAW PACT as counter to NATO.
North Atlantic Council decides to equip NATO forces with nuclear weapons.

1966   France announces its withdrawal from military integration with NATO and that NATO facilities must be removed from France.

1967   SHAPE is moved to Casteau, near Mons, Belgium.
NATO headquarters is moved to Brussels, Belgium.
NATO Defense College is opened in Rome, Italy.
HARMEL REPORT approved and strategy of FLEXIBLE RESPONSE adopted.

1979   NATO dual-track decision to deploy CRUISE and PERSHING MISSILES and to seek arms control.

1982   Spain joins NATO.

1986   REYKJAVIK SUMMIT shocks European allies.

1987   United States and Soviet Union sign INF TREATY.

1990   London Declaration issued at London Summit.

1991   New force structures approved consisting of rapid reaction forces, main defense forces, and augmentation forces.
NATO announces new strategic concept, which abandons flexible response and emphasizes crisis management and conflict prevention.
Rome Declaration on Peace and Cooperation held out promise for a new relationship with the former Soviet Union and the states of Eastern Europe through the NORTH ATLANTIC COOPERATION COUNCIL.

North Atlantic Union   An alternative model for the future of the Atlantic Alliance in the form of a political and military union of North Atlantic Treaty Organization member nations, including the United States.

northern flank of NATO   Norway, and particularly northern Norway, where Soviet territory and troops were nearer to vital North Atlantic Treaty Organization interests than anywhere except on the CENTRAL FRONT in Germany. Prior to the end of the Cold War, the particular importance of northern Norway was that aircraft based there could command the sea approaches to the Kola inlet, which was vital for Soviet naval deployment.

Northern Ireland   The United Kingdom province established in 1921, encompassing the six northernmost counties of the island of Ireland; also known as ULSTER. The division of Ireland has been the crux of the dispute between the Protestant majority in the north and the overwhelmingly Catholic Republic of Ireland in the south. This division is complicated by the fact that the Catholics in Northern Ireland have higher unemployment rates and overall lower living standards because of what they perceive to be anti-Catholic discrimination on the part of the Protestant majority. The Catholics, with some justification, feel that their lives would be better in a united Ireland. Thus Irish nationalists, most visibly those in the IRISH REPUBLICAN ARMY, an anti-British, anti-partition Catholic organization, have waged a bloody and thus far futile campaign of terror against the British government and the Protestant population of Northern Ireland. Protestants in the north (particularly the ULSTER DEFENSE ASSOCIATION) and the British security forces have responded in kind. The 1920s and 1930s witnessed the initial wave of IRA violence. The current wave of violence, which has killed about 3,000 people, can be traced to the late 1960s. Since that time the conflict has typified the ACTION-REACTION model of violence, with revenge providing justification for both sides.

Northern Tier   Afghanistan and the four Asian members of the former Baghdad Pact: Iran, Iraq, Pakistan, and Turkey. In the 1950s the Western powers viewed these states as a barrier to the expansion of Soviet power in the Middle East. Since then the barrier has disintegrated.

north-south   A reference to the division of the world between generally more industrialized and prosperous states north of the equator and the generally less industrialized and less prosperous states south of the equator. The term often is used in the context of issues relating to the economic development of the THIRD WORLD states of the south.

North-South dialogue   Economic discussions between the North (the rich, industrialized countries generally located in the Northern Hemisphere) and the South (the poor agricultural countries located mainly in the Southern Hemisphere), sometimes informal and sometimes formalized in groups such as the CONFERENCE ON INTERNATIONAL ECONOMIC COOPERATION. The essence of the North-South dialogue was summed up by U.S. President John F. Kennedy in his inaugural address of January 20, 1961: "To those peoples in the huts and villages of half the globe struggling to break the bonds of mass misery, we pledge our best efforts to help them help themselves, for whatever period is required—not because the Communists may be doing it, not because we seek their votes, but because it is right. If a free society cannot help the many who are poor, it cannot save the few who are rich." In practice,

though, the dialogue has not always been harmonious. Nor have the states from the South succeeded in achieving many of their objectives, such as the establishment of a NEW INTERNATIONAL ECONOMIC ORDER.

note   1. A diplomatic letter from the head of a foreign ministry to the head of a foreign mission (and vice versa).   2. A battle, siege, or other act of war. According to Karl von Clausewitz in *On War* (1832): "Thus war became essentially a regular game in which time and change shuffled the cards; but in its significance, it was only diplomacy somewhat intensified, a more forceful way of negotiating, in which battles and sieges were the diplomatic notes."

note circulaire   French for "a circular letter"; a diplomatic note sent by a foreign minister to all of the foreign missions in a capital on something of interest to the entire diplomatic corps.

note collective   French for "a common (mutual) letter"; a diplomatic message that usually expresses disapproval of some action, jointly signed by states that are formally or informally allied on the same side of an issue. This is seldom considered a friendly mode of communication.

note diplomatique   French for "a diplomatic letter"; the most formal of communications between states. It is usually written in the third person in the manner of one government to another.

note identique   French for "an identical letter"; diplomatic communications from two or more states to another state that are identical in substance, but not necessarily identical word for word.

note verbale   French for "a verbatim letter"; a communication written in the third person that summarizes or confirms a conversation between diplomats. Usually delivered by hand to the other party, it is neither addressed nor signed.

notionals   Fake organizations or businesses created as fronts for intelligence agencies.

NSC   *See* NATIONAL SECURITY COUNCIL.

NSC-68   U.S. National Security Council memorandum Number 68, approved by President Harry S Truman in 1950. Shocked by the Soviet nuclear test in 1949 as well as by the fall of China and apprehensive about its implications, Truman ordered the NSC to reevaluate United States policy toward the Communist bloc. The result was this seminal document of U.S. Cold War strategy. NSC-68, mainly written by PAUL H. NITZE, presented a very sober—some would say alarmist—assessment of the Soviet threat based on the notion that the superpower relationship was a Manichean struggle between the forces of freedom and those of tyranny. Moreover, it not only argued that the Communist assault on free institutions was worldwide but also that a defeat of free institutions anywhere was a defeat everywhere. If it crystallized the assessment of threat as both global and largely military in character, NSC-68 also displayed a concern with credibility and suggested that the United States could enhance this through devoting about 20 percent of its gross national product to defense. The year 1954 was predicted to be the one of greatest danger; by then the Soviet Union would have amassed enough atomic weapons to strike the United States. The problem at this stage would be both the Soviet capacity for surprise attack and Moscow's coercive power. Against this threat, U.S. military strength appeared inadequate. Consequently, NSC-68 recommended a buildup of U.S. and allied military strength to provide defense against air attacks on North America and air and surface attacks on Western Europe and other areas of U.S. interest. In an argument that would be crystallized later into the strategy of FLEXIBLE RESPONSE, Nitze and his coauthors argued that the United States should be able to respond to Soviet aggression at any level of military force and anywhere it took place. In essence, they provided a blueprint for the United States rearmament program and for the militarization of CONTAINMENT. Whether this would have taken place without the outbreak of war in Korea is uncertain. The Korean War, however, did seem to provide considerable support for NSC-68 and led to the adoption of many of its recommendations. As both a clarion call to arms and the intellectual rationale for the transformation of containment, NSC-68 was of immense importance and highly controversial.

GEORGE KENNAN ON NSC-68

[Policy Planning Staff Director George] Kennan strongly objected to NSC-68. He argued that [Joseph] Stalin had no grand scheme for world conquest, that the Soviet sphere of influence lay in Eastern Europe, and that American diplomacy was already too rigid and militaristic. But [U.S. Secretary of State Dean] Acheson and [President Harry S] Truman were watching the home front too. Wary of domestic rumblings over apparent Soviet successes, they overrode Kennan's objections and used NSC-68 to quadruple defense spending and accelerate United States military build-up, including development of the hydrogen bomb. NSC-68, a durable document, lived on to become the rationale for America's intervention in the Vietnam War.

SOURCE: John Patrick Diggins, *The Proud Decades* (1988).

Nth country   Any addition to the states possessing nuclear weapons—the next state of a series to develop nuclear capabilities. The Nth country problem was how strategists discussed the problem of nuclear PROLIFERATION.

nuclear blackmail   A term used to describe coercion though nuclear threats. It is very similar to the concept of COMPELLENCE and to THOMAS C. SCHELLING'S BARGAINING THEORY. In some respects "blackmail" is the wrong term; nuclear coercion may be open and very public, as when the Soviet Union threatened France and Great Britain in the Suez Crisis. The term is suitable in that a threat is made and there is a possibility that it will be implemented unless the party on the receiving end behaves in accordance with demands.

nuclear club   A reference to those states that have developed their own independently controlled nuclear weapons. Other states may have the technical capacity to "join" the club but have yet to publicly announce that they have a deliverable nuclear weapons system.

nuclear disengagement   The idea of reducing the potential for conflict tied specifically to nuclear weapons. The notion is that a mutual pullback of nuclear weapons will ease the military confrontation. In a sense the INF TREATY of 1987, which agreed to the elimination of all nuclear missiles in Europe with a range between 500 and 5,500 kilometers, can be understood as an exercise in partial nuclear disengagement.

nuclear freeze   A policy of stopping the development and deployment of nuclear weapons by all sides. The U.S. House of Representatives approved a resolution calling for an "immediate, mutual, and verifiable freeze" in 1983; but all nuclear-freeze motions have been defeated in the Senate. Other states sought to inhibit the deployment of nuclear weapons by creating a NUCLEAR-FREE ZONE or a ZONE OF PEACE.

nuclear-free zone (NFZ)   **1.** A state or region the armed forces of which do not have nuclear weapons. A declaration of nuclear-free zone status is sometimes seen as a way of inhibiting other states from using nuclear weapons in the zone in the event of war. Some cities have municipal laws declaring their jurisdictions to be nuclear-free zones, but this is more an expression of revulsion toward nuclear weapons than foreign policy, which only the national government makes.   **2.** A political demand that nuclear deployments in a certain area of the globe to be banned by treaty. For example, the New Zealand government has demanded a Pacific Ocean NFZ. **3.** An area that is free of nuclear weapons by treaty or other international understandings. Nuclear-free zones in this sense can be seen as additional constraints on the PROLIFERATION of nuclear weapons. A nuclear-free zone was established in Antarctica with the Treaty of 1959. There also has been an attempt to establish a nuclear-free zone in Latin America through the 1968 Treaty of Tlatelolco, which prohibited nuclear weapons in Latin America and has been signed by some countries that did not sign the Nuclear Non-Proliferation Treaty. A South Pacific Nuclear Free Zone was established in 1985 by the South Pacific Nuclear Free Zone Treaty signed by Australia, New Zealand, and 13 other island states. *Compare to* ZONE OF PEACE.

nuclear hostage   A major target that is not attacked in a first (or subsequent) strike during a nuclear war. By attacking military targets while leaving cities undamaged, the attacker effectively holds the cities HOSTAGE.

nuclearism   A term coined by Jay Lifton and Richard Falk in *Indefensible Weapons: The Political and Psychological Case against Nuclearism* (1982) to refer to what the authors describe as a "psychological, political and military dependence on nuclear weapons" and a tendency to see these weapons as a solution to a variety of problems, including security.

nuclear nation   **1.** A military nuclear power. **2.** A state that uses nuclear power for civilian energy purposes.

nuclear nonproliferation   The policy of forestalling the spread of nuclear weapons to states that do not yet have such weapons. The United States, since 1945, has followed a policy of nonproliferation, seeking to reduce the incentives for nonnuclear states to adopt nuclear weapons and seeking to control the flow of weapons-grade nuclear materials. Yet the United States also has helped Great Britain and, at times, France with the development and deployment of strategic nuclear capabilities. While the states of the former Soviet Union and China have not transferred specific nuclear weapons technology to their allies, they have (just as the United States, Great Britain, and France have) aided allies and Third World states in developing civilian nuclear power plants. But this civilian technology often makes it possible for states to develop the related weapons capabilities.

Nuclear Non-Proliferation Treaty   The 1968 treaty to inhibit the spread of nuclear weapons initially signed by 62 states and subsequently signed by at least 74 additional states. It calls for nuclear states not to transfer nuclear weapons and for nonnuclear states not to adopt them. The uses of nuclear energy for peaceful purposes are not covered by the treaty. But peaceful nuclear programs were to be subject to a safeguards system arranged by the INTERNATIONAL ATOMIC ENERGY AGENCY. The treaty has been important but its power is limited. Key states refused to sign; for example, China and France (both of which had already developed nuclear weapons) and India, Israel, Pakistan, and South Africa (all of which subsequently developed nuclear weapons). Other nonnuclear powers that had any desire to build such weapons simply refused to sign it. And some that signed it have ignored it. In 1995, the twenty-fifth anniversary of the treaty coming into force, the signatories must decide whether to extend it beyond its initial 25 years.

nuclear parity   *See* PARITY, NUCLEAR.

nuclear plenty   The condition of having enough nuclear weapons to use them for both tactical and strategic purposes and to target everything regarded as an important asset of the adversary.

nuclear proliferation   *See* PROLIFERATION.

nuclear safeguards   The system of international protections created by the International Atomic Energy Agency requiring that "countries must file with the Agency regular detailed reports on their civilian nuclear activities and must allow international inspectors to visit their nuclear facilities to verify the reports and to ensure that there has been no diversion of materials from civilian to military purposes." The 1968 Nuclear Non-Proliferation Treaty provides a framework within which the international safeguards are supposed to operate.

nuclear stalemate   A condition in which the comparative strength and mutual invulnerability of opposing nuclear forces results in mutual DETERRENCE against the use of nuclear weapons.

nuclear stockpile   **1.** The totality of a state's nuclear weapons. In this context it includes differing nuclear weapons suitable for all manner of delivery systems, such as artillery, bombs, land mines, missiles, and so on. **2.** Those specific nuclear weapons available to an individual military commander.

nuclear superiority   *See* STRATEGIC SUPERIORITY.

nuclear terrorism   The term applied generally to the threat that would be posed by the use of nuclear materials as a terrorist's weapon. Discussions of nuclear terrorism fall into three primary categories: terrorist access to existing nuclear weapons, terrorist development of nuclear weapons, and terrorist attacks upon nuclear reactors. The level of terror and destruction that the potentiality of nuclear terrorism would inspire has remained a major concern of experts, governments, nuclear facility administrators, and the public. *Compare to* TERRORISM.

nuclear threshold   That point at which nuclear weapons of any sort are introduced during a war, in addition to or instead of conventional arms. As such it is one of the fire-breaks discussed in the theory of ESCALATION and is of critical importance to strategic planners. Although the nuclear threshold is a psychological construct as much as a physical one, it is something that has been emphasized by the long tradition of nonuse of nuclear weapons since the end of World War II. One of the points about durable thresholds is that they are highly salient, thereby making it relatively easy for states to recognize and observe them. As THOMAS C. SCHELLING noted in *Arms and Influence* (1966), thresholds are more effective where they relate to qualitative distinctions rather than quantitative differences. In the North Atlantic Treaty Organization during the 1980s, there was a major debate about raising the nuclear threshold. When examined closely it is clear that this debate used the concept of the threshold in a loose if not confused way. What its advocates really meant was that NATO should make efforts to build up its conventional forces so that in the event of a Soviet attack, it could resist for longer and at a higher level of conventional intensity without resorting to the first use of nuclear weapons.

nuclear umbrella   An informal way of describing the protection extended to Western Europe and Japan by U.S. extended deterrence. This nuclear guarantee was part of the policy of the North Atlantic Treaty Organization from the 1950s MASSIVE RETALIATION to the current doctrine of FLEXIBLE RESPONSE. Ever since the late 1950s, when it became clear that the United States was or would soon be vulnerable to Soviet missiles, doubts have been cast on the credibility of this umbrella or nuclear guarantee. These doubts were voiced most frequently by French President Charles de Gaulle, who was fond of asking: Would the United States be prepared to destroy Washington or New York for London, Paris, or Bonn? The doubts became even more insistent in the beginning of the 1970s when the Soviet Union achieved strategic parity with the United States. Indeed, a desire to assuage these doubts and reaffirm the validity of extended deterrence or the nuclear guarantee was one element in the NATO decision of December 1979 to deploy cruise and Pershing missiles in Europe. The credibility issue, however, was much more a problem in theory than in practice, as the Soviet Union would have to have gambled that nuclear weapons would not be used in the event of a large-scale attack on Western Europe. Indeed, the credibility of extended deterrence may have stemmed simply from the possibility that events might get out of control and that even if there was an attempt to limit a conflict in Europe, it might escalate nonetheless. In this sense deterrence in Europe rested on what Thomas Schelling in *Arms and Influence* (1966) described as "threats that leave something to chance." The Soviet Union, in effect, also extended a nuclear umbrella over its WARSAW PACT allies. However, this was never a major issue between them because the Eastern European satellites of the Soviet Union never had the option of developing independent nuclear deterrents; their military policies were dictated to them by Moscow.

nuclear warfare 1. War in which nuclear weapons are used on a large scale. This was the focus of HERMAN KAHN's *Thinking about the Unthinkable* (1962), in which Kahn looked at the prospects for limiting nuclear war. Kahn attempted to get away from the notion that nuclear war had to be what he called a spasm war and contended that it was important to think about how, if a nuclear war started in spite of the best efforts to prevent it, it could be controlled, limited, and terminated. 2. The specter that helped to keep the COLD WAR cold by making sure that both the Soviet Union and the United States behaved with great prudence. During the Cold War Soviet and U.S. troops never met in combat, and in their dealings with each other the superpowers never actually crossed the line between coercion and overt violence.

nuclear weapon A complete weapon assembly in its intended ultimate configuration that, upon completion of the prescribed arming, fusing, and firing sequence, is capable of producing a nuclear reaction and concomitant release of energy, along with varying levels of FALLOUT, all factors capable of

killing many people. Nuclear weapons come in a variety of sizes and shapes, ranging from small weapons that could be used on the battlefield to much larger weapons that could be used to destroy cities. What is most interesting about nuclear weapons is not their physics but the psychology surrounding them. Indeed, much of the debate about nuclear weapons during the last ten years has centered around the issue of whether they have any utility beyond deterring their use by the adversary. Some, such as former U.S. Secretary of Defense Robert McNamara, have argued that nuclear weapons have no utility apart from deterring nuclear use. Others, particularly those who believe in what is sometimes termed existential deterrence, contend that nuclear weapons deter a much wider range of contingencies than this. Two concerns about the fate of nuclear weapons in the future have become increasingly salient. The first is that there will be a loss of control over some of the weapons in the former Soviet Union. The second surrounds their PROLIFERATION to other states that may be more reckless in their attitude and have neither the resources nor the inclination to impose strict controls over them.

nuclear weapon, clean A nuclear weapon that causes damage largely by explosive force; radioactive by-products or FALLOUT are kept to a minimum. It is designed to do more harm to things than to people.

nuclear weapon, dirty A nuclear weapon that causes damage (in addition to explosion and radiation emission) with radioactive by-products or FALLOUT. Also known as a *salted weapon,* it is designed to do more harm to people than to things. Initially most nuclear weapons were dirty because the technology to make "clean" weapons did not exist, a situation that is no longer the case today.

nuclear weapon, tactical *See* TACTICAL NUCLEAR WEAPON.

nuclear weapon exercise An operation performed with or on a nuclear weapon not directly related to immediate readiness. It includes removal of a weapon from its normal storage location, preparing it for use, delivery to an employment unit, and movement in a ground training exercise to include loading aboard an aircraft or missile and return to storage. It may include any or all of these operations but does not include launching or flying operations.

nuclear winter   A theorized change in the earth's climate that would be caused by the effects of smoke and FALLOUT from a full nuclear exchange among the superpowers. The freezing conditions resulting from the blotting out of most sunlight for weeks or months after a nuclear war by debris would destroy most plant and animal life that survived the initial blast. The theory is a very controversial one, based on certain projections about the amount of smoke that is emitted when different kinds of material burn. Some critics argue that nuclear winter is unlikely and that in fact a GREENHOUSE EFFECT is more likely in the aftermath of a nuclear war. Whatever the case, the overall impact of the nuclear winter theory was not very great. It added to concerns that the Third World would suffer from the consequences of any U.S.-Soviet conflict, even though it was not directly involved. This might have intensified slightly the pressure on Moscow and Washington to do something about the arms race. But if it helped to make the idea of large-scale nuclear war slightly more abhorrent, this was not a significant development: Nuclear war is an appalling prospect even without nuclear winter.

nuclear yield   The energy released in the detonation of a nuclear weapon, measured in terms of the kilotons or megatons of trinitrotoluene (TNT) required to produce the same energy release.

Number 10 Downing Street   The official residence of the British prime minister in London. It is the architectural embodiment of the bureaucratic institution of the office of the prime minister; thus British foreign policy is often said to come from this building.

nuncio   A diplomat from the Vatican who represents the pope in his capacity as the sovereign of Vatican City, not in his capacity as head of the Roman Catholic Church.

nuncio, Apostolic   The diplomatic agent of the pope who represents him both in his capacity as sovereign of Vatican City and as head of the Roman Catholic Church. In many traditionally Catholic states, the Apostolic nuncio is ex officio the dean of the Diplomatic Corps. However, this may be a courtesy precedence; often the actual function of such a dean are still performed by the senior ambassador.

Prime Minister Margaret Thatcher and U.S. Vice President George Bush at the entrance to Number 10 Downing Street in 1983. (British Information Services)

Nuremberg defense   The often used excuse of those caught undertaking illegal acts for political or military superiors: "I was only following orders." Both the term and the tactic originated with the war crimes trials in Nuremberg, Germany, of top NAZI leaders in the aftermath of World War II. The fallacy of this defense is that no soldier (or civilian employee) can be required to obey manifestly illegal orders. Indeed, as was shown in the MY LAI massacre of the Vietnam War, a soldier (or civilian employee) has a positive obligation to disobey such orders.

Nuremberg laws   The racial laws of Nazi Germany promulgated in 1935 at the NUREMBERG RALLY of that year. These laws made a distinction between ARYAN and non-Aryan German citizens and deprived Jews of the right to practice a profession or to marry non-Jews. Because the Nuremberg laws helped pave the way for the murder of millions of Jews in the HOLOCAUST and because Nuremberg, through the rallies, had become a symbol of Nazi ascendency, the city was chosen by the Allies as the site of trials for Nazi war criminals.

Nuremberg principles   The general legal principles, the norms of INTERNATIONAL LAW, established by Article 6 of the 1945 Charter of the International Military Tribunal, which enumerated the WAR CRIMES for which individuals would be held accountable.

Nuremberg rallies   Mass meetings of the NAZI party held in the northern Bavarian city of Nuremberg, Germany, from 1933 to 1938. They were known for their visual effect of thousands of robot-like Nazis marching to Richard Wagner's operatic music. The highlight of each rally was a major display of oratorical histrionics by ADOLF HITLER. The widely distributed films of these rallies were a major element of Nazi PROPAGANDA.

Nuremberg trials   1. The November 1945–October 1946 WAR CRIMES trials of the most prominent surviving NAZIs. While there were a variety of other war crimes trials at Nuremberg and in other locations throughout what was once German-occupied territory, this trial of the 21 top Nazi leaders remains the best known. The verdicts included 11

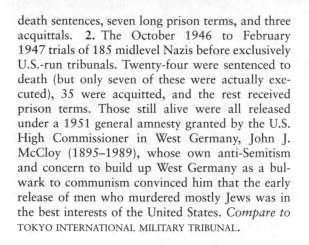

German war criminals in the defendants' dock at the 1945–1946 Nuremberg Trials. (National Archives)

death sentences, seven long prison terms, and three acquittals. **2.** The October 1946 to February 1947 trials of 185 midlevel Nazis before exclusively U.S.-run tribunals. Twenty-four were sentenced to death (but only seven of these were actually executed), 35 were acquitted, and the rest received prison terms. Those still alive were all released under a 1951 general amnesty granted by the U.S. High Commissioner in West Germany, John J. McCloy (1895–1989), whose own anti-Semitism and concern to build up West Germany as a bulwark to communism convinced him that the early release of men who murdered mostly Jews was in the best interests of the United States. *Compare to* TOKYO INTERNATIONAL MILITARY TRIBUNAL.

Nye, Joseph (1937–   )   The Harvard University professor and Carter Administration national security expert who has made major contributions to the analysis of international relations in both security and international political economy. Nye was the coauthor with Robert Keohane of *Power and Inter-* *dependence* (1977), which showed how states in the international system had become increasingly interdependent and examined the impact of this on international relations. Nye also was active on security issues and was one of the key participants in a Harvard study group on avoiding nuclear war, which led to a volume entitled *Hawks, Doves and Owls* (1985). This study looked at the ways in which nuclear war might occur and considered how the prospects for this might be reduced. In the late 1980s Nye focused much of his attention on challenging the view, put forward most fully and explicitly by Paul Kennedy in *The Rise and Fall of the Great Powers* (1987), that the United States was in decline. In *Bound to Lead* (1990) Nye refuted the argument about U.S. decline, contending that there was nothing inexorable about it. In his view the critical question was whether the United States had the political leadership and strategic vision to translate its substantial and comprehensive power resources into "real influence in a transitional period of world politics." *See also* CO-OPTIVE POWER; SOFT POWER.

O

OAPEC (Organization of Arab Petroleum Exporting Countries)   An association of the oil-producing states in the Arab world (Algeria, Iraq, Kuwait, Libya, Qatar, Saudi Arabia, and United Arab Emirates) that seeks to coordinate the members' petroleum economic policies, to exchange expertise, to provide training and employment for each other's citizens, and to undertake joint projects. Most OAPEC members also belong to OPEC.

OAS   **1.** ORGANIZATION OF AMERICAN STATES. **2.** *Organisation de l'Armee Secrete* (Secret Army Organization), a terrorist group of European settlers in Algeria, violent in their opposition to the loss of French sovereignty in that northern African country. In the early 1960s the OAS launched terrorist attacks against the Muslim Algerian population both in Algeria and in France; the mayor of Evian, France, the town in which a negotiated settlement to the Algerian question was being discussed, was killed in an OAS bomb attack. Many members of the French military were active in the OAS. Four French generals, in rebellion against French policy, led the abortive April 1961 OAS takeover of Algiers. In the spring of 1962, after the Evian accord on independence was reached between the government of CHARLES DE GAULLE and the Algerian nationalists, the OAS attempted to thwart enactment of the agreement by conducting a massive campaign of murder and destruction. These acts of terrorism, though tragic, proved ineffectual and prompted a violent National Liberation Front (FLN) backlash and eventually the flight of much of Algeria's European population after the ALGERIAN WAR OF INDEPENDENCE.

OAU   *See* ORGANIZATION OF AFRICAN UNITY.

observer   **1.** A person, state, or organization allowed to attend the functions of an international organization without being a full member. For example, the Palestine Liberation Organization has been given observer status by the General Assembly of the United Nations.   **2.** A military person sent by the United Nations to an area of potential conflict to determine if truce terms are being complied with, to report back on conditions to the UN, or to inhibit the escalation of tensions by maintaining a UN presence.

occupation   **1.** The temporary possession by a hostile military force of land captured in battle with the intention of returning it to the previous owners following a peace treaty and the normalization of diplomatic relations.   **2.** The permanent possession of land captured in battle without the sanction of a peace treaty or normal diplomatic relations with the state from whom the land was taken.   **3.** The historic means by which states extended their sovereignty over virgin territories. This concept is not applicable to the modern world because all land is currently spoken for or in dispute.

occupied territories   Land taken over by Israel after the 1967 SIX-DAY WAR and still retained by it (except for the Sinai Peninsula, which was returned to Egypt by a 1979 peace treaty). This includes the WEST BANK, the GAZA STRIP, the GOLAN HEIGHTS, and East Jerusalem. The last two areas were annexed by Israel in 1981 and 1967, respectively. According to the prime minister of Israel, Yitzhak Shamir: "We don't recognize and we don't accept the term 'occu-

Anonymous French citizens weep as they watch German soldiers occupy Paris on June 14, 1940. (National Archives)

pied territories.' We have never 'occupied' territories. We have never occupied territories of a foreign country's. There was never in the Middle East a Palestinian country. Therefore, we have never occupied territories that do not belong to us" (*Pittsburgh Post-Gazette,* November 25, 1991). The Palestine Liberation Organization and the Arab states take a different point of view, and this difference is at the heart of the Arab-Israeli dispute.

occupied territory   Land under the authority and effective control of a belligerent military force. The term is not applicable to territory being administered pursuant to peace terms, treaty, or other agreement, express or implied, with the civil authority of the territory.

Ocho Rios Declaration   A 1982 statement by the heads of government of the 12 CARIBBEAN COMMUNITY AND COMMON MARKET states, plus the Bahamas, at the conclusion of their third summit meeting held in Ocho Rios, Jamaica. It reaffirmed their commitment to regional integration and the expansion of trade within the area; affirmed the civil, cultural, economic, and political rights of the peoples of the region in accordance with the Universal Declaration of Human Rights; reaffirmed support for Belize in its territorial dispute with Guatemala; urged Venezuela and Guyana to continue efforts to reach a peaceful settlement of their border dispute; and stated that U.S. aid, as proposed in the CARIBBEAN BASIN INITIATIVE, should be given in consultation with the recipient countries.

October Manifesto   Czar NICHOLAS II's formal response to the RUSSIAN REVOLUTION OF 1905; an October 17, 1905, document that promised a constitution, civil liberties, and a duma (parliament) elected by a broad suffrage. This manifesto and associated economic reforms satisfied moderates and allowed czarist autocracy to survive until the RUSSIAN REVOLUTION OF 1917.

October revolution   *See* RUSSIAN REVOLUTION OF 1917.

October surprise   1. A development so late in a U.S. presidential campaign that the opposition does not have time to respond to it adequately before the November election.   2. A reference to the allegation that agents of the Ronald Reagan–George Bush presidential election campaign of 1980 made a secret deal with Iran not to have the U.S. embassy hostages released until after the November presidential election of that year. In 1991 the Congress started a formal investigation into the allegation. The IRANIAN HOSTAGE CRISIS was one of the major factors in President Jimmy Carter's defeat for reelection. One factor that made the October surprise charge more plausible than it otherwise might have been is the fact that during the IRAN-CONTRA AFFAIR, representatives of the Reagan-Bush Administration did in fact during 1985 and 1986 make secret deals with Iran to trade arms for U.S. hostages then held in Lebanon. However, in January 1993 a report released by the U.S. House of Representatives October Surprise Task Force concluded that while Ronald Reagan's 1980 campaign operatives were "operating on the outer limits of propriety," there was no truth to the October surprise allegation.

October War *See* YOM KIPPUR WAR.

Oder-Neisse Line The border between Germany and Poland. The Oder, a river in Central Europe, originates in the Silesia Mountains and flows into the Baltic Sea; the Neisse River is a major tributary of the Oder. German territory up to the Oder-Neisse line was occupied by Poland in 1945. The Soviet Union unilaterally established this shift to compensate Poland for ceding 70,000 square miles of its territory to the Soviet Union. This border was variously recognized by governments of both East and West Germany. Finally a unified Germany confirmed the Oder-Neisse border via a November 14, 1990, treaty with Poland.

OECD *See* ORGANIZATION FOR ECONOMIC COOPERATION AND DEVELOPMENT.

OECS *See* ORGANIZATION OF EASTERN CARIBBEAN STATES.

offer list Concessions offered by a country in trade negotiations, or a list of selected commodities on which a country offers to make concessions. The actual list submitted during the negotiations may cite exceptions to the agreed formula for tariff reductions or be an offer to accept expanded coverage under a proposed code of conduct.

Office of Strategic Services (OSS) The civilian intelligence, espionage, and sabotage organization of the United States during WORLD WAR II. It was created by presidential executive order in 1942 and directed all its life by WILLIAM J. DONOVAN. OSS agents were famous for operating behind enemy lines in both the European and Pacific theaters of war. They trained partisans, rescued downed Allied airmen, conducted sabotage, and provided raw intelligence. Nevertheless, the OSS engendered bureaucratic rivalries with the U.S. State Department, War Department, and Federal Bureau of Investigation. Thus it was abolished as an independent entity by President Harry S Truman in 1945. Its functional units were then divided between the State and War departments. Because these units and many of the former OSS employees became part of the CENTRAL INTELLIGENCE AGENCY when it was created in 1947, the OSS has always been considered the predecessor agency to the CIA.

OH, SO SOCIAL!

Gen. "Wild Bill" Donovan—of the Office of Strategic Service, sometimes called the "Cloak and Dagger Club," or "Oh, So Social," will miss [President Franklin D.] Roosevelt terribly. Donovan ran the giant espionage outfit which tried to find out what was going on behind enemy lines, and he had accumulated the most bizarre assortment of female spies, social-register bluebloods, and anti-Roosevelt haters ever seen in Washington. As an old personal friend, Roosevelt gave him free rein, including grandiose plans for a postwar-espionage service. [President Harry S] Truman does not like peacetime espionage and will not be so lenient.

SOURCE: Drew Pearson, *Washington Post,* April 27, 1945.

Official Development Assistance (ODA) According to the ORGANIZATION FOR ECONOMIC COOPERATION AND DEVELOPMENT, "those flows [of money] to developing countries and multilateral institutions provided by official agencies, including state and local governments, or by their executive agencies, each transaction of which meets the following tests: a) it is administered with the promotion of the economic development and welfare of developing countries as its main objective and b) it is concessional in character and contains a grant element of at least 25 percent." ODA may be in the form of SOFT LOANS, bilateral grants, or multilateral flows of various types. *See also* DEVELOPMENT DECADES; FOREIGN AID.

offset requirements Government-imposed conditions on foreign exporters that must be met if major sales agreements are to be approved. Such rules usually are made in an effort either to reduce the adverse balance-of-trade impact of a major sale or to gain specified industrial benefits for the importing country. Often an exporter may be required to purchase a specified amount of locally produced goods or services from the importing country. For example, a commercial aircraft manufacturer seeking sales to an airline in another country might be required to establish manufacturing facilities in the importing country, to source a specified percentage of the components used in manufacturing facilities in the importing country, or to source a specified percentage of the components used in manufacturing the product from established local manufacturers.

Okhrana Formally *Okhrannoye Otdelenie* ("security police"), the Russian secret police unit established in 1881 to combat the fledgling but rapidly expanding revolutionary movement in the major cities in czarist Russia. By the early 1900s the Okhrana had a pervasive presence, operating a vast net of informers and double agents in cities and smaller towns throughout the country. It was abolished in 1917. *Compare to* KGB.

OIC *See* ORGANIZATION OF THE ISLAMIC CONFERENCE.

oil embargo The 1973–1974 effort by the Arab members of OPEC to change Western policies toward the Middle East by refusing to export oil to those states that supported Israel during the October 1973 YOM KIPPUR WAR. At first only the United States was embargoed; then the Netherlands, Portugal, Rhodesia, and South Africa. Then OPEC announced a cutback on oil production of 25 percent. Because this would have hurt all industrialized states, the European Community and Japan almost immediately caved in and called for Israeli concessions to the Arabs. At the same time OPEC quadrupled the price of oil from $3 to $12 U.S. a barrel.

The embargo, which always "leaked," was lifted a few months later.

The embargo had several lasting effects. First, the price increase started a massive shift of wealth from the oil-hungry West to the Arab world. Second, it moderated in some cases and undermined in others Western support for Israel. Third, it highlighted the bargaining power of those Third World states with control over crucial resources. And finally, it started an inflationary spiral that hurt the advanced industrialized states but had an even more damaging impact on developing states. In addition, it encouraged the industrialized states to accelerate the search for alternative sources of fuel such as in the North Sea (by Great Britain and Norway) and in Alaska (by the United States).

Okinawa, Battle of The last major U.S. amphibious invasion of a Japanese-held Pacific Ocean island in WORLD WAR II. From April to June of 1945 an estimated 130,000 Japanese defenders died (another 7,000 surrendered) resisting overwhelming U.S. forces. The United States had over 50,000 casualties (including 12,000 dead)—many of them caused by kamikaze, or suicide, attacks by Japanese pilots on the U.S. naval fleet. Okinawa was scheduled to be the major base of operations for the expected U.S. invasion of the Japanese main islands that was forestalled by the ATOMIC BOMB. Because Okinawa and the islands in the Ryukyu chain traditionally belonged to Japan, in 1972 the United States returned them but retained its military bases.

Olympic Games The revival of the ancient Greek sporting event that, since 1896, has brought most of the states of the world together to compete in athletic events and score propaganda points for their governments. The games, essentially held every four years except during World War I and II, have always had political overtones. For example, the 1936 games in Berlin were designed to make Nazi Germany look respectable to the world; the 1972 Munich games were marred when Arab terrorists murdered Israeli athletes; and the 1980 Moscow games were not attended by most Western states in protest of the 1979 Soviet invasion of Afghanistan.

OLYMPIC GAMES—SUMMER		
Year	Location	Number of States Attending
1896	Athens, Greece	13
1900	Paris, France	22
1904	St. Louis, U.S.A.	12
1906	Athens, Greece	20
1908	London, England	23
1912	Stockholm, Sweden	28
1920	Antwerp, Belgium	29
1924	Paris, France	44
1928	Amsterdam, the Netherlands	46
1932	Los Angeles, U.S.A.	37
1936	Berlin, Germany	49
1948	London, England	59
1952	Helsinki, Finland	69
1956	Melbourne, Australia	67
1960	Rome, Italy	83
1964	Tokyo, Japan	93
1968	Mexico City, Mexico	112
1972	Munich, West Germany	122
1976	Montreal, Canada	92
1980	Moscow, U.S.S.R.	81
1984	Los Angeles, U.S.A.	141
1988	Seoul, South Korea	160
1992	Barcelona, Spain	173

OLYMPIC GAMES—WINTER		
Year	Location	Number of States Attending
1924	Chamonix, France	16
1928	St. Moritz, Switzerland	25
1932	Lake Placid, U.S.A.	17
1936	Garmisch-Partenkirchen, Germany	28
1948	St. Moritz, Switzerland	28
1952	Oslo, Norway	30
1956	Cortina D'Ampezzo, Italy	32
1960	Squaw Valley, U.S.A.	30
1964	Innsbruck, Austria	36
1968	Grenoble, France	37
1972	Sapporo, Japan	35
1976	Innsbruck, Austria	37
1980	Lake Placid, U.S.A.	37
1984	Sarajevo, Yugoslavia	49
1988	Calgary, Canada	57
1992	Albertville, France	64

OMA *See* ORDERLY MARKETING AGREEMENT.

on-site inspection The verification of compliance with the terms of an ARMS CONTROL agreement through physical access to those forces or weapons subject to limitations, either by representatives of the parties involved or by mutually acceptable neutral agents. Until the late 1980s all such forms of intrusive verification were rejected by the Soviet Union. Thus remote-sensing devices known as NATIONAL TECHNICAL MEANS (such as reconnais-sance satellites and seismic-sensing equipment) had to be used. The Stockholm Agreement of 1986 was the first international security accord to permit the signatory states to inspect forces on the ground for purposes of compliance. The Intermediate Nuclear Forces (INF) Treaty of December 1987 took this process a stage further in establishing processes for the elimination of an entire class of nuclear weapons. This treaty even included the right for "challenge inspections" on short notice.

OPEC (Organization of Petroleum Exporting Countries) An association of many of the world's oil-producing states, formed in 1960 by Iran, Iraq, Kuwait, Libya, Saudi Arabia, and Venezuela; members joining subsequently were Qatar, Indonesia, United Arab Emirates, Algeria, Nigeria, Ecuador, and Gabon. OPEC seeks to coordinate the petroleum policies of its members. During the Arab-

Israeli YOM KIPPUR WAR of October 1973, Arab OPEC members placed an embargo on oil exports to Western states supporting Israel in order to encourage them to change their policies toward the Middle East. OPEC's Special Fund was established in May 1976 as a multilateral source of loans and assistance to developing states that suffered extreme economic problems from the rise in oil prices. *See* OAPEC; OIL EMBARGO; PETROCURRENCIES.

OPEC siege   The December 21–23, 1975, kidnapping of 11 Organization of Petroleum Exporting Countries' oil ministers, along with almost 60 other hostages, at a conference in Vienna, Austria, by the POPULAR FRONT FOR THE LIBERATION OF PALESTINE. Terrorists stormed the Vienna OPEC headquarters, killing three persons in the process; then barricaded themselves and 70 hostages inside and demanded $5 million U.S. in ransom, television and radio broadcasts of Palestinian propaganda, and safe passage to Tripoli, Libya. After 36 hours, the government of Austrian Chancellor Bruno Kreisky conceded to the demands. The terrorists first flew to Algiers, Algeria, and then to Tripoli, only to fly once again to Algiers, where some of them surrendered. Since millions in ransom money was given to associates not directly involved with the attack, those arrested soon were able to buy their way to freedom. It is not publicly known how much ransom money in what currencies the kidnappers finally received. Estimates range from $5 million to $50 million U.S.

open city   A tenet of INTERNATIONAL LAW that allows an occupying army to withdraw its troops from a city and declare it an "open city" so that incoming opposition forces do not have to fight their way in, in the process destroying much of the city and its people. For example, when defeat by Germany was inevitable in 1940, France declared Paris an "open city." Under international law, further defense of the city by French troops would have constituted a crime.

open door   1. A policy that was adopted by the United States in relation to China and was embodied in a series of notes issued by U.S. Secretary of State JOHN HAY in 1899 and 1900 that attempted to establish the principle of equal economic opportunities for external powers. The notes sought to guarantee U.S. access to the Chinese markets that were being carved out as SPHERES OF INFLUENCE by France, Germany, Great Britain, Italy, Japan, and Russia. 2. A term that has been used in neo-Marxist interpretations of United States foreign policy to describe the U.S. desire for access to markets. According to this theory, it was the loss of markets in Eastern Europe in the latter half of the 1940s that made the United States so hostile to the Soviet Union and helped to bring about the Cold War. 3. A synonym for FREE TRADE that also is used to describe the policy or policies designed to bring this about. 4. General principles governing a country's foreign policy, characterized by a positive and welcoming attitude toward other countries' political, economic, social, and cultural influences. 5. The official foreign policy of the Chinese government under the leadership of DENG XIAOPING since 1978. The Chinese government decided to modernize its country by opening to the West and attracting new technology and investment and by encouraging JOINT VENTUREs inside Chinese borders. A key policy decision was to carve out parts of China that have relatively high economic development and pools of skilled workers as Special Economic Zones, where foreign businesses are given preferential treatment in terms of taxes and foreign currency conversion. As a result the Chinese economy is more integrated with the rest of the world than at any time in the past four decades under the Communist rule, and there has been great improvement in the standard of living for the Chinese people. The 1989 TIANANMEN SQUARE democracy movement and the subsequent government crackdown briefly interrupted the further opening up. Since then the Chinese government has been keeping tight political control while maintaining economic liberalization.

open skies proposal   The United States government's 1955 plan for the mutual and continuous aerial photo surveillance by the United States and the Soviet Union. This would have been accompanied by a full exchange of blueprints of U.S. and Soviet military installations in order to forestall fears of a FIRST STRIKE by either side. U.S. President Dwight D. Eisenhower made this proposal at the July 1955 Geneva Four-Power Summit Conference to reduce the likelihood of an East-West military confrontation in Europe. The

Soviet Union rejected the idea. Since then, however, what is effectively an open skies policy has been put in place not by diplomacy but by technology, especially military surveillance satellites. Nevertheless, the open skies idea came up again as the COLD WAR was about to wind down. U.S. President Ronald Reagan formally proposed it in 1989 to Soviet President Mikhail Gorbachev. After several years of negotiating, an Open Skies Treaty was agreed to in 1992 by all of the North Atlantic Treaty Organization states plus Belarus, Bulgaria, Czechoslovakia, Hungary, Poland, Romania, Russia, and Ukraine.

operation   The execution of a military or intelligence mission; the implementation of a strategic or tactical plan of action. Operations are often given CODE NAMES to summarize all of the integrated activities associated with them. For example, Operation Barbarosa was the German invasion of the Soviet Union in World War II; Operation Overlord was the World War II D Day invasion of France by the Allies.

Operation Ajax   The 1953 U.S. CENTRAL INTELLIGENCE AGENCY covert operation directed by Kermit Roosevelt (1916–   ) that fomented a successful coup d'état in Iran, unseating Prime Minister MOHAMMAD MOSSADEGH and reinstating MOHAMMED REZA PAHLEVI in the throne. Kermit's grandfather was U.S. President Theodore Roosevelt.

operational arms control   ARMS CONTROL that aims at regulating not the force structures and quantitative and qualitative characteristics of the military establishments but the activities of military forces—such as maneuvers or alert status.

operational code   The underlying core political beliefs of an individual or state that constantly influence its decision making. This notion was first enunciated by Nathan Leites in his *Study of Bolshevism* (1953) and adapted and developed by subsequent scholars, most notably ALEXANDER L. GEORGE. The focus on the belief systems of policymaking elites stemmed from the behavioralist approach to politics and international relations, and has subsequently become a central element in foreign policy analysis. Alexander George in "The 'Operational Code': A Neglected Approach to the Study of Polit-

ical Leaders and Decision-Making" (*International Studies Quarterly* 13, June 1969) argues that the operational code does not refer to a "set of recipes for political action" but to

> a set of general beliefs about fundamental issues of history and central questions of politics as these bear in turn on the problem of action. The actor's beliefs and premises . . . serve . . . as a prism that influences the actor's perceptions and diagnoses of the flow of political events, his definitions and estimates of particular situations. These beliefs also provide norms, standards, and guidelines that influence the actor's choice of strategy and tactics, his structuring and weighing of alternative courses of action.

George developed the concept much more broadly than Leites; it has served as the basis for several studies of key policymakers and the way they made decisions.

operational environment   The environment that actually exists, as opposed to the *psychological environment* that is perceived by decision makers. This concept, widely used in foreign policy analysis, was coined by HAROLD and MARGARET SPROUT. The distinction between the psychological and the operational environments is sometimes used in analyses of decision making to highlight possible discrepancies between the world as it exists and the world as it is seen by foreign policymakers.

operational policy   *See* DECLARATORY POLICY.

operational strategy   A specific plan for a military or diplomatic initiative. It can be as small as a pre-planned negotiating ploy used at an international conference, or as massive as the detailed planning for the military invasion of a neighboring state.

Operation Barbarosa   *See* BARBAROSA.

Operation Blast Furnace   A military operation by United States forces in Bolivia in 1986 that was directed against cocaine-processing laboratories. The operation, which involved six helicopters, 160 soldiers, and U.S. Drug Enforcement Agency personnel, led to some seizures, although the difficulties of keeping the operation a secret ensured that these were very modest. While the short-run disruption to processing activities was significant, the long-term effect was negligible. Moreover, the political consequences for the government of Bolivia were quite serious. The government lost popularity and was condemned by other Latin American governments, including Mexico and Colombia, for permitting the operation. The experience highlighted the difficulties the United States faces as it attempts to deal with drug trafficking from Latin America.

Operation Moses   The secret evacuation by air of 8,000 Ethiopian Jews, known as *Falashas,* by Israel in 1984 and 1985. These black African Jews were then resettled in Israel. In 1991 toward the end of the ETHIOPIAN CIVIL WAR, most of the rest of the Falashas were flown to new homes in Israel.

Operation Overlord   *See* D-DAY.

Operation Sea Lion   The planned German cross-channel invasion of Great Britain in WORLD WAR II. It began with the Luftwaffe bombardment known as the Battle of BRITAIN in August 1940, which lasted until the spring of 1941. The resistance of the Royal Air Force and the British people repulsed the German attack. By the late fall of 1940 the Germans, realizing that they could not obtain air superiority, called off Operation Sea Lion, and by early 1941 Adolf Hitler was looking to his planned annihilation of the Soviet Union in Operation BARBAROSA.

operations officer   A military officer who assists a unit commander with the detailed planning of operations. For example, an air force operations officer will pick crews and allot them targets and routes to accomplish the general mission selected by the squadron commander.

Opium Wars   Two trading wars in the nineteenth century between Western powers and preindustrial China, the first between Great Britain and China (1839–1842) and the second between Great Britain and France on the one side and China on the other (1856–1860). At the beginning of the nineteenth century, British traders began illegally importing opium into China in exchange for Chinese tea, silk, and porcelain. In 1839 the Qing dynasty, after a decade of unsuccessful anti-opium campaigns, adopted drastic prohibitory laws against the opium trade. The Emperor Tao-Kuang (1782–1850) dispatched a commissioner, Lin Zexu (1785–1850), to Canton, who detained the entire foreign community there and confiscated and destroyed some 20,000 chests of illicit British opium. The British retaliated with a punitive expedition. The ill-equipped Chinese forces were disastrously defeated. The Treaty of Nanking (1842) was signed in which the Chinese gave many concessions, including the cession of Hong Kong to Britain, opening ports, and granting British nationals EXTRATERRITORIALITY. In 1856 the British and French initiated hostilities again to extend their trading privileges in China, which resulted in a series of treaties between the Western trading nations. The Chinese later called these agreements "Unequal Treaties." All these factors were major reasons for the Chinese hostility and resentment of the West that was evident in the BOXER REBELLION, in the Communist revolutionary movement of the post–World War II era, and in the CULTURAL REVOLUTION.

opposite number   One who has an equal status and rank in another organization. Diplomatic and military officers are often said to deal "with their opposite numbers" in other governments.

Oran attack   The July 4, 1940, sinking of French warships in the harbor of Oran, Algeria, by the British Navy during the early stage of WORLD WAR II. After the British futilely pleaded with the French commanders to sail for the West Indies or voluntarily scuttle their ships to prevent their capture by the Germans (who had just occupied much of France and set up the VICHY government for the rest), the British attacked, in the process killing 1,300 French sailors. While this denied the ships to the German war effort, it also poisoned French attitudes toward the British and provided justification for many French citizens to collaborate with the Germans.

order   A communication—written, oral, or by signal—that conveys instructions from a superior to a subordinate. In a general sense, the terms order and COMMAND have the same meaning. However, an order implies discretion as to the details of execution whereas a command is more general and may consist of broader strategies. It is critical that orders be clear and unambiguous. Helmuth von Moltke (1800–1891), the founder of the German General Staff in the last century, was fond of saying: "Remember, gentlemen, an order than can be misunderstood will be misunderstood." Orders tend to be restricted to the military. Diplomats also take orders, but they call them "instructions."

ON STANDING ORDERS

At the time of my first stay in St. Petersburg in 1859 . . . it was then the custom for everyone connected with the court to promenade in the Summer Garden. . . . There the Emperor had noticed a sentry standing in the middle of a grass plot; in reply to the question why he was standing there, the soldier could only answer, "Those are my orders." The Emperor therefore sent one of his adjutants to the guard-room to make inquiries; but no explanation was forthcoming except that a sentry had to stand there winter and summer. The source of the original order could no longer be discovered. The matter was talked of at court, and reached the ears of the servants. One of them, an older pensioner, came forward and stated that his father had once said to him as they passed the sentry in the Summer Garden: "There he is, still standing to guard the flower; on that spot the Empress Catherine once noticed a snowdrop in bloom unusually early, and gave orders that it was not to be plucked." This command had been carried out by placing a sentry on the spot, and ever since then one had stood there all the year round.

SOURCE: *Bismarck, the Man and Statesman, Being the Reflections and Reminiscences of Otto, Prince von Bismarck,* translated by A. J. Butler (1899).

---

orderly marketing agreement (OMA)   A formal trade agreement between the United States and a foreign country in which the latter voluntarily agrees to limit for a specified period of time its exports of a particular industrial commodity to the United States. This form of import relief is an alternative to the imposition of quotas or higher tariffs as a method of protecting domestic industry, and is preferred by the exporting country because it is assured at least some share of the market. However, OMAs are opposed as being protectionist devices that raise domestic prices, reduce world output, and

freeze potential producers of the commodity out of the market. The European Community employs a similar device called a VOLUNTARY RESTRAINT AGREEMENT. *Compare to* EXPORT QUOTA; PROTECTIONISM; VOLUNTARY EXPORT RESTRAINTS.

order of battle   The strength and disposition of any military force; a list of the units in a military force deployed to take part in any imminent or ongoing conflict. The uncovering of the enemy's order of battle is a major task of military intelligence, because knowing exactly which units, with their specific capabilities, are scheduled for combat can tell an intelligence analyst much about the tactics and strategy the enemy has planned. In past wars the order of battle was a highly prized secret, but the development of signals intelligence and other technical means of intelligence gathering, such as satellite observation, has made disguising the order of battle much less possible.

Organization for Economic Cooperation and Development (OECD)   The only international organization comprising all industrial democracies; often called the "club of rich nations." Members include all the states of the North Atlantic Treaty Organization plus Austria, Finland, Sweden, and Switzerland in Europe, and Australia, Japan, and New Zealand in the Pacific. Founded in 1960 to replace the Organization for European Economic Cooperation, the organ of the MARSHALL PLAN for European recovery, the OECD extended international economic consultation beyond Europe to North America and the Pacific. The OECD provides for joint analysis of economic trends and for efforts to harmonize international economic practices and improve assistance to the developing countries. According to its secretary general, Jean-Claude Paye: "The OECD is not a supranational organization but a place where policymakers can meet and discuss their problems, where governments can compare their points of view and their experience. The secretariat is there to find and point out the way to go, to act as a catalyst. Its role is not academic; nor does it have the authority to impose its ideas. Its power lies in its capacity for intellectual persuasion" (*The Economist,* January 30, 1988). The OECD headquarters are in Paris, France. *See also* DEVELOPMENT ASSISTANCE COMMITTEE.

Organization for European Economic Cooperation
The organization established by recipients of the MARSHALL PLAN to supervise allocations of U.S. aid and to facilitate coordination among states receiving it.

Organization of African Unity (OAU)   A body consisting of the 51 independent states of Africa (with the exception of South Africa), organized to promote unity and solidarity among African nations. Created in 1963, with a secretariat located in Addis Ababa, Ethiopia, its annual meetings for heads of state are held in various African locations. The OAU serves as a sounding board for African opinion on colonialism, economic issues, and racial discrimination. It has tended to avoid interfering in the internal affairs of its member states.

Organization of American States (OAS)   The world's oldest regional association, created to promote the peaceful resolution of disputes and encourage the economic development of member states. Since the first international congress of American countries held in the United States in Washington, D.C., in 1889, the Western Hemisphere republics have maintained a system of cooperation in cultural, economic, political, and social fields. The 1948 treaty creating the OAS intensified this cooperation and reaffirmed the mutual defense commitment undertaken in the INTER-AMERICAN TREATY OF RECIPROCAL ASSISTANCE (Rio Treaty) signed in 1947. The 34 member states of the OAS are supposed to subscribe to the principles of pacific settlement of disputes, mutual assistance in the event of external aggression, nonintervention in the internal affairs of other nations, the importance of "representative democracy" to the "solidarity of American states," the need for economic cooperation, and the recognition of basic individual human rights without regard for race, nationality, creed, or sex. The OAS, which includes every major state in the Western Hemisphere except Cuba, has its headquarters in Washington, D.C.

Organization of Arab Petroleum Exporting Countries   See OAPEC.

Organization of Eastern Caribbean States (OECS)
An international group comprised of Antigua and Barbuda, Dominica, Grenada, Montserrat, St. Kitts and Nevis, St. Lucia, and St. Vincent and the Grenadines, created by a treaty in 1979 that came into force 1981. OECS members also belong to the CARIBBEAN COMMUNITY AND COMMON MARKET. The OECS aims to promote cooperation and solidarity among member states; to defend their territorial integrity and independence; to coordinate their foreign policies; and to promote economic integration. Following a military coup in Grenada in October 1983, the five members of the OECS, plus Barbados and Jamaica, acted to request U.S. military intervention on that island. See CARIBBEAN BASIN INITIATIVE; OCHO RIOS DECLARATION.

Organization of Petroleum Exporting Countries
See OPEC.

Organization of the Islamic Conference (OIC)   A continuing conference of Islamic foreign ministers created in 1972 in Jiddah, Saudi Arabia. It aims to promote Islamic solidarity; cooperation among member states; opposition to racial discrimination and colonialism; coordination of all efforts to safeguard Islamic holy places; and support for the Palestinian people. The OIC holds conferences of foreign ministers annually and summit conferences every three years; its headquarters are in Jiddah.

Organization of the Oppressed on Earth   A SHI'ITE Muslim extremist organization thought to be involved with the overarching HEZBOLLAH movement of radical Shi'ites in Lebanon. The group claimed responsibility for the June 1985 skyjacking of a TWA jetliner that resulted in the death of a U.S. Navy enlisted man. It also asserted responsibility for the February 1988 abduction and subsequent murder of William Higgins, head of the United Nations observer force in Lebanon.

orientation   1. A set of attitudes and policies that are reflected in the foreign policy of a state.   2. A general sense of direction in a state's foreign policy.   3. A broad approach to foreign policy. K. J. HOLSTI in *International Politics* (1983) identifies three kinds of orientation: ALLIANCE, NONALIGNMENT, and ISOLATIONISM.

Orlando, Vittorio Emanuele (1860–1952)   The premier of Italy at the end of World War I who led the Italian delegation to the PARIS PEACE CONFER-

ENCE. He initially supported BENITO MUSSOLINI, but in 1925 he publicly retired from politics to protest the fascist government. After fascism's defeat in World War II he returned to politics and served as a senator from 1948 until his death.

Orr, John Boyd (1880–1971) The British physician and nutritionist who won the 1949 Nobel Peace Prize for his work in creating and directing the Food and Agriculture Organization of the United Nations.

Ortega Saavedra, Daniel (1945–   ) The Communist president of Nicaragua from 1985 to 1990. After military training in Cuba, Ortega became a leader of the SANDINISTA guerrilla movement that opposed the dictatorial regime of Anastasio SOMOZA. After the Sandinistas took power in 1979,

he became part of the ruling junta until elected president. His administration, plagued by a civil war against the United States–backed CONTRAS, brought economic chaos to Nicaragua. Defeated in free elections by VIOLETA CHAMORRO in 1990, Ortega peacefully handed over power but remained leader of the political opposition.

Orwell, George (1903–1950) The British writer who created the classic satire on the Russian Revolution, *Animal Farm* (1945), and the famous novel of totalitarian oppression, *1984* (1949).

Osgood, Robert Endicott (1921–1986) A scholar and commentator on strategic issues and United States security policy. His study *Limited War: The Challenge to American Strategy* (1957) identified the prerequisites for limitation as well as the pressures for

Daniel Ortega on the day he is sworn in as president of Nicaragua, January 10, 1985. (U.S. Naval Institute)

expansion of conflicts. It also highlighted the tensions between LIMITED WAR thinking and the traditional U.S. approach to warfare. Subsequently Osgood reexamined some of the themes of this volume in *Limited War Revisited* (1979). He wrote a number of other important works, including *NATO: The Entangling Alliance* (1962), which provided a definitive analysis of the North Atlantic Treaty Organization during its first decade. Although Osgood's main interest was in security affairs, he also wrote on contemporary policy issues and covered such varied topics as alliances and ocean politics. In the early 1970s he edited an influential book entitled *Retreat from Empire? The First Nixon Administration* (1973) in which he encapsulated the NIXON DOCTRINE as involving "military retrenchment without political disengagement."

Osirak The site of an Iraqi nuclear reactor near Baghdad that Israel bombed and destroyed in 1981, believing it was being used to produce nuclear weapons that could threaten Israeli territory. This first attack, which was without prior warning, on any state's nuclear facilities was widely condemned. However, by the time of the PERSIAN GULF WAR in 1991, most of the states that had condemned the attack were grateful for it. Had the Israelis not bombed Osirak, Iraq might very well have had an operational nuclear weapon prior to its 1990 invasion of Kuwait. This could have radically altered the nature and outcome of the war.

OSS *See* OFFICE OF STRATEGIC SERVICES.

Ostpolitik West Germany's policy of accommodation with the Eastern bloc and reconciliation with East Germany, initially developed by Chancellor WILLY BRANDT in 1969. It followed French President Charles de Gaulle's rapprochement with Moscow in 1968 with a vision of a new international system. Brandt received the Nobel Peace Prize in 1971 for his Ostpolitik efforts, which he also called the "European Peace Order." This policy softened the 1955 Hallstein Doctrine, which denied West German recognition to all states that recognized East Germany and to all Communist states except the Soviet Union. Ostpolitik was formalized by a series of agreements: a 1970 nonaggression treaty between Bonn and Moscow, a 1970 Bonn-Warsaw pact, the

1971 Four Power Treaty on Berlin (the BERLIN TREATY), a Basic Treaty signed by the two Germanys in 1972 (ratified in June 1973), and in 1973 a Bonn-Prague treaty. Ostpolitik allowed for divided German families to visit each other, if not to be reunited; for an increase in trade between West Germany and Eastern Europe; and for the simultaneous admission to the United Nations of both East and West Germany in 1973. Ostpolitik was a critical stepping-stone that helped pave the way for GERMAN REUNIFICATION. *See also* ABGRENZUNG.

Ottoman Empire The Islamic Empire, which, beginning in the thirteenth century, grew out of Turkish tribes in Anatolia, absorbed the ruins of the Byzantine Empire, and proceeded by conquest to extend its rule throughout the Middle and Near East and North Africa and into Europe as far north as Hungary. The empire reached its height under Sulayman the Magnificent (1494–1566). It started to decline in the eighteenth century as the rise of NATIONALISM impelled its various subject peoples to seek independence. Known as the SICK MAN OF EUROPE prior to World War I, its participation in that war on the side of Germany led to its final dismemberment. After the war all of its land, except for Turkey itself, was lost in Balkan border adjustments or taken over by Great Britain and France as MANDATES from the League of Nations. Defeated, shorn of most of its former territory, and partially occupied by forces of the victorious European states, the Ottoman structure was repudiated by Turkish nationalists who rallied under the leadership of MUSTAPHA KEMEL ATATURK. After a bitter war, the nationalists expelled invading Greek forces from Anatolia. The sultanate and caliphate, the temporal and religious ruling institutions of the old empire, were abolished, and Turkey became a republic in 1923.

Outer Space Treaty A trilateral 1967 agreement among the United States, the Soviet Union, and Great Britain that bans the placement of nuclear weapons or "weapons of mass destruction" not only in orbit around the earth and in outer space, but also on the moon or any other celestial body. It also prohibits the use of the moon or any other celestial body for military purposes of any kind, including weapons testing, maneuvers, or the con-

out of area

U.S. Representative to the United Nations Arthur Goldberg (sitting, third from right) signs the Outer Space Treaty. To his left are Secretary of State Dean Rusk and President Lyndon B. Johnson. (Library of Congress)

struction of military installations. Under the treaty there are also rights of inspection. Although about 90 countries subsequently signed the treaty, it highlights the old adage that the easiest things to prohibit are those that no one wants to do anyway: It has never been challenged or broken.

out of area   A reference to contingencies and crises that occur outside the North Atlantic Treaty Organization's formal sphere of responsibility. There has been periodic discussion about broadening NATO's mandate to include responsibility for dealing with crises in non-NATO states. But several member states have objected and, without unanimity, any expansion of the mandate is impossible. Nevertheless, NATO has developed habits of cooperation that make it easier for its members to work together informally in responding to such crises as that in the Persian Gulf in 1990–1991. And in 1992 NATO, largely in response to the civil war in Yugoslavia, agreed that it could deploy peacekeeping forces in non-NATO European states.

overkill   A general description of the excessive levels of nuclear weaponry maintained by the military superpowers, used particularly during the Cold War. Evidence for the existence of overkill usually is presented in the form of statistics that show that the United States or the former Soviet Union has a nuclear capability far in excess of what is needed to

destroy any enemy or even the entire population of our planet. The excess weapons are thus considered to have no legitimate function, and their deployment is attributed not to real military preparedness but to ARMS RACE dynamics or the influence of a MILITARY-INDUSTRIAL COMPLEX. Of course, some of the weaponry considered to be overkill can be justified by the need to maintain a credible nuclear deterrent. The need for redundancy in case forces are destroyed preemptively or fail to operate as expected accounts for another major share of this alleged excess capacity to kill.

Overlord   The code name for D-DAY, the June 6, 1944, invasion of Nazi-occupied France by the Allies during World War II.

overt operations   The gathering of INTELLIGENCE information openly, without concealment. *Compare to* COVERT OPERATIONS.

owl   Term used to categorize one who does not fall neatly into either the HAWK or the dove category and who is concerned primarily about a possible loss of control leading to a crisis or conventional war that escalates to the nuclear level. As Joseph Nye, Graham Allison, and Albert Carnesale wrote in *Hawks, Doves and Owls: An Agenda for Avoiding Nuclear War* (1985), "Owls are . . . impressed by World War I, the assassination at Sarajevo, the leader's misperception of the military situation, and the inadvertent escalation caused by interlocking mobilization plans. Owls believe that crises or conventional war could create an environment for unintended nuclear war." *See also* SARAJEVO SYNDROME.

OXFAM Founded in 1942 as the Oxford Committee on Famine Relief, this international relief organization continues to raise and distribute funds to alleviate poverty, especially in THIRD WORLD states.

ozone layer That part of the earth's upper atmosphere that screens out ultraviolet radiation from the sun. The depletion of the ozone layer caused by manufactured chlorofluorocarbons (CFCs), which are used in refrigeration and aerosol cans, has become a major international issue. Because severe ozone depletion will increase human cancer rates and threaten the food chain, most of the industrialized states of the world have agreed, in the MONTREAL PROTOCOL, to cut in half the production and use of CFCs by the end of the century. This United Nations–sponsored agreement was signed in 1987.

P

Pacem in Terris   Latin for "peace on Earth"; the 1963 Encyclical of Pope John XXIII issued shortly after a period of Cold War concern with the Cuban Missile and Berlin crises. This was a call for peace and disarmament that condemned thermonuclear warfare. John XXIII asserted that the world was entering a new moment in history in which humans would share the conviction that all are equal by reason of their natural dignity, and the world would become "conscious of spiritual values, understanding the meaning of truth, justice, charity and freedom." He urged the protection of basic human rights and encouraged dialogue with Communist leaders while holding that communism was doomed to failure over the long term.

pacification   1. A military mission to obtain control over an area so that no enemy military action is possible there.   2. The terrorization or extermination by a modern military force of an indigenous population that usually possesses only primitive weapons. In this context pacification has been one of the main techniques by which the European powers traditionally put down colonial rebellions.   3. Peace negotiations.

Pacific Basin Community   An economic community that would encompass the states in the Pacific Ocean and on the Pacific rim. Although it can be traced back to 1917, this idea took on greater prominence in the 1980s as a result of the advocacy of Australian Prime Minister Bob Hawke and U.S. President Ronald Reagan's assertion that the twenty-first century would be the "century of the Pacific." The members of ASEAN have also endorsed the idea, while over 400 companies from various states in the region have formed the Pacific Basin Economic Council to promote trade and investment. Yet there are still many divisions in the region, and the general notion of a Pacific Basin Community has not yet been translated into a significant political and economic grouping. Indeed, given the diversity of the nations located in and around the Pacific, it is questionable whether this will happen.

Pacific century   A phrase that implies that the economic power of the PACIFIC RIM states will make them major influences in world politics in the twenty-first century.

Pacific Rim   The coastal and island region extending from Japan and South Korea through the South China Sea, including Taiwan, China, Hong Kong, the Philippines, Malaysia, Singapore, Thailand, Indonesia, Australia, and New Zealand. It covers an area twice the size of Europe and the United States combined.

pacific settlement of disputes.   *See* PEACEFUL SETTLEMENT OF DISPUTES.

Pacific War   The part of WORLD WAR II fought in Asia and the Pacific Ocean.

pacifism   Opposition to and refusal to participate in war. In essence, pacifism means that no stakes can be seen as being worth killing for. Pacifists find war abhorrent and refuse to support any state that goes to war, even their own. Pacifism is sometimes linked with socialism or with religious ideals and has been articulated most formally by the Quakers (the Society of Friends). Pacifists argue that nonviolent solutions are almost always available; if not, they prefer nonviolent resistance. The most famous proponent of pacifism and nonviolent resistance in the twentieth century was MOHANDAS GANDHI. Though he used such methods with success, it has been argued that the kind of tactics he used would have been far less successful against a more ruthless power than Great Britain. Pacifism was one of the contributing factors to the European peace movements that developed after both world wars and during the Cold War. For all its importance as an approach to issues of war and peace, however, pacifism is criticized by those who believe that there are values that are worth fighting to defend. Those who adhere to a JUST WAR approach are sometimes scathing about pacifism, as they believe that there are certain conditions under which war is virtually a moral imperative.

pacifist   1. An individual who is opposed to war in general. World War II cartoonist Bill Mauldin advised in *Up Front* (1945): "The surest way to become a pacifist is to join the infantry." Even U.S. General Dwight D. Eisenhower asserted that: "There is no greater pacifist than the regular officer" (*New York Times,* June 20, 1945). 2. An individual who is opposed to military establishments in peace or in war. Socialists who consider war to be inspired by capitalism traditionally have been pacifists. This is why George Orwell wrote: "The Socialist who finds his children playing with soldiers is usually upset, but he is never able to think of a substitute for the tin soldiers; tin pacifists somehow won't do" (*New English Weekly,* March 21, 1940). 3. One who will not defend her- or himself no matter what the provocation. 4. An individual who is unpatriotic. U.S. President Theodore Roosevelt attacked the patriotism of pacifists in a speech at Kansas City, Missouri, on May 30, 1916: "The professional pacifist is merely a tool of the sensual materialist who has no ideals, whose shriveled soul is wholly absorbed in automobiles, and the movies, and money making, and in the policies of the cash register and the stock ticker, and the life of fatted ease." 5. An individual who is against a particular war. This is not a correct

usage. But in the United States, people who were opposed to the Vietnam War in the 1960s were often called pacifists. This led Vietnam War opposition leader Dr. Benjamin Spock to this denial: "I am not a pacifist. I was very much for the war against Hitler and I supported the intervention in Korea. But in this war, we went in to steal Viet Nam" (*Time,* January 12, 1968).

pact   A treaty or international agreement. Since the term has slightly pompous connotations, it tends to be used for especially solemn agreements.

pacta sunt servanda   The Latin phrase that means "treaties must be observed." The sense that there is a duty to respect or observe treaties is one of the main bases of INTERNATIONAL LAW. The Declaration of London in 1871 by the major European powers stated: "It is an essential principle of the Law of Nations that no Power can liberate itself from the engagements of a treaty nor modify the stipulations thereof, unless with the consent of the contracting parties by means of an amicable understanding." This sentiment has been subsequently reinforced by the 1919 covenant of the League of Nations, by the 1945 Charter of the United Nations, and by the 1969 Vienna Convention on the Law of Treaties.

pacta tertiis nec nocent nec prosunt   The Latin phrase that means "agreements should neither harm nor benefit third states." This is the principle of INTERNATIONAL LAW now embodied in Article 34 of the 1969 Vienna Convention on the Law of Treaties: "A treaty does not create either obligations or rights for a Third State without its consent."

pactum de contrahendo   Latin meaning "an agreement to contract," an initial agreement to be made final at a later date. Under INTERNATIONAL LAW such a preliminary treaty is binding if it contains sufficiently detailed terms.

Pahlevi, Mohammed Reza (1919–1980)   The last shah (or king) of Iran who came to power during World War II after the British forced the abdication of his pro-German father in 1941. The young shah's government was friendly to Western interests until MOHAMMED MOSSADEGH became prime minister in 1951 and sought to nationalize the British-owned oil

Mohammed Reza Pahlevi and his wife. (Library of Congress)

known as the shah's White Revolution. The core of this program was land reform. Modernization and economic growth proceeded at an unprecedented rate, fueled by Iran's vast petroleum reserves, third largest in the world. By the 1970s the United States was equipping the shah's military forces with sophisticated weapons to allow Iran to replace Great Britain as the chief peacekeeper in the Persian Gulf. But Muslim fundamentalists were opposed to the Pahlevi dynasty; they detested his secular policies and the Western lifestyle of his entourage. Increasingly disenchanted with his repressive practices and government corruption, the opposition forced him into exile in 1979 by means of massive street demonstrations that became known as the IRANIAN REVOLUTION. After seeking medical treatment in the West, he died of cancer in Egypt the following year.

Pahlevi, Reza (1878–1944)   The Iranian officer of the Persian Coassack Brigade who seized control of the government in a 1921 military coup. In 1925 he became shah (king) and ruled as Reza Shah Pahlevi for almost 16 years. During his reign, Iran began to modernize, and the central government reasserted its authority over the tribes and provinces. Because of his close ties to Nazi Germany, both Soviet and British troops occupied Iran in 1941. Reza Shah was then forced to abdicate in favor of his son, MOHAMMED REZA PAHLEVI.

Palestine   The land on the western coast of the Mediterranean Sea that was part of the Ottoman Empire until World War I, when it was conquered by British and Arab forces. After the war the League of Nations made Palestine a British-mandated territory that included what is now Israel, the West Bank, the Gaza Strip, and Jordan. Because of constant Arab-Jewish tensions, the British Peel Commission of 1937 recommended that the area be partitioned between Arab and Jewish states. (This was in accord with the BALFOUR DECLARATION.) In 1947 the British turned the problem over to the United Nations, which recommended the same. The British announced that they would withdraw on May 14, 1948, despite the fact that the two sides could not reach a mutually acceptable agreement on partition. Thereupon the Jewish inhabitants declared themselves to be the State of Israel (reborn after two millennia) and the surrounding Arab states

industry. In 1953 the shah sought to oust Mossadegh's Communist-supported government with a coup that failed. Forced to flee the country, he got his throne back three days later when a U.S. Central Intelligence Agency–engineered coup, OPERATION AJAX, had the army take over and Mossadegh arrested. The shah, who had previously been a kind of playboy king, then assumed a more authoritarian role. In 1961 Iran initiated a series of economic, social, and administrative reforms that became

attacked, leaving the boundaries of Israel to be determined by cease-fire lines. The basic issue is still in serious contention: Hard-line Arabs hold that the Israelis are Western colonists brought to Palestine by the twentieth-century movement of ZIONISM who have no right to the land and have displaced the PALESTINIAN people. The Israelis feel that this is the biblical land of the Jewish people that was continuously inhabited by Jews since ancient times, the land from which the Jews were exiled in the DIASPORA after Roman conquest in 135, and to which all the Jews of the world are now welcome to return. The tension over this issue has manifested itself in the ARAB-ISRAELI WARS, the INTIFADA, and acts of TERRORISM. *See* ABDULLAH I.

Palestine Liberation Front   A splinter group of the POPULAR FRONT FOR THE LIBERATION OF PALESTINE—GENERAL COMMAND organized in 1977 by ABU ABBAS. It was recognized as an independent group in 1981 when it gained seats on the PALESTINIAN NATIONAL COUNCIL. In addition to attempting guerrilla infiltrations of Israel, it is best known for the 1985 hijacking of the *ACHILLE LAURO* cruise ship.

Palestine Liberation Organization (PLO)   The umbrella organization for PALESTINIAN nationalist political and guerrilla groups founded in 1964 by Ahmed al-Shukeiry. In February 1969, as a result of the upheavals that followed the resounding defeat of the Arab nations in the 1967 SIX-DAY WAR, the PLO turned to YASIR ARAFAT and his al-FATAH organization for leadership. Arafat has remained ensconced in the role of chairman since that time, and Fatah retains a majority on the powerful executive committee of the PALESTINIAN NATIONAL COUNCIL, the policymaking body for the PLO. The PLO, through its constituent organizations, carried out numerous raids into Israel in the mid- to late-1960s from its bases in Jordan. In September 1970 King Hussein of Jordan, concerned over the development of a state within his state, expelled the Palestinian guerrilla groups, and the PLO shifted its bases from Jordan to Lebanon and Syria. Dissension in the ranks scarred the PLO following the 1973 Arab-Israeli war, as the "moderate" faction led by Arafat supported PLO participation in peaceful efforts to secure a homeland, while the more radical groups dismissed any partial or negotiated approaches to

the problem. In 1976 the PLO split when the moderate majority indicated that they would accept a Palestinian state limited to the WEST BANK and GAZA STRIP as part of a negotiated settlement, while those who opposed any compromise with Israel formed the Palestinian REJECTION FRONT.

Since 1974 the mainstream PLO led by Arafat has refused to endorse publicly terrorist activity outside Israel and the occupied territories. Its "legitimization" began at the seventh summit of ARAB LEAGUE members, held in Rabat, Morocco, in 1974, which declared the PLO to be the sole legitimate representative of the Palestinian people. In October 1974 the United Nations General Assembly also recognized the PLO as the representative of the Palestinians and granted the PLO permanent observer status at the General Assembly. The PLO became a full member of the Arab League in 1976. Arafat addressed the UN in 1974, which granted the PLO legitimacy in the international arena. In 1975 and 1976 the PLO became embroiled in the LEBANESE CIVIL WAR, battling the Lebanese Christians. In 1982 the PLO was driven from its camps in southern Lebanon and its strongholds in Beirut by the Israeli Army's invasion. Following the Israeli siege of Beirut, PLO troops withdrew in September and took refuge in Syria and Tunisia. In 1988 King Hussein of Jordan made the surprising move of transferring his claims to the territories occupied by Israel to the PLO, thus putting pressure and responsibility on the PLO to arrive at some political approach to the Palestinian question. In Algiers, Algeria, on November 15, 1988, the PALESTINIAN NATIONAL COUNCIL declared an independent Palestinian state in the West Bank and the Gaza Strip, and accepted United Nations RESOLUTIONS 242 and 338, which implicitly recognize the existence of Israel. Arafat even explicitly stated on December 7, 1988, that the PLO accepts Israel's right to exist. But PLO support for Iraq during the 1991 Persian Gulf War angered many of the gulf states that previously supported the PLO. Consequently, when ARAB-ISRAELI PEACE TALKS began in Madrid, Spain, in late 1991, the PLO at Israeli insistence was not formally present. *See also* BLACK SEPTEMBER.

Palestine Question   1. Historically, the puzzle of what the British should have done with their League of Nations MANDATE in Palestine. In 1947 the British asked this question of the League's successor organization, the United Nations. It voted to partition the land into an Arab state, a Jewish state, and an international city, Jerusalem. The Arabs rejected this plan, the British announced that they would withdraw their forces in 1948 anyway, Israel declared its independence, and the first ARAB-ISRAELI WAR commenced. **2.** Sometimes used to describe the current problem of the OCCUPIED TERRITORIES.

Palestinian National Council The policymaking body that acts as a Palestinian parliament in exile and sets the course for PALESTINE LIBERATION ORGANIZATION policy. The organization meets approximately once a year. It is dominated by an executive committee of about 15 members, chaired by YASIR ARAFAT, whose al-FATAH organization has the largest number of committee seats among the Palestinian groups represented. In 1988 the PNC declared an independent Palestinian state in the OCCUPIED TERRITORIES of the West Bank and the Gaza Strip. In 1991 it authorized a delegation of Palestinian residents in the occupied territories to join the Jordanian delegation at the initial meeting of the ARAB-ISRAELI PEACE TALKS in Madrid, Spain, which were sponsored by the United States and the Soviet Union.

Palestinians **1.** The Arabs who live in Israel and in the OCCUPIED TERRITORIES, or who once lived there. **2.** All of the people who now live in the area that was once part of the British mandate of Palestine—Israel, the occupied territories, and Jordan. **3.** The Jewish population of the British mandate of Palestine prior to Israeli independence in 1948. For the first part of the twentieth century "Palestinian" was a synonym for "Zionist."

Palme, Olaf (1927–1986) The prime minister of Sweden (1969–1976; 1982–1986) who was an active international voice on disarmament and Third World economic development. He was a major critic of U.S. involvement in the Vietnam War. His assassination on a Stockholm street is a murder that has never been solved.

Palme Commission The independent international Commission on Disarmament and Security Issues,

created in 1981 and headquartered in Stockholm, Sweden, which sought to complement the work of the BRANDT COMMISSION "by concentrating on security and disarmament measures that could contribute to peace." Chaired by OLAF PALME of Sweden, with members from 18 countries, the commission's 1982 report, *Common Security: A Blueprint for Survival,* asserted that no country could win a nuclear war and argued against reliance on nuclear DETERRENCE. It recommended a nuclear-free zone in Central Europe, continued adherence to the ABM TREATY, and a more active peacekeeping role for the United Nations Security Council in the Third World. It also developed the idea of MUTUAL SECURITY.

Panama Canal The waterway that transverses the Isthmus of Panama in Central America and allows shipping to travel between the Atlantic and Pacific oceans. From 1880 to 1900 a French company, under Ferdinand de Lesseps (1805–1894), the man who built the Suez Canal in Egypt, attempted unsuccessfully to construct a sealevel canal on the site of the present Panama Canal. In November 1903, after Colombia rejected a treaty permitting the United States to build a canal, Panama proclaimed its independence and concluded the HAY-VARILLA TREATY with the United States. In 1914, after ten years of construction, the U.S. Army's Corps of Engineers completed the 83-kilometer (52-mile), six-lock canal. However, with the development of supertankers in the post–World War II period, the canal is no longer as strategically important today as it once was.

Panama Canal Treaties **1.** The 1977 agreements between the Republic of Panama and the United States that transferred ownership of the Panama Canal from the United States to Panama by the year 2000 and that guaranteed the permanent neutrality and operation of the canal. The treaties were ratified by a plebiscite in Panama in 1977 and by the U.S. Senate in 1978. *See also* DECONCINI RESERVATION. **2.** The HAY-VARILLA TREATY OF 1903. Under this treaty the United States had unilateral control of canal operations and administered the Panama Canal Zone—a 1,438-square-kilometer (553 square mile) area in which Panama had titular sovereignty but the United States had all the rights, power, and authority that it would have possessed had it been sovereign of the territory. In Panama, this arrangement was deeply resented from its outset. In January 1964 Panamanian dissatisfaction came to a head when riots against the United States resulted in the deaths of more than 20 persons. Later that month Panama suspended diplomatic relations with the United States. After relations were reestablished in April 1964, both governments agreed to appoint ambassadors to seek prompt resolution of the situation, and U.S. President Lyndon B. Johnson committed the United States to negotiation toward an entirely new treaty that would eliminate the causes of conflict between the two states. In June 1967 U.S. and Panamanian negotiators completed their work on three draft treaties dealing with the existing canal, a possible sealevel canal in Panama, and defense matters. These treaties were not acted on by either government, however, and in 1970 the new Panamanian government publicly rejected them. Negotiations resumed in June 1971 and continued intermittently until 1977. On September 7, 1977, U.S. President Jimmy Carter and Panamanian chief of government OMAR TORRIJOS signed the two new treaties at a ceremony at the headquarters of the Organization of American States in Washington, D.C.

Panama intervention The United States' military invasion of Panama, beginning on the night of December 19–20, 1989, to rid that state of its dictator. General MANUEL NORIEGA became the sole dictator of Panama in 1983. After diplomatic efforts by the U.S. failed to remove him from power, Noriega escalated tensions with the United States throughout 1989. U.S. intervention came as the result of increasing evidence that Noriega was in league with Colombia's MEDELLIN CARTEL, his indictment on drug charges by a grand jury in the United States, and his use of terroristic violence against the Panamanian people. On May 10, 1989, television news cameras captured the horror of Panamanian repression when they filmed the brutal beatings of Panama's duly elected president and dual vice presidents. The beatings took place in broad daylight and in full view of Panamanian Defense Force troops and police, who did nothing to intervene. Only three days before Noriega had voided the election results in which these men had been selected. On December 15, 1989, he declared that Panama was in a state of war with the United States. The following

---

WHAT THE 1977 PANAMA CANAL TREATIES CONTAIN

The first of the new treaties (formally called "Panama Canal Treaty") terminates and supersedes previous treaties related to the canal. It also spells out ways in which the canal is to be operated and defended until the year 2000:

> The United States retains primary responsibility for canal operations and defense until the end of the century, but with increasing Panamanian participation.
>
> The Canal Zone as an entity ceases to exist, and Panama assumes general jurisdiction over the area. The United States retains the right to use all land and water areas and installations necessary for the operation, maintenance, and defense of the canal until the end of the century. Until then, the United States retains bases to provide full security for the canal.
>
> The canal is to be operated by a U.S. government agency called the Panama Canal Commission, with five American and four Panamanian directors. After 1990 the canal Administrator (chief executive officer) will be Panamanian with an American deputy.
>
> The two countries agree to study the feasibility of constructing a sea-level canal in Panama.
>
> The treaty provides for payments to Panama from canal revenues.

The second treaty is entitled "Treaty Concerning the Permanent Neutrality and Operation of the Panama Canal." Under this regime of neutrality the canal is to remain open to merchant and naval vessels of all nations indefinitely, without discrimination as to conditions or tolls. The neutrality treaty does not give the United States the right to intervene in the internal affairs of Panama, an independent sovereign state. It does, however, give the United States and Panama responsibility to ensure that the canal remains open and secure to ships of all nations at all times. Each of the two countries shall have the discretion to take whatever action it deems necessary, in accordance with its constitutional processes, to defend the canal against any threat to the permanent regime of neutrality.

SOURCE: Adapted from U.S. Department of State, *Background Notes: Panama* (March 1992).

---

day his troops murdered a U.S. Marine, and four days after that U.S. President George Bush ordered U.S. forces forcibly to remove the Noriega regime from power. Noriega escaped immediate capture and hid in the Vatican embassy in Panama City.

After ten days in the embassy he surrendered to U.S. Drug Enforcement Agency personnel and was immediately taken to the United States to face criminal charges in connection with his drug activities.

The invasion was widely popular with both the U.S. and the Panamanian public; it came about only after gross abuses of human rights and the electoral process in Panama and repeated efforts by the United States to resolve the problem by diplomatic means. Columnist George F. Will assured the nation that "this intervention is a good-neighbor policy. America's role in Panama . . . is an act of hemispheric hygiene" (*Washington Post National Weekly*, December 25–31, 1989).

PRESIDENT BUSH EXPLAINS WHY THE U.S. INVADED PANAMA

Last night I ordered U.S. military forces to Panama. . . . For nearly two years, the United States, nations of Latin America and the Caribbean have worked together to resolve the crisis in Panama. The goals of the United States have been to safeguard the lives of Americans, to defend democracy in Panama, to combat drug trafficking, and to protect the integrity of the Panama Canal Treaty. Many attempts have been made to resolve this crisis through diplomacy and negotiations. All were rejected by the dictator of Panama, Gen. Manuel Noriega, an indicted drug trafficker.

Last Friday, Noriega declared his military dictatorship to be in a state of war with the United States and publicly threatened the lives of Americans in Panama. The very next day forces under his command shot and killed an unarmed American serviceman, wounded another, arrested and brutally beat a third American serviceman and then brutally interrogated his wife, threatening her with sexual abuse. That was enough.

SOURCE: President George Bush, address to the nation, December 20, 1989.

Pan Am Flight 103 The Pan American Airlines Boeing 747 that exploded in midair, killing all 259 persons on board, on December 21, 1988, while en route from London to New York. The wreckage, scattered over a large area of southwest Scotland, was most concentrated in the village of Lockerbie, where 11 more people were killed by a large piece of the aircraft that fell on houses. The bombing was the work of terrorists who concealed a time bomb in a radio-cassette player packed inside a suitcase and stowed in the aircraft's forward baggage compartment. The terrorists' intention was that the plane would disintegrate over the Atlantic Ocean, leaving no clues; but the plane, which took off from London's Heathrow Airport, exploded before it had cleared the British coast. The large volume of physical evidence allowed investigators to piece together the crime. In 1991 the United States and Great Britain indicted two Libyan intelligence agents in the bombing and demanded their extradition for trial. In 1992 the United Nations voted to impose limited economic sanctions on Libya if it did not turn over the suspects.

Pan-Arab Socialism The foundation of the foreign policy of Egyptian President GAMAL ABDAL NASSER that called for the unity of the Arab world in a socialist confederation led by Nasser. *Pan* means "across," so a pan-Arab movement meant "across all international borders." This movement, which had considerable appeal to the Arab masses, had its greatest popularity after the SUEZ CRISIS of 1956 when Nasser appeared to have been successful in defying Western interests. But the movement was a function of Nasser's popularity and seems to have died after Egypt's defeat in the SIX-DAY WAR of 1967.

***Panay* incident** The 1937 attack by Japanese aircraft on the U.S. gunboat *Panay* as it sailed down the Yangtze River near Nanking, China. Two Americans were killed, others injured, and the ship was sunk. While many thought the attack was an intentional effort to minimize U.S. influence in China, the Japanese officially apologized for a "terrible blunder," and that ended the incident.

Pancasila The set of five principles upon which the state of Indonesia is based. These principles were enunciated by future Indonesian President ACHMED SUKARNO in a June 1945 speech before the investigating committee for the preparation of independence. As amended and embodied in the Preamble of the 1945 Constitution, they consist of belief in God, humanity, unity of Indonesia, democracy based on the wisdom of a representative process, and social justice for all the people of Indonesia. The importance of Pancasila lay in the fact that it

Colonel James Murray, Jr., USMC, and Colonel Chang Cun San, of the North Korean Communist Army, initial maps showing the north and south boundaries of the demarcation zone during the Panmunjon cease-fire talks. (National Archives)

helped to transcend serious differences about the nature of the new state and, in particular, whether it should be secular or religious. The declaration of independence established a unitary republic based on Pancasila and the notion of "unity in diversity." In one sense, Pancasila was an appropriate response to the divergences, given that it was broadly conceived and avoided commitment to any particular ideology. *See also* DUAL FUNCTION.

Panmunjon   The city in North Korea that was the site of truce talks between the United Nations forces and the Communist forces involved in the KOREAN WAR. The talks, which began in 1951, took place first in the South Korean city of Kaesong. An armistice was signed on July 26, 1953. Many analysts believe that both the death of Soviet President Joseph Stalin and the indirect threats by the newly installed administration of U.S. President Dwight D. Eisenhower to use atomic weapons to end the military stalemate were pivotal factors in getting North Korea finally to sign an armistice.

pan-nationalism   A form of NATIONALISM that goes beyond a particular state or nation and seeks to unite a people who share certain common characteristics. For example, pan-Arabism is a form of nationalism that seeks to unite Arabs whether they live in Egypt, Jordan, Saudi Arabia, or elsewhere.

The essence is that the members of particular states identify first and foremost with the overall Arab nation. The difficulty in practice is that the existing political units or states have their own narrow interests that often diverge from this larger notion. Attempts to provide leadership of the Arab world and create a genuine pan-Arab movement have been tried by various leaders—most notably GAMAL ABDAL NASSER of Egypt and SADDAM HUSSEIN of Iraq—but have all failed.

paper tiger   A Chinese expression for a person or institution that is not as strong or powerful as appearances and reputation would suggest—or is as strong as it seems but cannot marshal the political will to use its full strength. During the Cold War the Chinese often used this expression about the United States and its nuclear weapons. Nevertheless, after the KOREAN WAR China was unwilling to follow this belief up with direct challenges to United States' interests.

para bellum   Latin meaning "prepare for war"; the notion that the best way to secure peace is to be ready for war. There are many assumptions underlying this notion, the most important of which is that the weak are more likely to be tempting targets than the strong. This belief provided much of the rationale for DETERRENCE strategies during the Cold War.

paramilitary organization **1.** An organization that operates with or in place of a regular military organization. In this capacity, it is often clandestine and semiofficial. For example, private paramilitary organizations called DEATH SQUADS have been utilized by some Latin American governments to terrorize left-wing and liberal elements in extralegal ways that official government forces do not wish to be associated with overtly. In this way, paramilitary organizations often have been used to buffer governments from accusations of state-sponsored TERRORISM. **2.** An illegal nongovernmental organization that adopts the discipline, orientation, and structure of a regular military organization, generally to actively oppose governmental authorities. **3.** A legal uniformed, disciplined, and lightly armed adjunct to a political party in a fascist state. **4.** A police or fire department.

Pareto, Vilfredo (1848–1923) The Italian economist and sociologist who pioneered the application of mathematical techniques to the study of political and social problems. Pareto, who wrote widely of the inevitability of elites and masses in any society, became a significant intellectual influence on the development of Italian FASCISM. Pareto's most important work on politics, *The Mind and Society* (1916, 1923), dealt with his theory of the circulation of elites. Ruling elites seek to perpetuate themselves by closing off power from new talent from the masses. This frustrated leadership talent eventually organizes the masses to overthrow the old elite and becomes the new elite. Then the cycle repeats.

Paris, Pact of *See* KELLOGG-BRIAND PACT.

Paris Agreement **1.** The 1954 protocols with West Germany by France, the United Kingdom, and the United States, that formally ended the post–World War II military occupation. However, military forces of these powers remained in West Germany as part of the North Atlantic Treaty Organization. **2.** The 1973 cease-fire between the United States and North Vietnam. This was the culmination of years of negotiations (1968 to 1973) that finally gave the United States a diplomatic fig leaf to hide behind as it withdrew its forces to end the VIETNAM WAR. In 1975, after the U.S. troops were withdrawn, North Vietnam completed its conquest of the South. The leading negotiators for each side, HENRY A. KISSINGER of the United States and LE DUC THO of North Vietnam, were jointly awarded the 1973 Nobel Peace Prize for their efforts. Kissinger accepted. Le Duc Tho refused, saying that peace had still not been achieved in Vietnam.

Paris Conference **1.** The 1947 meeting of 16 European states and the United States to develop economic programs to be funded by MARSHALL PLAN aid. **2.** The 1954 nine-power meeting that determined that Italy and West Germany should join the BRUSSELS PACT and that this pact would be renamed the WESTERN EUROPEAN UNION.

Paris Peace Conference The post–WORLD WAR I peace conference that opened in January 1919 and continued until August 1920. All victorious belligerents were present but not the defeated Central Powers and Bolshevik Russia. The victors did not want to repeat what they saw as a mistake of the CONGRESS OF VIENNA of 1815 in which the defeated nation participated in discussions. Although several dozen states attended this conference, the Council of Four—President WOODROW WILSON from the United States, Prime Minister DAVID LLOYD GEORGE of Great Britain, Prime Minister GEORGES CLEMENCEAU of France, and Prime Minister VITTORIO ORLANDO of Italy—made the peace. Orlando played only a minor role, and hence the name "Big Three" was applied to the others. In the negotiations Wilson was a moderating voice who wanted his FOURTEEN POINTS to be guiding principles, while Lloyd George and Clemenceau wanted a harsh peace. Japan, which was then recognized as a power, was important in discussions. The Paris Conference issued a series of peace treaties, including that of VERSAILLES with Germany, SAINT-GERMAIN with Austria-Hungary, TRIANON with greater Hungary, NEUILLY with Bulgaria, and SÈVRES with the Ottoman Empire. These names refer to the suburbs of Paris, where each treaty was signed. In these treaties Turkish and German territories became mandates of Western powers. Seeking to avoid the national pressures that had hampered the results of the Congress of Vienna, these treaties followed national SELF-DETERMINATION in east-central Europe, as Czechoslovakia, Poland, and Yugoslavia became sovereign nations.

Paris Summit Conference of 1960 The COLD WAR superpower meeting intended to transform the conciliation of the 1959 Camp David meeting between U.S. President Dwight D. Eisenhower and Soviet Premier Nikita Khrushchev into a comprehensive settlement for remaining Cold War issues. The U-2 INCIDENT, which occurred shortly before the conference, caused Khrushchev to demand a formal apology before he would allow the summit to conduct any serious business. The United States refused to be put into what it considered a humiliating position. Thus the meeting was prematurely adjourned and the Cold War got colder. *See also* CAMP DAVID, SPIRIT OF.

parity **1.** Equality; ESSENTIAL EQUIVALENCE of nuclear forces. Used in this sense, it provided the basis for arms control agreements during the Cold War. The assumption was that parity meant that neither side had any significant advantage over the other in terms of STRATEGIC WEAPONS. **2.** The equivalent value of a state's currency to a given standard, such as gold or the HARD CURRENCY of another state.

parity, effective A measure of the balance of nuclear weapons between states. One state might, for example, have greater strength in launchers and megatons, another in warheads and accuracy. If both states actually implemented their respective nuclear war plans, this situation could represent effective parity. The term is most often used, however, to recognize that in an era when the major nuclear powers have a capacity for mutual assured destruction (MAD), most asymmetries in numbers or force structure are relatively insignificant.

parity, nuclear A rough equivalency in nuclear forces. If a nuclear power "goes below parity," it is yielding "superiority" to the other side, something that both the United States and the Soviet Union during the Cold War stated they would never tolerate for themselves. U.S. President Richard Nixon wrote in *RN: Memoirs* (1978) that "It was clear to me by 1969 that there could never be absolute parity between the U.S. and the U.S.S.R. . . . Consequently, at the beginning of my administration I began to talk in terms of *sufficiency* rather than *superiority* to describe my goals for our nuclear arsenal." Soviet President Mikhail Gorbachev agreed: "Everybody must realize and agree: Parity

in the potential to destroy one another several times over is madness and absurdity" (*The Christian Science Monitor,* March 18, 1987). The best analysis of nuclear parity is found in Richard Betts's *Nuclear Blackmail and Nuclear Balance* (1987), which identified four distinct meanings of nuclear parity and four corresponding periods as to when it arrived: "If it meant mutual vulnerability to unacceptable damage, parity came in the mid-1950s; if it meant nearly equal levels of civil damage, it arrived by the early 1970s; if equality in missiles or delivery vehicles, by the mid-1970s; if the measure is the balance of forces as a whole or of counterforce capacity, by the late 1970s." The counterpart of this argument is that in the 1970s the strategic balance was not moving from parity to Soviet superiority, as many conservative critics in the United States contended, but from one form of parity to another.

parlementaire The representative of a military commander who, carrying a white flag, enters enemy lines to negotiate with the enemy commander. The *parlementaire* and associates (a driver or flag bearer, for example) are protected from harm by international law unless they use their status for treachery.

Parliamentary Assembly *See* COUNCIL OF EUROPE.

parliamentary system A means of governance whose power is concentrated in a legislature (the parliament), which selects from among its members a PRIME MINISTER and his or her cabinet officers. In a parliamentary system, the legislative and the executive branches of government are one. The prime minister represents the legislature and, through them, the voters. The government—that is, the prime minister and the cabinet—stays in power so long as it commands a majority of the parliament. The major check on the prime minister's power is the constant possibility that his or her party will lose its working majority. If the prime minister gets too far out of step with sentiment in the party or is seen as a liability, then the party will demand the government's resignation. When the government loses its majority by losing a VOTE OF CONFIDENCE, new elections must be held within a prescribed time period. In some systems, such as that of Great Britain, elections must be held once every five years even if no vote of confidence has been called and lost. Most of the democratic countries of the world use parliamentary systems of government. *Compare to* CABINET GOVERNMENT.

parochialism A narrow, provincial, or local frame of mind; limiting one's horizons to only what is found in one's own country as opposed to a great interest in the world. *Compare to* COSMOPOLITANISM.

Partial Test Ban Treaty The 1963 agreement that prohibits its signatories, the Soviet Union, the United Kingdom, and the United States, from testing nuclear weapons in the atmosphere, in space, or under the sea. Further restrictions on nuclear testing were agreed upon by the nuclear superpowers in 1974 and 1976. First, the THRESHOLD TEST BAN TREATY prohibited underground nuclear tests of more than 150 kilotons and prescribed specific testing sites. Two years later the U.S.-Soviet PEACEFUL NUCLEAR EXPLOSIONS TREATY retained the 150-kiloton limit but also included the provisions for limited on-site inspections. Neither of these last two agreements were ratified by the U.S. Senate; nevertheless, neither the United States nor the Soviet Union (or its successor, the Commonwealth of Independent States) has taken any action to violate them. *Compare to* COMPREHENSIVE TEST BAN TREATY.

Partido Revolucionario Institucional See INSTITUTIONAL REVOLUTIONARY PARTY.

partisan warfare A term that is sometimes used almost synonymously with GUERRILLA WARFARE or REVOLUTIONARY WARFARE. Used in reference to the RUSSIAN CIVIL WAR that followed the 1917 revolution, the term also is associated directly with WORLD WAR II, in which residents of territory occupied by Nazi Germany were encouraged to harass the occupiers. The most famous example of World War II partisan warfare was in Yugoslavia, where JOSIP BROZ TITO and his followers not only fought off the Axis powers but eventually formed the postwar government.

partition 1. A division. 2. The creation of two (or more) independent autonomous states from what was once a unified state or territory. For example, India was partitioned into two states (India and Pakistan) upon achieving independence from Great Britain in 1947.

passive defense See ACTIVE MEASURES.

TOLSTOY ON PARTISANS

One of the most conspicuous and advantageous departures from the so-called rules of warfare is the independent action of men acting separately against men huddled together in a mass. Such independent activity is always seen in a war that assumes a national character. In this kind of warfare, instead of forming in a crowd to attack a crowd, men disperse in small groups, attack singly and at once fly, when attacked by superior forces, and then attack again, when an opportunity presents itself. Such were the methods of the guerrillas in Spain; of the mountain tribes in the Caucasus, and of the Russians in 1812.

War of this kind has been called partisan warfare.

SOURCE: Leo Tolstoy, *War and Peace* (1865–69).

---

passive legation See LEGATION, RIGHT OF.

passport A document issued by a state to its nationals to identify them as citizens with the right to return after traveling abroad. Professional diplomats have special passports that allow them to avoid customs inspections and qualify them for DIPLOMATIC PRIVILEGES AND IMMUNITIES. Passports as documents that simply permit safe passage are very old indeed. For example, William Shakespeare in *Henry V* (Act IV, scene iii) has King Henry say:

> *That he which hath no stomach to this fight,*
> *Let him depart. His passport shall be made,*
> *And crowns for convoy put into his purse.*
> *We would not die in that man's company*
> *That fears his fellowship to die with us.*

Passy, Frédéric (1822–1912) The French lawyer and economist who shared the first Nobel Peace Prize in 1901 (with Jean Henry Dunant) for advancing the cause of international arbitration and founding the INTERPARLIAMENTARY UNION.

Pathet Lao The military arm of the Communist Party in Laos. In 1953 the leftist nationalist group in Laos formed an alliance with the Viet Minh, the Communist-controlled insurgents in Vietnam. Very quickly, the Pathet Lao gained control of the two northern provinces of Laos. Under the terms of the Southeast Asian Peace Treaty signed at Geneva in 1954, the Pathet Lao were restricted to the two northern provinces, but the Pathet Lao ceased cooperating with the government in 1964 and the LAOTIAN CIVIL WAR resumed. After South Vietnam was overrun by the Communists from North Vietnam in 1975, the Pathet Lao gained virtual control of all of Laos. *See also* LAOS ACCORDS.

patrimonial sea What some states call their TERRITORIAL WATERS after declaring that they have extended them 200 miles into the ocean. The United Nations–sponsored Law of the Sea Treaty, signed by more than 100 mostly Third World states in 1982, grants coastal states sovereignty extending 12 miles out to sea plus the rights to natural resources up to 200 miles out. The United Kingdom, the United States, and many other industrialized states, seeking to protect mining and fishing rights, have not signed this treaty.

patrimony 1. An inheritance. 2. A state's natural resources. The use of this term implies that stewards of the natural patrimony, such as oil or mineral wealth, have an obligation to manage it in the interests of generations to come.

patriot 1. A loyal citizen who loves and would defend his or her country. 2. One who demands benefits from a country because of some prior, often military, service. It is in this context the British Prime Minister Robert Walpole in a famous speech explained to the House of Commons on February 13, 1741, how he could "raise" patriots: "A patriot, sir! Why, patriots spring up like mushrooms! I could raise fifty of them within the four and twenty hours. I have raised many of them in one night. It is but refusing to grant an unreasonable or an insolent demand, and up starts a patriot."

patriotism 1. Love and loyalty toward one's state. 2. The belief that one's state is better than all others just because of the accident of being born within it. U.S. economist John Kenneth Galbraith (1908–   ) complained about this attitude when he wrote in *A Life in Our Times* (1981): "I have never understood why one's affections must be confined, as once with women, to a single country." 3. According to U.S. novelist Mark Twain (1835–1910), patriotism "is a word which always commemorates a robbery. There isn't a foot of land in the world which doesn't repre-

sent the ousting and re-ousting of a long line of successive owners" (*Mark Twain's Notebooks*, 1935). 4. According to English novelist H. G. Wells (1866–1946), "Patriotism has become a mere national self-assertion, a sentimentality of flag-cheering with no constructive duties" (*The Future in America*, 1906). 5. The uncritical attitude most famously expressed by a toast offered by U.S. naval officer Stephen Decatur (1779–1820) at Norfolk, Virginia, April 4, 1816: "Our country! In her intercourse with foreign nations, may she always be in the right; but our country, right or wrong." Samuel Flagg Bemis, in *John Quincy Adams and the Union* (1956), quotes U.S. President John Quincy Adams (1767–1848) in an August 1, 1816, letter to his father (former U.S. President John Adams) concerning Decatur's toast: "I can never join with my voice in the toast which I see in the papers attributed to one of our gallant naval heroes. I cannot ask of heaven success, even for my country, in a cause where she should be in the wrong. . . . My toast would be, may our country be always successful, but whether successful or otherwise, always right."

patron A state that has a CLIENT STATE to which it gives arms and/or other kinds of support. During the COLD WAR this kind of patronage was a major factor in competition between the United States and the Soviet Union. For example, in the Middle East the United States extended its influence by becoming the patron of Egypt and Israel, while the Soviet Union was patron of Iraq and Syria.

patron-client relations A relationship between two states in which there is a great disparity of power, but in which the larger power supports the smaller for reasons to do with its own competition with other large powers. Such relationships were prevalent during the Cold War. According to Christopher Shoemaker and John Spanier's *Patron-Client State Relationships* (1984), the CLIENT STATE relies on the PATRON for its security, but also "plays a prominent role in patron competition. The more advantage the patron gains over its competitor through its association with its client, the more the patron will value the relationship." Other states also recognize the nature of the relationship. In fact, such relationships are very complex, with clients sometimes manipulating their patrons more than they are manipulated by them and exerting REVERSE INFLUENCE. As Shoemaker and Spanier summed up: "Instead of rigid interaction between two states, patron-client state relationships are in reality fuzzy, fluid, fluctuating partnerships, subject to constant change and only becoming sharply defined in the context of a crisis."

Pauling, Linus Carl (1901–   ) The U.S. California Institute of Technology professor who won the 1954 Nobel Prize in chemistry and later won the 1962 Nobel Peace Prize for his advocacy of nuclear disarmament. He is only the second person to win two Nobel prizes; the other was MARIE CURIE.

Pax Americana   1. The "American peace"; the term used to describe the international order established by the United States in the aftermath of World War II. Key elements in this order were a global U.S. military presence and a liberal economic order in which FREE TRADE was the dominant theme. The term has its origins in the PAX BRITANNICA of the nineteenth century in which peace was imposed in Europe by the British (and was itself inspired by the term PAX ROMANA). In the period after World War II, the United States clearly emerged as the successor to Great Britain not only in Europe, where U.S. military presence became the key to maintaining the balance of power, but also in regions such as the Middle East, where U.S. influence replaced British. Because of the existence of the countervailing power of the Soviet Union, however, and the global nature of the international system, there were clearly limits to the Pax Americana. Yet the idea that the United States is the POLICEMAN OF THE WORLD still has an attraction for some. There were elements of this notion in the U.S. response to the Iraqi invasion of Kuwait and in the pronouncements by U.S. President George Bush on the NEW WORLD ORDER. **2.** The notion that the United States is the world's policeman and must be prepared to uphold international order.

Pax Britannica The "British peace"; the phrase favored by British statesman Joseph Chamberlain (1835–1914) to refer to the international order maintained by British rule of the world's seas in the aftermath of the CONGRESS OF VIENNA of 1815. The order rested on British naval power, the role of Great Britain as the key state in maintaining the BAL-ANCE OF POWER in Europe, its overseas empire, and Britain's industrial might. The wider importance of the Pax Britannica was that it provided the basis for the growth of international trade and commerce. As Michael Mandelbaum, in *The Fate of Nations* (1988), pointed out: "The Pax Britannica underpinned the first global expansion of the free market. Within its far-flung imperial boundaries, Britain was the government. The Royal Navy ensured uninterrupted seaborne commerce and on occasion enforced proper commercial behavior far from the British Isles." The decline of the British economy, however, coupled with the rise of other major powers, especially Germany, brought the Pax Britannica to an end around the turn of the twentieth century.

Pax Romana The "Roman peace"; the peace enforced within the ancient Roman Empire by its imperial legions.

Pax Sovietica   1. The "Soviet peace"; the peace that was imposed by the former Soviet Union on its Eastern European satellites during the COLD WAR. **2.** The peace the Soviet Union imposed on its own constituent republics. Now that the Soviet Union has broken up and nationalist fighting has begun in Armenia, Azerbaijan, and Georgia, we can see how effective the Pax Sovietica really was.

peace The absence of war. Making peace means bringing war to an end. A peace settlement refers to the arrangements agreed upon to bring war to an end. Peace is generally regarded as a positive condition of international politics, although not an absolute one. Realists in particular argue, as future U.S. Secretary of State Henry Kissinger did in *A World Restored* (1957) that: "whenever peace—conceived as the avoidance of war—has been the primary objective of a power or a group of powers, the international system has been at the mercy of the most ruthless member. . . . Whenever the international order has acknowledged that certain principles could not be compromised even for the sake of peace, stability based on equilibrium of force was at least conceivable."

peace, stable A term developed by KENNETH BOULDING in *Stable Peace* (1979), in which war is regarded as unlikely not because of threats of mutual annihilation but because of general satisfaction with the prevailing political situation.

Peace Corps The U.S. government program created by the Peace Corps Act of 1961 to help peoples of less developed states to meet their needs for skilled workers. The Peace Corps was the most successful and lasting of the foreign policy initiatives of the Kennedy Administration. It consists of a Washington, D.C., headquarters; three recruitment service centers supporting six area offices; and overseas operations in more than 60 countries. To fulfill the Peace Corps mandate, U.S. citizens of all ages and skills are trained in the appropriate local language, the technical skills necessary for their particular job, and the cross-cultural skills needed to adjust to a society with traditions and attitudes different from their own. Volunteers serve for two years, living among the people with whom they work. In 1990 the Peace Corps sent volunteers to Eastern Europe for the first time. In its early years the Peace Corps recruited young liberal arts graduates who were sent overseas to teach English and encourage community development. But in recent years the organization, in response to requests by the foreign states it serves, has sought more mature volunteers with specific technical skills in a wide variety of fields.

peace dividend **1.** The money once earmarked for military expenditures and now to be used for domestic purposes that is supposed to become available to NORTH ATLANTIC TREATY ORGANIZATION states due to the winding down of the COLD WAR. The post–Cold War peace dividend has been an especially important public policy issue in the United Kingdom and the United States. **2.** A similar fiscal windfall in the U.S. budget that was supposed to have become available at the end of the VIETNAM WAR. Neither materialized. U.S. Senator William Proxmire of Wisconsin complained in a speech in the Senate (February 3, 1971): "The military budget is going up while the Vietnam War is being wound down. The cruel fact is that there is no peace dividend. It is the only time in American history that we will spend more for the military at the end of a war than while the war was still going strong."

peace for our time *See* CHAMBERLAIN, NEVILLE.

peaceful change **1.** A redrawing of an international border without war. **2.** APPEASEMENT. Prior to World War II, Nazi Germany called for "peaceful changes" in the international status quo—and was granted many of them. **3.** A COLD WAR term for Western efforts to adjust borders in Eastern Europe. This was sometimes used as a euphemism for GERMAN REUNIFICATION. **4.** Large-scale political change that is not accompanied by large-scale violence, such as occurred during Czechoslovakia's VELVET REVOLUTION of 1989.

peaceful coexistence *See* COEXISTENCE.

peaceful nuclear explosions The use of the explosive power of nuclear weapons for nonmilitary purposes; military weapons technology applied to civilian-run excavation and mining. However, problems associated with radioactive FALLOUT have led to the abandonment of all such efforts. Theoretically, the peaceful use of nuclear explosions is still possible. It was ostensibly for this purpose that India exploded a "peaceful nuclear device" in 1974, though many outside observers were skeptical of this. (India has made no further nuclear explosions for this or any other purpose since then.)

Peaceful Nuclear Explosions Treaty A 1976 treaty signed by the United States and the Soviet Union as a companion to the THRESHOLD TEST BAN TREATY of their nuclear weapons sites; these tests are, therefore, considered to be for peaceful purposes. The U.S. Senate has not ratified this treaty, which was supported by the Carter Administration but opposed by the subsequent Reagan Administration because of inadequate VERIFICATION provisions. Nonetheless, its terms have not been violated.

peaceful settlement of disputes The resolution of contentious international issues by negotiation, mediation, or adjudication instead of a resort to force. That all possible efforts should be made toward peaceful (or pacific) settlement of disputes is a tenet of international law incorporated into a variety of international agreements since the 1899 Hague Conventions. The United Nations Charter contains specific clauses relating to the peaceful settlement of disputes. Article 1 of the charter states that one of the aims of the UN is to settle disputes that might lead to a breach of the peace, while Article 2 contains an injunction that member states settle their differences by peaceful means. In practice, of course, not all disputes are subject to peaceful settlement. In certain circumstances, military force will play a crucial role as the ultimate arbiter of disputes.

Peace Institute   *See* UNITED STATES INSTITUTE OF PEACE.

peace instruments   1. Treaties and other international agreements that inhibit war. **2.** International organizations that facilitate peace, such as the United Nations or the Organization of American States. **3.** Diplomats in general.

peacekeeping   A term used to describe the activities of third parties who intervene in civil wars and sometimes in international wars to help establish or maintain peace between actual or potential belligerents. Peacekeeping activities can take place either in an effort to prevent hostilities or as a preliminary to an effort to provide a settlement. They can include mediation and the deployment of what are termed *interposition forces* to keep potential belligerents apart. Peacekeeping often is done through the United Nations, which has its own PEACEKEEPING FORCE, generally involving military units from smaller nations. The difficulties of peacekeeping or peacemaking were underlined in the early 1990s by the United Nations' efforts to end the YUGOSLAVIAN CIVIL WAR.

peacekeeping force   A military unit of the UNITED NATIONS (but made up of soldiers from neutral states) or another international organization deployed to separate hostile parties. Troops in such units usually have small arms for personal protection but do not engage in combat; their role is simply to maintain a buffer between the belligerents. In 1988 the United Nations' peacekeeping forces were awarded the Nobel Peace Prize because they "represent the manifest will of the community of nations to achieve peace through negotiations and the forces have, by their presence, made a decisive contribution toward the initiation of actual peace negotiations." Peacekeeping forces are stationed in such places as the India-Pakistan border, the Golan Heights, in Lebanon, in Cyprus, and the Iran-Iraq border. With the end of the Cold War and a greater

international desire to solve regional conflicts, peacekeeping forces have been in greater demand than ever before and recently have been sent to Angola, Cambodia, El Salvador, the Iraq-Kuwait border, and the former Yugoslavia.

peace movement   1. The term used to describe the protest movement that developed in Europe and the United States in the late 1970s against the deployment of Cruise and Pershing missiles in Europe and an intensification of the ARMS RACE by the United States. The peace movement had diverse roots, ranging from PACIFISM, to European Protestantism, to simple fear about the possibility of nuclear war. **2.** The European movement, manifest mostly by the efforts of private individuals and organizations, to prevent war that began in the late nineteenth century and continued into the twentieth. After World War I the main efforts of this disparate movement focused on the LEAGUE OF NATIONS.

United Nations peacekeepers in the Sinai Desert. (U.S. Naval Institute)

peace research   The study of the causes of peace, designed to find policy prescriptions that can lead to and perpetuate conditions of peace. Peace research (or *peace studies*) is often contrasted with SECURITY STUDIES, or STRATEGIC STUDIES, in which the focus is on security and the uses of force rather than peace. Peace researchers generally are interested not simply in the management of conflict and war but in its elimination.

peace settlement   The process of bringing a war to an end and establishing the basis for subsequent relations between the previous belligerents. According to Robert Randle's *The Origins of Peace* (1973), it usually consists of two stages. The first includes the cessation of hostilities and the arrangements for a cease-fire. The second concerns the negotiations about the basis for the reestablishment of peaceful relations between the parties. Peace settlements and peacemakers always are criticized. The classic comment belongs to U.S. statesman Benjamin Franklin (1706–1790), who wrote in an October 12, 1781, letter to John Adams: "I have never known a peace made, even the most advantageous, that was not censured as inadequate, and the makers condemned as injudicious or corrupt. 'Blessed are the peacemakers' is, I suppose, to be understood in the other world; for in this they are frequently cursed."

peace studies   *See* PEACE RESEARCH.

peace treaty   A formal document that ends a war between two or more parties. All treaties facilitate peace; only peace treaties can terminate a state of war.

peace with honor   A peace treaty or condition of nonbelligerency in which national honor is questionable. Political figures never talk of "peace with honor" if the honor of the state is not in doubt. The phrase has a long lineage: English statesman Oliver Cromwell (1599–1658), in a speech to Parliament on September 4, 1654, said: "Peace is . . . desirable with all men, as far as it may be had with conscience and honor!" British Prime Minister Benjamin Disraeli (1804–1881), speaking of the Treaty of Berlin, said in the House of Commons on July 16, 1878: "Lord Salisbury and myself have brought you back peace—but a peace I hope with honor." Prime Minister Neville Chamberlain echoed Disraeli upon his return from making the MUNICH AGREEMENT: "For the second time in our history, a British Prime Minister has returned from Germany bringing peace with honor. I believe it is peace for our time" (*New York Times,* October 1, 1938). But this agreement was at once denounced as dishonorable; history has made it a classic example of dishonorable diplomatic dealings. Peace with honor seemed to become the goal of U.S. policy during the latter years of the Vietnam War. U.S. President Richard M. Nixon, in a speech to the nation on January 23, 1973, said: "As this long and difficult war [Vietnam] ends, I would like to address a few special words to . . . the American people: Your steadfastness in supporting our insistence on peace with honor has made peace with honor possible." But by that time "peace with honor" merely meant that the United States had found a diplomatic fig leaf by which it could retreat from Vietnam with a minimum of embarrassment.

Pearl Harbor   The United States' Pacific Fleet headquarters in Hawaii where, on Sunday, December 7, 1941, over 350 aircraft from six Japanese aircraft carriers launched an attack against the U.S. Navy ships moored in the harbor. This attack sank three battleships, capsized another, and heavily damaged four more. While many other ships were destroyed or damaged, the three U.S. aircraft carriers based there were at sea and missed the attack. Over 250 aircraft were also destroyed, almost all on the ground. Overall there were about 5,000 casualties, half of them deaths. This attack brought the United States into WORLD WAR II. On the following day when U.S. President Franklin D. Roosevelt asked Congress for a declaration of war, he called it "a day that will live in infamy."

The Pearl Harbor attack incensed the U.S. public not because it was a surprise, which is to be expected in war, but a sneak attack when there was no state of war. Indeed, Japanese emissaries were in Washington at the same time purportedly negotiating in good faith to resolve United States–Japanese differences. The Japanese government had intended to notify the United States that a state of war existed one-half hour before the attack. But because of decoding difficulties, the war message was not delivered until after the attack was well under way. This time difference was the difference between honor

The USS Arizona *burns after the Japanese surprise attack on Pearl Harbor on December 7, 1941. (National Archives)*

and dishonor. Fifty years later Japan's foreign minister, Michio Watanabe, almost apologized for the attack when he said: "This is the 50th anniversary of Pearl Harbor, and we feel a deep remorse about the unbearable suffering and sorrow Japan inflicted on the American people and the peoples of Asia and the Pacific during the Pacific war, a war that Japan started with the surprise attack on Pearl Harbor. Japan waged war against the United States because of the reckless decision of our military. . . . We can't get over our deep sorrow" (*Newsweek*, December 16, 1991). Japanese plans for a more formal apology were junked by Japan's parliament when U.S. President George Bush said there was no reason for the United States to apologize for HIROSHIMA.

Pearson, Lester B. (1897–1972)   The prime minister of Canada from 1963 to 1968. As a diplomat he was one of the founders of the United Nations in 1945, ambassador to the United States (1941–1946), and minister of external affairs (1948–1957). In this last capacity he played major roles in resolving the Palestine crisis of 1947–1948 and the SUEZ CRISIS of 1956. For this he was awarded the Nobel Peace Prize in 1957.

Pearson Commission   The 1968 Commission on International Development created by the INTERNATIONAL BANK FOR RECONSTRUCTION AND DEVELOPMENT to study the history of international cooperation for development assistance and make recommendations for a global strategy for development assistance in the 1970s. The commission, headed by LESTER B. PEARSON of Canada, published a report entitled "Partners in Development" that recommended that the percentage of gross national product of donor countries devoted to aid be increased to 0.7 percent, that 10 to 20 percent of official aid should come through multilateral channels, and that aid should not be considered a replacement for direct foreign investment and expanded world trade in furthering development. While the Pearson Commission's recommendations generated much debate on the role of foreign aid and the nature of Third World economic development, the specific suggestions for action were overwhelmingly ignored. *Compare to* BRANDT COMMISSION.

Peenemünde The northwest Germany site on the Baltic Sea that came to notice in World War II as the place where the Germans developed and tested jet aircraft engines and liquid fuel rockets, the V-WEAPONS. Modern ICBMs as well as space rockets have their origins in Peenemünde, for the scientists who worked there would later continue the development of rocketry for either the United States or the Soviet Union.

PEN (Poets, Essayists, Novelists) A worldwide federation of writers from over 50 states that, since 1921, has used its GOOD OFFICES to publicize the plight of persecuted or censored literary figures.

penetrated state A concept associated with JAMES ROSENAU that holds that the boundaries between national political systems and the international environment are becoming increasingly obscured and irrelevant to a whole range of processes. As Rosenau wrote in *The Scientific Study of Foreign Policy* (1971): "A penetrative process occurs when members of one polity serve as participants in the political processes of another" and play a part in the allocation of values within that other society. Examples of such penetration include foreign aid missions and the representatives of private corporations. Not all states are equally penetrated, of course, but in few if any cases can the borders of the state be regarded as impermeable.

Pentagon 1. The building that has become the symbol of the United States Department of Defense.

Construction was finished on January 15, 1943. The five-story, five-sided building has five concentric rings connected by ten spokelike corridors ranging out from the inner, or A, ring. The combined length of the corridors is 17.5 miles, and the total floor space is more than 6 million square feet. About 28,000 people, both civilians and military, work at the Pentagon. 2. Figuratively, either the high command of the U.S. military forces, especially the Joint Chiefs of Staff, or the civilian authorities in the Department of Defense.

pentagonal group *See* HEXAGONAL GROUP.

Pentagon Papers The unedited classified record of the step-by-step decisions that brought U.S. involvement in Vietnam to its peak by the end of the Johnson Administration. This essentially shapeless body of raw data became a cause célèbre when 47 volumes of them were leaked in 1971 to the *New York Times* and the *Washington Post* by Daniel Ellsberg (1931–), a former Department of Defense employee. The papers were published beginning June 13, 1971. The Nixon Administration got an injunction to prevent their publication, but the Supreme Court dissolved the injunction. The chairman of the Senate Foreign Relations Committee, J. William Fulbright, said of the papers: "Most of the material should not have been secret in the first place. . . . I still don't see the harm that came from it, other than the fact that there is involved a violation of the law. . . . I can disapprove of the leaking of documents, but at the same time I disapprove just as heartily of the abuse of the classification power" (*The Christian Science Monitor,* July 18, 1973).

people's republic A term used by Communist states to describe themselves. Such a term, as used in China, was designed to convey the impression that the regime was directly responsible to the people; in fact this often masked great authoritarianism on the part of such governments.

people's war A term that is often used as a synonym for REVOLUTIONARY WARFARE. The concept developed in China and stems from MAO ZEDONG's notion that the key to victory was the support of the people. For Mao the guerrilla fighters were the fish and the population provided the water from which

The Pentagon (Department of Defense)

the fish draw sustenance. In this sense, Mao recognized that revolutionary struggles were as much about political LEGITIMACY as about military force. This is reflected in Mao's comment in *Selected Military Writings* (1963) that "War cannot for a single moment be separated from politics . . . politics is war without bloodshed, while war is politics with bloodshed." If China provides the main example of successful people's war, however, Vietnam was equally important. Indeed, VO NGUYEN GIAP popularized the term in *People's War, People's Army* (1962) in which he argued that there are many different battlefronts in a revolutionary war.

perception   The psychological process that enables people to make sense of their environment; it is related both to the notion of information processing and to belief systems. Basically it involves how people see the world. A notion developed in psychology, it has become the basis for much analysis of foreign

policy decision making. As well as being interested in how policymakers perceive reality, however, analysts also have been concerned with the kinds of misperceptions that can occur. The classic study on all this with regard to foreign policy and international relations is ROBERT JERVIS's *Perception and Misperception in International Politics* (1976).

perestroika   **1.** Restructuring; the one word that encompassed MIKHAIL GORBACHEV's efforts to reform the economic, ideological, and sociopolitical aspects of the Soviet society. This word literally means rebuilding, reorientation, or reorganization but has taken on the additional meaning of setting a new trend toward creating a more democratic society with mutual feedback between the people and the state. It is inextricably intertwined with GLASNOST. During the Gorbachev years, *perestroika* was a move for greater self-criticism and democratization in the Communist Party and government, a stronger working relationship among the ruling apparatus, the intelligentsia, and the people. The word was conceptually accepted by many at first. But when applied to actual reform programs, it proved to be too little and too late to save the Soviet Union.   **2.** By analogy, any major reorganization effort.

Pérez de Cuéllar, Javier (1920–   )   The Peruvian diplomat who was his country's ambassador to the Soviet Union (1969–1971) and representative to the United Nations (1971–1975). After serving as a UN undersecretary, he became the fifth secretary-general of the United Nations (1982–1991). During his tenure the influence of the UN vastly expanded as the Cold War dissipated.

Pérez Esquivel, Adolfo (1931–   )   The Argentine human rights activist who won the 1980 Nobel Peace Prize for his late 1970s opposition to political repression by the military junta that controlled Argentina.

perimeter defense   *See* CONTAINMENT.

Permanent Court of Arbitration   *See* ARBITRATION, PERMANENT COURT OF.

Permanent Court of International Justice   The judicial arm of the LEAGUE OF NATIONS, which functioned poorly. It was dissolved in 1945 and replaced by the WORLD COURT.

Permanent International Peace Bureau   The organization based in Berne, Switzerland, that won the 1910 Nobel Peace Prize for its work as a clearinghouse for the pacifist movement. It still functions under the name of International Peace Bureau.

permissive actions links   Control mechanisms intended to prevent the accidental or unauthorized use of nuclear weapons. A variety of what are in effect electromechanical combination locks have been devised for this purpose.

Peron, Juan Domingo (1895–1974)   The army colonel who became president of Argentina (1946–1955; 1973–1974) and was the founder and leader of the Peronist movement there. In 1943 Peron and other military officers overthrew the civilian president, Edelmiro J. Farrell (1887–1980). Rising though the ranks as secretary of labor and social welfare, minister of war, and vice president, Peron garnered support from diverse sectors of the population. Aided by his charismatic wife, Eva "Evita" Duarte de Peron (1919–1952), he won the presidential elections of 1946. Peron advocated industrialization, NATIONALIZATION of existing industry, a nonaligned foreign policy, and extended workers' rights. Peron, who was an admirer of Adolf Hitler, made Argentina a safe haven for Nazis escaping a defeated Germany. According to Gerald L. Posner, "Peron set aside more than 10,000 blank passports and identity cards for Nazi fugitives" (*New York Times,* November 13, 1991). But these were not poor refugees. Peron allowed them secretly to ship to Argentina six U-boats full of gold, diamonds, and other liquid assets with which to start a new life and enrich him and his cronies. Peron was popular, especially among workers and the poor, but he alienated many Argentines because of the corruption and repression of his regime as well as high inflation. Overthrown in 1955, he settled in Spain, but returned to Argentina in 1973 and was elected president in a special election after Peronist supporters had won majorities in the legislature and presidency. Upon his death

in 1974, his third wife and vice president, Isabel Martinez de Peron, became president until a coup led by Jorge Rafael Videla (1925–   ) and a military junta took control of the country in 1976. *See also* ARGENTINE FASCISM.

perpetual peace   *See* KANT, IMMANUEL.

Pershing, John J. (1860–1948)   The United States general who commanded U.S. troops in Europe during WORLD WAR I. He was designated a five-star "General of the Armies" by the U.S. Congress in 1919. (So that his title would remain unique, each of the United States' World War II five-star generals was merely a "General of the Army.")

Pershing Missile   A mobile nuclear missile once deployed by the U.S. Army. The Pershing I was a medium-range ballistic missile with a single nuclear warhead designed for use against tactical battlefield targets. More than 800 of these were deployed in West Germany in the 1960s. In 1979 the decision was made to replace the Pershing I with the Pershing II, a solid-propellant medium-range ballistic missile designed for use in Europe. Its accuracy and range was such that it had the ability to strike COMMAND AND CONTROL facilities around Moscow in the Soviet Union. The INF TREATY of 1987 called for the elimination of the Pershing II and comparable Soviet missiles.

Persian Gulf Crisis   The period that followed the Iraqi invasion of Kuwait on August 2, 1990, and preceded the outbreak of the PERSIAN GULF WAR on January 16, 1991. Iraq justified its invasion by its long-standing claim that Kuwait was historically part of Iraq and by asserting that Kuwait was being unreasonable about adjusting disputed border areas. After the invasion, the United States, working through the United Nations, assembled a worldwide coalition to put pressure on Iraq to withdraw. At the same time it deployed military forces to prevent Iraq from extending its conquest into Saudi Arabia. There are two possible interpretations of U.S. and UN policy during this period. One is that the policy was an attempt at BRINKMANSHIP that failed as SADDAM HUSSEIN refused to withdraw from Kuwait; the other is that the United States actually wanted the opportunity to reduce Iraq's power and therefore attempted to manipulate the situation in ways that made war inevitable.

Persian Gulf War   1. The war that started on January 16, 1991, after Iraq had refused to remove its occupying military forces from Kuwait, and ended on February 27, 1991, when U.S. President George Bush declared victory for the allied forces. While the war was a major military success (only 166 coalition soldiers died in battle compared to an estimated 100,000 Iraqi dead), it was an equally important diplomatic victory. Immediately after the Iraqi invasion on August 2, President Bush, working through the United Nations, began assembling the diplomatic coalition that evolved into the military coalition against Iraq. The industrialized states of the West were concerned that Iraq, with the largest military establishment in the Arab world, was poised to take over the entire Arabian peninsula—and thereby control about half of the world's oil reserves. This prospect encouraged Saudi Arabia formally to invite the West to defend the kingdom. Thus, under UN sanction, Saudi Arabia became the main staging area for the assault on Iraqi forces in Kuwait. Critical to this effort was the earlier ending of the COLD WAR with the Soviet Union. This made it possible to bring the Soviets into the diplomatic (although not the military) coalition against Iraq even though they had supplied and trained the Iraqi military. (The United States had also helped Iraq obtain arms for its military, especially during the IRAN-IRAQ WAR; but the U.S. help was mainly financial.) The military coalition led by the United States included major units from Canada, Egypt, France, Italy, Saudi Arabia, Syria, and the United Kingdom. In addition, more than two dozen other states provided financial, humanitarian, or military assistance to the effort.

The war was immensely popular in the United States. It made national heroes out of General Colin Powell, the chairman of the Joint Chiefs of Staff, and General H. Norman Schwarzkopf, the field commander. It was the first war since World War II in which the U.S. people were, for the most part, enthusiastic and became all the more popular once it was evident that U.S. casualties were low.

The military campaign called for the most extensive bombing of any nation since World War II Germany. It proved that high-technology weapons did work and could save allied lives. And it showed that Iraqi leader SADDAM HUSSEIN's million-man army (once the world's fourth largest) was a PAPER TIGER when confronted with high-technology FIRST WORLD forces. As President Bush, gloating over victory, said: "By God, we've kicked the VIETNAM SYNDROME once and for all" (*Newsweek,* March 11, 1991).

The war also sent President Bush's domestic popularity to new, if temporary, highs. Critics of Bush's actions contended that he single-handedly sent more than half a million United States troops in harm's way without any formal approval of Congress. While Congress, at the last minute, gave the president legal authority to commit troops to combat (which he did on January 15, 1991), he asserted that he did not really need it—that his authority as COMMANDER IN CHIEF was sufficient. While the war was a clear military defeat for the Iraqi government, it ended before Saddam Hussein was weakened enough to be overthrown by internal opposition. The fact that Saddam Hussein was still in power long after the war, and able militarily to crush internal revolts by Kurds in the north and Shi'ites in the south, has taken much of the glow off the initial military victory.   2. The IRAN-IRAQ WAR of 1980–1988.

U.S. General H. Norman Schwarzkopf briefs troops during the Persian Gulf War. (Department of Defense)

PERSIAN GULF CRISIS AND WAR
A Chronology

1990

August 2	Iraq invades Kuwait. United Nations Security Council condemns the invasion and demands immediate Iraqi withdrawal.
August 5	U.S. President Bush declares Iraqi invasion "will not stand."
August 6	UN Security Council orders sweeping trade and financial boycott of Iraq and occupied Kuwait.
August 8	U.S. forces deployed in Saudi Arabia at request of Saudi government; Operation "Desert Shield" commences.
August 9	U.S. and allied naval forces begin a blockade on Iraqi trade.
August 20	Iraq announces it is moving U.S. and other Western hostages to military sites to serve as human shields against attack.
August 30	President Bush announces that he is requesting financial aid from allies to help pay cost of military buildup.
September 24	Iraq announces it will attack Israel with chemical weapons if Iraq is attacked by any state.
October 1	Israel announces it will distribute gas masks to all citizens.
November 8	President Bush announces that more than 150,000 additional troops will be sent to the gulf so that the United States will have an offensive option.
November 19	Iraq announces it will free all Western hostages.
November 29	United States Security Council authorizes the United States–led coalition forces to "use all necessary means" to expel Iraq from Kuwait if Iraq has not voluntarily withdrawn by January 15, 1991.

1991

January 12	U.S. Congress adopts resolution authorizing President Bush to take military action to expel Iraq from Kuwait.
January 15	United Nations deadline passes with no indication of Iraqi withdrawal from Kuwait.
January 16	United States and allied forces commence air bombardment of Iraq and Iraqi forces in Kuwait, Operation "Desert Storm" begins.
February 24	The 100-hour land war begins; United States and allied forces liberate Kuwait with astonishingly low allied casualties.
February 27	President Bush orders a cease-fire and declares the war won.

persona non grata   **1.** Informally, someone who is out of favor.   **2.** In DIPLOMACY this term has a very specific meaning: a diplomat formally declared to be "persona non grata" must leave the host country. The expulsion can be caused by the diplomat's own behavior, or the diplomat can be entirely innocent and be expelled for larger foreign policy considerations.

THE RULES ON PERSONA NON GRATA STATUS IN THE VIENNA CONVENTION ON DIPLOMATIC RELATIONS

1. The receiving State may at any time and without having to explain its decision, notify the sending State that the head of the mission or any member of the diplomatic staff of the mission is *persona non grata* or that any other member of the staff of the mission is not acceptable. In any such case, the sending State shall, as appropriate, either recall the person concerned or terminate his functions with the mission. A person may be declared persona non grata or not acceptable before arriving in the territory of the receiving State.
2. If the sending State refuses or fails within a reasonable period to carry out its obligations under paragraph 1 of this Article, the receiving State may refuse to recognize the person concerned as a member of the mission.

SOURCE: Article 9 of the Convention on Diplomatic Relations, adopted April 14, 1961, by the United Nations Conference on Diplomatic Relations and Immunities meeting in Vienna, Austria.

Peru coup   The 1992 "self-coup" by Peruvian President ALBERTO FUJIMORI that dissolved the legislature, suspended civil liberties, and created government by decree. The *autogolpe* (Fujimori's term for the self-coup) initially had widespread public support and was undertaken to enable the government to marshal the support and resources necessary to fight the SENDERO LUMINOSO insurgency. Fujimori has pledged to defeat the guerrillas by 1995, but many observers think the fight could go the other way. Nevertheless, during the fall of 1992 the government had captured, tried, and sentenced to life imprisonment the top leadership of the insurgency.

Pétain, Philippe (1856–1951)   The World War I French general, famous for his 1916 defense of VERDUN, who, in WORLD WAR II, collaborated with the German occupation forces. For heading the puppet VICHY government, he was tried and convicted of treason after the war. His sentence was death but this was converted to life imprisonment. It was often said of Pétain that, unlike CHARLES DE GAULLE, he loved Frenchmen more than he loved France—and that this helped to explain (but not excuse) his collaboration with the Nazis.

petrocurrencies   **1.** The monetary reserves of oil-rich states.   **2.** The money that oil-rich states keep in Western banks.

PFLP   *See* POPULAR FRONT FOR THE LIBERATION OF PALESTINE.

Philby, Kim (1912–1988)   A member of the CAMBRIDGE SPY RING who passed secret documents to the Soviet Union, beginning in 1940 when he joined the British Secret Intelligence Service (MI6) until he was exposed and fled to Moscow in 1963—where he continued to work for the KGB.

Philippine Insurrection   **1.** The 1896–1898 revolt against the corrupt Spanish colonial government of the Philippines.   **2.** The 1899–1902 guerrilla war against the new colonial power, the United States, which had acquired the Philippines from Spain under terms of the 1898 Treaty of Paris ending the SPANISH-AMERICAN WAR. At first U.S. President William McKinley did not want to keep the islands. But then he reversed himself. According to Stanley Karnow: "Unaware that the Filipinos were Roman Catholic, he later explained that God had instructed him to 'uplift and Christianize them' " (*New York Times,* April 1, 1989). The ensuing war claimed the lives of over 100,000 Filipinos and almost 5,000 U.S. troops. It ended only after insurrection leader Emilio Aquinaldo (1869–1964) was captured and forced to swear allegiance to the United States. The insurrection is also known as the Philippine-American War.

Philippine Invasion   The WORLD WAR II Japanese conquest of the Philippines that began the day after PEARL HARBOR, December 8, 1941. By May 6, 1942, the Japanese had defeated all regular U.S. and Filipino forces on the islands; guerrilla activity against the Japanese, however, continued. The fight to regain the Philippines began when U.S. forces under General DOUGLAS MACARTHUR landed on the island of Leyte on October 20, 1944. Filipinos and Americans fought together until the Japanese surrender in September 1945. The capital, Manila, was destroyed during the final months of the fighting. An estimated 1 million Filipinos lost their lives in the war with the Japanese. *See also* BATAAN.

MACARTHUR'S CALL TO ARMS

People of the Philippines: I have returned. By the grace of Almighty God, our forces stand again on Philippine soil—soil consecrated in the blood of our two peoples. . . . The hour of your redemption is here. Your patriots have demonstrated an unswerving and resolute devotion to the principles of freedom. . . . I now call upon your supreme effort that the enemy may know, from the temper of an aroused people within, that he has a force there to contend with no less violent than is the force committed from without. Rally to me. Let the indomitable spirit of Bataan and Corregidor lead on. As the lines of battle roll forward to bring you within the zone of operations, rise and strike. Strike at every favorable opportunity. For your homes and hearths, strike! For future generations of your sons and daughters, strike! In the name of your sacred dead, strike! Let no heart be faint. Let every arm be steeled.

SOURCE: General Douglas MacArthur, radio address to the people of the Philippines as American forces invaded Leyte, October 20, 1944, reprinted in his *Reminiscences* (1964).

This World War II poster encouraged Filipino opposition to the Japanese invaders. (National Archives)

Philippine Revolution The 1986 events in the wake of a presidential election won by incumbent President FERDINAND E. MARCOS after widespread election fraud. The actual winner, CORAZON AQUINO, led a peaceful civilian-military uprising supported by the United States that resulted in Marcos's exile to Hawaii and Aquino's installation as president.

Phillips curve The graphic presentation (first put forth in 1958 by the British economist A. W. Phillips) that demonstrates a direct relationship between unemployment and inflation; as unemployment declines, wages and prices can be expected to rise and vice versa.

Phoenix program A campaign of COUNTERINSURGENCY terrorism during the VIETNAM WAR mounted by the South Vietnamese military, the U.S. CENTRAL INTELLIGENCE AGENCY, and the U.S. Army Special Forces (Green Berets). The Phoenix program ran from 1968 to 1971 and was an effort to use the VIET CONG's own tactics—assassinations, kidnappings, and intimidation—against them. Francis Fitzgerald wrote in *Fire in the Lake* (1972) that the Phoenix "program in effect eliminated the cumbersome category of 'civilian'; it gave . . . license and justification for the arrest, torture, or killing of anyone in the country, whether or not the person was carrying a gun. And many officials took advantage of that license."

phony war **1.** The period of WORLD WAR II after the German conquest of Poland in September 1939 until April of 1940 when Germany attacked Denmark and Norway and battle was finally joined. During this time there was so little fighting, even though Great Britain and France had declared war on Germany, that the press dubbed it a "phony war." **2.** Any situation in which states are formally at war with each other but take no hostile military action toward each other. *See also* SITZKRIEG.

physical quality of life index (POLI) The scale of national economic health devised by the Overseas Development Council to replace the GROSS NATIONAL PRODUCT as the main indicator of economic prosperity. The POLI is a composite of three indicators (life expectancy, infant mortality, and literacy) selected because they reflect the effects of income, health, education, and the sharing of national wealth at all levels of society. A measure of the rate of progress that a country is making toward closing the gap between its current POLI (or any component thereof) and the best projected performance in the year 2000 is called the Disparity Reduction Rate (DRR).

Pilsudski, Józef K. (1867–1935) The provisional president and marshal of Poland from 1918 to 1921. He became minister of war and premier after he led a 1926 coup and ruled as dictator until his death in 1935. After his death Poland returned to a period of turbulent parliamentary democracy with prime ministers changing every year until the 1939 German conquest, which started WORLD WAR II in Europe.

Pinochet Ugarte, Augusto (1915–) The leader of the military junta that overthrew the government of President SALVADOR ALLENDE of Chile in September 1973. Pinochet, a military officer who served as army chief of staff and commander in chief of the armed forces, assumed the presidency following the coup and stifled all opposition to the new military regime. International human rights groups accused the Chilean military government of allowing DEATH SQUADS to murder thousands of citizens, and the United States cut off most aid to Chile in 1979. Pinochet returned Chile to a free market economy, now one of the healthiest in Latin America. A new constitution in 1981 called for a PLEBISCITE in 1988 that would decide if the ruling military junta should stay in office. The plebiscite went against the junta and called for a return to civilian rule. In the 1989 election for president, Patricio Aylwin Azócar (1919–) of the center left Coalition of Parties for Democracy won, becoming the first democratically elected president in Chile since 1970. But Pinochet remains head of the military, and the 1980 constitution written by the Pinochet government protects the military from being prosecuted for human rights violations (such as murder) and prohibits the civilian government from removing any of the four heads of the military department—including Pinochet—until 1998. When Aylwin was asked by British Prime Minister John Major what it was like being president with Pinochet still in charge of the army, he replied: "It's a unique experience. . . . Imagine what it would be like to be President of Spain with Franco still alive. I am with my Franco. It's General Pinochet" (*New York Times,* April 30, 1992). *See also* DINA.

Pire, Dominique Georges (1910–1969) The Belgian priest who won the 1958 Nobel Peace Prize for his efforts at resettling displaced persons after World War II.

place in the sun International importance; to be a major player in world politics. The phrase is most associated with Germany prior to World War I. For example, Kaiser WILLIAM II asserted: "Our navy should be further strengthened, so that we may be sure that no one can dispute with us our place in the sun that is our due" (*New York Times,* August 28, 1911).

Plan Orange The United States Navy's war plan, developed in 1921, which saw Japan as the United States' most likely adversary. It projected that the U.S. fleet would sweep westward from Pearl Harbor, liberate the Philippines, demolish the Japanese navy, and blockade Japan's home islands. One reason the U.S. Navy was able to defeat the Japanese so effectively in WORLD WAR II was that, using Plan Orange, the navy had repeatedly studied the problem in the two decades prior to the war.

Platt Amendment U.S. Senator Orville H. Platt's (1827–1905) amendment to a 1901 military appropriations bill that, after it was incorporated into a 1903 Treaty of Relations between the United States and Cuba, restricted the treaty-making power of Cuba and allowed U.S. military intervention to protect Cuban independence and domestic order. This amendment, which also was made part of the Cuban constitution, effectively made Cuba a PROTECTORATE of the United States. The Platt Amendment was used to justify U.S. military intervention in Cuba in 1906, 1912, and 1924. As part of U.S. President Franklin D. Roosevelt's GOOD NEIGHBOR POLICY it was abrogated by a new treaty with Cuba in 1934.

Plaza Accord An agreement reached by the finance ministers and central bankers of the GROUP OF FIVE at a 1985 meeting held at the Plaza Hotel, New York, in the United States. The participants agreed that: (1) additional measures were urgently required to reduce the U.S. budget deficit, which they identified as a major imbalancing factor in the world economy; (2) protectionist pressures should be resisted; and (3) they would cooperate to drive down the value of the U.S. dollar. U.S. Secretary of the Treasury James A. Baker III had sought this agreement in order to increase the COMPETITIVENESS of U.S. goods, reduce the U.S. foreign trade deficit, and head off congressional pressure for protectionist measures.

plebiscite 1. A vote on a major issue by the entire voting public of a state. For example, in a 1905 plebiscite Norway decided to separate from Sweden; in 1935 the citizens of the Saar valley voted, under League of Nations supervision, to join Germany; and in 1992 the white citizens of South Africa voted to end apartheid. 2. Any means of expression for popular opinion. In this sense, even a REFERENDUM on a new law is a plebiscite. **3.** Informally, a vote for a party or an individual associated with a particular policy. For example, some historians have contended that the 1920 national election, when the Democrats supported U.S. membership in the League of Nations (and lost the election) while the Republicans opposed it (and won), was a plebiscite on whether the United States should join the League.

plenary session   Any meeting of an assembly, a legislature, a convention, and the like, with all members present.

plenipotentiary   An agent, especially a DIPLOMAT, given full power to conduct business on behalf of the person(s) represented. Thus plenipotentiaries are diplomats fully empowered to negotiate.

Pleven Plan   *See* EUROPEAN DEFENSE COMMUNITY.

PLO   *See* PALESTINE LIBERATION ORGANIZATION.

pluralism   **1.** Overall cultural diversity in a political jurisdiction stratified along racial or ethnic lines. This concept was used first in the twentieth century by historians to describe the inherently unstable colonial rule of an alien minority over an indigenous majority. **2.** Any political system in which there are multiple centers of legitimate power and authority. For example, the United States has three branches of government (executive, legislative, and judicial); each has power in different spheres of society. Modern theories of government attempt to reaffirm the democratic character of society by asserting that open, multiple, competing, and responsive groups preserve traditional democratic values in a mass industrial state. Traditional democratic theory thus is transformed into a model that emphasizes the role of competitive groups in society. Pluralism assumes that power will shift from group to group as elements in the mass public transfer their allegiance in response to their perceptions of their individual interests. *Compare to* ELITE THEORY.

pluralism, cultural   **1.** The belief that a state's interests are best served by preserving ethnic cultures rather than by encouraging the integration and blending of cultures. This is in contrast to belief in assimilation, that all immigrants should be incorporated into the dominant culture. **2.** A social and political situation within a jurisdiction by which diverse racial and ethnic groups live in comparative peace and harmony.

pluralism, hyper-   A political condition wherein so many groups or parties compete for political power so successfully that power itself becomes fractionated and little can get done.

pluralism, political   A governing system with a constitutional separation of powers. The United States is an example. Because power is distributed among several entities, which can check each other if necessary, no single branch of government is all powerful or sovereign.

pogrom   One of the many attacks against Russian Jews by armed mobs, sponsored in part by the Russian government, between 1881 and the RUSSIAN REVOLUTION OF 1917. Similar state-condoned and abetted violent ANTI-SEMITISM was later undertaken by Nazi Germany against Jewish communities in Germany and the rest of Europe before and during World War II. The word literally means "massacre" and has come to signify any type of mass brutality against any ethnic, political, national, or religious minority.

Poincaré, Raymond (1860–1934)   The French premier (1912–1913) who strengthened the Allied diplomatic coalition that successfully fought WORLD WAR I, and who became the wartime president of France (1913–1920). From 1922 until his retirement in 1929, he would be premier twice more (1922–1924; 1926–1929). Claiming that Germany had defaulted on war REPARATIONS, he ordered the French occupation of the RUHR in 1923.

Point Four   The foreign aid program proposed by U.S. President Harry S Truman in his inaugural address in 1949 and then implemented by Congress in September 1950 to provide U.S. technical assistance to help raise production and living standards in underdeveloped areas, mainly Latin America. The program at its inception was administered through the International Development Fund, then by the Technical Cooperation Administration, and then by the Mutual Security Agency. It was phased out by the end of the 1950s. Many of its functions were taken over by the AGENCY FOR INTERNATIONAL DEVELOPMENT.

Poland, invasion of   The September 1, 1939, attack by Nazi Germany on the western border of Poland that marked the onset of WORLD WAR II. On September 17, 1939, the Soviet Union also invaded Poland, but from the east. The attackers then partitioned Poland according to the secret protocols of the NAZI-SOVIET NONAGGRESSION PACT. The country remained under either German or Soviet occupation until the end of the war but maintained a government in exile first in Paris, France, and later in London, England.

polarity   A term used to describe the fact that the international system tends to revolve around the most powerful states, which, in effect, provide "poles." The number of poles or great powers determines whether the system is characterized as having BIPOLARITY (two main powers), TRIPOLARITY (three great powers), or MULTIPOLARITY (usually five great powers).

polemology   **1.** The analysis of human conflict. **2.** The scientific study of the issues of war and peace.

police action   **1.** Military INTERVENTION by a state with a proclaimed purpose of upholding international law. **2.** The KOREAN WAR, because the war was fought with the approval and under the flag of the United Nations.

policeman of the world   A role the United States has sometimes played with its foreign policy. The first major instance of this in the twentieth century was President THEODORE ROOSEVELT's 1904 statement in his corollary to the MONROE DOCTRINE that called for the United States to exercise "an international police power." Both the Korean and Vietnam wars have often been described as policing efforts. Analyst Jeane J. Kirkpatrick wrote in *Commentary* (November 1979): "Vietnam presumably taught us that the United States could not serve as the world's policeman; it should also have taught us the dangers of trying to be the world's midwife to democracy when the birth is scheduled to take place under conditions of guerrilla war." But according to General Colin Powell, chairman of the U.S. Joint Chiefs

of Staff: "I certainly agree that we should not go around saying we are the world's policeman. But guess who gets called when suddenly someone needs a cop?" (*New York Times*, August 17, 1990).

THE WORLD'S NANNY

Observers have faulted our intervention in Vietnam as evidence of American arrogance of power—attempts by the United States to be the World's Policeman. But there is another dimension to American arrogance, the international version of our domestic Great Society programs where we presumed that we knew what was best for the world in terms of social, political, and economic development and saw it as our duty to force the world into the American mold—to act not so much the World's Policeman as the World's Nanny. It is difficult today to recall the depth of our arrogance.

SOURCE: Harry G. Summers, Jr., *On Strategy* (1982).

---

police state   **1.** A totalitarian society in which citizens are heavily supervised by police forces, both open and secret. A police state is an inherent tyranny, which rules by explicit or implied terror and which denies its citizens many civil liberties. In a police state, sheer force replaces the legal system and due process of law. **2.** A critical reference to a democratic state when an observer feels that the government is violating the basic freedoms of citizens. **3.** A state that lacks LEGITIMACY and depends solely on coercion to maintain not only domestic order but sometimes even its very existence.

Policy Planning Staff (PPS)   The U.S. Department of State's organizational unit responsible for making recommendations on long-range foreign policy. The PPS was created in 1947 by U.S. Secretary of State George Marshall at a time when the United States was coming to grips with a new international role in the aftermath of World War II and the development of the Cold War. Initially it consisted of five members whose task was to "formulate long-term programs for the achievement of U.S. foreign policy objectives," anticipate problems, evaluate current policies, and coordinate planning activities in the State Department. Under its first director, GEORGE F. KENNAN, the PPS played a major role in formulating the MARSHALL PLAN for European Economic Recovery. Kennan resigned in 1949 when it became clear that the PPS papers were no longer being directly considered by the secretary of state. The views of Kennan's successor PAUL H. NITZE coincided much more closely with those of new Secretary of State Dean Acheson, and the influential study NSC-68, which advocated large-scale conventional rearmament by the United States, began under the auspices of the planning staff. The PPS was abolished as an independent entity in 1969 and incorporated within the office of the secretary of state. It had never really fulfilled the function of long-range planning, partly because of the intrinsic nature of foreign policy but also because of the desire of the staff to influence day-to-day policies. As Robert Rothstein noted in *Planning, Prediction, and Policymaking in Foreign Affairs* (1972), the PPS was increasingly dominated by "the operator's ethos" with the result that "planning, prediction, and a concern for the significance of long-range developments were honored rhetorically and ignored in practice."

Polish corridor   The strip of territory taken from Germany after World War I to give Poland access to the Baltic Sea and the port city of DANZIG. This land, which separated East Prussia from the rest of Germany, was reincorporated into Germany after its 1939 conquest of Poland. After World War II the "corridor" and much other land that was once Germany's reverted to Poland. Then the corridor, in the sense of a narrow access to the sea, ceased to exist.

Politburo   A contraction for "Political Bureau of the Communist Party," an elite group within a Communist party organization where ultimate power is concentrated. Practiced in the former Soviet Union and still functioning in the Chinese Communist Party, the Politburo and the even more select Politburo's Standing Committee makes major policy decisions concerning the party and the whole nation. In China, the Politburo usually has two dozen or so members with two or three alternate members; the Standing Committee, the innermost circle of power, consists of about half a dozen people. Both bodies are supposedly elected by the Central Committee of the party.

political asylum   *See* ASYLUM.

political commissar   1. In the former Soviet Union, a civilian assigned to a military unit to ensure that its commanders follow the policies of the government.   2. By analogy, any representation of a central executive assigned to bureaucratic agencies to ensure that new employees and their policies are politically acceptable.

political development   The gradual evolution of a more effective, and presumably more democratic, political system in a state. The end result, especially in the context of DEVELOPING COUNTRIES, is a government better able to mobilize the resources of a state to improve the welfare of the citizens.

political economy   The conjunction of politics and economics; the study of relations between the economy and the state.

political integration   *See* INTEGRATION, POLITICAL.

political risk   In foreign investment, the possibility of loss due to such causes as currency inconvertibility, government action preventing entry of goods, EXPROPRIATION or confiscations, war, and terrorism. This is the chance a company takes by engaging in business in a politically unstable state; the business could be expropriated or social upheavals might make it impossible to operate—employees could even be killed. In response to this problem, political risk insurance does a thriving trade.

political stability   The ability of a POLITICAL SYSTEM to maintain an equilibrium, to retain the support of its citizens for government policies within a stable range, and to avoid radical and sudden changes in the underlying premises of its political and economic systems.

political system   The institutions and structures of a state that allow its citizens to make, implement, and change public policies. A political system essentially consists of those interactions through which values (such as equality and security) are allocated authoritatively for a society. The political system can be thought of as an input-output box, which takes in political demands and supports and puts out public policies, such as laws, court decisions, and regulations. These outputs then return, to influence the system as FEEDBACK.

political warfare   **1.** A competitive election campaign.   **2.** The aggressive use of diplomacy and other political means to gain national objectives; a policy of taking political action against the interests of another state in the expectation that the opposing state eventually will be worn down by the constant demands of internal and international political problems. Political warfare was a major weapon during the COLD WAR.   **3.** A key element in revolutionary warfare that accompanies the military component and that is designed to undermine the LEGITIMACY of the government in power.

politics   **1.** Governance; the means by which the will of a society is derived and implemented; the actions of a government, politician, or political party.   **2.** The pursuit and exercise of political power necessary to make binding policy decisions for a society.   **3.** The policymaking aspect of government, as opposed to its administration.   **4.** The interpersonal negotiations that lead to consensus within, and action by, groups.   **5.** A profession engaged in by those who seek to advance from one political office to another moving toward ever greater responsibility and power.   **6.** According to Ambrose Bierce's *Devil's Dictionary* (1906): "A strife of interests masquerading as a contest of principles. The conduct of public affairs for private advantage."

polity   **1.** An organized political jurisdiction, such as a state.   **2.** The government of a society.   **3.** The CONSTITUTION, written or unwritten, that governs a group.

Pollard, Jonathan (1954–   )   A civilian employee of the U.S. Navy who in 1987 was convicted of spying for Israel and sentenced to life in prison. The "Pollard affair" put severe strains on the U.S.-Israel relationship. It also strained relations between Israel and its traditionally supportive U.S.-Jewish community, many of whom thought it was ill-considered that Israel should recruit a Jewish-American, Pollard, to spy on his own country.

Pol Pot (1928–   )   The name taken by Saloth Sar, prime minister and dictator of Cambodia from 1975 to 1979. As head of the KHMER ROUGE, he renamed the state Kampuchea and attempted to remake it according to his own Communist vision.

In the process between 1 and 3 million of his people were killed. Deposed in 1979 by the invading Vietnamese Army and currently living in hiding, Pol Pot's troops still inspire fear among Cambodians as they continue to conduct guerrilla operations out of refugee camps along the Thai-Cambodian border. In 1991 United Nations–sponsored negotiations led to the establishment of a coalition government that included the Khmer Rouge upon the withdrawal of Vietnam's occupation army. There is great concern by democratic factions that Pol Pot will emerge once again as a problem for any new regime headed by NORODOM SIHANOUK.

polyarchy   **1.** A term (closely related to DEMOCRACY and PLURALISM) that means "government by the many," as opposed to government by a small elite.   **2.** A term used by Seyom Brown in *New Forces, Old Forces and the Future of World Politics* (1988) to describe a complex configuration of world politics in which there are multiple bases of alignment and antagonism and several subsystems, of which the nation-state system is only one.

polycentric   Literally, having many centers. This term—coined by Palmiro Togliatti (1893–1964), the leader of the Italian Communist Party—was used to describe the increasing tendencies toward fragmentation in the Communist bloc in the 1950s and 1960s. The split between Yugoslavia's Tito and the Soviet Union's Stalin in 1948 had suggested that the Communist world was hardly monolithic, but the fragmentation became much more apparent through the 1960s as the SINO-SOVIET SPLIT between Communist China and the Soviet Union widened from ideological bickering to include border clashes.

polycentrism   A situation in which there are many centers of decision and action. Polycentrism is complex and untidy—and contrasts greatly with the neatness of BIPOLARITY. Polycentrism differs from MULTIPOLARITY in that with the latter, there are only a comparatively few major centers of power.

Pompidou, Georges (1911–1974)   The World War II aide to General Charles de Gaulle who, when de Gaulle became president of France, became prime minister (1962–1968). Pompidou played major roles in negotiating an end to the Algerian War of

Independence and in drafting the constitution of the FIFTH REPUBLIC. After succeeding de Gaulle as president in 1969, he ended France's veto of British membership into the EUROPEAN COMMUNITY. Otherwise he continued most of de Gaulle's policies until he died in office.

pool reporter   The journalist who represents all the news media when it is impractical for a large number of individuals to go with a political figure on an airplane, to a meeting, and so on. Pool reporters are then obligated to share their information with their media colleagues.

Pope   The spiritual leader of the Roman Catholic Church. He is also the temporal ruler of Vatican City in Rome, Italy. He is elected after the death of his predecessor by a meeting of the College of Cardinals.

THE POPE'S DIVISIONS

[In 1935 Soviet President Joseph] Stalin and [Prime Minister V. M.] Molotov were, of course, anxious to know above all else what was to be the strength of the French Army on the Western Front; how many divisions? What period of service? After this field had been explored, [French Premier Pierre] Laval said: "Can't you do something to encourage religion and the Catholics in Russia? It would help me so much with the Pope." "Oho!" said Stalin. "The Pope! How many divisions has he got?"

SOURCE: Winston Churchill, *The Second World War: The Gathering Storm* (1948). According to John Colville in *The Fringes of Power* (1985), Churchill responded to Stalin by "replying that the fact they could not be measured in military terms did not mean they did not exist."

This seems to have been a favored phrase of Stalin's. At the Potsdam Conference of July 1945 U.S. Admiral William D. Leahy (in his 1950 memoir, *I Was There*), an advisor to President Harry S Truman, remarked that Stalin's response to pleas from Winston Churchill to consider the rights of Polish Catholics was: "How many divisions has the Pope?" U.S. President Dwight D. Eisenhower is quoted in the *New York Times* (May 10, 1965) as saying: "Communists only respect force. You remember the remark attributed to Stalin at the Yalta Conference when he was told of the importance of the views of Pope Pius XII. 'How many divisions does Pope Pius command?' Stalin asked at the time. That shows us the Communist mentality clearly."

Popular Front   The 1930s coalitions of left-wing and center political parties in France and Spain created to oppose right-wing fascist parties.

Popular Front for the Liberation of Palestine (PFLP)   Created in 1967 by GEORGE HABASH as a Marxist/Leninist Palestinian guerrilla group organized as an ideologically based alternative to AL-FATAH. The PFLP staged one of the most spectacular hijacking incidents ever in 1970, when it directed three jetliners to DAWSON'S FIELD in Jordan, where it blew them up. In 1972 the group organized a JAPANESE RED ARMY attack known as the LOD AIRPORT MASSACRE in Tel Aviv, Israel, in which 27 persons were killed. In 1976 it staged the hijacking of an Air France jetliner that ended with the Israeli raid at ENTEBBE. The PFLP also hijacked a Lufthansa plane in 1977 and directed it to Mogadishu, Somalia. West German commandos then conducted a successful rescue operation. The PFLP is noted for its working relationship with Ilyich Ramirez Sanchez, better known as CARLOS. Opposed to any compromise on the Palestinian issue, the PFLP has criticized the Palestine Liberation Organization leadership for pursuing what it calls "partial" solutions.

Popular Front for the Liberation of Palestine—General Command (PFLP-GC)   A splinter group of the PFLP established in 1968 by Ahmed Jabril (a former Syrian military officer) that is committed to the destruction of Israel and the establishment of an independent Palestinian state in its place. *See also* PALESTINE LIBERATION FRONT.

populism   Mass political movements that started in both Europe and the United States toward the end of the nineteenth century. Populism is known for mobilizing the poor, especially rural people who have suffered from the dislocations of industrialization and urbanization. In this sense, both twentieth-century Italian fascism and German Nazism have their beginnings in populist movements—which, however, came under control of despotic charismatic leaders. But any political movement that has mass support and is generally perceived to be acting in the interests of the people can be called populist.

Portsmouth, Treaty of   The 1905 agreement that ended the RUSSO-JAPANESE WAR. It was signed in Portsmouth, New Hampshire, in the United States, after being brokered by U.S. President Theodore Roosevelt. It signaled that the United States was a major player among the great powers of the world and won Roosevelt the Nobel Peace Prize for 1906.

port visit A docking of a warship in the harbor of a friendly or allied state. This has traditionally been seen as a gesture of goodwill, a symbol of support, and a way of exercising some influence through "showing the flag." In the 1980s, however, port visits by ships of the United States Navy became very controversial in the ANZUS PACT countries of Australia and New Zealand where there was strong antinuclear sentiment, because the United States refused to confirm or deny whether particular ships were nuclear armed.

position paper A formal statement of opinion or of proposed policies on political or social issues; often issued by candidates for public office, public interest groups, unions, and so on.

positivism The belief that INTERNATIONAL LAW is limited to treaties and other binding documents that states have specifically agreed to. Positivism denies that any aspect of international law is to be found in NATURAL LAW.

postinternational politics A term used by JAMES ROSENAU in *Turbulence in World Politics* (1990) to describe the fact that there is an "apparent trend in which more and more of the interactions that sustain world politics unfold without the direct involvement of nations or states." Postinternational "suggests the decline of long-standing patterns without at the same time indicating where the changes may be leading. It suggests flux and transition even as it implies the presence and functioning of stable structures. It allows for chaos even as it hints at coherence."

postmodernism An approach to social theory that is gradually coming into the field of international relations; also known as poststructuralism. The designation "postmodern" is applied to such areas as semiotics, deconstruction, feminist psychoanalytic theory, and intertextualism—all of which are concerned with the way knowledge and meaning are understood. Postmodern theorists share the belief that many so-called facts are really conventions of knowledge, which are supported by particular power structures. Postmodern thinkers argue, for example, that REALISM is simply a particular intellectual construct that restricts the way international politics is studied and understood. A useful collection of essays that develops these themes is edited by James Der Derian and Michael J. Shapiro and entitled *International/Intertextual Relations: Postmodern Readings of World Politics* (1989).

Potsdam Conference The last of the BIG THREE wartime summits, held in the Berlin suburb of Potsdam in July of 1945 ten weeks after Germany's surrender in WORLD WAR II. But the cast of leaders had changed. Joseph Stalin still represented the Soviet Union, but Harry S Truman had replaced Franklin D. Roosevelt as president of the United States, and Clement Attlee replaced Winston Churchill as British prime minister during the conference itself. At Potsdam it was decided to divide Germany into four occupation zones, and begin a DEMONTAGE program, to start a denazification program, to reallocate some German territory to Poland and the Soviet Union, to arrange for REPARATIONS, to resettle millions of German-speaking people from Eastern Europe to Germany, and to set up the International Military Tribunal to provide for war crimes trials. It was here that Truman first told Stalin of the ATOMIC BOMB.

Potsdam Declaration The joint proclamation of the United States, Great Britain, and China issued on July 26, 1945 during the POTSDAM CONFERENCE which stated that now that Germany had been "laid waste . . . the full application of our military power, backed by our resolve, will mean the inevitable and complete destruction of the Japanese armed forces and just as inevitably the utter devastation of the Japanese homeland." It then called "upon the government of Japan to proclaim now the unconditional surrender of all Japanese armed forces, and to provide proper and adequate assurances of their good faith in such action. The alternative for Japan is prompt and utter destruction." Tokyo did not respond, perhaps because the Japanese mistook this threat simply as wartime propaganda.

POW *See* PRISONER OF WAR.

Powell, Colin L. (1937–   )   The career United States Army officer who, after serving as National Security Advisor in the Reagan Administration, was made chairman of the Joint Chiefs of Staff in the Bush Administration in 1989. As chairman Powell was the highest-ranking United States military officer during the Panama intervention and the PERSIAN GULF WAR. Because Powell is an African-American, a gifted speaker, and a victorious general, he is mentioned often as a candidate for various U.S. political offices.

power   1. The ability or the right to exercise authority.   2. A national strength, such as a strong military or healthy economy.   3. Formal responsibility for government decisions. In this context power is value neutral. As playwright George Bernard Shaw wrote in *Major Barbara*, Act 3 (1905): "You cannot have power for good without having power for evil too. Even mother's milk nourishes murderers as well as heroes."   4. A single state; traditionally, a great power has a strong military, a small power docs not.   5. Military forces in general.   6. That which makes one person attractive to others, who hope some perceived influence will rub off. This is what U.S. Secretary of State Henry A. Kissinger meant when he said: "Power is the ultimate aphrodisiac" (*New York Times*, October 28, 1973).   7. That which corrupts when it is unlimited. The most famous statement on this come from Lord Acton (John Dahlberg): "Power tends to corrupt, and absolute power corrupts absolutely. Great men are almost always bad men. . . . There is no worse heresy than that the office sanctifies the holder of it" (letter to Bishop Mandell Creighton, April 5, 1887, reprinted in *Life and Letters of Mandell Creighton*, 1904).   8. That which, according to Chinese leader Mao Zedong, "grows out of the barrel of a gun" (*Quotations from Chairman Mao*, 1966). The power of regimes historically has been a function of their military prowess: their ability to coerce their populations internally and to defend themselves from external threats. In the late twentieth century economic power has taken at least an equal place with military.

Power implies a hierarchy of control of stronger over weaker. John R. P. French and Bertram Raven, in "The Bases of Social Power" (*Studies in Social Power*, ed. Dorwin Cartwright, 1959), suggest that there are five major bases of power: (1) expert power, which is based on the perception that the leader possesses some special knowledge or expertise; (2) referent power, which is based on the fol-

Colin Powell (Department of Defense)

lower's liking, admiring, or identifying with the leader; (3) reward power, which is based on the leader's ability to mediate rewards for the follower; (4) legitimate power, which is based on the follower's perception that the leader has the legitimate right or authority to exercise influence over him or her; and (5) coercive power, which is based on the follower's fear that noncompliance with the leader's wishes will lead to punishment. Subsequent research on these power bases has indicated that the first two are more positively related to subordinate performance and satisfaction than the last three. The word power causes confusion partly because it refers both to capabilities and what is, in effect, influence. In the former sense it refers to physical attributes; in the latter it is about the ability to use those capabilities to make another person or another state take action that would otherwise not be taken. In this second sense, it is relational. Interestingly, in French there are two terms for power: *pouvoir* (power) and *puissance* (influence). Part of the key in conducting successful international relations is to turn one's power into influence.

power, corridors of The official places, the bureaucracy, where political actors make decisions binding on the rest of society. The phrase comes from the title of a 1964 C. P. Snow novel.

power, two faces of The theory that real power is not always overt—that it is frequently covert and exercised in ways that are not readily observable. The other, hidden, face of power is often far more influential than its public face, exemplified by elected officials. The classic analysis of the two faces of power, "neither of which the sociologists see and only one of which the political scientists see," is Peter Bachrach and Morton S. Baratz's article "Two Faces of Power" (*American Political Science Review* 56, December 1962).

power behind the throne 1. Informal rulers; the most influential of a chief executive's advisors: traditionally, those who advised, or dictated to, a king. 2. The spouse of a formal ruler. 3. A POWER BROKER.

power broker 1. A person who has influence over others in power—influence that will be used for a price. The price in this case could be a promise of appointive office, the acceptance of a specific policy, the placement of a favored candidate on a ticket, or cash. 2. Someone who is so trusted by the contesting sides of an issue that he or she can mediate an agreement between them. 3. An *éminence grise*—one who runs government from behind the scenes. *Compare to* HONEST BROKER.

power politics A translation of the German word *Machtpolitik*, referring to an aggressive foreign policy that substitutes threats and the actual use of military power for international law; in short, the notion that might makes right. According to Ely Culbertson's *Must We Fight Russia?* (1946): "Power politics is the diplomatic name for the law of the jungle." *Compare to* REALISM; REALPOLITIK.

power projection *See* FORCE PROJECTION.

Powers, Francis Gary *See* U-2 INCIDENT.

powers that be People who must be obeyed; those who control a state, a company, or any other institution. This expression implies that there are always individuals, forces, or groups that exercise control, regardless of the legal or constitutional basis of formally established power. Historian David Halberstam used the phrase to describe the masters of U.S. newspaper empires in *The Powers That Be* (1979). But it comes from the Bible (Romans 13:1): "Let every soul be subject unto the higher powers. For there is no power but of God: the powers that be are ordained by God."

PQLI *See* PHYSICAL QUALITY OF LIFE INDEX.

Prague Spring The democratic reforms begun in Czechoslovakia following the election of ALEXANDER DUBCEK as the first secretary of the Communist Party of Czechoslovakia in January 1968. Dubcek's reform program, which was referred to as "socialism with a human face," initiated the momentum for radical changes within Czechoslovakia. Dubcek permitted the kind of intellectual freedom and political discussion that was still suppressed in the Soviet Union. But the Soviet government became suspicious that these changes would lead to Czechoslovakia's withdrawal from the WAR-

SAW PACT and thus invaded on August 20, 1968. The invasion caused the reforms to be terminated and Dubcek to be replaced with the authoritarian leadership of GUSTAV HUSAK, based on the Soviet model, that lasted for 20 more years—until the VELVET REVOLUTION of 1989. *See also* CZECHOSLOVAKIAN INVASION.

Pravda   Russian for "truth"; the name of the official newspaper of the Communist Party of the Soviet Union. Since the RUSSIAN REVOLUTION OF 1917 it was known for its censored news and sanitized reporting. It ceased publication in early 1992.

Prebisch Report   The 1964 report of the secretary-general of the UNITED NATIONS CONFERENCE ON TRADE AND DEVELOPMENT (UNCTAD), Argentinean economist Raul Prebisch (1901–1986), entitled *Towards a New Trade Policy for Development.* It was considered an attack on orthodox trade policy and became the basic policy document of the GROUP OF 77 at UNCTAD I. According to Prebisch's analysis, the economies of the developing countries can develop properly only if export earnings can be increased, and this can happen only if international measures are taken in the areas of international commodity agreements, compensatory finance, and tariff preferences. The measures are intended to replace FREE TRADE with FAIR TRADE.

precedence   1. The right to be first in formal ceremonies; the order observed by heads of state and diplomats of differing ranks. It was first agreed at the 1815 Congress of Vienna that diplomats in each class would be ranked according to their date of arrival at their post. This subsequently has been codified into international law by Articles 16 and 17 of the 1969 Vienna Convention on Diplomatic Relations.

precursor chemicals   1. Those chemical materials necessary for the development of chemical weapons.   2. Those chemical materials necessary for the processing of the drug cocaine. The waste products from this process have caused major environmental problems in states in which there is extensive cocaine processing.

preemption   *See* WAR, PREEMPTIVE.

preference   More favorable than usual TARIFF treatment granted by one state to another (or to a group of states). For example, members of the Organization for Economic Cooperation and Development grant nonreciprocal preferences in many categories of products from developing countries. *Compare to* REVERSE PREFERENCE.

premature antifascists   Those international volunteers who fought with the republican side against the fascists during the SPANISH CIVIL WAR. They were "premature" because they were against the fascists before World War II began—before it was more fashionable and politic to be so.

premier   *See* PRIME MINISTER.

preparedness   A military posture of being ready for war. This has been a continual theme in world history. Indeed the most famous sentiment on preparedness is usually credited to Vegetius, the fourth-century Roman military analyst: "Let him who desires peace, prepare for war" (*De Re Militari,* 378 A.D.). This idea has been echoed by political leaders ever since. U.S. President George Washington stated in his first annual message to Congress, on January 8, 1790: "To be prepared for war is one of the most effectual means of preserving peace." U.S. President Theodore Roosevelt maintained in a speech in New York City on November 11, 1902: "We need to keep in a condition of preparedness, especially as regards our navy, not because we want war, but because we desire to stand with those whose plea for peace is listened to with respectful attention." Chinese leader Mao Zedong said on June 15, 1949, shortly after his Communist forces prevailed over the Nationalists in the Chinese Civil War: "Just because we have won victory, we must never relax our vigilance against the frenzied plots for revenge by the imperialists and their running dogs" (*Quotations from Chairman Mao,* 1966). The issue of preparedness has taken on new dimensions as a result of the end of the Cold War; the problem lies in deciding what kinds of contingencies or threats the state should be prepared to meet and the level of preparedness that is required. This latter issue is multifaceted and encompasses the need to maintain strategic forces at a reasonable level of alert, the ability to deploy military forces rapidly and effectively in a crisis, the ability to reconstitute high levels of forces in the event of a major threat to security, and the capacity to provide the equipment and weapons systems that are necessary through the maintenance of an effective defense industrial base.

ADMIRAL FISHER ON PREPAREDNESS

My sole object is peace. . . . If you rub it in both at home and abroad that you are ready for instant war with every unit of your strength in the first line, and intend to be first in and hit your enemy in the belly and kick him when he is down, and boil your prisoners in oil (if you take any!), and torture his women and children, then people will keep clear of you.

SOURCE: Admiral Sir John Fisher (1841–1920) quoted in Ruddock F. Mackay, *Fisher at Kilverstone* (1973).

---

presidencies, two   American political scientist Aaron Wildavsky's (1930–   ) division of U.S. presidential powers into two separate spheres of influence: foreign policy and domestic policy. Wildavsky asserted that presidential leadership in foreign policy would generally find greater public support than leadership in domestic matters. His analysis, which first appeared in "The Two Presidencies" (*Trans-Action*, December 1966), has been tested by many scholars using different methods and has always held up. This means that even if a U.S. president is weak in terms of achieving his or her domestic agenda, formal and informal presidential powers regarding foreign policy matters are not likely to be impaired.

presidency, imperial   A phrase that suggests that the president of the United States has become the head of an international empire as well as the head of a domestic political state. It implies that the presidency has grown too powerful and has assumed more authority than is justified by its limited constitutional powers. The phrase is usually credited to the 1973 book of the same title by Arthur Schlesinger, Jr., which came out just as the Watergate scandal broke and all of the excesses of the Nixon Administration were bared to the world. While Schlesinger's phrase was a convenient way to summarize Nixon's corruption of the presidential office, the book, written before the scandal really broke, was not an attack on

Nixon but rather an analysis of the gradual enhancement of presidential powers in modern times. Schlesinger wrote: "The American democracy must discover a middle ground between making the President a czar and making him a puppet. The problem is to devise means of reconciling a strong and purposeful Presidency with equally strong and purposeful forms of democratic control. Or, to put it succinctly, we need a strong Presidency—but a strong Presidency *within the Constitution.*"

president   1. The head of state in a republic. The powers of presidents vary greatly. The presidents of France and the United States, because they are also the head of the government, have great powers. In contrast, most other presidents, such as those in Germany and Israel, have mainly ceremonial and informal authority.   2. An individual appointed or elected to preside over a formal assembly.   3. A chief executive officer of a corporation, board of trustees, university, or other institution.

TWENTIETH-CENTURY U.S. PRESIDENTS*

Name	Term of Office
Theodore Roosevelt	1901–1909
William Howard Taft	1909–1913
Woodrow Wilson	1913–1921
Warren G. Harding	1921–1923
Calvin Coolidge	1923–1929
Herbert Hoover	1929–1933
Franklin D. Roosevelt	1933–1945
Harry S Truman	1945–1953
Dwight D. Eisenhower	1953–1961
John F. Kennedy	1961–1963
Lyndon B. Johnson	1963–1969
Richard M. Nixon	1969–1974
Gerald R. Ford	1974–1977
Jimmy Carter	1977–1981
Ronald Reagan	1981–1989
George Bush	1989–1993
William J. Clinton	1993–

*See individual entries for each.

---

president for life   A DICTATOR. No self-respecting republic would ever tolerate this favored title of THIRD WORLD despots.

Presidential Directive 59 (PD–59) The nuclear strategy adopted by the Carter Administration in the summer of 1980, after a thorough review of existing nuclear targeting policy. Known as the COUNTERVAILING STRATEGY, it was embodied in Presidential Directive 59 (PD-59) and in Nuclear Weapons Employment Policy 1980 (NUWEP-80). The underlying logic for the new strategy was enunciated by Walter Slocombe, then deputy under secretary for defense, who argued that it was crucial, in an era of strategic parity, to ensure that "the Soviet Union, applying its own standards and models, would recognize that no plausible outcome of aggression would represent victory on any plausible definition of victory." Thus "the United States must have countervailing strategic options such that, at a variety of levels of exchange, aggression would either be defeated or would result in unacceptable costs that exceed gains" (*International Security,* Spring 1981). In large part this represented the same kind of logic that had led to the earlier emphasis that the Nixon Administration had placed on ESSENTIAL EQUIVALENCE. Indeed, in many respects the countervailing strategy was a refinement of the SCHLESINGER DOCTRINE that had been developed by President Richard M. Nixon's Secretary of Defense, James Schlesinger. Yet there also were important differences, especially in targeting priorities. The countervailing strategy gave a lower priority to Soviet recovery assets than Schlesinger had done, concentrating instead on "the things the Soviets value most—political and military leadership and control, military forces both nuclear and conventional, and the economic and industrial capacity to sustain military operations." A key theme of PD-59 was that a nuclear war between the superpowers might be protracted. Consequently, a program was initiated to improve the COMMAND, CONTROL AND COMMUNICATIONS (C3) capacity of the United States in ways designed to enable it to fight a nuclear war over an extended period. The Reagan Administration took this strategy a stage further and went from countervailing to PREVAILING.

presidential power 1. Executive power. For example, Article II of the U.S. Constitution vests the executive power in the president. There is considerable dispute over whether this power consists solely of those presidential powers listed in the Constitution, or whether it includes also those powers that are only implied. 2. Persuasion. Richard E. Neustadt's *Presidential Power* (1960) asserts that a president's real powers are informal, that presidential power is essentially the power to persuade. Neustadt quotes President Harry S Truman contemplating General of the Army Dwight D. Eisenhower becoming president: "He'll sit here, and he'll say, 'Do this! Do that!' *And nothing will happen.* Poor Ike—it won't be a bit like the Army. He'll find it very frustrating."

pretender 1. A person who claims to be the ruler of a state instead of another person presently occupying the throne in question. 2. A person who claims to be the rightful monarch of a state that often, by revolution, has abolished the monarchy. Many of the states of Eastern Europe, such as Bulgaria, Romania, and Russia, have pretenders, direct descendants of previous monarchs, living in exile and just waiting to be called back to power.

pre-theory A term used by JAMES ROSENAU in *The Scientific Study of Foreign Policy* (1971) to describe the process of preliminary identification of variables that he hoped would thereby be made comparable and subsequently would be developed into a theory of foreign policy. Rosenau identified five main variables that have an impact on foreign policy behavior: individual, role, governmental, societal, and systemic. He then assessed their relative impact or ranking in various types of societies based on the distinctions between large and small countries, developed and underdeveloped economies, open and closed political systems, penetrated and nonpenetrated systems, and in different issue areas.

prevailing strategy Plans developed by the Reagan Administration in relation to nuclear war. Whereas the Jimmy Carter Administration's COUNTERVAILING STRATEGY had emphasized the need to convince the Soviet leadership that it could not win a nuclear war, the Reagan Administration went a major step further and suggested that it was necessary for the United States to be able to prevail in a nuclear war. Although it denied that this meant winning, the implication was that the United States should ensure that it came out of any nuclear war in a better state and with more postwar power than the Soviet Union. In part, of course, the prevailing doctrine was enunciated to justify the Reagan defense buildup. Furthermore, Reagan's STRATEGIC DEFENSE INITIATIVE was fully in accord with this as it was intended to limit damage to the United States. The goal of prevailing strategy was established in National Security Decision Directive 13 and in Nuclear Weapons Employment Policy-82. The concept was very controversial. Not only was it widely seen as aggressive in character, but even senior military officers believed that it was an unobtainable goal, and one that would divert resources from more important military roles and functions.

Prevention of Nuclear War Agreement   The 1973 agreement between the United States and the Soviet Union in which they established procedures to help contain situations that might increase tensions and thereby the risk of nuclear war. This started as a Soviet effort to get the United States to agree to a NO FIRST USE of nuclear weapons declaration but, with British assistance, was rechanneled into a rather different agreement by the United States.

prime minister   The head of a government in a PARLIAMENTARY SYSTEM elected by the party with a majority of seats (or a coalition of parties). As such he or she is both the leader of the legislature and the chief executive who administers the government's various offices and agencies. The word *premier* is often used interchangeably with prime minister.

primogeniture   *See* DYNASTY.

Princip, Gavrilo (1894–1918)   The assassin of Archduke FRANZ FERDINAND of Austria and his wife, Countess Sophie. Princip, a Bosnian, was the only successful marksman in the group of five young nationalist members of "Young Serbia" that attacked the royal motorcade on June 28, 1914. All five were arrested and found guilty in an Austrian court but were spared execution because of their ages. Princip died of tuberculosis while in prison.

prisoners' dilemma   *See* GAME THEORY.

BRITISH PRIME MINISTERS*	
Name	*Term of Office*
Arthur James Balfour	1902–1905
Henry Campbell-Bannerman	1905–1908
Herbert Henry Asquith	1908–1916
David Lloyd George	1916–1922
Andrew Bonar Law	1922–1923
Stanley Baldwin	1923–1924
James Ramsay MacDonald	1924
Stanley Baldwin	1924–1929
James Ramsay MacDonald	1929–1935
Stanley Baldwin	1935–1937
Arthur Neville Chamberlain	1937–1940
Winston Churchill	1940–1945
Clement Richard Attlee	1945–1951
Winston Churchill	1951–1955
Anthony Eden	1955–1957
Harold Macmillan	1957–1963
Alec Douglas-Home	1963–1964
Harold Wilson	1964–1970
Edward Heath	1970–1974
Harold Wilson	1974–1976
James Callaghan	1976–1979
Margaret Thatcher	1979–1990
John Major	1990–

*See individual entries for each.

prisoner of war (POW)   A person who has been captured as a result of hostilities between states. There have been efforts to ensure that the treatment of these prisoners is regulated, and a historical trend has been discerned in the normal treatment of POWs from execution through enslavement, to ransom and gradually to regularized exchanges. This development of a more humanitarian approach was embodied in a series of international conventions formulated by successive conferences in Brussels, Belgium (1874); The Hague, the Netherlands (1899 and 1907); Copenhagen, Denmark (1917); and Geneva, Switzerland (1929 and 1949). As a result of these conventions, prisoners were defined as in the power of governments rather than individual captors, governments were responsible for the humane treatment of prisoners who also were to be "insulated" from participation in the war. In return, prisoners were to provide identification of themselves and their rank. The usual practice is that at the end of a war prisoners are repatriated. Since the end of the Vietnam War, however, there have been rumors that Vietnam was still holding U.S. prisoners of war, and the unwillingness of Hanoi to provide details of U.S. soldiers who were missing in action or prisoners of war became a major irritant in Vietnam's relations with the United States.

private international law See INTERNATIONAL LAW, PRIVATE.

private visit See STATE VISIT.

privileged sanctuary A place of safety from which one can launch military attacks but into which enemy forces cannot come. For example, during the Korean War the Chinese forces fighting as "volunteers" on behalf of North Korea had a privileged sanctuary just over the Chinese border. And during the Vietnam War, the North Vietnamese forces used Cambodia as a privileged sanctuary from which to stage attacks on South Vietnam. (This is why U.S. President Richard Nixon authorized the CAMBODIAN INCURSION.)

THE FIRST PRIVILEGED SANCTUARY

United Nations forces are now being attacked from the safety of a privileged sanctuary. Planes operating from bases in China cross over into Korea to attack United Nations ground and air forces and then flee back across the border. . . . The pretext which the Chinese Communists advance for taking offensive action against United Nations forces in Korea from behind the protection afforded by the Sino-Korean border is their professed belief that these forces intend to carry hostilities across the frontier into Chinese territory. The resolutions and every other action taken by the United Nations demonstrate beyond any doubt that no such intention has ever been entertained.

SOURCE: President Harry S Truman, press release, November 16, 1950. According to Frazier Hunt's *The Untold Story of Douglas MacArthur* (1954), this "was the first time that the phrase 'privileged sanctuary' had been used in a public document."

---

procès-verbal 1. French term meaning "verbal process," the official minutes of a meeting at an international conference. 2. The record of an agreement reached by empowered diplomatic agents. This is a kind of PROTOCOL and is drawn up as a formal document and signed by the parties.

proconsul 1. A governor of an ancient Roman province. 2. The highest administrator of a colonial or occupying power.

Profumo affair The 1963 scandal concerning British War Minister John Profumo (1915–   ), who was sharing a prostitute with a naval attaché of the Soviet embassy. This did not cause any compromise to national security, but when the liaison came to light Profumo was asked about it in the House of Commons. On March 23, 1963, he told the House that while he was acquainted with Christine Keeler, the woman in question, no impropriety had occurred. The scandal was less about sex than the fact that Profumo had lied to the House of Commons. Profumo finally admitted to the House on June 4, 1963, that he had lied. He thereupon resigned as war minister and from Parliament. Prime Minister HAROLD MACMILLAN was politically weakened by this scandal, and it was a contributing factor in his resignation shortly thereafter.

proletariat The poorest of the poor in ancient Rome. Karl Marx, in the nineteenth century, used it to refer to the working class in general. Marx wrote in the *Communist Manifesto* (1848): "Let the ruling classes tremble at a communist revolution. The proletarians have nothing to lose but their chains. They have a world to win. Working men of all countries, unite!" Because of the word's association with MARXISM, it should not be used to refer simply to workers, but only to "oppressed" workers. *Compare to* BOURGEOIS.

proliferation The spread of weapons to countries that did not previously possess them. Traditionally the word has been associated with nuclear weapons, hence the term nuclear proliferation; but it has increasingly been used to refer to the spread of ballistic missile technology and chemical weapons as well. A distinction is sometimes made between vertical and horizontal nuclear weapons proliferation. The former term refers to increases in existing nuclear arsenals; the latter refers to the acquisition of nuclear weapons by states that did not previously have them. There is considerable argument over the effects of nuclear proliferation. One school of thought contends that proliferation will increase stability; that more may be better because of the DETERRENT EFFECT of nuclear weapons. But the more usual view is that proliferation to states involved in regional conflicts and to states that do not have the necessary economic and technological means to ensure the safety of such weapons is far from likely to enhance stability. *See also* NONPROLIFERATION.

proliferation, managed An approach to nuclear weapons PROLIFERATION that starts from the assumption that little or nothing can be done to stop the further spread of nuclear weapons and therefore considers ways its more dangerous consequences might be mitigated. Among options to be considered as part of the management process is that major nuclear powers might help smaller powers develop such things as PERMISSIVE ACTIONS LINKS that would reduce the chances of an unauthorized or accidental use of nuclear weapons. The difficulty with this idea is that it undermines the continued efforts to prevent further proliferation, not least because any assistance to new nuclear powers could be interpreted all too easily as a reward rather than as simply a stabilizing mechanism.

pro memoria Latin meaning "for memory"; the formal record of a conversation between a foreign minister (or agent) and the head of a diplomatic mission (or agent). This is usually written in the third person but not signed, only initialed.

pronunciamiento Spanish for "proclamation"; a manifesto or edict typically issued by a newly installed revolutionary government in Latin America.

propaganda **1.** A government's mass dissemination of true information about its policies and the policies of its adversaries. **2.** A government's dissemination of similar information that is untruthful, or information that purports to come from a source other than the true one (sometimes called *black propaganda*). *White propaganda* is issued by a government and comes from identified sources; *gray propaganda* does not. Propaganda has a long and respectable history. Genghis Kahn (1162–1227),

for example, used exaggerated rumors of the strength of his army to terrorize populations and leaders into surrender. The term itself stems from the Congregation of Propaganda set up by the Roman Catholic Church in 1622 to propagate its views and to refute those of Protestants and heretics. The growth of democracy and mass political awareness presented new possibilities for propaganda. So too has the development of the mass media, which all governments use to influence their publics. Ever since World War II, when the German Ministry of Propaganda under JOSEPH GOEBBELS broadcast one lie after another, the term has taken on a sinister connotation. Goebbels advised others to "Think of the press as a great keyboard on which the government can play" (*Time,* March 27, 1933). Propaganda became so associated with the Nazis that Harrison E. Salisbury, writing of the period immediately following the United States' entry into the war in *A Journey for Our Times* (1983), said: "It is almost impossible to locate an offensive-minded, realistic, hard-boiled thinker in the [U.S.] army high command. To a suggestion that propaganda might be utilized as a military weapon, they throw up their arms in horror, exclaiming: 'Of course, we wouldn't think of using a Nazi method!' " **3.** The manipulation of people's beliefs, values, and behavior by using symbols (such as flags, music, or oratory) and other psychological tools. J. B. Priestley wrote in *Outcries and Asides* (1974), "Almost all propaganda is designed to create fear. Heads of governments and other officials know that a frightened people is easier to govern, will forfeit rights it would otherwise defend, is less likely to demand a better life, and will agree to millions and millions being spent on 'Defense.' " **4.** According to Sir Ian Hamilton, *The Soul and Body of an Army* (1921), making the "enemy appear so great a monster that he forfeits the rights of a human being." This makes it emotionally easier to kill the enemy. Hamilton further observes that since the enemy cannot bring a libel action, "there is no need to stick at trifles."

proportionality *See* JUST WAR THEORY.

prorogation **1.** A mutually agreed upon extension of time on the expiration date of an international agreement. **2.** Any extension of a deadline for an adjournment, a debate, and so on.

protecting power A neutral state (or an international organization such as the Red Cross) that agrees to look after the interests of a state after it has severed diplomatic relations with another state. Such interests include looking after the physical grounds and office of the former embassy and inspecting or taking custody of prisoners of war.

protectionism Legislatively influencing the prices of foreign goods on domestic markets; a government policy of high tariffs or low import quotas to protect domestic industries. Protectionism is the opposite of a FREE TRADE policy. Protectionist legislation is almost invariably proposed by members of a legislature from districts whose industries are adversely affected by foreign imports. Laid-off factory workers do not want to be told about the theoretical benefits of free trade; they want protectionist legislation that would put import duties on the foreign-made products that have cost them their jobs. *Compare to* MERCANTILISM.

protectorate The status of a small state or territory that is under the protection of a more powerful state. Protectorates were common during the period of COLONIALISM. An example of a continuing formal protectorate is Andorra in the Pyrenees Mountains, which is a joint protectorate of France and Spain. An example of an informal protectorate is Syria's domination of Lebanon.

protest A diplomat's formal objection to the actions of a state that are harmful to the protesting state or world peace in general.

protocol 1. The internationally accepted practices of diplomatic courtesy that have evolved over time; codes prescribing strict adherence to set etiquette, precedence, and procedure between diplomats and among military services. 2. A supplement to an international agreement; an annex to a treaty. 3. An early draft of a treaty. 4. The conventions of computer software that allow different parts of a computer system and different computer systems to communicate. 5. The records or minutes of a diplomatic meeting.

protocol, chief of The foreign ministry officer who is the in-house expert on the rules of diplomacy and ceremony.

protracted conflict 1. An inter- or intranational struggle that lasts for a long time and in which there are periodic outbreaks of full-scale war, as with the Arab-Israeli conflict. 2. A strategy related to guerrilla war, especially in Asia, where revolutionary forces have clearly believed that if they could avoid losing militarily they would win politically by outlasting any counterinsurgency forces, especially where these were provided by an outside power. The Vietnam War is an example of this strategy.

Provisional Irish Republican Army (PIRA) The Irish Catholic terrorist organization that formed in 1969 when the dormant IRISH REPUBLICAN ARMY (IRA) split into two wings, the Official and the Provisional. Initially both wings were aggressively militant, but in 1972 the Officials renounced terrorism. Most PIRA adherents, particularly in the rural areas, are traditional Irish nationalists ("Republicans"), as are older veterans of the movement. However, a group of younger leaders, primarily from NORTHERN IRELAND, profess radical leftist tendencies and now dominate the more traditional and conservative Republicans. PIRA terrorism is designed to move the people of Northern Ireland and Great Britain to pressure the British government to withdraw from Northern Ireland and let the Catholic and Protestant Irish settle the conflict without British interference. By using violence, the Provos, as they are informally called, also hope to focus worldwide attention on the struggle against British "oppression" and thereby generate broader international pressure on the British government. From the inception of the PIRA, the group has focused its energy on creating casualties. The more than 1,000 who have died at their hands are grim testimony to the PIRA's determination to "wash the British out of Ireland on a wave of blood." Favored PIRA targets include the British Army, Ulster security forces, prison and judicial officials, and Loyalist political party members. Most attacks have occurred in Northern Ireland, but occasionally actions have been carried out in the Republic of Ireland, Great Britain, and other West European nations.

provocation 1. An unplanned international incident that exacerbates an already tense diplomatic situation. 2. A deliberately planned international incident specifically designed to trigger a dispute or cause a war. For example, on the eve of the German 1939 invasion of Poland that started World War II, the Nazis staged a phony incident suggesting that Polish soldiers were attacking Germany.

Provos   *See* PROVISIONAL IRISH REPUBLICAN ARMY.

proximity talks   A process that has mediating diplomats travel between the delegations of differing parties located in nearby hotel or conference rooms. This is used when the parties to an issue are unwilling or unable to talk to each other directly. *Compare to* DIPLOMACY, SHUTTLE.

proxy   **1.** A person who acts for another in a formal proceeding.   **2.** A political candidate who represents not him- or herself but another candidate. For example, a military junta might select a civilian politician to front for it in a presidential election, or a governor's wife might run for his office if he is constitutionally ineligible to succeed himself.   **3.** A state, usually small, that acts on behalf of another state, usually much larger. Actions taken by proxies are less threatening than actions taken by the great power itself and therefore are less likely to be challenged. For example, during the 1970s Cuba functioned as the Soviet Union's proxy in Africa by sending troops to Angola.

proxy war   An armed conflict in which great powers are involved on differing sides as suppliers, supporters, and advisors to smaller states that are the actual combatants. Many of the Arab-Israeli wars of the last several decades have been classified as proxy wars because the United States was supporting and supplying Israel while the Soviet Union was doing the same for the Arab nations. Proxy wars may have had one beneficial side effect. According to Abba Eban in his book *The New Diplomacy* (1983): "A strong case can even be made for the proposition that peace in the northern industrial sector has been achieved by the export of limited wars to areas in which vital superpower interests have not been vitally engaged."

psychological environment   *See* OPERATIONAL ENVIRONMENT.

public good   A thing or service that which, if made available, benefits all the members of a group and not simply those who have contributed toward its production or helped to pay for it. Security, for example, is a public or *collective* good. This issue comes up in the context of an alliance like the North Atlantic Treaty Organization where the United States is the main provider of security and where other states consume more of it than they produce. This is why there are arguments over BURDEN-SHARING. In a situation of power asymmetry in an alliance and in which it is in the preponderant power's own interest to provide for security, the incentive for others to make what would be only marginal contributions is very low. This leads to the problem of the FREE RIDER. *Compare to* COMMON GOOD.

public opinion   **1.** The total of the individual feelings of a political society on a given issue; a force of such great intangible power that it sets informal limits on what a government can do.   **2.** The attitudes of an ill-informed public manipulated by the mass media.   **3.** Elite opinion. As George F. Kennan wrote in *American Diplomacy, 1900–1950* (1951), "What purports to be public opinion in most countries that consider themselves to have popular government is often not really the consensus of the feelings of the mass of the people at all but rather the expression of the interests of special highly vocal minorities—politicians, commentators, and publicity-seekers of all sorts: people who live by their ability to draw attention to themselves and die, like fish out of water, if they are compelled to remain silent." Public opinion in relation to foreign policy may be generally divided into the mass public, which is basically ignorant of foreign policy issues and uninterested in them, and the attentive public, which does have a sustained interest and some structured knowledge. There are many questions about the impact of public opinion on foreign policy, or what is sometimes termed the opinion policy relationship. Bernard Cohen argued in *The Public's Impact on Foreign Policy* (1973) that most officials define as public opinion the opinions of their colleagues, family, and friends. This suggests that for career officials, as opposed to elected politicians, mass public opinion is irrelevant on most issues. For the politician in a democratic society, of course, public opinion tends to have more impact as it is crucial to reelection. Yet even here it is clear that public opinion is influenced more by policymakers than policymakers are influenced by public opinion. It is the elite and the policymakers who provide the cues, who define issues in a particular way, and who provide both the information and the judgments that influence the public debate. This is not to deny that when it becomes aroused, even the mass public can have an impact—although it tends to do so by establishing constraints through its "moods," as described by theorist GABRIEL ALMOND.

Public Without Violence   *See* VELVET REVOLUTION.

Pueblo **incident**   The 1968 seizure of the USS *Pueblo,* a U.S. naval electronic intelligence-gathering ship by North Korean ships while it was in international waters off the Korean coast. After 11 months of imprisonment and torture, 82 surviving crew members were released; but only after a U.S. representative signed a document admitting that the *Pueblo* had been engaged in espionage in North Korean territorial waters. The document was signed but then repudiated as soon as the crew was free. Nevertheless, the ship was confiscated by North Korea. Lyndon B. Johnson, president of the United States during the incident, said in his memoirs, *The Vantage Point* (1971), that the *Pueblo* seizure was probably a Communist feint undertaken to increase tensions so that South Korea would bring back home some of the troops it had sent to South Vietnam.

Puerto Rican terrorists   Separatists who seek independence for the Caribbean island U.S. Commonwealth of Puerto Rico, the most violent domestic U.S. terrorist movement. Since 1898, when the United States acquired the island of Puerto Rico as a result of the Spanish-American War, there has been violence directed against the U.S. government and the private sector on the island, and against private corporations and other targets on the U.S. mainland. In the 1980s more than a third of terrorist incidents perpetrated in the United States and its territories were committed by Puerto Rican separatists. A variety of clandestine Puerto Rican–based groups have been waging this intermittent armed struggle for independence from the United States. The largest of these groups is Los MACHETEROS. Others include the *Organizacion de Voluntarios Para la Revolusion Puertorriqueña* (Organization of Volunteers for the Puerto Rican Revolution) and the *Comandos Armados de Liberacion* (Armed Liberation Commandos). On the U.S. mainland, the *Fuerzas Armadas de Liberacion Nacional Puertorriqueña* (Puerto Rican Armed Forces of National Liberation), known as the FALN, has been the most active and has been responsible for more than 150 acts of violence since the group first emerged in 1974.

Pugwash Conferences   COLD WAR–era meetings of scientists of differing political opinions in a cordial atmosphere where it was hoped that the scientific spirit would help them find a greater degree of agreement than their politicians had found possible. First held in 1957 in Pugwash, Nova Scotia, Canada, later meetings, although held elsewhere around the world, kept the name of the first site. Pugwash Conferences, which were closed to the press and the public, served as a forum for exchanges of views between East and West. They were particularly useful during times when relations between the United States and the Soviet Union were so strained that formal dialogue had been broken off. Although the end of the Cold War has diminished the importance of the Pugwash Conferences, it is possible that such gatherings will continue, although with a broader range of topics, such as environmental degradation.

punitive strategy   *See* WAR, PUNITIVE.

punitive war   *See* WAR, PUNITIVE.

Punta del Este Charter   *See* ALLIANCE FOR PROGRESS.

puppet state   **1.** A state whose basic policies are decided by another state. The modern use of the term dates from World War II, when the Germans established what the Allies called puppet governments in the states they conquered.   **2.** In the perception of a great power, any small state aligned with an opposing great power.

purge   To clean out or remove something. In politics this cleaning out usually refers to one's political rivals within one's own party. Thus when a group gains control of a political party, it sometimes purges (gets rid of) its rivals. In totalitarian states purges often have deadly implications. For example, JOSEPH STALIN periodically purged (meaning

murdered or imprisoned) those members of the COMMUNIST PARTY OF THE SOVIET UNION who seemed to question or oppose his power or policies. *See* GREAT PURGE.

putsch   The German word for a sudden revolt or attempt to overthrow a government. The difference between a putsch and a COUP D'ÉTAT is that the latter is undertaken by people already in government while the former is undertaken by outsiders. The most famous failed putsch is Adolf Hitler's BEER HALL PUTSCH.

puzzle palace   **1.** A military headquarters, such as the United States' Pentagon.   **2.** In the United States, the National Security Agency, because its primary mission is code breaking.   **3.** A confusing or complicated bureaucracy. U.S. President Ronald Reagan stated in a speech to the Iowa legislature in Des Moines on February 9, 1982, that: "If we do nothing else in this Administration we're going to convince that city that the power, the money and the responsibility of this country begin and end with the people, and not in some puzzle palace on the Potomac."

Pyrrhic victory   **1.** A military victory that leads to a defeat later on. In 280 B.C. Pyrrhus, king of Epirus, lost 15,000 men winning a battle over the Romans. According to Plutarch's *The Lives* (A.D. 106), as Pyrrhus was being congratulated, he said: "If we are victorious in one more battle with the Romans, we shall be utterly ruined."   **2.** An apparent victory that is not what it seems.

Q

Qaddafi, Muammar al- (1942–   )   The head of state of Libya who has been one of the foremost proponents of state-sponsored international TERRORISM. As an army colonel he came to power in a bloodless military coup in 1969 while the weak King IDRIS I was vacationing in Turkey. Qaddafi's early years of rule were characterized by an emphasis on Islamic law and a wave of revolutionary POPULISM. His government was looked upon favorably by the United States and most Western nations because he initially assumed a vocal anti-Communist stance and kept oil exports high. After the Arab OIL EMBARGO of 1973, which vastly increased Libya's oil revenues, Qaddafi started buying significant quantities of arms from the Soviet Union. Qaddafi is thought to have been the financier of many BLACK SEPTEMBER operations, including the 1972 MUNICH MASSACRE and the August 5, 1973, killing of five TWA passengers in the terminal at Athens airport. On December 17, 1973, two Arab terrorists under Qaddafi's sponsorship attacked a U.S. airliner at Rome airport, leaving 33 persons dead. Qaddafi gave his support to the December 1975 OPEC SIEGE. In 1975 the colonel severed ties with YASIR ARAFAT and the Palestine Liberation Organization. He has been a generous sponsor to the more radical Palestinian organizations such as the POPULAR FRONT FOR THE LIBERATION OF PALESTINE. In 1985 the U.S. government imposed sanctions against Libya, accusing Qaddafi of complicity with the Abu Nidal organization in the Vienna airport attack on December 27, 1985, in which two people were killed, and the Rome airport attack on the same day that left 15 dead. Libya was again implicated in state-sponsored terrorism in connection with the April 5, 1986, bombing of LA BELLE DISCO in West Germany. Qaddafi has denied any responsibility for these attacks. Nonetheless, the U.S. took military action against Libya in April 1986, attacking the cities of Tripoli and Benghazi and destroying Libyan ships in the Gulf of Sidre. Reports said that Qaddafi narrowly escaped death when U.S. pilots targeted his quarters; his four-year-old adopted daughter died in the attack. Since that time Qaddafi has cooled his direct involvement in international terrorism, except for the alleged involvement of Libyan agents in the bombing of PAN AM FLIGHT 103.

Quadragesimo Anno   The 1931 papal encyclical whose title literally means "Forty Years Having Passed" (that is, since the issuance of *RERUM NOVARUM*). This encyclical was written two years into the Great Depression, when the Roman Catholic Church was struggling with Italian dictator BENITO MUSSOLINI over the subject of Catholic social action. It sought to bring the central principles of *Rerum Novarum* up to date. It condemned a heartless and exploitative capitalist order, supported state intervention to correct abuses, and saw labor unions as necessary for mutual protection and improvement. In proposing a "reconstructing [of] the social order," it offered a Catholic third way between collectivism and radical individualism. It emphasized intermediate groups in society and developed two ideas: the principle of subsidiarity, which recognizes the priority of the person; and the notion of solidatism (or corporatism), which rejects both traditional liberalism and socialism.

Quadripartite Agreement on Berlin   *See* BERLIN, TREATY OF.

Quai d'Orsay The wharf on the south bank of the Seine River in Paris, France, on which the French Ministry of Foreign Affairs is located. The ministry itself is often referred to as the Quai d'Orsay.

Quakers, the This "Religious Society of Friends" was awarded the 1947 Nobel Peace Prize for relief and rehabilitation work for victims of war. The Quakers' two major relief organizations are the Friends Service Council headquartered in London, England, and the American Friends Service Committee headquartered in Philadelphia, U.S.A.

quantitative restrictions (QRs) Explicit limits, usually based on volume, on the amount of a specified commodity that may be imported into a country, sometimes also indicating the amounts that may be imported from each supplying country. Compared to TARIFFS, the protection afforded by QRs tends to be more predictable, being less affected by changes in competitive factors. QUOTAS have been used at times to favor preferred sources of supply. The GATT generally prohibits the use of quantitative restrictions, except in special cases, such as those cited in Article XX (which permits exceptions to protect public health, goods of archaeological or historic interest, and a few other special categories of goods), Article XXI (which permits exceptions in the interest of "national security"), or for SAFEGUARD purposes, when appropriate GATT-sanctioned procedures have been followed. *Compare to* RESIDUAL RESTRICTIONS.

quarantine 1. The compulsory isolation of people, animals, or products for a specified period of time, until it can be ascertained they do not carry disease. 2. A term that was used as a more acceptable substitute for BLOCKADE during the 1962 CUBAN MISSILE CRISIS, partly because a blockade is traditionally seen as an act of war.

Quarantine Doctrine U.S. President Franklin D. Roosevelt's suggestion that the fascist regimes of Germany, Italy, and Japan be isolated as if they had a contagious disease. In October 5, 1937, he said in a speech in Chicago, "There must be a return to a belief in the pledged word, in the value of a signed treaty. There must be a recognition of the fact that national morality is as vital as private morality . . . It seems unfortunately true that the epidemic of world lawlessness is spreading. When an epidemic of physical disease starts to spread, the community . . . joins in a quarantine of the patients in order to protect the health of the community against the spread of the disease. . . . War is a contagion, whether it be declared or undeclared." Roosevelt's call for a quarantine of aggressors fell on deaf ears internationally. According to James Chace and Caleb Carr's *America Invulnerable* (1988), "At the time of the Quarantine Speech . . . he was trying to urge the nations of the world to find new ways of controlling aggression and at the same time to get a reading of American public opinion on the subject. Though many American citizens . . . liked the overall tone of his speech, few were ready to support programs that might lead to war. Roosevelt would later remark of this period that 'It's a terrible thing to look over your shoulder when you are trying to lead—and to find no one there.' "

quarters 1. Housing for military personnel. 2. Housing for diplomatic personnel.

BELLS AND QUARTERS

[British] Bomber Command [during World War II] is in the building of a famous old school for girls. . . . When the Americans arrived . . . the famous story about the bells originated. The men moved into the girls' dormitory, and after they had retired the first night, the officers heard buzzes and bells ringing in their quarters, they being in the old administrative offices. They roused themselves and traced the calls until they found their origin, which was in the sleeping rooms formerly occupied by the girl students. In these rooms were little signs above the push buttons, reading, "If mistress is desired, ring bell."

SOURCE: Captain Harry C. Butcher, *My Three Years with Eisenhower* (1946).

Quebec Conference 1. The 1943 Anglo-American summit during WORLD WAR II at which plans were made for the Normandy invasion on D-DAY as well as for the campaigns in Italy and Burma. 2. The 1944 Anglo-American summit during World War II at which British Prime Minister Winston Churchill tentatively agreed with U.S. President Franklin D. Roosevelt to implement the MORGENTHAU PLAN (the recommendation of U.S. Secretary of the Treasury Henry Morgenthau that Germany's industrial plant be destroyed in the postwar world so that, as an agricultural state, Germany could never wage war again) and made plans to shift naval forces to the Pacific theater of operations for the final assault on Japan.

Quebec Liberation Front (FLQ)   *Front de Liberation du Quebec,* a violent separatist movement advocating the secession of the French-speaking province of Quebec from the largely English-speaking Canada. It was founded in the early 1960s and has been responsible for a campaign of bombings against Canadian public and governmental buildings since 1963.

Quebec Libre   French phrase meaning "free Quebec," the slogan of Parti Quebecois, the Canadian separatist movement that emerged in the mid-1960s under the leadership of René Levesque (1922–1987). When the movement gained control of the provincial government of Quebec in 1976, it promised to hold a referendum on loosening ties with the national government of Canada. The vote was held on May 20, 1980, and soundly rejected the notion of secession.

Quebec Separatism   The movement of French-speaking Quebecers, who make up one-quarter of Canada's population, to gain political independence of their province from the rest of English-speaking Canada. The issue of whether Quebec would remain part of Canada has been in the forefront of Canadian politics since the beginning of the 1960s. In October 1992 Canada held a national REFERENDUM on whether to change its constitution so that Quebec could remain a "distinct society" within the Canadian federation; the referendum lost at the polls, leaving the future of United Canada in some doubt.

Quemoy Crises   The crises that occurred in 1954–55 and 1958 over two small islands, Quemoy and Matsu, in the straits between Taiwan and Communist China; also known as the Taiwan crises. They raised not only the danger of hostilities between China and the United States, which was protecting the Nationalist government of Taiwan, but also the possibility of a direct superpower confrontation, given that Communist China was still allied with the Soviet Union at the time. The crises

were managed very effectively as Beijing and Washington observed certain tacit rules to keep the situation from getting out of control. The outcome was that the status quo was maintained. In 1958 U.S. Secretary of State John Foster Dulles engaged in SABER RATTLING over the Communist shelling of these islands, which raised the prospects, especially in the minds of North Atlantic Treaty Organization allies, of a nuclear showdown. The 1958 crisis, in particular, may have placed considerable strain on Sino-Soviet relations, as Beijing did not receive the level of support it wanted from Moscow, which seemed more sensitive to the risks. This contributed to the growing SINO-SOVIET SPLIT between the two great Communist powers.

Quidde, Ludwig (1858–1941)   The German historian and pacifist who won the 1927 Nobel Peace Prize (with FERDINAND BUISSON) for opposing German militarism, advocating Franco-German RAPPROCHEMENT, and supporting Germany's entry in the LEAGUE OF NATIONS.

quid pro quo   Latin meaning "something for something"; initially meaning the substitution of one thing for another. In politics and negotiations it refers to actions taken because of some promised action in return for the first.

Quisling, Vidkun (1887–1945)   A NAZI sympathizer in Norway whose treason assisted the Germans in their April–May 1940 conquest of Norway. While the Nazis allowed him to rule as prime minister in Norway in Hitler's name, he had few true followers. After the Allied victory in WORLD WAR II, Quisling was condemned to die and executed. His name has become a synonym for "traitor."

quorum   The number of individuals who must be in attendance to make valid the formal votes and other actions of an organized group. This may be a majority, or a certain preagreed percentage of the full membership.

quota   In the context of international trade, the quantity of goods of a specific kind that a country permits to be imported without restriction or imposition of an additional DUTY.

R

Rabin, Yitzhak (1922–   )   The first native-born prime minister of Israel who served from 1974 to 1977 when he succeeded GOLDA MEIR, and again since 1992 when his Labor Party–led coalition forced YITZHAK SHAMIR into retirement. Earlier Rabin had been chief of staff of the Israeli military during the SIX-DAY WAR of 1967 and ambassador to the United States (1968–1973). His party's 1992 electoral victory gave new impetus to the ARAB-ISRAELI PEACE TALKS.

radical tradition   A tradition of dissent from the main precepts and practices of British foreign policy. As A. J. P. Taylor noted in *The Troublemakers* (1957), the dissenter from British foreign policy "repudiates its aims, methods and principles. He claims to know better and to promote higher causes." Taylor also argues that the dissenters of today become the realists of tomorrow. Probably the best recent example of this tradition in Great Britain was the emergence of the CAMPAIGN FOR NUCLEAR DISARMAMENT, which criticized the British government's emphasis on strategic nuclear deterrence. Some members of CND even contended that Britain should withdraw from the North Atlantic Treaty Organization.

Rahman, Tunku Abdul (1903–   )   The first prime minister of an independent Malaya (1957–1963); then the first prime minister of the Federation of Malaysia (1963–1970). Popular sentiment for independence swelled in the Southeast Asian colony during and after World War II, and in 1957 the Federation of Malaya, established from the British-ruled territories of Peninsular Malaysia

in 1948, negotiated independence from the United Kingdom under the leadership of Rahman, who became prime minister. The British colonies of Sabah (North Borneo), Sarawak, and Singapore joined the Federation of Malaya to form Malaysia in 1963. Singapore withdrew in 1965 and became an independent republic. Neighboring Indonesia objected to the formation of Malaysia and pursued a program of economic, political, diplomatic, and military CONFRONTATION against the new country. The confrontation policy ended only after the fall of Indonesia's President ACHMED SUKARNO in 1966. Rahman held his federation together because of his skillful dealings with the Chinese, Indian, and Malay communities. But once massive communal rioting occurred in 1969, his ability to govern was compromised and he retired in 1970.

raid   **1.** An offensive military operation, usually small scale, involving a swift penetration of hostile territory to secure information, confuse the enemy, or destroy installations. As it is inherently temporary, it ends with a planned withdrawal upon completion of the mission.   **2.** Any attack, even of major scale, by strategic bombers.

Rainbow Warrior   A GREENPEACE ship destroyed on July 10, 1985, while at port in Auckland, New Zealand, by French government agents. The vessel had been engaged in efforts to interfere with France's nuclear weapons testing in the Pacific Ocean. One crew member was killed during the incident. The French government later apologized for the attack and agreed to assume some financial responsibility for the death of the crewman. Two

French agents were convicted and given brief jail terms for their part in the sabotage.

raison de guerre   French for "reason of war"; a doctrine, similar to the concept of RAISON D'ÉTAT, that justifies unusual actions in war. *Raison de guerre,* by analogy, is the doctrine that the vital necessity of winning a battle may, at times, justify behavior, such as TERRORISM, that would not normally be acceptable even in the context of the already less-constrained standards of morality that exist in war. While *raison d'état* has long been recognized in international law, *raison de guerre* is much less well established.

raison d'état   French for "reason of state"; for the good of the country. This Machiavellian concept is sometimes a critically important motive for otherwise unjustified government action, one that violates ordinary moral and legal codes but is undertaken for the greater interest and good of the state. As NICCOLÓ MACHIAVELLI wrote in *The Discourses* (1531): "When it is a question of saving the fatherland, one should not stop for a moment to consider whether something is lawful or unlawful, gentle or cruel, laudable or shameful; but putting aside every other consideration, one ought to follow out to the end whatever resolve will save the life of the state and preserve its freedom." If the life of the state is in question, raison d'état is then the rationale to do anything, no matter how otherwise illegal, to save it. Raison d'état, sometimes even used to justify TERRORISM, is a notion that is very closely related to REALISM and NEOREALISM.

raj   The Hindu word for "sovereignty," which in English refers to the time of British rule over India that ended in 1947.

RAND Corporation   A think tank created by the U.S. Air Force in 1947 and located in Santa Monica, California. The name is an acronym for "Research and Development." RAND has been concerned with the application of scientific and social science methods to the problems of strategy and security in the nuclear age. It became a key institution in the development of civilian expertise on nuclear strategy and functioned as the incubator for the work of many civilian strategists, including

such figures as BERNARD BRODIE, HERMAN KAHN, KLAUS KNORR, and THOMAS C. SCHELLING. The civilian strategists examined the impact of nuclear weapons on international politics, but in the process produced many highly controversial ideas, such as limited nuclear war. Ideas generated at RAND were central to the "golden age" of nuclear strategy from the mid-1950s to the mid-1960s. RAND remains one of the most important think tanks on national and international security issues.

Rapacki Plan   A 1957 proposal by Polish Foreign Minister Adam Rapacki (1909–1970) to establish a denuclearized zone in East and West Germany, Poland, and Czechoslovakia. This idea became a common theme in many proposals from the Soviet bloc at this time during the COLD WAR. While the ideas received sympathy from the peace movements in Western Europe, North Atlantic Treaty Organization governments were strongly opposed. They viewed NUCLEAR-FREE ZONE proposals as part of an overall Soviet diplomatic offensive designed to undermine NATO's reliance on nuclear weapons. With the ending of the Cold War and the new climate in East-West relations, such proposals appear more attractive and are bound to be discussed seriously.

Rapallo, Treaty of   The 1922 bilateral agreement signed in the Italian city of Rapallo that normalized relations between Germany and Russia after WORLD WAR I. The two states mutually repudiated war costs and damage claims. Russia renounced REPARATIONS from Germany. Germany renounced claims from the NATIONALIZATION of German property in Russia. This treaty ended the isolation of both states after World War I and put the rest of Europe on notice that friendly economic and diplomatic relations were possible. During the Cold War there were fears in North Atlantic Treaty Organization states that the Soviet Union might try to repeat Rapallo and woo the Federal Republic of Germany away from the Western Alliance by holding out the promise of GERMAN REUNIFICATION.

rapid deployment force   **1.** Any military force that is maintained on a significantly high level of readiness so that it is capable of being deployed very quickly against an enemy.   **2.** The U.S. Central Command established by President Jimmy Carter as a response to the potential need to intervene in the Persian Gulf region (known to U.S. planners as SOUTHWEST ASIA). During the 1970s the United States had relied on the shah of Iran to protect Western interests in the gulf. With his overthrow in 1979, it became necessary for Washington to consider the possibility of direct intervention to protect world oil supplies. In December 1979, in the midst of the IRANIAN HOSTAGE CRISIS, U.S. Secretary of Defense Harold Brown announced the establishment of the Rapid Deployment Force. All resistance to this idea disappeared after the Soviet invasion of Afghanistan and the proclamation of the CARTER DOCTRINE that the United States would protect its vital interests in the gulf by military force if necessary. This same Central Command led U.S. and allied forces in the 1991 PERSIAN GULF WAR.

Rapoport, Anatol (1911–) A U.S. scholar who has done extensive research on mathematical psychology, mathematical sociology, and conflict resolution. His *Fights, Games and Debates* (1960) was an important contribution to the development and the popularization of GAME THEORY. In this and subsequent writings, Rapoport attempted to use game theory to illustrate the dynamics of cooperation and conflict resolution. More generally Rapoport explored systems theory and in 1983 published *Mathematical Models in the Social and Behavioral Sciences*. One of his most famous books was *Strategy and Conscience* (1964). In this and in other works Rapoport made some vitriolic comments on the writings of HERMAN KAHN and other nuclear strategists. (On one occasion he even asked Kahn if, in the event he survived a nuclear war, he would be prepared to stand trial for advocating GENOCIDE.) He criticized Kahn and other strategic analysts for approaching nuclear strategy in Clausewitzian terms and argued that Karl von Clausewitz's conception of war as an instrument of policy should not obscure the fact that war also could be seen as a disease or as a crusade. Rapoport's critique of nuclear strategy was powerful, if not entirely compelling, and he remained concerned with having an impact on policy. In his study of Soviet and American perceptions of each other, *The Big Two* (1971), he highlighted some of the problems that typically arose at the level

of perception that exacerbated tensions between the United States and the Soviet Union.

rapprochement 1. The reestablishment of diplomatic ties between previously warring states. 2. Any warming of diplomatic relations between previously estranged governments. For example, after U.S. President Richard Nixon's 1972 visit to China, a rapprochement began that led to the reestablishment of normal diplomatic relations between the United States and China in 1979.

Rasputin, Grigori (1871–1916) The Russian Orthodox priest who, because he was able (through hypnotism) to stop the bleeding of Czar NICHOLAS II's hemophilic son, Alexis, became a close confidant of the boy's mother, the Empress Alexandra. During World War I, when Nicholas took direct command of the army in 1915, Alexandra and Rasputin were, in effect, left in charge of the government. Rasputin became notorious for shifting ministers at whim or to benefit his friends. But it was his personal behavior with drinking and sexual excesses with the female members of the aristocracy that aroused opposition. Thus in 1916 two grand dukes murdered him. The actions of Rasputin, sometimes called the "mad monk," did not cause the RUSSIAN REVOLUTION OF 1917, which followed his death and destroyed the monarchy. But he did so help discredit the institutions of the czar that he made the job of the revolutionaries that much easier.

ratification The authority of a legislature or sovereign to approve or reject TREATIES, constitutional amendments, or even a new CONSTITUTION itself.

rationality 1. The application of reason to decision making. 2. The idea that decision making is based on calculations of probable gains and losses (or costs and benefits) and that the decision maker will generate alternatives, assess them, and choose the one that promises to maximize values (i.e., give the best ratio of gains to losses). In this sense it is related to the notion of the "economic human," who is supposedly always concerned with value maximizing. 3. An abstract and idealized version of what decision making should be like but rarely is in practice. Limits on time, intellect, and information mean that policymakers rarely clarify all their values and interests or generate the whole universe of possible alternatives for achieving their values or objectives. Instead, they focus on the major values and choose the first alternative that promises to satisfy their requirements, even though it may fall far short of the optimum. This was described by Herbert Simon in *Administrative Behavior* (1947) as "satisficing" as opposed to maximizing. In practice, therefore, there are all sorts of limitations on the achievement of rationality in decision making. The idea of rationality was crystallized by GRAHAM T. ALLISON in what he termed the Rational Actor Model; he suggested that although it was used as the implicit model for explaining foreign policy decisions, it was an artificial construct that ignored the fact that most decisions were the product of bureaucratic bargaining among different groups with different interests and perspectives or the output of large organizations working according to standard operational procedures.

rationalization   1. Administrative actions that increase the effectiveness of military units through the more efficient use of resources. Rationalization includes standardization, INTEROPERABILITY, greater cooperation, and so on.   2. The wartime merging of industrial plants in given industries in a capitalist economy to achieve greater efficiency and lower production costs. This almost total government regulation of otherwise private business enterprises is possible only during a TOTAL WAR. 3. A false explanation for a policy decision that was taken for reasons that are not outwardly defensible.   4. Justification for an action after the fact. This may or may not have been the reason for the action.

ratline   1. The rope rigging on the masts of sailing ships that allows sailors to climb to the top of the masts.   2. By analogy, an organized effort for moving personnel and/or material by clandestine means across a denied area or border.

reactionary   An individual who would go back to outmoded ideas of former times. The term is a derogatory reference to those political activists who are so discontent with maintaining the current status quo that they desire a previous status quo.

readiness   A general measure of how well prepared military units are for immediate combat. Readiness covers such elements as ammunition and fuel stocks, training levels, mobilization plans, and, sometimes, the availability of reserves. The stress on weapons acquisition, always emphasized by the MILITARY-INDUSTRIAL COMPLEX, tends to undermine all aspects of readiness. Air forces, for example, always would prefer to buy more aircraft than to allow their pilots more flying time to train on the aircraft that they already have. Armies let their ammunition stocks run down and restrict the number of training rounds tank crews can fire in order to procure more tanks. Readiness and administration have always been in conflict. U.S. Admiral ALFRED THAYER MAHAN wrote in *Naval Administration and Warfare* (1908): "There has been a constant struggle on the part of the military element to keep the end—fighting, or readiness to fight—superior to mere administrative considerations. . . . The military man, having to do the fighting, considers that the chief necessity; the administrator equally naturally tends to think the smooth running of the machine the most admirable quality." But the whole issue was best summed up by U.S. Joint Chiefs of Staff Admiral Thomas H. Moorer: "If we continue [training] at a lowered tempo, there will be progressive deterioration of combat readiness. We're just like a football team, and if you don't practice during the week, you may not be able to play the game on Saturday" (*Time,* December 10, 1973). The issue of readiness has taken on a new importance with the end of the Cold War. There are various dimensions of readiness. The most important, though, will continue to be the strategic deterrent forces and some capacity to respond fairly rapidly at the conventional level.

Reagan, Ronald W. (1911–   )   The president of the United States from 1981 to 1989. Reagan, a movie actor, became involved in the ill-fated 1964 presidential campaign of Barry Goldwater. This made Reagan a major voice in national Republican politics, which led to his election as governor of California (1967–1975) and eventually to his successful 1980 presidential campaign against Jimmy Carter, whose presidency was crippled by the IRANIAN HOSTAGE CRISIS. As president, Reagan initiated a program of unparalleled deficit spending for a

Ronald Reagan (U.S. Naval Institute)

House Communications Director Patrick Buchanan: "The doctrine says we don't have to resign ourselves to the fact that once a country has become a member of the socialist or Communist camp it must remain there forever. Where genuine national-liberation movements seek to recapture their country from a Communist tyranny imposed from without, America reserves the right—and may indeed have the duty—to support those people" (*U.S. News & World Report,* January 27, 1986). Critic Michael Kinsley found the Reagan Doctrine to be "a specific rejection of international law as the illogical elevation of sovereignty over more important values such as democracy and freedom" (*The New Republic,* October 1, 1990). President Reagan's policy of giving support to right-wing wars of national liberation against Marxist-Leninist governments in the Third World can be understood as an updated version of the Republican notion of liberation or ROLL-BACK. The success of the Reagan Doctrine is a matter of some controversy, although proponents would argue not only that the help given by the United States to the rebels in Afghanistan was crucial in the Soviet withdrawal but also that the additional pressure this more competitive approach placed on the Soviet Union was an additional strain on the Soviet economy and ultimately a factor in its disintegration.

military buildup that supporters contend both brought domestic prosperity on credit and broke the back of communism in the Soviet Union and Eastern Europe. Critics argue that it created an artificial prosperity at the cost of enormous debt and was very dangerous internationally.

Reagan was masterful at using the media. His stage-managed public appearances rightfully earned him the title of the "Great Communicator." After the middle of his second term his reputation began to suffer as the IRAN-CONTRA AFFAIR unraveled. Nevertheless, he retired with his popularity largely intact, the first president successfully to complete two terms in office since DWIGHT D. EISENHOWER in the 1950s.

Reagan Doctrine The Reagan Administration's policy of militarily supporting guerrilla insurgencies against Communist governments in Third World countries, such as Afghanistan, Angola, Cambodia, and Nicaragua. According to White

realism An approach to INTERNATIONAL RELATIONS that accepts that struggle is an endemic feature of life in the international system, either because of the innate imperfectibility of humans or because of the anarchic nature of the international system. The realist school of thought has been attacked, however, because of its obsession with power and its relative indifference to domestic sources of state behavior or to considerations of morality. Yet it has deep roots going back to THUCYDIDES, NICCOLÓ MACHIAVELLI, THOMAS HOBBES, and JEAN-JACQUES ROUSSEAU, all of whom had interesting things to say both about power and about the relations among independent political units. Machiavelli, in particular, was concerned with amassing, maintaining, and using power. As he put it in *The Prince* (1532), "There is simply no comparison between a man who is unarmed and one who is not. It is unreasonable to expect that an armed man should obey one who is not or that an unarmed man should remain safe and secure when his servants are armed." A similar sense of the role of power is evident in the writings of Hobbes. There also is something of the same pessimism about human nature. Yet perhaps Hobbes's most important contribution was his contrast between relations among men in a society controlled by the state or Leviathan and the relations among men—and more particularly sovereigns—where there is no Leviathan to maintain order. For Hobbes, the relationship among sovereigns is akin to that in the STATE OF NATURE (before the formation of the state) in which life is "solitary, nasty, brutish and short." As he contends, sovereigns are in a state of continual jealousies and in the posture of gladiators with their weapons pointing toward one another. If such analyses provide the intellectual antecedents for the development of realism, contemporary realism also arose out of a sense of frustration with the idealism of the interwar period. This was evident in the writings of E. H. CARR, the British historian who, in *The Twenty Years' Crisis* (1939), offered a biting critique of idealist thinking and especially any idea that there was a natural harmony of interests among states. It was HANS J. MORGENTHAU, however, who really crystallized realism. Starting from the assumption that international politics, like all politics, was a struggle for power, Morgenthau argued that states defined their national interest in terms of power and that this was the key to understanding both international politics and foreign policy. Critics argued that Morgenthau relied too heavily on an elusive concept of human nature, that he failed to define his core concepts such as power and interest, and that he oscillated between prescriptive and descriptive theory. Although there were inconsistencies between Morgenthau's contention that state behavior could be understood as the pursuit of interests defined in terms of power and his criticisms of United States foreign policymakers for pursuing ideological objectives, his attack on ideological foreign policy does highlight the pragmatism that is an inherent part of realism. Subsequently the theory of realism has been modified; the emphasis increasingly has been placed on international anarchy and the structure of the system as the central features of international politics. The emphasis has moved from realism to NEOREALISM thanks largely to the writings of KENNETH WALTZ, who argues that the distribution of power in the international system is the main determinant of state behavior. *See also* NATIONAL INTEREST.

MORGENTHAU'S SIX PRINCIPLES OF POLITICAL REALISM

1. Political realism believes that politics, like society in general, is governed by objective laws that have their roots in human nature. . . .
2. The main signpost that helps political realism to find its way through the landscape of international politics is the concept of interest defined in terms of power. . . .
3. Realism assumes that its key concept of interest defined as power is an objective category which is universally valid, but it does not endow that concept with a meaning that is fixed once and for all. . . .
4. Political realism is aware of the moral significance of political action. It is also aware of the ineluctable tension between the moral command and the requirements of successful political action. . . .
5. Political realism refuses to identify the moral aspirations of a particular nation with the moral laws that govern the universe. . . . There is a world of difference between the belief that all nations stand under the judgment of God . . . and the blasphemous conviction that God is always on one's side. . . .
6. Intellectually, the political realist . . . thinks in terms of interest defined as power, as the economist thinks in terms of interest defined as wealth. . . .

SOURCE: Hans J. Morgenthau, *Politics Among Nations,* 5th ed. (1973).

---

realpolitik   A German word first applied to the practices of Camillo Cavour (1810–1861) and OTTO VON BISMARCK in the nineteenth century as they led the unification of their nation-states of Italy and Germany, respectively, mainly through tough industrial and military policies. It is now absorbed into English, meaning realist politics or the politics of reality. The term is applied to politics—whether of the organizational or societal variety—premised on material or practical factors rather than on theoretical or ethical considerations. It is the politics of REALISM; an injunction not to allow wishful thinking or sentimentality to cloud one's judgment. It has taken on more sinister overtones, particularly in modern usage. At its most moderate realpolitik is used to describe an overcynical approach, one that allows little room for human altruism, that always seeks an ulterior motive behind another actor's statements or justifications. At its strongest it suggests that no moral values should be allowed to affect the single-minded pursuit of one's own or one's country's self-interest, and an absolute assumption that any opponent will certainly behave in this same way.

reassurance 1. A process that is generally regarded as necessary to ensure that DETERRENCE strategies do not excessively frighten either one's own public or the adversary, who might thereby be provoked into the very action one wants to avoid. 2. An effort to give an adversary confidence that one does not intend to do harm. The process of providing reassurance can help to mitigate the SECURITY DILEMMA—although the adversary may be concerned that it is a trick.

rebellion *See* REVOLUTION.

rebus sic stantibus Latin for "fundamental change of circumstances"; a clause in a TREATY that allows a government to avoid performing its obligations under the treaty because the basic conditions that led to the treaty have changed in a substantial way. The doctrine holds that all treaties are concluded with the implied condition that they are binding only if circumstances remain relatively constant.

recall, letter of The formal notification from one head of state to another that a diplomatic representative is being returned home. It has now become normal that the succeeding envoy delivers his or her predecessor's letter of recall when he or she presents his or her own CREDENTIALS upon arrival.

reciprocal trade agreement A formal understanding concluded by a state with one or more other states under which TARIFFS or other trade barriers are reduced in return for reductions of foreign barriers against the goods of the first state.

reciprocity 1. The granting of privileges to the citizens of one state by the government of another, and vice versa. 2. A mutuality in the terms of trade between two states. This usually refers to the negotiated reduction of a state's import duties or other trade restraints in return for similar concessions

from another state. Because of the frequently wide disparity in their economic capacities and potential, the relationship of concessions negotiated between developed and developing countries is generally not one of equivalence. Thus the phrase *relative reciprocity* is used to characterize the practice of developed countries seeking less than full reciprocity from developing countries in trade negotiations. 3. One of the key norms in a legislature, whereby members exchange favors in order to further their own, their constituents', and the public's interests. 4. The basis for tacit codes of conduct that help to manage great power rivalry. 5. An approach to the development of international cooperation.

recognition 1. A term used to refer to acknowledgment of the existence of a state, with a government that has control over its territory and population. The withholding of recognition, when it is obvious that there is a state which meets these conditions, is generally motivated by political considerations. Indeed, as Michael Akehurst has argued in *A Modern Introduction to International Law* (1987), "Recognition is one of the most difficult topics in international law. It is a confusing mixture of politics, international law and municipal law. The legal and political considerations cannot be disentangled: when giving or withholding recognition, states are influenced more by political than by legal consideration, but their acts do have legal consequences." Another complication is in the usage of the terms DE JURE and DE FACTO recognition. The former is what is usually meant by recognition. The latter is less than recognition but more than not being recognized. For example, the United States since 1979 has not had de jure recognition of Taiwan and vice versa. However, the extensive relations between these two states is maintained by de facto recognition administered not by embassies but by the U.S. American Institute on Taiwan and Taiwan's Coordination Council in the United States. The act of external recognition can be crucial to the viability of a new state, as was evident in the case of the BALTIC STATES, which were recognized as states rather than as Soviet republics in the aftermath of the failed RUSSIAN COUP in August 1991. This meant that other states considered the Baltic states to be independent and would consequently view any Soviet effort to reincorporate the Baltic states into the Soviet Union as an act of international aggression. **2.** Acknowledgment of the fact that one state has extended territorial rights outside its original area of jurisdiction. *See also* DIPLOMATIC RECOGNITION; ESTRADA DOCTRINE.

red A Communist, because the red flag is the traditional symbol of communism and revolution. This is why someone thought to be leaning toward communism might be called "pink" or a "pinko," particularly in the United States.

Red Army The army of the Soviet Union created by V. I. LENIN from the RED GUARDS, which helped the Bolsheviks seize power in 1917. LEON TROTSKY, as commissar for war (1918–1925), gave the army discipline, organization, and victory during the RUSSIAN CIVIL WAR. Because Trotsky had to rely on former officers of deposed Czar Nicholas II, POLITICAL COMMISSARS were attached to all major units. This system of effective dual command continued throughout the Red Army's history. Despite widespread purges of officers during the GREAT PURGE in the mid-1930s, the army recovered to defeat the Germans on the Eastern Front during World War II. After the war its official name was changed to the Soviet Army, though informally it remained the Red Army until the breakup of the Soviet Union in 1991.

Red Army Faction (RAF) *Rote Armee Fraktion,* a German leftist terrorist organization that originated in the student unrest of the late 1960s. The group, founded by Andreas Baader (1943–1977) and Ulrike Meinhoff (1934–1976), was known as the Baader-Meinhof Gang in its early years, when it mounted a campaign of "armed resistance to U.S. imperialism and West German complicity." The RAF described itself as part of an international movement aimed at bringing about a worldwide revolution that would topple the existing power structures in the capitalist world. But in 1990 it came to light that it was really under the control of the East German government all along. Now all of its seemingly anarchist terrorist incidents have to be reevaluated as state-sponsored TERRORISM.

Red Berets A unit of the secret police of Czechoslovakia that was supposedly designed to fight terrorists but that, according to *U.S. News &* *World Report* (December 18, 1989), provided Mideast terrorist gangs with training, safe havens, and technical assistance as well as arms and explosives during the COLD WAR.

Red Brigades An Italian terrorist organization that grew out of the student unrest of the late 1960s and the radical wing of the Italian labor movement. One of the most lethal of the major European terrorist groups, it has conducted an extensive number of violent attacks; preferred targets have been members of the Italian "establishment" whom it considers to be the "oppressors of society." The group's campaign of kidnappings and violence reached its zenith with the kidnapping and murder of former Italian Prime Minister ALDO MORO in 1978. While initially concentrating on the Italian targets, in 1981 it "declared war" on the North Atlantic Treaty Organization and kidnapped U.S. General JAMES DOZIER.

Red China The informal name often used for the People's Republic of China to distinguish it from the Republic of China (Taiwan).

Red Crescent In many Muslim states, the national branch of the INTERNATIONAL RED CROSS.

Red Cross *See* INTERNATIONAL RED CROSS.

redemocratization The process of renewing democratic institutions in a society that has gone through a period of political repression. Sometimes this happens peacefully, as in Poland in the late 1980s or in Spain after the death of Francisco Franco in 1975. And often this happens after a war, as with Germany and Japan after World War II.

Red Guards **1.** The armed workers' militia that helped the BOLSHEVIKS come to power during the RUSSIAN REVOLUTION OF 1917. They later formed the nucleus of the RED ARMY that won the RUSSIAN CIVIL WAR. **2.** Groups of militant college and high school students organized at the encouragement of MAO ZEDONG, the CHINESE COMMUNIST PARTY chairman, during the CULTURAL REVOLUTION. Their mission was to eliminate all the remnants of the old culture in China and purge bourgeois elements within the party and government. In the mid-1960s several million Red Guards journeyed from all over the country to Beijing in eight massive demonstrations to meet Chairman Mao. Soon the Red Guards were engaged in factional fighting that killed many and destroyed much property. They also attacked diplomats and paralyzed all economic activities. Beginning in 1967 Mao cajoled the Red Guards to settle down in the countryside. Faced with bleak futures in poor, isolated rural China, most former Red Guards became demoralized and disillusioned. They later called themselves a "lost generation."

red line A line of demarcation that, if crossed by hostile forces, will bring a military response by those who established the line. Red is traditionally the color that indicates "danger" or "stop."

red scare 1. Any time of great fear of Communist subversion. 2. In the United States, the period immediately following World War I and the RUSSIAN REVOLUTION OF 1917, when U.S. hysteria over anarchists, Communists, and radicals resulted in the wholesale arrest and often the deportation of people thought to be subversive. The best-known aspect of the red scare of this period was the "Palmer raids," conducted by agents of U.S. Attorney General A. Mitchell Palmer (1872–1936), in which thousands of U.S. citizens as well as aliens were arrested. The raids were famous for their lack of due process and violations of civil liberties. They ended, along with Palmer's presidential ambitions in 1920, when Palmer's predicted uprising of "reds" in an effort to overthrow the government of the United States never happened. 3. The period of MCCARTHYISM after World War II.

red terror The BOLSHEVIK effort to secure its regime after the RUSSIAN REVOLUTION OF 1917 through mass arrests and summary executions of political opponents. This occurred as part of the RUSSIAN CIVIL WAR. *Compare to* GREAT PURGE.

red terrorism *See* BLACK TERRORISM.

reductionist theory A system of analysis that attempts to understand the whole through the study of its parts. Kenneth Waltz in *Theory of International Politics* (1979) claims that the focus on decision makers or bureaucratic factors to explain international political phenomena is an example of reductionism. But he argues that a focus on the international system and its structure instead is much more appropriate and leads to a far more compelling theory of international politics.

referendum The submission of proposed laws or constitutional amendments to voters for their direct approval or rejection. A referendum is much like a PLEBISCITE except that the former is routine and normal while the latter implies a highly unusual event in a state's history.

reflagging An exercise during the IRAN-IRAQ WAR in the Persian Gulf whereby the United States identified Kuwaiti tankers as belonging to the United States, thereby taking over responsibility for their safety. The ships were then protected by U.S. naval forces. *Compare to* FLAG OF CONVENIENCE.

reformism The belief that political change can occur incrementally without violence, as opposed to a belief that only the bloody overthrow of an existing regime can bring real change.

The USS Hawes *leads the reflagged tanker* Gas King *through the Persian Gulf in 1987. (U.S. Naval Institute)*

refugee   A person who, because of real or imagined danger, moves of his or her own volition, spontaneously or in violation of a stay-put policy, irrespective of whether the move is within his or her own country (in the case of *national refugees*) or across international boundaries (*international refugees*). A large increase in the number of refugees in a region is a major consequence of many wars or revolutions. This was evident with the Persian Gulf War and also has been evident in Europe as a result of the changes in the Soviet Union and Eastern Europe. In fact, there are those who argue that one of the main security problems for Western Europe through the rest of the 1990s will be that posed by refugees from the East.

regent   The person who is given the authority to function as a MONARCH because the monarch is too young, too ill, or temporarily too far away. For example, after World War I Admiral NIKOLAUS HORTHY ruled Hungary as regent.

regime   1. A type of government (democratic, totalitarian, and so on). 2. A government presently in power; the group of people that constitutes an administration. 3. A system of governance, as opposed to ANARCHY. 4. Any generally accepted or customary set of procedures. 5. A term that has been used increasingly in international relations to explain cooperation even in the absence of a state with HEGEMONY. In this sense "regime" has been defined by Stephen Krasner and others in *International Regimes* (1983) as "sets of implicit or explicit principles, norms, rules, and decision-making procedures around which actors' expectations converge in a given area of international relations. Principles are beliefs of fact, causation, and rectitude. Norms are standards of behavior defined in terms of rights and obligations. Rules are specific prescriptions or proscriptions for action. Decision-making procedures are prevailing practices for making and implementing collective choice." Regime has become one of the central concepts for understanding contemporary international relations. Although less widely used in relation to international security, it has been applied to some security issues. It is fairly common to refer, for example, to the nonproliferation regime.

region   1. A group of states that are geographically contiguous or at least in close geographical proximity. 2. More loosely, a particular area (such as the Middle East region) or what is sometimes termed a SUBSYSTEM in international relations.

regional development   Economic and social growth and improvement efforts in THIRD WORLD states approached on an area as opposed to a country-by-country basis.

regional influentials   States that play a major role in regional subsystems of the international system but also aspire to taking a role beyond the region.

regional integration   The process of political and economic combination that takes place in a particular part of a continent. Western Europe provides an excellent example of regional integration, as its states have not only established a single market but also are moving toward political union via the European Community.

regionalism   1. A sense of identity and outlook that characterizes a particular region, whether within a state or between two or more states. Whether regionalism is internal or external, it poses a challenge to the dominance of the nation. The greater the affiliation and sense of identity with the region, the less likely it is that the nation or state can evoke the same kind of loyalty. 2. An approach to solving international problems that is contrasted with GLOBALISM. Regionalism recognizes that certain problems are best dealt with on a region-by-region basis, taking account of the variations that exist from one geographical area to another. 3. The creation of formal ties among states at the regional level through the growth of international organizations. 4. A belief that peace can be promoted best if states in a given geographical area create cooperative structures to deal with economic, military, and political problems.

regional organizations   Associations of nearby states for economic or military purposes. For example, see individual entries for ASEAN, EUROPEAN COMMUNITY, and OAS. While the United Nations is worldwide and thus not a regional organization, it does have within it a variety of regional economic and social commissions.

regional power   A state that is one of the leading economic, military, and political forces in its part of the world. For example, South Africa in southern Africa, Brazil in South America, or Iran in the Persian Gulf. *Compare to* MIDDLE POWER.

regional security   **1.** The issue of DEFENSE in a particular geographical area.   **2.** Used to distinguish the scale of defense problems in the sense that regional security problems, for the most part, are less significant than global problems.

regular army   A permanent military force maintained in peace as well as in war; a standing professional army, as opposed to an emergency-only *militia*. Regular military forces do not include reserves that may be called up in time of war or other natural emergency.

Reich   *See* GERMAN REICH.

Reichstag fire   **1.** The burning of the building in which Germany's parliament was located from 1871 to 1945. On February 27, 1933, the building was set ablaze. The Nazis had planned to burn it so that they could blame the Communists. But before they could implement their plan, a genuine Communist, the mentally deranged Marinus van der Lubbe, committed the arson. He was quickly captured, tried, and executed. The Nazis then exploited the situation. Chancellor ADOLF HITLER, asserting that this lone action was part of a Communist plot, used this as an excuse to suspend civil liberties and proclaim a state of emergency—which lasted until 1945. The fire also was the excuse to invoke the Enabling Act of March 23, 1933, by which the Reichstag (meeting in a different building) effectively delegated all power to Hitler.   **2.** By analogy, any artificially created political event used as an excuse for dramatic action.

reign   **1.** The period of time a government holds power; traditionally, the time period during which a given monarch rules.   **2.** The final source of power, authority, or law in a polity. This is what Alexis de Tocqueville meant in *Democracy in America* (1835) when he said: "The people reign over the American political world as God rules over the universe."

Rejection Front   A coalition of PALESTINE LIBERATION ORGANIZATION groups that in 1982 broke from the PLO mainstream to oppose what it considered to be the defeatist policies of YASIR ARAFAT. These groups included the POPULAR FRONT FOR THE LIBERATION OF PALESTINE and the POPULAR FRONT FOR THE LIBERATION OF PALESTINE—GENERAL COMMAND, the Arab Liberation Front, the Popular Struggle Front, and the Palestine Liberation Front. The Rejection Front was encouraged by Iraq, Libya, and Syria, and stands against any negotiated settlement with Israel. Its goal is the total destruction of Israel so that its land area can be incorporated into a Palestinian state. *See also* CONFRONTATION STATES.

The Reichstag burns in 1933. (National Archives)

relative reciprocity   *See* RECIPROCITY.

RENAMO   *Resistencia Nacional Mocambicana* (Mozambican National Resistance), a guerrilla insurgency against the Marxist government of Mozambique in southern Africa. RENAMO, originally known as the National Resistance Movement, was established in 1976 under the sponsorship of Rhodesia's security forces, which recruited Mozambicans opposed to the socialist regime set up by FRELIMO (Front for the Liberation of Mozambique), the ruling party. In 1982 the group changed its name to RENAMO. Beyond its aim to overthrow the government of Mozambique, it has publicly enunciated only a vague anti-Communist political program. It conducts military operations against government as well as civilian targets, and frequently and increasingly runs cross-border operations into Malawi, Zambia, and Zimbabwe; it has murdered over 100,000 Mozambican civilians and forced 2 million more to flee to neighboring states in what has become known as the Mozambique Civil War. In October 1992 RENAMO and FRELIMO leaders meeting in Rome, Italy, signed a peace agreement that calls for a new national army made up of equal numbers from each side. But since neither side fully controls the soldiers, it is difficult to say whether the peace will hold.

Renault, Louis (1843–1918)   The French professor of international law who shared the 1907 Nobel Peace Prize (with ERNESTO T. MONETA) for his work in advancing international arbitration and codifying the rules of naval warfare.

reparations   Monetary compensation for damage done in war that is given by the vanquished to the victor. The most famous example of reparations was Germany's agreement in the post–World War I armistice of November 11, 1918, to provide "reparation for damage done." It had a strong punitive element and appealed to nationalist sentiment that had been whipped up by the war. In Great Britain's general election of December 1918 there were demands from some candidates to "squeeze the German lemon till the pips squeak." In fact, David Lloyd George, the British prime minister, was a force for moderation at the peace conference in Ver-

sailles, France. Even so, heavy financial reparations were imposed on Germany, which became a major issue in the interwar period. After the end of the World War II, reparations from Germany became one of the elements dividing the United States and the Soviet Union. Both the Soviet Union and France wanted to impose a punitive peace, but the United States was more concerned with German rehabilitation. In the end, the Soviet Union took reparations from the eastern part of Germany, which was under its control.

repatriation   Returning someone to the state in which he or she is a citizen. This is commonly done to displaced persons after a war. More recently it has referred to forcibly sending back to their native land the BOAT PEOPLE from Vietnam seeking refuge in Hong Kong, or from Haiti seeking refuge in the United States.

reprisal   **1.** Generally, an action taken in retaliation for some deed.   **2.** A coercive measure taken by one state against another in reaction to an injury. Examples include breaking diplomatic relations, curtailing trade, freezing assets, and so on.   **3.** A wartime act of vengeance, such as the shooting of hostages or other kinds of collective punishment. The Geneva Convention of 1949 severely restricts reprisals in time of war. But military reprisals are not always limited to wartime. For example, the Israelis tend to engage in military reprisals for terrorist attacks on their population in the hope that such actions will deter further attacks.   **4.** In international law, a specific concept related to SELF-HELP that allows the state to take an otherwise illegal action in response to a prior wrong against it. This action, however, must be proportionate to the initial wrong. For example, if state A sinks a warship of state B, then state B could sink a comparable warship of state A.

republic   A Latin word meaning "the public thing"; the state and its institutions; a form of government in which sovereignty is placed in the people who choose agents to represent their will in political decision making. *Compare to* DEMOCRACY.

republic, banana   An unstable national government, often a REPUBLIC; one that changes its laws, leaders, and constitutions too casually. The phrase is a pejorative way of referring to Latin American states because of the historically unstable nature of many of their regimes.

Republic of China (ROC)   The island of Taiwan. The Nationalist Party or KUOMINTANG (KMT) ruled China between 1929 and 1949, interrupted by the Japanese invasion during 1937 to 1945. With the Japanese surrender at the end of World War II, the Chinese Nationalists and Communists found themselves in the full-scale CHINESE CIVIL WAR for the dominance of China. The Nationalists lost and retreated to the island of Taiwan in December 1949. The island had been ceded to Japan by China in 1875. Returned to China in the wake of World War II, the Kuomintang administered it with extreme corruption and repression. Thus the native Taiwanese resented the Nationalists, even before they brought 2 million refugees with them when they fled the mainland. In Taiwan the leaders of the Republic of China, wiser from the lessons of their loss of the mainland, began concentrating their attention to reforming the economy, providing for people's welfare if not freedom, expanding education, and cultivating talent to set Taiwan on the road to modernization. The government's successful land reform between 1949 and 1953, followed by export expansion in the early 1960s, transformed Taiwan from a basically agricultural labor-intensive economy to a highly industrial and capital-intensive one. Along with economic prosperity, the KMT government gradually welcomed political participation by the indigenous population. In 1989 an opposition party, the Democratic Progress Party, captured 65 out of 293 contested seats in a national parliamentary election. In the 1970s Taiwan suffered a series of diplomatic setbacks when the People's Republic of China on the mainland was admitted to the United Nations to replace Taiwan and when a number of important nations, such as Japan and the United States, established diplomatic relations with the PRC at the expense of their formal diplomatic ties with Taiwan. Today, after 40 years of hostility across the Taiwan Straits, tensions between the two governments have relaxed somewhat and contacts are now broader and more frequent.

Rerum novarum   The 1891 encyclical of Pope Leo XIII; called "the flagship of Catholic social doctrine." Written at a time of major contention between liberalism and socialism in Europe, it addressed specific social issues: supporting private property, permitting workers to organize labor unions, paying just wages, improving working conditions, and arguing the need for rest. It condemned socialism and rejected the Marxist concept of class warfare. It sought an alternative to both socialism and competitive capitalism. It suggested that the state must aid poorer citizens and that employers and workers must cooperate in settling differences in a spirit of Christian brotherhood. On the basis of Leo XIII's encyclical, democratic Catholic parties and Catholic trade unions sprang up throughout Europe. *See also* QUADRAGESIMO ANNO.

reserve   **1.** That portion of a military force which is deep to the rear, or withheld from action at the beginning of an engagement, available to be thrown decisively against the enemy. Any force not engaged or lightly engaged also may be designated or employed as a reserve. The timely use of one's operational reserves is one of the most important aspects to the art of command. As Karl von Clausewitz wrote in *On War* (1832): "Fatigue the opponent, if possible, with few forces and conserve a decisive mass for the critical moment. Once this decisive mass has been thrown in, it must be used with the greatest audacity."   **2.** Members of military services who are not in active service but who are subject to call to active duty at the discretion of their government.   **3.** That portion of the funds of a governmental appropriation or contract authorization held or set aside for future operations or contingencies.

reserve assets   **1.** The cash (or liquid cash equivalents) that banks retain to pay the reasonably expected demands of depositors. Levels of these reserve assets are frequently mandated by law and periodically adjusted by CENTRAL BANKs.   **2.** The funds used by a state to finance BALANCE OF PAYMENTS deficits. These funds, also known as international reserves, can include cash, gold, foreign exchange, and SPECIAL DRAWING RIGHTS.

reserve currency   Any state's money that is acceptable by others to settle international debts. The U.S. dollar and the British pound have long been reserve currencies. Since World War II the Japanese yen and the German mark also have become reserve currencies.

resident foreign advisor   An administrative, economic, or social development expert sent for a lengthy tour of duty to a THIRD WORLD state from a more developed nation. His or her job is to train or provide technical expertise to local counterparts.

residual restrictions   QUANTITATIVE RESTRICTIONS that have been maintained by governments since before they became contracting parties to GATT and hence permissible under the GATT "grandfather clause." Most of the residual restrictions still in effect are maintained by developed countries against imports of agricultural products.

resistance   1. An organized effort by some portion of the civil population of a country to oppose militarily the formally established government of an occupying power. The Resistance in WORLD WAR II consisted of all those civilians in states occupied by Germany that in one way or another fought the Nazis, and particularly those in France. After the war the Geneva Convention of 1949 provided that captured members of formally organized resistance groups should be treated as prisoners of war.   2. Any effort by one state or power to oppose the demands or the moves of another power.

resolution   1. An act of a legislature.   2. An act approved by a majority of the representatives of an INTERGOVERNMENTAL ORGANIZATION.

Resolution 242   The United Nations resolution adopted after the 1967 SIX-DAY WAR that called for Israeli withdrawal from occupied territories and respect for "the sovereignty, territorial integrity and political independence of every state in the area."

Resolution 338   The United Nations Resolution that called for a cease-fire during the 1973 YOM KIPPUR WAR. It supplemented Resolution 242 by reaffirming it.

THE MEANING OF RESOLUTION 242

Resolution 242 . . . calls on the parties to make peace and allows Israel to administer the territories it occupied in 1967 until "a just and lasting peace in the Middle East" is achieved. When such a peace is made, Israel is required to withdraw its armed forces "from territories" it occupied during the Six-Day War—not from "the" territories, nor from "all" the territories, but from some of the territories, which included the Sinai Desert, the West Bank, the Golan Heights, East Jerusalem, and the Gaza Strip.

Five and a half months of vehement public diplomacy in 1967 made it perfectly clear what the missing definite article in Resolution 242 means. Ingeniously drafted resolutions calling for withdrawal from "all the territories" were defeated. . . . Speaker after speaker made it explicit that Israel was not to be forced back to the "fragile" and "vulnerable" Armistice Demarcation Lines, but should retire once peace was made to what Resolution 242 called "secure and recognized" boundaries, agreed to by the parties.

SOURCE: Eugene V. Rostow, *The New Republic* (October 21, 1991).

---

restricted area   1. An airspace of defined dimensions, usually above the land areas or territorial waters of a state, within which the flight of aircraft is restricted in accordance with certain specified conditions.   2. An area in which special measures are employed to prevent or minimize interference between friendly military forces.   3. An area under military jurisdiction in which special security measures are employed to prevent unauthorized entry.

retaliation   1. A military strike in response to an earlier action of those now being attacked. This word often is used in the context of nuclear DETERRENCE or nuclear war; then it refers to the notion of inflicting UNACCEPTABLE DAMAGE on an adversary in response to an attack upon oneself. The logic is that if one is capable of inflicting unacceptable damage in a retaliatory or SECOND STRIKE, then any potential enemy is likely to be deterred from starting a war.   2. Action taken by one state against another because of the imposition of a TARIFF or other trade barrier. Retaliation can take a number of forms, including the imposition of higher tariffs or import restrictions, or withdrawal of trade concessions previously agreed to. According to GATT, restrictive action by one country legally entitles the aggrieved party to compensatory action. *See also* SELF-HELP.

retorsion Any perfectly legal but decidedly UNFRIENDLY ACT taken in SELF-HELP by one state against the interests of another in response to an earlier unfriendly act. Retorsion never involves military force; it is limited to expelling diplomats, curbing fishing rights, banning exports, and the like.

retrenchment **1.** A retreat to a position of safety. In military fortifications a retrenchment was a trench to which the soldiers would retreat once their forward trenches had been overrun. **2.** By analogy, a foreign policy position that moves a state back to a position of relative safety as opposed to a more adventurous and exposed position.

revanchism The efforts or desires of states to recover lost territories. If a state is said to have revanchist aspirations, the implication is that it will make an effort, perhaps by means of military force, to recover territories it previously controlled.

reverse engineering A way of obtaining design and manufacturing knowledge through taking an item and dismantling it to see how it was put together. This is why it is so useful to obtain a new weapons system or its plans from a potential adversary. By reverse engineering weapons improvements can be discovered to thwart the enemy's capabilities.

reverse influence The persuasive force that a small CLIENT STATE can exert on its large patron. Some of this influence comes from the fact that as a result of tying itself to the small state, the patron cannot afford to see it collapse. For example, during the 1973 Yom Kippur War Egypt and Syria, because they were being defeated on the battlefield by Israel, sought direct military intervention from the Soviet Union. If the United States had not put its forces on worldwide alert to discourage the Soviets from intervening, they might have entered the war on the side of the Arabs.

reverse preferences A tariff advantage once offered by developing states to imports from certain developed states that granted them PREFERENCES. Reverse preferences characterized the YAOUNDE CONVENTIONS and other trading arrangements between the European Community and some developing states prior to the advent of the GENERALIZED SYSTEM OF PREFERENCES and the signing of the LOMÉ CONVENTION.

revisionism **1.** An approach to foreign policy that attempts to bring about changes in the territorial STATUS QUO. Revisionist states accept the main elements of the existing system—something that differentiates them from REVOLUTIONARY STATES, which want to overthrow the existing international system. The goal of a revisionist state is to advance its own position and expand its territory within the present context. **2.** Interpretations that challenge the orthodox or conventional wisdom. For example, in the United States Cold War Revisionism challenged the view that the Soviet Union was primarily responsible for the Cold War. Revisionism on the origins of the Pacific War argues that U.S. President Franklin D. Roosevelt knew about the impending Japanese attack on Pearl Harbor but was content to let it happen in order to bring the United States into World War II. Historical revisionism of this kind is almost invariably very controversial.

revolution **1.** Any social, economic, agricultural, intellectual, or political movement involving significant transformations of fundamental institutions. Those institutions may be class structures, economic systems, ideas and approaches to knowledge (as in a scientific revolution), methods of producing food supplies (as in a GREEN REVOLUTION), or systems of governance. Political events in which one group uses violence to take power from another group without really changing the political system also are often called revolutions, although the use of the term since the eighteenth century has tended to be confined to fundamental structural changes rather than to changes of personalities at the top. **2.** A right of the citizens of a society to overthrow bad, incompetent, or unjust rulers—by violence if necessary—to establish a better government. The leaders of the English Revolution of 1688 and the American Revolution of 1776, heavily influenced by JOHN LOCKE, believed this strongly. U.S. founder Thomas Jefferson wrote in a letter to William Stevens Smith on November 13, 1787, that "the tree of liberty must be refreshed from time to time with the blood of patriots and tyrants. It is its natural manure." In this context, revolution is a right that helps ensure proper government and threatens only the government of tyrants. The right of revolution serves as a continuous check on potential tyrants. According to U.S. President Abraham Lincoln in his first Inaugural Address, on March 4, 1861: "This country, with its institutions, belongs to the people who inhabit it. Whenever they shall grow weary of the existing government, they can exercise their constitutional right of amending it, or their revolutionary right to dismember or overthrow it."

Revolution must be contrasted with *rebellion*. Theoretically, those in rebellion seek power for its own sake. In seeking domination, they violate the structures of a civil society. In this context, the worst rebels are tyrannical rulers who have violated both their personal honor and their political mandates and thus deserve to be overthrown. The ability of those fighting to overthrow a government to sustain their cause ultimately affects whether history calls them "revolutionaries" or "rebels"—as the Confederate States of America discovered when they lost the American Civil War.

Revolutionary Guards   The personal militia of the AYATOLLAH KHOMEINI and his Iranian Revolution. Established to monitor and police the revolution in Iran, they have a history of brutally enforcing Khomeini's interpretation of the Koran and Islamic law. They have also been very active in the export of the revolution, providing both indigenous and foreign "volunteers for martyrdom" in Iraq, Lebanon, and other states with explosives and weapons training.

revolutionary state   1. A state that actively seeks to overthrow the existing international order and replace it with a new order of its own conception. Napoleonic France and Nazi Germany were revolutionary states. The Soviet Union also appeared to be a revolutionary state, but in the nuclear age, it became increasingly willing to accept the STATUS QUO—at least under those circumstances where it was clearly very dangerous to try to change it.   2. A state in which the government has recently come to power through revolution. *Compare to* REVISIONISM.

revolutionary warfare   Efforts by citizens of a state to overthrow and replace an existing government by military action. Because of its internal nature, a revolutionary war is inherently a CIVIL WAR even though outside assistance is often a factor. While it can involve clashes of traditionally organized armies, as happened during the English Civil War (1642–1648) and the American Revolution (1776–1783), in the twentieth century revolutionaries were more apt to use GUERRILLA WARFARE, as in the Chinese Civil War and the Vietnam War—at least until they were strong enough to confront their enemies with traditionally organized military units. *Compare to* PARTISAN WARFARE; PEOPLE'S WAR.

revolution of rising expectations   The changing attitudes of the people of traditionally poor countries now that the modern mass media have made them realize just how poor they are relative to the industrialized states of the West.

Reykjavik Summit   The United States–Soviet Union summit in Reykjavik, Iceland, that was held between U.S. President Ronald Reagan and Soviet Premier Mikhail Gorbachev in October 1986 and at which the two leaders reestablished a sense of vision in ARMS CONTROL. Prior to the meeting there was an effort to play its importance down. While it was intended as a preliminary meeting for the summit to take place in Washington a few months later, the discussions were far-reaching. Not only did the two leaders discuss going down to zero in INTERMEDIATE-RANGE NUCLEAR FORCES, but they also discussed far-reaching changes in strategic forces, such as the abolition of all BALLISTIC MISSILES. This created great consternation among strategic analysts because it became an element in the discussion even though no serious studies had been done prior to the meeting about its possible consequences. In the end no agreement was reached because Reagan was unwilling to accept the kind of restrictions on the STRATEGIC DEFENSE INITIATIVE program that Gorbachev wanted. The Reykjavik meeting was one of the major milestones on the road to defusing the COLD WAR because it led to subsequent agreements such as the INF TREATY. European governments were relieved that no arms control agreement had been reached: They did not want the U.S. NUCLEAR UMBRELLA suddenly lifted. It was perhaps the first and only time that the

Syngman Rhee (Library of Congress)

West European allies appreciated the value of Reagan's Strategic Defense Initiative. The best comment on Reykjavik was by journalist M. Benson in the *Newark Star Ledger* of October 20, 1986, when he wrote: "The summit that wasn't a summit ended in a failure that wasn't a failure with a deal that wasn't a deal because the superpowers disagreed over a weapon that isn't a weapon."

Rhee, Syngman (1875–1965)   The first president of the Provisional Korean Republic (in exile) from 1919 to 1941. (Korea was then under Japanese occupation.) Rhee, who had a doctorate from Princeton University (1910), spent most of World War II lobbying in Washington, D.C., for a postwar independent Korea. After the war the United States installed Rhee, a right-wing nationalist (and the only Korean leader well known to the Americans), as president of the Republic of Korea (South Korea). In 1948 he outlawed political opposition and ruled as a dictator. Following the North Korean invasion of the South in 1950, the United States and the United Nations (with the Soviet Union absent) agreed "to provide the Republic of Korea with all necessary aid to repel the aggressors." Thus the KOREAN WAR became part of the U.S. policy of CONTAINMENT of communism. Following electoral fraud by Rhee and widespread student revolts in 1960, he was forced into exile and lived in Hawaii until his death.

Rhineland   A German region along the Rhine River. After World War I the Rhineland was demilitarized by the 1919 Treaty of VERSAILLES. Germany's remilitarization of the Rhineland in 1936 constituted a formal rejection of the treaty by ADOLF HITLER's Germany. The small German forces that conducted the reoccupation were under specific orders to retreat if challenged by the French military. But all the French and British government did was issue diplomatic notes. Hitler learned that he could bluff and win—as he would do again in the MUNICH AGREEMENT.

Ribbentrop, Joachim von (1893–1946)   The German foreign minister under Adolf Hitler from 1938 to 1945. He concluded the 1939 NAZI-SOVIET NONAGGRESSION PACT and helped plan the attack on Poland in September 1939, which started World War II in Europe. He was found guilty of war crimes at the Nuremberg Trials and hanged.

Richardson, Lewis F. (1881–1953)   A U.S. scholar who was interested in the frequency and distribution of wars both geographically and temporally and who was one of the first to apply mathematical modeling to the study of international conflict. Richardson was author of *Statistics of Deadly Quarrels* (1960) and *Arms and Insecurity* (1960). His work on conflict modeling has been frequently cited by many subsequent analysts and also applied and developed by those who believe that quantification is a particularly illuminating approach to the study of conflict. *See also* WAR-WEARINESS HYPOTHESIS.

Rickover, Hyman G. (1900–1986)   The U.S. Navy admiral who is considered the "father" of nuclear power. Building on the scientific discoveries of the MANHATTAN PROJECT, he was the guiding force in creating both the first nuclear-powered navy ships and the first civilian nuclear power plants for generating electricity. He led the team that launched the *Nautilus*, the first nuclear-powered submarine, in 1955. He then dominated the nuclear navy until he was finally forced to retire because of age in 1982—after having served for 63 years, longer than any other officer in the history of the U.S. Navy.

Ridgway, Matthew Bunker (1895–   )   The U.S. World War II paratrooper general who is perhaps best known for his contribution to the KOREAN WAR when he replaced the dismissed General Douglas MacArthur in 1951 and turned the demoralized forces of the United States into an effective fighting force that was able to push back North Korean and Chinese troops. Ridgway subsequently became Supreme Allied Commander Europe (1952–1953) and Chief of Staff of the U.S. Army (1953–1955). In this capacity his advice was very important in 1954 in convincing U.S. President Dwight D. Eisenhower that the French position in Vietnam required intervention by U.S. troops if it was to be saved, and that the United States should not get directly involved in what would become the Vietnam War.

right of self-defense   *See* SELF-DEFENSE.

rimland   A key theme in the literature on GEOPOLITICS developed by NICHOLAS J. SPYKMAN, who identified an area that he described as the "inner crescent" or the "Eurasian rimland." In Spykman's view this zone included Western and Central Europe, the plateau countries of the Near East, Turkey, Iran and Afghanistan, Tibet, China and Eastern Siberia, and the three peninsulas of Arabia, India, and Burma-Siam. Spykman wrote in his major work, *America's Strategy and World Politics* (1942): "Who controls the Rimland rules Eurasia; who rules Eurasia controls the destinies of the world." He argued that, with a few exceptions, the

Hyman Rickover and a laughing President Jimmy Carter in 1977. (U.S. Naval Institute)

rimland was where most of the great civilizations of the world had developed. The Soviet Union dominated the Eurasian heartland and pursued a foreign policy of attempting to dominate and eventually break through the rimland and reach warm-water ports. These geopolitical ideas formed part of the basis for the post–World War II strategy of containing Soviet power. Although George F. Kennan did not explicitly talk about the rimland, his recommended CONTAINMENT of the Soviet Union around its periphery rested at least implicitly on the ideas of Spykman. The rimland concept was in part a reaction to the emphasis placed by HALFORD J. MACKINDER on the HEARTLAND THEORY.

Rio Summit   *See* EARTH SUMMIT.

Rio Treaty   *See* INTER-AMERICAN TREATY OF RECIPROCAL ASSISTANCE.

ripeness   A point at which a dispute is ready for resolution and at which outside mediation or intervention is likely to have most impact.

risk analysis 1. The process of studying and assessing the chances of war during normal or crisis conditions. 2. Analysis undertaken for private companies doing business (or considering doing business) in politically unstable states. Risk analysts seek to assess the chances of EXPROPRIATION or social upheavals.

Rogers, William P. (1913–   ) The attorney general of the United States (1957–1961) under President Dwight D. Eisenhower who, as secretary of state (1969–1973) under President Richard M. Nixon, was most noted for having his function as the nation's chief diplomat eclipsed by HENRY A. KISSINGER, the national security advisor, who eventually succeeded Rogers as secretary of state.

Rogers Act of 1924 *See* CALVIN COOLIDGE.

role 1. A position undertaken by an individual that has certain traditions, responsibilities, and expectations associated with it and that sets some limits to the impact of personality. The notion can be understood at a very general level since all foreign policy decision makers have a role as custodians of the NATIONAL INTEREST. It also can be understood in relation to very specific responsibilities that attach to particular positions. 2. A bureaucratic position that leads the individual who fills it to take a particular view on foreign policy issues.

role theory An approach to foreign policy analysis that emphasizes the importance of national role conceptions as a way of understanding foreign policy behavior. Such conceptions include the notion of the state as "faithful ally," as "mediator," or as "regional protector." The notion was initially developed by K. J. HOLSTI in "National Role Conceptions in the Study of Foreign Policy" (*International Studies Quarterly* 14, 1970).

rollback 1. A military tactic that calls for the progressive destruction and/or neutralization of the opposing defenses, starting at the periphery and working inward, to permit deeper penetration of succeeding defense positions. 2. A phrase used during the early years of the COLD WAR to describe what the United States should do to push Soviet influence out of Eastern Europe. This was in contrast to the U.S. policy of containing the Soviet Union inside its current area of influence. Although the Eisenhower Administration came to office having campaigned on the theme of liberation or rollback, it actually embraced the existing CONTAINMENT policy.

Romanov Dynasty The ruling family of Imperial Russia from 1613 to 1917. Contrary to popular impression, all the Romanovs were not all executed by the Bolsheviks during the RUSSIAN REVOLUTION OF 1917. A Romanov PRETENDER to the Russian throne still exists. Only Czar NICHOLAS II and his immediate family were murdered in 1918; many of the other relatives fled into exile.

Rome, Treaty of The treaty establishing the European Economic Community (COMMON MARKET) that was signed in Rome on March 25, 1957. Although a treaty establishing a European Atomic Energy Community (EURATOM) was also signed in Rome the same day, the Treaty of Rome refers only to the EEC Treaty. The Treaty of Rome was intended to establish a closer union of the states and peoples of Western Europe. The two overriding goals were gradually eliminating all legal restrictions on trade, labor migration, and capital movement in the EEC and establishing common external tariffs, so that there would be free movement of goods, services, capital, and peoples within the market. The original EEC Treaty had only six signatories: the EUROPEAN COAL AND STEEL COMMUNITY states of France, Great Britain, Italy, and the BENELUX countries. Great Britain had decided not to be part of this process, thereby marginalizing itself from European cooperation and establishing an ambiguous position regarding moves toward European unity that is still evident even though it is now a full member of the EEC. *See also* SINGLE EUROPEAN ACT.

Rome-Berlin Axis *See* AXIS.

Romero, Oscar (1917–80) The archbishop of San Salvador, El Salvador, assassinated while celebrating mass on March 24, 1980. Archbishop Romero, a Nobel Peace Prize nominee, was an internationally respected opponent of the regime in El Salvador and an outspoken critic of that country's right-wing DEATH SQUADS. At the archbishop's funeral on

March 30, government troops also opened fire on the huge crowds, killing 40 mourners and wounding many others.

Rommel, Erwin (1891–1944)   The best-known of Germany's WORLD WAR II generals. A loyal Nazi who once commanded Adolf Hitler's bodyguard, he later distinguished himself as a tank division commander during the 1940 Battle of FRANCE. Given the command of the Afrika Corps in 1941, he drove the British out of Libya and well into Egypt, earning the nickname of "Desert Fox." In 1942 he was decisively defeated by the British at EL ALAMEIN and retreated across North Africa until he was ordered to abandon his defeated (and soon-to-be-captured) army and return home. As the commander of the German forces in France during the Normandy invasion that began with D-DAY in 1944, he was unable to halt the Allied advance. Wounded in a random air raid on July 17, 1944, he was at home recuperating when he was implicated in the July 20 plot to assassinate Hitler. Because Rommel was Germany's most popular field marshal, Hitler's agents allowed him to take poison on October 14 instead of being tried and executed. In this way Rommel saved his family's reputation and had a state funeral. According to Max Hastings, *Overlord* (1984): "The myth of Rommel as a good German hostile to Nazism prevailed in the west for many years after the war. In reality, the C-in-C of Army Group B remained passionately devoted to Hitler until he became convinced that the war was militarily unwinnable."

ROMMEL THE ARCHAEOLOGIST

The story that [Rommel] had kept up his classics and was a keen archaeologist who spent his scanty leisure in digging for Roman remains was a production of the propagandists. [General] von Esebeck was responsible for it. "Some of us had been scratching about and had turned up some bits of Roman pottery," he told me. "We were looking at them when Rommel came along. What he actually said, when we showed them to him, was: 'What the hell do you want with all that junk?' But you can't tell that from the photograph!"

SOURCE: Desmond Young, *Rommel* (1950).

Rommel, Manfred (1928–   )   The son of ERWIN ROMMEL who, as a Christian Democrat, has been the mayor of Stuttgart, Germany, since 1974. While he initially won the election on his father's good name—the field marshal, unlike many other Nazi officers, was never implicated in war crimes—Manfred Rommel was very popular in his own right. He has even shown some political courage in defending the rights of immigrants in today's Germany. When he ran for reelection in 1990, the major opposition party did not even put up a candidate. Only a local GREEN party opposed him. Its slogan: "Send Rommel to the desert" (*New York Times*, November 24, 1991).

Roosevelt, Franklin Delano (1882–1945)   The president of the United States (1933–1945) who led his nation through the GREAT DEPRESSION of the 1930s and to victory against Germany in WORLD WAR II. Roosevelt entered public life as a member of the New York Senate (1910–1913). He became assistant secretary of the navy (1913–1920) in the Wilson Administration, the unsuccessful Democratic nominee for vice president in 1920, and governor of New York (1929–1933). Roosevelt reached the height of political power despite the fact that, after 1921, when he contracted polio, he was basically confined to a wheelchair. Yet because he was able to stand (with braces) to give speeches and because reporters were not allowed to take pictures that made him appear to be disabled, much of the U.S. public was unaware of his condition. Some of Roosevelt's foreign policy was very controversial. Critics argue that he was overly anxious to get the United States into the war in Europe, while others contend that he did not act decisively enough. Judgments about his postwar intentions of cooperation with the Soviet Union also run the spectrum from those who believe that this was a necessity to those who believe that he gave far too much away on Eastern Europe and that there was a sell-out at YALTA. Some observers also believe that had he lived longer, the opportunities for postwar cooperation between the United States and the Soviet Union would have been enhanced.

Roosevelt, Theodore "Teddy" (1858–1919)   The president of the United States from 1901 to 1909. After serving in the New York state legislature (1882–1884), managing a ranch in North Dakota (1884–1886), serving on the U.S. Civil Service

Roosevelt, Theodore "Teddy" (1858–1919)

Franklin D. Roosevelt signs the declaration of war against Japan on December 8, 1941. (National Archives)

FDR ON REFORMING THE U.S. NAVY

You should go through the experience of trying to get any changes in the thinking . . . and action of the career diplomats and then you'd know what a real problem was. But the Treasury and the State Department put together are nothing as compared with the Na-a-vy. . . . To change anything in the Na-a-vy is like punching a feather bed. You punch it with your right and you punch it with your left until you are finally exhausted, and then you find the damn bed just as it was before you started punching.

SOURCE: President Franklin D. Roosevelt quoted in Marriner Eccles, *Beckoning Frontiers* (1951).

Commission (1889–1895), heading the New York City Police Department (1895–1897), and serving as the assistant secretary of the navy (1897–1898), he became the colonel who led the Rough Riders in Cuba during the 1898 SPANISH-AMERICAN WAR. He was elected governor of New York on the basis of his war record and was made the Republican vice president under William McKinley by the party bosses, who wanted him out of New York because he was too much of a reformer. He became president after an assassin shot McKinley in 1901. Roosevelt, who won election to the presidency in his own right in 1904, took an expansive view of the presidency and thus set the tone for most of the presidents to follow. His BIG STICK poli-

Theodore Roosevelt (Library of Congress)

Our system makes no adequate provision for the directing brain which every army must have to work successfully. Common experience has shown that this cannot be furnished by any single man without assistants, and that it requires a body of officers working together under the direction of a chief and entirely separate from and independent of the administrative staff of an army (such as the adjutants, quartermasters, commissaries . . .). This body of officers, in distinction from the administrative staff, has come to be called a general staff.

SOURCE: Secretary of War Elihu Root argues for a general staff for the U.S. Army in *The Annual Report of the Secretary of War for the Year 1902.*

cies gave the United States the Panama Canal and made the United States a major player on the world scene. For his brokering an end to the RUSSO-JAPANESE WAR, he was awarded the Nobel Peace Prize in 1906.

Root, Elihu (1845–1937)   The U.S. secretary of war from 1899 to 1904 under Presidents McKinley and Roosevelt and secretary of state from 1905 to 1909 under Roosevelt. After the chaotic administration of the SPANISH-AMERICAN WAR, Root worked to reform the United States Army by introducing the GENERAL STAFF system. He won the Nobel Peace Prize in 1912 for efforts to create better relations with Latin America and his furtherance of international arbitration of disputes.

Rosecrance, Richard N. (1930–   )   The American analyst of international relations who is per-

haps best known for his work dealing with the structure of the international system, which is enunciated most fully in *Action and Reaction in World Politics: International Systems in Perspective* (1963) and *International Relations: Peace or War?* (1973). Rosecrance also has analyzed the changing nature of power and the relationship between military and economic instruments of policy in *The Rise of the Trading State: Commerce and Conquest in the Modern World* (1986). He has written on a wide range of other subjects, including Australian-Japanese relations, British defense policy, and strategic nuclear deterrence.

Rosenau, James Nathan (1924–   )   The American author of a major series of books and articles that attempted to apply scientific methods to the study of foreign policy and international relations. He argued that the key was always to ask one question about any foreign policy behavior: "Of what larger pattern is this behavior an instance?" An important conceptual study, *Public Opinion and Foreign Policy* (1961), was followed by a much more empirical approach, coauthored with OLE R. HOLSTI, dealing with the beliefs of American elites in the post-Vietnam era, entitled *American Leaders in World Affairs: Vietnam and the Breakdown of Consensus* (1984). One of Rosenau's most famous studies was "Pre-theories and theories of foreign policy" in *The Scientific Study of Foreign Policy*

(1980), which identified key INDEPENDENT VARIABLES (such as systemic, societal, role, individual, and governmental) and attempted to show how they influenced foreign policy in different kinds of states. He also developed the MULTICENTRIC WORLD idea and the concepts of the PENETRATED STATE and POSTINTERNATIONAL POLITICS.

Rosenberg, Julius (1918–1953) and **Ethel** (1915–1953) Members of a United States spy ring that passed information on the U.S. atomic bomb program to the Soviet Union. After a trial marked by controversy over their role in the acquisition by the Soviets of U.S. atomic bomb data, they were convicted of treason in 1951 and executed in 1953. They were the only U.S. citizens ever to be executed for peacetime espionage. Many historians attribute their death sentence to the anti-Communist feelings heightened by MCCARTHYISM.

Rostow, Walt Whitman (1916–) The economist and analyst of international affairs who served in the U.S. Office of Strategic Services during World War II and became President Lyndon Johnson's national security advisor, replacing McGeorge Bundy in 1966. As national security advisor, he is generally seen as having confirmed Johnson's willingness to escalate U.S. involvement in Vietnam. He also is regarded as someone who protected Johnson from dissenting views and opinions and transformed the post of NSA from being that of manager into that of advocate. His most famous book, which looked at the problems of economic development in the Third World, was *The Stages of Economic Growth* (1960).

round A cycle of multilateral trade negotiations under GATT, culminating in simultaneous agreements among participating countries to reduce tariff and nontariff trade barriers; for example, the Kennedy Round.

Rousseau, Jean-Jacques (1712–1778) The Swiss-born French Enlightenment political philosopher whose writings on democracy and the SOCIAL CONTRACT were major influences on the American and French revolutions. His most famous book, *The Social Contract* (1762), opens with the poignant:

Jean-Jacques Rousseau (Library of Congress)

"Man is born free, and everywhere he is in chains." To Rousseau, people in the STATE OF NATURE, or "noble savages," were good; but civilization and the institutions of society had corrupted them. The only form of social organization that could get humanity back to the state of natural liberty was radical direct democracy. Only this kind of popular sovereignty offered legitimacy; only the general will as expressed by the people could make valid law. Rousseau's notions fell on fertile intellectual ground. His basic ideas—that ordinary people had the right to govern themselves and had the right to overthrow kings who claimed a competing divine or hereditary right—can be found in the U.S. Declaration of Independence and in the U.S. Constitution. In his thinking about the relations among states, Rousseau has generally been seen as one of the forerunners of modern REALISM. Although this has been questioned by some analysts, in *A Lasting Peace through the Fed-*

eration of Europe (1782) Rousseau seemed to share the pessimism about international politics that characterizes most proponents of realism. This is evident in his comment:

> Every community without laws and without rulers, every union formed and maintained by nothing better than chance, must inevitably fall into quarrels and dissensions. . . . The historic union of the nations of Europe has entangled their rights and interest in a thousand complications; they touch each other at so many points that no one of them can move without giving a jar to all the rest. . . . Let us admit then that the Powers of Europe stand to each other strictly in a state of war, and that all the separate treaties between them are in the nature rather of a temporary truce than a real peace.

This statement is in many respects typical of Rousseau's thinking about peace and war. Because of his skepticism about the prospects for a lasting peace, Rousseau is often bracketed with THOMAS HOBBES in his thinking about international politics.

Royal Institute of International Affairs *See* CHATHAM HOUSE.

Royal Ulster Constabulary (RUC) The civilian police force of NORTHERN IRELAND. The RUC, with 13,000 members, has suffered about 300 deaths since 1969. Largely a Protestant institution, it has been attacked by Irish Catholics as a symbol of British occupation and anti-Catholic authority.

Ruhr The valley that, because of its rich coal deposits, has traditionally been the industrial heartland of Germany. In 1923 France claimed that Germany had defaulted on coal shipments from the Ruhr owed as REPARATIONS. A French and Belgian military force then occupied the area. The WEIMAR REPUBLIC government ordered miners and railway workers there not to cooperate and continued to pay their salaries for their passive resistance. Nevertheless, despite British and U.S. objections to the occupation, France obtained some additional coal as reparations. The occupation ended in 1925 on the eve of the LOCARNO treaty. The Ruhr occupation was one of the major

factors that led to the hyperinflation in Germany during the mid-1920s: The German government kept printing money to pay Ruhr workers who, for almost a year, were told not to work.

rules of engagement 1. Military or paramilitary orders that define the circumstances and limitations under which force can be used. For example, soldiers might be told to shoot only if they are fired upon first, or police might be told to use deadly force only when lives (as opposed to property) are in immediate danger. 2. Directives from a military headquarters that delineate the circumstances and limitations under which troops will initiate and/or continue combat operations. Rules of engagement are intended to govern the behavior of military forces in certain specified contingencies, ranging from crises through military interventions, to limited wars. Specific rules are often highly classified (secret); they reflect a desire to ensure civilian control over military operations—that conflict should not be initiated or escalated as a result of unauthorized actions. Rules of engagement may be general or detailed, stringent or permissive. Finding the appropriate balance, however, can be difficult. If the rules are too specific, military commanders may be robbed of discretion; on the other hand, if

---

COUNTING AND THE RULES OF ENGAGEMENT

You are a young lieutenant in Vietnam. The rules of engagement say that you can call in air support if you are confronted with more than twenty of the enemy. Less than twenty enemy you and your men have to handle by yourselves. One morning you count fifteen "Charlies" advancing through the rice paddy in front of you. I can tell you with total assurance that Lieutenant Future General claims he sees thirty enemy, calls in an air strike, kills the enemy with less effort, and saves his men. The overall war effort may suffer because somewhere else Lieutenant Total Honesty, facing nineteen Viet Cong, is still counting and hoping to get twenty. . . . And those who condemn Lieutenant Future General as they read this had best ask themselves quickly which officer they would prefer to walk with on patrol.

SOURCE: Arthur T. Hadley, *The Straw Giant* (1986).

---

they are too general, they will provide insufficient guidance. Closely related is the issue of how restrictive the rules are. The importance of this can be seen in United States naval involvement in the Persian Gulf in the late 1980s. In the aftermath of the 1987 attack on the USS *Stark* by an Iraqi aircraft, the rules of engagement were made more permissive. This was an important factor in the shooting down of a civilian Iranian passenger jet by the USS *Vincennes* during hostilities in 1988.

rules of the game   A term that is sometimes used in international politics to describe the normative restraints and regulatory principles that influence the conduct of states. According to Raymond Cohen in *International Politics: The Rules of the Game* (1981), the term can be used to cover a spectrum of rules, from tacit codes of conduct and the spirit of agreements to formalized international agreements, treaties, and norms.

rules of war   *See* LAW OF WAR.

Rummel, Rudolf J. (1932–   )   The U.S. analyst who developed the concept of the dimensionality of nations in *The Dimensions of Nations* (1972), in which he examined how differences in the characteristics of pairs of nations influenced the probable outcome of conflict between them. Rummel collected data for 236 variables about 82 nations, which were then subjected to a technique known as FACTOR ANALYSIS. He found that there was no close relationship between domestic conflict behavior and foreign conflict behavior.

running dog   A political stooge; a Chinese Communist term of derision for someone subservient to capitalist masters.

rural guerrilla warfare   *See* GUERRILLA WARFARE, RURAL.

ruse   A trick designed to deceive the enemy, thereby obtaining an advantage. (It is sometimes seen in its full French usage, *ruse de guerre* or "ruse of war.") It is characterized by deliberately exposing false information to the collection means of the enemy. Sun Tzu advised in *The Art of War* (fourth century B.C.): "When capable, feign incapacity;

A CLASSIC *RUSE DE GUERRE*

As to new stratagems, when the armies are engaged in conflict, every captain should endeavor to invent such as will encourage his own troops and dishearten those of the enemy. . . . In proof of which I will cite the example of the Roman Dictator C. Sulpicius, who, being about to come to battle, with the Gauls, armed all the teamsters and camp-followers, and mounted them upon the mules and other beasts of burden, and supplied them with standards, so as to seem like regular cavalry. These he placed behind a hill, with orders to show themselves to the enemy at a given signal during the heat of battle. The artifice, being carried out as ordered, so alarmed the Gauls as to cause them to lose the day.

SOURCE: Niccolò Machiavelli, *The Discourses* (1517).

---

when active, inactivity; when near, make it appear that you are far away; when far away, that you are near. Offer the enemy a bait to lure him; feign disorder and strike him. . . . Keep him under strain and wear him down. When he is united, divide him. Attack where he is unprepared; sally out when he does not expect you. These are the strategist's keys to victory."

Rush-Bagot Agreement of 1817   The treaty between the United States and the United Kingdom that demilitarized the border between the United States and Canada. It was first established as an executive agreement, then formally ratified as a treaty.

Rushdie, Salman (1947–   )   The Indian-born British author of the controversial novel *The Satanic Verses* (1988), which made him a target of fundamentalist Islamic furor because of its perceived blasphemy. In 1989 Iran's AYATOLLAH KHOMEINI called on Muslims to kill Rushdie for the defamation of Islam and the Prophet Muhammad. The ayatollah's death sentence, a *fatwa*, was accompanied by the promise of a huge financial reward for the successful assassin. This triggered a sweeping international reaction. Great Britain and Iran broke off diplomatic relations. The winner of the 1988 Nobel Prize for literature, Naguib Mahfouz of Egypt, called Khomeini's actions "intellectual terrorism." After Khomeini's death later in 1989, the Iranian government reaffirmed the *fatwa*. Western commentators debated the appropriateness of proposed responses to what was widely considered to be a terroristic attack on free speech and civil liberties. Some bookstores in the United States and the United Kingdom pulled the book from the shelves, only to be criticized for bowing to terrorist-inspired fear. The basis of these fears was confirmed by bombings of some bookstores that carried the book and by the murder of the book's Japanese translator and severe wounding of its Italian translator in a knife attack. Rushdie remains in hiding, surfacing only to give speeches on his ordeal to surprised and sympathetic audiences. Rushdie has always maintained that his novel is "a whimsical tale" that in no way insults Islam.

Rusk, Dean D. (1909–   )   The U.S. secretary of state throughout the administrations of John F. Kennedy and Lyndon B. Johnson (1961–1969). He was previously assistant secretary of state for Far Eastern affairs (1950–1952) and president of the Rockefeller Foundation (1952–1961). While a fine administrator, as secretary of state he allowed advocacy of major foreign policy decisions to become the domain of the president's national security advisors. His role in getting the United States involved in the VIETNAM WAR as well as his constant defense of the war to the Congress and the public so ruined his personal credibility and popularity that it was impossible for him, upon leaving office, to obtain employment in any major institution. Consequently, friends arranged for him to teach at the University of Georgia in his native state. There he has remained.

RUSK THREATENS BRITAIN

[Dean] Rusk was an Anglophile and a former Rhodes scholar, who was deeply distressed by the British attitude [about the Vietnam War]. According to Louis Heren, a British correspondent in Washington, Rusk asked him at a cocktail party why the British couldn't manage [to send to Vietnam] "just one battalion of the Black Watch?" Patiently Heren explained British policy. Rusk glowered: "When the Russians invade Sussex, don't expect us to come and help you."

SOURCE: David Dimbleby and David Reynolds, *An Ocean Apart* (1988).

Russell, Bertrand Arthur (1872–1970)   The English mathematician and philosopher who became notorious during World War I as an outspoken pacifist. This attitude got him dismissed from his teaching post at Trinity College of Cambridge University and a short prison term. He later wrote in his *Autobiography* (1967): "I discovered to my amazement that average men and women were delighted at the prospect of war. I had fondly imagined what most pacifists contended, that wars were forced upon a reluctant population by despotic and Machiavellian governments." Between the world wars he earned an international reputation as a radical social reformer and progressive educator. He so hated fascism that he suspended his pacifist beliefs for World War II. During the Cold War he became one of the leaders of the CAMPAIGN FOR NUCLEAR DISARMAMENT in Great Britain and in the 1960s an outspoken critic of the VIETNAM WAR. In 1950 he was awarded the Nobel Prize for literature.

Bertrand Russell (Library of Congress)

Russian Civil War   The merciless internal warfare and RED TERROR within the Russian Empire during consolidation of the Bolshevik regime from 1917 to 1922. There was immediate opposition to the new Communist government from other socialist parties, the military, czarists, numerous nationalities, and the liberals. The BOLSHEVIKS, with their newly created RED ARMY, were able to fend off advances of the White and Green armies, the coalition of anti-Bolshevik military forces. The conservative Whites had no coherent economic, political, or social policies, failed to gain support of the peasantry (the Greens), and were plagued by disjointed action. Outside allied intervention on behalf of the Whites was halfhearted and uncoordinated. The civil war was won in 1923 when the Red Army established Bolshevik control in almost all the lands of the former empire, including many non-Russian nationalities. Then the Union of Soviet Socialist Republics was proclaimed. The only parts of czarist Russia that escaped immediate inclusion into the new Soviet Union were Finland and the BALTIC STATES.

Russian Coup of 1991   The failed attempt by Kremlin hard-liners to reverse the democratic reforms of Soviet President MIKHAIL GORBACHEV and reassert the supremacy of the Communist Party. The coup began on August 18 when representatives of the coup leaders detained Gorbachev, his family, and several aides at Gorbachev's vacation home in the Crimea.

On August 19 *Tass,* the official Soviet news agency, announced that Gorbachev was "ill" and that Vice President Gennadi Yanayev and seven other officials from the "State Committee for the State of Emergency" had assumed leadership of the country. "Acting President" Yanayev said Gorbachev was "very sick" but could someday possibly return to office. Troops and tanks surrounded the Russian parliament building in Moscow where elected Russian President BORIS YELTSIN and his government were located. Several tanks defected to the opposition, and officers refused orders to attack the parliament building. Yeltsin then called for a general strike and demanded the return of Gorbachev. U.S. President George Bush stated that the United States would not recognize the legitimacy of the new government and called for Gorbachev's return.

On August 20 Yeltsin spoke with both Bush and British Prime Minister John Major. Leaders of the republics of Kazahkstan and Ukraine also denounced the coup. Former Soviet Foreign Minister Eduard Shevardnadze joined the crowd outside the parliament building in Moscow. Rallies in support of Gorbachev and Yeltsin were held in Leningrad, Moscow, and other cities. When armored vehicles sent by the coup leaders cautiously approached the Russian parliament building, thousands of protesters blocked them, which resulted in the deaths of three defenders. However, the tanks pulled back. The European Community froze more than $1 billion U.S. in food and technical aid that had been promised to the Soviet Union. On August 21 the coup collapsed. Tanks withdrew from Moscow and the Baltic Republics and returned to their bases. The Presidium of the Supreme Soviet voided the decrees of the emergency committee. On August 22 Gorbachev arrived back in Moscow. While he was still president, power in the Soviet Union had shifted to Yeltsin. The coup was the pivotal event that led to the total dissolution of the Soviet Union by the end of the year. It failed because the plotters could not depend on the loyalty of the military, because they did not cut the opposition's fax and telephone communications, and because they were not ruthless enough to kill or detain opposition leaders immediately. The plotters were rightly and derisively called the "gang that couldn't coup straight."

Russian Provisional Government   The government of Russia immediately after the abdication of Czar NICHOLAS II in 1917. It continued until it was overthrown by the BOLSHEVIKS under V. I. LENIN later that year. Civil liberties such as freedom of speech, press, and assembly were granted by the Provisional Government; but even though it received diplomatic recognition from abroad, its power was slight and only held in a few cities. At the local level the separate SOVIETs provided leadership. The government's failure to give land to the peasants, control the military, improve the economy, or solve nationality problems, together with its unsuccessful summer military offensive against the invading Germans, left it helpless. During uprisings in July ALEKSANDR KERENSKY became prime minister but was too weak to forestall the Bolsheviks or the RUSSIAN CIVIL WAR.

Russian Revolution of 1905   The largely spontaneous uprising against czarist autocracy that began on BLOODY SUNDAY (January 9, 1905) when a peaceful demonstration of factory workers in St. Petersburg was attacked by czarist troops. These revolutionary workers, intellectuals, ethnic minorities, and peasants found the government repressive and unbearable since the country was controlled by Czar Nicholas II, the nobility, the church, and the army. By October the czar was forced to grant the "October Manifesto" limiting his autocratic power, granting limited civil freedoms, and establishing a new legislative body, the Duma. While disturbances continued until 1907, the government was able to reassert control. V. I. LENIN deemed these events a "dress rehearsal" for 1917.

Russian Revolution of 1917   The March 1917 overthrow of Czar NICHOLAS II and the Romanov dynasty, which had ruled the Russian Empire for more than 300 years. During World War I several factors, including food shortages, lack of coal for heating in the cities, inept conduct of the war, strikes, and sheer war-weariness, eroded what little support the monarchy had. Events fed on each other and snowballed into a general strike in February 1917 in Petrograd and other cities. Thousands of soldiers joined the ranks of the protesters in a social revolution that was spontaneous in character and surprised all radical parties. In March, when Nicholas II abdicated, representatives of the national legislature (the Duma) formed the RUSSIAN PROVISIONAL GOVERNMENT. But the new government continued its participation in World War I, which led to widespread economic and social dislocation and popular discontent. A social revolution continued on two fronts: In the cities SOVIETs were formed with the people themselves taking charge; in the villages peasants expropriated estates. On November 7, 1917, the provisional government was overthrown by a revolutionary group known as the BOLSHEVIK ("Majority") wing of the Russian Social Democratic Party. V. I. LENIN, leader of the Bolsheviks, was named head of the first Soviet government. The new regime accepted the harsh treaty of BREST-LITOVSK with Germany and the other Central Powers on March 3, 1918, ending Russia's participation in World War I. The Soviets declared all land the property of the state, and a rapid succession of decrees nationalized banks, factories, railroads, and other sectors of the economy. The bitter RUSSIAN CIVIL WAR ensued, but by 1923 the Bolsheviks had consolidated their power.

THE AUTHOR OF
THE RUSSIAN REVOLUTION

I always regard myself as the real author of the Russian Revolution, because I said that the best thing the soldiers could do in the 1914–18 war was to shoot their officers and go home; and the Russians were the only soldiers who had the intelligence to take my advice.

SOURCE: George Bernard Shaw quoted in Hesketh Pearson, *G.B.S.: A Postscript* (1951).

Russo-Finnish War   *See* FINNISH-RUSSIAN WAR.

Russo-Japanese War   A 1904–5 war between Japan and Russia over dominance in China's Manchuria and Korea. In 1904 Japan launched a surprise attack on the Russian forces at Port Arthur after Russia had reneged on its agreement to withdraw from Manchuria. In a series of battles at Port Arthur and Mukden, the Russian forces were soundly defeated. The Japanese fleet bottled up the local Russian fleet and defeated Russia's Baltic fleet when it reached the Tsushima Strait between Korea and Japan. In the 1905 Treaty of PORTSMOUTH, brokered by U.S. President Theodore Roosevelt, Japan got the Russian lease to Port Arthur and the Liaotung Peninsula, a position of privilege in Manchuria, and Korea (which became a protectorate). The Russo-Japanese War was a watershed, because it was the first war in modern times when a non-Western nation defeated a European power. This brought a shift in the balance of power in Europe and made Russia seek a rapprochement with France and Great Britain, hence the TRIPLE ENTENTE.

S

SA The *Sturmabteilung* (stormtroopers) or "brown-shirts" of NAZI Germany; a paramilitary group created by the Nazi Party in 1921. Their beatings and intimidation of opponents aided ADOLF HITLER's rise to power. After Hitler became chancellor the regular German Army demanded that the SA, with over half a million men, be curtailed. Hitler himself had come to fear its leaders. In what became known as the "night of the long knives" (June 30, 1934), he had the SA leadership group, possibly as many as 1,000 men, murdered. Thereafter an unarmed SA would never be even a remote threat to the regular military. But its rival, the notorious SS under HEINRICH HIMMLER, developed into a military force parallel to the army—and it was the SS that operated the CONCENTRATION CAMPS and committed many of the atrocities of World War II.

Saar A heavily industrialized state in southwestern Germany now known as Saarland. In the settlement after World War I, the Saar with its coal mines was detached from Germany and placed under French military protection, although Germany retained some limited autonomy. In a 1935 plebiscite, the inhabitants chose to return to Germany. Following World War II, the Saar was once again occupied by France. After a popular referendum in 1955, the inhabitants voted overwhelmingly to rejoin Germany.

Saavedra Lamas, Carlos (1878–1959) Argentina's minister of foreign affairs (1932–1938) who won the 1936 Nobel Peace Prize for his mediation of the 1935 truce that ended the CHACO WAR between Bolivia and Paraguay.

Sabah An area of northern Borneo (previously known as British North Borneo) that was incorporated into Malaysia in the 1960s and also is claimed by the Philippines. The government of the Philippines protested Sabah's incorporation into Malaysia on the grounds that Sabah originally belonged to the Philippines and had been sold illegally to Great Britain by the sultans of Brunei and Sulu in the nineteenth century. The British government as well as the United Nations was satisfied that the majority of the inhabitants approved their incorporation into Malaysia in 1963. The Philippines, however, maintained its claim to the area. In 1986 both Malaysia and the Philippines asserted that they wanted to resolve the Sabah issue and created a joint panel of foreign ministry officials to adjudicate. The difficulty remained that the claim to Sabah was included in the constitution of the Philippines. In 1987 the government sought but failed to get amending legislation. While the continuing territorial dispute over Sabah retains the potential for mischief between Malaysia and the Philippines, the issue seems to have diminished in importance.

saber rattling Any implied threat to use military power; a figurative shaking of a sword (or saber) at an adversary.

sabotage **1.** The deliberate destruction of property. **2.** The slowing down of work in order to damage a business. During a 1910 French railway strike, the strikers destroyed some of the wooden shoes (sabots) that held the rails in place. Thus "sabotage" came into the English language in the

A 1944 Italian antisabotage poster. (Library of Congress)

context of industrial warfare. During World War II the word became popular as a description of the efforts of secret agents to hinder an enemy's industrial military capabilities.

BUREAUCRACY THWARTS SABOTAGE

The sense of bungling and futility cast a shadow over Washington and over political life generally. In the country at large, said one observer, a profound cynicism had developed toward "the system." [President Franklin D.] Roosevelt was still popular, but not the major political and economic institutions which affected people's lives. In the late months of 1942 a joke was being told of a Japanese spy sent to discover which agencies of American government could be sabotaged and thereby cripple the American war effort. He reported back: "Suggested plan hopeless. Americans brilliantly prepared. For each agency we destroy two more are already fully staffed and doing exactly the same work."

SOURCE: Geoffrey Perrett, *Days of Sadness, Years of Triumph: The American People 1939–1945* (1973).

Sabra and Shatila PALESTINIAN refugee camps in Lebanon in which refugees were slaughtered by members of the CHRISTIAN PHALANGE militia in 1982. No accurate figures of the number killed is known, but the victims are thought to number several thousand. The Israeli minister of defense, Ariel Sharon, was criticized for allowing the Phalangists into the camps while his troops remained outside. Sharon resigned his position when an Israeli government investigative panel, the Kahan Commission, found him partially responsible for the bloodshed.

SACEUR Supreme Allied Commander Europe; the top military commander of the NORTH ATLANTIC TREATY ORGANIZATION's land and air forces in Europe. SACEUR has so far been a U.S. Army general, in part because of the need to seek authority for the use of nuclear weapons from the U.S. president but also as recognition of the large U.S. contribution to NATO.

Sadat, Anwar al- (1918–1981) President of Egypt from 1970 to 1981. As an Egyptian Army officer during World War II, Sadat was court-martialed and imprisoned by the British for collaborating with the Nazis. In 1952 he participated in the coup that deposed King Farouk. Thereafter he served as Egyptian President GAMAL ABDAL NASSER's aide and vice president of Egypt (1964–1966; 1969–1970). In 1970 he succeeded to the presidency upon Nasser's death and initiated the 1973 Arab-Israeli YOM KIPPUR WAR. Afterward he sought a rapprochement with the United States and Israel. In a dramatic gesture he visited Jerusalem in 1977 and addressed the Israeli parliament. This led to the CAMP DAVID ACCORDS and the formal Egyptian-Israeli peace treaty of 1979. For this Sadat shared the 1978 Nobel Peace Prize with Israeli Prime Minister MENACHEM BEGIN.

Anwar Sadat (Library of Congress)

Sadat was assassinated in 1981 as he reviewed a military parade in Cairo. As army vehicles passed the reviewing stand, one halted and four men in military fatigues leapt out of the back and stormed the presidential dais, firing automatic rifles and throwing hand grenades. The assassins were members of TANZIM AL-JIHAD, an Islamic fundamentalist group that considered Sadat to be overly influenced by the West and a traitor to the Arab cause, in large measure because of his participation in the Camp David Accords. Sadat was succeeded by his vice president, HOSNI MUBARAK, who oversaw the trial and execution of Sadat's assassins.

saddle point   A concept from GAME THEORY to describe the point that neither side in a zero-sum situation can improve upon by independent movement.

safe conduct   A document similar to a PASSPORT, issued by a military authority, that a person must have to enter or remain in a restricted area; it guarantees passage, without hindrance or harm, through a military or conflict zone. A safe conduct also may enable the holder to move goods to or from places within the area and to engage in trade there, which would otherwise be forbidden.

Historically, the right of free passage for the envoys (or heralds) of the enemy was a long-accepted practice between belligerents. This allowed for the passing of messages between the opposing forces, necessary to allow for peace and/or surrender negotiations and to reach agreement on when and where the armies should meet for battle. While the changing nature of warfare and communications has made safe conducts unnecessary for some of these roles, the principle is still valid under the RULES OF WAR and may even have some relevance during civil wars. Forces of the Palestine Liberation Organization, for example, were accorded safe conduct from Lebanon in 1982 after the Phalangist massacre of Palestinian inhabitants of the Sabra and Shatila refugee camps.

safeguard   1. A temporary or emergency international trade action, such as import quotas or higher tariffs, designed to protect industries that are suddenly threatened by a large volume of imports. A country's right to impose import controls or other temporary trade restrictions to prevent commercial injury to a domestic industry, and the corresponding right of exporters not to be arbitrarily deprived of access to markets, are what is meant by the term multilateral safeguard system. Provisions to this effect exist in the GATT and, in particular, in Article XIX, which is entitled: "Emergency Action on Imports of Particular Products." Temporary measures—which may take the form of higher tariffs, tariff quotas, QUANTITATIVE RESTRICTIONS, or VOLUNTARY RESTRAINT AGREEMENTS—are designed to reduce the amount or speed of the internal economic adjustments required when domestic industries are faced with increased foreign competition and rapidly rising imports. GATT Article XIX permits a country whose domestic industries or workers are adversely affected by increased imports to withdraw or modify concessions it had earlier granted or to impose new import restrictions if it can establish that a product is "being imported in such increased quantities as to cause or threaten serious injury to domestic producers," and to keep such restrictions in effect "for such time as may be necessary to prevent or remedy such injury."

2. Agreements and verification procedures concerning the peaceful use of atomic energy enforced by the INTERNATIONAL ATOMIC ENERGY AGENCY.

safe house An innocent-appearing house or apartment used by an INTELLIGENCE AGENCY to hide defectors or agents.

Saint-Germain, Treaty of The 1919 peace treaty that ended World War I between Austria and the Allies, dismembered the Austrian-Hungarian Empire, and created the Austrian Republic. Austria lost huge amounts of territory to Czechoslovakia, Italy, Poland, Romania, and Yugoslavia, had its army limited to 30,000 men and its navy dismembered. In addition, it was forced to pay reparations and forbidden to unite with Germany. *See also* ANSCHLUSS.

Sa'iqa, al- **1.** A PALESTINIAN group formed in 1968 to represent Syrian interests in the Palestinian struggle; its name means "thunderbolt." It is the Palestinian wing of the Syrian Baath party. **2.** The name of Egypt's antiterrorist hostage rescue unit.

Sakharov, Andrei Dmitrievich (1921–1989) The Russian physicist known as the "father" of the Soviet Union's nuclear bomb. During the LEONID BREZHNEV years he became the Soviet Union's best-known DISSIDENT because of his objections to atmospheric testing of nuclear bombs and his unrelenting demand for U.S.-Soviet cooperation in limiting the PROLIFERATION of nuclear arms and in dealing with problems of the Third World. He campaigned for the Soviet government to allow freedom of speech and the open circulation of information. His crusade against human rights violations in the Soviet Union earned him the Nobel Peace Prize in 1975, but cost him his position at the Lebedev Physics Institute. In 1980 he was stripped of his state honors and exiled to the city of Gorky until 1986, when General Secretary MIKHAIL GORBACHEV invited him back to Moscow. Sakharov continued his opposition to the Soviet government, especially against the Communist Party of the Soviet Union as the only power within the Soviet constitution. Not until March 1990, three months after Sakharov's death, did the CPSU agree to eliminate its guaranteed monopoly and did the changes within the Soviet Union that the man known as the "conscience of the nation" had sought for three decades actually begin to take place.

salami tactics One slice at a time; any military or negotiating campaign that seeks to wear down an opponent little by little.

Salazar, Antonio (1899–1970) The fascist dictator of Portugal from 1932 until 1968 when the military who brought him to power brought him down. While he supported the AXIS during World War II, he kept Portugal neutral. This technical neutrality allowed him to lead Portugal into the North Atlantic Treaty Organization in 1949.

salience Something that is prominent and around which actors can focus expectations and behavior. In limiting war, for example, the limitations tend to be focused around salient factors such as a geographical boundary or a river. This notion is developed by THOMAS C. SCHELLING in *Arms and Influence* (1966).

Salinas de Gortari, Carlos (1948–) The president of Mexico since 1988. He has implemented major economic reforms, making Mexico more economically competitive and attractive to foreign investment. In 1992 he concluded the NORTH AMERICAN FREE TRADE AGREEMENT with Canada and the United States.

SALT (Strategic Arms Limitation Talks) The negotiations between the United States and the Soviet Union to promote balanced and verifiable limits on strategic nuclear weapons. SALT I started in 1969; after two and a half years of negotiating, the parties signed the ABM TREATY and an interim agreement, which presumably froze offensive weapons at existing levels for five years. The agreement restricted the Soviet Union to 2,347 launchers and the United States to 1,710—an asymmetry that was offset by the U.S. deployment of multiple warheads (MIRVs) on its missiles. SALT II, which began in 1972, sought to achieve a comprehensive agreement to replace the interim agreement. A SALT II treaty was signed by the United States and the

Soviet Union in 1979, but U.S. Senate ratification of the treaty was postponed indefinitely in January 1980 in response to the late December 1979 Soviet invasion of Afghanistan. Nevertheless, the United States abided by the terms of the treaty until 1986, when President Ronald Reagan asserted that Soviet violations made it impossible for the United States to continue doing so. Reagan told a news conference on June 11, 1986: "The Soviet regime, for seven years, has been violating the restraints of the treaty. . . . the treaty was really nothing but the legitimizing of an arms race. It didn't do anything to reduce nuclear weapons or the nuclear threat. All it did was regulate how fast and how much we could continue increasing the number of weapons. So I was always hostile to that particular treaty because it did not reduce weapons." As the nuclear superpowers increasingly agree on significant reductions in strategic forces after the end of the COLD WAR (via START), the SALT agreements have become irrelevant.

salted weapon   *See* NUCLEAR WEAPON, DIRTY.

samizdat   Russian term for secretly produced and privately circulated written materials, including journals and books, deemed critical of the state or its laws. This was a major means by which Soviet DISSIDENTs communicated with each other prior to GLASNOST.

Sanchez, Ilyich Ramirez   *See* CARLOS.

sanction   1. The penalties connected to a law to encourage individuals to obey it.   2. Ratification by a higher (or simply another) authority.   3. Foreign policies that range from the suspension of diplomatic or economic relations to outright military intervention, designed to force another nation to change its behavior. Article 41 of the Charter of the United Nations provides that:

The Security Council may decide what measures not involving the use of armed force are to be employed to give effect to its decisions and it may call upon the Members of the United Nations to apply such measures. These may include complete or partial interruption of economic relations and of rail, sea, air, postal, tele-

graphic, radio and other means of communication, and the severance of diplomatic relations.

If these peaceful sanctions are not sufficient, Article 42 provides:

Should the Security Council consider that measures provided for in Article 41 would be inadequate or have proved to be inadequate, it may take such action by air, sea, or land forces as may be necessary to maintain or restore international peace and security. Such action may include demonstrations, blockade, and other operations by air, sea, or land forces of Members of the United Nations.

Note that the word sanction does not appear in the Charter of the United Nations. That is because such measures were notoriously unsuccessful when used by the LEAGUE OF NATIONS in the Abyssinian-Italian War in 1935 and 1936. Instead the charter refers to "effective collective measures" (Article 1) and "preventive or enforcement action" (Article 2). Nevertheless, when the United Nations imposed "effective collective measures" on Iraq in 1990 in the Persian Gulf Crisis, the rest of the world called them sanctions. And ever since the 1970s the UN General Assembly has routinely called on the Security Council to impose economic sanctions on South Africa to end APARTHEID. Indeed, in 1981 and 1986 the UN even sponsored International Conferences on Sanctions Against South Africa. This perennial call for sanctions only diminished in the later 1980s when the United States and the European Community joined many Third World states by imposing sanctions that, now that South Africa is on the road to dismantling apartheid, are beginning to be lifted.

sanctuarization   The theory that nuclear weapons are not usable against other nuclear powers, because a state with even a small nuclear force has an effective deterrent in that it has the potential to do unacceptable damage to an attacker. Thus a nuclear power may become a "sanctuary" in time of war. The United States has never admitted that sanctuarization was the basis of its nuclear policy because the FLEXIBLE RESPONSE strategy of the North Atlantic Treaty Organization depends on the U.S. nuclear guarantee. However, many respected ana-

General César Augusto Sandino (center) and staff. (National Archives)

lysts would argue that nuclear PARITY, combined with the possibility of uncontrolled ESCALATION from any nuclear use, in reality means that the only function nuclear weapons really serve is to deter one nuclear power from attacking another.

sanctuary   **1.** A safe location.   **2.** A sacred or religious place.   **3.** The traditional protection offered by churches to individuals fleeing the secular law because of political or other crimes.   **4.** A movement to help illegal immigrants from Central America find refuge in the United States.   **5.** A state or area near or contiguous to a combat area that by TACIT AGREEMENT between the warring states is exempt from attack and therefore serves as a refuge for logistic, staging, or other activities of the combatant states. *Compare to* ASYLUM.

Sandinista   A member of the *Frente Sandinista de Liberacion Nacional* (Sandinista National Liberation Front), a major Nicaraguan political party founded in 1962, named for anti-imperialist César Augusto Sandino (1893–1934) who, in the 1920s, organized armed resistance to the U.S. forces that had occupied the country. The Sandinistas took power in 1979 in the aftermath of the NICARAGUAN CIVIL WAR. During the administration of President Ronald Reagan, the U.S. government began a campaign to undermine the Sandinista government because of its ties to Cuba and the Soviet

Union, its military buildup, and its export of revolution to other Central American countries. The U.S.-sponsored CONTRAS, an insurgent force composed of former SOMOZA regime army officers and disillusioned Sandinistas, fought to topple the Sandinistas, forcing the government to devote large portions of its budget to defense and to enact wartime measures. A U.S. economic boycott, lack of private initiative, and high cost of defense led to a dismal economic situation in Nicaragua. These economic difficulties caused the Sandinistas' popularity to decline, and in 1990 National Opposition Union candidate VIOLETA BARRIOS DE CHAMORRO defeated incumbent Sandinista President DANIEL ORTEGA.

Sands, Bobby (1954–1981)   The imprisoned IRISH REPUBLICAN ARMY member who died as a result of a highly publicized hunger strike in March 1981 at Maze Prison in Northern Ireland. During the hunger strike, Sands was elected to the British Parliament as a SINN FEIN candidate.

San Francisco Conference   The 1945 UNITED NATIONS Conference on International Organization where representatives from 50 countries met in San Francisco to discuss the UN Charter based on the proposals put forward by the representatives of China, the Soviet Union, the United Kingdom, and the United States. The charter was signed on June 26,

1945, by the representatives of the 50 countries. (Poland, which was not present at the conference, signed it later and thus became one of the original 51 member states.) By October 24 a majority of the signatories had ratified the charter and the United Nations officially came into existence. Ever since, this date has been observed as United Nations Day each year.

sanitize 1. To clean, sterilize, or disinfect. 2. To revise a document to prevent the identification of (a) sources, (b) the actual individuals and places concerned, or (c) the means by which it was obtained. Intelligence reports often are sanitized before they are distributed.

Sarajevo The garrison town and capital of Bosnia-Herzegovina, where on June 28, 1914, a Serbian extremist assassinated Archduke FRANZ FERDINAND, heir to the Austrian and Hungarian thrones, and his wife. Contrary to extremist expectations, this act did not spark a rebellion in Bosnia against the Austrian-Hungarians. When Austria issued an ultimatum demanding a voice in the internal affairs of Serbia in finding the conspirators, Serbia refused. WORLD WAR I began as Austria declared war on Serbia on July 28, 1914. Sarajevo once again dominated the international news in the early 1990s when it was besieged by Serbian forces during the YUGOSLAVIAN CIVIL WAR.

Sarajevo Syndrome A preoccupation with the possibility that in a nuclear age crisis, events might get out of control rather like they did in the Sarajevo Crisis, which led to World War I. While such concerns may be warranted, some of those who examined the Sarajevo Syndrome—most notably Robert McNamara, in *Blundering into Disaster* (1987)—tended to exaggerate them and to downplay the capacity of governments to deal with crises. *Compare to* OWL.

SAS (Special Air Service) An elite British army regiment created during World War II to conduct penetration missions behind enemy lines. It has been used extensively in Northern Ireland as an antiterrorist force and in London as a hostage rescue unit. In 1980 the SAS stormed the Iranian embassy in London where anti-Khomeini Iranians were holding 21 hostages. Five of the six terrorists and two hostages were killed during the raid.

Satanic Verses See RUSHDIE, SALMAN.

satellite 1. A small object within the orbit of a larger one; a subservient attendant or follower. 2. A state informally dominated by another state. For example, the Communist states of Eastern Europe were generally considered to be satellites of the Soviet Union during the Cold War. However, no self-respecting country would ever formally admit to being a satellite, because that would imply that it is has less than full SOVEREIGNTY.

Sato, Eisaku (1901–1975) The prime minister of Japan (1964–1972) who shared the 1974 Nobel Peace Prize (with SEAN MACBRIDE) for improving relations among the states of Asia and for maintaining Japan's policy of eschewing nuclear weapons.

SAVAK The acronym, in Persian, for *Sazemane Etelaat va Aminate Kechvar* (Iranian Security and Intelligence Organization); the secret police of the shah of Iran that sought to eliminate his political enemies through violence and physical intimidation. During the 1970s the organization began to pursue the regime's opponents outside Iran, including Iranian students studying abroad. SAVAK is believed to have been responsible for the 1977 death of the son of AYATOLLAH RUHOLLAH KHOMEINI, one of the events that sparked the 1979 IRANIAN REVOLUTION.

Savimbi, Jonas See ANGOLAN CIVIL WAR.

scapegoating 1. The Old Testament practice of selecting a goat to be sent into the wilderness, symbolically carrying the sins of a whole community. 2. By analogy, shifting the blame for a problem or failure to some other person, group, or organization—a common bureaucratic and political tactic. Often an elected official functions as a scapegoat. As President John F. Kennedy told in a press conference on June 15, 1962: "I know when things don't go well, they like to blame the President, and that is one of the things Presidents are paid for." But sometimes entire ethnic or religious groups are blamed for a society's problems and persecuted as were the Jews in Nazi Germany.

BRITISH PUBLIC MADE SCAPEGOATS

Sir John French, to conceal his failure in the 1915 Battle of Neuve Chapelle, complained that he was short of shells. The government in their turn blamed the munition workers, who were alleged to draw high wages and to pass their days drinking in public houses. Legislation was hastily introduced to restrict the hours when public houses were open and, in particular, to impose an afternoon gap when drinkers must be turned out. Those restrictions, still with us, rank with Summer [Daylight Savings] Time as the only lasting effects of the First World War on British life. Anyone who feels thirsty in England during the afternoon is still paying a price for the battle of Neuve Chapelle.

SOURCE: A. J. P. Taylor, *The First World War* (1963). The "afternoon gap" was finally abolished by parliament in 1988.

---

scenario   **1.** An imaginary but usually quite feasible situation that is used for heuristic, planning, and exercise purposes. One of the virtues of a scenario is that it compels thinking about responses should the government actually be faced with such a situation. In this sense it can be understood as a useful way to think about possible options. As a basis for exercises or simulations, scenarios provide an opportunity to become familiar with the procedures that would be used in a crisis or a war.   **2.** A way of thinking about nuclear war, something of which there can be no practical experience. HERMAN KAHN used scenarios for nuclear war and for ESCALATION in his books on these subjects, which he described as "thinking about the unthinkable."

Schelling, Thomas C. (1921–   )   The U.S. economist who in the late 1950s was associated with the RAND CORPORATION. In a series of very influential and well-known studies he applied some of the insights from GAME THEORY to the analysis of conflict. Schelling highlighted the issue of rational choice in situations where the outcome also depended on the choice of the adversary. Many of his insights into conflict behavior, developed in *The Strategy of Conflict* (1960), were dazzling, although he was sometimes criticized for being a theoretical strategist rather than an empirical one. In *Arms and Influence* (1966) Schelling looked at the various forms that coercive bargaining could take and defined BARGAINING THEORY, tactics designed to make an adversary back down. He also was one of the main pioneers in developing the concept of ARMS CONTROL as a way of stabilizing nuclear DETERRENCE, ideas that were articulated in his *Strategy and Arms Control* (with Morton Halperin, 1961). Although he has written less about strategy recently, he is still renowned as one of the most important strategic thinkers of the nuclear age.

Schlesinger Doctrine   The idea of LIMITED NUCLEAR OPTIONS first developed by James Schlesinger (1929–   ) while he was U.S. secretary of defense under President Richard M. Nixon from 1973 to 1975.

Schleswig-Holstein Question   The mid-nineteenth–century dispute between Denmark and Prussia over the ducal states of Schleswig and Holstein. It is still famous today because of what British Prime Minister Lord Palmerston (1784–1865) flippantly said about this matter in 1863: "There are only three men who have ever understood it: one was Prince Albert, and he is dead; the second was a German professor who became mad; I am the third and I have forgotten about it." In 1864 Prussia went to war with Denmark over these duchies. Austria joined the Prussians, and the two were victorious. They jointly governed the duchies until 1866, when Prussia declared war on Austria-Hungary, on the grounds of disagreements over Austrian military crossings of Prussia and the administration of Schleswig-Holstein. Since then, Schleswig-Holstein has been the northernmost state within Germany.

Schlieffen Plan   Germany's battle plan at the beginning of WORLD WAR I. Devised by Alfred von Schlieffen (1833–1913), the head of the German GENERAL STAFF from 1892 to 1906, it was a rapid way to overcome the two-front threat from the Franco-Russian ENTENTE. It called for a flanking attack against France, proceeding through neutral Belgium and swinging around Paris in a scythelike movement. Assuming that France would fall in six weeks, the Germans would have time to move against Russia, which needed a great deal of time to mobilize. The Schlieffen Plan did not bring quick victory. In fact, the German invasion of neutral Belgium on August 4, 1914, brought Great Britain into the war, thus expanding its scope.

Schmidt, Helmut (1918–   )   The chancellor of West Germany from 1974 to 1982. A leader of the Social Democrats who had held important government positions including minister of defense and minister of finance, he succeeded WILLY BRANDT as chancellor. He kept West Germany's inflation and unemployment rates the lowest in the West and its currency the strongest. His government even reduced consumption of foreign oil. His excellent English and his economic expertise made him a worldwide spokesman for international economics in general and the new Germany in particular. Schmidt was one of the key figures in the decision of the North Atlantic Treaty Organization to modernize its long-range theater nuclear forces through the deployment of cruise and Pershing missiles, although he also insisted that this be accompanied by a second arms control track. In fact, the idea of the zero option, which eventually became the basis for the INF TREATY, is sometimes attributed to Schmidt. He had poor personal relations with U.S. President Jimmy Carter and intensely disliked the United States' reversion to Cold War policies in the late 1970s and early 1980s under Carter and Ronald Reagan. He saw this shift in U.S. policy as a threat to the West German OSTPOLITIK. Schmidt was forced out as chancellor in 1982 when his Social Democrat Party–led coalition government dissolved over economic issues. He was then succeeded by the leader of the Christian Democrats, HELMUT KOHL. As well as being a prominent statesman, Schmidt also has been a talented analyst and commentator on international affairs and strategic issues. His works include *Defense or Retaliation* (1962) and *A Grand Strategy for the West* (1985).

school solution   A CONVENTIONAL WISDOM approach to dealing with a diplomatic or military problem, so called because such solutions represent the answers expected by instructors at military academies or command and staff colleges.

EPITAPH TO THE SCHOOL SOLUTION

Here lie the bones of Lieutenant Jones,
A product of this institution.
In his very first fight,
He went out like a light,
Using the School Solution!

SOURCE: Anonymous.

Schuman Plan   The plan devised by JEAN MONNET and announced by French Foreign Minister Robert Schuman (1886–1963) in May 1950 for the creation of the EUROPEAN COAL AND STEEL COMMUNITY. The ECSC, established by the 1951 Treaty of Paris, effectively removed the coal and steel industries of the signatories from national control and subordinated them to a SUPRANATIONAL authority. Significantly, Great Britain refused to accept this element of supranationalism and, in what was to become a pattern throughout the 1950s, stayed on the sidelines of the process of European integration.

The Schuman Plan was motivated partly by aspirations for European integration and was the first step toward that objective. It also was motivated by fear of a resurgent Germany. The ECSC tied German heavy industry to European industry, thereby removing from German control a principal source of military power. Schuman's stated objective was to make war not merely unthinkable but materially impossible.

Schumpeter, Joseph Alois (1883–1950)   The Austrian-born U.S. economist who developed theories of economic development and business cycles. While he maintained that the most frequently criticized aspects of CAPITALISM were largely responsible for rapid advances in productivity and technology, he also predicted that pure capitalism would eventually disappear—because the traditional entrepreneur becomes obsolete when the political factors that protect unrestrained capitalism are destroyed by reformers. According to Richard Swedberg in *Schumpeter* (1992), Schumpeter was the first to observe: "Catch a parrot, teach him to say 'supply and demand' and you have an economist." Schumpeter's major work is *Capitalism, Socialism and Democracy* (3d ed., 1950).

Schwarzkopf, H. Norman   *See* PERSIAN GULF WAR.

Schweitzer, Albert (1875–1965)   The Alsatian-German medical missionary in Africa who won the 1952 Nobel Peace Prize for his life's work as a humanitarian and philosopher.

Scowcroft, Brent (1925–   )   The career U.S. Air Force officer who was the national security advisor to U.S. President Gerald R. Ford (1975–1977) and again to President George Bush (1989–1993). He also was a member of the Tower Commission, which investigated the IRAN-CONTRA AFFAIR. Scowcroft is considered a prime architect of Bush's NEW WORLD ORDER and the conduct of the PERSIAN GULF WAR.

Scowcroft Commission   The U.S. presidential panel (headed by Brent Scowcroft) that reported in 1983 on the vulnerability of United States strategic forces. As well as arguing that the United States should proceed with the deployment of MX missiles in existing silos, the commission also proposed the design of a single-warhead small missile, the MIDGETMAN, which would be less attractive as a target and less threatening to Soviet missiles. In addition, it advocated a more serious search for ARMS CONTROL agreements with an emphasis on warhead rather than launcher limits. Although the deployment mode of the small ICBM was not specified, the commission was particularly interested in hardened mobile launchers and wanted to move away from multiple warheads and back to single-warhead missiles as a means of enhancing strategic stability. Overall the Scowcroft Commission helped to justify U.S. President Ronald Reagan's decision to vastly expand and modernize U.S. strategic weapons. This, in turn, it is often argued, encouraged the Soviets to get more serious about ARMS CONTROL efforts, which, in turn, led to the INF and START TREATIES. *See also* TRIAD.

Scramble for Africa   1. The period from 1876 to 1912 when Belgium, France, Germany, Great Britain, and Italy competed militarily and diplomatically to carve up the African continent into their respective colonies.   2. The geopolitical competition of the 1970s between the United States and the Soviet Union (assisted by Cuba) for influence in Africa, especially Angola and the HORN OF AFRICA.

SDI   *See* STRATEGIC DEFENSE INITIATIVE.

sea-air-land team (SEAL)   A U.S. Navy commando-type force specially trained and equipped for conducting unconventional and paramilitary operations, including surveillance and reconnaissance in and from restricted waters, rivers, and coastal areas, and to train personnel of allied nations in such operations. Commonly referred to as a SEAL team. Such forces are especially skilled at infiltrating enemy territory by sea in small boats or as frogmen, by air from helicopters or by parachute, and by land in ranger patrols.

Seabed Treaty   *See* CONTROL OF ARMS ON THE SEABED TREATY.

sea-launched cruise missile (SLCM)   The most numerous of all CRUISE MISSILES, which may be fired from both submarines and surface ships. The Soviet Navy armed its ships with cruise missiles of varying degrees of technical sophistication since the late 1950s, and the U.S. Navy has made them general equipment since the early 1980s. Most of the SLCM (pronounced "slickum") inventories carry only conventional warheads, intended for ship-to-ship combat, but an undeterminable portion are nuclear armed and capable of striking targets over 2,000 kilometers inland.

sealed orders   Secret or confidential orders in a sealed envelope, given to a diplomat or military commander with instructions not to open them until a given time or on arrival at a specified destination.

sealift   The capacity to move troops, equipment, and supplies rapidly to a conflict zone by ship. While the limitations of AIRLIFT potential is often discussed, traditional sealift capacity faces equally serious problems. A major reason for sealift shortfall is that navies are prone to concentrate their attention on the more "glamorous" business of acquiring combat ships and to focus on what they see as their primary single-service tasks, rather than supporting army and air force needs, which they may regard as marginal due to the effects of INTER-SERVICE RIVALRY. Sealift inadequacies are common, in fact, to all Western nations with a need or desire for FORCE PROJECTION. The old-fashioned troop carriers of the two world wars have not been replaced in naval inventories, and supply and amphibious warfare craft are in short supply in all navies. Of even more pressing concern is the fact that countries such as the United Kingdom and the United States have experienced a very serious shrinkage in the size of their merchant navies. Thus, in any sustained future war, the ability of either government to rely on conscripting civilian ships and crews, as has been the pattern in the past, will be much reduced.

SEATO (Southeast Asia Treaty Organization) The now-expired mutual security organization created by the 1954 Manila Pact signed by Australia, France, New Zealand, Pakistan, the Philippines, Thailand, the United Kingdom, and the United States. SEATO was part of the post–World War II U.S. strategy of CONTAINMENT; it was designed to be an Asian counterpart of the North Atlantic Treaty Organization. In contrast to NATO, the members lacked a geographical focus, a common appreciation of the threat, and a unified command structure. There was never any serious effort to respond to crises in a concerted fashion. In the 1970s the irrelevance of SEATO became increasingly apparent. Pakistan left the group in 1972. By then France had ceased to participate in SEATO's military activities (it continued to make a financial contribution until 1974). In 1975 the member states agreed to dissolve the organization, effective 1977.

secession 1. The withdrawal of one's membership in an organization. 2. The withdrawal of a polity from a larger politician union. Secessionist movements are more likely in federal or confederal states because such states, by their very nature, maintain the idea and symbolism of autonomy and because they usually do not have a history of unity sufficient to prevent separatist tendencies. Secession almost never is seen as a legitimate cause, especially in the Third World, where it poses a challenge to NATION-BUILDING. The political question that often must be answered is: Where does national SELF-DETERMINATION end and secession begin? Secession, which is usually inspired by NATIONALISM, can occur peacefully or through CIVIL WAR. Recent peaceful examples of secession include the 1990 secession of the BALTIC NATIONS from the Soviet Union and the 1992 secession of Slovakia from Czechoslovakia. Less-than-peaceful secession examples include the Kurdish effort to achieve independence from Iraq in the wake of the 1991 Persian Gulf War and the desire of Bosnia to be independent of Serbia in the Yugoslavian Civil War. *See also* CONFEDERATION; FEDERALISM.

second decision center thesis During the Cold War, a major justification for Great Britain's independent nuclear DETERRENT. According to the argument, because the Soviets might not believe in the firmness of the U.S. NUCLEAR UMBRELLA covering Western Europe, it might conclude that it could safely use its nuclear weapons to intimidate or destroy European targets. But if Great Britain was known to have nuclear weapons and to be prepared to use them in the case of a Soviet attack on North Atlantic Treaty Organization states, the uncertainty of what response it might face would deter the Soviet Union. This is an example of deterrence through uncertainty.

second front The term that referred to the forthcoming Allied invasion of Western Europe during the latter part of WORLD WAR II. The "first" front was the eastern or Soviet front. Stalin wanted a second front as soon as possible to take pressure off the Soviet Union. See also D-DAY.

Second International *See* INTERNATIONAL, THE.

second strike 1. An attack on an enemy after it has attacked. This is always a disadvantageous position because of the losses incurred in the original offensive. Consequently, when international tensions are high between states, there is always the temptation that a war will start with a FIRST STRIKE so that the instigator can avoid the disadvantages of having to suffer losses before attacking. 2. The launching of a nuclear attack in retaliation to such an attack.

second-strike capability The ability to survive a first military strike with sufficient resources to deliver an effective counterblow. This concept usually is associated with nuclear weapons. The key to effective and stable nuclear DETERRENCE is not the total number of nuclear weapons possessed by one side but the residual capability that would be left after a first strike by an enemy. This capacity to survive and retaliate is crucial. The nuclear powers' preoccupation with the survivability of missiles, either through emplacement in hardened silos or through the concealment and mobility inherent in submarine-launched systems, derives from a desire to maintain an effective second-strike capability. *Compare to* FIRST-STRIKE CAPABILITY.

Second World   A Cold War–era term for the then-socialist countries of Eastern Europe plus the Soviet Union. Now that the Cold War is over, this term is obsolete except in the sense of the "former Second World." As yet there is no commonly accepted replacement phrase for these developing states of Eastern Europe. *See also* FIRST WORLD; THIRD WORLD; FOURTH WORLD.

secretariat   **1.** The office responsible for the administrative affairs of a legislature or an international organization. It is headed by a secretary-general. **2.** In particular, the UNITED NATIONS Secretariat, whose secretary-general is appointed to a five-year term of office by the GENERAL ASSEMBLY upon the recommendation of the SECURITY COUNCIL. It is the administrative unit of the United Nations that services other organs of the organization and administers their policies and programs. The Secretariat, an international staff of more than 25,000 men and women from different countries and regions, carries out the day-to-day work of the United Nations both at headquarters in New York and in offices and centers around the world.

secretary   **1.** A diplomatic rank for those in positions that support the activities of the chief of a mission. For example, a first secretary is a career foreign service officer who is second in command to the AMBASSADOR, the second secretary is third in command, and so on. Diplomatic secretaries should not be confused with clerical assistants.   **2.** A service person whose function is defined by an executive whom he or she supports. While such functions are often considered stenographic or clerical, the association of a secretary with an executive is a major relationship in carrying out the responsibilities of the executive as well as in controlling access to executive judgment and responsibilities. The word comes from the Latin *secretarius,* meaning

"confidential officer, one who can be trusted with secrets."   **3.** The head of a cabinet agency of the U.S. government; for example, the secretary of state, the secretary of defense.

secretary-general   The chief administrator of a SECRETARIAT. The most famous secretary-general is that of the UNITED NATIONS. Since the beginning of the United Nations, this office has been filled by a career diplomat from a country perceived as relatively neutral by both the Western alliance and the Soviet bloc. The secretary-general may bring to the attention of the SECURITY COUNCIL any matter that, in his or her judgment, threatens international security and peace, and may use GOOD OFFICES to help in resolving international disputes. A recent example was Secretary-General Javier Perez de Cuellar's unsuccessful attempt to get invading Iraqi forces out of Kuwait before U.S.-led allied forces, with the approval of the United Nations, concluded the Persian Gulf War in 1991.

**THE SECRETARIES GENERAL OF
THE UNITED NATIONS***

Name	Country	Tenure
Trygve Lie	Norway	1946–1953
Dag Hammarskjöld	Sweden	1953–1961
U Thant	Burma	1961–1972
Kurt Waldheim	Austria	1972–1982
Javier Perez de Cuellar	Peru	1982–1991
Boutros Boutros Ghali	Egypt	1992–present

*See individual entries for each.

---

secretary of state   The senior cabinet member and chief foreign policy officer of the United States. The secretary of state (who is fourth in line of succession to the presidency after the vice president, the speaker of the House of Representatives, and the president pro tempore of the Senate) is the administrator of the Department of State responsible for all diplomatic missions abroad. While personally in charge of foreign policy bureaucracy, all post–World War II secretaries of state have had to, in effect, share power with other institutional and personal influences on the foreign policymaking process. Recent secretaries have often found themselves competing for foreign policy dominance with the secretary of defense, the head of the Central Intelligence Agency, and the president's national security advisor. Overall, the secretary of state is only as strong or as influential as a president allows him or her to be. The only postwar secretaries to dominate the foreign policymaking process vis-à-vis the other actors were DEAN ACHESON under Harry S Truman, JOHN FOSTER DULLES under Dwight D. Eisenhower, and HENRY A. KISSINGER under Richard M. Nixon and Gerald Ford.

Securitate   The heavily armed secret police force of Romania under dictator NICOLAE CEAUȘESCU. This force remained loyal to Ceausescu until the very end of his regime by opening fire on the general populace as well as on regular forces. There is no official number of its membership, but it has been estimated at 70,000. Although some members have been brought to trial since the overthrow of Ceausescu in 1989, many are unknown and have slipped easily into new jobs with the army, police, or elsewhere.

security   **1.** Being safe; a condition that results from protective (usually military) measures that ensure a state's inviolability from hostile acts. **2.** A key objective of states in the anarchic international system. A state is relatively secure if its physical survival, territorial integrity, and political independence and values are not under threat or they are well protected.   **3.** The certainty that certain basic needs or requirements will be met. In this connection Caroline Thomas in *In Search of Security* (1987) suggested that in relation to Third World nations, the concept needs to be broadened to include such things as health security and food security—not simply safety from military attack. **4.** With respect to classified matter, a condition that prevents unauthorized persons from having access to safeguarded information or things. *Compare to* NATIONAL SECURITY.

security assistance   The programs of various governments relating to international defense cooperation. Security assistance (sometimes called *military assistance*) has five components: (1) military assistance in which defense articles and defense services are provided to eligible foreign governments on a

U.S. PRESIDENTS AND THEIR SECRETARIES OF STATE SINCE WORLD WAR II

President	Term	Secretary of State
Franklin D. Roosevelt	1933–1945	Cordell Hull (1933–1944)
		Edward R. Stettinius, Jr. (1944–1945)
Harry S Truman	1945–1953	Edward R. Stettinius, Jr. (1945)
		James F. Byrnes (1945–1947)
		George C. Marshall (1947–1949)
		Dean G. Acheson (1949–1953)
Dwight D. Eisenhower	1953–1961	John F. Dulles (1953–1959)
		Christian A. Herter (1959–1961)
John F. Kennedy	1961–1963	Dean Rusk (1961–1963)
Lyndon B. Johnson	1963–1969	Dean Rusk (1963–1969)
Richard M. Nixon	1969–1974	William P. Rogers (1969–1973)
		Henry A. Kissinger (1973–1974)
Gerald R. Ford	1974–1977	Henry A. Kissinger (1974–1977)
Jimmy Carter	1977–1981	Cyrus R. Vance (1977–1980)
		Edmund Muskie (1980–1981)
Ronald Reagan	1981–1989	Alexander M. Haig, Jr. (1981–1982)
		George P. Shultz (1982–1989)
George Bush	1989–1993	James A. Baker III (1989–1992)
		Lawrence Eagleburger (1992–1993)
William J. Clinton	1993–	Warren Christopher (1993–)

grant basis; (2) international military education and training, which provides military training to foreign military and civilian personnel; (3) foreign military sales, which provides credits and loan repayment guarantees to enable eligible foreign governments to purchase defense articles and defense services; (4) security supporting assistance, which promotes economic and political stability in areas where a government has special foreign policy security interests; and (5) direct military INTERVENTION.

security certification   The formal indication that a person has been investigated and is eligible for access to CLASSIFIED INFORMATION to the extent stated in the certification.

security check   **1.** An investigation into the loyalty of a potential or current employee (or agent) by a government agency.   **2.** A secret sign in a message from an intelligence agent that indicates that the message is genuine.

security classification   A category to which secret information and material is assigned to denote the amount of harm that unauthorized disclosure would cause. Three such categories are top secret, secret, and confidential.

security clearance   An administrative assessment that an individual is eligible to have access to CLASSIFIED INFORMATION.

security community   A group of states in which the use of military force is effectively excluded as an instrument of policy in relations among the members. Force or the threat of force may still be an instrument of policy in dealings with states that are not members of the community. The notion was developed by KARL DEUTSCH on the basis of a study of the North Atlantic region and has increasingly been applied to the EUROPEAN COMMUNITY. For a security community to come into being, three preconditions have to be met: The states have to share values that are broadly compatible with each other; they have to be responsive to each other's needs; and their policy goals must be relatively predictable.

security complex   A concept developed by Barry Buzan in *People, States and Fear* (1983) to describe "a group of states whose primary security concerns link together sufficiently closely that their national security cannot realistically be considered apart from one another."

Security Council   The most powerful of the elements created by the UNITED NATIONS Charter for dealing with questions of international peace and security. The Security Council has five permanent members (China, France, Russia, the United Kingdom, and the United States, commonly known as the Big Five) and representatives of ten other nations, five of which are chosen each year for two-year terms. Each of the permanent members has a VETO over all decisions, which provides the major powers with protection against majority decisions in the larger UN GENERAL ASSEMBLY, where each member nation has only one vote. If a permanent member does not support a decision but does not wish to block it, it can abstain from voting. Resolutions by the Security Council are legally binding to all member states. Among the means the Security Council may employ to maintain international peace and security are dispatching PEACEKEEPING FORCES, applying economic SANCTIONs such as trade embargoes, and taking collective military actions. Until recently, the Security Council was paralyzed on major issues of international peace and security because of the superpower rivalry. But with the end of the COLD WAR, the United States succeeded in 1990 in getting its approval of using military force against Iraq during the PERSIAN GULF WAR. There has been considerable discussion in recent years of revamping the Security Council to add Germany and Japan to its permanent membership so that it more appropriately reflects the power relationships of the current world. But any attempt to do so would require a redrafting of the UN Charter—something that many states are reluctant to do for a wide variety of reasons. For example, it can be expected that the Third World would demand a vast expansion of the permanent members of the Security Council to reflect its interests. But even if that were agreed to, it is not known how the United Nations could select one state to represent such vast regions as Africa, South America, or South Asia. The potential political problems are so great that they create an inhibition toward dealing with them at all.

security dilemma   **1.** A situation in which one state takes action to enhance its security only to have this action seen as threatening by other states. The result is that the other states engage in countermeasures that intensify the first state's insecurity.

The dilemma arises from the fact that because of this process, actions taken to enhance security can actually end up diminishing it. There also is a dilemma for the second state in that if it regards the first state's action as defensive and takes no countermeasures, it leaves itself vulnerable, whereas if it responds vigorously, it will exacerbate the first state's insecurity. The problem often is seen as inherent in a system that lacks a central overriding authority and in which there is a lack of trust among states. The concept was developed most fully by John Herz, in *International Politics in the Atomic Age* (1959). HERBERT BUTTERFIELD, in his *History and Human Relations* (1952), developed a similar theme, which he termed "the predicament of Hobbesian fear." Although the security dilemma is a feature of ANARCHY, it can be exacerbated by ideological considerations and by perceptions based on an INHERENT BAD FAITH MODEL. Moreover, it can create its own dynamic in which there is a spiral of conflict. The difficulty is that states often find themselves in a security dilemma but do not recognize it as such, with the result that they attribute innate aggressiveness to states that are responding to them defensively. Indeed, recognition of the security dilemma is the first step toward mitigating it. While it is difficult to transcend the security dilemma in a state of anarchy, merely recognizing that one's actions are proving counterproductive can go a long way toward halting them. For this reason, MIKHAIL GORBACHEV's greatest contribution to the end of the Cold War may have been his recognition that certain Soviet actions were not seen as legitimate acts of self-defense by others but rather as evidence of hostile intent on the part of the Soviet Union. **2.** The term is sometimes used more loosely, and not very accurately, to describe the general security challenges facing a particular state. *Compare to* MUTUAL SECURITY; REASSURANCE. *See also* THUCYDIDES.

security interest A NATIONAL INTEREST of a state that has implications for its safety. Security interests can vary in intensity but unless they are marginal interests, it is likely that the state will protect them through the use of force. On occasion, however, there is intense debate about the importance of security interests in a particular region and about whether these interests are worth going to war for.

security risk **1.** A government employee thought to be so susceptible to the possible influence of foreign agents that he or she cannot be trusted with continued access to sensitive information. **2.** Any disloyal citizen.

security studies **1.** Research and teaching on matters relating to domestic, national, and international security, or anything that involves threats of, and the actual or potential use of, force by a state. The main focus of security studies is on conflict rather than cooperation, although security analysts also are interested in cooperation to manage conflicts. **2.** A term that is used almost interchangeably with STRATEGIC STUDIES—the study of military strategy. Arguably, the field of security studies is wider than that of strategic studies. Moreover, it is something that may be widened further as new items on the international agenda, such as narcotics trafficking and environmental problems, come under the purview of security studies.

security umbrella Protection from military attack that a major power offers a small state usually by means of a treaty or ALLIANCE. For example, during the Cold War the United States offered a security umbrella to Taiwan to deter mainland China from invading.

security zone A geographical area that GREAT POWERS consider crucial to their safety. Because they regard the presence or intrusion of other powers in the zone as threatening, they often attempt to dominate the area either directly or indirectly. Since 1945 both the United States and the Soviet Union developed extended security zones. The United States, concerned about Communist penetration of Latin America, often has intervened to prevent the establishment of Communist governments there. The Soviet Union had a concept of security that was both ideological and territorial. Thus it dominated Eastern Europe and intervened when necessary to ensure ideological orthodoxy. With the end of the COLD WAR, however, the Soviet Union took a more relaxed view of its European security zone.

sedition The act of advocating resistance to or rebellion against a legally established government.

While sedition once included actual REBELLION, in recent centuries it has been limited to speaking and writing. By this modern definition it cannot be a crime in states that have freedom of speech, unless the speaker advocates violence or lawbreaking. However, in totalitarian states sedition can be tantamount to TREASON.

selective strike An attack on a precise and carefully delimited military target, chosen so as to maximize military value, or to send a very clear signal, while minimizing the risks of ESCALATION. As such, selective strikes are at the heart of the more general concept of LIMITED NUCLEAR OPTIONS. The concept is not limited to nuclear warfare, however. The essential point is that a selective strike is as much a matter of signaling to the enemy as of achieving purely military goals. The trouble is that the FOG OF WAR usually makes strikes much less selective than intended. Some military thinkers like to talk about the SURGICAL STRIKE, with the implication that such a use of violence is analogous to removing a tumor for the benefit of the whole body. Yet this is seldom achieved even with the target acquisition capacity of modern weapons, and COLLATERAL DAMAGE often occurs; for example, a hospital might be bombed in a raid meant only to destroy a terrorist headquarters.

self-censorship *See* CENSORSHIP.

self-defense **1.** In terms of international law, the basic right of a state to fight back against military attacks by other states. This right was recognized in Article 51 of the United Nations Charter, which stated that "Nothing in the present Charter shall impair the inherent right of individual or collective self-defense if an armed attack occurs against a member of the United Nations, until the Security Council has taken the measures necessary to maintain international peace and security." There has been much argument about whether this right of self-defense is anticipatory or whether it allows for preemption—whether it is necessary, legally, to wait until after the attack has occurred. **2.** Actions taken by a state designed to prevent it from being attacked by others. This can range from conscription by which large citizen armies are created, to the development of special weapons that have a DETERRENT EFFECT, to joining an ALLIANCE with other

similarly situated states, to issuing a DECLARATORY POLICY about what would happen if an aggressor attacked.

self-determination Literally, the right to choose one's own fate; in world politics, used in relation to collectivities rather than individuals. According to Michael Akehurst in *A Modern Introduction to International Law* (6th ed., 1987), self-determination means "the right of a people living in a territory to determine the political and legal status of that territory—for example, by setting up a state of their own or by choosing to become part of another state." Groups that feel that they have a national identity, which is not expressed in the existing arrangements, often demand such *national self-determination*. Article 1 of the Charter of the United Nations asserts that one of the purposes of this international organization is "friendly relations among nations based on respect for the principle of equal rights and self-determination of peoples." The difficulty with self-determination as a guiding force of international law is that its expression within an existing state can lead to SECESSION or CIVIL WAR. For example, self-determination has lead to the breakup of the Soviet Union and to the Yugoslavian Civil War. And it is the basic problem underlying the Arab-Israeli Wars over who—which group of people—has the right to Palestine. The principle of self-determination was popularized by U.S. President Woodrow Wilson during World War I and afterward at the PARIS PEACE CONFERENCE.

self-fulfilling prophecy An action or statement based on fear of a particular development that contributes to the development actually occurring. Treating another state as a threat or potential enemy and taking precautions against it may provoke that state into behaving in a hostile way in response. *See also* SECURITY DILEMMA.

self-help **1.** The notion that independent states in an anarchic international system have only themselves to depend on for security and well-being. This is a defining characteristic of the international system, and one that is central to theories of REALISM in international politics. **2.** In international law, self-help is the ultimate SANCTION in the hands of a state that has been injured by another. If the other state refuses to provide REPARATIONS or come before a tribunal, self-help is the only means available. It encompasses RETORSION, a lawful act designed to injure the other state, and REPRISAL, an act that is normally illegal but that is made legal by the prior illegal act of the other state. Reprisals should be proportionate to the initial act to which they respond.

self-restraint   The exercise of compassion in dealings with adversaries so that one does not always try to maximize one's gains at their expense. The problem with this strategy is that it can be seen as a symptom of weakness by adversaries or by powerful domestic constituencies within the state. Self-restraint can pay off in the long run, however. For example, after World War II the United States demonstrated tremendous self-restraint in dealing with Germany and Japan. Consequently, instead of punishing them as states, punishment was confined to a relatively few high-level officials who had committed WAR CRIMES. Then the United States helped to rebuild their economies and turned states that were hated enemies into close political friends as well as economic rivals.

self-sufficiency   Minimal or no DEPENDENCE on other states for goods, resources, or services. A state can attempt to achieve self-sufficiency across the board or in relation to a few critical resources. Self-sufficiency minimizes a state's vulnerability to outside forces, but the more goods that are encompassed by it the more likely it is to be achieved at the expense of the international trading system. *See also* AUTARCHY.

senate   1. The Latin word for "a group of old men"; the governing body of the ancient Roman Republic.   2. The upper (or smaller) chamber of a bicameral national legislature.

Sendero Luminoso   "The Shining Path," formed in 1969 as an Indian left-wing guerrilla group in Peru. It has become the most dangerous and unpredictable terrorist and insurgency group in Latin America, responsible for an estimated 15,000 deaths since 1980. The group's name is taken from an early Peruvian Communist's statement that hailed MARXISM as the "shining path to the future." It is dedicated to the violent overthrow of the government of Peru and its replacement with a revolutionary Marxist peasant regime. Influenced both by Inca traditions and by MAOISM, the movement aims to destroy all modern political and economic institutions, and to replace them with those of an idealized, premodern past. Sendero Luminoso seeks to enlist the support or acquiescence of the Native American peasants by a twin strategy of TERRORISM and exploitation of their political and economic grievances. Their activities provoked severe governmental reaction in 1992: the PERU COUP, which suspended civil liberties and dissolved the legislature to enable the government to battle the guerrillas with fewer encumbrances. The Sendero Luminoso suffered a major defeat when, in September 1992, government forces captured or killed most of its top leadership, including the group's founder and intellectual force, Manuel Abimael Guzman (1934–   ). Now that Guzman and his immediate staff are all in jail, it is estimated that the government has a window of opportunity to address the root causes of rural poverty before the movement flares up again.

Sendic, Raul   *See* TUPAMAROS.

senior service   A country's oldest armed service. For example, in the United States the senior service is the army; in the United Kingdom, it is the Royal Navy. The senior service may sometimes be given precedence over the other services at formal diplomatic events.

sensitive position   A government position necessitating access to classified (secret) documents and other information bearing on NATIONAL SECURITY. Candidates for such positions usually are required to have a SECURITY CLEARANCE.

sensitive products   Goods whose costs of production are such that any reduction in TARIFF or in NON-TARIFF BARRIERS to imports can threaten the continued viability of the domestic industry. Since significant changes in the competitive situations of these industries could dislocate large number of workers and cause major economic and political problems, the products of these industries are likely to be excepted from tariff reduction formulas in trade negotiations. Steel and textiles are examples of products that are considered sensitive in many states.

separatist movement   A group that desires to secede from a given state, either to form a new state or to attach its territory to a neighboring state to which it feels strongly tied. A separatist group's motivation is often a sense of NATIONALISM, a belief that it is culturally distinct from the majority of the population in its current state. Separatist movements such as those that exist in the Basque region of northern Spain, the French island of Corsica, and the U.S. island of Puerto Rico have as their goal SECESSION and independence.

September, Dulcie (1943–1988)   The Paris representative of the AFRICAN NATIONAL CONGRESS who was assassinated at her office in 1988 by attackers believed to be agents of the government of South Africa. South African government sources denied responsibility and suggested that dissension among the ANC ranks may have led to her shooting.

service   1. The armed forces of a state.   2. A military unit that provides combat support and/or administration for a larger unit; for example, the finance corps, quartermaster corps, and so on. 3. A branch of the military whose primary function is to render noncombatant support rather than to engage in combat.   4. All activities of a military command other than combat.   5. One of the components of the armed forces of a nation (army, navy, etc.).   6. In communications, notes covering routing instructions, time of delivery or receipt, radio frequency used, the operator's identifying sign, or similar information, all written on a message blank by the sending and receiving operators. 7. A designation for a civil agency, such as the U.S. Foreign Service.

session   1. The time between the opening and the closing of a legislature or court. This can be a few weeks, a few months, or almost all year.   2. The daily meetings of a legislature or court. Thus a session can last many months and at the same time begin anew at 9:00 A.M. each morning.

Sèvres, Treaty of   The 1920 settlement between Turkey and the Allies that was part of the PARIS PEACE CONFERENCE after World War I. It established the new boundaries of Turkey without its Middle Eastern empire and provided that "the navigation of the straits, including the Dardanelles, the Sea of Marmara and the Bosporus, shall in future be open, both in peace and war, to every vessel of commerce or of war and to military and commercial aircraft, without distinction of flag."

shah   The Persian word for "king." The last shah of Iran was MOHAMMED REZA PAHLEVI.

Shamir, Yitzhak (1915–   )   The Polish-born prime minister of Israel (1983–1984; 1986–1992). He migrated to Israel in the mid-1930s, joined first the IRGUN and then the STERN GANG, and was a leading terrorist prior to Israel's independence in 1947. As foreign minister in the MENACHEM BEGIN government (1980–1983), he was well positioned to succeed Begin in 1983. He was again foreign minister from 1984 to 1986 as part of a coalition government. Shamir has been sharply criticized for allowing U.S.-Israeli relations to deteriorate, largely because his policy of expanding Israeli settlements on the WEST BANK was in direct contradiction to U.S. efforts to broker a negotiated peace with the Palestinians. His

Yitzhak Shamir (Embassy of Israel)

lack of progress toward peace and the economic turmoil caused by the massive migration of Jews from the former Soviet Union caused his Likud Party to lose the 1992 elections. He was then succeeded by YITZHAK RABIN.

Shanghai Communiqué A joint Sino-U.S. document describing the new state of relations between China and the United States signed in 1972 by Chinese Premier Zhou Enlai and U.S. President Richard Nixon. Nixon's dramatic trip to China following National Security Advisor Henry Kissinger's secret visit to Beijing marked a rapprochement between two former enemies. At the conclusion of Nixon's talks with the Chinese leaders in Beijing, the two sides could not reach agreement on some important bilateral issues. Nixon and his entourage flew to Shanghai as his last stop before he headed for home. In Shanghai, the two parties issued a joint COMMUNIQUÉ that contained some purposeful ambiguities which allowed the two countries to set aside some differences, especially on the TAIWAN issue, and begin the process of normalizing relations.

SHAPE Supreme Headquarters Allied Powers Europe; the headquarters of the entire European North Atlantic Treaty Organization military command under the direct authority of SACEUR. Located near Mons, Belgium, it is largely an administrative headquarters, not a command location.

Sharpeville incident The event that led the AFRICAN NATIONAL CONGRESS to abandon its policy of nonviolence in its struggle for civil rights: On March 21, 1960, 69 blacks were killed and over 200 wounded when South African police opened fire with automatic weapons on a peaceful throng of anti-apartheid demonstrators in this township near Johannesburg.

Shatung question The concern at the PARIS PEACE CONFERENCE of 1919 over what should be done with Shatung, the province in northeastern China that was controlled by Germany. The Japanese, who occupied this territory early in World War I and were promised it in various secret treaties, were given indefinite control. This prompted much criticism in China, the United States, and elsewhere. After World War II Shatung was returned to China.

sherpa An assistant who helps a political executive get to a SUMMIT meeting by negotiating with counterparts on the other side just what the summiteers will do and sign. A real "sherpa" is a Tibetan guide who assists outsiders in climbing to the mountain summits of the Himalayas.

Shevardnadze, Eduard (1928–) The foreign minister of the Soviet Union from 1985 until he dramatically resigned in December 1990 amid his publicly announced fears of a coming crackdown and dictatorship. Although he began his career as a product of the Communist Party, Shevardnadze became one of its best-known reformers. After his resignation, he remained a highly visible advocate for the policies of new thinking, defined, then nearly abandoned, by Soviet President MIKHAIL GORBACHEV. He even helped to create a party of prominent liberals in mid-1991 to oppose the Communist Party and to create a two-party system. After the failed RUSSIAN COUP of August 1991, Shevardnadze, who helped to defeat the coup plotters, reemerged as foreign minister of what he called "the former Soviet Union." He chose to resume his old post because "the place of democrats and reformists at this moment must be at the barricades" (*New York Times,* November 21, 1991). After he helped dissolve the Soviet Union and create the Commonwealth of Independent States, he returned in early 1992 to his native state of Georgia (which had been embroiled in fighting the GEORGIAN CIVIL WAR) to reintroduce democratic stability as head of its State Council pending elections. In December 1992 he was elected to the chairmanship of the Georgian Parliament, the top political office in Georgia.

Shi'ite A sect of Islam that split from the mainstream SUNNI group during the seventh century over a dispute about the leadership of the faith. Shi'ites believe that the mantle of leadership belongs to the descendants of Ali, cousin and son-in-law of the Prophet Muhammad. Ali's son Hussein is the forefather of today's Shi'ites, having died in battle to maintain leadership of Islam within the family of the Prophet. Shi'ites see in Hussein the virtues of righteous rebellion, militancy, and martyrdom. Shi'ites comprise perhaps a tenth of the world's Islamic population, and their minority status and theological differences with the majority have brought them much persecution in the Sunni states of Iraq, Kuwait, and Saudi Arabia. Only in Iran, where they form a majority population, have Shi'ites seized power and instituted a government according to the precepts of their faith. Since the rise of revolutionary Iran in 1979, fundamentalist Shi'ites have attempted to spread their revolutionary religious fervor through widespread acts of terror committed by such groups as AMAL and HEZBOLLAH.

Shining Path   *See* SENDERO LUMINOSO.

ship of state   A nautical metaphor for a national government, one of the oldest of such metaphors. In *The Prince* (1532) Niccolò Machiavelli uses it— "the ship of state has need of help"—and it was old then. While this phrase has been used by a great many writers since Machiavelli, Henry Wadsworth Longfellow's usage of it as a reference to the United States in "The Building of the Ship" (1849) may be the most famous:

> *Thou, too, sail on, O Ship of State!*
> *Sail on, O Union, strong and great!*
> *Humanity with all its fears,*
> *With all the hopes of future years,*
> *Is hanging breathless on thy fate!*

shot across the bow   **1.** In traditional naval warfare a cannon fired just in front of another ship to indicate that if it did not stop, it would be sunk. **2.** A possible strategy for an early use of nuclear weapons in a war. A small strike, possibly using only one warhead, would be made in order to give the other side a chance to halt its attack. Only if the warning is ignored would a full-scale nuclear war begin. *Compare to* DEMONSTRATION.

show of force   The display of military force to coerce, intimidate, or deter another state. The essence of an effective show of force is that it establishes CREDIBILITY for much more drastic action should it be deemed necessary. Actions such as the Reagan Administration's use of large naval guns against targets in Lebanon in the 1980s was taken partly for its direct military effect, but also as a show of force for purposes of intimidation. (In this particular case, it did not work very well.)

Shukairy, Ahmed al- (1907–1980)   Founder of the PALESTINE LIBERATION ORGANIZATION in 1964. The PLO initially was an umbrella group for various guerrilla movements opposed to any settlement with Israel. In 1969 one of these guerrilla groups, al-FATAH, under YASIR ARAFAT, grew so strong that it took over the PLO. Then Shukairy faded into obscurity.

Shultz, George P. (1920–   )   U.S. secretary of labor from 1969 to 1970, director of the Office of Management and Budget from 1970 to 1972, secretary of the treasury from 1972 to 1974, and secretary of state from 1982 to 1989. During his tenure as secretary of state, Shultz helped to reestablish DÉTENTE with the Soviet Union and to conclude significant ARMS CONTROL measures even though he was opposed by hard-liners in the Reagan Administration. When it came to the use of force, however, Shultz was a hard-liner, arguing that if the United States was unwilling to use force, its diplomacy would lack CREDIBILITY. He also took a very strong line on terrorism as stated in the SHULTZ DOCTRINE.

Shultz Doctrine   As stated by U.S. Secretary of State George Shultz in October 1984, the idea that U.S. policy toward terrorism "should go beyond passive defense to consider means of active prevention, preemption, and retaliation."

shuttle diplomacy   *See* DIPLOMACY, SHUTTLE.

SICBM   *See* MIDGETMAN.

sick man of Europe   **1.** Turkey prior to World War I because its OTTOMAN EMPIRE was crumbling from corruption and the restlessness of the peoples it held captive. **2.** Great Britain in part of the post–World War II period because it was not as economically successful as other European states such as France and Germany. **3.** A metaphor for any European country with chronic economic or political problems.

Sicily, invasion of   The July-to-August 1943 Allied amphibious attack on the German-occupied Italian island of Sicily during WORLD WAR II. It came after the Allied North Africa campaign and was a prelude to the invasion of Italy.

Siegfried Line The military defenses on the western border of Germany during WORLD WAR II.

signals intelligence (SIGINT) INTELLIGENCE information comprising all communications intelligence, electronics intelligence, and telemetry intelligence. The activity consists of monitoring all the radio wavelengths used by an opponent (or at times an ally), transcribing them, and attempting to decode its messages. The earliest use of SIGINT in a significant way was the British Admiralty's radio monitoring service, which gave advance notice that the German Grand Fleet was putting to sea just before the Battle of Jutland in 1916. It was the failure of the U.S. Navy to take seriously signals intelligence reports of Japanese naval movements in December 1941 that led to their Pacific fleet being surprised at Pearl Harbor. It is not always necessary to be able to decode the enemy's radio communications to gain useful information; changes in the location, pattern, and volume of radio messages by themselves can give vital clues. *See also* ELECTRONIC INTELLIGENCE.

Sihanouk, Norodom (1922–   ) The king of Cambodia (1941–1955) who assumed the throne upon the death of his father. He worked steadily for his country's independence from France and finally, in 1953, realized this goal. Sihanouk then gave up his throne in 1955 so that he could become active in politics, took the title of crown prince, and became prime minister. He was overthrown in a 1970 U.S.-backed military coup (led by LON NOL) after failing to keep his country out of the turmoil of the VIETNAM WAR. After the coup he took refuge in China, where he set up a government in exile and lent his name to the Communist guerrilla movement, the KHMER ROUGE. In 1975 when they and their leader POL POT took over Cambodia, they made him a figurehead president. But in that same year, as they began the CAMBODIAN HOLOCAUST, they arrested Sihanouk; he was released in 1979 as invading Vietnamese troops approached the capital of Phnom Penh. Once again he took up residence in China and North Korea and set up another government in exile. Even though the Khmer Rouge killed five of his children and 14 of

Norodom Sihanouk during his term as prime minister. (Library of Congress)

his grandchildren, beginning in 1982 he sought to form a coalition government in exile with them and other factions. Working under the auspices of the United Nations, he and others negotiated an agreement by which the Vietnamese troops would withdraw and a coalition government would rule pending elections. Under a UN-sponsored peace plan, Sihanouk returned to Cambodia (whose name had been changed to KAMPUCHEA in 1976 but back to Cambodia in 1989) in 1991 as president to lead a transitional Supreme National Council composed of previously warring factions, including the Khmer Rouge. Under the terms of the peace plan, he must stand for election in 1993.

Sikhs   A religious minority in northern India, historically in conflict with Hindus and the Hindu-dominated Indian government. The Sikhs developed in the sixteenth century as a warrior class whose monotheistic beliefs were a synthesis of Islam and Hinduism. Traditional Sikh men wear turbans and never cut their hair. The more than 10 million Sikhs in India tend to be better educated and economically more prosperous than most Indians. This conflict has in recent years been marked by rampant acts of terrorism by radical Sikhs. Sikh extremism is especially prevalent in the northern state of PUNJAB, where desecration of Hindu shrines, murders, and bombings occur frequently. A small but violent movement emerged in 1981 when Sant Jarnail Singh Bhindranwale began preaching Sikh fundamentalism and urging the Sikh community in India to pressure the government for an independent Sikh state. Bhindranwale's followers and supporters adopted terrorism as one of their tactics. An upswing in the level of Sikh violence has followed the Indian government's 1984 attack on the GOLDEN TEMPLE OF AMRITSAR, the most revered of Sikh holy places and the site of Bhindranwale's headquarters. In response to the assault of the Golden Temple, Sikhs assassinated Indian Prime Minister INDIRA GHANDI in October 1984. One of the most tragic episodes of Sikh terrorism was the bombing of an Air India jetliner in June of 1985, in which 329 people were murdered. Sikhs have denied responsibility for the incident; most experts believe otherwise. The goal of Sikh terrorism is the formation of an independent Sikh state of Khalistan, which would be located in the present Indian state of Punjab.

silo   The basing mode for ICBMs, a hole in the ground protected with a concrete and steel wall, inside which a missile is placed. For further protection it has a heavy concrete cover that can be opened automatically.

Silver Triangle   A term sometimes used to describe the three South American countries of Peru, Colombia, and Bolivia, which grow and process much of the illegal cocaine used in North America and Europe. Peru and Bolivia provide the main cultivation regions; most of the refining is done in Colombia. *Compare to* GOLDEN TRIANGLE.

Sinatra Doctrine   *See* BREZHNEV DOCTRINE.

Sinai   The desert peninsula that separates Egypt and Israel. It was the site of major battles between these two states during the SUEZ CRISIS of 1956, the SIX-DAY WAR of 1967, and the YOM KIPPUR WAR of 1973. Israel temporarily occupied the Sinai until it signed the 1979 Peace Treaty with Egypt in the wake of the CAMP DAVID ACCORDS, which called for its phased withdrawal. This was completed in 1982. Since then an international peacekeeping force of U.S. and European states has remained as a buffer between Egypt and Israel. *See also* TABA.

sine qua non   Latin for "without which not"; an indispensable condition. If such a condition is not accepted then there is no deal.

single-column tariff   *See* TARIFF, SINGLE-COLUMN.

Single European Act   An act signed in February 1986 by the members of the EUROPEAN COMMUNITY, which revised certain aspects of the 1957 Treaty of ROME and added provisions on political cooperation. The act was significant for a variety of reasons. It allowed decisions on certain matters that had hitherto required unanimity to be made through majority voting; it formalized the EC's concern with research and development and with the environment; and it devised "cooperation procedures" for giving the EUROPEAN PARLIAMENT a greater say but without making it an equal of the COUNCIL OF MINISTERS. More important were the measures to establish political cooperation and those to achieve a single European market by the end of 1992. The achievement of the single market requires the elimination of all constraints on the circulation not only of goods and services but also of capital and people. This decision to work toward a real opening of the frontiers has raised concerns about the free flow of drugs and criminals but has also helped to reinvigorate the movement toward West European unity. *See also* MAASTRICHT TREATY.

single integrated operations plan (SIOP)   The major nuclear targeting and war-fighting plan of the United States, developed to provide the operational dimension of U.S. nuclear strategy against the Soviet Union. It has gone through numerous changes and refinements since the first SIOP of December 1960. The SIOP first emerged as an important factor in the Kennedy Administration. In 1962 Secretary of Defense Robert McNamara enunciated a counterforce nuclear strategy based on the assumption that DETERRENCE would be best achieved if the United States approached nuclear war in the same way that it had approached wars in the past—with the enemy's military forces (which now were predominantly nuclear forces) as the primary targets. The logic was that if the United States hit only Soviet missiles, it could keep enough forces in reserve to deter Soviet retaliation against U.S. cities. This new strategy was embodied in the Single Integrated Operational Plan known as SIOP-63. This plan had several categories of targets and five major attack options, ranging from an attack on Soviet strategic nuclear forces to an all-out spasm (all nuclear weapons fired at once) attack that would target Soviet urban and industrial centers. All these attack options envisaged fairly large-scale strikes. In the mid-1960s McNamara publicly moved away from the COUNTERFORCE strategy and replaced it with an emphasis on MAD, or mutual assured destruction; the SIOP, though, continued to reflect the emphasis on counterforce. The plan was modified by the Nixon Administration to remedy its insufficient flexibility, especially in the size of options. A revised SIOP was adopted in 1976; it added a series of smaller selective and more discrete alternatives that would give the president far greater flexibility than in the past. Although the Carter Administration further refined U.S. nuclear-weapons thinking with its emphasis on COUNTERVAILING STRATEGY, the next major change in the SIOP came in October 1983 to bring it into line with the Reagan Administration's notion of PREVAILING STRATEGY. With the end of the Cold War and the demise of the Soviet Union, the SIOP is less important today than it was in the past. Yet because some of the successor states to the Soviet Union have inherited its nuclear armory, the United States will need to retain an overall plan for use of nuclear weapons.

Sinn Fein   The legal political wing of the outlawed paramilitary IRISH REPUBLICAN ARMY. The organization, founded in 1905 and headquartered in Belfast, NORTHERN IRELAND, advocates a united Ireland, espouses a left-wing political ideology that decries foreign economic investment in Ireland, supports the withdrawal of Ireland from the European Community, and envisions NATIONALIZATION of industry and collectivization of farms. Many Sinn Fein members have been implicated in IRA acts of terrorism, and the group's leadership has often voiced support for PROVISIONAL IRISH REPUBLICAN ARMY actions.

Sino-   A term to describe things Chinese; thus Sinology is the study of Chinese issues and history.

Sino-Indian Conflict   The 1959–1962 border war between China and India that failed to resolve conflicting border claims in the Himalayas. Negotiations since then have been interrupted by occasional border clashes. Both sides currently maintain a huge military presence in the border region with combined forces of 400,000 troops. China has a vital military interest in maintaining control over the region that links Xizang (Tibet) and the Xingjiang autonomous regions, whereas India's primary interest lies in the Indian state of Arunachal Pradesh. Tensions remain high between the two countries, although neither has ruled out further negotiations of their dispute. Most observers believe that the mountainous terrain, high-altitude climate, and concurrent logistical difficulties make it unlikely that a protracted or large-scale war would erupt on the Sino-Indian border.

Sino-Japanese Wars   Two wars between China and Japan. The first one was fought in 1894–1895 after decades of disputes between the two powers over dominance in Korea. Japan had sided with the more radical modernizing forces within the Korean government, while China had continued its support of the conservative Korean royal family. War was declared on August 1, 1894, after a pro-Japanese Korean leader had been lured to Shanghai and assassinated there. Despite the massive numbers of Chinese soldiers deployed, the modernized Japanese forces scored overwhelming victories both on land and at sea. In March 1895 the Japanese troops successfully invaded Shantung and Manchuria. China sued for peace. The subsequent Treaty of Shimonoseki contained huge Chinese concessions to Japan, including the cession of Taiwan and the Liaotung peninsulas in Manchuria, the grant of trading privileges, and the payment of a large indemnity.

The second war was formally started in 1937 when China began full-scale resistance against the Japanese invasion of Manchuria, China, in 1931, and when Japanese troops barbarically attacked NANKING. The Nationalist and Communist forces formed a temporary alliance in their joint fight against Japan. The war ended in 1945 when Japan surrendered to the Allies of World War II. *See also* CHINESE CIVIL WAR; MANCHURIAN CRISIS.

Sino-Soviet Bloc   A loose term for the group of nations, all of them with more or less Communist regimes, which were dominated by or under the HEGEMONY of the Soviet Union or Communist China (the People's Republic of China) during the period when these two countries adhered to the SINO-SOVIET TREATY of 1950. In general, the group was considered to include the WARSAW PACT nations of Eastern Europe and those countries in the Far East, such as North Korea and North Vietnam, which at the time were under the strong influence of Communist China. As the Soviet Union and the People's Republic of China drifted apart in the late 1950s, the term was less and less used.

Sino-Soviet border dispute   The diplomatic bickering over and military actions taken by China and the Soviet Union along their mutual borders. Russia and China shared a long common frontier, the details of which were laid down in treaties signed in 1858, 1860, 1864, and 1881 during a period of Chinese weakness and Russian assertiveness. Although the Bolshevik government that seized power in 1917 renounced these unequal treaties,

the CHINESE CIVIL WAR effectively placed territorial issues in abeyance. Furthermore, after the victory of the Chinese Communists in 1949, China and the Soviet Union in 1950 signed the SINO-SOVIET TREATY, a 30-year pact of friendship, alliance, and mutual assistance. The Sino-Soviet dispute, which became increasingly discernible in the early 1960s, reflected Chinese dissatisfaction with the post-Stalinist leadership of the Soviet Union. MAO ZEDONG of China, as an original revolutionary leader, did not regard NIKITA S. KHRUSHCHEV of the Soviet Union as having a legitimate claim to leadership of the international Communist movement. Furthermore, by emphasizing that there were separate roads to socialism and that China was farther toward this goal than the Soviet Union, Beijing initiated a frontal challenge for the ideological leadership of the Marxist movement. Against this background the territorial disputes (over parts of Siberia, inner Mongolia, and the Heilungklang province, e.g.), which had hitherto appeared relatively trivial, took on greater significance, if only as a symptom of the underlying differences and tensions and as a manifestation of the Chinese desire to be treated by the Soviet Union as an equal.

After several border incidents in the early 1960s, an attempt was made to clarify the boundaries by negotiations. These efforts made little progress and were suspended in 1965. The CULTURAL REVOLUTION in China sparked mass demonstrations on the frontier supporting Chinese claims. In February 1967 the Soviet embassy in Beijing was besieged. By this time it is estimated that there were 40 Soviet divisions and even more Chinese divisions on the frontier. During late 1967 and throughout 1968 fighting broke out on several occasions around what the Soviets knew as Damansky Island and what the Chinese called Zhenbao Island in the Ussuri River. These clashes escalated significantly in March 1969. After Chinese troops ambushed a Soviet patrol, the Soviet Union responded by killing hundreds of Chinese soldiers in what was a clear display of military superiority. Further incidents led to more fighting in 1969, and the Chinese announced that full-scale war might break out at any time. Not surprisingly, each side blamed the other for this escalation. The Soviet Union was concerned about the possibility of a large-scale Chinese incursion. There is even some evidence that in late 1969, the

Soviet Union seriously considered launching a preventive strike against Chinese nuclear installations. Whether the military preparations were intended as coercive measures or as preliminaries to an attack remains uncertain. Whatever the case, they encouraged China to discuss the issues in an attempt to defuse what was clearly the most dangerous crisis of the postwar period in the Pacific.

The Soviet Union was careful to ensure that its coercive actions were accompanied by conciliatory gestures and a willingness to negotiate. In 1969 Soviet Prime Minister Alexei Kosygin flew to Beijing for talks with Mao. The two leaders agreed to discussions on the border issues, which continued until 1978, but little progress was made.

Major changes came with the emergence of Mikhail Gorbachev as the Soviet leader in 1985. There was a tacit, probably reciprocal, relaxation in the military confrontation along the border. China not only removed troops from the frontier but in the mid-1980s cut its armed forces by 1 million soldiers. The Soviet Union placed its border divisions on a lower level of readiness. Against this background, Gorbachev's 1986 visit to Beijing held out considerable promise. It was the first Sino-Soviet Summit for three decades and reflected the new détente that had been reached through the 1980s. Gorbachev confirmed that Moscow wanted a full demilitarization of the 4,000-mile border, stating that, with joint efforts, the frontier could be turned into a "border of peace." A commission was to be set up to promote this objective. The Chinese issued a communiqué stating that the two sides had "agreed to take measures to cut the military forces in the areas along the Sino-Soviet boundary to a minimum level commensurate with the normal, good neighborly relations between the two countries" and to speed up discussions aimed at settling the border line. With the demise of the Soviet Union in 1991, China now has the opportunity to resolve all border disputes with the former Soviet republics (such as Russia and Kazakhstan) that are its new neighbors.

Sino-Soviet split   The estrangement of the two major Communist powers from the mid-1950s to the late 1980s. After the founding of the People's Republic of China in 1949, the Chinese leaders'

priority was the consolidation of their power, ensuring national security and economic development. Partly because of U.S. hostility as a result of the defeat of the Chinese Nationalist government and involvement in the Korean War, China leaned toward the Soviet Union to achieve its objectives. The 1950 SINO-SOVIET TREATY of Friendship, Alliance, and Mutual Assistance set the tone of the relationship for the next five years, during which China gave the Soviet Union the right to use military bases and recognized Soviet leadership of the international Communist movement in exchange for economic, military, and technological assistance. In the late 1950s NIKITA S. KHRUSHCHEV's de-Stalinization within the Soviet Union and his conciliatory foreign policy toward the West upset China's MAO ZEDONG, who favored a more militant policy toward the West and accused Khrushchev of being a revisionist. The Sino-Soviet relationship took a turn for worse when China abandoned its attempt to copy the Soviet economic model and the Soviet Union withdrew all its advisors in 1960. In the 1960s the ideological split led to the territorial SINO-SOVIET BORDER DISPUTE, culminating in 1969 in bloody armed clashes on their borders. In the 1970s China's foreign policy became more moderate even though the Soviet Union was still regarded as its main threat. In 1982 both sides resumed twice-a-year consultations on normalizing bilateral relations. China insisted, however, that the Soviet Union withdraw from Afghanistan, cease its support of Vietnamese occupation of Cambodia, and decrease its forces along the Chinese border. The changes in the Soviet leadership in the 1980s gave new impetus to the normalization of relations. Soviet President Mikhail Gorbachev's visit to China in May 1989, despite the goodwill it meant to convey, led to a democracy movement and subsequent military crackdown in TIANANMEN SQUARE that caused the international ostracization of China for several years. In the meantime, the dismantling of the Soviet Union and the formation of a new Commonwealth of Independent States became a cause of deep concern to the Chinese leaders. They are relieved to see a long-term threat disappearing over the northern border, but are worried about the impact of the Soviet rejection of communism upon the Chinese people.

Sino-Soviet Treaty The 1950 agreement that called for the Soviet Union to come to the assistance of China if it was attacked by Japan or an ally of Japan (a clear reference to the United States). The Soviet Union then bolstered Communist China's military strength during the 1950s. The two nations drifted apart toward the end of the decade, however, and eventually became bitter rivals over the SINO-SOVIET BORDER DISPUTE.

Sino-Vietnamese conflict The deterioration of Vietnam's relations with China after Vietnam strengthened its alliance with the Soviet Union in the mid-1970s. This led to incidents of violence along the border of the two countries. When the pro-Beijing POL POT regime in Cambodia (then Kampuchea) was ousted by invading Vietnamese troops in December 1978, China viewed the action as Vietnam's attempt to seek regional dominance. In February 1979 China launched a limited military campaign involving only ground troops along the entire Sino-Vietnamese border to teach Vietnam "some necessary lessons," according to Teng Hsiao-ping, the Chinese deputy prime minister (*New York Times*, February 10, 1979). In March Beijing declared that its objectives had been achieved and unilaterally withdrew all its troops from the Vietnamese territories. Sino-Vietnamese relations remained sour until recently, when a United Nations–sponsored cease-fire among the warring factions of Cambodia paved the way for talks on resumption of diplomatic relations between China and Vietnam.

Sitzkrieg German for "sitting war"; a situation in which war has been declared but no military action has been taken. This term is generally applied to the winter of 1939–1940, when there was very little military action after the German conquest of Poland; also known as the PHONY WAR.

Six, the The first European states that signed the 1957 Treaty of ROME and established the European COMMON MARKET.

Six-Day War The third major ARAB-ISRAELI WAR. In May 1967, after tensions had increased between Syria and Israel, Egyptian President Gamal Abdal Nasser moved armaments and about 80,000 troops into the Sinai Peninsula and ordered withdrawal of United Nations peacekeeping troops from the armistice line and Sharm El-Sheikh. Nasser closed the Strait of Tiran to Israeli ships, blockading the Israeli port of Eilat at the northern end of the Gulf of Aqaba. On May 30 Jordan and Egypt signed a mutual defense treaty. Hostilities broke out on June 5. In a preemptive strike, the Israelis launched air attacks that destroyed the Egyptian Air Force. After six days of fighting, when all parties had accepted the cease-fire called for by UN Security Council Resolutions 235 and 236, Israel controlled the Sinai Peninsula, the Gaza Strip, the Kuneitra (Golan) sector of Syria, and the formerly Jordanian-controlled West Bank of the Jordan River, including East Jerusalem. On November 22, 1967, the Security Council adopted Resolution 242, the "land for peace" formula, which called for the establishment of a just and lasting peace that should be based on Israeli withdrawal from territories occupied in 1967 in exchange for the end of all states of belligerency, respect for the sovereignty of all states in the area, and recognition of the right to live in peace within secure, recognized boundaries. The Israelis returned the Sinai to Egypt in 1982. The remaining areas obtained during the Six-Day War, known collec-

---

SIX-DAY WAR OF 1967
A Chronology

June 5	Israeli Air Force, in a surprise attack, effectively destroys the air force of Egypt. Israeli troops engage Arab forces in Sinai.
6	Egypt closes the Suez Canal (it would remain closed until 1975); claims United States and Great Britain were aiding Israelis.
7	Israeli forces advance into the Sinai, the Gaza Strip, and the West Bank. Jordan agrees to a cease-fire.
8	Egypt agrees to a cease-fire. Israeli Air Force attacks U.S. intelligence-gathering ship *Liberty*.
9	Egyptian President Nasser offers his resignation, but it is rejected by the Egyptian National Assembly.
10	Soviet Union severs diplomatic relations with Israel and pledges assistance to Arab states. Israel captures Golan Heights. Syria agrees to cease-fire and war ends.

tively as the OCCUPIED TERRITORIES, have been a continuing point of tension between Israel and the Arab world ever since.

skinheads   Violent white males, characteristically with shaved heads or very closely cropped hair, who have been responsible for racially motivated gang violence in Europe and the United States. Many skinheads espouse NEO-NAZI philosophy and wear Nazi insignia. Skinhead violence in the United States, concentrated on the West Coast, has been directed against blacks, Asians, Hispanics, Jews, and homosexuals; skinheads in European nations, especially Germany, Great Britain, and Hungary, have targeted immigrants, Jews, and Muslims.

skyjacking   Using force to take an airliner and its passengers hostage for personal or political motives. Modern skyjacking, or *air piracy*, dates from 1961 when a U.S. airliner was hijacked to Cuba. In the early 1970s skyjacking became the modus operandi of the POPULAR FRONT FOR THE LIBERATION OF PALESTINE to publicize the Palestinian cause. Some of the most celebrated cases were the skyjacking of an Air France airliner to ENTEBBE in July of 1976 and the diversion of a number of European airliners to DAWSON'S FIELD in Jordan in 1970. Elaborate airport security procedures implemented since then have dramatically reduced the number of skyjackings.

SLBM (submarine-launched ballistic missile)   The naval model of an intercontinental ballistic missile (ICBM). Carried on nuclear-powered submarines known as SSBNs, SLBMs have ranges varying from 2,000 kilometers for the first version of the U.S. Polaris missile to between 9,000 and 11,000 kilometers for the most advanced Soviet and U.S. weapons. For much of their brief history submarine-carried missiles were much less accurate than land-based ICBMs and could be used only for countervalue strikes against urban-industrial targets. The great value of this leg of the TRIAD was that submarines on patrol are virtually undetectable, so that the SLBM part of a nation's nuclear deterrent could ensure its SECOND-STRIKE CAPABILITY. When these missiles were both MIRVed and given longer ranges, the importance of the SSBN fleets—especially for the United States—

increased greatly. SLBMs will continue to be important for the United States even though the numbers will go down considerably as a result of the arms accord between U.S. President George Bush and Russian President Boris Yeltsin reached in June 1992. *See* START II.

SLCM   *See* SEA-LAUNCHED CRUISE MISSILE.

sleepers   Terrorists or intelligence agents who maintain a low profile so as to be in a position to provide aid to their more active brethren. Sleepers may provide safe houses, forged identification and documents, weapons, vehicles and transport, money, information, and other valuable forms of assistance.

sleeping dictionary   A diplomat's lover in a foreign country; so called because such social arrangements have facilitated learning the local language.

SLORC   State Law and Order Restoration Council; the name that Burma's (now Myanmar's) ruling military junta adopted for itself in 1988.

Slovakia   A new state in what was the eastern part of Czechoslovakia. The Germans forced the creation of a Slovak state in 1938 to divide a conquered Czechoslovakia. While Slovakia was reincorporated into Czechoslovakia in 1945, separatist tensions remained. After the VELVET REVOLUTION and end of Communist rule in 1989, the tensions flared up. In mid-1992 the Czechoslovakian legislature peacefully voted itself out of existence. On January 1, 1993, independent Czech and Slovak republics were born.

small intercontinental ballistic missile   *See* MIDGETMAN.

small powers   1. A state that, according to Marshall Singer in "The Foreign Policies of Small Developing States" (in J. Rosenau, K. Thompson, and G. Boyd, eds., *World Politics*, 1976) lacks one of the four basic components of power: wealth (human and material), organization (formal and informal), status (ascribed and acquired), and will (conscious and unconscious). 2. States that are the objects of international politics because they are small and weak. *Compare to* GREAT POWERS.

SMERSH The special assassination agency of the Soviet Union whose job was the liquidation of enemies who lived on foreign soil. SMERSH is an acronym for *Smert Shpionam* ("death to spies"). SMERSH's most famous victim was LEON TROTSKY, who was murdered in Mexico City in 1940. Because SMERSH, a World War II unit of the KGB, figured prominently in Ian Fleming's James Bond novels, many people think the agency was fictional; but it was real.

SMICE An updated acronym for the various factors that motivate someone to turn traitor and spy on his or her own county: sex, money, ideology, compromise, and ego. *See also* MICE.

Smith, Ian *See* ZIMBABWE CIVIL WAR.

Smith, Walter Bedell (1895–1961) The career U.S. Army officer who was General Dwight D. Eisenhower's chief of staff during World War II; U.S. ambassador to the Soviet Union (1946–1949) and the director of the Central Intelligence Agency (1949–1953).

Smithsonian Agreement *See* BRETTON WOODS SYSTEM.

Smuts, Jan Christiaan (1870–1950) The South African guerrilla leader during the BOER WAR who later became one of the leading proponents of cooperating with Great Britain. He led the South African World War I campaign in German East Africa, helped create the British Royal Air Force, and was a strong advocate of the LEAGUE OF NATIONS at the Paris Peace Conference in 1919. After the war he became prime minister (1919–1924) and deputy prime minister (1933–1939) of South Africa. In 1939 he became prime minister again and strongly supported British efforts in World War II. (He was made a field marshal in 1941.) In 1945 he attended the San Francisco Conference where he helped create the United Nations. In 1946 he tried unsuccessfully to persuade the United Nations to allow South West Africa (Namibia), then a MANDATE territory under South African rule, to be incorporated into South Africa. In the 1948 election Smuts's Unionist Party was defeated by the Nationalist Party led by Daniel Malan (1874–1959). The Nationalists then implemented APARTHEID. Smuts did not favor separate development; he was content with white supremacy. Smuts then served as chancellor of Cambridge University, England, until his death.

Snake, the The range of variance of European Economic Community currencies agreed to in 1972 to limit fluctuations of their various currencies so that the margin between the strongest and weakest currency would not be more than 4.5 percent. The name snake was attached to the scheme because on a graph, the narrow band of permitted fluctuation over time resembled a snake. In 1979 the Snake was superseded by the EUROPEAN MONETARY SYSTEM.

Snyder, Glenn H. (1924–   ) A U.S. scholar who has produced two germinal works in the field of national and international security studies. His *Deterrence and Defense* (1961) was one of the most rigorous contributions to strategic analysis. His dissection of the various subtleties of the relationship between DETERRENCE and DEFENSE is a classic of systematic and incisive analysis. He subsequently turned his interest to international crises, and his volume coauthored with Paul Diesing entitled *Conflict Among Nations: Bargaining and Decision Making in International Crises* (1977) provided a brilliant analysis of crises from the nuclear age and earlier. The book dealt with crises from a decision-making perspective as well as from the perspective of the international system. Because it also offered a comprehensive discussion of BARGAINING THEORY in crises, it is one of the most frequently cited works on the subject.

Snyder, Richard (1916–   ) A U.S. pioneer of the decision-making approach to foreign policy, which emphasized motivational analysis as a major factor in international relations. The Snyder decision-making approach initially appeared in the early 1950s and was published as *Foreign Policy Decision Making* (1962). It was not only an innovative study but also was central to the development of foreign policy analysis as an academic discipline. By focusing on the individuals who made policy and looking at the organizational and domestic context in which they make it, Snyder moved decisively away from the BLACK BOX APPROACH to foreign policy. His emphasis on both the rigor of the social science approach and the insights that could be gleaned from psychology and sociology, as much as the details of the decision-making approach itself, opened the way for subsequent scholars to build on the decision-making approach in a systematic fashion. While the Snyder schema for studying foreign policy decision making was applied only by Glenn Paige in *The Korean Decision* (1968), it nevertheless is significant.

Soccer War   *See* FOOTBALL WAR.

Social Charter   1. The 1989 nonbinding pledge by all of the governments of the EUROPEAN COMMUNITY (except Great Britain) to improve working conditions and rights of workers. The charter proposes putting issues such as equal employment opportunity, minimum wages, and union rights on a statutory basis. 2. The 1965 agreement by member states of the COUNCIL OF EUROPE guaranteeing minimal rights to all workers.

social contract   1. The philosophic notion that the obligations that individuals and states have toward each other originate in a theoretical agreement they have tacitly made with each other. If the state breaks the social contract, then grounds for revolution exist. This was an important consideration in the U.S. Declaration of Independence. 2. The social welfare policies of a government. They are considered a contract because citizens have grown to expect and depend on them. *Compare to* STATE OF NATURE.

social Darwinism   British naturalist Charles Darwin's (1809–1882) concept of biological evolution applied to the development of human social organization and economic policy. British sociologist Herbert Spencer (1820–1903) spent much of his career applying Darwin's concepts of "natural selection" and "survival of the fittest" to the social sciences. Social Darwinism heavily influenced European attitudes toward COLONIALISM and WAR.

social defense   Seeking to protect a state by making it extremely difficult for an enemy invader to occupy it. This kind of DETERRENCE ranges all the way from passive civil disobedience to large-scale guerrilla warfare. It is premised on the belief that no

occupying power can subdue a population that thoroughly resists it. The obvious problem with this approach is that history shows COLLABORATION with an occupying enemy is certainly as common as organized opposition to it.

social democrats   Centrist to left political parties in many West European states. For example, in Germany, Portugal, and the United Kingdom, they are centrists, while in Denmark, Iceland, and Switzerland they are left wing. *Compare to* CHRISTIAN DEMOCRATS.

social indicator   A statistical measure that aids in the description of conditions in the social environment; for example, measures of health, income distribution, physical environment, or poverty. *Compare to* STATIC INDICATORS.

socialism   A system of government in which most of the means of producing and distributing things are owned or managed by the government, and in which BASIC HUMAN NEEDS are defined by and provided for directly by the government. Socialism may or may not be democratic. All of the industrialized states of the West offer a variety of socialistic programs to their citizens; examples include food stamps, national health insurance, and unemployment insurance. Because they combine elements of both socialism and CAPITALISM, they are known as MIXED ECONOMIES. *Compare to* MARXISM.

socialism in one country   Soviet dictator JOSEPH STALIN's policy that the socialist state be built first in the Soviet Union, as opposed to LEON TROTSKY's idea of INTERNATIONALISM: pressing for continuous contemporary socialist revolutions throughout the world. Stalin wrote in *Problems of Leninism* (1926): "First of all there is the question: Can Socialism possibly be established in one country alone by that country's unaided strength? The question must be answered in the affirmative." This was a reversal of Stalin's position of two years earlier, when he had agreed with Trotsky that socialism could not be achieved in one country alone. Stalin reversed himself for two main reasons: (1) He did not want needlessly to threaten his capitalist neighbors with revolution and encourage them to take military action against him, and (2) he asserted as a matter of doctrine that the Soviet Union could create a viable socialist state on its own—without the help of socialist revolutions in other states.

socialism with a human face   *See* DUBCEK, ALEXANDER.

socialist commonwealth   A vague term that referred to all of the Communist states of the world that were within the Soviet Union's SPHERE OF INFLUENCE. It was a Communist counterpart to FREE WORLD during the COLD WAR.

Socialist International   *See* INTERNATIONAL, THE.

Söderblom, Nathan (1866–1931)   The Swedish archbishop who won the 1930 Nobel Peace Prize for being one of the architects of the twentieth-century ecumenical movement, which seeks to unify all Protestant churches and ultimately all Christians.

SOE   *See* SPECIAL OPERATIONS EXECUTIVE.

soft currency   Money that cannot be converted easily to the currency of other states. Generally speaking, because the currencies of the industrialized states of the West are readily acceptable as payments for goods and debts in international trade, they are considered to be HARD CURRENCY. Because the currencies of many developing countries are not convertible, they are considered "soft." *Compare to* CONVERTIBLE CURRENCY.

soft kill   *See* HARD KILL.

soft loans   Low-interest or no-interest loans made to developing countries by international lending institutions such as the INTERNATIONAL DEVELOPMENT ASSOCIATION.

soft power   Relatively intangible forms of power, such as an attractive ideology or an intriguing culture that can provide a state with considerable influence and help to co-opt others. A term used by security theorist Joseph Nye, it is closely related to the notion of CO-OPTIVE POWER.

soft target   *See* HARD TARGET.

solidarity   1. A feeling of common purpose. 2. Labor union unitedness; the common responsi-

bilities and interests of union members.   3. The independent Polish labor union confederation (in Polish, *Solidarnösc*) founded by LECH WALESA in 1980 following a negotiated agreement between the Polish government and a committee representing striking shipyard workers in Gdansk. The national discontent underlying the strikes was intensified by revelations of widespread corruption and mismanagement. At the sixth Central Committee Plenum of the Polish United Workers' (Communist) Party (PZPR) in September 1980, EDWARD GIEREK was replaced by Stanislaw Kania as first secretary. Alarmed by the rapid deterioration of the PZPR's authority following the Gdansk agreement, the Soviet Union proceeded with a massive buildup of its military forces along Poland's border in December 1980. In February 1981 Polish Defense Minister General WOJCIECH JARUZELSKI assumed the position of prime minister as well, and in October 1981 he also was named party first secretary. At the first Solidarity national congress in September–October 1981, Lech Walesa was elected national chairman of the union. When Solidarity called for democratic elections and a referendum on the Communist Party's continued dominance of the state, the regime declared MARTIAL LAW on December 12, 1981. The army and police were used to crush the union. Virtually all Solidarity leaders (including Walesa, who was temporarily jailed) were arrested or detained, as were many affiliated intellectuals. Still, this union, which later evolved into a political party, led the movement for Polish freedom from Communist rule. Solidarity remained underground until it was again legalized in 1989 following the strikes of 1988. In 1990 Solidarity's candidate, TADEUZ MAZOWIECKI, was appointed prime minister. However, since the election of Walesa to the presidency, Solidarity's internal problems, having to do with tactical differences about the best way to create a viable free market economy, have caused it to fragment into many splinter groups.

Solidarity, Declaration of   The strong condemnation of international communism adopted at the tenth Inter-American Conference, held in Caracas, Venezuela, in 1954, by the American republics. They declared that domination or control of any American republic by Communists was a threat to political independence and would not be tolerated.

Solzhenitsyn, Alexander Isaevich (1918–   )   The Russian author and uncompromising critic of Soviet socialism. He was exiled internally to Kazahkstan because, while serving in the army during World War II, he referred to Soviet leader Joseph Stalin critically in letters to a friend. He was restored to citizenship in 1956 and began to write. His best-known books are *One Day in the Life of Ivan Denisovich* (1962), *The First Circle* (1968), *August 1914* (1971), and *The Gulag Archipelago: 1918–1956*, 3 vols. (1973–1975). He won the Nobel Prize for literature in 1970. After his 1974 expulsion from the Soviet Union, he moved to the United States. In 1990 his Soviet citizenship was restored, just before the dissolution of the Soviet Union in 1991.

Somalian Civil War   The anarchy that began when Somalia (located in the HORN OF AFRICA) attacked Ethiopia in 1977. By 1982 Ethiopian forces, in a major counterattack, invaded Somalia, creating a massive refugee problem. While fighting with Ethiopia ended even before the conclusion of the ETHIOPIAN CIVIL WAR in 1991, a decade-long drought and internal tribal warfare has caused a massive problem of starvation. Between war and famine Somalia has lost a million out of its 8 million citizens since 1980. And because conditions degenerated to a THOMAS HOBBES–like STATE OF NATURE with no government to maintain order and distribute emergency food supplies from the United Nations and other international agencies, millions more were at risk. By late 1992 six differing warring clans each controlled parts of the capital of Mogadishu, and it was almost impossible for relief agencies to distribute food to the countryside. Finally in December the United States, at the request of the United Nations Security Council, led a multinational peacekeeping relief effort. Approximately 28,000 U.S. troops landed in the capital of Mogadishu to restore order and secure relief supply routes into rural areas. There was little fighting and U.S. forces began to withdraw in early 1993. While peace talks have begun between the rival factions, the economy of Somalia has been so damaged that it will be many years before it can function to the extent of preventing widespread starvation without international relief.

Somme, Battle of   **1.** The five-month-long 1916 WORLD WAR I battle of ATTRITION between Anglo-French and German forces along a 20-mile stretch of the Somme River in France. It left more than a million dead and wounded but ended in a stalemate.   **2.** A 1918 battle in the same area by the same sides. This time the Allies, with help from U.S. troops, prevailed. After the 1918 battle the 1916 battle became the "First Battle of the Somme" and the 1918 battle became the "Second. . . ."

Somoza   The Nicaraguan family of dictators who dominated that country's politics for 46 years. General Anastasio "Tacho" Somoza Garcia (1896–1956) became commander of Nicaragua's army, the National Guard (*Guardia Nacional*), in 1934. He was responsible for the death of Nicaraguan revolutionary César Augusto Sandino (1893–1934). In 1936 Somoza became president and ruled directly or indirectly until 1956, when he was assassinated. His vice president and son, Luis Somoza Debayle (1922–1967), assumed the presidency, holding office from 1956 to 1963. In 1967 his brother, Anastasio Somoza Debayle (1925–1980), was elected president, controlling the country until 1979 even though his presidency (1967–1972; 1974–1979) was interrupted by a two-year period of military junta rule. Overall Somoza was an authoritarian but not a totalitarian dictator. After the bloody but popular SANDINISTA revolution forced him into exile in 1979, he was assassinated while in Paraguay.

The U.S. government had supported the Somoza regimes, which had done much to build a Nicaraguan middle class, but human rights violations and corruption led U.S. President Jimmy Carter to cut U.S. aid to Somoza Debayle's government in 1979. After all, this was the man who responded to charges of ballot-rigging by saying: "Indeed, you won the elections, but I won the count" (*Guardian*, June 17, 1977).

Songgram, Pibul (1897–1964)   The founder of modern Thailand, one of the leaders of the 1932 coup that changed his country from an absolute to a constitutional monarchy. Upon becoming prime minister of Siam in 1938, he changed the name of the country to Thailand. In World War II when the Japanese invaded the area, Songgram saw the wis-

Anastasio Somoza (Library of Congress)

dom of collaborating with them. He was removed from power in 1944, but in 1948, in a bloodless revolution, he became prime minister again. As such he changed the country's orientation from pro-Chinese and anti-West to pro-West and anti-Chinese leanings. He sent troops to fight in the Korean War, and he allowed SEATO to have its headquarters in Bangkok. In September of 1957 he was overthrown by a coup.

Sonnenfeldt Doctrine   A term that was used to describe a 1975 statement by Helmut Sonnenfeldt, then chief advisor to U.S. Secretary of State Henry Kissinger, in which he suggested that it was in the interest of the United States to encourage the development of "organic links" between the Soviet Union and the states of Eastern Europe. Speaking in Lon-

don at a meeting of U.S. ambassadors stationed in Eastern and Western Europe, Sonnenfeldt suggested that there were dangers in a situation in which the only link between the states of Eastern Europe and the Soviet Union was Soviet military domination. According to the official State Department summary of the remarks (published in the *New York Times* on April 6, 1976), Sonnenfeldt stated that the United States should "strive for an evolution that makes the relationship between the Eastern Europeans and the Soviet Union an organic one . . . our policy must be a policy of responding to the more clearly visible aspirations in Eastern Europe for a more autonomous existence within the context of a strong Soviet geopolitical influence." This was interpreted as a demand to recognize and accept Soviet domination over Eastern Europe, and as such it created considerable controversy in the United States, where it was seen as another example of the POWER POLITICS approach to foreign policy followed by Kissinger. In fact, both Kissinger and U.S. President Gerald Ford complained that Sonnenfeldt had been misunderstood and that the United States had no intention of recognizing the Soviet sphere of influence in Eastern Europe as legitimate.

Soong, T. V. (also spelled Sung Tsu-Wen) (1894–1971)   Financier of the Chinese Nationalist Government who served as minister of finance (1925–1928) and minister of foreign affairs (1941–1945) under CHIANG KAI-SHEK. Educated in the United States at Harvard University, Soong played a key role in reforming China's taxation system, restoring Chinese tariff autonomy, and negotiating the end of extraterritoriality rights—the right of foreigners to govern themselves while on Chinese soil. When the Communists took over the mainland in 1949, Soong moved to the United States where he remained active in business and banking. He was the brother of SOONG CH'IN-LING and SOONG MEI-LING.

Soong Ch'in-ling (also spelled Song Qinling) (1892–1981)   Wife of the Chinese revolutionary and KUOMINTANG founding father SUN YAT-SEN. She became politically active after her husband's death and broke away from CHIANG KAI-SHEK's Kuomintang, which she denounced as having betrayed the ideals of Sun Yat-sen. After the Communists formed the People's Republic, Soong Ch'in-ling remained in China's mainland and joined the government as the leader of a left-wing Kuomintang group.

Soong Mei-ling (also spelled Song Meiling) (1899–   )   Wife of Chinese Nationalist President CHIANG KAI-SHEK and sister of SOONG CH'IN-LING and T. V. SOONG. Educated in the United States, Soong Mei-ling was often quoted as saying "The only thing oriental about me is my face." She served as a crucial link between her husband's cause and the West, where she helped him obtain financial and military support. She was known in the West as Madame Chiang Kai-shek.

sortie   *See* AIR STRIKE.

source   1. The raw data from which INTELLIGENCE information is derived.   2. In clandestine activities, a person (an agent), normally a foreign national, in the employ of an intelligence agency.   3. In interrogation, any individual who furnishes intelligence information, with or without the knowledge that the information is being used for intelligence purposes. In this context, a *controlled source* is in the employment or under the control of the intelligence agency and knows that the information is to be used for intelligence purposes. An *uncontrolled source* is a voluntary contributor of information and may or may not know that the information is to be used for intelligence purposes.   4. In academic work, a source of information, which is generally acknowledged in a reference.

South   The developing states of the THIRD WORLD, because so many of them are below the equator or, at least, south in relation to the industrialized states of the FIRST WORLD, or the North. *See also* NORTH-SOUTH.

South African apartheid   *See* APARTHEID.

South African War   *See* BOER WAR.

Southern Cone   The southern part of Latin America, which includes Brazil, Chile, Paraguay, Uruguay, and Argentina.

Southern Flank   A North Atlantic Treaty Organization term for its southernmost members, those on the Mediterranean Sea. Because the region includes Greece and Turkey, which are enemies in the conflict on Cyprus, it is regarded as one of NATO's weakest areas.

South Pacific Forum   An organization established in 1971 to provide an informal opportunity for heads of government in the south Pacific region to discuss a variety of common problems and issues. Current members include Australia, the Cook Islands, Fiji, Kiribati, Nauru, New Zealand, Niue, Papua New Guinea, the Solomon Islands, Tonga, Tuvalu, Vanuatu, and Western Samoa. The South Pacific Bureau for Economic Cooperation, located at Suva, Fiji, is its official secretariat.

South Pacific Nuclear Free Zone Treaty The 1985 agreement by Australia, Fiji, Kiribati, New Zealand, Niue, Papua New Guinea, Tuvalu, and Western Samoa not to manufacture, acquire, or control nuclear explosive devices; to allow the stationing or testing of such devices within their territories; or to allow the dumping of nuclear waste. No restrictions were imposed on access to the region by nuclear-powered or nuclear-armed ships and aircraft. The treaty contained protocols that the five major nuclear powers were called on to sign through which they would pledge not to use or threaten the use of nuclear weapons against any of the signatories and not to test nuclear weapons within the zone. China and the Soviet Union signed; France, Great Britain, and the United States refused. In effect, the treaty did little more than underline the acceptance of the principle of NONPROLIFERA-TION among states that lacked the inclination, and in most cases the ability, to become nuclear powers.

Southwest Asia A term used by the United States for military planning purposes; generally seen as the region centered on the Persian Gulf. Southwest Asia is generally understood to overlap both the Middle East and South Asia and includes Kenya, Sudan, Egypt, Saudi Arabia, Iraq, Iran, Afghanistan, and Pakistan. It was a key part of what in the late 1970s was termed the ARC OF CRISIS. Southwest Asia was the main focus of the RAPID DEPLOYMENT FORCE.

sovereign 1. The highest authority in a state. In a monarchy this is a king or queen; in a republic it is the people. 2. The government of a state. 3. The person with the greatest power in a state. 4. Having to do with royalty or supreme rank.

sovereign immunity 1. A government's freedom from being sued in its own courts for damages in all but those situations in which it passes specific statutes allowing for it. As a SOVEREIGN entity, only rarely can a government be charged in a lawsuit within its own borders. The traditional essence of sovereign immunity is summed up in the phrase "the KING CAN DO NO WRONG." However, to overcome the inherent inequity of this, many states enact laws that allow citizens to sue or petition their governments for damages done to them. 2. The

INTERNATIONAL LAW legal principle that one state is not subject to the legal processes of another state; states cannot sue each other.

sovereign independence *See* INDEPENDENCE.

sovereignty 1. Being highest in power, rank, or authority. In a republic such as the United States, the people are sovereign and government is considered their agent. In a monarchy such as the United Kingdom, the queen or king is sovereign and the people are her or his subjects. But some monarchs are more sovereign than others. The king of Saudi Arabia, because he has fewer constitutional restrictions than does the queen of the United Kingdom, has far greater control over his subjects. 2. The fact that a state recognizes no higher constitutional authority than itself. In this sense, sovereignty is a legal concept. The interesting discussions that are often cast in terms of limiting sovereignty, however, are really about independence, which is essentially a political as opposed to a legal concept and is relative rather than absolute. 3. The basis for the notion of international society that is predicated on the expectation that a state's sovereignty will be respected by others. The concomitant of sovereignty is the principle of NONINTERVENTION in the internal affairs of states.

soviet 1. A Russian word for "council." Soviets initially arose in the Urals among striking workers to direct their activities during the RUSSIAN REVOLUTION OF 1905. The BOLSHEVIKs adroitly used the slogan "All Power to the Soviets," and once in control they used these soviets, with a pyramidal arrangement of local, provincial, and republic-wide councils, as the theoretical basis of the new government to extend their control. An All-Russian Congress of Soviets (which in 1936 was renamed the Supreme Soviet) became the highest authority of the state. 2. A citizen of the UNION OF SOVIET SOCIALIST REPUBLICS from 1923 (when the nation was created) through 1991.

Soviet bloc A COLD WAR term for those Eastern European states that were more or less under the control of the Soviet Union and governed by Communist parties. It was usually understood to include Bulgaria, Czechoslovakia, East Germany, Hungary, Poland, and Romania.

sovietologist   A scholar or policy analyst who studies the UNION OF SOVIET SOCIALIST REPUBLICS. With the passing of this political entity in 1991, a field that once had great currency has become the domain of historians.

Soviet space program   The COLD WAR efforts of the SOVIET UNION to explore the earth's atmosphere and beat the United States in the SPACE RACE. Using some of the German scientists who helped to develop the V-weapons toward the end of World War II, the Soviets with *SPUTNIK I* put the first satellite in earth orbit in 1957 and the first man in space, YURI GAGARIN, in 1961. While the Soviets never put men on the moon as the United States did in 1969, they continued with many earth-orbit flights throughout the 1970s and 1980s. Thus their cosmonauts on the whole logged more time in space than did U.S. astronauts. In 1975, as part of DÉTENTE, the United States and the Soviet Union had their only Cold War–era joint mission with the APOLLO-SOYUZ flight. After the demise of the Soviet Union in 1991, it was widely expected that there would be many more joint missions with the U.S. NATIONAL AERO-NAUTICS AND SPACE ADMINISTRATION.

Soviet studies   1. The study of the Soviet Union, which took many forms, all of which were concerned with unwrapping the mysteries of Soviet foreign policies and domestic politics.   2. A defunct field of study, unless one is a historian.

Spaak, Paul-Henri (1899–1972)   The Belgian politician and diplomat who was premier of Belgium (1938–1939, 1946; 1947–1949) and secretary general of the North Atlantic Treaty Organization from 1957 to 1961. A strong advocate of a united Europe, Spaak then returned to the Belgian government and was deputy prime minister for foreign and African affairs from 1961 to 1966.

space race   The COLD WAR competition between the United States and the Soviet Union to explore outer space that began when the Soviets launched *SPUTNIK I* in 1957 and intensified when U.S. President John F.

Kennedy told a joint session of Congress on May 25, 1961: "I believe that this nation should commit itself to achieving the goal, before this decade is out, of landing a man on the moon and returning him safely to the earth." The United States won the race to the moon in 1969. *See also* NATIONAL AERONAUTICS AND SPACE ADMINISTRATION.

Spaceship Earth   A concept from the environmental movement that suggests that the planet earth is a single fragile ecosystem whose resources need better management by its human caretakers.

Spandau   The sixteenth-century fortress in Berlin that from 1947 to 1987 was an Allied-operated prison for World War II NAZI war criminals.

Spanish-American War   The 1898 war between the United States and Spain that began when the U.S. battleship *Maine* mysteriously exploded in the harbor of Havana, Cuba, a Spanish colony. Without serious military opposition the United States took control from Spain of Cuba, Guam, the Philippines, and Puerto Rico. These acquisitions plus a strong naval construction program gave the United States the status of an imperial power.

Spanish Civil War   The 1936 to 1939 conflict that has been called a "rehearsal for World War II" because it pitted elected republican forces aided by Communists against a fascist army aided by Italy and Germany. The Western democracies, through thousands of volunteers who formed INTERNATIONAL BRIGADES, fought with the republicans against the fascists aided by German CONDOR LEGION troops and planes.

The war began when the Spanish drove out their king in 1936 and elected a POPULAR FRONT government of centrists and leftists. The FALANGE, a party of Spanish fascists, refused to accept the results of the ballots. The Spanish Army, led by General FRANCISCO FRANCO, rebelled against the Popular Front government. Following the victory of his nationalist forces in 1939, Franco ruled a nation that was exhausted both politically and economically. Spain was officially neutral during World War II but followed a pro-AXIS policy.

During the civil war an estimated 600,000 perished, and Franco put another 1 million in concen-

Colonel Theodore Roosevelt with his Rough Riders in Cuba at the top of San Juan Hill after its capture, July 1898. (Library of Congress)

tration camps afterward. The victorious Allies of World War II isolated Spain at the beginning of the postwar period, and the country was not allowed to join the United Nations until 1955.

Spanish Law of Succession   The 1947 Spanish legislation that declared Spain a monarchy, named FRANCISCO FRANCO as acting regent and chief of state, and provided for a Council of Regents to name Franco's successor. In 1969 Franco designated Prince JUAN CARLOS DE BOURBON as his successor. Juan Carlos became king and chief of state following Franco's death in 1975.

Spartan analogy   The parallel drawn by some analysts between the priority that was given to defense spending in the city-state of Sparta in ancient Greece and in the twentieth-century Soviet Union. In both cases the effort to treat military spending as a special case undermined the economy and led to the collapse of the state.

Spaso House   The residence of the U.S. Ambassador in Moscow, Russia.

Special Air Service   *See* SAS.

special drawing rights (SDRs)   International monetary reserve units created by the INTERNATIONAL MONETARY FUND in 1969 to supplement the limited supplies of gold and dollars that had been the prime stable international monetary assets. SDRs have been used between members to settle BALANCE OF PAYMENTS accounts and as both reserve assets and reserve credits. The SDR is pegged to a BASKET OF CURRENCIES.

special economic zones   Small coastal areas in China demarcated by the reform-oriented Chinese government in 1979 to promote economic development and the introduction and adoption of advanced technology from more industrialized nations through foreign investment (either totally or in partnership with local financing). Special preferential terms and facilities are offered to outside investors in terms of taxation, land-use fees, and entry and exit controls for both JOINT VENTURES and foreign-owned enterprises. Special economic zones have greater decision-making power in economic activities than do other administrative units in China's cities or provinces. *Compare to* FREE TRADE ZONE.

special forces   Military units trained for unconventional operations, especially COUNTERINSURGENCY warfare. The U.S. Army Special Forces, often called the Green Berets because of their official headgear, was formed in 1952. Originally they were designed to organize guerrilla bands behind enemy lines. During the early 1960s they began to evolve into a major counterinsurgency force; in this capacity they provided significant service during the Vietnam War. Special forces of other states include the British SAS and the German GSG-9.

specialized agencies   Task-oriented organizations associated with the UNITED NATIONS but autonomous in their operations. They function in relation to particular areas of activity such as public health and economic development. The 16 current specialized agencies work with the United Nations and each other through the coordination of the ECO-

---

THE UNITED NATIONS SPECIALIZED AGENCIES*

Food and Agriculture Organization of the United Nations (FAO)
International Bank for Reconstruction and Development (IBRD)/World Bank
International Civil Aviation Organization (ICAO)
International Development Association (IDA)
International Finance Corporation (IFC)
International Fund for Agricultural Development (IFAD)
International Labor Organization (ILO)
International Maritime Organization (IMO)
International Monetary Fund (IMF)
International Telecommunication Union (ITU)
United Nations Educational, Scientific and Cultural Organization (UNESCO)
United Nations Industrial Development Organization (UNIDO)
Universal Postal Union (UPU)
World Health Organization (WHO)
World Intellectual Property Organization (WIPO)
World Meteorological Organization (WMO)

*See individual entries for description.

NOMIC AND SOCIAL COUNCIL. They are often referred to as "part of the United Nations family."

Special Operations Executive (SOE)   The British government's secret organization to carry out SABOTAGE in Nazi-occupied Europe during WORLD WAR II. SOE specialized in training and equipping underground RESISTANCE groups.

special relationship   1. The cultural, historic, military, and nostalgic ties between the United States and the United Kingdom that have emerged since World War II. The special relationship has always had more resonance in London than in Washington, which is hardly surprising given the disparity in power of the two states. In intelligence, for example, British capabilities and facilities complement the global capabilities of the United States, and there is a long tradition of cooperation between the intelligence services of the two countries. A second area where cooperation has been unusually close has been in the relations between the armed forces of the two countries, especially their navies. A third area has been the close nuclear cooperation, manifested in the fact that Great Britain acquired both its Polaris and Trident nuclear missiles from the United States. The most striking point about such cooperation is that it has been institutionalized and therefore has been fairly consistent. At the level of top political leadership, however, the special relationship has had some ups and downs. The relationship between British Prime Minister Harold Wilson and U.S. President Lyndon Johnson in the 1960s, for example, was not very close, whereas that between Prime Minister Margaret Thatcher and President Ronald Reagan in the 1980s was extremely close. The special relationship also has been sustained by the fact that the United States was acting as Great Britain's "proxy" in maintaining the BALANCE OF POWER in Europe against the Soviet Union. In return, Great Britain almost invariably was on the side of the United States when it came to disputes with the continental Europeans in the North Atlantic Treaty Organization. In the first half of 1990, it appeared that Germany was taking Great Britain's place as the United States' closest ally in Europe. The Persian Gulf Crisis of 1990–1991, however, restored Great Britain's position as the favored ally, especially given Germany's unwillingness to participate in the hostilities against Iraq. Nevertheless, with the end of the Cold War, the special relationship, at least in the military sense, could well decline in importance.   **2.** In the general context of international relations, any interchange between states in which one of them expects special treatment from another because of cultural, geographical, historical, or political ties.

specific duty   *See* DUTY, SPECIFIC.

specific limitations on trade   Measures imposed by governments that restrict imports or exports of a product to an explicitly stated volume or value, or require separate government authorization for each export on import transaction.

specific tariff   *See* TARIFF, SPECIFIC.

spectrum of war   A term that describes the full range of conflict, from cold war to limited war to general warfare.

Spengler, Oswald (1880–1936)   The German historian whose *The Decline of the West* (1918) proposed that Western civilization had reached a period of decadence comparable to old age in the biological life cycle. Vital forces such as faith and social discipline were disappearing. Western civilization, in his view, was thus beyond its cultural flowering. The book became a best-seller, in part because it seemed to explain the catastrophe that Germany had just experienced, and it fit the mood of Germany's intellectuals after the defeat of their nation in World War I.

sphere of influence   **1.** A geographic region dominated by one major power; tacit or formal agreements inhibit other powers from intruding. For example, the United States has long considered Central and South America to be within its sphere of influence, as enunciated in the MONROE DOCTRINE.   **2.** A tactic of traditional IMPERIALISM whereby dominant states received commercial and legal privileges in other states without direct political and military involvement. China, for example, was divided into spheres of influence ruled by Belgium, France, Germany, Great Britain, Japan, and Russia in the late nineteenth century.

spillover effects   Benefits or costs that accrue to a party other than the buyer of a product or service; also known as *externalities*. For the most part, the benefits of private goods (such as a truck) and services (such as child care) inure exclusively to the buyer. In the case of public goods, however, the benefit or cost usually "spills over" onto third parties. A new airport, for example, benefits not only airline passengers but spills over onto the population at large in both positive and negative ways. Benefits might include improved airline service for a city, increased tourism, and attraction of new businesses, while costs might include noise pollution and traffic congestion.

spillover terrorism   The term applied to the extension of regional conflict into other, geographically removed areas in the form of terroristic episodes. For example, Western Europe has been an attractive site for spillover terrorism because of its proximity to the Middle East, its available sources of cooperative personnel, its easy terrorist targets, and its heavy concentration of media sources.

spin control   All efforts by a government or an individual political actor to manipulate the mass media to contain, deflect, and minimize an unraveling scandal or other embarrassing or politically damaging revelation. The goal is to put a positive face, or "spin" on the situation. The political assistants and public relations consultants who influence the "spin" are often called the "spin patrol." One important aspect of spin control is DENIABILITY.

spirit of agreement   **1.** The essence of a TREATY as opposed to its formal text.   **2.** The interpretation placed on a written text or treaty.   **3.** According to Raymond Cohen's *International Politics: The Rules of the Game* (1981), the general meaning or intent of a document derived from the constituent convergence of interests or purposes underlying its creation. The spirit of agreement occasionally can cause problems when the two sides have different interpretations of what it involves. During the 1970s, for example, there was a sense in Washington, D.C., that the Soviet Union, by deploying new strategic nuclear missiles, was not abiding by the spirit of the SALT I accord, even though certain new deployments were permitted under the accord.

spoils 1. Historically rape, pillage, and plunder; whatever normally illegal things military commanders allow troops to do in a conquered area. 2. Political appointments to the staff of international organizations; individuals selected not on the basis of merit and objective qualifications but because of the influence of a political patron—whether an individual or a state.

spook 1. A ghost. 2. Any spy, domestic or foreign, from one's own state or from another state. 3. Any employee of any intelligence agency. 4. A ghostwriter; an anonymous political speechwriter.

sports boycott *See* BOYCOTT, SPORTS.

spot exchange The purchase or sale of FOREIGN EXCHANGE for immediate delivery.

Spratly Islands A widely dispersed group of islets, coral reefs, and sandbars in the South China Sea claimed, in whole or in part, by the People's Republic of China, Taiwan, Vietnam, the Philippines, and Malaysia. The islands provoke such controversy partly because they occupy an important strategic position in the passage from Japan to Singapore and partly because of the belief that the seas around them are rich in oil and other mineral resources. Both China and Taiwan claim that they were traditionally under Chinese sovereignty. The fact that they were annexed by France (which then ruled Vietnam) in 1933 has provided Vietnam with a claim. In 1956 the Philippines also claimed a group of these islands, though not Spratly Island itself.

Sprout, Harold (1901–1980) and **Margaret** (1903–) U.S. analysts who saw geographical factors as a key element in international politics but who also departed from the DETERMINISM that had characterized earlier geopolitical theories. The Sprouts explicitly rejected determinism, arguing instead that geography provided both constraints and offered opportunities for states. In their most famous work, *The Ecological Perspective on Human Affairs with Special Reference to International Politics* (1965), they argued that the relationship between a person and his or her milieu was crucial at two levels: the level of perceptions (the psychological environment) and the milieu as it

actually exists (the OPERATIONAL ENVIRONMENT). Perceptions of the milieu would influence what was attempted, but the milieu as it really existed would determine what was achieved. The Sprouts were sensitive to the impact of technology on thinking about geopolitical influences and had some very important ideas about national CAPABILITY, arguing that capacities for action could best be analyzed in relation to specific operational undertakings compared to what the decision makers were trying to achieve. Their work was important not only for the specific insights it yielded but also because of the way in which it combined ideas from such different fields as psychology and geography.

Sputnik I The first artificial earth-orbiting satellite, launched by the Soviet Union on October 4, 1957. *Sputnik* is a Russian word for "a companion or fellow traveler"; by extension, a planetary satellite. The Soviets derived enormous prestige around the globe from this event, which marked the entry of the world into the Space Age and the beginning of the SPACE RACE. The United States responded by creating the National Aeronautics and Space Administration (NASA) and putting greater emphasis on science education.

spy An INTELLIGENCE agent. The spy has fallen on hard times. While long a staple of fiction, in the real world he or she is a fading occupational specialty because of increasing advances in technology. In modern international snooping ELECTRONIC INTELLIGENCE and NATIONAL TECHNICAL MEANS have become far more important in generating hard intelligence than the proverbial spy. But while declining in numbers, there will always be a role for the spy because, as MATA HARI knew, there were some things beyond the capabilities of new technology.

Spykman, Nicholas J. (1893–1943) A U.S. theorist of GEOPOLITICS whose main focus was what he termed the inner crescent or the Eurasian RIMLAND. This was a region that, historically, has been of profound significance. As he wrote in *America's Strategy in World Politics* (1942): "Between the center of the Eurasian land mass and the circumferential maritime route lies a great concentric buffer zone. It includes western and Central Europe; the plateau countries of the Near East, Turkey, Iran and

Afghanistan, Tibet, China and eastern Siberia, and the three peninsulas of Arabia, India, and Burma-Siam. In this border zone have developed all the great civilizations of the world except Egypt and Carthage . . . and the early civilization of Sumatra and Java." Spykman saw Soviet foreign policy largely in terms of the geopolitical imperative of breaking through the rimland area and obtaining control over warm water ports. He shared with HALFORD J. MACKINDER an appreciation of the importance of the struggle between land powers and sea powers, but differed from him in terms of the crucial region. Indeed, in *The Geography of Peace* (1944) he amended Mackinder's famous dictum about the heartland and stated: "If there is to be a slogan for the power politics of the Old World, it must be who controls the Rimland rules Eurasia; who rules Eurasia control the destinies of the world." The implication of this was that the United States had to maintain a position on the Eurasian rimland, a notion that provided the geopolitical underpinnings for the American policy of CONTAINMENT enunciated in the late 1940s.

squeezers In the United States, hard-liners in the Reagan Administration of the 1980s who wanted to exert pressure on the Soviet Union rather than negotiate with Moscow. They were opposed by the DEALERS. Although the dealers won in the sense that ARMS CONTROL agreements with Moscow were reached, the squeezers argued that the subsequent collapse of the Soviet Union vindicated their position.

Sri Lankan Civil War The rampant ethnic TERRORISM that has plagued the Indian Ocean island state of Sri Lanka since 1983. Since the island gained independence from Great Britain in 1948, the TAMIL ethnic minority feared that the Sinhalese majority would abuse Tamil rights. By the mid-1970s Tamil politicians were demanding a separate Tamil state— "Tamil Eelam"—in northern and eastern Sri Lanka. Other groups, particularly the LIBERATION TIGERS OF TAMIL EELAM, sought an independent state by force. In 1983 the death of 13 Sinhalese soldiers at the hands of Tamil militants unleashed the largest outburst of communal violence in the country's history. Hundreds of Tamils were killed in the capital city of Colombo and elsewhere, tens of thousands were left homeless, and more than 100,000 fled to south India. In the north and east of the island, security forces attempted in bloody battles to suppress the LTTE and other militant groups. Each side in the conflict accused the other of violating human rights. Terrorism so disrupted the political system that in 1987 the government requested that Indian Army "peacekeeping" troops neutralize Tamil separatist rebels there. Many viewed the Indian Army as an occupation force. An Indian–Sri Lankan political settlement that met many of the Tamil separatist demands was signed in July 1987. This agreement includes the establishment of a new Northeast Province, the boundaries of which approximate the embattled Tamil homeland. Also included in the agreement is the establishment of Tamil as an official language of Sri Lanka. Despite such political momentum, ethnic violence has continued to plague the nation. For example, Sinhalese antigovernment violence during the February 1989 parliamentary elections left at least 56 persons dead.

SS 1. The letter designation for submarines in the United States Navy. 2. Supersonic, as in the SST (supersonic transport). 3. A steamship. 4. *Schutzstaffel;* the elite security unit of Nazi Germany, commanded by HEINRICH HIMMLER, that oversaw the organization of a totalitarian POLICE STATE. It carried out blood purges of the Nazi Party and was responsible for countless war crimes, such as the shooting of U.S. prisoners of war during the Battle of the BULGE and the operation of CONCENTRATION CAMPS in which millions of innocent civilians were murdered. *See also* SA; SS MISSILE.

SSBN (Sub-Surface, Ballistic Nuclear) A term used in the United States and British navies for nuclear-powered submarines such as the Trident and Poseidon that carry ballistic missiles. The missiles they carry are known as submarine-launched ballistic missiles (SLBMs). The Russians have a variety of similar submarines. These weapons are the most secure leg of the nuclear TRIAD. Given the current state of the art in antisubmarine warfare, they are almost undetectable. They leave port on secret patrols of three months or longer, during which they never broadcast. As they are nuclear powered, they need never surface, and the range of their missiles is such that they have a huge area of sea in which to hide.

SS missile A "surface-to-surface" missile. The prefix "SS" was used by the North Atlantic Treaty Organization to identify different Soviet land-based BALLISTIC MISSILES. These prefixes were assigned numbers in ascending order in the sequence in which new missiles were discovered by Western intelligence agencies. For example, the SS-18 was the largest Soviet ICBM. Similarly, "SA" is the prefix given to surface-to-air missiles; "AS" to air-to-surface missiles; and "SS-N" to naval missiles. When a prefix included an "X," as in "SA-X-12," this meant that the missile system was still experimental and not yet deployed.

SSN The naval acronym for a nuclear-powered submarine that does not carry ballistic missiles (as opposed to an SSBN). SSNs are variously described as attack submarines, fleet submarines, and hunter-killer submarines. Their wartime mission is to protect the surface fleet against enemy submarine attack, to destroy an enemy's SSBNs, and to sink the enemy's naval and merchant ships. France, Russia, the United Kingdom, and the United States all deploy SSNs. Only the United States does not use traditional diesel-powered submarines as well.

SSNP *See* SYRIAN SOCIAL NATIONALIST PARTY.

STABEX *See* LOMÉ CONVENTIONS.

stability A situation of military, political, or social equilibrium that is likely to be sustained. An international system exhibits stability if it is not prone to massive outbreaks of violence or to large-scale change that is likely to transform it. There has been much discussion about the stability of bipolar as opposed to multipolar systems. Stability, however, is not simply a function of the lack of instability but also of the capacity of the system to absorb periodic outbreaks of instability.

stability-instability paradox The theoretical notion of the Cold War that in U.S.-Soviet relations, stability at the nuclear level (which presumed that neither side could use its nuclear weapons against the adversary) would lead to instability at lower levels. The presumption was that the Soviet Union would take advantage of the nuclear stalemate to launch episodes of conventional aggression. This did not occur, partly because the possibility of ESCALATION to nuclear war undermined the logic of the stability-instability paradox and its assumption that levels of violence could be neatly compartmentalized.

stab in the back **1.** A political double-cross that occurs when someone does not hold to his or her word or presumed allegiance. **2.** A sneak or surprise attack, whether political or military. **3.** The lie espoused by the German Army and conservative German politicians as to why Germany lost World War I: Germany was betrayed by liberals on the home front. The truth is that the German Army was defeated in the field. It asked for an armistice specifically to forestall an Allied invasion of Germany. **4.** Italy's attack on France after it had already been essentially defeated by Germany during the World War II Battle of FRANCE. As U.S. President Franklin D. Roosevelt said in a June 10, 1940, speech: "On this tenth day of June, 1940, the hand that held the dagger has struck it into the back of its neighbor." *Compare to* SCAPEGOATING.

staff *See* GENERAL STAFF.

staff estimate A diplomatic officer's expert evaluation of how factors in his or her particular field of interest will influence the courses of action under consideration by diplomats or military commanders.

staff out The administrative process of soliciting from support personnel a variety of views or recommendations on an issue so that a decision maker will know of all reasonable options.

Stalin, Joseph Vissarionovich (1879–1953) General secretary of the Communist Party of the Soviet Union from 1922 until his death in 1953. While training to be a priest, young Stalin became a Marxist instead; he joined the BOLSHEVIKs in 1903. After an insignificant role in the October 1917 coup, Stalin became the people's commissar of nationality affairs and was involved in military affairs on various fronts during the RUSSIAN CIVIL WAR. In 1922 he was elected the general secretary of the Communist Party, a post that controlled the bureaucracy and allowed him to consolidate his power. After V. I. LENIN's death in 1924, Stalin, by controlling the party machinery, fended off attacks of LEON TROT-

SKY and others by playing them off one another, with the goal of ending collective leadership—a goal he achieved by 1927. Stalin presented himself as the champion of SOCIALISM IN ONE COUNTRY, rather than Trotsky's INTERNATIONALISM. Stalin's harsh leadership practices began in the late 1920s and continued until his death. Through the murder or exile of rich peasants (the *kulaks*) and COLLECTIVIZATION of farms (with disastrous results for agriculture), the GREAT TERROR and PURGEs in the party and the military, a pervasive secret police and concentration camps (GULAGS), rapid industrialization through FIVE-YEAR PLANS, and self-glorification, Stalin became the undisputed dictator of the Soviet Union by the late 1930s. As many as 60 million Soviet citizens died because of Stalin's murderous purges and collectivization programs.

In foreign affairs, Stalin ignored intelligence that forecast a German attack on the Soviet Union. Instead he seems to have believed that the NAZI-SOVIET NON-AGGRESSION PACT signed between the two countries in 1939 would hold. According to Robert Payne in *The Rise and Fall of Stalin* (1965), Stalin was so shocked by the 1941 German invasion that he "simply threw down the reins of government, absented himself from military headquarters, surrendered to despair and drank himself into a stupor. [Nikita] Khrushchev declared that . . . after the first severe disasters and reverses Stalin abandoned all hope, saying at a meeting of the Politburo: 'All that Lenin created we have lost forever.'" However, Stalin and the Soviet people recovered to defeat Nazi Germany on the Eastern Front. After the war Stalin created BUFFER STATES—new Soviet satellites in Central and Eastern Europe. The latter actions were viewed negatively by the United States, and thus the COLD WAR began. The extension of Soviet influence in Eastern Europe and Asia heightened tensions between the United States and the Soviet Union. Major crisis points included the BERLIN AIRLIFT (1948–1949) and the KOREAN WAR (1950–1953). Stalin died on March 2, 1953, on the verge of initiating another purge.

Almost as soon as he was dead the process of *de-Stalinization* began. At the 1956 Twentieth Congress of the Communist Party, he was denounced by new leader NIKITA S. KHRUSHCHEV for creating a CULT OF PERSONALITY. Kenneth P. O'Donnel in *Johnny, We Hardly Knew Ye* (1972) tells the story that when U.S. President John F. Kennedy met Khrushchev in Vienna, Austria, in 1961, Kennedy in a moment of exasperation during a heated debate asked Khrushchev, "Do you ever admit a mistake?" Khrushchev replied: "Certainly. In a speech before the Twentieth Party Congress, I admitted all of Stalin's mistakes." Stalin's mistakes were still being admitted by Soviet leaders up to the moment that the Soviet Union collapsed in 1991.

Stalin is the only person who can compete in the popular imagination with Adolf Hitler, his ally at the beginning of World War II, as the worst person of the twentieth century. They were both amoral murderers ultimately responsible for the deaths of tens of millions. More recent international villains such as Pol Pot or Saddam Hussein murdered on too small a scale to compete in this contest. Yet Stalin still has his admirers; he furthered an ideology that still has adherents.

LENIN REJECTS STALIN

Stalin is too rude, and this fault, entirely supportable in relations among us Communists, becomes insupportable in the office of General Secretary. Therefore, I propose to the comrades to find a way to remove Stalin from that position and appoint to it another man who in all respects differs from Stalin only in superiority—namely, more patient, more loyal, more polite and more attentive to comrades, less capricious, etc.

SOURCE: V. I. Lenin, letter to the Central Committee of the Communist Party, December 25, 1922; postscript of January 4, 1923, quoted in Robert Payne, *The Rise and Fall of Stalin* (1965).

Stalingrad, Battle of   The August 1942–to–February 1943 battle between Germany and the Soviet Union, which was the turning point of WORLD WAR II on the Russian front. This battle stopped the German advance toward the Caspian oil fields and began the German retreat—a retreat that ended only in April 1945 when the RED ARMY occupied Berlin. More Soviet men were killed at Stalingrad alone (about 250,000) than U.S. soldiers in all of World War II. The Germans suffered about 250,000 casualties in the battle. Of the approximately 93,000 who surrendered, only about 7,000 survived captivity.

Stalinism **1.** Communism as practiced by JOSEPH STALIN when he ruled the UNION OF SOVIET SOCIALIST REPUBLICS. **2.** A type of dictatorial, totalitarian, centrally controlled regime that is reflective of the brutal style in which Stalin governed the Soviet Union.

standard international trade classification A numerical coding system developed by the United Nations to classify commodities used in international trade.

stand down To descend to a lower level of ALERT or combat readiness.

standing army *See* ARMY, STANDING.

standoff **1.** A political or military tactical stalemate wherein neither side can gain an advantage. **2.** A desirable characteristic of a weapons system that permits a force to launch an attack on the target at a safe distance, usually outside the range of counter-fire. The CRUISE MISSILE is a standoff weapon.

The USS Stark *listing after being struck by Iraqi-launched Exocet missile. (U.S. Naval Institute)*

Stark **incident** The May 17, 1987, attack on the USS *Stark,* a United States Navy frigate, in the Persian Gulf. Thirty-seven U.S. sailors were killed when their ship was hit by a French-built Exocet missile fired by an Iraqi fighter plane. The Iraqi pilot was not monitoring the international radio frequency that would have identified the *Stark* as a neutral ship. The United States contends that the ship was not in an Iraqi-proclaimed "exclusive zone." Iraq says it was. This incident led the United States to adopt more permissive RULES OF ENGAGEMENT, which was a contributory factor to the subsequent shooting down of an Iranian civilian jumbo jet in the VINCENNES INCIDENT.

START I (Strategic Arms Reduction Treaty) The accord signed on July 31, 1991, by U.S. President George Bush and Soviet President Mikhail Gorbachev, formally ending a negotiation process that began in June 1982 and known as the *Strategic Arms Reduction Talks.* The treaty, along with its protocols and annexes on definitions, was over 700 pages long. The treaty established equal ceilings on the number of STRATEGIC NUCLEAR WEAPONS that could be deployed by the United States and the Soviet Union and imposed equality in terms of THROW-WEIGHT. The main provision of the START I Treaty is that neither side can deploy more than 1,600 strategic nuclear delivery vehicles (ICBMs, SLBMs and heavy bombers), 6,000 total accountable warheads, 4,900 warheads on ICBMs or SLBMs, and 1,100 warheads on mobile ICBMs. In addition, there is a limit of 1,540 warheads on 154 heavy ICBMs, which required a 50 percent cut in the Soviet heavy missiles force, and a limit on aggregate throw-weight of the ICBMS and SLBMs, which required close to 50 percent cuts in Soviet throw-weight. The treaty also established highly intrusive VERIFICATION procedures, with provisions for 12 different types of inspection. Moreover, each side has to notify the other of activities associated with its strategic forces. Although the treaty was criticized in both Washington and Moscow for giving away too much to the other side, the failed 1991 coup in the Soviet Union meant that emerging technical and strategic judgments were less important than broad political assessments of the treaty. In the last few months of 1991 one argument was that the treaty was moot: With the collapse of the Soviet Union it was no longer needed. Another view was that the treaty provided at least a partial framework for dealing with what might be termed the problem of "internal proliferation" in the former Soviet Union. Not surprisingly, the Bush Administration appeared much closer to the latter view than the former. Even so, in the period following the failed coup, as Gorbachev's efforts to hold the union together came to naught, U.S. leaders recognized that the START agreement was far from a comprehensive framework to deal with the future of the Soviet nuclear armory.

START II The second Strategic Arms Reduction Treaty that grew out of the June 1992 accord between U. S. President George Bush and Russian President Boris Yeltsin. The treaty, signed early in January 1993, provides for a two-thirds reduction in the nuclear arsenals of both sides. By the year 2003 each side would be limited to less than 3,500 warheads and all long-range land-based missiles with multiple warheads would be banned. Because the treaty is designed to make it impossible for either side to launch a successful FIRST STRIKE, it is thought to lower the risk of nuclear war. The treaty's ultimate ratification may be dependent on whether other former Soviet republics that have nuclear weapons, especially Ukraine, also agree to its terms.

star wars *See* STRATEGIC DEFENSE INITIATIVE.

Stasi Nickname for the *Ministerium Für Staatssicherheit,* the East German Ministry for State Security. This organization, created in 1950, consisted of a vast network for internal and external espionage that employed nearly 85,000 agents and several million part-time informers. Stasi was so despised that it was the first institution to be abolished following the peaceful revolution of 1989.

state 1. A political jurisdiction possessing territory, population, and SOVEREIGNTY over its internal and external policies. While it is true, as future U.S. President Woodrow Wilson wrote in *The State* (1889), that "The state exists for the sake of society, not society for the sake of the state," the U.S. economist William Graham Sumner asserted in *Commercial Crises* (1879), "When all the fine phrases are stripped away, it appears that the state

is only a group of men with human interests, passions, and desires, or, worse yet, the state is only an obscure clerk hidden in some corner of a governmental bureau. In either case the assumption of superhuman wisdom and virtue is proved false." 2. The main actors in INTERNATIONAL POLITICS. Relations among states form the basis for international society with its system of rules and norms. 3. A component government in a federal system, such as a U.S. state government. 4. One of the 50 states of the United States. In many federal laws, the term also includes the District of Columbia, the Commonwealth of Puerto Rico, and any territory or possession of the United States. 5. A short form of reference to the U.S. Department of State. 6. An abstract concept referring to the ultimate source of legal authority. *Compare to* NATION.

state, department of *See* SECRETARY OF STATE and STATE, U.S. DEPARTMENT OF.

state, secretary of *See* SECRETARY OF STATE.

State, U.S. Department of The United States federal government agency whose primary objective is the execution of foreign policy to promote the long-range security and well-being of the nation. The Department of State is the oldest of all cabinet departments first created in 1789. Consequently, the secretary of state is the ranking (or senior) cabinet member.

state-centrism An approach to international politics or international relations that sees the state as the central actor. This view is often associated with theories of REALISM or NEOREALISM and has been challenged by those who highlight the emergence of nonstate actors such as multinational corporations and the development of cross-national links among societies that transcend the state.

statecraft 1. The art and science of governance, of leadership, and of politics. 2. Machiavellian cunning or duplicity in government. 3. Diplomacy.

state department, little The foreign policy advisors of the president of the United States who work as part of the White House staff.

state dinner   The most formal of dining experiences when heads of state ceremonially dine with each other while wearing some of their best clothes and most valuable jewelry. State dinners, which as a tradition date from ancient times, often are the highlight of a state visit. If the visit lasts for more than a day, the visitor often reciprocates with a comparable dinner for the host state staged at the visitor's embassy. Very little real business gets accomplished at such formal occasions, but they are important opportunities for the leaders and their staffs to socialize.

state enterprise   A business, industry, or utility owned and operated by a government or a government-owned corporation.

stateless person   An individual who is not a NATIONAL of any particular state; no state is obligated under its laws to allow him or her to live within its borders. Statelessness is often a problem with refugees who because of war have been driven out of a state that no longer wants them back. It also is the status of many people who are born to GUESTWORKERS in states that do not accept that citizenship is determined by where one is born.

state of nature   What some political theorists assumed to be the condition of humankind before the establishment of a SOCIAL CONTRACT and organized government. THOMAS HOBBES found life in it to be "nasty, brutish, and short." (Contemporary proponents of REALISM regard international politics as being very close to Hobbes's conception of the state of nature.) JEAN-JACQUES ROUSSEAU thought it idyllic. And JOHN LOCKE wrote that "the state of nature has a law of nature to govern it, which obliges every one; and reason, which is that law, teaches all mankind who will but consult it, that, being all equal and independent, no one ought to harm another in his life, health, liberty or possessions."

state of war   1. A time of military conflict between states.   2. The legal status of one state being at war with another; this may or may not be preceded by a formal DECLARATION OF WAR and may or may not actually involve military clashes. For example, at the beginning of World War II, Great Britain and France were "at war" with Ger-

---

THOMAS HOBBES DESCRIBES THE STATE OF NATURE

In such condition, there is not place for industry, because the fruit thereof is uncertain; and consequently no culture of the earth; no navigation nor use of the commodities that may be imported by sea; no commodious building; no instrument of moving, and removing, such things as require much force; no knowledge of the face of the earth; no account of time, no arts, not letters, no society, and which is worst of all, continual fear, and danger of violent death; and the life of man, solitary, poor, nasty, brutish, and short.

SOURCE: Thomas Hobbes, *Leviathan* (1651).

---

many for many months before the real fighting began. And many Arab states have been technically at war with Israel during long periods of informal peace.   3. The duration of an armed conflict.   4. A military emergency declared within a state to fight off insurrectionists such as guerrillas. This has also been declared when the insurrectionists have been peaceful. For example, a state of war was declared by General Wojcïech Jaruzelski in Poland in 1981 as a result of the counterrevolutionary intentions of Solidarity and the possibility that the Soviet Union might intervene to restore strong Communist rule. This declaration resulted in the internment of thousands of Solidarity activists, the closing of many social associations, and strict political discipline. The declaration was lifted after a few weeks.

state responsibility   The international law concept that states are to be held accountable for violations of their obligations under treaties or other sources of international law. Paralleling civil law, a state that illegally causes an injury may be required to make REPARATIONS. The perennial problem is the adjudication of such issues and enforcing payments in a world that is still essentially anarchic.

statesman/stateswoman   A political leader of considerable national or international reputation. The word is so inherently vague and has been used to describe such a variety of persons that it hardly means anything at all. According to U.S. President

Harry S Truman, "A statesman is a politician who's been dead ten or fifteen years" (*New York Telegram and Sun,* April 12, 1958). According to British Prime Minister Harold Macmillan, "When you're abroad you're a statesman; when you're home, you're just a politician" (*The Observer,* July 28, 1983). And according to French President Georges Pompidou, "A statesman is a politician who places himself at the service of the nation. A politician is a statesman who places the nation at his service" (*The Observer,* December 30, 1973).

state-sponsored terrorism TERRORISM aided by governments, as opposed to acts perpetrated by independent terrorist groups. States use terrorism as a foreign policy tool when they want to destabilize another government without risking a direct military confrontation. *See also* IRANIAN TERRORISM; SYRIAN TERRORISM.

state system **1.** An international arrangement involving regular interactions among independent political units. **2.** A synonym that is sometimes used very loosely to refer to the international community of nations. **3.** The modern international community that is generally regarded as having begun with the 1648 Treaty of Westphalia and that is still in existence today. Many of the features of the contemporary state system can be seen as developments of the European state system of the nineteenth century.

state trading nations Communist or dictatorial regimes that rely heavily on government entities, instead of private corporations, to conduct trade with other countries.

state visit An official visit, attended by appropriate ceremonies, by one head of state (or government) to another. This is in contrast to a *private visit,* when a head of state travels to another country for personal reasons without any fanfare.

static indicators **1.** Those elements of a state's power that are relatively slow to change. **2.** The military balance between two states in terms of basic indices of capability (such as tanks and planes). They do not take any account of the possible dynamic of conflict, which could have a sig-

nificant bearing on an outcome. *Compare to* SOCIAL INDICATORS.

statism **1.** A belief in the SOVEREIGNTY of individual states. **2.** Oppressive policies on the part of a government that crush civil liberties and increase the social and economic powers of the state. Statism in this sense was one of the major tenets of fascist Italy and Germany: that individuals existed to serve the state.

status of forces agreement A formal arrangement between a state that has armed forces stationed on another's soil, and the state in which those forces are stationed. Such agreements cover administrative matters, financial remuneration, and judicial questions raised as a result of the presence of foreign troops. For example, the United States signed status of forces agreements with the West European states in which military bases were established and troops deployed as part of the U.S. commitment to the North Atlantic Treaty Organization in the early 1950s.

status quo **1.** A Latin term meaning "the existing state of affairs." **2.** In world politics, a term used to describe policies designed to maintain the existing distribution of power. States that want to maintain the status quo are generally regarded as being very satisfied with it, perhaps to the point of being smug. They are often regarded as the "haves" of international politics, whereas the "have nots" are most anxious to bring about change. *Compare to* UTI POSSIDETIS.

status quo ante bellum Latin for "the state of affairs before a war." This is what an aggrieved state frequently fights for—the restoration of its borders as they were before the war began. Indeed, this has often become the goal of a war: to expel invaders. Of course, if the initial aggressors are pushed back into their own territory, then restoring the *status quo ante bellum* begins to look like a reasonable war aim for them as well.

status quo post bellum Latin for "the state of affairs at the end of a war." Sometimes it provides the basis for an agreement on which hostilities can be brought to an end. This would then amount to a cease-fire in place, which can be temporary or permanent pending a peace settlement.

Steel, Pact of   The military alliance of Germany and Italy concluded on May 22, 1939, that bound the two AXIS nations. It was an expansion of the military cooperation begun with the ANTI-COMINTERN PACT of 1936.

stereotype   1. A standard perception of something.   2. A simplified and established perception of another state or people that may be used to explain behavior when in fact it is far from an appropriate explanation. For example, it is not true that all Germans seek domination or that all of the French are obsessed with food. But the persistence of these and other stereotypes inhibits intercultural communications nonetheless. *Compare to* NATIONAL CHARACTER.

Stern Gang   A Zionist terrorist organization (formally, *Lohame Herut Yisra'el,* or Lehi, meaning "Fighters for the Freedom of Israel") that was a splinter group of the IRGUN and formed in 1940 by Abraham Stern (1907–1942), who had helped to found the Irgun. Lehi, a small, radical group, used assassination and terrorism to achieve its political ends. Stern was shot and killed by British police in Palestine on February 12, 1942. Lehi's leadership then resided in a triumvirate that included YITZHAK SHAMIR, who later became prime minister of Israel. The organization is best known for its 1948 assassination of the United Nations mediator for Palestine, Count FOLKE BERNADOTTE, whom Lehi considered an enemy of ZIONISM. Lehi joined with the Irgun and HAGANA during the 1948–1949 Israeli War of Independence.

Stettinius, Edward R., Jr. (1900–1949)   The industrialist and war resources administrator who became U.S. secretary of state in 1944. He resigned in 1945 to become the first U.S. representative to the United Nations (1945–1946).

Stevenson, Adlai E., II (1900–1965)   The governor of Illinois (1948–1952) who was the Democratic Party's nominee for U.S. president in 1952 and 1956. (He lost both times to Dwight D. Eisenhower.) Throughout the 1950s Stevenson was a leading U.S. voice for liberalism and international-

Adlai Stevenson II (Copyright The Washington Post; *reprinted by permission of the D.C. Public Library)*

ism. He ended his career as the United States ambassador to the United Nations (1961–1965), an organization he helped to found in 1946.

Stimson, Henry L. (1867–1950)   U.S. secretary of war (1911–1913) for President William H. Taft; secretary of state (1929–1933) under President Herbert Hoover; and secretary of war (1940–1945) during World War II for President Franklin D. Roosevelt. Stimson, a well-known Republican, was brought into Roosevelt's cabinet to help give a bipartisan tone to defense efforts.

Stimson Doctrine   The policy espoused by U.S. Secretary of State Henry Stimson in 1932 to not recognize Japanese rule in Manchuria or any other area Japan might take over by military conquest. *See also* MANCHURIAN CRISIS.

Stinger   A lightweight, shoulder-fired surface-to-air missile that can shoot down low-altitude aircraft. The Stinger is that rare example of a tactical weapon that has had strategic significance. Supplied to the Afghan resistance fighters indirectly by the United States after the 1979 Soviet invasion of Afghanistan, this weapon allowed the Afghans, without any air force of their own, to gain the local air superiority necessary for success on the ground. Unfortunately Stingers could be equally useful as terrorist weapons and there is a great concern that some may be used against civilian airliners.

Stockholm Agreement   The 1986 Document of the Stockholm Conference on Confidence and Security Building Measures. The participating states included the members of the North Atlantic Treaty Organization and the Warsaw Pact and the neutral and nonaligned nations in Europe. The agreement provides (1) 42 days' advance notification of military activities in the zone of application (which was the whole of Europe) when exercises involved at least 13,000 troops or 300 battle tanks, or whenever there were amphibious landings or parachute jumps involving 300 troops or more; (2) one-year advance notification of exercises involving more than 40,000 troops as part of an exchange of annual calendars of notifiable military activities; and (3) mandatory invitations to all other nations to observe exercises involving more than 17,000 troops. In addition to these provisions for notification and observation of certain military activities, there was also provision for VERIFICATION of compliance by up to three challenge on-site inspections per year. Although some observers were skeptical of the achievement at Stockholm, it was in fact an important step toward greater military TRANSPARENCY in Europe.

Stockholm Syndrome   The psychological phenomenon of aggressor identification; a tendency for victims of terrorist aggression to sympathize with those who have abused them. The term comes from the experiences of Swedish hostages in a 1973 bank robbery who, after being subjected to a week of physical and mental duress inside a Stockholm bank vault, voluntarily placed themselves between their police rescuers and the men who had taken them hostage in order to prevent the police from harming their captors.

stockpile   1. Strategic or critical materials stored for use in times of emergency.   2. Stores of special ammunition, such as nuclear weapons.

Stolypin, Piotr (1862–1911)   The Russian official under Czar NICHOLAS II who, as chairman of the Council of Ministers, was a staunch advocate of suppressing dissidents. His name then became synonymous with brutal repressive and summary executions (he was partial to mass hangings) in Russia. He was assassinated in 1911 in Kiev.

Strait of Hormuz   The body of water that connects the Indian Ocean with the Persian Gulf, bordered by Iran on the one side and Oman on the other. Because most of the oil from the gulf has to come through the strait, it is probably the most important strategic CHOKEPOINT in the world. It also places Iran in a very significant strategic position. During the IRAN-IRAQ WAR, Iran was able to threaten shipping coming through the Strait of Hormuz with Silkworm missiles it had obtained from China.

Straits, Turkish   The Bosporus, Sea of Marmara, and DARDANELLES, collectively known as the Turkish Straits. They connect the Mediterranean Sea to the Black Sea.

Strasbourg   The city in eastern France in which the EUROPEAN PARLIAMENT is situated, and consequently an informal means of referring to that body.

strategic   1. Of or relating to STRATEGY. According to U.S. Rear Admiral J. C. Wylie in *Military Strategy* (1967): "There is more truth than jest in the statement that, to any soldier, what he does is tactical and what his next senior does is strategic. This is generally expressive from the private all the way up to the theater commander."   2. Anything necessary to or important to initiate, conduct, or complete a strategy.   3. Anything required for a war effort but not available domestically; thus it is important to create a STOCKPILE of strategic materials.   4. Of great importance to a larger plan.   5. Long range and powerful in the context of military planning. Thus an ICBM is a strategic missile because it can hit targets across continents and has a nuclear warhead.   6. Concerning nuclear war.

strategic advantage   The state of power relations between opponents that enables one side effectively to control a military or political situation.

Strategic Air Command (SAC)   The part of the U.S. Air Force that operated part of the United States' nuclear deterrent, both with its bomber squadrons and the land-based ICBM force, during the COLD WAR. Created in the early 1950s, the hallmark of SAC was its constant alert status. In 1991 U.S. President George Bush decided that the danger of a surprise attack from the Soviet Union had so subsided that he ordered SAC to stand down from its alert status. SAC itself is going out of business—to be replaced by a reduced and unified multiservice command. The ultimate judgment on SAC may be that, because it never fired its nuclear weapons, it lived up to its slogan: "Peace is our profession."

strategic analysis   1. The art and science of evaluating military options.   2. Examining the various uses of nuclear weapons. This is a major area of military policy in which civilians have always played a large role. Indeed, in the West all of the major writers in this area—such as BERNARD BRODIE, HERMAN KAHN, HENRY A. KISSINGER, and ALBERT WOHLSTETTER—have been civilians. This has often created friction with military leaders. For example, U.S. Admiral Carlisle A. H. Trost, chief of naval operations, offered a typical attack: "Much of the criticism concerning today's Navy stems from career-academic strategists and so-called 'defense analysts' who have never set foot on a Navy deckplate. It is folly for these individuals, who have the responsibility neither to deploy a military force nor face the threat, to attempt to determine military requirements" (*Philadelphia Inquirer,* August 22, 1987). In response to just this kind of criticism Alain Enthoven, a former Pentagon systems analyst, is quoted in Fred Kaplan's *The Wizards of Armageddon* (1983) as saying: "General, I have fought just as many nuclear wars as you have."

Strategic Arms Limitation Talks   *See* SALT.

Strategic Arms Reduction Talks   *See* START.

strategic assessment   1. An evaluation of a situation or conflict in ways designed to determine its overall importance for national or international security.   2. A synonym for any overall assessment of military power. *Compare to* NET ASSESSMENT.

strategic balance   The comparative destructive capability of the military forces of two states (such as the United States and Russia) or rival alliances (such as the North Atlantic Treaty Organization and the Warsaw Pact). *Compare to* BALANCE OF POWER.

strategic bombardment   Bombing undertaken to destroy the enemy's industry, especially its war-related industrial plants, and thereby to shorten or even directly end the war. A strategic bombardment also may be aimed directly at killing the enemy population to destroy civilian morale and therefore the NATIONAL WILL to fight. The destruction of anything that will help this end, for example by hampering food supplies, is a legitimate strategic aim.

strategic bombing   *See* AIR WARFARE.

Strategic Bombing Survey   An attempt by the United States to assess the results of its STRATEGIC BOMBARDMENT campaigns against Germany and Japan during WORLD WAR II. Although immense resources were put into this campaign by both Great Britain and the United States, its effectiveness was not clear. In 1944 plans for establishing a survey were discussed in the United States, and in June it was agreed by the Joint Chiefs of Staff that an impartial and expert study should be undertaken by the U.S. Air Force with assistance from civilian specialists. In the next few months a team of specialists was put together that included PAUL NITZE, who was to be one of the most influential figures in the evolution of United States foreign and security policies during the Cold War. Twelve different areas were identified for the study with a division of the survey responsible for each one: Aircraft, Area Studies, Civilian Defense, Equipment, Military Analysis, Morale, Munitions, Oil, Overall Economic Effects, Physical Damage, Transportation, and Utilities. The European survey involved over 1,500 personnel, both civilian and military. As the liberation of Europe took place, the survey teams moved in to pursue their investigations through direct examination of the evidence, interrogations, and questionnaires. The intent was to provide guidance for the continuing air attacks being waged against Japan. In July 1945, however, it was decided that the survey should be extended to Japan. After Japan surrendered, survey members moved rapidly from Europe to the Pacific theater. In the case of Japan, however, there were differences among the U.S. Army Air Corps and the Navy as to their relative contributions to the strategic bombing campaign. This dispute was exacerbated by the fact that it so clearly had implications for defense priorities and the relative status of the U.S. Air Force and Navy in the postwar period. *The Summary Report on the European War* came out in September 1945 and the *Chairman's Report on the Pacific War* appeared in July 1946. The report on Europe acknowledged the failures as well as the successes of the campaign against Germany and emphasized how important it was to achieve total AIR SUPERIORITY to ensure effective strategic bombing. In the case of Japan, the survey concluded that as a result of the strategic bombing campaign, Japan would have been unable to fight beyond the end of 1945 even if the two atomic bombs had not been dropped. The Strategic Bombing Surveys provided the basis for much postwar thinking about AIR POWER.

THE REAL IMPORTANCE OF THE AIR WAR

Accounts of the bombing that I have so far seen . . . [put] emphasis on the destruction that air raids inflicted on German industrial potential and thus upon armaments. In reality the losses were not quite so serious. . . . The real importance of the air war consisted in the fact that it opened a second front long before the invasion of Europe. That front was the skies over Germany. . . . Defense against air attacks required the production of thousands of anti-aircraft guns, the stockpiling of tremendous quantities of ammunition all over the country, and holding in readiness hundreds of thousands of soldiers. . . . As far as I can judge from the accounts I have read, no one has yet seen that this was the greatest lost battle on the German side.

SOURCE: Albert Speer, *Spandau: The Secret Diaries* (1976). Speer (1905–1981), the Nazi in charge of German war production, was convicted of war crimes at the Nuremberg Trials and spent 20 years in Spandau prison.

---

strategic capability   **1.** The ability of a state or alliance to bring military force to bear against another state or alliance.   **2.** The ability of a state to project its power, to send its military forces considerable distances from their homeland. *Compare to* FORCE PROJECTION.

strategic command and control The system for maintaining control over strategic nuclear forces by the political leadership of a state so that this leadership can determine if and when these weapons should be released. It is sometimes discussed in terms of COMMAND, CONTROL AND COMMUNICATIONS (C^3) or COMMAND, CONTROL, COMMUNICATIONS AND INTELLIGENCE (C^3I). In the case of the United States, this involves a complex set of command structures, communication networks, and rules and safeguards designed to ensure that there is no unauthorized use of nuclear weapons. The system is supposed to be responsive to any presidential decision to retaliate in the event of an attack on the United States or those allies protected by extended nuclear DETERRENCE. For a long time strategic command and control was one of the neglected aspects of the strategic force structure. It is not something that is central to service roles and missions and was therefore not given funds commensurate with its importance. Nevertheless, because strategic command and control is necessary to give the order to retaliate in the event of an attack on the United States, its importance was recognized gradually. Beginning in the latter half of the 1970s, there was great concern that the Soviet Union might, because of the greater accuracy of new missiles, be able to destroy U.S. COMMAND AND CONTROL systems and thereby prevent retaliation. One of the major concerns was what was termed a DECAPITATION STRIKE, in which the political leadership would be destroyed. Other concerns were that certain kinds of nuclear explosions might disrupt communications between the president and the strategic forces—a problem sometimes described as that of CONNECTIVITY. The Carter and Reagan administrations both responded to these concerns by introducing measures to upgrade the United States' command and control system.

strategic deception 1. Hiding strategic weapons from a potential enemy. The problem with hiding these weapons during peacetime is that, if they are not known to a potential foe, they lose their DETERRENT EFFECT. 2. Cheating on arms control agreements to maintain greater strategic forces than formally allowed or agreed to. 3. Gaining a military victory through deceit (sometimes termed *military deception*). NICCOLÒ MACHIAVELLI's words from

The Discourses (1517) are still valid today: "Although deceit is detestable in all other things, yet in the conduct of war it is laudable and honorable; and a commander who vanquishes an enemy by stratagem is equally praised with one who gains victory by force."

strategic defense initiative (SDI) The Reagan Administration's effort to create a space-based "astrodome" defense against enemy missiles, popularly known as "Star Wars" because the purported capabilities of the final defense system sounded (to its critics) so much like a high-technology fantasy. It signaled a reversal in U.S. policy, which had previously rejected the strategy of building a BALLISTIC MISSILE DEFENSE (BMD) when the United States and the Soviet Union signed the Anti-Ballistic Missile (ABM) TREATY as part of the SALT I talks in 1972. BMD had been given a low priority by the United States because it was felt to be technically and economically impossible. This changed, however, when President Reagan in a March 23, 1983, speech offered a vision of the future in which the United States would move from a strategy based on nuclear DETERRENCE to one that would "intercept and destroy strategic ballistic missiles before they reached our own soil or that of our allies." Reagan then initiated a major program of research and development on space-based defensive systems. According to McGeorge Bundy, George F. Kennan, Robert S. McNamara, and Gerard Smith in "The President's Choice: Star Wars or Arms Control" (*Foreign Affairs*, Winter 1984–1985): "The inescapable reality is that there is literally no hope that Star Wars can make nuclear weapons obsolete. . . . [But] as long as the American People believe that Star Wars offers real hope of reaching the President's asserted goal, it will have a level of political support unrelated to reality." Even Dick Cheney, secretary of defense in the succeeding Bush Administration, had to admit: "During the Reagan Administration [SDI] was described in terms that, frankly, I think oversold the concept" (*New York Times*, March 29, 1989). But Reagan was probably correct in what he said in a speech in Washington, D.C. on March 23, 1987: "[The SDI] has been a singularly effective instrument for bringing the Soviets to the bargaining table." While the Bush Administration continued the SDI program at lower funding levels than the Reagan Administration had, the program, transformed into GPALS, was severely cut by the Clinton Administration in 1993.

SDI AS VISUALIZED IN 1945

As soon as they signal a flight of offensive rockets speeding towards them, the defensive rockets will automatically be released by radar, to speed into the heavens and explode in whatever cubic space in the stratosphere radar decides the enemy's offensive rockets will enter at a calculated time. Then, hundreds of miles above the surface of the earth, noiseless battles will be fought between blast and counter-blast. Now and again an invader will get through when up will go London, Paris or New York in a 40,000 feet high mushroom of smoke and dust. . . . Then should any life be left on earth, a conference will undoubtedly be held to decide who was victor and who was vanquished, the latter being forthwith liquidated by the former as war "criminals."

SOURCE: J. F. C Fuller, *Armament and History* (1945).

---

strategic doctrine   1. A principle or DOCTRINE for the development, deployment, and use of nuclear weapons. **2.** *Declaratory strategy* (what a state says it will do), which is not always the same as OPERATIONAL STRATEGY (what a state actually does). **3.** A set of ideas about military force and how it should be used that is often based on distinct historical experiences and ethnocentric attitudes. For example, at the beginning of World War I the French Army believed in the "cult of the offensive," that French soldiers were most effective when attacking the enemy. This was essentially true until the invention of the machine gun. Because this faulty strategic doctrine did not adjust to evolving military technology, France suffered enormous casualties until the doctrine was revised. The German World War II doctrine of BLITZKREIG is a good example of a doctrine that matched military missions and technology.

strategic envelopment   *See* INDIRECT APPROACH.

Strategic Framework for the Asian Pacific Rim   A 1990 report by the U.S. Department of Defense that outlined the Bush Administration's plans for the United States' military presence and strategy in Asia. The report announced that the United States would retain its FORWARD PRESENCE in the region but would make incremental reductions in U.S. forces in Japan, the Philippines, and South Korea. It provides the broad framework for the gradual process of U.S. retrenchment in Asia, although the removal of U.S. forces from the Philippines was subsequently hastened both by the 1991 failure of the Philippines to renew the Subic Bay base agreement and by the volcanic explosion that effectively destroyed Clark Airbase.

strategic goods   The raw materials that are essential to the functioning of an industrialized state's economy in peacetime, or to the continuation of its military effort in wartime. Petroleum is an obvious example. Indeed, it is the dependence of Western Europe, Japan, and to a lesser degree the United States on Persian Gulf oil supplies that has made this region a continuing concern for Western strategic planners. Other strategic materials include minerals such as aluminum, chromium, cobalt, manganese, tin, and titanium, all of which have widespread defense applications. All industrialized states are dependent to one degree or another on such imports. For example, the United States has become at least 50 percent dependent on foreign sources for 23 strategic materials. And for some of these (such as bauxite and alumina, cobalt, columbium, graphite, manganese, mica, and strontium), it is almost totally dependent on imported supplies. Thus the vulnerability of these supplies to disruption is a major concern. But vulnerability also depends on whether a state has accessible reserves, the size of its strategic stockpiles, and the availability of either alternative sources or of substitutes.

strategic nuclear weapons   Those NUCLEAR WEAPONS that are designed for use against an adversary's homeland. This distinguishes them from TACTICAL (or theater) NUCLEAR WEAPONS.

strategic petroleum reserve   The millions of barrels of oil that an oil-importing state holds in storage as an "insurance policy" against a disruption of the flow of foreign oil. Most of the major industrialized states (such as Germany, Japan, and the United States) have significant reserves.

strategic plan A plan for the overall conduct of a war, its OPERATIONAL STRATEGY.

strategic planning 1. The identification and examination of an organization's future opportunities and threats and their consequences; the process of analyzing an organization's environment and developing compatible objectives along with the appropriate strategies and policies capable of achieving those goals. 2. Arranging for the possible use of nuclear weapons.

strategic reserve 1. An external reinforcing military force that is not committed in advance to a specific combat operation, but that can be deployed later in response to circumstances. 2. A quantity of material placed in a particular geographic location due to military considerations or in anticipation of major interruptions in the supply or distribution system.

strategic retaliatory capability The ability to perform a SECOND STRIKE.

strategic stability A situation of potential conflict in which the incentives for any of the participants to take drastic or dangerous action are minimal. The concept, which was developed primarily in relation to superpower relationships, has three separate components: arms race stability allowing each superpower to feel relatively confident that the actions and policies of the other would not upset the balance between them; deterrence stability in which each side has survivable retaliatory forces, leaving little incentive for a FIRST STRIKE; and CRISIS STABILITY or an absence of incentives to act in haste or to strike first against the adversary. Strategic stability is a concept that is equally applicable to conventional and nuclear warfare situations.

strategic studies 1. That branch of the study of INTERNATIONAL POLITICS that focuses on the actual or potential use of military force in the relations among states. According to John Garnett in *Contemporary Strategy* (1976), strategic studies is "not a discipline in its own right. It is a subject with a sharp focus—the role of military power—but no clear perimeter, and it is parasitic upon arts, science and social science subjects for the ideas and concepts which

its practitioners have developed." 2. A synonym for SECURITY STUDIES, although "strategy" is actually much narrower than "security," which can be achieved through a variety of means, not all of which involve military force. 3. The study of STRATEGY in the nuclear age, a study that looks not only at the use of force but also at its nonuse and the threat of its use.

strategic superiority The possession of military forces, usually nuclear, in such numbers as to be able to overwhelm any potential enemy. This concept has lost much of its meaning in the nuclear era because both of the major nuclear powers have a SECOND-STRIKE CAPABILITY. U.S. Secretary of State Henry Kissinger once said in exasperation: "What in the name of God is strategic superiority? What is the significance of it, politically, militarily, operationally, at these levels of numbers? What do you do with it?" (*Department of State Bulletin,* July 29, 1974). Soviet President Mikhail Gorbachev felt that "any striving for military superiority means chasing one's own tail. It can't be used in real politics" (*Perestroika,* 1987). Nevertheless, U.S. President Richard Nixon wrote in *The Real War* (1980): "Nuclear superiority was very useful to us when we had it."

strategic theory 1. Concepts about warfare that developed in the nuclear age. 2. A set of core concepts that were developed in the 1950s and 1960s in relation to ARMS CONTROL, CRISIS MANAGEMENT, DETERRENCE, ESCALATION, and LIMITED WAR. These concepts were elucidated primarily in the United States by a group of analysts at the RAND Corporation and various universities who were interested not in abstract concepts but in developing arguments and recommendations whereby the United States could fight the COLD WAR more effectively. Many of their writings were primarily policy oriented, yet out of these it was possible to distill intellectually rigorous concepts and arguments. Although some of the strategic concepts developed during the Cold War may have wider applicability, most were seen in terms of two-power competition and suffered from ethnocentric biases. The Soviet Union, because of the vast conventional arms superiority of the WARSAW PACT, never had the West's obsession with using nuclear weapons to stop a conventional attack. Its declared policy was that it would never use nuclear weapons first. Therefore its publicly stated strategic theory emphasized retaliation. **3.** A derogatory usage that emphasizes that "theory" about nuclear war is not empirically based. On occasions, this was the military response to the arguments of civilian practitioners of STRATEGIC ANALYSIS.

strategic vulnerability   The susceptibility of vital ELEMENTS OF NATIONAL POWER to being seriously decreased or adversely changed by the application of actions within the capability of another nation. Strategic vulnerability may pertain to economic, geographic, military, political, scientific, or sociological factors.

strategic warning   **1.** A notification of the imminence of enemy-initiated hostilities; a war alert. **2.** Warning signs of preparation for a major surprise attack that an enemy would necessarily give off.

strategic weapon   **1.** Any weapon that is powerful enough to help decide the outcome of a military campaign or war. These weapons change over time with advances in technology. Thus the machine gun was a strategic weapon in World War I; the tank, designed to counter the machine gun, became a strategic weapon by the end of that war. **2.** Any NUCLEAR WEAPON. *See also* STRATEGIC NUCLEAR WEAPONS.

strategy   The overall conduct of a war or other major enterprise. Strategy is basically planning; it is what French General Antoine Henri Jomini in his *Summary of the Art of War* (1838) called "the art of making war upon the map." *Compare to* TACTICS.

strategy, grand   **1.** The overall military policies of a state or alliance. All military strategy logically follows from this overall national strategy. **2.** Military planning at a higher level than that used for one THEATER OF WAR or one campaign.

strategy, punitive   *See* WAR, PUNITIVE.

stratified crisis interaction   A term coined by Joseph F. Bouchard in *Command in Crisis* (1991) to reflect the fact that interactions in a CRISIS do not

---

THE PARADOXICAL LOGIC OF STRATEGY

Consider an ordinary tactical choice, of the sort frequently made in war. An advancing force can move toward its objective on one of two roads, one good and one bad. . . . Only in the conflictual realm of strategy would the choice arise at all, for it is only if combat is possible that a bad road can be good *precisely because it is bad* and may therefore be less strongly held or even left unguarded by the enemy. Equally, the good road is apt to be bad because it is the better road, whose use by the advancing force is more likely to be anticipated and opposed. In this case, then the paradoxical logic of strategy reaches the extreme of a full reversal.

SOURCE: Edward N. Luttwak, *Strategy* (1987).

---

take place between two monolithic governments but rather occur at a variety of levels. Bouchard argues that "interactions between the two sides in a crisis will have a tendency to become stratified into separate political, strategic and tactical interactions." Consequently, "political interaction occurs between the top-level decision makers in each nation; strategic interaction between the strategic nuclear forces and major military commands on each side; and tactical interaction between the operational units."

Stresemann, Gustav (1878–1929)   The chancellor of Germany's WEIMAR REPUBLIC during four months in 1923. As foreign minister from 1923 until his death, he negotiated a reduction in Germany's World War I REPARATIONS and gained Germany's admission to the League of Nations. For his work on the LOCARNO PACT OF 1925, he shared the 1926 Nobel Peace Prize with ARISTIDE BRIAND of France.

stress   The anxiety or fear felt by a person in a situation where there is a high threat to the things he or she values. Stress is exacerbated too if there are time pressures or if the situation is full of uncertainties. To assess the impact of stress on the quality of decision making, considerable attention has been given in foreign policy analysis to CRISIS situations in which there are generally high levels of stress. *See also* INVERTED U-CURVE.

strike   *See* SELECTIVE STRIKE; SURGICAL STRIKE.

strike force   1. A military unit organized specifically to undertake an offensive mission.   2. By analogy, a civilian effort to attack a major problem; a term commonly used by police and public prosecutors, as in a "crime strike force."

structural change   Alterations in the relative significance of the productive components of a national or international economy that take place over time. Expansion in the economy as a whole or temporary shifts in the relationship of its components as a result of cyclical developments would not be considered structural changes. Since the Industrial Revolution, structural change in most states has resulted principally from changes in COMPARATIVE ADVANTAGE associated with technological advance, but also to a lesser degree from changes in consumer preference. It has involved shifts from subsistence agriculture to commercial agriculture, a reduction in the percentage of the labor force engaged in agriculture, an increase in the relative significance of manufacturing, and, at a later stage, a further shift toward service industries. Other major structural changes involve shifts in the economic importance of various industries, shifts of influence among regions of large national economies, and changes in the composition of exports and imports.

Structural Impediments Initiative   The overall United States effort to coax Japan into changing its methods of doing business to make them more compatible with Western business practices. For example, some Japanese retail outlets will buy only products of Japanese origin, even when imported goods are less expensive. This is especially true with agricultural products. The Structural Impediments Initiative, begun in 1989, is the responsibility of the U.S. International Trade Commission, which conducts bilateral negotiations with the Japanese Ministry of International Trade and Industry and the Ministry of Foreign Affairs.

structuralism   1. Any approach that emphasizes the design of a system as the major explanation of its behavior. MARXISM, for example, provides structural explanations of the behavior of capitalist states.   2. An approach to explanations of the international system, most closely associated with KENNETH WALTZ, which emphasizes the importance of the anarchic structure of the international system and the distribution of power among the constituent units.

structural realism   *See* NEOREALISM.

structural violence   *See* GALTUNG, JOHAN.

Subic Bay Naval Station   The United States Navy's main Southeast Asian base during the post–World War II era. Located about 50 miles from Manila, in the Philippines, it was closed in 1992 after the Philippine government refused to extend its lease. There was widespread feeling in the Philippines that this massive U.S. presence inhibited the independent development of the Philippine political culture and economy.

subject   1. An individual who takes part in a scientific experiment or opinion survey.   2. A resident in a monarchy who owes allegiance to a king or queen. *Compare to* CITIZEN.

submarine launched ballistic missiles   *See* SLBM.

submarine warfare   The use of undersea vehicles as a means to attack an enemy. The attempt by air, surface, and subsurface forces to disrupt such operations is known as *antisubmarine warfare* (ASW). Modern military submarines have two distinct roles: as a platform for launching strategic nuclear ballistic missiles and as "hunter-killers" to attack other seagoing vessels, both merchant and naval. During World War II submarine warfare played a major role in the Battle of the ATLANTIC, when German U-Boats nearly choked off Great Britain's merchant shipping lifeline for food and war materiel.

subsidy   Payments, direct or indirect (such as tax advantages or other benefits), from a government to individuals or corporations to encourage specific business activities. Subsidies are widely used to encourage exports, which, in turn, helps overall economic development. However, when subsidies are considered unfair (or in violation of trade agreements), the importing state may respond with a COUNTERVAILING DUTY.

subsystem   A small part of a large grouping of related things. For example, while the international system consists of all of the states in the world, a subsystem of this would be Central America, Eastern Europe, or the Middle East. Foreign policy analysis often focuses on subsystems.

subversion   The performance of acts helpful to individuals, groups, or organizations that advocate the overthrow of an existing government by force and violence. All willful actions that are intended to be detrimental to the best interests of a government and that do not fall into the categories of ESPIONAGE, SABOTAGE, SEDITION, or TREASON can be considered subversive.

Sudetenland   The northern portion of Czechoslovakia that was inhabited mainly by ethnic Germans prior to World War II. The main issue of the 1938 MUNICH AGREEMENT was Adolf Hitler's demand that the Sudetenland be given to Germany. It was.

Suez Crisis   The 1956 conflict that pitted France, Great Britain, and Israel against Egypt. Although the roots of the conflict extended over decades, the proximate cause was the withdrawal by Great Britain and the United States in July 1956 of their offers of loans to help Egypt finance the construction of the ASWAN HIGH DAM. This refusal followed Egypt's conclusion of an arms-for-cotton exchange agreement with Czechoslovakia, which provided massive Soviet-made armaments to Egypt. On July 26, 1956, Egyptian President GAMAL ABDAL NASSER further responded by nationalizing the Suez Canal. After unsuccessful attempts to negotiate a settlement, Israel (by secret agreements with the British and French) invaded the Egyptian Sinai Peninsula. (Ships flying the Israeli flag and all cargo bound to and from Israel had been refused passage through the canal since 1948.) Thereupon France and Great Britain, as planned, dropped paratroops into Port Said, Egypt. As a cover, France and Great Britain ostensibly claimed a desire to separate the Egyptian and Israeli armies to assure the defense and continued operation of the canal. British Prime Minister ANTHONY EDEN pointedly told the House of Commons on November 4, 1956: "We are not at war with Egypt. We are in an armed conflict." War had not actually been declared. Hostilities ceased after the United Nations, under vigorous pressure from the United States, condemned the attack. France, Great Britain, and Israel withdrew, and the Egyptians retained the canal. After this fiasco, Eden had to resign as prime minister. The crisis demonstrated that it was now impossible for France and Great Britain to play power politics with other parts of the world without the support of the United States or the Soviet Union. The story persists that Eisenhower telephoned Eden during the crisis and literally yelled at him. This is partly true. According to Chester L. Cooper in *The Lion's Last Roar: Suez, 1956* (1978), Eisenhower "did call Downing Street, but mistook one of the Prime Minister's aides, who answered the call, for Eden himself. By the time Eden got to the phone, Ike had finished his tirade and hung up."

THE EFFECT OF EDEN'S ILLS ON THE SUEZ CRISIS

[Anthony Eden] had been physically weakened for some time—his intestines had stopped working, and . . . he came to America for an operation. The surgeons inserted a strip of plastic tubing, leaving the melancholy thought that the only relic of the British Prime Minister that would survive decomposition under ground would be a piece of American plastic.

The contempt with which [U.S. President] Eisenhower and [U.S. Secretary of State] Dulles treated Eden throughout the crisis probably owed something to his increasing derangement. (He threw an old ink stand at the distinguished military commentator Basil Liddell Hart, who was advising him on how to conduct the operation, and with ink spreading over his suit, Liddell Hart retaliated by shoving a wastepaper basket over the Prime Minister's head.) This certainly provided Eden's subordinates with an excuse to defect. Among the Cabinet ministers who supported Eden in planning the operation, and then deserted him in face of the American opposition and advised him to pull out a day after he had gone in, were Harold Macmillan . . . and R. A. Butler, his foreign secretary. . . . About six months after the fiasco . . . I asked Butler whether Britain would have completed the job if Eden had been well during Suez. Butler replied, "Oh yes."

SOURCE: Henry Fairlie, "Ike at Suez" (*The New Republic*, December 8, 1986).

Suharto (1921–   )   The president of Indonesia since 1967. His single name is also spelled Soeharto. As army chief of staff he crushed an attempted Communist coup in 1965 and led his own coup against President ACHMED SUKARNO in 1967. As President Suharto ended CONFRONTATION with Malaysia, restored Indonesia to a capitalist economy, expanded Indonesia through the EAST TIMOR OCCUPATION, and continues to suppress all domestic opposition. *See also* GOLKAR; NATIONAL RESILIENCE; NEW ORDER.

Sukarno, Achmed (1901–1970)   The president of the Republic of Indonesia from 1945 until 1967. Leader of the INDONESIAN WAR OF INDEPENDENCE, in 1957 he gave up the attempt to maintain representative party government in Indonesia and established a dictatorial regime to provide his people with GUIDED DEMOCRACY. His international stature reached its peak in 1955 when Indonesia hosted the BANDUNG CONFERENCE. His Cold War of CONFRONTATION with Malaysia and general economic stagnation caused the army to become disenchanted with him. Thus in 1967 he was overthrown by a military coup led by SUHARTO.

Sullivan principles   Fair employment practice principles drafted by Pennsylvania clergyman Leon H. Sullivan in 1977 and subsequently signed on a voluntary basis by many U.S. corporations doing business in South Africa. The principle called for nonsegregation of the races in eating, comfort, and work facilities; equal pay for equal work; and an increase in management training for nonwhites. In 1987 Sullivan rejected his own code and called for a total economic boycott to end APARTHEID.

summit   1. A meeting of the top executives of independent organizations, usually governments. The word in its diplomatic sense may first have been used by Walter Bagehot in *The English Constitution* (1867): "The old-world diplomacy of Europe was largely carried on in drawing-rooms, and, to a great extent, of necessity still is so. Nations touch at their summits." But British Prime Minister Winston Churchill is generally credited with popularizing the modern use of the word in the early 1950s. There is a great tendency to personalize the outcomes of summits—to believe that newfound interpersonal relations suddenly become more important than continuing national interests. But former U.S. Secre-

tary of State Henry Kissinger warned: "This reflects a profound American temptation to believe that foreign policy is a subdivision of psychiatry and that relations among nations are like relations among people" (*Time*, June 17, 1985). This is why some analysts such as U.S. Senator Barry M. Goldwater in *Why Not Victory?* (1962) have concluded: "The only summit meeting that can succeed is the one that does not take place." The COLD WAR summits between the United States and the Soviet Union were portentous and dramatic because they were meetings of adversaries, meetings of two sides that

U.S.–U.S.S.R. SUMMITS 1960–1990

Date	Leaders	Site
June 1961	Kennedy and Khrushchev	Vienna, Austria
June 1967	Johnson and Kosygin	Glassboro, N.J.
May 1972	Nixon and Brezhnev	Moscow, U.S.S.R.
June 1973	Nixon and Brezhnev	Washington, D.C., U.S.A.
June–July 1974	Nixon and Brezhnev	Moscow, U.S.S.R., Yalta, U.S.S.R.
November 1974	Ford and Brezhnev	Vladivostok, U.S.S.R.
June 1979	Carter and Brezhnev	Vienna, Austria
November 1985	Reagan and Gorbachev	Geneva, Switzerland
October 1986	Reagan and Gorbachev	Reykjavik, Iceland
December 1987	Reagan and Gorbachev	Washington, D.C., U.S.A.
May–June 1988	Reagan and Gorbachev	Moscow, U.S.S.R.
December 1988	Reagan and Gorbachev	New York, N.Y., U.S.A.
December 1989	Bush and Gorbachev	Malta
May–June 1990	Bush and Gorbachev	Washington, D.C., U.S.A.
September 1990	Bush and Gorbachev	Helsinki, Finland

had good reason to feel hostile toward each other. Now that the Cold War is over and relations between the United States and Russia are friendly, summits as we have known them may no longer be possible. During the Cold War, summits seemed to have more form than substance and occasionally— as with the Vienna Summit between U.S. President John F. Kennedy and Soviet President Nikita Khrushchev—seemed to exacerbate tensions rather than reduce them. It is noteworthy though that the DÉTENTE of the early 1970s and that of the latter half of the 1980s were characterized by an increase in the frequency with which Soviet and U.S. leaders met on a face-to-face basis. **2.** Any meeting between heads of government. For example, when the Council of the North American Treaty Organization meets at the heads-of-government level, this is generally termed a NATO Summit.

summit, economic Since 1975, the annual meeting of the leaders of the seven major industrialized countries (known as the Group of 7 or G-7): Canada, France, Germany, Great Britain, Italy, Japan, and the United States—plus the president of the EUROPEAN COMMISSION. Some summits have been more stimulating than others. Journalist Maureen Dowd reported that as the Italian leader read the final communiqué at the 1987 economic summit in Venice, "all the other heads of state in the Group of Seven, except Prime Minister Brian Mulroney of Canada, snoozed on stage" (*New York Times*, November 11, 1989).

SUMMIT SUMMATION

What really happens at even the most serious . . . summit conference where there are significant issues to be discussed? Though little serious conversation takes place at the banquet table, the time consumed in eating and drinking is appalling. . . .

Thus, in trying to measure the period permitted for a substantive exchange of views during ten hours of top-level propinquity, one should deduct at least four hours for eating and drinking. Another hour or two for small talk . . . then divide the remainder by two and one half for the translation. What is left is about two or three hours.

SOURCE: George Ball, *Diplomacy for a Crowded World* (1976).

Sunni From the Arabic *sunna* meaning "the traditional way"; the name given the orthodox Islamic majority sect. Most Arab states are dominated by Sunnis, giving rise to political as well as religious rivalry with the SHI'ITE minority.

Sun-Tzu (fourth century B.C.) The ancient Chinese writer whose essays, published as *The Art of War*, have influenced all Western military analysts since they were first available in Europe in the late eighteenth century. Sun-Tzu was the first writer to formulate a rational basis for the conduct and planning of military operations. He believed that rulers and generals needed a systematic thesis to guide and direct them in war and that skillful strategists should be able to beat adversaries without engaging them, to take cities without destroying them, and to overthrow states without bloodshed. He advocated the use of secret agents—spies and intelligence—to keep leaders informed and to make them able to plan better. His essays emphasize how to conduct a war of maneuver. According to James Coates and Michael Kilian's *Heavy Losses* (1985), in World War II a military aide of Nationalist General Chiang Kai-shek stated that "in Chiang's army, Sun Tzu's *The Art of War* was considered a classic but out of date. A few years later Chiang fell to Sun Tzu's tactics—employed at the hands of Mao."

Sun Yat-sen (1866–1925) Founding father of KUOMINTANG (the Chinese Nationalist Party), first provisional president of the Republic of China (1911–1912), and de facto ruler from 1913 to 1925. While in his teens, Sun studied in a British missionary school and a U.S. school in Honolulu, Hawaii. Later he studied medicine in Canton and Hong Kong. Troubled by the imperialistic exploitation China suffered at the hands of technologically advanced Western nations, he gave up medicine for politics. Sun's following expanded after 1905 when he became head of a revolutionary coalition, the League of Common Alliance, which was based on three principles: nationality (which was directed against Western imperialism), livelihood (which called for equalizing landholdings and nationalizing industries), and people's rights (which argued for a constitutional democracy in China). He was often in exile in Japan. After a rash of Manchu reforms failed, China's Republican Revolution of

1911–1912 caused the Manchu dynasty collapse. Taken by surprise by the start of the revolution, Sun returned to China from the United States to serve briefly as provisional president in Nanking. He resigned shortly thereafter when General Yuan-shi-kai promised to support and lead the new republic. Yuan thus withdrew support from the boy emperor P'u yi, who abdicated in 1912 formally ending the 2,100-year Manchu rule in China. Sun's revolutionary alliance and four smaller parties in 1912 formed the Kuomintang, or National Party, supporting representative democracy. Meanwhile Sun's international support shifted from Japan to the Soviet Union, which encouraged the Chinese Communists to cooperate with Sun's reorganized Nationalists. Despite the bloody CHINESE CIVIL WAR that ensued between the Nationalists and the Communists, the CHINESE COMMUNIST PARTY still considers Sun a pioneer of its revolution. *See also* SOONG CH'IN-LING.

superpowers   A term generally used to differentiate the United States and the Soviet Union of the COLD WAR from GREAT POWERS of the past. The term itself was coined by William T. R. Fox in *Super-Powers* (1944) and rested on the fact that the United States and the Soviet Union had "great power plus great mobility of power." In this sense, they seemed much more formidable than traditional great powers such as Great Britain or Germany. The term seemed particularly appropriate in the 1950s as the two states developed extensive nuclear arsenals in addition to their large conventional forces. The United States in particular also seemed to be a global power, something to which the Soviet Union increasingly aspired and finally became in the 1970s, although at the expense of domestic needs. In fact, it was often argued that the United States was the only true superpower because it was economically strong while the economy of the Soviet Union was more comparable to that of a developing country. As long ago as 1835 French historian Alexis de Tocqueville (1805–1859) in *Democracy in America* observed that: "There are now two great nations in the world which, starting from different points, seem to be advancing toward the same goal: the Russians and the Anglo-Americans." But the central

superpower dilemma of the atomic age was most succinctly put by J. Robert Oppenheimer (1904–1967), the American scientist in charge of inventing the atomic bomb: "We may be likened to two scorpions in a bottle, each capable of killing the other, but only at the risk of his own life" (*Foreign Affairs,* July 1953). Now that both the Cold War and the Soviet Union are over, the United States is clearly the world's only superpower.

supranational   An institution or organization that literally is above nations or states. Bruce Russett in *Trends in World Politics* (1965) notes that in a supranational organization, decisions are taken by majority vote and are binding on all members. In fact, most international institutions are intergovernmental rather than supranational and give members the right of veto. The EUROPEAN COMMUNITY, however, increasingly has some supranational characteristics, which are likely to develop further with acceptance of the principle of majority voting. Although supranational institutions are sometimes held up as ideals, states still guard their SOVEREIGNTY and independence, with the result that such institutions are relatively rare in international politics. The United Nations, for example, has very limited supranational authority. *Compare to* INTERGOVERNMENTAL ORGANIZATIONS.

Supreme Soviet   The highest-level legislature in the Soviet Union from 1936 to 1988. Until the MIKHAIL GORBACHEV era, it was largely an instrument for the will of the ruling POLITBURO. Constitutional reforms in 1988 placed it under the USSR Congress of Peoples' Deputies whose 2,250 members chose from their ranks the two coequal houses (the Soviet of the Union and the Soviet of Nationalities) of the Supreme Soviet with 271 members each. The Supreme Soviet ceased to exist with the demise of the Soviet Union at the end of 1991.

surgical strike   The destruction of a target by means of carefully controlled force so as to minimize COLLATERAL DAMAGE. It can refer to the use of conventional force—for example, a bombing raid on a terrorist headquarters intended to spare all innocent civilians nearby. It also can be used in nuclear strategy, where a surgical strike might be considered as a LIMITED NUCLEAR OPTION against a set of missile silos. However, surgical strikes rarely can be as clean as planned, and the notion of such an attack using nuclear weapons is absurd. *Compare to* SELECTIVE STRIKE.

surprise attack   An attack on the enemy when and where it is least prepared. Surprise in combat can bring success out of all proportion to the numbers involved. Surprise does not necessarily mean that the enemy is taken unaware; simply that it is unable to react effectively. This term generally refers to an attack that catches the defender by surprise. It has been discussed in terms of a nuclear attack in which the purpose is to destroy the adversary's retaliatory capabilities. It also has been discussed in relation to the possibility of a Soviet attack on North Atlantic Treaty Organization member states (or vice versa) using forces already in place. This has become a far less serious contingency with the 1991 dissolution of the Soviet Union. Historically, while surprise attacks have damaged the party being attacked, they have not necessarily been decisive for the final outcome of the war. Germany's 1941 invasion of the Soviet Union caught the Soviets by surprise but was not decisive. And the Japanese attack on Pearl Harbor in 1941 did not stop the United States from eventually defeating Japan. Often the problem of surprise is not one of information. In many cases, including the two cited above as well as the Arab attack on Israel in the 1973 Yom Kippur War and the Chinese entry into the Korean War, warning signals were visible but were dismissed—partly because they were not unequivocal, partly because they were surrounded by ambient noise, and partly because they ran counter to the preconceptions of key decision makers. Although steps can be taken to reduce the possibility of surprise, it is not something that can be eradicated. Sun Tzu summarized the theory of military surprise in his *The Art of War* (fourth century B.C.): "The enemy must not know where I intend to give battle. For if he does not know where I intend to give battle, he must prepare in a great many places. . . . If he prepares to the front his rear will be weak and if to the rear, his front will be fragile. If he prepares to the left, his right will be vulnerable and if to the right, there

will be few on his left. And when he prepares everywhere he will be weak everywhere."

surrender   An action taken during hostilities that involves capitulation to most or all the enemy's demands in return for a cessation of the fighting. Surrender or CAPITULATION is one way of bringing wars to an end. *Compare to* UNCONDITIONAL SURRENDER.

suspension of arms   A short truce arranged by local commanders in a theater of war for a special purpose, such as to collect the wounded, to bury the dead, or to arrange for an exchange of prisoners.

sustainable development   Economic activity that can be continued indefinitely (sustained) because it does not use up or destroy natural resources in the process. For example, power generated by wind is sustainable as opposed to power generated by fossil fuels that will eventually be exhausted.

Suttner, Bertha von (1843–1914)   The Austrian baroness whose novel, *Lay Down Your Arms* (1889), heavily influenced the PEACE MOVEMENT. She won the 1905 Nobel Peace Prize for her work as a peace activist—and for influencing Alfred Nobel in establishing the peace prizes.

Suu Kyi, Aung San (1945–   )   The leader of the political opposition to the ruling Burmese military junta who, after several years under close house arrest, was awarded the Nobel Peace Prize in 1991. The Nobel Committee was not allowed to communicate the news directly to her. She was awarded the prize in part to call attention to her plight and to show support for her efforts to use nonviolence to resist a brutal regime. Suu Kyi, who had lived in England with her British husband, returned to Burma (renamed Myanmar by the junta) in 1988 to care for her ailing mother. But she entered politics actively when the party she supported, the National League for Democracy, had an election victory negated by the ruling military junta. The junta has offered to allow her to return to England if she would promise to stay out of politics. But she refuses to leave until political power is transferred to the NLD. Suu Kyi is the daughter of U. Aung San (1914–1947), the founder of the modern Burmese

Army who fought with the Japanese against the British in World War II. When it became obvious that the Japanese were losing, he joined the Allies. He was to be the first prime minister of an independent Burma (after the British had announced their withdrawal), when he was assassinated in 1947. Her father's special status in Burmese history is probably why the junta has not simply murdered Suu Kyi as it has so many other opposition leaders. In April 1992, partly because of all the international attention created by the Nobel Prize, the military government allowed Suu Kyi's husband and two sons to visit her.

swallow   An INTELLIGENCE AGENCY term for a combination spy and prostitute who uses sex to pry secrets out of influential or knowledgeable foreigners or sets up individuals so that photographs can be taken that can later be used for blackmail.

SWAPO (South West African People's Organization)   A left-wing guerrilla organization committed to NAMIBIAN INDEPENDENCE from South Africa. Supported by Cuba, the Soviet Union, and a number of African states, SWAPO sought to maintain a low-intensity conflict against South African forces, prior to the negotiated settlement of 1988. In April 1989 the group was accused of breaking the negotiated truce. In late 1989 SWAPO emerged from the United Nations–monitored elections as the legitimate spokesman for Namibian nationalism.

SWAT   **1.** Strategy Without a Threat; a phrase that has frequently been used in relation to security and military planning of the United States and its allies now that the Soviet threat has disappeared. Although the term is sometimes used in a critical way as part of the argument that there is no longer much need for strategy, most users argue that military strategy is still required even though there is no longer a single threat to plan against. Some of those who advocate SWAT contend that there are generic contingencies for which it is necessary to plan—and that planning no longer needs to be threat-based the way it was during the Cold War. **2.** Special Weapons and Tactics; specially trained police, hostage rescue, or antiterrorist paramilitary or military forces.

Swiss neutrality   Switzerland's traditional policy of avoiding alliances that might entail military, political, or direct economic action. While the 1815 Congress of Vienna recognized permanent Swiss NEUTRALITY, the Swiss have been able to maintain it ever since by astute diplomacy and by a defense-only militia army in which all physically fit Swiss males must serve. In recent years the Swiss have broadened the scope of activities in which they feel able to participate without compromising their neutrality. In 1986 a national referendum rejected membership in the United Nations by a 2–1 margin. However, Switzerland maintains an observer at UN headquarters, is party to the Statute of the International Court of Justice, and belongs to most UN SPECIALIZED AGENCIES. The Swiss imposed economic sanctions against Iraq after its 1990 invasion of Kuwait. Switzerland has furnished military observers and medical teams to several UN operations and also is an active participant in the CONFERENCE ON SECURITY AND COOPERATION IN EUROPE. Switzerland maintains diplomatic relations with almost all countries and historically has served as a neutral diplomatic intermediary. For example, since 1980 it has represented U.S. interests in Iran. It is a tenet of Swiss foreign policy that Switzerland has a moral obligation to undertake economic, humanitarian, and social activities that contribute to world peace and prosperity. This is manifested by Swiss bilateral and multilateral diplomatic activity, assistance to developing countries, and support for the extension of international law, particularly humanitarian law. Geneva, Switzerland, is the headquarters of many international governmental and nongovernmental organizations, including the International Committee of the Red Cross (whose symbol is based on the design of the Swiss flag, with colors reversed; the Red Cross has historically been a Swiss organization).

Sykes-Picot Agreement   The 1916 confidential agreement between the diplomats of France and Great Britain (with Russian consent) that determined the post–World War I borders of the former OTTOMAN EMPIRE. Mark Sykes (1879–1919) represented British interests and François Georges Picot (1870–1951) represented French interests. The notable absence of Arab representation in the determination of the borders has led to conflicts that continue to this day.

Syrian Social Nationalist Party (SSNP) An organization dedicated to the establishment of the state of Greater Syria, incorporating all the land between the Euphrates and Nile rivers, as well as the island of Cyprus. The SSNP has a history of more than 50 years of terrorist activity, making it perhaps the oldest active terrorist organization in the world.

Syrian terrorism State-sponsored TERRORISM by one of the world's most active supporters of terrorism and subversion against other states. Syria is one of the "charter members" of the U.S. government's terrorism list, which was first compiled in 1979. Syrian personnel were directly involved in terrorist operations from the mid-1970s until 1983. These operations were directed primarily against other Arabs, such as Syrian dissidents, "moderate" Arab states such as Jordan, and pro-FATAH Palestinians. Israeli and Jewish interests also were major targets. By late 1983 the Syrian government had begun to rely on terrorist groups made up primarily of non-Syrians who were supported and trained in Syria and in Syrian-controlled regions of Lebanon. The most notorious of these are the ABU NIDAL organization and the POPULAR FRONT FOR THE LIBERATION OF PALESTINE.

systems analysis 1. Collecting, manipulating, and evaluating data on social units (as small as an organization or as large as a polity) to determine how to improve their functioning and to assist policymakers in selecting from among alternative courses of action. The systems approach views social units as complex sets of dynamically intertwined, interconnected (and often unknown) elements, including inputs (the people or things in the system), processes (what they do), outputs (the results of what they do), FEEDBACK loops, and the environments in which they operate. A change in any element of the system inevitably causes changes in its other elements. Norbert Wiener's (1894–1964) classic model of an adaptive system, from his 1948 book *Cybernetics,* epitomizes the basic theoretical perspectives of the systems school. *Cybernetic,* a Greek word meaning "steersman," was used by Wiener to mean the multidisciplinary study of the structures and functions of control and information-processing systems in animals and machines. The basic concept behind cybernetics is self-regulation—biological, social, or technological systems that can identify problems, do something about them, and then receive feedback to adjust themselves automatically. Wiener, a mathematician, developed the concept of cybernetics while working on antiaircraft systems during World War II. 2. The development and use of mathematical models as an aid in decision making. But this can be dangerous if nonquantifiable factors are not also taken into account. As Edward N. Luttwak wrote in "The American Style of Warfare" (*Survival,* March/April 1979), "Even though the historical record of war shows quite conclusively that superior firepower is often associated with defeat, and that winners more often than not were actually inferior in firepower, these mathematical models continue to be devastatingly influential because they capture all that is conveniently measurable about warfare. Thus bookkeepers may fancy themselves strategists." The classic example of this is the U.S. experience in Vietnam. The systems analysis techniques introduced by Secretary of Defense ROBERT S. MCNAMARA in the early 1960s were based on mathematical models that treated warfare as a cumulative exchange of firepower. The story is often told that a frustrated general in the Pentagon of 1968 fed into a computer all of the known data about the Vietnam War, then asked when the United States would win. The computer answered: "You won in 1964." But neither war nor the real world always responds rationally to superior resources or good intentions.

T

Taba A small portion of the SINAI Peninsula that remained in dispute after the CAMP DAVID ACCORDS because of disagreement over the exact border drawn between Egypt and Palestine in 1906. After direct negotiations failed to bilaterally resolve the dispute over these 250 acres on the Gulf of Aqaba, in 1986 both Egypt and Israel agreed to abide by the decision of a panel of arbitrators. Taba, on which the Israelis had built a hotel and resort complex, was awarded to Egypt. The Egyptians agreed to pay Israel compensation for the hotel.

table of organization *See* ESTABLISHMENT.

tacit agreement An informal understanding, often called a *tacit rule*, on the part of governments to do or not do something, such as not intrude upon each other's spheres of influence.

tactical nuclear weapon A relatively small and short-range nuclear artillery shell, missile, or bomb that can be useful on a large battlefield, as opposed to the longer-ranged and more powerful strategic nuclear weapons. It was once thought, as U.S. President Dwight D. Eisenhower said in a news conference on March 16, 1954, that there is "no reason why [such weapons] shouldn't be used just exactly as you would use a bullet or anything else." However, the political and military implications of going nuclear are so immense that such weapons would be used only in the most desperate circumstances. When U.S. President Ronald Reagan, speaking to newspaper editors in Washington, D.C., on October 16, 1981, said, "I could see where you could have the exchange of tactical [nuclear] weapons

against troops in the field without it bringing either one of the major powers to pushing 'the button,'" he was soundly criticized. It is no longer politically acceptable to consider these little nuclear weapons as just an extension of regular arms. Typical of such weapons are nuclear shells fired by artillery pieces, with ranges between approximately 15 and 25 kilometers, or missiles having a range of about 110 kilometers. Such weapons may have yields of less than 1 kiloton to perhaps 10 kilotons. More modern types of battlefield weapons in fact have what is called a dial-a-yield capacity, so that the field commander can select the explosive power to better suit the tactical situation. In 1991 U.S. President George Bush announced that all North Atlantic Treaty Organization stocks of battlefield nuclear weapons (there were more than 5,000 warheads in this category) would be withdrawn.

tactical weapons Short-range and local military means, as opposed to long-range STRATEGIC WEAPONS. Tactical weapons can decide the outcome of a battle but not necessarily the outcome of a war. This is an inherently vague concept because as technology advances with time, the nature of tactical weapons changes. Thus the machine gun, a strategic weapon in World War I, was so overcome in importance by other weapons (such as the tank) that by World War II it was reduced to a tactical weapon.

tactics 1. The maneuvering of aircraft, ships, or troops in preparation for immediate combat. By analogy, a tactical weapon (as opposed to a strategic one) is any device available to a military leader during the course of a battle. Nuclear weapons, while normally designed for strategic purposes, also have been designed for tactical use. 2. Short-term political actions; the day-to-day decisions that have to be made by political leaders. *Compare to* STRATEGY.

Taft, William Howard (1857–1930)   The only person to be both president of the United States (1909–1913) and chief justice of the U.S. Supreme Court (1921–1930). His foreign policy, which favored big business, came to be known as DOLLAR DIPLOMACY. While THEODORE ROOSEVELT's secretary of war (1904–1908) and handpicked successor, Taft quickly lost Roosevelt's support once in office. Roosevelt found him so unacceptably conservative that both men competed for the Republican nomination in 1912. When Roosevelt won the primaries but lost the nomination to Taft, he ran for president as a "Bull Moose" Progressive. This split the Republican vote and allowed WOODROW WILSON, the Democrat, to win.

Taiwan   The island on which the Republic of China is situated; previously known as Formosa, its colonial Portuguese name. In 1949, toward the end of the CHINESE CIVIL WAR, the defeated KUOMINTANG government under CHIANG KAI-SHEK moved offshore to Taiwan. The U.S. commitment to Taiwan developed the next year because of the KOREAN WAR, which Washington interpreted as part of a wider conflict between the free world and the Communist bloc. On June 27, 1950, two days after the war began, U.S. President Harry S Truman announced that he had ordered the U.S. Navy not only to prevent any attacks on Taiwan by Communist China but also to ensure that the Taiwan government ceased air and sea operations against the mainland. In 1954 the United States declared that the U.S. Navy would protect not only Taiwan but also other offshore islands that were crucial to Taiwan's security. A few weeks later the Communists began the bombardment of one of those islands, Quemoy, in response to which Chiang's forces launched attacks against the mainland. It was against the background of these QUEMOY CRISES that the United States moved to formalize its security relationship with Taiwan. On December 1, 1954, the two governments signed a mutual security treaty in which the United States agreed to defend Taiwan, the Pescadores (islands belonging to Taiwan), and

"such other territories as may be determined by mutual agreement" against armed attack. This did nothing to defuse the crisis, however, and in January 1955 both chambers of the U.S. Congress passed the Formosa Resolution authorizing the president to use armed force to defend Taiwan and the Pescadores.

The United States commitment to Taiwan was a significant element in the COLD WAR in Asia. As the Cold War receded, however, and the United States reappraised its relationship with Beijing in the early 1970s, it was inevitable that the relationship with Taiwan would be affected. The reappraisal stemmed from the desire of the Nixon Administration to exploit the SINO-SOVIET SPLIT by establishing closer links with the People's Republic of China, which, it was believed, could help to contain Soviet power in Asia. The process of normalization continued throughout the 1970s, not least because the United States was anxious to play its CHINA CARD in the competition with the Soviet Union. In 1978 the administration of U.S. President Jimmy Carter announced that full diplomatic relations between Washington and Beijing were to be established on January 1, 1979. The implications for Taiwan appeared ominous as the United States acknowledged that there was but one China and that Taiwan was part of it, announced that the mutual defense treaty of 1954 would be terminated, and stated that the remaining American military personnel in Taiwan would be withdrawn.

Taiwan was not completely abandoned. The United States also announced that its people would "maintain cultural, commercial and other unofficial relations with the people of Taiwan." Moreover, the United States made clear that it expected the Taiwan issue to be settled peacefully. In March 1979 the United States, through the Taiwan Relations Act legislation, declared that defensive arms would be supplied so that Taiwan would "maintain the capacity . . . to resist any resort to force or other forms of coercion that would jeopardize the security, or the social or economic system, of the people on Taiwan." It also emphasized that the United States would "consider any effort to determine the future of Taiwan by other than peaceful means, including by boycotts or embargoes, a threat to the peace and security of the Western Pacific area and of grave concern to the United States." Although the lack of official relations meant there could be no official embassies, the United States established the American Institute in Taiwan, staffed with U.S. Foreign Service officers who were said to be temporarily on leave. Some military advisors also remained in Taiwan, although with civilian status. In 1982 Washington and Beijing agreed that U.S. arms sales to Taiwan would be reduced. But arms sales restrictions were compensated by nongovernmental sales and by agreements that enabled Taiwan itself to produce sophisticated equipment under license. In spite of the demise of a formal United States commitment to Taiwan, therefore, the bilateral relationship remains a very real one, although one that is likely to diminish in importance in the future.

Taiwan crises *See* QUEMOY CRISES.

Tal, Wasfi al-, (1920–1971) The prime minister of Jordan (for five time periods between 1962 and 1971) who was assassinated by BLACK SEPTEMBER in 1971. Radical Palestinians considered Al-Tal to be their mortal enemy for his role in the September 1970 expulsion of the Palestinian guerrilla forces from Jordan. His murderers were convicted in Jordanian courts. Initially sentenced to death, their sentences were commuted to life imprisonment. But in 1973 they were released under a general amnesty.

Talal (1909–1972) The king of Jordan from 1951 to 1952. He became king upon the assassination of his father, ABDULLAH I. He was deposed after the Jordanian parliament declared him to be mentally ill. The crown passed to his son, HUSSEIN, the current king. Talal spent the rest of his life in an Istanbul, Turkey, mental institution.

Taleghani Center The name applied by Western intelligence agencies to the building in Tehran from which Iran administers its worldwide COVERT OPERATIONS. Many terrorist acts have been conceived, planned, and financed there.

Tamil A South Asian ethnic group found in Burma, India, Indochina, Thailand, and the West Indies. The Tamils of Sri Lanka are largely Hindu. Their numbers were substantially increased by the British during the nineteenth and early twentieth century when Tamils from India were imported into

Sri Lanka to work on plantations. The majority of Sri Lankans, who are Buddhist, have historically considered the minority Tamils a remnant of British colonial rule. This ethnic tension was a main cause of the SRI LANKAN CIVIL WAR.

Tamil Tigers *See* LIBERATION TIGERS OF TAMIL EELAM.

Tannenberg, Battle of A decisive WORLD WAR I battle fought in August 1914 on the Eastern Front. The Russians invaded East Prussia near Tannenberg, where the Germans, under PAUL VON HINDENBURG and ERICH LUDENDORFF, so soundly defeated them that the Russians were never again able to invade German territory during the war.

Tanzim al-Jihad In Arabic, "the Holy War Organization," an Egyptian fundamentalist group sometimes simply referred to as "al-Jihad." Four of its members staged the assassination of President ANWAR SADAT of Egypt in 1981. He was targeted as a symbol of modern secular Egypt and because he was considered to have compromised Arab and Islamic ideals in his relations with Israel and the United States.

tariff 1. Any bill or charges due. 2. The formal list of duties (taxes) imposed on imports or exports. *See also* DUTY.

tariff, double-column A schedule of taxes on imports listing two DUTY rates for some or all commodities. Imports may be taxed at a higher or lower rate depending on the importing state's trade relationship with the exporting states. In the past the United Kingdom maintained a double-column tariff in order to provide more favorable tariff treatment to the members of its commonwealth. *Compare to* TARIFF, SINGLE-COLUMN.

tariff, internal A tax on goods shipped between members of regional trade groupings, such as the European Community and the European Free Trade Association. These two organizations have eliminated internal tariffs.

tariff, single-column A TARIFF schedule listing only one duty rate for each imported commodity, regardless of the amount being shipped or its country of origin. Single-column tariffs hardly exist today because so many states have special tariff arrangements with so many trading partners. *Compare to* TARIFF, DOUBLE-COLUMN.

tariff, specific   A schedule of import taxes levied on the basis of some physical unit, as so many cents a bushel, pound, or yard. *See also* DUTY, SPECIFIC.

tariff escalation   A situation in which import taxes on manufactured products are relatively high, tariffs on semiprocessed items are moderate, and tariffs on raw materials are nonexistent or very low. Such "escalation"—which exists in the TARIFF SCHEDULES of most developed states—is said to discourage the development of manufacturing industries in developing countries, though it is done to encourage production and sales of domestic goods.

tariff quotas   Application of a higher tariff rate to imported things after a certain amount of the item has entered the state at the usual rate during a specified period.

tariff schedule   A comprehensive list of the goods that a state may import and the import duties imposed on each.

task force   1. A temporary gathering of disparate military units under a single commander to undertake a given mission.   2. By analogy, any temporary interdisciplinary team within a larger organization charged with accomplishing a specific goal. Task forces typically are used in government when a problem crosses departmental lines.   3. A temporary government COMMISSION charged with investigating and reporting on a problem. This meaning of task force has come into fashion at the expense of the more traditional government commission, because the name implies a more aggressive, more action-oriented, approach to seeking solutions to difficult problems.

tax haven   A state or territory in which foreigners can deposit funds, create holding companies, or otherwise engage in businesses that allow them to legally avoid taxes that they would be obligated to pay if they did the same things in their native states.

Team A/Team B   The two groups that formulated the 1976 United States National Intelligence Estimate. Team A consisted of the regular intelligence officers from the Central Intelligence Agency normally given the annual task of preparing the NIE. Team B, a group of nongovernment specialists, was mandated by President Gerald Ford's Foreign Intelligence Advisory Board to analyze independently the same raw data available to Team A. Team B concluded that Team A had "underestimated the Soviet threat" and it asserted that "the Russians were seeking overall military superiority and a war-fighting capability." This was not surprising. Team B was full of hard-liners who, in effect, interpreted the evidence to fit with their preconceptions. Later evidence reinforced the sense that the regular CIA assessment, that of Team A, had been fairly accurate.

Team Spirit   The joint MILITARY EXERCISES by the United States and South Korea that have taken place annually ever since 1976. The exercise, which usually involves over 200,000 troops, has become a source of dispute and tension between North and South Korea. Although the United States and South Korea both emphasize that the exercises are defensive in character and intended simply to enhance DETERRENCE, North Korea vehemently denounces them. While they are clearly an irritant to the North, the annual Team Spirit exercises have been important in reaffirming the U.S. commitment to South Korea. But as tensions have eased on the peninsula—partly in response to the changes in great power relations—the annual exercises have become rather less significant. As the dialogue deepens, it seems likely that they will be cancelled altogether.

Technetronic Age   A term coined by future U.S. National Security Advisor Zbigniew Brzezinski to describe an era in which societies are shaped decisively by the impact of technologies and electronics, especially computers and other new technologies of communication and information processing. He saw this as moving the world from the industrial to the postindustrial age. Brzezinski developed this argument in various places, including "America in the Technetronic Age" (*Encounter,* January 1968).

technology transfer   1. The application of methods developed in one area of research to another, often involving a concomitant shift in institutional setting (e.g., from one government agency to another). Examples include the application of space technology developed under the auspices of the National Aeronautics and Space Administration to the problems of mass transit or weather prediction. Claims regarding the future possibilities for transfer are often factors in decisions concerning continued financial support for the technology under development.   2. The movement of new methods from one state to another. All governments traditionally have been concerned with restricting the flow of new technologies in particular to potential enemies because of their possible military applications. Technology may be transferred in many ways: by giving it away (in technical journals, conferences, emigration of technical experts, technical assistance programs); by stealing it (industrial espionage); or by selling it (through patents, blueprints, industrial processes, and the activities of multinational corporations). Technology transfer issues between North and South are largely concerned with the actual cost of the technology; the suitability of the technology for the developing country's supply of labor, capital, and natural resources; and the fact that the seller often retains the decision-making power over the use of the technology.

Tehran Conference   The first meeting during WORLD WAR II of the BIG THREE—British Prime Minister Winston Churchill, U.S. President Franklin D. Roosevelt, and Soviet Premier Joseph V. Stalin—held in the capital of Iran in November 1943. As the Soviet counteroffensive gained against the retreating Germans, the leaders met to plan the proposed SECOND FRONT against Germany. Churchill, ever mindful of the slaughter in France during World War I, wanted an Anglo-American landing in the Balkans; but Stalin and Roosevelt were set on a cross-channel invasion on France's Normandy coast. Stalin also stated that the Soviet Union would retain the territories it had acquired from 1939 to 1941 (the Baltic States and parts of Poland) when it was allied to Germany. The other two leaders agreed grudgingly. The ATLANTIC CHARTER's idealism thus succumbed to the REALPOLITIK of war. *See also* FOUR POLICEMEN.

Edward Teller (Library of Congress)

Teller, Edward (1908–   )   The Hungarian-born physicist who helped build the atomic bomb for the United States when he worked on the MANHATTAN PROJECT (1943–1945). For his later research in nuclear fusion, Teller after 1952 became known as the "father of the hydrogen bomb." But Teller, who was a professor of physics at the University of California at Berkeley (1953–1975), did not restrict his advocacy of nuclear weapons to the laboratory. Since the beginning of the nuclear era, he has been in the forefront of those who publicly advocated that the United States build ever more sophisticated nuclear weapons systems. Consequently he opposed the limited TEST-BAN TREATY with the Soviet Union. He was one of the prime architects of U.S. President Ronald Reagan's STRATEGIC DEFENSE INITIATIVE and is generally credited with convincing Reagan of SDI's feasibility and desirability.

territorial imperative   1. A thesis put forward in *The Territorial Imperative* (1966) by U.S. anthropologist and playwright Robert Ardrey (1908–1980), who argued that human beings are essentially animals possessive of their land. Ardrey argued that territoriality is "a characteristic of our species as a whole, to be shaped but not determined by environment and experience, and to be a consequence not of human choice but of evolutionary inheritance." In essence, he believed that there is an innate compulsion to possess and defense physical space, and that humans, like other animals, have this compulsion. The ferocity with which states defend their territory appears to support this hypothesis. **2.** A term that is sometimes used rather loosely to justify expansionist policies. *Compare to* LORENZ, KONRAD.

territoriality principle A rather vague term that is based on the notion that legal consequences from state actions are valid only within the territory of that state. Put differently, the public law of other states is generally regarded as invalid or inapplicable within any individual state. This is why it is so difficult for states that want to expropriate property to obtain control over it when it is located in another state. *Compare to* EXPROPRIATION; EXTRATERRITORIALITY.

territorial waters The oceanic areas bordering a state's coast, over which that state exercises SOVEREIGNTY and regulates navigation. *See also* PATRIMONIAL SEA.

terrorism **1.** Violence against randomly selected civilian targets designed to create a pervasive sense of fear and thus affect government policies. The word itself dates back to the "reign of terror" in revolutionary France (1793–1794) when more than 17,000 citizens were officially executed and many thousands more perished under less formal circumstances. Modern terrorism is made possible by the modern mass media. It is essentially what the nineteenth-century French writer Paul Brouss (1844–1912) first called "propaganda by deed" and what U.S. historian Daniel Boorstin (1914–   ) would call a "pseudoevent"—something that would not have occurred had it not been for the potential of media coverage. Consequently, modern terrorists seek to commit crimes so despicable that they engender maximum publicity for their cause. As U.S. Senator John Glenn of Ohio said: "International publicity is the mother's milk of terrorism" (*U.S. News & World Report,* July 8, 1985). **2.** Violence against representatives (diplomats, police, politicians) of a state by those who wish to overthrow its government; in this sense, terrorism is REVOLUTION—thus the cliché that one person's terrorist is another's freedom fighter. Just as the branding of an act as terrorism is subjective, a moral judgment grounded in cultural and political mores, so is the act of defining terrorism. All people tend to reserve the word for politically motivated violence of which they do not approve. **3.** Covert warfare by one state against another; in effect, STATE-SPONSORED TERRORISM. Several states

The U.S. Marine barracks in Beirut, Lebanon, after a terrorist bombing in 1983. (U.S. Naval Institute)

have found that their sponsorship of shadowy terrorist organizations provides an effective vehicle for covert operations that offer minimal expense and an enormous DENIABILITY. Some states have used terrorist organizations to such a degree that they constitute a kind of war by proxy. Syria's utilization of Palestinian organizations such as the POPULAR FRONT FOR THE LIBERATION OF PALESTINE, Iran's influence over Lebanese Shi'ite groups such as HEZBOLLAH, and Libya's sponsorship of the ABU NIDAL organization and other groups are leading examples of this phenomenon. **4.** The acts of a regime that maintains itself in power by random or calculated abuse of its own citizens; in this sense, all oppressive and dictatorial regimes are terroristic. In many respects, it is a misnomer to use the word terrorism to describe the terror of a state against its own people, which may take the form of repression, torture, murder, and even GENOCIDE. Comparing the terrorism of small groups with the terrorism of national security organizations is certainly a case of comparing grapes and watermelons. But if the actions of states are excluded from discussions of terrorism, then by far the largest component of the world's immoral political violence is ignored arbitrarily. This is especially true when the boundaries between state terror and the terrorism of small groups becomes blurred, as in the case of Latin American regimes that have been implicated in the terrorist activities of right-wing DEATH SQUADS. *Compare to* NARCO-TERRORISM.

terrorism, enforcement The guerrilla practice of inspiring fear in the populace, to terrify it into supporting the rebel cause. At a minimum, enforcement terrorism seeks to prevent people from collaborating with the government. This term has been used to describe the SENDERO LUMINOSO's massive violence against the Peruvian *campesinos*, who are ostensibly the people that the group is dedicated to "liberating." The term similarly may be applied to inter-Palestinian terrorism, in which terrorist violence is used to eliminate and/or intimidate rivals.

tertiary Descriptive of the THIRD WORLD.

Test-Ban Treaty *See* PARTIAL TEST BAN TREATY.

Tet Offensive A 1968 battle of the VIETNAM WAR. On January 30, 1968—the start of the Lunar New Year, or Tet—VIET CONG guerrillas and North Vietnamese troops launched a surprise attack against Saigon and four provincial capitals in South Vietnam. In Saigon they entered the presidential palace and the U.S. embassy. They had hoped to spark an uprising in the South, but were driven back by a U.S.–South Vietnamese counterattack. In a strict military sense, the insurgents lost. Forty-five thousand Communist troops were killed compared to 1,000 U.S. soldiers and 2,000 South Vietnamese. But psychologically it was a Communist victory that caused U.S. domestic support for the war to erode. According to Don Oberdorder's *Tet!* (1971): "The Tet Offensive shocked a citizenry which had been led to believe that success in Vietnam was just around the corner. Tet was the final blow to the sagging credibility of the Johnson Administration and to the waning patience of the American people with this remote and inconclusive war." No longer could the U.S. government claim imminent victory—and be believed.

THE FAMOUS TET QUOTE

A sense of disaster pervaded the United States, sharpened by the most widely quoted remark of the war: "It becomes necessary to destroy the town in order to save it." The American major meant that the town had to be razed in order to rout the Viet-Cong, but his phrase seemed to symbolize the use of American power—destroying the object of its protection in order to preserve it from Communism.

SOURCE: Barbara W. Tuchman, *The March of Folly* (1984). The anonymous major was interviewed by Peter Arnett of the Associated Press during Tet. The story had the dateline: Ben Tre, Vietnam, February 7, 1968.

Thalweg German for "road in a valley"; the deepest part of a river or other navigable water channel. This is often used as an international boundary so that both sides have usable navigation rights, even when the deepest part is not exactly in the middle.

Thant, U (1909–1974) The Burmese representative to the United Nations (1957–1961) who was the third secretary general of the UN from 1961 to 1971. He was a neutralist on most Cold War issues and stressed Third World concerns and needs. His

Prime Minister Margaret Thatcher waving to the crowd at the 1979 Conservative Party Conference. (British Information Services)

withdrawal of UN peacekeeping forces from the Sinai Peninsula and the Gaza Strip at the request of Egypt in 1967 was widely criticized for helping to precipitate the Six-Day War in 1967.

Thatcher, Margaret (1925–   ) The conservative prime minister of Great Britain from 1979 to 1990. Elected as the first female prime minister in British history, she then held that office longer than any other twentieth-century British politician. Her championing of free market economic policies, coupled with an assertive role in world affairs, created an ideological style of leadership that came to be known as "Thatcherism." Her leadership during the 1982 FALKLANDS WAR made her a major actor on the international stage. While a stern Cold Warrior whose policies were right in step with those of her contemporary in office, U.S. President Ronald Reagan, she was also one of the first Western leaders to recognize that MIKHAIL GORBACHEV was a radical departure from previous Soviet leaders. Her oft-used nickname, "the Iron Lady," dates from a speech she gave before she became prime minister in which she warned a Conservative Party meeting on January 19, 1976, of the continuing Soviet threat.

This led *Red Star,* a journal of the Soviet Ministry of Defense, to write on January 23, 1976: "The Iron Lady of British politics is seeking to revive the cold war." The term might have been forgotten had not Thatcher, a week later in a speech in Finchley, England, played it up by saying: "I stand before you tonight in my green chiffon evening gown, my face softly made up, my fair hair gently waved . . . the Iron Lady of the Western World. Me? A cold war warrior? Well, yes—if that is how [the Soviet Press] wish to interpret my defense of values and freedoms fundamental to our way of life" (*The Times* [London], February 1, 1976).

In 1990 she staunchly encouraged U.S. President George Bush as he assembled the worldwide coalition that would rebuff the Iraqi invasion of Kuwait during the PERSIAN GULF WAR, but domestic problems of high inflation, high unemployment, and high trade deficits and her waning personal popularity made her party fearful that it could not win a fourth consecutive general election with her at the helm. Conservative Party insurgents staged what amounted to an intraparty coup, deposed Thatcher, and replaced her with JOHN MAJOR. A significant issue in the coup was Thatcher's opposition to full economic integration with the rest of Europe. While she generally supported the EUROPEAN COMMUNITY, she was largely alone in her strong opposition to full European monetary union. After the Conservative Party won a fourth term in the 1992 general election, her deposition was seen as a shrewd exercise of political self-renewal. However, at the time it seemed more like the crew of a sinking ship voting to throw their captain overboard. Thatcher thereupon retired to the back benches of the House of Commons and made herself available, for substantial fees, to the worldwide lecture circuit. In 1992 she was made a baroness and left the House of Commons for the House of Lords.

theater of war A major geographical area of conflict (or potential conflict) that is included in a unified military command. The classic definition comes from General Antoine Henri Jomini's (1779–1869) *Summary of the Art of War* (1838): "The theater of a war comprises all the territory upon which the parties may assail each other, whether it belong to themselves, their allies, or to weaker states who may be drawn into the war through fear or interest. When the war is also maritime, the theater may embrace both hemispheres. . . . The theater of a war may thus be undefined, and must not be confounded with the theater of operations [which] . . . embraces all the territory it [an army] may desire to invade and all that it may be necessary to defend." Paul Fussell wrote in his 1975 book *The Great War in Modern Memory:* "The most obvious reason why 'theater' and modern war seem so compatible is that modern wars are fought by conscripted armies, whose members know they are only temporarily playing their ill-learned parts."

theater nuclear forces (TNF) EUROMISSILES; INTER-MEDIATE-RANGE NUCLEAR FORCES; any of a range of nuclear armed ballistic and CRUISE MISSILES that were deployed by the North Atlantic Treaty Organization and the Warsaw Pact for nuclear strikes inside Europe. Through the INF TREATY and mutual agreement by NATO and Russia, all theater nuclear forces, including nuclear artillery, are being removed from Europe.

THE FIRST USE OF "THEATER OF WAR"

[Candide] clambered over heaps of dead and dying men and reached a neighboring village, which . . . the Bulgarians had burned in accordance with international law. Here, old men dazed with blows watched the dying agonies of their murdered wives who clutched their children to their bleeding breasts; there, disemboweled girls who had been made to satisfy the natural appetites of heroes gasped their last sighs; others, half-burned, begged to be put to death. Brains were scattered on the ground among dismembered arms and legs. Candide fled to another village as fast as he could; it belonged to the Bulgarians, and Arabian heroes had treated it in the same way. Candide, stumbling over quivering limbs or across ruins, at last escaped from the theater of war.

SOURCE: Voltaire, *Candide* (1759).

---

theology of liberation *See* LIBERATION THEOLOGY.

thermonuclear Having to do with nuclear fusion weapons, more commonly called H-bombs or HYDROGEN BOMBS.

think tank An organization whose sole function is research, usually in the policy and behavioral sciences. Some of the better-known U.S. think tanks include the Brookings Institution, the Heritage Foundation, and the RAND Corporation. The purpose of think tanks is to identify options, assess policies, and generally contribute to the debate over public policies in ways that improve the quality of those policies. They began, at least on a large scale, as a particularly American phenomenon; but in Southeast Asia, for example, there are many institutes dealing with aspects of foreign policy and security in the region. These include the Center for Strategic and International Studies in Indonesia, the Institute for South East Asia Studies in Singapore, and the Institute of Strategic and International Studies in Malaysia. There are also many think tanks in Europe. The Royal Institute of International Affairs (CHATHAM HOUSE) in London, England, is a good example. There are similar institutes of international affairs in Bonn, Germany, The Hague, the Netherlands; Paris, France; and Rome, Italy. Cooperative linkages among these institutions grew considerably in the 1980s. London also acts as the base for the International Institute for Strategic Studies, which adopts an international rather than British perspective and focuses on security issues.

third-generation rights A term stemming from the argument that concern about human rights has gone from an initial emphasis on civil and political rights or the exercise of liberty, through an emphasis on economic and social rights through the promotion of equality, to a third generation of concerns involving the rights of particularly deprived groups—what George Shepherd in "The Tributary States and People's Rights in Africa" (*Africa Today* 32, nos. 1–2, 1985) describes as "the right to live and to achieve certain basic standards of existence" including peace, development, and a healthy environment.

Third International *See* INTERNATIONAL, THE.

Third Reich Germany from 1933 to 1945 when it was ruled by ADOLF HITLER and his NAZI party. *Reich* is German for "empire or nation." The first Reich was the medieval Holy Roman Empire, which was abolished by Napoleon I in 1806. The second Reich began in 1871 when Prussia united modern Germany. Hitler proclaimed a Third Reich to imply the beginning of a new era in Germany history—but at the same time to imply its historical continuity with the previous Reichs. As a regime the Third Reich set back the progressive course of European history. It was the direct cause of WORLD WAR II in Europe, of the terrorization of the European continent during the OCCUPATION, and the murder of millions of innocents through the HOLOCAUST. No fourth Reich has followed because "Reich" now implies the kind of aggressive militarism that is no longer internationally acceptable—at least in a rhetorical sense.

Third Republic The constitutional government of France between its defeat in the Franco-Prussian War of 1870 and the establishment of the FOURTH REPUBLIC in 1946 after defeat and occupation in World War II. After barely surviving the strain of victory in World War I, the Third Republic exhibited great instability during the interwar years (1918–1939) with 44 governments headed by 20 different prime ministers, including POINCARÉ,

BRIAND, LAVAL, DALADIER, BLUM, and REYNARD. After the German conquest in 1940, the republic was effectively suspended.

Third World **1.** Those states with underdeveloped but growing economies and low per capita incomes, often with colonial pasts. "Third World" is often used interchangeably with or as a synonym for LDCs (less developed countries), "the South," DEVELOPING COUNTRIES, or "underdeveloped countries." Ecuador, India, Morocco, and Nigeria are examples. In the 1970s a FOURTH WORLD was distinguished from the Third World to include those developing countries with little economic growth, few natural resources, slight financial reserves, and extremely low per capita incomes. Bangladesh, Ethiopia, and Sudan are examples. Third World has been commonly used since the BANDUNG CONFERENCE of 1955. **2.** The non-Western and non-Japanese world in general. The problem with this conception of the Third World is that it lumps relatively rich states, such as Singapore and South Korea, with the poor ones. Now that the Cold War is over and the SECOND WORLD of Communist Eastern Europe and the Soviet Union is seeking to break out into the FIRST WORLD of industrialized Western societies, the use of the term Third World is being challenged. Given the backwardness of the economies of many of the former Soviet republics, it is arguable that they have joined the Third World rather than provided potential candidates for the First World.

thirty-eighth parallel The line (latitude 38 degrees north) that divides North and South Korea. It was first established at the YALTA CONFERENCE in 1945 as a "temporary" division prior to unification. The Soviet Union accepted the surrender of the Japanese and established a military government north of the thirty-eighth parallel. The United States accepted the Japanese surrender south of the dividing line and also established an occupation regime. The selection of the thirty-eighth parallel as the dividing line between the Soviet occupation forces and those of the United States occurred almost as a spur-of-the-moment agreement on the part of the U.S. and Soviet commanders involved. Later, separate governments emerged on both sides of this line. During the KOREAN WAR it became U.S. and United Nations

The Thirty-eighth Parallel in Korea in 1950. (National Archives)

policy to prevent any successful invasion by the North Koreans south of the thirty-eighth parallel and eventually to restrict advances of UN forces north of the line to movements essential to maintaining their military position. After the signing of the Korean War cease-fire in July 1953, the thirty-eighth parallel remained the dividing line between North and South Korea.

Thirty-Five, the The members of the CONFERENCE ON SECURITY AND COOPERATION in Europe, which included the European members of the North Atlantic Treaty Organization and the Warsaw Pact as well as Canada and the United States. With the reunification of Germany the number of members was reduced to 34; but with the subsequent disintegration of the Soviet Union the CSCE increased to around 50 members.

Tho, Le Duc (1911–   ) The chief negotiator for the North Vietnamese at the Paris peace talks that led to the 1973 agreement between North Vietnam and the United States which ended the latter's role in the VIETNAM WAR. Both Tho and the chief U.S. negotiator, HENRY A. KISSINGER, were awarded the Nobel Peace Prize for 1973. But Tho declined to accept citing that peace in Vietnam was yet to be achieved.

threat 1. A danger posed by another state or alliance. Generally a threat in this sense results from the fact that another actor has hostile intentions, or at least a hostile disposition, together with the capabilities actually to inflict some kind of harm. 2. An expression of one's intent to do harm to another state or individual. DETERRENCE is based on the notion of a threat that will be implemented if certain actions regarded as prohibited or undesirable are taken by another state, especially if that state is already seen as an adversary. 3. The anticipated inventory of enemy weapons and capabilities. In the superpower context, the inventory is of nuclear weapons and their delivery systems as well as of decoys, penetration aids, and other countermeasures. Smaller powers also represent a threat, but on a different scale. Instead of major war the threat might be LOW-INTENSITY CONFLICT, TERRORISM, or a few nuclear weapons.

threat assessment Calculating the danger presented by another state; or more specifically, the threat posed by a particular action of that state. Such assessments are usually made on a worst-case basis. *Compare to* NET ASSESSMENT.

threshold *See* NUCLEAR THRESHOLD.

Threshold Test Ban Treaty A 1974 treaty signed by the United States and the Soviet Union that limited the size of nuclear devices that could be tested underground (the "threshold"). This agreement, reached at the conclusion of the first SALT talks, did not impose real limitations on the superpowers because most of the nuclear devices tested were nuclear-trigger mechanisms that create relatively small explosions. While the treaty had an initial duration of five years, it was never ratified by the U.S. Senate. But both sides have observed the treaty's limitations. *See also* PARTIAL TEST BAN TREATY; PEACEFUL NUCLEAR EXPLOSIONS TREATY.

throw-weight A measure of a missile's capacity to carry a military payload on a ballistic trajectory capable of hitting a target. The throw-weight that the missile can carry determines the size of its bus (or front end), and therefore the size and number of the warheads it physically can carry. Throw-weight is necessarily a very small part of the total weight of a missile; the bigger the missile, however, the greater is its throw-weight.

Thucydides (455–400 B.C.) An Athenian historian and political analyst whose *Peloponnesian War* remains one of the greatest studies of war and politics ever written. As a young man Thucydides probably took part in the war between Athens and Sparta, which began in 431 B.C. In 424 he was appointed general but failed to save the Athenian colony of Amphipolis from the Spartans. As a result of this failure, he was exiled for 20 years. It was during this period that he wrote the work for which he is still remembered. It provides not only a full account of the war between Athens and Sparta but also some immensely incisive and timeless observations on the great issues of war and peace, including one of the most famous observations on the basic cause of war: "What made war inevitable was the growth of Athenian power and the fear which this caused in Sparta." This one sentence recognizes what has subsequently been termed the SECURITY DILEMMA. There are, however, many other important elements in Thucydides' account of the war, including the famous MELIAN DIALOGUE and an analysis of power. It was he who observed that "into the discussion of human affairs the question of justice only enters where there is equal power to enforce it" and then concluded that "the powerful exact what they can, and the weak grant what they must." *See also* HEGEMONIC WAR.

Tiananmen Square A large open area in the middle of Beijing, China, where official ceremonies are often held. The square gained notoriety in the West in 1989 when the Chinese military brutally crushed a pro-democracy demonstration being held there. The student demonstration initially was occasioned by the funeral of HU YAOBANG in April 1989, Chinese Communist Party secretary general, whom the students considered a champion for reform and democracy. This sparked mass student demonstrations against party corruption, worsening living conditions at universities, and hyperinflation. The demonstrations soon escalated into a popular pro-democracy movement in Beijing, Shanghai, and other provincial centers. Despite government appeals to disperse, the demonstrations gathered strength during the summit visit of the Soviet President MIKHAIL GORBACHEV (May 15–17) and culminated in a sit-in and hunger strike in Tiananmen Square. Army units were then sent in. At first they confronted the demonstrators peacefully. On the dawn of July 4, however, the troops opened fire and tanks rolled into the square to disperse the crowd. It was estimated that 2,000 died and 9,000 were injured. Hundreds of students and workers were arrested and sentenced to long jail terms. The West was outraged. The U.S. and other Western governments temporarily applied economic sanctions against the Chinese government, including suspension of military sales.

tied development loan Money borrowed by THIRD WORLD governments from FIRST WORLD governments that, while it has lower than market interest rates, requires recipients to accept conditions on how the funds will be spent. For example, X percentage of the loan must be spent on goods in the lending state or shipped in the lending state's aircraft or ships.

TIGER (Terrorist Intelligence Gathering Evaluation and Review) A British government organization that seeks to centralize and coordinate antiterrorist operations in Great Britain. TIGER was established by Prime Minister Margaret Thatcher in 1984 and focuses on intelligence initiatives against the IRISH REPUBLICAN ARMY.

Tigers *See* LIBERATION TIGERS OF TAMIL EELAM.

tilt A foreign policy by which a third party leans toward one of two parties in a conflict without formally taking sides. During the 1980–1988 Iran-Iraq War, for example, the United States tilted toward Iraq at various junctures because it did not want Iran to win, take over the wealth of the Iraqi oil fields, and thus be in a position to threaten the oil-rich states of the Persian Gulf. Thus the United States indirectly made it possible for Iraq to get the military supplies and intelligence it needed to forestall a victory by Iran. A "tilt" is an inexpensive way of participating in a war without risking troops and maintaining a position of DENIABILITY in case the other side wins.

Titanic The British passenger liner that sank on its maiden voyage across the Atlantic Ocean after striking an iceberg on the night of April 14–15, 1912. One of many reasons why 1,563 of the 2,224 passengers drowned was that the ship did not carry enough lifeboats for all passengers. The disaster resulted in the 1913 International Convention for Safety of Life at Sea, which required all ships to have enough lifeboat space for each passenger, required lifeboat drills, and required that ships maintain a 24-hour radio watch (to hear distress signals).

Tito, Josip Broz (1892–1980)　The leader of Yugoslavia from 1945 until his death. After gaining military experience on the winning side of the Russian Revolution of 1917 and then the losing side of the Spanish Civil War, Tito, a lifelong Communist organizer, was in an excellent position to organize the partisan opposition to German occupation of Yugoslavia in World War II. His National Liberation Front was the only local guerrilla army in Europe to liberate itself from the Germans. Yugoslavia then became the only European country to create a one-party Communist state on its own, without aid and support from the Soviet Union. In 1945 Tito became premier and minister of national defense in a new coalition government. His emphasis on an umbrella Yugoslav nationalism led to the country's expulsion from the SOVIET BLOC of Eastern European countries by Soviet Premier Joseph Stalin in 1948. Defying Stalin's orders, Tito devised a governing system that encouraged worker participation and self-management, instead of relying on more rigid socialist practices. Tito, who became president of Yugoslavia in 1953, emerged as a major neutralist leader and a founder of the NONALIGNED MOVEMENT. While he established a collective leadership to succeed him, a decade later the federation of Yugoslavia—which had been held together by Tito's strong personality—degenerated into the YUGOSLAVIAN CIVIL WAR.

Titoism　The unique version of socialism developed in Yugoslavia under JOSIP BROZ TITO. Domestically Titoism, in contrast to the totalitarian control espoused by Soviet-style MARXISM, emphasized worker participation in the management of factories and in many other aspects of economic and social life. Internationally, Titoism, again against the wishes of the Soviet Union, became a policy of neutralism pursued by a small country in an international world dominated by great powers.

Josip Broz Tito (Library of Congress)

Tlatelolco, Treaty of　The treaty that prohibited nuclear weapons in Latin America, signed by 21 Latin American states at Tlatelolco, Mexico, in 1967. It forbids the development or deployment of nuclear weapons in Latin America, the Caribbean, and the territorial waters of the states concerned. The treaty established an *Organismo para la Proscripcion de los Armas Nucleares en la América Latina* ("Agency for the Prohibition of Nuclear Weapons in Latin America," or OPANAL) in Mexico City to supervise compliance with its terms. States outside the region were excluded from the treaty proper, but the nuclear powers were invited to adhere to two added protocols. Protocol I requested them not to place nuclear weapons in their dependencies within the treaty zone. In Protocol II, outside powers were asked to respect Latin

America as a NUCLEAR-FREE ZONE. The United States became a party to Protocol II in 1971 and to Protocol I in 1981. France also signed both protocols. All the other major nuclear powers (China, the Soviet Union, and the United Kingdom) have signed Protocol II. Tlatelolco was the first treaty to ban nuclear weapons from an inhabited part of the world.

TNC *See* MULTINATIONAL CORPORATION.

Tōjō, Hidocki (1884–1948) The Japanese general who, upon becoming prime minister of Japan in October 1941, approved war plans against British, Dutch, French, and United States territories in the Pacific, which began with the attack on Pearl Harbor of December 7, 1941. After being tried by the postwar International Military Tribunal for the Far East, he was executed as a war criminal in 1948.

Tokyo Convention The 1963 international agreement, signed by more than 100 states, that requires the safe release of hijacked aircraft and the crew and passengers aboard them. It did not specifically deal with the punishment of the hijackers. *Compare to* MONTREAL CONVENTION.

Tokyo International Military Tribunal The International Military Tribunal for the Far East, created in 1946 to try WORLD WAR II Japanese war criminals. This Pacific region counterpart to the NUREMBERG TRIALS convicted 25 Japanese military and political leaders. Seven of the defendants were executed in 1948; all others were included in an amnesty granted by U.S. General Douglas MacArthur. The chief justice of the tribunal, William Webb of Australia, in his sentencing statement of November 4, 1948, noted his regret that Japanese Emperor HIROHITO, at U.S. insistence, did not stand trial as well: "The emperor perhaps did not want war, but he approved of it and everything else depended on it. He misused his duties, even if it were true that in case of his refusal he was to be murdered. A ruler has to risk his life if he is willing to save his people and country from a war. Thus, the Emperor has to be recognized as the most guilty of the crime." According to Chuo University (Japan) history professor Yoshiaki Yoshimi, "At the Tokyo trials, only a small number in the military and the bureaucracy were tried for their part in the war, leaving the majority of wartime leaders either immune from prosecution or freed from custody. By thrusting the full responsibility onto the few who were executed, the Japanese effectively absolved themselves of any blame" (*New York Times,* March 11, 1992).

Tokyo Rose (1916–) The nickname of a U.S. woman, Iva Ikuko Toguri D'Aquino, who broadcast Japanese radio propaganda during WORLD WAR II to U.S. troops in the South Pacific. Convicted of treason in the United States after the war's end, she was sent to prison for six years. Decades later U.S. President Gerald Ford formally pardoned her, believing that she had been forced to make the broadcasts.

TOKYO ROSE IN ACTION

The battle of Okinawa began on Easter Sunday, April 1st [1945]. [Our U.S. Air Force squadron] heard about it . . . standing around outside of the ready room, where a loudspeaker had been hung on palm tree. Tokyo Rose told us that the assault forces had landed, but had been repulsed; many ships had been sunk. On the second day she addressed our squadron specifically; she knew that 232 was coming, she said, but they would be ready for us. I felt ridiculously melodramatic, standing there being threatened on the radio; it was like stumbling onto the set of a B-grade spy movie, where an Oriental hisses, "Yankee dog, you die!" But I also felt a bit important—at least in Tokyo they had heard of us.

SOURCE: Samuel Hynes, *Flights of Passage* (1988).

Tokyo Round The GATT trade negotiations formally initiated by the 1973 Tokyo Declaration but actually held in Geneva, Switzerland. The Tokyo Round, also called the "Multilateral Trade Negotiations," differed from the previous GATT negotiations in that more states, including several Eastern European ones, attended and greater efforts were made to eliminate, reduce, or discipline nontariff measures that restrict trade as well as tariffs—especially those that impeded the expansion of international trade in agricultural goods. The agenda for the talks, which were attended by over 90 states, placed special emphasis on the export needs of DEVELOPING COUNTRIES and also included discussions on NONTARIFF BARRIERS to trade, trade in agricultural goods, and trade PROTECTIONISM. The talks were concluded on April 12, 1979, when 23 states initialed a comprehensive trade agreement designed to reduce tariffs an average of 33 percent over the following eight years and that established new codes of conduct regarding nontariff barriers to trade.

Tonkin Gulf Resolution *See* GULF OF TONKIN RESOLUTION.

Tonton Macoute In Haitian Creole, "Uncle Knapsack," a folk figure who steals children; the nickname of the *Voluntaires de la Sécurité* ("Volunteers for National Security") of Haiti. Established by Haitian strongman François "Papa Doc" DUVALIER upon his ascent to power in 1957, it was originally to provide an alternative source of armed power to the army. But soon the Tonton Macoute became more powerful than the regular military forces. The brutally violent force traditionally has been used to keep both the military and political opposition in check. The organization was officially disbanded in 1985 but still exists in secret groups, emerging intermittently to commit heinous acts of TERRORISM.

Torrijos, Omar (1929–1981) The military dictator of Panama (1968–1981) who negotiated the PANAMA CANAL TREATIES that will return the control of the Canal Zone to Panama by the end of this century. Torrijos's death in a plane crash deprived Panama of a charismatic leader whose populist domestic programs and nationalist foreign policy had broad appeal. He was succeeded by a military triumvirate headed by MANUEL NORIEGA.

totalitarianism A system of government in which a dominating elite holds all power and controls all aspects of society. Opposition is not allowed; power is maintained by internal terror and secret police. The early twentieth century saw a rise of totalitarianism with Nazi Germany, the Soviet Union under Joseph Stalin, and Fascist Italy as examples of totalitarian states. *Compare to* AUTHORITARIANISM; FASCISM; MARXISM.

TOTALITARIAN LIES

From the totalitarian point of view, history is something to be created rather than learned. A totalitarian state is in effect a theocracy, and its ruling caste, in order to keep its position, has to be thought of as infallible. But since, in practice, no one is infallible, it is frequently necessary to rearrange past events in order to show that this or that mistake was not made. . . . Then again, every major change in policy demands a corresponding change of doctrine and a reevaluation of prominent historical figures. This kind of thing happens everywhere, but is clearly likelier to lead to outright falsification in societies where only one opinion is permissible at any given moment. Totalitarianism demands, in fact, the continuous alteration of the past, and in the long run probably demands a disbelief in the very existence of objective truth.

SOURCE: George Orwell, *Inside the Whale and Other Essays* (1940).

---

total war 1. A conflict that threatens the survival of a nation in which all weapons are used. 2. A war effort that mobilizes all sectors of a state's economy. KARL VON CLAUSEWITZ first used this term in this sentence from his *On War* (1832): "The whole art of war is being transformed into mere prudence, with the primary aim of preventing the uncertain balance from shifting suddenly to our disadvantage and half-war from developing into total war." The term has come to be used to describe the kinds of wars that occurred during World War I and II. Total wars are most often contrasted with LIMITED WARS, which are fought for very specific military objectives and involve limited means. A major problem with the use of these terms is that of perspective. From the viewpoint of the United States, the VIETNAM WAR was limited; but from the perspective of North Vietnam, it involved all the energies of the state and, at least in relation to South Vietnam, was fought for the overthrow of the enemy. Similarly the IRAN-IRAQ WAR was more or less a total war from the perspective of the two states involved, but from the perspective of the international system it was clearly limited. It was B. D. Liddell Hart in *The Revolution in Warfare* (1946) who first made the case that total war is no longer possible for major powers: "When both sides possess atomic power, '*total* warfare' makes nonsense. Total warfare implies that the aim, the effort, and the degree of violence are unlimited. Victory is pursued without regard to the consequences. . . . Any unlimited war waged with atomic power would be worse than nonsense; it would be mutually suicidal."

tour d'horizon 1. A French term for a general overview of something. 2. A diplomatic meeting that covers most or all of a large number of all possible topics.

tous azimuts French for "all horizons." The French use this term to indicate that its nuclear weapons are pointed "in all directions." This doctrine was first pronounced in 1967 when the FORCE DE FRAPPE was first being deployed, and France was pulling out of the integrated military organization of the North Atlantic Treaty Organization. The French believed that because nuclear weapons were a major source of influence in the world, France had to have the capability to threaten the use of them on a large scale to enhance its reputation. Although based on President Charles de Gaulle's political and diplomatic thought, the military strategy itself was developed by General Charles Ailleret (1907–1968). For this reason it is sometimes called the *Ailleret Doctrine*. Rather than orienting French missiles in a specific direction, Ailleret explained that they had to "be capable of intervening everywhere, or as we say in our military jargon, at every point of the compass (*tous azimuts*)" (*New York Times,* December 1, 1967). Throughout the COLD WAR French nuclear capabilities continued to be directed primarily at the Soviet Union, and it was clear that *tous azimuts* had more to do with political independence than military planning. Now that the Cold War is over, France can be expected to develop a new targeting policy.

Tower Commission The President's Special Review Board established by U.S. President Ronald Reagan in the fall of 1986 to investigate the IRAN-CONTRA AFFAIR and the operations of the National Security Council. The commission, named for its chairman, John G. Tower (1925–1990), former U.S. senator from Texas, found that President Reagan had been "disengaged" and "did not seem to be aware" of the White House foreign policy process; that the National Security Council had indeed arranged to trade arms for hostages with Iran and sought to use funds from the arms sale to illegally aid the CONTRAS in Nicaragua; and that certain members of the White House staff sought to cover up these facts as the Iran-contra affair evolved.

Toynbee, Arnold J. (1889–1975) The British historian whose *A Study of History* (12 vols., 1934–1961) attempted to account for the rise and fall not of nations but of civilizations. Toynbee explained this largely in terms of civilizations' responses to challenges and subsequent lack of creativity, which makes them vulnerable to a new rising civilization on the periphery. He recommended that this could be prevented in today's world by a revitalization of Christianity, which would provide the basis for the establishment of a world state and world civilization. Toynbee's analytic construct, once extremely popular, has since fallen out of fashion.

trade, balance of *See* BALANCE OF TRADE.

trade adjustment assistance *See* ADJUSTMENT ASSISTANCE.

trade credits Loans by banks, corporations, or governments to finance the purchase of specific exports.

trade deficit *See* BALANCE OF TRADE.

trade diversion A shift in the source of an import, which occurs as a result of altering a state's import policies or practices without regard for any increase in importation of the item or items involved. For example, the establishment of a customs union will cause states participating in the new economic unit to import goods from other states in the union that previously were imported from states outside the union. According to some trade theorists, if the "trade creation" resulting from the customs union—that is, the new trade taking place that would not have taken place otherwise—exceeds the "trade diversion" it creates, the customs union will raise the general welfare, because it will entail a more efficient allocation of resources.

tradeoff A situation in which a decision maker pursues objectives or values that are not completely compatible and in which a little of one must be sacrificed in order to achieve a little more of the other. Tradeoffs are generally made at the margin, so that some combination of the objectives is still achieved.

trade restriction Anything that governments do to inhibit the free flow of goods across international borders, such as embargoes, health and safety regulations, quotas to protect domestic industries, tariffs, and so on.

trade surplus *See* BALANCE OF TRADE.

traditionalism An approach to INTERNATIONAL RELATIONS that values the study of history, that places great emphasis on wisdom and intuition, and that rejects many of the approaches that developed in the United States as a result of the emphasis on the behavioral sciences. In essence this was an argument over methodology. It also is sometimes referred to as the *classical approach* to international politics. Although the debate between the scientists and the traditionalists, which came to a head in the late 1960s, was more polarized than was warranted, it did highlight the fact that not all scholars thought applying scientific methods to the study of international relations was particularly appropriate or profitable. The traditionalist argument was expressed most forcefully by Hedley Bull in "International Theory: The Case for a Classical Approach" (*World Politics* 18, April 1966), who argued that by emphasizing quantification, strict logic, and scientific proof and denying themselves the benefits of intuition or wisdom, the proponents of the scientific approach would remain "as remote from the substance of international politics as the inmates of a Victorian nunnery were from the study of sex." Bull's remarks were directed at foreign policy analysts who viewed quantification, BEHAVIORISM, and SYSTEMS ANALYSIS as important means of obtaining greater knowledge about international relations.

tragedy of the commons A story used to illustrate the principle that the maximization of private gain will not result in the maximization of social benefit. When herders sought to maximize their individual gain by adding ever increasing numbers of cattle to a common pasture, the common was overgrazed. The resulting tragedy was that no one was able to use the common effectively for grazing. The concepts involved with the tragedy of the commons apply to societal problems such as pollution and overpopulation and the idea of the COMMON GOOD. Garrett Hardin, in "The Tragedy of the Commons" (*Science,* December 13, 1968), wrote: "Ruin is the destination toward which all men rush, each pursuing his own best interest in a society that believes in the freedom of the commons. Freedom in a commons brings ruin to all."

traitor *See* TREASON.

transaction flows Communications that proceed from one political system to another. Generally included are such things as mail, migration, student exchanges, telephone traffic, tourism, and trade. These transactions have been studied by KARL DEUTSCH and others in relation to integration in Western Europe in *The Integration of Political Communities* (1964).

transaction statement A trading document that delineates the terms and conditions agreed upon between an importer and an exporter.

transborder data flow The transportation of large volumes of information over great distances and across national boundaries, made possible by the merger of modern computer and communications technologies. Activities such as the booking of international airlines reservations, the making of international banking transfers, and the management of multinational corporations depend heavily on rapid international communication. Many states have enacted data protection laws to regulate both governmental and international access to their citizens' business and private records stored in computers. The Organization for Economic Cooperation and Development and the Council of Europe are attempting to establish international standards for transborder data flows; in the United States, the Congress, the State Department, the Department of Commerce, and the computer and communications industries also have been active in the consideration of these issues.

transboundary pollution Environmental contamination that originates within the borders of one state while its damage falls on the people and their physical surroundings in another state. The common types of transboundary pollution include ACID RAIN, export of hazardous wastes, release of stratospheric ozone-depleting chemicals, and emission of greenhouse gases that are thought to cause GLOBAL WARMING.

transformation *See* ADOPTION, DOCTRINE OF.

transgovernmental relations Relations between government departments in one state and those in another, which tend to remain informal even though they are fairly regular. Such relations cut across the traditional distinction between domestic and foreign policies, and help the participating departments deal with the increasingly complex issues that face them. For example, Interpol facilitates transgovernmental relations by helping criminal investigative agencies exchange information.

transit duty *See* DUTY, TRANSIT.

transit zone A port of entry in a coastal state that is established as a storage and distribution center for the convenience of a neighboring state that lacks adequate port facilities or access to the sea. It is so administered that goods in transit to and from the neighboring state are not subject to the customs duties, import controls, or many of the entry and exit formalities of the host state. For example, the Baltic nations seek to serve as transit zones between Western Europe and Russia. A transit zone is a more limited facility than either a FREE PORT or a FREE TRADE ZONE.

Transjordan The Arab emirate created by Great Britain in 1921 from parts of the former Ottoman Empire on the eastern bank of the Jordan River. Great Britain exercised power there under the MAN-DATES SYSTEM of the League of Nations. After the expiration of the mandate in 1946, Transjordan became an independent kingdom. In 1949 it changed its name to the Hashemite Kingdom of Jordan, the name it retains today under King HUSSEIN IBN TALAL.

transnational **1.** Descriptive of an enterprise, entity, idea, movement, or religion that crosses national boundaries and provides some kind of linkage between individuals, groups, or organizations in one state and individuals, groups, or organizations in another. Because things that are transnational cross the boundaries of a state, they are not easy for governments to control. **2.** A term used to describe actors in international relations who operate across state boundaries, usually in a specific area of activity or in relation to a particular function. Such actors include terrorist groups, corporations that have their headquarters in one country but operate in others, religious movements such as Islam or the Roman Catholic Church, and drug traffickers based in South America or Southeast Asia who sell their products in many different nations. *Compare to* NONGOVERN-MENTAL ORGANIZATIONS.

transnationalism **1.** The growing importance in international relations of TRANSNATIONAL actors, forces, and interactions. **2.** An emphasis on transnational factors in the study of international relations.

transnational relations The sum of the interactions between private individuals and groups that cross international boundaries.

transnational terrorism International TERRORISM; terrorism created by citizens of one state in another state; terrorism that crosses borders without the help of governments. If a government helps the terrorists, it then becomes state-controlled or STATE-SPONSORED TERRORISM.

transparency A term relating to military actions taken in an open way and subject to observation and monitoring, thereby providing reassurance to other states that there is no attempt to achieve strategic or tactical surprise. In the latter half of the 1980s emphasis was placed on making military activities in Europe increasingly transparent, thereby adding to security and stability.

treason   1. Violating the allegiance one owes to one's state. A person who does this is known as a *traitor*. 2. Rebellion; seeking to overthrow one's own state's legitimate government.   3. Treachery and disloyalty of various kinds. Treason was first defined by statute in the English Treason Act of 1351, which made it a crime punishable by death to conspire to or actually harm the sovereign (or his or her spouse and heirs), to levy war against the sovereign, to murder certain high government officials (such as the chancellor or the treasurer), or to sexually violate the women of the royal family. While amended in 1795, 1848, and 1945, this, in essence, is still the law in the United Kingdom. Treason is the only crime defined by the U.S. Constitution. Article III, Section 3, states that it "shall consist only in levying War against [the United States], or in adhering to their enemies, giving them aid and comfort. No person shall be convicted of treason unless on the testimony of two witnesses to the same overt act, or on confession in open court." The precise description of the offense in this document reflects an awareness that persons holding merely unpopular views might be branded as traitors. Recent experience in other states (such as NAZI Germany or the Soviet Union under JOSEPH STALIN) with prosecutions for conduct loosely labeled as treason confirms the wisdom of the authors of the Constitution in expressly stating what constitutes this crime and how it shall be proved. It was John Harington (1561–1612), an Elizabethan courtier in Great Britain, who wrote the famous epigram on treason:

> *Treason doth never prosper:*
> *what's the reason?*
> *For if it prosper, none dare*
> *call it treason.*

treason, high   Violating the allegiance one owes to one's state, as opposed to petit (meaning small) treason—the killing of someone to whom one would traditionally owe obedience (such as a husband or overlord). Petit treason, never a specific crime in the United States, was abolished in the United Kingdom in 1828. Ever since, such crimes have been treated as any other murder.

treaty   A formal agreement between two or more states that establishes both rights and obligations for the parties. There are two schools of thought on treaties: The interest school asserts, as Napoleon I said in his *Military Maxims* (1827): "Treaties are observed as long as they are in harmony with interests." Washington Irving, U.S. diplomat and author, agreed; he wrote in *Diedrich Knickerbocker's History of New York* (1809) that: "Treaties at best are but complied with so long as interest requires their fulfillment. Consequently, they are virtually binding on the weaker party only; or, in plain truth, they are not binding at all." Richard Humble in *Hitler's Generals* (1974) quotes Adolf Hitler: "There has never been a sworn treaty which has not sooner or later been broken or become untenable. . . . Why should I not make an agreement in good faith today and unhesitatingly break it tomorrow . . . ?" And President Charles de Gaulle of France took a more philosophic view: "Treaties are like roses and young girls. They last while they last" (*Time,* July 12, 1963).

Then there are those statesman who rebel at the stain on national honor that the breaking of a treaty implies. The classic example comes from the beginning of World War I. German Chancellor Theobald von Bethmann-Hollweg, speaking to British Ambassador Sir Edward Goshen on August 4, 1914, on Britain's declaration of war against Germany because of the German invasion of neutral Belgium, said: "Just for a word—'neutrality,' a word which in wartime has so often been disregarded—just for a scrap of paper, Great Britain is going to make war on a kindred nation which desires nothing better than to be friends with her" (*New York Times,* August 19, 1914). This scrap-of-paper image has been a constant theme in international relations ever since. For example, U.S. President Dwight D. Eisenhower said in a speech on March 16, 1959: "We have no intention of forgetting our rights or of deserting a free people. Soviet rulers should remember that free men have, before this, died for so-called 'scraps of paper' which represented duty and honor and freedom." President Ronald Reagan took a slightly different approach in a speech at West Point on May 27, 1981: "No nation that placed its faith in parchment paper, while at the same time it gave up its protective hardware, ever lasted long enough to write many pages in history."

The essential problem with obligations to honor the terms of a treaty is that they are inherently unenforceable without resorting to international sanctions or the threat of war. Unlike with a domestic business contract, the negligent party—a sovereign state—cannot be forced into compliance by a court order. International law does apply. Thus treaties that violate the obligations of member states under the United Nations Charter, much like contracts to commit a crime, are invalid. But unless a state agrees to ARBITRATION, it is free to interpret treaty terms in its interests. The desirability for international COMITY means that almost all states will meet their treaty obligations—but there is no legal process to force them to do so.

Once a treaty is negotiated, typically it is signed subject to ratification by a legislature or monarch. At that point TREATY RESERVATIONS, changes in the text, can be added. If a treaty is not ratified, it does not take effect and has no legal force. However, such as with the THRESHOLD TEST-BAN TREATY, both sides may comply with a treaty that is not formally ratified because it is in their interest to do so.

LLOYD GEORGE DENOUNCES THE DOCTRINE OF THE SCRAP OF PAPER

What is a treaty, says the German Chancellor, but a scrap of paper? Have you any £5 notes about you? Have you any of those neat little Treasury one-pound notes? If you have, burn them. They are only scraps of paper. What are they made of? Rags! What are they worth? The whole credit of the British Empire. . . .

Treaties are the currency of international statesmanship. German merchants, German traders have the reputation of being as upright and straightforward as any traders in the world, but if the currency of German commerce is to be debased to the level of that of her statesmanship no trader from Shanghai to Valparaiso will ever look at a German signature again. That is the doctrine of the scrap of paper; that is the doctrine which is proclaimed by Bernhardi—that treaties only bind a nation as long as it is to its interest. It goes to the root of all public law. It is the straight road to barbarism. . . . There is only one way of putting it right. If there are nations that say they will only respect treaties when it is to their interest to do so, we must make it to their interest to do so.

SOURCE: David Lloyd George, speech at Queen's Hall, London, on September 21, 1914.

Treaty of . . . *See* location of treaty negotiation. For example, for the Treaty of Rome *see* ROME, TREATY OF.

treaty reservation An annex to a treaty that states that it is being ratified only with certain conditions not contained in the original document. International law is unclear whether all of the other parties to the treaty must then agree to the reservation.

trench warfare The extended positioning of opposing armies in parallel protective earthworks over a wide front. This kind of warfare, by which troops would go "over the top" of their trenches to attack enemy trenches across "no-man's land," was used extensively in World War I. The essential stalemate in Western Europe for the first years of the war was caused by the fact that trenches on both sides proved to be extremely effective defensive positions—especially when machine guns prevented the enemy from getting across no-man's land. The modern tank was invented specifically to break this kind of stalemated warfare.

Trevi group The popular name of the EUROPEAN COMMUNITY's working group of interior and justice ministers, formed at the suggestion of former British Prime Minister Harold Wilson at the 1975 European Council at Trevi, Italy. The group, which now includes a delegation from the United States, deals with issues of extradition, organized crime, and terrorism.

triad 1. The three parts of the U.S. nuclear deterrent: land-based intercontinental ballistic missiles, submarine-launched ballistic missiles, and long-range strategic bombers. This diversification was originally intended to ensure the strongest possible defense and to disperse the attention of the enemy, the Soviet Union; each system was thought to be capable of an independent retaliatory counterstrike against the enemy. But the increasing number and sophistication of Soviet nuclear weapons in the late 1970s reopened the discussion of the ability of each part of the triad to withstand a Soviet first strike. The SCOWCROFT COMMISSION report, in effect, defined the problem away. The Soviet Union's nuclear deterrent force relied mainly on land-based intercontinental ballistic missiles and submarine-launched ballistic missiles. While it had long-range bombers, it never developed a nuclear bomber force comparable to the U.S. STRATEGIC AIR COMMAND. **2.** The North Atlantic Treaty Organization's array of strategic nuclear forces, theater nuclear forces, and conventional forces.

Trianon, Treaty of   The 1920 peace agreement between the victorious allies of World War I and the new republic of Hungary by which three-quarters of the territory that belonged to Hungary when it was part of the AUSTRO-HUNGARIAN EMPIRE was distributed to Czechoslovakia, Italy, Poland, Romania, and Yugoslavia. Thus the population of Hungary dropped from 21 to 8 million. The treaty also made Hungary responsible for REPARATIONS and mandated that the Hungarian Army could not exceed 35,000 men. The treaty was deeply resented by Hungarians. Consequently, Hungary's interwar foreign policy focused on revising it. *See also* PARIS PEACE CONFERENCE.

tributary state   A concept used by George Shepherd in "The Tributary States and People's Rights in Africa" (*Africa Today* 32, nos. 1–2, 1985) to refer to the status of most African states, which he sees as caught in the rivalry between the United States and the Soviet Union and also as suffering from the inequalities that result from the international capitalist system. The argument is that African states have very limited control over the forces that influence their economies and their security. In Shepherd's view, "They have enormous power over the lives of their own citizens in an increasingly military and repressive way; but their capacity to restructure their economies and to provide for their own security is dependent upon the centers of world power." Critics argued that Shepherd's argument exaggerated the impact of the Cold War on Africa, especially given the fact that—apart from Angola and conflict between Ethiopia and Somalia—the continent has not been a major focus of superpower competition. Although it is possible to agree with Shepherd about the conditions faced by most African states, this is more a result of the colonial legacy than the Cold War. Consequently, the end of the Cold War is unlikely to have much impact on those conditions. *Compare to* NEOCOLONIALISM.

trickle-down development   *See* BOTTOM-UP DEVELOPMENT.

Trident   The most recent development of U.S. submarine-launched ballistic missiles. It can carry multiple independently targeted reentry vehicles (MIRVs) and has greater accuracy than earlier SLBMs. The Trident missile, initially known as the Undersea Long Range Missile System (ULMS), has two variants. The first is the Trident 1 or the C4 missile, which has a range of around 7,400 kilometers and carries up to eight 100-kiloton warheads. The second variant is the Trident D5 which has a range close to 10,000 kilometers, a capacity to carry 14 warheads, and considerably improved accuracy. Because it was capable of destroying Soviet ICBMs, liberal critics argued that it was a COUNTERFORCE weapon. One result of U.S. President George Bush and Russian President Boris Yeltsin's 1993 START II agreement, however, is that a ceiling of 1,750 warheads on SLBMs is to be met by the year 2003. This will require that the United States cut its number of SLBM warheads by over 50 percent.

trigger thesis   A justification for the role of small strategic forces, such as those of France and Great Britain, against the charge that they were too insignificant to have credibility as deterrents. The argument went that these small forces got their power not from what they could do themselves in a battle with the Soviet Union, but by their ability to "trigger" a supporting strike by the United States. The trigger thesis made sense during the COLD WAR but has become irrelevant with its end.

Trilateral Commission   An organization based in New York in the United States of several hundred private citizens from Japan, North America, and Western Europe that was created in 1973 for the purpose of debating the common economic, political, and security issues of the three regions. Many of the commission's activities make use of the number three: It meets for three days every nine months, rotating among the trilateral regions; its newsletter is called the *Trialogue;* and its task force produces reports called Triangle Papers. The commission's overall goal is to foster economic cooperation and improve public understanding of the problems that each region faces. It has been a strong supporter of the URUGUAY ROUND of the GATT and constantly explores issues, such as Third World development, on which the elites of the three regions can cooperate.

trilateralism **1.** The totality of the economic and security relationships among Japan, the United States, and Western Europe. This partnership is based on the assumption that coordination among these industrialized countries is necessary to counter the demands of the NORTH-SOUTH DIALOGUE and the possibility of threats from anywhere in the world. Trilateralism has been manifest in the Organization for Economic Cooperation and Development and in the economic summits of the mid-1970s. **2.** A reference to the political and strategic triangle in the Middle East of Egypt, Saudi Arabia, and Syria.

Tripartite Declaration A joint 1950 statement by France, Great Britain, and the United States that dealt with the right of both Israel and the surrounding Arab countries to maintain prescribed military force levels, limitations on arms transfers to Middle East states, and maintenance of official armistice boundaries in the area. This was relevant only in the immediate post–World War II period when France, Great Britain, and the United States were the only external powers that could project military force into the Middle East. The actions of France and Great Britain during the 1956 SUEZ CRISIS effectively nullified the declaration; these two states conspired with Israel to violate the international borders of Egypt, which the declaration said should be respected.

Tripartite Pact *See* AXIS.

Triple Alliance The agreement among Austria-Hungary, Germany, and Italy that was created in 1882 and renewed every five years until WORLD WAR I. It grew out of an 1879 alliance between Austria-Hungary and Germany for mutual aid in case either was attacked by Russia. While Italy, which wanted to pursue colonial expansion, joined in 1882, in 1914, at the beginning of World War I, it reneged on its treaty commitment and joined the opposing group of allies (the TRIPLE ENTENTE).

Triple Entente The pre–WORLD WAR I military alliance of France, Great Britain, and Russia. In 1894

France and Russia joined in a mutual defense alliance that ended French diplomatic isolation. At the time, some were surprised that archconservative czarist Russia would join with liberal France. This defensive alliance required each party to aid the other if Austria or Germany was an aggressor against either. Amid a tense naval race with Germany, Britain entered an Entente Cordiale with France in 1904. With this agreement, the British left the naval defense of the Mediterranean to French forces. In 1907 the French brought Britain together with Russia to resolve issues over Afghanistan and Iran. Taken together, the agreements of 1894, 1904, and 1907 created the Triple Entente, which faced the Central Powers of Germany and Austria-Hungary in World War I.

tripolarity A situation in which three great powers dominate global politics. It is contrasted with BIPOLARITY, where there are two great powers, and MULTIPOLARITY, which is usually used to refer to a situation of five or more great world powers. The term was sometimes used to describe the rise of China to join the Soviet Union and the United States as SUPERPOWERS. Although there was some expectation that the bipolar system might evolve into a tripolar one, this never really happened because China remained so far behind the other two powers, technologically and economically. Some analysts of the international system argue that a tripolar international system is the least stable kind, as there would always be a temptation for two of the powers to ally against the third. But in historical fact, such a system has never existed—so no one really knows for sure.

tripwire **1.** A wire connected to explosives and so placed that an approaching enemy will hit it accidentally and thus be injured or alert one's forces. **2.** By analogy, a military force situated on a line of defense that is not expected to be able to hold off a major enemy assault but whose function is to buy time so that reserves can be brought into the battle or decisions can be made to use tactical or strategic nuclear weapons. The U.S. forces stationed in Europe and Korea are often referred to as tripwires. C. L. Sulzberger in *The Last of the Giants* (1970) quotes British Field Marshal Bernard L. Montgomery speaking on March 22, 1963, on just how a "tripwire" would work: "It would be a good idea to have just a few Americans and British in the front line to get killed right away if the Russians attack, just to bring everybody in immediately. I used to say when I was at [the North Atlantic Treaty Organization] that I would shoot an American myself if a war started, just to make sure." **3.** The NATO COLD WAR strategy that called for a nuclear response by the United States if the Soviets invaded Western Europe. This notion was based on the assumption that NATO was, first and foremost, a unilateral guarantee pact in which the United States provided a NUCLEAR UMBRELLA for Western Europe. This assumption was contrasted with the capacity for sustained conventional resistance—a concept based on the assumption that NATO is not a unilateral guarantee pact but a collective defense organization in which deterrence was best achieved not through threats of nuclear escalation but by the ability to deny the Soviet Union its objectives at the same level as its initial aggression.

triumvirate **1.** The joint leadership of Antony, Lepidus, and Octavian in ancient Rome. **2.** By analogy, joint rule by any three persons. *Compare to* TROIKA.

troika A Russian word for "a carriage drawn by three horses," which has come into English to mean any leadership shared by three people, three organizations, three countries, and so on. In 1960 the Soviet Union advocated that a three-person troika replace the office of the secretary general of the United Nations. Since this proposal was essentially made only to oppose the policies of then–Secretary General DAG HAMMERSKJÖLD, it was dropped after his death in 1961. *Compare to* TRIUMVIRATE.

Trojan horse **1.** From Homer's epic poem *The Iliad*, a large, hollow wooden horse that Greek soldiers hid inside as it was pulled within the walls of the city of Troy. At nightfall the Greek soldiers came out of the horse, opened the gates of the city to their allies waiting outside, and conquered Troy. Ever since, the Trojan horse has been a symbol of wily deception. **2.** A state that sabotages an international organization from inside. French President Charles de Gaulle claimed in the 1960s that Great Britain would be America's Trojan Horse in the EUROPEAN COMMUNITY. This was one reason de Gaulle vetoed Britain's first application to join the Community in 1963.

Trotsky, Leon (1879–1940) The Russian revolutionary (born Lev D. Bronstein) who founded and led the RED ARMY during the RUSSIAN CIVIL WAR. He was the principal opponent to JOSEPH STALIN following the death of V. I. LENIN. Trotsky held the position of people's commissar for foreign relations (1917–1918) in the new Soviet government and then was commissar for war (1918–1925) until Stalin dismissed him. Formally exiled from the Soviet Union in 1929, Trotsky eventually moved from Europe to Mexico, where he worked to oppose Stalin and Stalinism both within and outside the Soviet Union and attempted to establish a Fourth INTERNATIONAL. Trotsky was a strong advocate of INTERNATIONALISM and consequently opposed to Stalin's idea of SOCIALISM IN ONE COUNTRY. He was assassinated by Stalinist agents of SMERSH in Mexico City in 1940.

Trotskyite **1.** An adherent to Leon Trotsky's view that Communist revolutions should be continuously pressed worldwide. Joseph Stalin, in contrast, believed it was more expedient to advocate the principle of SOCIALISM IN ONE COUNTRY at a time. **2.** Someone who holds far-left political views. Trotskyites, or "trots," tend to be the most uncompromising of Communists.

truce A short ARMISTICE. An armistice usually denotes a complete end to hostilities; a truce is usually of much shorter duration and may involve little more than a temporary suspension of hostilities. A truce can occur for various reasons, such as to allow enemy forces to remove their wounded or to facilitate negotiations about the possible cessation of hostilities.

trucial states A former name for the present Persian Gulf confederation of the United Arab Emirates. They were called "trucial" because in the nineteenth century the British negotiated treaties among their various rulers.

Trudeau, Pierre Elliott (1919–) The Canadian Liberal Party prime minister (1968–1979; 1980–1984) who was a strong opponent of QUEBEC SEPARATISM. A French Canadian by birth, Trudeau was convinced that an independent Quebec would be disastrous for Quebec as well as for the rest of Canada. He significantly influenced the citizens of Quebec to reject independence in a May 20, 1980, referendum. Trudeau succeeded LESTER PEARSON in office and temporarily (from June 1979 to February 1980) lost power to Joe Clark (1939–) of the Progressive Conservative Party. In foreign policy Trudeau was a strong supporter of the North Atlantic Treaty Organization and the United Nations, opened diplomatic relations with China in 1970, sought closer ties to the Soviet Union and the European Community, and arranged for the United Kingdom in 1982 to amend the British North American Act of 1867 (which made Canada a British DOMINION) to grant Canada complete national sovereignty.

Truman, Harry S (1884–1972) The Democratic president of the United States (1945–1953) who (as vice president) became president when FRANKLIN D. ROOSEVELT died in office. It was Truman who decided to use the first ATOMIC BOMB on Japan to quickly end WORLD WAR II, whose foreign policy of Communist CONTAINMENT was the strategy that eventually won the COLD WAR, and whose MARSHALL PLAN led to the economic recovery of Western Europe after World War II. Truman had a clear sense of presidential responsibility and was often very decisive. He placed great store in key advisors, especially GEORGE MARSHALL and DEAN ACHESON, who were his successive secretaries of state. He also oversaw the creation of the Cold War security structure in the United States and was prepared to use force to stop Communist expansion as in Korea. Under Truman, the United States went from its initial desire to return to normalcy after the war, to containment through rebuilding its allies, to military containment in which U.S. forces were deployed in Asia and Europe for deterrence and defense against the Communist threat.

Truman Doctrine The policy of U.S. President Harry S Truman's administration that extended

President Harry S Truman (Library of Congress)

military and economic aid to those countries seeking to resist "totalitarian aggression," specifically Greece and Turkey. Truman presented this idea in 1947 in his address to a joint session of the U.S. Congress in support of the Greek-Turkish aid bill. The Soviet Union was at the time putting pressure on Turkey for free passage through the straits from the Black Sea to the Mediterranean Sea, and on Greece through support of a guerrilla war. The development of the Truman Doctrine was precipitated by Great Britain's reluctant decision that it could no longer afford to aid Greece and Turkey. If the United States did not assume this burden, it was argued, both Greece and Turkey would fall into the Communist camp. The Truman Doctrine became the cornerstone of the U.S. policy of CONTAINMENT.

THE TRUMAN DOCTRINE

The peoples of a number of countries of the world have recently had totalitarian regimes forced upon them against their will. The government of the United States had made frequent protests against coercion and intimidation in violation of the Yalta agreement, in Poland, Romania, and Bulgaria. I must also state that in a number of other countries there have been similar developments.

At the present moment in world history nearly every nation must choose between alternative ways of life. The choice is too often not a free one.

One way of life is based upon the will of the majority, and is distinguished by free institutions, representative government, free elections, guaranties of individual liberty, freedom of speech and religion, and freedom from political oppression.

The second way of life is based upon the will of a minority forcibly imposed upon the majority. It relies upon terror and oppression, a controlled press and radio, fixed elections, and the suppression of personal freedoms.

I believe that it must be the policy of the United States to support free peoples who are resisting attempted subjugation by armed minorities or by outside pressures.

I believe that we must assist free peoples to work out their own destinies in their own way.

I believe that our help should be primarily through economic and financial aid which is essential to economic stability and orderly political processes.

The world is not static, and the status quo is not sacred. But we cannot allow changes in the status quo in violation of the Charter of the United Nations by such methods as coercion, or by such subterfuges as political infiltration. In helping free and independent nations to maintain their freedom, the United States will be giving effect to the principles of the Charter of the United Nations.

SOURCE: President Harry S Truman, address to a joint session of Congress, March 12, 1947.

---

trustee The role that elected representatives adopt when they vote according to their conscience and best judgment rather than according to the narrow interests of their immediate constituents. This concept was famously put forth by British legislator Edmund Burke (1729–1797) in his 1774 "Speech to the Electors of Bristol." Burke asserted that he would be a trustee in Parliament as opposed to a delegate, one bound by prior instructions from a constituency. Most DIPLOMATIC AGENTS are delegates in the sense that they operate according to instructions from their governments. Only when it is not possible to communicate with their governments have diplomats been able to function as trustees and make independent policy decisions.

trusteeship A term used to refer to a system in which there is international supervision of colonial territories. This was first tried at the end of World War I, when there was greater recognition than ever before of the right to national SELF-DETERMINATION but also a belief that some nations were not yet ready for self-government. The idea was embodied in Article 22 of the League of Nations Charter, and the MANDATES SYSTEM was established in which colonial territories of the defeated states that were not yet deemed ready for independence were placed under the supervision of a major power. Great Britain, for example, was given a mandate over Iraq and encouraged and facilitated the moves toward Iraqi independence that finally occurred in 1932. Although not all the mandates were equally successful, a similar system was established at the end of World War II through the United Nations. This time the provisions for international supervision were more stringent and were exercised through the TRUSTEESHIP COUNCIL. Although the emplacement of Namibia under the supervision of South Africa was to prove troublesome, this system worked very well. Of the 11 territories under the trusteeship system, all but the Pacific Islands under the United States have become independent.

Trusteeship Council The United Nations agency in charge of supervising the administration of trust territories placed under the TRUSTEESHIP system. At the end of World War II, the international status of many territories were undetermined. The trusteeship system was to promote the advancement of the inhabitants of these territories and their progressive development toward self-government or independence. With the independence of many new nations, mostly from Africa and the Pacific, the goal of the trusteeship system has been largely fulfilled.

Tshombe, Moise *See* CONGOLESE CIVIL WAR.

tuna war The 1971–1972 dispute between U.S. tuna fishing boat owners and the government of

Ecuador, occasioned by Ecuador's extension of its TERRITORIAL WATERS to 200 nautical miles from its shore. Although the United States claims jurisdiction for the management of coastal fisheries up to 200 miles from its coast, its policy excludes highly migratory species such as tuna. Ecuador, on the other hand, claims the same 200-mile-wide territorial sea with no exceptions for the catch of migratory species. In the early 1970s Ecuador seized about 100 foreign-flagged boats (many of them from the United States) and collected fees and fines of more than $6 million. After a dropoff in such seizures for some years, several U.S. tuna boats were again detained and seized in 1980 and 1981. The U.S. Magnuson Fishery Conservation and Management Act then triggered an automatic prohibition of U.S. imports of tuna products from Ecuador. The prohibition was lifted in 1983, but the fundamental difference between Ecuadorean and U.S. legislation still exists.

Tupamaros   The left-wing Uruguayan urban guerrilla group founded in the early 1960s by Raul Sendic (1925–1989). The name Tupamaros is derived from the name of eighteenth-century Inca chieftain Tupac Amaro, who battled Spanish invaders. Early Tupamaros actions revolved around bank robberies and bombings against institutional targets. Beginning in 1966 the group turned to urban guerrilla tactics in the capital of Montevideo. It carried out an agenda of exposing institutional corruption and vied for mass support through such "Robin Hood" tactics as turning over loot from robberies to the poor. Frequent targets of violence included the offices of multinational corporations and members of the Uruguayan security forces. U.S. Agency for International Development employee Dan Mitrione was murdered in 1970 by Tupamaros who claimed that Mitrione was a Central Intelligence Agency agent. In 1971 the group abducted British Ambassador Geoffrey Jackson and held him for eight months. The Uruguayan government, in an all-out campaign against the group in 1972, arrested more than 2,500 persons. While the Tupamaros never recovered, their previous efforts had so weakened the democratic government of Uruguay that the military took power in 1973. Civilian rule resumed in 1984. Released in a general AMNESTY declared by the government in 1985, Sendic converted the Tupamaros into a legal political party. *See also* GUERRILLA WARFARE, URBAN; MARIGHELLA, CARLOS.

turbulence   A term used by JAMES ROSENAU in *Turbulence in World Politics* (1990) to describe the kinds of changes that are not contained by the boundaries of a system. Turbulence "is manifested in technological breakthroughs, authority crises, consensus breakdowns, revolutionary upheavals, generational conflicts, and other forces that restructure the human landscape in which they erupt." Turbulence obscures or destroys existing patterns, regularities, rules, and boundaries and involves changes in the basic parameters of world politics. It also moves very rapidly and tends to have a cascading effect.

turbulent field   A concept developed by ERNST HAAS in "Turbulent Fields and the Theory of Regional Integration" (*International Organization,* Spring 1976), to explain why POLITICAL INTEGRATION processes have run into difficulties. A turbulent field, according to Haas, stems from a situation in which there are many actors who find themselves faced with great complexity, who have confused and clashing perceptions, who are unsure of the trade-offs between objectives, and who are tied into a network of interdependencies yet can obtain some objectives without cooperation. "A turbulent field . . . is a policy space in which this type of confusion dominates discussion and negotiation." It can be subnational, national, regional, interregional, and global—and all at the same time.

Turkish Straits   *See* DARDENELLES.

Turnhalle Conference   A constitutional convention for Namibia called by South Africa and held at a former German drill hall called the "Turnhalle" in Windhoek, Namibia, from 1975 to 1977. A draft constitution that called for a weak confederation of ethnic states with voting along tribal and ethnic lines was rejected by the United Nations and by SWAPO (South West Africa People's Organization). *See also* NAMIBIAN INDEPENDENCE.

Turtle Bay   **1.** The area next to the East River in New York in the United States along which the United Nations is situated. **2.** By analogy, the United Nations itself.

tutelage   The process whereby military regimes establish and oversee democratic procedures that effectively bring the military government to an end. For example, in recent decades this has happened in Chile under AUGUSTO PINOCHET and in Spain under JUAN CARLOS.

Tutu, Desmond (1931–   )   The South African Anglican Church archbishop who was awarded the 1984 Nobel Peace Prize for his advocacy of nonviolent opposition to APARTHEID.

TWA Flight 847   The Trans World Airlines flight with 152 passengers on board that was hijacked by two Lebanese SHI'ITE gunmen while en route to Athens from Rome on June 14, 1985. In the process of making two round trips from Beirut to Algiers during the next three days, the hijackers allowed all but 40 of the hostages to be freed, and took on board additional terrorists. Passenger Robert Stethem, a U.S. Navy diver, was murdered and his body dumped onto the Beirut airport tarmac on June 15, in full view of the international media. On June 17 the remaining hostages were deplaned and dispersed to a number of Shi'ite strongholds in Beirut. Extensive negotiations were brokered by Nabbih Berri (1939–   ), leader of the AMAL militia, although the terrorists were believed to be affiliated with the HEZBOLLAH movement. A complex set of exchanges finally was arranged, including the release of some prisoners in Israeli jails. The terrorists held the aircraft and the remaining hostages for 17 days before they were released unharmed.

twin-track decision   The 1979 North Atlantic Treaty Organization decision to modernize its LONG-RANGE THEATER NUCLEAR FORCES in Europe, while at the same time offering to open negotiations with the Soviet Union to cover these new systems and the comparable Soviet SS MISSILES. The deployment decision was partly a response to concerns over coupling between the United States and its European allies in an era of strategic PARITY, partly a reflection of the need to modernize NATO's nuclear forces, and partly a response to the Soviet deployment of SS-20s. There also was a concern that DÉTENTE should not be abandoned. Most West European governments wanted to continue the arms control dialogue with the Soviet Union that had been proceeding primarily at the strategic level in SALT. Without the negotiation track—the "twin"—it is doubtful that NATO would have obtained a consensus in favor of deployment of the modernized nuclear weapons. While deployment proceeded apace, so did the negotiations, which

finally led to the INF TREATY that led to the removal of the missiles in question by both sides.

two-person rule   A procedure designed to prevent access by any one individual to nuclear weapons and certain of their designated components by requiring the presence at all times of at least two authorized persons, each capable of detecting incorrect or unauthorized procedures with respect to the task to be performed. Also referred to as the two-person concept or two-person policy.

two presidencies   See PRESIDENCIES, TWO.

Tyminski, Stanislaw (1948–   )   The Polish-born Canadian businessman who made millions in the West, and then ran against and lost to LECH WALESA in Poland's 1990 presidential race. Tyminski promised that he could turn the country's economy around without hurting anyone, advocated arming Poland with 100 medium-range nuclear missiles to ward off aggression, and revived traditional feelings of ANTI-SEMITISM by blaming Poland's infinitesimally small number of Jews (15,000 out of a population of 38 million) for oppressing the Polish people. While his Party "X" gained 23 percent of the votes, it captured only three of the 460 seats in parliament in the 1990 elections.

tyranny   1. Oppressive government. **2.** Nonrepresentative government. Future U.S. President James Madison defined tyranny in *The Federalist* (no. 47, 1788): "The accumulation of all power, legislative, executive, and judiciary, in the same hands, whether of one, a few, or many, and whether hereditary, self-appointed, or elective, may justly be pronounced the very definition of tyranny." **3.** ANARCHY. William Pitt, British Earl of Chatham, in a famous speech in Great Britain's House of Lords on January 9, 1770, said: "Where law ends, tyranny begins." JOHN LOCKE said the same in his *Second Treatise of Government* (1690).

tyranny of small decisions   1. A system in which individual decisions appear to be rational but the result is the opposite of what was intended, largely because others have made the same or similar choices. **2.** Recognition of the fact that INCREMENTALISM can lock one into a course of action that has unforeseen and damaging consequences.

U

Ugandan Civil War The violence that began in 1971 when IDI AMIN DADA took over the government of Uganda in a military coup, declared himself president, dissolved the parliament, and amended the constitution to give himself absolute power. His eight-year rule was marked by economic decline, social disintegration, and an effective but bloody war against the Acholi and Langi tribes for their political opposition to his regime. By 1978 an estimated 100,000 Ugandans had been murdered during Amin's reign of terror. (Some authorities place the figure much higher.) In October 1978 the Tanzanian Armed Forces, with the backing of Ugandan exiles, waged a war of liberation against Amin's troops and the Libyan soldiers briefly sent to help him. By April 1979 the capital of Kampala was captured, and Amin fled to Saudi Arabia. After a series of weak governments the military took over in 1980 and sponsored elections that returned Milton Obote (1924–), the president (from 1966 to 1971) whom Idi Amin had ousted, to power. After failing to control tribal insurgents, stop government corruption, or regain economic prosperity, Obote was sent into exile by a military coup in 1985. But soon the insurgents, the National Resistance Army under Yoweri Museveni (1944–), captured the capital of Kampala. In 1986 they organized a new government with Museveni as president. Other insurgencies continue to harass government forces but do not seem to threaten the regime.

ugly American *See* AMERICAN, UGLY.

Ulbricht, Walter (1893–1973) Secretary general of the East German Socialist Unity (Communist) Party (and, as such, dictator of East Germany) from 1950 to 1971. A strong opponent of West Germany, he refused to normalize East German–West German relations as proposed by WILLY BRANDT until his state was recognized as sovereign. Brandt had proposed the OSTPOLITK, that Germany be viewed as "two states within one nation." Ulbricht was responsible for the decision to build the BERLIN WALL in 1961. The recalcitrant Ulbricht retired in 1971 and was replaced by ERICH HONECKER.

Ulster NORTHERN IRELAND; the six counties of Ireland that, because of their Protestant majority populations, remained part of the United Kingdom when Ireland was partitioned in 1922. The essential reason for the continuing civil unrest and TERRORISM there is the desire of the Catholic minority to have one united Ireland free of British rule, and the desire of the Protestant majority not to be a minority in a mostly Catholic united Ireland. *See also* ANGLO-IRISH ACCORD OF 1985.

Ulster Defense Association (UDA) An illegal NORTHERN IRELAND Protestant "defense" organization, formed in the early 1970s as a paramilitary vigilante group in response to the growth of IRISH REPUBLICAN ARMY activism. The UDA, thought to exceed 40,000 members, adamantly supports the continuance of British rule in Ulster and stands in violent opposition to any political compromise. It has a history of assassinations and beatings of Catholics, and members have been convicted of kidnapping and murder.

Ulster Freedom Fighters (UFF) A NORTHERN IRELAND Protestant organization, formed in the mid-

1970s as a radical splinter group of the Ulster Defense Association. Far more prone to violence than its parent group, it appears to be the primary source of anti-Catholic violence in Ulster.

Ulster Volunteer Force (UVF)   Formed in 1966 as "a secret Protestant private army" of ULSTER nationalists, it takes its name from an early home-rule organization that had a membership of 100,000 during 1911–1912. The UVF both supported and carried out violent reprisals against IRISH REPUBLICAN ARMY members and sympathizers until its 1976 public renunciation of violence. But many of the group's critics doubt the sincerity of the UVF's 1976 pledge and believe that it is still active in anti-Catholic violence.

ultima ratio   **1.** Latin for "the final argument." **2.** A synonym for the use of force, because traditionally cannons had engraved on them the inscription *ultima ratio regum* (the final argument of kings).

ultimatum   **1.** A formal communication from one state to another that if specifically requested action is not taken by a certain date, dire consequences (often war) will result. What distinguishes an ultimatum from other threats or coercive moves is that it involves the notion of the last chance or the final demand. If the ultimatum is not complied with, the state issuing it must either implement its threat or suffer a serious loss of CREDIBILITY. Thus an ultimatum is not something used lightly. World War I began in 1914 when Austria sent a humiliating ultimatum to Serbia after the assassination of Archduke Franz Ferdinand, then declared war when the Serbian response was considered unsatisfactory. The Persian Gulf War of 1991 began when Iraq did not respond to the ultimatum implicit in a United Nations resolution demanding that Iraq withdraw from Kuwait by January 15, 1991. While an ultimatum is not in itself compulsion, it often has the same effect. The ultimatum, which was once considered a last chance to avoid war, has gone out of diplomatic fashion. Now that the Charter of the United Nations requires that "all members shall refrain in their international relations from the threat or use of force . . ." (Article 2, Section 4), the classical ultimatum would seem to be obsolete. It is a relic of an age when wars were formally declared.

Nowadays both ultimata and wars tend to be declared informally. Perhaps the most famous informal ultimatum of the Cold War period was that given by U.S. Attorney General Robert Kennedy to the Soviet ambassador in Washington during the Cuban Missile Crisis. In effect, Kennedy told him that unless Moscow agreed to remove the Soviet missiles from Cuba, the United States would be compelled to use force to remove them. The Soviets thereupon removed the missiles—in exchange for an equally informal agreement not to invade Cuba and to remove U.S. missiles from Turkey.   **2.** The final offer in a diplomatic negotiation, the maximum concession one side is willing to make to reach an agreement; but no resort to force is either implied or contemplated if the offer is not accepted.

ULTRA   The code name for the British WORLD WAR II CRYPTOGRAPHY project that cracked Germany's military code. This gave the Allies a crucial intelligence advantage. The fact that the Allies were consistently reading German electronic signals traffic was a secret so closely held that it was not revealed until 1974. Then all of the assessments of Allied commanders had to be reevaluated in light of the fact that they were effectively "reading the mail" of the opposition almost from the beginning of the war.

ULTRA IN ACTION

The second battle of Alamein started on October the twenty-third [1942]. . . . On November the second Hitler sent his now famous signal to Rommel saying that "there could be no other course but that of holding out to the last man and that for the German troops there was only the choice, victory or death." Alamein was the first real German defeat of the war and also the first of this type of signal to come from Hitler. . . . This signal was immediately picked up by us and was in the hands of Montgomery and Churchill within minutes of its transmission by Hitler. Apparently Rommel had either got sand in his cypher machine or was deliberately stalling because, instead of acknowledging the signal, he sent a request for a repeat. It was probably only time that a British commander has received a signal from the enemy's commander-in-chief before the enemy's commander in the field had got it, or at least admitted that he had.

SOURCE: F. W. Winterbotham, *The Ultra Secret* (1974).

---

ultra vires   Latin for "beyond powers"; descriptive of the actions of a corporation or international organization that are outside the scope of powers granted by its charter or articles of incorporation.

umbrella   *See* NUCLEAR UMBRELLA.

unacceptable damage   Harm that a state or military force is not willing to bear; destruction to a state's infrastructure or people that will not be tolerated if there is any choice. The ability of military powers to inflict unacceptable damage on each other, especially with nuclear weapons, is the essence of DETERRENCE.

unanimity   The rule used in international organizations which is the main brake that keeps these organizations from taking on a SUPRANATIONAL dimension. The idea of unanimity carries with it an acknowledgment of the VETO power of members if they do not agree with a particular proposal or policy. Although ways are sometimes found to get around this rule (in North Atlantic Treaty Organization communiqués, for example, a footnote may state that a particular member does not accept certain specified elements or paragraphs in the document), it does mean that the operation of the organization can be obstructed. On the other hand, the unanimity principle is a great safeguard of the rights of individual members of the organization and also can act as a safety valve. For example, the veto in the United Nations Security Council was an important factor in keeping the UN viable in spite of the Cold War. This allowed both the United States and the Soviet Union to remain in the UN despite their international rivalry. Because of the veto that each possessed, the UN could never harm their vital interests and could be useful as a platform for propaganda. Besides, it was a useful diplomatic BACK CHANNEL for both sides.

UNCED   *See* EARTH SUMMIT.

UNCITRAL   *See* UNITED NATIONS COMMISSION ON INTERNATIONAL TRADE LAW.

Uncle Sam   The old man in the white beard and top hat who personifies the United States government. The name is traced back to the Troy, New York, *Post* of September 7, 1813. Political cartoon-

In this 1903 Puck *cartoon Uncle Sam warns Central America not to interfere with the building of the Panama Canal. (Library of Congress)*

ist Thomas Nast (1840–1902) popularized the modern version of an Uncle Sam with a top hat, frock coat, and striped trousers. The most famous Uncle Sam is James Montgomery Flagg's World War I "I Want You" recruiting poster. *Compare to* JOHN BULL; MARIANNE.

Uncle Sap   UNCLE SAM when he is a "sap"—one who permits others to take advantage of his generosity or good nature. Domestic opponents of U.S. aid to other countries often claimed that providing such aid made the United States look like "Uncle Sap."

Uncle Shylock   A pejorative reference to UNCLE SAM (the United States) based on the allegation that U.S. aid programs really were not intended to help other nations so much as they were designed to advance the unilateral interests of the United States. "Shylock" was the moneylender in William Shake-

German Field Marshal Wilhelm Keitel signing surrender terms at Soviet headquarters in Berlin on May 7, 1945. (National Archives)

speare's play *The Merchant of Venice* (1597) who demanded repayment of an outrageous debt in precise, exact form (literally a pound of the debtor's flesh) without allowing any deviation from the original loan agreement.

UNCLOS *See* LAW OF THE SEA.

unconditional surrender Putting a defeated military force, a military installation, or an entire nation into the hands of an enemy without terms of any kind. The demand for such an outcome in the U.S. Civil War caused the phrase to first gain wide currency. General U. S. Grant responded to the Confederate offer to surrender on terms during the 1862 battle for Fort Donelson by saying: "No terms except an unconditional and immediate surrender can be accepted." During World War II the unconditional surrender of Germany, Italy, and Japan was the ultimate war aim of the Allies. As U.S. President Franklin Roosevelt stated at the end of the January 1943 Casablanca conference: "The elimination of Germany, Japanese and Italian war power means the unconditional surrender by Germany, Italy and Japan. That means a reasonable assurance of future world peace. It does not mean the destruction of the population of Germany, Italy or Japan, but it does mean the destruction of the philosophies in those countries which are based on conquest and the subjugation of other people." The policy of unconditional surrender was intended partly to mobilize domestic energies in Great Britain, the Soviet Union, and the United States for the prosecution of the war. It also was a reaction to the nature of the fascist regimes and was intended to ensure that there was no repetition of the situation that occurred after World War I, when the myth developed in Germany that the war had been lost because of a STAB IN THE BACK rather than through defeat on the battlefield.

THE UNCONDITIONAL SURRENDER SIGNED BY REPRESENTATIVES OF JAPAN ON SEPTEMBER 2, 1945, ABOARD THE USS *MISSOURI* IN TOKYO DAY

We, acting by command of and on behalf of the Emperor of Japan, the Japanese Government and the Japanese Imperial General Headquarters, hereby accept the provisions set forth in the declaration issued by the heads of the Governments of the United States, China and Great Britain on 26 July 1945, at Potsdam. . . .

We hereby proclaim the unconditional surrender to the Allied Powers of the Japanese Imperial General Headquarters and of all Japanese armed forces and all armed forces under Japanese control wherever situated.

We hereby command all Japanese forces wherever situated and the Japanese people to cease hostilities forthwith, to preserve and save from damage all ships, aircraft, and military and civil property. . . . We hereby command the Japanese Imperial General Headquarters to issue at once orders to the Commanders of all Japanese armed forces and all forces under Japanese control wherever situated to surrender unconditionally themselves and all forces under their control.

We hereby command all civil, military and naval officials to obey and enforce all proclamations, orders and directives deemed by the Supreme Commander for the Allied Powers to be proper to effectuate this surrender and issued by him or under his authority and we direct all such officials to remain at their posts and to continue to perform their non-combatant duties unless specifically relieved by him or under his authority. We hereby undertake for the Emperor, the Japanese Government and their successors to carry out the provisions of the Potsdam Declaration in good faith. . . .

The authority of the Emperor and the Japanese Government to rule the state shall be subject to the Supreme Commander for the Allied Powers who will take such steps as he deems proper to effectuate these terms of surrender.

---

uncontrolled source   *See* SOURCE.

unconventional warfare   GUERRILLA WARFARE, subversion, sabotage, and other operations of a low-visibility, covert, or clandestine nature. *Compare to* CONVENTIONAL WARFARE.

UNCTAD   *See* UNITED NATIONS CONFERENCE ON TRADE AND DEVELOPMENT.

undeclared war   Any armed conflict between states in which a formal DECLARATION OF WAR has not been issued. The lack of such a declaration allows the parties to keep the war more limited than it might otherwise be. LOW-INTENSITY WARFARE and STATE-SPONSORED TERRORISM are major examples of strategies used in undeclared wars.

underdeveloped   An adjective used in connection with the poor countries of the THIRD WORLD. First used in the 1950s, it is now considered mildly offensive and has been replaced by the term developing, which does not seem as judgmental.

underground   1. Descriptive of political events and publications that are neither secret nor completely unknown, but that are of such limited interest or low circulation that they are almost invisible to the general public. Underground publications often are circulated by dissidents in totalitarian or oppressive regimes.   2. A covert UNCONVENTIONAL WARFARE organization established to operate in areas controlled by the enemy. During World War II the Allies supported extensive underground operations in German-occupied Europe. The various underground organizations were collectively known as the RESISTANCE.

POST WAR UNDERGROUND PLANNING

General WILLIAM J. DONOVAN, head of the OSS, and David Bruce (also of the OSS) were cowering before enemy fire in Normandy, France, on June 7, 1944. Donovan, the chief U.S. spymaster in Europe, says: "By the way, David, have you arranged to be buried in Arlington Cemetery?"

Bruce replies: "Why, no."

"Well, I have; that's where I want to be buried. David, you've got to get a plot near mine. Then we can start an Underground together."

SOURCE: Anthony Cave Brown, *The Last Hero* (1982).

UNDP   *See* UNITED NATIONS DEVELOPMENT PROGRAM.

UNDRO   *See* UNITED NATIONS DISASTER RELIEF COORDINATOR, OFFICE OF THE.

UNEP *See* UNITED NATIONS ENVIRONMENT PROGRAM.

UNESCO *See* UNITED NATIONS EDUCATIONAL, SCIENTIFIC AND CULTURAL ORGANIZATION.

UNFPA *See* UNITED NATIONS FUND FOR POPULATION ACTIVITIES.

unfriendly act The description by one state of actions by another state that might lead to SANCTIONS (the ultimate of which is war) by the offended state. *Compare to* RETORSION.

UNHCR *See* UNITED NATIONS HIGH COMMISSIONER FOR REFUGEES, OFFICE OF THE.

UNICEF *See* UNITED NATIONS INTERNATIONAL CHILDREN'S EMERGENCY FUND.

UNIDO *See* UNITED NATIONS INDUSTRIAL DEVELOPMENT ORGANIZATION.

unilateral An action taken by a country acting singly, and not dependent on or conditional on any action by another country. For example, unilateral nuclear disarmament would occur if one state divested itself of its nuclear weapons while other states did not.

unilateral declaration A formal policy statement communicated by one state to all others for their guidance. Examples include the BREZHNEV DOCTRINE and the MONROE DOCTRINE.

Unilateral Declaration of Independence The action taken by the white government of Rhodesia on November 11, 1965, by which it declared itself a sovereign state, independent of Great Britain. This went against the wishes of the Africans who constituted 94 percent of the population. Although British Prime Minister Harold Wilson's government briefly contemplated the use of force in response, the British public was too divided to make this a feasible option. Nevertheless, the declaration ran so much against the principles of DECOLONIZATION and SELF-DETERMINATION that the Security Council of the United Nations decided that the situation was a threat to peace. Consequently, economic SANCTIONS were imposed, but these were not uniformly upheld

and so did not have much immediate effect. As a result of the activities of several internal guerrilla groups and outside pressure, especially from the United States, the white government was eventually forced to relinquish power; Rhodesia became Zimbabwe in 1980. *See also* ZIMBABWE CIVIL WAR.

unilateralism **1.** A practice of acting alone, without consultation with allies. Used in this way, the term is contrasted with MULTILATERALISM. For example, the United States under the Reagan Administration in the 1980s was often criticized by its allies for unilateral actions and policies in which there was either no advance consultation or the preferences of allies were ignored. Although the term is often used pejoratively, others see it as a necessary and desirable feature of a state's FOREIGN POLICY. **2.** DISARMAMENT by one side in the expectation that an adversary will follow the example. Some Western peace activists during the Cold War called for unilateral nuclear disarmament. *Compare to* BILATERALISM.

Union of Soviet Socialist Republics (U.S.S.R.) The experiment in COMMUNISM that grew out of the RUSSIAN REVOLUTION OF 1917 and lasted until the end of 1991, when the Soviet Union was dissolved. After the BOLSHEVIKS under V. I. LENIN, with the aid of the RED ARMY and the RUSSIAN CIVIL WAR, consolidated their power, they created the Soviet Union in 1923. Lenin's death the next year intensified an interparty struggle for power between groups led by JOSEPH STALIN and LEON TROTSKY. Stalin defeated his rivals by the late 1920s and later had them all killed. Throughout the 1930s, Stalin enforced a mass COLLECTIVIZATION drive among the peasantry. Millions died during the formation of collective farms, and millions of others were sent to labor camps or to exile in Siberia, where many perished. In addition, between 1931 and 1933 millions died in a famine in the Ukraine that was exacerbated by Stalin's attempt to gain foreign exchange from the sale of grain abroad. During this period Stalin also pursued a policy of FIVE-YEAR PLANS for rapid industrialization. Untold numbers of other Soviet cultural, economic, military, and political leaders were imprisoned or sent to labor camps, and many died in the GREAT PURGES of the 1930s. In the interwar years, Soviet diplomacy was directed toward gaining acceptance by other European countries. It succeeded only partially because the Soviet-led third Communist INTERNATIONAL (Comintern), founded in 1919, attempted through local Communist organizations to undermine West European governments. The Soviet Union was finally recognized by many European countries in 1924; by the United States in 1933.

Through the NAZI-SOVIET NONAGGRESSION PACT of 1939 Stalin conspired with Germany's Adolf Hitler to carve up Poland. When Nazi Germany invaded Poland on September 1, 1939 (the Soviets followed on September 17), World War II began. The Soviet government then abrogated its nonaggression pact with Finland and invaded in November 1939. Peace negotiations concluded in 1940 led to the cession of a large part of eastern Finland. In June 1940 the independent nations of Estonia, Lithuania, and Latvia were forcibly incorporated. In July the Soviet Union also forcibly annexed two eastern provinces of Romania (Bessarabia and northern Bukovina). Hitler then turned on his newfound ally and invaded the Soviet Union in 1941. Four years of fighting and heavy casualties left widespread devastation in the European part of the Soviet Union. Approximately 20 million Soviet citizens perished in the conflict (half of them civilians or prisoners). However, the ultimate victory of the Allies in 1945 found Soviet forces in a dominant position in Eastern Europe. Profound differences over the postwar order in Europe led almost immediately to a deep chill in relations between the Soviet Union and Western powers. The United States responded with a policy of CONTAINMENT that in turn led to the MARSHALL PLAN to rebuild Europe and the development of the North Atlantic Treaty Organization. The victory of Communist forces in China in 1949, the Soviet explosion of an atomic bomb in September 1949, and the Soviet-sponsored invasion of South Korea by North Korea in June 1950 led to a further intensification of the COLD WAR.

When Stalin died in 1953 his successors modified some of the more repressive aspects of the regime but did not alter its totalitarian structure. NIKITA S. KHRUSHCHEV, installed as first secretary of the Communist Party in 1953, consolidated his power by 1957. In a secret speech to the Twentieth Party Congress in 1956, Khrushchev denounced Stalin as a despot who had sacrificed much of the

party's best talents through misdirected purges and mistaken military tactics. "De-Stalinization" was accompanied by reforms of the political system. Under Khrushchev's leadership the principle of "peaceful coexistence" with the West was given greater emphasis. After Khrushchev was ousted in 1964, LEONID BREZHNEV eventually emerged in 1971 as first among equals in a collective leadership. Although some attempt was made to repair the damage inflicted on Stalin's image during the Khrushchev era, there was no return to the mass terror of the Stalin period. In the early 1970s Soviet relations with the West improved and trade with the West expanded. DISSIDENTs emerged in large numbers. Brezhnev signed the HELSINKI ACCORDS in 1975, which committed the Soviet Union to observe certain human rights standards. Emigration from the Soviet Union increased dramatically. As the decade progressed, however, the regime initiated a gradual internal tightening of controls that coincided with a more aggressive Soviet arms buildup and foreign policy. Soviet and Soviet-proxy interference in the ANGOLAN CIVIL WAR and the HORN OF AFRICA, the invasion of Afghanistan in 1979, the suppression of SOLIDARITY in Poland, and a brutal crackdown on human rights in the Soviet Union itself led to a renewed chilly period in East-West relations.

Following the death of Brezhnev in 1982, YURI ANDROPOV, former head of the KGB, became general secretary. Andropov began a new program of economic reform but did not live long enough to implement it. East-West relations deteriorated further under his brief rule with the Soviet suspension of arms control talks and the attack on KOREAN AIRLINES FLIGHT 007. When Andropov died in 1984, the POLITBURO selected KONSTANTIN CHERNENKO to succeed him. Chernenko was also in poor health and died after barely one year in office. To succeed him, the Politburo promptly chose the much younger MIKHAIL GORBACHEV, who moved rapidly to consolidate his control over the party and governmental apparatus. Toward the end of 1986 Western monitors began to notice improvements in human rights observance. Censorship and overt repression diminished. Elections held in March 1989 were the first contested races in the Soviet Union since the earliest days of the Soviet regime. Reformers and ethnic nationalists defeated several prominent party and military officials for seats in the new Congress of People's Deputies. For the first time in Soviet history citizens' representatives conducted a free and lively debate. The new congress agreed to address many previously taboo subjects, including the forcible incorporation of the BALTIC NATIONS and the role of the KGB. The congress elected Gorbachev head of state with the title Chairman of the Supreme Soviet. It then selected 542 people from its own ranks to serve in the new bicameral Supreme Soviet. Gorbachev was committed to making the Soviet system more competitive economically and technologically with the West through his policies of GLASNOST (openness), PERESTROIKA (restructuring), and *demokratizatsia* (democratization).

The Soviet Union under Gorbachev ended the Cold War by freeing Eastern Europe from Soviet domination, curtailing support for regional conflicts, and seeking a new relationship with the West. Many analysts believe that because the Soviet Union's economy was in such chaos, its leadership had little real choice. All this was too much for some hard-line Communists in the KREMLIN. By means of a 1991 coup they sought to stifle the reforms that were threatening the very existence of the Communist Party. But because of the reforms already in place, the plotters could not control the military, and the coup failed. The response was a formal dissolution of the Soviet Union. By the end of 1991 the former constituent republics became a loose confederation known as the Commonwealth of Independent States. By general consensus the Russian experiment with communism had failed.

unipolarity   A term that is used to describe an international system in which there is only one great power. It was argued by Charles Krauthammer in "The Unipolar Moment" (*Foreign Affairs,* vol. 70, no. 1, 1990–1991) that the disintegration of the Soviet Union had resulted in the replacement of BIPOLARITY by what he described as a "unipolar moment" in which no other state can rival the United States in terms of its power. As he puts it, the true geopolitical structure of the post–Cold War world is "a single pole of world power that consists of the United States at the apex of the industrial West." Krauthammer acknowledges that this is only temporary and suggests that it will be replaced by MULTIPOLARITY, but also argues that this will take

another generation or so. The notion of a unipolar international system is not accepted by those who argue that Japan now rivals or even surpasses the United States in terms of economic power, and that this, not military power, is increasingly the main currency of international influence.

UNITA   *See* ANGOLAN CIVIL WAR.

unitary taxation   A government's policy of taxing a business on its worldwide profits, not just profits earned in the taxing jurisdiction's borders.

United Arab Republic   Egypt and Syria, after they merged in 1958. Syria withdrew in 1961, but the term remained as the formal designation for Egypt for another ten years. *See also* NASSER, GAMAL ABDAL.

United Arab States   The name of the confederation of Egypt and North Yemen that lasted from 1958 to 1961. This was a separate confederation between Egypt and North Yemen that was not part of the UNITED ARAB REPUBLIC between Egypt and Syria.

United Nations   1. The WORLD WAR II allied coalition of states led by the United States and the United Kingdom who defeated the Axis powers of Germany, Italy, and Japan. The phrase "united nations," credited to U.S. President Franklin D. Roosevelt, was first used in the multilateral Declaration of United Nations on January 1, 1942. In this declaration each of the states in the coalition promised to "employ its full resources" to defeat the Axis—and not to make a separate peace.   2. The international peacekeeping agency that replaced the LEAGUE OF NATIONS. After its proposal at DUMBARTON OAKS, the UN charter was signed on June 25, 1945, at the SAN FRANCISCO CONFERENCE by 50 states; the United Nations formally came into existence on October 24, 1945, after a majority of the signatory states had ratified the charter. It had an advantage over the old League in that both the United States and the Soviet Union were members. By the 1980s, it had a membership more than three times as large as the original 51-nation group. The United Nations' business is conducted primarily through its GENERAL ASSEMBLY, headed by the secretary general, and the SECURITY COUNCIL of five permanent members—the United States, Russia, the United Kingdom, France, and China—and ten rotating members. Each permanent member has VETO power. The UN is funded by ASSESSMENTS on its member states by means of an elaborate formula. Many UN activities are carried out by its SPECIALIZED AGENCIES, such as the International Atomic Energy Agency (founded in 1957), the International Civil Aviation Organization (founded in 1947), the International Labor Organization (founded in 1946), and the World Health Organization (founded in 1948). The General Assembly and Security Council are headquartered in the United States in New York; many other major cities around the world serve as headquarters for the various agencies.

The United Nations has always been controversial. But as U.S. President John F. Kennedy said in his State of the Union Message of January 11, 1962: "Our instrument and our hope is the United Nations, and I see little merit in the impatience of those who would abandon this imperfect world instrument because they dislike our imperfect world." UN official Brian E. Urquhart concluded: "The UN is the only place the U.S. can turn to in time of crisis, when there's the risk of a serious confrontation between the nuclear powers. It makes no sense to throw away the key to the shelter" (*New York Times Magazine,* December 19, 1982).

With the end of the Cold War the capacity of the United Nations to function as the world's broker for collective international measures has been vastly increased. Instead of being the major force for SUPERPOWER rivalry, it has become a focus for cooperation between the West and the former SOVIET BLOC. The UN PEACEKEEPING FORCES are now deployed throughout the world in efforts to resolve regional conflicts. Now that the superpowers are no longer sponsoring PROXY WARS against each other, the BLUE BERETS of the UN forces are in more demand than ever. The best illustration of this new cooperative spirit is the fact that in 1990, during the PERSIAN GULF CRISIS, the UN Security Council, for only the second time in its history (the other time being the KOREAN WAR), authorized the use of force against an aggressor state.

United Nations Commission on International Trade Law (UNCITRAL)   The commission created in 1966 to reduce the legal obstacles to international trade. Its goal is to promote the progressive HARMONIZATION of trade laws.

REASONS FOR THE UNITED NATIONS

The Purposes of the United Nations are:

1. To maintain international peace and security, and to that end: to take effective collective measures for the prevention and removal of threats to the peace, and for the suppression of acts of aggression or other breaches of the peace, and to bring about by peaceful means, and in conformity with the principles of justice and international law, adjustment or settlement of international disputes or situations which might lead to a breach of the peace;

2. To develop friendly relations among nations based on respect for the principle of equal rights and self-determination of peoples. . . .

3. To achieve international cooperation in solving international problems of an economic, social, cultural, or humanitarian character.

SOURCE: Article 1 of the Charter of the United Nations (1945).

United Nations Conference on Environment and Development   *See* EARTH SUMMIT.

United Nations Conference on the Law of the Sea   *See* LAW OF THE SEA.

United Nations Conference on Trade and Development (UNCTAD)   A quasi-autonomous permanent organ of the United Nations that is concerned with international economic relations and especially the steps that DEVELOPED COUNTRIES might take to accelerate the pace of economic development in the DEVELOPING COUNTRIES. It is primarily a forum for less developed countries to discuss trade and other matters of similar interest. UNCTAD was first convened in Geneva, Switzerland, in 1964.

United Nations Day   October 24 of each year; on that date in 1948 the United Nations Charter entered into force after it had been ratified by the permanent members of the SECURITY COUNCIL and by a majority of member state signatories.

United Nations Development Decades   *See* DEVELOPMENT DECADES.

United Nations Development Program (UNDP)
The largest international channel for multilateral technical and preinvestment cooperation. Active in almost all United Nations member states, UNDP coordinates DEVELOPMENT activities through five-year country and intercountry programs in virtually every economic and social sector. The main objective of UNDP's projects is to help DEVELOPING COUNTRIES make better use of their human and natural resources, improve living standards, expand productivity, and participate more fully in an expanding world economy. UNDP also helps mobilize capital investment and increased participation by the private sector. In addition, UNDP promotes economic and technical cooperation among the developing countries themselves. In recent years UNDP has been involved in the major developmental issues of external debt, implementation of structural adjustment policies, recovery from the drought and famine in Africa, increasing agricultural productivity, and efficient management of governmental institutions and enterprises, all at the request of the respective governments. All UNDP activities are financed by voluntary contributions from governments of the UN member states and UN-related agencies.

United Nations Disaster Relief Coordinator, Office of the (UNDRO)   With headquarters in Geneva, Switzerland, UNDRO was established in 1972 by the United Nations General Assembly as a response to a series of major disasters in the late 1960s. As a focal point and clearinghouse for information on relief needs and on the items donors are sending to meet such needs, UNDRO coordinates emergency relief assistance of various organizations of the UN system and of other donors. UNDRO also promotes the study, prevention, control, and prediction of natural disasters and provides governments that request it with assistance in predisaster planning.

United Nations Economic and Social Council   *See* ECONOMIC AND SOCIAL COUNCIL.

United Nations Economic Commissions   The five regional commissions, subsidiary bodies to the ECONOMIC AND SOCIAL COUNCIL, which coordinate the economic and social work of the United Nations and its SPECIALIZED AGENCIES at the regional level. They are the Economic Commission for Africa (headquartered in Addis Ababa, Ethiopia), the Economic and Social Commission for Asia and the Pacific (Bangkok, Thailand), the Economic Commission for Europe (Geneva, Switzerland), the Economic Commission for Latin America and the Caribbean (Santiago, Chile), and the Economic and Social Commission for Western Asia (Baghdad, Iraq).

United Nations Educational, Scientific and Cultural Organization (UNESCO)   A SPECIALIZED AGENCY of the United Nations, UNESCO was founded in 1946 to contribute to peace and security in the world by promoting collaboration among nations through communication, culture, education, and science. In education, UNESCO combines literacy programs with a drive to make primary education universal and eliminate illiteracy's root causes. In the natural sciences, in addition to scientific projects, UNESCO works to correct the imbalance in scientific and technological human resources, 90 percent of which is now concentrated in the industrialized countries. In the social sciences, UNESCO has sponsored studies on tensions leading to war and racism and the socioeconomic factors of DEVELOPMENT. In cultural fields, UNESCO promotes artistic creativity, conservation of the world's cultural inheritance (books, works of art, monuments), and preservation of cultural identities and oral traditions. In communications, UNESCO helps developing countries to set up infrastructures of communications. Efforts are made to broaden international cooperation in communications and assist regional news agencies with an aim to increasing the flow of Third World news. However, the push for UNESCO to sponsor a NEW INTERNATIONAL INFORMATION ORDER was viewed by some member states as being anti-West and slanted to Third World interests. This controversy as well as UNESCO's overall poor management led to withdrawal of Singapore, the United Kingdom, and the United States from the organization in 1984. The absence of U.S. financial backing put strong pressure on UNESCO for reform. The General Conference of UNESCO, headquartered in Paris, France, is composed of representatives of all member states. It meets every other year while its executive board, consisting of 50 members elected by the General

Conference, meets at least twice a year and is responsible for supervising the program adopted by the conference.

United Nations Environment Program (UNEP) The United Nations organization created in 1972 (headquartered in Nairobi, Kenya) to monitor significant changes in the environment and to encourage and coordinate sound environmental practices. To achieve these objectives, UNEP sets up programs such as a global environmental monitoring system, which provide governments with necessary information to understand, anticipate, and combat adverse environmental changes; and a computerized referral service and register of toxic chemicals, which provides scientific and regulative information on such materials. The 1985 Vienna Convention and 1987 Montreal Protocol on the protection of the earth's ozone layer were negotiated with the help of UNEP. Since 1987 UNEP has been cooperating with the WORLD METEOROLOGICAL ORGANIZATION in studying possible climate changes as a result of atmospheric accumulation of greenhouse gases. UNEP was a catalyst in mobilizing the international community to convene the EARTH SUMMIT (United Nations Conference on Environment and Development) in Rio de Janeiro, Brazil in June 1992.

United Nations Fund for Population Activities (UNFPA) The organization created in 1967 by the General Assembly to provide additional resources to the United Nations system for technical cooperation and other activities in the field of human population management. Now the largest internationally funded source of assistance to population programs in developing countries, UNFPA plays a crucial role in family planning projects in these countries, where other sources of technical help often are not available. In addition to family planning, UNFPA assists governments in other special programs for women, youth, the aged, and those with disabilities. It also serves as a documentation center and clearinghouse for relevant information. UNFPA is funded by voluntary governmental contributions. In 1987 UNFPA's name was changed to the United Nations Population Fund, but UNFPA was retained as the official acronym.

United Nations Groups The division of United Nations member states into four groups so that each group can have appropriate representation—that is, fill a fixed number of seats—on various UN agencies, such as the Trade and Development Board of the United Nations Conference on Trade and Development. Group A contains African and Asian states; Group B contains Western European and non-European industrialized countries; Group C contains Central and South American countries; Group D contains Eastern European countries. Groups A and C are sometimes called the GROUP OF 77 because they joined to issue a developing-countries declaration at UNCTAD's first meeting in 1964.

United Nations Headquarters A complex of four buildings situated along the East River in New York City in the United States. The United Nations Charter did not specify where its headquarters should be located. On February 14, 1946, the UN General Assembly accepted the unanimous invitation of the U.S. Congress to locate the United Nations headquarters in the New York City region. Later that year, on December 14, 1946, the General Assembly accepted the offer of John D. Rockefeller, Jr. (1874–1960) to pay $8.5 million for the present 18-acre site on Manhattan's East Side. The City of New York also donated some adjacent parcels of land. Plans for the buildings were approved in 1947, and the first meetings in the new buildings were held in 1952. While the headquarters site is international territory owned by the United Nations, the laws of the United States, with the major exception of normal DIPLOMATIC PRIVILEGES AND IMMUNITIES, generally apply to it. Though UN headquarters are in New York, there are also major regional offices in Geneva, Switzerland; Vienna, Austria; and Nairobi, Kenya.

United Nations High Commissioner for Refugees, Office of the (UNHCR) An agency established by the United Nations General Assembly in 1950 to protect REFUGEES and promote durable solutions to their problems. UNHCR, which is descended from the post–World War I NANSEN INTERNATIONAL OFFICE FOR REFUGEES, depends totally on voluntary contributions from governments and other private sources for its operation. The basic function of UNHCR is to extend international protection to refugees who, by definition, do not enjoy the protection of their former home country. UNHCR

United Nations Industrial Development Organization (UNIDO)

seeks to ensure that refugees receive ASYLUM and are granted a favorable legal status in their asylum country. Material assistance also is essential to enable refugees or displaced persons to achieve permanent solutions to their problems, whether it is through voluntary repatriation, local settlement in the country of first asylum, or migration to another country. Resettlement of Latin American refugees (from the 1980s civil wars in El Salvador and Nicaragua to other states in North and South America) and Indo-Chinese refugees (fleeing, often as BOAT PEOPLE, the oppression of the Communist governments of Vietnam and Cambodia and seeking resettlement anywhere) are examples of instances where UNHCR played a role in negotiating with relevant governments to encourage the admission of refugees or displaced persons into their territories. UNHCR was awarded the Nobel Peace Prize in 1954 and 1981.

United Nations Industrial Development Organization (UNIDO)   The central coordinating body for the United Nations for industrial development. Established by the UN General Assembly in 1966 as an organ to promote and accelerate the industrialization of the DEVELOPING COUNTRIES and to coordinate UN activities in this field, UNIDO was converted to a fully autonomous SPECIALIZED AGENCY in 1986. It promotes cooperation between industrialized and developing countries in accelerating world industrial development; provides a forum for contacts, consultations, and negotiations between them; encourages investment activities; and facilitates TECHNOLOGY TRANSFER. UNIDO also helps bring the public and private sectors together in the planning of regional industrial development. In addition, the organization provides technical assistance in industrial development, organizes industrial training programs, helps countries obtaining external financing, and serves as clearinghouse for industrial information. Headquartered in Vienna, Austria, UNIDO has a General Conference that determines its general policy, a 53-member Industrial Development Board that reviews conference-approved programs and makes recommendations, and a 27-member Program and Budget Committee.

United Nations International Children's Emergency Fund (UNICEF) An agency created by the United Nations General Assembly during its first session in 1946 to meet the emergency needs of children in postwar Europe and China for food, drugs, and clothing. In 1950 the General Assembly changed UNICEF's mandate to cover all programs of long-term benefit to the children of DEVELOPING COUNTRIES. Its name was changed to the United Nations Children's Fund in 1953, but the well-known acronym UNICEF was retained. UNICEF cooperates with the national governments of the developing countries in their efforts to protect children and enable them to develop their full potentials. Its activities include long-term planning; training of personnel in health care, education, nutrition, and child welfare; and delivering supplies such as textbooks, medical equipment, and clean water pumping machinery. UNICEF depends entirely on voluntary contributions to finance its activities. Nearly three-quarters of its income comes from governments; the remaining portion comes from greeting card sales and fund-raising campaigns. UNICEF was awarded the Nobel Peace Prize in 1965.

United Nations Military Staff Committee The military chiefs of staff from each of the five permanent members of the United Nations Security Council—China, France, Great Britain, Russia, and the United States. Under the UN charter, the Military Staff Committee is the council's advisor on military matters and is to give "strategic direction" on such matters. Not used during the Cold War, it was revived in 1990 as a symbolic consultative panel during the PERSIAN GULF WAR.

United Nations Narcotics Convention A treaty adopted in Vienna, Austria, in 1988 and signed by more than 80 states that attempted to codify INTERNATIONAL LAW in the area of narcotics control. (The full name of the treaty is the UN Convention against Illicit Traffic in Narcotics, Drugs and Psychotropic Substances.) The convention establishes several measures for combating drug trafficking. It obligates the parties to criminalize each link in the drug trade—production, processing, and distribution as well as money laundering. It facilitates the removal of bank secrecy and makes it easier to seize assets of drug traders. It requires controls on the international flow of the precursor chemicals that are essential to the processing of drugs by monitoring their manufacture and distribution. In addition, the convention mandates unprecedented cooperation in the investigation and prosecution of trafficking offenses. Finally, it facilitates EXTRADITION of drug traffickers to stand trial, something that the United States has seen as particularly important. The convention was, in fact, advocated by the United States and represents an attempt by Washington to get other governments to accept the same legal standards and approach to the drug problem as the United States.

United Nations Observers Another name for the PEACEKEEPING FORCES of the United Nations.

United Nations Peacekeeping Forces *See* PEACEKEEPING FORCES.

United Nations Relief and Works Agency for Palestine Refugees in the Near East (UNRWA) Established by the United Nations General Assembly in 1949 to help the refugees who lost their homes and livelihood as a result of the Arab-Israeli conflict in PALESTINE in 1948, UNRWA provides education and training, health and relief services to Arab refugees from Palestine in Jordan, Lebanon, Syria, and the OCCUPIED TERRITORIES of the West Bank and Gaza Strip. UNRWA depends on voluntary contributions, mainly from governments, for both its normal and its emergency operations.

United Nations System The United Nations Organization plus its 16 SPECIALIZED AGENCIES and other associated organizations and programs.

United Nations Truce Supervision Organization (UNTSO) A group of military observers appointed by the United Nations Security Council in 1948 to broker an end to the hostilities between the Arab states and the new State of Israel. Armistice agreements were signed in 1949 by Israel and four Arab countries—Egypt, Jordan, Lebanon, and Syria. UNTSO supervised the application and observance of the terms of the agreements.

United Nations Trusteeship Council *See* TRUSTEESHIP COUNCIL.

United States Arms Control and Disarmament Agency *See* ARMS CONTROL AND DISARMAMENT AGENCY.

United States–Canada Free Trade Agreement of 1989 The bilateral treaty designed to eventually remove all TARIFFs between Canada and the United States by 1998. While many trade issues remain unresolved, the treaty provided mechanisms for dealing with them. While the economic advantages for both sides are generally recognized, there was considerable opposition to this agreement in Canada because of fears that Canada might eventually lose its distinct national identity by becoming, in effect, the "fifty-first state" of the United States. But such fears were not enough to threaten seriously the agreement, which was the first step toward the NORTH AMERICAN FREE TRADE AGREEMENT of 1992.

United States Institute of Peace The U.S. government corporation created in 1984 to support research on the peaceful resolution of international conflict mainly through a program of grants and fellowships. According to an editorial in *The New Republic* (November 11, 1991) recommending its dissolution, the institute is "an advisory body whose advice no one in the State Department needs or wants. . . . It survives today as a welfare hotel for political scientists who can't get grants from private foundations, and as a retirement home for aging arms control negotiators." Such a judgment, however, may be far too harsh. The institute provides a forum for the discussion of these issues and has published some particularly useful works on diplomacy, force, and international relations.

United States of Europe The name proposed in 1930 by French Prime Minister Aristide Briand for all of the European members of the LEAGUE OF NATIONS. His proposal was premature. However, by the 1990s, this name was widely, if informally, applied to the European Community.

United States v Curtiss-Wright Export Corporation The 1936 U.S. Supreme Court case defining the U.S. president's constitutional role in foreign policymaking. In 1934 the Congress adopted a joint resolution authorizing the president by proclamation to prohibit the sale (within the United States) of arms to some South American states. President Franklin D. Roosevelt issued such a proclamation. Curtiss-Wright sought to remove this constraint on its business in federal court on the grounds that the joint resolution constituted an unconstitutional delegation of legislative authority to the president. The U.S. Supreme Court eventually upheld the resolution and proclamation on the grounds that the Constitution created the "very delicate, plenary and exclusive power of the president as the sole organ of the federal government in the field of international relations" and that, in the international sphere, the president must be accorded "a degree of discretion and freedom from statutory restriction which would not be admissible were domestic affairs alone involved."

unit veto A term used by U.S. analyst Morton Kaplan (1921–   ) to describe a hypothetical international system in which 20 or so states would have nuclear weapons capable of a FIRST STRIKE. In Kaplan's view, states still would be reluctant to initiate first strikes under such a system, as this would leave their arsenals depleted and make them vulnerable to attack by a third nation. He also contends that there would be little need for alliances in this system, and that those that might develop would be nonideological. In addition, there would be few military interventions, partly because the great powers would tend to be isolationist in orientation.

unity of command 1. The principle of management that each person in an organization should be accountable to a single superior. 2. The concept that a military unit must be led by a single commander. This has long been known. In 1517 Niccolò Machiavelli wrote in *The Discourses:* "It is better to confide any expedition to a single man of ordinary ability, rather than to two, even though they are men of the highest merit, and both having equal ability." Napoleon would later agree: "Nothing is more important in war than unity in command. When, therefore, you are carrying on hostilities against a single power only, you should have but one army acting on one line and led by one commander" (*Military Maxims,* 1827).

Universal Declaration of Human Rights The December 10, 1948, proclamation of the United Nations General Assembly establishing a common standard of achievement for all peoples and all nations. Two years later the General Assembly decided that December 10 of each year should be observed as Human Rights Day all over the world. Articles 1 and 2 of the declaration state that "all human beings are born free and equal in dignity and rights" and are entitled to all the rights and freedoms set forth in the Declaration, "without distinction of any kind, such as race, color, sex, language, religion, political or other opinion, national or social origin, property, birth or other status." The remaining articles set forth the civil and political rights as well as the economic, social, and cultural rights to which all human beings are entitled. Two international covenants were adopted in the 1970s to put into binding legal form the rights proclaimed in the declaration: the International Covenant on Economic, Social and Cultural Rights and the International Covenant on Civil and Political Rights. *See also* HUMAN RIGHTS.

Universal Postal Union (UPU) The SPECIALIZED AGENCY of the United Nations that facilitates the flow of mail across international borders. Created in 1875 by the Berne Treaty, it became a United Nations specialized agency in 1948. UPU forms a single postal territory of countries for the reciprocal exchange of letter-post items. Its objectives are to secure the organization and improvement of the postal services; to take part in postal technical assistance sought by the member countries of the union; and to promote international collaboration in postal matters. Every member state of UPU agrees to transmit the mail of all other members by the best means used for its own mail. The Universal Postal Congress,

composed of representatives of all member countries, is the supreme authority of UPU. It meets every five years to review the Universal Postal Convention and its subsidiary agreements. The Executive Council, composed of 40 members elected by the congress with due regard for equitable geographical distribution, meets annually to ensure the continuity of the work of the union between congresses. The UPU is headquartered in Berne, Switzerland.

UNRWA *See* UNITED NATIONS RELIEF AND WORKS AGENCY FOR PALESTINIAN REFUGEES IN THE NEAR EAST.

UNTSO *See* UNITED NATIONS TRUCE SUPERVISION ORGANIZATION.

urban guerrilla warfare *See* GUERRILLA WARFARE, URBAN.

Uruguay Round The multilateral trade negotiations held under the auspices of GATT. It is called the Uruguay Round because it was initiated by the trade ministers of GATT member states at a 1986 meeting in Punta del Este, Uruguay. However, most of the actual talks were held in Geneva, Switzerland. Over 90 states have participated in these negotiations, which focused on agricultural trade, intellectual property rights, and rules on foreign investment. While the round was scheduled to be completed within four years, it has dragged on into 1993 because of the lack of agreement over agricultural product duties between North America and Europe.

useful idiots A phrase usually attributed to V. I. LENIN that refers to those capitalist politicians and businessmen who can be duped into helping communism.

useful talks Futile diplomatic negotiations. According to John Kenneth Galbraith in *Foreign Service Journal* (1969): "There are few ironclad rules of diplomacy but to one there is no exception. When an official reports that talks were useful, it can safely be concluded that nothing was accomplished."

utilitarianism *See* BENTHAM, JEREMY.

uti possidetis **1.** Latin meaning "as you possess," the Roman law concept that the physical possession of property whose ownership was in dispute should remain with the current possessor until a formal legal determination of ownership could be made. 2. The INTERNATIONAL LAW principle that property not dealt with by a TREATY ending hostilities should remain in the possession of the side that had it when the fighting stopped. 3. The respective territories occupied by opposing armed forces at the end of a war. 4. The principle that the borders of a newly independent state that was formerly a colony should remain those set by the former colonial power. This usage first emerged in the nineteenth century when most of the states of South America gained their independence from Spain.

utopia 1. The Greek word meaning "nowhere." 2. A model of a society that meets the needs of all of its citizens as they perceive those needs; in their terms, the perfect society. 3. A literary form that posits a carefully designed polity that will, by its character, raise contrasts with reality. While conceptions of ideal societies go back to ancient times, it was Sir Thomas More's 1516 book, *Utopia*, that gave the concept its modern name.

utopianism An approach to INTERNATIONAL RELATIONS that focuses on the ideal and how to reach it rather than reality. Those who advocate such approaches tend to see certain changes in the international system as leading to PERPETUAL PEACE. They tend to emphasize the rule of law, the creation of world government, and the abolition of war from the international system.

U-2 incident The events that unfolded after a United States high-altitude "U-2" surveillance plane was shot down by an antiaircraft missile over the Soviet Union on May 1, 1960. Having been assured by the U.S. Central Intelligence Agency, which directed the operation, that the pilot could not have survived, President Dwight D. Eisenhower told the world a lie: that the aircraft was merely an off-course weather research plane. But the Soviets had both the plane wreckage and a live pilot, Francis Gary Powers (1927–1977). A summit meeting had been scheduled for Paris later that month, but armed with this evidence of U.S. surveillance, Soviet Premier Nikita Khrushchev called the spying operation a violation of Soviet air space and demanded an apology. When Eisenhower refused, Khrushchev walked out of the Paris summit. The brief rapprochement of the late 1950s between the two superpowers was over. Khrushchev later said, "I had thought the President sincerely wanted to change his policies and improve relations. Then, all of a sudden, came an outrageous violation of our sovereignty. And it came as a bitter, shameful disappointment. . . . Now, thanks to the U-2, the honeymoon was over" (quoted in Michael R. Beschloss, *Mayday*, 1986). Powers was tried in Moscow and sentenced to ten years in prison. In 1962 he was exchanged for a U.S.-held Soviet spy, RUDOLF ABEL. The whole incident made the COLD WAR colder and undermined Eisenhower's and thus the presidency's credibility with the U.S. public—because the president of the United States had been forced to admit that he had openly and willfully lied to the people.

EISENHOWER EXPLAINS HIS LIE

As to our government's initial statement about the flight, this was issued to protect the pilot, his mission, and our intelligence processes, at a time when the true facts were still undetermined.

Our first information about the failure of this mission did not disclose whether the pilot was still alive, was trying to escape, was avoiding interrogation, or whether both plane and pilot had been destroyed. Protection of our intelligence system and the pilot, and concealment of the plane's mission, seemed imperative. . . .

For these reasons, what is known in intelligence circles as a "covering statement" was issued. It was issued on assumptions that were later proved incorrect. Consequently, when later the status of the pilot was definitely established, and there was no further possibility of avoiding exposure of the project, the factual details were set forth.

SOURCE: President Dwight D. Eisenhower, address to the nation on the U-2 incident, May 25, 1960.

valuation The process of appraising the worth of imported goods; a DUTY is then assessed according to the TARIFF SCHEDULE of the importing country.

value added tax (VAT) A type of national sales tax imposed by almost all Western European countries as a major source of revenue. It is levied on the value added to an item at each stage of production and distribution. Everyone from manufacturer to retailer pays VAT on purchases and in turn charges VAT on sales to customers. Since each one is entitled to tax refunds for the VAT they pay, ultimately the tax is entirely passed on to the last customer—the consumer.

Vance, Cyrus Roberts (1917–   ) The U.S. secretary of the army (1962–1964) and deputy secretary of defense (1964–1967) who was secretary of state for the first three years of the Carter Administration (1977–1980). When Carter approved an ill-fated military rescue mission during the IRANIAN HOSTAGE CRISIS, Vance protested and said he would resign whether the mission succeeded or failed. His resignation on the heels of the failed rescue attempt made the Carter Administration look all the more pathetic in its foreign policy and enhanced Vance's reputation for integrity—especially because resignation in protest is so rare in the U.S. government. Although Vance was part of an administration that often seemed inept, he often proved to be right on key issues. There were many matters on which the recommendations of National Security Advisor ZBIGNIEW BRZEZINSKI were at odds with those of Vance. The two men clashed over DÉTENTE and the relationship between arms control and Soviet geopolitical behavior in the Third World. Vance argued that Soviet advances were unlikely to be enduring in the face of local nationalist sentiment. In retrospect, his views proved to be correct, and Soviet gains in Africa turned out to be ephemeral—as did the Soviet Union itself. Nevertheless, he was undercut by the national security advisor, and his departure reflected not only his dissent over the hostage rescue mission but also the fact that the policies he advocated had been rejected by President Carter in favor of a reversion to a Cold War stance. In the early 1990s Vance surfaced from his private law practice to help mediate the civil war in Yugoslavia.

Vandenberg, Arthur H. (1884–1951) The Republican U.S. senator from Michigan who was an isolationist before World War II but who subsequently became one of the key figures in supporting the Truman Administration's growing commitment to Europe in the latter half of the 1940s. Vandenberg was the chairman of the Senate Committee on Foreign Relations in 1947 and 1948 and helped mobilize domestic support for the TRUMAN DOCTRINE and the MARSHALL PLAN. He also played a major role preparing the way for the North Atlantic Treaty (which created the North Atlantic Treaty Organization), signed in April 1949 and ratified by the Senate in July 1949. The 1948 Vandenberg Resolution recommended U.S. association with regional COLLECTIVE SECURITY organizations based on the principle of self-help and mutual aid. Although the Vandenberg Resolution is generally seen as the green light for the United States to join an entangling alliance with the states of Western Europe, in fact, Vandenberg's role went far beyond support of the resolution. While advocating a growing commitment to Europe, he actually was restraining the Truman Administration from going ahead much faster. Nevertheless, his contribution to the creation of the postwar security system was immense, and he was the key figure in establishing a degree of bipartisan support for the Truman Administration's initiatives. It is no accident that his illness and absence from the Senate in 1950 and 1951 coincided with the breakdown of BIPARTISANSHIP and a Senate Republican assault on Truman's decision to send U.S. troops to Europe.

Vargas, Getulio Dornelles (1883–1954)   Provisional president (1930–1933), elected president (1934–1937), dictator (1937–1945), and elected president (1950–1954) of Brazil, known for his social and economic policies. Under Vargas, Brazil emerged as a world power. Best known for creation of the *Estado Novo* ("New State") upon assuming dictatorial powers in 1937, Vargas modeled his government after fascist regimes, copying their repressive tactics but also passing progressive social legislation and facilitating industrial growth. As a result, both labor and the middle class supported him. In international affairs, he maintained an independent third position between the Western allies and fascist Europe. Nevertheless, in 1945 he was overthrown by a military coup d'état. But after a new constitution was adopted and representative government was restored, he again won election as president in 1950. However, Vargas could not deal effectively with a restless middle class, a multiparty system, or the restriction of presidential powers in a democratic government, and in 1954, amid demands that he resign, he committed suicide.

variable levy   A TARIFF subject to change as world market prices fluctuate, the changes being designed to assure that the import price after payment of duty will equal a predetermined "gate" price. The variable levy of the European Community, for example, equals the difference between the target price for domestic agricultural producers and lower offers for imported commodities.

Vatican City   The few acres around St. Peter's Basilica within Rome, Italy, that houses the Papacy and Curia of the Roman Catholic Church. Vatican City gained independence from Italy and the pope became its temporal leader by the terms of the 1929 LATERAN TREATY.

Vattel, Emerich de (1714–1767)   The Swiss jurist whose *Law of Nations* (1758) provided one of the most comprehensive analyses of the state of INTERNATIONAL LAW. In this study Vattel contended that "justice is the basis for all society" and is even more important between states than between individuals. As he put it: "All nations are . . . under a strict obligation to cultivate justice towards each other, to observe it scrupulously, and carefully to abstain from every thing that may violate it." Vattel does not assume, however, that this will always be the case, and he explicitly acknowledges that each state has a right not to suffer any of its rights being taken away. Moreover, it can lawfully and legitimately resort to force in order to protect this right. Vattel had a robust view of the use of military force and believed that without force to protect their rights, "the just would soon be at the mercy of avarice and injustice, and all their rights would soon become useless." Part of the significance of Vattel's work lies in the way in which it combined ideas from NATURAL LAW theory with deep insight into the nature of the behavior of sovereigns.

V-E Day   May 8, 1945; the day WORLD WAR II ended in Europe when Germany surrendered unconditionally to the Allies. *Compare to* V-J DAY.

Velvet Revolution   1. The peaceful autumn 1989 movement in Czechoslovakia that overthrew the Communist government. The roots of the revolution went back to the PRAGUE SPRING of 1968 and to 1977, when more than 250 people signed a manifesto called CHARTER 77 that criticized the government for its failure to implement human rights provisions of documents it had signed such as its own constitution and the HELSINKI ACCORDS. Charter 77 functioned as a citizens' lobby to induce the Czechoslovakian government to observe its formal obligations to respect the human rights of its citizens. The Communist government responded by subjecting Charter 77 signatories and other dissident groups to periodic harassment, persecution, and imprisonment. As political tensions in neighboring

Poland mounted during the 1980s activities of SOLI-DARITY, the government, fearing a spillover effect, became increasingly repressive. Charter 77 and other new groups critical of the government launched a series of peaceful demonstrations attended by thousands of citizens in Prague in late 1988 and early 1989. Those drew worldwide attention, especially when the regime forcibly dispersed a series of demonstrations in January 1989 and subsequently imprisoned several prominent human rights activists, including dissident playwright VACLAV HAVEL. In November 1989 these disparate groups united to become CIVIC FORUM, an umbrella group championing bureaucratic reform and civil liberties. Civic Forum quickly gained the support of millions of Czechs, as did its Slovak counterpart, Public Without Violence. Faced with overwhelming repudiation by the population, the Communist Party all but collapsed. Its leaders resigned in December 1989 and a new non-Communist government elected Havel as president. The new government ended the Communist Party's leading role in political life, eliminated restrictions on travel abroad, and passed legislation guaranteeing freedom of speech, of assembly, and of conscience. All political prisoners were freed, and work began in earnest on democratic political and economic reform. Ironically, this flowering of reforms and reawakening of political freedom eventually led to the CZECHOSLOVAKIAN DISSOLUTION. **2.** All of the revolutions against Communist governments that occurred in Eastern Europe in the latter half of 1989 and that involved relatively little bloodshed. *See also* GERMAN REUNIFICATION; SOLIDARITY; UNION OF SOVIET SOCIALIST REPUBLICS.

vengeance weapons *See* V-WEAPONS.

Venice Declaration on the Middle East   A 1980 declaration by the COUNCIL OF MINISTERS of the European Community, issued at the conclusion of the council's Venice, Italy, meeting, which affirmed the right of all states in the Middle East to existence and security within recognized and guaranteed borders; announced the willingness of the nine governments represented by the council to participate in international guarantees of a comprehensive settlement; called for self-determination for the Palestinian people and for the involvement of the PALESTINE LIBERATION ORGANIZATION in peace negotiations; opposed any unilateral initiative to change the legal status of Jerusalem; and stated that any future agreement regarding Jerusalem should guarantee freedom of access to the Holy Places.

Verdun, Battle of   The 1916 WORLD WAR I battle of ATTRITION in which the French and Germans suffered an estimated 1 million casualties. The 300-day attack against the French fortress of Verdun on the Meuse River was designed by the head of the German General Staff, General Erich von Falkenhayn (1861–1922), "to bleed France white" by massive attacks on this one key fortress. While PHILIPPE PÉTAIN became a French national hero for his successful defense of Verdun, it was French General Robert Nivelle's defiant statement, "They shall not pass," that became the motto of the defenders. According to Alistair Home's *The Price of Glory* (1962), "Nivelle's . . . irradiating self-confidence . . . really swept people away. His square shoulders gave a potent impression of strength and audacity. His face burned with ruthless determination, and when he expressed an intent his audience was somehow made to feel that it was already fait accompli. It was he, not Pétain as is sometimes thought, who gave birth to the immortalized challenge at Verdun: *'Ils ne passeront pas!'* "

Vereeniging, Treaty of   The 1902 treaty that ended the BOER WAR. The generous terms of the treaty allowed Boer leaders to support cooperation with the victorious British. This in turn led to the South Africa Act of 1910, which made South Africa a dominion under predominantly Boer influence.

verification   **1.** Ascertaining of the accuracy of something.   **2.** A formal statement which confirms the truth of a theory or fact.   **3.** A key element in many ARMS CONTROL agreements. This is a two-step process involving (a) a determination before a treaty of whether the other side could violate the treaty and evade detection and (b) the continuous monitoring of compliance after a treaty is signed and ratified. Verification is important because arms control agreements are generally made by governments that do not fully trust each other. Thus significant arms control measures must be accompanied by adequate provisions for ensuring that each side abides by the agreement, whether through

NATIONAL TECHNICAL MEANS or through negotiated arrangements for more intrusive measures such as ON-SITE INSPECTIONS. Opponents of arms control often use arguments about the difficulties of verification to cast doubt upon the whole process. Increasingly, however, it has become clear that although verification can never be foolproof, it can detect significant violations of a treaty. Since the INF TREATY there also has been a trend toward on-site inspections, something that the Soviet Union under Mikhail Gorbachev and Russia under Boris Yeltsin has been far more willing to accept than ever before.

TRUST—BUT VERIFY

My view is that President Gorbachev is different from previous Soviet leaders. I think he knows some of the things wrong with his society and is trying to fix them. We wish him well. And we'll continue to work to make sure that the Soviet Union that eventually emerges from this process is a less threatening one.

What it all boils down to is this: I want the new closeness to continue. And it will be as long as we make it clear that we will continue to act in a certain way as long as they continue to act in a helpful manner. If and when they don't—at first pull your punches. If they persist, pull the plug.

It's still trust—but verify.

It's still play—but cut the cards.

SOURCE: President Ronald Reagan, farewell address, January 11, 1989.

Versailles, Treaty of   The agreement between Germany and the victorious Allies of WORLD WAR I that was signed in the Hall of Mirrors in the Versailles Palace outside Paris, France, on June 28, 1919. It had territorial, military, and economic clauses. Germany had to surrender 13 percent of its prewar area, give up all colonies as mandates to others, and recognize the independence of Austria. (The last feature was meant to prevent an *ANSCHLUSS*.) The Treaty of Versailles further required the Germans to disarm. They were not to have large artillery, submarines, or an air force. The army was limited to 100,000 volunteers, the GENERAL STAFF was dissolved, and the navy was limited to six battleships; but rather than surrender their fleet, the Germans scuttled it. Germany had to allow French occupa-

tion of the RHINELAND and SAAR regions and was ordered to pay REPARATIONS later set at 33 billion marks, which it could not afford. Many Germans considered the treaty a humiliating DIKTAT. At first their representatives refused to sign but the Entente powers insisted. The Treaty of Versailles also contained the war guilt clause (ARTICLE 231) and the Covenant of the LEAGUE OF NATIONS. *See also* PARIS PEACE CONFERENCE.

Verwoerd, Hendrik F. (1901–1966)   The prime minister of South Africa from 1958 until his death. Educated in Germany, he became a professor of sociology at South Africa's University of Stellenbosch (1927–1937) until he resigned to protest the admission of Jewish refugees from Nazi Germany. He then edited an Afrikaner Nationalist newspaper that attacked "British-Jewish imperialism" and opposed South African participation in World War II. Becoming minister of native affairs in 1950, he was responsible for enforcing and expanding APARTHEID. When he became prime minister in 1958, he outlawed the AFRICAN NATIONAL CONGRESS, imprisoned NELSON MANDELA, and withdrew South Africa from the British COMMONWEALTH OF NATIONS. In 1966 he was stabbed to death on the floor of the parliament by a white government employee. He was succeeded by BALTHAZAR VORSTER.

veto   **1.** Latin for "I forbid"; the right of any of the five permanent members of the United Nations SECURITY COUNCIL (China, France, Russia, the United Kingdom, and the United States) under Article 27 of the UN charter to prevent any decision by withholding agreement. This was a necessary element in ensuring that a split between the great powers did not lead to a breakdown in the organization itself.   **2.** The disapproval of proposed legislation by any chief executive who has formal authority to do so.

Vichy   The WORLD WAR II collaborationist French government created in 1940 by the French National Assembly in the spa town of Vichy to administer that part of France (and its colonies) unoccupied by Germany. The Nazi puppet regime was headed by the World War I hero of VERDUN, Marshal PHILIPPE PÉTAIN, who was given autocratic powers. With Vichy as its capital, the new regime banned strikes

Jacob A. Malik, Soviet representative on the UN Security Council, raises his hand to veto a resolution calling on the Chinese Communists to withdraw troops from Korea, December 1950. (National Archives)

and trade unions, suppressed the RESISTANCE, sent French slave laborers to Germany, and cooperated with the GESTAPO in rounding up Jewish French citizens for deportation to CONCENTRATION CAMPS. The Vichy regime was never recognized by the Allies and soundly denounced after the war. Its leading members, Pétain and PIERRE LAVAL, were later tried for and convicted of treason. However, since most of France collaborated anyway, the regime, when it was in power, was not as unpopular as hindsight would suggest.

Victor Emmanuel III   The king of Italy from 1900 to 1946. When parliamentary democracy was in disarray in 1922, he invited the fascists under BENITO MUSSOLINI to form a government. While the fascists reduced him to a figurehead, they did make him, albeit briefly, the emperor of Ethiopia (1936–1943) and the king of Albania (1939–1943). In 1943, when the Italians seemed to be on the losing side in World War II, he dismissed Mussolini, concluded an armistice with the Allies, then declared war on Germany. When the future of the Italian monarchy was put to a national referendum in 1946, he abdicated in favor of his son, Umberto II, three weeks before the polling. Nevertheless, the monarchy was abolished. Victor Emmanuel died in exile in Egypt the following year.

Vienna Congress   *See* CONGRESS OF VIENNA.

Vienna Convention on Consular Relations   The United Nations–sponsored multinational agreement initially signed by 92 states in Vienna, Austria, in 1963, that created the currently operable international norms on the status, privileges, and immunities of consular officials. Until this time consular relations were negotiated by bilateral treaties and regional agreements.

Vienna Convention on Diplomatic Relations   The United Nations–sponsored multinational agreement initially signed by 81 states in Vienna, Austria, in 1961, that created the currently operable international norms on diplomacy and DIPLOMATIC RELATIONS. In addition to dealing with the status, privileges, and immunities of diplomatic officials, the convention codifies procedures for ACCREDITATION, *AGRÉMENT*, establishing DIPLOMATIC MISSIONS, and so on. This was the first comprehensive international revision of these practices since the 1815 CONGRESS OF VIENNA.

Vienna Summit Conference   1. The 1961 Soviet-U.S. conference where new U.S. President John F. Kennedy first met the Soviet first secretary of the Communist Party, Nikita Khrushchev. The main issue was the BERLIN CRISIS. Khrushchev told Kennedy that "Berlin is a cancerous sore in the throat that has to be cut out" (*Newsweek*, June 19, 1961). Kennedy reaffirmed the United States' determination to defend West Berlin. Because the two men did not get on well, COLD WAR tensions increased. **2.** The 1979 meeting between U.S. President Jimmy Carter and Soviet Premier Leonid Brezhnev where the SALT II treaty was signed.

Vienna Treaty Convention The Vienna Convention on the Law of Treaties, which was produced in 1969 and which came into force in January 1980. Although not all states became parties to it, the convention attempted to codify the existing customary law on treaties and in some cases to engage in "progressive development" of the law. It deals with the conclusion of treaties, which covers adoption of the text, the consent of the parties to be bound by a treaty, its entry into force, and the issue of reservations. The convention also deals with the application of treaties, the issue of invalidity, and the termination of treaties by mutual consent and otherwise. *See also* TREATY.

Viet Cong The Communist insurgents in South Vietnam during the VIETNAM WAR. Formally the *Viet Nam Cong San* ("National Liberation Front of Vietnamese Communists"), in the early 1960s, with the support of the government of Communist North Vietnam, they initiated a major effort to overthrow the U.S.-supported government of South Vietnam. After failing to succeed by using traditional guerrilla and terror tactics, they launched a full-scale offensive during the Tet holiday in 1968 and were virtually wiped out by South Vietnamese and U.S. forces. Thereafter, most of the fighting by the Communists was done by military units of North Vietnam. The TET OFFENSIVE was significant for the Viet Cong, however, in that it helped to break the U.S. will to continue with the war.

Viet Minh The principal guerrilla group headed by HO CHI MINH, which opposed the Japanese occupation of French Indochina in World War II. After the war the Viet Minh, increasingly dominated by Communists, resisted all French efforts to establish Vietnam as a free state within the French Union. The ensuing warfare became intense, and the French chose to withdraw from Vietnam after their defeat at DIEN BIEN PHU. Vietnam was then partitioned into South and North. The Viet Minh operating in the South fled to the North. Soon thereafter, under direct control of the North Vietnamese gov-

A Viet Cong prisoner of war, captured during the Tet Offensive in 1968. (National Archives)

ernment, they began returning to the South, where they and their South Vietnamese collaborators came to be designated as VIET CONG and fought the United States in the VIETNAM WAR. They formed the spearhead of the North Vietnamese invasions of the South, which ultimately resulted in the takeover of South Vietnam by the North Vietnamese in 1975.

Vietnamization U.S. President Richard M. Nixon's 1969–1975 face-saving policy of withdrawing U.S. forces from the VIETNAM WAR by gradually transferring the combat burden to South Vietnamese troops. Commentator Walter Lippmann almost immediately saw the flaw in the policy: "This must be just about the first time in the history of warfare that a nation has thought it could prevail by withdrawing combat troops and reducing its military presence" (*Newsweek,* December 1, 1969). Senator George S. McGovern testified before the U.S. Senate Committee on Foreign Relations on February 4,

U.S. troops in Vietnam in 1969. (Department of Defense)

1970, and said, "The policy of Vietnamization is a cruel hoax designed to screen from the American people the bankruptcy of a needless military involvement in the affairs of the Vietnamese people." But Vietnamization worked—assuming that its goals were mainly to extricate U.S. troops in an orderly fashion. The South Vietnamese Army held off the North (or the North allowed itself to be held off) until the U.S. presence was essentially gone. The fact that the North then promptly conquered the South does not detract from the success of a policy that was in effect premised upon a tacit agreement by the North to allow the Americans just to leave.

Vietnam syndrome The perceived reluctance of the U.S. citizenry to see their armed forces involved in a long, drawn-out war for no purpose that they could understand or support overwhelmingly. It was interpreted by many to be a general unwillingness to see U.S. forces used in any foreign conflict. However, in the wake of the PERSIAN GULF WAR, U.S. President George Bush on March 1, 1991, would proudly announce: "It's a proud day for Americans and, by God, we've kicked the Vietnam syndrome once and for all."

Vietnam War The 1956–to–1975 war between the non-Communist Republic of Vietnam (South Vietnam) and the Communist Democratic Republic of Vietnam (North Vietnam), which resulted in the victory of the North over the South and the unification of the two countries into the Communist Socialist Republic of Vietnam on July 2, 1976. The United States first offered financial support to South Vietnam during the Eisenhower Administration, after the French withdrawal following their 1956 defeat at DIEN BIEN PHU. Military assistance began with the Kennedy administration in 1961. By 1963 the United States had 16,000 military ADVISORS in South Vietnam. In 1964 the GULF OF TONKIN RESOLUTION allowed the administration of Lyndon B. Johnson to expand U.S. involvement in spite of the fact that Johnson had promised, notably in a campaign speech in Akron, Ohio, on October 21, 1964: "We are not about to send American boys nine or ten thousand miles away from home to do what Asian boys ought to be doing for themselves." Johnson lied about his intentions, but he had his reasons. He told his biographer Doris Kearns in 1970: "I knew that Harry Truman and Dean Acheson had lost their effectiveness from the day that the

Communists took over in China. I believed that the loss of China had played a large role in the rise of Joe McCarthy. And I knew that all these problems, taken together, were chickenshit compared with what might happen if we lost Vietnam" (*Lyndon Johnson and the American Dream*, 1976).

By 1968 the United States had over 500,000 men engaged in the most unpopular foreign war in U.S. history. As a direct result, the Democrats lost control of the White House to Republican Richard M. Nixon. The Nixon Administration's policy of VIET-NAMIZATION called for the South Vietnamese gradually to take over all the fighting from the U.S. soldiers. The United States continued to pull out, and the South held off the North for a while. As U.S. forces dwindled, the North became more aggressive and successful. Finally, the North's January 1975 offensive led to the South's unconditional surrender by April.

More than 58,000 U.S. soldiers died in the Vietnam War; another 150,000 were wounded. The views of the war held in the United States still diverge very considerably. Some believe that if the war had been fought without being micromanaged from Washington, United States forces would have been much more successful. This view was represented by President Ronald Reagan when he said on February 24, 1981, that U.S. soldiers "came home without a victory not because they had been defeated but because they had been denied permission to win." A similar view was evident in the comment of Graham A. Martin, the last U.S. ambassador to South Vietnam, who was quoted in the *New York Times* (April 30, 1985) as saying: "In the end, we simply cut and ran. The American national will had collapsed." On the other side are those who believe that the war was a profound strategic and moral blunder, that the United States extended CONTAINMENT to a region in which it was far less applicable, attempted to frustrate genuine nationalist aspirations of the Vietnamese, backed a succession of governments that lacked LEGITIMACY, and essentially fought an illegitimate and unwinnable war. President George Bush in his Inaugural Address of January 20, 1989, observed: "That war cleaves us still. But, friends, that war began in earnest a quarter of a century ago; and surely the statute of limitations has been reached. This is a fact: The final lesson of Vietnam is that no great nation can long afford to be sundered by a memory." Yet memories of Vietnam had a major impact on U.S. policy in the confrontation with Iraq in 1990 and 1991. U.S. military leaders, represented most articulately by the chairman of the Joint Chiefs of Staff, Colin Powell, were anxious to avoid the mistakes of Vietnam and made clear that if force was to be used, it should be used massively and decisively. This is what occurred, and the war against Iraq was fought without political interference in day-to-day operations.

VIETNAM WAR
A Chronology

1959	January	North Vietnam adopts a policy of "armed struggle" to take over South Vietnam.
	April 4	U.S. President Dwight D. Eisenhower, in a speech at Gettysburg College, commits the United States to support South Vietnam as an independent state.
	July 8	First two U.S. military "advisors" killed by Viet Cong.
1960	December	Vietnamese Communists form the National Liberation Front.
1961	June 9	South Vietnam requests U.S. troops for training mission.
	December 15	U.S. President John F. Kennedy renews U.S. commitment to independence of South Vietnam.
1962	February 6	U.S. Military Assistance Command located in Saigon. Major buildup of U.S. advisors begins.
1963	November 22	President Kennedy assassinated; over 16,000 U.S. military personnel in South Vietnam.
1964	August	U.S. Congress passes GULF OF TONKIN RESOLUTION.
1965	February	After Viet Cong attack on U.S. military in South Vietnam, United States bombs North Vietnam for the first time.
	March	First U.S. ground combat troops arrive in South Vietnam.
	December	By end of year 184,300 U.S. military personnel in South Vietnam; 636 killed in action since war began.

1966	September	U.S. announces it is using defoliants (Agent Orange) to destroy enemy ground cover.
	December	By end of year 385,300 U.S. military personnel in South Vietnam; 6,644 killed in action since war began.
1967	October 31	Fifty thousand antiwar protesters stage a "March on the Pentagon."
	December	By end of year 485,600 U.S. military personnel in South Vietnam; 16,021 killed in action since war began.
1968	January 30	TET OFFENSIVE begins.
	January 31	U.S. embassy in Saigon attacked.
	March 16	MY LAI massacre.
	March 31	U.S. President Lyndon B. Johnson announces he will not seek reelection.
	May 12	Peace talks with North Vietnam begin in Paris.
	August 28	Massive antiwar protests at Democratic National Convention in Chicago.
	November 5	Republican Richard M. Nixon, asserting that he has a plan to end the war, defeats Vice President Hubert H. Humphrey in the presidential election.
1969	December	By end of year 536,100 U.S. military personnel in South Vietnam; 30,641 killed in action since war began.
	March 26	Secretary of Defense Melvin Laird announces VIETNAMIZATION of war.
	June 8	President Nixon announces first U.S. troop withdrawals.
	July 25	NIXON DOCTRINE promulgated.
	November 15	Quarter-million people demonstrate in Washington against Vietnam War.
	December	By end of year 475,200 U.S. military personnel in South Vietnam; 40,024 killed in action since war began.
1970	April 30	CAMBODIAN INCURSION announced.
	December	By end of year 334,600 U.S. military personnel in South Vietnam; 44,245 killed in action since war began.
1971	March 29	Lt. William Calley, Jr., found guilty of murder at MY LAI.
	June 13	New York Times begins publishing PENTAGON PAPERS.
	December	By end of year 156,800 U.S. military personnel in South Vietnam; 45,626 killed in action since war began.
1972	April	Massive antiwar demonstrations throughout United States.
	December	By end of year 24,200 U.S. military personnel in South Vietnam; 45,926 killed in action since war began.
1973	January 27	PARIS AGREEMENT signed.
	March	North Vietnam releases 590 U.S. prisoners of war.
	December	By end of year only 50 U.S. military personnel in South Vietnam; 46,163 killed in action since war began; almost 10,000 more died in noncombat incidents.
1975	January	North Vietnam launches major offensive to take over South.
	April	North Vietnam conquers South Vietnam. Vietnam is unified and war is over.

vigilantism   The actions and underlying beliefs of *vigilantes*, private citizens who undertake to redress through extralegal violent action the perceived or actual failure of legal law enforcement authorities. Vigilante groups commonly have been active in states where police and government authorities have been unable to prevent or control TERRORISM; they arise out of frustration with the state's ineffectiveness and the desire to exact revenge. The Ulster Defense Forces in Northern Ireland and Latin American death squads are well-known examples of vigilante groups that, through illegal and extremely violent means, have utilized terrorism themselves. Vigilante terrorist groups often are identified with the political status quo and many times have included "off-duty" policemen whose illegal activities have tacit government approval. In such state-condoned cases, vigilante groups may be seen as elements of covert STATE-SPONSORED TERRORISM, in which "independent" groups are encouraged to carry out illicit operations with which the state does not wish to be associated publicly.

Villa, Francisco (Pancho Villa) (1874–1923) The political radical and military leader of masses of peasants in northern Mexico during the MEXICAN REVOLUTION. His followers demanded structural reform of both the government and land ownership. His raids across the border into New Mexico gave U.S. President Woodrow Wilson reason to send U.S. troops into Mexico in a futile mission to capture Villa in the MEXICAN BORDER CAMPAIGN.

***Vincennes* incident** The accidental shooting down of Iran Air Flight 655 by the USS *Vincennes* in the Persian Gulf on July 3, 1988. The warship believed it was under attack by an Iranian military plane; its high-technology radar could not distinguish that this was in fact a commercial passenger plane. The *Vincennes* then fired antiaircraft missiles, which killed all 290 civilians on the aircraft. Many believe that the bombing of PAN AM FLIGHT 103 later that year was sponsored by Iran to avenge this incident.

violation 1. The breaking of a law, rule, or agreement. 2. An action that does not accord with the behavior that is expected as a result of a treaty or other international obligation.

Violencia, La The period of extreme domestic violence in Colombia that extended from approximately 1946 to 1958, during which more than 200,000 persons were killed. From 1946 to 1950 alone, it is estimated that 112,000 persons died. Most of the deaths of La Violencia were attributable to civilian violence; there has been much debate about its underlying causes. While it was essentially a rural conflict between conservatives and would-be reformers, it was made all the more intense by banditry and personal feuds. *La Violencia* was eventually suppressed by the 1953–1957 brutal dictatorship of General Gustavo Rojas Pinilla (1900–1975), although sporadic rural violence has continued ever since.

Visa A document, usually in the form of a stamp in a PASSPORT, that allows a citizen of one state to visit another.

Visegrad nations Czechoslovakia, Hungary, and Poland, which agreed to cooperate on economic, foreign, and military policy in a meeting held at

A U.S. Navy sailor and a nurse celebrate the surrender of Japan with a kiss in Times Square, New York. (National Archives)

Visegrad, Hungary, in early May 1992. However, this regional effort at international cooperation may have been stillborn because after Czechoslovakia broke up later in 1992, Slovakia and Hungary began a bitter dispute over Slovakia's intention to divert the waters of the Danube River.

V-J Day September 2, 1945; the day WORLD WAR II ended in the Pacific when Japan surrendered on the USS *Missouri* anchored in Tokyo Bay. *Compare to* V-E DAY.

Vladivostok Accord An ARMS CONTROL agreement reached in November 1974 in Vladivostok (a Russian Pacific Ocean port) at the summit meeting between U.S. President Gerald Ford and Soviet Premier Leonid Brezhnev. This provided much of the framework for the final agreement on a SALT II

Treaty that was signed five years later. The Vladivostok Accord established an aggregate ceiling of 2,400 launchers and heavy bombers for each of the superpowers and permitted a sublimit of 1,320 launchers with multiple independently targeted warheads (MIRVs). Although the accord appeared to have gone a long way toward a new strategic arms control treaty, progress was slow in the aftermath of this summit. In part this was because the Vladivostok Accord was criticized by those who argued that it did little or nothing to constrain the THROW-WEIGHT of Soviet missiles. Moving from the accord to final agreement also was made more difficult by the appearance of new weapons systems, such as the CRUISE MISSILE on the U.S. side and the Backfire bomber on the Soviet side. Additionally, the negotiations were interrupted by the deep defense cuts proposed by the Carter Administration in 1977 that ignored the framework agreed upon in Vladivostok. This agreement was all the more disconcerting to the Soviet leadership because the accord had not been popular with the Soviet military anyway. According to one Soviet official, as reported by Strobe Talbott in *Endgame* (1979), "Brezhnev had to spill blood to get the Vladivostok accords."

Voice of America   The United States Information Agency's radio broadcasting service that transmits U.S. news, public affairs, and cultural and musical programs to overseas audiences in 41 languages; founded in 1942 for the purpose of combatting enemy PROPAGANDA and explaining the United States' wartime goals and disseminating its own propaganda to the world. It was continued after World War II as part of an information program designed to foster world understanding of the United States and its policies. In 1953 it became a part of the U.S. Information Agency, which had overall responsibility for administering U.S. information programs abroad. In 1978 USIA (including the Voice of America) and several other agencies were absorbed into the new International Communication Agency. The ICA was established as an independent federal agency, but its policy guidance comes from the secretary of state.

volte-face   A French term meaning a diplomatic "about-face"; a sudden reversal of a previously enunciated policy.

voluntary export restraint   Import relief measures taken outside the GATT framework by states wishing to protect domestic industries from injury by foreign competition. In the United States such devices are called ORDERLY MARKETING AGREEMENTS; in the EUROPEAN COMMUNITY they are called voluntary restraint agreements. *See also* EXPORT QUOTAS.

voluntary restraint agreement (VRA)   An informal bilateral or multilateral agreement in which exporters voluntarily limit exports of specified goods to a particular state in order to avoid economic dislocation in the importing state and the imposition of mandatory import restrictions. Unlike an ORDERLY MARKETING AGREEMENT, a VRA is both informal and has no definite time limit. *See also* EXPORT QUOTA.

Vo Nguyen Giap   *See* GIAP, VO NGUYEN.

Vorster, Balthazar (1915–1983)   The prime minister of South Africa from 1966 to 1978. Jailed for pro-Nazi involvement during World War II, he later became a Nationalist Party member of parliament. He was minister of justice (since 1961) when Prime Minister HENDRIK F. VERWOERD was assassinated. Succeeding him as prime minister, Vorster continued his predecessor's strict APARTHEID policies. Ill health forced his resignation in 1978. He left public life altogether the following year (1979) amid a scandal about his government's misuse of public funds. He was succeeded by PIETER W. BOTHA.

vote of confidence   In a PARLIAMENTARY SYSTEM, the formal approval that a party needs from a majority of the legislature if it is to continue in office. A legislative majority that has become disenchanted with the current administration may call for a vote of no confidence to force the government to resign or to call an election. If the government wins the vote of confidence, it stays in office.

Vranitzky, Franz (1937–   )   The Federal chancellor of Austria since 1986. Trained as a banker, he joined the government as finance minister in 1984 and was elected chancellor two years later. He has accepted responsibility for the role of many Austrian citizens in the ANTI-SEMITISM that produced the HOLOCAUST, supports HEXAGONAL GROUP relations with neighboring Alpine Danubian countries, and has led Austria's efforts to gain admission to the European Community.

vulnerability **1.** A sense of weakness. **2.** The susceptibility of a state or military force to any action by any means through which its war potential or combat effectiveness may be reduced or its will to fight diminished. **3.** The characteristics of a system that cause it to suffer a definite degradation (incapability to perform the designated mission) as a result of having been subjected to a certain level of effects in an unnatural hostile environment. **4.** A weakness that may be exploited by an adversary. Threats by others are often seen in terms of one's own weaknesses. **5.** A situation in which it is impossible to provide defense. During the Cold War, for example, the populations of the United States and the Soviet Union were in a position of vulnerability to the other side's strategic missile force, although threats of retaliations mitigated the effects of this vulnerability and made it unlikely that there would be any attempt to exploit it. *See also* WINDOW OF VULNERABILITY.

V-weapons The "vengeance" rocket weapons developed by the Germans at PEENEMÜNDE under the direction of WERNHER VON BRAUN toward the end of World War II. The V-1, or flying "buzz bomb," was first used against the civilian population of London in June 1944. The V-2, also used against London as well as other cities beginning in September 1944, was the first ballistic missile of the modern era. The V-weapons' developers formed the nucleus of both the U.S. and Soviet ICBM programs in the postwar era.

Waldheim, Kurt (1919–   )   The Austrian career diplomat who was the secretary general of the United Nations from 1972 to 1981 and president of Austria from 1986 to 1992. It was during his successful bid to be elected Austria's president in 1986 that his role as a junior officer in the WEHRMACHT during World War II was uncovered. Waldheim had always admitted that he served briefly in the German Army. But what he hid, lied about, and later admitted was that he had served as a lieutenant in the Balkans with a German Army unit that was guilty of widespread atrocities. These revelations did not prevent the Austrians from electing him president. But in that role he was ostracized by most of the other governments of the world. The Reagan Administration even barred him from traveling to the United States. The U.S. Justice Department said that while there was no definite proof that Waldheim had committed war crimes, the "evidence collected establishes a prima facie case that Kurt Waldheim assisted or otherwise participated in the persecution of persons because of race, religion, national origin or political opinion" (*Time,* May 11, 1987).

WALDHEIM ON REPRISALS

The reprisal measures imposed in response to acts of sabotage and ambush have, despite their severity, failed to achieve any noteworthy success, since our own measures have been only transitory, so that the punished communities or territories soon have to be abandoned once more to the [partisan] bands. On the contrary, exaggerated reprisal measures undertaken without a more precise examination of the objective situation have only caused embitterment and have been useful to the bands.

SOURCE: Lieutenant Kurt Waldheim, report on enemy activities in Greece sent to the chief of the general staff of Army Group E, May 25, 1944; quoted in Robert Edwin Hertzstein, *Waldheim: The Missing Years* (1988). Hertzstein notes that [Waldheim] "didn't argue that the German policy of reprisals was evil or criminal, merely that it was counterproductive. And whatever motivated it, there is no evidence that Waldheim ever openly criticized or otherwise protested against Nazi brutality on any other occasion."

Waldheimer's disease   Forgetting you were once a NAZI. This is a play on the term Alzheimer's disease, which causes loss of memory. Now whenever an old man who has denied a Nazi past is exposed, he is said to be suffering from Waldheimer's disease—named for KURT WALDHEIM, the most famous person who seemed to have this "medical" problem.

Walesa, Lech (1943–   )   The president of Poland since 1990; the electrician who, starting as a member of a trade union and instigator of strikes, quickly rose to become the father of SOLIDARITY in Poland. In 1980 the National Coordination Commission of Solidarity was created; the government recognized it in November of that year as a national union. Walesa was elected Solidarity chairman, but served only briefly because of his 11-month internment due to the installation of the STATE OF WAR. He was awarded the 1983 Nobel Peace Prize for his efforts at peaceful reform. In the presidential election in 1990, he defeated his once-close Solidarity trade union ally, former Prime Minister TADEUSZ MAZOWIECKI, as well as the "Dark Horse" challenger, emigré businessman STANISLAW TYMINSKI. Walesa waged a pugnacious and populist campaign against the Mazowiecki government he had largely created, while promising the public higher wages and better working conditions. Since entering office in November 1990, Walesa has abandoned his election platform and continued the strict economic reform policy created by the Mazowiecki government. Despite some economic progress, Walesa is faced with continuing economic hardship, the complete disintegration of the Solidarity party, a threat from Tyminski and his growing party, and (less seriously) pressure to lose weight to look more like a "western head of state."

WALESA ANSWERS THE QUESTION
"Has Communism Failed?"

It depends on the way you measure the concept of good, bad, better, worse, because, if you choose the example of what we Polish have in our pockets and in our shops, then I answer that Communism has done very little for us. If you choose the example of what is in our souls, instead, I answer that Communism has done very much for us. In fact our souls contain exactly the contrary of what they wanted. They wanted us not to believe in God and our churches are full. They wanted us to be materialistic and incapable of sacrifices; we are anti-materialistic, capable of sacrifice. They wanted us to be afraid of the tanks, of the guns, and instead we don't fear them at all.

SOURCE: *The Sunday Times* (London) March 22, 1981.

---

walk back the cat   A slang phrase for a retreat from a negotiating position; going from a hard-line stand to one more open to compromise.

walk in the woods   The initial arms control discussions that eventually led to the INF TREATY. Strobe Talbott describes how it came about in *The Master of the Game* (1988): "The climactic session occurred on the rainy afternoon of July 16, 1982. [Paul] Nitze and [Yuli] Kvitsinsky drove into the . . . mountains outside the village of Saint-Cergue near the French border. There, on a wooded mountainside where Geneva-based diplomats often went to ski cross-country, the two men went for a long walk. Eventually they sat on a log and, sheltering their papers against the drizzle, put the finishing touches on what they called 'a joint exploratory

package for the consideration of both governments.' It became known as the 'walk in the woods' formula." In 1988 a play by Lee Blessing entitled *A Walk in the Woods* and based on this actual event premiered on Broadway in New York.

Waltz, Kenneth (1924–   )   One of the leading U.S. figures in the study of international relations in the period since World War II. Kenneth Waltz has provided the intellectual arguments that became the basis for what has become known as NEOREALISM. The essence of the neorealist position is that the distribution of power within the international system has a major impact on both the stability of the system and the actions of the units (the states) within it. The importance of the international system has been a major theme in Waltz's analyses of international relations. In his first major book, *Man, the State and War: A Theoretical Analysis* (1959), he concluded that the anarchic nature of the international system was the most important cause of war. The structural realism theme is developed most fully in *Theory of International Politics* (1979). The other notable thing about Waltz is that he often turns conventional wisdom on its head. In *Foreign Policy and Democratic Politics: The American and British Experience* (1967), for example, he challenged the orthodoxy that the British parliamentary system was better at making foreign policy than the U.S. system based on the separation of powers. He did something similar in *The Spread of Nuclear Weapons: More May Be Better* (1981). Not surprisingly, therefore, his work has received considerable attention.

Wannsee Conference   A January 1942 meeting in a villa near Berlin, Germany, where NAZI officials met to discuss the best ways for the extermination of the Jews of Europe. This meeting did not initiate the HOLOCAUST (which was well underway); it was basically a business meeting of Nazi FINAL SOLUTION executives.

war   **1.** Violence and destruction inflicted by one state upon another in an effort to gain complete domination or a lesser political goal.   **2.** Diplomacy using force. According to KARL VON CLAUSEWITZ's *On War* (1832): "War is not merely a political act, but also a political instrument, a continuation of

A 1936 antiwar cartoon. (Library of Congress)

political relations, a carrying out of the same by other means." **3.** Anarchy; a state of nature without law. As Thomas Hobbes wrote in *Leviathan* (1651): "During the time men live without a common power to keep them all in awe, they are in that condition which is called war: and such as is of every man against every man." **4.** "An organized bore," according to Oliver Wendell Holmes, Jr. (1841–1935), the U.S. Supreme Court justice who served in the Civil War as a Union officer (quoted in C. Bowen, *Yankee from Olympus,* 1944). He expressed the common frustration that so much of military action is inaction—specifically, waiting. This definition has been confirmed in many other accounts. For example, Harry G. Summers, Jr.,

wrote in *On Strategy* (1982): "As every combat veteran knows, war is primarily sheer boredom punctuated by moments of stark terror." **5.** "The unfolding of miscalculations," according to Barbara Tuchman's *The Guns of August* (1962). **6.** Hell, according to U.S. General William Tecumseh Sherman. In a famous speech at the Michigan Military Academy on June 19, 1879, he said: "I am tired and sick of war. Its glory is all moonshine. It is only those who have neither fired a shot nor heard the shrieks and groans of the wounded who cry aloud for blood, more vengeance, more desolation. War is hell." **7.** "A biological necessity," according to German General Friedrich von Bernhardi in *Germany and the Next War* (1911). **8.** "An immense art which comprises all others," according to Napoleon I (quoted in J. Christopher Herold, *The Mind of Napoleon,* 1955). Common to all definitions of war is use of large-scale violence by one group against another. While this captures the essence of war, however, there are many distinctions and gradations to the concept that are also important. Many of these are very obvious, such as the distinction between CIVIL WAR and INTERNATIONAL WAR, between CONVENTIONAL WARFARE and NUCLEAR WARFARE, and between TOTAL WAR and LIMITED WAR. Nevertheless, by introducing such distinctions it is possible to obtain a fuller appreciation of the forms that war can take. Currently a major question concerns the future of war, particularly at the international level. Some analysts argue that international war has lost both its legitimacy and its utility. In terms of legitimacy, it is argued that democracies have been able to fight legitimate wars because they have been pitted against autocratic states. As democratization becomes increasingly global, however, there are some suggestions that this will make it even more difficult to resort to war, as modern democracies have never fought each other. Another dimension of the obsolescence thesis is that territorial gains no longer have the same value as they did in the past and that economic developments within states have become more important than territorial aggrandizement. A third argument is that the growth of economic interdependence has made it more difficult for states to go to war with each other. This argument is used predominantly in relation to Western Europe. While these arguments are persuasive, the idea that war will fade away is not wholly persuasive, at least so long as there is an international system without a central overriding authority.

FDR ON WAR

I have seen war. I have seen war on land and sea. I have seen blood running from the wounded. I have seen men coughing out their gassed lungs. I have seen the dead in the mud. I have seen cities destroyed. I have seen two hundred limping, exhausted men come out of the line—the survivors of a regiment of a thousand that went forward 48 hours before. I have seen children starving. I have seen the agony of mothers and wives. I hate war.

SOURCE: U.S. President Franklin D. Roosevelt, speech at Chautauqua, New York, August 14, 1936.

---

war, accidental   A war begun not by the leader of either side but because of a technical malfunction or the actions of insubordinate underlings. The nuclear age has brought about a pervasive fear of a nuclear war started by accident. Accidental war is a concept that is sometimes confused with inadvertent war. Whereas an inadvertent war would be one that resulted from a sequence of crisis moves that lead to hostilities even though the participants are anxious to avoid war, the notion of accidental war is narrower in focus. The idea is that some kind of malfunction of the nuclear DETERRENCE systems of a major powers could precipitate hostilities. These malfunctions could be the result of human error or irrationality, of technical problems such as false warnings, or more simply of accidents such as collisions that result in a nuclear explosion. Such events could have a particularly malevolent effect in times of crisis, as they might contribute to the belief on the part of the other side that war had begun.

war, broken-backed   The combat that might continue after a nuclear war between nuclear powers had stopped. In this highly theoretical concept it is assumed that any surviving military units would be conventional in nature and thoroughly disorganized. This was a fashionable concept in the 1950s but quickly faded into obscurity.

war, brushfire   1. A brief regional war that does not involve outside powers.   2. Local wars whose opposing sides become surrogates for, in effect proxies of, outside powers.

war, catalytic   See CATALYTIC WAR.

war, civil   An armed conflict between military units within the same state or political entity. Most of organized warfare since World War II has been civil war. Examples include the Korean War, the Vietnam War, Nicaragua in the 1980s, and Northern Ireland.

war, controlled counterforce   A military conflict in which one or both sides concentrates on destroying the armed forces of the enemy and makes a special effort to avoid harming civilian targets.

war, conventional   See CONVENTIONAL WARFARE.

war, dirty   See DIRTY WAR.

war, general   An armed conflict involving major powers and their allies in which all resources are used and national survival is at stake.

war, guerrilla   See GUERRILLA WARFARE.

war, hot   An active war in which nations engage each other in combat, as opposed to a COLD WAR in which bluster, rhetoric, and maneuver are the main armaments.

war, inadvertent   A war that results from an error of judgment, a miscalculation of opposition intentions, a misinterpreted threat or false intelligence. The classic example is World War I, which historian Barbara W. Tuchman described in *The Guns of August* (1962) as "the unfolding of miscalculations."

war, internal   See CIVIL WAR.

war, law of   See LAW OF WAR.

war, limited   See LIMITED WAR.

war, local   A war that is confined to a specific region or state, such as Vietnam or Afghanistan, even though some participating states may be from outside the area. A local war can be contrasted to a regional war (which involves a variety of states in the same region), which, in turn, can be contrasted to a world war (which involves many states on various continents.) *Compare to* LIMITED WAR.

war, low-intensity   *See* LOW-INTENSITY WARFARE.

war, phony   *See* PHONY WAR.

war, preemptive   A military attack launched in the belief that the adversary is poised to attack and that it is advantageous to strike first. Preemption is inherently related to the issue of survivability of military forces. The less survivable one's forces, the less able they are to ride out an enemy attack, the more incentive there is to strike preemptively. If both sides have highly vulnerable forces, the situation is doubly unstable. Temptations for preemptive actions during a crisis between the nuclear superpowers were a cause for concern at various junctures during the Cold War. This explains why there was an emphasis on making strategic nuclear forces invulnerable to a FIRST STRIKE. Crisis stability depends on there being no incentive for preemption. The most famous example of a preemptive strike at the conventional level was the Israeli attack on the Egyptian air force at the beginning of the 1967 Six-Day War. Feeling that it was about to be attacked, Israel decided that it would strike first and obtained a major military advantage by doing so. A preemptive strike is not necessarily illegal under international law. As far back as 1625 Francis Bacon wrote in his *Essays* ["Of Empire"] that: "A just fear of imminent danger, though there be no blow given, is lawful cause of war." *Compare to* WAR, PREVENTIVE.

A PREEMPTIVE GENERAL

"If I see that the Russians are amassing their planes for an attack," [U.S. General Curtis] LeMay continued, "I'm going to knock the shit out of them before they take off the ground."

[Robert C.] Sprague [a National Security Council advisor] was thunderstruck by the revelation. . . . Most startling was LeMay's final bit of news [as SAC commander in the late

1950s], that he would order a preemptive attack against Soviet air bases.

"But General LeMay," Sprague said, "that's not national policy."

"I don't care," LeMay replied. "It's my policy. That's what I'm going to do."

SOURCE: Fred Kaplan, *The Wizards of Armageddon* (1983).

---

war, preventive   Hostilities initiated in the belief that war, while not necessarily imminent, is inevitable, and that delay would pose an even greater risk. There is a thin line between preventive and preemptive action; the difference is essentially one of time. In a preventive war, hostilities are intended to stop not an impending attack but one that is deemed likely to occur at some time in the future. The idea of a preventive war against the Soviet Union was seriously considered by the United States during the early part of the COLD WAR. A preventive strike against Soviet nuclear installations was advocated when it was apparent that the United States was about to lose its nuclear advantage, but the idea was rejected as being inconsistent with the principles of a democratic state. For example, no less a figure than Francis P. Matthews, U.S. secretary of the navy, speaking on August 25, 1950, stated that "[A preventive war against the Soviet Union] would win for us a proud title—we would become the first aggressors for peace" (*The Nation*, September 9, 1950). Shortly thereafter Matthews was appointed ambassador to Ireland by President Truman. *Compare to* WAR, PREEMPTIVE.

war, proxy   *See* PROXY WAR.

war, psychological   The use of PROPAGANDA and other techniques to influence the attitudes, emotions, opinions, and ultimately the behavior of enemy military forces or populations in an effort to secure national objectives. Often involving an attempt to undermine enemy morale, it may be conducted simultaneously with open warfare or be used before or after the hostilities. Its many forms range from airdrops of leaflets to radio broadcasts to enemy-conveyed misinformation. Prior to World War II, Germany was especially adept at exaggerating its military capability to intimidate other European powers. Psychological warfare also was widely used during World War II. For example, Allied troops in the Far East were appealed to by TOKYO ROSE, while German attempts to undermine British morale included radio broadcasts by the traitor Lord Haw Haw. During the Falklands War psychological warfare was used by the British against Argentina: They broadcast popular music with messages in Spanish telling of anxious Argentine mothers and of the superiority of the British troops.

war, punitive   A war that is said to be waged solely to punish another state for a real or alleged wrong-doing. This should be distinguished from a *punitive strategy*, which is designed to hurt the other side in the war and bring about surrender or at least greater willingness to bargain.

war, push-button   1. A military conflict fought at such a high degree of sophistication in weapons technology that, quite literally, there is no hand-to-hand fighting; instead some sort of missiles are released by the push of a button. Push-button warfare describes the use of antitank or antiaircraft weapons at the conventional level, a full-scale exchange of strategic nuclear weapons, or anything in between.   2. A vague term for what is seen as an unhealthy and unnatural detachment from traditional warfare caused by modern weapons. Those who complain about push-button warfare bemoan the loss of heroism that characterized wars in the past. This sense of detachment is particularly poignant with regard to the possible use of nuclear weapons: the removal of the operators of the technology from the consequences of their actions, in terms of their awareness of that destruction or their exposure to similar danger, reduces the meaning of their actions so as to make the process automatic and technical.

war, spasm   Nuclear retaliation against an enemy with all possible weapons without special concern for military targets or war aims—just total vengeful destruction. This might well be the end of humanity. However, as Desmond Morris observed in *The Naked Ape* (1967): "There is a strong chance that we shall have exterminated ourselves by the end of the century. Our only consolation will have to be that, as a species, we have had an exciting term of office." Fortunately the end of the Cold War means that the possibility of a spasm war is now more remote.

war, tanker   That phase of the IRAN-IRAQ WAR in which each side launched attacks on the other's oil tankers or on the tankers of other Persian Gulf states that were shipping oil. This action led the United States to decide to escort Kuwaiti tankers in a REFLAGGING exercise. No "tanker war" was ever declared. This was just the informal name given to these events by the world press.

war, thermonuclear   A conflict involving the use of the HYDROGEN BOMB. Although there has been much discussion by strategic analysts about whether such a war could be limited, policymakers during the Cold War saw it as something to be avoided at all costs. Indeed the specter of thermonuclear war was one of the considerations that helped to keep the Cold War cold.

war, total   *See* TOTAL WAR.

War Communism   The economic system and policy of the Russian BOLSHEVIKS from 1918 to 1921. The aims of War Communism were to gain sufficient Communist control over the populace and economy to win the RUSSIAN CIVIL WAR. After the BREST-LITOVSK TREATY there was increasing centralization of power by the BOLSHEVIKS at the expense of local units. Along with the increasing exclusion of other groups, the party was being transformed from a revolutionary nucleus into an administrative one-party apparatus. A famine in the spring of 1918 enveloped the cities and countryside. Riots and a breakdown of transportation threatened Bolshevik authority. Thus stringent controls, such as the nationalization of industry, control of foreign trade, and the concentration of economic power at the center, known as War Communism, were implemented in early 1918. Many aspects of these unpopular policies were replaced in 1921 by the NEW ECONOMIC POLICY.

war correspondent   A reporter assigned by his or her news medium to a theater of operations. Modern war correspondents are products of modern journalism. While initially they were able to send only letters (or correspondence) back to their papers, since the advent of the telegraph they have been relatively instant sources of war news. Their main occupational frustration, besides occasionally being killed by the warring parties either purposely or accidentally, is military censorship. Today's archetypical war correspondent is more likely to be a television reporter and a camera team than a traditional print journalist. Richard Harding Davis (1864–1916), who covered six wars, was the journalist who set the pattern for the modern war correspondent. When TV journalists don a bush jacket and describe a battle in purple prose, they are paying homage to him.

HEMINGWAY'S INFLUENCE

It is impossible to realize how much of Ernest Hemingway still lives in the hearts of men until you spend time with the professional war correspondents. Most of the Americans are stuck in the Hemingway bag and they tend to romanticize war, just as he did. Which is not surprising: unlike fighting in the war itself, unlike big-game hunting, working as a war correspondent is almost the only classic male endeavor left that provides physical danger and personal risk without public disapproval and the awful truth that for correspondents, war is not hell. It is fun.

SOURCE: Nora Ephron, "The War Followers" (*New York* magazine, November 12, 1973).

---

war crime   **1.** A criminal act that remains illegal even when it is committed during war and under orders. Thus many German and Japanese officers were convicted of war crimes after World War II because their conduct went beyond what was considered allowable in war—especially when it involved the murder of prisoners of war or the systematic killing of whole populations of innocent, noncombatant civilians.   **2.** An act that the victor determines to be illegal after a war is over. As analyst Garry Wills said, "Only the winners get away with their lies, as only the winners decide what were the war crimes" (*New York Times,* July 10, 1975).   **3.** War itself. Voltaire wrote, "War is the greatest of all crimes; and yet there is no aggressor who does not color his crime with the pretext of justice" (*The*

Ignorant Philosopher, 1767). Ernest Hemingway, two centuries later, found the same: "Never think that war, no matter how necessary, nor how justified, is not a crime. Ask the infantry and ask the dead" (*Treasury of the Free World,* 1946).   **4.** A violation of an international peace treaty. For example, the Treaty of Versailles held Kaiser William II of Germany guilty of crimes against peace "for the highest affront to international morality and to the holy inviolability of treaties."

war crimes trials   *See* NUREMBERG TRIALS; TOKYO INTERNATIONAL MILITARY TRIBUNAL.

warfare, political   *See* POLITICAL WARFARE.

warfare, unconventional   *See* UNCONVENTIONAL WARFARE.

war-fighting   **1.** Combat, as opposed to DETERRENCE.   **2.** A nuclear war that follows a slow, controlled path of ESCALATION involving periods of cease-fire (or firebreaks) for intrawar bargaining. This highly theoretical concept is very unpopular because it implies fighting a nuclear war to win. However, according to former U.S. Secretary of Defense Robert S. McNamara (quoted in Gregg Herken's *Counsels of War,* 1985), "American nuclear policy has been a stated policy of warfighting with nuclear weapons from the beginning." Nuclear war theorist HERMAN KAHN agreed: "If we want to deter war, we must prepare for the chance that deterrence may fail—meaning we must be ready to actually fight a nuclear war and win. I call this 'thinking the unthinkable.' If we are unwilling to make this leap of imagination, our deterrent system is not credible" (*U.S. News & World Report,* September 21, 1981).

War for Nigerian Unity   *See* BIAFRA.

war game   **1.** A rehearsal of military strategy and tactics; a simulation, by whatever means, of a military operation involving two or more opposing forces, using rules, data, and procedures designed to depict an actual or assumed real-life situation. Traditionally, the term war game was used to describe MILITARY EXERCISES. Since World War II it also has been used to describe computer-generated crises or war simulations involving nuclear powers. These simulations may be used as teaching devices for military officers or diplomats engaging in role-playing and decision making about how to respond to the crisis. Alternatively, they have been used by systems analysts to help predict possible contingencies and to identify means of dealing with them. **2.** A commercial game sold in toy stores and hobby shops that allows players to refight, on a game board (or computer screen), a famous battle. **3.** War itself conceptualized as a game. It was KARL VON CLAUSEWITZ in *On War* (1832) who first observed that "war became essentially a regular game in which time and chance shuffled the cards."

war guilt clause   *See* ARTICLE 231.

warhead   That part of a missile, torpedo, or other projectile that contains the materials intended to do damage; very simply, the "business end" of a missile or other delivery vehicle, whether it be a submarine torpedo or smart bomb.

war of attrition   A war wherein the aim is primarily the killing of the enemy's forces and destroying its military materiel. The problem with this is that the enemy may be doing the same to the other side. World War I became the classic war of attrition when both sides were stalemated on the Western Front to the point of exhaustion. The stalemate was ended when one side, the Allies, had a large infusion of new troops (from the United States) and a new weapon (the tank), which allowed for maneuver. According to military expert Edward N. Luttwak, attrition is "war in the administrative manner . . . in which the really important command decisions are in fact logistic decisions. The enemy is treated as a mere inventory of targets, and warfare is a matter of mustering superior resources to destroy his forces by sheer firepower and weight of materiel" (*Survival*, March/April 1979).

war of national liberation   A Communist phrase for an INSURGENCY that attempts to overthrow an established non-Communist regime. The concept of wars of national liberation was related to the idea of the international CLASS STRUGGLE and reflected the Soviet Union's support for any movement, revolution, or uprising in the developing world that was

seen as weakening the West. This also was a major means by which the Soviets responded to the United States policy of CONTAINMENT without directly provoking the North Atlantic Treaty Organization allies. In 1961 Soviet Premier Nikita Khrushchev made a major speech in which he emphasized that the Soviet Union would support "wars of national liberation." In the United States, this was seen by the Kennedy Administration as a major and direct challenge. Consequently, the United States placed considerable emphasis on developing a capacity for COUNTERINSURGENCY, which was designed to ensure that wars of national liberation were unsuccessful. In the 1980s the roles were reversed as the United States supported what could be termed right-wing wars of national liberation against Marxist-Leninist governments.

war plans   **1.** Aggressive intentions by one state toward another. **2.** The logistical and staff planning undertaken prior to the commencement of a military opertion. **3.** The strategies and tactics used by a military leader.

CLAUSEWITZ ON WAR PLANS

War plans cover every aspect of a war, and weave them all into a single operation that must have a single, ultimate objective in which all particular aims are reconciled. No one starts a war—or rather, no one in his senses ought to do so—without first being clear in his mind what he intends to achieve by that war and how he intends to conduct it. The former is its political purpose; the latter is operational objective.

SOURCE: Karl von Clausewitz, *On War* (1832).

---

war powers   The legal authority to initiate war. In a republican form of government this power usually resides with the elected representatives of the people in a national legislature, such as the U.S. Congress or the British House of Commons. However, the practice has been that such republican regimes allow their presidents or prime ministers effectively to commit forces for limited actions without consultation. Some see this as an executive usurpation of legislative authority. Others view it as a prudent response to the conditions of the modern world. In traditional monarchies or dictatorial regimes war powers effectively reside with whoever controls the armed forces.

War Powers Resolution of 1973   The United States law that seeks to clarify the respective roles of the president and the Congress in cases involving the use of military forces without a declaration of war. The law specifies that the president "in every possible instance" shall consult with the Congress before introducing troops and shall report to the Congress within 48 hours of doing so. The use of the armed forces is to be terminated within 60 days (with a possible 30-day extension by the president) unless the Congress acts during that time to declare war, enacts a specific authorization for use of armed forces, extends the 60- to 90-day period, or is physically unable to meet as a result of an attack on the United States. At any time before the 60 days expires, the Congress may direct by concurrent resolution that U.S. military forces must be removed by the president. The War Powers Resolution was a direct response to presidential abuses of war-making authority during the Vietnam War. In one sense the resolution has been a failure: It has not been able to remedy the fact that presidents routinely ignore Congress in matters of foreign policy. On the other hand, the desire to avoid putting the resolution to the test has led administrations to be somewhat more responsive to Congress than they might otherwise have been. The Reagan Administration, for example, withdrew United States forces from Lebanon when it became clear that there was little congressional or public support for the action there. *See also* DECLARATION OF WAR; UNDECLARED WAR.

war-proneness   The propensity of a particular state or international system to go to war. It is widely argued, for example, that democracies are less prone to going to war than are authoritarian states. Moreover, much of the debate about the relative STABILITY of bipolar as opposed to multipolar international systems revolves around the issue of which type is the more war-prone.

war reserve   Stocks of materiel amassed in peacetime to meet military requirements in time of war. War reserves are intended to provide the interim support essential to sustain operations until resupply can be effected.

war room   **1.** That part of a military headquarters where current information is maintained on situation maps, charts, and computers. (The war room at the U.S. Pentagon is called the National Military Command Center.)   **2.** By analogy, a political headquarters organized for rapid responses to an evolving political campaign or crisis situation.

THE U.S. WAR ROOM DESCRIBED

Deep in the Pentagon behind heavy oak doors is a super secret room. . . . Shifts of officers from all four branches of the military maintain a round-the-clock vigil in this two-story chamber. A red telephone provides a direct link to the White House. Lifting a beige phone instantly establishes contact with any U.S. military commander anywhere in the world. One wall is covered with huge computer-fed display screens which flash the readiness of all American forces. A touch of a button will provide an item-by-item inventory of strategic weapons "on target." This is the War Room—the National Military Command Center; nerve center for the most potent military force in the world—control room for the modern automated war.

SOURCE: Robert C. Aldridge, *First Strike!* (1983).

Warsaw Ghetto Uprising   The April–May 1943 revolt of the Jews of Warsaw, Poland, who had all been forced to live in or relocated to a 3.5-square-mile area of the city during the German occupation of WORLD WAR II. After over 400,000 Jews of the ghetto had been deported by the Germans to CONCENTRATION CAMPS, the approximately 60,000 remaining, who by then knew of the gas chambers awaiting them, chose to fight rather than go quietly to their deaths. Those who did not die in the fighting were either burned alive as the ghetto was set ablaze or captured and transported to the Treblinka death camp. Only a handful survived the war. They remain the major example of Jewish civilians mounting an organized resistance to German efforts to kill them—by killing a significant number of Germans (at least 300) in return.

Warsaw Pact   A multilateral military alliance formed by the 1955 Treaty of Warsaw comprised of the Soviet Union, Bulgaria, Czechoslovakia, East Germany, Hungary, Poland, and Romania. The pact was ostensibly created as a Communist counterpart to the NORTH ATLANTIC TREATY ORGANIZATION and to counter the threat of a remilitarized West Germany. In fact, the parties already were integrated into the Soviet military system through standard treaties of alliance concluded between 1945 and 1948. The pact had a joint command under Soviet leadership, and all forces came under Soviet command in wartime. But as Soviet forces began their withdrawal from Eastern Europe in 1989–1990 and the two Germanys reunited, the pact for all practical purposes disintegrated. Although the pact was treated in some respects as the counterpart to NATO on the Soviet side, there were important differences. Whereas NATO was a voluntary alliance, the Warsaw Pact was, in part at least, a means of maintaining and enhancing Soviet control over the states of Eastern Europe. It also was used to provide a multilateral forum for Soviet actions such as the invasion of Czechoslovakia. Indeed, it was commonly joked that the difference between the two alliance systems was that, to keep their allies in order, the United States threatened to pull troops out, whereas the Soviet Union threatened to send them in. For all of its weaknesses the Warsaw Pact appeared to be a formidable military force—and when calculations of the military balance in Central Europe were made, it was almost invariably regarded as quantitatively superior to NATO. Without an underlying voluntary consensus, however, the Warsaw Pact was highly vulnerable to political change. In the aftermath of the revolutions of 1989 and the reunification of Germany in 1990, there was little role for the Warsaw Pact. It was formally dissolved in 1991.

Warsaw rising   The August-to-October 1944 attempt by Polish underground forces in Warsaw, Poland (known as the Home Army), to expel the occupying Germans from their capital. They were defeated; all were killed or captured. In response to the 10,000 casualties that the Germans suffered, they destroyed all of the major buildings of the city and forcefully resettled (to CONCENTRATION CAMPS and elsewhere) most of the surviving inhabitants. The rising was an effort by the anti-Communist Home Army to take control of its capital as the RED ARMY advanced from the east. But Soviet leader Joseph Stalin specifically halted the advance on the city to give the Germans time to destroy the only major anti-Communist group in Poland. The Red Army finally took the city in January 1945, and Poland remained under Soviet domination for over 40 years after that.

war trap   An approach to the analysis of war that looks at the conditions under which states go to war and focuses largely on the expected utility, the perceived advantages, for a stronger state to initiate a war against what appears to be a militarily weaker one. It is a trap because these expected utilities or advantages often fail to materialize. This concept was developed by Bruce Bueno de Mesquita in *The War Trap* (1981).

war-weariness hypothesis   The argument that war induces in its participants a desire to avoid further war for several years. For example, the United States after the Vietnam War was reluctant to get involved in further military action in the Third World. Similarly, France and Great Britain after World War I were reluctant to go to war once again and are often cited as examples of states suffering from war-weariness. LEWIS F. RICHARDSON is generally credited with one of the early systematic statements of the war-weariness hypothesis; he argued that long and costly bouts of fighting make those who have experienced them very reluctant to experience them again and immune to any attractions resort to war may appear to have. Although there is a strong prima facie case that the war-weariness hypothesis is correct, empirical studies have generally not found evidence to substantiate it.

Washington Naval Conference   The winter 1921–1922 meeting where the major maritime nations agreed to limit the naval arms race and to reduce tensions in the Pacific Ocean. Its principal agreements were the FIVE POWER TREATY, which set a tonnage limit for the capital ships of France, Great Britain, Italy, Japan, and the United States; the Four Power Treaty, by which France, Great Britain, Japan, and the United States agreed to respect each other's Pacific holdings and agreed not to build new fortifications in the Pacific except for Singapore and Pearl Harbor, the chief forward bases of Great Britain and the United States; and the Nine Power Treaty (by the first five plus Belgium, China, the

Netherlands, and Portugal), which guaranteed the territorial integrity of China. Japan, which signed all the treaties, ignored them shortly thereafter. *See also* LONDON NAVAL CONFERENCE.

Watergate The political scandal that eventually led to the resignation of U.S. President RICHARD M. NIXON. The Watergate is a hotel-office-apartment complex in Washington, D.C. When persons connected with the Republican Party's Committee to Reelect the President were caught breaking into the Democratic National Committee Headquarters (then located in the Watergate complex) in 1972, the resulting coverup and evolving scandal was condensed into one word—Watergate. The term has grown to refer to any political crime or scandal that undermines the public's confidence in its governing institutions.

Wazir, Khalil al- (1936–1988) Also known as Abu Jihad ("Father of the Holy War"); the Palestine Liberation Organization military chief assassinated on April 16, 1988, when a nine-man commando team stormed his headquarters in Tunis. Israel's government is believed to have organized the attack on Wazir, who was thought to have been leading the PLO's supporting effort in the INTIFADA.

weapon of last resort How successive British governments have described Great Britain's nuclear force. This emphasizes the point that the British independent nuclear deterrent has no war-fighting role; that it would not be part of a strategic ESCALATION. Therefore, it exists only for use "in the last resort," presumably to retaliate against a nuclear strike on Great Britain itself. Yet the British nuclear force is officially dedicated to the North Atlantic Treaty Organization and is supposed to come under the targeting plans developed by SACEUR (whose plans are based on the possible early use of nuclear weapons). If this casts doubt on the term, however, in another sense it is appropriate—it is very difficult to conceive of nuclear weapons being used in any way other than as a last resort.

weapons of mass destruction In ARMS CONTROL usage, devices that are capable of the greatest possible destruction; generally nuclear, chemical, and biological weapons.

weapons system A general term for an armament and all those component parts necessary for its operation. It can be as small as a pistol and its ammunition or as large as a manned battle tank and its support trucks. Much of the argument over defense spending deals with which weapons systems should be purchased and how many.

Weber, Max (1864–1920) The German sociologist who produced an analysis of an ideal-type bureaucracy that is still the most influential statement—the point of departure for all further analyses—on the subject. Weber also pioneered the concepts of the Protestant ethic, charismatic authority, and a value-free approach to social research. *See also* CHARISMA; LEGITIMACY. For Weber's major works, see Max Weber, *Protestant Ethic and the Spirit of Capitalism*, trans. Talcott Parsons (1904–5, 1958); H. H. Gerth and C. Wright Mills, eds., *From Max Weber: Essays in Sociology* (1946).

Wehrmacht 1. German meaning "defense force"; the German Army. 2. The entire German military establishment.

Weimar Republic The government of Germany that arose from the defeat of its imperial army in World War I and the revolution against the monarchy that culminated in the abdication of Kaiser WILLIAM II. It lasted from 1919 to 1934. Its constitution, written at Weimar (because Berlin was in turmoil), had provisions for a president, chancellor, and bicameral parliament. Its constitution was enlightened, guaranteeing civil liberties and having direct elections of the president and *Reichstag* (a legislature) by universal suffrage. The Weimar government had to immediately accept the humiliating Treaty of VERSAILLES and cope with both REPARATIONS and hyperinflation. The republic enjoyed some stability from 1923 to 1929 with the DAWES PLAN, which reduced reparations, and the LOCARNO PACT of 1925, which recognized borders with Germany's neighbors. When the GREAT DEPRESSION hit in 1929, unemployment soared in Germany. It was the worst in Europe. The Nazis rose to power and the republic effectively ended in 1933 shortly after ADOLF HITLER became chancellor of Germany; it formally ended in 1934 after the death of its last president, PAUL VON HINDENBURG. The only other president was FRIEDRICH EBERT, who served from 1919 to 1925.

Weinberger, Caspar W. (1917–   )   The U.S. secretary of defense (1981–1987) under Ronald Reagan, during a period in which the United States engaged in a massive military buildup in response to concerns over the Soviet threat and what was seen as a DECADE OF NEGLECT in the 1970s. Weinberger's tenure at the Pentagon was marked by considerable controversy, and critics contended that he was neither manager nor strategist. He was, however, a single-minded advocate of higher defense spending and of the STRATEGIC DEFENSE INITIATIVE. He also took a very strong line in opposing ARMS CONTROL agreements with the Soviet Union. Weinberger lost the battle on arms control as the second Reagan Administration gradually moved toward a new détente with the Soviet Union under Mikhail Gorbachev. Nevertheless, he did succeed in establishing the principle that certain preconditions have to be met before the United States should resort to military force, conditions that became known as the WEINBERGER DOCTRINE.

Weinberger Doctrine   A set of conditions that U.S. Secretary of Defense CASPAR W. WEINBERGER suggested should be met before the United States used military force in any circumstance. These six conditions were outlined in a speech to the National Press Club on November 28, 1984: (1) The United States should not commit forces to combat unless it was a matter of vital interest; (2) if forces were committed this should be done wholeheartedly and with the intention of winning; (3) there should be clearly defined political and military objectives; (4) there should be a continual reassessment of the situation; (5) there should be reasonable assurance that the use of force would have the support of Congress and the public; and (6) it should be a last resort. The speech was part of Weinberger's bureaucratic struggle with Secretary of State GEORGE P. SHULTZ, who wanted to use force in support of diplomacy and placed less emphasis on military victory and more on flexibility.

Weizmann, Chaim (1874–1952)   The Russian-born British chemist who became the first president of Israel from 1948 until his death. In 1916 Weizmann helped Great Britain solve a major problem in producing cordite, an ingredient in explosives and a requirement during World War I. In part because of this notable contribution to the war effort, Weizmann, then long active in the Zionist movement, became a major influence in the negotiations that led to the BALFOUR DECLARATION.

West Bank   Those lands on the West Bank of the Jordan River occupied by Israel since the 1967 SIX-DAY WAR. The West Bank is a locus of the Israeli-Palestinian struggle. In recent times it has been embroiled in the youth uprising known as the INTIFADA. In November 1988 the West Bank was declared part of an independent Palestinian state by the PALESTINIAN NATIONAL COUNCIL. It is U.S. policy that the final status of the West Bank and the Gaza Strip has yet to be determined. In the view of the United States, the term West Bank describes all of the area west of the Jordan River under Jordanian administration before the 1967 Arab-Israeli war. However, with respect to negotiations envisaged in the CAMP DAVID ACCORDS, it is U.S. policy that a distinction must be made between Jerusalem and the rest of the West Bank because of the city's special status and circumstances. Therefore, a negotiated solution for the final status of Jerusalem could be different in character from that of the rest of the West Bank.

Western European Union (WEU)   An organization that aims to strengthen the peace and security of Western Europe and to promote unity by means of cooperation in defense, economic, and political matters. This body is the successor to the BRUSSELS PACT whose original members were Belgium, France, Great Britain, Luxembourg, and the Netherlands. Following the accession of Germany and Italy in 1955, the organization was renamed the Western European Union. In 1988 Spain and Portugal became members. With headquarters in London, the chief organs of WEU are the council and the assembly: The council is the supreme authority, and consists of the foreign ministers, or the ambassadors resident in London; the assembly, which meets twice a year in Paris, consists of the delegates of the member countries to the Parliamentary Assembly of the COUNCIL OF EUROPE. *See also* EUROPEAN DEFENSE COMMUNITY; EUROPEAN DEFENSE IDENTITY.

Western Front Germany's defensive battle line against allied forces on its western border (mainly in France) during both world wars. This was in opposition to the *Eastern Front,* which faced the forces of Russia in World War I and the Soviet Union in World War II. The senseless brutality along the Western Front during World War I was immortalized in Erich Maria Remarque's 1929 novel, *All Quiet on the Western Front.*

Westminster, Statute of *See* COMMONWEALTH OF NATIONS.

Westpolitik A term that was used by the Federal Republic of Germany in the early 1970s to counterbalance its policy of *OSTPOLITIK.* The argument was that while Bonn was attempting to improve relations and establish closer links with the Soviet Union and the Soviet bloc countries, it was firmly rooted in the Western Alliance. The concept was meant to reassure those in the West who were apprehensive about the implications of Ostpolitik for Western cohesion and for West German loyalty.

Whitehall 1. The center of government in the United Kingdom. 2. That area of London, England, between Trafalgar and Parliament squares in which government buildings have historically (since the time of Henry VIII) been concentrated. 3. By analogy, the most senior members of the British civil service.

White House The official residence of the president of the United States and the architectural embodiment of the bureaucratic institution that is the modern U.S. presidency; thus U.S. foreign policy is often said to come from this building, which, indeed, is painted white. It is located in Washington, D.C.

white man's burden 1. The notion that Europeans and North Americans have special obligations to control the nonwhite world for its betterment. Author Rudyard Kipling (1865–1936) used this title for an 1899 poem to justify late nineteenth-century IMPERIALISM. It advocated the Victorian concept that Europeans had a duty to educate "backward" races in European culture and ways. In the wake of the Spanish-American War, it urged the United States, which had just acquired the Philip-

pine Islands, to assume the work of empire too. Today the term "white man's burden" is considered inherently racist and is not used except in a historical or sarcastic sense. 2. By analogy, the obligation of the industrialized nations to aid in the economic development of the THIRD WORLD.

IMPERIAL POLICY

Take up the White Man's burden—
Send forth the best ye breed—
Go bind your sons to exile
To serve your captives' need;
To wait in heavy harness
On fluttered folk and wild—
Your new-caught, sullen people,
Half-devil and half-child.

SOURCE: Rudyard Kipling, *The White Man's Burden* (1899).

---

white paper An official statement about a government policy, with appropriate background documentation.

white propaganda *See* PROPAGANDA.

WHO *See* WORLD HEALTH ORGANIZATION.

widening *See* EUROPEAN COMMUNITY WIDENING.

Wiesel, Elie (1928–   ) The Rumanian-born U.S. novelist and essayist who was liberated from BUCHENWALD concentration camp in 1945. In 1986 he was awarded the Nobel Peace Prize for a wide-ranging body of work that bears witness to the HOLOCAUST.

Wilhelmstrasse The street in Berlin, Germany, on which the German Foreign Ministry was located from 1871 to 1945; thus it became the metaphor for German foreign policy.

William (Wilhelm) II (1859–1941) Germany's posturing KAISER (1888–1918) who was the grandson of Great Britain's Queen Victoria. After dismissing OTTO VON BISMARCK as chancellor in 1890, he aggressively campaigned to establish a world role for Germany. To achieve his dream of a power-

William (Wilhelm) II (1859–1941)

The kaiser (center) in 1917 with Generals Hindenburg (left) and Ludendorff (right). (National Archives)

ful German Navy, he embarked on a naval race with the British. This race, along with such acts as congratulating the Boers in South Africa for resisting the British, severely antagonized Great Britain. His government's failure to renew a treaty with Russia allowed it to ally with France; this would eventually force Germany into a two-front war in 1914. Although William attempted to stop the beginning of WORLD WAR I in 1914, his actions up to that time had helped make war likely. While the kaiser played little part in the war itself, he was the symbol of arrogant German MILITARISM. He didn't even say the most memorable thing credited to him. On October 1, 1914, *The Times* (London) quoted him as saying: "It is my royal and imperial command that you . . . exterminate first the treacherous English, and . . . walk over [British] General French's contemptible little army." But according to Paul Fussell's *The Great War in Modern Memory* (1975), "It is now known that the phrase emanated not from the German side but from the closets of British propagandists, who needed something memorable and incisive to inspirit the troops. The phrase was actually devised at the [British] War Office by Sir Frederick Maurice and fathered upon the Kaiser." (This is why British troops in World War I sometimes called themselves, with affection,

the "old contemptibles.") William was forced to abdicate and go into exile in the Netherlands in November 1918. The Dutch government, not being part of the war nor party to the Paris Peace Conference, refused to hand him over as requested for trial by the allies. When he died in the German-occupied city of *Doorn* in 1941, German leader Adolf Hitler insisted that his passing be given minimal publicity.

WILLIAM THE INADEQUATE!

William II had none of the qualities of the modern dictators, except their airs. He was a picturesque figurehead in the center of the world stage, called upon to play a part far beyond the capacity of most people. . . . His undeniable cleverness and versatility, his personal grace and vivacity, only aggravated his dangers by concealing his inadequacy. He knew how to make the gestures, to utter the words, to strike the attitudes in the Imperial style. He could stamp and snort, or nod and smile with much histrionic art; but underneath all this posing and its trappings, was a very ordinary, vain, but on the whole well-meaning man, hoping to pass himself off as a second Frederick the Great.

SOURCE: Winston Churchill, *Great Contemporaries* (1937)

Williams, Betty   *See* CORRIGAN, MAIREAD.

Wilson, (James) Harold (1916–   )   The Labour Party prime minister of Great Britain from 1964 to 1970, and again from 1974 to 1976. He became leader of the Labour Party upon the death of HUGH GAITSKELL in 1963 and prime minister a year later. Domestically he was plagued with economic problems and was forced to devalue the pound in 1967. Internationally he was unable to prevent Rhodesia (now Zimbabwe) from issuing a UNILATERAL DECLARATION OF INDEPENDENCE in 1965, and his government's sanctions on the white minority government proved ineffective. Wilson's refusal to condemn the U.S. role in the VIETNAM WAR alienated him from the far left of his party, while his refusal to send troops there and to broker a peace angered the Johnson Administration in the United States—which was even more displeased in 1968 when Wilson announced Great Britain's withdrawal EAST OF SUEZ. After leading his party to slender victory in 1974, he again became prime minister but retired unexpectedly shortly after his sixtieth birthday in 1976.

Wilson, (Thomas) Woodrow (1856–1924)   The Democratic president of the United States from 1913 to 1921. Previously he had been president of Princeton University (1902–1910) and governor of New Jersey (1911–1913). Domestically he championed progressive reforms such as the Federal Reserve System, the Federal Trade Commission, and the modern income tax. Internationally he initially sought to keep the United States out of WORLD WAR I and broker a peace between the belligerents. Indeed his second-term campaign slogan in 1916 was "He kept us out of war." But Germany's use of unrestricted submarine warfare, the sinking of the *LUSITANIA*, and the ZIMMERMAN TELEGRAM forced him reluctantly to bring the United States into the war on the side of France and Great Britain. After the war he became the foremost advocate of the LEAGUE OF NATIONS and was frustrated by his inability to get the U.S. Senate to agree to U.S. participation. But for his efforts he was awarded the Nobel Peace Prize for 1919. Wilson is perhaps most famous for his FOURTEEN POINTS and for the IDEALISM he brought to United States foreign policy. Indeed, it is sometimes argued that there is a Wilso-

Woodrow Wilson (Library of Congress)

nian tradition in the U.S. approach to foreign relations. This was perhaps best exemplified in recent years in the foreign policy of JIMMY CARTER with its emphasis on HUMAN RIGHTS.

Wilson Doctrine   The policy of the United States during the administration of President WOODROW WILSON that it would militarily intervene in Latin America when U.S. interests were at stake. While there was never any formally promulgated doctrine on this policy, Wilson's actions (e.g., in sending U.S. forces to occupy Haiti in 1915 and the Dominican Republic in 1916) have allowed historians to impute such a doctrine to him. The doctrine was used most famously to justify the U.S. intervention in Mexico, the MEXICAN BORDER CAMPAIGN, in April 1914. This action was very much in accord with U.S. policies toward Latin America both before and since.

window 1. A diplomatic, military, or political term for a period of time when there is either a chance for achievement or a risk of danger. International events often create a WINDOW OF OPPORTUNITY for diplomatic action. A new weapon system may be developed to close a WINDOW OF VULNERABILITY. 2. Metal reflective material used to confuse enemy radar.

window of opportunity 1. A time frame when something significant can be achieved on a diplomatic or military front because of an opportune confluence of circumstances. 2. Historically, the notion that developed in the late 1970s in conjunction with concerns over a WINDOW OF VULNERABILITY and that predicted that the Soviet Union would use its strategic advantage over the United States as the basis for more assertive and expansionist policies, especially in the Third World. Conservative commentators in the United States believed that such policies were evident in Soviet geopolitical activity in the late 1970s, although arguably that had more to do with Soviet exploitation of the United States' VIETNAM SYNDROME than with Moscow's perceptions of the strategic balance.

window of vulnerability The belief that developed in the late 1970s that the Soviet Union was deploying increasingly accurate strategic forces at such a rate that Moscow would soon be in a position to place the land-based component of the U.S. strategic TRIAD at risk. Until the United States deployed new systems of its own and thereby closed this window, many U.S. strategic analysts felt that Moscow would become much more assertive and would have a psychological advantage in a crisis. Although the window never really materialized, it was important in U.S. domestic politics as the idea was popularized, particularly by the COMMITTEE ON THE PRESENT DANGER.

WIPO *See* WORLD INTELLECTUAL PROPERTY ORGANIZATION.

Wirtschaftswunder German for "economic miracle"; the recovery of West Germany from the devastation of World War II. The economy recovered because of currency reform, the MARSHALL PLAN, and a market economy, free from state planning but combined with welfare and social security programs.

WMO *See* WORLD METEOROLOGICAL ORGANIZATION.

Wohlstetter, Albert (1913–   ) A U.S. physicist who became one of the most important U.S. strategic analysts since World War II. While working at the RAND Corporation, he was asked to do a study of overseas basing for the Strategic Air Command. His study went far beyond a focus on overseas bases to deal with the whole question of the vulnerability of U.S. strategic forces. Wohlstetter's essential argument, influenced perhaps by the 1941 Japanese attack on Pearl Harbor, was that deterrent forces also could be a tempting target—especially in the nuclear age. Consequently, it was essential for strategic forces to be invulnerable, capable of riding out a surprise attack by the enemy and still being able to strike back afterward. Although Wohlstetter had some difficulty in persuading the Strategic Air Command to accept the need for invulnerability, this idea, and the concomitant distinction between first- and second-strike forces, gradually became the strategic orthodoxy. His views were summarized in a famous article, "The Delicate Balance of Terror," which appeared in *Foreign Affairs* (January 1959). Subsequently, Wohlstetter became a champion of strategic defenses as a way of adding extra survivability to ICBMs emplaced in hardened but fixed SILOS. In the mid-1980s Wohlstetter was a key figure in the President's Commission on Integrated Long Term Strategy that produced a report entitled *Discriminate Deterrence* (1988). This somewhat controversial report argued that in planning for future threats, especially in the Third World, the United States should place greater emphasis on precision guided weapons with an impressive capability for target acquisition and discrimination and a high lethality. Wohlstetter, one of the most important makers of American nuclear strategy, thus created ideas that continue to resonate.

Wolfers, Arnold (1892–1968) A Swiss-born U.S. scholar of international politics who wrote on several themes, including the Anglo-American tradition in foreign policy, alliances in international relations, and British and French foreign policies during the interwar period. In his most notable work, *Discord and Collaboration* (1962), he discusses national security as an "ambiguous symbol" and draws the distinction between those objectives of a state that are about power and acquisition (possession goals) and those that are about modifying the international environment (milieu goals). Wolfers was an important figure because he almost invariably dealt with fundamental issues and highlighted the ways in which the international system compelled states to behave in similar ways in spite of internal differences. Consequently his arguments are still quoted.

WOMP *See* WORLD ORDER MODELS PROJECT.

working funeral Diplomatic activities undertaken when leading political actors meet at the funeral of a head of state. West Germany's foreign minister, Hans-Dietrich Genscher, "claims to have invented the 'working funeral' when he met with U.S. Secretary of State George Shultz and Great Britain's Sir Geoffrey Howe after the state burial of Pakistan's President Mohammad Zia ul-Haq late last summer" (*Newsweek,* December 12, 1988). Then U.S. Vice President Dan Quayle agreed that funerals are unique venues for diplomatic exchanges: "There is ceremony for the funerals, but you can also do a lot of work. You can meet a lot of people. You can have some meetings and you'd be surprised at the kind of information and contact that is made beyond the ceremonial requirements" (*Los Angeles Times,* December 1, 1988).

World Bank *See* INTERNATIONAL BANK FOR RECONSTRUCTION AND DEVELOPMENT.

World Bank Group An integrated group of international institutions that provides financial and technical assistance to DEVELOPING COUNTRIES. The group includes the INTERNATIONAL BANK FOR RECONSTRUCTION AND DEVELOPMENT (or World Bank), the International Development Association, and the INTERNATIONAL FINANCE CORPORATION.

World Court The colloquial name for the International Court of Justice established by the United Nations Charter in 1945. The current World Court succeeded the Permanent Court of International Justice, established in 1920 by the League of Nations. Located in The Hague, the Netherlands, the World Court consists of 15 judges elected by the UN, each from a different country. The judges, who have nine-year terms and are eligible for reelection, are chosen on the basis of qualifications and political sponsorship. Some care is taken to ensure that the world's principal legal systems are all represented in the court. Because the court has no powers of enforcement, it usually considers only cases brought before it by the disputing nations themselves. Consequently, the World Court is not really a court but rather a panel for the ARBITRATION of minor international disputes. By "minor" is meant that the cases are of such insignificance to a state's vital interests that the state is willing to let an "objective" third party resolve it. In 1986 the World Court ruled against the United States in a case concerning the CONTRAS brought before it by the government of Nicaragua. But since the United States did not recognize the court's jurisdiction in this matter, the ruling had no effect—except that it was of considerable rhetorical value to the government of Nicaragua. This case highlights the basic problem with the World Court: It has no ability to compel states to do anything—even something as simple as attendance. Thus the United States, as many other states have done on other matters, simply ignored the court's effort to resolve the dispute. States participate in the court's proceedings only when they deem it in their interest to do so.

world government The idea of a single, central overriding authority or SUPRANATIONAL body that would direct the affairs of states and have a legitimate monopoly on the use of military force. The idea of a world government often is discussed alongside proposals for GENERAL AND COMPLETE DISARMAMENT and is equally unrealistic at the present time.

World Health Organization (WHO) One of 16 SPECIALIZED AGENCIES of the United Nations. Because it was created on April 7, 1948, when its constitution was ratified by UN member states, this date has since been observed annually as World Health Day. WHO's objective is the attainment by all peoples of the highest possible level of health. Its strategy to reach this goal emphasizes eight elements: education concerning prevailing health problems; proper food supply and nutrition; safe water and sanitation; maternal and child health, including family planning; immunization against major infectious diseases; prevention and control of local diseases; appropriate treatment of common diseases and injuries; and provision of essential drugs. In addition to WHO's role in building health infrastructures in member countries, WHO leads a worldwide campaign to provide effective immunization for all children to prevent the major communicable diseases of childhood. In collaboration with other UN agencies, WHO is actively pursuing global research programs involving tropical diseases and AIDS. With its headquarters in Geneva, Switzerland, WHO is governed by the World Health Assembly on which all member states are represented. Meeting only annually, the assembly has an executive board of 31 members as its executive arm.

World Intellectual Property Organization (WIPO) One of the United Nations' SPECIALIZED AGENCIES since 1974 whose principles date back to the 1883 Paris Convention for the Protection of Industrial Property and the 1886 Berne Convention for the Protection of Literary and Artistic Works. WIPO promotes respect for intellectual property throughout the world, helps stimulate creative activity, and facilitate the transfer of technology and the dissemination of literary and artistic works. Most important, it aids in wider acceptance of treaties and national legislation that are aimed at protecting both industrial property (chiefly inventions), trademarks, and industrial designs as well as copyrights (chiefly for literary, musical, artistic, photographic and cinematographic works). Headquartered in Geneva, Switzerland, WIPO has a conference of all member states and a general assembly, which is composed of those member states that are also members of the Paris and Berne unions. Policy matters are decided upon by joint sessions of the two bodies.

world law A notion that is closely linked to the idea of WORLD ORDER and WORLD GOVERNMENT. World law would go well beyond INTERNATIONAL LAW, which traditionally has been applied to state interactions at the political and strategic levels, and would apply to individuals and to social and economic issues and be drawn up by the world community. The problem with this idea is that it depends on the existence of such a world community, which does not yet exist. Indeed, transcending the existing international law and creating a new system of world law will prove very difficult.

World Meteorological Organization (WMO) Created in 1873 as the International Meteorological Organization (it changed to its current name in 1950 when it became one of the United Nations' SPECIALIZED AGENCIES), WMO works to provide meteorological and hydrological observations and services through establishing networks of stations and centers. It facilitates rapid exchange of meteorological and related information; promotes standardization of information, observation, and statistics in circulation and publication; encourages better application of meteorology to aviation, navigation, water, and agricultural activities; and fosters research and training in meteorology and related fields. In recent years, WMO has been called upon by the UN General Assembly to work closely with the UNITED NATIONS ENVIRONMENT PROGRAM in the area of global climate change. The World Meteorological Congress, which meets every four years, is the policymaking arm of WMO. All member states are represented by the heads of their meteorological services. An executive council of 36 directors from national meteorological or hydrological services serving in an individual capacity meets annually to supervise programs approved by the congress. WMO's headquarters are in Geneva, Switzerland.

world order 1. The existing order (the arrangement of sovereign states) in the global international system. 2. The minimum conditions for existence or COEXISTENCE in the international system. HEDLEY BULL in *The Anarchical Society* (1977) uses it in this sense and describes it as "those patterns or dispositions of human activity that sustain the elementary or primary goals of social life among mankind as a whole." 3. A normative or value-laden conception of the conditions for the good life. In fact, most analysts who are interested in a world order approach to the study of international relations seek to move beyond the preoccupation with the state, placing far more emphasis on the importance of the individual. Perhaps the most carefully articulated statement of this third approach is by RICHARD FALK, whose conception of world order entails examining the extent that a "given past, present or future arrangement of power and authority is able to realize a set of human values that are affirmed as beneficial for all people and apply to the whole world and that have some objectivity by their connection with a conception of basic human needs, as required for the healthy development of the human person" (*The End of World Order,* 1983). This conception of world order seeks to transform the existing system and replace it with one that does meet basic human needs. Some of the ways whereby this might be done are developed in the WORLD ORDER MODELS PROJECT.

World Order Models Project (WOMP) A project initiated in 1966 by the Institute for World Order that focused on ways to transform the existing international system to one in which human needs are likely to be met rather more fully. The project involves groups of scholars from different regions and key nations. Africa, Europe, India, Japan, Latin America, Russia, and the United States were all represented in the project. According to Richard Falk (one of the key figures in the project) in his *The End of World Order* (1983): "The WOMP group, through periodic interaction, evolved a framework of world order values that were general enough to command consensus within its membership and yet distinctive enough to establish an identity. The values agreed upon as suitable criteria for world order appraisal were minimization of collective violence; maximization of economic well-being; maximization of social and political justice; and maximization of ecological quality." In the first phase each group developed what was termed a "relevant utopia," which involved plans for restructuring power, wealth, and prestige on a world scale. A second phase, as described by Falk, attempted to "link the present to the future" through studies of global policy issues such as nuclear nonproliferation, human rights, and the NEW INTERNATIONAL ECONOMIC ORDER. It also involves an attempt to create a TRANSNATIONAL consensus on the direction and shape of an acceptable world order solution to

global problems. Although those involved in WOMP are concerned with providing practical guidance for changing the system, they are sometimes dismissed as utopian idealists. In a world that has become increasingly interdependent, however, and in which there are problems that can be dealt with only on a global level, the WOMP project offers an important and distinct perspective.

world politics 1. A loosely used synonym for the relations among states. 2. A more all-embracing term that is used to cover not only relations among states but also nonstate actors and actions and transnational relations and movement. 3. A term that is used implicitly to differentiate the kind of politics that occurs within states where there is a central overriding authority and that which occurs among states in which such an authority is lacking.

world public opinion A nebulous concept that is sometimes used to suggest the idea of a broad consensus in the international community that certain kinds of action are legitimate while others are not. Although there may be something to arguments that world public opinion is outraged by particular kinds of actions, the term often is used in a cynical way as part of an effort to legitimize particular policies and to add weight to condemnations of the actions of others. Although it is possible to see the voting in the United Nations GENERAL ASSEMBLY as some kind of expression of world public opinion, such votes really reflect the views of governments rather than peoples. Overall, therefore, world public opinion is a very unsatisfactory concept that is better used in PROPAGANDA than in analysis.

world society An approach to international relations, associated most closely with JOHN W. BURTON, which argues that the state-centric and power politics models of international politics have been outmoded by the growth of TRANSNATIONAL forces and interactions. As a result, Burton argues, it is more appropriate to treat the international system as a single global society in which the old emphasis on interests should be replaced by a new emphasis on needs.

world system An approach that emphasizes the world as a single economic and political organism.

Sometimes presented as a fourth level of analysis (following the individual, state, and international levels), the world system approach treats the globe as a single, holistic system. Associated most with Immanuel Wallerstein (1930–   ) who, in *The Modern World System* (1976), developed a neo-Marxist perspective to explain the development of the contemporary world system, this approach tends to emphasize the division of the world into "core" and "periphery" areas. The core consists of secondary producers of manufactured goods who dominate the primary producers of raw materials (the periphery) through the systematic use of violence and also engage in power competition among themselves. Some of the analyses deal with relations between the core and the periphery, whereas others focus on the struggle for dominance within the core itself.

World War I The global conflict, originally known as the Great War, that began in 1914 and ended in 1918 after 10 million people were killed, 20 million wounded, and the monarchies of Austria-Hungary, Germany, and Russia were overthrown. Its deepest causes were embedded in the Western State system. Prominent among them were the shift in the European BALANCE OF POWER with the unification of Germany and Italy by 1871 and the struggle between "have" and "have-not" nations for wealth, prestige, and territory. Other causes were the weakening of the Ottoman Empire with its Balkan tinderbox; chauvinistic nationalistic public opinion between Germany and Great Britain over economic competition; French desire for revenge for its loss of ALSACE-LORRAINE to Germany in 1871; a glorification of war based on SOCIAL DARWINISM; and the German-British naval race that led to the building of ever larger BATTLE-SHIPS. From 1905 to 1914 the two chief alliances—the TRIPLE ENTENTE (France, Great Britain, and Russia) and the TRIPLE ALLIANCE (Austria-Hungary, Germany, and Italy) grew more rigid, as they argued over trading rights in Morocco and local wars in the Balkans, where Austria-Hungary and Russia vied for control.

The June 28, 1914, assassination of Archduke FRANZ FERDINAND, heir to the Austrian throne, in Sarajevo by a Bosnian nationalist with Serbian support was the incident that ostensibly led to the beginning of the war. After the Germans gave the Austrian-Hungarian ambassador a "blank check" in responding to Serbia, Austria-Hungary issued an ULTIMATUM to Serbia to allow the Austrians to pursue the conspirators within Serbia. Serbia was generally conciliatory, but when not all terms of the ultimatum were met, Austria-Hungary partially mobilized and declared war on Serbia on July 28. Despite Germany's HALT IN BELGRADE PROPOSAL, by August 4 all parties in the two rigid alliances, except Italy, had declared war on each other. A wave of xenophobia and a near-carnival atmosphere swept Europe. In Austria and Germany troops were pelted with flowers in marching to train stations, and crowds cheered in London on learning of the outbreak of war. Few expected the horrors of the long war that would follow.

On the Western Front, Germany commenced the war with the SCHLIEFFEN PLAN. The Germans invaded neutral Belgium and attempted a scythe movement around Paris. Their effort to avoid a two-front war by rapidly winning in the West failed. The Belgians slowed the German advance and the British joined the French, who fought the Germans to a standstill at the first Battle of the MARNE east of Paris. Almost spontaneously soldiers began to dig trenches from which to hold the line. By November 1914 the WESTERN FRONT was fixed in opposing trenches from the English Channel to the Swiss frontier. Between the trenches were barbed-wire barriers and no man's land strips. For the next three years the western front moved less than ten miles either way.

In contrast to the west, the war on the Eastern Front had mobility. Although the Russians inflicted heavy losses on the Austrians and Hungarians, the German Army under HINDENBURG and LUDENDORFF defeated Russian armies at TANNENBERG and Masurian Lakes in 1914. The next year the CENTRAL POWERS drove into the Baltic states and western Russia. The Russians would be on the defensive for the rest of their war.

Both sides sought new allies. The Triple Entente gained Japan, which was eager to take German possessions in China and in the central Pacific. More important, Turkey and Bulgaria joined the Central Powers. The Entente powers also supported national autonomy for the Slavic peoples under Austrian-Hungarian rule and pushed for Arab independence from Turkey in the Near East. In an alliance shift in 1915, Italy entered the war on the Entente side after the secret LONDON TREATY promised it the Austrian Tyrol and Trieste.

As the war progressed, control of the sea grew in importance. The British, ignoring international law, imposed a strict BLOCKADE on Germany that did not distinguish between war supplies and peaceful cargo, seeking to starve the Germans out. Germany responded with SUBMARINE WARFARE meant to destroy British shipping and, in turn, starve the British. When the British liner *LUSITANIA* was sunk and 1,200 passengers, including U.S. citizens, drowned in 1915, U.S. President WOODROW WILSON warned the Germans that the United States would not accept a repetition. Although the Germans had built up their navy, it was still no match for that of the British. The only large-scale sea battle of World War I was off JUTLAND (or Skagerrak) in May of 1916. While the Germans inflicted more damage, the battle was a standoff and the Germans had to retreat to port. The British won, in effect, because they remained in command of the North Sea.

By the winter of 1916–1917, the strains of war were visible across Europe and major changes had occurred on the home front. TOTAL WAR gave women greater roles in industrial production and brought progressive centralization of political authority, economic regimentation, and restrictions on civil liberties. Three events in 1917 changed the course of the war. In February the Germans resumed unrestricted submarine warfare. That decision and pressure from U.S. financiers who had loaned the Entente $2.3 billion led the United States to declare war on the Central Powers on April 6. The euphoria over the United States' entrance into the war in Entente countries was tempered by a third event: the RUSSIAN REVOLUTION. After the Bolshevik coup against the provisional government in late 1917, Russia withdrew from the fighting (eventually signing a separate peace with Germany, the harsh Treaty of BREST-LITOVSK).

The Great War ended after two further campaigns in 1918. From March to June the Germans gambled everything on a final offensive with some success, but exhausted their reserves and again were stopped at the Marne River. By late spring the Germans had met all their wartime aims in the east, with control over vital natural resources and foodstuffs in East-ern Europe. Their situation in the west, however, deteriorated. In August, with newly invented tanks and fresh U.S. troops, the Allied armies swept forward. By October the Austrian-Hungarian army was disintegrating. The Austrian government signed an armistice on November 3. With his country on the brink of revolution, the German kaiser, WILLIAM II, abdicated on November 9. German representatives agreed to an armistice with fighting to cease on the eleventh hour of the eleventh day of the eleventh month in 1918. The Allies never invaded Germany, which later led German conservatives and Nazis to claim that the Germans had not lost the war but suffered a STAB IN THE BACK.

World War I was a watershed in Western history. Its carnage was the greatest to that date in European history. Added to this, an influenza epidemic swept a cold and weakened world in 1918 and 1919, killing twice as many people as had the war. Material destruction from the war was enormous in France, and three empires—Austria-Hungary, Germany, and Russia—disintegrated or were transformed. The great losses in lives and property put pressure on the Entente leaders for a vengeful treaty at the PARIS PEACE CONFERENCE.

The war had significant political and economic consequences. Pensioners and the middle class struggling with the postwar inflation, especially in Central Europe, looked to extreme political solutions in the form of TOTALITARIANISM. In this environment the FASCISM of BENITO MUSSOLINI and ADOLF HITLER took root—and would eventually lead to WORLD WAR II. As a result of war purchases by France and Great Britain, the United States (still a debtor nation in 1914) became the chief creditor nation in the world. Europe's economic and political domination of the world was stifled. Many historians consider the end of World War I to be simply a truce and term World Wars I and II as a replay of the Thirty Years War of 1618 to 1648.

WORLD WAR I A Chronology		
1914	June 28	Archduke FRANZ FERDINAND assassinated.
	July 28	Austria-Hungary declares war on Serbia.
	August 1	Germany declares war on Russia.

	August 3	Germany declares war on France.
	August 4	Germany invades Belgium.
		Great Britain declares war on Germany.
	August 5	Turkey closes DARDANELLES.
	August 6	Austria-Hungary declares war on Russia.
	August 12	Great Britain and France declare war on Austria.
	August 23	Japan declares war on Germany and starts to occupy German Pacific island possessions.
	August 26	Battle of TANNENBERG begins.
	September 5	First Battle of the MARNE begins. Germans halted; trench warfare starts.
1915	April 22	Germans use poison gas for the first time at second Battle of Ypres.
	April 25	Allies land at GALLIPOLI.
	May 7	*LUSITANIA* sunk.
	May 23	Italy declares war on Germany and Austria after secret agreements of Treaty of LONDON.
1916	February 21	Battle of VERDUN begins.
	May 31	Battle of JUTLAND begins.
	June 5	ARAB REVOLT against Turkey begins.
	June 6	KITCHENER drowns when his ship sinks.
	July 1	First Battle of the SOMME begins.
	August 29	HINDENBURG appointed chief of German GENERAL STAFF.
	December 7	LLOYD GEORGE becomes British prime minister.
1917	March	NICHOLAS II forced to abdicate.
	April 6	United States declares war on Germany.
	June 26	U.S. troops begin to arrive in France.
	July 6	T. E. LAWRENCE and Arabs take Aqaba from Turks.
	October 15	MATA HARI shot as spy.
	November 7	BOLSHEVIKS take over Russian government.
	November 17	CLEMENCEAU becomes French premier.
	November 20	Battle of Cambrai begins; first large-scale use of tanks.
	December 9	British forces enter Jerusalem.
1918	January 8	Woodrow Wilson states FOURTEEN POINTS.
	March 3	Russians leave war with BREST-LIVTOSK Treaty.
	March 21	Second Battle of the Somme begins.
	July 15	Second Battle of the MARNE begins.
	October 1	British and Arab forces enter Damascus.
	October 30	Armistice with Turkey.
	November 4	Armistice between Italy and Austria.
	November 9	Revolution in Germany overthrows monarchy and creates a republic. WILLIAM II abdicates and goes into exile. Austrian emperor Charles I abdicates.
	November 11	Armistice on Western Front.

World War II   The most destructive war in human history, which, from 1939 to 1945, killed 50 million people and devastated much of the heartland of civilization. It pitted the ALLIES (France, Great Britain, and, in time, the United States and the Soviet Union) against the fascist AXIS powers of NAZI Germany, Italy, and Japan.

The final diplomatic event preceding combat in Europe was the NAZI-SOVIET NONAGGRESSION PACT of August 23, 1939, the cynical agreement between opposing ideological groups that stunned Europe and seemed to allow the Germans to avoid a two-front war—unlike WORLD WAR I. Thus, a week later on September 1, 1939, the Germans started World War II in Europe with an unprovoked attack against Poland. Although France and Great Britain, through their policy of APPEASEMENT, had not opposed German leader ADOLF HITLER's dismemberment of Czechoslovakia, the THIRD REICH's conquest of Poland, whose territorial integrity had been guaranteed by the French and British, meant war. On September 17 the Soviets attacked Poland from the east. Poland formally surrendered on September 27 and ceased to exist as a state when it was partitioned between Germany and the Soviet Union.

World War II consisted of three phases. Phase one lasted from the invasion of Poland until April 1940. This was a time of eerie quiet, known as the PHONY WAR. The British sent troops to France and fought the Germans at sea. The Soviet Union took over the BALTIC NATIONS and invaded Finland, which put up a heroic resistance before conceding significant territory.

Phase two lasted from April 1940 to the summer of 1942, when the Axis armies conquered most of Europe and eastern Asia. As the British were sowing mines in the North Sea to prevent iron ore from neutral Sweden from reaching Germany, the Germans conquered Denmark and Norway. In May the Germans turned against Belgium and the Netherlands. On May 13, 134 German divisions attacked an equal number of Allied divisions in France, but German BLITZKREIG tactics, superior training, and a 3-to-1 advantage in airpower allowed them to defeat the Allies in a few weeks. The Allies, trapped at the French port of DUNKIRK, mounted a massive effort to evacuate 200,000 British and 130,000 French soldiers across the English Channel to England. The Germans marched into Paris on June 14, 1940. France formally surrendered on June 22 and was divided into VICHY and occupied France. General CHARLES DE GAULLE led the Free French RESISTANCE effort from England. In the west, Great Britain stood alone against Hitler's menace. The Battle of BRITAIN that followed prevented the Germans from gaining the COMMAND OF THE AIR necessary for the invasion force to cross the English Channel. This air battle pitted the German *Luftwaffe* against the British Royal Air Force (RAF). The British had superior planes (the Hurricane and Spitfire) and the newly invented radar, and had cracked the German military code. The Germans made the critical mistake of shifting their bombing raids from the airfields to the cities. Thus, while London endured the BLITZ, the RAF recovered, defeated the *Luftwaffe,* and prevented a German invasion. British Prime Minister WINSTON CHURCHILL praised the RAF pilots when he told the House of Commons on August 20, 1940: "Never in the field of human conflict was so much owed by so many to so few."

Italy was the weak link in the Axis forces. In October 1940 Italy invaded Greece but failed to defeat it. On February 1941 Hitler sent the Afrika Corps under ERWIN ROMMEL to help the Italians in Libya hold back the British forces attacking from Egypt. In May Hitler had to send troops to save Italy from defeat in Greece. The Germans crushed Yugoslavia when they were refused transit rights. This diversion in the Balkans delayed German plans to invade the Soviet Union, which proved costly in the long run.

With most of Continental Europe under his control, Hitler, who despised the BOLSHEVIKS and wanted land to the east, struck against the Soviet Union in June 1941, the nonaggression pact notwithstanding. The German divisions ripped through Soviet lines and proceeded in three prongs toward Leningrad, Moscow, and the Ukraine. The Germans laid siege to Leningrad, which lasted 900 days and reduced the city to starvation but not surrender. Soviet Marshal GEORGI ZHUKOV stopped the second German prong in the suburbs of Moscow in December 1941 with fresh troops from Siberia. Roughly a million Axis soldiers died on the road to Moscow or from the intense cold of the Soviet winter, for which they were poorly prepared. In the Ukraine, the German armies at first were welcomed as liberators from the yoke of JOSEPH STALIN's communism, but brutal treatment by the Nazis soon changed that perception. The Soviets resisted the Germans in STALINGRAD, thereby preventing German forces from reaching the oil of the Caucasus. Over a two-year period, the Soviet Union absorbed and broke the Nazi German armies, inflicting roughly four-fifths of their total of ten million World War II casualties.

The attack on the Soviet Union by Germany and that on the United States by Japan at PEARL HARBOR on December 7, 1941, made World War II a global war. In his request to Congress to declare war on Japan, U.S. President Franklin D. Roosevelt called the Pearl Harbor attack "a day that will live in infamy." Pearl Harbor united U.S. citizens as little else had done. ISOLATIONISM dissipated. After Pearl Harbor Hitler declared war on the United States and brought the full force of U.S. industrial and military might into the war in Europe. Germany's alliance with Japan obligated Germany to aid Japan only if Japan was attacked. Thus Hitler's declaration of war on the United States was completely gratuitous and extraordinarily stupid. Of course, the United States had already become the ARSENAL OF DEMOCRACY, sending LEND-LEASE ACT supplies to Great Britain across an Atlantic Ocean harassed by German submarines. The United States would quickly recover from its losses at Pearl Harbor. Meanwhile, in the Pacific theater Japan conquered Indochina, Indonesia, Malaya, and the Philippines. This so weakened the old colonial empires that the movement toward DECOLONIALIZATION was accelerated after the war.

The Japanese delegation arrives aboard the USS Missouri *to surrender formally, September 2, 1945. (National Archives)*

Phase three of the war began in the late spring of 1942. In the Pacific, the tide turned with the United States' naval victories at MIDWAY and CORAL SEA and on land at GUADALCANAL. In North Africa, British forces under BERNARD MONTGOMERY and U.S. forces under DWIGHT D. EISENHOWER drove back Erwin Rommel and the Afrika Corps. The German armies at Stalingrad surrendered in early 1943. By spring 1943 the Allies won the Battle of the ATLANTIC. In 1942 the Allies sank 87 German U-boats. In 1943 they sank 237 U-boats, and the wolfpacks (teams of U-boats) were on the defensive. Allied shipping was relatively secure. Soviet armies were soon to move west, and the Allies, after successfully invading Sicily, moved up the Italian boot. Italy's BENITO MUS-SOLINI was deposed but briefly reinstated by the Germans in the Italian puppet state in the north. It took the Allies until June 1944 to reach Rome.

For two years, Stalin had insisted on a SECOND FRONT to breach Hitler's FORTRESS EUROPE. On June 6, 1944, or D-DAY, Allied forces under Eisenhower crossed the English Channel with 4,000 ships, 10,000 aircraft, and 500,000 men. Except for a brief German counterattack in December, known as the Battle of the BULGE, the movement was eastward. With the end of the war in sight, the Allied leaders—Churchill, Roosevelt, and Stalin—met at YALTA to plan for the postwar world.

In 1945 Allied armies poured into Germany on two fronts, the Anglo-French-American forces from the west and the Soviet forces from the east. They found where the racial ideology of the Nazis had led in the CONCENTRATION CAMPS at AUSCHWITZ, Belsen, BUCHENWALD, and Dachau. Hitler's FINAL SOLUTION attempted to destroy European Jewry. Six million Jews and another 6 million Slavs and minorities, such as Gypsies and homosexuals, died from overwork, starvation, disease, and the gas chambers. BERLIN fell to the RED ARMY at the start of May 1945. Hitler had committed suicide on April 30. The Germans formally surrendered "unconditionally" on May 7, 1945 (which became known as

V-E DAY), but sporadic fighting continued through the summer.

The war took longer to end in the Pacific. In January 1945 American forces under General DOUGLAS MACARTHUR liberated the Philippines. At the POTSDAM CONFERENCE a formal declaration by the Allied leaders warned Japan to surrender unconditionally. Instead, the Japanese sent out large numbers of kamikaze pilots on suicide missions against U.S. ships. Refusing to lose large numbers of U.S. troops during an invasion of the Japanese home islands, President HARRY S TRUMAN ordered the dropping of the new ATOMIC BOMB on HIROSHIMA on August 6 and Nagasaki three days later. Japan capitulated on August 14. On September 2, 1945, Japan formally surrendered aboard the battleship USS *Missouri*.

Politically the age of European supremacy was over for the moment, as Europe was now dominated by two peripheral powers—the United States and Soviet Union. The ravaged continent had millions of DISPLACED PERSONS to resettle and an industrial base to rebuild. The alliance that led to victory was shattered after Yalta with the United States and Britain on one side and the Soviet Union on the other. The second portion of what some historians describe as a modern Thirty Years War was over, but a COLD WAR had begun that would last another 45 years. Thus the world war that began in 1914 (with a two-decade peace from 1918 to 1939) would not in this sense be over until 1991, when the Soviet Union, a creature of World War I, dissolved.

WORLD WAR II
A Chronology

1939	September 1	Germany invades western Poland.
	September 3	Great Britain and France declare war on Germany.
	September 17	Soviet Union invades eastern Poland.
	September 30	Germany and Soviet Union partition Poland.
	November 30	Soviet Union invades Finland.
1940	March 12	Finland buys peace with Soviet Union by ceding territory.
	April 9	Germany invades Norway and Denmark.
	May 10	Winston Churchill becomes British prime minister. Germany invades Luxembourg, the Netherlands, Belgium, and France.
	May 29	DUNKIRK evacuation begins.
	June 10	Italy attacks southern France.
	June 14	Germany occupies Paris.
	June 17	Soviet Union occupies Baltic States.
	June 22	France surrenders. Battle of BRITAIN begins.
	July 3	Britain sinks the French fleet in the ORAN ATTACK.
	September 22	Japan invades Indochina.
	October 12	Germans, unable to gain air superiority, cancel invasion of Great Britain.
	October 28	Italy invades Greece.
1941	February 6	Afrika Corps under ROMMEL sent to aid Italians in their fight against British in North Africa.
	March 11	LEND-LEASE ACT approved by U.S. Congress.
	April 6	Germany invades Greece and Yugoslavia.
	June 22	Operation BARBAROSA, the German invasion of the Soviet Union, begins.
	December 7	Japanese attack PEARL HARBOR and British Malaya.
	December 8	United States and Great Britain declare war on Japan.
	December 10	Japanese invade Philippines.
	December 11	Germany and Italy declare war on United States.
1942	February 15	Singapore surrenders to Japanese.
	April 9	BATAAN surrenders.
	April 18	DOOLITTLE RAID on Tokyo.
	May 4	Battle of CORAL SEA begins.
	June 4	Battle of MIDWAY begins.
	June 6	Germany destroys LIDICE.
	August 7	Battle of GUADALCANAL begins.
	October 23	Battle of EL ALAMEIN begins.
	November 8	Allied invasion of North Africa begins.
1943	January 14	Allies at CASABLANCA CONFERENCE call for UNCONDITIONAL SURRENDER.
	January 31	Germans defeated at STALINGRAD.
	July 5	Battle of KURSK begins.
	July 10	Allied invasion of Sicily begins.
	July 26	Mussolini deposed.
	September 3	Allies land in Italy.
	November 22	CAIRO CONFERENCE begins.
	November 28	BIG THREE meet at TEHRAN CONFERENCE.

1944	June 6	D-DAY.
	August 1	WARSAW RISING.
	August 25	Paris liberated.
	September 17	Battle of ARNHEM begins.
	October 20	U.S. troops invade the Philippines.
	December 16	Battle of the BULGE begins.
1945	January 17	Soviet Union takes Warsaw.
	February 4	YALTA CONFERENCE begins.
	February 13	DRESDEN bombed.
	February 19	Battle of IWO JIMA begins.
	April 20	Red Army reaches Berlin.
	April 28	Mussolini killed by partisans.
	April 30	Hitler commits suicide.
	May 8	V-E DAY.
	August 6	ATOMIC BOMB dropped on HIROSHIMA.
	August 9	Atomic bomb dropped on Nagasaki.
	August 14	Japan surrenders.
	September 2	Japan signs formal surrender on USS *Missouri*.

HOW THE WORLD WARS GOT NAMED

U.S. Secretary of War Henry L. Stimson in this September 10, 1945, letter to President Harry S Truman recommends that the title "World War II" be made official. Truman approved.

Dear Mr. President:

President Wilson, under date of July 31, 1919, addressed a letter to Secretary of War Baker which read, in part, as follows:

"It is hard to find a satisfactory 'official' name for the war, but the best, I think, that has been suggested is 'The World War,' and I hope that your judgment will concur."

Subsequently, under date of October 7, 1919, War Department General Orders No. 115 directed:

"The war against the Central Powers of Europe, in which the United States has taken part, will hereafter be designated in all official communications and publications as 'The World War.' "

As a matter of simplicity and to insure uniform terminology, it is recommended that 'World War II' be the officially designated name for the present war covering all theaters and the entire period of hostilities. . . .

Respectfully yours,

HENRY L. STIMSON

Secretary of War

---

worst case analysis 1. A term used to describe military planning based on the possibility that a putative adversary will actually initiate military action and that its military systems will have an optimum performance. 2. A term often used to describe military planning based solely on the enemy's capabilities (i.e., the capacity to do harm) which ignores the political context or the political intentions that determine whether there is a real probability that hostile action will be taken. 3. A pejorative term that is used to describe military analysis which takes place in a political vacuum. A good example of worst case analysis can be found in U.S. concerns in the late 1970s over the vulnerability of the U.S. land-based missile force. The argument was that the Soviet Union could destroy 95 percent of the Minuteman missiles in a first strike, and in a crisis might be tempted to do so. In fact, this assessment was based on outrageously optimistic assumptions about the performance of the Soviet missiles. Some of those who engaged in worst case analysis of this kind actually worked back from capabilities to intentions and argued that because the Soviet Union had the capacity for a strike of this kind, it would actually be tempted to initiate such a strike under certain circumstances. While it can be argued that the military has to plan on what an adversary is capable of rather than its intentions, it is clear that worst case analysis can exacerbate the SECURITY DILEMMA and perpetuate tensions.

Wright, Quincy (1890–1970) The U.S. author of an interdisciplinary classic, *A Study of War* (1942), which marked the beginning of what is now called PEACE STUDIES. A revised edition in 1965 brought the study up to date by including wars that occurred after World War II. Quincy Wright amassed an immense amount of information about wars and classified them as balance-of-power wars, civil wars, defensive wars, and imperialistic wars. His work provided much of the inspiration for some of the more quantitative approaches to research on war that subsequently appeared, especially the COR-RELATES OF WAR PROJECT. *See also* FIELD THEORY.

WTO The Warsaw Treaty Organization; the WAR-SAW PACT.

xenophobia An unreasonable fear or hatred of things that are foreign. This is a prejudice that is often created or reinforced by government policy. For example, until the middle of the nineteenth century Japan maintained a xenophobic attitude toward the outside world until it decided to adopt Western military and industrial technology. In this century the xenophobia of ALBANIAN ISOLATIONISM helped to make it the poorest state in Europe. All totalitarian regimes tend to be xenophobic to one degree or another because they fear the free flow of people and ideas. But as the demise of the SOVIET BLOC has shown, xenophobia always leads to economic stagnation and hardship.

Yalta Conference The last wartime meeting of JOSEPH STALIN of the Soviet Union, WINSTON CHURCHILL of Great Britain, and FRANKLIN D. ROOSEVELT of the United States, held at a Crimean resort on the Black Sea in February 1945. The basic postwar settlement was worked out here, including the temporary division of Germany with the Soviet army east of the Elbe River and the United States, Great Britain, and France in the rest of Germany (Churchill insisted on U.S. participation in this division, fearing otherwise that Great Britain would face the Soviets alone.) The issue of REPARATIONS was controversial and was submitted to a commission for recommendations. Secret provisions of the Yalta agreement were made public only after the war. They included a Soviet promise to declare war against Japan soon after the defeat of Germany; in return, the Soviet Union was to remain the dominant influence in Outer Mongolia and was to regain territories lost during the RUSSO-JAPANESE WAR of 1904–1905. Most of the later Western criticism of the Yalta agreement centered on the fact that it authorized the Soviet Union to take over a portion of Poland, with the understanding that Eastern Europe would thereafter be regarded as a Soviet SPHERE OF INFLUENCE or buffer zone, thus letting Eastern Europe fall to the Communists. But the primary U.S. goal of getting the Soviets to join the war against Japan was achieved.

Yalu River The boundary between China and North Korea. During the KOREAN WAR, the U.S. government expressed an unofficial policy of not allowing its military forces to cross the Yalu River into Communist China. The Chinese air and ground forces therefore used the Chinese side of the river as a PRIVILEGED SANCTUARY, even though they were fighting in Korea. U.S. air crew members occasionally intruded into the sanctuary in HOT PURSUIT of fleeing Chinese fighter aircraft, and some U.S. air crew members, forced to abandon their aircraft, came to ground across the river and became prisoners of the Communist Chinese (rather than of the North Koreans).

Yanikian, Gurgen (1900–1984) The retired Armenian engineer living in California whose 1973 assassinations of two Turkish diplomats marked the beginning of contemporary ARMENIAN TERRORISM. Yanikian invited the two representatives of the Turkish mission in Los Angeles out to lunch. After dining, he pulled out a handgun and shot them to death. At his trial he stated that the shootings were in revenge for the sufferings of his family during the ARMENIAN GENOCIDE of 1915 to 1922. Since these murders, more than 50 Turkish diplomats around the world have been killed by Armenian terrorists, many of whom look to Yanikian as the unwitting father of their movement. As for Yanikian, he was sentenced to life in prison for first-degree murder. He died in prison of natural causes in 1984.

yankees 1. The United States in general; all U.S. citizens. 2. The northerners during the American Civil War. 3. Residents of New England.

During the Cold War, "Yankee Go Home" became an oft-used slogan for those in the THIRD WORLD who favored Soviet models of economic and social development.

Churchill, Roosevelt, and Stalin at Yalta. (Library of Congress)

Yaounde Conventions   Trade agreements between the European Economic Community and 18 African countries signed at Yaounde, Cameroon. They involved mechanisms such as REVERSE PREFERENCES. The first Yaounde Convention was signed in 1963; the second in 1969. The Yaounde Conventions were replaced by the LOMÉ CONVENTIONS.

Yellow Rain   Term describing the chemical agents first used in the late 1970s by the Soviet Union in Afghanistan and by Moscow's ally Vietnam in Laos. To the victims the gas resembled "yellow rain." In 1981 a book by Sterling Seagrave, *Yellow Rain,* made allegations about this Soviet-sponsored CHEMICAL WARFARE. The scientific community in the West, however, was divided about the issue, with

some arguing that bee excrement was a more likely cause of the yellow rain than chemical weapons. While the Soviets never admitted to using Yellow Rain, there have been no reported instances of its use since the mid-1980s.

Yeltsin, Boris Nikolaevich (1931–   )   First president of the Russian Republic, elected in May 1990. He began his career with the Communist Party of the Soviet Union in 1961 and continued to move up the bureaucratic ladder despite his growing criticisms of central leadership. When he spoke out once too often in 1987, it cost him his membership in the Moscow party secretaryship and, shortly thereafter, his membership within the POLITBURO. Yeltsin then held the relatively minor position of first deputy chairman of the State Construction Committee until, again, his outspoken views drew too much attention. However, by this time he enjoyed a large public following. When he ran for a position in the Congress of People's Deputies in March 1989, he won 89 percent of the vote. The victory placed him in the new Supreme Soviet. One year later he was overwhelmingly elected to the presidency of the Russian Republic. In August 1991, after an attempted coup by Communist hard-liners failed, President Yeltsin emerged as the hero after publicly denouncing the plotters and putting his life on the line to defeat them. Following the coup attempt, the Soviet Union disintegrated and MIKHAIL GORBACHEV resigned as president, leaving Yeltsin to lead the most powerful republic in the former Soviet Union and to act as the symbolic leader of the COMMONWEALTH OF INDEPENDENT STATES. His tough economic reform program, combined with an ongoing dispute with the president of the Ukrainian Republic over who controls what from the former Soviet military, have caused Yeltsin's popularity to decline substantially. In a June 1992 visit to the United States Yeltsin agreed to dramatic reductions in nuclear arms and solicited financial aid to help transform the Russian economy. *See also* RUSSIAN COUP OF 1991.

YELTSIN BEFORE THE U.S. CONGRESS

The idol of communism, which spread everywhere social strife, animosity, and unparalleled brutality, which instilled fear in humanity, has collapsed. . . . I am here to assure you, we will not let it rise again in our land. . . .

You will recall August 1991, when for three days Russia was under the dark cloud of dictatorship. I addressed the Muscovites who were defending the White House of Russia. I addressed all the people of Russia. I addressed them standing on top of the tank whose crew had disobeyed criminal orders.

I will be candid with you. At that moment, I feared. But I had no fear for myself. I feared for the future of democracy in Russia and throughout the world. Because I was aware what could happen if we failed to win.

Citizens of Russia upheld their freedom, and did not allow the continuation of the 75 years of nightmare. From this high rostrum I want to express our sincere thanks and gratitude to President Bush and to the American people for their invaluable moral support for the just cause of the people of Russia. . . .

We must carry through unprecedented reforms in the economy, that over the seven decades has been stripped of all market infrastructure, lay the foundations for democracy, and restore the rule of law in the country that for scores of years was poisoned with political strife and political oppression. . . .

We have no right to fail in this most difficult endeavor, for there will be no second try, as in sports. Our predecessors have used them all up. The reforms must succeed. . . .

SOURCE: Boris Yeltsin before a joint session of the U.S. Congress, June 17, 1992.

Yom Kippur War   The October 1973 war that began on the Jewish holiday of Yom Kippur when Egypt and Syria attacked Israel in the GOLAN HEIGHTS and along the Suez Canal in the SINAI; also known as the *October War*. The surprise attack by Egypt and Syria was initially quite successful, but the Israelis soon recovered the initiative. With the aid of an airlift of weapons from the United States, Israeli forces outflanked the Egyptian Third Army and crossed the Suez Canal into Egypt proper. Israel's army, however, was overextended, and Israel was diplomatically more isolated than ever because of the Arab OIL EMBARGO. (The Arab states used the embargo to pressure Western states to, in turn, pressure Israel to be more accommodating to the Arab states.) U.S. Secretary of State Henry Kissinger mediated a disengagement of the opposing forces. After three weeks of fighting the most intense tank battles since World War II, all sides agreed to a United Nations–administered cease-fire. The United States in effect became the guarantor of the disengagement between Egypt and Israel. The short-lived Egyptian success in the war immensely increased the domestic stature of Egyptian President ANWAR SADAT and made it politically possible for him to make peace with Israel later.

YOM KIPPUR WAR
A Chronology

October	6	War begins when Egyptian troops surprise Israeli defenses and force a bridgehead on the eastern bank of the Suez Canal in the Sinai. At the same time Syria attacks Israel on Golan Heights.
	7	Israel counterattacks.

	10	Egyptians force Israelis to withdraw back into Sinai.
	12	Israeli troops rebuff Syrian attack on Golan Heights and advance toward Damascus.
	15	U.S. military resupply of Israel announced as a response to massive Soviet airlift to Egypt.
		Israeli forces cross Suez Canal into Egypt.
	17	Egyptian President Sadat proposes cease-fire to pre-1967 borders while largest tank battle since World War II continues.
	18	Arab states announce cut in oil production.
	21	Arab oil embargo of the United States announced.
	22	Egypt and Israel agree to a U.S.-Soviet–sponsored United Nations cease-fire resolution but sporadic fighting continues.
	24	Sadat requests intervention by Washington and Moscow to save the Egyptian Third Army.
		Brezhnev threatens unilateral intervention by the Soviet Union.
	25	United States increases military alert status. United States puts more pressure on Israel to observe the cease-fire.
		U.S. Secretary of State Henry A. Kissinger publicly states that the Soviet Union had taken no irrevocable action and was generally conciliatory. This helps defuse the superpower confrontation.
	29	Syria accepts cease-fire.
November	11	Israel and Egypt sign a cease-fire accord.
	15	First prisoners of war exchanged by Egypt and Israel.
January	17	Through shuttle diplomacy Kissinger arranges a disengagement of forces in the Sinai.
May	29	A similar disengagement is arranged on the Golan Heights with Syria.

Young, Oran (1941–) The U.S. international relations scholar whose *Politics of Force* (1968) was a pioneering comparative study of crises. It developed a number of hypotheses and applied them to the Berlin Crises of 1948 and 1961, the Cuban Missile Crisis of 1962, and the Quemoy Crisis of 1958 and then assessed their validity in the light of the evidence from these crises. Young also wrote on third-party intervention in international crises in *The Intermediaries* (1967). Subsequently

he contributed to the theory of international REGIMES, especially in relation to resources and their management on which he wrote extensively. His views on this were developed in *International Cooperation: Building Regimes for International Cooperation and the Environment* (1989).

Young Plan The 1929 financial arrangements devised by U.S. lawyer Owen D. Young (1874–1962) that lowered German World War I REPARATION payments, established new terms for how long they had to be repaid, and removed Germany completely from outside control. After the DAWES PLAN proved defective for making reparations payment, the Young Plan was proposed in 1926 and finally ratified in 1929. France was the last of the former Allies to agree to this plan, and only after sufficient German reparations to cover France's own debt to the United States were promised.

young Turks **1.** The army officers, mostly of junior rank, who sought reforms in the OTTOMAN EMPIRE in the decade prior to World War I. After the war MUSTAPHA KEMEL ATATURK emerged as the leader of these reformers. **2.** The new members of an organization or political party who seek to reform it significantly.

Yugoslavian Civil War The conflict within the six republics that until 1991 were part of Yugoslavia: Bosnia-Herzegovina, Croatia, Macedonia, Montenegro, Serbia, and Slovenia. Prior to World War I, the area that became Yugoslavia comprised the kingdoms of Montenegro and Serbia plus parts of the Ottoman and Austrian-Hungarian empires. Serbia led the movement for unification, and in December 1918 the Kingdom of the Serbs, Croats, and Slovenes emerged from the war a new nation. In 1929 its name was changed to Yugoslavia. Between the two world wars, Yugoslav politics were dominated by nationalistic conflicts between the Serbs and the Croats. Beginning April 6, 1941, the armed forces of Bulgaria, Germany, Hungary, and Italy invaded Yugoslavia and forced the monarchy into exile.

During the war, the country was torn by invaders and by internal ethnic, religious, and political strife. A fascist, pro-Nazi, Croatian separatist group, the

Ustashe, seized power in Zagreb and, on April 10, 1941, established the so-called Independent State of Croatia (which included Bosnia and Herzegovina) that allied itself with the Axis. Resistance forces in Yugoslavia were split into the "Yugoslav Army in the Fatherland" (popularly known as the CHETNIKS) and the National Liberation Army (the Partisans), led by JOSIP BROZ TITO and the Communist Party. In vicious and tragic fighting against the occupiers and each other, the war cost close to 2 million Yugoslav lives, about half of them at the hands of fellow Yugoslavs.

The Partisans developed a broader, more active resistance to the invaders and established their own government in the areas they controlled in late 1943. Allied pressure induced formation of a coalition government in 1945, but Communist-controlled elections produced a provisional assembly that proclaimed the Federal People's Republic of Yugoslavia on November 29. On January 31, 1946, a Soviet-type constitution was adopted, and Yugoslavia officially became a "people's republic," headed by Tito. The ensuing Communist regime suppressed the underlying ethnic and religious conflicts in Yugoslavia—at least until Tito's death in 1980. After his death the main power in Yugoslavia resided with the presidents of the six republics.

Toward the later 1980s a resurgent nationalism encouraged separatist movements in Slovenia and Croatia. As independence movements grew in the Yugoslav republics, the Serbian Communist leader Slobodan Milosevic (1941–   ) transformed himself into an aggrieved ethnic socialist leader and played upon the hatreds left over from World War II that Tito had suppressed. In 1991 Slovenia and Croatia voted for independence, followed by Bosnia-Herzegovina in 1992. With these votes, Milosevic and the Yugoslav Army unleashed a civil war. They armed Serb minorities living in the newly independent republics. Serb hard-line leaders claim that the Yugoslav Army as well as irregular forces are merely protecting Serbs from potential massacres in the new states. This was not a totally unreasonable charge, for during World War II the Croats (allied with the Nazis) did massacre hundreds of thousands of Serbs, Jews, and others. But most observers agree that this "protection" is out of all proportion to the need. The 1990s war has brought tens of thousands of deaths with barbaric violations of the Geneva Convention, the mass murder of noncombatants, and the mutilations of victims. Millions of refugees have been forced to flee their homes. The goal seems to be the creation of a greater Serbia at the expense of the lives and lands of people in the other republics.

Under German prodding, the European Community recognized Bosnia, Croatia, and Slovenia. The United States belatedly agreed to recognize them also. After numerous truces have been broken and United Nations' humanitarian aid convoys attacked, the fighting continues. The UN has placed an embargo on Serbia and branded Milosevic and the Yugoslav Army the main aggressors.

The dissolution of the former Yugoslav state continued brutally through the spring of 1993. Catholic Croatians fought Orthodox Serbs, and in Bosnia both fought Slavic Muslims. While the mountainous Alpine republic of Slovenia gained its independence against the Serb-controlled former Yugoslav Army, the Croatian declaration of independence began a conflict in which Serb insurgents, armed by the former Yugoslav Army, captured a third of that republic. Negotiations throughout the conflict have suffered from false promises from Serbia and the inability of Serb insurgent leaders to control their forces. Only after massacres, ETHNIC CLEANSING, torture in CONCENTRATION CAMPS, the forced expulsion of peoples mainly by Serb irregulars, and the constant bombardment of the Bosnian capital of Sarajevo did widespread criticism of human rights abuses arise in the West. By late 1992 the UN suspended Serbia's membership in the United Nations and took the preliminary steps for WAR CRIMES trials of Serbian leaders.

Zaibatsu The CARTELS of large market-dominating industrial corporations that developed in Japan in the 1920s and 1930s and that encouraged the initiation of expansionist policies by the government and military leadership. They were outlawed during the U.S. occupation after World War II, but they have since come back to dominate the economic life of Japan—and indirectly much of the rest of the world.

Zapata, Emiliano (1879–1919) A leader of the MEXICAN REVOLUTION from 1910 to 1918 who rallied large followings of peasants in southern Mexico. His call for sweeping land reform set off widespread peasant confiscation of land.

zero option U.S. President Ronald Reagan's plan for stopping the scheduled deployment of some U.S. nuclear weapons in Europe in exchange for similar Soviet efforts, put forth in a speech of November 18, 1981: "The United States is prepared to cancel its deployment of Pershing II and GROUND-LAUNCHED CRUISE MISSILEs if the Soviets will dismantle their SS-20, SS-4 and SS-5 missiles." The zero option idea emerged in connection with the 1979 decision of the North Atlantic Treaty Organization to deploy CRUISE MISSILES and PERSHING MISSILES in Western Europe. This was part of a two-track approach that was to be accompanied by arms control negotiations which might result in a reduction in the number of missiles to be deployed. But West Germany went along with the decision only on the understanding that the deployment could be cancelled if the Soviets made sufficient concessions. So the Reagan Administration publicly proposed to abandon the deployment altogether if the Soviet Union eliminated its SS-20 missiles. This zero option, as it became known, was essentially a negotiating ploy made in the expectation of a Soviet rejection. This, it was hoped, would help legitimize the deployment—which indeed went forward. Arms negotiations with the Soviets were suspended throughout 1984 but resumed in 1985 when the new Soviet leader, MIKHAIL GORBACHEV, enunciated a vision of a nuclear-free world and seemed to be willing to make significant concessions. The bargaining positions of the nuclear superpowers became much closer. This eventually led to the INF TREATY.

zero out 1. The total destruction of something, such as a military target. 2. To eliminate the budget of a government program, thus destroying it.

zero-sum game 1. A contest in which all of the payoffs to the players total zero no matter what the outcome. 2. A perspective on international politics that views possible gains for one side as a loss for the other; for one state to win, another state must lose. This brings the overall outcome to zero. It was U.S. Secretary of State George Shultz who warned: "Foreign affairs is not always a zero-sum game. We do not necessarily advance our own vital interests at another nation's cost" (*USA Today,* June 15, 1987). Once used only in GAME THEORY, the idea of zero-sum conflict has gradually gained wider usage. Often the U.S. debate about Soviet gains in the Third World during the 1970s was cast in terms of whether the superpowers were engaged in a zero-sum conflict, or whether gains by the Soviets were not of any real significance for the United States. One example of a zero-sum situation is the fight for the control of disputed territories in the Arab-Israeli conflict. If one side has the land, then the other side is dispossessed. Zero-sum problems of this kind are the most difficult conflicts to resolve, as there is so little common ground between the parties.

Zhou Enlai (also spelled Chou En-lai) (1898–1976) Premier (1949–1976) and foreign minister (1949–58) of the People's Republic of China. Zhou Enlai played a leading role in the CHINESE COMMUNIST PARTY from its inception in 1921. In 1924 he took part in the National Revolution led by SUN YAT-SEN's KUOMINTANG (KMT, or the Nationalist Party) in Canton. After the KMT-CCP split in 1927, Zhou was one of the chief organizers of armed revolts in major Chinese cities, which failed repeatedly.

Zhou Enlai (Library of Congress)

During the LONG MARCH, MAO ZEDONG took over the control of the party apparatus with Zhou's unswerving support thenceforth. Zhou played a crucial role in forging a united front between the KMT and CCP during the SINO-JAPANESE WAR. In December 1945 Zhou, along with U.S. General George C. Marshall, worked out a cease-fire agreement; but it was not successfully carried out and the CHINESE CIVIL WAR ensued. Zhou won over a group of Chinese intellectuals and politicians who had become disenchanted with the KMT government, a crucial factor that led to CHIANG KAI-SHEK's downfall in 1949. As premier and concurrently as foreign minister for a time, Zhou was the chief architect of the PRC's foreign policy. After Henry A. Kissinger, U.S. President Richard Nixon's national security advisor, made a secret visit to Zhou in Beijing in 1971 that later led to the normalization of Sino-American relations, Zhou's reputation as a diplomat and negotiator became widely recognized by the West. Zhou meanwhile maintained his prominent position in the party. During the CULTURAL REVOLUTION, he was an important stabilizing force. Avoiding any thrust for supreme personal power, Zhou remained a trusted ally of Mao all his political life.

Zhukov, Georgi Konstantinovich (1896–1974) The Soviet general known in the West as "the Eisenhower of Russia" for his achievements as army chief of staff in WORLD WAR II. He led the defense of Moscow. After the war, however, he was sent into virtual exile by JOSEPH STALIN. After Stalin's death, he was reinstated as a party member in good standing and became defense minister from 1955 to 1957 under Nikita Khrushchev.

ZHUKOV ON DISCIPLINE

[Marshal Zhukov] was a harsh disciplinarian. Senior commanders who failed to measure up were often fired on the spot. . . .

Once during the Polish campaign of 1944 Zhukov had stood with Marshal Konstantin Rokossovskii and General Pavel Batov . . . watching the troops advance. Suddenly Zhukov, viewing the scene through binoculars, yelled at Batov: "The corps commander and the commander of the 44th Rifle Division—penal battalion!" Both Rokossovskii and Batov began to plead for the two generals. Rokossovskii was

Georgi Zhukov (National Archives)

able to save the corps commander. But Zhukov remained firm regarding the second officer. The general was immediately reduced in rank, sent to the front lines, and ordered to lead a suicidal attack. He was killed almost instantly.

SOURCE: Cornelius Ryan, *The Last Battle* (1966).

Zia ul-Haq, Mohammed (1924–1988) The president of Pakistan from 1978 to 1988. Zia was the general who led a military coup d'état against the government of ZULFIKAR ALI BHUTTO in 1977. After proclaiming himself president in 1978, he outlawed political opposition, censored the press, and ruled through martial law until 1985. The lifting of martial law allowed for a rebirth of political activity, including the return from exile of BENAZIR BHUTTO. After the Soviet Union's AFGHANISTAN INTERVENTION, massive numbers of Afghan refugees poured into Pakistan, and Zia allowed Pakistan to become the staging area for various Western efforts to aid the Afghan resistance. Zia died in a plane crash caused by a bomb planted by political opponents. He was eventually succeeded, after national elections, by Benazir Bhutto, the daughter of the man he had deposed.

Zimbabwe Civil War The guerrilla war that began in the self-governing British colony of Southern Rhodesia when the white electorate refused to accede to African demands for increased political participation in the early 1960s and ended in 1979 when the British negotiated a transition to black majority rule. Although prepared to grant independence to Rhodesia in the 1960s, the British insisted that the white minority first demonstrate their intention to move toward eventual black majority rule. Desiring to keep their dominant position, the white Rhodesians refused to give such assurances. In 1965, after lengthy and unsuccessful negotiations with the British government, Rhodesian Prime Minister Ian Smith (1919–   ) issued a UNILATERAL DECLARATION OF INDEPENDENCE from the United Kingdom. The British government considered the new Rhodesian government illegal but made clear that it would not use force to end the rebellion. Instead it imposed unilateral economic SANCTIONS and requested that other nations do the same. In 1966 the United Nations Security Council, for the first time in its history, imposed mandatory economic sanctions on a state. Following a 1974 coup in Portugal and the resulting shifts of power in neighboring Mozambique and Angola, pressure on the Smith regime to negotiate a peaceful settlement increased. In addition, sporadic antigovernment guerrilla activity, which began in the late 1960s, increased dramatically after 1972, causing a slump in white morale. In 1974 the major African nationalist groups—the Zimbabwe African People's Union and the Zimbabwe African National Union, which had split away from ZAPU in 1963—were reunited into the "Patriotic Front" and combined their military forces, at least nominally. By 1979 over 20,000 lives had been lost in the constant guerrilla fighting. The Smith regime sought a solution by installing a token black majority government. But this did not end the war. Shortly after British Prime Minister Margaret Thatcher's Conservative government took power in 1979, the British began a new round of consultations, which culminated in an agreement. By the end of the year the parties signed an agreement calling for a cease-fire, new elections, a transition period under British rule, and a new constitution implementing majority rule while protecting minority rights. The agreement specified that upon the granting of independence, the country's name would become Zimbabwe, after the ancient civilization that once thrived there. The UN Security Council endorsed the settlement and voted unanimously for member nations to remove sanctions. During the transition period, nine political parties campaigned for the preindependence elections supervised by the British. ROBERT MUGABE's ZANU Party won an absolute majority and formed Zimbabwe's first government in 1980.

Zimmerman telegram   The 1917 message from the German Foreign Minister Arthur Zimmermann (1864–1940) to the German ambassador in Mexico suggesting an alliance between Germany and Mexico if the United States entered WORLD WAR I. It was intercepted and deciphered by British Naval Intelligence and became a major factor in the United States' entry into the war. The telegram's publication in the U.S. press on February 24, 1917, radically changed isolationist feelings. On April 2, 1917, President Woodrow Wilson would ask Congress for a Declaration of War against Germany.

THE ZIMMERMAN TELEGRAM

We intend to begin unrestricted submarine warfare on the first of February. We shall endeavor in spite of this to keep the United States neutral. In the event of this not succeeding, we make Mexico a proposal of alliance on the following basis: make war together, make peace together, generous financial support, and an understanding on our part that Mexico is to reconquer the lost territory in Texas, New Mexico, and Arizona. The settlement in detail is left to you.

SOURCE: Arthur Zimmermann, German foreign minister, telegram of January 16, 1917; reprinted in Barbara W. Tuchman, *The Zimmermann Telegram* (1958).

Zionism   **1.** The late nineteenth- and early twentieth-century political movement that led to the reestablishment of the ancient State of Israel in 1948. "Zion" refers to the hill in Jerusalem that is

the site of the ancient Temple of Solomon, the spiritual center of Judaism. Attachment to the land of Israel is a recurrent theme in Jewish scripture and writing. The desire of Jews to return to their homeland was first expressed during their ancient Babylonian exile and became a universal Jewish theme after the destruction of Jerusalem by the Romans in the year 70 and the DIASPORA that followed. It was not until the founding of the Zionist movement by THEODORE HERZL at the end of the nineteenth century that practical steps were taken toward securing international sanction for large-scale Jewish resettlement in PALESTINE, then a part of the Ottoman Empire. The BALFOUR DECLARATION in 1917 asserted the British government's support for the creation of a Jewish homeland in Palestine. This declaration was supported by a number of other states, including the United States, and became more important following World War I, when the United Kingdom was assigned Palestine under the MANDATES SYSTEM of the League of Nations. Jewish immigration grew slowly until the 1930s, then increased substantially because of Nazi persecution in Europe. But restrictions were soon imposed—both from the Germans, when they decided they would rather kill the Jews than allow them to emigrate, and from the British, who did not want to antagonize the Arab peoples who were reluctant to have more Jewish neighbors. After World War II and the revelation of the near extermination of European Jewry by the Nazis in the HOLOCAUST, international support for Jews seeking to settle in Palestine overcame British efforts to restrict immigration. It is one of the ironies of history that the German attempt to murder all the Jews so affected the world political climate that the Zionist dream of the rebirth of Israel was fulfilled.   **2.** The continuing political efforts of Israel to be a place of refuge for Jews throughout the world.   **3.** The political movement within Israel that would annex all of the WEST BANK as part of modern Israel, because it includes areas that were once part of ancient Israel. However, the Palestinian Arabs who live in this area bitterly oppose all such intentions.   **4.** Another example of Western imperialism, from the point of view of the Arab world. They contend that the European Jews who led the Zionist movement were basically colonists for Western interests and culture.   **5.** The external political and financial support that Israel receives from Jewish communities throughout the world. 6. Racism, according to the 1975 United Nations General Assembly Resolution 3379, which asserted that "Zionism is a form of racism and racial discrimination." This was basically an Arab-sponsored insult to Israel, the main effect of which was to make it more difficult for the Israelis to deal with the United Nations as an unbiased intermediary. With the changing alignments in world politics since the end of the Cold War and the Persian Gulf War, the resolution was repealed at the end of 1991.

zone of peace An attempt by states in a given region to prohibit or minimize GREAT POWER military competition and involvement in their area. This concept, a natural extension of NONALIGNMENT, has become integrated with the idea of the NUCLEAR-FREE ZONE. The idea of a zone of peace has had particular appeal in the Indian Ocean, in Southeast Asia, and the South Pacific. In 1971 the Association of South East Asian Nations (ASEAN) advocated that Southeast Asia should become a ZONE OF PEACE, FREEDOM AND NEUTRALITY. The members hoped that they could establish a regional order, relatively free from the machinations of extraregional powers, in which the states of the region would work together. The issue of great power involvement loomed even larger in the Indian Ocean when it was declared a zone of peace by the United Nations General Assembly in 1971. The great powers were asked to remove "all bases, military installations, logistical supply facilities, disposition of nuclear weapons and weapons of mass destruction" from the region. But they have been reluctant to follow this recommendation. Closely related to the idea of zones of peace, and equally difficult to establish and maintain, have been proposals for nuclear-free zones. The states of the South Pacific in particular have declared their region a nuclear-free zone, a stance that was endorsed by the UN in December 1975. Once again the great powers have been unwilling to oblige. France has continued its nuclear testing in the South Pacific, while the United States cut off some military links with New Zealand (its ally in the ANZUS PACT) when that country refused to allow the visit of U.S. warships that might be nuclear armed. So while zones of peace are attractive in principle, their impact has been somewhat slight. **2.** Areas of the world where states have not fought each other for long periods of time. The concept, in this context, was developed by KENNETH BOULDING. In his "Peace and the Evolutionary Process" (in R. Vayrynen, ed., *The Quest for Peace,* 1987), Boulding wrote that zones of peace "probably began in Scandinavia after the Napoleonic Wars between Sweden and Denmark, spread to North America about 1870, to Western Europe, Japan, Australia and New Zealand after World War II. Now we have a great triangle of stable peace, stretching roughly from Australia to Japan, across North America to Finland, with about eighteen countries which have no plans whatever to go to war with each other."

Zone of Peace, Freedom and Neutrality (ZOPFAN) A concept enunciated by the ASEAN nations in the Kuala Lumpur Declaration of 1971 and based on the old Asian proverb: "When elephants or buffalo fight, it is the smaller animals who get hurt." The concept was developed initially by Malaysia against the background of the United States' involvement in the Vietnam War and the concern that GREAT POWER competition in Southeast Asia would impinge on the ASEAN members. The idea of ZOPFAN was an effort to prevent this by making clear that the ASEAN members wanted the region to be neutralized so that they could avoid entanglement in great power rivalries. It also provided certain ground rules for ASEAN members in their dealings with one another and with outside powers. These included a renunciation of the threat or use of force; a demand for the eventual removal of foreign bases from the region; a prohibition of the use, storage, passage, production, or testing of nuclear weapons in the ZOPFAN region; a pledge to avoid becoming proxies of the great powers; and a promise of enhanced regional cooperation. Part of the problem with ZOPFAN is that it is both a set of principles and a set of aspirations. Not surprisingly, it has not always been strictly observed by all ASEAN members. Singapore, for example, has offered the United States access to naval facilities. If the concept has been qualified in practice, however, the aspirations that gave rise to it still exist, and it provides a framework for continued cooperation among the ASEAN states.

Zulu Time *See* GREENWICH MEAN TIME.

Appendix

Key Concepts Organized by Subject

Africa

Abyssinian-Italian War
African Crisis
African National Congress
Algerian War of Independence
Alvor Accord
Amin Dada, Idi
Angolan Civil War
apartheid
Banjul Charter
Bantustan
Biafra
Biko, Stephen
Boer War
Bokassa, Jean-Bedel
Botha, Louis
Botha, Pieter W.
Boumedienne, Houari
Buthelezi, Mangosuthu Gatsha
Cameroon plebiscite
Chad Civil War
Congolese Civil War
constructive engagement
De Klerk, F. W.
Ethiopian Civil War
front line states
Haile Selassie
Horn of Africa
Inkatha Freedom Party
Libya coup
Mandela, Nelson
Mau Mau
Mugabe, Robert G.
Namibian Independence

Organization of African Unity
RENAMO
Scramble for Africa
Sharpeville incident
Smuts, Jan Christiaan
SWAPO (South West African People's Organization)
Tutu, Desmond
Ugandan Civil War
Unilateral Declaration of Independence
Zimbabwe Civil War

Central America and the Caribbean

Arbenz Guzmán, Jacobo
Arias Peace Plan
Batista, Fulgencio
Bay of Pigs
Caraballeda Declaration
Cárdenas, Lázaro del Rio
Caribbean Basin Initiative
Caribbean Community and Common Market
Caribbean Development Bank
Castro, Fidel
Chamorro, Violeta Barrios de
Contadora Group
contras
Cuban missile crisis
Cuban Revolution
DeConcini reservation

Dominican Civil War
Duvalier family
El Salvador Civil War
Football War
Grenada, invasion of
Guantanamo Bay
Guatemalan Coup
Guevara, Ernesto "Che"
Haitian Coup
Johnson Doctrine
Kissinger *Report*
Mariel boatlift
Mexican Revolution
Nicaraguan Civil War
Noriega, Manuel Antonio
Ocho Rios Declaration
Ortega Saavedra, Daniel
Panama Canal
Panama intervention
Platt Amendment
Sandinista
Somoza
Tonton Macoute

Central and South-Central Asia

Afghanistan intervention
ahimsa
Amritsar Massacre
Ataturk, Mustapha Kemel
Bandaranike, Sirimavo
Bandung Conference

743

Appendix

Bangladesh War of
 Independence
Bhopal disaster
Bhutan-India Treaty
Bhutto, Benazir
Bhutto, Zulfikar Ali
Bindranwale, Sant Jarnail
 Singh
Boland Amendment
Colombo Plan
Dalai Lama
Gandhi, Indira
Gandhi, Mohandas Karamchand
Golden Temple of Amritsar
Indian partition
Jinnah, Mohammed Ali
Kashmir dipute
Mother Theresa
Nehru, Jawaharlal
rimland
Sikhs
Sino-Indian Conflict
Sri Lankan Civil War
Suu Kyi, Aung San
Zia ul-Haq, Mohammed

China

Anglo-Chinese Treaty of 1984
Boxer Rebellion
Chiang Kai-shek
Chinese Civil War
Chinese Communist Party
Chinese-Taiwanese Conflict
Chinese–United States rap-
 prochement
cultural revolution
Deng Xiaoping
Gang of Four
great leap forward
Hong Kong
Korean War
Kuomintang
Little Red Book
Liu Shaoqi
Long March

Manchurian Crisis
Mao Zedong
Mukden Incident
Nanking, Rape of
Opium Wars
Quemoy Crises
Red Guards
Republic of China
Shanghai Communiqué
Sino-Japanese Wars
Sino-Soviet border dispute
Sino-Soviet split
Sun Yat-sen
Taiwan
Tiananmen Square
Yalu River
Zhou Enlai

Cold War

Acheson, Dean Gooderham
Austrian State Treaty
bargaining theory
Berlin Blockade
Berlin crises
Berlin Wall
Birch, John
brinkmanship
Carter Doctrine
Central Treaty Organization
Charter of Paris for New Europe
China card
coexistence
cold war
Cold War critics
Cold War revisionists
collective security
Committee on the Present
 Danger
containment
cordon sanitaire
Cuban missile crisis
defection
détente
domino theory
Dulles, John Foster

East-West
evil empire
Forrestal, James V.
Glassboro
Greek Civil War
Iron Curtain
Kennan, George F.
Kirkpatrick Jeane
Kissinger, Henry A.
Korean Airlines Flight 007
Korean War
missile gap
new world order
Nitze, Paul H.
North Atlantic Treaty
 Organization
open skies proposal
Paris Summit Conference of
 1960
Pax Americana
Pax Sovietica
rollback
space race
superpowers
Truman Doctrine
Warsaw Pact

Diplomacy

accord
accreditation
agrément
ambassador
American Academy of
 Diplomacy
archives
attaché
back channel
breaking relations
Chancellery
chargé d'affaires
clientitis
communiqué
concordat
confidence-building measures
Congress of Vienna

consul
courtesy call
declaration
demarche
diplomacy
diplomat
doctrine
embassy
entente
Estrada Doctrine
Excellency, your
exchange of notes
exequatur
final act
foreign office
foreign secretary
foreign service
frank and candid exchange of
    views
high commissioner
hot line
interests section
laissez-passer
legation
mediation
minister
negotiations
nonaggression pact
note
nuncio
passport
peace with honor
persona non grata
plenipotentiary
protocol
rapprochement
ratification
recognition
sanctuary
summit
treaty
truce
ultimatum
Vienna Convention on Consular
    Relations
Vienna Convention on Diplo-
    matic Relations
working funeral

East Asia and the Pacific

Agent Orange
ANZUS Pact
Aquino, Corazon
ASEAN
Australia Group
Bao Dai
Cambodian holocaust
Cambodian incursion
Diem, Ngho Dinh
Dien Bien Phu
East Timor occupation
Five Power Defense Arrange-
    ments
Fukuda Doctrine
Giap, Vo Nguyen
Golden Triangle
Greater East Asia Co-Prosperity
    Sphere
Gulf of Tonkin Resolution
Hirohito
Ho Chi Minh
Huks
Inchon invasion
Indochina
Indonesian War of Independence
Japanese Peace Treaty
Khmer Rouge
Kim Il-Sung
Korean War
Lansing-Ishii Agreement
Laos Accords
Laotian Civil War
Lon Nol
Lytton Commission
Marcos, Ferdinand E.
My Lai
Pacific Basin Community
Paris Agreement
Pathet Lao
Pearl Harbor
Philippine Revolution
Pol Pot
Pueblo incident
Rahman, Tunku Abdul
Rhee, Syngman
Russo-Japanese War

Shatung Question
Sihanouk, Norodom
Suharto
Sukarno, Achmed
Tet Offensive
Viet Cong
Viet Minh
Vietnam War

Eastern Europe

Aegean dispute
Albanian isolationism
Ataturk, Mustapha Kemel
Balkan question
Benes, Eduard
Brezhnev Doctrine
Ceauşescu, Nicolae
Charter 77
Chetniks
COMECON
Curzon line
Czechoslovakian coup of 1918
Czechoslovakian invasion
Danube Dam
Danzig
Djilas, Milovan
Dubcek, Alexander
European Bank for Reconstruc-
    tion and Development
Finnish-Russian War
Georgian Civil War
Gomulka, Wladyslaw
Havel, Vaclav
Honecker, Erich
Hungarian Uprising
Jaruzelski, Wojciech
John Paul II
Kadar, Janos
Little Entente
Masaryk, Jan
Nagy, Imre
Oder-Neisse Line
Ottoman Empire
Pilsudski, Józef K.
Polish corridor

Algerian War of Independence
Alsace-Lorraine
Blum, Léon
Briand, Aristide
Clemenceau, Georges
Cresson, Edith
Daladier, Edouard
de Gaulle, Charles
Dreyfus Affair
Fifth Republic
Force d'Action Rapide
force de frappe
Fourth Republic
France, Battle of
Franco-German brigade
Gaullism
Laval, Pierre
Mendes-France, Pierre
Mitterand, François
OAS
Pétain, Philippe
Poincaré, Raymond
Pompidou, Georges
Rainbow Warrior
Third Republic
Vichy

Germany

Abgrenzung
Adenauer, Konrad
Agadir crisis
Anschluss
Aryan
Beer Hall Putsch
Berlin crises
Bismarck, Otto von
Bitberg
Bonn-Moscow Treaty
book burning
Brandt, Willy
Creditanstalt
Dawes Plan
Drang Nach Osten
Erhard, Ludwig
German question
German reunification

Gestapo
Goebbels, Joseph
Hallstein doctrine
Hindenburg, Paul Ludwig von
Hitler, Adolf
Holocaust
Huns
Kohl, Helmut
Kristallnacht
Lebensraum
Locarno Pacts
London Debt Accord of 1953
Luxembourg Agreement
Munich Agreement
Nazi
Nuremberg laws
Ostpolitik
Potsdam Conference
Rapallo, Treaty of
Reichstag fire
Rhineland
Ruhr
Saar
Schmidt, Helmut
Weimar Republic
Westpolitik
William II
Young Plan

Intelligence and Espionage

active measures
agent
asset
Cambridge Spy Ring
Casey, William Joseph
Central Intelligence Agency
Church Committee
classified information
code name
covert operations
disinformation
Donovan, William Joseph
electronic intelligence
espionage
fifth man
Fuchs, Klaus

honest broker
human intelligence
intelligence
Mata Hari
MI5
MI6
mole
Mossad
need to know
Office of Strategic Services
propaganda
Pueblo incident
Rosenberg, Julius and Ethel
sabotage
signals intelligence
sleepers
SMERSH
SMICE
source
Team A/Team B
ULTRA
underground
U-2 incident

International Law

abrogation
accession
adjudication
administered territories
admission
adoption
ad referendum
advisory opinion
asylum
autolimitation
belligerency
Berne International Copyright
  Convention
blockade
boundary
boycott
Calvo clause
casus belli
conflict of laws
contraband
crimes against humanity

Appendix

Drago Doctrine
exclusion zone
exclusive economic zone
extradition
extraterritoriality
genocide
Grotius, Hugo
higher law
human rights
international law
just war theory
Law of Nations
law of the sea
law of war
nationality
neutrality
Nuremberg trials
open city
pacta sunt servanda
patrimonial sea
peaceful settlement of disputes
right of self-defense
self-determination
spirit of agreement
state of war
state responsibility
Tokyo International Military
  Tribunal
treason
treaty
Universal Declaration of Human
  Rights
uti possidetis
Vattel, Emerich de
war crime
World Court
world law

International Organizations

admission
Amnesty International
assessments, scale of
Economic and Social Council
Economic Community of West
  African States
EURATOM

EUREKA
European Parliament
General Assembly
Greenpeace
intergovernmental organization
International Atomic Energy
  Agency
International Bank for Recon-
  struction and Development
International Monetary Fund
international organization
International Red Cross
Interparliamentary Union
League of Nations
OPEC
Organization for Economic
  Cooperation and
  Development
Organization of African Unity
Organization of American States
OXFAM
secretariat
secretary-general
Security Council
specialized agencies
Trilateral Commission
United Nations
World Court
World Health Organization

International Relations Theorists

Allison, Graham T., Jr.
Almond, Gabriel
Angell, Norman
Apter, David E.
Arendt, Hannah
Aron, Raymond
Boulding, Kenneth
Brecher, Michael
Brinton, Crane
Brzezinski, Zbigniew
Buchan, Alastair
Bull, Hedley
Burton, John W.
Butterfield, Herbert

Carr, Edward Hallett
Clausewitz, Karl Maria von
Cobden, Richard
Deutsch, Karl Wolfgang
Etzioni, Amitai
Falk, Richard
Galtung, Johan
George, Alexander L.
Gramsci, Antonio
Haas, Ernst
Halperin, Morton H.
Haushofer, Karl
Hegel, George Wilhelm
  Friedrich
Herz, John
Hobson, John A.
Hoffmann, Stanley
Holsti, Kalevi J.
Holsti, Ole R.
Ikle, Fred
Jervis, Robert
Kant, Immanuel
Keohane, Robert O.
Kissinger, Henry A.
Knorr, Klaus
Lasswell, Harold D.
Lippmann, Walter
Lorenz, Konrad Z.
Mackinder, Halford J.
Modelski, George A.
Morgenthau, Hans J.
Niebuhr, Reinhold
North, Robert C.
Nye, Joseph
Osgood, Robert Endicott
Rapoport, Anatol
Richardson, Lewis F.
Rosecrance, Richard N.
Rosenau, James Nathan
Rummel, Rudolf J.
Schelling, Thomas C.
Snyder, Glenn H.
Snyder, Richard
Sprout, Harold and Margaret
Spykman, Nicholas J.
Thucydides
Waltz, Kenneth
Wohlstetter, Albert
Wolfers, Arnold

Wright, Quincy
Young, Oran

International Relations Theory

absolute gain
accommodation
actor
alternative world futures
balance of power
bargaining chip
bilateralism
billiard ball model
bipolarity
bipolycentric crisis
bolstering
buffer
choke points
collegial model
concert system
crisis management
Dollard hypothesis
end game
English School
ethnocentrism
factor analysis
field theory
force
functionalism
game of nations
game theory
geographical determinism
geopolitics
global integration
Great Man Theory of
    History
habit-driven actor
heartland theory
hegemonic stability theory
hegemony
high politics
incrementalism
influence
interdependence
internationalism
international relations

international system
irredentism
isolationism
level of analysis
long cycle
Melian Dialogue or Debate
middle power
militarism
modernist school
multilateralism
multipolarity
nation
national character
neorealism
nongovernmental organization
open door
operational code
patron-client relations
polarity
policeman of the world
postmodernism
power
rationality
realism
reductionist theory
regionalism
revisionism
sanction
satellite
security dilemma
special relationship
sphere of influence
stability
superpowers
technology transfer
traditionalism
transnational
trilateralism
world order
zero-sum game

International Trade

balance of payments
Bretton Woods system
Cancun Summit
Caribbean Basin Initiative

Caribbean Community and
    Common Market
central bank
COCOM
common market
comparative advantage
Consensus of Cartagena
debt crisis
debt relief
devaluation
dumping
duty
exchange rate
exclusive economic zone
export
fair trade
foreign exchange
foreign investment
free trade
free trade zones
GATT
gold standard
Group of Seven
Group of 20
Group of 24
hard currency
harmonization
import
industrial policy
joint venture
loan guarantee
Lomé conventions
managed trade
most favored nation
multinational corporation
North American Free Trade
    Agreement
open door
orderly marketing agreement
Plaza Accord
protectionism
quantitative restrictions
reciprocal trade agreement
reciprocity
reserve currency
soft currency
special economic zones
Structural Impediments Initiative
summit, economic

damage control
damage limitation
declaration of war
defense
deterrence
disarmament
Douhet, Giulo
escalation
fog of war
force
force multiplier
force projection
friction
general defense
general staff
GRIT
guerrilla warfare
insurgency
insurrection
interservice rivalry
intervention
Joint Chiefs of Staff
just war theory
Liddell Hart, Basil H.
limited war
low-intensity conflict
Maginot Line
Mahan, Alfred Thayer
maritime strategy
military-industrial complex
Mitchell, William "Billy"
mobilization
national security
partisan warfare
people's war
preparedness
rapid deployment force
readiness
reserve
retaliation
rules of engagement
security
security dilemma
show of force
Strategic Bombing Survey
strategy
Sun-Tzu
tactics
theater of war

threat
war

North America

America First
arrogance of power
Baker, James A. III
big stick
bipartisanship
Bush, George Herbert Walker
Cárdenas, Lázaro del Rio
Carter, James Earl "Jimmy"
Chamizal Tract Dispute
Council on Foreign Relations
Eisenhower, Dwight David "Ike"
Federal Bureau of Investigation
Ford, Gerald R.
Fortress America
Fulbright, J. William
globalism
good neighbor policy
Haig, Alexander M., Jr.
Harriman, William Averell
Hull, Cordell
Institutional Revolutionary Party
Iran-contra Affair
Iranian hostage crisis
Jackson, Henry M. "Scoop"
Johnson, Lyndon B.
Kennedy, John Fitzgerald
King, Martin Luther, Jr.
McCarthyism
McNamara, Robert S.
Mansfield, Michael J. "Mike"
Mexican Border Campaign
Mexican Revolution
Monroe Doctrine
Mulroney, Brian
National Aeronautics and Space
    Administration
Nixon, Richard M.
Nixon Doctrine
North American Free Trade
    Agreement
Pax Americana
Peace Corps

Pentagon
policeman of the world
Policy Planning Staff
presidency, imperial
president
puzzle palace
Quebec Separatism
Reagan, Ronald W.
Reagan Doctrine
red scare
Roosevelt, Franklin Delano
Roosevelt, Theodore "Teddy"
Rusk, Dean D.
secretary of state
Tower Commission
Trudeau, Pierre Elliott
Truman, Harry S
Uncle Sam
United States–Canadian Free
    Trade Agreement of 1989
United States Institute of Peace
Vietnam syndrome
Vietnam War
Voice of America
Weinberger Doctrine
Wilson, (Thomas) Woodrow
Wilson Doctrine

North Atlantic Treaty Organization

Aegean dispute
Atlantic Community
Atlanticist
Belgian neutrality
burden-sharing
COCOM
decoupling
deep strike strategy
Eurogroup
Euromissile
European Defense Community
European Defense Identity
European Defense Initiative
European Fighter Aircraft
    Agreement
European NATO

Appendix

flexible response
great debate
Harmel Report
North Atlantic Assembly
North Atlantic Cooperation
   Council
North Atlantic Council
North Atlantic Treaty
   Organization
SACEUR
tripwire
Warsaw Pact

Nuclear Weapons Policy

Alamogordo
armageddon
ballistic missile
Bikini
Brodie, Bernard
build-down
Campaign for Nuclear Disarmament
Catholic Bishops' letter
central strategic warfare
countervailing strategy
countervalue
declaratory policy
doomsday machine
dual function (*Dwifungsi*)
dual key
Dulles, John Foster
Einstein, Albert
European Nuclear Disarmament
fail-safe
first strike
flexible response
football
GPALS
hard target
Hiroshima
hydrogen bomb
ICBM
intermediate-range nuclear forces
Kahn, Herman
launch on warning
McNamara, Robert S.

MAD
Manhattan Project
massive retaliation
missile gap
Nitze, Paul H.
no first use
NSC-68
nuclear-free zone
nuclear threshold
nuclear umbrella
nuclear warfare
nuclear weapon
nuclear winter
parity
Presidential Directive 59
proliferation
Rickover, Hyman G.
Schelling, Thomas C.
Scowcroft Commission
second strike
single integrated operations plan
strategic defense initiative
Teller, Edward
throw-weight
triad
verification
window of vulnerability

Political Economy

absolute advantage
adjustment assistance
balance of trade
beggar-thy-neighbor policy
Bretton Woods system
capitalism
central bank
comparative advantage
competitiveness
customs union
development
duty
economic determinism
economic growth
economic nationalism
gold standard
gross national product

guns and butter
Hayek, Friedrich August von
industrial policy
inflation
international political economy
Keynes, John Maynard
laissez-faire
Malthus, Thomas Robert
mercantilism
military-industrial complex
mixed economy
nationalization
Phillips curve
political economy
protectionism
public good
Schumpeter, Joseph Alois
socialism
structural change

Political Theory

absolutism
alienation
anarchism
Aquinas, Thomas
authoritarianism
autocracy
autonomy
Bakunin, Mikhail
behavioralism
Bentham, Jeremy
big brother
big lie
charisma
citizenship
civil disobedience
commonwealth
communism
confederation
democracy
dictator
divine right of kings
doctrine
fascism
federalism
garrison state

higher law
Hobbes, Thomas
Hume, David
ideology
influence
Kant, Immanuel
Kropotkin, Peter
legitimacy
Leninism
liberalism
Locke, John
Machiavelli, Niccolò
Malthus, Thomas Robert
Maoism
Marxism
Mill, John Stuart
nationalism
nihilism
pacifism
Pareto, Vilfredo
pluralism
populism
power
raison d'état
realpolitik
regime
revolution
Rousseau, Jean-Jacques
social contract
social Darwinism
sovereignty
state
state of nature
systems analysis
totalitarianism
tyranny
utopia
Weber, Max

Scandinavia

Arnoldson, Klas P.
Cod Wars
Kola Peninsula
Nordic Council
Nobel Prize
Quisling, Vidkun

Reykjavik Summit
Schleswig-Holstein Question
Stockholm Syndrome

South America

Allende, Salvador
Alliance for Progress
Andean Group
Argentine fascism
Beagle Channel Dispute
Belgrano
Cali cartel
Chaco War
death squads
dirty war
Falklands War
Letelier, Orlando
Letitia conflict
liberation theology
Lima group
Marighella, Carlos
Medellin Cartel
Peron, Juan Domingo
Peru coup
Pinochet Ugarte, Augusto
Sendero Luminoso
Tupamaros
Vargas, Getulio Dornelles
Violencia, La

Soviet Union

Andropov, Yuri Vladimirovich
apparatchik
Baltic nations
Beria, Lavrenti Pavlovich
Bolshevik
Brezhnev, Leonid Il'ich
capitalist encirclement
Chernobyl
COMECON
Comintern
Communist Party of the Soviet
   Union

correlation of forces
five-year plans
glasnost
Gorbachev, Mikhail Sergeyevich
Great Purge
Gromyko, Andrei Andreevich
gulags
International, The
Kerensky, Aleksandr
KGB
Khrushchev, Nikita S.
Kirov, Sergei
Korean Airlines Flight 007
Kremlin, the
Kronstadt
Lenin, Vladimir Ilyich
Leninism
Litvinov Agreement
Marxism
Mensheviks
Molotov, Vyacheslav M.
New Economic Policy
Nicholas II
Pax Sovietica
perestroika
Politburo
Rasputin, Grigori
Red Army
Russian Civil War
Russian Coup of 1991
Russian Revolution of 1917
Sakharov, Andrei Dmitrievich
Shevardnadze, Eduard
socialism in one country
Solzhenitsyn, Alexander Isaevich
soviet
Soviet space program
Stalin, Joseph Vissarionovich
Trotsky, Leon
Union of Soviet Socialist
   Republics
Yeltsin, Boris Nikolaevich

Spain

Basque terrorism
Condor Legion

Appendix

Falange
fifth column
Franco, Francisco
Gibraltar question
Ibarruri, Dolores
International Brigades
Juan Carlos
Spanish-American War
Spanish Civil War
Spanish Law of Succession

Terrorism

Abu Abbas
Abu Nidal
Achille Lauro
Armenian terrorism
assassination
Basque terrorism
black terrorism
Bonn Declaration
Brighton bombing
counterterrorism
death squads
Deir Yassin
Entebbe Raid
Euroterrorism
hostage
Iranian terrorism
Islamic Jihad
Japanese Red Army
King David Hotel incident
La Belle Disco
Letelier, Orlando
Ma'alot massacre
Moro, Aldo
Munich Massacre
narco-terrorism
OPEC siege
Pan Am Flight 103
Provisional Irish Republican
   Army
Puerto Rican terrorists
Red Army Faction
Red Brigades
Rushdie, Salman
skinheads

skyjacking
state-sponsored terrorism
Stockholm Syndrome
Syrian terrorism
terrorism
Tupamaros
Yanikian, Gurgen

Third World Development

ACP countries
Agency for International
   Development
Baker Plan
Bandung Conference
basic human needs
Brandt Commission
Brundtland Report
Cancun Summit
Charter of Economic Rights and
   Duties of States
colonialism
Committee of Twenty-Four
conditionality
debt crisis
decolonization
dependency theory
developing countries
development decades
Fanon, Frantz Omar
Fourth World
green revolution
Group of 77
Institute for International
   Finance
interdependence
International Development
   Association
landlocked and geographically
   disadvantaged states
lifeboat ethics
Lomé conventions
New World Information and
   Communications Order
Nonaligned Movement
north-south
Official Development Assistance

Palme Commission
Pearson Commission
physical quality of life index
Prebisch Report
regional development
Third World
white man's burden

Treaties and International Agreements

ABM Treaty
Amman Agreement
Anglo-Chinese Treaty of 1984
Anglo-French Channel
   Agreement
Anglo-German Naval Agree-
   ment of 1935
Anglo-Irish Accord of 1985
Anglo-Irish Treaty of 1921
Anglo-Soviet Treaty of 1942
Antarctic Treaty
Anti-Comintern Pact
ANZUS Pact
Austrian State Treaty
Bonn-Moscow Treaty
Brest-Litovsk Treaty
Caraballeda Declaration
Chapultepec, Act of
Comprehensive Test Ban Treaty
Consensus of Cartagena
Control of Arms on the Seabed
   Treaty
Conventional Forces Europe
   Treaty
Czechoslovakian-German Treaty
Geneva Conventions
Hague Convention of 1970
Helsinki Accords
INF Treaty
Inter-American Treaty of Recip-
   rocal Assistance
Kellogg-Briand Pact
Locarno Pacts
London Debt Accord of 1953
London Naval Conference
Luxembourg Agreement

United Kingdom

United Nations

World War I